D0673134

Poland

Neal Bedford

Steve Fallon, Marika McAdam, Tim Richards

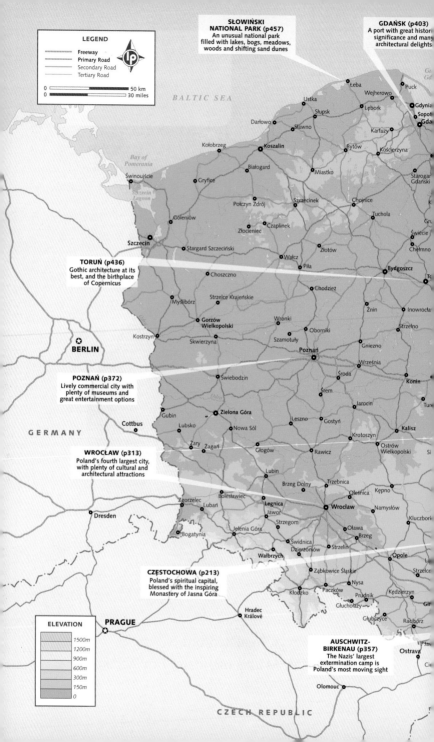

LEGEND

Freeway
Primary Road
Secondary Road
Tertiary Road

0   50 km
0   30 miles

SŁOWIŃSKI NATIONAL PARK (p457)
An unusual national park filled with lakes, bogs, meadows, woods and shifting sand dunes

GDAŃSK (p403)
A port with great historic significance and many architectural delights

BALTIC SEA

Łeba
Puck
Ustka
Wejherowo
Słupsk
Lębork
Gdynia
Darłowo
Sopot
Sławno
Gda
Kartuzy
Kołobrzeg
Koszalin
Bytów
Kościerzyna
Białogard
Miastko
Starogar
Gdański
Swinoujście
Gryfice
Szczecinek
Chojnice
Tucholska
Połczyn Zdrój
Gru
Czaplinek
Świecie
Goleniów
Złocieniec
Chełmno
Stargard Szczeciński
Złotów
Szczecin
Wałcz
Bydgoszcz
Piła

TORUŃ (p436)
Gothic architecture at its best, and the birthplace of Copernicus

Choszczno
Chodzież
To
Strzelce Krajeńskie
Myślibórz
Żnin
Inowrocła
Wronki
Gorzów Wielkopolski
Oborniki
Strzelno
Kostrzyn
Skwierzyna
Szamotuły
Poznań
Gniezno

BERLIN

Września

POZNAŃ (p372)
Lively commercial city with plenty of museums and great entertainment options

Świebodzin
Środa
Konin
Śrem
Jarocin
Ture
Gubin
Zielona Góra
Leszno
Gostyń
Kalisz
Cottbus
Lubsko
Nowa Sól
Krotoszyn

GERMANY

Żary
Żagań
Głogów
Rawicz
Ostrów Wielkopolski
Si

WROCŁAW (p313)
Poland's fourth largest city, with plenty of cultural and architectural attractions

Lubin
Brzeg Dolny
Trzebnica
Oleśnica
Kępno
Zgorzelec
Bolesławiec
Legnica
Wrocław
Namysłów
Dresden
Lubań
Jawor
Kluczbork
Strzegom
Jelenia Góra
Oława
Bogatynia
Brzeg
Świdnica
Dzierżoniów
Strzelin
Opole
Wałbrzych

CZĘSTOCHOWA (p213)
Poland's spiritual capital, blessed with the inspiring Monastery of Jasna Góra

Ząbkowice Śląskie
Strzelce
Nysa
Kłodzko
Paczków
Kędzierzyn
Prudnik
Gł
Hradec
Králové
Głuchołazy
Głubczyce
Racibórz

PRAGUE

ELEVATION

1500m
1200m
900m
600m
300m
150m
0

AUSCHWITZ-BIRKENAU (p357)
The Nazis' largest extermination camp is Poland's most moving sight

Ostrava
Ci

Olomouc

CZECH REPUBLIC

Bay of Pomerania

Szczecin Lagoon

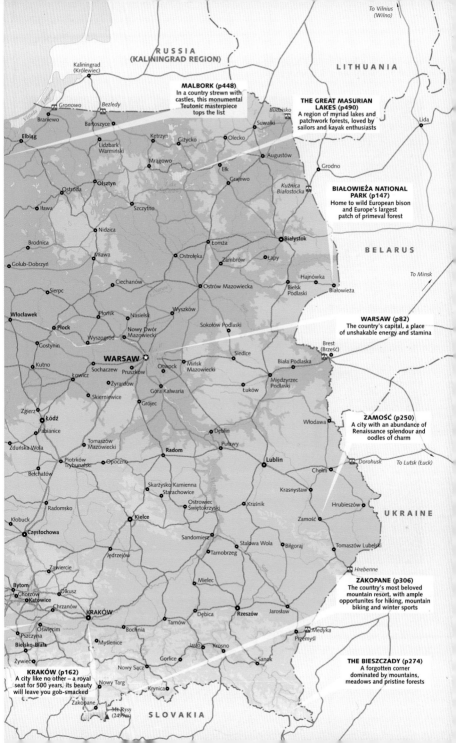

MALBORK (p448)
In a country strewn with castles, this monumental Teutonic masterpiece tops the list

THE GREAT MASURIAN LAKES (p490)
A region of myriad lakes and patchwork forests, loved by sailors and kayak enthusiasts

BIAŁOWIEŻA NATIONAL PARK (p147)
Home to wild European bison and Europe's largest patch of primeval forest

WARSAW (p82)
The country's capital, a place of unshakable energy and stamina

ZAMOŚĆ (p250)
A city with an abundance of Renaissance splendour and oodles of charm

ZAKOPANE (p306)
The country's most beloved mountain resort, with ample opportunites for hiking, mountain biking and winter sports

THE BIESZCZADY (p274)
A forgotten corner dominated by mountains, meadows and pristine forests

KRAKÓW (p162)
A city like no other – a royal seat for 500 years, its beauty will leave you gob-smacked

On the Road

NEAL BEDFORD Coordinating Author
A friend from university always said one drink is for girls, but I never bought into his philosophy. Still, two drinks seemed better than one at Wisłostrada, a rockin' arts and music festival on the banks of the Vistula in Warsaw. The next day I vowed to stick to one drink at a time.

MARIKA MCADAM I was sorry to be leaving Kazimierz Dolny with its quaint architecture and quirky tradition of baking rooster-shaped bread. If I had to leave, I was going to take advantage of the fact that there was no-one around at 6.30am and ride out of there on a rooster.

STEVE FALLON In the forest on the way to Muczne in the Bieszczady I encountered two sooty charcoal-burners. It takes 24 hours for the sycamore and beech logs to burn and another day for the charcoal to cool. It's hot, dirty work and the guys wanted to drink. I wanted to burn. We compromised.

TIM RICHARDS I had no idea that Poland could get so hot in spring, and was equally surprised by the old-fashioned charm of Kołobrzeg's beach. The beach chairs for hire, the fine white sand, and the beach vendor surreptitiously selling beer while chanting 'Tea! Coffee!' made for a fun break.

See full author bios page 541

Poland Highlights

With its eventful history, diverse landscapes, graceful cities and vibrant culture, Poland is a big country boasting a great deal of attractions. Here's what our authors, staff and travellers love most about it – share your Polish highlights at lonelyplanet.com\bluelist.

BRUCE BI

1 **NA ZDROWIE!**

Kraków (p162), the jewel of Poland. Also freezing cold. Find a dark pub off ul Floriańska, gather some new Polish friends, a round of vodka shots and be merry. This will also help solve any colds you've picked up along the way.

PetraJW, Bluelist contributor

KRZYSZTOF DYDYŃSKI

❷ WARSAW RISING MUSEUM

Air raid sirens, machine gun sprays and stomping boots pull you into a new (old) reality. The attention to detail makes it the best multimedia museum (p99) anywhere! This 'can't turn your eyes away' tribute to Warsaw's 63-day resistance fight against the Nazis stars ordinary people defending their city. I left with incredible respect for the indomitable Polish spirit.

Annie Larris, traveller, USA

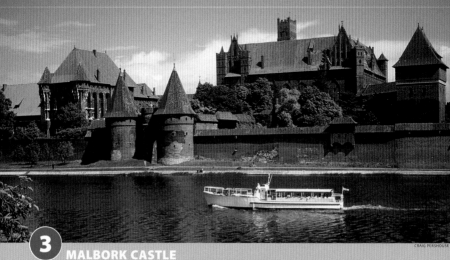

CRAIG PERSHOUSE

❸ MALBORK CASTLE

This 13th-century castle (p448) withstood Prussian devastation and the armies of the great Napoleon. Go and see where the origins of the Teutonic order began and gave rise to one of the nation's most attractive historic museums.

Izabela, Bluelist contributor

SUMMER EVENINGS IN ZAMOŚĆ

Sitting in the Rynek (p252) during an evening of the Zamość Theatre Summer, watching an open-air pantomime take place in front of the magnificently illuminated town hall. Nondescript tunes fill the square and ricochet off the flood-lit buildings as sheet-shrouded performers flap their arms to symbolise…something, or perhaps just to keep their balance on their teetering stilts. Fire is introduced into the spectacle and smoke engulfs the audience, who suddenly look panicked and uncertain about whether to applaud or drop and roll. And then something extraordinary happens – the waiter brings a thick, chilli-laced hot chocolate, which, in its glorious perfection, makes it official that this Renaissance town is something special.

Marika McAdam, author

KRZYSZTOF DYDYNSKI

4

SHOPPING FOR AMBER IN GDAŃSK

What I enjoyed most of all was shopping for amber jewellery in Gdańsk (p403). It was great fun scouring the lovely Old Town for the perfect orange earrings or green pendant. The prices are so good, why not buy one more amber brooch?

Fayette Fox, traveller, USA

KRZYSZTOF DYDYNSKI

5

GETTING HIGH IN THE TATRAS

Looking at the view (and trying not to look down) as you ride the cable car high above spruce trees to the top of Mt Kasprowy Wierch (p309), near Zakopane, the Tatras.

Sam Trafford, Lonely Planet, Australia

FCL PHOTOGRAPHY / ALAM

6

GRACEFUL KALISZ

Kalisz (p396) was somewhere I'd never even heard of, but it turned out to be a great little regional centre and definitely off the mainstream tourist track. The elegant buildings in the centre look different to those in most Polish cities' Old Town areas – more graceful and streamlined – and that's because the city was entirely rebuilt in the 1920s after being destroyed in WWI.

Tim Richards, author

KRZYSZTOF DYDYNSKI

7

JASNA GÓRA: PILGRIMAGES FOR ALL

Joining in the crowds of pilgrims making their way towards the Monastery of Jasna Góra (p215) is a fascinating Polish pilgrimage, even for non-believers. Initially, the stark contrast between Catholic devotion and the chic new shopfronts lining the pilgrimage route seems incongruous, but by the time you reach the chapel you realise that Our Lady of Częstochowa is just as revered and relevant today as she was when she first made Częstochowa the spiritual heartland of Poland.

Marika McAdam, author

KRAKÓW'S JEWISH LEGACY

Eating smoked chicken in wine sauce and other traditional Jewish food with my friend Kevin while listening to live *klezmer* (traditional Jewish music) on the main square of Kazimierz (p186), Kraków's ancient Jewish quarter, which was emptied by the Nazis in 1943 – it's eerie and ineffably sad.

Richard Samson, Lonely Planet, England

MARK DAFFEY

10 TOP POLISH PEAK

Mt Rysy (p304): one of the jewels of the Tatras and the highest peak in Poland.

Jayjaywallace, Bluelist contributor

KRZYSZTOF DYDYNSKI

11 ROAMING THE BIESZCZADY

I tarried for a weekend in the extreme southeast corner of Poland, where I was joined by old friends. We toured Bieszczady National Park (p281) in the back of a Jeep, encountering Boyk and Lemk villages abandoned or destroyed after WWII, ancient cemeteries, peat reserves (complete with quicksand) and even a decapitated stag shot by poachers from over the border in Ukraine.

Steve Fallon, author

WROCŁAW: ISLAND CITY

Wrocław (p313) is really an interesting city with a lot of history, which shows in the buildings in the main square. The city is a maze of islands that are well connected but you can catch boats for a ride along the river.

jillm6355, Bluelist contributor

WITOLD SKRYPCZAK

12

LAKESIDE SOLITUDE

After a day rushing around, I spent the last two hours of sunshine paddling around Lake Wigry (p159) with only a few fishing birds and fishermen for company. I couldn't have wished for a better way to relax – in Poland's pristine outdoors, with hardly a soul in sight, and a warm sun on my back.

Neal Bedford, author

LOOKGALERIA / ALAMY

13

CZORSZTYN CASTLE

This ancient ruin served as a national fortress and refuge ground for fleeing royals. Czorsztyn castle (p303) invites you to see the walls that survived the Mongol invasion of 1241, but that later fell in a heap of ash after a bolt of lightning.

Izabel, Bluelist contributor

14

WITOLD SKRYPCZA

TORUŃ: COPERNICUS' BIRTHPLACE

Astronomer Copernicus was born in 1473 in the city of Toruń (p436). Toruń's Old Town is listed among the Unesco World Heritage sites. The house where Copernicus was born and spent childhood and the cathedral where he was christened are still standing in medieval Toruń.

Sihi, Bluelist contributor

15

CRAIG PERSHOUSE

Contents

Regional Map Contents

Pomerania p404
Warmia & Masuria p480
Mazovia & Podlasie p122
Wielkopolska p371
Warsaw p84
Silesia p314
Małopolska p211
Kraków p165
The Carpathian Mountains p260

Destination Poland

Overrun countless times by marauding aggressors, subjugated to overbearing foreign rule for centuries, and now told their beloved vodka can be made from *anything*, the Polish nation has endured more than most. Yet Poland, a country crushed flat so many times it has become indestructible, is shaking off the last vestiges of forced slumber and rushing with great abandon into a modern 21st century.

This massive land in the heart of Europe has become the epitome of a changing continent. Now a member of the EU, it is enjoying the rewards – and experiencing the challenges – of this exclusive club. Money has begun to flow into the country, repairing roads, building shopping malls and beautifying streets, but the progress is laboriously slow for some. Poland still has an unemployment rate twice as high as some of its EU compatriots, and its young, educated citizens are leaving in droves for wealthier pastures.

Despite the country's rush to embrace the future, its past cannot be ignored, particularly when it confronts you at every turn. Warsaw may be embracing New World cuisine, café culture and clubs that never close, but you'll still encounter peasant women selling bunches of flowers in its beautifully reconstructed Old Town. Drive across the country's northern expanse and you'll stumble upon a string of 14th-century Gothic castles, the last remnants of the once powerful Teutonic Knights. Catch a no-frills flight to Kraków or Wrocław and you'll arrive in magnificent medieval centres. Or choose almost any major city – and too many small towns – and you'll bear witness to extermination camps, derelict Jewish cemeteries, and dark political prisons, terrible reminders from the last 70 years.

While the country's cities rapidly modernise, its countryside continues to retain its rustic allure. In Poland's southern reaches, dominated by tree-clad mountains, the cliché of horse-drawn carts transporting hay from the fields still holds true. Bucolic splendour spreads from the outskirts of urban centres as far as the eye can see, and pockets of primeval forest in the northeast shelter herds of wild bison. The clear waters of the Great Masurian Lakes prove irresistible to sailors and kayakers, and the long, sandy beaches of the Baltic coast provide ample opportunity for summer seaside sojourns.

It is, however, in this rural expanse that Poland's populist politicians gained a groundswell of support, which swept a conservative coalition government to power in 2005. Internally some saw it as a step backwards, and the then government's anti-gay stance, ultra-Catholic bent and draconian intentions drew a rash of opprobrious criticism. Externally, Poland's political moves in the last two years have also caused headaches; relations with Germany sank to an all-time low since the fall of communism, and friction with Russia rose to unsettling levels. However, elections in October 2007 changed Poland's political landscape once again, with the liberal Civic Platform party winning the majority of votes. Many breathed a sigh of relief, not least other EU leaders, who will now deal with the more pragmatic and pro-EU Prime Minister Donald Tusk.

Yet Poland and its people should not be judged by the actions of its politicians. Poles remain doggedly warm and generous despite the massive upheavals, something many visitors can attest to. Even if you protest profusely, you will be forced to polish off a bottle of vodka or two, eat

FAST FACTS

Population: 38.9 million
(December 2005)

Area: 312, 685 sq km

GDP (per head):
US$15,900 (2007)

Inflation: 1.3% (2006)

Unemployment: 12%
(August 2007)

Number of lakes: 9000

Number of bison in the
wild: 700

Annual vodka spending:
US$2.6 million

Proportion of population who are practising Roman Catholics: 75%

Proportion of population who died in WWII: 20%
(UK 0.9%; USA 0.2%)

plate after plate of *bigos* (cabbage and meat stew), and join intense discussions on philosophy and politics, but it's comforting to know that it's all done with a love of life and an appreciation for the present, because no-one can be sure what tomorrow will bring. But don't take our word for it: spend some time here and you'll discover a unique land where East meets West and helpings of joy and sorrow have been served up in equal proportions. And you'll come away with new-found admiration for this unbreakable country.

Getting Started

Poland is a user-friendly country that even the most disorganised traveller should find relatively easy to navigate. While a little bit of planning never goes astray, at least to pinpoint a few must-see attractions, no huge amount of advance planning is needed. Plus anything you forget to pack can be picked up in-country, and English is widely spoken in the main tourist areas.

WHEN TO GO

A country this size has enough going on to make it a year-round destination, but most people visit when the weather is warmer, from May to October. The tourist season peaks in July and August, when schools and universities are on holiday and most Polish workers and employees take their annual leave. It's a time when things can get very crowded, particularly in tourist hot spots such as the Baltic beaches, Great Masurian Lakes and Carpathian Mountains. The likes of Kraków and Warsaw can also seem overrun with visitors during the peak.

See Climate Charts (p505) for more information.

Naturally, in July and August transport becomes more crowded too, and can get booked out in advance. Accommodation may be harder to find, and sometimes more expensive. Fortunately, a lot of schools, which are empty during the holidays, double as youth hostels, as do student dormitories in major cities. This roughly meets the demand for budget accommodation. Most theatres are closed in July and August.

If you want to avoid the masses, the best time to come is either late spring/early summer (mid-May to June) or the turn of summer and autumn (September to October), when tourism is under way but not in full flood. These are pleasantly warm periods, ideal for general sightseeing and outdoor activities such as walking, biking, horse riding and canoeing. Many cultural events take place in both these periods.

The rest of the year, from mid-autumn to mid-spring, is colder and darker. This doesn't mean that it's a bad time for visiting city sights and enjoying the cultural life as it's no less active than during the tourist season. Understandably, hiking and other outdoor activities – aside from skiing – are less prominent in this period. Most camping grounds and youth hostels shut up shop at this time.

The ski season runs from December to March. The Polish mountains are spectacular, but the infrastructure (hotels and chalets, lifts and tows, cable cars, transport etc) is still not well developed. Zakopane, Poland's winter capital, and the nearby Tatra Mountains have the best ski facilities.

COSTS & MONEY

Though not the bargain it used to be, Poland is still a relatively inexpensive country for travellers. Just how inexpensive, of course, depends largely on what degree of comfort you need, what hotel standards you are used to, what kind of food you eat, where you go, how fast you travel and the means of transport you use. If, for example, you are accustomed to hire cars and plush hotels, you can spend as much as you would in Western Europe.

A budget traveller prepared for basic conditions and willing to endure some discomfort on the road could get by on a daily average of around US$35 to US$40. This amount would cover accommodation in cheap hotels and hostels, food in budget restaurants, travel at a reasonable pace by train or bus, and still leave you a margin for some cultural events, a few beers and occasional taxis. If you plan on camping or staying in youth hostels and eating in cheap bistros and other self-services, it's feasible to cut this average down to US$25 per day without experiencing too much suffering. Cities are more expensive than the rural areas, with Warsaw and Kraków being the most expensive.

In general, Poland's admission to the EU has yet to have a marked effect on prices countrywide. In major centres, such as Warsaw, Kraków and Gdańsk, there has been a slight rise in costs across the board, but not to the extent seen in Western Europe.

READING UP

You will get far more out of your visit if you read up on the country before you go. There's no shortage of English-language books about Poland, though most deal with language, culture and customs rather than actual travel experiences.

The evocative writing of Bruno Schulz in *Street of Crocodiles* captures life in his small village of Drogobych (now in Ukraine) before WWII. His descriptions are gorgeous and quite brilliant.

In *The Bronski House,* accomplished travel writer Philip Marsden accompanies exiled poet Zofia Hinska on a return to her childhood village, now in Belarus. It's a magical retelling of life among the landed gentry of eastern Poland between the wars.

Ted Simon's account of his 2400km walk from Germany to Romania via Poland in *The Gypsy In Me* is a tale of travel through postcommunist Eastern Europe and a moving personal quest for family origins.

On Foot to the Golden Horn, by Jason Godwin, follows the journey of three friends on their walk from Gdańsk to Istanbul soon after the fall of communism. Although a tad dated, the book is a great snapshot of the time.

Despite there being little in the way of travel in *A Traveller's History of Poland* by John Radzilowski, it's still a fine read and a good introduction to the roller-coaster ride that is Poland's history.

Rising '44, by Norman Davies, provides an enthralling account of Warsaw's second uprising against the Nazis. The book's highlights are personal tales of Poles and Germans involved in the terrible battle.

For further background literature, look out for bookshops around the world specialising in Eastern Europe; **Polonia Bookstore** (www.polonia.com) in the USA, for example, stocks an extensive collection. Online, the **Instytut Książki** (The Book Institute; www.instytutksiazki.pl) has a wealth of information on Polish authors and literature in general.

HOW MUCH?

Double room in midrange hotel 200zł

Cinema ticket 16zł

1L of vodka 40zł

Tram ticket in Warsaw 2.40zł

100km bus trip 15-18zł

LONELY PLANET INDEX

1L of petrol 4.50zł

1.5L of bottled water 2.50zł

0.5L of Żywiec beer 5-7zł

Souvenir T-shirt 15zł

Zapiekanki (Polish pizza) 3.50zł

DON'T LEAVE HOME WITHOUT...

▪ your travel-insurance policy details (p510)

▪ a few words of Polish and a Polish phrasebook (p533)

▪ good walking shoes for urban and rural exploration

▪ a taste for vodka – Poles will expect you to join in

▪ a hangover remedy

▪ a smile, as you won't see many on the streets because smiling at strangers is seen as a sign of stupidity

▪ insect repellent in summer

▪ student card for cheap deals (p507)

TOP 10

Warsaw •

POLAND

Germany

POLES YOU SHOULD KNOW

Poland's history is filled with famous figures, but we've listed 10 who will keep popping up on your travels.

1 Frédéric Chopin (p53)

2 Nicolaus Copernicus (p481)

3 Marie Curie (p95)

4 Tadeusz Kościuszko (p33)

5 Jan Matejko (p56)

6 Adam Mickiewicz (p51)

7 Józef Piłsudski (p35)

8 Jan III Sobieski (p32)

9 Lech Wałęsa (p39)

10 Karol Józef Wojtyła/Pope John Paul II (p261)

MUST-SEE MOVIES

Films are a great way to gain an insight into a country's character, or at the very least a nice way to spend an evening. Here are our 10 best films by Polish directors; most are in Polish (except for *The Pianist* and *Three Colours: White*) but are available with English subtitles. See p52 for more on Polish cinema.

1 *Kanał* (Canal; 1957) Director: Andrzej Wajda

2 *Nóż w wodzie* (Knife in the Water; 1962)
   Director: Roman Polański

3 *Rejs* (The Cruise; 1970)
   Director: Marek Piwowski

4 *Człowiek z marmaru* (Man of Marble; 1976)
   Director: Andrzej Wajda

5 *Miś* (Teddy Bear; 1981)
   Director: Stanisław Bareja

6 *Przesłuchanie* (Interrogation; 1982)
   Director: Ryszard Bugajski

7 *Dekalog* (The Decalogue; 1987)
   Director: Krzysztof Kieślowski

8 *Three Colours: White* (1994)
   Director: Krzysztof Kieślowski

9 *Dług* (The Debt; 1999)
   Director: Krzysztof Krauze

10 *The Pianist* (2002) Director: Roman Polański

LITERATURE

The depth of Polish literature is immense. Here's a list of 10 of the best books, all of which are available in English. See p50 for more on Polish literature.

1 *A Minor Apocalypse* (1984) Tadeusz Konwicki

2 *Ashes and Diamonds* (1958)
   Jerzy Andrzejewski

3 *Dreams and Stones* (2004) Magdalena Tulli

4 *Pan Tadeusz* (1834) Adam Mickiewicz

5 *Prawiek and Other Times* (1996)
   Olga Tokarczuk

6 *Quo Vadis* (1905) Henryk Sienkiewicz

7 *Solaris* (1961) Stanisław Lem

8 *The Peasants* (1924)
   Władysław Reymont

9 *Under Western Eyes* (1911) Joseph Conrad

10 *View with a Grain of Sand* (1995)
   Wisława Szymborska

INTERNET RESOURCES

Experience Poland (www.experiencepoland.com) Offers a wide range of general information on travelling in Poland.

Lonely Planet (www.lonelyplanet.com) Check out the Thorn Tree bulletin board for fresh advice from travellers. The site also has general information and links to Poland-related sites.

Poland.pl (www.poland.pl) General directory site, an excellent place to start surfing.

Polish National Tourist Office (www.polandtour.org) Official site for general tourist information.

Polska (www.poland.gov.pl) Good, all-round site for tourists and businesspeople alike, run by the Ministry of Foreign Affairs.

Travel Poland (www.travelpoland.com) Reliable online accommodation-booking service.

Warsaw Voice (www.warsawvoice.pl) Covers Poland's current affairs.

TRAVELLING SUSTAINABLY

Since our inception in 1973, Lonely Planet has encouraged our readers to tread lightly, travel responsibly and enjoy the serendipitous magic independent travel affords. International travel is growing at a jaw-dropping rate, and we still firmly believe in the benefits it can bring – but, as always, we encourage you to consider the impact your visit will have on the global environment and the local economies, cultures and ecosystems.

In general Poland is still suffering the side effects of communist ideals. As one environmentalist put it, under communism everyone owned Poland, so in effect no-one owned Poland. Therefore no-one took responsibility, or accountability, for nature. The idea of sustainable development and tourism is slowly catching on, and the opportunities to support both the local economy and environment are growing year by year.

For more information on the environmental issues facing Poland, see the Environment chapter (p68).

Getting There & Away

If you're Europe-based, it's easy to travel to Poland by bus, train or boat. Of course it may be a long journey, but there's nothing like a trip across the continent. If air travel is your only option, or you simply can't face sitting in a bus or train for a day, consider offsetting your carbon emissions (the respected www.climatecare.org can organise this for you).

Local Transport

Poland may be a big country, but there's no real reason to use air-bound transport. Electric-powered trains, which leave no direct carbon footprint and are a wonderful way to see the country, extensively cover Poland, and it's no more than a day's train ride from one Polish town to another. And if trains don't go there, buses do. Cycling is an alternative option for travelling the country, as bicycles can be taken on trains, thereby allowing you to avoid long, arduous stretches on two wheels. Almost every town and city has an extensive public-transport system, employing buses, trolleybuses or electric trams; normally it's a far more convenient way to see a place than by car.

Accommodation & Food

Poland's accommodation range is wide, so it's generally an easy task to avoid the large, generic hotel chains and choose smaller, family-run places, thus ensuring your tourist dollar directly benefits the local community. Environmental awareness, however, is still a work in progress, with only a handful of hotels providing a choice to opt out of daily towel service, and even fewer separating their waste for recycling.

Agrotourist accommodation, pensions and private rooms are also excellent alternatives, where you can be sure your money remains with the owners.

It's simple to pick up local produce in Poland – most towns and cities have market days where farmers from the surrounding areas sell their homegrown fruit, vegetables and flowers. Unless it's certified organic there's no guarantee it's free of chemical sprays, but there's a good chance it is. Under communism, most farmers were unable to afford chemical pesticides or fertilisers so were inadvertently organic producers, and there has been a major increase in organic farming in the past few years.

As for eating responsibly, European bison (p149) is sometimes seen on menus. It's legal meat, but, considering the animal's tiny population, it shouldn't be and you're best to avoid it.

Responsible Travel Organisations

There are a number of organisations in Poland working towards the development of sustainable tourism. They include the following:

Association for Ecotourism Development (www.ekoturystyka.org)
European Bison Programme (www.zbs.bialowieza.pl/zubr)
Institute for Sustainable Development (www.ine-isd.org.pl)
Polish Environmental Partnership Foundation (www.epce.org.pl)
WWF Poland (www.wwf.pl)

Itineraries
CLASSIC ROUTES

HITTING THE HIGHLIGHTS   Two Weeks / Gdańsk to Kraków
This route runs north to south – with a detour to the northeast of the country –
and takes in Poland's top attractions.

Begin with a day in the grand old port city of **Gdańsk** (p403), then head
east to the **Great Masurian Lakes** (p490) for some water-based exploration
(or relaxation). On the way to the lakes, stop at **Malbork** (p448) to see the
celebrated castle.

From the lakes, it's an easy journey to **Białowieża National Park** (p147) and
its primeval forest and European bison herds, before heading to **Warsaw**
(p82). Spend at least two days discovering the capital city, then continue
south to Poland's 'other capital', **Kraków** (p162), which merits at least
another two days' exploration.

Kraków is a convenient base for day trips to two more top sights – the
strange, subterranean world of the **Wieliczka Salt Mine** (p192), and the chilling Nazi extermination camp at **Auschwitz-Birkenau** (p357) in Oświęcim,
40km to the west. Spend the final two or three days hiking amid the
stunning scenery of the **Tatra National Park** (p306).

This 1250km route
takes in Poland's
biggest sights,
starting in the far
north of the coun-
try and ending in
the far south. By car
it can be completed
in two weeks, in
three weeks if using
public transport.

ALONG THE VISTULA

Four Weeks / Kraków to Gdańsk

The Vistula is Poland's greatest river, winding its way from the foothills of the country's southern mountain range to the Baltic Sea. It passes through – or close to – a string of historical towns and imposing castles.

Begin upstream with two or three days at the former royal capital of **Kraków** (p162) and take a day tour to **Auschwitz-Birkenau** (p357) in Oświęcim. From Kraków it's 120km to **Baranów Sandomierski** (p228) and its beautiful Renaissance castle, and then only a short distance to **Sandomierz** (p224), a town with impressive architectural variety and few tourists. From here, it's worth taking a detour to the Renaissance masterpiece of **Zamość** (p250), one of Poland's finest historic towns.

Back on the path of the Vistula, stop in at picturesque **Kazimierz Dolny** (p241) before hitting **Warsaw** (p82) and indulging in its delights for a couple of days. Back on the road, call in at **Płock** (p134), Poland's art nouveau capital, then follow the river into Pomerania and through the heart of medieval **Toruń** (p436).

Soon after Toruń the river makes a sharp right and heads directly for the sea. In former times, the Vistula's path was guarded by one Teutonic stronghold after the next – today, these gothic gems silently watch the river pass by. You can see the Teutonic Knights' handiwork at **Chełmno** (p444), **Kwidzyn** (p447) and **Gniew** (p447), but the mightiest example resides at **Malbork** (p448), on the banks of one of the river's sidearms. End your journey at the port city of **Gdańsk** (p403), where river meets sea.

This road trip follows the Vistula River as it carves its way 2000km through Poland's lush landscape. It touches on some of the country's larger and lesser-known sights, and takes between three and four weeks to complete.

ROADS LESS TRAVELLED

THE EASTERN MARCHES   Three Weeks / Kraków to Suwałki

Poland's most popular sights lie along the Gdańsk–Warsaw–Kraków–Tatra axis that runs north–south through the country. To get off the beaten track, head for the eastern marches, borderlands running along the frontier with Ukraine and Belarus, where few visitors venture.

From **Kraków** (p162) head towards the southeastern corner of the country, stopping off at **Bóbrka** (p287), home to the world's first oil well. Make for **Sanok** (p274), with its skansen and icon museum, and devote a couple of days to exploring the remote **Bieszczady National Park** (p281).

Turn north, and take the back roads to the Renaissance town of **Zamość** (p250), by way of **Przemyśl** (p270) and its quirky Museum of Bells & Pipes. Continue to **Chełm** (p247), where you can explore the chalk tunnels beneath the town square, and then on to **Lublin** (p232).

Strike out north through the rural backwaters of eastern Poland to the pilgrimage site of **Grabarka** (p152), with its hill of 20,000 crosses, before making for **Hajnówka** (p146) and **Białowieża National Park** (p147).

Then it's north again to the provincial city of **Białystok** (p139), which provides a base for visiting the wooden **mosques** (p145) near the Belarusian border and the mysterious wetlands of **Biebrza National Park** (p143).

Finish with a short trip to the lake resort of **Augustów** (p153). From nearby **Suwałki** (p157) catch a train back to Warsaw, or on to Vilnius in Lithuania.

This 1200km trip is most easily done by car (allow two to three weeks), but it's also possible by public transport (which will take about four weeks). It would also make an interesting bicycle tour (six weeks for the whole route).

WESTERN WANDERINGS
Three Weeks / Wrocław to Szczecin

Poland's western expanse is largely ignored by tourists more eager to sample the country's big guns such as Kraków and the Great Masurian Lakes. This is, however, a vibrant place with one lively town after another and a coastline lined with sandy beaches right to the German border.

Base yourself in **Wrocław** (p313) for a few days and avail yourself of its eclectic architectural mix, full cultural calendar and selection of day trips, including the splendid **Książ Castle** (p332). From Wrocław it's an easy step to **Zielona Góra** (p367), Poland's only wine-producing town, and then on to **Poznań** (p372), Wielkopolska's commercial heart and bustling main city.

Visit the eccentric castle at **Kórnik** (p386), only 20km southeast of Poznań, then move on to **Gniezno** (p389), the cradle of the Polish state. Spend a day exploring the town and its mammoth Gothic cathedral, then head north to **Biskupin** (p394), a reconstructed Iron Age village. The sizable city of **Toruń** (p436) is the next port of call, followed by a visit to the Gothic fortifications at **Chełmno** (p444).

From here, it would be easy to make for Gdańsk, but just as rewarding is an exploration of Poland's Baltic coast. Head northwest to dune-filled **Słowiński National Park** (p457) and then follow the coastline west towards Germany and the popular seaside resort of **Kołobrzeg** (p462). Continue west and pull up just short of the border at **Świnoujście** (p468), another of Poland's summer playgrounds. It's only a short trip south to **Szczecin** (p471), a busy port with a mishmash of architecture.

Covering 1200km of Poland's western expanse, this road trip hits some intriguing towns and the best of the country's sandy coastline. Allow two to three weeks by car, four weeks by public transport.

TAILORED TRIPS

UNESCO WORLD HERITAGE SITES

Poland's numerous world heritage sites are mainly human-made efforts scattered the length and breadth of the country.

No less than four old town centres make the esteemed list. The painstakingly reconstructed centre in **Warsaw** (p91) is one, along with medieval **Toruń** (p436), Renaissance **Zamość** (p252) and the granddaddy of them all, **Kraków** (p172).

Poland is covered in castles, but none can compare to the magnificent example at **Malbork** (p448). The country isn't short of a church or two either, but the timber-and-clay Church of Peace at **Świdnica** (p329) and the sublime wooden churches of the Carpathian Foothills, including **Dębno Podhalańskie** (p303), **Haczów** (p287) and **Sękowa** (p291), will even wow heathens.

Within easy reach of Kraków is the pilgrimage site of **Kalwaria Zebrzydowska** (p259), the weird and wonderful **Wieliczka Salt Mine** (p192) and the Nazi extermination camp at **Auschwitz-Birkenau** (p357) in Oświęcim.

The newest addition to the list is Wrocław's **Centennial Hall** (p322), a landmark in the history of reinforced concrete, while more down-to-earth is the **Białowieża National Park** (p147), Mother Nature's only entry.

BEACHES & WATERWAYS

Water isn't the first thing to spring to mind when thoughts turn to Poland. But water aplenty there is, if you know where to look.

The Baltic coast is lined with a string of swimming beaches, starting at **Świnoujście** (p468) on the border with Germany and ending in the fashionable seaside resort of **Sopot** (p425). In between there's **Międzyzdroje** (p466), **Kołobrzeg** (p462), **Darłowo** (p461), **Ustka** (p460) and **Łeba** (p455), all of which offer clean, sandy seashores and a seaside lifestyle. Poking out into the Gulf of Gdańsk is **Hel Peninsula** (p433), with arguably the best beaches in Poland.

Heading inland to sweeter waters, the **Elbląg-Ostróda Canal** (p486) offers a unique boat trip, while the **Great Masurian Lakes** (p490) have all manner of water-bound possibilities. Further east, the **Augustów-Suwałki Region** (p152) has its fair share of waterways, such as **Lake Wigry** (p159), the **Czarna Hańcza River** (p154) and the **Augustów Canal** (p156).

Not to be outdone are the **Biebrza** (p143) and **Narew** (p144) national parks, which have gentle kayaking opportunities.

OUTDOOR ADVENTURE

With its wide-open spaces, pristine forests, thousands of lakes, long coast-line and southern mountain range, Poland has plenty for the outdoor enthusiast. The question then is not which activity to pursue, but where, and for how long?

The tall peaks and forest-clad slopes of the Carpathian Mountains area almost has it all, with some of the country's best trekking options in the **Tatras** (p304), an extensive array of mountain biking for all experience levels in the **Bieszczady** (p274), gentle rafting in the **Dunajec Gorge** (p301) and skiing, snowboarding and snowman-building in **Zakopane** (p306). Not to be outdone, the **Great Masurian Lakes** (p490) come up trumps with the best sailing and kayaking opportunities in the country; here you can spend weeks exploring the region's sparkling lakes and plethora of tributaries. The rivers in this area also provide a chance to enjoy watery adventures; two of the most celebrated, the **Krutynia River** (p481) and **Czarna Hańcza River** (p154) can be found in the far north. Salt-water junkies can get a fix with windsurfing and kitesurfing along the long, thin **Hel Peninsula** (p433), while those who prefer to be in, rather than on, the water can explore one of the many swimming beaches that line the coastal expanse of northern and western Pomerania – **Kołobrzeg** (p462) is among the most popular spots to take a dip.

Less strenuous but equally rewarding activities are spread throughout the Mazovia and Podlasie areas. It's pure soul-food cycling through age-old **Białowieża Forest** (p147) and **Augustów Forest** (p157), which spread east to the Belarusian border. There are enough paths here to keep cycling enthusiasts entertained for days, but if getting around on two wheels isn't your thing, they can just as easily be enjoyed on foot. Budding ornithologists can avail themselves of the ample bird-watching possibilities at **Biebrza National Park** (p143), which contains riverscapes, peat bogs, marshlands and damp forests within its borders.

History

Poland's history is an immense tale. Forever sandwiched between two powerful and aggressive neighbours, it has over the past millennium defended its freedom and sovereignty on innumerable occasions, only to be overrun and subjugated to occupation by foreign powers time and time again. It has gone from being the largest country in Europe to completely disappearing off the world map, and seen its population devastated in two world wars. Yet it is testament to the astounding resilience of the Polish people that Poland has not only bounced back from every crushing blow but also had the energy to hold strong to its own culture.

BEFORE THE POLES

The lands of modern-day Poland have been inhabited since the Stone Age, with numerous tribes from the east and west calling its fertile plains home. Archaeological finds from both the Stone and Bronze Ages can be seen in many Polish museums, but the greatest example of pre-Slavic peoples resides in Biskupin (p394); its fortified town from the Iron Age was built by the Lusatian tribe around 2700 years ago. The Celts, followed by the Germanic tribes and then the Baltic folk, all established themselves on Polish soil, but it wasn't until the coming of the Slavs that Poland began to shape itself into a nation.

SLAVIC ORIGINS

Although the exact date of the arrival of the first Slavic tribes is unknown, historians agree that the Slavs began settling the area between the 5th and 8th centuries. From the 8th century onwards, smaller tribes banded together to form greater conglomerations, thus establishing themselves more fully on the lands of the future Polish state. The country's name derives from one of these tribes, the Polanie (literally, 'the people of the fields, open-country dwellers'), who settled on the banks of the Warta River near present-day Poznań. Their tribal chief, the legendary Piast, managed to unite the scattered groups of the surrounding areas into a single political unit in the 10th century, and gave it the name Polska (later Wielkopolska, meaning Great Poland). It wasn't until the coming of Piast's great-great grandson, Duke Mieszko I, that much of Poland was united under one dynasty.

THE FIRST POLISH KINGDOM

After Duke Mieszko I converted to Christianity, he did what most early Christian rulers did and began conquering the neighbours. Soon the entire

TIMELINE

Before AD 500	966	970s
Establishment of the first Polish town, Gniezno, by Lech, one of three mythical brothers who in legend founded the three Slavic nations (Poland, Ruthenia and Bohemia).	Polska's first recorded ruler, Duke Mieszko I, converts to Christianity, possibly as a political move against Otto the Great. It marks the date of the formal birth of the Polish state.	Duke Mieszko I builds Poland's first cathedral at Gniezno, and a second at Poznań. The Catholic religion begins its long hold on the Polish people.

coastal region of Pomerania (Pomorze) fell under his sovereignty, along with Śląsk (Silesia) to the south and Małopolska (Little Poland) to the southeast. By the time of his death in 992, the Polish state was established within boundaries similar to those of Poland today, and the first capital and archbishopric were established in Gniezno. By that time, towns such as Gdańsk, Szczecin, Poznań, Wrocław and Kraków already existed. Mieszko's son, Boleslaw the Brave, continued his father's work, even pushing the Polish border as far east as Kyiv. His son, Mieszko II, was less successful in the conquering department, and during his reign the country experienced wars in the north and a period of internal fighting within the royal family. The administrative centre of the country was moved from Wielkopolska to the less vulnerable Małopolska, and by the middle of the 11th century, Kraków was established as the royal seat.

When pagan Prussians, from the region that is now the northeastern tip of Poland, attacked the central province of Mazovia in 1226, Duke Konrad of Mazovia called for help from the Teutonic Knights (p451), a Germanic military and religious order that had made its historic mark during the Crusades. The knights soon subjugated the pagan tribes but then bit the hand that fed them, building massive castles in Polish territory, conquering the port city of Gdańsk (and renaming it Danzig), and effectively claiming all of northern Poland as their own. They ruled from their greatest castle of all, at Malbork (p448), and within a matter of decades became a major European military power.

KAZIMIERZ III & REUNIFICATION

Not until 1320 was the Polish crown restored and the state reunified. It was under the rule of Kazimierz III Wielki (Casimir III the Great; 1333–70) that Poland gradually became a prosperous and powerful state, despite concessions being made to Bohemia in the southwest and the Teutonic Knights in the north. Kazimierz Wielki regained suzerainty over Mazovia, then captured vast areas of Ruthenia (today's Ukraine) and Podolia, thus greatly expanding his monarchy towards the southeast.

Kazimierz Wielki was also an enlightened and energetic ruler on the domestic front. Promoting and instituting reforms, he laid down solid legal, economic, commercial and educational foundations. He also passed a law providing privileges for Jews, thus establishing Poland as a safe house for the Jewish community for centuries to come. Over 70 new towns were founded, and the royal capital of Kraków flourished. In 1364 one of Europe's first universities was established at Kraków, and an extensive network of castles and fortifications was constructed to improve the nation's defences. There is a saying that Kazimierz Wielki 'found Poland built of wood and left it built of stone'.

1038	1241–42	1364
Under the rule of Piast Kazimierz I, the Polish capital is moved from Gniezno to Kraków. The southern city would remain the seat of royal Poland for the next 550 years.	Mongol invasions leave not only Poland, but also much of Europe, in ruin. This leaves room for German settlers to move east into Poland, but also Poland to expand eastwards into Ukraine.	Kraków University, Europe's second after Prague University, is established. It paves the way for higher learning in Poland.

THE JAGIELLONIAN DYNASTY (1382–1572)

The close of the 14th century saw Poland forge a dynastic alliance with Lithuania, a political marriage that increased Poland's territory five-fold overnight and that would last for the next four centuries. The union benefited both parties – Poland gained a partner in skirmishes against the Tatars and Mongols, and Lithuania received help in the fight against the Teutonic Knights. Under Władysław II Jagiełło (1386–1434), the alliance defeated the Knights and recovered eastern Pomerania, part of Prussia and the port of Gdańsk, and for 30 years the Polish empire was Europe's largest state, extending from the Baltic to the Black Sea.

Jews in Poland: a Documentary History, by Iwo Cyprian Pogonowski, provides a comprehensive record of half a millennium of Polish-Jewish relations in Poland.

Eastward Advance Checked

But it was not to last. Threat of invasion became apparent towards the end of the 15th century – this time the main instigators were the Ottomans from the south, the Tatars of Crimea from the east, and the tsars of Moscow from the north and east. Independently or together, they repeatedly invaded and raided the eastern and southern Polish territories, and on one occasion managed to penetrate as far as Kraków.

Poland's Golden Age

Despite this, the Polish kingdom's power was firmly established and the country advanced both culturally and spiritually. The early 16th century brought the Renaissance to Poland and during the reigns of Zygmunt I Stary (Sigismund I the Old; 1506–48) and his son Zygmunt II August (Sigismund II Augustus; 1548–72), the arts and sciences flourished. This was Poland's golden age, which spawned the likes of Nicolaus Copernicus (p481).

The bulk of Poland's population at this time was made up of Poles and Lithuanians but included significant minorities from neighbouring countries. Jews constituted an important and steadily growing part of the community and by the end of the 16th century Poland had a larger Jewish population than the rest of Europe combined.

On the political front, Poland evolved during the 16th century into a parliamentary monarchy with most of the privileges going to the *szlachta* (gentry, the feudal nobility), who comprised roughly 10% of the population. In contrast, the status of the peasants declined, and they gradually found themselves falling into a state of virtual slavery.

Hoping to strengthen the monarchy, the Sejm convened in Lublin in 1569, unified Poland and Lithuania into a single state, and made Warsaw the seat of future debates. Since there was no heir apparent to the throne, it also established a system of royal succession based on direct voting in popular elections by the nobility, who would all come to Warsaw to vote. In the absence of a serious Polish contender, a foreign candidate would be considered.

1410	1493	1541
Polish and Lithuanian forces defeat the Teutonic Knights at the Battle of Grunwald. The decisive victory is a major turning point for Poland, ridding the country of the Teutonic threat once and for all.	Poland's lower house of parliament, or Sejm, is established. The first Sejm consists of bishops and noblemen, and is largely present to keep an eye on the monarchy.	Nicolaus Copernicus proposes that the earth orbits the sun, and changes the course of science forever. Poles say that Copernicus 'stopped the sun and moved the earth'.

ROYAL REPUBLIC (1573–1795)

From the very beginning, the experiment proved disastrous. For each royal election, foreign powers promoted their candidates by bargaining and bribing voters. During this period, no fewer than 11 kings ruled Poland; only four were native Poles.

Alliances & Expansion

The first elected king, Henri de Valois, retreated to his homeland to take up the French crown after only a year on the Polish throne. His successor, Stefan Batory (Stephen Bathory; 1576–86), prince of Transylvania, was a much wiser choice. Batory, together with his gifted commander and chancellor Jan Zamoyski, conducted a series of successful battles against Tsar Ivan the Terrible and came close to forming an alliance with Russia against the Ottoman threat.

After Batory's premature death, the crown was offered to the Swede Zygmunt III Waza (Sigismund III Vasa; 1587–1632), and during his reign Poland achieved its greatest extent ever, more than three times the size of present-day Poland. Despite this, Zygmunt is best remembered for moving the Polish capital from Kraków to Warsaw between 1596 and 1609.

Eastern Interlopers & the Deluge

The beginning of the 17th century marked a turning point in Poland's fortunes. The increasing political power of the Polish nobility undermined the authority of the Sejm; the country was split up into several huge private estates, and nobles, frustrated by ineffective government, resorted to armed rebellion.

Meanwhile, foreign invaders were systematically carving up the land. Jan II Kazimierz Waza (John II Casimir Vasa; 1648–68), the last of the Vasa dynasty on the Polish throne, was unable to resist the aggressors – Russians, Tatars, Ukrainians, Cossacks, Ottomans and Swedes – who were moving in on all fronts. The Swedish invasion of 1655–60, known as the Deluge, was particularly disastrous.

The last bright moment in the long decline of the Royal Republic was the reign of Jan III Sobieski (John III Sobieski; 1674–96), a brilliant commander who led several victorious battles against the Ottomans. The most famous of these was the Battle of Vienna in 1683, in which he defeated the Turks and checked their advancement into Western Europe.

The Rise of Russia

By the start of the 18th century, Poland was in severe decline and Russia had evolved into a mighty, expansive empire. The tsars systematically strengthened their grip over the flailing country, and Poland's rulers effectively became puppets of the Russian regime. This became crystal clear during the reign of

1569	1573	1596–1609
The Kingdom of Poland and the Grand Duchy of Lithuania unite as a single state in an attempt to counteract the rising threat of the Moscow tsars. The union lasts until 1791.	Religious freedom is constitutionally established by the Sejm and equality of creeds guaranteed. Faiths such as Roman Catholicism, Eastern Orthodoxy, Protestantism, Judaism and Islam are able to coexist relatively peacefully.	After 550 years, Kraków loses the capital crown to Warsaw. The city is chosen as the seat of Polish power because of its central location, and closer proximity to Vilnius.

Stanisław August Poniatowski (1764–95), when Catherine the Great, empress of Russia, exercised direct intervention in Poland's affairs. The collapse of the Polish empire was just around the corner.

THE THREE PARTITIONS

As Poland languished, Russia, Prussia and Austria gained in strength. The end of the 18th century was a disastrous period for the country, with the neighbouring powers agreeing to partition Poland on no fewer than three separate occasions in a span of 23 years. The First Partition led to immediate reforms and a new, liberal constitution, and Poland remained relatively stable. Catherine the Great could tolerate no more of this dangerous democracy though, and sent Russian troops into Poland. Despite fierce resistance the reforms were abolished by force and the country was partitioned a second time.

Legendary lover Casanova spent some time in Warsaw in the 1760s but was forced to flee following a duel with a Polish aristocrat.

Enter Tadeusz Kościuszko, a hero of the American War of Independence. With the help of patriotic forces, he launched an armed rebellion in 1794. The campaign soon gained popular support and the rebels won some early victories, but Russian troops, stronger and better armed, defeated the Polish forces within a year. Resistance and unrest remained within Polish borders, which led the three occupying powers to the third and final partition. Poland disappeared from the map for the next 123 years.

Polish Resistance & Resilience

Despite the partitions, Poland continued to exist as a spiritual and cultural community, and a number of secret nationalist societies were created. Since revolutionary France was seen as their major ally in the struggle, some leaders fled to Paris and established their headquarters there.

The Ottoman Empire, though an ancient enemy of the Poles, was the only European power that never recognised the Partition of Poland.

In 1815 the Congress of Vienna established the Congress Kingdom of Poland, but Russian oppression continued. In response, armed uprisings broke out, the most significant of which occurred in 1830 and 1863. An attempted insurrection against the Austrians also occurred in 1846.

In the 1870s Russia dramatically stepped up its efforts to eradicate Polish culture, suppressing the Polish language in education, administration and commerce, and replacing it with Russian. However, it was also a time of great industrialisation in Poland, with cities like Łódź experiencing a booming economy. With the outbreak of WWI in August 1914, the fortunes of Poland changed once again.

WWI (1914–18)

WWI resulted in Poland's three occupying powers going to war. On one side were the Central Powers, Austria-Hungary and Germany (including Prussia); on the other, Russia and its Western allies. Most of the fighting was staged in Polish lands, resulting in staggering losses of life and livelihood. Since no formal Polish state existed, there was no Polish

1655–60	1683	1772
During the Deluge, Poland loses over a quarter of its territory, cities are burned and plundered, the countryside devastated and economy destroyed. From a population of 10 million, four million succumb to war, famine and bubonic plague.	Jan III Sobieski leads a Polish force in a battle against the Ottomans at the gates of Vienna. His victory saves the city and its rulers from the Turkish threat, but in turn weakens Poland's own military defences.	First Partition of Poland at the instigation of Catherine the Great. Russia, Prussia and Austria annex substantial chunks of the country, amounting to roughly 30% of Polish territory.

army to fight for the national cause. Even worse, some two million Poles were conscripted into the Russian, German or Austrian armies, and were obliged to fight one another.

Paradoxically, the war eventually brought about Polish independence. After the October Revolution in 1917, Russia plunged into civil war and no longer had the power to oversee Polish affairs. The final collapse of the Austrian empire in October 1918 and the withdrawal of the German army from Warsaw in November brought the opportune moment. Marshal Józef Piłsudski took command of Warsaw on 11 November 1918, declared Polish sovereignty, and usurped power as the head of state.

RISE & FALL OF THE SECOND REPUBLIC

Poland began its new incarnation in a desperate position – the country and its economy lay in ruins, and an estimated one million Poles had lost their lives in WWI. All state institutions – including the army, which hadn't existed for over a century – had to be built up from scratch.

The Treaty of Versailles in 1919 awarded Poland the western part of Prussia, providing access to the Baltic Sea. The city of Gdańsk, however, was omitted and became the Free City of Danzig. The rest of Poland's western border was drawn up in a series of plebiscites, which resulted in Poland acquiring some significant industrial regions of Upper Silesia. The eastern boundaries were established when Polish forces defeated the Red Army during the Polish-Soviet war of 1919–20.

When Poland's territorial struggle ended, the Second Republic covered nearly 400,000 sq km and had a population of 26 million. One-third was of non-Polish ethnic background, mainly Jews, Ukrainians, Belarusians and Germans.

After Piłsudski (opposite) retired from political life in 1922, the country experienced four years of unstable governments until the great military commander seized power once again in a military coup in May 1926. Parliament was gradually phased out but, despite the dictatorial regime, political repression had little effect on ordinary people. The economic situation was relatively stable, and cultural and intellectual life prospered.

On the international front, Poland's situation in the 1930s was unenviable. In an attempt to regulate relations with its two inexorably hostile neighbours, Poland signed nonaggression pacts with both the Soviet Union and Germany. Nevertheless, it soon became clear that the pacts didn't offer any real guarantee of safety.

On 23 August 1939 a pact of nonaggression between Germany and the Soviet Union was signed in Moscow by their foreign ministers, Ribbentrop and Molotov. This pact contained a secret protocol defining the prospective partition of Eastern Europe between the two great powers. Stalin and Hitler planned to carve up the Polish state between themselves.

Marshal Józef Piłsudski's most famous quotation was: 'To be defeated and not to submit, that is victory; to be victorious and rest on one's laurels, that is defeat.'

3 May 1791	**1793**	**1795**
The world's second written constitution (the first was that of the USA) is signed in Warsaw, by then a city of 120,000 inhabitants. It places peasants under direct protection of the government, and thereby attempts to wipe out serfdom.	Second Partition of Poland, with Russia and Prussia strengthening their grip by grabbing over half the remaining Polish territory. Poland shrinks to around 200,000 sq km and a population of four million.	Third Partition of Poland. The country ceases to exist completely, and only becomes a republic after the end of WWI.

PIŁSUDSKI – PATRIOT, SOLDIER, STATESMAN

Father of the Polish republic, military mastermind of the Miracle on the Vistula, and victor over the might of the Soviet army, Marshal Józef Piłsudski is revered in Poland as a patriot, soldier and statesman.

Piłsudski was born in 1867 in the Russian-occupied Vilnius region and joined the anti-tsarist movement while still a teenager. He spent many of his formative years in prison – first five years in Siberia, then a brief stint in Warsaw's Citadel before being sent to a jail in St Petersburg. After escaping from St Petersburg, he returned to Poland and began, with the help of *acquired* Russian funds, to develop the Polish Legions, the military force that fought under his leadership during WWI. At the end of the war Marshal Piłsudski entered Warsaw, took power on 11 November 1918, and proclaimed Poland a sovereign state. The Russian Revolution, however, had created a new enemy in the east.

In 1919 Piłsudski launched a massive offensive towards the east, capturing vast territories that had been Polish before the 18th-century partitions. A Soviet counteroffensive reached as far as Warsaw, but in the Battle of Warsaw in August 1920, the Polish army, under Piłsudski, outmanoeuvred and defeated the Red Army.

Once an independent Poland was safely back on the map and a modern democratic constitution had been adopted in 1921, Piłsudski stepped down in 1922. Disillusioned with economic recession and governmental crisis, he reappeared on the political scene in May 1926. In a classic coup d'etat, he marched on Warsaw at the head of the army, resulting in three days of street fighting that left 400 dead and over 1000 wounded. After the government resigned, the National Assembly elected Piłsudski as president but he refused to take the post, opting instead for the office of defence minister, which he maintained until his death. There are few doubts, though, that it was Piłsudski who ran the country behind the scenes until he died in 1935. Despite his dictatorial style, he was buried with ceremony among Polish kings in the crypt of Kraków's Wawel Cathedral.

WWII (1939–45)

WWII began at dawn on 1 September 1939 with a massive German invasion of Poland. Fighting began in Gdańsk (at that time the Free City of Danzig) when German forces encountered a stubborn handful of Polish resisters at Westerplatte. The battle lasted a week. Simultaneously, another German line stormed Warsaw, which finally surrendered on 28 September. Despite valiant resistance there was simply no hope of withstanding the numerically overwhelming and well-armed German forces; the last resistance groups were quelled by early October. Hitler's policy was to eradicate the Polish nation and Germanise the territory. Hundreds of thousands of Poles were deported en masse to forced-labour camps in Germany, while others, primarily the intelligentsia, were executed in an attempt to exterminate spiritual and intellectual leadership.

The Jews were to be eliminated completely. At first they were segregated and confined in ghettos, then shipped off to extermination camps scattered around

One of the great myths of WWII is that Polish cavalry charged against German tanks in the opening stages. In reality a Polish cavalry regiment destroyed a German infantry division, and was then counter-attacked by German armour. Nazi propaganda tried to twist the event into a symbol of Polish backwardness.

1807	**1810**	**1815**
Napoleon Bonaparte establishes the Duchy of Warsaw after crushing the Prussians on Polish soil. After Napoleon's defeat at the hands of the Russians, the duchy returns to the Russian and Prussian fold.	Birth of Frédéric Chopin, Poland's most beloved musician and a perennial favourite around the world.	Congress Kingdom of Poland is established at the Congress of Vienna. The Duchy of Warsaw is swept away and Poland once again falls under the control of the Russian tsar.

Auschwitz – The Nazis and the Final Solution is a BBC documentary that attempts to deal with the horrific events at Auschwitz.

the country. Almost the whole of Poland's Jewish population (three million) and roughly one million Poles died in the camps. Resistance erupted in numerous ghettos and camps, most famously in Warsaw (see boxed text, p99).

Soviet Invasion

Within a matter of weeks of the Nazi invasion, the Soviet Union moved into Poland and claimed the country's eastern half. Thus, Poland was yet again partitioned. Mass arrests, exile and executions followed, and it's estimated that between one and two million Poles were sent to Siberia, the Soviet Arctic and Kazakhstan in 1939–40. Like the Nazis, the Soviets set in motion a process of intellectual genocide; see below for more information.

A Surplus of Memory: Chronicle of the Warsaw Ghetto Uprising, by Yitzhak Zuckerman, is a detailed narrative of this heroic act of Jewish resistance.

Government-in-Exile & Homegrown Resistance

Soon after the outbreak of war, a Polish government-in-exile was formed in France under General Władysław Sikorski, followed by Stanisław Mikołajczyk. It was shifted to London in June 1940 as the front line moved west.

The course of the war changed dramatically when Hitler unexpectedly attacked the Soviet Union on 22 June 1941. The Soviets were pushed out of eastern Poland by the onslaught and all of Poland lay under Nazi control.

MASSACRE AT KATYŃ

In April 1943, German troops fighting Soviet forces on the eastern front came across extensive mass graves in the forest of Katyń, near Smolensk, in present-day Belarus. Exploratory excavations revealed the remains of several thousand Polish soldiers and civilians who had been executed. The Soviet government denied all responsibility and accused the Nazis of the crime. After the Communists took power in Poland the subject remained taboo, even though Katyń was known to most Poles.

It wasn't until 1990 that the Soviets admitted their 'mistake', and two years later finally made public secret documents showing that Stalin's Politburo was responsible for the massacre. Meanwhile, in the summer of 1991, further mass graves of Polish soldiers were discovered in Myednoye and Kharkov, both in central Russia.

The full horror of Katyń was finally revealed during exhumations of the mass graves by Polish archaeologists in 1995–96. Soon after their invasion of Poland in September 1939, the Soviets took an estimated 180,000 prisoners, comprising Polish soldiers, police officers, judges, politicians, intellectuals, scientists, teachers, professors, writers and priests, and crammed them into various camps throughout the Soviet Union and the invaded territories. On Stalin's order, signed in March 1940, about 21,800 of these prisoners, including many high-ranking officers, judges, teachers, physicians and lawyers, were transported from the camps to the forests of Katyń, Myednoye and Kharkov, shot dead and buried in mass graves. The Soviet intention was to exterminate the intellectual elite of Polish society, and eliminate the driving force and the leadership of the nation.

No-one has been brought to trial for the atrocity, as Russia states that Katyń was a military crime rather than a genocide, war crime, or crime against humanity.

1830	1863	19th Century
First of a number of insurrections against the ruling Russians, known as the November Insurrection. Within a year the rebellion is defeated, and executions and deportations of Poles to Siberia begins.	January Insurrection against Russian rule. The insurgency is ruthlessly crushed, and Russia abolishes Congress Poland, or the Kingdom of Poland. Polish lands and its citizens are incorporated directly into the Russian Empire.	At the end of the century around four million Poles, from a total population of 20 to 25 million, emigrate to avoid harsh Russian rule. Most go to the USA, thus laying foundations for the large Polish communities that exist there today.

The Führer set up camp deep in Polish territory (see boxed text, p492), and remained there for over three years.

A nationwide resistance movement, concentrated in the cities, had been put in place soon after war broke, to operate the Polish educational, judicial and communications systems. Armed squads were set up by the government-in-exile in 1940, and these evolved into the Armia Krajowa (AK; Home Army), which figured prominently in the Warsaw Rising (see boxed text, below).

Amazingly, considering the Soviet treatment of Poles, Stalin turned to Poland for help in the war effort against the German forces advancing eastwards towards Moscow. The official Polish army was re-formed late in 1941, but was largely under Soviet control.

The Tide Turns

Hitler's defeat at Stalingrad in 1943 marked the turning point of the war on the eastern front, and from then on the Red Army successfully pushed westwards. After the Soviets liberated the Polish city of Lublin, the pro-Communist Polish Committee of National Liberation (PKWN) was installed on 22 July 1944 and assumed the functions of a provisional government. A week later the Red Army reached the outskirts of Warsaw.

When God Looked the Other Way, by Wesley Adamczyk, is a gripping and terrible tale of a Polish family deported to southern Siberia in WWII.

THE WARSAW RISING

In early 1944, with German forces retreating across Poland in the face of an advancing Soviet army, the Polish resistance (AK; Armia Krajowa) in Warsaw was preparing for the liberation of their city. On 1 August 1944, orders were given for a general anti-German uprising, with the intention of establishing a Polish command in the city before the Red Army swept through.

The initial rising was remarkably successful and the AK, creating barricades from ripped-up paving slabs and using the Warsaw sewers as underground communication lines, took over large parts of the city. They hoped to control the city until support came from both the Allies and the Soviets. But none arrived. The Allies were preoccupied with breaking out of their beachhead in Normandy after the D-day landings, and the Red Army, which was camped just across the Vistula River in Praga, didn't lift a finger. On learning of the rising, Stalin halted the offensive and ordered his generals not to intervene or provide any assistance in the fighting, instead allowing the Germans to break the back of any potential Polish resistance to a Communist takeover of the country.

The Warsaw Rising raged for 63 days before the insurgents were forced to surrender; around 200,000 Poles were killed. The Nazi revenge was brutal – Warsaw was literally razed to the ground, and, on Hitler's orders, every inhabitant was to be killed. It wasn't until 17 January 1945 that the Soviet army finally marched in to 'liberate' Warsaw, which by that time was little more than a heap of empty ruins.

For the Poles, the Warsaw Rising was one of the most heroic – and most tragic – engagements of the war. The events of the rising are commemorated in the Warsaw Rising Museum (p99) and the Monument to the Warsaw Uprising (p93).

1903	1914	11 Nov 1918
Warsaw-born Marie Curie wins the Nobel prize for physics. She is the first woman to win the acclaimed prize, and becomes the first person to win two when she is awarded a second in 1911, this time for chemistry.	Start of WWI. The occupying powers – Germany and Austria to the west and south, Russia to the east – force Poles to fight each other on Polish soil.	Founding of the Second Republic, so named to create a symbolic bridge between itself and the Royal Republic that existed before the partitions. The new republic's borders are not fixed until 1922, after the end of the Polish-Russian War.

Winston Churchill
observed that 'Poland
was the only country
which never collaborated
with the Nazis in any
form and no Polish units
fought alongside the
German army'.

Warsaw at that time remained under Nazi occupation. In a last-ditch attempt to establish an independent Polish administration, the AK attempted to gain control of the city before the arrival of the Soviet troops (see boxed text, p37), with disastrous results. The Red Army continued its westward advance across Poland, and after a few months reached Berlin. The Nazi Reich capitulated on 8 May 1945.

At the end of WWII, Poland lay in ruins. Over six million people, about 20% of the prewar population, lost their lives, and out of three million Polish Jews in 1939, only 80,000 to 90,000 survived the war. Its cities were no more than rubble; only 15% of Warsaw's buildings survived. Many Poles who had seen out the war in foreign countries opted not to return to the new political order.

POSTWAR: SOVIET CONTROL

At the Yalta Conference in February 1945, Roosevelt, Churchill and Stalin agreed to leave Poland under Soviet control. They agreed that Poland's eastern frontier would roughly follow the Nazi–Soviet demarcation line of 1939. Six months later, Allied leaders set Poland's western boundary along the Odra (Oder) and the Nysa (Neisse) Rivers; in effect, the country returned to its medieval borders.

You can find a library of
wartime photographs
chronicling the horror
and destruction of the
Warsaw Rising at www
.warsawuprising.com.

The radical boundary changes were followed by population transfers of some 10 million people: Poles were moved into the newly defined Poland while Germans, Ukrainians and Belarusians were resettled outside its boundaries. In the end, 98% of Poland's population was ethnically Polish.

As soon as Poland formally fell under Soviet control, Stalin launched an intensive Sovietisation campaign. Wartime resistance leaders were charged with Nazi collaboration, tried in Moscow and summarily shot or sentenced to arbitrary prison terms. A provisional Polish government was set up in Moscow in June 1945 and then transferred to Warsaw. General elections were postponed until 1947 to allow time for the arrest of prominent Polish political figures by the secret police. After rigged elections, the new Sejm elected Bolesław Bierut president; Stanisław Mikołajczyk, accused of espionage, fled back to England.

The website www.polish
roots.org/genpoland
/polhistory.htm shows
how Poland's borders
have shifted over the past
200 years since Partition.

In 1948 the Polish United Workers' Party (PZPR), henceforth referred to as 'the Party', was formed to monopolise power, and in 1952 a Soviet-style constitution was adopted. The office of president was abolished and effective power passed to the first secretary of the Party Central Committee. Poland became an affiliate of the Warsaw Pact.

Bread & Freedom

Stalinist fanaticism never gained as much influence in Poland as in neighbouring countries, and soon after Stalin's death in 1953 it all but disappeared. The powers of the secret police declined and some concessions were made

August 1920	1 Sep 1939	17 Sep 1939
Poland defeats the Red Army in the Battle of Warsaw, known as the Miracle on the Vistula. The decisive battle helps to secure large portions of land that once resided in what is now Belarus and Ukraine.	Nazis use the Gleiwitz incident – a staged attack on a German radio station by Germans dressed as Polish soldiers – as grounds for invading Poland. The invasion on 1 September starts WWII.	The Soviet Union fulfils its side of the Molotov-Ribbentrop Pact, a blueprint for the division of Eastern Europe between it and Nazi Germany, and invades eastern Poland. Within a matter of weeks the country is swallowed up by its old enemies.

to popular demands. The press was liberalised and Polish cultural values were resuscitated.

In June 1956 a massive industrial strike demanding 'bread and freedom' broke out in Poznań. The action was put down by force and soon afterward Władysław Gomułka, a former political prisoner of the Stalin era, was appointed first secretary of the Party. At first he commanded popular support, but later in his term he displayed an increasingly rigid and authoritarian attitude, putting pressure on the Church and intensifying persecution of the intelligentsia. It was ultimately an economic crisis, however, that brought about his downfall; when he announced official price increases in 1970, a wave of mass strikes erupted in Gdańsk, Gdynia and Szczecin. Again, the protests were crushed by force, resulting in 44 deaths. The Party, to save face, ejected Gomułka from office and replaced him with Edward Gierek.

Another attempt to raise prices in 1976 incited labour protests, and again workers walked off the job, this time in Radom and Warsaw. Caught in a downward spiral, Gierek took out more foreign loans, but, to earn hard currency with which to pay the interest, he was forced to divert consumer goods away from the domestic market and sell them abroad. By 1980 the external debt stood at US$21 billion and the economy had slumped disastrously.

By then, the opposition had grown into a significant force, backed by numerous advisers from the intellectual circles. When, in July 1980, the government again announced food-price increases, the outcome was predictable: fervent and well-organised strikes and riots spread like wildfire throughout the country. In August, they paralysed major ports, the Silesian coal mines and the Lenin Shipyard in Gdańsk.

Unlike most previous popular protests, the 1980 strikes were nonviolent; the strikers did not take to the streets, but stayed in their factories.

> In 1944 Stalin was quoted as saying 'fitting communism onto Poland was like putting a saddle on a cow'.

SOLIDARITY

On 31 August 1980, after long, drawn-out negotiations in the Lenin Shipyard, the government signed the Gdańsk Agreement. It forced the ruling party to accept most of the strikers' demands, including the workers' right to organise independent trade unions, and to strike. In return, workers agreed to adhere to the constitution and to accept the Party's power as supreme.

Workers' delegations from around the country convened and founded Solidarity (Solidarność), a nationwide independent and self-governing trade union. Lech Wałęsa, who led the Gdańsk strike, was elected chair.

It wasn't long before Solidarity's rippling effect caused waves within the government. Gierek was replaced by Stanisław Kania, who in turn lost out to General Wojciech Jaruzelski in October 1981. However, the trade union's greatest influence was on Polish society. After 35 years of

> Learn more about the communist years at www.ipn.gov.pl, the website of the Institute of National Remembrance.

19 April 1943	1 August 1944	Feb–Aug 1945
Start of Ghetto Uprising in Warsaw. The Jewish resistance fighters hold out against overwhelming German forces for almost a month.	Start of the Warsaw Rising. The entire city becomes a battleground, and after the uprising is quelled, Warsaw is systematically razed.	Poland's borders are redrawn. The Soviet Union annexes 180,000 sq km to the east, while the Allies return 100,000 sq km of Poland's western provinces after centuries of German rule.

restraint, the Poles launched themselves into a spontaneous and chaotic sort of democracy. Wide-ranging debates over the process of reform were led by Solidarity, and the independent press flourished. Such taboo historical subjects as the Stalin-Hitler pact and the Katyń massacre could, for the first time, be openly discussed.

The Polish Revolution: Solidarity 1980-82, by Timothy Garton Ash, is an entertainingly written insight into a 16-month period that undermined the whole communist system.

Not surprisingly, the 10 million Solidarity members represented a wide range of attitudes, from confrontational to conciliatory. By and large, it was Wałęsa's charismatic authority that kept the union on a moderate and balanced course.

The government, however, under pressure from both the Soviets and local hardliners, was loath to introduce any significant reforms and systematically rejected Solidarity's proposals. This only led to further discontent and, in the absence of other legal options, more strikes. Amid fruitless wrangling, the economic crisis grew more severe. After the unsuccessful talks of November 1981 between the government, Solidarity and the Church, social tensions increased and led to a political stalemate.

MARTIAL LAW & ITS AFTERMATH

When General Jaruzelski unexpectedly appeared on TV in the early hours of the morning of 13 December 1981 to declare martial law, tanks were already on the streets, army checkpoints had been set up on every corner, and paramilitary squads had been posted to possible trouble spots. Power was placed in the hands of the Military Council of National Salvation (WRON), a group of military officers under the command of Jaruzelski himself.

Mad Dreams, Saving Graces: Poland, a Nation in Conspiracy, by Michael T Kaufman, is a trip through the dark times of martial law and the gloomy period up until 1988 – as readable as it is informative.

Solidarity was suspended and all public gatherings, demonstrations and strikes were banned. Several thousand people, including most Solidarity leaders and Wałęsa himself, were interned. The spontaneous demonstrations and strikes that followed were crushed, military rule was effectively imposed all over Poland within two weeks of its declaration, and life returned to the pre-Solidarity norm.

In October 1982 the government formally dissolved Solidarity and released Wałęsa from detention, but the trade union continued underground on a much smaller scale, enjoying widespread sympathy and support. In July 1984 a limited amnesty was announced and some members of the political opposition were released from prison. But further arrests continued, following every public protest, and it was not until 1986 that all political prisoners were freed.

COLLAPSE OF COMMUNISM

The election of Gorbachev in the Soviet Union in 1985 and his *glasnost* and *perestroika* programmes gave an important stimulus to democratic reforms all through Eastern Europe. By early 1989 Jaruzelski had softened his position and allowed the opposition to challenge for parliamentary seats.

1947	1953	June 1956
Despite Stanisław Mikołajczyk – the government-in-exile's only representative to return to Poland after the war – receiving over 80% of the popular vote in elections, 'official' figures hand power to the communist government.	Ruling communists arrest Cardinal Stefan Wyszyński, the primate of Poland's Catholic Church. He is first imprisoned then placed under house arrest in the Bieszczady Mountains. Wyszyński is finally released three years later.	Poland's first industrial strike, at Cegielski factories in Poznań. Around 100,000 people take to the streets; the Soviet Union crushes the revolt with tanks, leaving 76 dead and over 900 wounded.

Semifree elections were held in June 1989, in which Solidarity succeeded in getting an overwhelming majority of its supporters elected to the Senat, the upper house of parliament. The communists, however, reserved for themselves 65% of seats in the Sejm. Jaruzelski was placed in the presidency as a stabilising guarantor of political changes for both Moscow and the local communists, but the noncommunist prime minister, Tadeusz Mazowiecki, was installed as a result of personal pressure from Wałęsa. This power-sharing deal, with the first noncommunist prime minister in Eastern Europe since WWII, paved the way for the domino-like collapse of communism throughout the Soviet bloc. The Party, haemorrhaging members and confidence, historically dissolved itself in 1990.

Free Market

In January 1990 the government's finance minister Leszek Balcerowicz introduced a package of reforms to change the centrally planned communist system into a free-market economy. His shock-therapy economics allowed prices to move freely, abolished subsidies, tightened the money supply, and sharply devalued the currency, making it fully convertible with Western currencies.

The effect was almost instant. Within a few months the economy appeared to have stabilised, food shortages became glaringly absent, and shops filled up with goods. On the downside, prices skyrocketed and unemployment exploded. The initial wave of optimism and forbearance turned into uncertainty and discontent, and the tough austerity measures caused the popularity of the government to decline.

LECH WAŁĘSA'S PRESIDENCY

In November 1990 Wałęsa won the first fully free presidential elections and the Third Republic of Poland was born. During his statutory five-year term in office, Poland witnessed no fewer than five governments and five prime ministers, each struggling to put the newborn democracy back on track.

After his election, Wałęsa appointed Jan Krzysztof Bielecki, an economist and his former adviser, to serve as prime minister. His cabinet attempted to continue the austere economic policies introduced by the former government but was unable to retain parliamentary support and resigned after a year in office. No less than 70 parties contested the country's first free parliamentary elections in October 1991, the result of which placed Prime Minister Jan Olszewski at the head of a centre-right coalition. Olszewski lasted only five months, falling prey to a no-confidence vote, and was replaced by Hanna Suchocka of the Democratic Union in June 1992. Suchocka was the nation's first woman prime minister, and became known as the Polish Margaret Thatcher. Her coalition government managed to command parliamentary majority, but was in increasing discord over many issues, and failed to survive a no-confidence vote in June 1993.

1970	1978	November 1980
West German chancellor Willy Brandt signs the Warsaw Treaty, a document that formally recognises the country's borders. Brandt famously kneels in front of a monument to the victims of the Warsaw Ghetto Uprising.	Karol Wojtyła, archbishop of Kraków, becomes Pope John Paul II. His election and triumphal visit to his homeland a year later dramatically increase political ferment.	Solidarity, the first noncommunist trade union in a communist country, formally recognised by the government. Its membership numbers 10 million (60% of the workforce), a million of which comes from the Party's ranks.

Communist Comeback

The impatient Wałęsa stepped in, dissolving parliament and calling a general election. His decision was a gross miscalculation, with the postcommunist opposition succeeding in swaying public opinion with accusations of mismanagement and indifference to the social cost of reforms by the Solidarity-led coalition. The pendulum swung to the left, and the election resulted in a coalition between the Democratic Left Alliance (SLD) and the Polish Peasant Party (PSL), both reformed Communist parties from the pre-1989 era.

The new government, headed by PSL leader Waldemar Pawlak, continued with general market reform, but the economy began to slow. Continuous tensions within the coalition caused its popularity to fall, and its running battles with the president brought further change in February 1995, when Wałęsa threatened to dissolve parliament unless Pawlak was replaced. The fifth and final prime minister of Wałęsa's presidential term was Józef Oleksy, yet another former Communist Party official.

Wałęsa's presidential style and his accomplishments were repeatedly questioned by practically all political parties and the majority of the electorate. His quirky behaviour and his capricious use of power prompted a slide from the favour he had enjoyed in 1990 to his lowest-ever level of popular support in early 1995, when polls indicated that only 8% of the country preferred him as president for the next term. Despite this, Wałęsa manoeuvred vigorously and, in a miraculous comeback, went close to achieving a second term.

POSTCOMMUNISTS IN POWER

The November 1995 election was essentially a tight duel between the anticommunist folk figure, Lech Wałęsa, and the much younger, one-time communist technocrat and SLD leader, Aleksander Kwaśniewski. Kwaśniewski finished ahead, but only by a margin of 3.5%.

Włodzimierz Cimoszewicz, another former Communist Party official, took the post of prime minister. In effect, the postcommunists gained a stranglehold on power, controlling the presidency, government and parliament – a 'red triangle', as Wałęsa warned. The centre and the right – almost half of the political nation – effectively lost control over the decision-making process. The Church, much favoured by Wałęsa during his term in the saddle, also lost out and didn't fail to caution the faithful against the danger of 'neopaganism' under the new regime.

Balance Returned

By 1997 the electorate apparently realised things had gone too far. Parliamentary elections in September were won by an alliance of about 40 small Solidarity offshoot parties, collectively named the Solidarity

13 Dec 1981	April 1989	1990
Martial law declared in Poland. It is debatable whether the coup is Soviet driven or an attempt by the Polish Communists to prevent Soviet military intervention. Martial law lasts until 22 July 1983.	Poland becomes the first Eastern European state to break free of communism. In so-called round-table negotiations, Poland's opposition is allowed to stand for parliament and Solidarity is re-established.	Not a great year for Polish Communists. The Party dissolves, the first democratic presidential election takes place, the country becomes a free market economy, and bananas become freely available.

Electoral Action (AWS). The alliance formed a coalition with the centrist liberal Freedom Union (UW), pushing ex-communists into opposition. Jerzy Buzek of AWS became prime minister, and the new government accelerated the country's privatisation.

President Kwaśniewski's political style sharply contrasted with that of his predecessor, Wałęsa. Kwaśniewski brought political calm to his term in the post, and was able to cooperate successfully with both the left and right wings of the political establishment. This gained him a remarkable degree of popular support, and paved the way to another five-year term in office.

No fewer than 13 people contested the presidential election in October 2000, but none came close to Kwaśniewski, who won a sweeping victory, capturing 54% of the vote. The centrist businessman Andrzej Olechowski came a distant second, with 17% support, while Wałęsa, trying his luck for the third time, suffered a disastrous defeat, collecting just 1% of the vote.

TOWARDS EUROPE

On the international front, Poland had been granted full NATO membership in March 1999, while back home the September 2001 parliamentary election changed the political axis once again. SLD staged its great second comeback, taking 216 seats in the Sejm, just 15 short of an outright majority. The party formed a coalition with the PSL, repeating the shaky alliance of 1993, and former senior Communist Party official Leszek Miller took up the position of prime minister.

Poland's biggest move in the 21st century was its inclusion into the EU fold on 1 May 2004. The next day, Miller resigned due to a string of corruption scandals and amid mounting popular unrest over high unemployment and poor living standards. His replacement, respected economist Marek Belka, lasted until elections in September 2005, when the conservative Law and Justice (PiS) party and the liberal-conservative Citizens Platform (PO) party swept to power. Combined, the two gained 288 out of the 460 Sejm seats; in comparison, SLD won only 55. PiS member Kazimierz Marcinkiewicz was nominated prime minister, and one month later another PiS member, Lech Kaczyński, secured the presidential seat.

POLAND TODAY

Unsurprisingly, Marcinkiewicz didn't last long, resigning in July 2006 over a reputed rift with PiS leader Jarosław Kaczyński. Jarosław, the twin brother of the president, was quickly appointed to the position. The new prime minister soon set about upsetting both Russia and Germany, attempting to derail the EU's reform treaty, loading public media with his supporters, and alienating many young Poles with his national rhetoric.

Norman Davies' two-volume *God's Playground: a History of Poland* is beautifully written, easy to read and a perfect key to understanding 1000 years of the Polish nation. *The Heart of Europe: a Short History of Poland* is a condensed version, with a greater emphasis on the 20th century.

1995	1997	1999
Aleksander Kwaśniewski wins the presidential election over legendary figure Lech Wałęsa by the slimmest of margins (51.7% to 48.3% in a second round of voting), despite his adversary polling poorly in the lead-up to the election.	New constitution passed in October to replace the Soviet-style document in force since 1952 (though amendments had been made in 1992 to correspond with the postcommunist status quo).	Poland becomes a member of NATO. The country has come full circle, moving from the Warsaw Pact with the former Soviet Union to an alliance with the powers of the West.

However, his reign was short-lived – in a snap election in October 2007 Jarosław lost out to the more liberal and EU-friendly Donald Tusk and his Civic Platform party.

Despite the myriad reforms and coalitions, Poland is still floundering in the political and economic stakes, and looks as though it will for some years to come. But considering its tumultuous past, the country has found some stability, and is relishing its self-governance and peace.

1 May 2004	July 2006	October 2007
Poland joins the EU. Despite massive support, there is a fear that the country is swapping one foreign governing power for another, and EU membership will spark a wave of emigration, particularly by the young and well educated.	Twin brothers Lech and Jarosław Kaczyński occupy the presidential and prime minister seats respectively. Their nationalistic and conservative policies alienate many people.	Donald Tusk's liberal Civic Platform party wins a snap election against Jarosław Kaczyński's conservative PiS party. Pro-EU supporters, both within Poland and across Europe, breathe a sigh of relief.

The Culture

THE NATIONAL PSYCHE

Polish people are a resilient bunch – even the briefest glance at the country's history shows this to be true. They exude an age-old spirit of independence, and are remarkably adaptable and inventive, with each person forming their own solution for any dilemma, whether within the family or within the nation. This isn't always a good combination, as sometimes explanations on how things work in the country are not always forthcoming. This can be seen as indifference or an assumption of intelligence; knowing the Poles, it's probably a little of both.

Poles are not always realistic, and can be charmingly irrational and romantic at times. This penchant for dreaming could partly explain the country's astounding record in the fields of arts and science. They are often far more concerned with the present than the future, which is not always optimal (ie populist politics often wins the day). However this is changing, with a rising number of Poles taking an active part in the preservation of their cultural and natural heritage. For example, interest in Poland's Jewish culture is on the rise, and Polish people turned out in force to help save the Rospuda River (p158).

You'll rarely see Poles wearing bright colours or flashing a stranger a smile (the latter is seen as a sign of stupidity), yet at dinner, in a train carriage, or out in a group, they can be lively, boisterous, expressive, and ready to enjoy life to the fullest. Once you break the ice with most Poles, you'll find them warm and hospitable, and if you're lucky enough to make Polish friends, they will normally be extremely generous and open-handed. There's a traditional saying that 'a guest in the house is God in the house'. While they love jokes and are generally easy-going, they may suddenly turn serious and hot-blooded when it comes to an argument.

Homophobia is still rife in the country, and at times it can be shocking to hear homophobic comments loudly proclaimed in public, even by well-educated people. Officials have gone as far as to call for a psychological evaluation of the effect of Teletubbies' handbag-carrying Tinky Winky on the nation's children (he's a boy), although the matter has been treated fairly light-heartedly by most. Drinking in public is socially acceptable, and drunks stumbling around at 9am are a daily occurrence.

Not surprisingly, given Poland's history, the past, especially the events of WWII, still has a firm grip on the Polish national psyche. Every family has been directly affected by the Nazi occupation or communist regime, and there are physical reminders of terrible events in many towns and cities across the country. Entry into the EU is, even in a tiny way, helping to heal the wounds, with some Poles believing that the country is back in the European family. A fatalistic streak still haunts the population though, the result of Poland's past upheavals.

By and large, Poles are more conservative and traditional than Western Europeans, and the Roman Catholic religion plays an important role in this conservatism. For Poles, the Church's leading figure is still Pope John Paul II, who retains cult status in the country.

Polish men are passionate about handshaking, and always extend a hand when greeting friends, sometimes before a word is spoken. Women, too, often shake hands with men, but the man should always wait for the woman to offer her hand first. Older men may go so far as to greet a woman by kissing her hand; here, again, it's the woman who suggests such a form by a perceptible

By EU declaration, vodka can now be made of any agricultural material provided it is appropriately labelled. The ruling hasn't gone down well with the Poles, who argue that vodka can only be made from potatoes, grain and molasses.

rise of her hand. Flowers have a special place in Polish culture, and men love to give them to women. The rose was traditionally the flower reserved for special occasions, but there're no strict rules these days. What does still seem to be widely observed, however, is the superstition of presenting an odd, not an even, number of flowers. Flowers are especially important on name days, which is usually the Catholic feast day of the patron saint who shares your name, and less holy names have a date too. It's traditional for friends to give at least a single bloom on such days.

Poles aren't always strict about time. You may find yourself waiting a bit for your Polish friend to turn up for an appointed meeting; it's not rude, it's just the way it is. Likewise, if you are invited to dinner or a party in someone's home, don't arrive exactly on time or, God forbid, turn up early.

DAILY LIFE

Since the fall of communism, daily life in Poland has rapidly been converging with Western patterns. Shopping streets are now lined with high street brand names, TVs blare the latest American and German dramas and sitcoms, and no-one leaves home without their *komórka* (mobile phone). There is a huge appetite for self-improvement, and plenty of ambition to take advantage of the new opportunities offered by EU membership. City walls and lampposts are plastered with posters advertising courses in English, German and Russian, and diplomas in business studies and computer programming.

There is also a widening culture gap between the urban and rural communities. The old country ways are still very much alive in rural areas, where you'll see the family milk cow grazing by the roadside, people cutting and stacking hay by hand, and goods going to the market by horse and cart. Despite their urban existence, city dwellers still like to retain some connection with the countryside, and many escape to the hills or lakes at the weekends to enjoy a touch of rural lifestyle.

One habit that will probably never die is the country's devotion to the Roman Catholic Church. It plays a prominent role in the lives of most – Poland is one of Europe's most religious countries, with 75% of the population describing themselves as practising Catholics (the corresponding figure for France is 12%). On weekends many churches countrywide are filled to overflowing – even in Warsaw it can be standing room only, while in the countryside people, dressed in their Sunday best, use whatever means necessary (horse, cart, tractor, bicycle) to attend services. On weekdays Mass can still be half full. Even for nonreligious Poles, the Church remains important: it is the glue that binds many small communities together, and it has the eternal gratitude of the nation for leading the opposition against the communist regime.

Note that Poles don't appreciate intrusions during Mass, so unless you're there to pray, it's best to wait until it's over before entering a church.

ECONOMY

Since 1990, Poland has pursued a policy of economic liberalisation, and purely looking at the figures, it's paying off. The country's GDP has steadily risen since 2000, foreign investment is up (mainly through EU funds), exports are booming, and inflation is among the lowest in the EU. While the economy currently looks rosy, it may not be sustainable in the long term due to Poland's greatest economic hurdle, unemployment. The official figure sits at 12% but soars to 35% in some parts of the country and among Poland's youth.

Polish Customs, Traditions & Folklore (1996) by Sophie Hodorowitz Knab describes Poland's customs month-by-month, and is a useful resource for anyone wishing to understand the country better.

If you see a chimney sweep in Poland, the tradition is to grab another person's button, wait until you see someone wearing glasses, then make a wish.

POPULATION

Poland's population is one of the most ethnically homogenous in the world, with 96.7% of a population of just under 39 million claiming Polish ancestry. Of the remaining 3.3%, 0.4% is German, 0.1% Ukrainian, 0.1% Belarusian, and the final 2.7% is composed of a mixture of Russians, Jews, Lithuanians, Tatars, Roma (Gypsies), Lemks, Boyks and a dozen other groups. The smaller minorities barely rate a presence in Poland, as most groups total less than 5000 members.

The ethnic make-up is largely a result of massive migratory movements in Poland during the aftermath of WWII (see p38). However, Poland was for centuries one of Europe's most cosmopolitan countries, with quite a mixed and varied population. It was also home to the continent's largest Jewish community (see p35), but today Polish Jews only number between 5000 and 10,000.

Population density varies considerably throughout the country, with Upper Silesia being the most densely inhabited area, while the northeastern border regions remain the least populated. Over 70% of the country's inhabitants now live in towns and cities, compared with 30% in the 1930s. Warsaw is by far the largest Polish city (1.7 million), followed by Łódź (768,000) and Kraków (752,700).

SPORT

Like most European countries, *piłka nożna* (soccer) stands head and shoulders above other sports in Poland. Millions play the game, at least at a social level. The country's national team is, by European standards, fairly mediocre today, but in the '70s and '80s it was a force to be reckoned with, taking third place in the World Cup competitions of 1974 and 1982. At a national league level, Wisła Kraków (www.wisla.krakow.pl) and Legia Warszawa (www.legia.com in Polish) rank among the best.

Poles are also passionate about volleyball. Like its soccer compatriot, the men's national volleyball team was strong in the 1970s, capturing the World Championships in 1974 and Olympic gold in 1976. In recent years there has been a resurgence in the sport, with the men's team taking silver in the 2006 World Championships. Other sports on the fringes of nationwide support include basketball, cycling, athletics, kayaking and rowing. Poland's youth has discovered urban street sports in recent years; you'll encounter a rising number of teenagers on skateboards and bikes in the city centres, or trying their hand (and feet) at free running.

The website www.soccer way.com/teams/poland lists every soccer club in Poland and provides a link to their individual websites.

EMIGRATION & IMMIGRATION

According to rough estimates, between five and 10 million Poles live abroad, the result of two major episodes of emigration – one at the beginning of the 20th century and another during WWII. Emigration continued on a smaller scale after the war, particularly during the economic hardships of the '80s and '90s. The largest Polish émigré community lives in the USA; Chicago alone is reputed to be home to one million people of Polish extraction.

POLAND'S WINTER HERO

The winter sport of ski jumping has produced one of Poland's greatest sporting legends, Adam Małysz. At the end of the 2006–07 season, the quiet man from Wisła in the Silesian Beskids had won 38 World Cup competitions (the second-highest number ever), four World Cup trophies, and a silver and a bronze at the 2002 Winter Olympics in Salt Lake City. He is also the only person to win three World Cup championships in a row.

Since Poland's accession to the EU in 2004, approximately one million Poles have left the country, mainly destined for the UK and Ireland in search of higher paying jobs, or a job at all. Of these, around 80% are under the age of 34, taking with them skills that are proving difficult to replace. The construction and computer industries are hardest hit, and many workers from Belarus have crossed the border to fill the manual labour shortage. Workers are also being tempted from Asia and India, and after the 2008 Beijing Olympics there should be a marked increase in Chinese labour – their skills will be required to prepare the country's inadequate football venues for the 2012 UEFA European Championships.

MEDIA

Poland has the largest and most diverse broadcasting market in Eastern Europe and the country has had freedom of press since the fall of communism. Its TV and radio broadcasting is regulated by state-run Krajowa Rada Radiofonii i Telewizji (KRRiT, the National Council of Radio Broadcasting and Television). In theory a politically independent organisation, KRRiT has in the past few years been dogged by political scandal, most notably during the 2001 elections, when a number of its members were accused of falsifying laws and attempting to gain control over private media.

Around 300 newspapers are published in Poland. The country's largest-selling paper is German-owned *Fakt* (Fact), a tabloid-style daily with a readership of around seven million. In second place is *Gazeta Wyborcza* (Election Gazette), a liberal, opinionated newsprint owned by Polish publishing house Agora. Despite its highly independent slant, it has failed to escape political scandal (although it was the innocent party): in 2003 the paper was involved in an attempted bribery case, when Lew Rywin, a film director, allegedly solicited a bribe of $US17.5 million from editor Adam Michnik in exchange for an amendment in a media bill in favour of the paper. Rywin was accused of working on behalf of then prime minister Leszek Miller. Other popular rags include the moderately conservative *Rzeczpospolita* (the Republic), and weeklies *Wprost, Gazeta Polska,* and *Polityka*.

Telewizja Polska (TVP; Polish Television) is Poland's public TV broadcaster, operating two national channels (TVP1 and TVP2), a range of regional services, and the satellite channel TV Polonia. Its main competitor is Polsat, a commercial operator; other private TV networks include TVN and French-owned Cyfra+.

Radio doesn't have the influence that broadsheets and TV has over Poles. Polski Radio is the country's public sender, with five national stations and 17 regional ones. Outranking it in the popularity stakes is RMF FM, a privately run commercial station; Radio Zet, Warsaw's first private radio after communism ended, is another nationwide broadcaster with a solid commercial agenda. The country's most controversial radio station is Radio Maryja, an ultra-Catholic broadcaster accused of xenophobic and anti-Semitic rhetoric. It's reputedly the fifth most listened-to station in the country, with almost 900,000 people tuning in on a daily basis. The station and its founder, Catholic-nationalist Father Tadeusz Rydyzk, frequently make political ties – in 2004 the station heavily backed the League of Polish Families (LPR), and in 2007 President Lech Kaczyński and Prime Minister Jarosław Kaczyński put their weight behind the station in the run-up to the October 2007 elections.

RELIGION

Poland is a deeply religious country, with 95% of the population identifying as Roman Catholics. Minority faiths, including the Orthodox Church, Protestantism, Judaism, and Old Believers, make up the remaining 5%.

www.culture.pl is a website with news, profiles, essays, articles and listings on Polish culture.

POLAND'S CATHOLIC CHURCH TODAY

Following the collapse of communism in 1989, Poland's Roman Catholic Church moved swiftly to fill the vacuum left by the communist government, claiming land, power and the role of moral arbiter of the nation. When Lech Wałęsa became president he was the Church's most prominent supporter, and never went anywhere without a priest at his side.

The Church's interference in politics created marked changes in political priorities. In the early 1990s the crusade against abortion soared to the top of the agenda and pushed economic issues into the background. Abortion had been legalised in 1956 during the communist era, and served, in practice, as a common form of birth control. Even though only about 10% of the population supported a total ban on abortion, the Church achieved its aim and the parliament duly voted for an anti-abortion law, which was introduced in 1993. Moderates did manage to have amendments attached requiring that contraceptives be made available and that Polish schools begin providing sex education for the first time.

The Church also turned its attention to the younger generation, pressing for the reintroduction of religious instruction in schools. Voluntary religious education was introduced in primary schools in 1990 and became mandatory in 1992. A glut of young men studying for the priesthood led to a surplus of clergy, and priests became a new export item – many Catholic priests throughout Europe today are of Polish origin.

From around 1994, however, the Church began to lose some of its popular support, as a result of a gathering backlash against its early successes. The more liberal segments of the population began to feel a growing resentment at the compulsory religious instruction in public schools, the strong anti-abortion laws and the numerous privileges accorded to the Church, such as special treatment in the granting of electronic-media licences.

This unpopularity was compounded in 1995 when the Church contributed to the return to power of former communist politicians. This alienated a fair number of voters, who turned against the clerical militancy backed by Lech Wałęsa and voted instead for Aleksander Kwaśniewski in the 1995 presidential elections.

It took a long time for the Polish Church to make up its mind about Poland's accession to the EU. Despite the Polish Pope John Paul II being in favour, the Church only lent its support to the government campaign to promote EU membership on condition that Poland's existing abortion law remain in place.

In past times, Polish territory spanned the borders between Rome and Byzantium, and the Catholic Church (Kościół Katolicki) had to share its influence with other creeds, particularly the Orthodox Church (Kościół Prawosławny). In 1596 the Orthodox hierarchy in Poland split with Russian Orthodoxy and accepted the supremacy of the pope in Rome. This created the so-called Uniat Church (Kościół Unicki), often referred to as the Greek-Catholic Church (Kościół Greko-Katolicki). Despite the doctrinal change, the Uniat Church retained its traditional Eastern rites and liturgical language.

After WWII Poland's borders shifted west, and consequently the Orthodox Church is now present only along a narrow strip on the eastern frontier; its adherents number a little over 1% of the country's population, yet it is the second-largest creed after Roman Catholicism. Orthodox churches are recognisable by their characteristic onion-shaped domes.

The Uniat Church has an even smaller number of believers (at most 0.5%), mostly Ukrainians and Lemks who are scattered throughout the country because of forced resettlement imposed by the communist authorities in the aftermath of WWII.

Poland's Muslim community numbers only 500, most of whom live near two of the country's three mosques at Kruszyniany and Bohoniki (p145). The mosques were built by the Muslim Tatars in the 18th century.

WOMEN IN POLAND

Polish women have generally always been independent, resourceful, forthright, and they have a reputation for beauty. Traditionally, their role in society was that of mother and homemaker, but this attitude has slowly changed over the past few decades and the country's younger demographic is no longer satisfied with this conventional view. Nowadays women have the same study opportunities as their male counterparts (since the early 1980s in fact), are well represented in the white-collar workforce, and more and more are entering male-dominated sectors, such as the police force. But prejudice dies hard: some employers can be reluctant to employ younger women, afraid they'll soon get pregnant, often the top jobs are reserved for men, and politics is almost solely a male domain. The Church's sanctification of the family – and women's traditional place in it – still strongly influences Poland's social fabric, although this is also diminishing, particularly in the younger generation.

ARTS
Literature

In Poland, as in many Eastern European countries, literature holds a special place in the hearts of the citizens. It has served as the only outlet for resentment against foreign rule during occupation, and has often captured the spirit of a struggling country.

Poland's rich literary history dates back to the 11th century, but it wasn't until the 1500s that works in the Polish language gained a semblance of popularity. By the 1700s Latin literature had completely given way to Polish prose.

NOVELISTS

The Nobel prize for literature was first awarded in 1901, and it was only four years later that Henryk Sienkiewicz (1846–1916) became the first of several Polish writers to be so honoured. Sienkiewicz took the prize for *Quo Vadis?*, an epic novel chronicling the love affair between a pagan Roman and a young Christian girl in ancient Rome. The book was the world's first 'bestseller' and has been translated into dozens of languages; a century after its first publication it is still in print. Novelist and short-story writer Władysław Reymont (1867–1925) became another Nobel prize winner in 1924 for *The Peasants* (Chłopi), a four-volume epic about Polish village life.

Between the wars several brilliant avant-garde writers emerged who were only fully appreciated after WWII. They included Bruno Schulz (1892–1942), Witold Gombrowicz (1904–69) and Stanisław Ignacy Witkiewicz (also known as Witkacy; 1885–1939). Witkacy, an unusual talent in many fields (including painting, literature and photography), was the originator of unconventional philosophical concepts, such as the 'theory of pure form', and creator of the Theatre of the Absurd long before Ionesco made it famous. Only in the 1960s were Witkacy's plays, such as *Mother* (Matka), *Cobblers* (Szewcy) and *New Deliverance* (Nowe Wyzwolenie), discovered internationally. Despite penning only a handful of books, Schulz is regarded as one of Poland's leading literary lights; his *The Street of Crocodiles* is a good introduction to his ingenious, imaginative prose. As a Jew caught in the maelstrom of WWII, he stood little chance of surviving the Nazi occupation.

The postwar period presented Polish writers with a conundrum: adopt communism and effectively sell out, or take a more independent path and risk persecution. Czesław Miłosz (1911–2004), who broke with the communist regime, offered an analysis of this problem in *The Captive Mind* (Zniewolony Umysł). Miłosz, a long-time émigré who spent the last 40

The website www .polishwriting.net is a guide to around 20 contemporary Polish novelists whose works are available in English, and includes short biographies, interviews, articles and extracts from their works.

years of his life in the USA, occupies the prime position in Polish postwar literature, and the Nobel prize awarded to him in 1980 was recognition of his achievements.

Novelist, screenwriter and film director Tadeusz Konwicki (b 1926) is another remarkable figure of the postwar literary scene. A teenage resistance fighter during WWII, Konwicki's pre-1989 works had the communist censors tearing their hair out. He has written more than 20 novels, among which the best known are the brilliant *A Minor Apocalypse* (Mała Apokalipsa) and *The Polish Complex* (Kompleks Polski).

Stanisław Lem (1921–2006) is without doubt Poland's premier writer of science fiction. Around 27 million of his books, translated into 41 languages, have been sold around the world. Of the more than 30 novels he has written, the most famous is *Solaris,* which was made into a movie twice, the latest one starring George Clooney in 2002.

Look in the window of any large Polish bookshop and you will see the latest best-selling offerings from a younger generation of writers that includes Gdańsk-based journalist and novelist Pawel Huelle (b 1957), Olga Tokarczuk (b 1962) and psychologist and translator Magdalena Tulli (b 1955). Katarzyna Grochola (b 1957), whose pointedly humorous novels are about a woman's life in modern Poland, has been compared to Helen Fielding, author of *Bridget Jones's Diary.*

In *Solaris* (1961) by Stanisław Lem, a psychologist is sent to investigate a space station where the crew are haunted by figures from their past. Like all the best sci-fi, the story uses a futuristic setting to explore what it is to be human.

POETS

The 19th century produced three exceptional poets: Adam Mickiewicz (1798–1855), Juliusz Słowacki (1809–49) and Zygmunt Krasiński (1812–59). Known as the Three Bards, they captured a nation deprived of its independence in their romantic work. The greatest of the three, Mickiewicz, is to the Poles what Shakespeare is to the British, and is as much a cultural icon as a historical and creative figure. Born in Navahrudak, in what is now Belarus, he was a political activist in his youth and was deported to central Russia for five years. He left Poland in the 1830s, never to return, and served as a professor of literature in Lausanne and Paris. His best works, written while he was in

POLISH PROSE IN EXILE

A number of Polish émigrés have made a name for themselves outside the country's borders.

Józef Teodor Konrad Nałęcz Korzeniowski (1857–1924) was born into a family of impoverished but patriotic gentry in Berdichev, which is now in western Ukraine. He left the country in 1874 and, after 20 years travelling the world as a sailor, settled in England. Though fluent in his native Polish, he dedicated himself to writing in English. He is known throughout the world by his adopted name of Joseph Conrad, and his novels (*Heart of Darkness* and *Lord Jim,* to name but two) are considered classics of English literature.

Nobel prize winner Isaac Bashevis Singer (1902–91) spent his formative years in Poland before moving to the USA in 1935 in the face of rising fascism. Singer originally wrote in his native tongue of Yiddish, before translating his work into English for an American audience. Two of his most memorable stories are *Enemies, a Love Story* and *Yentl;* the latter was made into a film starring Barbra Streisand.

During the late '60s and early '70s, Ryszard Kapuściński (1932–2007) was one of Poland's only foreign correspondents, mostly covering wars and revolutions in Africa, Asia and the Americas. He went on to pen literary works of some standing, including *Imperium,* dealing with the last days of the Soviet Union, and *The Emperor,* covering the demise of Haile Selassie's Ethiopian regime.

Despite controversy surrounding the authenticity of some of Jerzy Kosiński's (1933–91) works, the author is known for his two highly regarded novels, *The Painted Bird* and *Being There.* Kosiński was born Josek Lewinkopf in Łódź and emigrated to the USA in 1957.

exile, have, not surprisingly, a strongly patriotic theme. Mickiewicz' most famous poem, known to all Polish schoolchildren, is the epic, book-length *Pan Tadeusz* (1834). It is a romantic evocation of a lost world of 18th-century Polish-Lithuanian gentry, torn apart by the Partition of 1795. There is an exhibition dedicated to Mickiewicz in Warsaw's Literature Museum (p91) and a first edition of the poem resides in Płock's Diocesan Museum (p135).

Polish literature's most recent Nobel prize was awarded in 1996 to Wisława Szymborska (b 1923), a Kraków poet little known beyond the borders of her motherland. The Swedish academy described her as 'the Mozart of poetry' with 'something of the fury of Beethoven'. For those intending to sample her work, a good introduction is the volume entitled *View with a Grain of Sand,* published in 1995. It's a selection of 100 poems, translated into English, that span nearly 40 years of her work.

Cinema

Though the invention of the cinema is attributed to the Lumière brothers, some sources claim that a Pole, Piotr Lebiedziński, should take some of the credit; he built a film camera in 1893, two years before the movie craze took off.

The first Polish film was shot in 1908, but large-scale film production only took off after WWI. Little work produced between the wars reached international audiences; the country's greatest contribution to world cinema at the time was actress Pola Negri, a star of Hollywood's silent flicks of the 1920s.

During the first 10 years following WWII, Polish cinematography didn't register many significant achievements, apart from some semidocumentaries depicting the cruelties of the war. One such remarkable example is *The Last Stage* (Ostatni Etap), a moving documentary-drama directed by Wanda Jakubowska (1901–98), an Auschwitz survivor.

THE POLISH SCHOOL

Polish cinema came to the fore from 1955 to 1963, the period known as the Polish School. The school drew heavily on literature and dealt with moral evaluations of the war – its three greatest prodigies, Andrzej Wajda (b 1926), Roman Polański (b 1933) and Jerzy Skolimowski (b 1938), all attended the Łódź Film School and went on to international acclaim.

Wajda produced arguably his best work during this time, the famous trilogy *A Generation* (Pokolenie), *Canal* (Kanał) and *Ashes and Diamonds* (Popiół i Diament). Since then, the tireless Wajda has produced a film every couple of years, the best of which include *Man of Marble* (Człowiek z Marmuru), its sequel *Man of Iron* (Człowiek z Żelaza), and *The Promised Land* (Ziemia Obiecana), which was nominated for an Oscar.

Polański and Skolimowski began their careers in the early '60s; the former made only one feature film in Poland, *Nóż w Wodzie* (Knife in the Water), before continuing his career in the West. The latter shot four films, of which the last, *Ręce do Góry* (Hands Up), made in 1967, was kept on the shelf until 1985. He also left Poland for more receptive pastures, and while he gained an international following, it was nothing compared to the recognition Polański received. Polański's body of work includes such remarkable films as *Cul-de-Sac, Rosemary's Baby, Chinatown, Macbeth, Bitter Moon* and *The Pianist*.

AFTER THE POLISH SCHOOL

Poland's filmmakers never reached the heights of the Polish School after 1963, yet they continued to make exemplary works. The communist era

Check out the Polish Film Institute's website at www.pisf.pl for up-to-date information on the Polish film industry.

Roman Polański's Oscar-nominated debut feature *Nóż w Wodzie* (Knife in the Water; 1963) is a consummate piece of film-making. A tense battle of wits between two men over a pretty woman, it's set on a yacht on the Great Masurian Lakes.

produced a string of important directors, including Krzysztof Zanussi, Andrzej Żuławski and Agnieszka Holland, and in 1970 Marek Piwowski shot *The Cruise* (Rejs), Poland's first cult film. Krzysztof Kieślowski (1941–96), director of the extraordinary trilogy *Three Colours: Blue/White/Red*, started in 1977 with *Blizna* (Scar), but his first widely acclaimed feature was *Amator* (Amateur). After several mature films, he undertook the challenge of making the *Dekalog* (Decalogue), a 10-part TV series that was broadcast all over the world. The postcommunist period has witnessed a rash of young directors, but none has yet proved to be of the class of Polański or Wajda.

More recently, Poland has produced a number of world-class cinematographers, including Janusz Kamiński, who was awarded two Oscars for his work on Steven Spielberg's *Schindler's List* and *Saving Private Ryan*. Allan Starski is another Pole to win an Oscar for *Schindler's List*, this time for art and set direction.

Lesser known but perhaps no less talented are several other Polish cinematographers responsible for various acclaimed Hollywood productions, including Adam Holender *(Midnight Cowboy)*, Andrzej Bartkowiak *(Verdict, Jade, Terms of Endearment, Prizzi's Honor)*, Andrzej Sekuła *(Pulp Fiction)* and Piotr Sobociński *(Marvin's Room, Ransom)*.

Music
CLASSICAL
The foremost figure in the history of Polish music is Frédéric Chopin (1810–49), who crystallised the national style in classical music, taking inspiration from folk or court dances and tunes such as *polonez* (polonaise), *mazurek* (mazurka), *oberek* and *kujawiak*. No-one else in the history of Polish music has so creatively used folk rhythms for concert pieces, nor achieved such international recognition.

The Pianist (2002), the harrowing true story of a Warsaw Ghetto survivor, won three Oscars (including Best Actor and Best Director) and two BAFTAs for Roman Polański.

Chopin was not the only composer inspired by folk dances at the time. Stanisław Moniuszko (1819–72) used his inspiration to create Polish national opera; two of his best-known pieces, *Halka* and *Straszny Dwór*, are staples of the national opera-house repertoire. Henryk Wieniawski (1835–80), another remarkable 19th-century composer, also achieved great heights in the world of Polish music.

A discussion of traditional Polish music cannot be complete without a mention of Oskar Kolberg (1814–90). The pioneering Kolberg spent much of his life recording songs and dances from across the country, and by the time of his death he had amassed a substantial collection. Unfortunately it was destroyed during WWII, but the collection was begun again in 1945.

By the beginning of the 20th century, Polish artists were beginning to grace the world stage. The first to do so were the piano virtuosos Ignacy Paderewski (1860–1941) and Artur Rubinstein (1886–1982), the latter performing right up until his death. Karol Szymanowski (1882–1937) was another musical

---

THE CHOPIN TRAIL

There are several places in and around Warsaw that are associated with Poland's national composer, Frédéric Chopin.

■ Chopin Museum (p97) – a small museum housed in the headquarters of the Chopin Society

■ Holy Cross Church (p96) – where Chopin's heart is buried

■ Warsaw University (p96) – from 1826 to 1829 Chopin studied at the school of music here

■ Żelazowa Wola (p120) – Chopin's birthplace; the house where he was born has been restored as a museum

personality of the first half of the 20th century; his best-known composition, the ballet *Harnasie*, was influenced by folk music from the Tatra Mountains, which he transformed into the contemporary musical idiom.

In the 1950s and 1960s a wealth of talent began to emerge once more, including Witold Lutosławski, with his *Musique Funèbre* and *Jeux Vénitiens*, and Krzysztof Penderecki, with his monumental dramatic forms such as *Dies Irae, Ubu Rex, Devils of Loudun, Seven Gates of Jerusalem* and *Credo*.

Originally eclipsed by the aforementioned masters, Henryk Górecki developed his own musical language. His Symphony No 3 (also known as *Symphony of Sorrowful Songs*), written in 1976, became a worldwide phenomenon in 1992 when it was recorded by Dawn Upshaw and the London Sinfonietta. The huge success of the third symphony shed light on the composer's other works, notably his String Quartets Nos 1 and 2, written for, and exquisitely performed by, the Kronos Quartet.

JAZZ

Jazz entered Polish airwaves in the 1930s, and the biggest name of the time was trumpet virtuoso Eddie Rosner. By the early 1950s it was relegated to an underground movement, when musicians would jam behind closed doors away from the eyes and ears of the ruling communists. Krzysztof Komeda (1931–69), the legendary pianist, became Poland's first jazz star and an inspiration to many musicians that followed, including Michał Urbaniak (violin, saxophone), Zbigniew Namysłowski (saxophone) and Tomasz Stańko (trumpet), all of whom became pillars of Polish jazz in the 1960s and remain active today. Urbaniak opted to pursue his career in the USA, and is the best-known Polish jazz musician on the international scene.

Of the younger generation, Leszek Możdżer (piano) is possibly the biggest revelation thus far, followed by several other exceptionally skilled pianists such as Andrzej Jagodziński and Włodzimierz Pawlik. Other young jazz talents to watch out for include Piotr Wojtasik (trumpet), Maciej Sikała (saxophone), Adam Pierończyk (saxophone), Piotr Baron (saxophone) and Cezary Konrad (drums).

POLISH HIP-HOP

Poland's music scene encompasses a broad spectrum of artists, playing everything from folk and jazz to punk and rock, but turn on any music TV and all you'll see is home-grown hip-hop. Whether it's thanks to the restrictions of the communist era or the current high levels of youth unemployment, since 1990 a whole generation has enthusiastically embraced the 'money, guns and hos' gangsta philosophy, and the recent worldwide commercial explosion of the genre has opened things up wide for Poland's many urban crews and posses.

Little of what you'll hear is revolutionary in a musical sense, but the point is that you'll hear it – hip-hop is firmly ensconced in the mainstream in Poland. It's also virtually the only form of Polish-language music to make it out of the country, and while it's never going to outsell Eminem, you can already find Polish rap nights in clubs as far afield as London. Unsurprisingly, the heaviest presence is in Germany, where a large expat population and an equally active hip-hop scene provide a booming market.

Names to look out for include 52 Dębiec, Ascetoholix, ZIP Skład, WWO, Slums Attack, Grammatik, Fisz, Kaliber 44 and OSTR; tune into radiostacja (101.5FM in Warsaw) or pick up one of its compilation CDs to get a taste of what's hot in the scene. If you don't speak any Polish you won't make much sense of anything, but there's the usual sprinkling of American slang and you should at least recognise the term *kurwa* after a while – it is of course the f-word, proving that some things in hip-hop transcend national boundaries.

ROCK & POP

Unlike most countries, pop plays third fiddle to rock and hip-hop (see boxed text, opposite) in Poland. The country's first rock pioneer was Tadeusz Nalepa (1943–2007), who began his career in the late 1960s and went on to nationwide success. Other veterans of the rock-pop scene include Lady Pank, Republika, Budka Suflera, Maanam, Bajm, T.Love and Hey. Recent years have seen a rash of productions covering just about every musical genre and style from salsa to rap. Brathanki and Golec u Orkiestra are both popular groups that creatively mix folk and pop rhythms, and the likes of Wilki, Dżem and Myslovitz are currently keeping the country's rock traditions alive.

Architecture

Poland's architectural styles have basically followed Western Europe over the centuries. The earliest style to enter the country was Romanesque, which dominated from the late 10th to the mid-13th centuries. Its functional, austere style generally employed round-headed arches, semicircular apses and symmetrical layouts, all in sturdy stone. The remnants of Polish Romanesque are few, but there are some precious examples, including the collegiate church at Tum (p133).

GOTHIC

The Gothic style made its way into Poland in the first half of the 13th century, but it was not until the early 14th century that the so-called High Gothic became universally adopted. Elongated, pointed arches and ribbed vaults were characteristic of the style. Brick replaced stone, and the buildings, particularly churches, tended to reach impressive loftiness and monumental size. Gothic left behind countless churches, town halls and burghers' houses, but the mightiest examples are the Teutonic Knights' castles scattered across northern Poland. Specific examples of Gothic architecture include the magnificent Malbork Castle (p448), Wawel Cathedral and Castle in Kraków (p168), the Cathedral of St John the Baptist in Wrocław (p321), Gniezno's cathedral (p391), and many buildings in the towns of Lublin (p232) and Toruń (p436).

RENAISSANCE

In the 16th century a new fashion transplanted from Italy began to supersede Gothic as the dominant style. More delicate and decorative, Renaissance architecture focused on perfect proportions and a handsome visual appearance. In contrast to Gothic, brickwork was almost never openly shown. Much attention was paid to both detail and decoration, which included bas-reliefs, gables, parapets, galleries, round arches and stucco work. There are a number of Renaissance buildings in Poland – notably Wawel Castle and the Sigismund Chapel in Kraków (p168), and the castles at Baranów Sandomierski (p228) and Ogrodzieniec (p213) – though many of them were later 'adorned' by the subsequent architectural fashion, the Baroque. However the pearl of Renaissance in Poland is the town of Zamość (p250), which has remained relatively unchanged since the 16th century.

BAROQUE

As with the rest of Europe, Baroque entered Poland in the 17th century and swept almost all other styles aside. Lavish and highly decorative, it placed a strong imprint on existing architecture by adding its sumptuous décor, which is particularly evident in church interiors and the palaces of the aristocracy. The most prominent figure of the period was Tylman van Gameren, a Dutch

The Polish Way: a Thousand-Year History of the Poles and their Culture (1988) by Adam Zamoyski is one of the best accounts of Polish culture from its birth to recent past. It is fully illustrated and exquisitely written.

architect invited to Poland after the Deluge (p32). His finest masterpieces include Krasiński Palace (p93) in Warsaw, the Palace of Nieborów (p131), the Church of St Anne in Kraków (p183) and the Royal Chapel in Gdańsk (p414). Also worthy of note is the exemplary Baroque church in Święta Lipka (p489). In the 18th century Baroque culminated in French-originated Rococo, but this style didn't make much of a mark on Poland, which by then was swiftly sliding into economic and political chaos.

THE 'NEOS' & ART NOUVEAU

At the beginning of the 19th century, a more complex phase of architectural development started in Poland, which might be characterised as a period of the 'neo', or a general turn to the past. This phase comprised neo-Renaissance, neo-Gothic and even neo-Romanesque styles. The most important of all the 'neo' fashions, though, was neoclassicism, which used ancient Greek and Roman elements as an antidote to the overloaded Baroque and Rococo opulence. Monumental palaces adorned with columned porticoes were erected in this period, as well as churches that looked more like Roman pantheons. Italian architect Antonio Corazzi was very active in Poland in this period, and designed several massive neoclassical buildings, including the Teatr Wielki (Grand Theatre; see p95) in Warsaw, the town where neoclassicism left its strongest mark.

The second half of the 19th century was dominated by eclecticism – a style that profited from all the previous trends – but it didn't produce any architectural gems. More innovative was Art Nouveau, which developed in England, France, Austria and Germany, and made its entrance into Poland at the beginning of the 20th century. It left behind some gems, including the City Art Gallery in Łódź (p124), Płock's cathedral interior (p134), and the Hotel Royal in Kraków (p198). After WWI, neoclassicism took over again but lost out to functionalism just before WWII.

SOCIALIST REALISM & BEYOND

The postwar period started with a heroic effort to reconstruct destroyed towns and cities, and the result, given the level of destruction, is truly impressive. Social realism, the oppressive architectural style of the communist regime, entered Poland at this time; Warsaw's Palace of Culture & Science (p97) and Plac Konstytucji (p99) are classic examples.

Since the 1960s Polish architecture has followed more general European styles, though with one important local distinction: almost all major cities have been ringed by vast suburbs of anonymous concrete apartment blocks, a sad consequence of massive urbanisation and the architects' lack of imagination. In Poland's defence, it didn't have the necessary cash flow to accommodate aesthetic values. Nor did Poland receive external assistance from the Marshall Plan, which helped some other Western European nations to rebuild after the war. Only after the fall of communism was there a trend towards the construction of homes on a more human scale and modern-style architecture.

Painting

The country's first major painter was no Pole at all. Bernardo Bellotto (c 1720–80) was born in Venice, the nephew (and pupil) of that quintessential Venetian artist, Canaletto. He specialised in *vedute* (town views) and explored Europe thoroughly, landing the job of court painter in Warsaw during the reign of King Stanisław August Poniatowski (1764–95). An entire room in Warsaw's Royal Castle (p87) is devoted to his detailed views of the city, which proved invaluable as references during the re-

Poles who became household names include Antoni Patek (cofounder of watchmakers Patek Philippe & Co), Max Factor (the father of modern cosmetics) and the four Warner brothers (founders of Warner Bros).

construction of the Old Town after WWII. Bellotto often signed his canvases *'de Canaletto'*, and as a result is commonly known in Poland simply as Canaletto. Also on display in the castle are works by Marcello Bacciarelli (1731–1818), the king's favourite portraitist, who captured seminal moments in Polish history on canvas.

DEVELOPMENT OF POLISH ARTISTS

By the middle of the 19th century, Poland was ready for its own painters. Born in Kraków, Jan Matejko (1838–93) created stirring canvases that glorified Poland's past achievements. He aimed to keep alive in the minds of his viewers the notion of a proud and independent Polish nation, during a time when Poland had ceased to exist as a political entity. His best-known work is *The Battle of Grunwald* (1878), an enormous painting that took three years to complete. It depicts the famous victory of the united Polish, Lithuanian and Ruthenian forces over the Teutonic Knights in 1410 and is displayed in Warsaw's National Museum (p100). The likes of Józef Brandt (1841–1915) and Wojciech Kossak (1857–1942) also contributed to the documentation of Polish history at this time; Kossak is best remembered as co-creator of the colossal *Racławice Panorama*, which is on display in Wrocław (p318).

The closing decades of the 19th century saw the development of Impressionism in Europe, but it was met with much reserve by Polish artists. Even though many of the first-rank national painters of this period, such as Aleksander Gierymski (1850–1901), Józef Chełmoński (1849–1914), Władysław Podkowiński (1866–95), Leon Wyczółkowski (1852–1936) and Julian Fałat (1853–1929) were in some way, or for some time, influenced by the new style, they preferred to express themselves in traditional forms and never completely gave up realism. This is particularly true of their Polish landscapes, an important part of their work.

On the other hand, the revolution in European painting influenced those Polish artists who lived and worked outside Poland, particularly those in Paris. Among them were Olga Boznańska (1865–1940), whose delicate portraits were painted with notable hints of Impressionism, and Tadeusz Makowski (1882–1932), who adopted elements of Cubism and developed an individual, easily recognisable style.

POST WWII

From the end of WWII until 1955, the visual arts were dominated by socialist realism. It was also a time when poster art came to the fore, building on a tradition dating back to the turn of the century. One of the most influential artists was Tadeusz Trepkowski (1914–54), who produced his best posters after WWII; his works, and those by other poster artists, can be seen at Warsaw's Poster Museum (p102).

From 1955 onwards, Poland's painters began to experiment with a variety of forms, trends and techniques. Zdzisław Beksiński (1929–2005) is considered one of the country's best contemporary painters; he created a unique, mysterious and striking world of dreams in his art. The career of Tadeusz Kulisiewicz (1899–1988) began before WWII, but he reached mastery in his delicate drawings in the postwar period, while Tadeusz Kantor (1915–90), who famously founded Cricot 2 Theatre, was also very creative in painting, drawing and other experimental forms. The work of Jerzy Nowosielski (b 1923) is strongly inspired by the religious iconography of the Orthodox Church; he has decorated the interiors of several churches, including the Orthodox Church of the Holy Trinity (p146) in Hajnówka.

For a comprehensive look at the last 100 years of Poland's poster art, log on to www.theartof poster.com.

POLAND'S SKANSENS

'Skansen' is a Scandinavian word referring to an open-air ethnographic museum. Aimed at preserving traditional folk culture and architecture, a skansen gathers together a selection of typical, mostly wooden, rural buildings (dwellings, barns, churches, mills) collected from the region, and often reassembles them to look like a natural village. The buildings are furnished and decorated in their original style, incorporating a range of traditional household equipment, tools, crafts and artefacts, and offer an insight into the life, work and customs of the period.

The concept of open-air museums emerged in the late 19th century in Scandinavia and became popular in Europe during the interwar period. Poland's first skansen was established in 1906 in Wdzydze Kiszewskie (p435), near Gdańsk, and focussed on Kashubian folk culture. The next, dedicated to traditional Kurpie culture, appeared in 1927 in Nowogród (p143), in northern Mazovia. Both were almost totally destroyed during WWII but later reconstructed.

There are currently about 35 skansens in Poland focusing on distinctive regional traits. They are sometimes called *muzeum budownictwa ludowego* (museum of folk architecture), *muzeum wsi* (museum of the village) or *park etnograficzny* (ethnographic park), but the term 'skansen' is universally applied.

Although most skansens have been established by reassembling regional buildings, there are also some small *in situ* skansens, including one in Kluki (p457) and another in Bóbrka (p287). It's hard to form a hard-and-fast 'skansen top 10' list, but at the very least you shouldn't miss the ones in Sanok (p277) and Nowy Sącz (p294).

Folk Arts & Crafts

Poland has long and rich traditions in folk arts and crafts, and there are significant regional distinctions. Folk culture is strongest in the mountainous regions, especially in the Podhale at the foot of the Tatras, but other relatively small enclaves, such as Kurpie and Łowicz (both in Mazovia), help to keep traditions alive.

Industrialisation and urbanisation have increasingly encroached on traditional customs, though. People no longer wear folk dress except for special occasions, and the artefacts they make are mostly for sale as either tourist souvenirs or museum pieces; in any case, they are not used for their original purposes. The growing number of ethnographic museums is an indicator of the decline of traditional folk art; these museums are the best places to see what is left. One interesting type of ethnographic museum is the skansen (open-air museum; see boxed text, above), created to preserve traditional rural architecture.

Despite the decline there's still a lot to see outside the museums and skansens. The Polish rural population is conservative and religious, which means that traditions don't die overnight. The further off the beaten track you get, the more you'll see. New folk art pops up in the country every now and then; the Folk Museum at Sromów (p132) has some prime examples. Traditions periodically spring to life around religious feasts and folk festivals, and these events offer the best opportunity to get a feel for how deep the folk roots go.

Theatre

Although theatrical traditions in Poland date back to the Middle Ages, theatre in the proper sense of the word didn't develop until the Renaissance period and initially followed the styles of major centres in France and Italy. By the 17th century the first original Polish plays were being performed on stage. In 1765 the first permanent theatre company was founded in Warsaw and its later director, Wojciech Bogusławski, came to be known as the father of the national theatre.

Theatre development was hindered during Partition. Only the Kraków and Lviv theatres enjoyed relative freedom, but even they were unable to stage the great Romantic dramas, which were not performed until the beginning of the 20th century. By the outbreak of WWI, 10 permanent Polish theatres were operating. The interwar period witnessed a lively theatrical scene with the main centres situated in Warsaw and Kraków.

After WWII, Polish theatre acquired an international reputation. Some of the highest international recognition was gained by the Teatr Laboratorium (Laboratory Theatre), which was created in 1965 and led by Jerzy Grotowski in Wrocław. This unique experimental theatre, remembered particularly for *Apocalypsis cum Figuris*, was dissolved in 1984, and Grotowski concentrated on conducting theatrical classes abroad until his death in early 1999. Another remarkable international success was Tadeusz Kantor's Cricot 2 Theatre of Kraków, formed in 1956. Unfortunately, his best creations, *The Dead Class* (Umarła Klasa) and *Wielopole, Wielopole,* will never be seen again; Kantor died in 1990 and the theatre was dissolved a few years later.

Among existing experimental theatres, the most powerful and expressive include the Gardzienice (p239), based in the village of the same name near Lublin, the Teatr Witkacego (Witkacy Theatre) in Zakopane and the Wierszalin in Białystok.

In the mainstream, the most outstanding theatre company in Kraków is the Stary Teatr (Old Theatre; p205). There are several top-ranking theatres in Warsaw (p114), including the Teatr Ateneum, Teatr Powszechny and Teatr Dramatyczny.

Polish theatre directors to watch out for include Jerzy Jarocki, Jerzy Grzegorzewski, Kazimierz Dejmek, Andrzej Wajda, Krystian Lupa and Maciej Prus.

Prominent among other forms of theatre are Wrocławski Teatr Pantomimy (Pantomime Theatre of Wrocław; p325) and Polski Teatr Tańca (Polish Dance Theatre; p385) based in Poznań.

The 2006 Miss World pageant in Warsaw was the first held in a European city other than London.

Food & Drink

Food has played a pivotal role in keeping the Polish nation on track. During the more than 120 years or so in the wilderness, when Poland ceased to exist politically, Poles found a source of unity in their language, their religion and their cuisine. And while many of the dishes are uniquely its own, this cosmopolitan country has borrowed heavily from the cuisines of its neighbours and nations further afield. The Jewish, Russian, Ukrainian, Hungarian, German and even Italian traditions have all left their mark.

For the most part, Polish food is hearty and filling – a favourite saying is *'Jedzcie, pijcie, i popuszczajcie pasa'* ('Eat, drink, and loosen your belt'). Food is rich in meat and game, thick soups and sauces proliferate, and potatoes and dumplings are abundant. Some of the preparations and tastes (such as the ubiquitous sweet-sour one) are unusual; favourite seasonings include marjoram, dill and caraway seeds.

Poles wish each other *smacznego* (smach-*nay*-go), the Polish equivalent of *bon appetit*, at the start of the meal and end the same meal by saying *dziękuje* (djen-*koo*-ye) to one another, which means thank you.

STAPLES & SPECIALITIES

Chleb (bread) has always meant more than mere sustenance to Poles. Bread is a symbol of good fortune and is sacred to many; some older people kiss a piece of bread if they drop it on the ground. Traditional Polish bread is made with rye flour, but bakeries nowadays turn out a bewildering array of loaves, including those flavoured with sunflower, poppy and sesame seeds as well as raisins and nuts.

Rye is a staple ingredient of another favourite Polish dish, *żurek*. This traditional soup is made with beef or chicken stock, bacon, onion, mushrooms and sour cream, and is given a distinctive, tart flavour through the addition of *kwas* (a mixture of rye flour and water that has been left to ferment for several days). It's often accompanied by hard-boiled egg or *kiełbasa* (Polish sausage) and served inside a hollowed-out loaf of bread.

As Polish as *żurek*, but perhaps not as unique is *barszcz* (or *barszcz czerwony*), a red beetroot soup known in Russia as borscht that can be served as *barszcz czysty* (clear borscht), *barszcz z uszkami* (borscht with tiny ravioli-type dumplings stuffed with meat) or *barszcz z pasztecikiem* (borscht with a hot meat- or cabbage-filled pastry).

Pierogi (or 'Polish ravioli') are square- or crescent-shaped dumplings made from dough and stuffed with a whole range of fillings, including cottage cheese, potato and onion, minced meat, sauerkraut or even fruit. They are usually boiled and then served doused in melted butter.

The Polish street snack of choice is *zapiekanki*, the 'Polish pizza' made up of half a stale baguette split lengthwise and topped with melted cheese, chopped mushrooms and ketchup and best (or only) eaten after a heavy night on the town.

Main dishes include the iconic *bigos* (see opposite), *gołąbki* (cabbage leaves stuffed with beef, onion and rice and baked in tomato sauce), *golonka* (boiled pig's knuckle) served with horseradish and sauerkraut, and the ubiquitous *kotlet schabowy* (breaded pork chops). More elaborate preparations are *schab wieprzow* (roast loin of pork) – or preferably *dzik* (wild boar) – with caraway seeds and chopped marjoram rubbed into the skin before roasting, and *kaczka z jabłkami* (roast duck with apples).

Main courses are usually accompanied by *ziemniaki* (potatoes), which are served in many forms – boiled, roasted, fried or mashed. One of the more distinctively Polish recipes is *placki ziemniaczane* (potato fritters) – patties of grated potato and onion fried until crisp and often served with sour cream. Another traditional Polish grain is buckwheat, which is often served as a side dish in the form of *kasza* (or *kasza gryczana;* buckwheat groats).

Poles have always taken advantage of the abundant wild food that grows in field and forest and a favourite summer pastime, even for city folk, is

---

TRAVEL YOUR TASTEBUDS

If there is one dish more genuinely Polish than any other, it's *bigos*. It's made with sauerkraut, fresh chopped cabbage and meat, including one or more of pork, beef, game, sausage and bacon. All the ingredients are mixed together and cooked over a low flame for several hours, then put aside to be reheated a few more times. As with French cassoulet, this process enhances the flavour. The whole operation takes a couple of days and the result can be nothing short of mouthwatering. Every family has its own well-guarded recipe as far as the ingredients, seasonings and cooking time go, and you will never find two identical dishes. One of our neighbours in southern Poland once let slip that the sauerkraut had to be rinsed no fewer than three times before adding it to the pot. This made all the difference to ours.

Because it's so time-consuming, *bigos* does not often appear on a restaurant menu and the version served in cheap eateries and cafés is often not worth its name. The best place to try *bigos* is at someone's kitchen table – if you ever happen to get such an invitation, don't pass it up. *Bigos* is at its most delicious when washed down with liberal quantities of vodka, so bring along a bottle.

---

gathering wild mushrooms and berries. The necessity in times past of making abundant summer food last through the long, cold winters means that Polish cuisine is rich in pickles, preserves and smoked fish and meat. The most famous Polish preserves are sweet and fragrant *ogórki kiszone* (dill-pickled cucumbers), often sold from wooden barrels at fruit and vegetable markets.

There are regional specialities across the country – freshwater fish dishes in the north, aromatic duck preparations in Wielkopolska, large dumplings called *kluski* in Silesia that are often served with bacon (*kluski śląskie ze słoniną*) – but nowhere are specialities so well defined as in the Podhale region at the foot of the Tatras. Among some of the things to try here are *kwaśnica* (sauerkraut soup), *placki po góralsku* (potato pancakes with goulash) and the many types *oscypki* (smoked sheep's cheese) that come in oblong shapes with distinctive stamps on the rind. These are sometimes sliced, baked and served with *żurawiny* (preserved cranberries).

Mushroom-picking is almost a national pastime in the hills and forests of Poland in autumn.

DRINKS
Tea & Coffee

Poles are passionate tea drinkers. *Herbata* (tea) is traditionally served in a glass, not a cup, and never drunk with milk. Instead, a slice of lemon is added plus sugar to taste.

Kawa (coffee) is another popular drink, especially with the arrival of trendy international chains such as Starbucks and Costa in the larger cities. The traditional Polish way of preparing coffee is *kawa parzona*, a concoction made by putting a couple of teaspoons of ground coffee beans directly into a glass and topping it with boiling water. *Kawa po turecku* (Turkish-style coffee) is strong boiled coffee.

Beer & Wine

There are several brands of locally brewed Polish *piwo* (beer), the best of which include Żywiec, Tyskie, Okocim and Lech. Beer is readily available in shops, cafés, bars, pubs and restaurants – virtually everywhere – and is almost always lager. Not all bars chill their beer, so if you want a cold one ask for *zimne piwo* (cold beer). It is very popular among young people to drink *piwo z sokiem* (beer mixed with fruit cordial or juice) with a straw.

Poland doesn't have much of a tradition of wine drinking but that is changing – and fast. The average annual wine consumption, while small at just 5.46L per head of population (compared with just under 60L for France), is growing by 10% to 15% a year, and wine could soon rival beer and vodka in popularity.

The country produces almost no *wino* (wine) of its own. Poles generally prefer seasoned and sweet wines, and their market is dominated by lower-priced products from Hungary and Bulgaria. Western European wines, particularly French, German and Spanish, are now widely available in shops and restaurants.

Spirits

Poland has virtually no wine industry apart from a miniscule amount produced every year at Zielona Góra in Silesia.

The No 1 tipple in Poland – indeed, the one almost synonymous with the country – is *wódka* (vodka). And while the jury is still out on who actually invented the stuff – Poland or its old adversary to the east – most people agree that Polish vodka is superior to the Russian equivalent.

These days drinking habits in the cities are changing, with Poles increasingly turning to beer and wine instead of vodka. Yet, as soon as you go to a small town and enter the only local restaurant, you'll see those tipsy folk debating jovially over bottles of vodka. Old habits die hard; only Russians drink more vodka per capita than Poles.

Polish vodka comes in a number of colours and flavours. *Czysta* (clear) vodka is not, as is often thought in the West, the only species of the *wódka* family. Though clear vodka does form the basic 'fuel' for seasoned drinkers – *wyborowa* is the finest of the wheat-based clear vodkas and *żytnia* the rye-based ones – there is a whole spectrum of varieties, from very sweet to extra dry. These include *myśliwska* ('hunter's vodka' tasting not unlike gin), *wiśniówka* (flavoured with cherries), *jarzębiak* (rowan berries), *cytrynówka* (lemon), *pieprzówka* (pepper) and the famous *żubrówka* ('bison vodka', which is flavoured with grass from the Białowieża Forest on which the bison feed.

Annual vodka consumption in Poland stood at 641.5 million litres in 2008, or just under 17L per head nationwide.

Clear vodka should be served well chilled. Flavoured vodkas don't need as much cooling, and some are best drunk at room temperature. While all vodkas were traditionally drunk neat (see below) and – horror of horrors – *never* mixed as cocktails, that too is changing and some experiments have been very successful indeed. Like beef and claret, *żubrówka* and apple juice – known as a *tatanka* (buffalo) – is a match made in heaven.

Other notable spirits include *śliwowica* (plum brandy), *winiak* (grape brandy) and Goldwasser, a thick liqueur laced with flakes of real gold leaf. *Miód pitny* (mead) is considered the oldest Polish alcoholic drink. It has a very delicate, sweet taste, as it is made using honey, water and yeast. *Krupnik* is honey liqueur.

DRINKING VODKA POLISH-STYLE

In Poland vodka is usually dunk from a 50mL shot glass called a *kieliszek*. It's downed in a single gulp – *do dna* (to the bottom), as Poles say. A piece of a snack or a sip of mineral water is consumed just after drinking to give some relief to the throat. Glasses are immediately refilled for the next drink and it goes quickly. Poles say, 'The saddest thing in the world is two people and just one bottle.'

As you may expect, at this rate you won't be able to keep up with your fellow drinkers for long. Go easy and either miss a few turns or sip your drink in stages. Though this will be beyond the comprehension of a 'normal' Polish drinker, you as a foreigner will be treated with due indulgence. If you do get tipsy, take comfort in the fact that Poles get drunk too – and sometimes rip-roaringly so. There's a reason that the French describe anyone well under the weather as 'drunk as a Pole'. *Na zdrowie* (Cheers)!

WE DARE YOU...

Adventurous diners can start as soon as they sit down at most very traditional Polish eateries. On the table in a large bowl will be a massive helping of *smalec*, what we (don't) like to call 'heart attack in a dish'. It's fried pork fat (not chicken, that is Jewish schmaltz) topped with crackling and spread on large hunks of bread. Nasty but oh-so nice. Other even less appetising-sounding entries on the menu, most of which are absolutely delicious, include *nóżki w galarecie* (jellied calves' trotters), *flaki* (seasoned tripe cooked in bouillon with vegetables), *karp w galarecie* (carp in gelatine) and *czernina* (ducks'-blood broth with vinegar).

CELEBRATIONS

A deeply religious Roman Catholic country, Poland observes the most important feast days of the liturgical calendar with great piety.

The main meal on the night before Christmas begins with *barszcz wigilijny* (meatless Christmas Eve borscht) served with *uszka postne* (little mushroom packets). This is usually followed by carp in some form. It might be the standard *karp z masłem* (carp fried in butter) or even *karp po żydowsku* (Jewish-style carp), which sees the fish steamed with vegetables and served *w galarecie* (in aspic). But usually it's a more elaborate preparation such as *karp w szarym sosie*, where the fish is served with a delightful (but vile-sounding) 'grey' sauce of almonds, raisins, butter, caramelised sugar and sweet wine. The sweet of choice at Christmas is *piernik*, a dense honey and spice cake.

After *Rezurekcja*, the Easter Sunday morning Mass at daybreak, families traditionally go home to a brunch or early lunch of dishes and delicacies denied during Lent. Sometimes the meal begins with a *żurek wielkanocny*, which is a special Easter *żurek* with hard-boiled eggs and Polish sausage. This is followed mostly by cold dishes such as *szynka gotowana* (boiled ham), *kiełbasa* and *pasztet* (pâté). Desserts include the bread-like *babka* ('grandma's cake') and *sernik* (cheesecake).

WHERE TO EAT & DRINK

A *restauracja* (restaurant) is the main place for a meal with table service. They range from unpretentious eateries where you can have a filling meal for as little as 20zł, all the way up to luxurious establishments that may leave a sizable hole in your wallet. The menus of most top-class restaurants are in Polish with English and/or German translations, but don't expect foreign-language listings in cheaper eateries (nor waiters speaking anything but Polish).

Restaurants generally open around 11am (at 9am or 10am if they have a breakfast menu). Closing time varies greatly from place to place and from city to province but 10pm to 11pm is usually a safe bet in cities. In villages and smaller towns it may be pretty hard to find somewhere to eat after 9pm.

A Polish *bar mleczny* (milk bar) is a no-frills, self-service cafeteria that serves mostly meat-free dishes at very low prices. The 'milk' part of the name reflects the fact that a good part of the menu is based on dairy products. You can fill up for around 10zł to 15zł. Milk bars were created to provide cheap food for the less affluent and were subsidised by the state. The free-market economy forced many to close, but a number have survived by introducing meat dishes, upgrading standards and raising their prices.

Milk bars open around 8am and close at 6pm (3pm or 4pm on Saturday); only a handful are open on Sunday. The menu is posted on the wall. You tell the cashier what you want, then pay in advance; the cashier gives you a receipt, which you hand to the person dispensing the food. Once you've finished your meal, return your dirty dishes (watch where other diners

Flowers are *de rigueur* when visiting Poles at home and should always be swathed in lots of greenery and presented in uneven numbers (eg 11 or 13 roses).

TIPS ON TIPPING

Poles tip in an unusual way (well, for most of us anyway) in restaurants and cafés and never leave the money on the table, which they consider to be both rude and stupid. You should just tell the waiter how much you're paying in total. If the bill is, say, 45zł, you're paying with a 100zł note and you think the waiter deserves a gratuity of around 10% to 12%, just say you're paying 50zł or that you want 50zł back. And there is another important lesson to learn on the subject of tipping. When paying the *rachunek* (bill), do not hand the waiter a note and say 'thank you' at the same time. To a Pole, that means 'keep the change' – even if the bill was 18zł and you handed over 50zł. *Uwaga* (Be careful).

---

put theirs). Milk bars are very popular and there are usually queues, but they move quickly. Smoking is not permitted and no alcoholic beverages are served.

A *jadłodajnia* falls somewhere between a restaurant and a milk bar and serves (usually excellent) home-style dishes. They keep hours similar to milk bars.

In today's Poland, a *kawiarnia* (café) usually serves snacks and light meals along with hot and cold drinks. Generally speaking, the line between a café and a restaurant has become blurred. Cafés tend to open around 10am and close at any time between 9pm and midnight. Most cafés are smokers' territory and, given Polish smoking habits, the atmosphere can be really dense.

VEGETARIANS & VEGANS

Vegetarians won't starve in Poland but (and it must be said) they may lose weight. The cheapest place to go is a milk bar, but many new restaurants and salad bars have vegetarian dishes on the menu and you'll actually find dedicated vegetarian and even vegan restaurants in cities and large towns. Typical Polish vegetarian dishes include the following:

knedle z jabłkami – dumplings stuffed with apples
knedle ze śliwkami – dumplings stuffed with plums
kopytka – Polish 'gnocchi'; noodles made from flour and boiled potatoes
leniwe pierogi – boiled noodles served with cottage cheese
naleśniki – crepes; fried pancakes, most commonly *z serem* (with cottage cheese), *z owocami* (with fruit) or *z dżemem* (with jam), and served with sour cream and sugar
pierogi – dumplings made from noodle dough, stuffed and boiled; the most popular are *pierogi ruskie* ('Russian *pierogi*' with cottage cheese, potato and onion), *z serem* (with cottage cheese), *z kapustą i grzybami* (with cabbage and wild mushrooms), *z jagodami* (with blueberries) and *z truskawkami* (with strawberries)
placki ziemniaczane – fried pancakes made from grated raw potato, egg and flour; served *ze śmietaną* (with sour cream) or *z cukrem* (with sugar)
pyzy – ball-shaped steamed dumplings made of potato flour
ryż z jabłkami – rice with apples
serem i z makiem – dumplings with cottage cheese/poppy seeds

Accompaniments & Salads

Potatoes are the most common accompaniment to the main course and they are usually boiled or mashed. *Frytki* (chips) are also popular, as are steamed *kasza gryczana* and various dumplings. *Surówki* (or *sałatki*; salads) can come as a light dish on their own or as a side dish to the main course. The latter variety includes the following:

ćwikła z chrzanem – boiled and grated beetroot with horseradish
mizeria ze śmietaną – sliced fresh cucumber in sour cream
sałatka jarzynowa – 'vegetable salad'; cooked vegetables in mayonnaise, commonly known as Russian salad

sałatka z pomidorów – tomato salad, often served with onion
surówka z kapusty kiszonej – sauerkraut, sometimes served with apple and onion

EATING WITH KIDS

Children are welcome in most restaurants and milk bars, but it's rare to find a high chair or special children's menu, so you'll have to make do with smaller portions of the adult menu. For more information on travelling with children, see p505.

HABITS & CUSTOMS

Poles start off their day with *śniadanie* (breakfast), which is roughly similar to its Western counterpart and may include *chleb z masłem* (bread and butter), *ser* (cheese), *szynka* (ham), *jajka* (eggs) and *herbata* or *kawa*.

The most important and substantial meal of the day is *obiad* (lunch), usually eaten somewhere between 1pm and 5pm, either at home or in the *stołówka* (workplace canteen). *Obiad* is closer to a Western dinner, but the timing is more like lunch. You could say it's a dinner at lunchtime.

The evening meal is *kolacja* (supper). The time and menu vary greatly: sometimes it can be nearly as substantial as *obiad* but more often it's just sliced meats with a little bit of salad or even lighter – a pastry and a glass of tea.

For all you'll ever want to know about Polish cuisine (plus recipes!), visit the Food and Drink chat room of the Polish Forums website at www.polish forums.com/polish_food _drink-f8_1.html.

COOKING COURSES

The most famous cookery school in the land (partly because he has appeared on his own TV programme) is **Kurt Scheller's Cooking Academy** (☎ 022 626 8092; www.schelleracademy.com.pl; 5th fl, ul Piękna 68) in Warsaw. It has day, weekend and holiday courses available of many flavours and descriptions. A course in 'Traditional Polish Cuisine' lasts about four hours and costs 170zł. An extended weekend course on the same subject is 420zł.

EAT YOUR WORDS

If you want to twist your tongue around a little Polish as well as some *pierogi*, turn to the Language chapter on p533 for a bit of pronunciation practice.

Useful Phrases

Table for (four people), please.
   Proszę stolik dla (czterech osób).   pro·she sto·leek dla (chte·reh o·soop)
May I have a menu?
   Czy można prosić o kartę?   chi mozh·na pro·sheech o kar·te

---

THE ART OF READING POLISH MENUS

A Polish menu is normally split into several sections, including *zakąski* (hors d'oeuvres), *zupy* (soups), *dania drugie* or *potrawy* (main courses), *dodatki* (side dishes), *desery* (desserts) and *napoje* (drinks). The main courses are often split further into *dania mięsne* (meat dishes), *dania rybne* (fish dishes), *dania z drobiu* (poultry dishes) and *dania jarskie* (vegetarian dishes).

The name of the dish on the menu is accompanied by its price and, in milk bars in particular, by its weight or other quantity. The price of the main course doesn't normally include side orders such as potatoes, chips and salads; these must be chosen from the *dodatki* section. Only when all these items are listed together is the price that follows for the whole plate of food.

Also note that for menu items that do not have a standard portion size – most commonly fish – the price given is often per 100g. When ordering, make sure you know how big a fish (or piece of fish) you're getting. To avoid surprises in the bill, study the menu carefully and make things clear to the waiter.

What's the speciality here?
> *Jaka jest specjalność zakładu?*   ya·ka yest spe·*tsyal*·noshch zak·*wa*·doo

What do you recommend?
> *Co by pan/pani polecił/iła?*   tso bi pan/*pa*·nee po·*le*·cheew/po·le·*chee*·wa (m/f)

Are the side dishes included in the price?
> *Czy dodatki są wliczone w cenę?*   chi do·*dat*·ki som vlee·*cho*·ne ftse·ne

Can I have the bill, please?
> *Proszę o rachunek?*   *pro*·she o ra·*hoo*·nek

Among classic Polish cookbooks available in English is *Polish Cookery* by Marja Ochorowicz-Monatowa, the bible of Polish cookery and first published in 1911.

Food Glossary

barszcz or **barszcz czerwony**	barshch cher·vo·ni	clear beetroot broth (borscht)
bażant	ba·zhant	pheasant
befsztyk	bef·shtik	beef steak
befsztyk tatarski	bef·shtik ta·tar·skee	raw minced beef accompanied by chopped onion, raw egg yolk and often chopped dill cucumber and anchovies
botwinka	bot·feen·ka	soup made from the stems and leaves of baby beetroots; often includes a hard-boiled egg
bryzol	bri·zol	grilled beef (loin) steak
budyń	boo·din'	milk pudding
chłodnik	khwod·neek	chilled beetroot soup with sour cream and fresh vegetables; served in summer only
ciastko	chyast·ko	pastry, cake
dorsz	dorsh	cod
dzik	jeek	wild boar
gęś	gensh	goose
gołąbki	go·womb·kee	cabbage leaves stuffed with minced beef and rice, sometimes also with mushrooms
grochówka	gro·khoof·ka	pea soup, sometimes served *z grzankami* (with croutons)
indyk	een·dik	turkey
kaczka	kach·ka	duck
kapuśniak	ka·poosh·nyak	sauerkraut and cabbage soup with potatoes
karp	karp	carp
kotlet schabowy	kot·let skha·bo·vi	a fried pork cutlet coated in breadcrumbs, flour and egg, found on nearly every Polish menu
krupnik	kroop·neek	thick barley soup containing a variety of vegetables and small chunks of meat
kurczak	koor·chak	chicken
lody	lo·di	ice cream
łosoś wędzony	wo·sosh ven·dzo·ni	smoked salmon
melba	mel·ba	ice cream with fruit and whipped cream
pieczeń cielęca	pye·chen' chye·len·tsa	roast veal
pieczeń wieprzowa	pye·chen' chye·len·tsa vye·psho·va	roast pork
pieczeń wołowa	pye·chen' vo·wo·va	roast beef
pieczeń z dzika	pye·chen' zjee·ka	roast wild boar

polędwica	po·len·dvee·tsa	'English-style beef; roast fillet
po angielsku	po ang·yel·skoo	of beef
pstrąg	pstrong	trout
rosół	ro·soow	beef or chicken (*z wołowiny/z kury*)
		bouillon, usually served *z makaronem*
		(with noodles)
rumsztyk	room·shtik	rump steak
sarna	sar·na	roe deer, venison
schab pieczony	skhab pye·cho·ni	roast loin of pork seasoned
		with prunes and herbs
śledź w oleju	shlej v o·le·yoo	herring in oil with chopped onion
śledź w śmietanie	shlej v shmye·ta·nye	herring in sour cream
stek	stek	steak
sztuka mięsa	shtoo·ka myen·sa	boiled beef with horseradish
zając	za·yonts	hare
zrazy zawijane	zra·zi za·vee·ya·ne	stewed beef rolls stuffed with
		mushrooms and/or bacon and
		served in a sour-cream sauce
zupa grzybowa	zoo·pa gzhi·bo·va	mushroom soup
zupa jarzynowa	zoo·pa ya·zhi·no·va	vegetable soup
zupa ogórkowa	zoo·pa o·goor·ko·va	cucumber soup, usually
		with potatoes and other vegetables
zupa pomidorowa	zoo·pa po·mee·do·ro·va	tomato soup, usually served
		either *z makaronem* (with noodles)
		or *z ryżem* (with rice)
zupa szczawiowa	zoo·pa shcha·vyo·va	sorrel soup, usually served with
		hard-boiled egg

Environment

THE LAND

With primeval forest, sand dunes, coastal lakes, beaches, islands, caves, craters, a desert, and a peninsula called 'Hel', it's fair to say that the Polish landscape is varied.

Its neighbours are interesting too: Poland is bordered by seven countries and one sea. Its northwest border is the 524km Baltic coastline; in the west Poland shares 460km with Germany, to the south it borders the Czech Republic and Slovakia (1310km), and to the east it shares borders with northeast Ukraine, Belarus, Lithuania and Russia (1244km).

The total area of Poland is 312,685 sq km – more than twice the size of Nepal and four times the size of the Czech Republic. Some 52% of the land is agricultural, and almost 30% is forested. Poland's landscape was largely forged during the last ice age, when the Scandinavian ice sheet advanced southward across the Polish plains and receded some 10,000 years later. Now there are five discernable landscape zones: the Sudetes and Carpathian Mountains in the south, the vast central lowlands, the lake belt, the Baltic Sea in the north, and the north-flowing rivers.

Southern Mountains

The southern mountains stretch from the Sudetes Mountains in the southwest, through the Tatra to the Beskids in the southeast. The Sudetes are geologically ancient hills, their rounded forms reaching their highest point at the summit of Śnieżka (1602m) in the Karkonosze range (p336). Poland's highest point is Mt Rysy (2499m) in the Tatras (p304), a jagged, alpine range on the border with Slovakia.

To the north of the Tatra lies the lower but much larger, densely forested range of the Beskids, with its highest peak being Babia Góra (1725m). The southeastern extremity of Poland is taken by the Bieszczady (p274), which is part of the Carpathians and arguably the most picturesque mountain range in the country.

Mt Rysy is reputed to have been climbed by Nobel prize winner Marie Curie and Russian revolutionary Lenin (on separate occasions). A red hammer and sickle symbol is painted on a rock where the latter is believed to have rested.

Central Lowlands

The central lowlands stretch from the far northeast all the way south, 200km shy of the border. The undulating landscape of this, the largest of Poland's regions, comprises the historic areas of Lower Silesia, Wielkopolska, Mazovia and Podlasie. Once upon a time, streams flowing south from melting glaciers deposited layers of sand and mud that helped produce some of the country's most fertile soils. As a result, the central lowlands are largely farmland and Poland's main grain-producing region. In places, notably in Kampinos National Park (p119) to the west of Warsaw, fluvioglacial sand deposits have been blown by wind into sand dunes up to 30m high – some of the largest inland dune complexes in Europe.

Fuel for the 19th century industrial revolution was extracted from the vast coal deposits of Upper Silesia in the western part of the lowlands.

THE WATER
Lake Belt

The lake zone includes the regions of Pomerania, Warmia and Masuria. The latter contains most of Poland's 9300 lakes – more than any other European country except Finland. The gently undulating plains and strings of post-glacial lakes were formed by sticky clay deposited by the retreating ice sheet, leaving

THE ACCIDENTAL DESERT

Near Katowice in Upper Silesia lies Błędowska Desert (Pustynia Błędowska), the only desert in Poland.

Theories abound as to how this 32-sq-km patch of sand (with an average thickness of 40m) found its way to Poland. One theory attributes it to drifting sand and gravel in the ice age. Another is that Błędowska is the accidental child of urbanisation, perhaps born when its forests were stripped to provide wood to nearby Olkusz around the 13th century and developed further when the land was assaulted by mining. The more plausible explanation, offered by Polish folklore, is that a devil who was casually flying through the area with a bag of sand (and why not?), inadvertently tore it on a church spire and the sand that gushed from the bag formed Błędowska.

The size of Błędowska has decreased since successful revegetation efforts of the '50s and '60s. In the summer, the sand can reach temperatures of up to 70˚C, but climatologists question whether Błędowska really qualifies as a desert. The German Afrika Korps reportedly trained in Błędowska under the notorious Nazi commander Erwin Rommel (the 'Desert Fox') before their deployment to Africa.

clay-rich soil that is now forested. The lake region boasts the only remaining *puszcza* (primeval forest) in Europe, making Białowieża National Park (p147) and the wildlife inhabiting it one of the highlights of the country.

Baltic Coast

The Baltic coast stretches across northern Poland from Germany to Russia (Kaliningrad region). The coastal plain that fringes the Baltic Sea was shaped by the rising water levels after the retreat of the Scandinavian ice sheet and is now characterised by swamps and sand dunes. These sand and gravel deposits form not only the beaches of Poland's seaside resorts but also the shifting dunes of Słowiński National Park (p457), the sand bars and gravel spits of Hel (p433) and the Vistula Lagoon.

Rivers

Poland's rivers drain northwards into the Baltic Sea. The biggest is the mighty 1090km-long Vistula (Wisła; p435), originating in the Tatra mountains. Along with its right-bank tributaries – the Bug and the Narew – the Vistula is responsible for draining almost half of the country and is known as the 'mother river' of Poland, given its passage through both Kraków and Warsaw. The second largest river, the Odra, and its major tributary, the Warta, drains the western third of Poland and forms part of the country's western border. Rivers are high when the snow and ice dams melt in spring and are prone to flooding during the heavy rains of July.

WILDLIFE
Animals

There is a rich bounty of zoological and ornithological treasure in Poland. Its diverse topography supports a range of mammal species, including wild boar, red deer, elk and lynx in the far northeast, and brown bears and wildcats in the mountain forests. Rare bird species found in Poland include thrush nightingales, golden eagles, white-backed and three-toed woodpeckers, and hazel grouses, among 200 other species of nesting bird.

Of the 110 species of mammal and 424 species of bird known to inhabit Poland, 12 of each are considered threatened.

BISON

Białowieża National Park (p147) is home to hundreds of European bison, the largest mammal in Europe (bulls can reach almost 2m tall and 3m long)

THE BISON – BACK FROM THE BRINK

The European bison (Bison bonasus) is called żubr in Polish and is the biggest European mammal, its weight occasionally exceeding 1000kg. These large cattle, which live for as long as 25 years, look pretty clumsy but can move at 50km/h when they need to.

Bison were once found all over the continent, but the increasing exploitation of forests in Western Europe began to push them eastwards. In the 19th century the last few hundred bison lived in freedom in the Białowieża Forest. In 1916 there were still 150 of them in the forest but three years later they were totally wiped out. By then, only about 50 bison survived in zoos throughout the world.

It was in Białowieża that an attempt to prevent the extinction of the bison began in 1929, by bringing several animals from zoos and breeding them in their natural habitat. The result is that today there are more than 300 bison living in freedom in the Białowieża Forest alone and about 350 more have been sent to a dozen other places in Poland. Many bison from Białowieża have been distributed among European zoos and forests, and their total current population is estimated at about 2500.

and a stoic survivor. In the 15th century, the bison teetered on the brink of extinction, despite King Sigismund's introduction of the death penalty for poachers. The last wild Polish bison was shot in 1919. A decade later, through breeding programmes in Białowieża National Park, the species was resurrected and – thanks to the Russian and German use of the death penalty to deter poachers – survived WWII. Breeding programmes have since been so successful that Białowieża National Park now contains the largest concentration of European bison in the world.

WOLVES

Grey wolves, the largest members of the canine family, are individually distinct animals who travel and hunt in hierarchical units. In the days of old, wolf hunting was a favourite pastime of Russian tsars. This, and diminishing habitats, drove their numbers into the red until wolves had all but disappeared in Poland a decade ago. After specialised legislation to protect them was passed in 1998, the wolf census conducted in 2001 revealed that the numbers are climbing. Though official numbers are higher, scientists estimate that there are around 650 wolves in Poland.

After the invasion of Poland, Nazis stole herds of tarpans and transported them into Germany with the intention of breeding the pure Aryan wild horse.

HORSES

Poles and horses go way back. Poland has a long tradition of breeding Arabian horses (see boxed text, opposite) and the Polish plains were once home to wild horses. Several species of wild horse have been preserved in zoos, including the tarpan, which is extinct in the wild. Luckily, Polish farmers used to crossbreed tarpans with their domestic horses. The small Polish konik horse is a result of this mix and has kept the tarpan genes alive. Konik horses are now being used to breed the tarpan back. The hucul pony is a direct descendant of the tarpan living in the Carpathians.

Keen ornithologists can get in touch with the Polish Society for the Protection of Birds via its website at www.otop .org.pl/.

BIRDLIFE

The diverse topography of Poland is like flypaper for a range of bird species and orni-tourists. The vast areas of lake, marsh and reed bed along the Baltic coast, and the swampy basins of the Narew and Biebrza Rivers, are home to many species of waterfowl, and are visited by huge flocks of migrating geese, ducks and waders in spring and autumn. A small community of cormorants lives in the Masurian lakes. Storks, which arrive from Africa in spring to build their nests on the roofs and chimneys of houses in the countryside, are a much loved part of the rural scene. The expression 'every fourth stork is Polish' is based on the fact that Poland welcomes around one quarter of Europe's 325,000 white storks each year, most of which make their summer homes in Masuria and Podlasie in the northeast.

The *orzeł* (eagle) is the national symbol of Poland and was adopted as a royal emblem in the 12th century. Several species can be seen, mostly in the southern mountains, including the golden eagle and short-toed eagle, as well as the rare booted eagle, greater spotted eagle and lesser spotted eagle. The white-tailed eagle, supposedly the inspiration for the national emblem, lives in the Słowiński (p457) and Wolin (p467) National Parks.

RSPB Birds of Britain and Europe is a chunky tome by Rob Hume, covering around 500 species with one bird per page. Bird-watching amateurs and aficionados will enjoy the revised 2006 edition.

Plants

Poland contains the only surviving fragment of the forest that covered much of Europe in prehistoric times. This primeval forest of Białowieża National Park (p147) is still home to majestic five-century-old oak trees and a range of flora that is, quite literally, ancient.

The most common plant species in Poland is the pine, which covers 70% of the total forested area, but the biological diversity and ecological resilience of forests are increasing because of the proliferation of deciduous species such as oak, beech, birch, rowan and linden. The forest undergrowth hosts more than 600 varieties of moss and 1500 varieties of fungi. There are also some 2250 species of seed plants in Poland.

In the highest mountain regions, coniferous forests of dwarf mountain pines are capable of resisting harsher climates, while the lowlands and highlands are hospitable for dry-ground forests and marsh forests. Distinctly Polish plants include the Polish larch *(Larix polonica)* and the birch *(Betula oycoviensis)* in the Ojców region. One third of all European plant species can be found in the Carpathians.

Those interested in botany may want to peruse the 2007 hardcover Atlas of Seeds and Fruits of Central and East-Europe Flora: The Carpathian Mountains Region by Vít Bojnanský and Agáta Fargasová.

CONSERVATION AREAS

Currently 28% of Poland is forested and the majority of forests are administered by the state. Around 23% of the country is under some sort of protection as a national park, landscape park or other type of conservation area. The area of land that is forested is gradually growing and is anticipated to reach 30% by 2020 and 33% in 2050.

National Parks

There are 23 *parki narodowe* (national parks) in Poland, covering about 3200 sq km – around 1% of the country's surface area. Other than a concentration of six in the Carpathian Mountains, they are distributed fairly evenly and

---

POLISH ARABIANS

Many important international horseracing championships have been won by Polish-bred Arabians. Breeding Arabians commenced in the 16th century, when waves of external aggressors revealed the prowess of their steeds and captured horses were retained as prizes of war. Originally owned by ancient Slavic tribes, Arabian horses (known as 'oriental whites' in history and legend) were bred by the Polish aristocracy and became a coveted asset in European cavalry.

Poles have repeatedly shown their commitment to the breed by evacuating and hiding their Arabians during times of hostility. After WWI, only 25 mares and seven fillies remained in Poland, and many were lost or stolen during WWII. Today, beyond its success on the racetrack, the Polish-bred Arabian is loved for its courage and endurance, Polish qualities that have ensured the survival of the breed to the present day. Polish-bred Arabians are only sold for export during the annual auction following the Polish National Horse Show.

A STORK OF GOOD LUCK!

In addition to their baby-delivery service, *bociany* (storks) are also known in Poland to bring good luck. For this reason, Poles will often place wagon wheels and other potential nesting foundations on their roofs to attract the white stork. Telecommunications companies even go to lengths to ensure that their structures are stork-friendly.

Storks are the heroes of many Polish legends and folktales. One story goes that when animals became too numerous in God's dominion, they were placed in a sack which God requested a man dispose of in the sea. As it always does, curiosity got the better of the humble human and after he took a peek in the sack, God zapped him into a stork so he could hunt for the animals that escaped in the commotion.

The black trimming at the end of the stork's wings (which can span 2m) are also the work of God. When the stork refused to graciously board Noah's ark like the other refugees of the animal kingdom, God tainted the tips of her wings as a melancholy mark of her arrogance. While the other animals were grateful to have been given a dry refuge from the floods, the stork longed for her former home in Africa and still wanders restlessly between Poland and Egypt, always longing for whichever one she's left.

therefore exhibit the range of landscapes, flora and fauna in the country. The parks have been administered by the Ministry of Environment since 2004.

No permit is necessary to visit the parks, but most have entry fees of between 4zł and 6zł, payable at the park office or entry points. Extra fees often apply for camping (only allowed in specific areas) and entry into various museums and exhibitions.

Białowieża (p147), the oldest national park in Poland, was established in 1932 and inscribed on the Unesco World Heritage List in 1979.

Prize-winning children's book *Bocheck in Poland* by Josepha Contoski is a beautifully rendered story of the relationship between white storks and Polish people.

Landscape Parks

In addition to Poland's national parks, the *parki krajobrazowe* (landscape parks) also play a key role in conservation efforts. As well as their aesthetic contribution, landscape parks are often of key historic and cultural value.

The first landscape park was created in 1976; today there are more than 100. Suwałki Landscape Park (p160) spans 63 sq km of elegant land formations and truly charming lakes. The 7km walk around Lake Jaczno is definitely worth undertaking. This and other walks begin in the village of Smolniki, which along with other villages in the Suwałki region, offers a glimpse into traditional architecture.

Reserves

Finally, Poland has a number of *rezerwaty* (reserves) – usually small areas containing a particular natural feature such as a cluster of old trees, a lake with valuable flora or an interesting rock formation. Nine biosphere reserves have been recognised by Unesco for their innovative approach to sustaining various ecological elements. Zwierzyniec, in Roztocze National Park (p257), protects a range of animals including the bison and tarpan, and fauna such as fir and beech.

Łuknajno Reserve (p499) is home to Europe's largest community of swans.

ENVIRONMENTAL ISSUES

The communist regime in Poland wasn't too concerned with protecting the country's environment; decades of intensive industrialisation turned rivers into sewers and air into smog. It wasn't until 1990, after the regime crumbled, that the Ministry of Environmental Protection was established to develop an environmental policy to clean up the mess. Today, Poland's environment is improving, but in some areas it still looks more grey then green.

National park	Features	Activities	Best time to visit	Website	Page
Białowieża	primeval forest; bison, elk, lynx, wolf	wildlife-watching, hiking	spring, summer	www.bpn.com.pl	p147
Biebrza	river, wetland, forest; elk, great snipe, aquatic warbler	bird-watching, canoeing	spring, autumn	www.biebrza.org.pl	p143
Kampinos	forest, sand dunes	hiking, mountain-biking	summer	www.kampinoski -pn.gov.pl	p119
Karkonosze	mountains; dwarf pine, alpine flora	hiking, mountain-biking	summer, winter	http://kpnmab.pl/	p336
Narew	river, reed beds; beaver, waterfowl	bird-watching, canoeing	spring, autumn	www.npn.pl	p144
Ojców	forest, rock formations, caves; eagles, bats	hiking	autumn	www.opn.pan .krakow.pl	p210
Roztocze	forest; elk, wolf, beaver, tarpan	hiking	spring, autumn	www.roztoczan skipn.pl	p257
Słowiński	forest, bog, sand dunes; white-tailed eagle, waterfowl	hiking, bird-watching	all year	www.slowinskipn .pl	p457
Tatra	alpine mountains; chamois, eagle	hiking, climbing, skiing	all year	www.tpn.pl	p304
Wolin	forest, lake, coast; white-tailed eagle, bison	hiking, bird-watching	spring, autumn	www.wolinpn.pl	p467

Environmental issues that have been hitting the headlines in recent years include the development of the Via Baltica Expressway and logging threats to the Białowieża Forest. Poland is also coping with global environmental concerns such as global warming, water shortage and pollution, and waste management.

Białowieża Forest

Currently only 17% of the immense Białowieża Forest is protected as a national park. The remaining 83% is administered at the state level and threatened by logging. Various organisations, with the Polish WWF at the helm, are working to extend the blanket of protection to the entire forest. They are campaigning for a 50% reduction in the amount of wood obtained from the forest, the reinforcement of the ban on felling trees more than 100 years old, and a dedicated approach to managing tourism in the forest.

Via Baltica Expressway

The Via Baltica is a road-transport project aiming to link Warsaw to Helsinki through the Baltic states. Proposed bypasses of this multilane freeway are fraught with controversy. While Polish authorities stress that congestion would be drastically relieved in the area and that bypasses would cause minimal damage (being a bridge over the valley rather than a ground-level highway), conservation groups are concerned about the irreparable damage the development would cause to protected lands and animal species.

Polish authorities gave the official go-ahead to the Augustów bypass in February 2007 – a move that will violate the Rospuda valley in northeast Poland. Relentless pressure from a network of Polish nongovernmental

Keep your eye on the Via Baltica issue via the Via Baltica website at www .viabalticainfo.org.

and international organisations (including Birdlife International, WWF and the Polish Society for the Protection of Birds), prompted the European Commission to request that the European Court of Justice issue an urgent order suspending the work. On 18 April 2007, the European Court ordered that Poland turn off its power saws. Authorities sought to recommence work in August of the same year, but their actions were again blocked by the European Commission requesting the European Court issue an interim measure to prevent it until it gives a final ruling on the issue.

The website of the Ministry of the Environment (www.mos.gov.pl/kzpn) provides details on environmental protection, water management and national parks.

Global Warming

Poland is ranked the 21st most polluting country in the world and the sixth highest in Europe, accounting for 1.2% of the world's carbon dioxide emissions. Though its per-capita emissions are not substantially higher than the European average, emissions per unit of GDP highlight the extreme inefficiency of the energy sector, with pollution concentrated around industrial sources. The area of Upper Silesia, for example, produces more pollutants than Warsaw. Polluted areas, referred to as 'ecological hazard zones', cover some 10% of the country.

Poland reduced its emissions by 30% in the decade leading up to the millennium. Its ambitious goal is to continue this trend with a further 30% to 40% reduction by the year 2020. The World Bank is assisting the country to reduce carbon dioxide emissions, though, ironically, the main benefactors are the major polluters themselves: big, fat, flatulent power plants. In its 2007 'Dirty Thirty' report, the WWF listed the 30 most polluting power plants in Europe – four of them were Polish.

Poland is a signatory to key environmental conventions including the UN Framework Convention on Climate Change and the Kyoto Protocol. Recent years have seen an escalation in pressure from the European community for Poland to honour its commitments.

Water Shortage & Pollution

Poland's natural water supplies are limited, with the figures for available water per capita among the lowest in Europe. At the same time, the utilisation of the country's water resources is inefficient, with high per-capita consumption.

The water supply of half the population is polluted, largely due to poor waste-water treatment. There are still some water-treatment practices remaining in Poland from the communist era. Only half of Polish households are connected to municipal sewerage systems, compared to over 90% in some European countries. Many industrial plants are known to discharge water directly into rivers without running waste-water treatment plants.

Added to this is the additional problem that the vast majority of Polish rivers flow into the Baltic Sea, a relatively stagnant body of water that is highly sensitive to pollution.

Waste Management

Poland is one of Europe's largest sources of industrial waste (mainly from coal mining and heavy industry), and less than 1% of it is treated. Only 23% of Poland's hazardous waste is treated, and treatment of municipal waste is also minimal; virtually all of it ends up in landfills. However, the environmental situation in Poland is improving. Issues like waste management are slowly, but surely, being addressed.

Activities

Poland is not widely known as a haven for adrenalin junkies, but perhaps it should be. Poles have been partaking in adventure sports and outdoor activities for decades and foreign travellers are starting to get in on the action. Tour operators are increasingly catering for the demands of adventurers from all over the world, offering steadily improving tourist infrastructure and serving up a wider range of adrenalin hits.

Increasing sports-extremism in Poland means that the country is up for almost anything these days. Keep your eye out for new adventure sports and activities in your travels. And if you prefer a more traditional approach, there are plenty of trekking and cycling options too.

Happily, despite an increased number of adventurers in Poland since its admission to the EU, it is still possible to trek, cycle, kayak or ski without coming across crowds of other people doing the same – for the moment.

TREKKING

Poland's mountainous areas can all be explored on foot. There are around 2000km of walking trails sliced through the country's national parks and many are well-signed and well-equipped with shelters. Nature's repertoire of heights, gradients, climates and terrains is showcased in Poland: trekking options range from week-long treks for the hardcore hiker to hour-long rambles for the ascent-adverse.

Carpathian Mountains

The Tatra Mountains in the south is the most notable region for trekking in Poland. The West and the High Tatras offer different scenery; the latter more challenging and as a result more spectacular. One of the most popular climbs in the Tatras is Mt Giewont (1894m). The cross at the peak attracts many visitors, though the steep slopes deter some. For information on Mt Giewont and various other hikes in the Tatras, see boxed text, p306.

The valleys around Zakopane (p306) offer walks of varying lengths for walkers of varying fitness (some take less than an hour). Similarly, trails around nearby Pieniny (see boxed text, p302) and the Bieszczady (see boxed text, p282) in the east offer terrific trekking experiences – even for those who prefer to stroll. Another great option is Beskid Sądecki (p291), which has convenient paths dotted with mountain hostels. Muszyna (p298) or Krynica (p296) are popular bases to access this region.

The lower Beskid Niski mountain range offers less arduous walks and less spectacular views; see boxed text, p290, for more information.

Two commendable, practical walking guides for the Tatras are *High Tatras: Slovakia and Poland* by Colin Saunders and Renáta Nározná, and Sandra Bardwell's *Tatra Mountains of Poland and Slovakia.*

Sudetes Mountains

The Karkonosze National Park (p336) offers a sterling sample of the Sudetes. The ancient and peculiar 'table top' rock formations of the Góry Stołowe (p344) mountains are among the highlights of the Sudetes. The area is easily accessed from the town of Szklarska Poręba (p337) at the base of Mt Szrenica (1362m) and there is a choice of walking trails from Karpacz (p338) to Mt Śnieżka (1602m). Further south, the village of Międzygórze (p348) is another well-kitted base for Sudetes sojourns. Tourist offices in the region stand ready to point you to suitable trails and mountain hostels.

SAFETY GUIDELINES FOR WALKING

To ensure that you enjoy your walk, put some thought into your safety before embarking on your adventure:

- Obtain reliable information about the conditions and characteristics of your intended route from local national park authorities

- Weather conditions can be unpredictable in Poland, so be prepared with appropriate clothing and equipment

- Pay any fees and get hold of any permits required from local authorities

- Be sure you are healthy and feel comfortable walking for a sustained period

- Choose routes within your capabilities or not far beyond them

- Be aware of local laws, regulations and etiquette about flora and fauna

- Be aware that terrain can vary significantly from one region, or even from one trail, to another

---

Other Regions

There are other tracks in the country that deserve a day or two if you are in the vicinity.

The Augustów Forest in the Augustów-Suwałki Region has 55 lakes and many well-paved roads and dirt tracks. Diverse wildlife can be found in various stretches of the forest. There are numerous bays and peninsulas to explore around nearby Lake Wigry in the Wigry National Park (p159) and the 63-sq-km Suwałki Landscape Park (p160) offers pretty views from its picturesque terrain.

There is also Kampinos National Park (p119) just outside of Warsaw with its famed sand dunes, Wielkopolska National Park (p388) in Wielkopolska, and the compact Wolin National Park (p467) in northwest Poland. The lowest (read: most foot-friendly) mountain range in the country is in Świętokrzyski National Park (p223) in Małopolska. In addition to these, Roztocze National Park (p257) offers a range of light walks through gentle terrain, and the landscape park surrounding Kazimierz Dolny (p244) offers some easy ambles.

Further Information

Tour operators offering guided treks through areas like the Tatras and Sudetes are becoming too numerous to mention. When deciding which company to trust with your złoty and your spirit of adventure, perhaps let their level of environmental responsibility be a deciding factor.

Check national park websites (see p71) for more information on trekking and cycling routes, but things change, so ask in person before you assume a particular route is open.

Information about environmentally friendly walking, cycling and horse-riding trails is available at www.green ways.pl and through the Polish Environmental Partnership Foundation (www.epce.org.pl), which promotes them.

CYCLING

Almost every region of Poland has bicycle routes, from small and comfortable circuits to epic international routes. It's possible to restrict yourself to the flat regions of the country and travel the rest by train, but if you're not deterred by gradients you can cycle some of the most riveting (and relatively unexplored) regions of the country.

Some epic bicycle adventures are waiting in the Bieszczady ranges (p274); these tracks will roll you through a montage of primeval forest and rippling meadows, opening up intermittently to postcard-perfect natural and architectural panoramas. The 70km Icon Trail near the village of Sanok rewards cyclists with old timber churches and castles. The Cross Border Cycle Route (p285) is a signposted route leading into Slovakia.

There are some enchanting routes (starting in Narewka) through the northern part of the Białowieża Forest, including detours into parts of Białowieża National Park. Bicycles are strictly forbidden in the protected areas beyond the western and northern areas of the forest.

Cycling in the Masuria region is also rewarding; the town of Węgorzewo (p494) on Lake Mamry is a convenient base to access 18 marked routes ranging from 25km to 109km circuits. The Augustów Forest and the areas around Suwałki are also satisfying, though bike hire is difficult in the latter region so it may be better to arrive equipped.

The Sudetes are a jackpot for mountain-bikers. Stretching to the Czech border, Karkonosze National Park (p336) offers varied bike paths and is popular with Polish extreme-sports enthusiasts.

The region around Zakopane is fun to explore on wheels. Certain parts of the Tatra National Park are accessible by bicycle (p309). Designated cycling areas can change, so always check which routes are open before you set off.

Safety

Where possible, stay on marked cycling trails; travelling on national roads can be hair-raising and occasionally life-threatening. Motorists in Polish cities (with the exceptions of Kraków and Gdańsk) are rarely cycle-conscious, so don't expect too much consideration for your space and safety. When leaving busy cities, it is often wise to travel along rivers rather than roads, even if you have to traverse unpaved areas. Be extra cautious in winter – ice can disguise hazardous and uneven paths and potholes.

Bikes are sometimes stolen and vandalised in Poland. Use a reliable lock, even when storing your bike in buildings and travelling on trains. The countryside poses less threat than built-up areas, but better to be safe than cycle-less. Check that your accommodation is accessible by bicycle; some places may not be because of street layout, traffic density and road conditions. If you're storing your bicycle in your room, check that elevators can accommodate your bike, or be prepared for an upper-body workout.

To find out more about Critical Mass gatherings (where groups of cyclists meet and ride together) in Poland go to www .rowery.org.pl/bicycles .htm.

Further Information

There are various laws concerning cycling in Poland that you should be familiar with before you pedal off. There are rules governing lights and reflectors, cyclists under 18, and drinking and cycling (don't mix them: a jail sentence can apply!). To familiarise yourself with road rules and regulations in Poland, check out **Rowery** (www.rowery.org.pl/bicycles.htm), an advocacy group trying to promote cycling in Poland and bring safety standards up to scratch. For more information on road rules see p524, and for general cycling information see p520.

Bring wet-weather gear – Poland can surprise you with long and heavy rains even in summer. Don't expect every bicycle shop to stock parts you need; basic parts for basic bikes are readily available, but if your bike is anything special expect that replacement parts will need to be ordered from afar.

The following websites may be useful for cyclists:

Cycling Poland (☎ +44 01536 738 038; www.cyclingpoland.com) A well-run cycling tour operator that caters for international tourists.

Cyklotur (www.cyklotur.com in Polish) Can help with parts and information.

EuroVelo (www.ecf.com) European Cyclists' Federation project to establish a 65,000km European Cycle Network throughout the continent. Five of the 12 proposed routes run through Poland.

Zielony Rower (www.zielonyrower.pl) Information about eco-friendly bike tours and tracks.

SKIING & SNOWBOARDING

If you haven't skied before, perhaps Poland is the place to start, if only because you'll pay less here for the privilege than elsewhere in Europe. Accommodation in ski-resort areas can range from 30zł for rooms in private homes, up to the more luxurious 300zł hotel options. Ski-lift passes cost around 70zł per day.

Southern Poland is well-equipped for cross-country and downhill skiers of all abilities and incomes, though there's nothing budget about the scenery. Snowboarding's popularity is also increasing on the slopes.

The Tatras is the most well-equipped skiing area and the country's winter-sports capital of Zakopane is the most popular place to ski (p309). The slopes of this region, which peak at Mt Kasprowy Wierch (1987m), are suitable for all skill levels, and Zakopane has good equipment and facilities. As well as challenging mountains (like Mt Kasprowy Wierch and Mt Gubałówka, with runs of 4300m and 1500m respectively) the varied terrain around Zakopane offers flat land for beginners and plenty of time to learn, with a generous ski season extending to May.

Another centre of outdoor action is Szklarska Poręba (p337) in Silesia, at the foot of Mt Szrenica (1362m). The city offers almost 15km of skiing and walking routes, and great cross-country skiing. The nearby town of Karpacz (p338) on the slopes of Mt Śnieżka (1602km) enjoys around 100 days of snow per year, and the town of Międzygórze (p348) also hosts ski-enthusiasts who are venturing out to the **ski centre** (☎ 074 814 1245; www.czarnagora.pl; 57-550 Stronie Śląskie) at the 'black mountain' of Czarna Góra.

The village of Szczyrk, at the base of the Silesian Beskids, has less severe slopes and far shorter queues than elsewhere in the country. Szczyrk is home to the Polish Winter Olympics training centre and has mild enough mountains for novice skiers and snowboarders. See Szczyrk's official website (www.szczyrk.pl) for information on ski routes, ski schools, equipment hire and tourist services.

CANOEING, KAYAKING & RAFTING

The Drawa Route is believed to have been a favourite kayaking journey of Pope John Paul II when he was a young man.

Choices of where to kayak in Poland flow freely: the lowlands of Masuria, Warmia and Kashubia in Poland's north offer literally thousands of lakes and rivers to chose from.

Great Masurian Lakes

The town of Olsztyn is a handy base for organising adventures on water, particularly kayaking (p481). **PTTK Mazury** (☎ 089 527 4059; www.mazurypttk.pl in Polish; ul Staromiejska 1; ☼ 8am-4pm Mon-Fri) organises trips, equipment and guides; seek advice at the regional tourist office (p479). From Olsztyn it's possible to canoe the Łyna River to the border of Kaliningrad, or spend a couple of laid-back hours floating closer to the city.

The town of Olsztynek (p484) is an under-utilised treasure offering access to some very attractive lakes and is home to a helpful tourist office that can help you explore them.

The most popular kayaking route in the Great Masurian Lakes area runs along the Krutynia River (p481), originating at Sorkwity and following the Krutynia River and Lake Bełdany to Ruciane-Nida (p500). Some consider Krutynia the most scenic river in the north and the clearest river in Poland. It winds through 100km of forests, bird reserves, meadows and marshes. This is the queen of the Masuria rivers and arguably the king of kayaking spots.

A commendable tour operator is **Masuren Koch** (☎ 089 752 2058; www.masuren2.de), operating from Hotel Koch in Kętrzyn, which can arrange all manner of adventures in the region.

Augustów-Suwałki Region

In the less-visited and far cooler Augustów-Suwałki Region (p152), the lakes are not connected as they are in the Great Masurian Lakes, but the waters are crystal clear. The river to paddle in these parts is the Czarna Hańcza (p154), generally from Augustów along the Augustów Canal, all the way to the northern end of Lake Serwy. This route takes in the 150-year-old Augustów Canal, the Suwałki Lake District and the Augustów Forest. Numerous tour operators cover this loop, but it is also possible to do this and other routes independently.

South of the Masurian Lakes, the Biebrza River runs through the scenic splendour of the Podlasie region and through Biebrza National Park (p143). Lake Wigry in Wigry National Park (p159) offers surprisingly pristine paddling. The knowledgeable **Mr Bogdan Łukowski** (www.wigry.info/kontakt.html) can help organise kayaking excursions in this area. Also in Podlasie, **Kaylon** (☎ 085 715 5308, www.kaylon.pl) organises canoeing and kayaking adventures through Narew National Park.

Pomerania

The most renowned kayaking river in Pomerania is the Brda, which leads through forested areas of Bory Tucholskie National Park and past some 19 lakes. For more information go to http://park.borytucholskie.info (website in Polish).

The Drawa Route, which runs through Drawa National Park, is an interesting journey for experienced kayakers. Information on accommodation, kayak hire and routes through Drawa National Park can be found at www.d pn.pl.

Carpathian Mountains

The organised rafting trip to do in Poland is the placid glide through Dunajec Gorge (p301) in the Pieniny. There's nothing wet and wild about it, but it's a tradition that started in the 1830s, and the scenery hasn't lost a fraction of its splendour since.

HORSE RIDING

It's worth spending some time in the saddle in Poland – a country that has enjoyed a long and loyal relationship with horses (see p71). National parks, tourist offices and private equestrian centres are becoming more proficient in marking routes and organising horseback holidays along them.

The **PTTK** (Polish Tourist Countryside Association; www.pttk.pl) can assist with organising independent horse riding through its Mountaineering and Horse Riding subcommittee. There are many state-owned and private stables and riding centres throughout the country, from rustic agrotourism establishments to luxurious stables fit for a Bond film. It is also possible to organise riding tours of a few hours, or a few days, with the many private operators. The cost of undertaking these experiences varies enormously depending on duration and level of luxury. A down-to-earth horseback ride on a hucul pony for a week can cost around €700, while a weekend at a fine estate with access to steed-studded stables can cost upwards of €400. Shop around until you find something that suits your taste, ability and budget.

For more horse-holiday information go to www .equinetourism.co.uk /worldwidehorseholidays /poland.htm.

The following are notable places to ride horses in Poland:

Białowieża National Park (p147) Offers the chance to ride (or use horse-drawn carriages and sleighs in winter) on non-designated routes through forests.

Bieszczady National Park (p274) Has the 600km Transbeskidy Route, where you can ride a hucul pony; it is the longest horse-riding route in the country.

Kraków–Częstochowa Upland (p210) Has a 250km Transjurajski Horse-Riding Route that takes in castle ruins and the Błędowska Desert (see boxed text, p69).

Lower Silesia (p361) Offers the 360km Sudety Horse-Riding Route.
Masurian Lake District (p490) Provides the opportunity to ride horses around the lakes.

SAILING, WINDSURFING & KITESURFING

For useful information on birding in Poland, including links to societies and clubs, go to www .fatbirder.com/links_geo /europe/poland.html.

There's an under-explored seafaring culture in Poland. It's possible to hire yachts or sailing ships complete with their own shanty-singing skipper. The Baltic coast attracts some sails, but the summer crowds testify to the sailing-suitability of the Great Masurian Lakes, which truly live up to their name. This sprawling network of lakes allows sailors to enjoy a couple of weeks on water without visiting the same lake twice.

You can hire sail boats and wind/kitesurfing gear in Giżycko (p495), Mikołajki (p498), Ruciane-Nida (p500) and several smaller villages.

Boat enthusiasts will get a particular thrill from boat excursions on the Elbląg–Ostróda Canal (p486) in the Olsztyn region. The 159km-long canal built between 1848 and 1876, has varied water levels (differing by almost 100m). An impressive system of slipways 'carries' boats across the dry land and drops them back into the water on the other side. There are few places in the world where one can travel by boat across 550m of land.

Where to Watch Birds in Eastern Europe by Gerard Gorman is an authoritative work with some information dedicated to bird-watching in Poland.

Baltic Sea sailing takes place on the bay at Szczecin (p471), shared by Germany and Poland. Sailors can visit Wolin Island and National Park (p467) when sailing this 870-sq-km bay. The bay in Gdańsk (p403) also offers access to sea harbours and quaint fishing towns.

The artificial Soliński Lake in the Bieszczady Mountains (p274) and Czorsztyńskie Lake in the Pieniny Mountains (p299) are both sailable.

Windsurfing and kitesurfing are mostly done in the same areas that attract sailors, but the true heartland is Hel (p433) – the Gulf of Gdańsk between Władysławowo and Chałupy along the Baltic coast. The arbitrary dance of wind and currents constantly changes the shape of the enticingly named Hel Peninsula. The Great Masurian Lakes may be popular, but there's no place like Hel.

BIRD-WATCHING

Poland has an incredible range and number of birds to see. The winged residents of Polish nature reserves are a diverse bunch, particularly around the lakes and wetlands in the northeastern part of the country. See p70 for more information about the country's birdlife.

The bird-watching movement in Poland is not yet commensurate with the quality of bird-watching on offer; there are only around 3000 bird-watchers and ornithologists, mainly organised in university departments that study bird movements and trends. National park visitor centres, like that at Biebrza National Park (p143), can assist bird-watchers.

Specialised and foreigner-friendly bird-tour companies in Poland include the following:

Bird Guide (www.birdguide.pl) Specialising in tours through the Białowieża and Biebrza Forests.
Birds Poland (www.birdspoland.com.pl) Well-informed birding tours in the Białowieża and Biebrza Forests, the Baltic coast, the Masurian lake district and the Odra River valley.

HANG-GLIDING & PARAGLIDING

Hang-gliding and paragliding are taking off in Poland, particularly in the southern mountains. A popular place from which to glide is the Nosal in Zakopane. Enquire at tourist offices and tour operators in Zakopane (p307).

Parachute jumping over the Tatras is also possible. The **Bieszczady Extreme Sports Group** (☎ 060 071 0106; www.extremalne.bieszczady.pl in Polish) organises paragliding over the Bieszczady mountains.

CLIMBING & CAVING

The Tatras offer climbing opportunities for beginner and advanced climbers. Contact the **Polish Mountain Guides Society** (www.pspw.pl in Polish) for further information and a list of qualified guides. There are more than 1000 caves in the country, but few are ready for serious spelunking. Bear's Cave (p349) in Kletno and Paradise Cave (p221) near Kielce are open to the public.

DIVING

Yes, diving. The fact that diving is possible in Poland is a little-known fact, but true all the same. The most popular place for scuba diving is the Great Masurian Lakes. Lake Hańcza in Suwałki Landscape Park (p161) in the country's northeast offers the deepest inland diving (108m) and some impressive vertical rock walls. **CK Diver** (☎ 087 428 4362; www.ckdiver.suw.pl; ul Mickiewicza 9) in Giżycko can assist.

There is some impressive shipwreck diving off the Baltic coast (see www .balticwrecks.com for details about the wrecks) and winter can create a fine coat of ice for ice diving.

Water in Poland can be cold; if you go below 6m to 7m temperatures can drop to 3°C or 4°C. Visibility depends on the usual variables, but where pollution is particularly bad, visibility can be down 1m or so.

By international standards, the cost of diving courses in Poland is reasonable. Basic courses are around 1000zł (often plus equipment hire), with exams for the Open Water Diving Certificate incurring additional fees. Specialist courses are offered by some operators in fields such as shipwreck diving and underwater photography; these courses range from 400zł to 600zł. If you want to do a course, **Scuba Schools International** (SSI Polska; www .ssi-polska.com) has a strong presence in Poland. Alternatively, **PADI** (Professional Association of Diving Instructors; www.padi.com) has a list of certified operators through which you can do courses.

Warsaw

Warsaw

Take a stroll through Warsaw's pristine Old Town and Royal Castle and you'd think the city had enjoyed a comfortable existence the past 200 years. But at the end of WWII they, and nearly the entire metropolis, lay in rubble and ruin. The fact that Varsovians picked themselves up and rebuilt almost everything is reason enough to pay the country's capital a visit.

Warsaw's unquenchable energy not only extends to construction. Today it is a thriving, dynamic and progressive city, the epitome of a Polish nation firmly fixed on the future. Its bar, clubbing and music scene is unmatched in the country, and its yearly calendar is filled with theatre productions, operas and art-house film premieres. If culture is your thing, then Warsaw is your place.

The city's museums are often testament to its terrible past; many, like the Warsaw Rising Museum, retell the devastation WWII wrought. But there are more light-hearted gems too, like the picture-perfect palaces at Łazienki and Wilanów. Shoppers will max out credit cards on handmade products, and diners can satisfy their hunger with quality Polish cuisine and an ever-increasing array of food from around the world.

True, Warsaw is an acquired taste, and the first impressions probably won't appeal – stepping off the train or airport bus at Warszawa Centralna train station and staring at the drab blocks lining Al Jerozolimskie may tempt you to hop straight back on. But the vibe and drive of Poland's greatest city is infectious, and if you give it a little of your time, you'll be richly rewarded.

HIGHLIGHTS

- Taking in Warsaw and beyond from the top of the **Palace of Culture & Science** (p97)
- Listening to first-hand accounts of WWII at the **Warsaw Rising Museum** (p99)
- Spending your hard-earned cash on **handmade products** (p115)
- Marvelling at the renovation work in the **Old Town** (p91)
- Taking in the regal splendour of the **Royal Castle** (p87)
- Tapping into the capital's **nightlife** (p112), whether it be bar hopping, clubbing, live jazz or highbrow entertainment
- Admiring Warsaw's palaces at **Łazienki Park** (p101) and **Wilanów** (p101)

Old Town ★
★
Royal Castle ★

Warsaw Rising Museum ★

★ Palace of Culture & Science

Łazienki ★ Park

★ Wilanów

- POPULATION: 1.7 MILLION
- AREA: 495 SQ KM

WARSAW IN...

One Day
What better place to start a tour of Warsaw than the **Royal Castle** (p87), a former Mazovian stronghold. Spend the rest of the morning exploring the back streets of the **Old Town** (p91), then head to the **New Town** (p92) for a spot of lunch. Let the food digest while wandering through the **Historical Museum of Warsaw** (p91) before crossing town to the **Warsaw Rising Museum** (p99). Wait until late afternoon to take in the view from the top of the **Palace of Culture & Science** (p97), then round the day off with dinner at one of many restaurants in and around **ul Nowy Świat** (p96).

Two Days
Begin with a wander down **ul Krakowskie Przedmieście** (p96) and **ul Nowy Świat** (p96), the upper section of the Royal Way. Stop for breakfast en route before spending a few hours exploring the cultural gems of the **National Museum** (p100). Lunch south of **Al Jerozolimskie** (p99), then pass the early afternoon in the beautiful **Łazienki Park** (p101). With the rest of the afternoon, explore Warsaw's **markets** (p115) or **handcraft stores** (p115) and end the two days with dinner and drinks, and perhaps a jazz concert in **Akwarium Jazzarium** (p113).

HISTORY

Warsaw's history has more ups and downs than a jejunum. But like the very essence of the Polish character, it has managed to return from the brink of destruction time and time again.

The first semblance of a town only sprang up around the beginning of the 14th century when the dukes of Mazovia built a stronghold on the site of the present Royal Castle. In 1413 the dukes chose Warsaw as their seat of power, and things went swimmingly for over 100 years until, in 1526, the last duke died without an heir. The burgeoning town – and the whole of Mazovia – fell under direct rule of the king in Kraków and was incorporated into royal territory.

Warsaw's fortunes took a turn for the better after the unification of Poland and Lithuania in 1569, when the Sejm (the lower house of parliament) voted to make Warsaw the seat of its debates, because of its central position. The ultimate ennoblement came in 1596 when King Zygmunt III Waza decided to move his capital from Kraków to Warsaw.

The Swedish invasion from 1655 to 1660 was not kind to Warsaw, but it swiftly recovered and continued to develop. Paradoxically, the 18th century – a period of catastrophic decline for the Polish state – witnessed Warsaw's greatest prosperity. A wealth of palaces and churches was erected, and cultural and artistic life flourished, particularly during the reign of the last Polish king, Stanisław August Poniatowski.

In 1795 the city's prosperity was again shattered – following the partition of Poland, its status was reduced to that of a provincial town. When Napoleon rolled into town in 1806 on his way to defeat in Russia, things started looking up – the warring Frenchman created the Duchy of Warsaw and the city became a capital once more. The celebrations were brief however, as in 1815 Warsaw, and the rest of Poland, fell under Russian rule. The Varsovians rebelled against their rulers in 1830 and 1864, but the city remained in Russian hands until WWI.

After WWI Warsaw was reinstated as the capital of independent Poland and the urban development and industrialisation begun in the late 19th-century continued. By 1939, the city had grown to 1.3 million, of whom 380,000 were Jews who had traditionally made up a significant part of Warsaw's community.

German bombs began to fall on 1 September 1939 and a week later the city was besieged; despite brave resistance, Warsaw fell within a month. The conquerors instantly set about terrorising the local population with arrests, executions and deportations, and a Jewish Ghetto was swiftly built. The city rebelled against the Germans twice, first in April 1943 (see boxed text, p99) and second in August 1944 (see boxed text, p37). Both rebellions were ruthlessly crushed.

At the end of the war the city of Warsaw lay in ruins and 800,000 people – more than half of the prewar population – had perished.

WARSAW

(By comparison, the total military casualties for US forces in WWII was 400,000, for UK forces 326,000.) A massive rebuilding project was undertaken soon after (see boxed text, p93) and despite over 40 years of communist rule the city once again regathered its strength and is now enjoying an unprecedented period of economic growth.

ORIENTATION

Warsaw is a large, sprawling city split into two uneven halves by the Vistula (Wisła) River. Most of the tourist action is on the western side of the river, which is centred on the modern financial district.

The financial district's centrepiece is the prominent Palace of Culture & Science, which

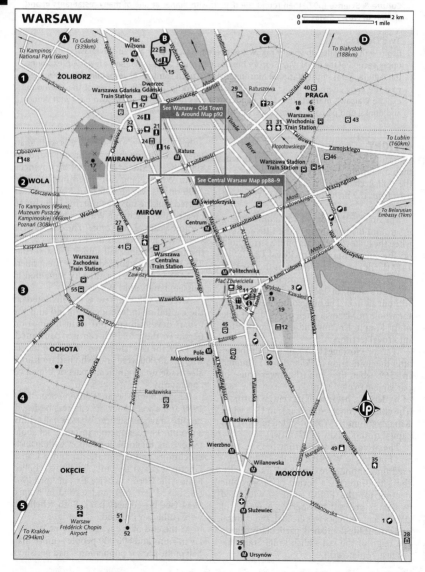

can be seen from almost anywhere in the city. Lying to the north of this area is the celebrated Old Town, and further north again is the New Town. West and northwest of the financial district is the former Jewish Ghetto.

An ancient processional route, known as the Royal Way (Trakt Królewski) leads south from the Old Town for 4km to Łazienki Park. Along the way it changes its name from ul Krakowskie Przedmieście to ul Nowy Świat and finally Al Ujazdowski. Wilanów, a royal retreat, lies even further south, around 6km from Łazienki Park.

Warszawa Centralna train station (also known as Dworzec Centralny), which lies southwest and in easy walking distance of the Palace of Culture & Science, is the city's main train hub. Warszawa Zachodnia bus terminal is 3km to its west, on Al Jerozolimskie, Warsaw's main east–west thoroughfare. The international airport is on the southwestern edge of the city.

INFORMATION
Bookshops
American Bookstore (www.americanbookstore.pl in Polish) Sadyba Best Mall (Map p84; ☎ 022 370 3173; ul Powsińska 31); ul Koszykowa (Map pp88-9; ☎ 022 660 5637; ul Koszykowa 55); ul Nowy Świat (Map pp88-9; ☎ 022 827 4852; ul Nowy Świat 61; ⊙ 10am-7pm Mon-Sat, 10am-6pm Sun) English-language publications, including travel guides.

Atlas (Map p84; ☎ 022 620 3639; Al Jana Pawła II 26; ⊙ 10am-7pm Mon-Fri, 10am-2pm Sat) Specialises in maps, atlases and travel guides; the best place in town for hiking and national park maps.

EMPiK (www.empik.com in Polish) ul Marszałkowska (Map pp88-9; ☎ 022 702 9402; ul Marszałkowska 116/122); ul Nowy Świat (Map pp88-9; ☎ 022 627 0650; ul Nowy Świat 15/17); Złote Tarasy (Map pp88-9; ☎ 022 222 0606; ul Złota 59) Has 15 stores Warsaw-wide; stocks a wide selection of British, German, French and US newspapers and magazines.

Marjanna (Map p92; ☎ 022 826 6271; ul Senatorska 38; ⊙ 11am-6pm Mon-Fri, 10am-2pm Sat) The city's best French-language bookshop, located in the Institut Français Varsovie.

Traffic Club (Map pp88-9; ☎ 022 692 1454; ul Bracka 25; ⊙ 10am-10pm Mon-Sat, 10am-7pm Sun) Multilevelled and multicoloured mega store with city maps on the 1st floor and English and German fiction on the 2nd.

Cultural Centres
The Centrala train station tourist office has a full list of cultural centres in Warsaw.

British Council (Map pp88-9; ☎ 022 695 5900; www .britishcouncil.pl; Al Jerozolimskie 59)

Goethe Institut Warschau (German Cultural Institute; Map pp88-9; ☎ 022 505 9000; www.goethe .de/warschau in German & Polish; ul Chmielna 11a)

WARSAW

Institut Français Varsovie (French Cultural Institute; Map p92; ☎ 022 505 9800; www.ifv.pl in French & Polish; ul Senatorska 38)

Istituto Italiano di Cultura (Italian Institute; Map pp88–9; ☎ 022 628 0618; www.iic.pl in Italian; ul Marszałkowska 72)

Internet Access

Internet cafés come and go as quickly as Polish politicians but this lot seem fairly stable.

Casablanca (Map pp88–9; ☎ 022 828 1447; ul Krakowskie Przedmieście 4/6; per 10min 1.50zł; ☉ 9am-1am)

Eccoms Internet (Map pp88–9; ul Warecka 1; per hr 5zł; ☉ 9am-11pm)

Internet Café (Map pp88–9; ☎ 022 826 6062; ul Nowy Świat 18/20; per hr 6zł; ☉ 9am-10pm Mon-Fri, 10am-10pm Sat & Sun)

Simple Internet Café (Map pp88–9; ☎ 022 628 3190; ul Marszałkowska 99/101; per hr 1-4zł; ☉ 24hr) Warsaw's biggest, with 150 terminals; highest rates from 9am to 7pm, cheapest from 2am to 7am.

Verso Internet (Map p92; ☎ 022 831 2854; ul Freta 17; per hr 5zł; ☉ 8am-8pm Mon-Fri, 9am-5pm Sat, 10am-4pm Sun) Enter off ul Koźla.

Internet Resources

www.e-warsaw.pl Official website of the city of Warsaw.

www.inyourpocket.com/city/warsaw.html Highly opinionated, but often amusing, coverage of the capital.

www.warsaw-life.com Eating, sleeping, drinking and shopping reviews.

www.warsawvoice.pl Online version of the English-language magazine.

Medical Services

For an ambulance, call ☎ 999, or ☎ 112 from a mobile phone. English-speaking dispatchers are rare, however, so you're probably better off phoning the following medical centres. For nonurgent treatment, you can go to one of the city's many *przychodnia* (outpatient clinics). Your hotel or your embassy (see p507) can provide recommendations.

There are plenty of pharmacies in Warsaw where you can get medical advice; look or ask for an *apteka*. There are always several pharmacies that stay open all night; a list is provided (in Polish) in the *Gazeta Wyborcza* newspaper (in the Supermarket section).

Apteka 21 (Map pp88–9; ☎ 022 825 3128; Warszawa Centralna train station, Al Jerozolimskie 54; ☉ 24hr) An all-night pharmacy at the central train station.

Damian Medical Centre (Map p84; ☎ 022 566 2222; www.damian.com.pl; ul Wałbrzyska 46; ☉ 7am-9pm Mon-Fri, 8am-8pm Sat, 10am-3pm Sun) A reputable private outpatient clinic with hospital facilities.

EuroDental (Map pp88–9; ☎ 022 627 5888; www .eurodental.com.pl; ul Śniadeckich 12/16; ☉ 8am-8pm Mon-Sat, 10am-4pm Sun) Private dental clinic with multilingual staff.

LIM Medical Center (Map pp88–9; ☎ 022 458 7000; www.cm-lim.com.pl; Marriott Hotel Bldg, Al Jerozolimskie 65/79; ☉ 7am-9pm Mon-Fri, 8am-8pm Sat, 9am-6pm Sun) Private clinic with English-speaking specialist doctors and its own ambulance service; carries out laboratory tests and arranges house calls.

Money

Kantors (currency-exchange offices) and ATMs are easy to find around the city centre. There are 24-hour *kantors* at the Warszawa Centralna train station and either side of the immigration counters at the airport, but exchange rates at these places are about 10% lower than in the city centre. Avoid changing money in the Old Town, where rates are shocking.

Amex (Map pp88–9; ☎ 022 581 5100; ul Chłodna 51; ☉ 9am-5pm Mon-Fri) Cashes its own travellers cheques as well as those of other major banks, but the rate may be lower than Bank Pekao.

Bank Pekao Marriott Hotel (Map pp88–9; Al Jerozolimskie 65/79); Plac Bankowy (Map p92; Plac Bankowy 2); ul Krakowskie Przedmieście (Map pp88–9; ul Krakowskie Przedmieście 1); ul Wilcza (Map pp88–9; ul Wilcza 70) Cashes travellers cheques and has more than a dozen offices in the city centre. Cash advances on Visa and MasterCard.

Western Union (Map pp88–9; ☎ general info 022 636 5688, 0800 120 224; Bank BPH, Al Jerozolimskie 27; ☉ 9am-5pm Mon-Fri) Money-transfer service, with branches at a number of locations; this is the main central office.

Post & Telephone

Main post office (Poczta Główna; Map pp88–9; ☎ 022 826 0303; ul Świętokrzyska 31/33; ☉ 24hr) One of over a hundred post offices in the city. Poste restante is at windows 41 and 42 (address c/o Poste Restante, Poczta Główna, ul Świętokrzyska 31/33, 00-001 Warszawa), and a rack of public phones is close by.

Tourist Information

The various branches of the city's official Tourist Information Centre provide free city maps and booklets (such as the handy *Warsaw in Short* and the *Visitor*), sell maps of other Polish cities, and will help you book a hotel room.

Free monthly tourist magazines worth seeking out include *Poland: What, Where, When; What's Up in Warsaw; Welcome to Warsaw;* and *Warsaw Point*. All are mines of information about cultural events and provide reviews of new restaurants, bars and night-clubs. They're available in the lobbies of most top-end hotels. The comprehensive monthlies *Warsaw Insider* (8zł) and *Warsaw in Your Pocket* (5zł) are also useful.

Tourist Information Centre (Centrum Informacji Turystycznej; ☎ 022 9431; www.warsawtour.pl) Airport (Map p84; Arrivals Hall Terminal 1; ☉ 8am-8pm May-Sep, 8am-6pm Oct-Apr; Etiuda Terminal; ☉ 8am-8pm May-Sep, 8am-6pm Oct-Apr); Old Town (Map p92; ul Krakowskie Przedmieście 39; ☉ 9am-8pm May-Sep, 9am-6pm Oct-Apr); Warszawa Centralna train station (Map pp88-9; ☉ 8am-8pm May-Sep, 8am-6pm Oct-Apr)

Travel Agencies

Almatur (Map pp88-9; ☎ 022 826 3512; www.almatur.com.pl; ul Kopernika 23; ☉ 9am-7pm Mon-Fri, 10am-3pm Sat) Handles student travel.

Kampio (Map p84; ☎ 022 823 7070; www.kampio.com.pl; ul Maszynowa 9/2; ☉ 8am-4.30pm Mon-Fri) Focuses on ecotourism, organising kayaking, biking, walking and bird-watching trips.

Orbis Travel (www.pbp.com.pl in Polish) Plac Konstytucji (Map pp88-9; ☎ 022 6288222; Plac Konstytucji 4; ☉ 10am-6pm Mon-Fri); ul Bracka (Map pp88-9; ☎ 022 827 7140; ul Bracka 16; ☉ 10am-6pm Mon-Fri) The largest agency in Poland, with five offices in town.

STA Travel (Map pp88-9; ☎ 022 626 0080; www.sonatatravel.com.pl; ul Krucza 41/43; ☉ 10am-6pm Mon-Fri, 10am-2pm Sat) Like Almatur, specialises in student travel.

DANGERS & ANNOYANCES

Warsaw is no more dangerous than any other European capital city, but you should take precautions while strolling about the streets at night, and watch your possessions on public transport and in other crowded places. Pickpockets are especially active on bus 175 (between the airport and the city centre), on

> ### WARSAW TOURIST CARD
> If you're planning to spend time in the city and want to see as much as there is to see, consider purchasing a Warsaw Tourist Card. It provides free or discounted access to most of the main museums, free public transport, and discounts at some theatres, sports centres and restaurants. Cards valid for 24 hours/three days cost 35zł/65zł and are sold at tourist information centres and some hotels.

the trams that run along Al Jerozolimskie, and in and around the central train station. Beware also of 'mafia taxis' (see p119).

Praga has a reputation as a rough area at night. Most locals use taxis as transport in and out of the neighbourhood, and so should you.

SIGHTS
Old Town & Around

Despite being a mere 40-odd years old, Warsaw's Old Town (Stare Miasto) looks 200 (see p93). It's the first (and sometimes the only) part of the city tourists hit, and with good reason; this small quarter holds the lion's share of Warsaw's historical monuments, including the Royal Castle, St John's Cathedral, and Citadel.

CASTLE SQUARE

A natural spot from which to start exploring the Old Town is triangular Castle Sq (Plac Zamkowy). Attracting snap-happy tourists by the hundreds each day is the square's centrepiece, the **Sigismund III Vasa Column** (Kolumna Zygmunta III Wazy; Map p92). This lofty 22m-high monument to the king who moved the capital from Kraków to Warsaw was erected by the king's son in 1644 and is Poland's second-oldest secular monument (after Gdańsk's Neptune). It was knocked down during WWII, but the statue survived and was placed on a new column four years after the war. The original, shrapnel-scarred granite column now lies along the south wall of the Royal Castle.

ROYAL CASTLE

It's a simple exercise moving on from Castle Sq to the **Royal Castle** (Zamek Królewski; Map p92; ☎ 022 355 5170; www.zamek-krolewski.com.pl; Castle Sq

WARSAW

CENTRAL WARSAW

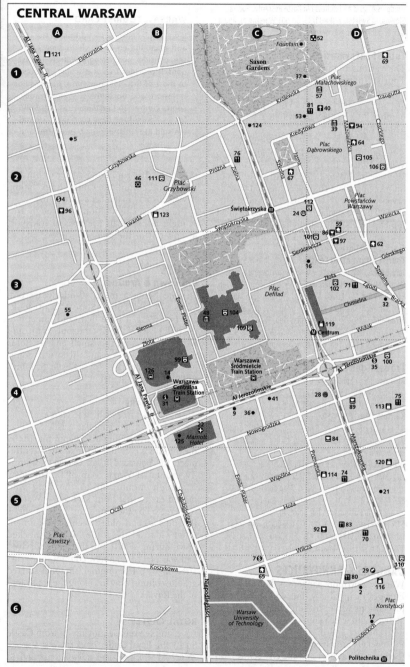

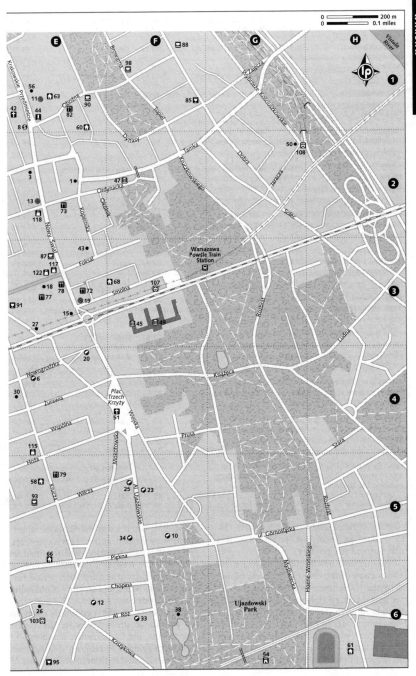

4; Route I adult/student 12/6zł, Route II 20/13zł, free Mon Jul-Sep; ⏰ 10am-6pm Tue-Sat, 11am-6pm Sun & Mon); just turn east and you're there.

This massive brick edifice, now a marvellous copy of the original that was blown up by the Nazis towards the end of the war (see boxed text, p93), began life as a wooden stronghold of the dukes of Mazovia in the 14th century. Its heyday came in the mid-17th century, when it became one of Europe's most splendid royal residences, and during the reign of Stanisław August Poniatowski

(1764–95), when its grand Baroque apartments were created. It then served the tsars, and in 1918, after Poland had regained its independence, it became the residence of the president. Today it is filled with period furniture, works of art, and an army of old ladies watching your every move.

Two floors of the castle are open to the public. Route I takes in the Court Apartments, the Parliament Chambers and the Crown Prince's Apartment, split between the ground and 1st floors, while Route II covers the Great Apartment and the King's Apartment on the 1st floor. Arguably the most impressive rooms are included in Route II, hence the price difference.

Dominating the Great Apartment is the magnificent **Great Assembly Hall**. It has more bling than P Diddy and has been restored to its 1781 décor of dazzling gilded stucco and golden columns. The enormous ceiling painting, *The Disentanglement of Chaos*, is a postwar re-creation of a work by Marcello Bacciarelli showing King Stanisław bringing order to the world. The king's face also appears in a marble medallion above the main door, flanked by the allegorical figures of Peace and Justice.

The neighbouring **National Hall** was conceived by the king as a national pantheon; the six huge canvases (surviving originals) depict pivotal scenes from Polish history. Surprisingly the ceiling has been left bare. A door leads off the hall into the smaller **Marble Room**, decorated in 16th-century style with coloured marble and trompe l'œil painting. The room houses 22 portraits of Polish kings, from Bolesław Chrobry to a large gilt-framed image of Stanisław August Poniatowski himself.

Further on from the National Hall is the lavishly decorated **Throne Room**. The dominant colour here is Regal Red, but there's also plenty of gold trimming, and 86 Polish eagles worked from silver wire. Connected to the Throne Room by a short corridor is the **King's Apartment**, the highlight of which is the **Canaletto Room** at the far end. An impressive array of 23 paintings by Bernardo Bellotto (1721–80), better known in Poland as Canaletto (he used the name of his more famous uncle), captures Warsaw in great detail from its heyday in the mid-1700s. The works were of immense help in reconstructing the city's historic monuments.

Overlooking Castle Sq from the 1st floor is the **Crown Prince's Apartment**. The lavishness of the rooms here is overshadowed by the collection of historical paintings by Jan Matejko; look for his most famous work, *The Constitution of the 3rd of May 1791*, which shows a triumphant King Stanisław being borne into the castle on the shoulders of a jubilant crowd.

Guided tours (☎ 022 355 5338; per group 85zł) of the castle are available in a number of languages; book in advance, though English- and German-speaking guides can usually be obtained at short notice.

OLD TOWN

The partially walled Old Town (Stare Miasto) is centred on **Old Town Sq** (Rynek Starego Miasta), which, for those with an eye for historical buildings, is the loveliest in Warsaw. It's lined with tall houses exhibiting a fine blend of Renaissance and Baroque with Gothic and neoclassical elements – aside from the façades at Nos 34 and 36, all were reconstructed after WWII. An 1855 statue of the **Mermaid** (Syrena), the symbol of Warsaw, occupies the square's central position, the site of the city's original town hall, demolished in 1817. On almost any given day, the square is swamped with tourists enjoying the pretty surrounds and numerous cafés and restaurants.

On the northern side of the square is the **Historical Museum of Warsaw** (Muzeum Historyczne Warszawy; Map p92; ☎ 022 635 1625; Old Town Sq 42; adult/student 6/3zł, Sun free; ☼ 11am-6pm Tue & Thu, 10am-3.30pm Wed & Fri, 10.30am-4.30pm Sat & Sun). It's a worthwhile introduction to the city, capturing seminal moments in Warsaw's history through photographs and documents. Its film covering the reconstruction of the city, screened several times daily (the English version is at noon), is fascinating. The nearby **Literature Museum** (Muzeum Literatury; Map p92; ☎ 022 831 4061; Old Town Sq 20; adult/student 6/5zł, Sun free; ☼ 10am-3pm Mon, Tue & Fri, 11am-6pm Wed & Thu, 11am-5pm Sun) features a permanent exhibition dedicated to Adam Mickiewicz (p51), Poland's most famous poet.

Back towards Castle Sq stands the restored neo-Gothic façade of **St John's Cathedral** (Katedra Św Jana; Map p92; ☎ 022 831 0289; ul Świętojańska 8; admission free; ☼ 10am-1pm & 3-6pm Mon-Sat, 3-6pm Sun). The oldest of Warsaw's churches, it was built at the beginning of the 15th century on the site of a wooden church, and subsequently remodelled several times. Razed during WWII, it regained its Gothic shape through postwar reconstruction. Look for the red-marble Renaissance tomb of the last dukes of Mazovia in the right-hand aisle, then go downstairs to the **crypt** (admission 1zł) to see more tombstones, including that of Nobel prize–winning writer Henryk Sienkiewicz.

Heading north out of the Old Town along ul Nowomiejska you'll soon see the redbrick **Barbican** (Barbakan; Map p92), a semicircular defensive tower topped with a decorative

Renaissance parapet. It was partially dismantled in the 19th century but reconstructed after WWII, and it's now a popular spot for buskers and art sellers.

NEW TOWN

The New Town (Nowe Miasto) is a bit of a misnomer, considering it was founded at the end of the 14th century and since 1408 has commanded its own jurisdiction and administration. It exudes similar architectural styles to those found in the Old Town, but lacks any defensive walls, probably due to the fact that historically it was inhabited by poor folk.

Ul Freta is the New Town's main street, leading north from the Barbican towards **New**

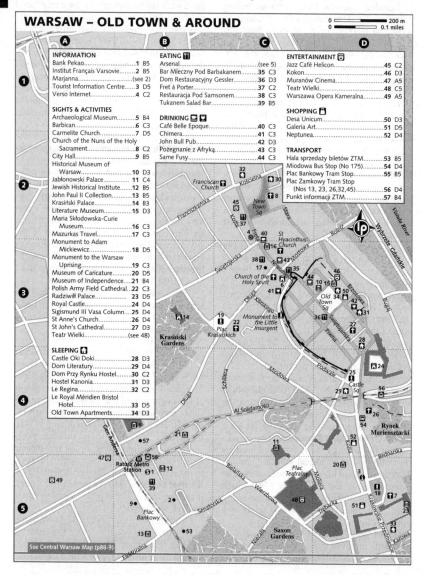

WARSAW – OLD TOWN & AROUND

0 ———— 200 m
0 ———— 0.1 miles

See Central Warsaw Map (p88-9)

A PHOENIX FROM THE FLAMES

Warsaw's Nazi occupiers did a good job of following Hitler's instructions to raze the city after the Warsaw Rising – at the end of WWII, about 15% of the city was left standing. So complete was the destruction that there were even suggestions that the capital should be moved elsewhere, but instead it was decided that parts of the prewar urban fabric would be rebuilt.

According to plan, the most valuable historic monuments were restored to their previous appearance based on original drawings and photographs. Between 1949 and 1963 work was concentrated on the Old Town, aiming to return it to its 17th- and 18th-century appearance – today not a single building in the area looks less than 200 years old. So complete was the restoration that Unesco granted the Old Town World Heritage status in 1980.

The Royal Castle took a little longer. It wasn't until 1971 that reconstruction began, and by 1984 the splendid Baroque castle stood again as if nothing had happened. Although the brick structure is a copy, many original architectural fragments have been incorporated into the walls.

The authorities also had to build, from scratch, a whole new city capable of providing housing and services to its inhabitants. This communist legacy is less impressive. The city centre was, until quite recently, a blend of bunkerlike Stalinist structures and equally dull edifices of a later era, while the outer suburbs, home to the majority of Warsaw's inhabitants, were composed almost exclusively of anonymous, prefabricated concrete blocks.

The city's skyline is still marred by ugly high-rises, but things have improved markedly since 1989. Newly constructed steel-and-glass towers have begun to break up the monotony, and the city outskirts are steadily filling up with aesthetically pleasing villas and family houses. Warsaw may never regain an architectural landscape that truly appeals, but considering all it's been through, it's doing one hell of a job rectifying things.

Town Sq (Rynek Nowego Miasta). Marie Curie (see boxed text, p95) was born in 1867 along ul Freta, and her former home now houses the **Maria Skłodowska-Curie Museum** (Map p92; ☎ 022 831 8092; ul Freta 16; adult/student 8/3zł, Thu free; 🕙 8.30am-4pm Tue, 9.30am-4pm Wed-Fri, 10am-4pm Sat, 10am-3pm Sun), which chronicles the life and work of this distinguished scientist.

Even by Polish standards, there are a lot of churches here. Of the six, the **Church of the Nuns of the Holy Sacrament** (Kościół Sakramentek; Map p92; ☎ 022 635 7113; New Town Sq 2) is the most intriguing; the work of prominent architect Tylman van Gameren, it has a fine Baroque exterior and clean white interior.

UL DŁUGA

Ul Długa leads southwest from ul Freta past the **Polish Army Field Cathedral** (Katedra Polowa Wojska Polskiego; Map p92; ul Długa 13/15), the soldiers' place of worship. There's no homage to the glory of war here; inside the main doors, which feature bas-reliefs of major battles fought by Polish forces, is a gruesome crucifix, with heads protruding from solid metal blocks on all sides of a ruined Jesus. Inside there are numerous plaques to fallen Polish soldiers.

Directly opposite the cathedral stands one of Warsaw's most important landmarks, the

Monument to the Warsaw Uprising (Pomnik Powstania Warszawskiego; Map p92). This bronze tableau depicts Armia Krajowa (AK; Home Army) fighters emerging ghostlike from the shattered brickwork of their ruined city, while others descend through a manhole into the network of sewers. The monument was unveiled on 1 August 1989, the 45th anniversary of the uprising (see boxed text, p37).

On the opposite side of ul Bonifraterska is the 1677 **Krasiński Palace** (Pałac Krasińskich; Map p92), designed by the ubiquitous Tylman van Gameren and considered one of the most splendid Baroque palaces in Warsaw. Today it's a branch of the National Library, and if you ask nicely you may be let inside.

CITADEL

Continuing north of the New Town you'll soon see the **Citadel** (Cytadela; Map p84), a massive 19th-century fortress overlooking the Vistula. Built by the Russian tsar to intimidate Warsaw following the November Insurrection of 1830, it served as a notorious political prison for years and nowadays is used by the military.

The huge gate overlooking the river is known as **Brama Straceń** (Gate of Execution; Map p84), a spot where political prisoners were executed all too frequently after the 1863 uprising. From the gate, a short cobbled road leads to the **Muzeum Pawilon-X** (Block 10 Museum; Map p84; ☎ 022 839 2383; ul Skazańców 25; admission free; 🕑 9am-4pm Wed-Sun), which preserves a wing of the old political prison. The cells are labelled with the names of the more famous prisoners who were incarcerated here, the best known being Józef Piłsudski, who did time in cell No 25 on the 1st floor; another cell contains the anvil on which prisoners were made to forge their own shackles. Inside are paintings by Alexander Sochaczewski (1843–1923), a former inmate who, along with 20,000 other anti-Russian insurgents, was transported to the labour camps of Siberia in 1866. The paintings, such as the huge *Pożegnanie Europy* (Farewell to Europe), depict the suffering of his fellow prisoners. In the museum grounds is an original *kibitka*, the closed prison carriage that was used to transport high-security prisoners to the east.

South of the Old Town

The area running south from Castle Sq to busy Al Jerozolimskie is the stomping ground of Warsaw's students, shoppers and socialites. This is nothing new, however; for much of the 19th century it was the commercial and cultural heart of Warsaw. During this time the city's university was founded here, as was Teatr Wielki, thought to be Europe's largest theatre.

PLAC BANKOWY

Like most of Warsaw's squares, Plac Bankowy (Bank Sq) is too big and busy to be appealing. This was once the financial district of 19th-century Warsaw, but the only reminder of this is spread along the western side of the square; here you'll see the imposing **City Hall** (Ratusz; Map p92) and the former stock exchange and Bank of Poland building, both grand neoclassical buildings designed by Antonio Corazzi

in the 1820s. The latter houses the **John Paul II Collection** (Kolekcja im Jana Pawła II; Map p92; ☎ 022 620 2725; Plac Bankowy 1; adult/student 11/5.50zł; 🕑 10am-5pm Tue-Sun), an art collection donated to the Catholic Church by the Carrol-Porczyński family. It's quite a surprise to find the likes of Dali, Van Gogh, Constable, Rubens, Goya and Renoir gracing the walls of a fairly nondescript museum, and to normally have them all to yourself. Polish artists are also represented, including Warsaw-born Wojciech Gerson (1831–1901), whose massive *Baptism of Lithuania* (1889), which beautifully captures Lithuania's conversion to Christianity, is highly expressive despite lacking colour.

The eastern side of the square was redeveloped after WWII and is now dominated by a blue skyscraper built on the site of a synagogue destroyed by the Nazis. The story goes that a local rabbi placed a curse on the site and, sure enough, the skyscraper was dogged by problems and took 30 years to build. Just behind it is the **Jewish Historical Institute** (Żydowski Instytut Historyczny; Map p92; ☎ 022 827 9221; www.jhi.pl; ul Tłomackie 3/5; adult/student 10/5zł; 🕑 9am-4pm Mon-Wed & Fri, 11am-6pm Thu), which houses a library and paintings, sculptures, and old religious objects related to Jewish culture. However it's the exhibition on the Warsaw Ghetto (p99) that sticks with you when you leave. Black-and-white photos and 40 minutes of original film footage from the Ghetto hit home – images of the atrocious conditions Jews were forced to endure, with starvation and death part of everyday life, tell a disturbing tale.

The northern end of the square is a busy intersection overlooked by the former Arsenal, a massive 17th-century building that now houses the **Archaeological Museum** (Muzeum Archeologiczne; Map p92; ☎ 022 831 3221; ul Długa 52; adult/student 6/3zł, Sun free; 🕑 9am-4pm Mon-Thu, 11am-6pm Fri, 10am-4pm Sun). Its permanent exhibition on the prehistory of Poland is periodically enlivened by temporary displays.

SYMBOL OF FAITH

All over Warsaw, on monuments and memorials, in museums and old photographs, you will see a distinctive monogram in the form of a 'P' stuck atop a 'W' in the shape of an anchor, the Catholic symbol of faith. This monogram – 'PW' stands for 'Polska Walczy' (Poland Fights) – was the symbol of the Armia Krajowa (AK; Home Army), the Polish resistance army that led the Warsaw Rising in 1944. Fortuitously, 'PW' can also stand for 'Powstanie Warszawskie' (Warsaw Rising), and the monogram has come to serve as a symbol of that tragic but heroic struggle.

MARIE CURIE

Warsaw-born Marie Curie (1867–1934) is a household name whose scientific achievements are staggering. She assisted in the discovery of the chemical elements radium and polonium – work that laid the foundations of radiography, nuclear physics and cancer therapy – and isolated pure radium. She was the first woman to be awarded a Nobel prize and the first person ever to win two Nobels.

Born Maria Skłodowska into a family of Polish teachers, she spent the first 24 years of her life in Warsaw before moving to Paris in 1891 to pursue a career in science, earning degrees in physics and mathematics at the Sorbonne. In 1895 she married French physical chemist Pierre Curie (1859–1906), and changed her name to Marie. Despite their laboratory being not much more than a barn, their scientific partnership proved to be extremely fruitful, resulting in the discovery in 1898 of two new radioactive elements, polonium (named after Marie's homeland) and radium. In 1903, they, together with Antoine Henri Becquerel, were awarded the Nobel prize for physics, for the discovery of natural radioactivity.

After Pierre's tragic death in a traffic accident in 1906, Marie devoted her energy to research and succeeded him as lecturer and head of physics at the Sorbonne – the first woman ever to teach at the 650-year-old university. Two years later she became a professor and in 1911 was awarded the Nobel prize for chemistry, for the isolation of pure radium.

Marie Curie was instrumental in founding the Radium Institute in Paris in 1914, which later became a universal centre for nuclear physics and chemistry. She also helped establish the Radium Institute in Warsaw in 1932.

In 1934 she died of leukaemia caused by prolonged exposure to radiation, and in 1995 her remains were reinterred in the Paris Panthéon, making her the first woman to receive this honour in recognition of her own achievements.

Stranded on a nearby traffic island in the middle of Al Solidarności is the **Museum of Independence** (Muzeum Niepodległości; Map p92; ☎ 022 826 9091; Al Solidarności 62; adult/student 5/3zł, Sun free; ☽ 10am-5pm Tue-Fri, 10am-4pm Sat & Sun), which has a small room devoted to the Solidarity movement and stages temporary exhibitions related to Poland's struggles for independence.

PLAC TEATRALNY

The broad expanse of Plac Teatralny (Theatre Sq) is bordered to the south by the colossal **Teatr Wielki** (p113). This neoclassical edifice was designed by Antonio Corazzi and constructed between 1825 and 1833. After it was burnt out during WWII, only the façade was restored; the rest was reshaped to suit modern needs. The theatre contains a small **museum** (admission free; ☽ 10am-2pm Tue-Fri). The neoclassical **Jabłonowski Palace** (Pałac Jabłonowskich; Map p92), opposite the theatre, served as the town hall from 1817 until WWII, when it was dismantled due to damage sustained. It was completely rebuilt in 1997.

SAXON GARDENS & AROUND

The magnificent **Saxon Gardens** (Ogród Saski; Map p92; admission free; ☽ 24hr) date from the early 18th century and were the city's first public park. Modelled on the French gardens at Versailles, the gardens are filled with chestnut trees and Baroque **statues** (allegories of the Virtues, the Sciences and the Elements), and there's an ornamental **lake** overlooked by a 19th-century **water tower** in the form of a circular Greek temple.

If it looks to you as though the gardens are missing a palace, you'd be right. The 18th-century Saxon Palace (Pałac Saski), which once occupied Plac Piłsudskiego (Piłsudski Sq), was, like so many other buildings, destroyed during WWII. All that survived were three arches of a colonnade, which have sheltered the **Tomb of the Unknown Soldier** (Grób Nieznanego Żołnierza; Map pp88–9) since 1925. The guard is changed every hour, and groups of soldiers marching back and forth between the tomb and the Radziwiłł Palace are a regular sight, though the big event is the ceremonial changing of the guard that takes place every Sunday at noon.

South across ul Królewska is the **Zachęta Gallery of Modern Art** (Map pp88–9; ☎ 022 827 5854; Plac Małachowskiego 3; adult/student 10/7zł, Thu free; ☽ noon-8pm Tue-Sun), a beautiful neoclassical temple that stages temporary exhibitions of contemporary art, mostly along the lines of video installations. Its bookshop has a fine collection of art books, but most are in Polish. Nearby, the circular dome of the 18th-century **Evangelical Church** (Map pp88-9; ☎ 022 827 6817; Plac Małachowskiego 3) proudly overlooks a busy junction. The dome is in fact the largest in Warsaw, and the church is renowned for its excellent acoustics and is the venue for a variety of musical events.

Across the street is the **Ethnographic Museum** (Muzeum Etnograficzne; Map pp88-9; ☎ 022 827 7641; ul Kredytowa 1; adult/student 8/4zł, Wed free; ◷ 9am-4pm Tue, Thu & Fri, 11am-6pm Wed, 10am-5pm Sat & Sun). The museum's top floor provides a good introduction into the country's rural heart, with a small but fine assembly of Polish folk art and crafts, but it's the portrait shots of indigenous people from around the world that steal the show.

UL KRAKOWSKIE PRZEDMIEŚCIE

This wide boulevard, running from Castle Sq to Nowy Świat, is the start of the Royal Way. It begins proudly with **St Anne's Church** (Kościół Św Anny; Map p92; ☎ 022 826 8991; ul Krakowskie Przedmieście 68), which is arguably the most ornate church in the city. It miraculously escaped major damage during WWII, which explains why it sports an original trompe l'œil ceiling, a Rococo high altar and gorgeous organ. The façade is also Baroque in style, although there are neoclassical touches here and there, and the detached **belfry** (adult/child 3/2zł; ◷ 10am-9pm) is thoroughly neo-Renaissance. At the top of the belfry is a viewing platform, which offers superb views over the Old Town.

Heading south you pass the **Monument to Adam Mickiewicz** (Map p92), author of *Pan Tadeusz*, before reaching the former **Carmelite Church** (Kościół Karmelitów; Map p92; ☎ 022 826 0531; ul Krakowskie Przedmieście 52/54). This church, too, escaped the ravages of war and, like St Anne's, has 18th-century fittings, including the high altar designed by Tylman van Gameren.

Set next to the church is the neoclassical **Radziwiłł Palace** (Pałac Radziwiłłów; Map p92), which is guarded by four stone lions and an equestrian **Statue of Prince Józef Poniatowski**. The prince was the nephew of the last Polish king, Stanisław August Poniatowski, and commander in chief of the Polish army of the Duchy of Warsaw created by Napoleon. Today the palace is the official residence of the president.

A short detour along ul Kozia leads to the quirky **Museum of Caricature** (Muzeum Karykatury; Map p92; ☎ 022 827 8895; www.muzeumkarykatury.pl; ul Kozia 11; adult/student 6/3zł, free Sat; ◷ 11am-5pm Tue, Wed & Fri-Sun, 11am-6pm Thu). The museum holds around 15,000 original works by Polish and foreign caricaturists dating from the 18th century onwards, plus satirical and humorous books, magazines, and the like. Displays are rotated on a regular basis.

Past the Bristol (p107) back on the Royal Way, a decorative gate topped with the Polish eagle marks a centre of studentdom. The central campus of **Warsaw University** (Uniwersytet Warszawski; Map pp88-9; ☎ 022 552 0000; www.uw.edu.pl; ul Krakowskie Przedmieście 26/28) was founded in 1816, although its oldest building, the Kazimierz Palace (Pałac Kazimierzowski), dates from 1634. With its leafy avenues and smiling students, it appears a peaceful place, but like any good university it has been a breeding ground for independent thought and the site of many student protests.

Because it's so close to the university, the **Holy Cross Church** (Kościół Św Krzyża; ☎ 022 826 8910; ul Krakowskie Przedmieście 3) has witnessed more student demonstrations and tear gas than any other church in Poland. During the Warsaw Rising, it was the site of heavy fighting between the insurgents and the Germans. It was seriously damaged, but some original Baroque altarpieces have survived and adorn its interior. Note the epitaph to Frédéric Chopin on the second pillar on the left-hand side of the nave. It covers an urn containing the composer's heart, brought from Paris after Chopin's death and placed here in accordance with his will.

The contemplative figure sitting on a plinth south of the university is a **Monument to Nicolaus Copernicus** (Pomnik Mikołaja Kopernika; Map p92), the great Polish astronomer.

UL NOWY ŚWIAT

Running from the junction of ul Świętokrzyska and ul Krakowskie Przedmieście to Al Jerozolimskie, **ul Nowy Świat** (New World St) is the busiest street in Warsaw outside the Old Town, but here it's generally Poles who make up the masses.

It's long been the city's fashionable shopping street, and is lined with restaurants, shops and cafés. Most of the buildings date from post-WWII, but the restoration here was so complete that the predominant style of architecture is 19th-century neoclassical. Aside from shopping, eating and drinking, the best thing to do here (and its side alleys ul Foksal and ul Chmielna) is find a comfy seat and watch the parade of Poles.

A short detour east along ul Ordynacka leads to **Ostrogski Palace** (Map pp88–9). Situated on a high fortified platform on the Vistula escarpment, the small Baroque palace (again designed by Tylman van Gameren) is today the seat of the Chopin Society, which hosts recitals and chamber music concerts in a lovely concert hall inside. There is also a small **Chopin Museum** (Map pp88–9; ☎ 022 827 5473; www.nifc.pl; ul Okólnik 1; adult/student 8/4zł, Wed free; ☺ 10am-6pm Tue-Sun) with static displays related to the great musician's life; there are a few interesting pieces, such as Chopin's last piano and death mask, but it's really only for fans. Guides are available for 100zł (English guides must be booked in advance).

Financial District

The open expanses and tall buildings bounded by ul Marszałkowska, Al Jerozolimskie, ul Jana Pawła II and Al Solidarności collectively constitute Warsaw's financial zone. Its dominating feature (and that of the city) is the **Palace of Culture & Science** (Pałac Kultury i Nauki, PKiN; Map pp88–9; ☎ 022 656 7136; www.pkin.pl; Plac Defilad 1; admission free; ☺ 9am-8pm Sun-Thu, 9am-11pm Fri & Sat), which rises high above the newly built skyscrapers that have begun to mark this area in the past 10 years.

Love it or hate it, every visitor to Warsaw should visit the PKiN. This 'gift of friendship' from the Soviet Union was built between 1952 and 1955 and at 231m high still remains the tallest building in Poland. It's never sat well with the locals, who have branded it with one uncomplimentary moniker after another; the Elephant in Lacy Underwear, a reference to both to the building's size and to the fussy sculptures that frill the parapets, is a particular favourite.

The massive structure is home to a huge congress hall, three theatres, a multiplex cinema and two museums, as well as hectares of office space. The basement levels are patrolled by a 50-strong pride of feral cats, who keep the building clear of rats and in return receive pampering from an official vet. However, the best feature of the building is the view it provides (Poles often joke that this is the best view of the city because it's the only one

that doesn't include the 'palace' itself). Take the high-speed lift (enter via the main entrance, facing ul Marszałkowska) to the 30th floor (115m) **viewing terrace** (adult/student 20/15zł; ☺ 9am-8pm Sun-Thu, 9am-11.45pm Fri & Sat) and take it all in – on a clear day the Mazovian plains are laid out before you. One-hour **guided tours** (☎ 022 656 63 45; per person 40zł; ☺ 10am & 2pm Mon-Sat Jun-Aug) of the palace allow you to visit the 2800-seat Congress Hall, former gathering place of the Communist Party faithful, impressive marble-lined chambers and meeting rooms, and former Soviet president Brezhnev's favourite chill-out room. Tours must be booked in advance, and there's a five-person minimum.

Photo and film buffs will be intrigued by the **Fotoplastikon** (Map pp88–9; ☎ 022 617 6173; www .fotoplastikon.stereos.com.pl; Al Jerozolimskie 51; adult/ student 20/10zł; ☺ 3-6pm Tue & Thu, 11am-3pm Sat), a late-19th-century forerunner of the cinema. It's reputedly the last working example of its kind in Europe, and consists of a large rotating drum set with individual eyepieces displaying stereoscopic 3D photos, some of them in colour. Each session consists of 48 pictures and takes about 20 minutes.

Former Jewish Ghetto

Before WWII, much of Warsaw's thriving Jewish community lived in Mirów and Muranów, two districts to the west of Al Jana Pawła II. It was here that the Nazis created the Warsaw Ghetto in 1940 (see boxed text, p99), which was razed after the 1943 Ghetto Uprising. Today the area is characterised by cheap, communist-era apartment buildings, but a few remnants of Jewish Warsaw still survive.

It is a large area to cover on foot, but fortunately the main sights are clustered together in the northern part. Take tram 16, 17, 19, 29 or 33 northbound on Al Jana Pawła II to the Anielewicza stop, and walk back south one block to the ugly concrete bunker of **Pawiak Prison Museum** (Map p84; ☎ 022 831 1317; ul Dzielna 24/26; admission free; ☺ 9am-5pm Wed & Fri, 9am-4pm Thu & Sat, 10am-4pm Sun). Built between 1830 and 1833, Pawiak was Poland's most notorious political prison, once used for incarcerating the enemies of the Russian tsar. During WWII it became even more notorious as the Gestapo's main prison facility – between 1939 and 1944 around 100,000 prisoners passed through its gates, of whom around 37,000 were executed on site and 60,000 transported to the gas chambers. It was blown up by the Nazis in 1944, but half of the mangled gateway, complete with rusting, original barbed wire, and three detention cells (which you can visit) survive, along with chilling memoirs of the horrors suffered by the inmates.

About 200m north of Pawiak, on the corner of ul Anielewicza and ul Zamenhofa, is a tree-lined park, which in summer is dotted with sunbathers. It's an incongruously peaceful setting for the **Ghetto Heroes Monument** (Map p84), a memorial to the thousands who lost their lives in the ill-fated Ghetto Uprising of 1943. The grey stone tower is built of Swedish granite, originally imported by the Nazis to build their own victory monument. On one side a bronze relief depicts a crush of doomed but defiant insurgents; on the other is a scene of martyrdom – a Jewish elder clutching a Torah scroll leads a group of his people, the sinister outlines of Nazi helmets and bayonets visible in the background. In the northwest corner of the park is **Skwer Willy Brandta** (Willy Brandt Sq), with another memorial marking the visit of German Chancellor Willy Brandt to this spot on 7 December 1970. Willy famously fell to his knees in a gesture of contrition for Germany's crimes against Poland.

Opposite the Ghetto Monument is the site of the proposed **Museum of the History of Polish Jews** (Muzeum Historii Żydów Polskich; Map p84; www .jewishmuseum.org.pl). The museum will be a multimedia and education centre, but as it's still in the design stage it's hard to know what will be included, or how the building will even look. At the time of writing, Finnish architects Lahdelma & Mahlamäki had been chosen for the design, and the entire project was expected to cost more than $US65 million.

From the Ghetto Heroes Monument head north along ul Zamenhofa, past a garden with a little mound topped by a simple limestone block, a **Monument to Mordechaj Anielewicz** (Map p84), leader of the Ghetto Uprising, who perished in a bunker on this site in 1943. At the northern end of ul Zamenhofa turn left along ul Stawki and cross the street at the tram stop. A little further along is the **Umschlagplatz Monument**, marking the site of the *umschlagplatz* (literally, 'taking-away place'), the railway terminus from which Warsaw's Jews were transported to Treblinka. The rectangular monument's marble walls are carved with more than 3000 Jewish forenames, from

Aba to Zygmunt, and the stark message: 'Along this path of suffering and death over 300,000 Jews were driven in 1942–43 from the Warsaw Ghetto to the gas chambers of the Nazi extermination camps'. Its shape is symbolic of the cattle trucks into which the prisoners were herded.

It's a 15-minute walk west along ul Stawki and then south on ul Okopowa to the **Jewish Cemetery** (Cmentarz Żydowski; Map p84; ☎ 022 838 2622; ul Okopowa 49/51; adult/student 4/2zł; ☺ 10am-4pm Mon-Thu, 9am-1pm Fri, 9am-4pm Sun). Founded in 1806, it suffered little during the war and still boasts more than 150,000 tombstones, the largest collection of its kind in Europe. Large parts are, however, neglected and very overgrown, making it a forlorn place. A notice near the entrance lists the graves of many eminent Polish Jews, including Ludwik Zamenhof, creator of the international artificial language Esperanto. Look also for the **tomb of Ber Sonnenberg** (1764–1822), one of Europe's finest funerary monuments; take the first paved path on the left beyond the ticket office and when you arrive at a junction on your right, look left: it's the roofed structure over by the wall. The marble relief on one side shows a walled city by a river and a Jewish cemetery; on the other side is the Tower of Babel and a forest hung with musical instruments, as well as a ship sinking in the river.

A five-minute walk northwest from the Palace of Culture & Science leads to Plac Grzybowski, the centrepiece of Warsaw's current Jewish community. Here, behind the **Teatr Żydowski** (Jewish Theatre; p114) is the **Nożyk Synagogue** (Map pp88-9; ☎ 022 620 4324; www .warszawa.jewish.org.pl; ul Twarda 6; admission 6zł; ☺ 9am-7pm Mon-Fri, 11am-6pm Sun May-Sep, 9am-5pm Mon-Fri, 11am-4pm Sun Oct-Apr), the city's only synagogue to survive WWII. Built between 1898 and 1902 in neo-Romanesque style, its interior features heavy metal chandeliers and tall vaulted colonnades. It's still used for religious purposes, and you may catch children reading from the Torah during the day.

Ul Próżna, a short street leading off Plac Grzybowski, opposite the Teatr Żydowski, is an eerie and incongruous survivor of WWII. Its crumbling, unrestored redbrick façades, the ornamental stucco long since ripped away by bomb blasts, are still pockmarked with bullet and shrapnel scars. A few blocks to the south, in the courtyard of an apartment building at ul Sienna 55, stands one of

THE WARSAW GHETTO

At the outbreak of WWII Warsaw was home to about 380,000 Jews (almost 30% of the city's total population), more than in any other city in the world except New York.

In October 1940 the Nazis established a ghetto in the predominantly Jewish districts of Muranów and Mirów, west of the city centre, sealed off by a 3m-high brick wall. In the following months about 450,000 Jews from the city and its surroundings were crammed into the area within the walls, creating the largest and most overcrowded ghetto in Europe. By mid-1942 as many as 100,000 people had died of starvation and epidemic diseases, even before deportation to the concentration camps had begun.

In a massive liquidation campaign in the summer of 1942, about 300,000 Jews were transported from the ghetto to the extermination camp at Treblinka. Then in April 1943, when only 50,000 people were left, the Nazis began the final liquidation of the ghetto. In a desperate act of defiance, the survivors took up arms in a spontaneous uprising, the first in any European ghetto.

From the outbreak of the uprising on 19 April it was clear that the Jews had little chance of victory against the heavily armed Nazis. German planes dropped incendiary bombs, turning the entire district into a chaos of burning ruins. Fierce fighting lasted for almost three weeks until, on 8 May, the Nazis surrounded the Jewish command bunker and tossed in a gas bomb.

Around 7000 Jews were killed in the fighting and another 6000 perished in fires and bombed buildings. The Nazis lost 300 men with another 1000 injured. The ghetto was razed to the ground except for a few scraps of wall, which survive to this day.

A number of personal accounts that have been written provide testament to the brutality of life within the ghetto walls. For further reading pick up a copy of any of the following: *A Square of Sky: A Jewish Childhood in Wartime Poland*, by Janina David, *Beyond These Walls: Escaping the Warsaw Ghetto*, by Janina Bauman, and *The Diary of Mary Berg: Growing Up in the Warsaw Ghetto*, by Mary Berg.

the few surviving fragments of the redbrick **wall** (Map pp88–9) that once surrounded the Warsaw Ghetto.

On the southwestern edge of the former ghetto stands the modern **Warsaw Rising Museum** (Muzeum Powstania Warszawskiego; Map p84; ☎ 022 539 7905; www.1944.pl; ul Przyokopowej 28; adult/concession 4/2zł, audio-guide 5zł; ☺ 8am-6pm Mon, Wed & Fri, 8am-8pm Thu, 10am-6pm Sat & Sun). The museum is housed in a beautifully restored redbrick power station and it traces the history of the Rising (see boxed text, p37) through three levels of interactive displays, photographs, film archives and the personal accounts of those who survived.

The sheer volume of material is overwhelming, but the museum does an excellent job of instilling visitors with a sense of the desperation Varsovians faced during the war. The ground floor begins with the division of Poland between Nazi Germany and the Soviet Union in 1939 and moves through the major events of WWII. A lift then whisks you to the 2nd floor and the start of the Rising in 1944. The largest exhibit, a *Liberator* bomber similar to the planes that used to drop supplies for insurgents during the Rising, fills much of the 1st floor. Be sure to take the lift towards the rear of the building that rises to a viewing platform; here pictures pinpoint the handful of buildings on the cityscape that survived the war.

A peaceful green park surrounds the museum and is home to the 'Wall of Remembrance', which records the names of the 10,000 insurgents who died during the Rising.

South of Al Jerozolimskie

Al Jerozolimskie is a big, ugly thoroughfare that creates a physical east–west border through the city. The area to its south was earmarked by the communists for post-WWII development, and some of the city's boldest socialist-realist architecture can be found here. Ul Marszałkowska, a broad avenue running south from near the financial district, contains the most impressive examples; its stretch between **Plac Konstytucji** (Constitution Sq) and **Plac Zbawciela** is lined with arcades bearing giant reliefs of heroic workers – the imposing scale and rigid, rectilinear forms are pinnacles of conformity and control. Constitution Sq itself is also worth a look for its two giant colonnades.

Not everything here has been bent to communist ideals. A few side streets close to Al Jerozolimskie still retain a semblance of pre-WWII charm, and are home to 19th-century houses, traditional workshops (p115), and cafés – **ul Wilcza** is particularly fine to stroll. Further south are remnants of the royal house of Poland in the form of Łazienki Park and Wilanów.

NATIONAL MUSEUM & POLISH ARMY MUSEUM

Containing almost 800,000 items in its permanent galleries, the **National Museum** (Muzeum Narodowe; Map pp88-9; ☎ 022 621 1031; www.mnw .art.pl; Al Jerozolimskie 3; permanent galleries adult/student 12/7zł, Sat free, temporary exhibitions 17/10zł, audio-guides 5zł; ☒ permanent galleries 10am-4pm Tue-Sun, temporary exhibitions 10am-4pm Tue & Wed, 10am-8pm Thu & Fri, 10am-5pm Sat & Sun) is the largest museum in the country. It's housed in a massive building, which is wheelchair accessible, at the western end of Al Jerozolimskie.

It's impossible to see the entire collection in one day, so it's best to choose your galleries wisely. With exhibits ranging from archaeology to 20th-century Polish art, choosing can be a hard task.

No-one should miss the **Faras Collection**, however. This display of early Christian art originates from a town on the banks of the Nile in what is now Sudan, and was rescued by Polish archaeologists from the rising waters of the Aswan High Dam. Frescoes and architectural fragments, dating from the 8th to 12th centuries, combine ancient Egyptian symbolism (winged sun discs and lotus flowers, for example) with Christian iconography, and include beautiful, expressive and often colourful images.

The gallery of **Medieval art** features a superb collection of religious painting and sculpture from all over Poland, with many gruesome renditions of the Crucifixion and scenes of grisly martyrdom. Most impressive is the huge Wrocław triptych depicting the *Martyrdom of St Barbara* (1447). The carved reliefs showing scenes from the saint's life and death are beautifully made despite their disturbing subject.

More **Polish art**, this time from the 16th to mid-20th centuries, is housed on the upper floors. Of the many, many paintings look for works by Jan Matejko, such as his epic *The Battle of Grunwald* (1878). The two main figures are the white-clad Ulric, grand master of the Teutonic Knights, to the left; and Witold, grand duke of Lithuania, dressed in red and sword raised in victory, perched atop a wild-eyed steed on the right. In the same room is Matejko's famous painting of *Stańczyk* (1862), the 16th-century court jester of King Sigismund the Old; here he represents the nation's conscience, meditating sadly on a major military defeat while the king and queen dance in the background.

Next door, and housed in the same building, is the **Polish Army Museum** (Muzeum Wojska Polskiego; Map pp88-9; ☎ 022 629 5271; Al Jerozolimskie 3; adult/student 12/7zł, Sat free; ☒ 10am-4pm Wed-Sun), which presents the history of the Polish army from the creation of the Polish state until WWII. Heavy armour, tanks and fighter planes from WWII are displayed in the park adjoining the museum.

AL UJAZDOWSKIE & AROUND

As the Royal Way leaves ul Nowy Świat it becomes Al Ujazdowskie, a wide, tree-lined boulevard with many an old mansion now home to an embassy of a foreign power. Near its northern section the road passes through Plac Trzech Krzyży (Three Crosses Sq), a square centred on 19th-century **St Alexander's Church** (Kościół Św Aleksandra; Map pp88–9), which is modelled on the Roman Pantheon.

As Al Ujazdowskie continues south it runs close to **Ujazdów Castle** (Zamek Ujazdowski; Map pp88–9), a fairytale-like edifice in its third incarnation. Erected in the 1620s for King Zygmunt III Waza as his summer residence, it was burned down by the Nazis in 1944, blown up by the communists in 1954 and eventually rebuilt in the 1970s. For the nonce it houses changing exhibitions of modern art from the **Centre for Contemporary Art** (Centrum Sztuki Współczesnej; Map pp88-9; ☎ 022 628 12 71; www.csw.art.pl; Al Ujazdowskie 6; adult/student 12/6zł, Thu free; ☒ 11am-7pm Tue-Thu, Sat & Sun, 11am-9pm Fri); a new centre is planned near the Palace of Culture & Science.

Immediately to the south of the castle are the **Botanical Gardens** (Ogród Botaniczny; Map p84; ☎ 022 628 7514; Al Ujazdowskie 4; adult/student 5/2.50zł; ☒ 9am-8pm Mon-Fri, 10am-8pm Sat & Sun Apr-Aug, 10am-7pm Sep, 10am-6pm Oct), established in 1818, and a short distance to the west of the gardens is the **Mauzoleum Walki i Męczeństwa** (Mausoleum of Struggle & Martyrdom; Map p84; ☎ 022 629 4919; Al Szucha 25; admission free; ☒ 9am-5pm Wed, 9am-4pm Thu & Sat, 10am-5pm Fri, 10am-4pm Sun), a branch of the

Pawiak Prison Museum. Like Pawiak, this building was used by the Gestapo for interrogation, torture and murder, and now stands as a memorial to the thousands of Poles who passed through its doors. With its depressing basement holding cells and Gestapo officer's interrogation room (complete with original bullwhips, coshes, knuckledusters etc), it's a hard place to visit.

ŁAZIENKI PARK

This **park** (Park Łazienkowski; Map p84; ☎ 022 625 7944; www.lazienki-krolewskie.pl; ul Agrykola 1; admission free; ☼ dawn-sunset) – pronounced wah-*zhen*-kee – is a beautiful place of manicured greens and wild patches. Its popularity extends to families, Sunday strollers, proud peacocks and the many red squirrels that call it home.

Once a hunting ground attached to Ujazdów Castle, Łazienki was acquired by King Stanisław August Poniatowski in 1764 and transformed into a splendid park complete with palace, amphitheatre and various follies and other buildings. The centrepiece of the park is the neoclassical **Palace on the Water** (Pałac na Wyspie; ☎ 022 625 7944; adult/concession 12/9zł; ☼ 9am-4pm Tue-Sun), the former residence of the king. It straddles an ornamental lake (gondola rides 6/4zł per adult/child) and like most other Łazienki buildings was designed by the court architect Domenico Merlini. During WWII the Nazis attempted to blow it up, but succeeded only in starting a fire that destroyed much of the 1st floor. Renovated and refurbished, the palace is open to guided tours – highlights include the 17th-century marble reliefs depicting scenes from Ovid's *Metamorphoses* gracing the original bathhouse (*łazienki* in Polish, hence the name), and the ornate ballroom.

Near the palace is the **Island Amphitheatre** (Amfiteatr na Wyspie), built in 1790 and based on the appearance of the Roman theatre at Herculaneum. It is set on an islet in the lake, allowing part of the action to take place on the water.

About halfway between the palace and Al Ujazdowskie is the circular **Water Reservoir** (Wodozbiór; admission free; ☼ 9am-4pm Tue-Sun), which stored water for distribution through wooden pipes to the palace and its fountain; it now houses an art gallery. Only a short walk north you'll find the **White House** (Biały Dom; adult/student 5/3zł; ☼ 9am-4pm Tue-Sun), which was erected in 1774 as a temporary residence

for the king until the palace was finished. It's incredibly small for a royal home and has managed to retain most of its original 18th-century interior.

A few other buildings are scattered throughout the park, the most architecturally intriguing of which is the 18th-century **Belvedere Palace** (Pałac Belweder; Map p84; ul Belwederska 52) at the southern limit of Al Ujazdowskie. It served as the official residence of Marshal Józef Piłsudski (from 1926 to 1935) and Polish presidents from 1945 to 1952 and 1989 to 1994, and now houses an upmarket restaurant.

WILANÓW

Warsaw's crowning glory in the park-palace arena is Wilanów (vee-*lah*-noof), some 6km south of Łazienki. Its origins date back to 1677, when King Jan III Sobieski bought the land and set about turning the existing manor house into an Italian Baroque villa (calling it in Italian '*villa nuova*' from which the Polish name is derived) fit for a royal summer residence.

Wilanów changed hands several times over the ensuing centuries, and with every new owner it acquired a bit of Baroque here and a touch of neoclassical there. Miraculously, it survived WWII almost unscathed and most of its furnishings and art were retrieved after the war.

The best place to start exploring the complex is **Wilanów Palace** (Map p84; ☎ 022 842 8101; www.wilanow-palac.art.pl; ul Wiertnicza 1; adult/concession 16/8zł, Polish guide 60zł, foreign-language guide 120zł, Sat free; ☼ 9am-6pm Sun, Mon & Wed, 9am-4pm Tue, Thu & Fri, 10am-4pm Sat May–mid-Sep, 9am-4pm Wed-Mon mid-Sep–Apr). Its highlights include the two-storey Grand Entrance Hall, the Grand Dining Room, and the Gallery of Polish Portraits, featuring a collection of paintings from the 16th to 19th centuries. Note the so-called coffin portraits – a very Polish feature – that are images painted on a piece of tin or copperplate personifying the deceased, then attached to the coffin during the funeral. The exterior of the palace is adorned with impressive murals, including a 17th-century sundial with a bas-relief of Chronos, god of time. As guides are expensive, you might be better off picking up an audio-guide (6zł).

The side gate next to the northern wing of the palace leads to the **gardens and parks** (adult/student 5/3zł, Thu free; ☼ 9.30am-sunset), which, like the palace itself, display a variety of styles.

The central part comprises a manicured, two-level Baroque Italian garden, which extends from the palace down to the **lake** (boat trips adult/concession 6/4zł), the south is Anglo-Chinese in design, and the northern section is an English landscape park.

The **Orangery** (Oranżeria; adult/student 5/3zł, Thu free; 10am-6pm Wed-Mon May–mid-Sep, 10am-4pm Wed-Mon Sep–mid-May), off the northern wing of the palace, features decorative art and sculpture from the 16th to 19th centuries.

Standing separately from the rest of the complex just outside the palace gates is the **Poster Museum** (Muzeum Plakatu; Map p84; ☎ 022 842 4848; www.postermuseum.pl; ul Kostki Potockiego 10/16; adult/student 9/5zł, Mon free; noon-4pm Mon, 10am-5pm Tue-Sun Jun-Sep, noon-4pm Mon, 10am-4pm Tue-Sun Oct-May). Its vaults house a massive 55,000 posters – one of the largest collections in the world – but only a fraction of this is shown at one time. Exhibitions change regularly, making it a museum to visit time and time again.

Get to Wilanów on bus 116 or 180 from any stop on ul Krakowskie Przedmieście, ul Nowy Świat or Al Ujazdowskie.

Praga

Crossing the Vistula from the Old Town into Praga, Warsaw's eastern suburb, is like entering another city. Clean, level streets and renovated buildings are replaced by broken roads and crumbling façades, and much of the populace is working class and poor.

Despite the grit, Praga is *the* place to be. The area is slowly being gentrified as artists, musicians and entrepreneurs move in, attracted by its pre-WWII buildings (as it was not directly involved in the battles of 1944, Praga didn't suffer much damage) and cheap rent. Ventures open and close on a regular basis but the list of established places grows steadily longer. **InfoPraga** (Map p84; ☎ 022 670 0156; www.infopraga .com.pl in Polish; ul Ząbkowska 36; 10am-6pm Mon-Fri, 10am-4pm Sat), the suburb's tourist and cultural information office, is handy for keeping pace with Praga developments.

Directly across from the Old Town and close to the river is the city's **Zoological Gardens** (Ogród Zoologiczny; Map p84; ☎ 022 619 4041; ul Ratuszowa 1/3; adult/student 12/6zł; 9am-6pm). Established in 1928, the zoo has some 3000 animals representing 280 species from around the world. Close by, rising from behind a clump of trees just off Praga's main thoroughfare, Al Solidarności, are the five onion-shaped domes

of the **Orthodox Church** (Cerkiew Prawosławna; Map p84; ☎ 022 619 0886; Al Solidarności 52). Built in the 1860s in Russo-Byzantine style, its small nave still retains original Byzantine portraits and gold upon gold.

Further into the neighbourhood is the disused redbrick **Koneser Vodka Factory** (Map p84; ul Ząbkowska 27/31), dating from the early 20th century. It houses two progressive galleries, **Luksfera** (☎ 022 619 9163; www.luksfera.pl; admission 2zł; 2-7pm Wed-Fri, 11am-5pm Sat & Sun) and **Klimy Bocheńskiej** (☎ 022 670 2190; www.bochenskagallery .pl; admission 2zł; noon-7pm Wed-Sun), the first of which specialises in photography and the second contemporary art from a wide range of media. Another kilometre east is **Fabryka Trzciny** (p113), a former marmalade factory that's become one of the city's leading art centres, hosting a broad range of events plus a gallery and restaurant.

Note that Praga is not safe to wander at night; it's best to travel from A to B by taxi.

WALKING TOUR

This short stroll through Warsaw's beautifully renovated Old Town takes in its big sights and back alleyways.

Start just west of the Old Town at the **Monument to the Warsaw Uprising (1**; p93), then head northeast along ul Długa and take the first right into ul Kilińskiego. At the far end are the redbrick fortifications of the Old Town; go right and then left into the garden below the walls to see the **Monument to the Little Insurgent (2)**, a memorial to the children who died in the Warsaw Rising. Follow the path northwards along the inside of the walls to the **Barbican (3**; p91).

Turn right and follow ul Nowomiejska to the **Old Town Sq (4**; p91). Stop to admire its gabled houses, then head diagonally across the square and go left down ul Celna, then right to a **viewpoint (5)** looking across the river to Praga. Go up the stairs to the left of the rear entrance to the John Bull Pub to reach the picturesque little square **Plac Kanonia (6)**; the cracked 17th-century bell in the middle was rescued from the WWII ruins of **St John's Cathedral (7**; p91). Beyond the bell, go through the arch on the right – the gallery above the arch was once a private passage linking the cathedral to the king's residence in the Royal Castle – and along the alley beside the cathedral, then left at the end to reach Castle Sq and the **Royal Castle (8**; p87).

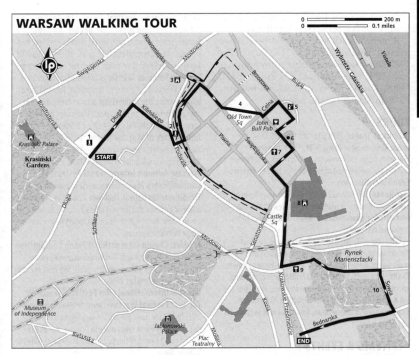

WARSAW WALKING TOUR

WALK FACTS

Start/Finish Plac Krasińskich/Royal Way
Distance 2km
Duration one hour

At the southern end of Castle Sq, climb the bell tower of **St Anne's Church** (**9**; p96) before taking the steps just north of the tower that lead to a cobbled path that slopes down and around behind the church. The path leads to the little square of Rynek Mariensztacki, which lies at the heart of the attractive **Mariensztat (10)** district. Rebuilt in 1948, with buildings inspired by Warsaw's 18th-century architecture, it was the city's first socialist housing development. Turn right along ul Sowia, then climb up the cobbled lane of ul Bednarska to finish on the Royal Way at ul Krakowskie Przedmieście.

COURSES

Many private schools offer Polish-language courses. Three-week intensive courses are around 1500zł to 2000zł. Personalised lessons cost anything from 30zł to 60zł an hour.

Academia Polonica (Map pp88-9; ☎ 0801 000 853; www.academiapolonica.com; Al Jerozolimskie 55/14)
IKO (Map pp88-9; ☎ 022 826 2259; www.iko.com.pl; ul Kopernika 3)
Polonicum (Centre of Polish Language & Culture for Foreigners at Warsaw University; Map p92; ☎ 552 1530; www.polonicum.uw.edu.pl; ul Krakowskie Przedmieście 26/28)
Schola Polonica (Map pp88-9; ☎ 022 625 2652; www .schola.pl; ul Jaracza 3/19)

WARSAW FOR CHILDREN

At first glance Warsaw doesn't appear the best place to bring children for a holiday, but there's enough here to keep them entertained. Topping the list of attractions is the Zoological Gardens (opposite), followed by the Polish Army Museum (p100) with its big tanks and planes, some of which can be climbed into.

Parks abound. Łazienki Park (p101) has plenty of space to run, plus egoistic peacocks to spot, hungry ducks to feed, and a boat trip to take, while Saxon Gardens (Map p95) and Ujazdowski Park (Map pp88–9) have good playgrounds. There are boat trips at Wilanów (p101) too.

WARSAW

The view from the Palace of Culture & Science (p97) is impressive for all ages.

A useful English-language guidebook aimed at expat families in Warsaw, *The Capital For Children* (28zł), is available from branches of EMPiK and American Bookstore (p85). Lonely Planet's *Travel with Children*, by Cathy Lanigan, is also a useful resource.

TOURS

Mazurkas Travel (Map p92; ☎ 022 635 6633; www .mazurkas.com.pl; ul Długa 8/14; ⏱ 9am-6pm Mon-Fri) Warsaw's major tour operator with morning sightseeing tours (140zł per person) of the city plus trips to Kraków, Gdańsk and Białowieża.

Our Roots (☎ 022 620 0556; our-roots.jewish.org.pl) Specialises in tours of Jewish sites; the Jewish Warsaw tour lasts five hours and costs 400zł. Other tours can be organised on request.

PiPiN (Map p84; ☎ 510 432 564; www.pipin.pl; ul Koński Jar 10/35) Vintage car and bicycle tours of the city's main sights, along with a few of its lesser-known corners.

Trakt (Map pp88-9; ☎ 022 827 8068; www.trakt.com .pl; ul Kredytowa 6; ⏱ 8am-7pm Mon-Fri, 9am-1pm Sat & Sun) Offers guided tours (930zł) in 20 languages, including English and German, for two to four persons, for up to four hours.

FESTIVALS & EVENTS

The following list of the city's main festivals is by no means exhaustive. Check Warsaw Tour's website (www.warsawtour.pl) for an extensive list.

Mozart Festival (www.operakameralna.pl) Staged annually from mid-June to the end of July and organised by the Warsaw Opera Kameralna. Features performances of all 26 of Mozart's stage productions plus a selection of his other works.

TOURS BY PUBLIC TRANSPORT

A single ticket on Warsaw's public transport system can go a long way, if you know which bus or tram to take. **Bus 180** runs the entire length of the Royal Way, connecting the Royal Castle with Wilanów Palace, while the double-decker **bus 100** passes the Old Town, Citadel, Palace of Culture & Science, Museum of Warsaw Rising and the zoo. On weekends and public holidays, a renovated historical tram, known as **Tram T**, covers much the same route as bus 100. For exact routes and times consult www.ztm.waw.pl (in Polish) or pick up a brochure at one of the city's tourist offices (p87).

Art of the Street Festival (Festiwal Sztuka Ulicy; www .sztukaulicy.pl) Held in early July, this five-day festival features street theatre, open-air art installations and 'happenings' staged unpredictably in public places such as Old Town Sq, the Royal Way, public parks and even bus stops.

Warsaw Summer Jazz Days (www.adamiakjazz.pl in Polish) This series of concerts, throughout July and August, brings leading international jazz stars to town, mixed in with performances by local talent. Major gigs are held in Congress Hall at the Palace of Culture & Science.

Anniversary of Warsaw Rising (www.1944.pl) Festivals and concerts commemorate the 1944 uprising against Nazi occupiers. A minute of silence is held at 5pm.

Warsaw Autumn International Festival of Contemporary Music (www.warsaw-autumn.art.pl) This 50-year-old festival, held over 10 days in September, is the city's pride and joy and offers a chance to hear the world's best avant-garde music, including new works by major Polish composers.

Frédéric Chopin International Piano Competition (www.konkurs.chopin.pl) This world-renowned piano competition takes place every five years; the next one is in September and October 2010.

Warsaw International Film Festival See opposite.

JVC Jazz Festival Warsaw (www.festivalproductions .net) One of the most prestigious jazz festivals in Europe, this three-day event takes place in October. Has already played host to most of the jazz greats, from Dizzy Gillespie to Miles Davis.

SLEEPING

While Warsaw has a variety of sleeping options, it still needs to go a long way to match its bar and restaurant selection. There's no real 'hotel district' either, with accommodation scattered the width and breadth of the city and the Old Town lacking a healthy choice of hotels, hostels and midrange places.

That's not to say things aren't improving. The number of independent hostels has begun to creep into the double-digit figures and there is a cluster of five-star hotels in and around the financial district. Midrange hotels remain a problem though – few exist for a city this size, and most lack charm and character. Note that many hotels offer cheaper rates than those quoted below on weekends.

The city's tourist information offices (p87) can help you to find and book accommodation if you so require.

Old Town & Around
BUDGET

Hostel Kanonia (Map p92; ☎ 022 635 0676; www.kanonia.pl; ul Jezuicka 2; dm/d 35/100zł; ▣) Kanonia is

FOCUS ON FILM FANATIC

Arguably Poland's largest film festival is the Warsaw International Film Festival (www.wff.pl). Entertaining the country's cinema buffs since before the fall of communism, this 10-day film extravaganza packs its programme with art-house film premieres, lectures and screen-writing workshops. The festival's director is Stefan Laudyn, who has overseen proceedings since 1991, and is in a good position to comment on Polish cinema – he is the founder of the Warsaw Film Foundation, and a board member of the European Film Academy. Author Neal Bedford asked him a few questions about the festival, Polish film and his home, Warsaw:

What's the focus of the festival? Has it always been international or did it begin as a vehicle for Polish cinema? It's always been international, but at some point I realised it can also be a great opportunity to promote Polish cinema – since 2000 we organise a sidebar event named Warsaw Screenings, presenting new Polish films to foreign professionals. Subsequently Polish movies are invited to leading international events.

Does the festival have a central theme? Does it change every year? Our motto is: films about people and for people. We create the programme having in mind our audience is interested in the culture of our neighbours from the region, our continent, and the world – in that order. We avoid being too mainstream, but at the same time experimental fare is not really our cup of tea. The programming team of 10 people watches hundreds and hundreds of films from all over the world to choose what we believe is the créme of current production.

Your thoughts on present Polish film? Are the bad old days of big-brother communism gone or are there still some restrictions in place? Ironically, the best Polish films were made in the old days – by Has, Polański, Munk, Wajda, early Kieślowski. Nowadays there's a shortage of good stories, but I believe there are young people somewhere as talented as their famous older colleagues.

If a person wanted an introduction to Polish film, what five films would you recommend? *Miś* (Teddy Bear), by Stanislaw Bareja, *Rejs* (The Cruise), by Marek Piwowski, *Jańcio Wodnik* (Johnnie the Aquarius), by Jan Jakub Kolski, *Człowiek z marmuru* (Man of Marble), by Andrzej Wajda, and *Amator* (Camera Buff), by Krzysztof Kieślowski.

Do you have a favourite Polish film, director, and actor/actress? Sure, but in the case of films it changes year to year – currently it's *Sztuczki* (Tricks), by Andrzej Jakimowski. Actress Krystyna Janda, who received Best Actress Award at Cannes in 1990 – I admire since last century. Actor Andrzej Chyra – I was there in 1999 when he became famous overnight after the first screening of *Dług* (The Debt).

Do you have a favourite Warsaw cinema? Kinoteka – a miniplex situated in the Palace of Culture. It has a spectacular location, nice interior and good programming. The Warsaw festival is held there.

One good thing about Warsaw? It has hidden jewels, off the tourist tracks, known mostly to locals.

One bad thing about Warsaw? That 1930s Warsaw doesn't exist. 'Hitler and Stalin did their job' as my old friend Muniek Staszczyk from T.Love sang.

Where can you buy tickets to the Warsaw International Film Festival? Presale starts a week before the event at EMPiK's ul Marszałkowska branch (p85). Many screenings are sold out before the festival commences so it's best to get in early. Last year we had over 92,000 admissions.

WARSAW

one of a new breed of private hostels setting up shop in Warsaw. Its location couldn't be better, tucked away in the heart of the Old Town, and with simple, functional rooms, a bar, and bike rental, it goes a long way in fulfilling most backpackers' needs.

Dom Przy Rynku Hostel (Map p92; ☎ 022 831 5033; www.cityhostel.net; Rynek Nowego Miasto 4; dm 50zł; ☺ Jul-Sep; ▣) Located in a quiet corner of the busy New Town, Przy Rynku is a neat, clean and friendly hostel occupying a 19th-century house. Its rooms sleep two to five persons and there's a big kitchen and laundry facilities for guest use.

MIDRANGE

Old Town Apartments (Map p92; ☎ 022 887 9800; www.warsawshotel.com; Old Town Sq 12/14; apt from 170zł) This agency rents out a range of apartments sleeping one to six people, with superb central locations on and around the Old Town's main square. All are attractively furnished and include bathroom and kitchen with cooker and fridge, but no phone.

Castle Oki Doki (Map p92; ☎ 022 425 0100; www.castleokidoki.pl; ul Świętojańska 2; dm 60-70zł, d 210-420zł; ▣) Owned and run by Oki Doki Hostel (see right), this newcomer to the Old Town's accommodation scene is housed in a 17th-century tenement house. All rooms overlook either Castle Sq or St John's Cathedral, and come in a range of playful styles – choose from 'Alice in Wonderland', 'Orient Express', 'Mermaid' and the like. The more expensive variety have four-star luxury.

Dom Literatury (House of Literature; Map p92; ☎ 022 635 0404; www.fundacjadl.com in Polish; ul Krakowskie Przedmieście 87/89; s/d from 180/300zł; ℗) In short, Dom Literatury is a plush hotel with a wonderful location and far too many stairs. It's also the headquarters of the Polish PEN Club, a writers' organisation. If you're happy enough to lug your bags to the 3rd floor, you'll enjoy views over the Old Town and rooms with formal décor, deep sofas and wooden beams on the ceiling.

TOP END

Le Regina (Map p92; ☎ 022 531 6000; www.leregina.com; ul Kościelna 12; rm from 1000zł; ℗ ✗ ▣ ⛲ ♿) Housed in a lovely arcaded 18th century–style palace just a few minutes' walk from the Old Town, the Regina manages a successful combination of traditional architecture and contemporary design. Rooms

are light and airy, decorated in shades of chocolate and vanilla, with lots of polished walnut, gleaming chrome and marble in the more expensive rooms. Check the website for specials – they can be as low as 50% of the rack rate.

South of the Old Town

BUDGET

Smolna Youth Hostel (Map pp88-9; ☎ /fax 022 827 8952; www.hostelsmolna30.pl; ul Smolna 30; dm from 36zł, s/d 65/120zł) A huge hostel popular with school groups, this central option complements its basic rooms with singles and doubles that have private bathrooms. While there's not a lot in the way of extra frills, it's clean and safe, and has a kitchen.

our pick Oki Doki Hostel (Map pp88-9; ☎ 022 826 5112; www.okidoki.pl; Plac Dąbrowskiego 3; dm 42-55zł, s/d from 115/145zł; ▣) Oki Doki has made excellent use of this former trade union building and created a hostel of some standing. Each of its bright, large rooms is individually named and decorated (like blue? ask for '7th Heaven'; reading? take 'Gazetka') and all contain lockers for guests. The owners are well travelled and know the needs of backpackers, providing a late-opening bar (where you can buy breakfast in the morning), a self-service laundry and bike rental.

Hostel Helvetia (Map pp88-9; ☎ 022 826 7108; www.hostel-helvetia.pl; ul Kopernika 36/40; dm from 43zł, s with/without bathroom 150/130zł, d 180/150zł; ▣) Another of Warsaw's quality hostels, Helvetia has spick-and-span rooms painted in warm, bright colours with wooden floors and a good amount of space. Bicycles and scooters are available for rent, laundry and kitchen facilities are in top order, and with only 38 beds, it's best to book ahead in summer.

MIDRANGE

Hotel Mazowiecki (Map pp88-9; ☎ 022 827 2365; www.hotelbelwederski.pl; ul Mazowiecka 10; s with/without bathroom 198/150zł, d 248/200zł) Once reserved as military accommodation, the Hotel Mazowiecki now offers its rooms to all and sundry. The shared bathrooms are a little worse for wear, but those in private rooms are of a far better standard.

Hotel Gromada (Map pp88-9; ☎ 022 582 9900; www.gromada.pl; Plac Powstańców Warszawy 2; s with/without bathroom 198/150zł, d 248/200zł; ℗ ✗) The 300-bed Hotel Gromada is an ugly blob on the

Warsaw skyline, but its rooms are in good condition and the Old Town and Nowy Świat are close at hand.

Hotel Harenda (Map p92; ☎ 022 826 0071; www .hotelharenda.com.pl; ul Krakowskie Przedmieście 4/6; s/d ste 300/380/520zł; P 🖳) Housed in an elegant neoclassical building, the Harenda boasts a quiet location close to the Old Town and an appealingly old-fashioned ambience. The single rooms are on the small side but the bathrooms are spotless; you're paying for the location here.

TOP END

Sofitel Victoria (Map pp88-9; ☎ 022 657 8011; www.sofitel .com; ul Królewska 11; r from 600zł; P ✕ 🖳 🕿 🕭) Conveniently located midway between the Old Town and the Palace of Culture & Science, the Sofitel is Warsaw's newest offering in hotel luxury. With all the bits and bobs you'd expect from a top hotel (great concierge service, full wellness centre, the occasional celebrity overnighting), it's a fine choice, and an even better one if you can secure a discount from the website.

Le Royal Méridien Bristol Hotel (Map p92; ☎ 022 551 1000; www.warsaw.lemeridien.com; ul Krakowskie Przedmieście 42/44; s/d from 750zł; P ✕ 🖳 🕿 🕭) Established in 1899 and restored to its former glory after a massive renovation, the Bristol is touted as Poland's most luxurious hotel. Its neoclassical façade, spectacularly floodlit at night, conceals a feast of original Art Nouveau features, and huge rooms that are both traditional and homy. Attentive staff cater to your every whim, and the Old Town is only a few minutes' walk away.

Financial District
MIDRANGE

Premiere Classe (Map p84; ☎ 022 624 0800; www .premiereclasse.com.pl; ul Towarowa 2; r 184zł; P ✕ 🖳) Rooms at this modern, purpose-built hotel are a little small, but standards are high for what you pay. It's also not very handy to the city's attractions, but it is on the bus 175 route between the airport and the Old Town.

Friends Guesthouse (Map pp88-9; ☎ 309 323 334; ul Sienkiewicza 4; s/d 190/240zł) This gay-friendly guesthouse offers three compact but smartly decorated rooms, each with a private shower, and shared toilet and kitchenette. Laundry facilities are free of charge, staff are friendly and professional, and the location is ideal. There's a two-night minimum stay.

Hotel Maria (Map p84; ☎ 022 838 4062; www.hotel maria.pl; Al Jana Pawła II 71; s/d 320/380zł; P 🖳) The family-friendly Maria is a modern, low-rise, 22-room hotel conveniently located for visiting the city's Jewish sights. Its rooms are mostly spacious, bright and cheerful, but a few are bland and unexciting so if possible have a look before booking.

South of Al Jerozolimskie
BUDGET

Nathan's Villa Hostel (Map pp88-9; ☎ 022 622 2946; www.nathansvilla.com; ul Piękna 24/26; dm from 45zł, s/d 130/160zł; ✕ 🖳) An established hostel set in a quiet courtyard, south of the centre. Like any good place, it has a kitchen, common room and reading room, but also provides free laundry and a simple breakfast. Take bus 131, 501, 505 or 525 from Warszawa Centralna train station to the Plac Konstytucji stop.

Biuro Podróży Syrena (Map pp88-9; ☎ 022 628 4978; www.kwatery-prywatne.pl; ul Krucza 17; s/d from 60/90zł, apt from 120zł; 🕑 office 9am-7pm Mon-Fri, 11am-7pm Sat, 2-7pm Sun) This agency offers rooms in private apartments, as well as whole apartments, for short-term rental. All the accommodation is in the city centre and one-night rental is accepted. The only hassle is picking up and dropping off the key.

Camping 123 (Map p84; ☎ 022 823 3748; camp123 @friko6.onet.pl; ul Warszawskiej 1920r 15/17; per person/car/ tent 12/12/12zł; P 🕿) Set in extensive grounds near the Warszawa Zachodnia bus terminal, Camping 123 has well-tended grass, tree-shaded areas and good facilities, including a tennis court and laundry. Wood-panelled, two-person bungalows (90zł) are also available, but beware, the walls are paper-thin.

MIDRANGE

Warsaw Apartments (Map p84; ☎ 022 550 4550; www .warsaw-apartments.com.pl; ul Augustówka 9; 1-/2-person apt 235/265zł; P) This agency manages three modern apartment blocks on the outskirts of Warsaw. All are in good order, and the apartments have phone, TV, cooker and refrigerator, which can be rented by the night; for stays of over a month the nightly rate falls by almost 50%.

Hotel Agrykola (Map pp88-9; ☎ 022 622 9110; www .hotelagrykola.pl in Polish; ul Myśliwiecka 9; dm from 50zł, s/d 249/300zł; P 🖳) Halfway between hostel and hotel, the Agrykola is a bright, modern place incorporating a sports centre. It has a restaurant, sauna and solarium, and there's no curfew. It's a little off the beaten track; take bus 107 from Al Jerozolimskie (the stop outside the Novotel, a block east of the central train station) to the Rozbrat stop; the entrance is back on the other side of the roundabout, beneath the overpass.

TOP END

our pick **Hotel Rialto** (Map pp88–9; ☎ 022 584 8700; www .hotelrialto.com.pl; ul Wilcza 73; r from 460zł; P ⊠ ⬜) Billed as Poland's first boutique hotel, this converted town house is a monument to early-20th-century design and craftsmanship. Each of the hotel's 44 rooms is individually decorated in Art Nouveau or Art Deco style, with antique and reproduction furniture, period light fittings and mosaic-tiled or marbled bathrooms. There are plenty of modern touches where it counts, with flat-screen TVs, power showers, and a sauna and steam room. The celebrated Kurt Scheller's Restaurant (p110) fills the ground floor.

Praga
MIDRANGE

Hotel Praski (Map p84; ☎ 022 818 4989; www.praski .pl; Al Solidarności 61; s/d 240/270zł; P) As hotels go, Praski won't excite too many travellers, but it's a solid midrange option little more than 1km from the Old Town. Rooms are decked out in appealing shades of burgundy, rose and green, and there are cheaper rooms with shared bathrooms (single 150zł, double 200zł) on offer.

Hotel Hetman (Map p84; ☎ 022 511 9800; www .hotelhetman.pl; ul Kłopotowskiego 36; s/d 330/380zł; P ⬜) Across the river but only just over a kilometre's walk or bus ride from the Old Town, the Hetman sports English-speaking staff, brand-new rooms decked out in soothing shades of pink and green, gleaming bathrooms, and a fitness room with Jacuzzi. It's in a quiet location, but buses and trams to all parts of the city stop nearby.

EATING

Of all the cities in Poland, you'll eat the best in Warsaw. It's not just hearty Polish cuisine on offer either – you'll find a growing selection of European, Southeast Asian, Indian and Japanese restaurants worthy of your hard-earned cash. Naturally prices have risen with the increased variety and the country's entry into the EU, but you can still find some good, cheap eats in the centre, particularly in the form of Poland's classic milk bars.

The largest concentration of eateries exists on and around Nowy Świat and south of Al Jerozolimskie. The Old Town generally houses expensive tourist traps, but there is a handful of quality spots if you take the time to look.

The price breakdown for Warsaw restaurants (based on the average cost of a main course) is: budget (less than 20zł), midrange (25zł to 50zł) and top end (more than 50zł).

Old Town & Around
BUDGET

Bar Mleczny Pod Barbakanem (Map p92; ☎ 022 831 4737; ul Mostowa 27/29; mains 3–8zł; ⏰ 8am-5pm Mon-Fri, 9am-5pm Sat & Sun) Just outside the Barbican, this popular milk bar looks as though it hasn't changed for decades. It serves cheap, unpretentious Polish standards in a location that would be the envy of many upmarket eateries.

MIDRANGE

Restauracja Pod Samsonem (Map p92; ☎ 022 831 1788; ul Freta 3/5; mains 15–30zł; ⏰ 10am-11pm) Situated in the New Town, Pod Samsonem is frequented by locals and tourists looking for inexpensive and tasty Polish food infused with a Jewish flavour – marinated herring, gefilte fish and *kawior po żydowsku* ('Jewish caviar' – chopped chicken liver with garlic). It's always busy and you may have to wait, especially for the popular outdoor tables.

Fret á Porter (Map p92; ☎ 022 635 3754; ul Freta 37; mains 25–56zł; ⏰ noon-11pm) Choose between the pavement terrace, with views of tree-lined New Town Sq, and the eccentric dining room with its modern art on rag-rolled brick walls and multicoloured napkins clashing with Regency-striped upholstery. The menu also indulges in bold contrasts, ranging from traditional Polish dishes (green lentil soup with mint, roast duck and grilled pork) to exotic offerings such as kangaroo and emu steaks.

TOP END

Dom Restauracyjny Gessler (Map p92; ☎ 022 831 4427; Old Town Sq 21/21a; mains 50–100zł; ⏰ 11am-midnight) Gessler has a well-founded reputation as the top restaurant on the Old Town's main square. Its two dining areas are quite distinct – the ground floor is an elegant, formal restaurant, while a rustic country inn fills labyrinthine brick-vaulted cellars below. With this kind of set-up the menu is of course dominated by traditional Polish dishes, ranging from *żurek* (traditional sour rye soup) to roast venison with cranberries. Reservations recommended.

South of the Old Town
BUDGET

Tukanem Salad Bar Plac Bankowy (Map p92; ☎ 022 531 2520; Plac Bankowy 2; salad portions 3-5zł; 8am-8pm Mon-Fri, 10am-1am Sat); ul Koszykowa (Map pp88-9; ☎ 022 630 8820; ul Koszykowa 54; 8am-7pm Mon-Fri, 10am-4pm Sat); ul Kredytowa (Map p92; ☎ 022 827 7119; ul Kredytowa 2; 10am-6pm Mon-Fri) The 'Toucan' works on three tried and tested principles: fresh food, low prices, and quick service. It offers a wide range of mainly vegetarian salads in simple surrounds, but fuller meals are also available, normally during lunch hours.

Vegabar (Map pp88-9; ☎ 022 211 3484; ul Obożna 9; soups 5.50-7.50zł, mains 7-18zł; 11am-9pm Mon-Fri, noon-9pm Sat, noon-7pm Sun) Imaginative vege-mains and soups are the stock products of Vegabar, a tiny establishment just off Krakowskie Przedmieście. Everything is freshly prepared daily, so you'll instantly feel those vitamins doing their job. Turn up for lunch and you can pick up a soup and main for around 20zł.

our pick Cô tú (Map pp88-9; Hadlowo-Usługowe 21; mains 10-14zł; 10am-9pm Mon-Fri, 11am-7pm Sat & Sun) The wok at this simple Asian diner never rests as hungry Poles can't get enough of the excellent dishes coming from the kitchen. The menu is enormous, covering all the main bases (seafood, vegetable, beef, chicken, pork), and you'll never have to wait more than 10 minutes for your food despite the queues. Hadlowo-Usługowe is accessed through the archway at Nowy Świat 26.

Qllinarnia (Map pp88-9; ul Zielna 5; mains around 12zł; 11am-7pm Mon-Fri, noon-4pm Sat) Don't expect friendly service or a warm welcome at this simple yet colourful milk bar. But do expect fast service, top-rate home-cooked Polish food (including a smattering of European classics, such as lasagne and quiche), and a packed house. Enter from ul Marszałkowska; it's easy to spot among the liquor stores and sex shops.

Bar Krokiecik (Map pp88-9; ☎ 022 827 3037; ul Zgoda 1; mains 7-19zł; 9am-8pm) Decent Polish food this close to Nowy Świat and the financial district isn't hard to find, but not at these prices. So there's no wonder it's sometimes hard to find a seat at Krokiecik, a modern take on the milk bar serving soups, salads and hot dishes such as *fasolka po bretońsku* (sausage and bean casserole), *strogonow z wołowiny*

(beef stroganoff) and *ragout z kurczaka* (chicken ragout).

MIDRANGE

Arsenał (Map p92; ☎ 022 635 8377; ul Długa 52; mains 15-35zł; 9am-11pm) Parents, children, pasta lovers and archaeological buffs will all be satisfied with Arsenał. It's located next to the Archaeological Museum (p94), serves scrummy home-made pasta with a range of sauces, and has a playground, playroom, and kids' menu for the little-uns.

Restauracja Polska (Map pp88-9; ☎ 022 826 3877; ul Nowy Świat 21; mains 25-50zł; noon-11pm) The Polska is a classic old-fashioned Polish restaurant of the type that Polish families favour for special occasions – folksy farmhouse décor, lacy tablecloths, bouquets of flowers everywhere, and smartly dressed, attentive staff. The menu is devoted to hearty home cooking – this is the place to try authentic *pierogi* (dumplings), *żurek*, *schab z dzika* (roast wild boar with crispy dumplings) and other *dania staropolskie* (old Polish dishes). The restaurant is set well back from the street – enter the gate at No 21 and go straight ahead until you see it on your right. Don't be put off by the scruffy exterior.

Sense (Map pp88-9; ☎ 022 826 6570; ul Nowy Świat 19; mains 20-60zł; noon-11pm Mon-Thu, noon-12.30am Fri & Sat, noon-10pm Sun) We're not sure why the menu is headed up with sexual references (we could make a few guesses, though), but the Asian fusion selections under 'foreplay', 'hardcore', and 'wet 'n' wild' will certainly give your tastebuds an orgasm. Sense is not only hugely popular for its food, but also for its cocktails, highballs and minimalist interior.

TOP END

Deco Kredens (Map pp88-9; ☎ 022 826 0660; ul Ordynacka 13; mains 35-75zł; 10am-11pm Mon-Fri, 11am-11pm Sat & Sun) This place flaunts an appealingly over-the-top Art Deco dining room, which looks for all the world like a 1930s bordello (minus the ladies). Fat armchairs tempt you to linger over a menu of Polish and international cuisine – the crispy roast duck, served on a wooden platter with potato pancakes, beetroot and baked apple, is superb.

South of Al Jerozolimskie
BUDGET

Greenway (Map pp88-9; ☎ 022 696 9321; ul Hoża 54; mains 5-10zł; 10am-9pm) One branch of a country-wide chain swept to popularity by its healthy food selection. Take your pick from the international menu, which includes Mexican goulash, Warsaw curry, samosas and enchiladas. Portions are hefty, and there's no table service.

Wook (Map pp88-9; ☎ 022 630 7474; Al Jerozolimskie 65/79; soups 4zł, mains 6zł; ☾ 11am-11pm) Despite its poor location in the bowels of the Marriott, Wook manages to attract plenty of hungry locals with dainty yet tasty portions of imaginative Asian food. Mix and match with a couple of choices (crispy duck followed by wan tan noodles with cabbage anyone?) and you'll come away satisfied.

MIDRANGE

Dżonka (Map pp88-9; ☎ 022 621 5015; ul Hoża 54; mains 10-30zł; ☾ 11am-7pm Mon-Fri, 11am-5pm Sat & Sun) With only six tables, 'petite' is no over-exaggeration for Dżonka's size. Small it may be, but big it is on Asian cuisine, serving up steaming Thai soups, Mandarin chicken and spicy (by Polish standards) beef Szechwan. Reservation recommended.

Warsaw Tortilla Factory (Map pp88-9; ☎ 022 621 8622; ul Wilcza 46; mains 15-30zł; ☾ noon-1am Sun-Thu, noon-2am Fri & Sat) This is the closest you'll come to authentic Mexican food in the city. And it does a decent job too of the burritos, enchiladas, nachos and tortillas. The décor of red brick, dark wood and steel isn't very Mexican, and neither is the 'hangover brunch' served till 5pm at weekends, but who cares when it's all accompanied by spiced-up Bloody Marys.

Tandoor Palace (Map p84; ☎ 022 825 2375; ul Marszałkowska 21/25; mains 25-50zł; ☾ noon-10.30pm) Billed as the best Indian restaurant in Poland, the Palace's food is prepared by experienced North Indian chefs using a genuine *tandoor* (clay oven). The extensive menu ranges from classics such as butter chicken, *shahi korma* (chicken or lamb in a mild, creamy sauce with crushed almonds) and biryani to Kashmiri balti dishes and sizzling platters.

India Curry (Map pp88-9; ☎ 022 438 9350; ul Żurawia 22; mains 30-46zł; ☾ 11am-11pm) The strong smells of India – the ones that churn, rather than turn, the stomach – wafting from the door are a good sign that this place does decent curry. The usual selection of tandoori chicken and rogan josh is available, and vegetarians will be happy with the likes of *malai kofta* (balls of cottage cheese stuffed with nuts in a coconut, herb and cashew sauce) and *aloo bhindi bhaji* (curried potato and okra).

Bacio (Kiss; Map pp88-9; ☎ 022 626 8303; ul Wilcza 43; mains 30-50zł; ☾ noon-midnight Mon-Fri, 1pm-midnight Sat & Sun) Romance is a wonderful thing, and if you like it shoved down your throat then you'll go weak at the knees over Bacio. The décor here is over the top, featuring a copy of Klimt's *The Kiss*, a portrait of Juliet, and more dried flowers, cat paraphernalia and horse pictures than a little girl could ever wish for. This shrine to amour also specialises in authentic Italian home cooking, from melt-in-the-mouth carpaccio to linguine with wild mushrooms.

TOP END

our pick **Kurt Scheller's Restaurant** (Map pp88-9; ☎ 022 584 8771; Hotel Rialto, ul Wilcza 73; mains 50-150zł; ☾ noon-10.30pm Sun-Fri, 5.30-10.30pm Sat) Swiss-born Mr Scheller whips up some of the city's most sought-after cuisine in this beautiful Art Deco restaurant. The menu is a trip for the taste-buds, swinging from Asian to Polish and back again, but always focusing on ingredients in season. There are also plenty of unusual morsels, such as creamy horseradish soup with veal tongue stripes, but be sure to save a little room for the wonderful desserts. Cooking courses are also offered (see p65).

Tomo (Map pp88-9; ☎ 022 434 2344; ul Krucza 16/22; mains 50-100zł; ☾ noon-11pm) You could do worse than spend an hour at Tomo's sushi bar, gazing at the little boats ferrying tiny morsels of sushi and maki in never-ending circles. The likes of tempura and teriyaki are also available, and staff are friendly and English-speaking.

DRINKING
Bars

Most drinking establishments open at 11am or noon and close when *ostatni gość* (the last guest) leaves – in practice, any time between midnight and 4am.

Chimera (Map p92; ☎ 022 635 6919; ul Podwale 29) Chimera is two bars in one – a basement filled with aging furniture and bric-a-brac, and an outside courtyard perfect for people watching. It's just outside the Old Town and a wonderful place to relax after a long wander.

John Bull Pub (Map p92; ☎ 022 831 0367; ul Jezuicka 4) Located in the cultural heart of the Old Town, and with views of the Vistula from the terrace, the John Bull is a comfortable and cosy spot to rest and sip a quiet ale. As far as the overseas British pub is concerned, this is a good one.

CONCENTRATED DRINKING

Warsaw's nightlife is as diverse as it is dispersed, but there are a few central points where bar hopping doesn't require taking the bus.

Dive through the archway at ul Nowy Świat 26 and you'll discover **Centrum Hadlowo–Usługowe** (Map pp88–9), a collection of bars, eateries and shops in stark contrast to the rapidly modernising face of 21st-century Warsaw. Here tiny drinking holes with names such as Pemek and Windigo fill a T-junction of squat concrete bunkers, attracting a young, bohemian crowd eager to avail of the relaxed vibe and cosy retro furniture. There's also outdoor seating, but the open-air party moves inside at 10pm due to city regulations. Lining the stomach is no problem either, with Turkish available from Kafefajka and Antalya, sushi from Besuto, and Asian from Cô tú (p109).

Close to the university at ul Dobra 33/35 is another concentration of bars, this time appealing to the city's student population. Here you'll find **Aurora** (Map pp88–9; ☎ 022 498 4565; ul Dobra 33/35), **Diuna** (Map pp88–9; ul Dobra 33/35) and **Jadłodajnia Filozoficzna** (Map pp88–9; ☎ 0501 040855; ul Dobra 33/35), all housed in what look like old construction-site offices. Each has its own distinctive musical flavour (live or DJ-supplied), whether it be punk/rock, experimental electronica, or reggae and jazz, but on almost any given night of the week the atmosphere is lively and the beer cheap.

Między Nami (Map pp88–9; ☎ 022 828 5417; www .miedzynamicafe.com in Polish; ul Bracka 20) A mix of bar, restaurant and café, 'Between You & Me' attracts a trendy set with its designer furniture, whitewashed walls and excellent vegetarian menu. There's no sign over the door; look for the Gauloises Blondes awnings.

NoBo (Map pp88–9; ☎ 022 622 4007; ul Wilcza 58a) A sumptuous mix of crimson and maroon décor and comfy sofas, all set to a chilled-out backbeat. Whether you're here to enjoy the fusion menu or an evening with friends, don't forget those mojitos.

Paparazzi (Map pp88–9; ☎ 022 828 4219; ul Mazowiecka 12) Paparazzi may have enjoyed a recent renovation, but it still remains a favourite with the trendy crowd. Its speciality is cocktails, and with a talented and friendly bar staff, it truly has raised the standards.

Plan B (Map pp88–9; ☎ 0508 316 974; www .planbe.pl in Polish; Al Wyzwolenia 18) This small bar squeezed into a stretched attic overlooking Plac Zbawiciela borders on dingy, but the mix of students and young office workers don't seem to mind. Find some couch space and relax to smooth beats from regular DJs.

The following are also worth stopping at:

Café Bar Lemon (Map pp88–9; ☎ 022 829 5545; ul Sienkiewicza 6; ⏱ 24hr) For late starters or the terminally energised. With a kitchen also open for morning refuels, it really does cover all the bases. Club, bar, café – you decide.

Sheesha Lounge (Map pp88–9; ☎ 022 828 2525; ul Sienkiewicza 3) Water pipes, belly dancers, henna tattooing and DJs spinning exotic tunes; a bar-restaurant with a modern Middle Eastern feast for all the senses.

Cafés

Café culture is a relatively new phenomenon to Warsaw, but locals adore it. You'll find places across the city, and new ones popping up on a regular basis.

Cafe Blikle (Map pp88–9; ☎ 022 826 4568; ul Nowy Świat 35; coffee from 9zł; ⏱ 9am-7pm Mon-Sat, 10am-6pm Sun) The mere fact that Blikle has survived two world wars and the pressure of communism makes it a household name. But what makes this legendary café truly famous is its donuts, for which people have been queuing up for generations. Join the back of the line and find out why.

Green Coffee (Map pp88–9; ☎ 022 629 8373; ul Marszałkowska 84/92; coffee 9zł, snacks 7-15zł; ⏱ 7am-11pm) The rich aroma of coffee pervades your senses as you enter this relaxed café on an otherwise nondescript section of Marszałkowska. The coffee is reputedly the best in town, and the food an inviting mix of cakes, quiches, sandwiches and muffins. Service apparently depends on the weather.

Pożegnanie z Afryką (Map p92; ☎ 022 831 4420; ul Freta 4/6; coffees 8-10zł, snacks 8-12zł; ⏱ 11am-9pm) 'Out of Africa' is a tiny café offering nothing but coffee – but what coffee! Choose from around 50 varieties, served in a little pot, and a range of tempting cakes. This is the original shop in a chain of about 20 branches scattered around Poland's major cities.

Coffee Karma (Map p84; ☎ 022 875 8709; Plac Zbawiciela 3/5; sandwiches & snacks 8-12zł; ⏱ 7.30am-10pm Mon-Fri, 10am-10pm Sat & Sun) 'Karma, you nuns and monks, are your intentions', so the Buddhist

COFFEE & A GOOD READ

Poles have had a long love affair with literature, but the new love is coffee. It was therefore only a matter of time before someone came up with the café-bookshop, thus providing locals with a practical *ménage á trois*. These intellectual establishments have sprung up across town, offering racks of books alongside coffee, tea and snacks. They're wonderful places to spend a few hours, dipping into a book or catching a literary event or concert, which many hold on a regular basis. Some of the more frequented places include the following:

Antykwariat (Map pp88-9; ☎ 022 629 9929; ul Żurawia 45; coffee 8zł; ⏱ 1-11pm Mon-Fri, 4-11pm Sat & Sun) Lovely sepia-tinted atmosphere, with all scuffed wood, mismatched furniture, old cushions and overflowing shelves of books. Best enjoyed in winter, as there's no garden.

Chłodna 25 (Map p84; ☎ 022 620 2413; ul Chłodna 25; ⏱ 8am-10pm Mon-Thu, 8am-midnight Fri, noon-midnight Sat, noon-10pm Sun) Bohemian haunt attracting journalists, artists, musicians and anyone else who can fit through the door. Concerts, films, debates and lecturers feature regularly; wine, beer and homemade cakes available.

Czuły Barbarzyńca (Map pp88-9; ☎ 022 826 3294; ul Dobra 31; ⏱ 10am-10pm Mon-Thu, 10am-midnight Fri & Sat, noon-10pm Sun) Stripped-back space where books, discussions and readings come first and coffee (albeit good) is just along for the ride. The 'Gentle Barbarian' was the city's first café-bookshop.

Kafka (Map pp88-9; ☎ 022 826 0822; ul Oboźna 3; ⏱ 9am-10pm) Quiet café serving healthy cakes, quiches and sweet-and-sour pancakes (3zł to 10zł). Choose from its massive selection of secondhand books and kick back on its low couches or outdoor seating.

Numery Litery (Map pp88-9; ☎ 022 622 0560; ul Wilcza 26; ⏱ 9am-9pm Mon-Fri, noon-8pm Sat & Sun) Small, peaceful pocket for quiet reflection or a chilled chat. Extensive coffee and tea collection and plenty of children's books and coffee-table tombs (mostly in English).

Tarabuk (Map pp88-9; ☎ 022 827 0819; ul Browarna 6; ⏱ 10am-10pm Mon-Fri, noon-10pm Sat & Sun) Cosy café that not only provides space for books and coffee, but also concerts, readings, lectures and vodka.

saying goes. Few truly religious folk frequent Karma, but at least the café owner's intentions are pure and simple – thick smoothies, strong coffee and an easygoing air. The intentions of guests are to secure an outdoor table in summer or a low couch behind large bay windows in winter, something that can often prove hard to do.

Café Belle Epoque (Map p92; ☎ 022 635 4105; ul Freta 18; tea 10zł, mains 10-20zł; ⏱ 1-11pm) This atmospheric café is a fairyland of chiffon, velvet and lacy lampshades, crammed with bric-a-brac and dusty antiques – you can buy pretty much anything you see here. An excellent range of speciality teas is accompanied by a menu of cakes, snacks and light meals.

Same Fusy (Only Tea Leaves; Map p92; ☎ 022 635 9104; ul Nowomiejska 10; tea 12-19zł, snacks 8-12zł; ⏱ 1-11pm) This place is a superbly designed surprise: an Oriental-style café on the 1st floor and a stylish tearoom downstairs. Over a hundred different types of tea, from the accepted norm to the 'out of the ordinary'.

ENTERTAINMENT

Warsaw's range of classical and contemporary entertainment options is the best in the country. The city is home to many classical music, opera and theatre venues, and the list of clubs and jazz bars grows longer every year. Film is also well represented in both mainstream and art-house cinemas.

Detailed listings of museums, art galleries, cinemas, theatres, musical events and festivals (in Polish only) can be found in the Friday edition of *Gazeta Wyborcza* and in the monthly cultural magazine *WiK* (Warszawa i Kultura). The free what's-on monthly *Aktivist* is distributed through restaurants, bars and clubs.

As for useful English-language listings, the monthly *Warsaw Insider* and the entertainment columns of the weekly *Warsaw Voice* provide some information on cultural events, as well as on bars, pubs and other nightspots.

Tickets for theatre, opera, musical events and visiting shows can be bought from **Eventim** (Map pp88-9; ☎ 022 621 9454; www.eventim.pl; Al Jerozolimskie 25; ⏱ 9am-7pm Mon-Fri) and some EMPiK stores (see p85).

Clubs

Balsam (Map p84; ☎ 022 898 2843; www.balsam.net.pl in Polish; ul Racławicka 99) A unique club, located inside an old military fort. It's good for lunch during the day but clubbers hold court at night and party hard under its vaulted ceilings.

Fabryka Trzciny (Map p84; ☎ 022 619 0513; www .fabrykatrzciny.pl; ul Otwocka 14) Located in a revamped factory in the heart of Praga, this art centre hosts a range of events, including well-patronised clubbing nights.

Harlem (Map p84; www.warsaw-harlem.com in Polish; ul Kolejowa 8/10) This converted warehouse that has become one of the most popular clubs in town. DJs pump out hip-hop, R & B and gangsta rap to a crowd dressed straight out of a blinged MTV video.

Klubokawiarnia (Map pp88–9; www.klubo.pl in Polish; ul Czackiego 3/5) Under the steady gaze of communist icons, dance the night away to great music with a chilled party crowd at this basement club. Regular fancy-dress events are held spice up an already funky night.

M25 (Map p84; ☎ 022 863 4567; www.m25.waw.pl in Polish; ul Mińska 25) 'In Electronica We Trust' is M25's motto, and in M25 we trust. This cavernous place has one of the best sound systems in town and is to the fore in dance and cultural events in Warsaw.

Stodoła (Map p84; ☎ 022 825 6031; www.stodola.pl; ul Batorego 10) Originally the canteen for builders of the Palace of Culture & Science, Stodoła is one of Warsaw's biggest and longest running student clubs. It hosts events, club nights and touring bands when they're in town.

Underground Music Café (Map pp88–9; ☎ 022 826 7048; www.under.pl in Polish; ul Marszałkowska 126/134) A swarm of students and backpackers pour into this basement club for its cheap beer, dark lighting and selection of music that varies from '70s and '80s to house, R & B and hip-hop.

The following are some other places worth noting:

Hybrydy (Map pp88–9; ☎ 022 822 3003; www.hybrydy .com.pl in Polish; ul Złota 7/9) Well-established student club with two rooms and a mix of acid jazz, soul, big beats and live music.

Luzztro (Map pp88–9; ☎ 022 826 6472; Al Jerozolimskie 6) Throwback to the dark underground clubs of old, with house, drum 'n' bass and electro.

Piekarnia (Map p84; ☎ 022 636 4979; www.pieksa.pl in Polish; ul Młocińska 11) Old fav' of the clubbing scene, with a packed dance floor. They don't call it 'The Bakery' for nothing.

Jazz

Akwarium Jazzarium (Map pp88–9; ☎ 022 620 5072; ul Złota 59) Reopened in August 2007, this was Warsaw's first jazz club. Only the white piano remains from the old days but with John Coltrane's eyes staring at you from one wall, you are left in no doubt that this place knows its heritage.

Jazz Café Helicon (Map p92; ☎ 022 635 9505; ul Freta 45/47) This small café-bar is a top-drawer jazz venue. A former music store, it still sells jazz and blues CDs and has added trumpets hanging over tables and black-and-white tiling on the floor.

Klub Tygmont (Map pp88–9; ☎ 022 828 3409; ul Mazowiecka 6/8) Hosting both local and international acts, the live jazz here is both varied and plentiful. Concerts start around 9pm but it fills up early, so either reserve a table or turn up at opening time (6pm). Dinner is also available.

Classical Music & Opera

Filharmonia Narodowa (National Philharmonic; Map pp88–9; ☎ 022 551 7128; www.filharmonia.pl; ul Jasna 5; ☽ 10am-2pm & 3-7pm Mon-Sat) Home of the world-famous National Philharmonic Orchestra and Choir of Poland, founded in 1901, this venue has a concert hall (enter from ul Sienkiewicza 10) and a chamber-music hall (enter from ul Moniuszki 5), both of which stage regular concerts. The box office entrance is on ul Sienkiewicza.

Warszawa Opera Kameralna (Warsaw Chamber Opera; Map p92; ☎ 022 831 2240; www.operakameralna.pl; Al Solidarności 76b; ☽ box office 9am-6pm Mon-Fri, 3 hours before performance Sat & Sun) The Warszawa Opera's repertoire ranges from medieval mystery plays to contemporary works, but it's most famous for its performances of Mozart's operas – the annual Mozart Festival (p104) is staged here.

Teatr Wielki (Grand Theatre; Map p92; ☎ 022 692 0208; www.teatrwielki.pl; Plac Teatralny 1; ☽ box office 9am-7pm Mon-Fri) This magnificent neoclassical theatre, dating from 1833 and rebuilt after WWII, is the city's main stage for opera and ballet, with a repertoire of international classics and works by Polish composers, notably Stanisław Moniuszko.

Chopin Society (Map pp88–9; ☎ 022 827 5473; www .nifc.pl; Ostrogski Palace, ul Okólnik 1) The society organises piano recitals in the beautiful auditorium in Ostrogski Palace (also home to the Chopin Museum, p97). Every Sunday from May to September, piano recitals are held at Chopin's birthplace in Żelazowa Wola (p120).

Cinemas

Most films (except for children's films, which are dubbed into Polish) are screened in their original language with Polish subtitles. Check

WARSAW

GAY & LESBIAN WARSAW

Warsaw's gay nightlife has been inching out of the closet since the mid-1990s, and there is now a fair selection of gay and lesbian venues. For a guide to all the latest places and events, check out the websites www.innastrona.pl, www.gay.pl and www.warsaw.gayguide.net.

Fantom (Map pp88-9; ☎ 022 828 5409; ul Bracka 20a; admission 15zł; ☽ 2pm-2am Mon-Thu, 2pm-3am Fri, 2pm-4am Sat, 6pm-2am Sun) Poland's longest-running gay club, Fantom has been on the go since 1994 and stages a huge party every Saturday starting at 10pm. It's a steamy, full-on experience, complete with sauna, Jacuzzi, sex shop and video lounge; the inconspicuous entrance (a black door with 'Fantom' stencilled on it) is in the courtyard behind Między Nami.

Kokon (Map p92; ☎ 022 831 9539; ul Brzozowa 37; admission 9zł; ☽ 4pm-3am) The Kokon is a four-floor gay club in the heart of the Old Town, done up with designer chic and featuring 1970s and '80s hits, 'gay house' music and a weekly drag show.

Rasko (Map pp88-9; ☎ 022 890 0299; ul Krochmalna 32a; ☽ 5pm-late) One of Warsaw's most popular gay and lesbian bars, Rasko is a cosy and welcoming little pub with regular karaoke and drag nights.

listings on www.kino.pl (in Polish only, but decipherable – click on 'Repertuar', then 'Warszawa', then the name of the cinema); admission ranges from 5zł to 20zł. Cinemas in Warsaw include the following:

Cinema City Sadyba (Map p84; ☎ 022 550 3333; ul Powsińska 31) Modern 12-screen multiplex with wheelchair access.

Iluzjon Filmoteki Narodowej (Map p84; ☎ 022 646 1260; www.fn.org.pl; ul Narbutta 50a) Home to the national film archive, and also Warsaw's main art-house cinema.

Kino Luna (Map pp88-9; ☎ 022 621 7828; www.kino luna.pl in Polish; ul Marszałkowska 28) Mainly art-house films from around the world.

Kinoteka (Map pp88-9; ☎ 022 550 7070; www.kino teka.pl; Plac Defilad 1) Multiplex housed in the Palace of Culture & Science; entrance faces Al Jerozolimskie.

Muranów Cinema (Map p92; ☎ 022 831 0358; ul Gen Andersa 1) Screens art-house films.

Theatre

Polish theatre has long had a high profile and continues to do so. Warsaw has about 20 theatres, including some of the best in the country. Most theatres close in July and August for their annual holidays. The leading playhouses, all of which lean towards contemporary productions:

Teatr Ateneum (Map pp88-9; ☎ 022 625 7330; www .teatrateneum.pl in Polish; ul Jaracza 2)

Teatr Dramatyczny (Map pp88-9; ☎ 022 656 6844; www.teatrdramatyczny.pl; Palace of Culture & Science, Plac Defilad 1)

Teatr Polonia (Map pp88-9; ☎ 022 622 2132; www .teatrpolonia.pl in Polish; ul Marszałkowska 56) Run by Krystyna Janda, winner of Best Actress at Cannes in 1990.

Teatr Powszechny (Map p84; ☎ 022 818 0001; ul Zamojskiego 20)

The **Teatr Żydowski** (Jewish Theatre; Map pp88-9; ☎ 022 620 7025; www.teatr-zydowski.art.pl; Plac Grzybowski 12/16) derives its inspiration from Jewish culture and traditions, and some of its productions are performed in Yiddish – Polish and English translations are provided through headphones.

SHOPPING

Like any modern Eastern European city, Warsaw has all the brand name stores and plethora of shopping malls you'd expect in the West. For the most part, prices are a little cheaper here, but things probably won't stay that way for long.

The upshot of all this commercialisation is the slow death of establishments that have existed since the communist era and beyond – a case of goodbye Marx, hello Marks & Spencer. Some still exist (see opposite) but whether they can weather the shopping storm is anyone's guess.

The main shopping area lies in the maze of streets between the Palace of Culture & Science and ul Nowy Świat, and along the eastern part of Al Jerozolimskie and the southern part of ul Marszałkowska.

Arts, Crafts & Souvenirs

Cepelia (www.cepelia.pl; ☽ stores 11am-7pm Mon-Fri, 10am-2pm Sat) Plac Konstytucji (Map pp88-9; ☎ 022 499 9703; Plac Konstytucji 5); ul Chmielna (Map pp88-9; ☎ 022 816 1481; ul Chmielna 8); ul Krucza (Map pp88-9; ☎ 022 499 9705; ul Krucza 23); ul Marszałkowska (Map pp88-9; ☎ 022 628 7757;

ul Marszałkowska 99/101) An established organisation dedicated to promoting Polish arts and crafts, Cepelia stocks its shops with woodwork, pottery, sculpture, fabrics, embroidery, lace, paintings and traditional costumes from various Polish regions.

Neptunea (Map p92; ☎ 022 826 0247; www.neptunea.pl; ul Krakowskie Przedmieście 47/51; 11am-7pm Mon-Fri, 11am-5pm Sat) Talk about a mish-mash of items. Neptunea is a purveyor of Polish jewellery, carved stoneware and crafts, along with furniture, shells and even musical instruments from across the globe.

Desa Unicum (www.desa.pl in Polish) Old Town Sq (Map p92; ☎ 022 621 6615; Old Town Sq 4/6; 10am-7pm Mon-Fri, 10am-4pm Sat); ul Nowy Świat (Map pp88-9; ☎ 022 827 4760; ul Nowy Świat 51; 11am-6.30pm Mon-Fri, 11am-5pm Sat) Desa Unicum is an art and antiques dealership that sells a range of old furniture, silverware, watches, paintings, icons and jewellery. Check customs regulations on p506 before purchasing anything.

Galeria Grafiki i Plakatu (Map pp88-9; ☎ 022 621 4077; ul Hoża 40; 11am-6pm Mon-Fri, 10am-3pm Sat) This small gallery stocks what is unquestionably the best selection of original prints and graphic art in Poland. It also has a good range of posters.

Galeria Art (Map p92; ☎ 022 828 5170; www.galeriaart.pl; ul Krakowskie Przedmieście 17; 11.30am-7pm Mon-Fri, 11.30am-5pm Sat) Owned by the Union of Polish Artists, this gallery offers a broad range of contemporary Polish art for sale, and an English-speaking manager who may – or may not – be of help.

Markets

Bazar na Kole (Map p84; ul Obozowa; early morning-2pm Sat & Sun) This huge antiques and bric-a-brac market, located in the western suburb of Koło, offers everything from old farm implements and furniture to WWII relics such as rusted German helmets, ammo boxes and shell casings. You will have to pick through the junk to find a bargain, but that's half the fun. Take tram 12, 13 or 24 to the Dalibora stop.

Hala Mirowska (Map p84; Al Jana Pawła II; dawn-dusk) Despite being converted into a modern supermarket, Hala Mirowska is worth visiting for its architecture alone. The redbrick pavilion of this 19th-century marketplace is in exceptional condition, and there's still a semblance of market atmosphere here; a few stalls selling fresh flowers and fruit and vegetables line its south and west sides.

Giełda Foto (Map p84; ☎ 022 825 6031; ul Batorego 10; 10am-2pm Sun) Camera buffs should have this market high on their list of things to do in Warsaw. Housed in the Stodoła student club, it has an incredible array of cameras and accessories, ranging from pre-WWII goods to the newest equipment. Most are in working order, and cheaper than can be found in retail outlets.

Shopping Centres

Arkadia (Map p84; ☎ 022 323 6767; Al Jana Pawła II 82; 10am-10pm Mon-Sat, 10am-9pm Sun) The largest shopping mall in Poland, with almost 200 stores under one roof. It's handy to the Dworzec Gdański metro station.

TRUE CRAFTSMANSHIP

Forget the shopping malls and generic shops, they're for kids. *Real* shoppers should take to the back streets of Warsaw, where the art of handmade products is still alive, and quality over quantity is paramount. Here are a few of the city's better spots:

Aniela (Map pp88-9; ☎ 022 628 9108; ul Żurawia 26; 11am-6pm Mon-Fri) Possibly the last corset maker in Warsaw; slim-lined, and tight fitting, since 1896.

Bracia Łopieńscy (Map pp88-9; ☎ 022 629 2045; ul Poznańska 24; 9am-5pm Mon-Fri) The oldest bronze-metal foundry in Warsaw has been in business since 1862. Pick up exceptional pieces in the shape of candleholders, mirror and picture frames, wall lamps etc.

Cafe Blikle (Map pp88-9; ☎ 022 826 4568; ul Nowy Świat 35; 9am-7pm Mon-Sat, 10am-6pm Sun) A Warsaw institution; producing cakes and pastries since 1869 (see p111).

Jan Kielman & Sons (Map pp88-9; ☎ 022 828 4630; www.kielman.pl; ul Chmielna 6; 11am-7pm Mon-Fri, 11am-2pm Sat) The Kielman clan has been making shoes since 1883. Their leather footwear starts at 1900zł, but you'll probably have them for life.

Wyrobów Oświetleniowych (Map pp88-9; ☎ 022 620 4376; www.oswietlenie.strefa.pl; ul Emilii Plater 36; 9am-5pm Mon-Fri) Need an exquisite chandelier? Pick up a Gothic or *fin-de-siécle* number here. Most end up in museums and palaces, but there are a few pieces available (wall lamps start at 700zł) for the average Joe.

THE RUSSIAN MARKET

Once Europe's biggest flea market, selling everything from ex-Soviet military items and illegal booze to power tools and underwear, this Warsaw institution was closed in August 2007 due to the rebuilding of Stadion Dziesięciolecia for the Euro 2012. At the time of writing it was homeless; consult the city's tourist information centres (p87) for more up-to-date details.

Galeria Centrum (Map pp88-9; ☎ 022 551 4517; ul Marszałkowska 104/122; ☺ 9.30am-9pm Mon-Fri, 9.30am-8pm Sat, 11am-5pm Sun) A privatised version of the formerly state-owned chain of Domy Towarowe shops, this department store sells mass-market men's, women's and children's clothing, accessories, shoes, cosmetics and jewellery.

Sadyba Best Mall (Map p84; ☎ 022 550 3000; ul Powsińska 31; ☺ 10am-9pm Mon-Sat, 10am-8pm Sun) A modern mall housing a wide range of fashion stores, shoe shops, jewellery and perfume stores, an American Bookstore branch, a multiplex cinema and a dozen different eating places.

Złote Tarasy (Map pp88-9; ☎ 022 222 2200; ul Złota 59; ☺ 10am-10pm Mon-Sat, 10am-8pm Sun) The latest mall to hit Warsaw, with almost every high street name you can think of. Its distinctive curved glass roof is clearly visible near the Palace of Science & Culture.

GETTING THERE & AWAY
Air
AIRPORT
Warsaw-Frédéric Chopin Airport (Port Lotniczy im F Chopina; Map p84; ☎ 022 650 4220; www.lotnisko-chopina.pl) lies in the suburb of Okęcie, at the southern end of ul Żwirki i Wigury, 10km south of the city centre; it handles all domestic and international flights.

In the Terminal 1 international arrivals (odloty) hall, there is a **tourist information desk** (☺ 8am-8pm May-Sep, 8am-6pm Oct-Apr), which sells city maps and can help visitors find accommodation. You will also find some **currency-exchange counters** (☺ 24hr), half a dozen ATMs, several car-hire agencies and a **left-luggage office** (per bag per day 5zł; ☺ 24hr). You can buy tickets for public transport from **Ruch newsagency** (☺ 5am-10pm).

The upper level of Terminal 1 houses international departures (przyloty), which has airline offices, a **bank** (☺ 8am-6pm Mon-Fri, 8am-1pm Sat), and a **post office** (☺ 8am-8pm Mon-Fri, 8am-2pm Sat).

Budget airlines, including Wizz, Germanwings, Ryanair, EasyJet and SkyEurope, use Terminal Etiuda (Map p84), a separate building that's a few minutes' walk south of the main terminal building. It's a basic, overcrowded place with few amenities, aside from a **tourist information desk** (☺ 8am-8pm May-Sep, 8am-6pm Oct-Apr).

Terminal 2 was still under construction at the time of writing, and will hopefully be open by the time it receives flights.

FLIGHTS
You'll find information about domestic routes and fares on p520. Tickets can be booked at **LOT** (Polish Airlines; Map pp88-9; ☎ 0801 703 703; www.lot.com; Marriott Hotel, Al Jerozolimskie 65/79; ☺ 9am-7pm Mon-Fri, 9am-3pm Sat) or at most travel agencies. The LOT timetable lists international flights to and from Poland on various airlines, along with LOT's own international and domestic flights.

Bus
Warsaw is home to two **Państwowa Komunikacja Samochodowa** (PKS; www.pks.warszawa.pl in Polish) bus terminals. **Warszawa Zachodnia bus terminal** (Map pp88-9; ☎ 022 822 4811; Al Jerozolimskie 144), west of the city centre, handles the majority of international routes and domestic routes south, north and west. **Warszawa Stadion** (Stadium Bus Terminal; Map p84; ☎ 022 818 1589; ul Zamojskiego 1), on the east side of the river, deals mainly with domestic and international bus traffic eastbound. Bus tickets are sold at the respective terminals. Some international services depart from the Warszawa Centralna bus terminal on the north side of Warszawa Centralna train station.

PKS operates several buses a day from Warszawa Zachodnia to Gdańsk (42zł to 48zł, five to seven hours), Częstochowa (35zł, 3½ hours), Kazimierz Dolny (22zł, 2½ hours), Kraków (38zł to 43zł, five to 5½ hours), Olsztyn (22zł to 34zł, 3½ to four hours), Toruń (32zł to 54zł, four hours), Wrocław (46zł to 50zł, five to 6½ hours) and Zakopane (54zł, 7¾ hours). Services from Warszawa Stadion include a few daily buses to Lublin (21zł to 40zł, three hours), Białystok (26zł, 3¾ hours), and Zamość (32zł, five hours).

Polski Express (www.polskiexpress.net, in Polish) coaches depart from Warsaw's Frédéric Chopin airport and pick up passengers at its own **bus stop** (Map pp88-9; Al Jana Pawła II), next to Warszawa Centralna train station. Tickets for Polski Express routes are available from either of its offices – the main office **Centralny Punkt Informacji i Sprzedaży Biletów** (Central Information & Ticket Sales Point; ☎ 022 854 0285; ⏰ 6.30am-9.30pm) is beside the bus stop – and from selected Orbis Travel outlets and **Almatur** (Map pp88-9; ☎ 022 826 2639; www.almatur.com.pl; ul Kopernika 23; ⏰ 9am-7pm Mon-Fri, 10am-3pm Sat). Polski Express buses travel to Białystok (41zł, four hours; one daily), Gdynia via Gdańsk (45zł to 59zł, seven hours, two daily), Kraków (83zł, eight hours, one daily), Lublin (41zł to 50zł, 3½ hours, seven daily), Szczecin (69zł to 83zł, 10 hours, two daily), and Łódź (36zł to 39zł, 2½ hours, seven daily).

For information on international bus routes, see the Land section in Getting There & Away in the Transport chapter (p518).

Car

All the major international car-hire companies have offices in Warsaw (p523), many of which are based at the airport. Polish companies offer cheaper rates, but may have fewer English-speaking staff and rental options. Dependable local operators include **Local Rent-a-Car** (Map pp88-9; ☎ 022 826 7100; www.lrc.com.pl; ul Marszałkowska 140), which offers an Opel Corsa in the summer months for €44 a day, or €238 a week, including tax, collision damage waiver (CDW), theft protection and unlimited mileage. **Gromada Rent a Car** (Map pp88-9; ☎ 022 846 5404; Plac Powstańców Warszawy 2), at Hotel Gromada, is another local option, with cars for as little as €30 a day.

Train

Warsaw has several train stations, but the one that most travellers use almost exclusively is **Warszawa Centralna train station** (Dworzec Centralny, Warsaw Central; Map pp88-9; Al Jerozolimskie 54); it handles the overwhelming majority of domestic trains and all international services. Refer to the Getting There & Away section in the destination chapters for information about services to/from Warsaw. For details of international trains, see the Land section in the Transport chapter (p518).

Remember, Warszawa Centralna is not always where domestic and international trains terminate, so make sure you get off the train sharply when it arrives.

The station's spacious main hall houses ticket counters, ATMs and snack bars, as well as a post office, newsagents (where you can buy public-transport tickets) and a tourist information desk (p87). Along the underground passages leading to the tracks and platforms are a dozen *kantors* (one of which is open 24 hours), a **left-luggage office** (⏰ 7am-9pm; per 24hr 5-10zł), luggage lockers (4zł per 24 hours), eateries, several other places to buy tickets for local public transport, internet cafés and bookshops.

Tickets for domestic trains are available from counters at the east end of the main hall (but allow at least an hour for possible queuing), and international train tickets are available from either the helpful **information office** (☎ 022 474 1760; ⏰ 9am-8pm) at the west end, one lonely counter at the east end, or from any major Orbis Travel office (p87). Tickets for immediate departures on domestic trains are also available from numerous, well-signed booths in the underpasses leading to Warszawa Centralna.

Some domestic trains also stop at **Warszawa Śródmieście train station** (Map pp88-9; Al Jerozolimskie), which is 300m east of Warszawa Centralna, at **Warszawa Zachodnia train station** (Map p84; Al Jerozolimskie), next to Warszawa Zachodnia bus terminal, and at Warszawa Wschodnia, in Praga, on the east bank of the Vistula.

GETTING AROUND
To/From the Airport

The cheapest way of getting from the airport to the city (and vice versa) is by city bus 175 (2.40zł, every eight to 15 minutes, 4.50am to 11.10pm), which will take you all the way to the Miodowa stop (Map p92; 30 to 40 minutes) in the Old Town, passing en route along Al Jerozolimskie, ul Nowy Świat and ul Krakowskie Przedmieście.

The night bus 611 replaces bus 175, connecting the airport with Warszawa Centralna train station every 30 minutes between 11pm and 5am. The bus stop is on a traffic island outside the international arrivals hall – look for the red-and-yellow bus shelter. There's a second stop outside Terminal Etiuda. Watch your bags closely – this line is a favourite playground for thieves and pickpockets. Don't forget to buy tickets at the airport's Ruch newsagency, located in the arrivals hall, and to validate them in one of the ticket machines when you board the bus.

The taxi stand is right outside the door of the arrivals hall and handles taxis run by MPT Radio Taxi, Sawa Taxi and Merc Taxi. They all have desks inside the terminal, so you can ask about the fare to your destination – it should be around 30zł to Centralna station and 40zł to the Old Town.

Bicycle

Cycling in Warsaw is a double-edged sword. The city is generally flat and easy to navigate, distances aren't too great, and cycle paths are on the increase. However, Warsaw drivers don't give a toss about cyclists and you'll soon be following the locals' lead and sharing the footpath with pedestrians. Bike hire is available from Oki Doki Hostel (p106) and Local Rent-a-Car (p117) for around 35zł per day, and Hostel Helvetia (p106) offers bike rental to guests.

Car & Motorcycle

Warsaw's streets are full of potholes – some more dangerous than others – so driving demands constant attention.

The local government has introduced paid parking on central streets. You pay using coins (usually 2zł per hour) in the nearest ticket machine (parkomat) and get a receipt that you display in the windscreen. For security, try to park your car in a guarded car park (parking strzeżony). There are some in central Warsaw, including one on ul Parkingowa, behind the Novotel (Map pp88–9).

PZM (☎ 022 849 9361, 9637; ul Kazimierzowska 66) operates a 24-hour road breakdown service (pomoc drogowa).

See p117 for local car-hire agencies.

Public Transport

Warsaw's integrated public-transport system is operated by **Zarząd Transportu Miejskiego** (City Transportation Board; ☎ 24hr info line 022-9484; www.ztm .waw.pl) and consists of a network of tram, bus and metro lines, all using the same ticketing system. The main routes operate from about 5am to about 11pm, and services are frequent and pretty reliable, though it's often crowded during rush hours (7am till 9am and 3.30pm till 6.30pm Monday to Friday). Friday and Saturday nights the metro runs until 2.30am. After 11pm several night bus routes link major suburbs to the city centre. The night-service

'hub' is at ul Emilii Plater, next to the Palace of Culture & Science, from where buses depart every half-hour.

It's best to buy a ticket before boarding buses, trams and metros; exact change is normally required when purchasing a ticket on buses or trams and drivers may refuse to sell them if they are running behind schedule. Tickets are sold at Ruch and Relay newsstands, hotels, post offices, metro stations and various general stores – look for a sign saying 'Sprzedaży Biletów ZTM'.

Tickets, timetables and information are available at the following ZTM information desks:

Hala sprzedaży biletów ZTM (Map p92; ul Senatorska 37; ☻ 7am-5pm Mon-Fri) Enter from Plac Bankowy.

Punkt informacji ZTM (Map p92; Pawilon 09, Ratusz metro station; ☻ 7am-8pm Mon-Fri)

Punkt informacji ZTM (Map p84; Pawilon 1002, Plac Wilsona metro station; ☻ 7am-8pm Mon-Fri)

A jednorazowy bilet (single-journey ticket) costs 2.40zł (3zł from driver; 1.25zł for school children aged seven or over; kids under seven ride free); these tickets are not valid for transferring between services. A 90-minutowy bilet (90-minute ticket) costs 6zł, and is valid for 90 minutes from the time of validation, with unlimited transfers. Also available are one-/three-/seven-day unlimited transfer tickets for Warsaw (7.20/12/24zł), and Warsaw and its surrounding suburbs, including all 700 and 800 buses (9.60/14.40/32zł). These tickets cover night buses; otherwise a single fare costs 4.80zł. Foreign students under 26 years of age who have an International Student Identity Card (ISIC) get a discount of 48% (in Warsaw only; no other Polish city gives ISIC student concessions).

There are no conductors on board vehicles. Validate your ticket by feeding it (magnetic stripe facing down) into the little yellow machine on the bus or tram or in the metrostation lobby the first time you board; this stamps the time and date on it (or the route number for single-fare tickets). Inspections are common and fines are high (120zł as an instant fine or 84zł within seven days at an information desk, plus 2.40zł for a ticket). Watch out for pickpockets on crowded buses and trams (especially airport bus 175 and trams running along Al Jerozolimskie).

The construction of Warsaw's metro system began in 1983 and so far only a single line is in operation, running from the southern suburb of Ursynów (Kabaty station) to Marymont via the city centre. A northern extension to Młociny should be complete by 2008, and there are long-term plans to build a second, east–west line. Yellow signs with a big red letter 'M' indicate the entrances to metro stations. Every station has a public toilet and there are lifts for disabled passengers. You use the same tickets as on trams and buses, but you validate the ticket at the gate at the entrance to the platform, not inside the vehicle. Trains run every eight minutes (every four minutes during rush hours).

Taxi

Taxis in Warsaw are easily available and not too expensive: around 6zł flag fall and 3/6zł per kilometre during the day/night. Reliable companies include **MPT Radio Taxi** (☎ 9191), which has English-speaking dispatchers, **Super Taxi** (☎ 9622), **Tele Taxi** (☎ 9627) and **OK! Taxi** (☎ 9628).

All are recognisable by signs on the taxi's roof with the company name and phone number. Beware of 'pirate' or 'mafia' taxis, which do not display a phone number or company logo – the drivers may try to overcharge you and turn rude and aggressive if you question the fare. They no longer patrol the airport, Centralna station, or luxury hotels, but still haunt tourist spots looking for likely victims.

All official taxis in Warsaw have their meters adjusted to the appropriate tariff, so you just pay what the meter says. When you board a taxi, make sure the meter is turned on in your presence, which ensures you don't have the previous passenger's fare added to yours. Taxis can be waved down on the street, but it is better to order a taxi by phone; there's no extra charge for this service.

AROUND WARSAW

KAMPINOS NATIONAL PARK

Popularly known as the Puszcza Kampinoska, the **Kampinos National Park** (Kampinoski Park Narodowy; off Map p84; ☎ 022 722 6001; kampinoski-pn.gov.pl) begins just outside Warsaw's northwestern administrative boundaries and stretches west for about 40km. It's one of the largest national parks in Poland, with around three-quarters of its area covered by forest, mainly pine and oak.

The park includes Europe's largest area of inland sand dunes, mostly tree-covered and up to 30m high, and it's a strange feeling to have sand between your toes so far from the sea. Other parts of the park are barely accessible peat bogs that shelter much of its animal life.

Elks, beavers and lynxes live in the park but are hard to spot; you are more likely to see other animals such as hares, foxes, deer and, occasionally, wild boars. The park is home to some bird life, including black storks, cranes, herons and marsh harriers.

Kampinos is popular with hikers and cyclists from the capital, who take advantage of its 300km of marked walking and cycling trails. The eastern part of the park, closer to the city, is more favoured by walkers as it's accessible by public transport; the western part is less visited. As well as half- and one-day hikes, there are two long trails that traverse the entire length of the park, both starting from Dziekanów Leśny on the eastern edge of the park. The red trail (54km) ends in Brochów, and the green one (51km) in Żelazowa Wola.

If you plan on hiking in the park, buy a copy of the Compass *Kampinoski Park Narodowy* map (scale 1:30,000), available from bookshops in Warsaw (p85).

On the southern boundary of the park around 1km west of the tiny village of Kampinos is a large wooden house that is the **Muzeum Puszczy Kampinoskiej** (Kampinos Forest Museum; off Map p84; ☎ 022 725 0123; Granica; admission free; ❂ 9am-4pm Tue-Sun). Inside, static displays wax lyrical on the park's flora and fauna, while outside there's a small exhibition (in English and Polish) on the country's national parks and a group of forest buildings which collectively create a small **skansen**.

Bivouac sites designated for camping are the only accommodation options within the park's boundaries, but there are hotels close by in Czosnów, Laski, Leszno, Tułowice and Zaborów. Warsaw's tourist information centres (p87) have a full list of places to stay near the park.

Getting There & Away

The most popular jumping-off point for walks in the eastern part of the park is the village of Truskaw. To get there from central Warsaw, take tram 4 or 36 northbound on ul Marszałkowska to Plac Wilsona, then city bus 708 (two or three an hour on weekdays, hourly on Saturday).

WARSAW

PKS buses run from Warszawa Zachodnia bus terminal to Kampinos (8.60zł, one hour, three daily).

ŻELAZOWA WOLA

If it wasn't for Poland's most famous musician, Żelazowa Wola (zheh-lah-zo-vah vo-lah) wouldn't be on the tourist map. This tiny village 53km west of Warsaw is the birthplace of Frédéric Chopin, and the house where he was born on 22 February 1810 has been restored and furnished in period style to create a **museum** (☎ 046 863 3300; adult/student museum & park ticket 12/6zł, park only 4/2zł, free Fri; manor house ☺ 9am-5.30pm Tue-Sun mid-Apr–mid-Oct, 9am-4pm Tue-Sun mid-Oct–mid-Apr, park 9am-5.30pm Mon, 9am-8pm Tue-Sun May-Aug, 9am-5.30pm Mar-Apr & Sep–mid-Oct, 9am-4pm mid-Oct–Feb). It's a lovely little country house with beautiful gardens, but there is little in the way of original memorabilia. Nonetheless, the tranquillity and charm of the place make it a pleasant stop.

Piano recitals, often performed by top-rank virtuosos, are normally held here each Sunday from the first Sunday in May to the last Sunday in September. There are usually two concerts, up to an hour long, at noon and 3pm; there's no fee other than the park entry ticket. The programme can be found on www.nifc.pl.

There's a restaurant opposite the entrance to the museum, but nowhere to stay overnight. The nearest accommodation is in Sochaczew, 6km away.

Getting There & Away

PKS buses run from the Warszawa Zachodnia bus terminal to Żelazowa Wola (10zł, 1¼ hours, three daily). There's a morning departure from Warsaw at 9.33am; a bus returning to Warsaw leaves Żelazowa Wola at 4.38pm.

Several travel agencies and the Chopin Museum (p97) in Warsaw put together organised tours for the Sunday concerts – a more comfortable option. Check with Warsaw's tourist information centres (p87) for details, or catch the 1.30pm bus from the Chopin Museum.

Mazovia & Podlasie

Travel only 30km from Warsaw's Old Town and you enter another Poland. Women bend double in fields, horse-drawn carts and tractors transport produce to market, wooden bridges and dirt roads await EU intervention, and castles and cathedrals dominate towns. Of course it's not all R&R (rural and rustic) in Podlasie and Mazovia (Mazowsze in Polish), but the locals do a good job of convincing you otherwise.

Mazovia's rolling landscape and rural bliss have a deceptively long history, but the telltale signs are easy to spot if you know where to look. Once a duchy, this province is dotted with castles, cathedrals and palaces, the biggest of which reside in the riverside towns of Płock and Pułtusk and the quiet village of Nieborów. Łódź is Mazovia's reigning capital, with more going for it than meets the eye. It's the country's second-largest metropolis and would easily win 'Poland's Ugliest City' if such a competition was held, but if you take the time to discover its palaces, art galleries and 19th-century redbrick textile factories, you'll be happy you made the effort.

Podlasie is the verdant green lungs of Poland. Aside from a few patches of urbanisation, this large province is a bucolic paradise of farmland, forest and lakes. Its four national parks are splendid – Narew and Biebrza for their marshlands and birdlife; Wigry for its peaceful lake, pockets of forest and Augustów Canal; and Białowieża for its primeval forest and king of Polish fauna, the bison. Humans also play their part, supplying a couple of splendid skansens (open-air museums of traditional architecture) at Nowogród and Ciechanowiec, a touch of Muslim culture in Kruszyniany and Bohoniki, and Jewish heritage at Tykocin.

HIGHLIGHTS

- Marvelling at the ugly streets and hidden gems of **Łódź** (p122)

- Harking back to a time when romance was all the rage at **Nieborów & Arkadia** (p131)

- Wondering how **Płock** (p134) got hold of so many Art Nouveau treasures

- Exploring the last remnants of Poland's Tatar culture at **Kruszyniany & Bohoniki** (p145)

- Searching primeval forest for a glimpse of the rare European bison at **Białowieża National Park** (p147)

- Relaxing the mind and exercising the body kayaking the **Rospuda** (p158) and **Czarna Hańcza** (p154) rivers

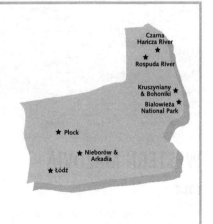

- POPULATION: NINE MILLION
- AREA: 76,118 SQ KM

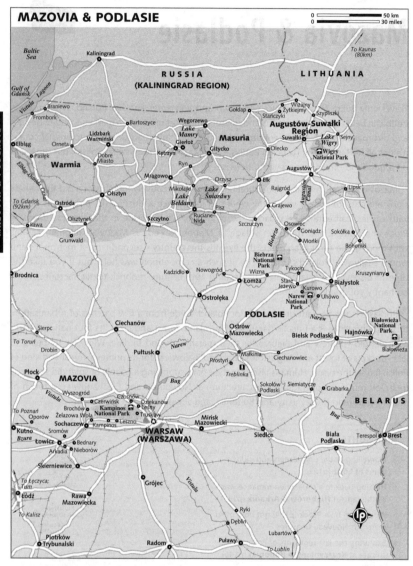

WESTERN MAZOVIA

ŁÓDŹ
pop 768,000

As Polish cities go, Łódź is about as strange as it gets. For starters, its name is pronounced 'Woodge'. Secondly, Łódź looks as though it's been dropped from a great height and left to lie where it fell – visually it could politely be called gritty. Thirdly, behind the obvious grime is a treasure-trove of delights: palatial mansions, Art Nouveau buildings, progressive galleries, gigantic 19th-century redbrick factories, and a creative energy that has not only reached Poland's stage, but the world's.

History

Although the first account of its existence dates from 1332, Łódź remained an obscure settlement until the beginning of the 19th century. In the 1820s the government of the Congress Kingdom of Poland – eyeing up the town's advantageous position at what was then the border of Russia and Prussia – embarked on a programme to industrialise the country, and Łódź was selected as a new textile centre.

Enterprising industrialists – Poles, Jews and Germans alike – rushed in to build textile mills, closely followed by thousands of workers. The wealthy mill owners built opulent palaces (the Historical Museum of Łódź, right, and the Cinematography Museum, p126, currently fill two), while workers occupied drab suburbs around the centre. By the outbreak of WWI, Łódź had grown a thousandfold, reaching a population of half a million. It had become Poland's second-largest city, a title it still holds today.

Following WWI the city's growth slowed, mainly because of the loss of the huge Russian market, but industrial sectors such as machinery and chemistry continued to expand. WWII was both cruel and kind to the city – the Nazis created Poland's first Jewish ghetto here but Łódź escaped major destruction. Today it continues to be Poland's textile capital, although production is dropping.

Orientation

Ul Piotrkowska is Łódź' 3.6km-long north–south backbone. Most of the city's tourist sights, hotels and restaurants are on or near it. The heart of Jewish Łódź lies to the northeast of ul Piotrkowska, and Manufaktura to the northwest. The main train station, Łódź Fabryczna, and the central bus station are next to each other, a few blocks east of the northern end of ul Piotrkowska. A second train station, Łódź Kaliska, lies 1.5km west of Piotrkowska, while a third, Łódź Widzew, is 5km east of Fabryczna.

Information

BOOKSHOPS

EMPiK ul Piotrkowska (☎ 042 631 1998; ul Piotrkowska 81; 🕑 9am-9pm Mon-Sat, 11am-7pm Sun); Manufaktura (☎ 042 664 8548; ul Jana Karskiego 5; 🕑 9am-9pm Mon-Sat, 11am-7pm Sun) Good range of foreign newspapers and magazines.

Księgarnia Oxpol (☎ 042 630 2013; ul Piotrkowska 63; 🕑 10am-6pm Mon-Fri, 10am-3pm Sat) Books in English.

INTERNET ACCESS

Mega Net Café (☎ 042 636 3376; Al Piłsudskiego 5; per hr 2zł; 🕑 11am-11pm) On the 3rd floor of Silver Screen.
Silver Zone (☎ 042 639 5800; Al Piłsudskiego 5; per hr 2zł; 🕑 11am-11pm) Comfy seats and fast connections.

MONEY

Bank Pekao (Al Kościuszki 47)

POST

Main post office (ul Tuwima 38; 🕑 24hr)

TOURIST INFORMATION

Cultural Information Centre (Centrum Informacji Kulturalnej; ☎ 042 633 9221; www.cik.lodz.pl in Polish; ul Piotrkowska 102a; 🕑 10am-6pm Mon-Fri, 10am-2pm Sat) The place for cultural events info.
Tourist Information Centre (Centrum Informacji Turystycznej; ☎ 042 638 5956; www.uml.lodz.pl; Al Piotrkowska 87; 🕑 9am-7pm Mon-Fri, 10am-2pm Sat May-Oct, 9am-6pm Mon-Fri, 10am-2pm Sat Nov-Apr) General tourist information; has a number of free booklets in English, including *Jewish Landmarks in Łódź*.

TRAVEL AGENCIES

Eurotravel (☎ 042 630 4488; Al Kościuszki 22; 🕑 9.30am-5.30pm Mon-Fri, 10am-1pm Sat) Youth travel, domestic and international bus tickets, Eurolines.
Fabricum (☎ 042 636 2825; www.fabricum.pl; ul Wigury 7; 🕑 9am-5pm Mon-Fri) Offers guided tours of Łódź, its surrounding region and Poland. Specialises in tours of Poland's Unesco sites.
Orbis Travel (☎ 042 636 6126; ul Piotrkowska 68; 🕑 9am-6pm Mon-Fri, 10am-2pm Sat) General travel.

Sights

UL PIOTRKOWSKA

The ramrod-straight ul Piotrkowska is the very heart of Łódź and, aside from Manufaktura, the only section of the city to have enjoyed well-needed rejuvenation in recent years. Mostly pedestrianised and lined with some of Poland's finest Art Nouveau façades, it's a pleasant street to wander. It also contains the lion's share of the city's shops, restaurants, pubs, open-air cafés and galleries, and is bedecked with bronze stars in honour of Poland's cinematic elite (see boxed text, p124).

HISTORICAL MUSEUM OF ŁÓDŹ

Housed in the magnificent palace of the Poznański family is the **Historical Museum of Łódź**

HOLLY-ŁÓDŹ BOULEVARD

Ul Piotrkowska began life in the 19th century as the road to Piotrków Trybunalski (hence its name), then the major town of the region. By the beginning of the 20th century Piotrkowska was an elegant boulevard, lined with Art Nouveau buildings and expensive restaurants, but in the wake of WWII it became a gloomy, grey street of soot-blackened façades and a handful of half-empty shops, much the same as city streets all over communist Poland. Its revival began in the 1990s, when the Piotrkowska Street Foundation was created by a group of local artists and architects with the aim of turning the derelict street into a lively European city mall. It has also become a sort of homage to locals done good, with statues and stars dedicated to the city's famous sons and daughters.

In front of the famous Hotel Grand is the **Aleja Gwiazd** (Avenue of the Stars), a series of bronze stars set in the pavement in imitation of Los Angeles' Hollywood Blvd, each dedicated to a well-known name in Polish film. Nearby, in front of the house (No 78) where the eminent Polish pianist Artur Rubinstein once lived, is **Rubinstein's Piano**, a bronze monument much loved by snap-happy tourists. A few paces down the street is **Tuwim's Bench** (at No 104), another unusual monument, this one created in memory of local poet Julian Tuwim. Touch his nose – it's supposed to bring good luck. The last of the series is **Reymont's Chest** (at No 135), showing the Nobel prize winner in literature, Władysław Reymont, sitting on a large travel trunk.

Although the northern half of ul Piotrkowska is pedestrianised, public transport is provided by a fleet of **bicycle rickshaws** (riksza); for around 4zł they will whisk you from one end to the other.

(Muzeum Historii Miasta Łodzi; ☎ 042 654 0323; ul Ogrodowa 15; adult/concession 7/4zł, free Sun; ☺ 10am-4pm Tue & Thu, 2-6pm Wed, 10am-2pm Sat-Mon). More like a prince's residence than a businessperson's home, the museum's opulent interior is a clear indication of the Poznańskis' wealth: it's bedecked with elaborate dark-wood wall panelling, delicate stained-glass windows and a suitably grand ballroom. Despite the exhibitions taking a back seat to the building, they're interesting all the same, covering Łódź' history, the Łódź ghetto, and famous citizens including pianist Artur Rubinstein, writer Jerzy Kosiński and poet Julian Tuwim. All three, of Jewish origin, were born in Łódź and deservedly have their own room(s) in the palace.

MUSEUM OF ETHNOGRAPHY & ARCHAEOLOGY

Forever with its eye on the former market place of Plac Wolności (Liberty Sq) is the **Museum of Ethnography & Archaeology** (Muzeum Archeologiczne i Etnograficzne; ☎ 042 632 9714; Plac Wolności 14; adult/concession 6/4zł, free Tue, 11am-6pm Thu, 9am-4pm Wed & Fri-Sun). Most displays are fairly standard, featuring archaeological finds from the Stone Age to the Middle Ages, but the money collection on the 1st floor is worthy of note – as late as 1991 the government was still producing 1,000,000zł bills. The bridal party on the top floor is by far the most engaging ethnography display, with the groom dressed in spiffy orange-and-green pants and the bride weighed down by a heavy headdress of flowers.

MODERN ART MUSEUM

Contemporary art lovers should make a detour two blocks west of ul Piotrkowska to the **Modern Art Museum** (Muzeum Sztuki; ☎ 042 633 9790; ul Więckowskiego 36; adult/concession 7/4zł, free Thu; ☺ 10am-5pm Tue, 11am-5pm Wed & Fri, noon-7pm Thu, 10am-4pm Sat & Sun). It contains an extensive collection of 20th-century paintings, drawings, sculpture and photography from Poland and abroad, as well as many works by contemporary artists. There are also works by Picasso, Chagall and Ernst (not always on display).

CITY ART GALLERY

Near the Modern Art Museum is the **City Art Gallery** (Miejska Galeria Sztuki; ☎ 042 632 7995; ul Wólczańska 31/33; adult/concession 4/2zł; ☺ 11am-5pm Tue-Fri, 11am-4pm Sat & Sun), housed in a fairytale 1903 Art Nouveau villa that once belonged to German industrialist Leopold Kindermann. While the building itself lacks colour, it's well worth a look for its attractive flower motifs, tree-trunk columns and wrought-iron work. Contemporary works by Polish artists are normally the focus of the gallery's temporary exhibitions.

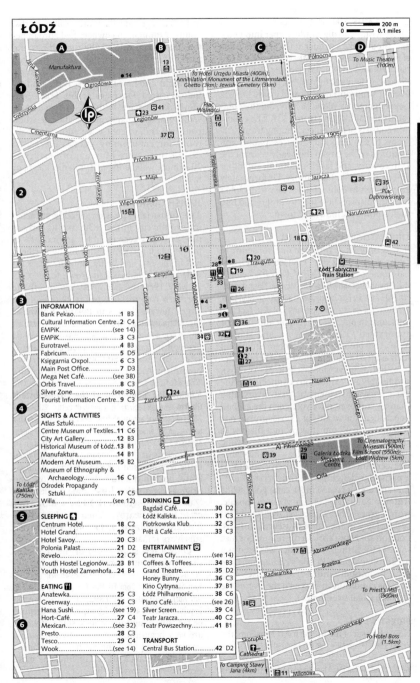

ŁÓDŹ

MAZOVIA & PODLASIE

CENTRE MUSEUM OF TEXTILES

Those wishing to dig a little deeper into Łódź' past should take a gander at the **Centre Museum of Textiles** (Centralne Muzeum Włókiennictwa; ☎ 042 683 2684; ul Piotrkowska 282; adult/concession 8/4zł, free Sat; 9am-5pm Tue, Wed & Fri, 11am-7pm Thu, 11am-4pm Sat & Sun). It's appropriately located inside Ludwig Geyer's gorgeous White Factory, the city's oldest textile mill, dating from 1839. The collection consists of machinery ranging from early looms to contemporary devices, photos and paintings of the city in the heady years of the 19th century, and fabrics, clothing and other objects related to the industry. Unfortunately everything's in Polish, but it's easy to decipher from the displays how the city progressed into such a powerful industrial town.

CINEMATOGRAPHY MUSEUM

If you only have time for one museum in Łódź, make it this one. Housed in the palatial home of 'Cotton King' Karol Scheibler, the **Cinematography Museum** (Muzeum Kinematografii; ☎ 042 674 0957; Plac Zwycięstwa 1; adult/concession 5/3zł; 10am-3pm Tue-Fri, 11am-3pm Sat & Sun) is in fact two museums in one. The basement and 1st floor are devoted to Polish cinema, and contain props, film posters, archaic camera equipment such as a 120-year-old photo-plasticon (a device that displays stereoscopic 3D photos), and temporary exhibitions connected to the city's illustrious cinematic past. Everything changes, however, once you reach the ground floor – here the wealth of 19th-century Łódź is plain to see. Room after room is filled with extravagant boiserie (elaborately carved wood panelling), dreamy ceiling frescoes and elaborate ceramic stoves. The 'Mirror Room' is a particular delight, with three crystal mirrors and angels coated in 24-carat gold, while Antonio Salviati's *Turkish Woman* mosaic, which graces the 'Office' stove, would sit comfortably in the finest museums in Paris, London or New York. You may recognise some of the fittings – the palace was used as a backdrop in Andrej Wajda's *Ziemia obiecana* (The Promised Land; 1975) because of its pristine condition (it survived the war as the Gestapo Chief's residence).

PRIEST'S MILL

Now a branch of the Modern Art Museum, the **Priest's Mill** (Księży Młyn; ☎ 042 633 9790; ul Przędzalniana 72; adult/concession 7/4.50zł; 10am-5pm Tue, noon-5pm Wed & Fri, noon-7pm Thu, 11am-4pm Sat & Sun) started life

in 1875 as a grand villa of the wealthy Herbst family. Although the owners fled abroad before the war, taking all the furnishings and works of art with them, the interior has been restored and furnished like the original, giving an insight into how the pre-WWII barons of industry lived. Once again, this 'home' was more like a palace, with red-carpeted stairwells, graceful chandeliers, elaborate wood panelling and, of course, an enormous ballroom for entertaining guests. It's 1.5km east of the Centre Museum of Textiles (a 20-minute walk along ul Tymienieckiego, or take bus 55).

JEWISH QUARTER

The industrial expansion of Łódź attracted Jews to the city in the 1830s and as early as the 1840s they accounted for around 20% of the population. Many settled in the northern half of the city, and by the time the Nazis invaded their numbers had grown to 230,000. In May 1940 the occupiers sealed off the northern part of Łódź to create one of the largest Jewish ghettos in Poland. Known as the **Litzmannstadt Ghetto**, after the German name for Łódź, around 200,000 Jews passed through its gates between then and August 1944; of these, 150,000 boarded trains bound for Auschwitz at Radegast Station. The station has now been turned into the **Annihilation Monument of the Litzmannstadt Ghetto** (Pomnik Zagłady Litzmannstadt Getto; ☎ 042 632 7112; ul Stalowa; admission free; 10am-6pm Mon-Thu, noon-8pm Sat & Sun May-Oct, 9am-5pm Mon-Thu, 10am-3pm Sat & Sun Nov-Apr), a powerful reminder of the horrors of the Holocaust. Three original cattle wagons used for deportations stand silently next to the now-defunct station, and original deportation lists (some headed with 'Zur Arbeit' – 'to work') line a long concrete tunnel nearby. When the Red Army liberated Łódź in 1945, only 880 Jewish survivors remained.

Only a few steps south of the station is the city's **Jewish Cemetery** (Cmentarz Żydowski; ☎ 042 656 7019; ul Bracka 40; admission 4zł; 9am-5pm Sun-Thu, 9am-3pm Fri May-Oct, 8am-3pm Sun-Fri Nov-Apr). Founded in 1892, it is the largest Jewish graveyard in Europe, with around 68,000 surviving tombstones, some of which are very beautiful. It is currently enjoying a partial cleanup, but the further you wander from the entrance off ul Zmienna the more overgrown and wild it becomes.

MANUFAKTURA

Izrael Poznański was a wise man. Not only did he have the vision and tenacity to build the second-largest textile factory in Łódź, he also built it within stumbling distance of his palatial residence (p123). At its peak, the enormous redbrick factory – a series of factories, in fact, constructed between 1852 and 1892 – employed 4000 workers and housed more than 80,000 spindles. Poznański died in 1900 but the factory lived on, churning out textiles through two world wars and communist occupation. The decades, however, took their toll on both the buildings and cotton sales, and in 1997 the spindles spun their last.

In 2000 French developers bought the site with an eye to transforming it into a cultural space for Łódź (and perhaps making a bit of dosh on the side). Work began in 2003, and by 2006 the factory was ready for public inspection. The result is **Manufaktura** (☎ 042 664 9260; www.manufaktura .com; ul Jana Karskiego 5), a massive shopping mall/entertainment venue containing a string of shops, restaurants, clubs and bars, along with a cinema and, in the future, a hotel. The restoration is impressive, with many factories restored to their former glory; some, however, still stand derelict and in stark contrast to their pristine surrounds. The only glitch in an otherwise exemplary job is the uncomplimentary modern steel-and-glass structure that fills the western end of the complex.

On the 2nd floor of the cinema is the excellent **Manufaktura Museum** (☎ 042 664 9293; ul Jana Karskiego 5; admission 2zł; ⊙ 9am-7pm Tue-Fri, 11am-7pm Sat, 10am-8pm Sun), where more information on the history and renovation of Manufaktura can be gleaned.

Both the cemetery and monument are about 3km northeast of the centre. Take tram 1 from ul Kilińskiego or tram 6 from Al Kościuszki.

GALLERIES

Łódź has a healthy art scene, with more than two dozen galleries in and around the city centre; pick up *Łódź the City of Art* from the tourist office for a complete list. Some of the better-known:

Atlas Sztuki (☎ 042 632 7750; ul Piotrkowska 114/116; adult/concession 4/2zł, free Thu; ⊙ 4-8pm Tue-Fri, 11am-5pm Sat & Sun) Focuses on Polish photographers, including the Łódź Kaliska group.

Ośrodek Propagandy Sztuki (☎ 042 674 1059; ul Sienkiewicza 44; adult/concession 4/2zł, free Thu; ⊙ 11am-6pm Tue-Fri, 11am-5pm Sat & Sun) Showcases local talent.

Willa (☎ 042 632 7995; ul Wólczańska 31; adult/concession 4/2zł, free Thu; ⊙ 11am-5pm Tue, Wed & Fri, 11am-6pm Thu, 11am-4pm Sat & Sun) Housed in the City Art Gallery – another that presents local artists.

Festivals & Events

Łódź is blessed with festivals year-round; here are but two of the biggest:

Łódź Ballet Meetings A dance and ballet festival that includes both Polish and foreign groups, and runs for two weeks in May every odd-numbered year. Performances are staged in the Grand Theatre.

Camerimage (www.camerimage.pl) An international cinematography festival held over seven days in late November/early December (see p129).

Sleeping

The low number of foreign tourists visiting the city means that Łódź' hotel scene is aimed mainly at the business and trade-fair market, and few places have anything in the way of character.

BUDGET

Youth Hostel Legionów (☎ 042 630 6680; www.ylodz .pl; ul Legionów 27; dm 18-30zł, s/d from 45/70zł; P ☒ ⬛) It looks a bit rough from the outside, but inside standards at Legionów are above par for a Polish hostel. Choose from rooms equipped with radio, TV and private bathroom, or cheaper versions with shared facilities. There's a café on the premises, secure parking, a kitchen for guests and a 24-hour reception (although curfew is 10pm). Legionów also runs Youth Hostel Zamenhofa (ul Zamenhofa 13), which usually handles the overflow.

Hotel Boss (☎ 042 672 4889; www.hotel-boss.pl; ul Tatrzańska 11; s/d from 55/118zł; P ☒) Boss is the choice of those with little money to spend on accommodation but who want to stay in a hotel. It's a bit of a soulless concrete box but some effort has been made to make the rooms feel homey. It's quite a hike from the centre – 10 minutes from central ul Piotrkowska on tram 7 or 13 – but comfortable and good value.

Hotel Urzędu Miasta (☎ 042 640 6613; ul Bojowników Getta Warszawskiego 9; s/d/tr 100/144/180zł) This hotel is run by the city council and provides basic, characterless accommodation, but at just 500m north of Plac Wolności it's not a bad trade-off.

Camping Stawy Jana (☎ 042 646 1551; ul Rzgowska 247; camping per tent/person/car 6/6/6zł, s/d 35/70zł; P) Stawy Jana is part of a sports centre, and offers a choice between your own tent and heated chalets. It's 5km south of the centre on the Piotrków Trybunalski road. Take tram 5 from ul Kilińskiego, near Łódź Fabryczna station, to the end of the line and continue walking south for 500m.

MIDRANGE

Polonia Palast (☎ 042 632 8773; www.hotelpolonia .com.pl; ul Narutowicza 38; s/d 110/180zł, with private bathroom 150/225zł) 'Palast' (palace) is certainly stretching it – rooms are stuck in the 1970s, and in need of a makeover. But they're adequate enough, and Polonia's big attraction is its plum location, just a few minutes' walk from both ul Piotrkowska and the train and bus stations.

Hotel Savoy (☎ 042 632 9360; ul Traugutta 6; s/d from 119/249zł) Don't be fooled by the name: this hotel has nothing on the original Savoy. What it does have is a great location just off ul Piotrkowska, standard rooms in communist brown and beige (in both colour and character), and a handful of 'retro' rooms (singles/doubles from 199/299zł) with pseudo antique furniture. Forgo breakfast and save 20zł on the room price.

Centrum Hotel (☎ 042 632 8640; www.hotelcentrum .com.pl; ul Kilińskiego 59/63; s/d from 190/270zł; P X 💻 👤) Towering over the Łódź Fabryczna train station, Centrum provides grand views of the city from its upper-floor rooms. It caters to a business crowd, with facilities such as a gym and sauna, and rooms with high standards but little character. One room, the David Lynch Suite, rises above them all, though: it's where Lynch stays when in town for the film festival, and comes with office, kitchen and lounge.

our pick Revelo (☎ 042 636 8686; www.revelo.pl; ul Wigury 4/6; s/d 250/280zł; P) Revelo does an excellent job of mixing old and new in a beautifully preserved villa dating from 1925. Staff greet you dressed in 1920s outfits and lead you up dark wood stairs to immaculate rooms with period furniture, brass bedsteads, plasma TVs and thoroughly modern bathrooms. Downstairs is filled by the boutique hotel's quality restaurant and attached garden. With only six rooms, it's best to book ahead.

TOP END

Hotel Grand (☎ 042 633 9920; logrand@orbis.pl; ul Piotrkowska 72; s 289-379zł, d 339-449zł; P X 💻 👤) The old-fashioned Grand is the city's longest-running hotel, slap bang in the middle of all the action on ul Piotrkowska. Opened in 1888 at the peak of the textile boom, it was the city's top hotel, hosting such distinctive guests as Pablo Casals and Isadora Duncan. The public areas retain a turn-of-the-century atmosphere, but the rooms, while comfortable, are mostly modern and bland.

Eating

Tesco (Al Piłsudskiego 15; 8am-9pm Mon-Sat, 9am-8pm Sun) Self-caterers can head for this supermarket in the huge Galeria Łódzka shopping centre.

Wook (☎ 042 633 2323; Manufaktura, ul Jana Karskiego 5; dishes 4-6zł; 11am-11pm) Like Warsaw, Łódź loves Asian food. Here the flavour's Chinese, and while the prices look spectacular, the servings are actually quite small. No matter: order a couple and dig in heartily – it's surprisingly good Asian cuisine considering you're in the middle of Poland.

Greenway (☎ 042 632 0852; ul Piotrkowska 80; mains 7.50-9zł; 10am-1am) Part of a chain currently sweeping Poland, Greenway is an attractive, modern café-bar serving a range of appealing dishes such as Mexican goulash (with beans and sweet corn), Indian vegetable kofta and spinach dumplings. Vegetarians will jump for joy at the choices. A second Greenway is in Manufaktura.

Presto (☎ 042 630 8883; ul Piotrkowska 67; pizzas 8.50-26zł; noon-11pm Sun-Thu, noon-midnight Fri & Sat) Presto is a simple trattoria with a pizza list almost as long as ul Piotrkowska, and a few pasta dishes thrown in for good measure. What makes it stand out from the crowd? The pizzas are cooked in a wood-fired oven. Yum.

Hort-Café (☎ 042 632 4498; ul Piotrkowska 106/110; mains 10-20zł; 9am-8pm Mon-Sat, 11am-8pm Sun) Part bakery, part café, this homy little place serves pastries, cream cakes, milk shakes, ice cream, light meals, salads and crepes in a pot plant- and flower-bedecked space. There's an outdoor summer terrace.

Anatewka (☎ 042 630 3635; ul 6 Sierpnia 2/4; mains 20-30zł; 11am-10pm) This Jewish restaurant just off Piotrkowska is often packed with expats and young Poles eager to sample excellent duck and goose mains. The atmosphere is warm and convivial, and the dining experience is rounded off with live music most nights.

Mexican (☎ 042 633 6868; ul Piotrkowska 67; mains 20-40zł; ☼ 11.30am-2am) The only place in town with anything resembling Latin American food. Expect plenty of Mexican favourites such as burritos, enchiladas and tacos, and the occasional Tex-Mex option. There's live Latino music from 7pm Tuesday to Saturday.

Hana Sushi (☎ 042 632 3255; ul Piotrkowska 72; mains 30-150zł; ☼ 11am-11pm) Hana Sushi is the Grand's restaurant offering, with a minimalist look and serene atmosphere. Choose from a menu filled with maki, sushi, sashimi, tempura and the like, and watch the comings and goings on ul Piotrkowska through the floor-to-ceiling windows. A less formal branch is located in Manufaktura.

Drinking

Łódź Kaliska (☎ 042 630 6955; ul Piotrkowska 102; ☼ 10am-2am Mon-Thu, 10am-4am Fri & Sat, 4pm-4am Sun) Łódź Kaliska's reputation as a must-see bar extends as far as Warsaw and possibly further. It draws a broad cross-section of Łódź society with its open-door policy, and the unusual décor – stripped-back walls are covered in fun, semi-erotic photos from the bar's namesake art group – goes well with the dim red lighting and slightly seedy atmosphere. In summer the crowds spill out onto an outdoor terrace above the alleyway.

Bagdad Café (☎ 042 639 9799; ul Jaracza 45; ☼ 9am-midnight Mon-Wed, 9am-6pm Thu-Sat, 10am-midnight Sun) Housed in the basement of a crumbling mansion, the Bagdad is the place to head for a cheap, booze-infested night out. The city's top DJs regularly feature on the decks, a motley crew of students ram the place to overflowing, and in summer table football is all the rage out back.

Pret á Café (☎ 042 632 9203; ul Piotrkowska 67; ☼ 10am-10pm Mon-Fri, 10am-2am Sat, noon-10pm Sun) Carrie Bradshaw and her cohorts would feel right at home in this café-bar/high-fashion store in an alley off ul Piotrkowska. The cool little corner of minimalist chic has framed designer dresses on the wall, fashion mags lying on the taupe leather banquettes, a minicatwalk for impromptu fashion shows, and a rack of fancy frocks to flick through.

Piotrkowska Klub (☎ 042 630 6573; ul Piotrkowska 97; ☼ 11am-midnight Mon-Sat, noon-midnight Sun) Easily recognisable by the two-storey, wrought-iron-and-glass drinking area that stands outside the front door, Piotrkowska Klub has great views up and down its namesake street. Inside it's more sedate, with wood panelling and cosy booths tucked into quiet corners.

Entertainment

Both the Cultural Information Centre and Tourist Information Centre (p123) have information on what's on, and can supply you with the monthly *042 Magazine*, which lists theatres, cinemas, art galleries and museums alongside upcoming events, concerts and club nights. It's in both English and Polish. The yearly *Łódź the City of Art* booklet is another great source of information. Otherwise go online to the Polish-only www.reymont.pl.

CINEMAS

As home to Poland's film industry, Łódź is well supplied with cinemas. These are the most convenient city-centre ones:

Cinema City (☎ 042 664 6400; ul Jana Karskiego 5) Brand-new cinema in Manufaktura with box-office hits.

Cinematography Museum (☎ 042 674 0957; Plac Zwycięstwa 1) Screens mainly independent films from

---

CENTRE FOR CINEMA

Łódź is the centre of Polish cinema. Its **film school** (ul Targowa 61/63) – which in 1948 opened here rather than Warsaw because much of the capital lay in ruins – is famous throughout Europe, and has produced some of the world's greatest directors. The country's world-renowned trio – Roman Polański, Krzysztof Kieślowski and Andrzej Wajda – all studied here, as did Poland's lesser-known (but equally talented) lights Andrzej Munk (*Czlowiek na torze*, Man on the Tracks; 1957), Jerzy Skolimowski (*Moonlighting;* 1982), and Marek Piwowski (*Rejs*, The Cruise; 1970).

The school, near the Cinematography Museum, can be visited throughout the year, but cinema lovers should time their visit with **Camerimage** (www.camerimage.pl), an international festival held over seven days in late November/early December. The festival celebrates the art of cinematography and is one of the biggest events on the city's cultural calendar, attracting both big names in the cinema business (David Lynch, Oliver Stone) and droves of mere mortals.

around the world, often free of charge. Children's films on Sunday.

Kino Cytryna (☎ 042 632 1859; ul Zachodnia 81/83) Mostly Hollywood blockbusters but a few art-house titles.

Silver Screen (☎ 042 639 5858; Al Piłsudskiego 5) Ten-screen multiplex with mainstream films.

CLUBS
Łódź is well known as Poland's centre for electronic music, but DJs regularly mix it up with hip-hop, house and drum 'n' bass. Aside from the clubs below, catch the best of the bunch at Bagdad Café (p129) and Łódź Kaliska (p129).

Piano Café (☎ 042 632 7114; ul Piotrkowska 80; ⏰ 4pm-midnight) This small brick-cellar establishment is a drinking hole that welcomes all types and doubles as a gallery for local artists.

Honey Bunny (☎ 042 633 0914; ul Piotrkowska 90; ⏰ 6pm-1am Wed & Thu, 6pm-5am Fri & Sat) The club to be seen at, with gorillas on the door and a bouncing dance floor.

Coffees & Toffees (☎ 042 637 6148; ul Tuwima 6/10; ⏰ 2-9.30pm Sun-Thu, 10am-5am Fri & Sat) More relaxed than Honey Bunny, with comfy sofas and local and international DJs.

OPERA, THEATRE & CLASSICAL MUSIC
Grand Theatre (Teatr Wielki; ☎ 042 633 9960; www .teatr-wielki.lodz.pl; Plac Dąbrowskiego; ⏰ box office noon-7pm Tue-Sat, 3-7pm Sun) The city's main venue for opera and ballet also stages festival events and visiting shows.

Łódź Philharmonic (Filharmonia Łódzka; ☎ 042 664 7979; www.filharmonia.lodz.pl; ul Piotrkowska 243; ⏰ box office 10am-6pm Mon-Fri, from 10am Sun) Stages regular concerts of classical music every Friday and occasionally on other days of the week.

The city has many other theatres, of which the following are highly rated:

Music Theatre (Teatr Muzyczny; ☎ 042 678 1968; ul Północna 47/51; ⏰ box office 11am-6.30pm Tue-Fri, from noon Sat, from 3pm Sun) Stages mostly operettas and musicals.

Teatr Jaracza (☎ 042 632 6618; ul Jaracza 27; ⏰ box office 8.30am-7pm Tue-Fri, noon-7pm Sat & Sun) Among the most respected drama theatres in Poland.

Teatr Powszechny (☎ 042 633 5036; www.teatr-pows zechny.lodz.pl; ul Legionów 21; ⏰ box office 9am-3pm Mon, 9am-7pm Tue-Fri, 5-7pm Sat & Sun) Polish drama.

Getting There & Away
BUS
The **central bus station** (Dworzec Centralny PKS; Plac Sałacińskiego 1) is right outside Łódź Fabryczna

train station. There are buses to Warsaw (24zł, three hours, five daily), Płock (20zł, three hours, nine daily), and Łowicz (10zł, 1½ hours, hourly). Polski Express buses run to Warsaw airport (36zł to 39zł, 2½ hours, seven daily), Gdynia (57zł, seven hours, one daily) via Gdańsk and Toruń, and Kraków (53zł, five hours, two daily) via Częstochowa and Katowice.

TRAIN
The city has three train stations. **Łódź Fabryczna** (Plac Sałacińskiego 1), which is a few blocks east of ul Piotrkowska, is the main station but **Łódź Widzew** (ul Adamieckiego) often has better connections to Warsaw (31zł, 2½ hours, seven daily). **Łódź Kaliska** (Al Unii Lubelskiej 3/5), to the west of the city centre, handles trains to Wrocław (42zł, four hours, up to five daily), Poznań (42zł, 4½ hours, four daily), Łowicz (11zł, two hours, two daily) and Kraków (46zł, 4½ hours, one daily).

Getting Around
Łódź' public-transport system is operated by **Miejskie Przedsiębiorstwo Komunikacyjne** (MPK; www.mpk.lodz.pl) and includes trams and buses, both of which use the same ticket system. A ticket becomes valid for a set length of time after you validate it in the machine on board, and remains valid for unlimited transfers between bus and tram lines. Tickets valid for 10/30/60/120 minutes cost 1.70/2.40/3.60/4.80zł; a 24-hour ticket costs 9.60zł.

Order a taxi through **MPT** (☎ 042 9191) or **Merc Radio** (☎ 042 650 5050). Bicycle rickshaws ply ul Piotrkowska and cost around 4zł to 10zł per trip (two passengers maximum).

ŁOWICZ
pop 30,300

For much of the year Łowicz (*wo*-veech) is a town close to slipping into a permanent coma, but when Corpus Christi (Boże Ciało) comes around it's *the* place to be. It can also boast a long and important connection to the Catholic Church – it was for over 600 years the seat of the archbishops of Gniezno, the supreme Church authority in Poland – and is a regional centre for folk arts and crafts, although you'll see little of it outside Łowicz' museum.

For information visit the **PTTK office** (☎ 046 830 9149; Stary Rynek 3; ⏰ 10am-5pm Tue-Sun).

Sights

The vast 15th-century **Łowicz Cathedral** (☎ 046 837 6266; Stary Rynek 24/30) dominates the Stary Rynek (Old Town Sq). Originally Gothic, it underwent several renovations and is now a mishmash of styles, including Renaissance, Baroque and Rococo. It isn't particularly attractive, but the locals seem to love it and bus in from around the country for Sunday mass. Twelve archbishops of Gniezno and primates of Poland are buried in the church.

On the opposite side of the square is **Łowicz Museum** (☎ 046 837 3928; Stary Rynek 5/7; adult/concession 7/4zł, free Sat; 🕐 10am-4pm Tue-Sun, closed days following public holidays), housed in a 17th-century missionary college designed by prolific Dutch architect Tylman van Gameren. The former priests' chapel, with its fading Baroque frescoes (1695) by Italian artist Michelangelo Palloni and finely carved ivory tusks, is the museum's highlight. The 1st floor comes a close second, with archaeological finds from the region such as Stone Age tools and more tusks, this time from mammoths. Colourful folk costumes, painted Easter eggs, traditional wooden furniture and photos of old farmsteads make interesting browsing on the 2nd floor. In the back garden of the museum are two old **farmsteads** from the region, complete with original furnishings, implements and decoration.

Festivals & Events

Corpus Christi (which falls on a Thursday in May or June), a feast in honour of the Holy Eucharist, is celebrated with gusto in Łowicz. It is marked by a large procession that circles the main square and the cathedral, and most of its participants dress in brightly coloured and embroidered traditional costumes and carry elaborate banners. This is the most solemn celebration of Corpus Christi in the country, and it's the best time to visit Łowicz and get a real feel for the devout Catholicism of rural Poland. The procession starts at around noon and takes roughly two hours to complete the whole circuit.

Sleeping & Eating

Hotel Aneta (☎ 046 837 0448; aneta@lowicz.com.pl; ul Powstańców 36; d/tr 45/60zł, d with bathroom 80zł) In a former workers' dormitory built from prefabricated panels, the small, basic rooms of this hotel are not the stuff of luxury, but will do in a pinch. It's about 1.5km south of the centre.

Hotel Zacisze (☎ 046 837 3326; www.zacisze.dt.pl in Polish; ul Kaliska 5; s/d/tr 95/135/165zł; P ⓧ) Located 300m south of the Stary Rynek and back from the road, this is a fairly comfortable place with basic rooms, '70s architecture and '80s music. It has its own reasonably priced restaurant, helpful staff with a little English, and a covered swimming pool.

Getting There & Away

The bus and train stations are side by side, about a five-minute walk east from the Stary Rynek. There are fast trains to Warsaw's Zachodnia station every two hours (20zł, one hour) but the train connection to Łódź is surprisingly slow; there are two trains daily between Łowicz and Łódź' Kaliska station (11zł, two hours). You're better off taking the bus (10zł, 1½ hours, hourly).

AROUND ŁOWICZ

Nieborów & Arkadia

pop 1500

It's hard to imagine anything of interest in the tiny, rural villages of Nieborów (nyeh-*bo*-roof) and Arkadia, 9km southeast of Łowicz. But hiding among the tree groves are two perfect backdrops for a Jane Austen novel.

Designed by Tylman van Gameren for Cardinal Radziejowski, archbishop of Gniezno and primate of Poland, the late-17th-century **Palace of Nieborów** is a classic example of Baroque architecture. In 1774 Prince Michał Hieronim Radziwiłł bought the palace, and he and his wife Helena set about cramming it with as much furniture and works of art as they possibly could. An imposing library was added, and an informal, English-style landscaped park, designed by Szymon Bogumił Zug, was laid out next to the old Baroque garden. A majolica (a type of porous pottery) factory, the only one in Poland at the time, was established on the grounds in 1881 and operated on and off until 1906.

In the 1920s the palace underwent its last important transformation, when a mansard storey was added to the building. The palace remained in the possession of the Radziwiłł family right up to WWII, after which, fortunately undamaged, it was taken over by the state and converted into a museum.

More than half of the palace rooms are now occupied by the **Nieborów Museum** (☎ 046 838 5635; www.nieborow.art.pl; adult/concession 15/6zł, park only 6/4zł, free Mon; 🕐 10am-4pm daily Mar & Apr, 10am-6pm daily May & Jun, 10am-4pm Mon-Fri, 10am-6pm Sat & Sun Jul-Sep, 10am-3.30pm Tue-Sun Oct, closed Nov-Feb). Part of the ground floor features 1st-century Roman sculpture and bas-reliefs collected by Helena, and highly unusual black-oak panelling from the late 19th century. The stairwell leading to the 1st floor, with its ornamental Dutch tiles dating from around 1700, is worth the entry fee alone.

The whole 1st floor was restored and furnished according to the original style and contains a wealth of *objets d'art*. Take note of the tiled stoves, each one different, made in the local majolica factory, and don't miss the two late-17th-century globes in the library, the work of Venetian geographer Vincenzo Coronelli.

The **French garden** (10am-dusk), on the southern side of the palace, has a wide central alley lined with old lime trees and is dotted with sculptures, statues, tombstones, sarcophagi, pillars, columns and other stone fragments dating from various periods. Many of them were brought from Arkadia. The **English landscaped park** (10am-dusk), complete with stream, lake, ponds and fishers, is to the west of the garden, behind an L-shaped reservoir.

With its overgrown ruins, peeling pavilions, temples and follies, **Arkadia** (adult/concession 6/4zł, free Mon, parking 8zł; 10am-dusk) is a romantic, pagan enclave in a sea of Catholicism. The landscaped park was laid out by Princess Helena Radziwiłł in the 1770s to be an 'idyllic land of peace and happiness', but after the princess's death the park fell into decay. Most of the works of art were taken to Nieborów's palace and can be seen there today, and the abandoned buildings fell gradually into ruin. Nowadays, the air of decay only adds to the charm of the place. Tree-shrouded ruins are dotted throughout the park, including a red-brick **Gothic House** (Domek Gotycki) perched above **Sybil's Grotto**, a 'Roman' aqueduct, and the impressive **Archpriest's Sanctuary** (Przybytek Arcykapłana), a fanciful mock ruin dominated by a classical bas-relief of Hope feeding a Chimera. The focus of Arkadia is **Diana's Temple** (Świątynia Diany), which overlooks the lake and houses a display of Roman sculpture and funerary monuments. It and the Archpriest's Sanctuary are the only two structures in the park to have enjoyed any kind of renovation.

Combined, the graceful palace and fanciful park make an excellent excursion from Łowicz – bring a picnic and spend the day.

GETTING THERE & AWAY

Arkadia is on the southern side of the Łowicz–Skierniewice road (No 70), 4km southeast of Łowicz; Nieborów is on the same road, a further 5km beyond Arkadia. Where the main road bends sharply to the right at Nieborów, keep going straight on – the palace is 300m ahead, on the right.

Slow trains from Warsaw (Warszawa Śródmieście, Warszawa Zachodnia and other commuter stations only, not Warszawa Centralna) to Łowicz stop at Mysłaków (12.50zł, 1¼ hours, seven daily), the last stop before reaching Łowicz. From the station it's a 10-minute walk to Arkadia, and another 5km (around 50 minutes' walk) to Nieborów. Warsaw–Łowicz trains also stop at Bednary, which is 4km from Nieborów.

There are up to 11 buses daily between Łowicz and Skierniewice, stopping at both Arkadia and Nieborów (both 4zł). The last bus to Łowicz from Nieborów leaves at 4.37pm; from Arkadia at 4.40pm.

Sromów
pop 800

Sromów (*sro*-moof) is a tiny rural hamlet with one big attraction – a private **Folk Museum** (Muzeum Ludowe; 046 838 4472; adult/concession 5/4zł; 9am-5pm Mon-Sat, noon-5pm Sun), founded by skilled artisan and passionate crafts collector Julian Brzozowski.

Set in a garden full of folksy statues, the museum is housed in four buildings, two of which feature animated tableaux of historic scenes and village life – a country wedding, a pageant of kings, a Corpus Christi procession in Łowicz, and the four seasons on the farm. A chapel featuring a dozen life-sized figures has been built next to the museum to commemorate the pope's visit to the region in 1999. The figures are all carved from wood and painstakingly painted and costumed. The animation, with synchronised music, is driven by concealed rods and shafts powered by 28 electric motors. All this is the result of 50 years of dedication and work by Mr Brzozowski and his family. Although a little kitsch, it's unique and fascinating and kids will love it.

The other buildings house a collection of about 30 old horse carts and carriages, assembled by the owner from the surrounding villages. Other exhibits include traditional paper cutouts, regional costumes, folk paintings, decorated wooden chests and embroidery. If the museum appears closed (as it sometimes is during quiet seasons), ask at Mr Brzozowski's house across the road, and he or someone from the family will open it and show you around.

Though only 65km from Warsaw, the village and surrounding area are very rural – there are old wooden houses, a few thatched roofs, cows grazing on the roadside and chickens foraging everywhere.

GETTING THERE & AWAY

Sromów, 10km northeast of Łowicz, is hard to find even on detailed, large-scale maps. Driving from Warsaw, follow road No 2 (E30) towards Poznań. The minor road to Sromów is on the right, about 16km after Sochaczew and 8km before Łowicz. The turn-off is marked by a petrol station and a small sign ('Sromów – Muzeum'); Ruszki is also signposted. The museum itself is about 3km from the main road; take the first turn on the left.

Public transport is difficult. Sporadic buses from Łowicz to Rybno will let you off on the Rybno road, 1km from the museum.

ŁĘCZYCA & TUM

pop 15,500 & 500

Łęczyca (wen-*chi*-tsah) may not look like much today, but from the Dark Ages to the 16th century this ordinary town played an important role in planting Poland's Catholic roots. Remnants of its illustrious past can be seen in its small castle and classic Romanesque church.

Łęczyca's 1500-year history began in the 6th century, when a stronghold was built 2km east of the present town site. By the 10th century a Benedictine abbey was established, and one of the first Christian churches in Poland was built. In the 12th century a monumental Romanesque collegiate church replaced the former one, and the settlement expanded. It was burned down by the Teutonic Knights in the early 14th century, and the town was then moved to its present location, where a castle and defensive walls were erected.

During the next two centuries Łęczyca prospered, becoming the regional centre and the seat of numerous ecclesiastical synods. Later on, however, due to wars, fires and plagues, the town slid into obscurity. In the 19th century the defensive walls and most of the castle were sold for building material.

The surviving structure was restored after WWII and turned into the **Łęczyca Museum** (☎ 024 721 2449; ul Zamkowa 1; adult/concession 6/3zł; free Thu; ☼ 10am-5pm Tue-Fri, 11am-5pm Sat & Sun). A modest archaeological section fills the basement, the highlight of which is fragments of Tum's church, while the upper level contains period furniture, medieval weapons, and an ethnographic section that features regional artefacts, mostly woodcarving.

The original site of Łęczyca grew into an independent village and was named **Tum**. The stronghold fell into ruin but the collegiate **church** was rebuilt. It's Poland's largest Romanesque church and a fine example of the architecture from that period. Although rebuilt several times, it has essentially preserved its original 12th-century form. It's a sizable defensive construction with two circular and two square towers, and two semicircular apses on each end, all built from granite and sandstone. The interior retains Romanesque features but is influenced by later Gothic remodelling, especially in the aisles. The Romanesque portal in the porch (the entrance to the church) is one of the finest in Poland. From the same period are fragments of frescoes in the western apse. If the church is locked, get the keys from the priest's house, 100m east of the church, on the opposite side of the road.

Directly opposite the Romanesque church is another fine example of religious architecture, this time in the form of a **wooden Orthodox church** (note the telltale onion-shaped dome).

Sleeping & Eating

Zajazd Senator (☎ 024 721 2404; ul Ozorkowskie Przedmieście 47, Łęczyca; d/tr 100/130zł) On the Łódź road, 1km from the centre, it offers large rooms and a decent restaurant for such a small hotel.

Stara Prochownia (Łęczyca; pizza 11-15zł; ☼ noon-10pm) Housed in the only building left standing in the castle grounds, this is a charming spot offering wood-oven-baked pizzas. It's decorated with black-and-white photos capturing Łęczyca in a bygone era and a hotchpotch of wooden furniture, and there are also outdoor tables. If only they could stop providing plastic cutlery.

There's nowhere to stay or eat in Tum.

Getting There & Away

The train station is on the southern outskirts of Łęczyca. Hourly trains run daily north to

Kutno (6.50zł, 35 minutes) and south to Łódź (9zł, one hour).

The bus terminal is close to the castle. There are plenty of buses to Łódź (12zł, one hour) and several to Kutno (25km).

Tum is only 30 minutes' walk through the fields from Łęczyca.

OPORÓW
pop 1000

The village of Oporów (oh-*po*-roof) lies well off the main tourist routes, but it's worth visiting for its diminutive Gothic **castle**. It's one of the few castles in Poland to have survived almost in its original form.

The fortified residence was built in the mid-15th century for Władysław Oporowski, the archbishop of Gniezno. Though it changed owners several times during its history, it underwent only a few alterations and today still retains its original simplified structure. The more important changes were the 17th-century wooden ceilings on the 1st floor, covered with Renaissance decoration, the enlargement of the windows and the construction of the terrace at the entrance.

Well restored after WWII, today the castle houses the **Oporów Museum** (☎ 024 285 9122; adult/concession 8/5zł; ☿ 10am-4pm Tue-Sun), which features a collection of exquisite furniture and paintings, French pistols and more medieval weaponry, and other objects dating from the 15th to the 19th centuries. The majority of exhibits are not directly connected with the castle's history, but were acquired from old palaces and residences in the region. A walk along the castle's parapets provides views of the surrounding moat and fine **park** (admission free; ☿ 8am-6pm).

Oporów is best visited using your own transport.

PŁOCK
pop 128,000

Most of Mazovia's mid-sized cities hold little interest for the average traveller, but not Płock (pronounced pwotsk). Dramatically perched on a cliff high above the Vistula, this pretty town has a long, varied history and a spruced-up old centre. It also can boast the remnants of a Gothic castle, a glorious cathedral, and the finest collection of Art Nouveau in the country.

Płock was a royal residence between 1079 and 1138 and the first Mazovian town to be given a municipal charter (in 1237). Its city walls were built in the 14th century and the town developed as a wealthy trading centre until the 16th century. The flooding of the Vistula in 1532, when half the castle and part of the defensive walls slid into the river, was merely a portent of further disasters to come, and the wars, fires and plagues that struck the town – and the region – in the following centuries brought its importance to an end.

Information

Bank Pekao (ul Kwiatka 6)

EMPiK (☎ 024 262 4916; Plac Narutowicza 5; ☿ 9am-6pm Mon-Fri, 9am-4pm Sat) Small section of English mags 'n' rags.

Main post office (ul Bielska 14b)

Tourist Information Centre (Centrum Informacji Turystycznej; ☎ 024 367 1944; cit.plock@ump.pl; Dom Darmstadt, Stary Rynek 8; ☿ 9am-6pm Mon-Fri, 10am-4pm Sat, 10am-2pm Sun May-Sep, 9am-4pm Mon-Fri Oct-Apr) Provides a wealth of information on the town and its region, and has free internet access.

Sights

After the large oil refinery and petrochemical plant on the southern side of the river, the dominating feature of Płock is two redbrick towers, the **Clock Tower** (Wieża Zegarowa) and the **Noblemen's Tower** (Wieża Szlachecka) – the last vestiges of the original Gothic **castle** that once protected the city. While both are impressive, it's the neighbouring **cathedral** (admission free; ☿ 10am-5pm Mon-Sat, 2-5.30pm Sun & public holidays) that will draw most people's attention. And rightly so. Despite losing most of its 12th-century Romanesque character during numerous transformations, it remains an imposing structure. The interior, topped with a Renaissance dome added in the mid-16th century, boasts a number of tombstones and altarpieces from various periods, and tasteful Art Nouveau frescoes. The royal chapel (at the back of the north aisle) holds the sarcophagi of two Polish kings, Władysław Herman and his son Bolesław Krzywousty, who lived in Płock during their reigns. Both are in immaculate condition (the tombs, not the kings).

Take time to note the bronze doors at the southern end of the cathedral – copies of the original 12th-century doors commissioned by the local bishops. The originals disappeared in mysterious circumstances and reappeared in Novgorod, Russia, where they are today. The magnificent doors depict scenes from

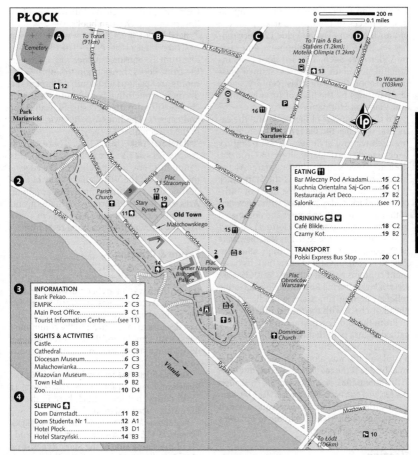

the Old Testament in extraordinary detail. The bronze relief in the tympanum above the doors shows the Adoration of the Magi, with a model of the cathedral (symbolically offered as a gift) below.

Next to the cathedral is the **Diocesan Museum** (Muzeum Diecezjalne; ☎ 024 262 2623; ul Tumska 3a; adult/concession 4/2zł; ⏰ 10am-3pm Tue-Sat, 11am-4pm Sun May-Sep, 10am-1pm Wed-Sat, 11am-2pm Sun Oct-Apr), housing a large collection of manuscripts, paintings, sculpture, vestments and tapestries. Naturally the overriding theme here is Catholicism, but the curators have had the good sense to include nonreligious items, such as the Charter of Płock from 1237, Stone Age archaeological finds, ceramics and coins from across the globe, and medieval weaponry. A few select pieces steal the show, though – look for the delicately gilded 12th-century ciborium from Czerwińsk and a 1st edition of Adam Mickiewicz' *Pan Tadeusz* (see p51). Guided tours are available for 10zł, but are normally only in Polish.

Art Nouveau aficionados will wet themselves upon entering the **Mazovian Museum** (Muzeum Mazowieckie; ☎ 024 364 7071; ul Tumska 8; adult/concession 8/4zł, free Thu; ⏰ 10am-5pm Tue-Sun May-Oct, 10am-3pm Tue, 10am-4pm Wed-Fri, 10.30am-4.30pm Sat & Sun Nov-Apr), not far north of the Diocesan Museum. Housed in an Art Nouveau residence dating from the early 1920s, the museum exhibits entire rooms (bedrooms, living rooms, dining rooms, studies, all perfectly colour-coded) of the splendid design on the

1st and 2nd floors. There are too many exquisite pieces to mention, but keep an eye out for the Henry van de Velde 12-piece dinner set, the Klingsor gramophone, and vases by Villeroy & Boch. The 3rd floor contains fanciful porcelain sculptures, stained glass from around the turn of last century, and a few paintings by the likes of Józef Mehoffer and Vlastimil Hofmann.

To the northwest of the castle and the cathedral stretches the **Old Town**. The dominating architectural style here is 19th-century neoclassical, particularly along ul Grodzka, the Old Town's main thoroughfare. At the northern end of Grodzka is the **Stary Rynek** (Old Town Sq), formerly the heart of 14th-century Płock; today it's lined with renovated 18th- and 19th-century houses and dominated by the neoclassical **town hall** (Ratusz). A short walk southeast of the Rynek is **Małachowianka** (ul Małachowskiego 1), the oldest high school in Poland (1180) and still in operation. Its basement contains a small **museum** (☎ 024 366 6600; admission free) featuring Romanesque and Gothic reliefs; opening times are sporadic so call ahead or check with the tourist office.

From the Old Town, you can return to the cathedral by a path that follows the clifftop – a pleasant walk with great views over the Vistula all the way along. To the east of the road bridge is the **zoo** (Ogród Zoologiczny; ☎ 024 366 0511; ul Norbertańska 2; adult/concession 5/3zł; ☽ 9am-7pm May-Sep, 9am-6pm Apr & Sep, 9am-5pm Mar & Oct, 9am-4pm Nov-Feb), which has a picturesque wooded setting above the river. It's home to Poland's largest snake collection.

Sleeping

Dom Studenta Nr 1 (☎ 024 366 5415; ul Nowowiejskiego 6; dm 30zł) Płock has three student hostels, including this year-round option just to the north of the old town. The simple, adequate rooms with shared facilities sleep three to four persons.

Motelik Olimpia (☎ 024 262 8426; ul Dworcowa 46; s/d 80/100zł; **P**) The big advantage of this basic 11-room motel is its location directly opposite the train and bus stations. There are also a garden and barbecue for guests.

Dom Darmstadt (☎ 024 367 1922; www.dd.pokis .pl; Stary Rynek 8; d 120zł) Ideally situated above the Tourist Information Centre in a historic townhouse, Dom Darmstadt is a quiet, cosy place with three double rooms (book in advance) sharing one bathroom and a kitchen.

German speakers can avail themselves of its library of 1500 German books.

Hotel Płock (☎ 024 262 9393; www.hplock.plocman .pl; Al Jachowicza 38; r 140zł; **P** **⌨**) The Płock looks dire from the outside, but once you're through the front doors things begin to improve. Its rooms are spacious and comfy, although the décor is something your grandma might choose (floral-patterned sheets, wallpaper and carpet). The hotel has its own brewery in the basement.

Hotel Starzyński (☎ 024 366 0200; www.starzynski .com.pl; ul Piekarska 1; s/d from 210/260zł; **P** **⌨**) This communist-era hotel perched on the edge of the cliff above the Vistula has quirky but appealing décor, reminiscent of, but not quite, Art Deco. Rooms are bright and modern, and the more expensive ones have superb views over the river, as does the hotel restaurant.

Eating & Drinking

Bar Mleczny Pod Arkadami (☎ 024 262 9521; ul Tumska 5; mains 4-8zł; ☽ 9am-6pm Mon-Fri, 9am-4pm Sat & Sun) If ever there was an archetypal milk bar, this is it. Pod Arkadami has managed to survive the political and economic upheavals of the past decades to retain an air of the communist days, with simple Polish fare, even simpler décor, and a steady stream of customers both young and old.

Kuchnia Orientalna Saj-Gon (☎ 024 268 7700; Plac Narutowicza 1; mains around 10zł; ☽ 11am-9.30pm) It looks dodgy, but locals flock here in droves for quick, cheap Asian food.

Restauracja Art Deco (☎ 024 268 5751; Stary Rynek 17; mains 15-40zł; ☽ 11am-11pm) Set in the middle of the sunny side of the Stary Rynek, this place has the comfiest outdoor tables on the square, and a menu of Polish favourites ranging from *czernina staropolska* (ducks'-blood soup) and a *pierogi* (dumpling) platter to roast duck, roast pork, and potato dumplings with pork crackling.

Salonik (☎ 024 268 5771; Stary Rynek 19; mains 20-40zł; ☽ 11am-11pm) Sister restaurant to Art Deco and similar in style, Salonik specialises in fish and Polish classics, but there's also a touch of French and Italian to the menu and vegetarians will be happy with the options. The *fin-de-siécle* décor includes sewing tables with foot pedal still attached.

Czarny Kot (☎ 0661 376 486; Stary Rynek 25; ☽ noon-midnight) The musically themed 'Black Cat' lazily occupies one corner of the Old Town's main square and provides comfy sofas and a small terrace for coffee- and beer-drinking guests. Enter on most Friday and Saturday nights and you'll be treated to live jazz and blues.

Cafe Blikle (☎ 024 268 3457; ul Tumska; ◷ 9am-6pm Mon-Sat, 10am-4pm Sun) An offshoot of Warsaw's famous café, this is the spot for cakes, coffee and ice cream.

Getting There & Away
The train and bus stations are nearly 2km northeast of the Old Town. At present only one train operates out of Płock, to Kutno (16zł, one hour) at 6.53am, but this may soon stop.

There are frequent PKS buses to Warsaw (25zł, two hours), two a day to Gdańsk and one a day to Toruń. Polski Express buses run to Warsaw (30zł, 1½ hours, up to 15 daily) and Torún (30zł, two hours, eight daily), leaving from opposite Hotel Płock. For Gdańsk, catch a bus to Torún and change there. Other operators, such as Ekobus and Baracuabus, also travel to Warsaw and often underbid PKS and Polski Express.

NORTHERN & EASTERN MAZOVIA

PUŁTUSK
pop 19,200
A sleepy town with a splendid castle and the longest market square in the country, Pułtusk (*poow*-toosk) is a fine place to stop for a few hours if your travels happen to lead you this way.

Today Pułtusk is just another dot on the Polish map, but the town's history is long and varied – its roots date back to the 10th century, making it one of Mazovia's oldest towns. It enjoyed its golden age in the 15th and 16th centuries, when it was the residence of the bishops of Płock and an important trade and cultural centre. In 1806 Napoleon's army fought one of its toughest battles in the campaign against Russia here, and in 1944 Pułtusk was on the front line for several months, during which time 80% of its buildings were destroyed.

Sights & Activities
The town's historic core, set on an island, is laid out around a 400m-long cobbled **Rynek**.

It still operates as a market place on Tuesday and Friday, when stallholders selling local farm produce and piles of junk overrun its northern half. In the middle stands the 15th-century brick tower of the town hall, today a **Regional Museum** (☎ 023 692 5132; adult/concession 4/3zł; ◷ 10am-4pm Tue-Sun). The so-so collection of archaeological finds (many from inside the castle grounds) is rather lame, but the views from the museum's tall tower certainly aren't. Nearby, at **house No 29**, Napoleon recuperated after the Battle of Pułtusk.

The northern end of the square is bordered by the **collegiate church** (*kolegiata*). Erected in the 1440s, the church underwent the usual architectural makeover every few centuries, and contains a dozen Baroque altars, Renaissance stucco decoration on the nave's vault, and aisles with original Gothic features. Note the 16th-century wall paintings in the chapel at the head of the right-hand aisle.

At the opposite end of the square stands the **castle**. Built in the late 14th century as an abode for bishops, it was rebuilt several times in later periods. It's now a plush hotel and conference centre. A cobbled road leads around the east side of the castle to a little harbour on the Narew river where you can hire **rowing boats** (15zł per hour) and **kayaks** (10/60zł per hour/day) and organise **boat trips** (30 minutes/one hour 75/150zł).

Sleeping & Eating
Hotel Baltazar (☎ 023 692 0475; www.hotel-baltazar .pl; ul Baltazara 41; s/d/tr 100/120/150zł; P) Hidden away at the end of a minor road, 1km north of the Rynek (signposted), this family-run hotel is an attractive, modern alternative to the Dom Polonii, with bright, spacious rooms and friendly service. Bicycles and kayaks are for hire, and there's a restaurant on the premises.

Dom Polonii (☎ 023 692 9000; www.dompolonii .pultusk.pl; ul Szkolna 11; s/d/tr/ste 250/330/390/530zł; P) Housed in the restored and much-converted castle, Dom Polonii offers atmospheric accommodation in sepia-tinted rooms redolent of past elegance, with creaky parquet flooring and archaic plumbing. There are cheaper rooms in other buildings in and around the castle grounds (singles/doubles from 140/220zł).

Pułtusk has a very weak culinary scene. The best restaurants are inside the castle, but they can be disappointing for what you pay. For lunch, try the riverside Taverna.

MAZOVIA & PODLASIE

Getting There & Away

Pułtusk lies on the road from Warsaw to the Great Masurian Lakes. There's no railway in town, but there are regular buses to and from Warsaw (14zł, 1½ hours, half-hourly). Pułtusk's **bus station** (☎ 023 692 2967; ul Nowy Rynek 3) is just off the main road through town, about 600m southwest of the Rynek.

TREBLINKA

In a peaceful clearing, hidden deep in the Mazovian pine forest, stands a granite monolith; around it is a field of 17,000 jagged, upright stones, many engraved with the name of a town or village. Beneath the grass, mingled with the sand, lie the ashes of some 800,000 human beings.

Treblinka, the site of the Nazis' second-largest extermination camp after Auschwitz, is another name that will forever be associated with the horror of the Holocaust. Between July 1942 and August 1943, on average more than 2000 people a day, mostly Jews, were gassed in the camp's massive gas chambers and their bodies burnt on huge, open-air cremation pyres.

Following an insurrection by the inmates in August 1943, the extermination camp was completely demolished and the area ploughed over and abandoned. The site of the camp is now the **Museum of Fighting & Martyrdom** (Muzeum Walki i Męczeństwa; ☎ 025 781 1658; admission incl museum 2zł; ⏰ 24hr). Access is by a short road that branches off the Małkinia–Sokołów Podlaski road and leads to a car park and a **kiosk** (⏰ 9am-7pm Apr-Oct, 9am-4pm Nov-Mar) that provides information and sells guidebooks. Across from the kiosk, the ground floor of a white building houses a small **museum** (⏰ 9am-7pm) with factual yet chilling explanations of the camp (for example, gas chambers could hold up to 5000 people at one time) and a handful of the personal belongings of prisoners found at the site.

It's a 10-minute walk from the car park to the site of the **Treblinka II** extermination camp, alongside a symbolic railway representing the now-vanished line that brought the cattle trucks full of Jews from the Warsaw Ghetto. The huge granite monument, 200m east of the ramp, stands on the site where the gas chambers were located. Around it is a vast symbolic cemetery in the form of a forest of granite stones representing the towns

and villages where the camp's victims came from. Unlike Auschwitz, nothing remains of the extermination camp, but the labels on the plan showing the original layout speak volumes: 'Building for Sorting Gold and Valuables'; 'Storehouse for Victims' Property (Disguised as Train Station)'; 'Barracks Where Women Undressed, Surrendered Valuables and Had Heads Shaven'; 'Approach to Gas Chambers'.

A further 20-minute walk leads to another clearing and the site of **Treblinka I**, a penal labour camp that was set up before Treblinka II, where remains of the camp, including the concrete foundations of the demolished barracks, have been preserved.

Getting There & Away

Treblinka is about 100km northeast of Warsaw, a two-hour drive away. Take Rte 8 towards Białystok, and 15km north of Wyszków turn right on road No 694 (signposted Ciechanowiec). When you reach Małkinia (26km from the main road), take the first turn on the right (again signposted Ciechanowiec), then go right again immediately after the railway (road No 677 to Przewóz). You cross a rickety wooden bridge over the Bug River, then cross a railway line to reach Treblinka village (4km from Małkinia). Continue for another 4km through the hamlet of Poniatowo; the entrance to the site is the first turn on the right after you cross the railway line again.

Małkinia lies on the Warsaw–Białystok railway line; there are hourly trains from Warszawa Centralna every two hours, and more frequent ones from Warszawa Wileńska station (14zł to 22zł, 1¾ hours). There are no buses to Treblinka so your only option (other than an 8km walk) is to take a taxi from the train station; reckon on paying between 60zł and 120zł, depending on how long you want the taxi to wait.

SOUTHERN PODLASIE

Southern Podlasie (pod-*lah*-sheh) fills a large swath of northeastern Poland, hogging much of the country's border with Belarus. More than any other region in this vast country, it is here that the influence of foreign cultures can be felt the strongest. The closer you get to the last dictatorship in Europe, the more onion-shaped Orthodox domes you'll see and Belarusian language you'll hear. You'll also be witness to remnants of 17th-century Tatar settlement (see p145). Jews, who once populated the region, have left traces of their presence too (see p142).

Despite its rich cultural make-up, the main attraction here is nature. Podlasie literally means 'the land close to the forest', a moniker it has for good reason. This part of the world was once covered in primeval forest, and while much of it has fallen to the woodcutter's axe, a rich pocket still remains within the Białowieża National Park. Southern Podlasie is also home to unique lowland marches, which fall under the protection of the Biebrza and Narew National Parks; both offer excellent kayaking opportunities.

BIAŁYSTOK
pop 292,000

Białystok (byah-*wis*-tok) is Podlasie's metropolis and a large, busy city for these parts. Attractions are few, but its close proximity to the region's national parks makes it a good base, and the mix of Polish and Belarusian cultures gives it a special atmosphere found in no other Polish city.

The city may have been founded in the 16th century but it didn't begin to develop until the mid-18th century, when Jan Klemens Branicki, the commander of the Polish armed forces and owner of vast estates – including the town – established his residence here and built a palace. A century later the town received a new impetus from the textile industry, and eventually became Poland's largest textile centre after Łódź. The textile boom attracted an ethnic mix of entrepreneurs, including Poles, Jews, Russians, Belarusians and Germans, and by the outbreak of WWI Białystok had some 80,000 inhabitants and more than 250 textile factories.

During WWII the Nazis practically destroyed the city, murdering half its population, including almost all the Jews, and razing most of the industrial base and central district. Postwar reconstruction concentrated on tangible issues such as the recovery of industry, infrastructure and state administration, together with the provision of basic necessities. As you can still see today, historic and aesthetic values receded into the background.

Information

Bank BPH (Rynek Kościuszki 7)
EMPiK (☎ 085 743 5068; ul Sienkewicza 3; ☒ 9am-7pm Mon-Fri, 9am-4pm Sat) Some English-language books, magazines and newspapers.
Main post office (ul Warszawska 10)
Piramida Café (☎ 085 742 1818; ul Grochowa 2; per hr 5zł; ☒ 8am-midnight Mon-Fri, 9am-midnight Sat & Sun) Internet access.
Tourist Information Point (Punkt Informacji Turystycznej; ☎ 085 732 6831; ul Malmeda 6; ☒ 8am-5pm Mon-Fri) Plenty of information on the region; gives advice on obtaining a Belarus visa.

Sights

The centre of the city is marked by the triangular Rynek Kościuszki, the former market square, with its 18th-century **town hall** in the middle. The town hall was rebuilt from scratch after the war and now houses the **Podlasie Museum** (Muzeum Podlaskie; ☎ 085 742 1473; Rynek Kościuszki 10; adult/concession 4/2zł; ☒ 10am-5pm Tue-Sun), which features a modest collection of Polish painting on the ground floor, including some important names such as Malczewski and Witkacy, and archaeological finds from a Viking village unearthed near Elbląg.

In Park Pałacowy to the east of the square stands the former residence of Jan Klemens Branicki, **Branicki Palace** (Pałac Branickich). Branicki, once a contender for the Polish crown, built the palace as a residence that would rival the king's in importance and luxury after losing to Stanisław August Poniatowski in royal elections. Burned down in 1944 by the retreating Nazis, the palace was restored to its original 18th-century shape, but the interior, which is off limits to the public, was largely modernised. The landscaped gardens are free to wander, however.

Across the road from the palace is a strange merger of two churches: a small 17th-century **old parish church** and, attached to it, a huge mock-Gothic **cathedral**. The latter was constructed at the beginning of the 20th century as an 'extension' of the former, the only way to bypass the tsarist bureaucracy that officially forbade Poles to build new Catholic churches.

It's worth making a detour outside the central area to the modern **Orthodox Church of the Holy Spirit** (Cerkiew Św Ducha; ☎ 085 653 2854; ul Antoniuk Fabryczny 13), 3km northwest of the centre (bus 5 from ul Lipowa in the centre will let you off nearby). Begun in the early 1980s, this monumental building is the largest Orthodox

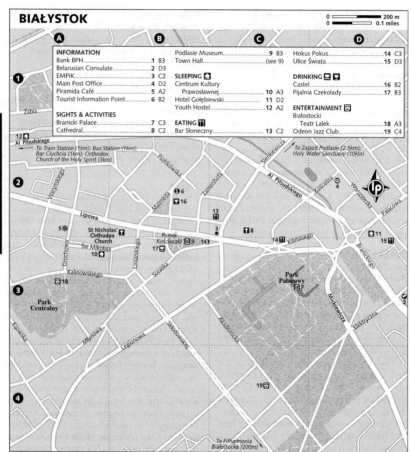

BIAŁYSTOK

| 0 | 200 m |
| 0 | 0.1 miles |

INFORMATION
Bank BPH....................................1 B3
Belarusian Consulate..................2 D3
EMPiK...3 C2
Main Post Office.........................4 D2
Piramida Café.............................5 A2
Tourist Information Point...........6 B2

SIGHTS & ACTIVITIES
Branicki Palace...........................7 C3
Cathedral....................................8 C2

Podlasie Museum........................9 B3
Town Hall...............................(see 9)

SLEEPING
Centrum Kultury
  Prawosławnej.........................10 A3
Hotel Gołębiewski...................11 D2
Youth Hostel............................12 A2

EATING
Bar Słoneczny.........................13 C2

Hokus Pokus...........................14 C3
Ulice Świata............................15 D3

DRINKING
Castel.......................................16 B2
Pijalnia Czekolady...................17 B3

ENTERTAINMENT
Białostocki
  Teatr Lalek...........................18 A3
Odeon Jazz Club......................19 C4

church in Poland. The huge, central, onion-shaped dome is topped with a large cross (weighing 1500kg) symbolising Christ, while 12 smaller crosses around it represent the apostles. The spacious interior boasts a spectacular main iconostasis and two smaller ones on either side, and a fantastic giant chandelier. The church is locked, except for daily morning services and Sunday Mass, but enquire at the **church office** (kancelaria kościelna; ☯ 8-11am & 3-5pm Mon-Fri) in the house behind the church, and somebody may open it for you.

Sleeping

Youth Hostel (☎ 085 652 4250; www.ssm.bialystok.ids.pl; Al Piłsudskiego 7b; dm 23-33zł; ☯ year-round; P) This modern hostel is housed in an old-style villa,

incongruously set amid concrete apartment blocks (it's tucked away from the street behind block No 7). It offers accommodation in pine bunk beds in wood-panelled dorms of six to 16 beds, with kitchen and 24-hour reception.

Zajazd Podlasie (☎ 085 675 0586; www.hotel podlasie.pl; ul 27 Lipca 24/1; s/d 120/135zł; P ▣) About 2.5km northeast of the centre, this purpose-built hotel comes with crisp, modern rooms and no-nonsense functional décor. There's also a restaurant on site and a bus stop in front of the main doors – take bus 3, 6 or 18 northbound from ul Sienkiewicza, or bus 18 from the train station.

Centrum Kultury Prawosławnej (☎ 085 744 3010; ckp@orthodox.bialystok.pl; ul Św Mikołaja 5; s/d 70/140zł; ✗) In a great location only a few minutes' stroll from the city centre is this cultural centre, run by the Orthodox Church community. It offers quiet, nonsmoking guest rooms, some with private bathrooms, to all comers.

Hotel Gołębiewski (☎ 085 678 2500; www.gole biewski.pl; ul Pałacowa 7; s/d 196/217zł; P ⊠ &) The almost unpronounceable Gołębiewski is a business-oriented hotel, a faceless multistorey block concealing spacious modern rooms and a swimming pool, sauna and Jacuzzi complex. There's a 30% discount on weekends.

Eating & Drinking

Hokus Pokus (☎ 085 740 3026; ul Kilińskiego 12; mains 10-20zł, pizzas 10-25zł; ⊗ 8am-11pm Mon-Sat, 10am-11pm Sun) Hokus Pokus doesn't quite get its décor right – chrome, sheepskin and stainless steel don't work well together – but its food is another matter. Excellent pizza, pasta, steaks and burgers keep locals coming back time and time again. It's family friendly and has top fruit drinks.

Ulice Świata (☎ 085 740 4161; ul Warszawska 30a; mains 10-20zł; ⊗ 1-11pm) The menu at this attractive two-level place offers a huge range of dishes from all over the world, from African and American to Mexican and Mediterranean.

Pijalnia Czekolady (☎ 085 742 0647; Rynek Kościuszki 17; ⊗ 9am-10pm Mon-Fri, 10am-10pm Sat & Sun) Serving fabulous chocolate in the form of drinks, cakes and sweets, Pijalnia is a chocolate-lover's dream come true. Willy Wonka would be proud of its chocolate fountain, and there's outdoor seating overlooking the main square.

Castel (☎ 085 732 6865; ul Spółdzielcza 10; ⊗ 11am-midnight Mon-Fri, noon-1am Sat & Sun) Castel is a hugely popular bar with two distinct sections – a romantic, dimly lit interior and a boisterous outdoor terrace. Grab your drink at the bar, otherwise you'll be waiting all night to be served.

Białystok has many cheap and cheerful eateries, including **Bar Słoneczny** (☎ 085 743 5815; ul Sienkiewicza 5; mains 6-10zł; ⊗ 9am-7pm Mon-Fri, 10am-5pm Sat, 11am-5pm Sun) and **Bar Ciuchcia** (ul Kolejowa; kebabs 8-11zł; ⊗ 9am-10pm); the former has a large outdoor patio while the latter churns out excellent kebabs from a dinky steam engine in front of the train station.

Entertainment

Odeon Jazz Club (☎ 085 742 4988; ul Akademicka 10/1; ⊗ noon-11pm Sun & Mon, noon-1am Tue-Thu, noon-3am Fri & Sat) The circular Odeon attracts a 30s to 40s

crowd with live jazz and blues on Friday and DJs spinning tunes from the '60s, '70s and '80s on Saturday.

Filharmonia Białostocka (☎ 085 732 2331; ul Podleśna 2; ⊗ box office 10am-5pm Tue-Thu, 10am-7pm Fri) Holds concerts of classical music every Friday, as well as hosting special events and visiting orchestras.

Białostocki Teatr Lalek (☎ 085 742 5031; ul Kalinowskiego 1) One of Poland's best puppet theatres, it stages children's shows, such as *Pinocchio* or *Punch and Judy* as well as traditional Polish stories, at least three or four times a week.

Getting There & Away

The Dworzec PKS **bus station** (ul Bohaterów Monte Cassino 10) and Dworzec PKP **train station** (ul Dworcowa 1) are next to each other, about 2km west of the central area. You can walk to the centre in 20 minutes, or take bus 2, 4 or 28 to Rynek Kościuszki.

BUS

There are regular PKS buses from Warsaw (Warszawa Stadion) to Białystok (26zł, 3¾ hours, seven daily), and Polski Express buses from Warsaw airport (41zł, four hours, one daily). Buses to Augustów (15zł to 18zł, two hours) leave seven times a day, to Olsztyn (28zł, five hours) three times a day, and to Gdańsk (44zł, nine hours) once a day at 6.10am.

TRAIN

The main intercity rail services are to Warsaw (Warszawa Wschodnia station; 35zł, 2½ hours, every two hours), and Gdańsk (49zł, 7½ hours, two daily) via Olsztyn. There is one direct overnight train to Kraków (54zł, eight hours); otherwise a change in Warsaw is required.

AROUND BIAŁYSTOK

About 20km north of Białystok is the **Holy Water Sanctuary** (Sanktuarium Święta Woda), where a miraculous spring has been a site of pilgrimage since the early 18th century. In 1997 the nearby hill was declared a Monument to the Third Millennium, or the Mountain of Crosses, and all heaven broke loose. Crowds of pilgrims have rushed to visit the site, leaving crosses of every shape and size. There are now more than 10,000 crosses and the number grows with every year.

MAZOVIA & PODLASIE

The site is next to the road to Sokółka, 2km north of Wasilków, opposite a yellow Pronar petrol station. To get there, take bus 100 from ul Bohaterów Monte Cassino opposite the PKS bus terminal in Białystok.

TYKOCIN
pop 1900

Like so many of the region's sleepy towns, Tykocin's (ti-*ko*-cheen) importance lies in its past. It started life as a stronghold of the Mazovian dukes, but its real growth didn't begin until the 15th century and was further accelerated after the town became the property of King Zygmunt II August in 1543. It was during this period that Jews started to settle in Tykocin, their community growing rapidly to define the town's character for the next four centuries. They also built the town's greatest monument, a 17th-century synagogue that miraculously survived WWII.

By the end of the 18th century Tykocin's fortunes had changed and the town gradually slid into decline. During WWII it lost all its Jews – half of the town's population – and then in 1950 it was deprived of its town charter, to become an ordinary village. It recovered its charter in 1994, but otherwise nothing has changed; only a few historic buildings survive as evidence of the town's illustrious past.

Sights

Tykocin's **synagogue** is one of the best-preserved in Poland, its four-square form dominating the western part of town, which was traditionally the Jewish quarter. This sober-looking edifice, erected in 1642, remained in use for religious services right up until WWII.

Renovated after the war, the synagogue is now the **Tykocin Museum** (☎ 085 718 1613; ul Kozia 2; adult/concession 5/3zł; ⏱ 10am-5pm Tue-Sun). The interior, with a massive almemar (raised platform on which the reading desk stands) in the centre and an elaborate Aron Kodesh (the Holy Ark where the Torah scrolls are kept) in the eastern wall, has preserved many of the original wall paintings, including Hebraic inscriptions. Adjacent to the former prayer room is a small exhibition containing photos and documents of Tykocin's Jewish community and objects related to religious ritual, such as elaborate brass and silver hanukiahs (candelabras), Talmudic books and liturgical equipment. There's an extension of the museum in the **Talmudic house**, right behind the synagogue, which is used mostly for temporary exhibitions. Tours of the synagogue leave at 10am and 5pm and are included in the cost of admission.

At the opposite end of the town stands the 18th-century Baroque **Holy Trinity Church** (Kościół Św Trójcy). Two symmetrical towers linked to the main building by arcaded galleries overlook the spacious Rynek (called Plac Czarnieckiego). In the middle of the square stands the **Monument to Stefan Czarniecki**, a national hero who distinguished himself in battles against the Swedes. The statue, from the 1760s, is one of the oldest secular monuments in Poland. Next to the church is the squat **Alumnat**, the world's first hospice for war veterans, dating from 1633. It still provides food and lodging, but nowadays for tourists.

Sleeping & Eating

Dom Pod Czarnym Bocianem (☎ 085 718 7408; www.czarnybocian.prv.pl; ul Poświętna 16; d 80zł) About 100m east of the Holy Trinity Church, the 'House Beneath the Black Stork' is a pleasant guesthouse run by a local couple in a modern villa on the bank of the Narew River. There are five double rooms with en suite bathrooms. Guests have use of the kitchen for fixing snacks and meals and can use kayaks free of charge.

our pick Kiermusy Dworek Nad Łąkami (☎ 085 718 7444, in Białystok 085 718 7444; www.kiermusy.com.pl; Kiermusy; s/d 190/250zł, house 450-800zł, castle apt from 900zł; P) The 'Manor House on the Meadow' is a small, rural village of wooden houses and accompanying countryside inn. The inn is decorated in traditional Polish style, while the houses have a distinctive rustic look, although they're modern where it counts (kitchen and bathroom). About 800m from the manor house and connected by a raised wooden walkway through reedy marshes is a faux-medieval castle that also has accommodation. Food is served in the inn. It is 3km northwest of Tykocin, on the road towards the village of Nieciece.

our pick Restauracja Tejsza (☎ 085 718 7750; ul Kozia 2; mains 10-20zł; ⏱ 10am-8pm) In the basement of the Talmudic house (enter from the back), this basic eatery serves excellent and inexpensive home-cooked kosher meals, including some of the best *pierogi* in the country. There's also an outdoor seating area.

POLAND'S STORK VILLAGE

Storks are a common sight in towns and villages across Podlasie, where artificial platforms are carefully constructed for the lanky white birds to build their nests upon. But **Pentowo**, a collection of farm buildings 2km northwest of Tykocin on the road to Kiermusy, holds the title of Poland's Stork Village. In 1991 a hurricane ripped through the village, snapping many of the trees like twigs, and over the ensuing years storks began to nest in the broken treetops. Storks are notoriously inept at building their homes, so the locals decided to give these bringers of happiness and babies a lending hand, and eight platforms were built.

Today Pentowo can boast 23 nests and at times more than 70 birds. The best time to see nesting storks is between April and August – by the time September comes around they're on their long journey south to Africa.

Getting There & Away

Tykocin is served by hourly buses from Białystok (9zł, one hour); buses stop at the Rynek, 100m from the synagogue.

NOWOGRÓD
pop 2000

Nowogród (no-*vo*-groot) is similar in every way to all the other small, rural towns in the western reaches of Podlasie, except two – it has a notable skansen and direct access to the Narew River. The town's inhabitants, known as the Kurpie, are also special in their own way. They have developed a distinctive style of dress, music and house decoration over the centuries, but are best known in Poland for their paper cutouts and weaving.

Founded in 1927, **Skansen Kurpiowski** (☎ 086 217 5562; ul Zamkowa 25; adult/concession 6/4zł; ◷ 8am-4pm Mon-Fri, 10am-5pm Sat & Sun May-Sep, 9am-2pm Mon-Fri Oct-Apr) is the second-oldest museum of its kind in Poland, spectacularly located on a wooded bank overlooking the Narew. Like the rest of the town, it was destroyed during WWII and rebuilt from scratch. Most of the buildings, however, are genuine 19th-century pieces of rural wooden architecture collected from all over the Kurpie region. There are 34 buildings, including cottages, barns, granaries and mills with fine architectural detail and elaborate decoration. One close to the river offers snacks and drinks. There's also a collection of charming beehives, including some fashioned from hollow tree trunks.

Sleeping options include the modern **Hotel Zbyszko** (☎ 086 217 5518; www.zbyszko.com; ul Obrońców Nowogrodu 2; s/d/tr 110/150/190zł; P ☒), beside the Narew on the road out of town to Zbójna. It's perfectly placed for trips up (if you're fit) and down the river; kayaks are available for 25zł per day.

The skansen is best visited with your own transport, as you'll need to travel to Łomża, the nearest sizable town, to find a bus connection (four daily). The bus stop is on the Rynek, a few minutes' walk from the skansen.

BIEBRZA NATIONAL PARK

The Biebrza (*byehb*-zhah) National Park (Biebrzański Park Narodowy) is Poland's largest and longest, stretching more than 100km from close to the Belarus border to the Narew River near Tykocin. Established in 1993, it's a relatively new park but a very important one, protecting the **Biebrza Valley**, Central Europe's largest area of natural bog.

The varied landscape consists of river sprawls, peat bogs, marshes and damp forests. Typical local flora includes numerous species of moss, reed grass and a range of medicinal herbs. The fauna is rich and diverse, and features mammals such as wolves, wild boar, foxes, roe deer, otters and beavers. The king of the park, however, is the elk: about half of the country's population, around 500 animals, live within the park's borders.

Bird-watchers flock to the Biebrza to glimpse the 270 or so bird species (over half of all species recorded in Poland) that call the park home. Storks, cranes, hawks, curlews, snipe, ruffs, egrets, harriers, crakes, sandpipers, owls, shrikes and at least half a dozen species of warblers are the more common varieties, while the great snipe, the white-winged black tern and the aquatic warbler are more rare.

Information

Entry to the park costs 4/2zł per adult/concession and can be paid at the **visitors information centre** (☎ 086 272 0620; www.biebrza.org.pl; Osowiec; ◷ 8am-7pm daily May-Sep, 8am-3pm Mon-Fri Oct-Apr) by the park's headquarters, just along the road from Osowiec-Twierdza train station. The helpful English-speaking staff will provide information about the park and its facilities. You'll be able to get details of where to stay and eat (or to buy food), and advice on the best spots for watching different bird species and how to get there. The centre provides information on where to find guides (35zł to 40zł an hour per group), kayaks (per hour/day 4/20zł) and canoes (5/30zł). The office is stocked with maps and brochures on the park, some of which are in English. The 1:100,000-scale *Biebrzański Park Narodowy* map (12zł) is among the best, with descriptions of half- and full-day hiking and kayaking trips in several languages.

Sights & Activities

The park can be broadly divided into three areas: the **Northern Basin** (Basen Północny), the smallest and least-visited area of the park; the **Middle Basin** (Basen Środkowy), stretching along the river's broad middle course and featuring a combination of wet forests and boglands; and the equally extensive **Southern Basin** (Basen Południowy), where most of the terrain is taken up by marshes and peat bogs. The showpiece is the **Red Marsh** (Czerwone Bagno) in the Middle Basin, a strictly protected nature reserve encompassing a wet alder forest that is inhabited by about 400 elks.

With over 200km of water trails crisscrossing the length of the valley, the best way to explore the park is by **boat**. The principal water route flows from the town of Lipsk downstream along the Biebrza to the village of Wizna. This 140km stretch can be paddled at a leisurely pace in seven to nine days. Bivouac sites along the river allow for overnight stops and food is available in towns on the way. The visitors information centre in Osowiec-Twierdza can provide maps and information. You can also hire a kayak for just a few hours or a day and cover part of the route; a handy two-hour stretch runs from Goniądz to Osowiec-Twierdza (kayaks can be rented from Goniądz' camping ground). Access to kayak trails costs 5.50zł for adults and 3.50zł for students and children per day on top of hire charges. The park is also connected to Augustów via the Augustów Canal (p156).

Despite its overall marshy character, large parts of the park can be explored relatively easily by **bicycle** and on **foot**. About 250km of signposted trails have been tracked through the most interesting areas, including nearly 50km through the Red Marsh alone. Dikes, boulders and dunes among the bogs provide access to some splendid bird-watching sites. Several viewing towers on the edge of the marshland allow for more general views of the park.

One of the most celebrated festivals in the park's calendar is the **National Championships in Scything Boggy Meadows for Nature**, held on the second weekend of September. Teams from all over the country turn up with scythes in hand, all eager to be the quickest to cut 100m of bog meadow. It's both a fun day out and ecologically sound – if the grass was left to grow, birds would have trouble nesting in the meadows.

Sleeping

There are several bivouac sites within the park and more outside its boundaries. The three most strategically located are in Osowiec-Twierdza (2km from the information centre), Grzędy (a gateway to the Red Marsh) and Barwik (close to the great snipe's habitat). All three are accessible by road and have car parks. You'll pay about 5zł per person per night to pitch your tent. There are also five rooms (for up to 16 people) in the **hunting lodge** (per person 30zł) in Grzędy.

The nearest camping grounds and hotels to the park are in Goniądz, Mońki and Rajgród. Youth hostels in the region include those in Goniądz, Grajewo, Osowiec-Twierdza and Wizna; all are open in July and August only. There are also about 70 **agrotourist farms** (d 30-35zł) in the region – the park's visitors information centre can provide details, as can its website (most listings are in the Polish-language section).

Getting There & Around

Osowiec-Twierdza is 50km northwest of Białystok, and sits on the railway line between Białystok (10zł to 16zł, one hour, five daily) and Ełk (9zł to 14zł, 40 minutes, five daily). The park office is just 200m from Osowiec-Twierdza station, and there are hiking trails and lookout towers within a few kilometres.

Having your own transport is a huge advantage, as you can easily access most of the park's major attractions.

NAREW NATIONAL PARK

Another marshland nature reserve, the Narew (*nah*-ref) National Park (Narwiański Park Narodowy) is just as interesting as Biebrza but not as geared towards visitors. The park protects an unusual stretch of the Narew River that's nicknamed the 'Polish Amazon', where the river splits into dozens of channels that spread out across a 2km-wide valley, forming a constellation of swampy islets in-between.

The park encompasses an area of about 73 sq km, 25% of which is bog and a further 3% water. Predictably, the most abundant flora and fauna species are those accustomed to aquatic conditions, including the omnipresent white-and-yellow water lilies. Among the 40 mammal species, the beaver is the most characteristic inhabitant, numbering at least 260 individuals living in about 70 lodges. The area is a favourite ground for birds, with as many as 180 species identified in the park, including about 150 species that breed here.

Sights & Activities

The most interesting area is the northwestern part of the park, where the watery labyrinth of channels is most extensive. The best way to get a taste of the marshland is by **kayak or boat** (trails adult/concession 4/2zł). Paddling through narrow, snaking channels and ponds with water so crystal clear you can see fish and plants to a depth of 2m is a highlight of a trip to the park. The best time for bird-watching is either early morning or late afternoon, when water birds are most active.

The main starting points for exploring the park are the tiny hamlet of Kurowo and the village of Uhowo. **Kurowo** sits on the left (western) bank of the Narew, connected to the outer world only by a rough road, which rarely sees a passing car. The central point of this tiny place is a late-19th-century country mansion that houses the **Narew National Park Headquarters** (☎ 085 718 1417; www.npn.pl; ♥ 7.30am-3.30pm Mon-Fri) and a small exhibition on the park's natural history. Here you can pay the park admission (adult/concession 5/1.20zł), camp near the building (per person 2.50zł; toilets but no showers) and rent kayaks (per hour/day 5/30zł). There's no restaurant so bring your own food or time your visit to coincide with the **Podlasie Honey Feast** on the last weekend of August. It's the biggest party on the national park's calendar, with beekeepers and local folk artists gathering to promote their wares.

Uhowo, near Łapy at the southern end of the park, is larger. This is the home base of **Kaylon** (☎ 050 250 8050; www.kaylon.pl; ul Kolejowa 8), an agency that organises canoeing expeditions

through the park from May to September. It charges 150zł per day for a guide, 26zł for kayak hire, 32zł for a three-person Canadian canoe and 1.40zł per km for transport.

Getting There & Around

There's no public transport to Kurowo, so without a car or bike you'll have a bit of a walk. The starting point is the village of Stare Jeżewo, 28km west of Białystok, on the main road (No 8) towards Warsaw. It's serviced by frequent buses from Białystok (every two hours). From Stare Jeżewo, walk 500m south on the road to Sokoły, and turn left at the first (unsigned) crossroads. Follow this side road for 3km until you reach another crossroads where the sealed surface ends. Take the road to the right (south) for another 1km until you see a large brick granary where the road divides. Take the left-hand fork for the last 1km to Kurowo. It takes a bit over an hour, but it's a pleasant walk through a bucolic landscape.

KRUSZYNIANY & BOHONIKI

These two small villages, close to the Belarusian border to the east and northeast of Białystok, are noted for their timber mosques, the only surviving historic mosques in Poland. They were built by the Muslim Tatars, who settled here at the end of the 17th century.

Kruszyniany (kroo-shi-*nya*-ni) is the larger of the two villages and also contains the larger of the two mosques. Its green **mosque** (☎ 0502 543 871; adult/concession 3/2zł; ♥ 9am-7pm May-Oct, by appointment Nov-Apr) is an 18th-century rustic wooden construction, in many ways similar to old timber Christian churches. You'll find it hidden in a cluster of trees, set back from the main road in the central part of the village.

The mosque's modest interior, made entirely from pine, is divided into two rooms, the smaller one designed for women, who are not allowed into the main prayer hall (unless they're a tourist). The latter, with carpets covering the floor, has a small recess in the wall, the mihrab, in the direction of Mecca. Next to it is the *minbar*, a pulpit from which the imam says prayers. The painted texts hanging on the walls, the Muhirs, are verses from the Quran.

The mosque is used for worship, and on the most solemn holy days there may not be enough room inside for all the congregation. Dress properly (no bare legs) and remove shoes before entering the prayer hall.

Kruszyniany's **Mizar** (Muslim cemetery) is located in the patch of woodland 100m beyond the mosque. The recent gravestones are Christian in style, showing the extent of cultural assimilation that has taken place, and are on the edge of the graveyard. Go deeper into the wood, where you'll find old tombstones hidden in the undergrowth. Some of them are inscribed in Russian, a legacy of tsarist times.

The **mosque** of **Bohoniki** is similar to Kruszyniany's mosque in its decoration and atmosphere, though the Bohoniki mosque is more modest and its new pinewood panelling has been left unpainted. It, too, can be visited; the keys are kept at the house across the road from the mosque. Bohoniki's **Mizar** is about 1km north of the mosque at the edge of a tree grove; walk to the outskirts of the village then turn left up a tree-lined dirt road. As in Kruszyniany, the old tombstones are further afield, overgrown by bushes and grass.

There is no accommodation or place to eat in Bohoniki, but Kruszyniany has both. **Dworek Pod Lipami** (☎ 085 722 7554; www.dworek podlipami.pl; ul Kruszyniany 51; s/d 50/100zł; **P**), almost opposite the mosque, is a lovely manor house with comfortable rooms and incredibly friendly staff. Traditional Tatar food and drink from the region is served, such as *babka ziemniaczana* (potato cakes) and *barsacz* (hot beetroot juice). Only a few doors down is **Tatarska Jurta** (☎ 085 749 4052; ul Kruszyniany 58; mains 10-20zł; 🕙 10am-8pm), a restaurant that also serves traditional Tatar dishes and wonderful homemade cakes; you can even watch as your host does the preparation and cooking. Take some time to check out its authentic Mongolian yurt in the back yard, which is held together by camel-hair rope.

The two villages are 37km apart, each about 50km from Białystok, and are best reached by car. Visiting by public transport is not feasible.

HAJNÓWKA
pop 22,200

Set on the edge of the Białowieża Forest, Hajnówka (high-*noof*-kah) is the main gateway for the Białowieża National Park. The town itself won't hold your attention for long, but its tourist office is an excellent place to pick up information on Białowieża and activities in the region.

Information

Białowieża Forest Regional Tourist Office
(Centrum Turystyki Regionu Puszczy Białowieskiej; ☎ 085 682 4381; www.powiat.hajnowka.pl; ul 3 Maja 45; 🕙 9am-5pm Mon-Sat May-Sep, 9am-5pm Mon-Fri Oct-Apr) Very knowledgeable and provides maps and booklets in English.

Sights

The **Orthodox Church of the Holy Trinity** (Cerkiew Św Trójcy; ☎ 085 873 2971; ul Dziewiatowskiego 13) is the town's major (well, only) sight and arguably one of the most beautiful modern Orthodox churches in Poland. Begun in the early 1970s and fully completed two decades later, the irregular structure, covered by an undulating roof, supports two slender towers, the main one 50m high. The bold, unconventional design, the work of Polish architect Aleksander Grygorowicz, has resulted in a powerful and impressive building. Its creators have also done a good job inside. The icons and frescoes include the work of Jerzy Nowosielski, and the stained-glass windows are from a Kraków workshop.

The **church office** (kancelaria kościelna; 🕙 10am-1pm & 2-5pm Mon-Sat) is in the house next to the church. If you enquire there during opening hours one of the priests will show you around the church. Otherwise try to time your visit to coincide with the services (10am Sunday, 8am weekdays).

Hajnówka's only other attraction is somewhat less spiritual, but probably more famous. **Bar U Wołodzi** (☎ 085 682 4626; ul 3 Maja 34a) is known throughout Poland for its bizarre collection of communist memorabilia and dozens of Soviet uniforms. It was closed at the time of research due to the owner's poor health but hopefully it will reopen soon.

Sleeping

Most people simply pass through Hajnówka on their way to or from Białowieża, but if you have to stay the night head for the bright and modern **Hotelik Orzechowski** (☎ 085 682 2758; www.hotel-orzechowski.com.pl; ul Piłsudskiego 14; s/d/tr 100/140/180zł; **P**), southeast of the tourist office.

Getting There & Away

The train and bus stations are next to each other, south of the main road junction and roundabout in the middle of town. There are

THE TATARS OF POLAND

In the 13th century large parts of Eastern Europe were ravaged by hordes of fierce Mongol horsemen from Central Asia. These savage nomadic warriors (commonly, though confusingly, referred to in Europe as the Tatars) came from the great Mongol empire of Genghis Khan, which at its peak stretched from the Black Sea to the Pacific. They first invaded Poland in 1241 and repeatedly overran and destroyed most of Silesia and Małopolska, the royal city of Kraków included. They withdrew from Europe as fast as they came, leaving few traces other than some folk stories. Not long after, the empire broke up into various independent khanates.

By the end of the 14th century, Poland and Lithuania faced an increasing threat from the north, from where the Teutonic order swiftly expanded southwards and eastwards over their territories. As a measure of protection, Lithuania (which was soon to enter into a political alliance with Poland) began looking for migrants eager to settle its almost uninhabited borderland fringes. It welcomed the refugees and prisoners of war from the Crimean and Volgan khanates, offspring of the once powerful Golden Horde state ruled by the heirs of Genghis Khan. The new settlers were Muslim Tatars of a different tribal background.

The Tatars' military involvement in Polish affairs began in 1410 at the Battle of Grunwald, where King Jagiełło defeated the Teutonic Knights; in this battle a small unit of Tatar horsemen fought alongside the Polish-Lithuanian forces. From that time the numbers of Tatar settlers grew, and so did their participation in battles in defence of their adopted homeland. By the 17th century, they had several cavalry formations reinforcing Polish troops in the wars, which were particularly frequent at that time.

In 1683, after the victory over the Turks at the Battle of Vienna, King Jan III Sobieski granted land in the eastern strip of Poland to those who had fought under the Polish flag. The Tatars founded new settlements here and built their mosques. Of all these villages, only Kruszyniany and Bohoniki have preserved some of their Tatar inheritance, though apart from their mosques and cemeteries not much else remains. The original population either integrated or left, and there are only a few families living here today who are true descendants of the Tatars.

Of a total of some 3000 people of Tatar origin in Poland, the majority found homes in large cities such as Warsaw, Białystok and Gdańsk. Nonetheless, they flock together in Kruszyniany and Bohoniki for important holy days, as Poland's only mosques (apart from one built in Gdańsk in the 1990s) are here. And they usually end up here at the local Tatar graveyards, two of only three still in use in the country (the other is in Warsaw).

hourly buses from Białystok to Hajnówka (8zł, two hours).

From Warsaw, you can take a fast train from Warszawa Wschodnia to Siedlce, and connect with the slow train to Hajnówka (32zł to 42zł, 3½ to four hours, two daily). There's also one direct train from Warsaw to Hajnówka (31zł, 3½ hours), which runs on Saturday year-round and daily in August.

BIAŁOWIEŻA NATIONAL PARK

The Białowieża (byah-wo-*vyeh*-zhah) National Park (Białowieski Park Narodowy) is the oldest national park in the country, and is famous as the place where the European bison was successfully reintroduced into the wild (see boxed text, p70). The park protects a small part of a much bigger forest known as the **Białowieża Forest** (Puszcza Białowieska),

which straddles the border between Poland and Belarus.

The *puszcza* (primeval forest) was once an immense and barely accessible forest stretching for hundreds of kilometres, but is now reduced to an area of about 1200 sq km, distributed approximately evenly between Poland and Belarus. In the 15th century it became a private hunting ground for Polish monarchs and later for Russian tsars. During WWI the Germans exploited it intensively, felling around five million cu metres of timber. The gradual colonisation and exploitation of its margins has also diminished the forest's area and altered its ecosystem. Even so, this vast forest, protected for so long by royal patronage, has preserved its primeval core largely untouched, and is the largest area of original lowland forest left in Europe.

Soon after WWI the central part of the *puszcza* was made a nature reserve, and in 1932 it was formally converted into a national park. Today the total area of the park is 105 sq km, of which 47 sq km is strictly protected. It is included on Unesco's World Heritage List. Unfortunately the region of forest outside the national park's borders is still under threat of logging – see the Environment chapter (p68) for more details.

Orientation

The starting point for excursions into the national park is the village of Białowieża, 85km southeast of Białystok. It has information points, accommodation, food and several travel agencies that can organise visits to the Strictly Protected Area of the park.

The village straggles along for about 3km on the southern edge of the national park, centred on the rectangular Park Pałacowy (Palace Park), which contains the Natural History Museum. The tourist office and Hotel Żubrówka are at the southern entrance to Park Pałacowy; the youth hostel is near its eastern entrance.

If you're arriving by bus from Hajnówka, there are three bus stops in Białowieża: one at the entrance to the village, one just after Hotel Żubrówka (closest to the PTTK office), and one at the post office (closest to the youth hostel and museum).

MAPS

The 1:85,000 *Białowieża Forest & Neighbourhood* map by CartoMedia has English-language information, street plans of Hajnówka and Białowieża, and marked cycle and walking paths through the forest. It's on sale in bookshops in Warsaw and Białystok, and at the PTTK offices in Hajnówka and Białowieża.

Information

MONEY

Hotel Żubrówka (☎ 085 681 2303; ul Olgi Gabiec 6) Has an ATM right outside its entrance.

TOURIST INFORMATION

National Park Information Point (☎ 085 681 2901; www.bpn.com.pl; Park Pałacowy; ☺ 8am-4pm Tue-Sun May-Sep) A small wooden hut at the eastern entrance to Park Pałacowy; information is also available at the Natural History Museum.

PTTK Tourist Service (Biuro Usług Turystycznych PTTK; ☎ 085 681 2295; www.pttk.bialowieza.pl; ul Kolejowa

17; ☺ 8am-4pm Mon-Fri, 8am-3pm Sat) Arranges guides, accommodation and bike hire (5/25zł per hour/day).

TRAVEL AGENCIES

Soon after your arrival check with a travel agency about visiting the Strictly Protected Area, as all visitors must be accompanied by a guide and it may take a while to arrange one or to gather a group to share the costs.

There are several agencies that organise trips. The major operator is PTTK Tourist Service, which organises English-, German- or Russian-speaking guides (165zł for up to three hours) for visits to the Strictly Protected Area, and trips by *bryczka* (horse-drawn cart) or sledge in winter (from 140zł for four people). Weekends are the best times to join English-speaking tours.

Other agencies with English-speaking guides:

Biuro Turystyki Ryś (☎ 085 681 2249; ul Krzyże 22)
Nature Tour (☎ 085 681 2007; naturetour@wp.pl; Park Dyrekcyjny 4/1)
Puszcza Białowieska (☎ 085 681 2898; bup@tlen.pl; Natural History Museum, Park Pałacowy)

Sights

STRICTLY PROTECTED AREA

Dating from 1921, the **Strictly Protected Area** (SPA, Obszar Ochrony Ścisłej; adult/child 6/3zł) is the oldest section of the national park, covering an area of around 4750 hectares, bordered to the north and west by the marshy Hwoźna and Narewka Rivers, and to the east by the Bielawiezskaja Primeval Forest National Park in Belarus.

The terrain is mostly flat, swampy in parts, and covered with mixed forest of oak, hornbeam, spruce and pine. Ancient trees reach spectacular sizes uncommon elsewhere, with spruce 50m high and oak trunks 2m in diameter; some of the oak trees are more than 500 years old. The forest is home to a variety of large mammals, including elks, stags, roe deer, wild boar, lynxes, wolves, beavers and the uncontested king of the *puszcza*, the bison. There are about 120 species of birds, including owls, cranes, storks, hazelhens and nine species of woodpecker.

The SPA can be entered only in the company of an official guide, who can be hired through travel agencies (opposite). You can hike, or travel by horse-drawn cart or, in winter, horse-drawn sledge. The standard tour takes about three hours, but longer routes, including some of the more remote areas, are also available (around six hours, 330zł).

Hiking is probably the best way to get a close feel for the forest, and the most popular with visitors. The normal route follows an 8km trail, which takes about three to four hours. The reserve gets pretty swampy in spring (March to April) and may at times be closed to visitors.

PALACE PARK
At the end of the 19th century, **Park Pałacowy** (Palace Park; admission free; 24hr) was laid out around a splendid palace built for the Russian tsar in 1894 on the site of an ancient royal hunting lodge once used by Polish kings. The **Russian Orthodox Church**, outside the eastern entrance to the park, was built at the same time. The southern entrance to Park Pałacowy, beside the PTTK office, leads across a fish pond past a stone **obelisk**, which commemorates a bison hunt led by King August III Saxon in 1752. The royal bag that day was 42 bison, 13 elks and two roe deer.

The avenue leads uphill past a redbrick **gate**, which is all that remains of the tsar's palace – it was burned to the ground by retreating Nazis in 1944. The palace site is now occupied by the **Natural History Museum** (Muzeum Przyrodniczo-Leśne; ☎ 085 681 2275; Park Pałacowy; adult/ concession 12/6zł; viewing tower & temporary exhibitions 6/3zł; 9am-4.30pm Mon-Fri, 9am-5pm Sat & Sun mid-Apr–mid-Oct, 9am-4pm Tue-Sun mid-Oct–mid-Apr), which features exhibitions relating to the flora and fauna of the park (mostly forest scenes with stuffed animals and a collection of plants), the park's history, and the archaeology and ethnography of the region. The permanent exhibition can be seen only by **guided tour** (up to 25 persons 55zł), which adds flavour to an otherwise static museum but is a tad expensive

if your group numbers are small. The viewing tower provides terrific views over the village, and just north of the museum you will find a grove of 250-year-old oaks.

BISON RESERVE
If you don't have time for a guided tour of the SPA, get a close look at some of the wildlife in the **Bison Reserve** (Rezerwat Żubrów; ☎ 085 681 2398; adult/concession 6/3zł; 9am-5pm daily May-Sep, 8am-4pm Tue-Sun Oct-Apr), a park where animals typical of the *puszcza*, including bison, elks, wild boar, wolves, stags and roe deer, are kept in large, ranch-style enclosures. You can also see the *żubroń*, a cross between a bison and cow, which has been bred so successfully in Białowieża that it is even larger than the bison itself, reaching up to 1200kg.

Another peculiarity is the tarpan (*Equus caballus gomelini*), a small, stumpy, mouse-coloured horse with a dark stripe running along its back from head to tail. The tarpan is a Polish cousin of the wild horse (*Equus ferus silvestris*) that once populated the Ukrainian steppes but became extinct in the 19th century. The horse you see is the product of selective breeding in the 1930s, which preserved the creature's original traits.

The reserve is 3km west of the Park Pałacowy (4.5km by road). You can get here on foot by the green- or yellow-marked trails, both starting from the PTTK office, or by the trail called Żebra Żubra (Bison's Ribs). You can also get there by horse-drawn cart – ask at the PTTK office for details.

ROYAL OAKS
About 3km north of the Bison Reserve are the Royal Oaks (Dęby Królewskie), a score of ancient trees, some over four centuries old. There is a short walking trail that winds its way among the venerable trunks. Each of the trees is named after a Lithuanian or Polish monarch; the biggest tree of the lot is Stefan Batory – 5.1m in circumference, 40m tall and 450 years old.

To get here, take the motor road from Białowieża towards Narewka (it begins beside the PTTK office, and has blue trail marks) for 5km to a crossroads. Turn right; the oaks are 200m along the dirt road. You can also hike north from the Bison Reserve on a yellow-marked trail (3km). If you take a cart to the Bison Reserve, you can visit the oaks on the same trip.

A BOOST FOR BISON

Krzysztof Niedziałkowski, a project coordinator at the **Mammal Research Institute** (www.zbs.bialowieza.pl) in Białowieża, is no stranger to conservation programmes. For a number of years he has been involved in the European Bison Programme (EBP), a programme aimed at sustainable regional development with bison as the focal point. Author Neal Bedford spoke to him about the programme and its big, hairy mascot:

What's EBP's main goal? The idea is to improve the situation of the European bison, and ensure the long-term conservation of the species. But we also want to foster the acceptance of bison in local communities, and promote it as a symbol for the region.

How are you doing this? We're attempting to create a European Bison Land, which would be an area that encompasses most of the sites where European bison currently live and could live in the future. The bison would be used as a symbol at the tourist attractions within the Bison Land, thus increasing awareness of the animals and in turn environmental issues in general. We're also pushing for the development of ecological corridors.

Ecological corridors? They are natural corridors, such as meadows, rivers and valleys, that animals use for migration. The idea is to connect the areas where bison live in the north of Poland, namely Białowieża, Kruszyniany and Borecka Forest near the Masurian lakes.

Had much success? We haven't had so many bison in Białowieża Forest for the last 100 years. The forest is utilised more evenly, as the bison have more places to forage. There's also evidence of migration tendencies being observed. Recently, bison have established themselves near Mielnik, 80km south of Białowieża. As for regional development, local communities have created an association, which aims at creating a European Bison Land.

What's the current bison population? There are about 400 at Białowieża, 50 near Kruszyniany, and 60 by the lakes. Belarus has about 200 to 250, and another 200 or so live in the Bieszczady Mountains. The Bieszczady bison come from a different line, and we don't want to crossbreed them with those in the north.

How do you keep track of the beasts? Some have collars with tracking devices, but around 30 now wear GPS collars. We receive SMS from the bison six times a day, which tell us where they are, if they're moving, feeding, lying down etc. It's an expensive system, but it's the best because the bison aren't disturbed by human presence.

Any poaching in the forest? Of bison, rarely. Wild boar and roe deer are normally the main targets. There is a yearly culling of the bison though, where between 10 and 40 animals are killed. In my opinion it's not needed as the forest can sustain a larger population, but the Polish Ministry of Environment thinks otherwise.

Sleeping & Eating

Białowieża has a good choice of accommodation options, most of which are inexpensive. Apart from the places listed here, the road approaching the village is lined with dozens of signs advertising *pokoje gościnne* (guest rooms) in private homes (25zł to 35zł per person), and the regional tourist office in Hajnówka (p146) has a list of around 40 *agroturystyczne* (agrotourist) options in and around the town.

Youth Hostel Paprotka (☎ 085 681 2560; www.paprotka.com.pl; ul Waszkiewicza 6; dm 19-24zł, q/d 24/40zł; P 🖵) This friendly youth hostel is set in an old timber house behind the mustard-coloured school building. There are dormitories that contain between six and 12 beds each, a couple of doubles and quads, a kitchen, and a lovely big common room that has a roaring fire at one end. But best of all, there is a washing machine (10zł) for guest use!

Dom Turysty PTTK (☎ 085 681 2505; Park Pałacowy; d/tr/q 80/105/128zł) This 19th-century redbrick pavilion operated by PTTK has an excellent location in Park Pałacowy. It offers small, basic rooms with private bathrooms, and a bistro serving simple, cheap meals. Note that it's popular with school and student groups, so it can occasionally be busy and noisy.

Pensjonat Unikat (☎ 085 681 2109; www.unikat .bialowieza.com; ul Waszkiewicza 39; s/d/tr/q 90/100/120/140zł; P) If you can handle the décor – a bison's head takes pride of place above the central fireplace and deerskins are nailed everywhere – Unikat is a good option a few hundred metres east of the National Park Information Point. This 50-bed timber guesthouse has clean, functional and sizable rooms, and a fine restaurant.

Hotel Białowieski (☎ 085 681 2022; www.hotel .bialowieza.pl; ul Waszkiewicza 218b; s 130-190zł, d 150-220zł, ste 410-440zł; P 🖳) The rooms at the child-friendly Białowieski are bright and modern and offer the same comfort level as the Żubrówka, but with a little less atmosphere. Many have balconies overlooking the garden. There's a play area at the back and bikes for hire (per hour/day 7/35zł).

Hotel Żubrówka (☎ 085 681 2303; www.hotel -zubrowka.pl; ul Olgi Gabiec 6; s/d 340/380zł, ste 500-900zł; P 🖳 👍) More dead bisons greet you upon entering Żubrówka, the town's plushest hotel. Rooms are suitably comfortable and modern, and suites have open fireplaces. There's also a spa centre and sauna on site.

Camping Grudki (☎ 085 681 2484; ul Grudkowska; per person/tent/car 6/3/5zł) This small camping ground, about 1km south of Białowieża on the road to Grudki, occupies a peaceful spot among a grove of trees. There's hot water, showers and bike hire (per hour/day 5/20zł), but no cooking facilities.

There are good restaurants at the Unikat, Białowieski and Żubrówka hotels, and also at the Natural History Museum (Restauracja Parkowa), but none compare to **Carska** (☎ 085 681 2119; ul Stacja Towarowa 4; mains 40-75zł; ⏲ 11am-10pm). This silver-service restaurant in the tsar's private railway station 1km south of the town, specialises in game, such as *szynka z sarny* (pickled wild-boar ham).

For cheap eats, there's a pizzeria across the road from Żubrówka, and a grill-bar beside the car park, behind the PTTK office. A number of small grocery shops are scattered throughout the town.

Getting There & Away
PKS buses run from stance No 2 at Hajnówka bus station (outside the train station) to Białowieża (4zł to 5zł, one hour, up to eight daily). The private company Oktobus also runs buses (seven daily) to Białowieża from the bus stop outside the prominent CTO store on Hajnówka's main street, ul 3 Maja.

There are also two buses daily direct from Białystok to Białowieża (12zł, two hours), run by KPO Victoria.

CIECHANOWIEC
pop 4900

Ciechanowiec (che-kha-*no*-vyets) would be of little importance to travellers if it weren't for its famous **Museum of Agriculture** (Muzeum Rolnictwa; ☎ 086 277 1328; ul Pałacowa 5; with guide adult/concession 10/5zł, without guide 6/3zł; ⏲ 8am-4pm Mon-Sat, 9am-6pm Sun May-Sep, 8am-4pm Mon-Sat, 9am-4pm Sun Oct-Apr). Set in the grounds of a former estate, it consists of an early-19th-century palace, stables, coach house and other outbuildings that are now exhibition halls. While these are attractions in their own right, it's the 40-odd wooden constructions that are the stars here, and collectively they constitute one of the country's finest **skansens**. The buildings, from across Mazovia and Podlasie, include the likes of simple peasant cottages, large manor houses, granaries, barns and working mills.

The guided tour takes you through the interior of several wooden houses, and you'll also be shown exhibitions featuring items such as old agricultural machinery, archaic tractors, primitive steam engines, peasants' horse-drawn carts and rudimentary tools. There's also a small botanic garden growing medicinal plants and a veterinary exhibition. The tour takes about two hours. Alternatively, you can do away with the tour and freely roam the grounds, but you cannot enter the buildings.

English- and German-speaking guides (50zł per group) may be available on the spot, but if you want to be sure call the museum in advance and book.

Sleeping
There's no better place to stay in town than the **museum** (r per person 50zł) itself. A number of beds are available in the palace and a few of the skansen buildings, such as the 1858 hunting lodge and the water mill. The standard

varies depending on where you stay, but the price remains the same.

Getting There & Away

The bus station is a few minutes' walk from the museum. There are eight buses daily from Białystok (17zł, 2½ hours), while from Warsaw (Warszawa Stadion) there are two fast buses (24zł, 2¾ hours) in the morning and one ordinary bus (18zł, four hours) in the afternoon.

GRABARKA

The **Holy Mountain of Grabarka** hardly means a thing to the average Roman Catholic Pole, yet it's the largest Orthodox pilgrimage centre in Poland. Remote from main roads and important urban centres, the 'mountain' (more of a wooded mound, really) lies 1km east of the obscure hamlet of Grabarka. The only town of any size in the region is Siemiatycze, 9km to the west.

The story of the **Grabarka crosses** goes back to 1710, when an epidemic of cholera broke out in the region and decimated the population. Amid utter despair, a mysterious sign came from the heavens, which indicated that a cross should be built and carried to a nearby hill. Those who reached the top escaped death, and soon afterwards the epidemic disappeared. The hill became a miraculous site and a thanksgiving church was erected. Since then pilgrims have been bringing crosses here to place alongside the first one, and today the hill is covered with around 20,000 crosses of different shapes and sizes.

A **convent** and a **church** are also hidden among woods on top of the hill. The 18th-century timber church went up in flames in 1990, but it was rebuilt in a similar shape to the previous one. The convent is more recent, established in the aftermath of WWII in an effort to gather all the nuns, scattered throughout the country, from the five convents that had existed before the war.

Grabarka's biggest feast is the **Spas** (Day of Transfiguration of the Saviour) on 19 August. The ceremony begins the day before at 6pm and continues with Masses and prayers throughout the night, culminating at 10am with the Great Liturgy, celebrated by the metropolitan of the Orthodox Church in Poland. Up to 50,000 people may come from all over the country to participate.

On 18 August the surrounding forest turns into a car park and camping ground. Cars and tents fill every space between the trees. Despite this wave of modernity, the older, more traditional generation comes on foot without any camping gear and keeps watch all night. The light of the thin candles adds to the mysterious atmosphere.

If you wish to experience this magical night, you have the same options – to pitch your tent or to stay awake. The commercial community is well represented, with plenty of stalls selling food and drink and a variety of religious goods, including CDs and cassettes of Orthodox church music.

Getting There & Away

Sycze train station (more of a halt with an empty platform) is a short walk from the hill; trains between Siedlce (11zł, one hour, four daily) and Hajnówka (10zł, one hour, two daily) stop here. There is one train direct from Warsaw (28zł, 2¼ hours) at 7.13am on Saturday and daily around the feast of Spas.

From the Sycze train platform, it's a little over 1km to the holy mountain. There are no obvious signs to indicate the direction but the yellow trail heading south will get you there. If you are coming from Hajnówka, go left from the platform down the road. From there the road veers right, but follow the track straight into the forest – you'll come across the trail and signs as you go.

THE AUGUSTÓW-SUWAŁKI REGION

The northern stretch of Podlasie, known as Suwalszczyzna, is an area of outstanding natural beauty, with large swaths of pristine forest and, towards the very north, rugged hills and deep valleys. Its defining feature, though, is water: it is a notable lakeland region, with around 200 lakes, and its rivers and canals are among the most paddled in the entire country.

Like the rest of Poland, the modern population here consists predominantly of Poles, but it was for centuries an ethnic and religious mosaic comprising Poles,

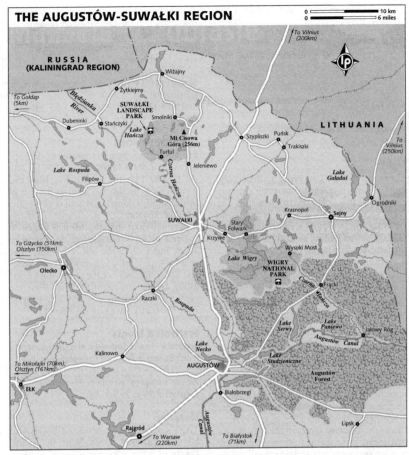

THE AUGUSTÓW-SUWAŁKI REGION

Lithuanians, Belarusians, Tatars, Germans, Jews and Russians. Traces of this complex cultural mix can still be found, at least in the local cemeteries.

Despite its natural beauty and historical ethnic make-up, the region attracts few visitors from outside Poland's borders. It is therefore the perfect place to avoid the summer crowds that swamp the Masurian lakes to the west, find your own peaceful pocket and kick back for a couple of days.

AUGUSTÓW
pop 30,000

Augustów (aw-*goos*-toof) is a small but sprawling town straddling the Netta River as it enters Lake Necko. It's the gateway to

Suwalszczyzna and, with its close proximity to a number of natural wonders, it's a popular base for holidaymakers.

The town itself has retained little historical character due to WWII effectively resetting the clock – during a two-month battle in 1944 the town switched hands several times and 70% of it was destroyed. Its history, however, dates back to the time of King Zygmunt II August, who in 1557 founded the town and modestly named it after himself. Despite the strategic location, its development only really began in the 19th century after the construction of the canal bearing the town's name, and was further boosted when the Warsaw–St Petersburg railway was completed in 1862. Today Augustów largely survives on tourism, booming in the summer and effectively dying in the winter.

Information

Atol tourist office (☎ 087 643 2883; www.augustow .pl in Polish; Rynek 44; 🕑 8am-8pm Mon-Fri, 10am-6pm Sat & Sun) Friendly and helpful, with information on the city and its surrounds.

Bank Pekao (ul Żabia 3)

Main post office (Rynek 3)

Wypożyczalnia Videomaniak (☎ 087 643 5339; ul 3 Maja 46; per hr 4zł; 🕑 10am-9pm) Internet access.

Sights

The most important (and pretty much the only) sight in town, the **regional museum** (Muzeum Ziemi Augustowskiej), is at two locations. The main section, featuring a small **ethnographic exhibition** (☎ 087 643 2754; ul Hoża 7; adult/concession 3/2zł; 🕑 9am-4pm Tue-Sun), is on the 3rd floor of the tatty, modern public library. There is also a more interesting section dedicated to the **history of the Augustów Canal** (☎ 087 643 2360; ul 29 Listopada 5a; adult/concession 3/2zł; 🕑 9am-4pm Tue-Sun), housed in a quaint, 19th-century wooden cabin in front of some council offices.

Activities

KAYAKING

Kayak trips are the best reason to visit Augustów, and while your arms may feel the strain, the scenery is well worth the aching muscles. Kayaking tours are organised by numerous local operators, including several hotels and hostels. They all run various routes on different rivers in the region, and can create personal itineraries according to your requirements and time availability. Alternatively, kayaks can be hired individually (20zł to 25zł per day), to head out on your own tour.

The **Czarna Hańcza River** is the most popular kayaking destination in the region. The traditional route normally starts at Lake Wigry (p159) and follows the river downstream through the Augustów Forest (p157) to the Augustów Canal (p156). The trip takes six to eight days, depending on how fast you paddle, and costs around 400zł. Various shorter trips are also available; for example, **Szot** (☎ 087 643 4399; www.szot.pl in Polish; ul Konwaliowa 2) organises weekend trips through arguably the most spectacular stretch of the Czarna Hańcza, the 25km journey from Frącki to Jałowy Róg (140zł).

Other rivers used for kayaking trips by tour operators include the Rospuda (four to six days; see boxed text, p158) and the Biebrza (seven to 10 days); some also offer trips to rivers in neighbouring Lithuania (seven days). Other kayak operators:

Sirocco (☎ 087 643 0084; www.siroccokajaki.pl in Polish; ul Zarzecze 3a)

Szekla Port PTTK (☎ 087 643 3850; www.szekla.pl in Polish; ul Nadrzeczna 70a)

BOAT EXCURSIONS

From May to September, pleasure boats operated by **Żegluga Augustowska** (☎ 087 643 2881; ul 29 Listopada 7) ply the surrounding lakes and a part of the Augustów Canal to the east of town. All trips depart from and return to the **wharf** (ul 29 Listopada).

Boats depart hourly from 9.40am to 5.45pm in July and August, and between 10am and 1.40pm the rest of summer. The shortest trips (15zł, one hour) ply Lake Necko and Lake Białe but not the canal. More interesting are the cruises further east along the canal system; the longest is currently a trip to Lake Studzieniczne (35zł, 3½ hours).

Festivals & Events

Augustów Theatre Summer Held in July and August.

Polish Sailing in Anything Championships (Mistrzostwa Polski w Pływaniu na Byle Czym) Highly bizarre and entertaining open event for homemade vessels, held at the end of July on the Netta River.

Sleeping

There's a range of year-round hotels and hostels scattered throughout the town. Plenty of holiday homes open in summer to accommodate individual tourists.

Gościniec Ostoja (☎ 087 643 0222; recepcja@ostoja .augustow.pl; ul Wojska Polskiego 53a; s/d 80/120zł; **P**) At the southern end of town, this family house provides excellent homey accommodation in a range of individually furnished rooms. It's spacious, the bathrooms are gleaming and breakfast is substantial – certainly enough to make up for minor niggles such road noise, a lack of curtains, and being a fair walk to the lakes.

Augur Usługi Hotelowe (☎ 0508 738 725; www .augur.pl in Polish; ul 3 Maja 1; s/d/tr 80/120/160zł, 6-bed r 260zł; **P**) Self-catering accommodation bang in the centre of town. Rooms are plain but have en suite and TV, and share a communal kitchen; character comes in the form of a

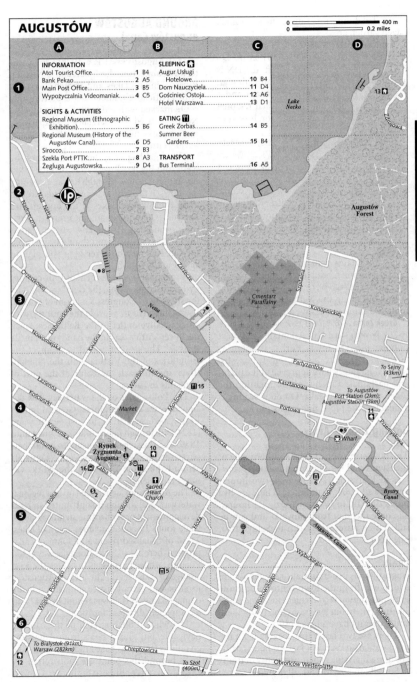

AUGUSTÓW

0 — 400 m
0 — 0.2 miles

INFORMATION
Atol Tourist Office..................1 B4
Bank Pekao..........................2 A5
Main Post Office....................3 B5
Wypożyczalnia Videomaniak........4 C5

SIGHTS & ACTIVITIES
Regional Museum (Ethnographic
　Exhibition)..........................5 B6
Regional Museum (History of the
　Augustów Canal)...................6 D5
Sirocco...............................7 B3
Szekla Port PTTK....................8 A3
Żegluga Augustowska................9 D4

SLEEPING
Augur Usługi
　Hotelowe.........................10 B4
Dom Nauczyciela...................11 D4
Gościniec Ostoja....................12 A6
Hotel Warszawa....................13 D1

EATING
Greek Zorbas........................14 B5
Summer Beer
　Gardens...........................15 B4

TRANSPORT
Bus Terminal.......................16 A5

MAZOVIA & PODLASIE

stone-clad dining/function room and a small paved garden area.

Dom Nauczyciela (☎ 087 643 2021; www.dn.augustow .pl in Polish; ul 29 Listopada 9; s/d/tr 90/130/150zł; P) Right by the pleasure-boat wharf, the DN is a neat and very reasonable option with high standards. It has its own restaurant and a travel agency offering all the usual regional activities. Bikes are available for hire (per hour/day 4/30zł).

Hotel Warszawa (☎ 087 643 2805; www.hotel warszawa.pl; ul Zdrojowa 1; s/d/tr/ste 260/360/430/650zł; P) The top digs near town, Warszawa is a quality three-star hotel with plenty of trimmings such as a restaurant, a bar, a sauna, bikes, boats and classic-car hire. Rooms are suitably comfortable and the entire complex is discreetly hidden among trees near the lake.

Eating

Augustów is fairly light on year-round restaurants. In summer, head to the semipermanent **beer gardens** (ul Mostowa), by the Netta bridge and strung out along the Netta River, for cheap food and drink in a festive atmosphere.

Greek Zorbas (☎ 087 643 2939; ul Kościelna 4; mains 10-27zł; ⏰ noon-11pm) Unaccountably the most popular place in town, Zorbas is about as Greek as Pavarotti, but the meaty maestro would doubtlessly have approved of the pizza-and pasta-based menu, not to mention the token slabs of moussaka. Outdoor seating is available if the piped music gets too loud.

Getting There & Away

BUS

The bus terminal is on the southern side of the Rynek and handles roughly hourly services to Białystok (15zł to 18zł, two hours) and Suwałki (8zł, 45 minutes). There are five buses directly to Warsaw (33zł, 4½ hours); all come through from Suwałki and can be full. Three buses a day run to Sejny (10zł, one hour).

TRAIN

Augustów has two train stations, but both are a long way from the town centre. Augustów Port train station is convenient for some of the lakeside hotels, but fast trains don't stop there and it doesn't have a ticket office.

There are two fast trains, leaving from the main station, to Warsaw (46zł, 4½ hours) daily, going via Białystok. There are plenty of trains to Suwałki (6.50zł to 12zł, 30 minutes).

AROUND AUGUSTÓW

Augustów Canal

Built in the 1820s, the Augustów Canal (Kanał Augustowski) is a 102km-long waterway connecting the Biebrza and Niemen Rivers. Linking lakes and stretches of river with artificial channels, it's a picturesque route marked with old locks and floodgates. No longer used commercially, it's experiencing a renaissance as a tourist attraction and kayak route.

The canal begins at the confluence of the Netta and Biebrza Rivers and flows for 33km north to Augustów through low and swampy meadows. It then continues eastwards through a chain of wooded lakes to the border with Belarus, where it extends into foreign territory for another 19km. This eastern part is the most spectacular, and should be included in your itinerary however long you plan to spend in the region.

A remarkable achievement of 19th-century hydraulic engineering, the canal was built by the short-lived Congress Kingdom of Poland. It was intended to provide the country with an alternative outlet to the Baltic Sea, since the lower Vistula was in the hands of a hostile Prussia. The project aimed to connect the tributaries of the Vistula with the Niemen River and to reach the Baltic at the port of Ventspils in Latvia.

The Polish part of the waterway was designed by an army engineer, General Ignacy Prądzyński, and built in just seven years (1824–30), though final works continued until 1839. The Russians were meant to build their part from the town of Kaunas up to Ventspils around the same time, but the work was never completed.

The Augustów Canal ended up as a regional waterway, and though it contributed to local development, it never became an international trade route. Its route includes 28km of lakes, 34km of canalised rivers and 40km of canal proper. There are 18 locks along the way (14 in Poland), whose purpose is to bridge the 55m change in water level. The lock in Augustów itself has an extra twist to its history: badly damaged in WWII, it was rebuilt in 1947 – in a completely different location!

The whole Polish stretch of the canal is navigable, but tourist boats from Augustów go only as far east as Lake Studzieniczne – the locks beyond this point are inoperative. By kayak, you can continue to the border. Contact tour companies (see p154) for information, tour options and kayak-hire conditions.

Augustów Forest

The Augustów Forest (Puszcza Augustowska) stretches east of Augustów as far as the Lithuanian–Belarusian border. At about 1100 sq km, it's Poland's largest continuous forest after the Bory Dolnośląskie in Lower Silesia. It's a remnant of the vast primeval forest that once covered much of eastern Poland and southern Lithuania.

The forest is mainly made up of pine and spruce, with colourful deciduous species such as birch, oak, elm, lime, maple and aspen. The wildlife is rich and diversified, and includes beavers, wild boar, wolves, deer and even some elks. Birds are also well represented and the 55 lakes abound in fish.

The forest was virtually unexplored until the 17th century, but today it is crisscrossed by paved roads, dirt tracks, and walking and cycling paths. Despite this, there are large stretches that are almost untouched, and if you want to get firmly off the beaten track in Poland then this is a great swath of nature to do it in.

You can explore part of the forest using private transport; roads will take you along the Augustów Canal to the border. Many of the rough tracks are perfectly OK for bikes and horses, and on foot you can get almost everywhere except the swamps. The Atol tourist office in Augustów (p154) can provide information on accommodation and bike rental, including brochures on cycle routes in the forest. A good general map with all roads, tracks and tourist trails in the forest is the detailed *Puszcza Augustowska* map (5zł, scale 1:70,000).

SUWAŁKI

pop 69,300

Suwałki (soo-*vahw*-kee) is the largest town in the region, and while a pleasant enough place to visit, it lacks the lakes and forests that popularised Augustów. There's also little in the way of tourism infrastructure, so if you view it as a gateway to the surrounding countryside rather than a destination in itself, you're pretty much on the right track.

The town first appeared on the map at the end of the 17th century as one of the villages established by the Camaldolese monks from Wigry. The small multinational community grew slowly; at different times it included Jews, Lithuanians, Tatars, Russians, Germans and Old Believers, a religious group that split off from the Russian Orthodox Church in the 17th century. Only the last are still present in Suwałki.

Information

Bank Pekao (ul Kościuszki 72)

Post office (ul Sejneńska 13)

Tourist office (☎ 087 566 5872; www.sirt.suwalki.com .pl in Polish; ul Kościuszki 82; ☺ 10am-6pm Mon-Sat May-Sep, 8am-4pm Mon-Fri Oct-Apr) Very helpful and well informed on the region's attractions; free internet access.

Sights

It might seem a bit grim as an attraction, but the local **cemetery** gives a good picture of the town's ethnic and religious history. It actually consists of several separate cemeteries for people of the different creeds – the religious tolerance of the community not extending to shared burial grounds.

You'll notice straight away the large size of the **Jewish cemetery** – at the beginning of the 20th century Jews made up half the town's population. Their cemetery was destroyed in WWII and only a memorial stands in the middle, assembled out of fragments of old grave slabs. The tiny **Muslim graveyard** is the last remnant of the Tatars, but the graves are now hardly recognisable.

At the back of the **Orthodox cemetery** is the **Old Believers' graveyard**; both are largely wild and unkempt. A dwindling handful of Old Believer followers still congregate on Sunday morning at the **church** (molenna; ul Sejneńska 37a) on the opposite side of town. The simple timber church dates from the beginning of the 20th century, but the icons inside are significantly older. Except for during Mass, you have little chance of seeing them. Within the graveyard mix you will also find a Catholic and a Protestant cemetery.

The main thoroughfare of the town, ul Kościuszki, retains some 19th-century neoclassical architecture. Here you'll also find the **Regional Museum** (☎ 087 566 5750; ul Kościuszki 81; adult/concession 5/3zł; ☺ 8am-4pm Tue-Fri, 9am-5pm Sat & Sun), which presents the little that is known of the Jatzvingians, the first settlers in this area. Its annexe, the **Museum of Maria Konopnicka** (combined ticket adult/concession 7/4zł), is dedicated to one of Poland's best-loved authors and poets.

Activities

The **PTTK office** (☎ 087 566 5961; ul Kościuszki 37; ☺ 8am-4pm Mon-Fri) operates kayak trips down the Czarna Hańcza (p154) and Rospuda (below) Rivers, and hires out kayaks (22zł per day) if you would rather do the trip on your own. **Forma-T** (☎ 087 563 7119; ul Noniewicza 93; ☺ 8am-4pm Mon-Fri) offers the same services but has newer kayaks.

Sleeping & Eating

Suwałki has a decent enough range of accommodation, but don't feel you have to stay in town – this is prime agrotourism territory, and the tourist office and local travel agencies will happily set you up with a rural idyll for a few nights.

Hotel Hańcza (☎ 087 566 6633; www.hotelhancza .com; ul Wojska Polskiego 2; s/d/tr 95/145/180zł; P) You wouldn't expect much from this huge block in the southern part of town, but actually it's not a bad choice, with lake views

and two budget restaurants. It is alarmingly popular with school groups in June and July, though.

Hotel Suwalszczyzna (☎ 087 565 1900; www.hotel suwalszczyzna.pl in Polish; ul Noniewicza 71a; s/d 140/170zł; P) Tucked away behind an unpromising façade, both the hotel and its ground-floor restaurant offer some of the best standards in town. The collection of framed, signed football shirts on the stairway suggests either an abiding passion for soccer or an unusual preponderance of sporting guests.

Restauracja Rozmarino (☎ 087 563 2400; ul Kościuszki 75; mains 10-25zł; ☺ 9am-midnight) Never has so much been crammed into so little space with so few negative results. As pizzeria–cum–piano bar–cum–art gallery–cum–restaurants go, this is an amazing place, boasting a two-tiered rainbow-coloured summer garden for live music, a menu that looks like a newspaper, and unusual treats such as crab claws and ostrich balls to shake up the usual Italian suspects.

THE ROSPUDA RIVER

At 102km in length, the Rospuda River is the second-longest river in the Suwalszczyzna region. Being in the firing line of the Via Baltica Expressway (p73), it's the most talked about waterway in the country.

The idea of running a massive concrete road through the middle of the river and its surrounding valley seems like madness. Putting aside the fact that it is part of the European Natura 2000 Network, and therefore protected under EU law, this unique wetland is home to a number of protected bird species such as the lesser spotted eagle, white stork, black woodpecker and hazel grouse, and more than a dozen rare orchids. Wolves, deer, foxes and beavers all use it as a natural migration corridor.

Of its 102km, just over 70km can be paddled (a six-day trip), from Lake Czarne near the Russian border to the town of Augustów. The river's flow changes as it progresses south: its upper reaches are similar to fast-flowing mountain streams, while further down it slows to a meander, weaving through tightly packed reeds. At its final stretch, before it enters Lake Necko, the river begins to widen and forested banks replace the reeds. One-day kayak trips, which start in the town of Raczki and end at Lake Necko, are run out of Augustów (see p154) or can be organised through **Bogdan Łukowski** (www.wigry.info/kontakt.html).

Not everyone thinks the Rospuda needs protecting, including some residents of Augustów. Hwy 8, the main road connecting the Baltic states with Poland (and Europe), passes directly through the town, and at times traffic congestion is horrendous. The Via Baltica would relieve Augustów of its traffic problem, making roads safer and cutting back on pollution.

The Rospuda and Via Baltica is therefore a highly contested issue, with both sides unwilling to back down. An alternative route suggested by NGOs and roading consultants, which would send the expressway northwest to Raczki and then northeast to Suwałki, thus circumnavigating Rospuda's protected area, is a highly viable option, but the government and Augustów locals are opposed to it because it will delay the project even further.

The Via Baltica is currently on hold. At the end of 2007 the Regional Administrative Court in Warsaw cancelled the environmental consent for an Augustów bypass, claiming the project did not fall into line with Polish nature conservation legislation. The Polish government continues to search for possible solutions to enable the project to proceed.

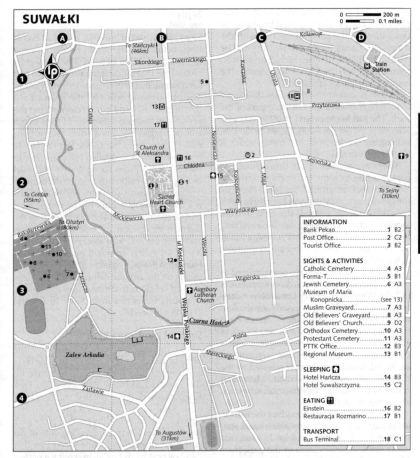

SUWAŁKI

MAZOVIA & PODLASIE

Einstein (☎ 087 563 0773; ul Kościuszki 82; mains 12-30zł; ❂ noon-midnight) Dine with the great physicist (his portraits and theoretical equations plaster the rich-red walls) at this modern eatery in the heart of town. The menu contains regional cuisine with a few European options thrown in to keep things contemporary. A cheap lunch menu is available during the week.

Getting There & Away

The train station is 1.5km northeast of the centre; the bus terminal is closer to the central area. Trains are useful mostly for longer journeys, with four daily departures to Białystok (18zł to 31zł, 2½ hours) and two to Warsaw (46zł, five hours); see p519 for information on travelling on to Lithuania.

Frequent buses run to Augustów (8zł, 45 minutes), Sejny (7zł, 45 minutes) and Białystok (25zł, 2¾ hours).

AROUND SUWAŁKI
Wigry National Park

On the northern fringes of Augustów Forest is arguably the most beautiful lake in Podlasie. At 21 sq km, **Lake Wigry** is also the largest in the region and one of the deepest, reaching 73m at its greatest depth. Its shoreline is richly indented, forming numerous bays and peninsulas, and there are 15 islands on the lake. The lake is the dominating feature of **Wigry National Park** (Wigierski Park Narodowy), a small park to the east of Suwałki whose dense forest belt and plethora of smaller lakes make it a popular destination for kayakers, cyclists and hikers. The Czarna Hańcza River flows through the park, connecting with the Augustów Canal further downstream. The park's wildlife is diverse, including wolves, lynxes, eagle owls and black cormorants; the beaver is the park's emblem.

Access is easiest from the Suwałki–Sejny road, which crosses the northern part of the park. The **park headquarters** (☎ 087 566 6322; www .wigry.win.pl; ⏰ 7am-3pm Mon-Fri, also 9am-5pm Sat & Sun Jul & Aug) are on this road, in Krzywe, which is 5km from Suwałki.

There are marked trails throughout the park, leading to some truly remote corners. You can walk all around the lake (49km by the green trail), provided you have three days. Lakeside camping grounds along the trail are located within reasonable day-long walking distances. The *Wigierski Park Narodowy* map shows all the necessary detail and is available at the park headquarters.

The park's attractions are not restricted to nature. Spectacularly located on a peninsula in Lake Wigry is a former **Camaldolese monastery**, built by the death-obsessed Camaldolese monks (p190) soon after they were brought to Wigry by King Jan II Kazimierz Waza in 1667. The whole complex, complete with a church and 17 hermitages, was originally on an island, which was later connected to the shore. It has now been turned into a hotel and restaurant, providing an atmospheric base for exploring the park.

Train lovers can get a fix riding the **narrow-gauge train** (☎ 087 563 9263; www.augustowska.pl; adult/ concession 20/14zł; ⏰ 10am, 1pm & 4pm Jul & Aug) that skirts the southern fringes of the park from Płociczno-Tartak to Krusznik. The trip takes about 2½ hours, passing through lush forest and providing views of Lake Wigry.

The park headquarters runs various lodges and camping grounds in the reserve itself, and there are several agrotourist farms nearby. The monastery peninsula is arguably the most atmospheric place to overnight. Here you'll find a few options, including **Dom Pracy Twórczej w Wigrach** (☎ 087 563 7000; dom@wigry.org; s/ d 120/160zł, apt 300zł; 🅿 ♿), with accommodation in the former monks' hermitages, and **Drażba** (☎ 087 563 7045; wigry6@op.pl; r 60zł; 🅿), a friendly homestay with kayak and bicycle hire.

The Suwałki–Sejny road is serviced by regular buses. If you want to go directly to the monastery, take the bus to Wigry (four daily buses in summer).

Sejny
pop 5000

Sejny, 30km east of Suwałki, is the last Polish town before the Ogrodniki border crossing to Lithuania, 12km beyond. The town grew around the Dominican monastery, which had been founded in 1602 by monks from Vilnius. The order was expelled by the Prussian authorities in 1804 and never returned, but the proud two-towered silhouette of their **church** still dominates the town from its northern end. It dates from the 1610s, but the façade was thoroughly remodelled 150 years later in the so-called Vilnius Baroque style. Its pastel interior has harmonious Rococo decoration.

At the opposite, southern end of the town is a large **synagogue**, built by the sizable local Jewish community in the 1880s. During the German occupation it served as a fire station and after the war as a storage room. Today it's an art gallery operated by the **Borderland Foundation** (Fundacja Pogranicze; ☎ 087 516 3400), focusing on the arts and culture of different ethnic and religious traditions from the region.

Hourly buses run from Sejny to Suwałki (7zł, 45 minutes).

Suwałki Landscape Park

About halfway between Suwałki and the Lithuanian border is a cluster of pristine lakes and rugged hills that collectively make up the Suwałki Landscape Park (Suwalski Park Krajobrazowy). It was the first nature reserve of its kind to be established (in 1976), and covers 63 sq km. A healthy portion of the park is either lakes (26 in all, totalling 10% of the park's area), patches of fine forest (another 24%) or peat lands (10%), making it a perfect place for walking or cycling.

The village of **Smolniki**, 20km north of Suwałki, is probably the most convenient base for the park. There are several marked trails passing through the village, and a handful of accommodation options; enquire at the Suwałki tourist office (p157) for details or contact the **park office** (☎ 087 569 1801; www.spk.org .pl in Polish; Turtul; ⏰ 8am-7pm Mon-Fri, 9am-5pm Sat Jul & Aug, 8am-3pm Mon-Fri Sep-Jun) on the southern edge of the park for more general information.

The Smolniki neighbourhood is rugged, largely wooded, and dotted with a dozen small lakes, and there are three good viewpoints in the village, which allow you to enjoy some of this landscape. One of the numerous walking options is an hour's walk west to **Lake**

TROUBLED WATERS?

The two bridges at Stańczyki were designed by the Italians and built by the Germans, in what was then the territory of East Prussia, as part of the Gołdap–Żytkiejmy railway track. The first bridge was constructed between 1912 and 1914; 12 years later the second, identical bridge was built parallel to it, just 15m to the south. Construction was interrupted by WWII, but the northern line was used until late 1944, when the Red Army dismantled the tracks and took them to the Soviet Union, leaving the bridges inoperable.

You don't need to be an architect to realise there are a lot of unanswered questions surrounding the bridges – it's unclear why anyone in their right mind would build not just one but two massive structures in such an awkward part of such a remote area, just to prop up an underused railway line (three services a day hardly justifies the massive effort involved). It all seems a far cry from the customary Prussian pragmatism.

Perhaps the authorities were seduced by the monumental classical form of the design itself – the bridges are undeniably attractive. Sadly, the structure isn't as solid as it looks, and the increase in tourism threatens to destroy both the bridges and the riverbank on which they stand. Bungee-jumping has already been banned here, but, unless a conservation plan is put in place, Stańczyki's bridges may soon be lost once again.

Hańcza, the deepest lake in the country. With its steep shores, stony bottom and amazing crystal-clear water, it's like being up in the mountains.

If you travel between Smolniki and Suwałki, it's worth stopping in **Gulbieniszki** at the foot of **Mt Cisowa Góra**. This 256m-high hill, just off the road, is cone-shaped and provides a fine view over the surrounding lakes.

The 1:50,000 map *Suwalski Park Krajobrazowy* (10zł) is good for exploring the area. It has all the hiking trails marked on it and good sightseeing information in English on the reverse.

Stańczyki
pop 200

Deep within the Romincka Primeval Forest Landscape Park (Romincka Puszcza Park Krajobrazowy), close to the Russian border, is an unusual sight – a pair of disused **railway bridges** rising out of the woods. Linking the steep sides of the valley of the Błędzianka River, 36m above water level, these two identical, 180m-long constructions were built as part of the Gołdap–Żytkiejmy train line. With their tall pillars supporting wide, elegant arches, they have the air of a Roman aqueduct. Now unused and without tracks, the bridges look like huge, surreal sculptures in the middle of nowhere.

You can walk on the top of both bridges and go down and look at them from below – it's really a weird sight. For a long time almost unknown and forgotten, they are now becoming an attraction, and a car park with some basic facilities was built and is attended in summer.

There are two daily buses from Suwałki (9zł, 70 minutes) in summer. Alternatively, there's access from the Gołdap–Wiżajny road, serviced by about six buses daily. Get off at the Stańczyki turn-off and walk 1.5km, and you'll see the bridges on your left.

Kraków

Kraków, which celebrated its 750th birthday in 2007, is by far Poland's biggest drawcard, and it's immediately apparent why. As the royal capital for 500 years, the city was able to absorb much history and talent over the centuries and is today a treasure trove of Gothic and Renaissance architecture. Miraculously, this jewellery box emerged largely intact after WWII. As a result, no other city in Poland can boast so many historic buildings and monuments or such a vast collection of artworks, with some 2.3 million registered.

Wawel Castle is Kraków's centrepiece and a must-see, but most visitors will find themselves drawn to the Old Town, with its soaring Gothic churches and gargantuan Rynek Główny (Main Market Sq), the largest in the nation. Just outside the Old Town lies the former Jewish quarter Kazimierz, its silent synagogues reflecting the tragedy of the recent past.

Kraków is well endowed with attractions and diversions of a more modern variety, with hundreds of restaurants, bars and music clubs tucked away down its cellars and narrow alleyways. Though hotel prices are above the national average, and visitor numbers are very high in summer, this vibrant, cosmopolitan city is an essential part of any visit to Poland.

Give yourself at least several days or even a full week to do Kraków justice. This is not a place to rush through; the longer you stay, the more captivating you'll find it. And without even trying, you'll discover something pretty, old, curious or tasty around every corner.

HIGHLIGHTS

- Enjoying an easy ride through Polish history at magnificent **Wawel Castle** (p169)
- Eyeballing odd elixirs and remedies at the wonderful **Museum of Pharmacy** (p184)
- Relaxing to the clip-clop of hooves on a tour of the Old Town from the back of a **horse-driven carriage** (p195)
- Getting down and, well, salty at the unique **Wieliczka Salt Mine** (p192)
- Meeting Copernicus face to face at the **Collegium Maius** (p183)
- Dining out on the views from and the fabulous cuisine at **Wentzl** (p202)
- Getting your head and feet around **Rynek Główny** (p172), Europe's largest medieval market square
- Witnessing both the sad past and hopeful future of Jewish Kraków at the **Galicia Museum** (p188) in Kazimierz

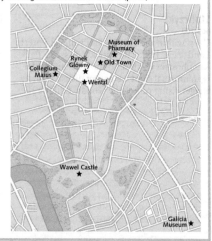

- POPULATION: 752,700
- AREA: 327 SQ KM

HISTORY

The first traces of Kraków's existence date from around the 7th century, but the earliest written record of the town dates from 966, when a Sephardic Jewish merchant from Cordova called Abraham ben Jacob (Ibrahim ibn Yaqub) visited and referred to the town in his account as a trade centre called Krakwa.

In 1000 Kraków was made a bishopric and 38 years later the capital of the Piast kingdom. Wawel Castle and several churches were built in the 11th century and the town, which had sprung up initially around Wawel Hill, grew in size and power.

The Tatars burned Kraków almost to the ground in 1241 but by 1257 the new town's centre had been set on a grid pattern, with a large market square in the middle.

Kraków rose to new prominence in 1364 when King Kazimierz Wielki, a generous patron of art and scholarship, founded the Kraków Academy, what would later be called Jagiellonian University, the second university in central Europe after the University of Prague founded four years earlier.

Kraków's economic and cultural boom led to a golden age of expansion in the 15th and 16th centuries. Kraków became a member of the Hanseatic League, which attracted craftspeople. Learning and science prospered – Nicolaus Copernicus, who would later develop his heliocentric view of the universe, studied here in the 1490s – and the population passed the 30,000 mark.

But all was not well in the royal city. In 1596 King Zygmunt III moved the capital to Warsaw, although Kraków remained the place of coronations and burials. The Swedish invasions, beginning in 1655, accelerated the decline; by the end of the following century the city's population had been reduced to 10,000. In the Third Partition of Poland (1795), Kraków was made part of the Austrian province of Galicia.

The city enjoyed reasonable cultural and political freedom under the Austrian landlords; by the close of the 19th century it had become a major centre for Polish culture and the spiritual capital of a country that officially no longer existed. The avant-garde artistic and literary movement known as Młoda Polska (Young Poland) was born here in the 1890s, and it was here that a national independence movement originated. The latter would go on to spawn the Polish Legions under the command of Józef Piłsudski.

By the outbreak of WWII the city had 260,000 inhabitants, 65,000 of whom were Jews. During the war, Kraków, like all other Polish cities, saw its Jewish citizens herded into a ghetto and transported to Nazi work and extermination camps; most of them would never be seen again. The city was thoroughly looted by Nazis but didn't experience major combat or bombings. As such, Kraków is virtually the only large Polish city that has retained its old architecture and appearance.

After the war, the communist government moved quickly to open a huge steelworks at the newly created suburb of Nowa Huta, just 10km east of the Old Town, in a bid to break the traditional intellectual and religious framework of the city. The social engineering proved less successful than its unanticipated by-product – ecological disaster. Monuments that had managed to survive invasions by the Tatars, Swedes and Nazis have been gradually eaten away by acid rain and toxic gas.

With the creation of Nowa Huta and other new suburbs after WWII, Kraków trebled in size to become the country's third-largest city, after Warsaw and Łódź. The historic core, though, has changed little and continues to be the political, administrative and cultural centre of the city.

ORIENTATION

Virtually everything you'll need to see or do is conveniently squeezed into the compact Old Town, measuring roughly 800m by 1200m and encircled by Planty, a narrow parkland that was once a moat. At the centre of the Old Town is Rynek Główny (Main Market Sq) while at its southern tip sits Wawel Hill and its castle. Further south stretches the district of Kazimierz.

The bus and train stations sit next to one another just beyond the northeastern border of the Old Town; from here it's about 600m to Rynek Główny. John Paul II International Airport is at Balice, 11km west of the city centre.

Maps

The free map from the tourist offices should be sufficient for a short visit. If you want something more detailed, one of the best is the 1:20,000 scale *Kraków Plan Miasta* (7.90zł), which is published by Copernicus, and includes a 1:10,000 scale map of the Old Town.

KRAKÓW

Demart's *Katowice + 3* (8zł) is similar but also has thumbnail maps of certain suburbs, including Wieliczka.

INFORMATION
Bookshops
Austeria (Map p187; ☎ 012 430 6889; High Synagogue, ul Józefa 38; ⏰ 9am-7pm) Best collection of Jewish-themed books and Judaica in Kraków.
EMPiK (Map p170; ☎ 012 429 4577; www.empik.com; Rynek Główny 5; ⏰ 9am-10pm) Best for newspapers and magazines.
Księgarnia Hetmańska (Map p170; ☎ 012 430 2453; Rynek Główny 17; ⏰ 9am-9pm Mon-Sat, 11am-9pm Sun) Impressive selection of English-language books on Polish history and culture.

Księgarnia Pod Globusem (Map p170; ☎ 012 430 0445; ul Długa 1; ⏰ 10am-7pm Mon-Fri, 10am-2pm Sat) All kinds of maps and travel guides.
Massolit Books & Café (Map p170; ☎ 012 432 4150; www.massolit.com; ul Felicjanek 4; ⏰ 10am-8pm Sun-Thu 10am-9pm Fri & Sat) City's best; sells new and secondhand English-language fiction and nonfiction, including Polish history and literature in translation.
Sklep Podróżnika (Map p170; ☎ 012 429 1485; ul Jagiellońska 6; ⏰ 11am-7pm Mon-Fri, 10am-3pm Sat) Sells a wide selection of regional and city maps, as well as Lonely Planet titles.

Cultural Centres
British Council (Map p170; ☎ 012 428 5932; 1st fl, Rynek Główny 6; ⏰ 8.30am-7pm Mon-Fri)

GREATER KRAKÓW

KRAKÓW

French Institute (Map p170; ☎ 012 424 5350; ul Stolarska 15; ☯ 9am-6.30pm Mon-Fri)

Goethe Institute (Map p170; ☎ 012 422 6902; Rynek Główny 20; ☯ 10am-4pm Mon-Thu, 10am-3pm Fri)

International Cultural Centre (Międzynarodowe Centrum Kultury; Map p170; ☎ 012 424 2899; www .mck.krkow.pl; Rynek Główny 25; ☯ 10am-6pm Tue-Sun) Promotes European culture through exhibits and research.

Italian Institute of Culture (Map p170; ☎ 012 421 8943; ul Grodzka 49; ☯ 9am-5.30pm Mon, 9am-4.30pm Tue-Fri)

Judaica Foundation (Map p187; ☎ 012 430 6449; www.judaica.pl; ul Meiselsa 17; ☯ 10am-5pm Mon-Fri, 10am-2pm Sat & Sun)

Internet Access

Cafe Internet e-network (Map p170; ☎ 012 431 2394; ul Sienna 14; per hr 4zł; ☯ 24hr)

Greenland Internet Café (Map p170; ☎ 012 422 0319; ul Floriańska 30; per hr 3zł; ☯ 9am-midnight)

Internet Café Hetmańska (Map p170; ☎ 012 429 1106; ul Bracka 4; per hr 4zł; ☯ 24hr)

Internet Klub Garinet (Map p170; ☎ 012 423 2233; ul Floriańska 18; per hr 4zł; ☯ 9am-midnight) The pick of the crop near the main square.

Klub Internetowy Pl@net (Map p170; ☎ 012 292 7685; Rynek Główny 24; 3zł; ☯ 10am-10pm) Right on the main square.

Labirynt Internet Art Klub (Map p187; ☎ 012 292 0514; ul Józefa 15; per hr 3,50zł; ☯ 10am-10pm) In Kazimierz.

Internet Resources

City of Kraków (www.krakow.pl) Good general information direct from city hall.

Cracow Life (www.cracow-life.com) Heaps of information on eating, drinking and entertainment.

Explore Krakow (www.explore-krakow.com) Information on sights and activities as well as accommodation.

Krakow Info (www.krakow-info.com) An excellent source for news and events.

Krakow Post (www.krakowpost.com) New English-language weekly online, with local news, interviews, features and listings.

Kraków Card

The excellent-value **Kraków Card** (www.krakowcard .com; 2-/3-day 50/65zł), available from tourist offices, travel agencies and hotels, offers free entry to 32 museums (though not those on Wawel Hill), unlimited travel on public transport, and discounts on organised tours and at certain restaurants.

Medical Services

The **US Consulate Department of Citizen Services** (☎ 012 429 6655) can provide a list of English-speaking doctors. Pharmacies are everywhere – the city counts more than 200 of them.

Apteka 24 (Map p165; ☎ 012 411 0126; ul Mogilska 21) This 24-hour pharmacy is east of the Old Town.

Dent America (Map p170; ☎ 012 421 8948; www.dent america.pl; 2nd fl, Plac Szczepański 3) A Polish-American dental clinic.

Falck (Map p170; ☎ 96 75; www.falck.pl) Attends house calls and has its own ambulance service.

Medicover (Map p165; ☎ 012 616 1000; www.medi cover.pl; ul Rakowicka 7) Has English-speaking specialist doctors and does lab tests.

Medicina (Map p165; ☎ 012 266 9665; www.medicina.pl; ul Barska 12) Oldest private health-care provider in Kraków.

Laundry

Most hostels now have washing machines (and sometimes even dryers) that you can use for free.

Betty Clean (Map p170; ☎ 012 423 0848; ul Zwi-erzyniecka 6; ☯ 7.30am-7.30pm Mon-Fri, 8am-3.30pm

Sat) Branch of a chain of laundries, near southeastern border of Old Town.

Money

Kantors (private currency-exchange offices) and ATMs can be found around the centre. It's worth noting that many *kantors* close on Sunday, and areas near Rynek Główny and the main train station offer poor exchange rates.

Bank Pekao (Map p170; Rynek Główny 31; ☉ 8am-6pm Mon-Fri, 8am-2pm Sat) Travellers cheques are probably best changed here. Cash advances on Visa and MasterCard are also obtainable here, either from the cashier inside or the ATM outside.

Post

Main post office (Map p170; ul Westerplatte 20; ☉ 7.30am-8.30pm Mon-Fri, 8am-2pm Sat)
Post office (Map p170; ul Lubicz 4; ☉ 7am-8pm Mon-Sat)

Telephone

MOBILE PHONES

Orange (Map p170; ☎ 012 432 6700; www.orange.pl; ul Wielopole 2; ☉ 10am-6pm Mon-Fri, 10am-2pm Sat)
Plus GSM (Map p187; ☎ 012 422 5971; www.plusgsm.pl; ul Krakowska 4; ☉ 10am-7pm Mon-Fri, 10am-2pm Sat)

Tourist Information

Małopolska Region Tourism Information Centre (Map p170; ☎ 012 421 7706; www.mcit.pl; Rynek Główny 1/3; ☉ 9am-7pm Mon-Fri, 9am-5pm Sat & Sun Apr-Sep, 9am-5pm Mon-Fri, 9am-2pm Sat Oct-Mar) Regional tourist office inside Cloth Hall.

Tourist offices Rynek Główny (Map p170; ☎ 012 433 7310; www.karnet.krakow2000.pl; Town Hall Tower, Rynek Główny; ☉ 9am-7pm Apr-Sep, 9am-5pm Oct-Mar) Old Town (Map p170; ☎ 012 421 7787; ul Św Jana 2; ☉ 10am-6pm Mon-Sat) Planty (Map p170; ☎ 012 432 0110; ul Szpitalna 25; ☉ 9am-7pm May-Sep, 9am-5pm

,Oct-Apr) Wyspiański 2000 Pavilion (Map p170; ☎ 012 616 1886; Wyspiański 2000 Pavilion, Plac Wszystkich Świętych 2; ☉ 10am-8pm) Kazimierz (Map p187; ☎ 012 422 0471; ul Józefa 7; ☉ 9am-5pm Mon-Fri) Tourist information offices in five key locations.

Travel Agencies

Orbis Travel (Map p170; ☎ 012 619 2459; www.orbis.pl; Rynek Główny 41; ☉ 9am-7pm Mon-Fri, 9am-3pm Sat) Sells transportation tickets (air, train, ferry and organises tours.

Travel Partner (Map p170; ☎ 012 429 51 65; www .travelpartner.pl; ul Św Tomasza 4; ☉ 10am-6pm Mon-Fri, 10am-1pm Sat) Cheap international air tickets.

Polish Travel Adventure (☎ 0693 648 525, 0605 231 923; www.cracow.tourism.pl) Well-regarded agency without address organises excursions and adventure travel in and out of Kraków.

DANGERS & ANNOYANCES

Kraków is generally a safe city for travellers, although as a major tourist hot spot it has its fair share of pickpockets; be vigilant in crowded public areas.

If you're staying in the centre of the Old Town, especially near the main square, you may experience late-night noise from the area's many restaurants, bars and clubs; ask for a room at the back if this is going to be an issue. In summer, the large numbers of tourists in town can be a little overwhelming and mean long queues for top sights such as Wawel Castle and scarce seating in the more popular restaurants. Keep an eye out for the many horse-driven carriages that cart tourists around the Old Town, including along the pedestrianised streets.

Be aware that if carrying a large suitcase or backpack on a Kraków city bus you must buy an extra ticket (2.50zł).

FOLLOW YOUR NOSE

Kraków is a wonderful city to explore on your own. The streets are well-marked, the buses and trams easy to negotiate, and the natives friendly. This book is designed to whet your appetite and to guide you when you arrive; by all means visit many of the sites and the museums listed in this chapter – they're part of the Kraków package. But at the risk of shooting ourselves in the feet *and* fingers, we'd like to remind you that this is a guidebook and not a handbook. Leave it in your room or backpack from time to time, and wander outside to make your own discoveries. Want to see a Kazimierz with real residents? Head south over the bridge to working-class Podgórze. Street fashion in action? Jump on tram 1 or 7 heading east to the Kraków Plaza, the city's biggest shopping mall. Or just go blindly into that great maze of streets and rail lines beyond the Old Town, poking your head into little shops, joining in a game of *piłka nożna* (football) in a park or having a beer in a local *piwnica* (pub). You've arrived in Kraków – for real.

SIGHTS
Wawel

The very symbol of the nation, the hilltop **Wawel** (*vah*-vel; www.wawel.krakow.pl) is more steeped in Polish history than any other place in the country. It was the seat of the kings for over 500 years from the early days of the Polish state, and even after the centre of power moved to Warsaw in the late 16th century, it retained much of its symbolic power. Today it is the silent guardian of a millennium of Polish history and the most visited site in the country.

The way to Wawel Hill begins at the southern end of ul Kanonicza, from where a lane leads uphill. Past the equestrian statue of Tadeusz Kościuszko, it turns to the left, leading to a vast open central square surrounded by several buildings, of which the cathedral and the castle are the major attractions.

Plan on at least four hours up here if you want anything more than just a glance over the place and be aware of the different opening hours of all the attractions. In summer, it's best to come early as there may be long queues for tickets later in the day. Alternatively, you can prebook your tickets (16zł) by phoning at least one day ahead by phone or in person at the **Tourist Service Office** (Map p170; ☎ 012 422 1697; Bldg 9, Wawel 5; ⊙ 9am-3pm Mon, Wed & Thu, 9am-4pm Thu-Sun). If possible, avoid weekends, when Wawel is besieged by visitors.

In the southwestern part of the complex you'll find a **visitors centre** (Map p170; ☎ 012 422 5155; ⊙ 9am-6pm) as well as a gift shop, post office and café with outside terrace.

WAWEL CATHEDRAL

This **cathedral** (Katedra Wawelska; Map p170; ☎ 012 422 2643; Wawel 3; royal tombs & bell tower adult/concession 10/5zł; ⊙ 9am-4pm or 5.15pm Mon-Sat, 12.15-4pm or 5.15pm Sun) has witnessed most of the coronations, funerals and entombments of Poland's monarchs and strongmen over the centuries, and wandering around the grandiose funerary monuments and royal sarcophagi is like a fast-forward tour through Polish history. Many outstanding artists have left behind a wealth of magnificent works of art. The cathedral is both an extraordinary artistic achievement and Poland's spiritual sanctuary.

The building you see is the third church on this site, consecrated in 1364. The original cathedral was founded sometime after the turn of the first millennium by King Bolesław Chrobry and was replaced with a larger Romanesque construction around 1140. When it burned down in 1305, only the Crypt of St Leonard survived.

The present-day cathedral is basically a Gothic structure, but chapels in different styles were built around it later. Before you enter, note the massive iron door and, hanging on a chain to the left, huge prehistoric animal bones. They are believed to have magical powers; as long as they are here, the cathedral will remain. The bones were excavated on the grounds at the start of the 20th century.

Once inside, you'll get lost in a maze of sarcophagi, tombstones and altarpieces scattered throughout the nave, chancel and ambulatory. Among a score of chapels, a highlight is the **Holy Cross Chapel** (Kaplica Świętokrzyska) in the southwestern corner of the church (to the right as you enter). It is distinguished by the unique 15th-century Byzantine frescoes and the red marble sarcophagus (1492) in the corner by Veit Stoss. The showpiece chapel, however, is the **Sigismund Chapel** (Kaplica Zygmuntowska) up the aisle and on the southern wall. It is often referred to as 'the most beautiful Renaissance chapel north of the Alps' and is recognisable by its gilded dome from the outside. Diagonally opposite is the **Tomb of St Queen Hedwig** (Sarkofag Św Królowej Jadwigi), a much beloved and humble 14th-century monarch whose unpretentious wooden coronation regalia are on display nearby.

In the centre of the cathedral stands the flamboyant Baroque **Shrine of St Stanislaus** (Konfesja Św Stanisława), dedicated to the bishop of Kraków, who was canonised in 1253 and is now the patron saint of Poland. The silver sarcophagus, adorned with 12 relief scenes from the saint's life, was made in Gdańsk between 1663 and 1691; note the engravings on the inside of the ornamented canopy erected about 40 years later.

Ascend the tower accessible through the sacristy via 70 steps to see the **Sigismund Bell** (Dzwon Zygmunta). Cast in 1520, it's 2m high and 2.5m in diameter, and weighs 11 tonnes, making it the largest historic bell in Poland. Its clapper weighs 350kg, and eight strong men are needed to ring the bell, which happens only on the most important church holidays and for significant state events. The views from here are worth the climb.

Back down in the nave, descend from the left-hand aisle to the **Crypt of St Leonard**, the only remnant of the 12th-century Romanesque cathedral extant. Follow through and you will get to the **Royal Crypts** (Groby Królewskie) where, along with kings such as Jan III Sobieski, many national heroes and leaders, including Tadeusz Kościuszko, Józef Piłsudski and WWII General Władysław Sikorski, are buried in a half-dozen chambers.

Diagonally opposite the cathedral is the **Wawel Cathedral Museum** (Muzeum Katedralne; Map p170; ☎ 012 422 2643; adult/concession 5/2zł; ⏰ 10am-3pm Tue-Sun), a treasury of historical and religious objects from the cathedral. There are plenty of exhibits, including church plate and royal funerary regalia, but not a single crown. They were all stolen from the treasury by the Prussians in 1795 and reputedly melted down.

WAWEL CASTLE

The political and cultural centre of Poland until the end of the 16th century, **Wawel Royal Castle** (Zamek Królewski na Wawelu; Map p170; ☎ 012 422 5155; Wawel 5; ⏰ grounds 6am-dusk) is, like the cathedral, the very symbol of Poland's national identity.

The original, rather small residence was built in the early 11th century by King Bolesław Chrobry beside the chapel dedicated to the Virgin Mary (known as the Rotunda of SS Felix and Adauctus). King Kazimierz Wielki turned it into a formidable Gothic castle, but when it burned down in 1499, King Zygmunt Stary commissioned a new residence. Within 30 years a splendid Renaissance palace, designed by Italian architects, was in place. Despite further extensions and alterations, the three-storey Renaissance structure, complete with a courtyard arcaded on three sides, has been preserved to this day.

Repeatedly sacked and vandalised by the Swedish and Prussian armies, the castle was occupied after the Third Partition by the Austrians, who intended to make Wawel a citadel. Their plan included turning the castle into barracks, and the cathedral into a garrison church, moving the royal tombs elsewhere. They never got that far but they did turn the royal kitchen and coach house into a military hospital and raze two churches standing at the outer courtyard to make room for a parade ground. They also enveloped the whole hill with a new ring of massive brick walls, largely ruining the original Gothic fortifications.

The castle was recovered by Poles after WWI and the restoration began immediately and continued up until the outbreak of WWII. The work was resumed after the war and has been able to recover a good deal of the castle's earlier external form and its interior decoration.

The castle is now a museum containing five separate sections, each requiring a different ticket that is valid for a specific time. There's a limited daily quota of tickets for some parts, so arrive early if you want to see everything or phone ahead to reserve. You will need a ticket even on 'free' days.

The **Royal Chambers** (Komnaty Królewskie; adult/concession 15/8zł, free Mon Apr-Oct, Sun Nov-Mar; ⏰ 9.30am-1pm Mon, 9.30am-5pm Tue & Fri, 9.30am-4pm Wed & Thu, 11am-6pm Sat & Sun), also known as the State Rooms, is the largest and most impressive exhibition; the entrance is in the southeastern corner of the courtyard, from where you'll ascend to the 2nd floor Proceed through the apparently never-ending chain of two-dozen rooms and chambers of the castle, restored in their original Renaissance and early Baroque style and crammed with period furnishings, paintings, tapestries and works of art.

The two biggest (and the most spectacular) interiors are on the 2nd floor. The **Hall of Senators**, which was originally used for senate sessions, court ceremonies, balls and theatre performances, houses a magnificent series of six 16th-century Arras tapestries following the story of Adam and Eve, Cain and Abel or Noah (they are rotated periodically). The **Hall of Deputies** has a fantastic coffered ceiling with 30 individually carved and painted wooden heads staring back at you. Meant to illustrate the life cycle of man, from birth to death, they are all that have survived from a total of 194 heads, which were carved in around 1535 by Sebastian Tauerbach. There's also a tapestry with the Polish insignia dating from 1560.

Enter the **Royal Private Apartments** (Prywatne Apartamenty Królewskie; adult/concession 20/15zł; ⏰ 9.30am-5pm Tue & Fri, 9.30am-4pm Wed & Thu, 11am-6pm Sun) at the middle of the eastern side of the courtyard, and go up marble steps to the 1st floor. In a way, it's a continuation of the previous trip, but it leads through somewhat more intimate interiors, thus giving an insight into how the monarchs and their families once lived. The dozen or so apartments are visited with a guide, which is included in the ticket

KRAKÓW

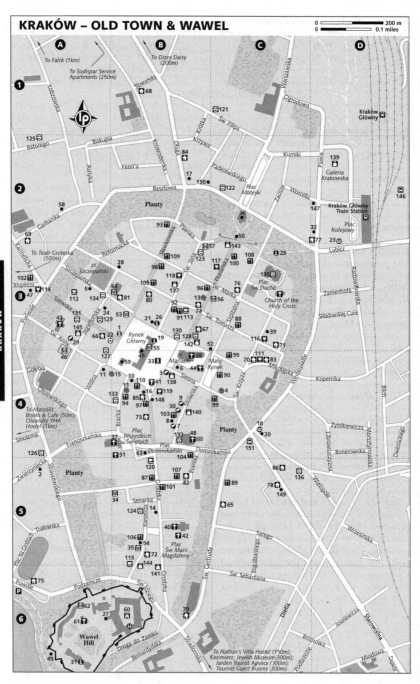

KRAKÓW – OLD TOWN & WAWEL

INFORMATION
Bank Pekao 1 B3
Betty Clean 2 A5
British Council 3 B4
Cafe Internet e-network 4 C4
Dent America 5 A3
EMPiK 6 B4
French Consulate 7 B4
French Institute 8 B4
German Consulate 9 B4
Goethe Institute 10 B4
Greenland Internet Café (see 117)
International Cultural Centre 11 A4
Internet Café Hetmańska 12 B4
Internet Klub Garinet 13 B3
Italian Institute of Culture 14 B5
Klub Internetowy Pl@net 15 B4
Księgarnia Hetmańska 16 B4
Księgarnia Pod Globusem 17 B2
Main Post Office 18 C4
Małopolska Region Tourism Information Centre 19 B3
Orange 20 C4
Orbis Travel 21 B3
Police Station 22 A3
Post Office 23 D2
Sklep Podróżnika 24 A3
Tourist Office 25 C3
Tourist Office (see 59)
Tourist Office (see 63)
Tourist Office 26 B3
Tourist Service Office 27 A6
Travel Partner 28 B3
UK Consulate 29 A3
US Consulate 30 B4
Visitors Centre 31 A6
Waweltur 32 D2

SIGHTS & ACTIVITIES
Adam Mickiewicz statue 33 B4
Archaeological Museum 34 B5
Archdiocesan Museum 35 B5
Barbican 36 C2
Basilica of St Francis 37 B4
Basilica of the Assumption of Our Lady 38 B4
Bird Service 39 C3
Church of SS Peter & Paul 40 B5
Church of St Adalbert 41 B4
Church of St Andrew 42 B5
Church of St Anne 43 A3
Church of St Barbara 44 B4
Cloth Hall 45 B4
Collegium Maius 46 A4
Cracow Tours 47 A3
Dominican Church of the Holy Trinity 48 B4
Dragon's Den 49 A6
Florian Gate 50 C2
Franciscan Monastery 51 B4
Hipolit House 52 B3
Kraków City History Museum 53 B3
Marco der Pole 54 B5
Małopolska Contemporary Art Collection 55 B3
Museum of Pharmacy 56 C3
Princes Czartoryski Museum 57 B3
School of Polish Lanquage & Culture 58 A2
Town Hall Tower 59 B4
Wawel Castle 60 B6
Wawel Cathedral 61 A6
Wawel Cathedral Museum 62 A6
Wyspiański 2000 Pavilion 63 B4
Wyspiański Museum 64 B3

SLEEPING
Cracow Hostel (see 16)
Hostel Centrum Kraków 65 C5
Hostel Flamingo 66 A3
Hostel Gardenhouse 67 B3
Hostel Giraffe 68 B1
Hotel Alexander 69 A2
Hotel Amadeus 70 C4
Hotel Campanile 71 C3
Hotel Copernicus 72 B5
Hotel Jan 73 B4
Hotel Pod Różą 74 B3
Hotel Pod Wawelem 75 A6
Hotel Pollera 76 C3
Hotel Polonia 77 D2
Hotel Pugetów 78 C5
Hotel Royal 79 B6
Hotel Saski 80 B3
Hotel Stary 81 B3
Hotel Wawel 82 B5
Hotel Wit Stwosz 83 C4
Jordan Guest Rooms 84 B2
Polonia House 85 B4
Wielopole Guest Rooms 86 C5

EATING
Balaton 87 B5
Bar Smaczny 88 C3
Bar Wegatariański Vega 89 C5
Casa della Pizza 90 C4
Cherubino 91 B3
Chłopskie Jadło 92 B3
Cyrano de Bergerac 93 B2
Gospoda CK Dezerter 94 B4
Greenway 95 C4
Gruzińskie Chaczapuri 96 B3
Gruzińskie Chaczapuri Branch 97 B4
Indus Tandoori 98 B3
Jadłodajnia 99 C4
Jama Michalika 100 C3
Metropolitan (see 80)
Miód Malina 101 B5
Nostalgia 102 A3
Orient Ekspres 103 B4
Paese 104 B4
Sakana Sushi Bar 105 B3
Smak Ukraiński 106 B5
Taco Mexicano 107 B5
U Babci Maliny 108 C3
U Babci Maliny Branch 109 B3
Wentzl 110 B4

DRINKING
Black Gallery 111 C4
Café Bunkier 112 A3
Café Camelot 113 B3
Ciemnia Club (see 68)
CK Browar 114 A3
Demmers Teahouse 115 B5
Light Box Gallery (see 129)
Nic Nowego 116 C3
Piwnica Pod Złotą Pipą 117 C3
Pod Papugami 118 B3
U Luisa 119 B4
Wiśniowy Sad 120 B5

ENTERTAINMENT
7 Club 121 C1
Academy of Music 122 C2
Caryca (see 136)
Cień 123 B3
Cricoteka 124 B5
El Sol 125 A2
Filharmonica Krakowska 126 A4
Harris Piano Jazz Bar 127 A4
Jazz Club U Muniaka 128 B3
Kitsch (see 136)
Music Bar 129 A3
Piano Rouge 130 B3
Piec' Art 131 A3
Prozak 132 B4
Rdza 133 B4
Stary Teatr w Krakowie 134 A3
Teatr im J Słowackiego 135 C3
Łubu-Dubu 136 C5

SHOPPING
Andrzej Mleczko Gallery 137 B3
Galeria Bukowski 138 B4
Galeria Krakowska 139 D2
Galeria Plakatu 140 B4
Jan Fejkiel Gallery 141 B6
Krosno 142 B3
Labirynt 143 C3
Mikołajczyki Amber 144 B5
Salon Antyków Pasja 145 A3

TRANSPORT
Bus Station 146 D2
Centrum Turystyki 147 D2
Eccentric Bike Tours & Rentals 148 B4
Joka Rent a Car 149 C5
Jordan (see 146)
LOT 150 B2
Minibuses to Wieliczka 151 C4

price. English-language tours depart at least once an hour.

As in the Royal Chambers, you'll see plenty of magnificent old tapestries, mostly northern French and Flemish, hanging on the walls. The collection, largely assembled by King Zygmunt August, once numbered 360 pieces, but only 138 survive. Even so, this is probably the largest collection of its kind in Europe, and one of Wawel's most precious possessions. Other highlights include the so-called **Hen's Foot**, Jadwiga's gemlike chapel in the northeast tower, and the sumptuous Gdańsk-made furniture in the **Alchemy Room** and annexe. The collection includes a 400kg cupboard.

The **Crown Treasury & Armoury** (Skarbiec Korony i Zbrojownia; adult/concession 15/8zł, free Mon Apr-Oct, Sun Nov-Mar; 9.30am-1pm Mon, 9.30am-5pm Tue & Fri, 9.30am-4pm Wed & Thu, 11am-6pm Sat & Sun) are housed in vaulted Gothic rooms surviving from the 14th-century castle on the ground floor of the northeastern part of the castle. The most famous object in the treasury is the Szczerbiec, or 'Jagged Sword' dating from the mid-13th century, which was used at all Polish coronations from 1320 onwards. Nearby are the shoes worn by King Zygmunt August at his coronation in 1530. The adjacent armoury features a collection of old weapons from various epochs – from crossbows, swords, lances and halberds from the 15th to 17th centuries to muskets, rifles, pistols and cannon from the 18th century onward.

The **Oriental Art Exhibition** (Wystawa Sztuka Wschodu; adult/concession 7/4zł; 9.30am-1pm Mon, 9.30am-5pm Tue & Fri, 9.30am-4pm Wed & Thu, 11am-6pm Sat & Sun) features a collection of 17th-century Turkish banners and weaponry, captured after the Battle of Vienna, displayed along with a variety of old Persian carpets, Chinese and Japanese ceramics, and other Asian antiques. The entrance is from the northwestern corner of the courtyard.

Lost Wawel (Wawel Zaginiony; adult/concession 7/4zł; 9.30am-5pm Tue & Fri, 9.30am-4pm Wed & Thu, 11am-6pm Sat & Sun), which was being renovated during our last visit, is an exhibition that's accommodated in the old royal kitchen. Along with the remnants of the late-10th-century Rotunda of SS Felix and Adauctus, which is reputedly the first church in Poland, you can see various archaeological finds (including colourful old ceramic tiles from the castle's stoves), as well as models of the previous Wawel churches, the foundations of which can still be seen in the central courtyard. The entrance to the exhibition is from the outer courtyard to the right of the Tourist Service Office.

DRAGON'S DEN

If you've had enough of high art and Baroque furnishings, complete your Wawel trip with a visit to the hokey **Dragon's Den** (Smocza Jama; Map p170; admission 3zł; 10am-6pm Jun-Aug, 10am-5pm Apr, May, Sep & Oct), former home of the legendary Wawel Dragon (Smok Wawelski), and an easy way to get down from the hill. The entrance

to the cave is next to the **Thieves' Tower** (Baszta Złodziejska) at the southwestern end of the complex. From here you'll get a good panorama over the Vistula River and the suburbs further west, including the Manggha Centre of Japanese Art & Technology (p185) on the opposite bank of the river, and the Kościuszko Mound (p189) far off on the horizon.

After you buy your ticket from a coin-operated machine at the entrance, you descend 130 steps into the cave, then stumble some 70m through its damp interior and emerge onto the bank of the Vistula next to a distinctive fire-spitting **bronze dragon**, the work of contemporary sculptor Bronisław Chromy.

Old Town

The layout of the Old Town was drawn up in the mid-13th century after devastation caused by the Tatar invasions and has survived more or less in its original form. The construction of the fortifications began in the 13th century, and it took almost two centuries to envelop the town with a powerful, 3km-long chain of double defensive walls complete with 47 towers and eight main entrance gates as well as a wide moat.

When this defence system became obsolete at the beginning of the 19th century it was demolished, except for a small section to the north. The moat was filled up and a ring-shaped park called Planty was laid out on the site, surrounding the footprint-shaped Old Town with parkland.

The Old Town has a surfeit of historical monuments, including a dozen museums and some 20 of the city's 120 churches – not to mention scores of other important sights.

The Old Town, which has been included on Unesco's World Heritage List since 1978, is pretty much car-free and the tram crosses it only once (along ul Dominikańska and ul Franciszkańska 150m south of Rynek Główny), so you can stroll largely undisturbed by traffic noise and pollution.

RYNEK GŁÓWNY

Measuring 200m by 200m, Kraków's **Rynek Główny** (Map p170; Main Market Sq) is the largest medieval town square in Europe and one of the finest urban designs of its kind. Its layout, based on that of a *castrum* (Roman military camp), was drawn up in 1257 and has

(Continued on page 181)

BEST OF POLAND

Stretching from the sandy shores of the Baltic to the rugged peaks of the Carpathians, Poland unfolds across the heart of Europe. It offers a welcoming glass of vodka, great nightlife, untouched wilderness, historical treasures and some decidedly peculiar attractions. Where else could you hope to encounter European bison on the hoof, sand dunes that 'walk' or ghosts in underground salt mines? With its Teutonic castles, the remote lakes of Masuria, medieval market towns and reminders of the horrors of WWII, Poland is breathtaking, awe-inspiring, poignant and exciting all at once.

City Life:
Urban Vibes & High Culture

Poland's heart may reside in the countryside, but its pulse races in the cities.
Kraków is the bastion of Polish culture and
the country's pre-eminent attraction, but
Warsaw is hip and happening and a string
of other cities offer intimate portraits of
Polish life.

① Poznań

Wear out your shoe leather taking in the sights and atmosphere of Poznań – from the town hall to the old whipping post – on one of the city's 10 self-guided walking tours (p380).

② Rynek Główny

Kraków's Rynek Główny (p172) is just the spot to settle in for coffee, lengthy chats and wonderful people-watching opportunities.

③ Warsaw's Palaces

Admire Warsaw's palaces: the ornate neo-classical confection at Łazienki Park (p101) and baroque splendor of Wilanów (p101).

④ Warsaw Old Town

The Old Town (p91) in Warsaw, recreated from WWII rubble with meticulous attention to detail, is testament to Polish resilience and pride.

⑤ Kraków Museum of Pharmacy

Eyeball the odd elixirs and remedies – and be thankful for modern medicine – at the wonderful Museum of Pharmacy (p184) in Kraków.

⑥ Zamość

The Italianate architecture in the Old Town (p252) of Zamość has seen it dubbed Poland's 'Padua of the North'.

⑦ Wrocław

The lively streets of Wrocław, and especially the area around the Rynek (p315), offer a smorgasbord of diverse architectural styles.

⑧ Gdańsk

You can pretend you are royalty as you pass along Gdańsk's Royal Way (p409), then enjoy the buzz of buskers, eateries and cafés along Długi Targ (p411).

The Great Outdoors: Lakeside, Seashore & Mountaintop

There is plenty of Poland to explore if you're after fresh air and adrenaline. Poland's mountains offer miles of walking trails and great skiing, while national parks, countless lakes and the Baltic coast offer opportunities for bird-watchers, sailors and sun seekers.

1 Tatra Mountains
Stride out and enjoy the crisp, cool, clear air in the Tatra Mountains (p304) above the fashionable resort of Zakopane.

2 Hel
Go to Hel (p433) to bask on the seashore or meet a rare grey seal at the Fokarium.

3 Dunajec Gorge
Snaking its way between steeply rising cliffs and rolling down gentle rapids, Dunajec Gorge (p301) attracts keen rafters.

4 Bison Spotting
In the primeval forest at Białowieża National Park (p147) keep an eye out for a glimpse of the rare European bison.

5 Sopot
Take a dip in the waterfront spa park or in the limpid waters of the Baltic at Sopot (p425) by day, then cruise with the crowds, buskers and ice cream vendors on ul Bohaterów Monte Cassino after dark.

6 Great Masurian Lakes
Set sail or paddle a kayak through the extensive system of canals and rivers of the Great Masurian Lakes (p490).

7 Bieszczady
Explore the natural beauty of the Bieszczady (p274), a wild realm of dense forests and open meadows.

8 Roztocze National Park
The might of Mother Nature is fully in evidence as you stand beneath the soaring fir and beech trees – the tallest in Poland – in Roztocze National Park (p257).

9 Cycling in Wielkopolska
The wide open spaces and broad vistas of the Wielkopolska countryside are ideal for cycling (p380).

10 Morasko
The peaceful forest at Morasko (p388) is home to 10,000-year-old meteorite craters.

Cultural Life: Tradition & Modernity

Poland boasts not just great vodka, but a robust cultural life, with famous names to match, including Joseph Conrad and Roman Polański. Catholic spirituality is strong, and age-old traditions remain, but Poland embraces the future with lively nightlife, great clubs and a thriving music scene.

1 Chapel of Skulls

Eyeball cranium after cranium at the macabre Chapel of Skulls (p343) near Kudowa-Zdrój.

2 Enjoying a Tipple

Down your vodka (p62) in one, but don't try to outdrink a Pole.

3 Icon Trail

Set out, by foot or cycle, to follow the Icon Trail (p278) from Sanok and visit the region's charming Uniat timber churches.

4 Częstochowa

Join throngs of Black Madonna pilgrims in Poland's spiritual heart at Częstochowa (p213).

5 Skansens

The traditional folk culture and architecture of pre-industrial Poland is preserved at skansens (p58) around the country.

6 Zalipie

The painted barns, cottages, tools and furniture of Zalipie (p265) must make it Poland's most colourful town.

7 Biskupin

The fortified village of Biskupin (pictured overleaf; p394) is your opportunity to backtrack 2700 years to the Iron Age.

8 Warsaw Nightlife

Warsaw's nightlife (p112) is a blast, whether you are into bar hopping, clubbing, live jazz or highbrow entertainment.

9 Tatar Culture

The last remnants of Poland's Tatar culture are in evidence at the villages of Kruszyniany and Bohoniki (p145).

(Continued from page 172)

been retained to this day, though the buildings have changed substantially over the centuries. Most of them now look neoclassical, but don't let the façades confuse you – the basic structures are much older, as can be seen by their doorways, architectural details and interiors. The cellars date from medieval times.

Dominating the square is the centrally positioned **Cloth Hall** (Sukiennice; Map p170; Rynek Główny 1), once the centre of Kraków's medieval rag trade. It was formed in the early 14th century when a roof was put over two rows of stalls and extended into a 108m-long Gothic structure in the second half of the 14th century. The hall was rebuilt in Renaissance style after a fire in 1555; the arcades were added in the late 19th century. The ground floor is still a trading centre but now one for crafts and souvenirs, while the upper floor is taken over by the **Małopolska Contemporary Art Collection** (Małopolskie Kolekcje Sztuki Nowoczesnej; Map p170; 012 422 1166; www.moma.pl in Polish; adult/concession 10/5zł; 11am-6pm Tue-Sat, 10am-3pm Sun), replacing the **Gallery of 19th-Century Polish Painting** (Galeria Sztuki Polskiej XX Wieku). That collection, with works by Józef Chełmoński, Jacek Malczewski, Aleksander Gierymski and the leader of monumental historic painting, Jan Matejko, has been moved to the Royal Castle at Niepołomice, 20km east of Kraków, for three years while Cloth Hall is renovated.

The **Town Hall Tower** (Wieża Ratuszowa; Map p170; 012 619 2320; adult/concession/family 6/4/12zł; 10.30am-6pm May-Oct), southwest of the Cloth Hall, is all that is left of the 15th-century town hall that was dismantled in the 1820s. The 70m-tall tower can be climbed in summer.

At the northern corner of the square, the 17th-century Krzysztofory Palace is home to the **Kraków City History Museum** (Muzeum Historyczne Miasta Krakowa; Map p170; 012 619 2300; www.mhk .pl; Rynek Główny 35; adult/concession/family 4/3.50/8zł, free Wed; 10am-5.30pm May-Oct, 9am-4pm Wed & Fri-Sun, 10am-5pm Thu Nov-Apr). Basically the story of Kraków from 1257 to WWII, the museum features a bit of everything related to the city's past, including old clocks, armour, paintings, Kraków's celebrated *szopki* (Nativity scenes), and the costume of the Lajkonik (see p196).

In the southern corner of the square is the small, domed **Church of St Adalbert** (Kościół Św Wojciecha; Map p170). One of the oldest churches in the Old Town, its origins date from the 11th century. You can see the original foundations in the basement, where a small **exhibition** (10am-4pm Mon-Sat May-Sep) also presents archaeological finds excavated from the Rynek.

A few steps north of the church is the **Adam Mickiewicz statue** (Map p170), surrounded by four allegorical figures representing the Motherland, Learning, Poetry and Valour. The *szopki* competition is held in early December (see p196).

KRAKÓW FOR FREE

- Walk up to Wawel Castle (p169) on Monday morning to see where and how Poland's royalty once lived.
- Stroll about the narrow cobbled streets of the Old Town and Rynek Główny (p172).
- Visit the Ethnographic Museum (p186) on Sunday, the day all its sections are free to visit.
- Watch out for Kraków's colourful buskers, often performing on Rynek Główny and the adjacent streets.
- Tour private art galleries to keep yourself up to date on Polish contemporary art.
- Admire the *Lady with an Ermine* gratis on Thursday at the Princes Czartoryski Museum (p183).
- Explore the city churches, all of which are free to visit, with the exception of the chancel of the Basilica of the Assumption of Our Lady.
- Watch the clock in the courtyard of the Collegium Maius (p183) go through its paces at 11am and 1pm daily.
- Climb and enjoy the view from the Piłsudski Mound (p191) in Las Wolski.
- Catch a free concert, show or exhibition around the centre; check the programme with a tourist office branch (p167).

The flower stalls, usually to the north of the statue and traditionally run by women, have been trading on this site since medieval times. The area in between is the 'pasture' for Kraków's pigeon population, which the city – unbelievably – encourages. The area is currently fenced off, as excavations for a possible underground shopping and entertainment complex are going on below the surface.

BASILICA OF THE ASSUMPTION OF OUR LADY

Overlooking the square from the northeast is the **Basilica of the Assumption of Our Lady** (Bazylika Wniebowzięcia Najświętszej Marii Panny; Map p170; Rynek Główny 4; adult/concession 6/4zł; ☯ 11.50am-6pm Mon-Sat, 2-6pm Sun), better known in these parts as the Mariacki. The first church on this site was built in the 1220s and, typically for the period, was 'oriented' – that is, its sanctuary pointed eastward. Following its destruction during the Tatar raids, the construction of a mighty basilica began, using the foundations of the previous church. That's why the church stands at an oblique angle to the square.

The façade is dominated by two towers of different heights. The lower one, 69m high and topped by a Renaissance dome, serves as a bell tower and holds five bells, while the taller one, which is 81m high, has traditionally been the city's property and functioned as a watchtower. It's topped with a spire surrounded by turrets – a good example of medieval craftsmanship – and in 1666 was given a 350kg gilded crown that's about 2.5m in diameter. The gilded ball higher up contains Kraków's written history. It is from this tower that the *hejnał* (bugle call; see boxed text, opposite) is sounded hourly around the clock.

The main church entrance, through a Baroque porch added to the southwest façade in the 1750s, is used by worshippers and the faithful; tourists must enter through the side door to the southeast, which leads into the chancel. The chancel is illuminated by the magnificent stained-glass windows dating from the late 14th century; the blue star vaulting of the nave is breathtaking. On the opposite side of the church, above the organ loft, is a fine Art Nouveau stained-glass window by Stanisław Wyspiański and Józef Mehoffer. The colourful wall paintings, designed by Jan Matejko, harmonise beautifully with the medieval architecture and are an appropriate background for the

high altar, which is acclaimed as the greatest masterpiece of Gothic art in Poland and allegedly acclaimed as the eighth wonder of the world by Pablo Picasso.

The altarpiece is a pentaptych (an altarpiece consisting of a central panel and two pairs of side wings), intricately carved in lime wood, then painted and gilded. The main scene, visible when the pentaptych is open, represents the Dormition (or Assumption) of the Virgin surrounded by the Apostles. The outside has a dozen sections portraying scenes from the life of Christ and the Virgin. The altarpiece is topped with the Coronation of the Virgin in Heaven and, on both sides, the statues of the patron saints of Poland, St Stanislaus and St Adalbert.

Measuring about 13m high and 11m wide, the pentaptych is the largest and most important piece of medieval art of its kind. It took a decade for its maker, the Nuremberg sculptor Veit Stoss (known to Poles as Wit Stwosz), to complete this monumental work before it was solemnly consecrated in 1489.

The pentaptych is opened daily at precisely 11.50am and closed at 6pm, except for Saturday when it's left open for the Sunday morning Mass. The altarpiece apart, don't miss the delicate crucifix on the Baroque altar in the head of the right-hand aisle, another work by Veit Stoss, and the still larger crucifix placed on the rood screen, attributed to pupils of the master.

To the south of the church is the small, charming **Plac Mariacki**, which until the early 19th century was a churchyard. The sombre 14th-century **Church of St Barbara** (Kościół Św Barbary; Map p170), bordering the square on the east, was the cemetery chapel and serves the Polish faithful (the Mariacki was for Germans) during the Middle Ages. Note the skull and crossbones on the north exterior; just inside the entrance is an open chapel featuring stone sculptures of Christ and three of the Apostles, also attributed to the Stoss school. On the square is **Hipolit House** (Kamienica Hipolitów; Map p170; ☎ 012 422 4219; www .mhk.pl; Plac Mariacki 3; adult/concession/family 6/4/10zł, free Wed; ☯ 10am-5.30pm Wed-Sun May-Oct, 9am-4pm Wed & Fri-Sun, noon-7pm Thu), a branch of the city history museum than contains faithful recreations of town house interiors from the 17th to early 19th centuries.

East of Plac Mariacki is the **Mały Rynek**, the 'Little Market Sq'. It was the meat market in medieval times.

FIRE COMPANY BUGLE BOYS

Every hour on the hour the *hejnał* (bugle call) is sounded four times on a trumpet from the higher tower of Mariacki (Basilica of the Assumption of Our Lady). Today a musical symbol of the city, this simple melody, based on only five notes, was played in medieval times as a warning call. Intriguingly, it breaks off abruptly in midbar. Legend links it to the Tatar invasions; when the watchman on duty spotted the enemy and sounded the alarm, a Tatar arrow pierced his throat midphrase. Because the town was awakened from its collective slumber and defended itself successfully, the tune has stayed that way ever since. The job is now done by a handful of firemen in costume – at least from the waist up. The *hejnał* is broadcast on Polish Radio every day at noon.

PRINCES CZARTORYSKI MUSEUM

The **Princes Czartoryski Museum** (Muzeum Książąt Czartoryskich; Map p170; ☎ 012 422 5566; www.muzeum -czartoryskich.krakow.pl; ul Św Jana 19; adult/concession/family 9/6/18zł, free Thu; ☼ 10am-4pm Tue & Thu, 10am-7pm Wed, Fri & Sat, 10am-3pm Sun May-Oct, 10am-3.30pm Tue, Thu & Sat, 10am-6pm Wed, Fri & Sun Nov Apr) is one of the richest collections in town, and is itself something of a museum of a museum. Originally established in 1800 in Puławy by Princess Izabela Czartoryska as the first historical museum in Poland, the collection was secretly moved to Paris after the November Insurrection of 1830 (in which the family was implicated) and in the 1870s brought to Kraków. The collection experienced another 'excursion' during WWII when the Nazis seized it and took it to Germany, and not all the works were recovered. Even so, there's a lot to see, including a fascinating collection of European painting, mainly Italian, Dutch and Flemish. The stars of the show are Leonardo da Vinci's masterpiece *Lady with an Ermine* (c 1482), one of only three da Vinci oil paintings extant, and Rembrandt's *Landscape with the Good Samaritan*, also known as *Landscape before a Storm* (1638). Other exhibitions include Greek, Roman, Egyptian and Etruscan art and Turkish weapons and artefacts, such as carpets, saddles and a campaign tent, recovered after the 1683 Battle of Vienna.

COLLEGIUM MAIUS

The **Collegium Maius** (Map p170; ☎ 012 422 0549; www .uj.edu.pl/muzeum; ul Jagiellońska 15; adult/concession 12/6zł, 6zł for all Sat; ☼ 10am-3pm Mon, Wed & Fri, 10am-6pm Tue & Thu, 10am-2pm Sat), built as part of the Kraków Academy (now the Jagiellonian University), is the oldest surviving university building in Poland, and one of the best examples of 15th-century Gothic architecture in the city. It has a magnificent arcaded courtyard and a fascinating university collection.

Inside you'll be shown half a dozen historic interiors, where you'll see rare 16th-century astronomical instruments used by star pupil Copernicus as well as some of his manuscripts, a fascinating alchemy room, old rectors' sceptres and, the highlight of the show, the oldest (and perhaps tiniest) existing globe (c 1510) showing the American continent. You'll also visit an impressive Aula, a hall with an original Renaissance ceiling, and crammed with portraits of kings, benefactors and rectors of the university (five of whom were sent to Sachsenhausen concentration camp in 1939). The treasury contains everything from copies of the 1364 university foundation papers and Jan III Sobieski's hammered silver table to film awards (including an Oscar) made to director Andrzej Wajda.

All visits are guided in groups; tours begin every half-hour and there's usually a couple of daily tours at 11am and 1pm in English. In summer it's advisable to reserve in advance, either personally or by phone. The **courtyard** (☼ 7am-dusk) can be entered free of charge. Try to visit at 11am or 1pm, when the 14th-century replica clock on the south side chimes and its cast of characters go through their paces.

Also here is an exhibition called **World of Senses** (Świat Zmysłów; ☎ 012 663 1521; adult/concession 7/5zł; ☼ 10am-1.30pm Mon-Sat), which has 40 interactive models that teach visitors how the five senses function (and can deceive us).

CHURCH OF ST ANNE

Around the corner from the Collegium Maius is the Baroque **Church of St Anne** (Kościół Św Anny; Map p170; ul Św Anny 11). Designed by the omnipresent Tylman van Gameren, and built in the late 17th century as a university church, the Church of St Anne was long the site of inaugurations of the academic year, doctoral promotions and a resting place for many eminent university professors and rectors. A spacious,

KRAKÓW

stark-white interior fitted out with fine furnishings, gravestones and epitaphs, and embellished with superb stucco work and murals – all stylistically homogeneous – puts the church among the best classical Baroque buildings in Poland.

MUSEUM OF PHARMACY

It might not sound like a crowd-pleaser but the Jagiellonian University Medical School's **Museum of Pharmacy** (Muzeum Farmacji; Map p170; ☎ 012 421 9279; www.cm-uj.krakow.pl; Floriańska 25; adult/concession 6/3zł; ☺ noon-6.30pm Tue, 10am-2.30pm Wed-Sun) is one of the largest museums of its kind in Europe and arguably the best. Accommodated in a beautiful historic town house worth the visit alone, it features a 22,000-piece collection, which includes old laboratory equipment, rare pharmaceutical instruments, heaps of glassware, stoneware, mortars, jars, barrels, medical books and documents. Several pharmacies dating back to the 19th and early 20th centuries, including one from Lesko, have been painstakingly recreated here, and the garret is crammed with elixirs and panaceas, including vile vials or dried mummy powder. Much attention is given to the 'righteous gentile' Tadeusz Pankiewicz (see boxed text, p190) and the Pharmacy Under the Eagle (see p189) he courageously kept in operation in the Jewish ghetto during the German occupation.

DEFENSIVE WALLS

The **Florian Gate** (Brama Floriańska; Map p170; adult/concession/family 6/4/12zł; ☺ 10.30am-6pm May-Oct) is the only one of the original eight gates in the city's *mury obronne* (defensive walls) that was not dismantled during the 19th-century 'modernisation'. It was built around 1300, although the top is a later addition. The adjoining walls, together with two towers, have also been left standing. To the north of the gate and included in the entry fee is the **Barbican** (Barbakan; Map p170; ☺ 10.30am-6pm May-Oct). The most intriguing remnant of the medieval fortifications, the Barbican is a powerful, circular brick bastion adorned with seven turrets. There are 130 loopholes in its 3m-thick walls. This curious piece of defensive art was built around 1498 as an additional protection of the Florian Gate, and was once connected to it by a narrow passage running over a moat. It's one of the very few surviving structures of its kind in Europe, and also the largest and perhaps the most beautiful.

ARCHAEOLOGICAL MUSEUM

This **museum** (Muzeum Archeologiczne; Map p170; ☎ 012 422 7100; www.ma.krakow.pl; ul Poselska 3; adult/concession 7/5zł, free Sun; ☺ 9am-2pm Mon, Wed & Fri, 2-6pm Tue & Thu, 10am-2pm Sun Jul & Aug, 9am-2pm Mon-Wed, 2-6pm Thu, 10am-2pm Fri & Sun Sep-Jun) presents Małpolska's history from the Palaeolithic period up until the early Middle Ages. Also on show is an absorbing collection of ancient Egyptian artefacts, including both human and animal mummies, and 4200 iron coins from the 9th century. The gardens, laid out with rose bushes, magnolia trees and contemporary sculptures, are a lovely place for a stroll afterwards. Make sure you ask for an audioguide.

BASILICA OF ST FRANCIS

The mighty **Basilica of St Francis** (Bazylika Św Franciszka; Map p170; Plac Wszystkich Świętych 5) was erected in the second half of the 13th century but was repeatedly rebuilt and refurnished after at least four fires, the last and the most destructive being in 1850 when almost all the interior was destroyed. Of the present decorations, the most interesting are the Art Nouveau stained-glass windows in the chancel and above the organ loft; the latter is regarded as among the greatest in Poland. All were designed by Stanisław Wyspiański, who also executed most of the frescoes in the sanctuary and side altars.

Adjoining the church from the south is the **Franciscan Monastery** (Map p170; Klasztor Franciszkanów; ul Franciszkańska 4), which preserves its original Gothic cloister, complete with fragments of 15th-century frescoes and portraits of Kraków's bishops. Enter the cloister from the transept of the church.

DOMINICAN CHURCH OF THE HOLY TRINITY

The equally powerful **Dominican Church of the Holy Trinity** (Kościół Dominikanów Św Trójcy; Map p170; ul Stolarska 12) was also built in the 13th century and badly damaged in the 1850 fire, though its side chapels, dating mainly from the 16th and 17th centuries, have been preserved in reasonably good shape. Monumental neo-Gothic confessionals and stalls topped with angels playing musical instruments are a later adornment. Note the original 14th-century doorway at the main (western) entrance to the church.

The monastery, just behind the northern wall of the church, is accessible from the street. The cloister there has retained its Gothic shape pretty well and boasts a number of fine epitaphs, tombs and paintings.

WYSPIAŃSKI MUSEUM

Dedicated to one of Kraków's most beloved sons and the key figure of the Młoda Polska (Young Poland) movement, the **Wyspiański Museum** (Muzeum Wyspiańskiego; Map p170; ☎ 012 422 7021; www.muzeum.krakow.pl; ul Szczepańska 11; adult/concession/family 7/5/14zł, free Thu; ☺ 10am-7pm Tue, Wed & Sat, 10am-4pm Thu & Fri, 10am-3pm Sun May-Oct, 10am-3.30pm Wed, Thu & Sat, 10am-3.30pm Sun Nov-Apr), on the 1st and 2nd floors of Szołayski House, reveals how many branches of art Stanisław Wyspiański explored. A painter, poet and playwright, he was also a designer particularly renowned for his stained-glass designs, some of which are in the exhibition. Among his never realised projects was Acropolis, a political, religious and cultural centre to be built on Wawel Hill. There's a model made according to his design – an amazing mix of epochs and styles, a Greek amphitheatre and a Roman circus included.

CHURCH OF SS PETER & PAUL

The first Baroque building in Kraków, the **Church of SS Peter & Paul** (Kościół Św Piotra i Pawła; Map p170; ul Grodzka 54) was erected by the Jesuits, who had been brought to the city in 1583 to do battle with supporters of the Reformation. Designed on the Latin cross layout and topped with a large skylit dome, the church has a refreshingly sober interior, apart from some fine stucco decoration on the vault. The figures of the 12 Apostles standing on columns in front of the church are copies of the statues from 1723.

CHURCH OF ST ANDREW

Built towards the end of the 11th century, **Church of St Andrew** (Kościół Św Andrzeja; Map p170; ul Grodzka 54) is one of Kraków's oldest, and has preserved much of its austere Romanesque stone exterior. As soon as you enter, though, you're in a totally different world; its small interior was subjected to a radical Baroque overhaul in the 18th century.

ARCHDIOCESAN MUSEUM

Located in a 14th-century town house, the **Archdiocesan Museum** (Muzeum Archidiecezjalne; Map p170; ☎ 012 421 8963; ul Kanonicza 21; adult/concession 5/3zł; ☺ 10am-4pm Tue-Fri, 10am-3pm Sat & Sun)

presents a collection of religious sculpture and painting, dating from the 13th to 16th centuries. Also on display is the room where Karol Wojtyła (the late Pope John Paul II) lived from 1958 to 1967 (he also lived next door from 1951 to 1958), complete with his furniture and belongings – including his skis. There's also a treasury of gifts he received here too.

Outside the Old Town

There are a couple of important sights worth the easy walk west from the Old Town.

MANGGHA CENTRE OF JAPANESE ART & TECHNOLOGY

The **Manggha Centre of Japanese Art & Technology** (Map p165; ☎ 012 267 2703; www.manggha.krakow.pl; ul Konopnickiej 26; adult/concession/family 10/6/16zł, free Tue; ☺ 10am-6pm Tue-Sun Sep-May, 10am-8pm Tue-Sun Jun-Aug), lying on the right bank of the Vistula diagonally opposite Wawel Hill, was the brainchild of the Polish film director Andrzej Wajda, who donated the US$340,000 Kyoto Prize money he received in 1987 for his artistic achievements to fund a permanent home for the National Museum in Kraków's extensive collection of Japanese art, ceramics, weapons, fabrics, scrolls, woodcuts and comics. The striking modern building, which opened in 1994, was designed by the Japanese architect Arata Isozaki. The bulk of the collection is made up of the 7000 or so pieces assembled by Feliks Jasieński (1861–1929), an avid traveller, art collector, literary critic and essayist, known by his pen name of Manggha. The centre regularly sponsors events relating to Japanese culture, including film, theatre and traditional music.

NATIONAL MUSEUM

The so-called Main Building (Gmach Główny) of the **National Museum in Kraków** (Muzeum Narodowe w Krakowie; Map p165; ☎ 012 295 5500; www.museum .krakow.pl; Aleja 3 Maja 1; adult/concession 18/12zł, free Thu; ☺ 10am-4pm Tue & Thu, 10am-7pm Wed, Fri & Sat, 10am-3pm Sun May-Oct, 10am-3.30pm Tue, Thu & Sun, 10am-6pm Wed, Fri & Sat Nov-Apr), 500m due west of the Old Town down ul Piłsudskiego, houses three permanent exhibitions: the Gallery of 20th-Century Polish Painting, the Gallery of Decorative Art, and Polish Arms and National Colours – plus various temporary exhibitions. The painting gallery has an extensive collection of Polish painting (and some sculpture) covering the period from 1890 until the present day. There are several stained-glass designs (including the ones for Wawel Cathedral) by Stanisław Wyspiański, and an impressive selection of Witkacy's paintings. Jacek Malczewski and Olga Boznańska are both well represented also. Of the postwar artists, take particular note of the works by Tadeusz Kantor, Jerzy Nowosielski and Władysław Hasior, to name just a few.

Kazimierz

Today one of Kraków's inner suburbs and located within walking distance south of Wawel and the Old Town, Kazimierz was for a long time an independent town with its own municipal charter and laws. Its colourful history was determined by its mixed Jewish-Polish population, and though the ethnic structure is now wholly different, the architecture gives a good picture of its past, with clearly distinguishable sectors of what were Christian and Jewish quarters. The suburb is home to many important tourist sights, including churches, synagogues and museums.

WESTERN KAZIMIERZ

The western part of Kazimierz was traditionally Catholic, and although many Jews settled here from the early 19th century until WWII – for example, the main Jewish hospital was on ul Skawińska – the quarter preserves much of its original character, complete with its churches.

Beginning at the base of Wawel Hill, walk south along the river bank. Just past the Grundwald Bridge you'll see the **Pauline Church of SS Michael & Stanislaus** (Kościół Paulinów Św Michała i Stanisława; Map p187; ul Skałeczna 15), commonly known to Poles as the Skałka (Rock) due to its location; it was built on a rocky promontory, which is no longer pronounced. Today's mid-18th-century Baroque church is the third building on the site, previously occupied by a Romanesque rotunda and later a Gothic church. It is associated with Bishop Stanisław (Stanislaus) Szczepanowski, canonised in 1253 and now patron saint of Poland. You can even see the tree trunk (on the altar to the left and encased in glass), believed to be the same one on which King Bolesław Śmiały (Boleslaus the Bold) beheaded the bishop in 1079.

The cult of the saint has turned the place into a sort of a national pantheon. The **crypt** (adult/concession 2.5/2zł; 🕐 9am-5pm) underneath the church shelters the tombs of 12 eminent Poles, including the composer Karol Szymanowski and painters Jacek Malczewski and Stanisław Wyspiański.

About 250m east sits the **Church of St Catherine** (Kościół Św Katarzyny; Map p187; ul Augustiańska 7). One of the most monumental churches in the city, and possibly the one that has best retained its original Gothic shape, it was founded in 1363 and completed 35 years later, though the towers have never been built. The church was once on the corner of Kazimierz's market square but the area was built up in the 19th century. The lofty and spacious whitewashed interior boasts the imposing, richly gilded Baroque high altar from 1634 and some very flamboyant choir stalls.

Continue east on ul Skałeczna, turn right into ul Krakowska, and you'll see the **former town hall** (Map p187) of Kazimierz on the opposite side of the street. Built in the late 14th century in the centre of a vast market square (Plac Wolnica is all that's left), it was significantly extended in the 16th century, at which time it acquired its Renaissance appearance. The **Ethnographic Museum** (Muzeum Etnograficzne; Map p187; ☎ 012 430 5563; www.mek.krakow.pl; Plac Wolnica 1; adult/concession 6.50/4zł, free Sun; 🕐 10am-5pm Mon & Wed-Fri, 10am-2pm Sat & Sun May-Sep, 10am-6pm Mon, 10am-3pm Wed-Fri, 10am-2pm Sat & Sun Oct-Apr) accommodated here after WWII has one of the largest collections in Poland but only a small part of it is on display over three floors. The permanent exhibition features the reconstructed interiors of traditional Polish peasant cottages and workshops (ground floor), folk costumes, craft and trade exhibits, extraordinary Nativity scenes (1st floor), and folk and religious painting and woodcarving (2nd floor).

In the northeastern corner of Plac Wolnica is **Corpus Christi Church** (Kościół Bożego Ciała; Map p187; ul Bożego Ciała 26). Founded in 1340, it was the first church in Kazimierz and for a long time the town's parish church. Its interior has been almost totally fitted out with Baroque furnishings, including the huge high altar, extraordinary massive carved stalls in the chancel and a boat-shaped pulpit. Note the surviving early-15th-century stained-glass window in the sanctuary and the crucifix hanging above the chancel.

JEWISH QUARTER

A tiny area of about 300m by 300m northeast of Corpus Christi Church, the Jewish sector

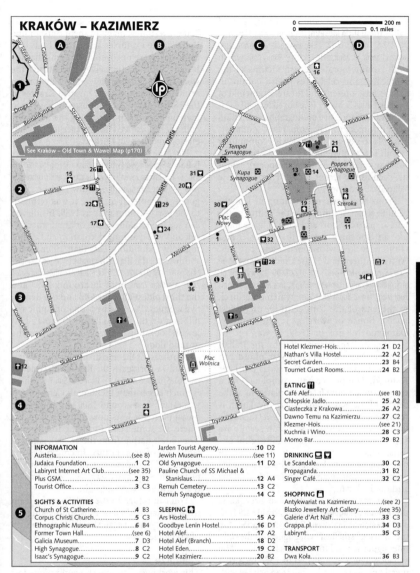

KRAKÓW – KAZIMIERZ

0 — 200 m
0 — 0.1 miles

See Kraków – Old Town & Wawel Map (p170)

KRAKÓW

INFORMATION
Austeria..(see 8)
Judaica Foundation..........................**1** C2
Labirynt Internet Art Club..............(see 35)
Plus GSM..**2** B2
Tourist Office..................................**3** C3

SIGHTS & ACTIVITIES
Church of St Catherine....................**4** B3
Corpus Christi Church......................**5** C3
Ethnographic Museum......................**6** B4
Former Town Hall............................(see 6)
Galicia Museum................................**7** D3
High Synagogue................................**8** C2
Isaac's Synagogue............................**9** C2

Jarden Tourist Agency....................**10** D2
Jewish Museum................................(see 11)
Old Synagogue................................**11** D2
Pauline Church of SS Michael &
  Stanislaus....................................**12** A4
Remuh Cemetery............................**13** C2
Remuh Synagogue..........................**14** C2

SLEEPING
Ars Hostel......................................**15** A2
Goodbye Lenin Hostel....................**16** D1
Hotel Alef......................................**17** A2
Hotel Alef (Branch)........................**18** D2
Hotel Eden....................................**19** C2
Hotel Kazimierz..............................**20** B2

Hotel Klezmer-Hois........................**21** D2
Nathan's Villa Hostel......................**22** A2
Secret Garden................................**23** B4
Tournet Guest Rooms....................**24** B2

EATING
Café Alef..(see 18)
Chłopskie Jadło..............................**25** A2
Ciasteczka z Krakowa....................**26** A2
Dawno Temu na Kazimierzu..........**27** C2
Klezmer-Hois..................................(see 21)
Kuchnia i Wino..............................**28** C3
Momo Bar......................................**29** B2

DRINKING
Le Scandale....................................**30** C2
Propaganda....................................**31** B2
Singer Café....................................**32** C2

SHOPPING
Antykwariat na Kazimierzu............(see 2)
Blazko Jewellery Art Gallery..........(see 35)
Galerie d'Art Naïf..........................**33** C3
Grappa.pl......................................**34** D3
Labirynt..**35** C3

TRANSPORT
Dwa Koła......................................**36** B3

of Kazimierz became, over the centuries, a
centre of Jewish culture equal to no other in
the country. With the mass deportation and
extermination of the Jewish people of Kraków
by the Nazis during WWII, all traces of the
folklore, life and atmosphere of the quarter
disappeared. Today only the architecture reveals that this was once a Jewish town, though

a handful of 'themed' restaurants, complete
with live *klezmer* music most nights, have
been opened on ul Szeroka. Miraculously,
seven synagogues survived the war, but only
one of them continues to function as a regular
place of worship.

Beginning your tour from the Corpus Christi
Church, walk east along ul Św Wawrzyńca

for 500m to what should be your first port of call – the **Galicia Museum** (Muzeum Galicja; Map p187; ☎ 012 421 6842, 012 422 1736; www.galiciajewishmuseum .org; ul Dajwór 18; adult/child 7/5zł; ☯ 9am-7pm), which both commemorates Jewish victims of the Holocaust and celebrates Jewish culture in Galicia past, present and future. Brainchild of the late Chris Schwarz (see boxed text, p164) it features an impressive photographic exhibition depicting modern-day remnants of southeastern Poland's once thriving Jewish community called 'Traces of Memory', video testimony of survivors and some seminal temporary exhibits, such as the recent 'Polish Heroes: Those Who Rescued Jews'.

From here walk north along ul Dajwór to ul Szeroka, traditionally the centre of the Jewish quarter. Short and wide, it looks more like an elongated square than a street and is often packed with tourists and coaches. At its southern end is the fine **Old Synagogue** (Stara Synagoga; Map p187; ☎ 012 422 0962; www.mhk.pl; ul Szeroka 24; adult/concession 7/5zł, free Mon; ☯ 10am-2pm Mon, 9am-3.30pm Wed-Sun), which dates back to the end of the 15th century, the oldest Jewish house of worship in the country. Damaged by fire in 1557, it was reconstructed in Renaissance style by the Italian architect Matteo Gucci. It was plundered and partly destroyed by the Nazis but later restored. The prayer hall, complete with a reconstructed *bimah* (raised platform at the centre of the synagogue where the Torah is read) and the original *aron kodesh* (the niche in the eastern wall where Torah scrolls are kept), houses an exhibition of liturgical objects; adjacent rooms are dedicated to Jewish traditions and art. Upstairs there's a photographic exhibit focusing on Jewish Kraków and the Holocaust.

Near the northern end of ul Szeroka is the **Remuh Synagogue** (Map p187; ☎ 012 429 5735; ul Szeroka 40; adult/concession 5/2zł; ☯ 9am-4pm Sun-Fri), the district's smallest synagogue and the only one regularly used for religious services. The synagogue was established in 1558 by a rich merchant, Israel Isserles, but is associated with his son Rabbi Moses Isserles, a philosopher and scholar.

The **Remuh Cemetery** (Map p187; ☯ 9am-4pm Sun-Fri) is just behind the synagogue. Founded in the mid-16th century, it was closed for burials in the late 18th century, when a new and larger graveyard was established. During WWII Nazis vandalised and razed the tombstones,

but during postwar conservation work some 700 gravestones, many of them outstanding Renaissance examples and dating back four centuries, were uncovered. It seems that the Jewish faithful themselves had buried the stones to avoid their desecration by foreign armies, which repeatedly invaded Kraków in the 18th century. The tombstones have been meticulously restored, making the place one of the best-preserved Renaissance Jewish cemeteries anywhere in Europe.

Near the southeastern edge of the cemetery is **Isaac's Synagogue** (Synagoga Izaaka; Map p187; ☎ 012 430 5577; ul Jakuba 25, enter from ul Kupa 18; adult/concession 7/6zł; ☯ 9am-7pm Sun-Fri), Kraków's largest synagogue. Completed in 1644, it was returned to the Jewish community in 1989. Inside you can see the remains of the original stuccowork and wall-painting decoration and a photography exhibition. Less than 100m to the southeast is the **High Synagogue** (Synagoga Wysoka; Map p187; ☎ 012 426 7520; ul Józefa 38; adult/concession 7/5zł; ☯ 9am-7pm), built in around 1560 and the third oldest after the Old and the Remuh Synagogues. It contains a photographic exhibition on the 1st floor and Kraków's best Jewish bookshop, Austeria (see p164), on the ground floor.

Northeast of the Jewish quarter and behind the railway bridge is the **New Jewish Cemetery** (Map p165; ul Miodowa 55; ☯ 8am-6pm Sun-Fri), which is much larger than the Remuh Cemetery. It was established around 1800 and is the only burial place for Jews now in use in Kraków. There are some 9000 surviving tombstones (the oldest dating from the 1840s), some of which are of great beauty. In contrast to the manicured Remuh Cemetery, this one is completely unkempt and overgrown, which makes it an eerie and very sad sight.

You can return to the Old Town by tram from ul Starowiślna, or walk south along the same street and over the bridge to the suburb of Podgórze.

Podgórze

This working-class suburb would pique few travellers' curiosities if it wasn't for the notorious role it played during WWII. It was here that the Nazis herded some 15,000 Jews into a ghetto and continued to empty it by way of deportations to the concentration camps, including one a short distance to the southwest in Płaszów. The centre of the ghetto was Plac Zgody, the ironically

---

KAZIMIERZ & ITS CHEQUERED PAST

Kazimierz was founded in 1335 by King Kazimierz Wielki on the southern fringe of Kraków. Thanks to numerous privileges granted by the king, the town developed swiftly and soon had its own town hall, a market square almost as large as Kraków's, and two huge churches. The town was encircled with defensive walls and by the end of the 14th century came to be Małopolska's most important and wealthiest city after Kraków.

The first Jews came to settle in Kazimierz soon after its foundation, but it wasn't until 1494, when they were expelled from within the walls of Kraków by King Jan Olbracht, that their numbers began to grow quickly. They settled in a prescribed area of Kazimierz, northeast of the Christian quarter, and the two sectors were separated by a wall.

The subsequent history of Kazimierz was punctuated by fires, floods and plagues, with both communities living side by side, confined to their own sectors. The Jewish quarter became home to Jews fleeing persecution from all corners of Europe, and it grew particularly quickly, gradually determining the character of the whole town. It became the most important Jewish centre of all Poland.

At the end of the 18th century Kazimierz was administratively incorporated into Kraków, and in the 1820s the walls were pulled down. At the outbreak of WWII Kazimierz was a predominantly Jewish suburb, with a distinct culture and atmosphere. But most Jews were killed by the Nazis in the extermination camps. Of the 65,000 Jews living in Kraków (most of whom lived in Kazimierz) in 1939, only about 6000 survived the war. The current Jewish population in the city is estimated at just under 200.

During communist rule, Kazimierz was largely a forgotten district of Kraków, partly because the government didn't want to touch the sensitive Jewish question. Then in the early 1990s along came Steven Spielberg to shoot *Schindler's List* and everything changed overnight.

In fact, Kazimierz was not the setting of the movie's plot – most of the events portrayed in the film took place in the Podgórze ghetto, Oskar Schindler's factory just outside it and the Płaszów extermination camp, all of which were further southeast, beyond the Vistula. Yet the film turned the world's attention to Kraków's Jewry as a whole, and since Kazimierz is the only substantial visual relic of Jewish heritage, it has benefited the most. 'Schindler tourism' now draws in crowds of visitors – Poles and foreigners alike – for all the right and all the wrong reasons.

---

named 'Peace Sq' that is today known as **Plac Bohaterów Getta**, (Map p165), where the process of selecting who would stay and who would be placed on the waiting train to one of the camps was completed. Today it is marked by a memorial by Kraków architects Piotr Lewicki and Kazimierz Latak consisting of 70 **empty chairs**, half of which are illuminated. They are meant to represent furniture and other remnants discarded on that very spot by the deportees.

On the south side of the square is the **Pharmacy Under the Eagle** (Apteka Pod Orłem; Plac Bohaterów Getta 18; ☎ 012 656 5625; adult/concession/family 4/3/8zł, free Mon; ☼ 10am-2pm Mon, 9.30am-5pm Tue-Sat) run by the non-Jew Tadeusz Pankiewicz (see boxed text, p190) during occupation and now a museum. Just south of the square are the remains of the **ghetto wall** (ul Lwowska 25-29) with a plaque marking the site. About 400km east of Plac Bohaterów Getta is **Oskar Schindler's enamelware factory** (Map p165; ul Lipowa 4).

Outer Kraków

Sights located both to the east and west of Kraków and just in (or just outside) the city limits are worth a half- or full-day excursion.

ZWIERZYNIEC

The prime attraction of the suburb called **Zwierzyniec** (Map p165), just under 3km west of the Old Town, is the **Kościuszko Mound** (Kopiec Kościuszki; Map p165; ☎ 012 425 1116; Aleja Waszyngtona; adult/concession/family 6/4/10zł, waxworks exhibition 8/6/12zł; ☼ 9am-dusk), erected between 1820 and 1823 soon after Kościuszko's death, to pay tribute to the man who embodied the dreams of independent Poland in times of foreign occupation. The mound stands 34m high, and soil from the Polish and American battlefields where Kościuszko fought was placed here. The views over the city are spectacular.

The entrance is through a small neo-Gothic chapel, which has an exhibition of memorabilia related to Kościuszko; there is a separate

KRAKÓW

WHEN THE SAINTS CAME MARCHING IN

At Jerusalem's Yad Vashem, a museum dedicated to the Holocaust, there is a row of trees called the 'Ave of the Righteous Among Nations'. They represent some of the 21,300-odd Gentiles (non-Jews) who either saved Jews during the Holocaust or came to their defence by putting their own lives at risk. Among those so honoured is Oskar Schindler, probably the best known of the so-called 'Righteous Gentiles' thanks to the book by Thomas Keneally originally titled *Schindler's Ark* (1982) and Steve Spielberg's mega-hit film based on the work, *Schindler's List* (1993). But Schindler, a heavy-drinking profiteer and something of an antihero, who originally managed to save the lives of Jews only because he needed their cheap labour at his enamelware factory (see p189) in Podgórze, is just one of some 6000 Poles – almost one-third of the worldwide total – named in this roll of honour. Much more altruistic and noble-minded – a man you'd much prefer to have over to dinner – was the pharmacist Tadeusz Pankiewicz, who cajoled the authorities into letting him keep his business, the Pharmacy Under the Eagle (see p189), open in the ghetto until the final deportation, dispensed medicines (often without charge), carried news from the 'outside world' and even allowed use of the establishment as a safe house on occasion. His harrowing memoir, *The Cracow Ghetto Pharmacy*, describes many of these deeds in measured detail without bravado or boast, and provides an eye-witness account of the short and tragic history of the Kraków ghetto from beginning to liquidation. In March 2006 an exhibit called 'Polish Heroes: Those Who Rescued Jews' opened at the Galicia Museum p188) in Kazimierz – it is now at the Auschwitz Jewish Centre (see p358) in Oświęcim – focusing on the lives and deeds of 21 Kraków residents who acted according to the most noble principles of humanity, either directly or behind the scenes, on behalf of Jews. If they canonised living people – and we think they should – you would be walking among saints in Kraków today. Come to think of it, you are.

waxworks exhibition called Polish Routes to Independence. The large brick fortification at the mound's foothill is a fortress built by the Austrians in the 1840s (now a hotel).

To reach the mound by public transport, take tram 1, 2 or 6 southwest to the end of the line; get off at Salwator and board bus 100, which will take you (every hour or so) directly to the entrance.

LAS WOLSKI

The 485-hectare **Las Wolski** (Wolski Forest; Map p165), west of Zwierzyniec, is the largest forested area within the city limits and a popular weekend destination for city dwellers.

The forest's hilly southern part facing the Vistula, known as Srebrna Góra (Silver Mountain), is topped with the mighty **Monastery of the Camaldolese Monks** (Klasztor Kamedułów; Map p165; ☎ 012 429 7610; www.kameduli .info in Polish). The order, part of the Benedictine family of monastic communities, was brought to Poland from Italy in 1603 and in time founded a dozen monasteries throughout the country. Today there are just two in Poland, including another in Masuria.

The order, with its very strict rules, attracts curiosity – and a few ironic smiles, particularly for its Memento Mori ('remember you must

die') motto – and its members' ascetic way of life. The monks live in seclusion in hermitages and contact each other only during prayers; some have no contact with the outside world at all. They are vegetarian and have solitary meals in their 'homes', with only five common meals a year. The hermits don't sleep in coffins as rumoured, but they do keep the skulls of their predecessors in the hermitages.

Kraków was the first of the Camaldolese seats in Poland; a church and 20 hermitages were established here between 1603 and 1642, and the whole complex was walled in. Not much has changed since. The place is spectacularly located and can be visited.

You approach it through a long walled alley that leads to the main gate, the ceiling of which is covered in naive frescoes. Once you are let in, you walk to the massive white limestone façade of the monastery church (50m high and 40m wide). A spacious, single-nave interior is covered by a barrel-shaped vault and lined on both sides with eight ornate Baroque chapels. The Baroque main altar is impressive

Underneath the chancel of the church is a large chapel used for prayers and, to its right, the crypt of the hermits. Bodies are placed into niches without coffins and then sealed. Latin inscriptions state the age of the deceased and the period spent in the hermitage. The niches are opened after 80 years and most of the remains moved to a place of permanent rest. It's then that the hermits take the skulls to keep in their shelters.

In the garden behind the church are 14 surviving hermitages where several monks live (others live in the building next to the church), but the area is off-limits to tourists. You may occasionally see hermits in the church, sporting long bushy beards and fine white cassocks.

Men can visit the church and crypt any day from 8am to 11am and 3pm to 4.30pm; guests are allowed in every half-hour. Women can enter the complex only on certain feast days, of which there are a dozen: Easter, Easter Monday, 3 May, Pentecost (two days), Sunday after 19 June, 2nd and 4th Sundays in July, first Sunday in August, Assumption of May (15 August), Mary's Birthday (8 September) and Christmas.

The hermitage is 7km west of the city centre. Take tram 1, 6 or 32 to the end of the line in Zwierzyniec and change for any westbound bus except the 100. The bus will let you off at the foot of Srebrna Góra, then it's a 200m walk up the hill to the church.

After visiting the monastery you can walk north for about 1km through the forest to the 20-hectare **Zoological Gardens** (Ogród Zoologiczny; Map p165; ☎ 012 425 3551; Aleja Kasy Oszczędności Miasta Krakowa 14; adult/concession 12/6zł; ☼ 9am-dusk), which is home to about 2000 animals representing 300 species from around the world.

About 1km further north is the **Piłsudski Mound** (Kopiec Piłsudskiego; Map p165; admission free; ☼ 24hr), the youngest and, at 35m, the tallest of the four city mounds. It was erected in honour of the marshal after his death in 1935 and was formed from soil taken from WWI Polish battle sites. Bus 134 from the zoo will bring you back to the city. You can also reach the Piłsudski Mound from the Kościuszko Mound on foot via a well-marked trail in about 2½ hours.

TYNIEC

A distant suburb of Kraków, 12km southwest of the centre, **Tyniec** (off Map p165) is the site of the **Benedictine Abbey** (Opactwo Benedyktynów; off Map p165; ☎ 012 259 5025; www.benedicite.pl; ul Benedyktyńska 37) dramatically perched on a cliff above the Vistula. The Benedictines came to Poland in the second half of the 11th century, and it was in Tyniec that they established their first base. The original Romanesque church and the monastery were destroyed and rebuilt in the 14th and 18th centuries. Today the church is essentially a Baroque building, though the stone foundations and the lower parts of the walls, partly uncovered and behind protected glass to the west of the church, show its earlier origins.

You enter the complex through a pair of defensive gates, resembling the entrance to a castle, and find yourself in a large courtyard. To the southwest is an octagonal wooden pavilion, which protects a stone well dating from 1620.

ICONIC LAJKONIK: KRAKÓW'S HORSEMAN

Another symbol of Kraków is the Lajkonik, a bearded man dressed in richly embroidered garments, a tall pointed hat and riding a hobbyhorse. He comes to life on the Thursday after Corpus Christi (late May or June) and heads a joyful pageant from the Premonstratensian Convent in Zwierzyniec to the Old Town's Rynek Główny.

Exact details of the Lajkonik's origins are hard to pin down, but one story involves a Tatar assault on Kraków in 1287. A group of raftsmen discovered the tent of the commanding khan on a foray outside the city walls and dispatched the unsuspecting Tatar leader and his generals in a lightning raid. The raftsmen's leader then wore the khan's richly decorated outfit back to the city.

The pageant, accompanied by a musical band, takes at least six hours to complete the trip, while the Lajkonik takes to dancing, jumping and running, greeting passers-by, popping into cafés en route, collecting donations and striking people with his mace, which is said to bring them good luck. Once the pageant reaches the main square, the Lajkonik is greeted by the mayor and presented with a symbolic ransom and a goblet of wine.

The Lajkonik's garb and his hobbyhorse were designed by Stanisław Wyspiański; the original design is kept in the Kraków City History Museum. It consists of a wooden frame covered with leather and embroidered with nearly a thousand pearls and coral breads. The whole outfit weighs about 40kg.

The monastery itself, home to 40 monks, cannot be visited but the church is open to all. Behind a sober façade, the dark interior is fitted out with a mix of Baroque and Rococo furnishings; up to the left are the remnants of early wall paintings. The organ is plain but has a beautiful tone, and concerts are held here in summer. Have a look at the exuberant Rococo pulpit.

To reach the abbey, take bus 112 from the Rondo Grunwaldzkie, the roundabout on the west side of Grunwald Bridge.

NOWA HUTA

The youngest and largest of Kraków's suburbs, **Nowa Huta** (New Steelworks; off Map p165; www.nh.pl in Polish) is a result of the postwar rush towards industrialisation. In the early 1950s a gigantic steelworks and a new town to serve as a bedroom community for its workforce, were built about 10km east of the centre of Kraków. The steel mill accounted for nearly half the national iron and steel output, and the suburb has become a vast urban sprawl, populated by over 200,000 people.

Because of increasing awareness of environmental issues, the industrial management was forced to cut production and reduce the workforce, yet the mammoth plant is still working despite the fact that it's unprofitable.

The steelworks can't be visited, but you may want to have a look around the suburb. Nowa Huta is a shock after the Old Town's medieval streets. Tram 4, 14 or 15 from Kraków Główny train station will drop you at **Plac Centralny**, the suburb's central square. Drop into the **tourist office** (off Map p165; Os Słoneczne 16; ☎ 012 643 0303; www.karnet.krakow2000.pl; ☼ 10am-2pm Tue-Sat) a couple of hundred metres north for a free map and to inspect the **Nowa Huta Museum** (off Map p165; www.mhk.pl; adult/concession 4/3zł, free Wed) inside. It doesn't matter where you start your sightseeing as the landscape varies little throughout the district. Most of the area is a grey concrete sea of Stalinist-style architecture, but fortunately, there are a few interesting sights in that sea.

In the northwestern part of the suburb, is the **Church of Our Lady Queen of Poland** (Kościół Najświętszej Marii Panny Królowej Polski; off Map p165; www.arkapana.pl in Polish; ul Obrońców Krzyża), otherwise known as the Arka Pana (Lord's Ark). This interesting, though rather heavy, ark-shaped construction was the first new church permitted in Nowa Huta after WWII, and

was completed in 1977 entirely by volunteer labourers. Up till then, Nowa Hutans used the two historic churches that had somehow managed to escape the avalanche of concrete. They are both on the southeastern outskirts of Nowa Huta, in the Mogiła suburb about 2.5km southeast of Plac Centralny (tram 15), and are worth a visit if you are in the area.

The small, shingled **Church of St Bartholomew** (Kościół Św Bartłomieja; off Map p165; ul Klasztorna) dates from the mid-15th century, which makes it Poland's oldest surviving three-nave timber church. If it's locked, enquire at the house at the back, and a nun may open it for you.

Across the street is the **Cistercian Abbey** (Opactwo Cystersów; off Map p165), which consists of a church and monastery with a large garden-park behind it. The Cistercians came to Poland in 1140 and founded abbeys around the country, including this one in 1222.

The church, open most of the day, has a large three-nave interior with a balanced mix of Gothic, Renaissance and Baroque furnishings and decoration. Have a look at the Chapel of the Crucified Christ (in the left transept), the polyptych in the high altar, and the beautiful stained-glass windows behind it.

WIELICZKA

Just outside the administrative boundaries of Kraków, some 14km southeast of the city centre, Wieliczka (vyeh-_leech_-kah) is famous for its ultra-deep **Salt Mine** (Kopalnia Soli; off Map p165; ☎ 012 278 7302; www.kopalnia.pl; ul Daniłowicza 10; adult/concession/family 46/31/174zł Jul & Aug, 45/30/168zł Sep-Jun; ☼ 7.30am-7.30pm Apr-Oct, 8am-5pm Nov-Mar), which has been in continuous operation for 700 years and can be visited. It's an eerie world of pits and chambers, and everything has been carved by hand from salt blocks. The mine was included on Unesco's World Heritage List in 1978.

The Wieliczka mine is renowned for the preservative qualities of its microclimate, as well as for its health-giving properties. An underground sanatorium has been established at a depth of 135m, where chronic allergic diseases are treated by overnight stays.

The mine has a labyrinth of tunnels, about 300km distributed over nine levels, the deepest being 327m underground. A section of the mine, some 22 chambers connected by galleries, is open to the public as a museum, and it's a fascinating trip.

You visit three upper levels of the mine, from 64m to 135m below the ground, walking

---

NOWA HUTA: SOCIALIST WET DREAM & NIGHTMARE

The postwar communist regime deliberately built Nowa Huta steelworks in Kraków to give a 'healthy' working-class and industrial injection to the strong aristocratic, cultural and religious traditions of the city. It was of no interest to city planners that Kraków had neither ore nor coal deposits and that virtually all raw materials had to be transported from great distances. The project also did not take into account that the site had one of the most fertile soils in the region, nor that construction of the complex would destroy villages that could trace their histories back to the early Middle Ages.

The communist dream hasn't materialised exactly as planned. Nowa Huta hasn't, in fact, threatened the deep traditional roots of Kraków. Worse, it actually became a threat to its creators, with strikes breaking out here as frequently as anywhere else, paving the way for the eventual fall of communism. The steelworks did, however, affect the city in another way: it brought catastrophic environmental pollution that threatened people's health, the natural environment and the city's historical monuments.

---

through an eerie world of pits and chambers, all hewn by hand from solid salt. Some have been made into chapels, with altarpieces and figures, others are adorned with statues and monuments – all carved out of salt – and there are even underground lakes.

The showpiece is the ornamented **Chapel of St Kinga** (Kaplica Św Kingi), which is actually a fair-sized church measuring 54m by 18m, and 12m high. Every single element here, from chandeliers to altarpieces, is of salt. It took over 30 years (1895) for one man and then his brother to complete this underground temple, and about 20,000 tonnes of rock salt had to be removed. Occasional Masses and concerts are held here. Other highlights are the salt lake in the **Eram Barącz Chamber**, whose water contains 320g of salt per litre, and the 36m-high **Stanisław Staszic Chamber** with its panoramic lift.

Included in the entry price is a visit to the **Kraków Saltworks Museum**, accommodated in 14 worked-out chambers on the third level of the mine, where the tour ends, but most visitors appear to be 'salted away' by then. From here a fast mining lift takes you back up to the real world.

Visitors are guided in groups and the tour takes about two hours. You walk about 2km through the mine – wear comfortable shoes. The temperature in the mine is 14°C. In July and August English-language tours depart every half-hour from 8.30am to 6pm. During the rest of the year there are between six and eight daily tours in English.

Minibuses (2.50zł) to Wieliczka depart Kraków every 10 minutes between 6am and 8pm from the northern end of ul Starowiślna, near the main post office, and drop passengers off at the bottom of the road leading up to the salt mine entrance. Trains between Kraków and Wieliczka (3zł, 15 minutes) leave every 45 minutes throughout the day, but the train station in Wieliczka is over a kilometre from the mine.

To avoid the tremendously long queues at Wieliczka itself, especially in season, you are strongly advised to buy your ticket from one of the tourist offices in Kraków (see p167) before setting out.

ACTIVITIES

Poland's largest water park, **Park Wodny** (Map p165; ☎ 012 616 3190; www.parkwodny.pl; ul Dobrego Pasterza 126; per hr adult/concession Mon-Fri 16/16zł, Sat & Sun 19/17zł, all day incl sauna weekdays 38/32zł, weekend 43/37zł; ⏰ 8am-10pm), is 2.5km northeast of the Old Town and accessible by bus 125, 128 and 152 from the train station. It boasts various pools, including one enormous one with hundreds of metres of water chutes and slides, climbing-walls, Jacuzzis, and various saunas, as well as video games, an internet café, a restaurant and a water bar.

Roughly 2km east of the city centre, **Fantasy Park** (Map p165; ☎ 012 290 9515; www.fantasypark.pl; Aleja Pokoju 44; ⏰ 10am-2am), in the Kraków Plaza shopping centre, is the perfect place to head on a rainy day. It has 20 ten-pin bowling lanes (54zł to 84zł per hour, depending on the time of day and day of the week), plus billiards, air-hockey, video arcades and even an internet café and bar. There's also a supervised kids' play area (10zł to 15zł per hour). You can get here on tram 1, 14 or 22.

Bird Service (Map p170; ☎ 012 292 1460; www.bird .pl; ul Św Krzyża 17) is Poland's No 1 specialist in bird-watching tours. It organises birding trips in eastern Poland, including the Białowieża and Biebrza National Parks and organises the Polish Bird Festival, held annually in the second week of May in northeastern Poland. This is a holiday package (from €400) that covers eight nights' accommodation in an optimal bird-watching location, half-board and information. Bird Service also offers week-long bicycle tours along the Dunajec River in the Carpathian Mountains (from €420).

WALKING TOUR

Start an easy, 'introductory' tour of Kraków outside the Mariacki, the **Basilica of the Assumption of Our Lady (1)** in Rynek Główny. Take a leisurely stroll around the main market

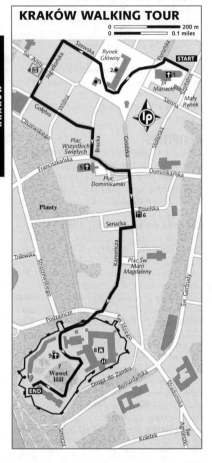

KRAKÓW WALKING TOUR

square, passing through the **Cloth Hall (2)** to browse the craft stalls. Head west past the **Town Hall Tower (3)**, which you might consider scaling for fabulous views of the square and city. Enter ul Szewska and follow it to the junction with ul Jagiellońska, then turn south and walk to the **Collegium Maius (4)** for at least a quick look at the famous courtyard and its clock. Carry on to the junction with ul Gołębia. Turn right and follow this road southeast as far as ul Bracka, then turn south past the **Basilica of St Francis (5)**, and join busy ul Grodzka, which is replete with eateries, including **Miód Malina (6; p201)**, should you fancy a bite. Go as far as ul Senacka, and from there turn south onto charming ul Kanonicza. This will lead you right to the foot of **Wawel Hill (7)**. Climb to the top to visit the stately **Wawel Royal Castle (8)** and **Wawel Cathedral (9)**, or just take in the stunning views across the river. If you want to get closer to the water, go to the entrance of the **Dragon's Den (10)** in the southwestern part of the Wawel complex and walk down the stairs.

KRAKÓW FOR CHILDREN

Kraków isn't the most child-friendly of cities, but there's enough going on in the vicinity to keep kids amused for a few days. The main attraction for younger children is undoubtedly **Park Wodny** (p193), a very modern and well-equipped water-park complex, with three pools, 800m of water slides and chutes and a 30m rapids labyrinth.

Fantasy Park (p193) has a supervised children's play area with climbing frames and the like to keep toddlers occupied, while older siblings can try their hand at bowling, billiards or video games.

Hands-on science is offered at the **Collegium Maius** (p183), where older children can explore the five human senses though interactive models. The swords, crossbows and suits of armour at **Crown Treasury & Armoury** (p172) in Wawel will keep some kids (especially boys) enthralled for longer than you may think.

The puppet shows that play regularly at **Teatr Groteska** (p205), though in Polish language, are a big hit with kids and adults alike.

WALK FACTS

Start/Finish Rynek/Dragon's Den
Distance approximately 1.5km
Duration around 1½ hours

Away from the city centre, the **Zoological Gardens** (p191) are an obvious choice for a day out with the kids, and there are pleasant grounds for a walk afterwards, including one to the eminently climbable **Piłsudski Mound** (p191) a kilometre to the north.

Around 2km northeast of the centre, **Anikino** (Map p165; ☎ 012 411 3007; www.anikino.pl; ul Nieduża 4; ☼ 9am-9pm), just off Aleja Jana Pawła II, is a supervised indoor play area for toddlers, with prices starting at 10/12zł for the first hour on weekdays/weekends, and 18/25zł for the day.

LANGUAGE COURSES

The granddaddy of all Polish language schools is Jagiellonian University's **School of Polish Language & Culture** (Szkoła Języka i Kultury Polskiej; Map p170; ☎ 012 421 3692; www.uj.edu.pl/Polonia/en; ul Garbarska 7a). It organises intensive two-week (50-hour) courses (€350) during the academic year, and courses lasting up to six weeks (€720) in summer. A private school that gets good reports is the **International School of Polish Language & Culture** (Map p165; ☎ 012 661 4030; www.polishcourse .org; 5th fl, ul Bronowicka 58), with courses lasting one/two weeks (25/50 hours) costing €170/260.

TOURS

The most romantic way to tour Kraków is in one of the many **horse-drawn carriages** (half-/full hr 100/200zł), which line up at the northern end of Rynek Główny and on ul Grodzka opposite the Church of St Andrew. You decide which route you want to take, or leave it up to the driver to take you for a trot round the sights of the Old Town or even down to Kazimierz.

Cracow Tours (Map p170; 012 430 0726; www.cracow tours.pl; ul Krupnicza 3) offers a four-hour bus tour of the city (adult/concession 120/60zł) and **Tour Bus** (☎ 0501 377 604; www.tourbus.pl; day ticket adult/concession 50/25zł) is a 'jump-on, jump-off' bus, but neither can get you into the Old Town and parts of Kazimierz like the little five-seat carts run by **Omega City Tour** (☎ 0506 832 999; www.omega.civ.pl/citytour) and **Krak Tour** (☎ 0886 664 999) can. Expect to pay about 170zł per person for an hour's run-around with taped commentary.

If you prefer to see the city on foot, several companies offer walking tours including **Marco der Pole** (Map p170; ☎ 012 430 2131; www .marcoderpole.com.pl; ul Kanonicza 15), with one of the Old Town departing at 10am daily and the tour of Kazimierz at 1.30pm between April and early November. Both last three hours and cost 45zł.

To our mind the best bicycle tour in town is that offered by **Krakow Bike Tours** (☎ 0663 731 515; www.krakowbiketour.com), whose four-hour spin on wheels around town (59zł) starts daily at 1pm and will take you to everything from Rynek Główny and Wawel to Oskar Schindler's factory in Podgórze. It has excellent guides and commentary. Two-hour Kraków by Night Tours (49zł) run May to September.

A 45-minute cruise on the Vistula River is available on the **Nimfa** (Map p165; ☎ 012 422 0855, 0663 165 910; adult/concession 15/10zł) berthed below Wawel Hill near Grunwald Bridge between five and seven times a day Monday to Saturday. If you want to get on the drink *with* a drink, jump aboard the ever-popular **Kraków Booze Cruise** (Map p165; ☎ 0500 597 050; www.krakow boozecruise.com), which departs from the same spot at 7pm every Wednesday, Friday and Saturday. The cost (60/90zł for women/men) gets you all the beer you can drink, all you can eat from the barbecue and vegetarian buffet, and a couple of hours on the water.

Theme tours include those run by **Crazy Guides** (☎ 0500 091 200; www.crazyguides.com), which offers entertaining tours of the city's communist-era suburbs, including a 2½-hour one to Nowa Huta (119zł), in a restored East German Trabant car. The **Jarden Tourist Agency** (Map p187; ☎ 012 421 7166; www.jarden.pl; ul Szeroka 2) specialises in Jewish-heritage tours. The most popular one, Retracing Schindler's List (two hours by car), costs 65zł per person. All tours require a minimum of three people and must be arranged in advance.

FESTIVALS & EVENTS

Kraków has one of the richest cycles of annual events in Poland. Ask any tourist-office branch (see p167) for more details or check the website www.krakow-info.com.

January

New Year's Concert (www.dkpodgorze.krakow.pl in Polish) Kraków ushers in the New Year with prestigious classical-music at **Teatr im J Słowackiego** (Map p170), which is at Plac Św Ducha 1, while plebs make do with fireworks and rock bands in Rynek Główny.

February

Shanties International Festival of Sailors' Songs (www.shanties.pl in Polish) Going strong for two dozen years, despite Kraków's inland location.

KRAKÓW

March

Bach Days n Music (www.amuz.krakow.pl) Baroque fugues and such for days at the **Academy of Music** (Map p170) at ul Basztowa 8.

April

Paka Cabaret Review (www.paka.pl in Polish) Of interest mostly to Polish speakers but plenty of one-offs around town for visitors too.

May

Juvenalia During this student carnival, students receive symbolic keys to the town's gates and take over the city for four days and three nights. There's street dancing, fancy-dress parades, masquerades and lots of fun.

Cracovia Marathon (www.cracoviamaraton.pl) An increasingly popular international running event.

Krakow International Film Festival (www.cracow filmfestival.pl) Film festival that's been going for almost half a century shows some 350 films from 20 countries.

June

Lajkonik Pageant (www.mhk.pl) Seven days after Corpus Christi (usually June but possibly late May). This colourful pageant headed by Lajkonik, a comical, oh-so-Cracovian figure disguised as a bearded Tatar riding a wooden horse, parades from a church in Zwierzyniec to the main market square accompanied by loud, high-pitched music.

Jewish Culture Festival (www.jewishfestival.pl) The biggest Jewish festival in Europe features a variety of cultural events including theatre, film, music and art exhibitions, and concludes with a grand open-air *klezmer* concert on ul Szeroka.

July

International Festival of Street Theatre (www.teatrkto.pl in Polish) Takes place on Rynek Główny.

Summer Jazz Festival (www.cracjazz.com) Featuring the best of Polish modern jazz.

August

Music in Old Kraków International Festival (www.capellacracoviensis.art.pl) Kraków's most important musical event goes for two weeks, spans five centuries of musical tradition, from medieval to contemporary, and is presented in concert halls, churches and other historic interiors.

September

Sacrum-Profanum Festival (www.sacrumprofanum.pl) Classical music festival dedicated to composers of different countries each year (Russia 2005, France 2006, USA 2007 etc).

Pierogi Festival (www.biurofestiwalowe.pl) Three-day fête honouring the king of dumplings.

October

Organ Music Festival (www.filharmonia.krakow.pl) With a tradition of over 30 years, this festival gives people a chance to listen to organ recitals, which take place in several city churches.

November

Zaduszki Jazz Festival (strszu@hot.pl) This popular festival, held in jazz clubs around the city, livens up an otherwise dull month.

December

Kraków Christmas Crib Competition (www.mhk.pl) Held on the main market square beside the statue of Adam Mickiewicz on the 1st Thursday of December, this contest attracts crowds of spectators. A sort of Nativity scene, but very different from those elsewhere in the world, Kraków's *szopki* are elaborate compositions built in an architectural, usually churchlike form, and made in astonishing detail from cardboard, wood, tinfoil and the like – some are even mechanised. The prize-winners are put on display until mid-February at a special exhibition in the Kraków City History Museum (see p181). You can see gold medallists from previous years at the Ethnographic Museum (see p186).

SLEEPING

Kraków is Poland's premier tourist destination, with prices to match. Here expect to pay up to 200zł for a budget double, up to 400zł for midrange, and anything over that for top end. There is an ever-increasing supply of accommodation options but advance booking during the busy summer season is recommended for the very central places. The Old Town is the main area for midrange and top-end hotels, as well as a few budget places, while cheaper, and sometimes better-value, options can be found outside the area bounded by the Planty.

Kazimierz also has a number of atmospheric midrange and top-end hotels, in a quieter location. Note that some of the more expensive hotels often quote prices in euros.

Modern hostels, geared towards the needs (and expectations) of Western backpackers are springing up everywhere, both inside and out of the city centre, while private rooms and apartments may be the answer, if you're intending to stay a bit longer. **Waweltur** (Map p170; ☎ 012 422 1921; www.waweltur.com.pl; ul Pawia 8; ⏰ 8am-7pm Mon-Fri, 8am-2pm Sat) arranges accommodation in private rooms (from 55zł per person) in private homes scattered around the city (so check the location carefully first). The apartments (studios from 140zł) are self-contained, and come with kitchens and bathrooms.

Good websites for apartment rentals include www.krakow-apartments.com and www.noce.pl.

Old Town & Surrounds

BUDGET

Kraków has a good supply of budget places, though the cheapest places are outside the centre so you will need to do some commuting. Bright, clean, modern hostels with multilingual staff and 'luxuries' like washing machines and dryers are a very welcome addition to the budget accommodation scene, while the older, cheaper, traditional hostels may be a bit basic for some. During holidays, the older hostels tend to fill up with noisy groups of school kids and readers have complained about standards of cleanliness. During the summer, several student hostels let out rooms on the outskirts of town, and these often have good on-site facilities.

Kraków has several camping grounds, all of which are pretty distant from the centre but are linked to it by public transport.

Oleandry YHA Hostel (Map p165; ☎ 012 633 8822; www.smkrakow.pl/eng; ul Oleandry 4; dm 22-34zł; ✗) About 1km west of the Old Town and just north of the Żaczek, this is a very big (and often very noisy) 330-bed place with basic dorms in need of updating (and/or a good wash) and lots of rules, including a midnight curfew. Take tram 15 from outside the main train-station building and get off just past Hotel Orbis Cracovia.

Hotel Studencki Żaczek (Map p165; ☎ 012 633 1914; www.zaczek.bratniak.krakow.pl; Al 3 Maja 5; s/d/tr from 90/110/165zł; ℗ 🖳) This student dormitory is just past the Main Building of the National Museum 1km west of the Old Town. It has a variety of accommodation on offer, including cheaper rooms with shared bathrooms. Breakfast is 10zł extra.

Trzy Kafki (Map p165; ☎ 012 632 8829; www.trzykafki.pl; Al Słowackiego 29; s/d/tr/q 60/80/100/120zł; 🖳) Roughly 1.5km northwest of the Old Town, this place is part of a chain of three establishments in Kraków, and has fairly simple but excellent-value rooms with modern shared bathrooms and kitchens. It offers a laundry service, and breakfast is 10zł to 15zł extra. Reach here from the Old Town on tram 3, 5, 7 or 19.

Dizzy Daisy (Map p165; ☎ 012 92 0171; www.hostel.pl; ul Pędzichów 9; dm 35-60zł, d 120-160zł, tr 150-210zł; ✗ 🖳) This rather stunning 52-bed hostel

is a bit out of the centre (500m north of the main market square) but has stunning modern décor, great facilities and attracts an international crowd of party people.

Cracow Hostel (Map p170; ☎ 012 429 1106; www.cracowhostel.com; Rynek Główny 18; dm 40-70zł; 🖳) Location, location, location. This all-dormitory hostel on three floors may not be the best in town, with somewhat cramped rooms of between four and 18 beds. But it's perched high above the main market square, with an amazing view from the comfortable lounge.

Stranger Hostel (Map p165; ☎ 012 634 2516; www.thestrangerhostel.com; ul Kochanowskiego 1/3; dm 30-60zł, d 120-160zł; ℗ 🖳) Recently included in the Lonely Planet Bluelist as one of the 10 hippest hostels in the world, this 32-bed place makes up for its off-centre location with parties, barbecues and DVD films on a 3m screen. Some people have been known to check in and never check out. Most rooms have eight to 12 beds, though there is one double.

Hostel Giraffe (Map p170; ☎ 012 430 0073; www.hostelgiraffe.com; ul Krowoderska 31; d 45-60zł, d 160zł; ℗ 🖳) This upbeat place north of the Old Town manages to be both laid-back and stylish at the same time. There are all the expected amenities – free laundry and internet, large kitchen etc – but the old piano in the bar is an extra.

Hostel Flamingo (Map p170; ☎ 012 422 0000; www.flamingo-hostel.com; ul Szewska 4; dm 55-80zł, d 170zł; ✗ 🖳) Any place that bills itself as 'run by flamingos for flamingos' gets our custom. We love the pink and lilac décor, the cheeky attitude and the great location just steps west of the main market square. Dorms have four to 10 beds.

Camping Clepardia (Map p165; ☎ 012 415 9672; www.clepardia.pl; ul Pachońskiego 28a; per person/tent 20/10zł, bungalows d/tr from 100/130zł; ⌚ Apr–mid-Oct; ℗ 🖳) Clepardia has tent space and several cabins with a bathroom, and guests have free access to the outdoor swimming pool next door. It's 4km north of the centre, and accessible by bus 115 from the main train station. The site is opposite the Elea department store.

Camping Nr 46 Smok (Map p165; ☎ 012 429 8300; www.smok.krakow.pl; ul Kamedulska 18; per person/tent 20/12zł, bungalows d/tr from 150/170zł; ℗) This quiet camping ground with 11 rooms is around 4km west of the Old Town in leafy Zwierzyniec. To get here from the train station, take tram 2 to the end of the line in Zwierzyniec and change for any westbound bus (except bus 100).

KRAKÓW

Kraków is awash with modern hostels that have all the amenities and a surfeit of good times. Among other good bets are the following:

Ars Hostel (Map p187; ☎ 012 422 3659; www.arshostel .pl; ul Koletek 7; dm 45-60zł; **P** □) This 40-bed hostel is famed as much for its name ('art' in Latin) as for its location below Wawel.

Hostel Centrum Kraków (Map p170; ☎ 012 429 1157; www.centrumkrakow.pl; ul Św Gertrudy; dm 45-60zł; □) Quiet all-dorm hostel on three floors convenient to both the Old Town and Kazimierz.

Hostel Gardenhouse (Map p170; ☎ 012 431 2824; www.gardenhouse.pl; 3rd fl, ul Floriańska 5; dm 50-65zł, d 150-160zł; □) This hostel has an enviable location in a 15th-century building behind the Mariacki.

MIDRANGE

Centrally located hostels with comfortable twins and doubles have become a realistic alternative for those looking for moderately priced accommodation. Many midrange hotels are located away from the heart of the city, but there are a few within easy walking distance of Rynek Główny and other major sights.

Jordan Guest Rooms (Pokoje Gościnne Jordan; Map p170; ☎ 012 421 2125; www.nocleg.jordan.pl; ul Długa 9; s/d/ tr 140/210/280zł; **P** ✕ □) Jordan is a reasonable and very modern place on the northern edge of the Old Town. The 20 rooms are on the upper floors but you book through the travel agency–cum–jewellery shop downstairs.

Hotel Campanile (Map p170; ☎ 012 424 2600; www.campanile.com.pl; ul Św Tomasza 34; s & d 219-329zł; ✕ □ &) Part of a French chain, this 106-room modern hotel has somehow succeeded in nestling in the Old Town, just a few blocks from the Rynek. It has attractive, bright rooms done out in 'corporate décor'.

Hotel Petrus (Map p165; ☎ 012 269 2946; www.petrus .net.pl; ul Pietrusińskiego 12; s €48-65, d €60-75; **P** &) Get away from the crowds at this beautifully appointed place close to Park Skały Twardowskiego and its lake, about 2km southwest of the city centre. The 27 rooms are cool and modern and there's a cosy lounge with a log fire, as well as a sauna, gym, restaurant and beer garden. Rates are 10% cheaper at the weekend.

Polonia House (Dom Polonii; Map p170; ☎ 012 422 4355; www.wspolnota-polska.krakow.pl; Rynek Główny 14; s/d 198/235zł, apt 267-348zł) You couldn't ask for a more central location than this. The Dom has just two high-ceilinged double rooms (over-

looking the Rynek) and one double suite, all on the top floor. Needless to say, it gets booked out far in advance.

U Pana Cogito (Map p165; ☎ 012 269 7200; www.pcog ito.pl; ul Bałuckiego 6; s/d/q 210/260/340zł; **P** ✕ □ &) White and cream seem to be the colours of choice at this friendly 14-room hotel in a lovely mansion about 1km southwest of the centre. All rooms have big bathrooms and refrigerators, and for extra privacy, the one apartment has a separate entrance. The hotel also has its own restaurant, also done out in fresh, minimalist white.

Hotel Royal (Map p170; ☎ 012 421 3500; www.royal .com.pl; ul Św Gertrudy 26-29; s 179-249zł, d 279-369zł, tr 399zł, ste 450-600zł; **P** □ &) This large and impressive Art Nouveau edifice is one of the surprisingly few hotels close to Wawel Hill. It's split into two sections; the 38 higher-priced two-star rooms are cosy and far preferable to the 69 fairly drab one-star ones at the back.

Hotel Saski (Map p170; ☎ 012 421 4222; www.hotel saski.com.pl; ul Sławkowska 3; s 250-320zł, d 290-390zł, tr 440zł; ✕ □) If you're in the mood for a touch of *belle époque* Central European style, but without the hefty price tag, the Saski may be the place for you. This grand old establishment occupies a historic mansion just off Rynek Główny. The uniformed doorman, rattling century-old lift and ornate furnishings lend the place a certain glamour, and though the rooms themselves are comparatively plain, most have very modern bathrooms, and the double set of doors is an unusual feature. Cheaper singles and doubles share a bathroom.

Hotel Pollera (Map p170; ☎ 012 422 1044; www .pollera.com.pl; ul Szpitalna 30; s 210-320zł, d 260-390zł, tr 330-470zł; **P** ✕ □ &) The Pollera is a classy place dating from 1834 with 42 large rooms crammed with elegant furniture. The singles are unexciting, but the doubles are far nicer, and it's central and quiet.

Hotel Polonia (Map p170; ☎ 012 422 1233; www.hotel -polonia.com.pl; ul Basztowa 25; s/d/tr/ste 260/303/350/450zł, without bathroom from 98/111/130zł; □) The Polonia occupies a grand old building near the train and bus stations. The rooms are light and modern but many overlook the noisy main road. The suites are particularly spacious and attractive though. Rooms without en suite are not so nice.

Wielopole Guest Rooms (Map p170; ☎ 012 422 1475; www.wielopole.pl; ul Wielopole 3; s 210zł, d 320-380zł; **P** ✕ □ &) Wielopole's 36 bright, modern rooms are housed in a renovated block with a great courtyard on the eastern edge of the Old Town, and all have spotless bathrooms. Breakfast (served in your room) costs 20zł extra.

Hotel Wit Stwosz (Map p170; ☎ 012 429 6026; www .wit-stwosz.com.pl; ul Mikołajska 28; s 275-295zł, d 330-370zł, tr 385-450zł, apt 490-550zł; ✄ 🖵) Wit Stwosz occupies a recently renovated 16th-century town house northeast of the Rynek. Its 17 rooms are fully modernised, though some are a bit plain. Overall it's comfortable, stylish and remarkably good value for its location.

Hotel Jan (Map p170; ☎ 012 430 1969; www.hotel -jan.com.pl; ul Grodzka 11; s 250-320zł, d 340-430zł, tr 460zł) Hotel Jan is a restored town house with 50 beds on a busy and often noisy pedestrian street, just a stone's throw from Rynek Główny. Rooms are pleasant and comfortable, and the cool medieval cellar makes an atmospheric setting for breakfast.

Hotel Pod Wawelem (Map p170; ☎ 012 426 2626; www.hotelpodwawelem.pl; Plac Na Groblach 22; s 240-420zł, d 340-560zł, apt 520-600zł; ℗ ✄ ✄ 🖵 ⴵ) This hotel, at the foot of Wawel and overlooking the river, has just been renovated and has a crisp and up-to-date feel to it. The 48 rooms are generously proportioned and look either onto the river or the castle. The view from the rooftop café is stunning.

TOP END

There are plenty of upmarket accommodation options in the Old Town and around, which is certainly Kraków's most atmospheric area in which to stay.

Hotel Alexander (Map p170; ☎ 012 422 9660; www .alexhotel.pl; ul Garbarska 18; s/d 340/420zł; ℗ ✄ ✄ ⴵ) The Alexander is a modern, if slightly anonymous, 38-room place, offering the usual standard of three-star comfort. It's on a shabby but quiet street, just west of the Old Town.

Hotel Wawel (Map p170; ☎ 012 424 13 00; www.hotel wawel.pl; ul Poselska 22; s 300zł, d 430-520zł; ✄ ✄ 🖵) Ideally located just off busy ul Grodzka, what was once the midrange Wawel-Tourist has undergone a major facelift and emerged as the Wawel. Its 40 rooms are large, comfortable and now very stylish. It's set far enough back from the main drag to avoid most of the Old Town noise.

Hotel Pugetów (Map p170; ☎ 012 432 4950; www .donimirski.com; ul Starowiślna 15a; s/d/tr/ste 250/510/ 600/790zł; ℗ ✄ ✄ 🖵) Kraków's first boutique hotel, the Pugetów stands proudly next to the

19th-century neo-Renaissance palace of that name and offers just seven rooms and suites with individual names (Conrad, Bonaparte) and identities. Think embroidered bathrobes, black-marble baths and a fabulous silver-service cellar restaurant.

Hotel Pod Różą (Map p170; ☎ 012 424 3381; www .hotel.com.pl/podroz; ul Floriańska 14; s/d/ste 550/650/750zł; ✄ 🖵) A hotel that has never closed, even in the dark, dreary days of communism, 'Under the Rose' offers antiques, Oriental carpets, a wonderful glassed-in courtyard restaurant and state-of-the-art facilities.

Hotel Amadeus (Map p170; ☎ 012 429 6070; www .hotel-amadeus.pl; ul Mikołajska 20; s/d/ste €160/170/ 240; ℗ ✄ ✄ 🖵) Amadeus, with its Mozartian flair, is one of Kraków's most refined hotels. Its 22 rooms are tastefully furnished (if somewhat small) and service is of a high standard. There's a sauna and a small fitness centre, and a well-regarded gourmet restaurant. Check out the photos of famous guests in the lobby.

our pick Hotel Stary (Map p170; ☎ 012 424 3400; www .stary.hotel.com.pl; ul Szczepańska 5; s/d/ste 700/850/950zł; ✄ ✄ 🖵 ⴵ ⴵ) Setting new standards for accommodation in Poland, the 53-room Stary is housed in an 18th-century aristocratic residence that exudes charm. But the only thing 'old' about this place is its name and the building it is in. The fabrics are all natural, the bathroom surfaces Italian marble and the free internet service ultra highspeed.

Hotel Copernicus (Map p170; ☎ 012 424 3400; www .hotel.com.pl/copernicus/; ul Kanonicza 16; s 700zł, d 850-950zł, ste from 1200zł; ✄ ✄ 🖵) Nestled in two beautifully restored buildings in one of Kraków's most picturesque and atmospheric streets, the 29-room Copernicus is arguably the city's finest and most luxurious hotel. The rooftop terrace, with spectacular views over Wawel, and the swimming pool, accommodated in a medieval vaulted brick cellar, add to the hotel's allure.

Kazimierz
BUDGET

Budget accommodation has finally arrived in Kazimierz as it grows in popularity as both a sightseeing and nightlife district.

our pick Goodbye Lenin (Map p187; ☎ 012 421 2030; www.goodbyelenin.pl; ul Berka Joselewicza 23; dm 30-60zł, d 120-140zł; ℗ ✄ 🖵) Just about our favourite hostel in Kraków, this 70-bed place with a cheeky Polish People's Republic theme and

Mediterranean colours is down a quiet street off ul Starowiślna. Most dorm rooms have four to six beds and we love the spacious downstairs lounge with a popular bar and pool table. The kitchen is open forever and tea and coffee are gratis.

Secret Garden (Map p187; ☎ 012 430 5445; ul Skawińska 7; dm 45zł, s/d/tr/q 80/120/165/200zł; ⊠ ⊠ ⊡) This 18-room hostel in Western Kazimierz has three wings decorated according to different themes – films, fruits and flowers – and 18 bright and colourful rooms. The only drawback is that there are no bathrooms en suite.

Tournet Guest Rooms (Tournet Pokoje Gościnne; Map p187; ☎ 012 292 0088; www.accommodation.krakow.pl; ul Miodowa 7; s 100-140zł, d 120-180zł, tr 220zł) This is an excellent-value neat pension in the centre of Kazimierz, offering simple but comfortable and quiet rooms. The bathrooms, however, are tiny. Check-in time is noon to 10pm.

Nathan's Villa Hostel (Map p187; ☎ 012 422 3545; www.nathansvilla.com; ul Św Agnieszki 1; dm 50-65zł, d/tw 160/180zł; ℗ ⊠ ⊡) The doyen of modern hostels in Kraków, Nathan's is located roughly halfway between the Old Town and Kazimierz. Comfy rooms (dorms have four to 10 beds), sparkling bathrooms, free laundry, a cellar bar and back garden with barbecue, and friendly, professional staff make this place a big hit with budget travellers.

MIDRANGE

Kazimierz has a small selection of interesting midrange hotels, some with a distinct Jewish flavour. It's a pleasant, peaceful and now fashionable place to stay.

Hotel Klezmer-Hois (Map p187; ☎ 012 411 1245; www.klezmer.pl; ul Szeroka 6; s 220-260zł, d 280-320zł, apt 500zł) This uniquely stylish little hotel has been restored to its prewar, Jewish character, and has 10 airy rooms, each decorated differently, though the cheaper rooms do not have private bathrooms. There's a good-quality Jewish restaurant (see p202) on site, as well as an art gallery, and live music every evening.

Hotel Kazimierz (Map p187; ☎ 012 421 6629; www.hk.com.pl; ul Miodowa 16; s €60-65, d €75-80, tr €90-95; ℗ ⊠ ⑤) This friendly inn in the heart of the Jewish quarter has 35 simple but modern, comfortable rooms above a popular restaurant. We love the stained glass.

Hotel Alef (Map p187; 012 424 3131; www.alef.pl; ul Św Agnieszki 5; s/d/tr €59/77/92; ℗ ⊠ ⊡) ul Szeroka (Map p187; ☎ 012 421 3870; ul Szeroka 17) This hotel

within the shadow of Wawel has 45 large, charming rooms, furnished with genuine antiques and delightful paintings. The tiny (four-room) branch at ul Szeroka has a good Jewish restaurant.

Hotel Eden (Map p187; ☎ 012 430 6565; www.hoteleden.pl; ul Ciemna 15; s/d/tr/ste 260/350/430/550zł; ⊠ ⊡ ⑤) Located in three meticulously restored 15th-century town houses, the Eden has 27 comfortable rooms and comes complete with a pub, a sauna and the only mikvah (traditional Jewish bath) in Kraków. Kosher meals are available on request.

EATING

By Polish standards, Kraków is a food paradise. The Old Town is tightly packed with gastronomic venues, serving a wide range of international cuisines and catering for every pocket.

Kraków has plenty of budget eateries called *jadłodajnia* (something like 'diner') and offer hearty Polish home-style meals at very low cost. Cheap takeaway fare can be found along ul Grodzka, while better-quality restaurants line the streets away from the main square. Kazimierz has a number of small restaurants, some of which offer Jewish-style cuisine and are worth the walk.

Old Town & Surrounds

BUDGET

Bar Smaczny (Map p170; ☎ 012 422 4220; ul Św Tomasza 24; mains 3.20-8.20zł; ⏲ 11am-7pm Mon-Fri, noon-5pm Sat & Sun) This simple place northeast of the Rynek claims to have the best *pierogis* (dumplings) in Kraków and we'll vouch for that assertion. There's a good choice of vegetarian ones.

Jadłodajnia (Map p170; ☎ 012 421 1444; ul Sienna 11; mains 3.60-10zł; ⏲ 10am-5pm Mon-Fri, 10am-3pm Sat) Probably the best of the old-style restaurants serving home-style food, this place dates back to 1934. Savoury soups and meat-and-potato dishes prevail.

Bar Wegetariański Vega (Map p170; ☎ 012 422 3494; www.vegarestauracja.com.pl in Polish; ul Św Gertrudy 7; mains 5-12zł; ⏲ 9am-9pm) Vega is an excellent, exclusively vegetarian place, serving tasty *pierogi*, crepes, tofu and salads in bright and pleasant surrounds.

U Babci Maliny (Map p170; ☎ 012 421 4818; www.kuchniaubabcimaliny.pl in Polish; ul Szpitalna 38; mains 5-14zł; ⏲ 11am-10pm) ul Sławkowska (Map p170; ☎ 012 422 7601; ul Sławkowska 17) 'At Granny Raspberry's' is a godsend for travellers on a budget, with hearty

Polish staples at giveaway prices served in an overwrought boudoir-like basement eatery. Love the boas and the chandelier.

Greenway (Map p170; ☎ 012 431 1027; www.greenway .pl; ul Mikołajska 14; mains 8-12.50zł; ⏰ 10am-10pm Mon-Fri, 11am-9pm Sat & Sun) Some of Kraków's best-value vegetarian and vegan fare is on offer at Green Way, with veggie burgers, enchiladas and salads on the menu.

Taco Mexicano (Map p170; ☎ 012 421 5441; ul Poselska 20; mains 12-16zł) If you hanker after something from 'south of the border' and Slovakian bread dumplings is not what you had in mind, this cantina is for you. It's popular with locals and visitors alike, and serves fairly authentic enchiladas, burritos and tacos.

Sakana Sushi Bar (Map p170; ☎ 012 429 3086; www .sakana.pl; ul Sławkowska 5/7; mains 9-30zł; ⏰ noon-11pm Mon-Sat, 1-10pm Sun) With sushi and sashimi floating around in little boats that loop around a 'canal' encircling a communal figure-eight table, the Sakana just has to be different. There's tempura too and some unusual soups.

Gruzińskie Chaczapuri (☎ 0501 223 183; www .chaczapuri.pl in Polish; mains 10-20zł; ⏰ 9am-midnight) ul Floriańska (Map p170; ul Floriańska 26) ul Grodzka (Map p170; ul Grodzka 3) If you have a hankering for something a little different, this cheap and cheerful chain of Georgian restaurants with five branches in Kraków serves up grills, salads and steaks and, the house speciality: cheese pie.

MIDRANGE

Gospoda CK Dezerter (Map p170; ☎ 012 422 7931; www .ck-dezerter.pl in Polish; ul Bracka 6; mains 12-25zł; ⏰ 9am-11pm Sun-Thu, 9am-midnight Fri & Sat) Dezerter is a pleasantly decorated place that focuses on traditional, meaty Galician specialities, including Austrian and Hungarian cuisine.

Smak Ukraiński (Map p170; ☎ 012 421 9294; www .ukrainska.pl; ul Kanonicza 15; mains 15-25zł; ⏰ noon-10pm) Hidden away below one of Kraków's most attractive streets, this little place presents authentic Ukrainian dishes in a cosy little cellar decorated with predictably folksy flair. Expect lots of dumplings, borscht (the Ukrainian variety) and waiters in waistcoats.

Indus Tandoori (Map p170; ☎ 012 423 2282; ul Sławkowska 13/15; mains 10-33zł; ⏰ 10am-midnight Mon-Fri, 10am-10pm Sat & Sun) By all accounts the best Indian restaurant in town, the Indus serves curries, tandoori dishes and *thalis* (metal trays with a selection of tasty treats), in a long narrow dining room.

Orient Ekspres (Map p170; ☎ 012 422 6672; www .orient-ekspres.krakow.pl; ul Stolarska 13; mains 15-33zł; ⏰ noon-11pm) Hercule Poirot might be surprised to find this elegant eatery here, well off the route of its railway namesake. The food is a mix of international dishes, served with wine by the glass. Mellow music, candlelight and the choo-choo-train theme make it a good place for a romantic tête-à-tête.

Jama Michalika (Map p170; ☎ 012 422 1561; www .jamamichalika.pl; ul Floriańska 45; mains 10-40zł; ⏰ 9am-10pm) If these walls could talk… Established in 1895, this cavernous place was traditionally a hang-out for writers, painters, actors and other artistic types and the birthplace of the Młoda Polska movement. Today it's a grand, Art Nouveau restaurant with a very green interior and lots of theatrical etchings adorning the walls. The traditional Polish food is reasonable value but the compulsory coat-check, and pay toilets are an annoying extra expense.

Balaton (Map p170; ☎ 012 422 0469; www.balaton .krakow.pl; ul Grodzka 37; mains 21-32zł; ⏰ noon-10pm) Balaton, with its shabby décor and uninspired wait staff, may not look inviting, but it's a very popular place for simple Hungarian food and seems to fill up quickly every night.

Nostalgia (Map p170; ☎ 012 425 4260; www.nostalgia .krakow.pl; ul Karmelicka 10; mains 17-37zł; ⏰ noon-11pm) A refined version of the traditional Polish eatery, Nostalgia features a fireplace, overhead timber beams, uncrowded tables and courteous service. Wrap yourself around Russian dumplings, pork loins in green pepper sauce, or veggie options such as potato pancakes. In warm weather there's an outdoor dining area.

Miód Malina (Map p170; ☎ 012 430 0411; ul Grodzka 40; mains 23-45zł; ⏰ noon-11pm) The charmingly named 'Honey Raspberry' serves 'enlightened' Polish dishes in colourful surrounds. Grab a window seat and order the forest mushrooms in cream and any of the duck or veal dishes.

Casa della Pizza (Map p170; ☎ 012 421 6498; Mały Rynek 2; mains 14-48zł; ⏰ 10am-late) As the name would suggest, this is an amenable and unpretentious place in the Little Sq, away from the bulk of the tourist traffic. It has a very long menu of pizza and pasta dishes and a lovely terrace with perfect views of the Mariacki towers. The downstairs bar section is the Arabian-styled Shisha Club (www.shisha .pl), serving Middle Eastern food.

Cherubino (Map p170; ☎ 012 429 4007; www .cherubino.pl; ul Św Tomasza 15; mains 22-49zł; ⏰ noon-midnight Mon-Sat, noon-11pm Sun) Cherubino, which bills itself as a restaurant and winery, offers lovely Italian dishes amid a charming, artsy interior. The antique carriages filling up the room are wonderful.

TOP END

Paese (Map p170; ☎ 012 421 6273; ul Poselska 24; mains 28-66zł; ☺ noon-11pm) The name hints at it but the Moor's head with a bandana confirms it: this is a Corsican, not a French restaurant. The thatched-cottage décor is comfortable and the dishes – duck in lavender sauce, veal with rosemary, saddle of venison – well chosen and redolent of the maquis. Fish and vegetarian options are also on the menu.

Metropolitan (Map p170; ☎ 012 421 9803; www .metropolitan-krakow.com; ul Sławkowska 3; mains 31-79zł; ☺ 7.30am-midnight Mon-Sat, 7.30am-10pm Sun) Attached to the Hotel Saski, the Metropolitan is a snazzy fusion restaurant with a distressed Mediterranean look to it. It has nostalgic B&W photos of international locales plastering the walls and is a great place for breakfast. It also serves pasta, grills and steaks, and more ambitious things like honey and orange roasted duck leg.

our pick Wentzl (Map p170; ☎ 012 429 5712; www .wentzl.pl; Rynek Główny 21; mains 53-66zł; ☺ 1-11pm) To our mind Kraków's finest restaurant, this eatery dating back to 1792 and perched high above the main market square has timbered ceilings above you, Oriental carpets and fine oil paintings all around. The food is sublime – foie gras, chanterelles in cream, duck marinated in żubrówka (bison grass vodka) – and service of a predictably high standard.

Cyrano de Bergerac (Map p170; ☎ 012 411 7288; ul Sławkowska 26; mains 40-90zł; ☺ noon-midnight) One of Kraków's top eateries, this restaurant serves fine, authentic French cuisine in one of the most beautiful cellars in the city. Artwork and tapestries add to the romance and in warmer months there's seating in a covered courtyard.

Kazimierz
BUDGET

Momo Bar (Map p187; ☎ 06096 85775; ul Dietla 49; mains 4-13zł; ☺ 11am-8pm) Vegans will cross the doorstep of this restaurant with relief – the majority of the menu is completely animal-free. The space is decorated with Indian craft pieces, and serves up subcontinental soups, stuffed pancakes and rice dishes, with a great range

of cakes. The *momo* (Tibetan dumplings; 12.50zł) are worth ordering.

MIDRANGE

Chłopskie Jadło (Map p187; ☎ 012 421 8520; ul Św Agnieszki 1; mains 18-55zł; ☺ 10am-10pm Sun-Thu, 10am-midnight Fri & Sat) Old Town (Map p170; ☎ 012 429 5157; ul Św Jana 3) This place, a short walk south of Wawel, looks like a rustic country inn somewhere at the crossroads in medieval Poland, and serves up traditional Polish 'peasant grub' (as its name says). Live folk music is performed here on Friday and Saturday, and seating in antique sleighs adds to the rustic atmosphere. We love the *żurek* (sour rye) soup in a bread loaf.

Kuchnia i Wino (Map p187; ☎ 012 430 6710; www .kuchniaiwino.eu; ul Józefa 13; mains 27-49zł; ☺ noon-10pm) The name – 'Cuisine and Wine' – may not suggest this bistro has a lot of imagination, but just try one of the delightfully inspired Mediterranean dishes on the short menu such as veal with basil. We love the sky-painted ceiling and the Tuscan tones.

A number of restaurants in and around ul Szeroka offer Jewish-inspired dishes such as *czulent* (bean casserole with beef and vegetables), *knyshe* (aka *knish*, a dumpling with the filling of potato, ground meat, sauerkraut, onions or buckwheat groats) and stuffed gooseneck. The best of the lot is **Dawno Temu na Kazimierzu** (Once upon a Time in Kazimierz; Map p187; ☎ 012 421 2117; ul Szeroka 17; mains 18-34zł; ☺ 10am-midnight), a blast from the past with sewing machines on the tables and old Jewish shop signs outside. You'll find similar dishes, décor and atmosphere at the following two places, which also feature live *klezmer* music nightly at about 8pm.

Café Alef (Map p187; ☎ 012 421 3870; www.alef.pl; ul Szeroka 17; mains 10-48zł; ☺ 10am-midnight)

Klezmer-Hois (Map p187; ☎ 012 411 1245; ul Szeroka 6; mains 16-46zł; ☺ 10am-9.30pm)

DRINKING

You'll be spoiled for choice when heading out for a drink in Kraków. The Old Town alone supposedly counts 400 bars and pubs, and ul Szewska, running west from the main market square, is a particularly fruitful hunting ground. Some offer snacks or meals, but most are just watering holes, many in vaulted cellars. For teetotallers and/or those in search of something hot, there are plenty of cafés and teahouses around too.

Pubs & Bars

OLD TOWN

Nic Nowego (Map p170; ☎ 012 421 6188; ul Św Krzyża 15; ☽ 7am-3am Mon-Fri, 10am-3am Sat & Sun) 'Nothing New', run by a genuine Paddy, is a 'modern Irish café-bar' and a welcome addition to the drinking scene in Kraków. It's a bright, modern place with a long bar, a great atmosphere and good food.

CK Browar (Map p170; ☎ 012 429 2505; ul Podwale 6/7; ☽ 9am-2pm Sun-Thu, 9am-4pm Fri & Sat) Serious tipplers will head for this microbrewery with its own cavernous drinking hall, and order the home brew in 3L tubes a metre high, which the wait staff bring to your table and fix onto special taps.

Ciemna Club (Map p170; ☎ 0692 651 311; ul Krowoderska 8; ☽ 6pm-2am Sun-Thu, 6pm-5am Fri & Sat) This is Kraków's premier gay bar with facilities intended for those seriously OFB (out for business). Ring and await appraisal/approval; this is Poland, after all.

Pod Papugami (Map p170; ☎ 012 422 8299; ul Św Jana 18; ☽ 1pm-2am) 'Under the Parrots' is a vaguely 'Irish' cellar pub decorated with old motorcycles, street signs, musical instruments and other junk. It's good to escape to, with its pool table and tunnel-like maze of rooms.

Piwnica Pod Złotą Pipą (Map p170; ☎ 012 421 9466; ul Floriańska 30; ☽ noon-midnight) The 'Pub under the Golden Pipes' is another inviting cellar bar. It's more sedate than most such places, better suited to conversation than listening to music.

Black Gallery (Map p170; ☎ 012 423 0030; ul Mikołajska 24; ☽ noon-6am Mon-Sat, 2pm-6am Sun) Underground pub-cum-nightclub with a modern aspect: split levels, exposed steel frame lighting and a metallic bar. It really gets going after midnight.

U Louisa (Map p170; ☎ 012 617 0222; Rynek Główny 13; ☽ 11am-1am Sun-Wed, 11am-4am Thu-Sun) This stylish pub is conveniently located below the main square as you enter from ul Grodzka. Big screens to watch sports and wi-fi throughout rounds out the picture.

KAZIMIERZ

Singer Café (Map p187; ☎ 012 292 0622; ul Estery 20; ☽ 9am-4am Sun-Thu, 9am-5am Fri & Sat) Louche hang-out of choice among the Kazimierz cognoscenti, this laid-back café-bar has nothing to do with music per se (is that Serbian pop we hear in the background?) but is a nod to all the sewing machines around. Great place.

Le Scandale (Map p187; ☎ 012 430 6855; Plac Nowy 9; ☽ 8am-3am) Smooth drinking hole with low black leather couches, ambient lighting and a gleaming well-stocked bar. Full of mellow drinkers sampling the extensive cocktail list.

Propaganda (Map p187; ☎ 012 292 0402; ul Miodowa 20; ☽ 11am-3am Sun-Thu, 11am-5am Fri & Sat) This is another one of those places full of communist nostalgia, but so real are the banners and mementoes here that we almost started singing the 'Internationale'. Killer cocktails.

Cafés & Teahouses

Wiśniowy Sad (Map p170; ☎ 012 430 2111; ul Grodzka 33; ☽ 11am-11pm Mon-Fri, 11am-midnight Sat & Sun) With its old furniture, lacy tablecloths and scattered antiques, the 'Cherry Orchard' evokes the world of Chekhov and serves Russian-style tea and pastries. Sip your Darjeeling to live piano recitals at 8pm from Thursday to Sunday.

Café Camelot (Map p170; ☎ 012 421 0123; ul Św Tomasza 17; ☽ 9am-midnight) For coffee and cake, try this genteel haven hidden around an obscure street corner in the Old Town. Its cosy rooms are cluttered with lace-covered candle-lit tables, and a quirky collection of wooden figurines featuring spiritual or folkloric scenes.

Ciasteczka z Krakowa (Map p187; ☎ 012 428 2890; ul Stradomska 19; ☽ 9am-9pm Mon-Sat, 10am-8pm Sun) This bakery-cum-café has some of the best cakes and pastries in Poland.

Café Bunkier (Map p170; ☎ 012 431 0585; Plac Szczepański 3a, ☽ 9am-1am Mon-Thu, 9am-2am Fri-Sun) The 'Bunker' is a wonderful café with a positively enormous glassed-in terrace tacked onto the Bunkier Sztuki (Art Bunker), a cutting-edge gallery northwest of the Rynek. It's one of the few modern buildings in the Old Town and looks just like its name suggests. Enter from Planty.

Demmers Teahouse (Map p170; ☎ 012 423 1660; ul Kanonicza 21; ☽ 11am-7pm) An outlet of the famous Viennese *teehaus*, this is the best place in Kraków for a cup of tea. It sells 130 varieties, many of which can be tried in an intimate tearoom in the 13th-century cellar of this lovely building with sgraffito.

ENTERTAINMENT

Kraków has a lively cultural life, particularly in theatre, music and visual arts, and there are numerous annual festivals. The comprehensive Polish and English monthly magazine *Karnet* (www.karnet.krakow.pl; 4zł), available at any branch of the tourist office (see p167), lists almost every event in the city.

Another free what's-on monthly magazine, *This Month in Kraków* (www.cracow .pl), has less-detailed coverage. The bimonthly *Kraków In Your Pocket* (www.inyourpocket .com), which has a cover price of 5zł but is often free at tourist-information offices, hotels and bars, has excellent coverage of entertainment, including bars, pubs and clubs.

In addition to the websites of Cracow Life (www.cracow-life.com) and Krakow Post (www.krakowpost.com), excellent online sources of information are www.krakow nightlife.com and, for club events and parties, www.kr-nightlife.pl and www.where2b.org.

Nightclubs

There are quite a number of nightclubs and discos in and around the Old Town. The following places are the best and most popular at the moment.

Rdza (Map p170; ☎ 06003 95541; www.rdza.pl; ul Bracka 3/5; ⏰ 7pm-6am) This basement club attracts some of Kraków's more sophisticated clubbers with its Polish house and exposed brick walls and comfy sofas. The more consistent door policy of late is welcomed.

7 Club (Map p170; ☎ 012 631 9500; Św Filipa 7; ⏰ 6am-2am Sun-Thu, 6am-5am Fri & Sat) Still hanging in there after all these years, Kraków's oldest gay venue is a dance club at the weekend, with strip and drag shows to boot (and we're *not* talking a dress code here).

El Sol (Map p170; ☎ 012 633 8835; www.elsol-krakow .pl; ul Batorego 1; ⏰ 7pm-midnight Sun-Thu, 7pm-3am Fri & Sat) This Latino club reverberates to the sound of salsa, merengue, samba and bossa nova nightly.

Prozak (Map p170; ☎ 012 429 1128; www.prozak.pl; Plac Dominikański 6; ⏰ 7pm-4am Sun-Thu, 7pm-6am Fri & Sat) A legend in its own lifetime, this nightlife giant was once celebrated for luring Kraków's rich and beautiful into its labyrinth of passageways, nooks and crannies. It still draws in the clubbing faithful, but too may (drunken) foreigners have scared away the local talent.

Cień (Map p170; ☎ 012 422 2177; www.cienklub.pl; ul Św Jana 15; ⏰ 8pm-5am Tue-Thu, 8pm-7am Fri & Sat) The enormous 'Shadow' attracts a perfect (as in fake tans) crowd with house sounds produced by DJs fresh in from Ibiza and great décor. A tough door policy will keep half your mates out.

Music Bar (Map p170; ☎ 012 422 2546; ul Szewska 9; ⏰ 11am-1am) Not for serious clubbers (you know who you are), this complex, with a large bar in a covered courtyard and the rather chichi Light Box Gallery (open 6pm to 4am Thursday to Sunday) up the glass stairs, mostly attracts a young crowd.

Grungy joint **Łubu-Dubu** (Map p170; ☎ 012 423 0521; www.lubududu.pl; 4th fl, ul Wielopole 15; ⏰ 4pm-2am Sun-Thu, 6pm-4am Fri & Sat) is an echo of the past, from the garish colours to the collection of objects from 1970s Poland. In the same building you'll also find the erstwhile gay **Kitsch** (Map p170; ☎ 012 422 5299; www.kitsch.pl), Kraków's popular last port of call, on the 2nd floor and the more trendy and musically risk-taking **Caryca** (Map p170; ☎ 012 431 0863) on the 1st floor.

Jazz

Kraków has a lively jazz scene and a number of clubs have live music (tickets around 20zł) year-round.

Jazz Club U Muniaka (Map p170; ☎ 012 423 1205; ul Floriańska 3; tickets 20zł; ⏰ 6.30pm-2am) Housed in a fine cellar, this is one of the best-known jazz outlets in Poland, the brainchild of saxophonist Janusz Muniak, who often performs here. There are concerts most nights from 9.30pm.

Harris Piano Jazz Bar (Map p170; ☎ 012 421 5741; www.harris.krakow.pl in Polish; Rynek Główny 28; ⏰ 9am-2am May-Oct, 1pm-2am Nov-Apr) Another active jazz haunt, Harris hosts jazz and blues bands most days of the week except Sunday at 9pm.

Pieć'Art (Map p170; ☎ 012 429 6425; www.piecart.pl in Polish; ul Szewska 12; ⏰ 1pm-3am) This cosy cellar club tends to stage acoustic jazz on Wednesday and irregular gigs on other days.

Piano Rouge (Map p170; ☎ 012 431 0333; www .thepianorouge.com; Rynek Główny 46; ⏰ noon-3am) This sumptuous jazz club and restaurant, in a cellar on the north side of the main market square, is decked out with classic sofas, ornate lampshades and billowing lengths of colourful silk. Live jazz every night at 9.30pm or 10pm.

Classical Music & Opera

Classical music concerts are staged in venues throughout Kraków in the summer months but especially at Polonia House (p198) and the Church of SS Peter & Paul (p185).

During the rest of the year the **Filharmonia Krakowska** (Kraków Philharmonic; Map p170; ☎ 012 422 4312; www.filharmonia.krakow.pl; ul Zwierzyniecka 1; ⏰ box office noon-7pm Tue-Fri, 1hr before performance Sat & Sun) is home to one of the best orchestras in the country.

The **Opera Krakowska** (Kraków Opera; ☎ 012 628 8101; www.opera.krakow.pl) performs at the **Teatr im J Słowackiego** (below) as there's no proper opera house in Kraków.

Cinemas

Kraków counts just under 20 cinemas, with many of them in the centre. The cinemas that may have some art-house and quality mainstream movies on their programme include **Kino Mikro** (Map p165; ☎ 012 634 2897; www.kinomikro .pl in Polish; ul Lea 5), **Kino Paradox** (Map p165; ☎ 012 430 0025; www.cmjordan.krakow.pl; ul Krowoderska 8) and the cinema at the **Rotunda Cultural Centre** (Map p165; ☎ 012 634 3412; www.rotunda.pl; ul Oleandry 1).

Theatre

Kraków has just over a dozen theatres and is second only to Warsaw in that department. **Cricoteka** (Map p165; ☎ 012 422 8332; www.cricoteka .com.pl; ul Kanonicza 5; ☷ 10am-2pm Mon-Fri 10am-2pm Wed, Fri & Sat, 2-6pm Tue & Thu) Cricoteka is the archive that documents the avant-garde (and now defunct) Cricot 2 theatre, created in 1955 by Tadeusz Kantor and the city's best-known theatre outside the national borders. Theatre buffs may be interested in visiting this place while the museum that will hold the documents is completed in Podgórze.

Stary Teatr w Krakowie (Kraków Old Theatre; Map p170; ☎ 012 422 4040; www.stary-teatr.krakow.pl; ul Jagiellońska 1; ☷ box office 9am-5pm Mon-Fri, 9am-1pm Sat) This is the best-known (and most beautiful) city theatre and has attracted the cream of the city's actors.

Teatr im J Słowackiego (Julius Słowacki Theatre; Map p170; ☎ 012 422 4022; www.slowacki.krakow.pl; Plac Św Ducha 4; ☷ box office 9am-5pm Mon-Fri, to 7pm performance days) This important theatre focuses on Polish classics and large-scale productions. It's in a large and opulent building (1893) that's patterned on the Paris Opera, and is southwest of Rynek Główny.

Teatr Groteska (Map p170; ☎ 012 633 3762; www .groteska.pl; ul Skarbowa 2; ☷ box office 8am-noon & 3-5pm Mon-Fri & 1hr before performance) The 'Grotesque Theatre' stages mostly puppet shows and is especially known for its creepy, wordless version of The Golem, the story of a Frankenstein-like clay creature brought to life by a Prague rabbi.

Scena STU (Map p165; ☎ 012 422 2744; www.scenastu .com.pl in Polish; Aleja Krasińskiego 16/18; ☷ box office 9am-7pm Mon-Fri & 2hr before performance Sat & Sun) The 'STU Stage' started in the 1970s as a politically involved student theatre and was immediately successful. Today it is a solid professional troupe performing avant-garde plays.

SHOPPING

Kraków's Old Town has a vast array of shops, selling everything from tacky T-shirts to exquisite crystal glassware, and all within a short walk from the main market square. Ul Grodzka and ul Floriańska are good places to start looking. If you're in a mall mood, the **Galeria Krakowska** (Map p170; ☎ 012 428 9900; www .galeria-krakowska.pl; ul Pawia), next to the train station, has 270 shops.

Antiques

For everything from rust to diamonds check out the two weekend flea markets in Kazimierz. The one on Saturday morning is held in Plac Nowy and the one on Sunday in the Hala Targowa (Market Hall) on ul Grzegórzecka northeast of the Jewish quarter.

Salon Antyków Pasja (Map p170; ☎ 012 429 1096; ul Jagiellońska 9; ☷ 11am-7pm Mon-Fri, 11am-3pm Sat) This is one of the most established antique salons in the Old Town, with clocks, maps and bric-a-brac.

Antykwariat na Kazimierzu (Map p187; ☎ 012 292 6153; ul Meiselsa 17; ☷ 10am-5pm Mon-Fri, 10am-2pm Sat & Sun) In the basement of the Judaica Foundation in Kazimierz, this Aladdin's cave is a jumble of antique china, glass, paintings, books and other assorted schlock.

Art

For a complete listing of art galleries in the city, get a hold of the free flyer Galerie (www.poland-art.com) produced every two months.

Labirynt (Map p170; ☎ 012 292 6080; www.galeria labirynt.and.pl in Polish; 1st fl, ul Floriańska 36; ☷ 10am-7pm Mon-Fri, 10am-3pm Sat) Labirynt No 2 (Map p187; ☎ 012 292 1300; ul Józefa 15; ☷ noon-6pm Mon-Fri, 11am-3pm Sat) The two 'Labyrinths' are more affordable places for art, and show a decent mix of both painting and sculpture.

Jan Fejkiel Gallery (Map p170; ☎ 012 429 1553; www .fejkielgallery.com; ul Grodzka 65; ☷ 11am-7pm Mon-Fri, 11am-3pm Sat) Fejkiel has one of the best collections of contemporary prints and drawings in Kraków.

Starmach Gallery (Map p165; ☎ 012 656 4317; www.starmach.com.pl; ul Węgierska 5; ☷ 11am-6pm Mon-Fri) One of the most prestigious art galleries in town, Starmach has renowned contemporary painting.

KRAKÓW

Galerie d'Art Naïf (Gallery of Naive Art; Map p187; ☎ 012 421 0637; http://artnaive.sky.pl; ul Józefa 11; ⌚ 11am-5pm Mon-Fri, 11am-3pm Sat) This Kazimierz gallery exhibits and sells the work of some of Poland's most celebrated Naive painters and sculptors, and folk artists.

Andrzej Mleczko Gallery (Map p170; ☎ 012 421 7104; www.mleczko.pl; ul Św Jana 14; ⌚ 11am-7pm Mon-Fri, 10am-3pm Sat) The gallery displays and sells comic drawings and other articles by Poland's most popular satirical cartoonist, Andrzej Mleczko (see boxed text, opposite).

Galeria Plakatu (Poster Gallery; Map p170; ☎ 012 421 2640; www.cracowpostergallery.com; ul Stolarska 8-10; ⌚ noon-5pm Mon-Fri, 11am-4pm Sat) Poland has always excelled in the art of poster making and this is the city's largest and best choice of posters, created by Poland's most prominent poster makers.

Gifts & Souvenirs

An obvious place to look for gifts and souvenirs (not always of the highest quality) is the arcaded **Cloth Hall** (p181), which houses dozens of little shops selling jewellery, wooden chess sets, glass, textiles, T-shirts and other reasonably priced items.

Krosno (Map p170; ☎ 012 421 5496; Plac Mariacki 1; ⌚ 10am-7pm Mon-Fri, 10am-3pm Sat) This small shop sells an attractive range of glassware made by Poland's famous Krosno factory.

Mikołajczyki Amber (Map p170; ☎ 012 422 3696; ul Kanoniczna 22; ⌚ 9am-9pm Mon-Sat, 9am-8pm Sun) Branch of a chain selling 'Baltic gold', Poland's most treasured semiprecious material. Unlike some amber shops, Mikołajczyki Amber includes a certificate of quality with each purchase.

Galeria Bukowski (Map p170; ☎ 012 433 8855; ul Sienna 1; ⌚ 10am-7pm Mon-Fri, 10am-6pm Sat) This unbearably cute shop specialises in *miś pluszowy* (teddy bears) of all shapes, sizes, hues and descriptions.

Blazko Jewellery Art Gallery (Map p187; ☎ 012 430 6731; Józefa 11; ⌚ 11am-7pm Mon-Fri, 11am-3pm Sat) Exceptionally well-designed and -crafted baubles from a young Kazimierz-based jeweller.

Sporting Goods

If you're going to play the game, you'll need the kit.

Grappa.pl (Map p187; ☎ 012 421 1778; www.grappa .pl in Polish; ul Dajwór 25; ⌚ 10.04am-6.04pm Mon-Fri, 10.04am-3.04pm Sat) This affable and helpful shop stocks everything you'll need to start hiking, trekking or climbing.

GETTING THERE & AWAY

Air

John Paul II International Airport (☎ 012 295 5800; www.lotnisko-balice.pl) is in Balice, about 11km west of the city. The only domestic flights from here are to Warsaw (up to 10 a day), which you can reach more cheaply centre to centre by train, and Gdańsk (twice daily). Kraków has direct international flight connections with up to four dozen mostly European cities including Dublin, Frankfurt, London, Paris, Rome and Vienna. There are also flights to Chicago (daily) and New York (twice weekly).

LOT (Map p170; ☎ 0801 703 703; ul Basztowa 15; ⌚ 9am-6pm Mon-Fri, 9am-3pm Sat) makes reservations and issues tickets.

Bus

The modern bus terminal is behind the city's main train station, Kraków Główny, just northeast of the Old Town. Travel by bus is particularly advisable to places like Zakopane (16zł, 2½ hours) as it's considerably shorter and faster than by train, and fast PKS buses go there roughly every half-hour. Two private companies, **Trans Frej** (www.trans-frej.com.pl) and **Szwagropol** (www.szwagropol.pl), also run buses to Zakopane, which are marginally cheaper and much faster (15zł, 1¾ hours). Tickets for Trans-Frej are available from **Waweltur** (Map p170; ☎ 012 422 1921; www.waweltur.com.pl; ul Pawia 8; ⌚ 8am-7pm Mon-Fri, 8am-2pm Sat); for Szwagropol, tickets are sold by **Centrum Turystyki** (Map p170; ☎ 012 422 2904; ul Worcella 1) opposite the train station. Both also go to Nowy Sącz (16zł) and Nowy Targ (14zł).

There are around six daily PKS departures to Częstochowa (15zł, three hours) and hourly ones to Oświęcim (8zł, 1½ hours). Other destinations include up to five buses a day to Lublin (35zł, 4½ hours), six to Zamość (21zł to 35zł, four to five hours) and 10 to Cieszyn (15zł, two hours) at the Czech border. There are also up to four buses a day to Warsaw (38zł to 43zł, five to 5½ hours). Other destinations are better served by train.

There are plenty of international buses run by **Eurolines** (www.eurolinespolska.com.pl), including those to Amsterdam (269zł, 20½ hours), Budapest (100zł, 7½ hours), London (349zł, 27 hours), Munich (231zł, 19 hours), Paris (349zł, 24 hours), Prague (115zł, 10 hours), Riga (194zł, 20 hours), Rome (350zł, 25 hours) and Vienna (130zł, 10½ hours).

NOT FROM THE DRAWING BORED

Andrzej Mleczko is Poland's foremost satirical cartoonist. His work appears regularly in the national media, including *Polityka*, Poland's biggest-selling news weekly. He lives in Kraków.

Local boy? I was born in Tarnobrzeg near Rzeszów in what we call 'Polska C' [small towns and villages in rural Poland]. I came to Kraków in 1967 to study architecture.

So a native by now then... Yes, but it took a long time. People here are very conservative by nature. They say that the only true Cracovian is one whose grandfather owned a *kamienica* (town house) on Rynek Główny!

Architecture to satire... How did that happen? I drew from the age of four and should have gone to the art academy. But when I applied, they examined my drawings and said as politely as they could that they were too 'mannerist'. I had to go where my drawing was needed, where it could be put to use.

Did you just wake up one day and decide to be funny? No, it just emerged. There wasn't one single event. But when I was 12 I sent some of my drawings in to a children's radio programme. 'Your drawing is very good,' said the show's moderator, 'but why are the pictures so sad?' This was an excellent review as it made me look at the way I did things.

How different was pursuing your line of work under the old régime? There was relative freedom under [Communist party secretary Edward] Gierek and you did as much as you could get away with. I could draw, say, [then Soviet leader] Brezhnev with a funny moustache as long as I did it in a polite, almost praising sort of way. The year under martial law was different. Artists boycotted the media.

Has the humour changed? Humour never changes – only reality does. The years since 1989 have affected the topics we laugh at, not the humour itself.

Some of your cartoons are a bit, well, language dependent, no? Not necessarily. Lots of my cartoons are without captions. Many have sexual references; everyone understands sexual eroticism and there's not much difference to it around the world. And some have little text. A nun being pursued by a baby penguin shouting 'Mama!' The funniest cartoon is still a man, a pavement and a banana peel.

Is there anything especially Polish about you humour? There seems to be a lot on politics, religion and sex. (Laughter) These are pretty universal themes! I just do what is in my head at the time. I just can't really analyse it like that. I guess that will have to be done after my death!

I can't live without... My work room at the lower end of ul Grodzka and particularly my table. I envy people who can draw anywhere.

One sight a visitor to Kraków cannot miss is... The metaphysical stained-glass windows in the Basilica of St Francis by Wyspiański. They're wonderful.

Information and tickets are available from Waweltur as well as **Jordan** (Map p170; ☎ 012 393 5266; www.jordan.pl; ☼ 8am-6pm Mon-Fri, 9am-3pm Sat) in the bus terminal. Check the website www.eurolinespolska.com.pl for the latest prices and timetable information.

Train

The lovely Kraków Główny (Kraków Central) train station, on the northeastern outskirts of the Old Town, handles all international and most domestic trains. The only other station of any significance is Kraków Płaszów, 4km southeast of the city centre, which operates a few trains that don't call at Kraków Główny. Local trains between the two stations run every 15 to 30 minutes. All trains listed here depart from the central station. Advance tickets for international and domestic trains can be booked directly at the station or from Cracow Tours (p195).

Each day from Kraków, 10 fast trains head for Warsaw (71zł to 89zł, 2¾ hours) and to Wrocław (34zł, 4½ hours). Count on six trains to Poznań (50zł, five to six hours), two to Lublin (40zł to 115zł, five hours) and eight to Gdynia via Gdańsk (105zł, 7¼ hours).

To Częstochowa (31zł, two hours), there are two morning fast trains as well as several afternoon/evening trains. Trains to Katowice (20zł, 1½ hours) run every half-hour to an hour. There are plenty of trains daily to Tarnów (13zł, 1½ hours). A dozen of these trains continue to Rzeszów (19.50zł, 2½ hours). To Oświęcim (11zł, 1½ hours), there are a couple of trains early in the morning and then nothing until the afternoon.

Internationally, there are daily direct trains to Berlin, Bratislava, Bucharest, Budapest, Hamburg, Kyiv, Odesa, Prague and Vienna.

GETTING AROUND
To/From the Airport
The airport can be reached on bus 192 (2.50zł, 40 minutes) from just north of the bus station. It runs once or twice an hour from about 5am to 11.30pm; night bus 602 then kicks in. You can also board the 192 (as well as the less frequent bus 208) at Plac Invalidów on the corner of Aleja Słowackiego and ul Królewska. Bear in mind you will be charged 2.50zł for a large suitcase or backpack.

Balice airport is now linked with Kraków by train (4zł, 20 minutes), which is faster and cheaper than the bus when you consider the additional baggage charge. Trains depart Kraków Główny once or twice an hour between 4am and 11.30pm. From the station at Balice you can walk 300m to the terminal or wait for the shuttle bus, which runs every half-hour.

A taxi between the airport and the city centre should cost about 50zł.

Bicycles
You can rent bicycles from several outfits in Kraków including **Eccentric Bike Tours & Rentals** (Map p170; ☎ 012 430 2034; ul Grodzka 2; per hr/5hr/day 6/25/40zł; ☺ 10am-8pm) in the Old Town and **Dwa Koła** (Two Wheels; Map p187; ☎ 012 421 5785; ul Józefa 5; 3hr/5hr/day 15/20/30zł; ☺ 9am-8pm) in Kazimierz.

Car & Motorcycle
With limited parking, and much of the Old Town a car-free zone, driving in Kraków will be more of a hindrance than a help. If you are travelling by car, the major route into the

city is the A4; note that a 5zł toll is paid when you enter and exit it. The Old Town is closed to traffic, except for access to two guarded car parks on Plac Szczepański (though this is likely to close very soon) and Plac Św Ducha if you can find a space. If not, use one of the guarded car parks in the surrounding area, including those along ul Karmelicka near the Stranger Hostel (Map p165), and ul Powiśle (Map p170) northeast of Wawel. Street parking in the area outside the Old Town, known as 'Zone C', requires special tickets (karta postojowa), which you buy from kiosks, mark with the correct month, day and time, and then display on your windscreen. They cost 3zł for one hour and must be displayed from 10am to 6pm Monday to Friday.

RENTAL
Many of the big international car-rental firms have offices in Kraków including **Hertz** (Map p165; ☎ 012 422 2939; www.hertz.com.pl; Hotel Orbis Cracovia, Aleja Focha 1; ☺ 8am-4pm Mon-Fri, 8am-noon Sat). However, you should get a better deal at one of the local firms that distribute their leaflets around town, including **Joka Rent a Car** (Map p170; ☎ 012 429 6630; www.joka.com.pl; ul Starowiślna 13) next door to the Hotel Pugetów.

Public Transport
Kraków is served by an efficient network of buses and trams that run between 5am and 11pm. Some night buses (which begin with a '6') run later.

Single-journey (2.50zł), one-hour (3.10zł) and one-/two-/three-day (10.40/18.20/25zł) tickets can be bought at street kiosks, and must be validated as soon as you board. Note that a single ticket is also required for bulky luggage. Tickets for night buses are 5zł. Most tourist attractions are in the Old Town or within easy walking distance, so you won't need buses or trams unless you're staying outside the centre.

Taxi
If you need one of Kraków's 3500 cabs, these are some of the better-known companies:
Barbakan Taxi (☎ 012 9661, 0800 404 400)
Euro Taxi (☎ 012 9664)
Express Taxi (☎ 0800 111 111)
Lajkonik Taxi (☎ 012 9628)
Radio Taxi (☎ 012 9696, 0800 500 919)

Małopolska

It's a mystery why Małopolska remains relatively unexplored by international travellers. Pilgrims walk for more than two weeks to pray before the sacred *Black Madonna* painting of Częstochowa, but if they just kept walking they would find a range of surprising attractions, from the quaint to the downright quirky.

This is a region where you can be haunted by a friendly ghost in an underground chalk tunnel, explore the ruins of a castle once connected to another by a sugar-coated corridor, and meet townsfolk who quarrel over who has the right to bake rooster-shaped bread.

While the rest of the continent loudly extols its attributes, this eccentric pocket of Poland is a modest region that quietly polishes its treasures: Renaissance towns, cobblestoned laneways, sidewalk cafés, labyrinthine museums, opulent palaces, alluring castles and primeval forest.

Modern-day Małopolska began to form its complexion centuries ago, and its ancestry is still apparent today. The botanical and zoological interests of 16th-century aristocrats led to the establishment of vast natural estates; today, these are national parks. Ancient trade routes sliced through the region, bringing demographic diversity along with economic prosperity; today there are some 19 ethnic groups among the three million inhabitants. In 1569 the region accounted for almost half the country and now Małopolska is literally 'Little Poland'; it takes up a sizable chunk of the country with 22 districts blanketed over 57 cities and 2630 villages.

Turbulent tides of history, entrenched religious veneration and waves of cultural cosmopolitanism have added colourful layers to the character of Małopolska. The fact that it has maintained its modesty through it all is just another reason to experience it.

HIGHLIGHTS

- Joining throngs of **Black Madonna** (p216) pilgrims in Częstochowa
- Blushing as portraits peer down at you in Kielce's **Palace of the Kraków Bishops** (p218)
- Revelling in the distilled grandeur of **Pieskowa Skała Castle** (p210) in Ojców National Park
- Wishing you had a better phrasebook as you chat to a ghost in the **Chełm Chalk Tunnels** (p248)
- Commenting that 'they don't make them like they used to' at the fairy-tale fantasy of **Krzyżtopór Castle** (p229) in Ujazd
- Wondering why it happened at **Majdanek Extermination Camp** (p237) in Lublin
- Being dwarfed by ancient nature in **Roztocze National Park** (p257)
- Forgetting you're in Poland in the Italian Renaissance town of **Zamość** (p250)

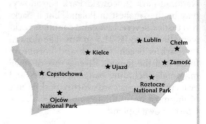

MAŁOPOLSKA

THE KRAKÓW– CZĘSTOCHOWA UPLAND

When Silesia fell to Bohemia in the mid-14th century, King Kazimierz III Wielki (Casimir III the Great, 1333–70) set about fortifying the frontier by building a chain of castles all the way from Kraków to Częstochowa. It is this 100km stretch that comprises the Kraków–Częstochowa Upland (Wyżyna Krakowsko–Częstochowska).

The plan worked; the wall of castles built on hilltops and ridges was never penetrated by the Bohemians. However, the 1655 Swede invasion destroyed many castles and changed the face of the upland. The conflicts of the turbulent 18th century completed the process of castle destruction, leaving some impressive ruins for the 21st-century traveller.

This upland region is also popularly known as the Jura, having been formed from limestone in the Jurassic period some 150 million years ago. Erosion left hundreds of caves and oddly shaped rock formations, which can still be enjoyed in Ojców National Park, most notably the 25m-high Hercules' club pillar at the base of resplendently restored Pieskowa Skała.

An excellent way to explore the upland is by hiking the Trail of the Eagles' Nest (Szlak Orlich Gniazd), which winds 164km from Kraków to Częstochowa past dramatic hills and countless castles. You needn't lug your camping gear – accommodation is never more than a day's walk away. Tourist offices in Kraków and Częstochowa can provide more information.

OJCÓW NATIONAL PARK

Perhaps size doesn't matter after all. Ojców National Park (Ojcowski Park Narodowy) may be the smallest in Poland, but it packs two castles, several caves and countless rock-formations into its 21.5 sq km. The flora in the park is beech, fir, oak and hornbeam forest and the fauna a diverse mix of small mammals including badgers, ermines and beavers. This postcard-worthy park is one of the most beautiful areas of the Kraków–Częstochowa Upland.

Orientation & Information

Most tourist attractions line the road running along the Prądnik River between Ojców and Pieskowa Skała. There is no direct bus connecting these villages, but the flat 7km between them is well worth walking. The Trail of the Eagles' Nest also follows this road.

Before you embark on your quest, buy a map of the park in Kraków. There are a couple of versions, but Galileo's *Ojcowski Park Narodowy* (scale 1:20,000, 5.90zł from EMPiK) stands out for detailing every trail, road and rock.

The small **PTTK office** (☎ 012 389 2010; http://ojcow.pttk.pl in Polish; Ojców 15; ☺ 9am-3pm May-Oct) is in the car park at the foot of Ojców castle.

Sights & Activities

The well-manicured village of Ojców is based in the national park, and is popular with day-trippers from Kraków. There are a couple of museums in town, but the true allure of Ojców is its access to the tourist trails running through the national park.

CASTLES & MUSEUMS

If you can only do one thing in Ojców National Park, visit 14th-century **Pieskowa Skała Castle** (☺ courtyard 7am-sunset), one of the best-preserved castles in the upland and one of the brightest feathers in Poland's Renaissance cap. To find the Pieskowa Skała Castle, follow the path up the hill into the national park. After WWII (during which it served as a refuge for orphans) the castle was restored to its present glory. Truly an extension of the magnificence of Kraków, Pieskowa Skała Castle was rebuilt in the 16th century in imitation of the royal residence of Wawel and now serves as a branch of the Royal Wawel Castle Museum. Give yourself plenty of time to revel in the richness of the **museum** (☎ 012 389 6004; adult/concession 10/7zł; ☺ 10am-4pm Tue-Thu, 10am-noon Fri, 10am-6pm Sat & Sun May-Aug, 10am-4pm Tue-Sun Oct-Apr, closed Mon), which spans the Gothic 15th century, through the Renaissance and Baroque periods, right up to 19th-century Art Nouveau.

From the castle, the red trail along the road towards Ojców takes you to a 25m-tall limestone pillar; it's called **Hercules' Club** (Maczuga Herkulesa), despite obvious temptations to name it otherwise.

Ojców Castle (☎ 012 389 2044; adult/concession 2.5/1.5zł; ☺ 10am-4.45pm Apr-May & Aug-Sep, 10am-5.45pm Jun & Jul, 10am-3.45pm Oct, 10am-2.45pm Nov, closed Mon) was deserted in 1826, and has since fallen into ruin. The 14th-century entrance gate and octagonal tower are original, but there's little

MAŁOPOLSKA

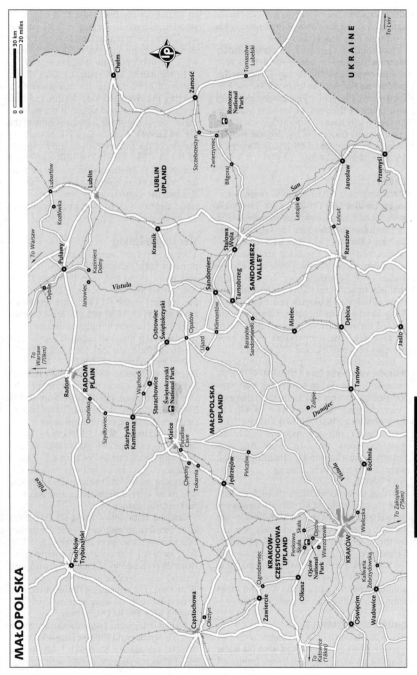

else to explore. The view of the wooden houses scattered across the slopes of Prądnik valley is worth the little money and effort.

Just south of the castle, the **Natural History Museum** (Muzeum Przyrodnicze; ☎ 012 389 2040; adult/concession 2.5/1.5zł; ☯ 9am-4.30pm Tue-Sun mid-May–mid-Nov, 8am-3pm Tue-Fri mid-Nov–mid-May) focuses on the geology, archaeology, flora and fauna of the park. A wooden mansion further south houses modest historical and ethnographic displays in the **Regional Museum** (Muzeum Regionalne; ☎ 012 389 2010; adult/concession 1.5/1zł; ☯ 10am-3pm Tue-Sun).

CAVES

Stretching over 270m through several passages, **Łokietek Cave** (☎ 012 419 0801; www.grotalo kietka.pl in Polish; Grota Łokietka; adult/concession 7/4.50zł; ☯ 9am-3.30pm Apr, 9am-6.30pm May-Aug, 9am-5.30pm Sep, 9am-4.30pm Oct, 9am-3.30pm Sat & Sun Nov-Mar) is accessible from the black trail heading southwards from Ojców Castle and can be visited on a 30-minute tour. Legend has it that before he became king in the 14th century, Władysław Łokietek hid from Czech King Vatzlav II in the cave. Chambers are named for the various uses made of them by Łokietek. The temperature of the cave remains between 7°C and 8°C all year.

Just outside the park boundaries, **Wierzchowska Górna Cave** (☎ 012 411 0721; adult/concession 12/10zł; ☯ 9am-4pm Apr, Sep & Oct, 9am-5pm May-Aug, 9am-3pm Nov) is in the village of Wierzchowie, 5km southwest of Ojców. At 950m long, Wierzchowska is the largest in the Kraków–Częstochowa highlands. Artefacts from the late Stone Age and pottery from the middle Neolithic period were uncovered here during excavations after WWII.

Other caves for enthusiasts include **Dark Cave** (Jaskinia Ciemna; ☎ 012 380 1011; www.ciemna .ojcow.pl in Polish; adult/concession 6/3zł; ☯ 10am-5pm Apr-Nov), close to Ojców and easily reached by the green trail, and the **Bat Cave** (Jaskinia Nietoperzowa; ☎ 012 389 5395; adult/concession 6/3zł; ☯ 10am-5pm), further away along the blue trail. The latter has yielded bones of Arctic animals from the early Stone Age and other animals including the majestic lemming.

CHURCHES & CHAPELS

About 200m north of Ojców Castle is the frequently photographed **Chapel upon the Water** (Kaplica na Wodzie), which was fashioned in 1901 from the bathhouse that originally stood in its place. In keeping with its exterior simplicity, the three altars inside are shaped as peasants' cottages. You may sneak a peek inside when the doors open for religious service.

In the hamlet of Grodzisko, 2km north, the road divides: take the left-hand fork skirting the river and look for the red trail branching off the road uphill to the right. It takes you to the small Baroque **Church of the Blessed Salomea**, built in the 17th century on the site of the former 13th-century convent of the St Clare order. The wall encircling the church is adorned with sandstone statues representing Salomea and her family. Behind the church is an unusual carved stone elephant (1686) supporting an obelisk on its back.

Sleeping & Eating

There are several sleeping and eating options in both Pieskowa Skała and Ojców, and more along the road between them. Ask about private rooms (30zł to 60zł per person) at the PTTK or the **Ojcowianin travel agency** (☎ 012 389 1466, 012 389 2089) in the Regional Museum building. Alternatively, wander along the road between Ojców and Pieskowa Skała and look for 'noclegi' signs.

Dom Wycieczkowy Zosia (☎ 012 389 2008; Ojców-Złota Góra 4; per person with shared/private bathroom 25/35zł) You can't beat the value or the vibe at this casual place, just 1km west up the hill from Ojców castle. It offers well-kept rooms, facilities and friendly common areas.

Zajazd Zazamcze (☎ 012 389 2083; Ojców 1B; www .zajazdzazamcze.ojcow.pl; s/d/tr 100/140/180zł; 💻) An easy walk from the Ojców turn-off, Zajazd Zazamcze offers bland but airy rooms. The restaurant turns out hearty and wholesome fare in its cosy dining room and boasts a park-worthy garden.

Camping Złota Góra (☎ 012 389 2014, 05023 84149; Złota Góra; per adult/under 10yr 5/3.5zł, tent/car/trailer/caravan/motorbike/power connection 4/5/8/10/3/7zł; ☯ 19 Apr-15 Oct) A few hundred metres from Dom Wycieczkowy Zosia, this camping ground has a bonfire at its heart and trees all around. The expanding dining area lures passers-by with its snug seating and fast-flowing beer. It's BYO tent only.

Half a kilometre from Pieskowa Skała Castle is **Agroturystyka Mirosław Glanowski** (☎ 012 389 6212; www.jura.tur.pl/glanowski in Polish; Pieskowa Skała, Podzamcze 2; per person 25-30zł), with a range

MAŁOPOLSKA

of clean rustic rooms, a simple restaurant and camping facilities.

The restaurant-café at **Pieskowa Skała Castle** (☎ 012 389 1103; ⊙ 10am-8pm) is accessible without a museum ticket; the restaurant interior is castle-kitsch but the upstairs terrace affords regal views.

Notwithstanding these options, the best place to dine is along the roadside where **home-grown eateries** turn out authentic Polish sausages, goulash, cakes and bread, all made from local produce and served without fuss by the babbling Prądnik River.

Getting There & Away

The company that once ran direct buses between Ojców and Kraków has fallen on hard times. Affected locals are working hard to reconnect their town, but in the meantime visitors can only get to Ojców by minibus.

The limited direct minibuses leave from the corner of Długa and Kelców streets (near the Drogeria on the corner) in Kraków and arrive at the PTTK office at the base of Ojców castle. At the time of writing, five minibuses departed from Kraków each weekday from 7.45am to 5.20pm, and four returned from Ojców between 6.35am and 6.20pm. Weekend timetables are the same, minus the first bus.

The alternative way to Ojców is via the nearby town of Skała (2.5zł, 30 minutes). From Kraków, take a direct or a Wolbrombound minibus to Skała from where regular minibuses leave for Olkusz between around 5am and 8.30pm, passing through Pieskowa Skała (1.5zł, 10 minutes). Ask to be let off at the turn-off to Ojców and walk the 3km into town or walk the picturesque 7km from Pieskowa Skała to Ojców after visiting the castle. To return to Kraków, either catch the direct minibus from the PTTK office, or make your way back via Skała.

It sounds more complicated than it is – don't be deterred.

OGRODZIENIEC

pop 4500

Claiming prime position on the highest hill of the upland (504m), the ruins of **Ogrodzieniec Castle** (☎ 032 673 2220; admission 3zł; ⊙ 9am-sunset Apr-Oct) look like they belong in a medieval-style fairytale. Incorporating natural rock in its foundations and parts of the walls, the fortress was built during the reign of King Kazimierz III Wielki but enlarged in the mid-

16th century by its owner, Seweryn Boner, a wealthy banker from Kraków. Boner employed Italian masters from the royal court to remodel the castle into a Renaissance residence. After exploring the nooks and crannies of this enormous complex, it's easy to believe reports that the castle was once as splendid as Wawel.

The Swedes started the process of ruination in 1655, and the abandonment of the castle by its owners in the 1810s led it to become a tourist attraction.

Getting There & Away

Buses make for Ogrodzieniec from the town of Zawiercie.

From Częstochowa, there are two buses per day to Zawiercie (6zł, 1½ hours, 6.50am and 2pm), from where you can change for a bus to Ogrodzieniec. Alternatively, take a bus passing Zawiercie on its way to another destination (such as Kielce, Kraków or Jędrzejów).

Trains bound for Katowice from Częstochowa also stop in Zawiercie.

CZĘSTOCHOWA

pop 246,225

Every year, Częstochowa (chen-sto-*ho*-vah) attracts four to five million visitors from 80 countries, who come to fall at the feet of the *Black Madonna*. Some walk for 20 days over hundreds of kilometres with offerings for the Virgin. Others take a bus from Kraków.

Poland's spiritual heartland is not just for the faithful. The Monastery of Jasna Góra is the country's national shrine and one of the highlights of the region. Since an influx of resources from the EU, renovations are working their way up the main thoroughfare towards the monastery, adding new pride to ancient reverence.

During pilgrimage times – particularly the day of Assumption on 15 August – hordes of devotees become a main attraction for people-watchers, and a deterrent for crowd-weary wanderers.

History

The first known mention of Częstochowa (believed to be named for the town's Slavic founder Czętoch) dates to 1220. Częstochowa's emergence as Poland's spiritual capital began with the arrival of the Paulite order from Hungary in 1382, who named the 293m hill in the western part of the city 'Jasna Góra'

CZĘSTOCHOWA

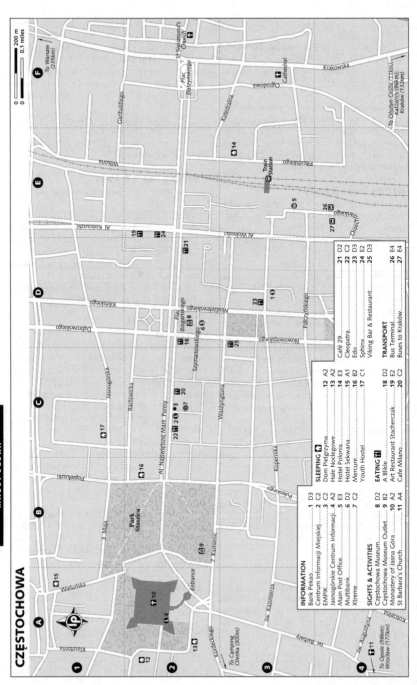

(Bright Hill) and erected a monastery on top. Believers were drawn to the site for the miracles credited to the *Black Madonna* painting. The fact that Jasna Góra was one of the few places in the country to survive Swedish aggression (1655–66) was attributed to the miraculous Virgin (despite her having being safely stowed in Silesia at the time).

The town's foundational charter was granted in the 14th century under German law by King Kazimierz III Wielki, placing Częstochowa on an important trade route from Russia. Agricultural and industrial development, aided by the Warsaw–Vienna railway line, saw Częstochowa evolve into an established industrial centre by the end of the 19th century. By the outbreak of WWII, the city had some 140,000 inhabitants. Częstochowa became a municipal district in 1933, and in 1998 became the first Polish city to be awarded the coveted European Council Prize of Europe.

Despite communist attempts to destabilise the town's religious spirit with a bout of intense industrialisation, Jasna Góra still proudly towers over the city, with the factory chimneys only slightly sullying the distant horizon.

Orientation

Social activity takes place along the wide thoroughfare, Al Najświętszej Marii Panny (Al NMP). At the western end is the Monastery of Jasna Góra.

At the time of writing, the spacious Al NMP was being further widened, and local proprietors of restaurants/cafés/shops were making special efforts to match this new elegance.

Information

There are a number of *kantors* (private currency-exchange offices) and ATMs on Al NMP.

Bank Pekao (ul Kopernika 19) Gives cash advances on Visa and MasterCard.

EMPiK (☎ 034 361 1717; Al NMP 63/65; 9am-8pm Mon-Fri, 9am-5pm Sat, 10am-5pm Sun) Bookshop with English-language collection.

Jasnogórskie Centrum Informacji (☎ 034 365 3888; www.jasnagora.pl; ul Kordeckiego 2; 7.30am-7pm May–mid-Oct, 8am-5pm mid-Oct–Apr) Information centre inside Jasna Góra Monastery.

Miejskie Centrum Informacji (City Information Centre; ☎ 034 368 2250; www.czestochowa.pl; Al NMP 65; 9am-5pm Mon-Sat) Maps and sights information.

Multibank (ul Szymanowskiego 1) Conveniently located 24-hour ATM.

Xtreme (Internet Cafe; ☎ 034 368 3689; www.xtreme .net.pl; Al NMP 65A; per hr 3zł; 7.30am-11pm)

Sights
MONASTERY OF JASNA GÓRA

Impressive though it is, the exterior of Jasna Góra gives little indication of the grandeur layered behind its walls. Exploring this functioning monastery gives a fascinating insight into its history, and a deep appreciation for its present-day relevance. Arrive early and take your time.

You are free to wander around the complex at your own leisure (crowds permitting). **Audio guides** (adult/concession 14/10zł in Polish, English, German & Italian) are available for four routes; the most important covers the main sanctuary and takes 45 minutes.

In the oldest part of the complex, the **Chapel of Our Lady** (Kaplica Cudownego Obrazu; 5am-9pm) contains the revered *Black Madonna* (see boxed text, p216). The picture is ceremoniously unveiled at 6am and 1.30pm (2pm Saturday and Sunday) and veiled at noon and 9.20pm (1pm and 9.20pm Saturday and Sunday). Be sure to note the walls displaying votive offerings brought by pilgrims. Adjoining the chapel is the impressive **basilica** (*bazylika*). Its present shape dates to the 17th century and the interior has opulent Baroque furnishings.

On the northern side of the chapel, paintings in the **Knights' Hall** (sala Rycerska) depict key events from the monastery's history; there's also an exact copy of the *Black Madonna*. Upstairs, the **Golghota Gallery** contains a series of unique paintings by celebrated local painter and cartoonist Jerzy Duda Gracz (1941–2004) whose evocative works are indicative of the monastery's ability to preserve its historical heritage while maintaining modern relevance.

The 106m **belltower** (admission 2zł; 8am-4pm Apr-Sep), the tallest historic church tower in Poland, offers views over the monastery complex and the expanse of Al NMP. After falling many times over history, the current tower dates to 1906.

The **600th Anniversary Museum** (Muzeum Sześćsetlecia; 9am-5pm summer, 9am-4pm winter) contains fascinating artefacts, including the founding documents of Jasna Góra from 1382 and a cross made from the steel of the World

MAŁOPOLSKA

THE BLACK MADONNA OF CZĘSTOCHOWA

Unlike other pilgrimage sites, Jasna Góra has never claimed the appearance of apparitions. Its fame is attributed to the presence of the *Black Madonna*, a 122cm by 82cm painting of the Virgin Mary with the Christ Child on a panel of cypress timber, which was crowned 'Queen of Poland' in 1717.

It is not known for sure when or where the *Black Madonna* was created, but some say she was painted by St Luke the Evangelist on a table in the house of the Holy Family. She is believed to have been brought to Częstochowa from Jerusalem via Constantinople. The painting arrived in Częstochowa in 1382.

In 1430, the face of the Madonna was slashed by Hussites. She still bears the scars either because they were left as a reminder of the sacrilegious attack or; as legend has it, because they continually reappeared despite attempts to repair them. Legends about the *Black Madonna's* role in saving Jasna Góra from the Swedish Deluge in 1655 and in keeping the Russians at bay in 1920 are still extolled today. Whatever the truth of the legends, the widespread belief in them is real, as is evident from the votive offerings – from crutches and walking canes to jewellery and medals – which are still presented to the Virgin by devoted pilgrims today.

Trade Centre, destroyed in New York on 11 September 2001. Particularly moving are rosaries made from bread crumbs by concentration camp prisoners. Lech Wałęsa's 1983 Nobel Peace Prize, donated by its recipient, can be found beyond the Father Kordecki Conference Room.

The **arsenal** contains military mementos including spoils of battle, offerings from soldiers and an impressive collection of Turkish weapons from the 1683 Battle of Vienna.

The 17th-century **treasury** *(skarbiec)* contains votive offerings dating back to the 15th century. Since the 17th century, records have been kept of gifts given to the Madonna.

Depictions of Saint Maximillian Kolbe wearing his Auschwitz uniform can be seen throughout the complex. This Franciscan priest was canonised by Pope John Paul II for his stalwart devotion during the Holocaust and the sacrifice of his life for another man.

The monastery's gates are open from 5.30am to 9.30pm.

OTHER CITY ATTRACTIONS

The 17th-century **St Barbara's Church** (Kościół Św Barbary; ul Św Barbary) is 1km south of the monastery. Its location is believed to have been determined by the spring that emerged here when the *Black Madonna* needed to be washed after it was vandalised (it's still bubbling away behind the church). This legend is depicted on the vault of the chapel.

In the neoclassical town hall, **Częstochowa Museum** (Muzeum Częstochowskie; ☎ 034 360 5631; www.mcz.net-galeria.art.pl; Plac Biegańskiego 45A; admission 3zł; ☺ 11am-5pm Tue-Sun), on Al NMP,

contains paintings of Polish artists as well as extensive documentation detailing the history of Częstochowa and the region at large. Some of the collection is housed in the **Częstochowa Museum outlet** (Park Staszica; ☺ 11am-5pm Tue-Thu, 11am-5.30pm Wed, Fri, Sat & Sun) close to the monastery.

OLSZTYN CASTLE

A visit to the Olsztyn castle ruins, 11km east of Częstochowa, is a refreshing trip out of town…if you find dungeons refreshing. The castle was built in the 14th century by King Kazimierz III Wielki and fell into ruins after it was destroyed by the Swedes in 1655.

Take city bus 58 or 67 from ul Piłsudskiego opposite the train station. Alternatively, walk along the Trail of the Eagles' Nests, which starts from Plac Daszyńskiego and leads via Olsztyn up to Kraków.

Festivals & Events

'Gaude Mater' International Festival of Religious Music (1–6 May) More than 1000 musicians perform in churches and concert halls for Częstochowa's biggest cultural event.

Marian feasts (3 May, 16 July, 15 August, 26 August, 12 September and 8 December) On these days the monastery is flooded by feasting pilgrims.

Assumption (15 August) Pilgrims have been travelling by foot to Jasna Góra for Assumption since 1711. Those from Warsaw leave on 6 August for the 250km journey.

Sleeping

During pilgrimage periods (such as the Marian feast days) book well ahead, or stay elsewhere and make a day trip into Częstochowa.

Hotel Polonia (☎ 034 324 2388; www.hotel-polonia
.czest.pl; ul Piłsudskiego 9; s/d/tr/q 80/100/130/160zł)
Polonia has an old-world foyer and old-
fashioned taste. The décor is out of style,
but over time its retro charm will kick in
and pink will make a comeback. It's clean,
quirky and nicely located near the train and
bus stations.

Hotel Sekwana (☎ 034 324 8954; sekwana@
sekwana.pl; ul Wieluńska 24; s/d/tr/q 120/150/180/200zł;
P ⌧ ⌖) On a quiet, lovely street near the
monastery, Sekwana offers a range of rooms,
some newer and more spacious than others.
Breakfast is included, and is served in the
family-friendly onsite Restauracja Francuska,
with its French-themed murals.

Mercure (Hotel Patria; ☎ 034 324 7001; mer.patria@
orbis.pl; ul Popiełuszki 2; s/d/ste/apt 295/340/450/550zł;
P ⌧ ▣) Renovations sweeping up Al NMP
would do well to turn right on Pułaskiego
and clean up the entrance of the Mercure.
Despite its hackneyed exterior, the Mercure
offers good-quality accommodation. Rooms
are standard international-hotel style; some
have bathtubs.

There are a couple of church-run places
that fill up fast despite their tepid tone
(feel at home but make sure you're back
in at 10pm). **Hale Noclegowe** (☎ 034 377 7224;
ul Klasztorna 1; dm 17zł; ☽ May–mid-Oct) is where
genders are divided and facilities shared,
while **Dom Pielgrzyma** (☎ 034 377 7564; ul
Wyszyńskiego 1/31; s 70zł, d 100-130zł, tr 105-126zł, q
140zł) has a bustling kiosk that gives it a true
summer-camp feel.

In summer, you can also try the **youth hostel** (☎ 034 324 3121; ul Jasnogórska 84/90; dm 20-36zł;
☽ Jul & Aug), two blocks parallel to Al NMP
(look for small green triangular sign). The
smiling green **Camping Oleńka** (☎ 034 360 6066;
camping@mosir.pl; ul Oleńki 22/30; car/tent 10/12zł, 4-person
bungalow with bathroom 120zł), behind the monastery, has space for around 400 people. Those
who forget to bring tents can enjoy great
value in the self-contained bungalows.

Eating

In addition to the cheap eateries near the
monastery, an eclectic modern range of
eateries have been introduced recently.

Edo (☎ 034 324 2233; www.edo.czwa.eu; ul Kopernika
22; mains 8-30zł; ☽ noon-11pm) Edo is a bold attempt at exoticism that seems to be paying
off. Modern Japanese décor adds flavour to
tempura, salads and sushi dishes, while Polish

waiters in Japanese attire are a new take on
the Far East.

Viking Bar & Restaurant (☎ 034 324 5768; ul
Nowowiejskiego 10; mains 8-30zł; ☽ 10am-10pm) This
casual corner bar offers great value meals of
pleasing proportions, and has a more refined
adjoining restaurant. There are a few outdoor
tables when the weather permits. You'll have
an English menu at *dzień dobry*.

Café 29 (☎ 034 361 2355; Al NMP 29; mains 10-30zł;
☽ 10am-10pm Mon-Thu, 10am-11pm Fri & Sat, noon-10pm
Sun) Warm on the inside, cool on the outside,
Café 29 attracts the sleek young things of
Częstochowa, who mellow over smoothies
(6zł) and pizzas (from 12zł).

Sphinx (☎ 034 366 4185; Al Kościuszki 1; mains 15-35zł;
☽ noon-11pm Mon-Fri, 11am-11pm Sat & Sun) Sphinx is
a reliable chain restaurant serving solid meat
and salad meals in the pleasant (though often
loud) surrounds of Egyptian bling.

Art Restaurant Stacherczak (☎ 034 369 3801; www
.artrestaurant.pl; Al Kościuszki; mains 15-40zł; ☽ 11am-11pm)
An attempt to blend cuisine with culture, the
Art Restaurant is a multitiered space offering
innovative Asian-inspired platters, standard
steaks and food of no particular genesis. The
vibe is turned up a treat on weekends with
musical performances. Check the website
for details.

There are several popular choices along
Al NMP:

A Blikle (☎ 034 368 0531; Al NMP 47/42; mains 10zł;
☽ 8am-7pm Mon-Thu, 8am-8pm Fri & Sat, 9am-8pm
Sun) Dangerously good pastries on the main thoroughfare
or in the courtyard.

Cafe Milano (☎ 034 365 4929; Al NMP 57/59; mains
10-25zł; ☽ 7am-11pm) Spanish-run, family-friendly café.

Cleopatra (☎ 034 368 0101; Al NMP 71; mains 15-20zł;
☽ 11am-11pm) Kebab, pizza and sandwich staples with
a prime view of the monastery.

Getting There & Away
BUS

The **bus terminal** (☎ 034 379 11 4950; www.pks-czesto
chowa.pl; ☽ information counter 7am-8pm) is close to the
central train station and serves many towns in
the region including Jędrzejów (10.50zł, two
hours) and Opole (11.50zł, two hours).

From Kraków (133km away), there are
many buses to Częstochowa (15.20zł, three
hours, eight per day, between 6.30am and
9.20pm). Alternatively, there is the faster
Polski Express bus (20zł, two hours, three
daily), which also heads from Częstochowa to
Warsaw (50zł, three hours, one daily).

MAŁOPOLSKA

Buses leave for Kielce (21zł, three hours) at 11.45am, 3.20pm and 5.55pm. For information on getting to Ogrodzieniec see p213.

TRAIN

The **train station** (Al Wolności) handles half a dozen daily fast trains to Warsaw (38zł, 3½ hours) and about the same number to Kraków (31zł, two hours).

There are five trains per day to Kielce (17zł, two hours 20 minutes) between 6.45am and 6.45pm.

Trains to Katowice (14zł to 17zł, 1½ hours) run every hour or so between 3am and 9pm, from where there are connections to Kraków and Wrocław. To Zakopane, there are only a few trains in the inconvenient wee hours (27zł, seven hours, between 1am and 4am).

THE MAŁOPOLSKA UPLAND

The Małopolska Upland is skirted by the Vistula and Pilica Rivers, but the centrepiece of this beautiful expanse is the Holy Cross Mountains (Góry Świętokrzyskie), repository of abundant natural beauty, witness to harrowing episodes in the country's history, and object of religious reverence. The main urban centre of Kielce, which sits at the foot of the mountains, is a convenient base to access this varied cultural landscape and the surrounding mountain ranges.

KIELCE
pop 206,461

Don't judge a town by its outskirts. The ring of postwar suburbs around the centre doesn't inspire exploratory enthusiasm, but Kielce (*kyel*-tseh) is growing into itself. Recent revamps of the main thoroughfare (ul Sienkiewicza) have injected new pride into Kielce, which is confidently flaunting its makeover.

In addition to key attractions – like the remarkable Palace of the Kraków Bishops – Kielce is a convenient base for nearby Chęciny, Jędrzejów and Świętokrzyski National Park.

Information
Internet cafés in Kielce seem to go bust before your 30 minutes are up. To compensate, some

hotels offer internet access. There are plenty of *kantors* on ul Sienkiewicza. The main post office is next to the train station, and there's another on Sienkiewicza.

Bank Pekao (ul Sienkiewicza 18; ☺ 8am-6pm Mon-Fri, 10am-2pm Sun) Advances on Visa and MasterCard.

Informacja Turystyczna (☎ 041 345 8681; www.um .kielce.pl/turystyka; Plac Niepodległości 1; ☺ 9am-5pm Mon-Fri, 10am-3pm Sat) Impressively helpful tourist office in an easy-to-miss corner on the 1st floor of the train station.

Raiffeisen Bank (ul Sienkiewicza 60A; ☺ 10am-6pm Mon-Fri)

Sights
Unless you have an unnatural interest in ugly bus terminals, *the* sight to see in Kielce is the **Palace of the Kraków Bishops** (Pałac Biskupów Krakówskich). Kielce was the property of the Kraków bishops from the 12th century through to 1789. This palace was built (from 1637 onwards) as one of their seats and remains a pristine testament to the richness of that era. The palace houses the **National Museum** (☎ 041 344 4014; www.muzeumkielce.net; Plac Zamkowy 1; adult/concession 10/5zł, free Sun; ☺ 10am-6pm Tue & Fri, 9am-4pm Wed, Thu & Sun, 10am-4pm Sat), where 17th- and 18th-century interiors are so alive you feel like you're trespassing in a bishop's boudoir. Keep an eye on the ornamental ceilings (plafonds) painted from 1641 by Venetian Tommaso Dolabella. The centrepiece is the former dining hall where the whole brood of bishops stare down from their 56 portraits. The upper and lower portraits of this evocative historical montage were painted two centuries apart. The rest of this captivatingly cavernous multilevel museum leads through collections of porcelain, historical armour and various centuries and genres of Polish painting.

The **cathedral** facing the palace looks nothing like the Romanesque church first erected here in 1171. The cathedral was rebuilt in the 17th century and later dressed in Baroque decorations. Pope John Paul II celebrated Mass here in 1999. The nearby **Museum of the Kielce Village** (Muzeum Wsi Kieleckiej; ☎ 041 344 9297; ul Jana Pawła II 6; admission 2zł; ☺ 10am-3pm Mon-Fri & Sun) is housed in the only 18th-century wooden mansion in Kielce.

The delightfully presented **Toy Museum** (Muzeum Zabawkarstwa; ☎ 041 344 4078; www.muzeum zabawek.kielce.pl; Plac Wolności 2; adult/concession 6/3zł; ☺ 10am-5pm Tue-Sun) offers the chance to remi-

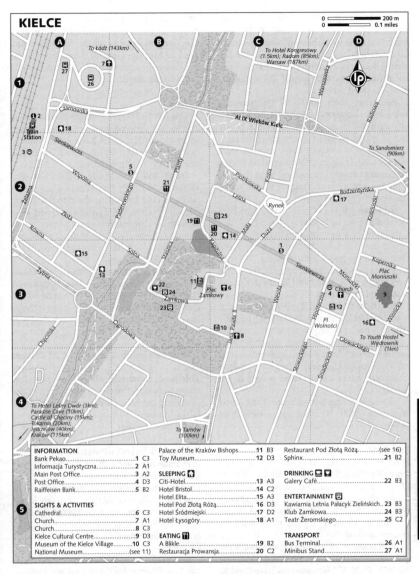

KIELCE

| 0 | 200 m |
| 0 | 0.1 miles |

To Łódź (143km)

To Hotel Kongresowy (1.5km); Radom (85km); Warsaw (187km)

Al IX Wieków Kielc

Train Station

To Sandomierz (90km)

Rynek

Bodzentyńska

Plac Zamkowy

Zamkowa

Plac Wolności

To Youth Hostel Wędrownik (1km)

To Hotel Leśny Dwór (3km);
Paradise Cave (10km);
Castle of Chęciny (15km);
Tokarnia (20km);
Jędrzejów (40km);
Kraków (115km)

To Tarnów (100km)

INFORMATION	
Bank Pekao	1 C3
Informacja Turystyczna	2 A1
Main Post Office	3 A2
Post Office	4 D3
Raiffeisen Bank	5 B2

SIGHTS & ACTIVITIES	
Cathedral	6 C3
Church	7 A1
Church	8 C3
Kielce Cultural Centre	9 D3
Museum of the Kielce Village	10 C3
National Museum	(see 11)

Palace of the Kraków Bishops	11 B3
Toy Museum	12 D3

SLEEPING	
Citi-Hotel	13 A3
Hotel Bristol	14 C2
Hotel Elita	15 A3
Hotel Pod Złotą Różą	16 D3
Hotel Śródmiejski	17 D2
Hotel Łysogóry	18 A1

EATING	
A Blikle	19 B2
Restauracja Prowansja	20 C2

Restaurant Pod Złotą Różą	(see 16)
Sphinx	21 B2

DRINKING	
Galery Café	22 B3

ENTERTAINMENT	
Kawiarnia Letnia Pałacyk Zielińskich	23 B3
Klub Zamkowa	24 B3
Teatr Żeromskiego	25 C2

TRANSPORT	
Bus Terminal	26 A1
Minibus Stand	27 A1

MAŁOPOLSKA

nisce about toys you forgot you wanted. The room full of frogs somehow makes sense when you're there.

Sleeping

Budget accommodation is hard to come by in Kielce, but there are abundant midrange options.

BUDGET & MIDRANGE

Hotel Bristol (☎ 041 366 3065; www.bristol.kielce.pl; ul Sienkiewicza 21; s/d/tr 120/150/170zł; P ☐) Centrally situated and appropriately priced, Bristol is a winning choice in its price category. Dark corridors look like an Agatha Christie crime scene, but the compact rooms are fresh and spotless with big windows.

Hotel Śródmiejski (☎ 041 344 1507; www.hotel srodmiejski.pl; ul Wesoła 5; s/d 130/150zł; P 🖵) In a quiet lane close to the heart of town, clean and compact Śródmiejski is hard to beat; the fact that it is so freshly refurbished makes prices seem like an opening special. Its restaurant also gets good reviews.

Hotel Leśny Dwór (☎ 041 362 1088; www.lesny dwor.com.pl; ul Szczepaniaka 40; s/d/ste 160/220/350zł; P) Roughly 3km southwest of the centre but a world away in every other respect, Leśny Dwór is a quaint hotel opposite Park Baranowski. It offers charming rooms and a restaurant capable of anything from roasting a pig for a party to serving vegetarian meals for a couple of travellers.

Citi-Hotel (☎ 041 343 5151; www.citipark.pl; ul Paderewskiego 4c; s/d/tr 180/250/300zł; P 🖵 🖳) Citi-Hotel is a new business centre with a professional air. Its 35 compact but sleek rooms enjoy good natural light. It's not nearly as personal as nearby Elita, but offers perks like a pool, sauna and Japanese/Korean restaurant downstairs.

Hotel Elita (☎ 041 344 2230; www.hotelelita.com.pl; ul Równa 4A; s/d/apt 180/260/360zł; P) Elita is a friendly (though not remotely wheelchair-friendly) place at a quiet end of town, which is small enough to feel cosy. Rooms and bathrooms are spacious and spotless. The generous 2pm checkout leaves ample time to get down the stairs.

The uninspiring but adequate **Youth Hostel Wędrownik** (☎ 041 342 3735; ul Szymanowskiego 5; dm 29zł) is 1.5km east of the centre.

TOP END

Hotel Pod Złotą Różą (☎ 041 341 5002; www.zlota roza.pl; Plac Moniuszki 7; s/d 240/350zł, ste 430-600zł; P 🖵) Small but meticulously refurbished rooms shine with rich brown finish. There's no unnecessary ostentatiousness here; it's just a compact, stylish place with an elegant restaurant.

Hotel Łysogóry (☎ 041 366 5500; www.lysogory.com .pl in Polish; ul Sienkiewicza 78; s 240-320zł, d 360-520zł, ste 450-760zł; P 🗶 🖵) Renovations have tried to work in an old-world feel, but the newness translates as modern sterility in the rooms. However, you certainly won't find anywhere newer (or nearer the train station) than this big, shiny establishment.

Hotel Kongresowy (☎ 041 332 6393; www.exbud .com.pl in Polish; ul Manifestu Lipcowego 34; s/d/ste Mon-Fri from 260/370/590zł, Sat & Sun from 182/259/470zł;

P 🗶 🖵) An established business hotel a couple of kilometres northeast of the centre, Kongresowy has all the facilities you'd need to host the General Assembly, assuming delegates were prepared to catch bus 4 or 34 to get there.

Eating

A Blikle (☎ 041 343 2324; www.blikle.pl; ul Sienkiewicza 29; mains 10zł; ⏰ 9am-8pm) A welcome addition to newly sophisticated Kielce, this bakery-café is pleasant for a high-calorie break and low-energy people-watching.

Sphinx (☎ 041 341 5134; www.sphinx.pl; ul Sienkiewicza 48/50; mains 15-35zł; ⏰ 11am-11pm Sat & Sun) A particularly cosy branch of the popular chain, friendly staff, an English menu and portions fit for a pharaoh make this inexplicably Egyptian-themed restaurant a safe choice for casual dining outside under the umbrellas or inside under the trees.

Restauracja Prowansja (☎ 041 344 1144; ul Sienkiewicza 25; mains 25zł; ⏰ 11am-11pm Mon-Fri, 11am-midnight Sat, 11am-10pm Sun) A relaxed Polish, French and Italian restaurant enjoyed by regulars, serving authentic courses including pigs trotters, frogs and snails (though vegetarians won't starve).

Restaurant Pod Złotą Różą (☎ 041 343 7880; www .zlotaroza.pl; Plac Moniuszki 7; mains 40zł; ⏰ 10am-11pm) This hotel restaurant offers upmarket dining in the wood-finished dining room or the charming cobblestoned courtyard. Cuisine is traditional Polish with a sprinkling of international dishes.

Drinking & Entertainment

Dom Środowisk Twórczych (☎ 041 368 2053; www .kielcedst.net in Polish; ul Zamkowa 5) One of the best venues in town offers temporary exhibitions and live music (classic through to rock and jazz) in a resplendent but relaxed open-air space at the foot of the palace. Check the online programme or wander past to see what's happening.

Galery Café (☎ 041 341 5223; ul Zamkowa; ⏰ 10am-late) This popular local hangout is a particularly nice place for an afternoon beer.

Klub Zamkowa (☎ 041 344 7226; www.zamkowa.pl; ul Zamkowa 2; ⏰ 11am-1am) A hit-and-miss clubbing experience with old Polish décor and a new Polish vibe.

In addition to these watering holes, stylish bars at pl Walności attract vibrant late-night crowds.

MAŁOPOLSKA

For more highbrow fare, see what the local art-house talents are up to at **Teatr Żeromskiego** (☎ 041 344 6048; www.teatr-zeromskiego .com.pl in Polish; ul Sienkiewicza 32).

Getting There & Away

BUS

The UFO-shaped bus terminal (landed by aliens from a planet entirely devoid of taste) is well organised and conveniently close to the train station.

Buses to Święty Krzyż (3.90zł, one hour, four daily) leave between 6.45am and 3.40pm; for Łódź (25zł to 27zł, 3½ hours, around 15 daily) between 6am and 8.20pm; for Sandomierz (18zł, two hours, 14 daily), between 7am and 7.40pm; and for Kraków (18zł to 23zł, 2½ hours, 13 daily) between 2am and 5.35pm. Check other destinations at the busy **information desk** (☒ 6am-8pm).

The minibus stand (opposite the bus terminal) clearly displays schedules. Minibuses to nearby destinations such as Chęciny (2.5zł, 20 minutes, every half-hour or so) are more constant and convenient than PKS buses. However, minibuses to Kraków (18zł, two hours, every half-hour from 5am to 8.10pm) can fill up fast – a normal bus is a better bet for this trip.

TRAIN

The train station (the key landmark at the western end of ul Sienkiewicza) services many destinations. There are around 15 trains per day to Radom (22zł, two hours), which continue on to Warsaw (36zł, 3½ hours); 14 trains to Kraków (31zł, three hours); four to Lublin (38zł, three hours); and five to Częstochowa (28zł, 1½ hours).

AROUND KIELCE

Castle of Chęciny

From a distance, the **Castle of Chęciny** (ul Przedborska 14; adult/concession 4/3zł; ☒ 9am-5pm) looks like a foreboding tri-chimneyed factory. Closer inspection reveals its impressive hilltop location presiding over the quaint town of Chęciny. The view from one of the towers reveals why the site was chosen as an all-seeing defensive position. Visitors can climb the tower to experience a great view of the surrounding region and pleasant town of Chęciny.

The castle is estimated to have come into existence around 1280, taking its name from the village. At the turn of the 13th century, the knighthood of the region would assemble here. In 1306, the castle was presented to the then Bishop of Kraków (Jan Muskata) who would later surrender it to royal power. After the death of King Władysław Łokietek (who used the castle as a venue for important political assemblies), Kazimierz III Wielki developed it into a fortress; it is believed that Kazimierz's second wife spent two years here after being repudiated by her husband. Over the years, the castle was used as a residence for widowed wives of Polish kings, a treasury and a jail for high-profile prisoners including the Teutonic Knights captured on the Grunwald battlefield.

In the 16th century, the castle was unable to support the bastions required by new defensive strategies, and so lost its impenetrability. It fell to ruin in the attacks that followed (notably the Swedish onslaught of 1707) and under Austrian rule, which saw parts of the castle demolished. Legend has it that a ghostly 'white lady' can still be seen strolling along the castle walls. She is believed to be an apparition of Queen Bona who once lived at Chęciny Castle.

Today the castle conjures up all of this history. On a gloomy day, clambering along the heavy stone walls is an evocative experience, it's well worth the short trip from Kielce.

GETTING THERE & AWAY

Regular minibuses leave Kielce every 20 minutes or so on their way to various destinations. Ask to be let off at the Rynek in Chęciny (2.5zł, 20 minutes) for the castle, which is about 25km from Kielce. Check minibuses bound for Bolmin (13 per day between 6.30am and 7pm), Łukowa (26 per day between 6.10am and 7.30pm), Ostrów (four per day between 9.10am and 5.25pm), Wolica (five per day between 9.10am and 5.25pm) and Zajączków (10 per day between 5.50am and 5.20pm).

To get to the castle, walk the 800m from the Rynek around behind the castle and enter from its rear. From the car park there is a pleasant unpaved and sometimes rocky path through a small patch of atmospheric forest.

Paradise Cave

If you haven't seen caves before, you'll enjoy **Paradise Cave** (Jaskinia Raj; ☎ 041 346 5518; www .lysogory.com.pl; tours 10zł; ☒ 10am-5pm Tue-Sun May-Aug,

10am-4pm Tue-Sun Mar, Apr & Sep-Nov). However, if you are an experienced spelunker, then a visit to Paradise Cave may be only marginally more thrilling than exploring your garage with a torch in winter.

The paved path through the cave makes for a sanitised 180m loop. The cave is only 8m at its highest point, but some of the larger chambers are truly impressive, not so much for the size of the stalactites but for their sheer density – as many as 200 per square metre.

The 40-minute tours (leaving every 15 minutes or so) are only conducted in Polish. Independent visitors must call in advance to reserve their place.

The entrance building shelters a small cafeteria, and a display depicting the use of the cave by primitive humans before they were required to make telephone bookings.

Beside the car park for the cave, **Zazard Raj** (☎ 041 346 5127; Dobrzączka 26-060 Chęciny; s/d/q 90/120/200zł) is a wholesome place to stay (and eat) with little around it other than the caves.

GETTING THERE & AWAY
Better than the irregular PKS buses are the regular minibuses leaving Kielce every 20 minutes or so on their way to various destinations. Ask to be let off at the Jaskinia Raj turn-off (1.5zł, 15 minutes) for the caves. Check minibuses bound for Bolmin (13 per day between 6.30am and 7pm), Łukowa (26 per day between 6.10am and 7.30pm), Ostrów (four per day between 9.10am and 5.25pm), Wolica (five per day between 9.10am and 5.25pm) and Zajączków (10 per day between 5.50am and 5.20pm).

For the caves (which are closer to Kielce than to the centre of Chęciny), walk the 900m from the turn-off on the main road to the well-signed cave entrance. On the way back, hail down a bus passing on its way to Kielce along the main road.

Tokarnia
In the village of Tokarnia, 20km from Kielce, is the 80-hectare **Open-Air Museum of the Kielce Village** (Muzeum Wsi Kieleckiej; ☎ 041 315 4171; www .mwk.com.pl in Polish; adult/concession 10/7zł; ⌚ 10am-6pm Tue-Sun Apr-Oct, 9am-4pm Mon-Fri Nov-Mar). The skansen (open-air museum of traditional architecture) includes many structures complete with interiors. Particularly interesting is the exhibition dedicated to local woodcarver Jan Bernasiewicz (1908–84).

Give yourself a couple of hours, or maybe more if you have children in tow. In summer there is a café at the entrance to the museum.

Several minibuses from Kielce pass Tokarnia on their way to other destinations, as do five normal buses (3zł, 30 minutes) between 10.40am and 8.40pm on their way to destinations such as Jędrzejów. Get off at the village of Tokarnia and continue on foot for around 1km to the entrance of the skansen.

Jędrzejów
pop 18,000
Records of Jędrzejów (yend-*zeh*-yoof) date back to the 11th century. The first Cistercian monastery in Poland was established here, but today the pride of Jędrzejów is its **Sundial Museum** (Muzeum Zegarów Słonecznych; ☎ 041 386 2445; Rynek 7/8; adult/concession 10/7zł; ⌚ 9am-4pm Tue-Sun May-Sep, 9am-3pm Oct-Apr, closed public holidays & day following). The sundial collection (reputedly the world's third-largest after Oxford and Chicago) belonged to Dr Tadeusz Przypkowski whose home became the museum upon his death in 1962. The collection crosses eras (the oldest dating to 1524 measures time at night using the position of the stars) and continents (from as far afield as China, Japan and Australia). Even those who don't know what 'gnomonics' means will find the museum interesting. What's not to like about a cannon-firing sundial? Beyond time-telling technology, the well-preserved lodgings of Dr Przypkowski are also on show throughout the labyrinthine house. Tours are conducted when there are tourists to conduct. This is not a weather-dependent excursion – all the sundials are indoors.

On the western outskirts of town is the **Sanctuary of the Blessed Wincenty Kadłubek** (Opactwo Cystersów; ul 11 Listopada), 2km from the Rynek, on the road towards Zawiercie and Częstochowa. Founded in 1140, the Cistercian Abbey and Church holds the distinction of having been attended twice by Cardinal Karol Wojtyła before he became Pope John Paul II. It was also here in Jędrzejów that Wincenty Kadłubek (1161–1223) completed his famed *Chronica Polonorum* (Chronicle of Poland); his remains are in a 17th-century Baroque coffin in the side chapel off the southern aisle.

The abbey was appropriated by the Russians in 1819 and it was only returned to the Cistercians after WWII.

GETTING THERE & AWAY

From Kielce, it's possible to travel the 44km to Jędrzejów by bus (6zł, 30 minutes, every two hours) or train (12zł, 20 minutes, every two hours).

The bus and train stations are next to each other, 2km west of the Rynek and linked to it by an urban bus, which continually loops from the Rynek (where the sundial museum is) to both stations (1.4zł, 10 minutes).

ŚWIĘTOKRZYSKI NATIONAL PARK

The Góry Świętokrzyskie (shfyen-to-*kshis-kee*) – literally, 'Holy Cross Mountains' – are not only blessed with natural beauty, but are also steeped in history spanning the ages. The hailed pilgrimage site of Święty Krzyż was first imbued with reverence in the era of paganism. The abbey survived the horror of Nazi occupation, and is one of the highlights of the park today (albeit slightly dishevelled). It features a couple of worthwhile museums.

The national park covers the 15km-long gentle mountain range known as Łysogóry (Bald Mountains), marked in the west by Mt Łysica (612m) and in the east by Mt Łysa Góra (595m). Between these lies a dense belt of fir and beech forest, which covers almost all of the 60 sq km park. Unusual piles of broken *gołoborza* (quartzite rock) on the northern slopes hint at how ancient this mountain range is. This is Poland's oldest mountainous geological formation (and lowest, due to erosion over more than 300 million years); it has witnessed the entirety of the country's tumultuous history, and deserves your attention for a full or half day.

Tickets into the **national park** (adult/concession 5/2.5zł) are valid all day and include entry into some museums.

Getting There & Away

The park is about 20km east of Kielce. You can get there by bus from the city to three different access points: the village of Święta Katarzyna at the western end at the foot of Mt Łysica; the Święty Krzyż abbey on the top of Mt Łysa Góra; and the village of Nowa Słupia, 2km east of Święty Krzyż.

Generally, visitors to the park enter via Nowa Słupia and walk the 18km trail from there to Święta Katarzyna via Święty Krzyż. Most of the museums are around Nowa Słupia and nearby Święty Krzyż; if you start

in Święta Katarzyna you'll need to ramble quite quickly to get to the museums before they close.

Buses leave every hour or so from Kielce to Święta Katarzyna (6zł, 30 minutes) roughly between 5am and 7pm, stopping at Święta Krzyż on the way. To get to Nowa Słupia (6zł, one hour), take a bus bound for either Jeziórko or Rudki (around 10 per day until 6pm or so).

There are frequent buses from both Nowa Słupia (6zł, one hour) and Święta Katarzyna (6zł, 30 minutes) back to Kielce, but from Święty Krzyż there are only buses every few hours; it may be best to walk along the red trail back to Święta Katarzyna for onward transport.

Nowa Słupia

Nowa Słupia and the surrounding region is the largest ancient metallurgical centre discovered in Europe so far. The **Museum of the Holy Cross Ancient Metallurgy** (Muzeum Starożytnego Hutnictwa Świętokrzyskiego; ☎ 041 317 7018; ul Świętokrzyska 59; adult/concession 5/2zł; ⏰ 9am-5pm) was established on the site where primitive 2nd-century smelting furnaces (*dymarki*) were discovered in 1955. Since 1967 the process of melting iron in *dymarki* stoves has been demonstrated in Nowa Słupia in late August every year.

The **Tourist Information Centre** (Informacja Turystyczna; ☎ 041 317 7626; ul Świętokrzyska 18) in the centre of town can arrange budget rooms in private houses. The PTSM **youth hostel** (☎ 041 317 7016; ul Świętokrzyska 61; dm per person 14zł, d 25-30zł), next to the museum, has 60 beds in double and dorm rooms.

From the museum, the 2km King Way path (Droga Królewska) leads to Święty Krzyż (by car, it's a 16km detour).

Święty Krzyż

Święty Krzyż (Holy Cross) mountains take their name from the **Benedictine monastery of Holy Cross**, so called for the segment of Jesus' cross that was supposedly kept here. The abbey is at the top of Łysa Góra (595m) – the second-highest mountain in the range, after Łysica (612m).

The Święty Krzyż abbey has a fascinating history. Most sources estimate that it was built in the 11th century on a site of pagan worship from the 8th and 9th centuries. With the abolition of the Benedictine Order by the

MAŁOPOLSKA

Russians in 1819, the abbey was converted into a prison. After a brief period of restoration, the Nazis reconverted the buildings into prisons. The Gestapo tortured many monks here before transporting them to Auschwitz and thousands of Soviet prisoners were executed and buried in mass graves near the peak. Under communism, the abbey was transferred to the national park and renovations commenced.

The monastery now houses the small **Missionary Museum** (Muzeum Misyjne; ☎ 041 317 7021; admission included in park price; ☽ 9am-noon & 1-5pm Mon-Sat, noon-4pm Sun) featuring some objects collected by missionaries over the years.

On the western side of the abbey, facing a 157m TV tower (the largest free-standing TV tower in Poland), is the **Natural History Museum** (Muzeum Przyrodniczo-Leśne; ☎ 041 317 7087; ☽ 9am-5pm, closed public holidays & day following), focusing on the park's geology, flora and fauna. Just beyond the TV mast, to the right, a short side path leads to some quartzite rocks.

The abbey's **Holy Cross Church** (☽ 9am-5pm Mon-Sat, noon-5pm Sun & holidays) was rebuilt several times over the years. The present-day church and its mainly neoclassical interior date to the late 18th century.

On the access road near the car park, 2km before Święty Krzyż, is **Jodłowy Dwór** (☎ 041 302 5028; fax 041 302 6146; d/tr 150/180zł), a pleasant hotel and restaurant. The Tourist Information Centre in Nowa Słupia (p223) can assist with budget accommodation in private rooms.

The Trail

The 16km trail between Święty Krzyż and Święta Katarzyna is a physically comfortable and scenically rewarding four-hour walk.

From Święty Krzyż the trail follows the road for the first 2km to the car park (where Jodłowy Dwór is), before branching off and running west along the edge of the forest for around 9km. It then enters the woods, ascends the peak of Mt Łysica and winds down for 2km to Święta Katarzyna.

Święta Katarzyna

This small village is developing into a local holiday centre with several simple places to stay and eat including the **youth hostel** (☎ 041 311 2006; ul Kielecka 45; dm/d 16/50zł), which offers simple lodging in four- to eight-bed dorms in pleasant grounds. Some double rooms have bathrooms.

The former Dom Wycieczkowy PTTK, **Ośrodek Wypoczynkowy Jodełka** (☎ 041 311 2111; fax 041 311 2112; ul Kielecka 3; s with shared bathroom 50zł, d/tr/q with private bathroom 120/165/195zł), offers a range of revamped rooms and a pleasant onsite restaurant.

THE SANDOMIERZ VALLEY

The Sandomierz Valley (Kotlina Sandomierska) covers an extensive area in and around the fork of the Vistula and San Rivers. In the heart of the valley is Sandomierz – an underrated gem of Gothic grandeur. Nearby are the fantastic fairy-tale ruins of Ujazd castle.

SANDOMIERZ
pop 24,778

Tourists really should be rolling down the sloping Rynek of Sandomierz and piling up at the town hall. But the grandeur of the old town, with the impressive Gothic town hall propped upright in its centre, remains relatively undiscovered. Immaculate buildings of multiple architectural flavours line undulating laneways as locals nonchalantly wander by, apparently oblivious to their good fortune in not being overrun by hordes of visitors.

History

No-one is certain of precisely when Sandomierz came to life, but as far back as the 11th century the town was classified (by chronicler Gall Anonim) as a major settlement of the Kingdom, along with Kraków and Wrocław.

In the 13th century, repeated assaults by Tartar raiders meant that Sandomierz had to be resurrected several times, most significantly in 1260 when it was rebuilt uphill at the site it occupies today. During the reign of Kazimierz III Wielki (1333–70), Sandomierz became a significant trade hub and saw the construction of the Royal Castle, Opatów Gate and the town hall. The town prospered until the mid-17th century, the same era that saw the arrival of the Jesuits and the invasion of the Swedes – an onslaught from which it never completely recovered.

After having survived WWII with its historic architecture relatively unscathed, the

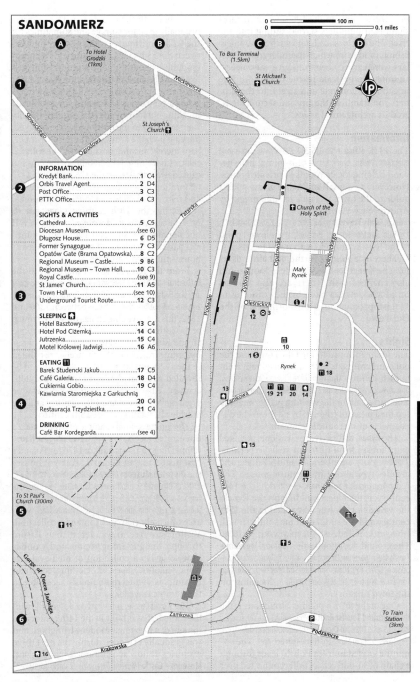

SANDOMIERZ

0 — 100 m
0 — 0.1 miles

To Hotel Grodzki (1km)

To Bus Terminal (1.5km)

St Michael's Church

St Joseph's Church

Church of the Holy Spirit

Mały Rynek

Rynek

INFORMATION
Kredyt Bank................................1 C4
Orbis Travel Agent.......................2 D4
Post Office.................................3 C3
PTTK Office...............................4 C3

SIGHTS & ACTIVITIES
Cathedral...................................5 C5
Diocesan Museum.....................(see 6)
Długosz House...........................6 D5
Former Synagogue.....................7 C3
Opatów Gate (Brama Opatowska)....8 C2
Regional Museum – Castle............9 B6
Regional Museum – Town Hall.....10 C3
Royal Castle..............................(see 9)
St James' Church......................11 A5
Town Hall................................(see 10)
Underground Tourist Route.........12 C3

SLEEPING
Hotel Basztowy........................13 C4
Hotel Pod Ciżemką....................14 C4
Jutrzenka................................15 C4
Motel Królowej Jadwigi..............16 A6

EATING
Barek Studencki Jakub................17 C5
Café Galeria............................18 D4
Cukiernia Gobio........................19 C4
Kawiarnia Staromiejska z Garkuchnią
....20 C4
Restauracja Trzydziestka.............21 C4

DRINKING
Café Bar Kordegarda................(see 4)

To St Paul's Church (300m)

Gorge of Queen Jadwiga

To Train Station (3km)

MAŁOPOLSKA

next threat came in the 1960s when its most significant buildings started sliding into the river. The soft loess soils on which Sandomierz is built (and from which its underground cellars were carved) began to give way, necessitating a large-scale rescue operation. The injection of concrete and steel into the slippery soil stabilised the city and securely tethered its architectural assets.

Information

The **PTTK office** (☎ 015 832 2305; www.pttk-sando mierz.pl in Polish; Rynek 12) is of minimal help beyond helping locate rooms in private homes. However, it does sell an English glossy pocket guide to the town (*A guide to Sandomierz* by Andrzej Sarwa, 10zł).

An **Orbis Travel Agent** (☎ 015 832 3040; Rynek 12; 🕑 8am-5pm Mon-Fri, 9am-1pm Sun), at the lowest point of the Rynek, can help with travel tickets.

There is a *kantor* in the **post office** (Rynek 10). The **Kredyt Bank** (Rynek 5) a few doors south also changes cash. There are also *kantors* on ul Mickiewicza close to the corner of ul 11 Listopada, about 1km northwest of the Old Town.

Sights

The main entrance to the Old Town and the only surviving gate of the four originally built is 14th-century **Opatów Gate** (Brama Opatowska; ul Opatowska; adult/concession 3/2zł; 🕑 9am-4.30pm summer). You can climb to the viewing platform at the top for a pleasant (though by no means bird's-eye) view of surrounding terrain.

The **Rynek**, distinctive for its slope, is ringed with houses from different stylistic periods. Today, only numbers 10 and 27 have the arcades typical of 16th-century houses. The red rectangular **town hall**, erected in the 14th century, is the oldest building on the Rynek; the white clock tower was added in the 17th century and the sundial on the southern wall (the work of Tadeusz Przypkowski) in 1958. The ground floor houses the **Regional Museum – Town Hall** (Muzeum Okręgowe – Ratusz; Rynek; adult/concession 4/3zł; 🕑 10am-5pm Tue-Sun May-Sep, 9am-4pm Tue-Fri & 10am-3pm Sat & Sun Oct-Apr), focusing on the town's history.

One of the town's premier attractions is the **Underground Tourist Route** (Podziemna Trasa Turystyczna; ☎ 015 832 3088; ul Oleśnickich; adult/concession 7/4zł; 🕑 10am-5.30pm May-Sep, 10am-4pm Oct-Apr). The 40-minute guided tour (in Polish) leads through a chain of 30-odd cellars tidily connected over

500m beneath the Old Town. The cellars – originally used for storage and sometimes for shelter during times of conflict – were built between the 13th and 17th centuries. The deepest point is about 12m below ground, but feels like more, because of disorienting twists, turns and Escher-esque staircases. There is an interesting legend about a local girl who tricked the invading Tatar army into the tunnels; the city was saved when the entrances were blocked, burying both the army and the heroic (or perhaps merely misunderstood) girl. The soft-soil cellars undermined the stability of the city and caused near-disaster in the 1960s; the 1964–77 restoration programme reinforced the cellars and reinvented them as a tourist attraction.

Nearby, the 18th-century **synagogue** (ul Żydowska) was virtually destroyed during WWII but remains of 18th- and 19th-century murals partially survived. The former synagogue houses the town's archives.

From the Rynek, take ul Mariacka to the **cathedral** (☎ 015 832 7343; www.katedra.sandomierz.opoka .org.pl in Polish; ul Mariacka; 🕑 10am-2pm & 3-5pm Tue-Sat, 2-4pm Sun & public holidays). Built between 1360 and 1382, this massive church has preserved much of its Gothic exterior, apart from the Baroque façade added in the 17th century. The Russo-Byzantine frescoes in the chancel were painted in the 1420s but later whitewashed, only to be revealed again at the beginning of the 20th century. Also note the impressive Baroque organ gallery of the late 17th century and the marble altar dating to the 18th century.

The quintessential example of Sandomierz's underrated assets, the medieval **Długosz House** (Dom Długosza) was built in 1476 for Poland's first historian, Jan Długosz. Today it houses the **Diocesan Museum** (Muzeum Diecezjalne; ☎ 015 832 2304; ul Długosza 9; adult/concession 4/3zł; 🕑 9am-4pm Tue-Sat & 1.30-4pm Sun & public holidays Apr-Oct, 9am-3pm Tue-Sat & 1.30-3pm Sun & public holidays Nov-Mar), with an exquisitely rich and romantic collection. Visitors are free to wander at their leisure through the glistening rooms and wonder how so lavish a collection of medieval artwork, sculpture, tapestries, clothing, coins and ceramics is so unceremoniously accessible to the humble traveller.

The **Royal Castle**, a few steps downhill from the cathedral, was built in the 14th century on the site of a previous wooden stronghold and was gradually extended during the next three centuries. It now accommodates the **Regional Museum – Castle** (Muzeum Okręgowe – Zamek; ☎ 015 832

---

365 REASONS NOT TO BE MARTYRED

The interiors of Sandomierz Cathedral give a pleasant first impression, but focus on the details beyond the initial ostentatiousness and you discover the macabre side of Sandomierz.

The paintings on the walls of the cathedral are by 18th-century artist Karol de Prevot (1708–37), who was apparently not of a cheery disposition. The four paintings on the back wall under the organ depict historic scenes such as the 1656 destruction of Sandomierz castle by the Swedes. But it is the series of 12 paintings on the side walls that are a real argument for checking ID at the door of this cathedral.

The series, *Martyrologium Romanum,* depicts the martyrdom of the Dominican Fathers and other people of Sandomierz at the hands of the Tartars between 1259 and 1260. The unfortunate subjects are being sawn, burned, hanged, whipped, quartered, sliced, diced and otherwise discourteously treated.

The 12 paintings are supposed to symbolise the 12 months of the year; next to each image of torture a number represents the day of the month. Legend has it that if you find the day and month on which you were born, you'll discover how you're going to die. Happy Deathday to you.

2265; www.republika.pl/mosandomierz in Polish; ul Zamkowa 14; adult/concession 7/5zł; ☏ 10am-5pm Tue-Fri & 10am-6pm Sat & Sun May-Sep, 9am-4pm Tue-Fri & 10am-3pm Sat & Sun Oct-Apr) containing modest ethnographic, archaeological and art collections.

Dating from the 1230s, **St James' Church** (Kościół Św Jakuba; ☏ 015 832 7343; www.sandomierz.dominikanie .pl in Polish; ul Staromiejska; ☏ 10am-5pm Mon-Fri, 10am-6pm Sat & Sun) is the oldest building in town (but doesn't show its age) and is believed to be the first brick church in Poland. Among few historic objects remaining is the sarcophagus in the presbytery, carved in 1676 out of a single oak trunk. The belfry beside the church holds two of the oldest bells in Poland, cast in 1314 and 1389. The church is along cobblestoned ul Staromiejska.

Continue up ul Staromiejska as far as **St Paul's Church** (built in the 15th century and today a Gothic, Renaissance and Baroque mix) and left into the **Gorge of Queen Jadwiga** (Wąwóz Królowej Jadwigi), named for the queen who was reputedly fond of it. The gorge, with walls up to 10m, is the result of water carving the soft loess soil. Follow it to ul Krakowska or take the first path on the left back to St James' Church.

Sleeping
BUDGET & MIDRANGE
Jutrzenka (☏ 015 832 2219; ul Zamkowa 1; s/d/tr 50/100/100zł; [P]) Cluttered with colour and character, the breezy rooms at Jutrzenka are something special. Its proprietors have unconsciously gone all out to fill rooms with fun, each offering a different combination of cluttered bric-a-brac and mismatched

odds and ends. Some rooms have dining tables, another has a giant TV and all have conveniences like kettles. Price depends on variables like size, furniture and proximity to shared bathrooms.

Hotel Grodzki (☏ 015 832 2423; www.hotelgrodzki .pl; ul Mickiewicza 38; d with shared bathroom 120zł, s/d with private bathroom 150/190zł; [P]) Serviceable rooms in an uninteresting modern hotel, conveniently located near the bus station 1km northwest of the Old Town. Doubles on the top floor are great value with good light from sloping skylights, and a spotless shared bathroom. Unlimited breakfast is included.

Motel Królowej Jadwigi (☏ /fax 015 832 2988; www .motel.go3.pl; ul Krakowska 24; d 150-170zł, tr 220zł; [P]) The managers of this quirky motel, a little off the old town, couldn't be more enthusiastic about housing and feeding you. The reception/restaurant area is bric-a-brac on acid; antiques and kooky collectables teeter on every surface. The friendly couple who run it have refrained from injecting the same eccentricity into the tastefully reserved rooms. Inspect before you select; rooms vary in size and style within the same price category.

TOP END
Hotel Pod Ciżemką (☏ 015 832 0550; www.sando mierz-hotel.com.pl in Polish; Rynek 27; d/ste 250/300zł) Extensively refurbished, Pod Ciżemką is the grandest place in the Old Town. Set in a 400-year-old house, the stylish rooms are commendable renditions of old-world elegance, as is the onsite restaurant.

Hotel Basztowy (☏ 015 833 3450; www.hotel basztowy.pl; pl Ks J Poniatowskiego 2; s 170-220zł, d/tr/ste

MAŁOPOLSKA

270/330/400 zł; (P) (🖥)) Opened in 2003, business hotel Basztowy has maintained its freshness while still achieving a hint of ancient elegance. The restaurant has a fine wood finish, and the billiard room is a nice touch. Some rooms offer a pleasant view.

Eating & Drinking

Cukiernia Gobio (☎ 015 644 5922; Rynek 31a; snacks 3-8zł; 🕐 9am-7pm Mon-Fri, 9am to 8pm Sat & Sun) A cheap-as-chips café recommended here primarily for the quirkiness of its coffee offerings – anyone for Sandomierz coffee with fresh egg? If you are not feeling that brave, you can't go wrong with a standard coffee or hot chocolate to wash down good-value cakes, waffles or pita bread sandwiches. Far more benign is **Café Galeria** (☎ 0604 907 946; Rynek 25/26; 🕐 8am-10pm), which serves a range of teas in cosy quarters.

In the same building as the PTTK Office is the ever-popular **Café Bar Kordegarda** (ul Rynek 12; 🕐 10am-last customer), where the funky young things of Sandomierz descend on the Rynek for a casual drink and chat.

For a magical meal, go to **Motel Królowej Jadwigi** (☎ /fax 015 832 2988; www.motel.go3.pl; ul Krakowska 24) where the eccentric dining room is more like a scene from a fairytale than a motel restaurant.

Local favourite **Restauracja Trzydziestka** (☎ 015 644 5312; Rynek 30; mains 10-30zł; 🕐 lunch & dinner) offers full flavour and full plates. Similar, though a tad more downmarket, is **Kawiarnia Staromiejska z Garkuchnią** (☎ 015 832 3778; Rynek 28; mains 8-15zł; 🕐 9am-11pm), which offers simple staples and (an attempt at) an English menu.

Getting There & Away

BUS

The **PKS bus terminal** (☎ 015 832 2302; ul Listopada 22) is 1.5km northwest of the Old Town; frequent urban buses go there from Opatów Gate.

There are a dozen fast buses to Warsaw (50zł, three hours), which cost roughly the same as the train, and four buses per day to Kielce (17.60zł, two hours).

There are buses to Tarnobrzeg (4zł, 30 minutes, every half-hour) but suburban bus 11 (2.40zł) running along Michiewicza is more convenient and just as frequent. From Tarnobrzeg, frequent buses go to Baranów Sandomierski (4zł, 50 minutes).

For Ujazd, change at Opatów (5.20zł, 45 minutes, 30km) or Klimontów.

TRAIN

The train station, 3km southeast of the Old Town, on the other side of the Vistula, is served by city buses to/from Opatów Gate. Four trains run to Warsaw daily (41zł, four hours). There are also daily trains to Katowice (42zł, five hours, one morning train, 243km) and Zamość (33zł, three hours, one evening train, 153km).

BARANÓW SANDOMIERSKI

pop 1500

The pride of Baranów Sandomierski, beyond even its sulphur deposits, is **Baranów Castle** (☎ 015 811 8040; www.baranow.com.pl; ul Zamkowa 20; adult/concession 10/6zł; 🕐 castle park & courtyard 7am-10pm, museum 9am-5pm Tue-Sun, 9am-3pm low season). This Renaissance castle was built at the end of the 16th century for the Leszczyński family, though its tumultuous history spanning many residents means that the façade and interiors are largely the result of restoration work carried out in the 1960s. The architectural detail of Baranów Castle is thought to be the work of Santi Gucci (though only completed after his death) and the stuccowork still preserved on parts of the ceilings is credited to Giovanni Battista Falconi.

The castle was occupied by the Leszczyński family for more than 100 years from 1569 to 1677; the last resident Leszczyński bore a son who would later become King of Poland.

After the brief tenancy of Dymitri Winiowiecki, Prince Józef Karol Lubomirski took over ownership in 1682, and commissioned various alterations under the guidance of Tylman van Gameren. The 19th century brought two major fires to Baranów Castle, one of which caused damage its owners could not afford to repair. The house was sold at auction in 1867 to the Krasicki family, remaining in their hands until the outbreak of WWII. After the war, the castle was transferred to the state-owned Siarkopol sulphur-enterprise (hence the sulphur-extraction exhibit downstairs), and to the Warsaw-based Industrial Development Agency in 1997.

Today, many of the castle's 2nd-floor rooms are open to visitors (guided tours are conducted in Polish only). The cellar also displays archaeological finds, including the remains of the Gothic stronghold discovered during the castle's restoration process after WWII.

Sleeping & Eating

Hotel Zamkowy (☎ 015 811 8039; ul Zamkowa 20; s/d in hotel 180/280zł, s/d in castle 250/350zł, ste 300-700zł; P) In the building just west of the castle, Hotel Zamkowy offers pleasant rooms, though its castle rooms are preferable. Weekend rates are attractive, as are the sauna, gym, billiard table and the fact that the hotel can arrange fishing in the pond (for a fee).

Magnacka Restaurant (☎ 015 811 8040; ul Zamkowa 20; mains 20-30zł; ☯ 11am-11pm) In the basement of the castle, Magnacka Restaurant serves Polish food and modern European cuisine, with traditional feasts on Thursdays.

Getting There & Away

The train station is well out of the village so it's more convenient to travel by bus.

There's no direct transport to Baranów Sandomierski but minibuses from Sandomierz run to Tarnobrzeg (4zł, 30 minutes) regularly between 6.20am and 5.30pm. Even easier is city bus 11 (2.40zł). From Tarnobrzeg, both regular buses and minibuses pass through Baranów Sandomierski (3zł, 30 minutes) on the way to Mielec and Krasiczyn.

The bus station is close to the Rynek, from where the castle is an easy 1km walk. You shouldn't have to wait more than 30 minutes for a bus back to Tarnobrzeg; some pass the bus stop outside the castle.

UJAZD
pop 1600

Krzyżtopór Castle (☎ 015 860 1133; adult/concession 6/4zł; ☯ 8.30am-sunset), in the small village of Ujazd (oo-yahst), was commissioned by eccentric governor Krzysztof Ossoliński, and built on his fantastical imagination.

Ossoliński wanted his love of magic and astrology to be incorporated into every aspect of the castle. The architect commissioned to create Ossoliński's dream was Italian Lorenzo Muretto (known in Poland as Wawrzyniec Senes), who worked on the mammoth project between 1631 and 1644.

History and legend offer zany accounts of the castle. It was designed to embody a calendar, with four towers representing the four seasons, 12 halls for the 12 months of the year, 52 rooms for the 52 weeks, and 365 windows for 365 days – plus one to be used only during leap years.

Some of the cellars were used as stables for Ossoliński's 370 white stallions, and

are adorned with mirrors and black marble. The crystal ceiling of the great dining hall is believed to have been the base of an enormous aquarium.

Perhaps the most enchanting report is that concerning the tunnel that ran under it, linking to the castle of Ossoliński's brother. The 15km tunnel to Ossolin was believed to have been covered with sugar so the two brothers could visit each other on horse-drawn sledges, pretending they were travelling on snow.

Sadly, Ossoliński was barely able to enjoy a full calendar year in his playground; he died in 1645 – only a year after the castle was completed.

Among the few details to have survived the past four decades are the stone symbols at the gate: the krzyż (cross) representing religious devotion; and the topór (axe), as depicted on the Ossoliński family coat of arms. Spend long enough clambering over and under these enormous ruins, and you will be able to imagine the other details.

After damage done by the Swedes in the 1650s and the abandonment of the castle by its subsequent owners in 1770, this dreamland fell to ruin. Since WWII, talk of converting the castle into a military school or hotel has petered out, leaving Krzyżtopór Castle as a landscape for the daydreams of its visitors.

Getting There & Away

There is no direct transport to Ujazd from major towns like Sandomierz. The major points of access are Opatów (5zł, 40 minutes, 28km) or Klimontów (5zł, 40 minutes, 28km).

From Opatów, there are several buses daily. At the time of writing, buses passing Ujazd left Opatów at 5.50am, 6.20am, 8.30am, 11.20am, 12.30pm, 1.10pm and 3.20pm. Or a taxi to the castle and back costs around 60zł, including half-an-hour waiting time.

THE RADOM PLAIN

The Radom Plain (Równina Radomska) extends between Małopolska to the south and Mazovia in the north. This gentle area is seldom visited by tourists, but it does attract wanderers who are tuned in to the ebb and flow of artistic movement (the creative refuge of the Centre of Polish Sculpture is here). One of the most expansive skansens in Małopolska is just outside the maturing town of Radom.

MAŁOPOLSKA

RADOM

pop 225,149

Unlike most Polish towns, the heart of Radom doesn't beat at its Rynek. Rather, it is to the main thoroughfare of ul Żeromskiego that Radomites go to show that their industrial town does not have an industrial attitude.

The biannual Radom Air Show (during the last weekend of August of every other year) sets the town and the sky above it abuzz with activity.

Little remains of its historical heritage – dating to the Middle Ages – but Radom seems too occupied with its future to be missing its past.

There's a **tourist office** (☎ 048 363 5775; ul Traugutta 3; ⏲ 10am-5pm Mon-Fri, 11am-1pm Sat) opposite the train station (near Hotel Poniatowski), which may be able to give you some general guidance.

Sights

On the southern side of the run-down Rynek is the **Jacek Malczewski Museum** (Muzeum im Jacka Malczewskiego; ☎ 048 362 2114; www.muzeum.edu.pl; Rynek 11; adult/concession 5/3zł; ⏲ 9am-3pm Tue-Thu, 10am-3pm Fri, 10am-4pm Sat & Sun), named for the Radom-born painter. It contains a large collection of the namesake's work, as well as art by other painters and a small archaeological collection.

The most significant relic of Radom's earliest years is the **St Waenceslaus church** in the Old Town Sq. Built originally in the 13th century from wood, it was the first parish church of Old Radom. It was used for various purposes (such as a military hospital and psychiatric ward) and completely restored in the 1970s. The main parish **Church of St John the Baptist** was founded by Kazimierz III Wielki in 1360 and altered by numerous people up to the present. The church is located behind Jacek Malczewski Museum.

Some 8km from the centre of town and 1km off the Kielce Rd is the **skansen** (Muzeum Wsi Radomskiej; ☎ 048 332 9281; www.muzeum-radom.pl in Polish; ul Szydłowiecka 30; adult/concession 8/5zł; ⏲ 9am-5pm Tue-Fri, 10am-8pm Sat & Sun), which is extensive enough to justify bringing a picnic lunch. Furnished interiors showcase styles from the whole region. Urban buses 5, 17 and K will get you to the turn-off, from where you walk 1km to the entrance. Returning to Radom, turn left back onto the highway; the bus stop is in a small side street 20m or so past the turn-off.

Sleeping & Eating

Hotel Iskra (☎ 048 383 8745; www.hoteliskra.radom.pl in Polish; ul Planty 4; s/d/tr 110/160/165zł, with breakfast 125/130/210zł; P) Hidden by Poniatowski Hotel, the Iskra offers bright, well-maintained rooms big enough to stretch out in. Conveniently located near the train and bus stations.

Hotel Glass (☎ 048 340 2585; www.hotelglass.radom .pl; ul Prażmowskiego 17; s/d/ste 108/160/215zł; P ▢) This friendly hotel is named for its glass exterior (it would have been Hotel Pink if it was named for its interior). Standard rooms are unremarkable, but apartments offer distinct sleeping and sitting areas.

Hotel Gromada (☎ 048 368 9100; radomhotel.centrum @gromada.pl; ul Narutowicza 9; s/d 200/220zł, apt 300-400zł; P ✕ ▢ ⅁) This generic business hotel has spacious rooms and an onsite restaurant and bar. Apartments are reasonable value given their terrace and kitchen annex. Another branch is located 2.5km west of the town centre.

Pleasant eateries line ul Żeromskiego. For a late afternoon beer, try a café in Park Tadeusz Kościuszki at the eastern end of the pedestrian strip. Closer to the train station, the restaurant at **Hotel Glass** (☎ 048 340 2585; ul Prażmowskiego 17; mains 10–30zł; ⏲ 7am-midnight) offers surprisingly tasty Polish fare in its ambient (read: dimly lit) restaurant.

Getting There & Away

The train and bus stations are next to each other, 2km south of the city's main street, ul Żeromskiego.

Daily, there are at least 15 trains to Kielce (22zł, 1½ hours, 85km) and around a dozen to Warsaw (22zł, 2½ hours, 100km). For more information, ask at the **information counter** (⏲ 6am-10pm) in the train station.

Most buses bound for Warsaw and Kraków (192km) depart in the afternoon. There are around 10 buses leaving for Łódź (135km) between 6am and 6.30pm, as well as several daily buses to Lublin (13zł, 2½ hours) and Puławy (8zł, 1½ hours).

Normal buses pass through Szydłowiec or Orońsko on their way to destinations further afield. More convenient minibuses leave from an area opposite the car park between the bus and train stations.

OROŃSKO

pop 1200

A time-slowing slice of historical charm and contemporary creativity, the **Centre of**

Polish Sculpture (Centrum Rzeźby Polskiej; ☎ 048 618 4516; www.rzezba-oronsko.pl; ul Topolowa 1; adult/concession 5/3zł; ☯ indoor exhibitions & palace 8am-4pm Tue-Fri & 10am-6pm Sat & Sun May-Oct, 7am-3pm Tue-Fri & 8am-4pm Sat & Sun Nov-Apr, park until sunset) is supported by the Józef Brandt Foundation and is established in that esteemed painter's 19th-century estate.

The centre comprises the manor house of Józef Brandt (1841–1915), the museum of contemporary sculpture, and a hotel for creatively inclined visitors.

The Italian neo-Renaissance **Manor House of Józef Brandt** remains as it was when he lived and worked here…assuming he lived and worked extremely tidily. Impeccable interiors are adorned with works by Brandt and his colleagues of the era.

The **museum of contemporary sculpture** is spread throughout the landscaped garden, in the former chapel, orangery and coach house, and the more recently constructed exhibition hall. Temporary exhibitions throughout the grounds are mostly the works of contemporary artists. It is possible to watch resident sculptors at work in the open-air workspace from the terrace of the canteen.

Sleeping & Eating

Sculptor House (☎ /fax 048 618 4516; ul Topolowa 1; s/d/tr 45/60/70zł; **P**) The centre's Sculptor House in the former granary can accommodate 24 people. There is also a small restaurant for resident artists, and a canteen open to all.

Getting There & Away

Orońsko lies on the Radom–Kielce highway and the bus service is frequent (there's no railway). The centre is an easy walk from the bus stop on the highway, from where you can take urban bus K, a PKS bus coming from Szydłowiec, or a passing minibus (2.50zł to 4zł, 30 minutes) back to Radom. Any of these will also let you off at the turn-off for Radom's skansen. For Kielce you will need to change in Skarżysko Kamienna or double back to Radom.

SZYDŁOWIEC
pop 12,074

The town of Szydłowiec (shi-*dwo*-viets) achieved its municipal status in 1470, and until the 19th century was the property of the aristocratic Sapieha and Radziwiłł families. Under their influence, the town prospered through

the excavation of sandstone used in construction – the church being a prime example.

Sights

The attractive Renaissance **town hall** seems disproportionately large for the size of the Rynek. It has the look of an impressive white-washed castle, right down to the towers and decorative parapets.

Presiding proudly over the Rynek from its southern side is the 15th-century **church**. The Gothic exterior, built partly from local sandstone, contrasts vividly with its colourful Renaissance interior. Original details to note include the high wooden altar, the polyptych depicting the Assumption and the impressive flat wooden ceiling of the nave, all of which date back to the beginning of the 16th century.

About 500m northwest of the Rynek is a small 16th-century **castle** surrounded by a picturesque moat. Some of its rooms house the **Museum of Polish Folk Musical Instruments** (Muzeum Polskich Ludowych Instrumentów Muzycznych; ☎ 048 617 1789; ul Sowińskiego 2; adult/concession 4/3zł; ☯ 9am-3.30pm Mon-Fri, 9.30am-5pm Sat & Sun). There is no information in English, but there are some lovely instruments to admire all the same. Unfortunately there is nothing interactive for the kids to bang or clang.

Before WWII, 70% of the population of Szydłowiec was Jewish. The town's **Jewish cemetery** is one of the largest in Poland, yet today is a quarter of the size it was when it was founded in 1788. Most of the 2000-odd tombstones are from the 19th century (the oldest from 1831). To get there from the Rynek, head east along ul Kilińskiego, left onto ul Kościuszki (the road to Radom) and after 250m turn right onto ul Spółdzielcza. The cemetery is 100m ahead.

Sleeping & Eating

Youth Hostel (☎ 048 617 5955; ul Kolejowa 16; dm 25-30zł) The only place to stay in Szydłowiec is the youth hostel, 1km southeast of the Rynek, beyond a colony of dull apartment blocks. Look for the '*noclegi*' sign in front of the pleasant house.

Piwnica Szydłowiecka (☎ 048 617 0224; Rynek 1; mains 10-20zł; ☯ lunch & dinner) For some central and historical dining, head to this restaurant in the cellar of the town hall.

Getting There & Away

The bus terminal (which looks like an abandoned gas station along Route 66) is 1km north from the Rynek. Only a few buses go straight to Kielce (6.80zł, 1½ hours, three or more daily). If you're going to Radom (2.5zł, 45 minutes, every half-hour), minibuses are preferable; they leave from behind the PKS building and pass Orońsko on the way.

Forget the train – the station is 5km east of town.

THE LUBLIN UPLAND

Stretching east of the Vistula and San Rivers up to the Ukrainian border is the Lublin Upland (Wyżyna Lubelska). Lublin, its biggest city, still bears the scars of WWII but carries itself with dignity these days. The area also boasts (though not loudly enough) Kazimierz Dolny, a quaint town on the banks of the Vistula that attracts weekenders looking to escape the city – and the 21st century. Also worth visiting are the town of Zamość and the nearby village of Zwierzyniec, both built on the Renaissance dreams of Jan Zamoyski.

LUBLIN
pop 362,247

Lublin's centre has emerged into the new century with revived confidence, and the locals are out in droves to enjoy it. The Rynek is ringed with bars, cafés and restaurants, which have new-world attitude while still respecting their old-world location. Step through Krakowska Gate to pick up the pace on ul Krakowskie Przedmieście, with its parade of pepped-up Poles and perky holidaymakers.

After many years spent lagging behind other towns of equivalent size, Lublin has relaunched itself as the bustling leader of its region. After its painful history, Lublin's ability to laugh again is a testament to its character as a true survivor.

History

Not only has this city witnessed some of history's most harrowing chapters, it has also been the instigator of social movements, and the setting for some of the country's most landmark events.

The area was likely settled as early as the 6th century, becoming an important trade centre and fortification by the 10th and 11th centuries. The city was destroyed and rebuilt many times in efforts to protect Poland from invading Tatars, Lithuanians and Ruthenians. The city received its municipal charter in

1317, and the castle was built soon afterwards by Kazimierz III Wielki. It was in Lublin in 1569 that the union between Poland and Lithuania was formed, creating the largest state in Europe at the time.

In November 1918, the first independent government of Poland was formed here, which soon handed power over to Józef Piłsudski. Lublin became a Nazi headquarters for Operation Reinhardt, the beginnings of Hitler's 'Final Solution'. It was also in Lublin that the provisional communist government was installed by the Soviets in July 1944 during the last stages of WWII. Lublin is considered by some to be the true birthplace of Solidarity – the avalanche of strikes against the communist regime that spread throughout Poland in 1980, eventually leading to the Gdańsk agreements. Since WWII, Lublin has expanded threefold to become the biggest city in Małopolska and the most significant industrial and academic centre in Eastern Poland.

Orientation

Your explorations are likely to be limited to the compact Old Town. The New Town stretches west along the main thoroughfare, ul Krakowskie Przedmieście.

The train station is 2km south of the centre, but the busy PKS and minibus terminals are next to each other on the northern edge of the Old Town, a skip from the castle.

Information

Plenty of *kantors* and ATMs line ul Krakowskie Przedmieście and adjacent streets.

Bank Pekao ul Krakowskie Przedmieście (Map p233; ul Krakowskie Przedmieście 64; 8am- 6pm Mon-Fri, 10am-2pm Sat); ul Królewska (Map p235; ul Królewska 1) Cash advances on Visa and MasterCard.

EMPiK (Map p233; 081 534 8286; Galeria Centrum, ul Krakowskie Przedmieście 40; 9.30am-8pm Mon-Fri, 9.30am-6pm Sat, 10.30am-4pm Sun) Abundant travel information (in Polish), ample maps, and English-language novels, newspapers and magazines.

LOIT Tourist Information Centre (Map p235; 081 532 4412; www.loit.lublin.pl; ul Jezuicka 1/3; 9am-6pm Mon-Fri, 10am-4pm Sat, 10am-3pm Sun May-Sep, 10am-5pm Mon-Fri, 10am-3pm Sat Oct-Apr) Extremely helpful English-speaking staff, souvenirs for sale and lots of brochures, including handy city walking-route companion tourist routes of Lublin.

Main post office (Map p233; ul Krakowskie Przedmieście; 9am-5pm)

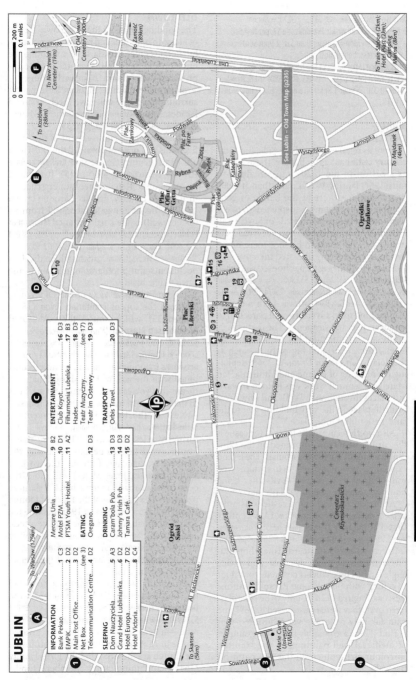

LUBLIN

INFORMATION	
Bank Pekao.....................................1	C3
EMPiK..2	D2
Main Post Office............................3	D2
Net Box....................................(see 3)	
Telecommunication Centre...........4	D2

SLEEPING	
Dom Nauczyciela............................5	A3
Grand Hotel Lublinianka...............6	D2
Hotel Europa...................................7	D2
Hotel Victoria.................................8	C4

Mercure Unia..................................9	B2
Motel PZM...................................10	D1
PTSM Youth Hostel.....................11	A2

EATING	
Oregano.......................................12	D3

DRINKING	
Caram'bola Pub............................13	D3
Johnny's Irish Pub.......................14	D3
Tamara Café.................................15	D2

ENTERTAINMENT	
Club Koyot..................................16	D3
Filharmonia Lubelska..................17	B3
Hades..18	D3
Teatr Muzyczny....................(see 17)	
Teatr im Osterwy........................19	D3

TRANSPORT	
Orbis Travel.................................20	D3

MAŁOPOLSKA

Net Box (Map p233; ☎ 081 532 5220; www.net box.end.pl; ul Krakowskie Przedmieście 52; per hr 4.5zł; ☺ 9am-9pm Mon-Fri, 10am-9pm Sat, 2-9pm Sun) Internet access, behind post office.

Post office (Map p235; ul Grodzka; ☺ 9am-4pm)

www café (Map p235; ☎ 081 442 3580; 3rd fl, Rynek 8; per hr 3zł; ☺ noon-8pm) Internet access. Follow signs to PTTK.

Sights

CASTLE
Despite its relatively friendly façade, the 14th-century **castle** has a grim history. It was rebuilt as a prison in the 1820s and remained so until 1954. During WWII more than 100,000 people suffered here at the hands of Nazi occupiers before being transported on to extermination camps. Hundreds of Jewish and Polish political prisoners had survived here until July 1944, only to be shot mere hours before the Red Army liberated the city.

Since 1957, the castle has housed the **Lublin Museum** (Map p235; ☎ 081 532 5001; www.zamek.lublin .pl; ul Zamkowa 9; adult/concession 6.50/4.50zł, free Sat; ☺ 9am-4pm Wed-Sat, 9am-5pm Sun), with a collection ranging from silverware and porcelain to woodcarvings and weaponry. The particularly impressive art includes big names (such as Jacek Malczewski) and big pictures, such as the detail-rich *Lublin Union of 1569*, depicting the merging of Poland and Lithuania. Jan Matejko's seminal work was hidden in various places throughout WWII, and now takes pride of place in the very building where the landmark union took place.

Also worth seeing in the foyer of the castle is the curious **Devil's Paw**, imprinted on the 17th-century table of the Royal Tribunal. The legend explaining its existence relates to a widow who was avenged by a team of devils after being unjustly treated by the Royal Tribunal.

At the eastern end of the castle is its most prized asset – the exquisite 14th-century **Chapel of the Holy Trinity** (Map p235; adult/concession 6.50/4.50zł; ☺ 10am-5pm Tue-Sat, 10am-6pm Sun), featured on many postcards (the photographers must have snuck in a flash and a wide angle lens). The chapel is covered from floor to ceiling with polychrome Russo-Byzantine frescoes. Painted in 1418, only to be later plastered over, they were rediscovered in 1897 and painstakingly restored over a hundred-year period. These are possibly the finest examples of medieval wall paintings in the country, so colour-rich you could lick the paint off the walls.

OLD TOWN
The winding streets of the Old Town are full of life, with new cafés and restaurants opening, but don't wander after dark. Areas around the bus stop and bus terminal should also be approached with caution in the early hours.

Some of the buildings in the historic quarter surrounding the Rynek have lovely restored façades. At the Rynek's centre is the 1781 neoclassical **Old Town Hall** (Map p235).

The only significant remnant of the fortified walls that once surrounded the Old Town is the 14th-century Gothic-style **Krakowska Gate** (Brama Krakowska; Map p235). It received its octagonal Renaissance superstructure in the 16th century, and its Baroque crown in 1782. Inside the gate (accessed from its eastern wall) is the small **Historical Museum of Lublin** (Muzeum Historii Miasta Lublina; Map p235; ☎ 081 532 6001; Plac Łokietka 3; adult/concession 3.50/2.50zł; ☺ 9am-4pm Wed-Sat, 9am-5pm Sun), which displays documents and photographs relating to the town's civic history.

For an expansive view of the Old Town, climb to the top of **Trinitarian Tower** (1819; Map p235), which houses the underrated **Archdiocesan Museum** (Muzeum Archiecezjalne; Map p235; ☎ 0695 475152; Plac Katedralny; adult/concession 5/3zł; ☺ 10am-5pm Apr-Oct). The chaotic layout of artworks in hidden nooks and crannies, combined with the lack of English explanations, means that you can discover ancient artefacts in the haphazard manner of Indiana Jones.

Next to the tower is the 16th-century **cathedral** (Map p235; Plac Katedralny; ☺ dawn-sunset), formerly a Jesuit church. There are many impressive details to behold, including the Baroque *trompe l'oeil* frescoes (the work of Moravian artist Józef Majer) and the 17th-century altar made from a black Lebanese pear tree. The painting of the Black Madonna is said to have shed tears in 1945, making it a source of much reverence for local devotees. The acoustic vestry (so called for its ability to project whispers) and the **treasury** (skarbiec; ☺ 10am-2pm & 3-5pm Tue-Sun) behind the chapel are also worth some attention.

Originally a Gothic complex founded by King Kazimierz III Wielki in 1342, the **Dominican Priory** (Kościół Dominikanów; Map p235; ☎ 081 532 8990; www.domikikanie.lub.pl in Polish; ul Złota 9) was rebuilt in Renaissance style after it was ravaged by fire in 1575. Two historic highlights inside the church are the Chapel of the Firlej Family (1615), containing family members' tomb-

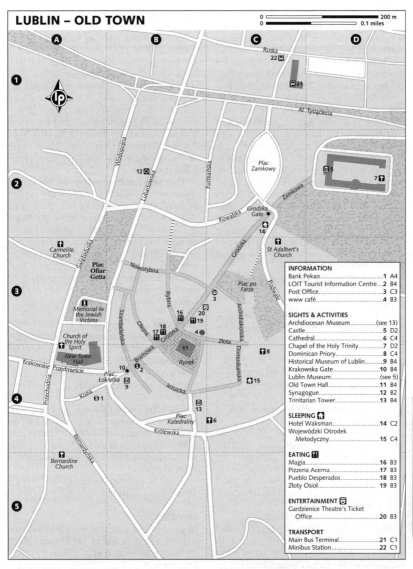

LUBLIN – OLD TOWN

INFORMATION
Bank Pekao	**1** A4
LOIT Tourist Information Centre	**2** B4
Post Office	**3** C3
www café	**4** B3

SIGHTS & ACTIVITIES
Archdiocesan Museum	(see 13)
Castle	**5** D2
Cathedral	**6** C4
Chapel of the Holy Trinity	**7** D2
Dominican Priory	**8** C4
Historical Museum of Lublin	**9** B4
Krakowska Gate	**10** B4
Lublin Museum	(see 5)
Old Town Hall	**11** B4
Synagogue	**12** B2
Trinitarian Tower	**13** B4

SLEEPING
Hotel Waksman	**14** C2
Wojewódzki Ośrodek Metodyczny	**15** C4

EATING
Magia	**16** B3
Pizzeria Acerna	**17** B3
Pueblo Desperados	**18** B3
Złoty Osioł	**19** B3

ENTERTAINMENT
Gardzienice Theatre's Ticket Office	**20** B3

TRANSPORT
Main Bus Terminal	**21** C1
Minibus Station	**22** C1

stones; and the Tyszkiewicz Chapel (1645–59), with impressive Renaissance stuccowork. For an insight into 18th-century Lublin, note the large historical painting, *The Fire of Lublin*, which depicts the 1719 fire (in the Szaniawski family chapel to your right as you enter the church). The Dominian Basilica was closed by the Russians in 1886; the monks returned just before the outbreak of WWII only to be expelled again by the postwar communist regime. The building was finally returned to the Dominicans in 1993.

MAJDANEK

Some 4km southeast of Lublin's centre is Majdanek extermination camp, where tens of thousands were murdered. The site is now the **Majdanek State Museum** (Państwowe Muzeum na Majdanku; off Map p233; ☎ 081 744 1955; www.maj danek.home.pl; Droga Męczenników Majdanka 67; admission free; ⊙ 8am-6pm Apr-Oct, 8am-3pm Nov-Mar), founded only four months after the camp's liberation – the first of its kind in the world. Unlike other extermination camps, the Nazis went to no effort to conceal Majdanek. Coming from the main road, the sudden appearance of time-frozen guard towers and barbed-wire fences interrupting the sprawl of suburbia is disquieting. The details are all the more confronting; gas chambers are open to visitors, and many of the prisoners' possessions are on display. The 5km walk through the museum starts at the Visitor's Centre, passes the foreboding Monument of Fight & Martyrdom, through parts of the barracks and finishes at the guarded mausoleum containing the ashes of many victims. Children under 14 are not permitted to visit the museum.

A short film (3zł) can be viewed at the visitor's centre when there is a minimum of five people.

Trolleybuses 23 and 156 (2zł) along ul Królewska, slightly south of Plac Łokietka, go to the entrance of Majdanek.

JEWISH RELICS

The first census in 1550 shows that 840 Jews lived in Lublin; 200 years later they had grown into the third-largest Jewish population in Poland, and before WWII around 30% of Lubliners were Jews.

The climax of the time-old plight of the Jewish community in Lublin came when the Nazis entered the town on 18 September 1939. A visit to Majdanek extermination camp (opposite) will help you understand what happened next. Of approximately 42,000 Jewish Lubliners, only a few hundred are believed to have survived the Holocaust.

There is a marked tourist route dedicated to monuments and buildings of relevance to Lublin's Jewish heritage. Ask the tourist information office for further information.

The only **synagogue** (Map p235; ☎ 081 532 0922; ul Lubartowska 8; ⊙ exhibition 1-3pm Sun, other times by appointment) to survive of the 38 that functioned before WWII is in an early 20th-century building, which bears no distinguishing features of a synagogue. It contains a modest exhibition of old photographs, books in Hebrew and ritual objects. Enter the gate from the street

and take the door on the right leading upstairs to the 1st-floor synagogue.

The **old Jewish cemetery** (off Map p233), established in 1541, has 30-odd readable tombstones. The oldest dates from 1641 and is the oldest Jewish tombstone in Poland in its original location. The graveyard is on a hill between ul Sienna and ul Kalinowszczyzna, a short walk northeast of the castle. It is surrounded by a high brick wall and the gate is locked. Contact **Mrs Honig** (☎ 081 747 8676; Apt 7, ul Dembowskiego 4) at her home, 200m north of the cemetery; she lets visitors in (leave a donation).

The **new Jewish cemetery** (off Map p233; ul Walecznych), founded in 1829, is the resting place of 52,000 Jews buried here until 1942. The cemetery was destroyed by the Nazis during WWII (who used tombstones in the construction of parts of Majdanek extermination camp) and is still in the process of being restored. Broken tombstones form a wall around the cemetery. The graveyard and the small museum can be visited during daylight hours. There is a 24-hour guard on duty.

SKANSEN

The well-designed **skansen** (Muzeum Wsi Lubelskiej; off Map p233; ☎ 081 533 8513; www.skansen.lublin .pl; ul Warszawska 96; adult/concession 8/4zł; ⊙ 9am-6pm), 5km west of the centre on the Warsaw road, covers an undulating terrain of 25 hectares. Appearing as a traditional village of numerous buildings with fully equipped interiors, there is a fine manor house, a windmill, an Orthodox church and a carved timber gate (1903) designed by Stanisław Witkiewicz. The skansen hosts various temporary displays and cultural events.

To get there from the centre, take bus 18, 20 or 5 from Al Racławickie.

Sleeping

In a recent bid to attract more international tourists, many hotels in Lublin have given themselves an extra coat of polish.

BUDGET

PTSM Youth Hostel (Map p233; ☎ /fax 081 533 0628; ul Długosza 6; dm/tr 26/35zł) A modest, well-run, all-year hostel 2km west of the Old Town (accessible by trolleybus 150 from the train station, and buses 5, 10, 18 and 57 from the bus terminal). You will find the youth hostel 50m up a lane off ul Długosza in the heart

---

THE EXTERMINATION CAMP OF MAJDANEK

Majdanek was built in 1941 under the orders of Heinrich Himmler in a bid to further Hitler's plans of eastern expansion. Over the following years it was extended (by a prisoner workforce); Jewish Lubliners were transported there from the Lublin ghetto in early 1942. The camp was run by the SS, and acted as a training ground for many of its most notorious members, including some of the most infamous female SS storm troopers.

The camp was initially intended to hold 250,000 prisoners at a time. The defeat of the German army on the eastern front thankfully meant that only 20% of the project was completed. And yet Majdanek came to be one of the Nazis' largest extermination camps. Estimates vary, but most recent research suggests that 80,000 people from some 30 countries lost their lives at Majdanek – most but not all were Jews. Gas chambers were the primary means of murder, followed by starvation, exhaustion and mass executions, the most unfathomable of which took place on 3 November 1943.

Perhaps more confronting than the scale of death are the horrific details; bodies were initially burned on open-air grates made of truck chassis, until a purpose-built crematorium was completed in 1943, capable of cremating up to 1000 bodies a day. All possessions were confiscated from prisoners upon entering the camp, gold and silver teeth were removed from dead bodies, human ashes were used to fertilise the camp's field, Jewish tombstones were used to pave roads, and 730kg of human hair left Majdanek for use in the manufacture of fabrics.

When the Red Army entered the camp on 23 July 1944, the Nazis only had time to destroy the crematorium; thousands of inmates and copious evidence of Nazi atrocities remained, making it the most well-preserved extermination camp. Majdanek was opened as a museum before many others had ceased operating.

---

of the university district. Bed clothes cost 6zł extra.

Wojewódzki Ośrodek Metodyczny (Map p235; ☎ 081 532 9241; www.wodn.lublin.pl in Polish; ul Dominikańska 5; beds 50zł) Not strictly a hotel, the Teacher Training Centre sometimes lends a bed to travellers. Good-value rooms (with two to five beds) are quickly snapped up, so book ahead. Look for the 'Wojewódzki Ośrodek Doskonalenia Nauczycieli' sign outside.

Dom Nauczyciela (Map p233; ☎ 081 53 8285; ul Akademicka 4; s/d/tr/q from 90/110/195/148zł) Nauczyciela offers you quaint, adequately furnished rooms with basins and clean, comfortable shared bathrooms. The overall atmosphere is that of a safe, open and bright college dorm.

Camping Marina (off Map p233; ☎ 081 745 6910; www.graf-marina.pl in Polish; ul Krężnicka 6; camping per tent 8zł, vehicle 3zł, chalet for up to 5 people 100zł; ☺ May-Sep) The Marina is serenely located on a man-made lake in a recreation area 8km south of the Old Town. Bus 8 from the centre takes you there.

Far away from Lublin's good bits, only use **Hotel Piast** (off Map p233; ☎ 081 532 2516; ul Pocztowa 2; s/d/tr 45/62/81zł) in the event of late arrival or early-morning departure. It's 2km south of the centre.

MIDRANGE & TOP END

Motel PZM (Map p233; ☎ 081 533 4232; motel@pzm .lublin.pl; ul Prusa 8; s/d/tr/apt 120/160/249/350zł; P ▢) The carpeted corridors and dowdy exteriors of the PZM thankfully don't reflect the clean, bright and vigilantly maintained room interiors. The PZM is an easy walk to the bus station and the Old Town; it's hard to find this sort of value in the centre.

our pick **Hotel Waksman** (Map p235; 081 532 5454; www.waksman.pl; ul Grodzka 19; s/d 180/200zł, s/d apt 240/260zł; P ✕ ▢) Hotel Waksman deserves the blue ribbon for many reasons, not least of which is its location at the historic juncture of Grodzka Gate. Each standard room (named 'yellow', 'blue', 'green' or 'red' for its décor) deliberately has its own individual character; there's even a water bed in the red room. The two apartments occupying the top floor are very special; they offer ample space for lounging or working, and views over both the Old Town from the front of the building, and the castle from the back. Relative to its larger competition, the Hotel Waksman is good value.

Hotel Victoria (Map p233; ☎ 081 532 7011; www .hotel.victoria.lublin.pl; ul Narutowicza 58/60; s 190-280zł, d 220-350zł, s/d apt 280/350zł; P ✕ ▢) The 10-storey Hotel Victoria has to be admired. While the

MAŁOPOLSKA

rest of Lublin was renovating to create old-fashioned elegance, Victoria went the other way with bold modern design. The building exterior is grey, but the open foyer (containing a chic restaurant, 24-hour bar, ATM and a small shop) is a warm red. Rooms are clean but don't live up to the foyer – the standard rooms are on the small side. Wireless internet is only available in the foyer.

Grand Hotel Lublinianka (Map p233; ☎ 081 446 6100; www.lublinianka.com; ul Krakowskie Przedmieście 56; s/d economy 260/300zł, standard 380/420zł, ste 500/540zł; P ⊠ 🖳) What was the Commercial Chamber of Lublin 100 years ago is now the grandest place to stay in Lublin. The classic foyer of this four-star hotel isn't at all overbearing and the same stylish minimalism translates to the calming pastel rooms. Marble bathrooms in suites include bathtubs, but even the economy guest is entitled to use the Turkish bath and sauna. The terrace café in the open-air centre of the building is a plus.

Hotel Europa (Map p233; ☎ 081 535 0303; www.hoteleuropa.pl; ul Krakowskie Przedmieście 29; s/d/tr/ste 290/380/430/960zł; P ⊠ 🖳 ♿) Hotel Europa offers old-world charm without too many frills. The building dates to the 1860s, but high-ceilinged rooms have been tastefully renovated to incorporate refined furniture. The pleasant onsite restaurant and bar are assets, but hardly necessary given its bull's-eye location along energetic Krakowskie Przedmieście. Weekend rates can bring down the price by as much as 100zł.

Mercure Unia Lublin (Map p233; ☎ 081 533 2061; www.mercure.com; Al Racławickie 12; s/d standard 295/355zł, s/d superior 325/385zł; P ⊠ 🖳) There is nothing lacking in facilities, but lots lacking in character at the Mercure. Despite the drab exterior, people stay for the location and business conveniences in the pastel-pale rooms. Breakfast costs an extra 30zł.

Eating

For fine dining in the Old Town, see what's cooking around the Rynek. If you're in a more modern mood, take a walk along ul Krakowskie Przedmieście.

Złoty Osioł (Map p235; ☎ 081 532 9042; www.zlotyosiol.pl; ul Grodzka 5a; mains 10-25zł; ☾ noon-midnight) Just northeast of the Rynek, Złoty Osioł offers traditional ambience and extraordinarily good-value traditional meals. There are delicious fish dishes, slightly bizarre drink selections

(like hot dry wine with jelly), and daily meal sets for the indecisive. The restaurant is set in a candlelit cellar with an annexed cosy green courtyard. Folk music concerts are occasionally held here.

our pick Magia (Map p235; ☎ 081 532 3041; www.magia.lublin.pl; ul Grodzka 2/Rynek 1; mains 15-65zł; ☾ noon-last customer) Like its menu, Magia's atmosphere is eclectic; there are numerous vibes to choose from throughout the warren of dining rooms and its large outdoor courtyard, with each area decorated with a touch of magic. The chef uses only fresh ingredients to create dishes ranging from tiger shrimps and snails to deer and duck, with every sort of pizza, pasta and pancake between. Prices are spread through the spectrum of budgets, so you can venture through multiple courses or eat lightly just to rent yourself a piece of the atmosphere.

Oregano (Map p233; ☎ 081 442 5530; ul Kościuszki 7; mains 20-45zł; ☾ noon-11pm) This pleasant, upmarket restaurant specialises in Mediterranean cuisine, featuring pasta, paella and seafood. There is a well-organised English menu, and the chefs aren't scared of spice.

For some laid-back dining and pleasant people-watching in the Rynek, try the following places:

Pizzeria Acerna (Map p235; ☎ 081 532 4531; Rynek 2; pizza from 11zł; ☾ 11am-10pm Mon-Thu & Sun, 11am-midnight Fri & Sat) Popular pizza and pasta.

Pueblo Desperados (Map p235; ☎ 081 534 6179; Rynek 5; mains 10-27zł; ☾ 9am-10pm Mon-Thu, 9am-midnight Fri & Sat, 10am-midnight Sun) Mexican fare in the heart of old Poland.

Drinking

Tamara Café (Map p233; ☎ 081 532 1023; www.tamaracafe.pl in Polish; Krakowskie Przedmieście 36; mains 15-35zł; ☾ 11am-last customer). This café, restaurant, pub and wine bar takes the latter very seriously. The food is an indecisive mix of Mexican, Mediterranean and Asian fare lovingly infused with fresh flavour, but it's all just a prelude to alcohol. If you're a cultured wine connoisseur, just feel like a cocktail concoction in the courtyard, or are a hungry tippler who wants some vodka with (or in) your meal, this is the place to pull up a chair.

Johnny's Irish Pub (Map p233; ☎ 081 534 9566; www.johnnys.lublin.pl; ul Narutowicza 9; mains 15zł; ☾ 10am-late) Johnny's serves hearty pub food in a multi-level, partially open-air dining area crowded with jovial drinkers each night.

MAŁOPOLSKA

Caram'bola Pub (Map p233; ☎ 081 534 6380; ul Kościuszki 8; pizzas 16zł; ☼ 11am-midnight Mon-Thu, 11am-2am Fri & Sat, noon-midnight Sun) is yet another friendly place for a casual beer and some pub food.

Entertainment

The tourist office can tell you about events around town. Also, the free monthly *Lublin w Pigułce* and the local daily *Kurier Lubelski* contain event listings.

NIGHTCLUBS

Hades (Kawiarnia Artystyczna Hades; Map p233; ☎ 081 532 8761; www.hades-lublin.pl in Polish; ul Peowiaków 12; ☼ noon-11pm) This local entertainment venue offers live music some nights, a club night on Fridays and the annual Hades Jazz Festival every year. Before late-night spirits kick in, Hades is a restaurant (mains 10zł to 20zł).

Down a small courtyard off ul Narutowicza, **Club Koyot** (Map p233; ☎ 081 743 6735; www .clubkoyot.com; ul Krakowskie Przedmieście 26; ☼ noon-late Mon-Fri, 4pm-late Sat & Sun) features live music most nights.

THEATRES

The main drama venue in town, **Teatr im Osterwy** (Map p233; ☎ 081 532 4244; www.teatrosterwy .pl in Polish; ul Narutowicza 17; ☼ box office noon-7pm Tue-Sat, 6-7pm Sun) features mostly classical plays.

Filharmonia Lubelska (Map p233; ☎ 081 743 7824; www.filharmonialubelska.pl in Polish; ul Skłodowskiej-Curie 5) is a large auditorium that stages classical and contemporary music concerts. In the same building, **Teatr Muzyczny** (Map p233; ☎ 081 532 7613; www .teatrmuzyczny.pl in Polish; ul Skłodowskiej-Curie 5; ☼ ticket sales 1-5pm) hosts a range of musical events with a strong modern attitude.

Performances are in Polish at **Teatr im H Ch Andersena** (Map p235; ☎ 081 532 1628; www.teatr andersena.pl; ul Dominikańska 1; tickets 15zł) but the puppets of Hans Christian Andersen can be enjoyed in any language. Check the website for show times.

Founded in 1977, 28km southeast of Lublin, **Gardzienice Theatre** is renowned in artistic circles for energetic, heady performances. Under the guidance of artistic director and founder Włodzimierz Staniewski, dramatic montages derive inspiration from gatherings with indigenous communities throughout and beyond Poland. Check whether they are in town at the **ticket office** (Map p235; ☎ 081 532 9840; http://gardienice .art.pl; ul Grodzka 5A).

Getting There & Away

Numerous transport links make Lublin a convenient transport hub.

BUS

The main bus terminal (Map p235) is just north of the Old Town, across from the castle. Slightly west behind the main bus terminal on ul Ruska is the well-organised minibus station (Map p235), which dispatches buses all over the region and slightly beyond.

Normal buses go to Warsaw (21zł to 40zł, 3½ hours, every hour) between 3am and 10pm. Minibuses are faster and cheaper (30zł, three hours, every 30 minutes). Polski Express buses (41zł to 50zł, every two hours) go direct to Warsaw airport between 5am and 5pm .

Minibuses to Kazimierz Dolny (7zł, one hour, every 30 minutes, 60km) are more efficient than normal buses (18zł, 2½ hours, every 30 minutes). Normal buses to Puławy pass through Kazimierz Dolny. Minibuses also service Zamość (15zł, two hours, every 30 minutes or so).

There are around 10 daily buses to Sandomierz (15zł, 100km).

TRAIN

The main **train station** (off Map p233; ☎ 081 94 36; ul Gazowa 4) is linked to the Old Town by trolleybus 160 and several buses including 13 and 17.

There are around 16 trains per day to Warsaw (20zł, 3½ hours) and a couple to Kraków (40zł to 115zł, five hours). Tickets can be bought at the train station or at **Orbis Travel** (Map p233; ☎ 081 532 2256, ticket bookings 081 532 5402; ul Narutowicza 33A; ☼ 9am-6pm Mon-Fri, 9am-2pm Sat).

KOZŁÓWKA

The hamlet of Kozłówka (koz-*woof*-kah), 38km north of Lublin, is famous for the sumptuous late-Baroque **palace**, built in the mid-18th century. The residence was acquired by the Zamoyski family in 1799, and today houses the **Museum of the Zamoyski Family** (☎ 081 852 8300; www.muzeumzamoyskich .lublin.pl; adult/concession 16/8zł, free Mon; ☼ 10am-4pm Mon-Fri, 10am-5pm Sat & Sun Mar-Oct, 10am-3pm Nov & Dec). The museum features original furnishings (much of which was replicated from originals in Versailles) and an impressive collection of ancestral paintings, mostly from the 17th to 19th centuries. There are

MAŁOPOLSKA

SOCIALIST REALISM – ART AS A POLITICAL TOOL

According to official credo, socialist realism was 'a creative way of transferring Marxism into the realm of art'. According to history, it was the reduction of art to propaganda. Socialist realism originated in the Soviet Union in the 1920s and by the mid-1930s was the only accepted style in visual arts, architecture, film, music and literature. After WWII, it spread throughout the Soviet-controlled eastern bloc.

When the communist regime felt itself sufficiently entrenched in Poland, it formally implemented socialist realism in 1949. Though it remained official artistic doctrine only until 1955, an enormous collection of work was produced in this brief period.

The artwork was intended to promote communist ideology, and its creators strove to instil socialist culture through artistic means. Artists could not express themselves individually, and were obliged to transmit official dogma in pseudo-artistic form. Given that its intended audience was the masses, the messages it conveyed had to be widely accessible and inspire optimism and motivation for the new order. The most common images were of communist leaders and key historical events, but the glorification of labour was also popular; bricklayers were portrayed gallantly at work and young women smiled heroically as they drove tractors.

After Stalin's death in 1953, the lunacy quickly subsided in Poland. The central storage facility for the works – which were discreetly removed from public view – was at Kozłówka (the palace wasn't opened until 1977), where selected pieces can be viewed today.

---

20 hectares of park surrounding the palace, and the garden has the manicure of classical French design.

The complex is also noted for the **Socialist-Realist Art Gallery** (adult/concession 6/3zł, free Tue; ✪ 10am-4pm Mon-Fri, 10am-5pm Sat & Sun Mar-Oct, 10am-3pm Nov & Dec). It has an overwhelming number of portraits and statues of revolutionary communist leaders (mainly from the years 1949–56), and idealised proletarian scenes of farmers, factory workers and so on, striving for socialism.

You can stay at the agrotourist **Rzadcóka farm** (☎ 081 852 8220; ekkornaccy@wp.pl; d/tr 70/90zł); call ahead to confirm availability and current prices. Or you can stay in some rooms throughout the palace complex (☎ 081 852 8300), such as the old guardhouse. Call ahead for details and prices.

Getting There & Away

The usual departure point for Kozłówka is Lublin, but this is not as convenient as it could be, given that there is one morning bus at 8.30am (5zł, 50 minutes, 40km).

A bus heads back to Lublin at around 3.30pm, and another at around 6.30pm. Double-check bus timetables before you visit the museum so you can plan your departure accordingly.

If you get stuck, take a minibus to Lubartów from where there is more regular transport back to Lublin.

PUŁAWY
pop 49,295

There is very little of interest in Puławy (poo-*wah*-vi) beyond the park and palace complex, so it's best explored as a day trip from Kazimierz Dolny or Lublin.

The aristocratic Czartoryski family brought Puławy into its golden age at the end of the 18th century. Izabela Czartoryska, wife of Prince Adam Kazimierz Czartoryski, exhibited a collection of valuable items in Sibyl's Temple and the Gothic House, thus creating Poland's first museum in 1801. Izabela was so committed to imbuing Puławy with character that she is believed to have helped lay the bricks of Sybil's temple with her own hands, and even hired a hermit to dwell near the palace to lend it atmospheric authenticity!

The family was forced to flee Poland after the failed November Insurrection of 1830, abandoning its estate, which fell into the hands of the tsar. The art collection had been secretly moved to Paris, and was brought back to Poland in the 1870s; it now comprises the core exhibits of the Kraków Czartoryski Museum.

After WWII, a nitrate combine was erected near Puławy, making it something of a drab industrial town.

Information

Maps showing the location of important sights are displayed at entrances to the landscape

park. The **PTTK office** (☎ 081 886 4756; www.oddzial
.pulawy.pttk.pl in Polish; ul Czartoryskich 6A) at the entrance to the palace complex can help you get
your bearings in the extensive park grounds.

There are several *kantors* in the centre, including a few on ul Piłsudskiego. **Bank Pekao**
(Al Królewska 11A) is close to the palace.

Sights

The centrepiece of the complex is **Czartoryski
Palace**, built by Tylman van Gameren between
1676 and 1679. It was altered many times
before becoming the sober, late-neoclassical
rendition it is today. It's lost its regality in
recent years, and is now a functioning agricultural research institute that is not open
to visitors.

The **landscape park** (admission free; ☒ to sunset)
surrounding the palace was founded in the
late 18th century by Princess Izabela. It's a
typical romantic park of the era, incorporating several pavilions and buildings. The park
is pleasant enough, though more bedraggled
than many others. Northwest of the castle,
along the Vistula, are some **caves** (adult/concession
2.50/2zł; ☒ 9.30am-4.30pm Apr-Oct), created when
Izabela decided to enlarge the site of lime
rock excavation in 1791. Tickets and torches
are available at the PTTK Office.

The **Regional Museum** (☎ 081 887 8674; ul
Czartoryskich 6A; adult/concession 4.3zł; ☒ 10am-2pm Tue-
Sun), 200m north of the palace, features ethnographic and archaeological exhibits, plus
temporary displays, some of which are related
to the Czartoryski family. Between May and
October, parts of the museum's collection are
displayed in **Sybil's Temple** (Świątynia Sybilli)
and the **Gothic House** (Domek Gotycki), both
dating to the early 19th century.

About 200m to the west on ul Piłsudskiego,
Czartoryski Chapel (built 1801–03) was modelled on the Roman Pantheon. The domed
interior has lost its original furnishings
and decoration.

Sleeping & Eating

Puławy is best explored as an easy day trip. In
the centre are drab hotels of the concrete-box
persuasion.

Centrum Szkoleniowo-Kongresowe (☎ /fax 081
887 7306; www.hotel.iung.pulawy.pl; Al Królewska 17; s/d
without breakfast 120/150zł, apt with breakfast 235zł; Ⓟ)
A billion times better than the drab concrete
boxes is this bright business hotel with no-fuss
furniture and its own bistro-style restaurant.

It's conveniently located 250m from the gates
of the palace.

Youth Hostel (☎ 081 886 3367; fax 081 888 3656; ul
Włostowicka 27; dm 18-38zł) The 118-bed hostel is
2km from the centre on the Kazimierz Dolny
road. Rooms are a chaotic explosion of colours
and furniture; ask to see a few to choose one
that's bright and spacious. A few extra zloty
will get you your own bathroom or breakfast
and dinner. Very basic self-cooking facilities
are available. Don't come back into the centre
if you're heading for Kazimierz – catch the bus
near the hostel's entrance.

Getting There & Around
BUS

The PKS bus terminal is in the city centre.
Buses to Lublin (7zł, 90 minutes) depart every
half-hour, but less frequently to Warsaw (19zł,
three hours). Both destinations are also serviced by Polski Express, with seven departures
a day to each.

Other buses go to Radom (8zł, two hours,
five daily) and Łódź (17zł, 2½ hours, four daily).
There are four morning buses to Lubartów,
which will let you off at Kozłówka.

Kazimierz Dolny (3.20zł, one hour, every
hour) is well served by PKS. Minibuses (2zł, 50
minutes) are less frequent but faster. Check the
schedule of suburban bus 12 in front of the terminal and take whichever goes first. Similarly,
if you're headed for Janowiec, choose between
a normal bus and city bus 17.

TRAIN

The town has two train stations: Puławy and
Puławy Miasto. The latter is the main one
and is closer to the centre, though still 2km
northeast. It is serviced by city buses; otherwise use taxis.

Trains for Lublin (15zł, 1½ hours) leave virtually every hour, but centre-to-centre buses
are more convenient. Trains to Warsaw (31zł,
two hours) run every other hour. Several fast
trains go to Radom (18zł, two hours) and
on to Kielce (22zł, three hours), from where
transport to Kraków is regular. For Kraków
it is more efficient to change in Dęblin (10zł,
20 minutes, every half-hour).

KAZIMIERZ DOLNY
pop 4000

Kazimierz Dolny has various assets: it's picturesquely situated on the banks of the Vistula,
it's surrounded by dense green countryside,

MAŁOPOLSKA

it's tightly packed with historical buildings and it boasts bread in the shape of roosters.

The buildings in this Lilliputian land are so charming that they appear to have survived the tides of history untarnished. In truth, the town suffered greatly at the hands of various aggressors, but has now revived into a fashionable weekend destination for people seeking respite from the city.

History

Earliest accounts of settlement in the region refer to a wooden cloister along the Vistula in 1181. The town was formally founded in the 14th century by King Kazimierz III Wielki who built a castle and gave the town its municipal charter. The town was called Dolny (lower), to distinguish it from the town of Kazimierz upriver, which is today part of Kraków.

Kazimierz Dolny became a thriving trade centre, with grain, salt, wood and oxen being shipped to Gdańsk and further on for export. The 16th and 17th centuries were particularly prosperous, and a number of splendid mansions and granaries were constructed. By 1630, Kazimierz Dolny's population had risen above 2500.

High times came to an end with the Swedish Deluge, the Northern War and; later, the cholera epidemic of 1708. The displacement of the Vistula bed towards the west accelerated the town's economic decline, allowing Puławy to overshadow it in the 19th century as the trade and cultural centre of the region.

At the end of the 19th century attempts were made to revive Kazimierz Dolny as a tourist centre, but the two world wars caused serious damage to the town. Since the end of WWII (which all but annihilated the town's Jewish population), preservation efforts have gone a long way to restore the historical character of Kazimierz Dolny, which is believed to attract more than one million visitors each year.

Information

Useful amenities are at or near the Rynek. There's a *kantor* in the **post office** (ul Tyszkiewicza 2) and an ATM in the back wall of the same building. There is also an ATM diagonally opposite the PTTK Office (at the Houses of the Przybyła Brothers) and another on the wall of Piekarnia Sarzyński.

Biblioteka Miejska (☎ 081 881 0305; bibliotekaka zimierz@poczta.onet.pl; ul Lubelska 32/34; per hr 2zł; ☻ 9am-5pm Mon-Fri, 10am-2pm Sat) Internet access in local public library.

PTTK office (☎ 081 881 0046; pttk_kazimierz_dolny@ poczta.onet.pl; Rynek 27; ☻ 8am-5.30pm Mon-Fri & 10am-5.30pm Sat May-Sep, 8am-4pm Mon-Fri & 10am-2.30pm Sat Oct-Apr) Can assist with private rooms (30zł to 60zł), maps and brochures.

Sights

The main **Rynek** of Kazimierz is distinct not only for the wooden well at its centre, but also the diverse architecture around it. The finest of these merchants' houses are the two connecting **Houses of the Przybyła Brothers** (Kamienice Przybyłów), built in 1615 by brothers Mikołaj and Krzysztof with rich Renaissance mannerist façades. Decorations depict the brothers' patron saints, St Nicholas (guardian of traders) and St Christopher (guardian of travellers). Also on the Rynek are the Baroque-style **Gdańsk House** (Kamienica Gdańska) from 1795, and several characteristic arcaded houses with wooden-tiled roofs from the 18th and 19th centuries.

Though thriving market days of old have long since past, homage is still paid to Kazimierz's culture of commerce; a small market selling secondhand goods and tourist trinkets is in **Mały Rynek**, southeast of the Rynek. The town also hosts a farmers' market on Tuesdays and Fridays.

The **House of the Celej Family** (Kamienica Celejowska), built around 1635, contains the **Town Museum** (☎ 081 881 0104; ul Senatorska 11; adult/ concession 5/3zł; ☻ 10am-5pm Tue-Sun May-Sep, 10am-3pm Tue-Sun Oct-Apr, closed public holidays & day following). Quaint though the archaeological specimens are, the real highlight here is the gallery showing the town's artistic portrayal by artists who have returned over the years to refine their skills and share their perspectives on this small pocket of Poland.

The tiny **Museum of Goldsmithery** (Muzeum Sztuki Złotniczej; ☎ 081 881 0081; ul Zamkowa 2; adult/concession 6/4zł; ☻ 10am-1pm Mon & 10am-5pm Tue-Sun May-Sep, 10am-3pm Tue-Sun Oct-Apr) seems overpriced for its size, but some of the gold and silverwork collection is captivating. Jewellery lovers will be particularly enraptured with the unique modern designs upstairs.

The **Reformed Franciscan Church** (Kościół Reformatów; ☎ 081 881 0118), on the nearby hill, was built at the end of the 16th century but lost its original style with subsequent Baroque and neoclassi-

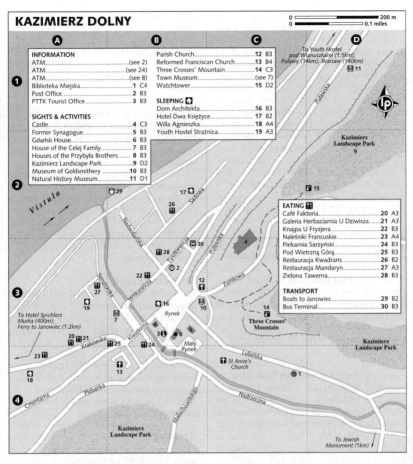

KAZIMIERZ DOLNY

0 — 200 m
0 — 0.1 miles

INFORMATION
ATM...(see 2)
ATM...(see 24)
ATM...(see 8)
Biblioteka Miejska...............................**1** C4
Post Office..**2** B3
PTTK Tourist Office............................**3** B3

SIGHTS & ACTIVITIES
Castle..**4** C3
Former Synagogue..............................**5** B3
Gdańsk House.....................................**6** B3
House of the Celej Family....................**7** B3
Houses of the Przybyła Brothers...........**8** B3
Kazimierz Landscape Park....................**9** D2
Museum of Goldsmithery.....................**10** B3
Natural History Museum......................**11** D1

Parish Church.....................................**12** B3
Reformed Franciscan Church................**13** B4
Three Crosses' Mountain......................**14** C3
Town Museum..................................(see 7)
Watchtower..**15** D2

SLEEPING
Dom Architekta..................................**16** B3
Hotel Dwa Księżyce.............................**17** B2
Willa Agnieszka..................................**18** A4
Youth Hostel Strażnica.........................**19** A3

To Youth Hostel
pod Wianuszkami (1.5km);
Puławy (14km); Warsaw (140km)

Kazimierz
Landscape Park
9

EATING
Café Faktoria......................................**20** A3
Galeria Herbaciarnia U Dziwisza...........**21** A3
Knajpa U Fryzjera...............................**22** B3
Naleśniki Francuskie............................**23** A4
Piekarnia Sarzyński.............................**24** B3
Pod Wietrzną Górą..............................**25** B3
Restauracja Kwadrans..........................**26** B2
Restauracja Mandaryn..........................**27** A3
Zielona Tawerna..................................**28** B3

TRANSPORT
Boats to Janowiec...............................**29** B2
Bus Terminal......................................**30** B3

Vistula

To Hotel Spichlerz
Murka (400m);
Ferry to Janowiec (1.2km)

Rynek
Mały
Rynek

St Anne's
Church

Three Crosses'
Mountain

Kazimierz
Landscape Park

Kazimierz
Landscape Park

To Jewish
Monument (1km)

Nadwiślańska • Sadowa • Puławska • Zamkowa • Tyszkiewicza • Witkiewicza • Senatorska • Klasztorna • Krakowska • Lubelska • Cmentarna • Piebanka • Małachowskiego • Nadrzeczna

cal decorations. The Franciscan brethren were compelled to leave the church twice in history: first between 1866 and 1928 when the tsar ordered the annulment of the order; and later under the Nazi occupation, when the Gestapo appropriated the complex.

The Gothic **parish church** presiding over the Rynek was built in the mid-14th century but remodelled when Renaissance taste swept through Poland. The ornate wooden organ from 1620 sounds as lavish as it looks; organ recitals are often held here. Note the Renaissance stalls in the chancel and the stucco decoration of the nave's vault, a classic example of the Lublin-Renaissance style typical of the region. Be sure to raise an eyebrow at the stag-antler chandelier.

Further along ul Zamkowa is what is left of the **castle** (adult/concession 2.20/1.60zł, including entry to watchtower). Originally built in 1341 as a stronghold against the Tartar incursion, the castle was extended in the 16th century and embellished further during the Renaissance. The castle fell into ruin after its partial destruction by the Swedes; the remaining fragments offer a pleasant view over the town and the Vistula. The **watchtower**, 200m uphill, was built a century before the castle and over the years served as a fortress, watchtower, lighthouse and prison. There is a panoramic view from the top of the 20m structure.

The path to the right slightly uphill from the parish church, leads to the **Three Crosses' Mountain** (Góra Trzech Krzyży; admission 1zł). If you're

244 THE LUBLIN UPLAND •• Kazimierz Dolny

coming from the watchtower, take the path to the left. There is some historical debate about the relationship between the crosses and the plague, which decimated the population of the town in 1708. It's doubtful whether human remains found at the site when the crosses were erected in 1852 belong to plague victims. Some historians believe that the site was referred to as 'cross mountain' long before the cholera epidemic. Whatever the origins of its name, the mountain affords sensational views.

The 18th-century **former synagogue** off Mały Rynek on ul Lubelska was originally wooden. It was rebuilt in brick in the 18th century and became a cinema after WWII. Just behind is the reconstructed wooden building, which once housed the kosher butcher. There is little to signify that this area was once the Jewish quarter.

The most overt reminder of the Jewish legacy of Kazimierz Dolny is the **Jewish Monument** in front of the old cemetery. The Nazis murdered some 3000 Jews from the town and its surrounds and desecrated the old cemetery. The Jewish Monument was assembled in 1984 from several hundred tombstone fragments collected here. The monument is just over 1km from the Rynek, on the road to Opole Lubelskie.

On the opposite side of town on the Puławy road, the **Natural History Museum** (Muzeum Przyrodnicze; ☎ 081 881 0326; ul Puławska 54; adult/concession 5/3zł; ☾ 11am-5pm Tue-Sun May-Sep, 10am-3pm Tue-Sun Oct-Apr, closed public holidays & day following) is housed in a large, finely restored granary from 1591. Though there is little information in English, kids will enjoy seeing the range of birds, animals and insects (albeit stuffed). Of particular interest is the video showing the process of taxidermy (animal stuffing, which, it turns out, is far less gruesome than it sounds) and a busy beehive whose occupants are blissfully oblivious to the fact that they live in a Big Brother beehive. Note the intricate wooden structure supporting the roof on the top floor; it's an exquisite example of 16th-century engineering, joining beams with pegs rather than nails.

Only a few **granaries** have survived out of nearly 60 built in the thriving 16th and 17th centuries during a boom in the grain trade. In addition to the one containing the Natural History Museum, there are two other fine examples. One on ul Puławska (containing Youth Hostel Pod Wianuszkami) was initially built in the 1780s from local rock but was rebuilt between 1978 and 1986 to serve its current purpose. The other on ul Krakowska (containing Hotel Spichlerz Murka) was built in 1636 but restored from 1949 to 1951 by architect Karol Siciński.

Activities

In 1979, the area around Kazimierz was decreed the **Kazimierz Landscape Park** (Kazimierski Park Krajobrazowy). Many walking trails have been traced in its 15,000 hectares, winding through the distinct gorges of the region.

There are three easy short trails known as *szlaki spacerowe* (walking routes) signposted in yellow, green and red, and three significantly longer treks called *szlaki turystyczne* (tourist routes) marked in blue, green and red. Almost all these routes originate in the Rynek. The tourist office sells maps of the park and its trails.

Festivals & Events

The highly acclaimed **Festival of Folk Bands & Singers** takes place in the last week of June. For more than 30 years, performers from the region have gathered at Mały Rynek in traditional garb to perform folk music from eras (and tastes) gone by.

The less raucous **Film & Art Festival** in late July lasts for around a week, and consists of musical concerts, art exhibitions and indoor and outdoor screenings of foreign and national films.

Sleeping

There are options aplenty in Kazimierz, but advanced bookings are essential on weekends in spring and summer. The most common accommodation is rooms in private houses (30zł to 60zł), some of which are run like small hotels. The PTTK office on the Rynek can help with this, or just wander through town looking for 'pokoje' (rooms) or 'noclegi' (accommodation) signs.

BUDGET

There are two efficiently run youth hostels in Kazimierz Dolny, which both include breakfast. **Youth Hostel Strażnica** (☎ 081 881 0427; www .straznica.kazimierzdolny.pl in Polish; ul Senatorska 25; dm 38zł) is a rare centrally located youth hostel a skip from the Rynek. Some double rooms offer good light and there are spacious common areas to spread out in. Larger and prettier but 1.5km out of town, **Youth Hostel pod Wianuszkami** (☎ /fax 081 881 0327; ul Puławska 80; dm/d 38/90zł) is located in an old granary.

MIDRANGE

Hotel Spichlerz Murka (☎ 081 881 0036; ul Krakowska 59/61; s/d 90/160zł) Divided over two buildings, with lush green surrounds, the Murka is replete with old wood and solid furniture and the larger Spichlerz is a converted granary that offers easy access to the Vistula, spartan but cosy rooms and barbecue facilities. Sometimes (depending on weather and mood) campers are allowed to stay in the grounds. The main Spichlerz building also boasts a restaurant and bar.

Willa Agnieszka (☎ 081 882 0411; willaagnieszka @wp.pl; ul Krakowska 41a; s/d 140/190zł; P) The intimate 12-room Willa Agnieszka is crisp and shiny. This place books out in a flash on weekends; call ahead. There's also an onsite restaurant.

Dom Architekta (☎ 081 883 5544; www.dom -architekta.pl; Rynek 20; d from 220zł; 🖳) This sleek establishment offers the style and atmosphere you would expect from an architecturally oriented hotel; there is plenty of open space to enjoy, sleek lines, soothing tones and a bull's-eye location right on the Rynek.

Hotel Dwa Księżyce (☎ /fax 081 881 0833; ul Sadowa 15; s/d/ste 220/250/420zł; P 🗙 🖳) The 'Two Moons' is a popular place on a quiet street where you can immerse yourself in the pace of Kazimierz Dolny. Some rooms are bigger than others in the same price category (with separate sitting areas), while apartment rooms in the main building have private balconies. The onsite restaurant often has live music. If you require internet access, request a room in the main building where wireless connection is more reliable. Prices include parking and breakfast.

Eating & Drinking

Kazimierz certainly has no shortage of cafés and restaurants; most are around the centre but not all are at the Rynek.

Piekarnia Sarzyński (☎ 081 881 0643; www.sarzynski .com.pl in Polish; ul Nadrzeczna 6; mains from 6zł; 🕑 breakfast, lunch & dinner) This bakery institution releases freshly baked aromas and trademark breaddough roosters into Kazimierz Dolny each day. From breakfast right through to dessert, Sarzyński bakery offers an epic range of pastries, breads, cakes and hearty meals.

Knajpa U Fryzjera (☎ 081 881 0426; ul Witkiewicza 2; mains 15-35zł; 🕑 9am-midnight) For funky flavour fusions in a weathered old hair-salon, U Fryzjera is a prime choice for breakfast, lunch or dinner. For the first meal of the day, perhaps try the 'Day After Sick Kitten' breakfast.

Pod Wietrzną Górą (☎ 081 881 0640; www.wietrzna gora.pl in Polish; ul Krakowska 1; mains 15-40zł; 🕑 breakfast, lunch & dinner) Right on the junction of ul Krakowska and Ul Cmentarna, Pod Wietrzną can be expensive; meal price is calculated by weight and the slices of meat are generous. Otherwise, the meals are pleasant, as is the popular beer garden.

Restauracja Mandaryn (☎ 081 881 0220; www .mandaryn.kazimierzdolny.pl in Polish; ul Senatorska 17; mains 20-30zł; 🕑 11am-late) Only vaguely oriental but all class, the Mandaryn serves Polish and international cuisine from one of the town's more varied menus.

Restauracja Kwadrans (☎ 081 882 1111; ul Sadowa 7a; mains 20-40zł; 🕑 10am-last customer) In a solid wooden building with a high-ceilinged terrace, Kwadrans demonstrates a love of clocks and heavy food. There are slim pickings for vegetarians but those more inclined towards venison will be pleased. There are some hearty breakfasts on offer.

Zielona Tawerna (☎ 081 881 0308; ul Nadwiślańska 4; mains 30-50zł; 🕑 noon-late) An old rustic house converted into a stylish restaurant with mismatched antique furniture, art on the walls, rugs on the floors and candles on the tables. There are many dining rooms to choose from throughout the creaking building and smooth tunes add a country-chic vibe to the 'Green Tavern'. Meals, from the meaty mains to the vegetable platter, are lovingly prepared. Ingeniously, half-sized dishes can be ordered at 70% of the full price. Desserts and drinks are creative too – hot beer anyone?

Two picture-perfect places that celebrate, nay, worship the decadence of hot beverages are **Galeria Herbaciarnia U Dziwisza** (☎ 081 881 0287; ul Krakowska 6; teas from 3zł; 🕑 breakfast & lunch) and nearby **Café Faktoria** (ul Krakowska 6B; coffee 4zł; 🕑 10am-9pm). The former is a civilised taste of an era when tea was a pastime; it boasts more than 100 varieties of tea leaf and an appealing range of calorie-rich accompaniments. In a similarly saccharine vein, Café Faktoria is a veritable temple to coffee and its loyal companion, chocolate; thrilling concoctions of both are brewing in various pots on the stove.

MAŁOPOLSKA

COCK-A-DOODLE-DOUGH

Spend any time in Kazimierz Dolny and you will soon wonder why its townspeople have such a proclivity for rooster-shaped bread. After seeing enough of it, you will find yourself wanting to try some. When you do, you will discover that bread tastes like bread no matter how it's shaped, and promptly return to your initial question: why?

Though its taste may be as bland as, well, bread, the rooster has an interesting history in Kazimierz. In the middle of last century, a rooster is believed to have averted certain disaster by warning the townsfolk of an approaching devil. This, combined with local bread-weaving traditions, resulted in the rooster's heroic portrayal in dough.

After a golden era in the 1950s, when rooster-shaped bread was baked all over town, tensions suddenly surfaced. In 1996, Piekarnia Sarzyński, convinced that its many years promoting the product and winning awards for its rooster renditions entitled it to exclusive rights, registered the rooster as its company trademark. The other bakers in town were outraged and demanded that the courts reinstate the rooster's status as the cultural (culinary?) property of the Kazimierz public.

Eight years later, the court released the rooster back into the public domain. But patent or not, no-one can bake a bird like Sarzyński's (p245).

Further along the road, **Naleśnicki Francuskie** (☎ 081 882 0335; ul Krakowska 26; crepes 4-10zł; ☺ noon-9pm Mon-Fri, 11am-10pm Sat, 11am-9pm Sun) offers sweet and savoury crepes in casual compact surrounds.

Getting There & Around

Kazimierz can be conveniently visited as a stop on your Lublin–Warsaw route, or as a day trip from Lublin. There's no railway in Kazimierz but there's a decent bus service.

Cyclists can acquire a map of bike routes in the area from the PTTK office and some small shops.

BOAT

In summer, pleasure boats run to Janowiec (one in the style of a Viking ship, minus oars and whips) on the opposite side of the Vistula – ask at the wharf at the end of ul Nadwiślańska.

There's also a **car and passenger ferry** (☎ 0602 858898; per person 3zł; ☺ 8am-8pm Mon-Fri & 8am-9pm Sat & Sun May-Sep), which takes five minutes and departs 1km west of Hotel Murka Spichlerz.

BUS

The PKS bus and minibus terminal is about 100m north of the Rynek. There are normal buses to Puławy (3.20zł, 45 minutes, every half-hour) and urban bus 12 can take you directly to the Puławy train station. The latter is more convenient because it stops closer to the castle than the minibus or PKS buses do.

There are around 14 minibuses per day to Lublin (7zł, 1½ hours, roughly every hour) between 6.20am and 5pm; and some to Zamość (10zł, 1¼ hours).

There are five or so daily fast buses to Warsaw (22zł, 3½ hours), or change for the train in Puławy. Private bus operators also run services from the bus station for Warsaw; tickets can be purchased on the bus for **Halo Express** (☎ 0602 664419), which has six buses to Warsaw daily; or **Anmar** (☎ 081 748 7335; www.anmar.info.pl in Polish), with four buses to Warsaw daily. Check times through the PTTK Office.

JANOWIEC
pop 1200

The village of Janowiec (yah-no-vyets), 2km upstream on the other side of the Vistula from Kazimierz Dolny, is best known for its **castle**, which is now part of the **Janowiec Museum** (☎ 081 881 5228; www.muzeumnadwislanskie .pl in Polish; ul Lubelska 20; adult/concession 8/6zł; ☺ 10am-5pm Mon-Fri, 10am-2pm Sat & Sun May-Oct, 10am-2pm Mon, 10am-5pm Tue-Fri, 10am-7pm Sat & Sun Nov-Apr). Inside the grounds of the castle, visitors can climb a few levels to viewing platforms offering a wide perspective of the castle and the surrounding countryside. Various rooms show exhibitions and contemporary 'art'.

The castle was built in the first half of the 16th century by Italian architect Santi Gucci Fiorentino, at the request of Mikołaj Firlej. It was furnished in 1537 and in the second half of the century Andrej Firlej converted the castle into a Renaissance residence. Through many years and owners (including the Tarło, Lubomirski and Osławski families), the castle grew to more than 100 rooms and became one of the most splendid in Poland. The Swedes began the process of ruination and two world wars completed the castle's demise. Under communism, it was the only private castle in Poland; it was finally handed over to the state in 1975 by its last owner, Leon Kozłowski.

The castle is still in ruins, but intense renovations have restored some rooms and revived external painted decorations. Upon entering the castle, note the red-and-white striped walls. This is not the work of a prankster graffiti artist; it is, apparently, how the castle was originally dressed.

In the park beside the castle is a **manor house** from the 1760s (another part of the museum), which offers insights into how Polish nobility lived. Among the outbuildings surrounding the manor is an old two-storey granary with an interesting **ethnographic exhibition** featuring old fishing boats, ceramics, tools and household implements.

It's also worth going down to the to Janowiec village at the foot of the castle to see its mid-14th-century Gothic **parish church**, extensively rebuilt in Renaissance style in the 1530s. Inside is the tomb of the Firlej family, carved in the workshop of Santi Gucci from 1586 to 1587.

Sleeping & Eating

The PTTK office in Kazimierz Dolny (see p242) will know about the availability of private rooms in Janowiec, but it's probably more rewarding to spend the night in Kazimierz.

The following are some delightful dining choices near the Rynek.

Maćkowa Chata (☎ 081 881 5462; ul Sandomierska 2; mains 10-15zł; ☒ 10am-10pm) A charming affair with an intimate terrace where passers-by and local fixtures idle. The *pierogi* (Polish dumplings) are particularly tasty.

Restauracja Serokomla (☎ 081 881 5240; ul Sandomierska 24/Rynek 12; mains 10-20zł; ☒ lunch & dinner) Less low key, Restauracja Serokomla sells souvenir-style condiments and decadent cakes (think chocolate, cheese, cookie and crumble) as well as solid meals in solid surrounds.

There is a kiosk and café inside the castle grounds and some eateries buried in the park in front of it.

Getting There & Away

Normal buses and urban bus 17 from Puławy (3.20zł, 40 minutes, every half-hour) drop you off at the Rynek. From there walk uphill

from the distinct pink parish and follow the discourteously small blue sign to the unpaved path to the castle.

You can visit Janowiec from Kazimierz Dolny by pleasure boat or **ferry** (☎ 0602 858898; tickets 3zł; ☒ 8am-8pm Mon-Fri, 8am-9pm Sat & Sun), which takes five minutes. From the ferry on the Janowiec side, the most straightforward way to the castle is to walk the flat 2.5km to Rynek. Returning to the ferry, you can follow the small trodden path (in front of you, to the right as you leave the castle) along the ridge of the park, walking towards the Vistula. When you reach the perplexing fork in the path (near a middle-of-nowhere restaurant), make your way down the steep rocks, where a rope has been tethered to assist your descent. If you're not game for this, return to the Rynek and take the main road to the Vistula (follow the signs to the 'Prom').

CHEŁM
pop 72,600

Chełm (pronounced hewm) isn't experiencing the same sort of facelift that other towns in the region are undergoing. It remains a quiet town with little accommodation on offer, so Chełm is best explored as an easy day or half-day trip from Zamość. Visitors come to experience its proudest asset – the chalk tunnels. The centre is compact and easy to explore on foot.

Chełm is about 70km east of Lublin, 25km from the Ukrainian border. Interestingly, the town sits on an 800m-thick layer of almost pure chalk, a natural phenomenon that has both wreaked havoc and been the source of the town's economic development. It has since been tamed into a tourist attraction. There is also a cathedral sanctuary, which is a pleasant place for a stroll.

Though Chełm's Jewish population was lost during WWII, the Jewish community has left its legacy in various ways. Curiously, the good people of Chełm once featured in Eastern European Jewish jokes in the same way the Irish were the protagonists of English jokes!

History

Chełm was founded in the 10th century and; like most towns along the eastern border, shifted between the Polish Piast crown and the Kyivan duchy on various occasions. King Kazimierz III Wielki eventually got hold of the area in 1366 and King Władysław Jagiełło established a bishopric here some 50 years later.

MAŁOPOLSKA

Around this time Jews began to settle in the town, and swiftly grew in numbers – by the end of the 18th century, 60% of the town's population was Jewish.

As happened elsewhere in the country, Chełm's golden era ended in the turbulent 17th century. Later came the Partitions, and the town fell under Austrian and later Russian occupation. It wasn't until WWI that Chełm began to recover as part of independent Poland, only to be cast down again by the horrors of WWII two decades later. This included the mass execution of Jews, whose population had grown by that time to about 17,000.

Information

Kantors and ATMs are in reasonable supply; try along ul Lwowska and Lubelska. The **main post office** (☎ 082 565 2236; ul Sienkiewicza 3; ☻ 10am-5pm Mon-Fri, 9.30am-2pm Sat) is north of Plac Łuczkowskiego. There is a smaller branch on the square itself.

Bank Pekao (Al I Armii Wojska Polskiego 41) South of the centre.

Chełmski Ośrodek Informacji Turystycznej (☎ 082 565 3667; www.itchelm.pl; ul Lubelska 63; ☻ 8am-4pm Mon-Fri, 9am-2pm Sat & Sun) Excellent source of local information, offering a number of very useful brochures.

EMPiK (☎ 082 564 0144; ul Lubelska 61; ☻ 10am-6pm Mon-Fri, 10am-4pm Sat & Sun) Sells some foreign-language books, newspapers, magazines and a good range of maps.

Internet Caffe (☎ 082 564 0980; ul Szkolna 51; per hr 3zł; ☻ 8am-9pm Mon-Fri, 8am-3pm Sat) Centrally located internet.

Sights

The city's star attraction is the **Chełm Chalk Tunnels** (Chełmskie Podziemia Kredowe; ☎ 082 565 2530; ul Lubelska 55A; adult/concession 9/6zł; ☻ 9am-5pm Mon-Fri, 10am-6pm Sat & Sun), an array of chalk passages hewn out by hand about 12m below ground level. The chalk mine – reputedly the only one of its kind in the world – began in medieval times. By the 16th century, the chalk extracted here was renowned throughout the country. Over the years, the tunnels expanded in size and complexity, and by 1939 a multilevel labyrinth of corridors had grown to 15km. During the 19th century, chalk extraction ceased and the tunnels were only explored by adrenalin junkies. Authorities decided to convert the tunnels into a tourist attraction, creating a 300m long passage for the purpose; unfortunately, these plans did not eventuate. During WWII the prepared route served as a

shelter for many of the town's Jews, but was eventually destroyed by the Nazis. Increased above-ground traffic in the 1960s served as a reminder of the tunnels' existence when parts of the street collapsed. Authorities reinforced sections, except for an 1800m stretch that was opened as a tourist route.

All visits are guided (in Polish only) in groups; tours depart at 11am, 1pm and 4pm daily and take less than an hour. The temperature in the tunnels is 9°C year-round, so come prepared. The friendly and endearingly matter-of-fact ghost haunts the tunnels (in Polish only), and is a quirky highlight of the tour.

The hill in the middle of Chełm (once the location of the first settlement and stronghold) is today crowned with the sparkling white **St Mary's Basilica** (Bazylika Mariacka). It's surrounded by a complex of religious buildings that were once a bishop's palace and a monastery. The gardens around the park are low-maintenance but widely used. The late-Baroque basilica was remodelled in the mid-18th century on the site of the 13th-century church that originally stood here. Handed to the Catholics in the interwar period, the St Mary's parish itself was founded in 1931. The sober interior lacks much decoration, except for the silver antependium at the high altar depicting Polish knights paying homage to Our Lady of Chełm. The icon of the Madonna overlooking the altar is a replica; the original was removed by the Russians during WWI and is now in Ukraine. The freestanding 40m-high **belfry**, originally built in the 19th century in the Orthodox style, was later given a partial neoclassical makeover.

Also wander past the former **Piarist Church** (Kościół Pijarski), off Plac Łuczkowskiego, a late-Baroque church built in the mid-18th century on an oval design. Once you enter the massive ornamented doors, you'll find yourself ensconced in colour. Wall paintings cover every square centimetre of the walls and vaults. This *trompe l'oeil* decoration was executed in 1758 by Józef Mayer – the same artist who embellished Lublin's cathedral – and the furnishings are all in Rococo style. Today it's the parish church.

The former monastery next door houses the **Chełm Museum** (Muzeum Chełmskie; ☎ 082 565 2693; ul Lubelska 55; adult/concession 3/2zł; free Thu; ☻ 10am-4pm Tue-Fri, noon-4pm Sat & Sun), containing modern Polish painting, natural-history displays and temporary exhibitions. Other outlets of the

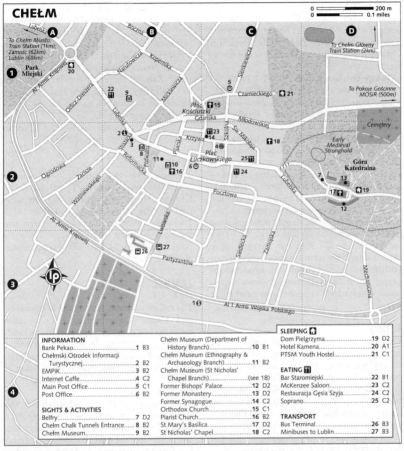

CHEŁM

MAŁOPOLSKA

museum open during the same hours and charge the same admission, or you can buy a combined ticket to all four sites (adult/concession 6/4zł). The **ethnography and archaeology branch** (ul Lubelska 56a) displays the museum's collection of archaeological finds dating from the Stone Age onwards and stages ethnography and temporary exhibitions. The **Department of History branch** (ul Lubelska 57) houses documents and photographs relating to Chełm's past. The third one, **St Nicholas' Chapel branch** (ul Św Mikołaja 4), showcases religious art from the 18th to the 20th centuries. Concerts of classical music are occasionally held here.

Of the scarce Jewish relics to have survived is the easy-to-miss **former synagogue** (ul Kopernika 8), on the corner of ul Kopernika and

ul Krzywa. There once was a larger synagogue in addition to this one, but it was destroyed in WWII. This remaining synagogue, built between 1912 and 1914, houses offices and is not open to the public. A few steps north on Plac Kościuszki is the neoclassical **Orthodox church**, built under tsarist rule from 1840 to 1852.

Sleeping

Chełm's accommodation options provide a strong argument for not staying overnight. It's better to day-trip from Lublin or Zamość. But if you do decide to stay, here are a few good budget options.

PTSM Youth Hostel (☎ 082 564 0022; ul Czarnieckiego 8; dm 30zł) This hostel has seen better days, but is pleasantly situated in a welcome patch of greenery. It's well signed by the green triangle symbol, but not well staffed. Outside 5pm to 10pm, Chełmski Ośrodek Informacji Turystycznej (the Tourist Information Office) may be able to contact someone to welcome you.

Pokoje Gościnne MOSiR (☎ 082 563 0286; ul I Pułku Szwoleżerów 15a; d/tr/q 65/77/90zł) A simple budget hotel next to the city stadium beyond Góra Katedralna, it offers basic rooms with shared bathrooms.

Dom Pielgrzyma (☎ 082 565 3656; ul Lubelska 2; dm/ s/d 25/50/100zł) An interesting accommodation choice within the cathedral sanctuary (which closes at 9.30pm), the 'Pilgrim House' – in a former Basilican Monastery – demands appropriate solemnity. If no-one answers the door, look for someone at the church.

Hotel Kamena (☎ 082 565 6401; www.hotelkamena .pl; Al Armii Krajowej 50; s 110-160zł, d 170-240zł, tr 210zł, apt 250-350zł; **P** 🖥 🛄) Kamena charges more than it should for rooms haphazardly strewn with furniture and lined with mud-brown carpet, but it's a straight-up, no-fuss, impersonal hotel, which is here if you need it for a night.

Eating

Plac Łuczkowskiego isn't particularly well used. Most of the main eating and drinking takes place along Lwowska where there are a few coffee bars, pizzerias and the like.

Bar Staromiejski (☎ 082 565 4340; ul Lubelska 68; mains 5-10zł; 🕙 9am-5pm Mon-Fri, 10am-4pm Sat & Sun) There's something comforting about the staying power of Staromiejski. This local favourite Polish-style milk bar serves cheap traditional fare in traditional Polish surrounds.

McKenzee Saloon (☎ 082 565 6464; ul Mikołaja Kopernika; mains 15-25zł; 🕙 9am-11pm) This shiny, new whip-cracker of a restaurant with attached kebab bar offers good quality and large quantities in prairie-inspired surrounds; you can eat your steak under the tarp of a wagon.

There's also a couple of vaulted cellar choices serving pizza and Polish fare:

Restauracja Gęsia Szyja (☎ 082 565 2321; ul Lubelska 27; mains 10-20zł; 🕙 lunch & dinner)

Soprano (☎ 082 565 0860; ul Lubelska 8; mains 10-30zł) Well thought-out ambience.

Getting There & Away
BUS

The bus terminal is on ul Lwowska, 300m south of Plac Łuczkowskiego. There are PKS buses to Lublin (10zł, 1½ hours, every 1½ hours), and more frequent private minibuses (9zł, one hour, every hour) departing from just outside the terminal. Half a dozen buses a day run to Zamość (10zł, 1½ hours), plus several private minibuses (9zł, 70 minutes). From Zamość there are regular minibuses to Chełm (9zł, 70 minutes) from 8am onwards. The last minibus back to Zamość leaves Chełm at around 6pm.

There are a couple of daily fast buses to Warsaw (30zł, four hours, 229km).

TRAIN

The town has two train stations: Chełm Miasto 1km west of the Old Town, and Chełm Główny 2km to the northeast. Both are serviced by urban buses. Trains to Lublin (11zł, 1½ hours, 70km) run every hour or two, and there are three fast trains per day to Warsaw (40zł, four hours, 247km); all these trains stop at both stations.

ZAMOŚĆ
pop 65,423

The self-proclaimed 'Pearl of the Renaissance' and 'Padua of the North', Zamość (zah-moshch) has never been known for its modesty. The latter name derives from its Italian designer, Bernando Morando, a Paduan native who brought his architectural vision to life in the middle of the Lublin Upland in the late 16th century.

Artistic exaggeration notwithstanding, this Renaissance town has earned its accolades; it escorted more than 100 architectural monuments through the ages relatively unharmed, it refused to surrender to Swedish invaders in the 17th century, it resisted being renamed 'Himmlerstadt' under Nazism and it earned a place on the Unesco World Heritage List in 1992. In short, Zamość is worth a visit.

History

Zamość began as something of a Renaissance-era housing estate. When Polish Chancellor and commander-in-chief Jan Zamoyski (1542–1605) decided to build a perfect city, he looked to Italy rather than neighbouring Russia for artistic inspiration. Architect Bernardo Morando was commissioned to build Zamoyski's dream, and in doing so created a model city showcasing leading Italian theories of urban design. The project began in 1580, and within 11 years 217 houses had

been built, with public buildings following soon afterwards.

By the end of the 16th century, the town's beauty – and its location on the crossroads of the Lublin–Lviv and Kraków–Kyiv trading routes – attracted international settlers including Armenians, Jews, Hungarians, Greeks, Germans, Scots and Italians.

The fortifications built to protect the city and its inhabitants were tested many times. The Cossack raid of 1648 proved little match for the strength of Zamość. Its impregnability was confirmed again in 1656, when Zamość boldly withstood the Swedish siege, along with Częstochowa and Gdańsk.

After a period of Austrian rule, Zamość fell to tsarism. It was during this time that the

city took its heaviest aesthetic beating. The Russians adapted many of the town's most splendid buildings for military purposes and almost entirely demolished the fortress walls in 1866, leaving only the ruined fragments that remain today. Zamość's modelling days were over.

Zamość was a key target of Hitler's plan for eastward expansion; German occupiers intended that some 60,000 Germans would be settled here before the end of 1943 (current German president Horst Köhler was born near Zamość after his parents had to resettle here). Due to fierce resistance by the Polish Underground, the determination of the people of Zamość, and eventually the arrival of the Red Army, the number of Germans to

MAŁOPOLSKA

relocate into the town barely reached 10,000. However, the Jewish population was brutally expelled from the town and its surrounds.

After Poland's admission to the EU in 2004, funds poured in and are being invested to enhance Zamość's appeal and ensure its longevity. The Old Market Hall and Bastion (No 7) are undergoing extensive renovations to make way for still more cafés and restaurants. There is even talk of restoring a segment of the moat and offering hot-air balloon rides over the Old Town. It's a big dream, but Zamość is no stranger to those – construction works taking place all over town suggest that this proud city might just pull it off.

Information

Most bank and internet facilities are located around the Rynek or not far from it.

Bank Pekao (ul Grodzka 2) Changes cash and advances on Visa and MasterCard.

Bar Muszelka (☎ 084 636 6009; ul Solna 7; per hr 3zł; ☽ 10am-8pm Mon-Fri, 11am-10pm Sat) Internet facilities.

Ela Travel (☎ 084 639 3001; licorbiszamosc@poczta .onet.pl; ul Grodzka 18; ☽ 9am-5pm Mon-Fri, 10am-1pm Sat) Can organise international bus, train and air tickets.

Usługi Ksero + Internet (☎ 084 639 2932; Rynek Wielki 10; per hr 3zł; ☽ 7.30am-5pm Mon-Fri, 10am-2pm Sat) Internet access.

Zamojski Ośrodek Informacji Turystycznej (☎ /fax 084 639 2292; Rynek Wielki 13; ☽ 8am-6pm Mon-Fri, 10am-4pm Sat, 10am-3pm Sun May-Sep, 8am-4pm Mon-Fri Oct-Apr) Very helpful tourist service in the town hall with maps, brochures and souvenirs. *Zamość – a short guidebook* (8zł), and the free brochure *A Walk around Zamość* are possibly worth picking up. Staff can arrange walking tours of the town in various languages. There is also a computer for respectful gratis internet use.

Sights

What with being a model city and all, Zamość is an ideal place to arbitrarily wander.

Don't get your hopes up about fortifications surrounding the town – the Russians turned the city walls to ruins. The best surviving segments are at the eastern end of town where intense renovations are under way to restore former glory.

RYNEK WIELKI

The Old Town is 600m long, 400m wide and surrounds a main square of exactly 100m by 100m. Look out for plaques on key buildings

around **Rynek Wielki**, which offer succinct information about the buildings' former use. The Italianate Renaissance Rynek is lined with arcaded burghers' houses (arcades were made compulsory by Jan Zamoyski himself). Each side of the Rynek (bar the northern side dominated by the lofty pink town hall) has eight houses bisected by two main axes of town; one runs west–east from the palace to the bastion, and the other joins the three market squares north to south.

The **town hall** was built between 1639 and 1651, and features were added and extended in the mid-17th century: its curving stairway came in 1768. Zamoyski didn't want the town hall to overshadow the palace or interrupt the view, and so unusually placed it on the northern side of the square rather than the centre. In summer, a bugle is played at noon from the 52m-high clock tower.

Originally, all the houses in the square were topped with decorative parapets, but these were removed in the 1820s; only those on the northern side have been (and still are being) restored. As these houses once belonged to Armenian merchants, you will find some distinct motifs on their façades. Two Armenian houses now shelter the **Zamość Museum** (Muzeum Zamojskie; ☎ 084 638 6494; www.museum-zamojskie.one .pl in Polish; Rynek 24/26; adult/concession 6/3zł; ☽ 9am-4pm Tue-Sun), with intriguing displays like a scale model of the 16th-century town and a letter to Jan Zamoyski from his architect, Bernardo Morando, with a hand-drawn plan of the square and names of the first occupants of each building. Also on display are archaeological finds such as Gothic treasures found in cemeteries in the Hrubieszów Valley. Note the original wooden ceilings and decorations around the windows and doors.

Continue walking through the arcades of the square to admire some other fine buildings; on the southern side take particular note of No 21, which dates back as far as 1590, and quintessentially Italian styled No 25. Also note the stuccowork in the vestibules, such as at No 10. The old pharmacy at No 2 dates back to 1609.

SOUTHWEST OF THE RYNEK

The **cathedral**, just southwest of the Rynek, was built by Morando (around 1587 to 1598) as a votive offering and mausoleum for the Zamoyskis. The exterior of the building changed dramatically in the 19th century, but the interior maintained many original features. Note the authentic Lublin-Renaissance-style vault, the stone and stuccowork, and the unusual arcaded organ loft. In the high altar is the rococo silver tabernacle of 1745. Jan Zamoyski's tomb is under the black marble in the chapel at the head of the right-hand aisle. The stairs next to the chapel lead to the family crypt.

Behind the church is the former vicarage from the 1610s with its splendid ornate doorway. It leads to the **Sacral Museum** (Muzeum Sakralne; ul Kolegiacka 2; admission 1zł; ☺ 10am-4pm Mon-Fri, 10am-1pm Sat & Sun May-Sep, 10am-1pm Sat & Sun only Oct-Apr), featuring a collection of religious art accumulated by the church.

Back outside the church, you can climb the freestanding **bell tower** (admission 1.5zł; ☺ 10am-4pm Mon-Sat May-Sep), though the terrace is not high enough to offer a bird's-eye view of the Old Town. This present tower was built from 1755 to 1775 after the original timber tower went up in flames. It contains three bells: Wawrzyniec (170kg), Tomasz (1200kg) and the largest, Jan (4300kg). You may need to ask for the key to the bell tower at the Sacral Museum.

WEST OF THE RYNEK

West from the collegiate church, the **Arsenal Museum** (Muzeum Arsenał; ☎ 084 638 4076; ul Zamkowa 2; adult/concession 5/2.50zł; ☺ 9am-4pm Tue-Fri) displays a modest collection of cannons, swords, muskets and other military hardware. Various temporary exhibitions are also held here.

In the 1830s, **Zamoyski Palace** (Pałac Zamoyskich) became a military hospital, but now houses government offices and is closed to the public.

NORTHWEST OF THE RYNEK

Just north across ul Królowej Jadwigi is the **Old Lublin Gate** (Stara Brama Lubelska), a partly ruined brick structure. Just after its construction in 1588 it was walled up in 1604 to commemorate a victorious event: Austrian Archduke Maximilian (a claimant to the Polish throne) was taken prisoner by Jan Zamoyski in the battle of Byczyna and triumphantly 'escorted' into the town through the gate. He is the last person to have walked through it.

To the east of the gate is the **Academy** (Akademia), recognised for making Zamość a thriving academic centre. The Academy was opened in 1595 with an impassioned appeal by Jan Zamoyski for young Poles to educate

themselves. The Baroque structure retained little character after tsarist times.

SOUTHEAST OF THE RYNEK

On the eastern edge of the Old Town is the **Hala Targowa**, the old Market Hall and prime site of massive renovation works to rejuvenate existing shops and cafés and add new attractions. The market is adjacent to the best surviving **bastion**, No 7. Walking tours of the walls can be arranged in various languages through Zamojski Ośrodek Informacji Turystycznej, but plans may be disrupted by renovation works. The entrance is by the **Lviv Gate** (Brama Lwowska), built in 1599 as the main eastern access gate. It still retains some original decorations, including a Latin inscription concerning the foundation of the town, and the Zamoyski family coat of arms.

Opposite the gate is the **Franciscan Church** (Kościół Franciszkanów; Plac Wolności). When it was built (between 1637 and 1655) it was reputedly one of the largest and most beautiful Baroque churches in the country. In 1784, the Austrian Empire abolished the Franciscan order, throwing the church into the hands of fate. It was converted to a hospital, an arms depot under the Russians, a museum and cinema between the two world wars, and an art college after WWII before finding its way back into the hands of the Franciscans in 1993.

Further south is the **former Orthodox Church**, built in the 1620s by Greek merchants and complemented by a fortified tower half a century later. The church was rebuilt several times but the original stucco decoration of the vault remains.

THE JEWISH QUARTER

The area around the Rynek Solny and ul Zamenhofa was once the heart of the Jewish quarter. Jews were granted permission to settle in Zamość in 1588, and by the mid-19th century accounted for 60% of the town's 4000 people. By the eve of WWII their numbers had grown to 12,000 (45% of the total population). In 1941 they were moved to the ghetto formed to the west of the Old Town, and by the following year most had been murdered in extermination camps.

One block east of Rynek Solny is the Renaissance **synagogue** (ul Pereca 14; donation appreciated; ☺ 9am-1pm Mon-Fri, 10am-5pm Sat & Sun) built between 1610 and 1618. One of the two side rooms off the main hall was destroyed during Nazi occupation, and the interior stripped of its fittings. The synagogue is the subject of a restoration project. Note the surviving stucco decoration and the reconstructed decorative parapets.

Interestingly, the site of **Jazz Club Kosz** was once a Jewish bathhouse – the large hall downstairs was once used for ritual bathing.

BEYOND THE OLD TOWN

Roughly 450m southwest of the Old Town is the **Rotunda** – a ring-shaped fort 54m in diameter surrounding a circular yard. The rotunda was built in the 1820s as part of the defensive infrastructure of the town, but during WWII the SS converted it into an interrogation centre. Some 8000 people from the Zamość area are believed to have been murdered here and their bodies burnt in the courtyard. The graveyard surrounding the rotunda is the resting place of people who were killed here, including Polish soldiers and members of the Polish underground. Since 1947, the rotunda has been the **Martyrdom Museum** (☎ 0606 952433; Droga Męczenników Rotundy; ⏰ 7am-8pm Mon-Fri, 8am-8pm Sat, 8am-10pm Sun May-Sep, 7am-3pm Mon-Fri Nov-Apr), containing various tributes to the victims of Nazi atrocities. Walking through the various cells (particularly by yourself) can be a disturbing and desolate experience.

Zamość has a small **zoo** (Ogród Zoologiczny; ☎ 084 639 3470; ul Szczebrzeska 8; adult/concession 5/3zł; ⏰ 9am-7pm Apr-Sep, 7am-3pm Oct-Mar) with small enclosures. There are some interesting exotic species, but many look homesick. A visit might be worthwhile if you have children in tow who need a break from all the history.

Festivals & Events

The **Zamość Theatre Summer**, organised by **Zamojski Dom Kultury** (☎ 084 639 2021; www.zdk .zamosc.pl in Polish), takes place from mid-June to mid-August with dramatic open-air performances on the Rynek in front of the town hall.

Every year, the manager of **Piwnica pod Rektorską** (☎ 0502 578442; www.kosz.zam.pl; Rynek 2) and formerly of Jazz Club Kosz, organises jazz and blues events in Zamość. They include the **International Meeting of Jazz Vocalists** in September (with performances and competitions between jazz singers from the region and far beyond); as well as **Jazz on the Borderlands** in May, and **New Cooperation** in August.

Sleeping

Though accommodation in Zamość caters for most budgets, the range isn't what you would expect from a town of this aesthetic fame. Nevertheless, there are some solid accomodation options available.

BUDGET

Camping Duet (☎ 084 639 2499; www.duet.virgo.com .pl in Polish; ul Królowej Jadwigi 14; s/d/tr/q 70/85/110/135zł; 🅿 🐾) This conveniently located camping ground, about 1.5km west of the Old Town, has neat bungalows for up to six people, tennis courts, a restaurant, a sauna and a Jacuzzi. In summer it can be crowded with happy holidaying families.

Pokoje Gościnne OSiR (☎/fax 084 638 6011; www .osir.zamosc.pl in Polish; ul Królowej Jadwigi 8; dm/s/d/tr/q incl breakfast 24/90/125/150/180zł; 🅿) Hardly a conventional place to stay, but the price is low and it's close to the centre. You may feel like you're trapped in a primary school sports day in the 1980s with a room overlooking a sports hall, but this can be a fun way of engaging with the real Poland. The onsite kiosk can also be handy.

The simple but functional **youth hostel** (☎ 084 638 9500; ul Zamoyskiego 4; dm 15-20zł; ⏰ Jul & Aug) is in a school not far from the bus terminal, 1.5km east of the Old Town.

MIDRANGE & TOP END

Hotel Jubilat (☎ 084 638 7630; www.hoteljubilat.pl in Polish; ul Wyszyńskiego 52; s/d/apt without breakfast 120/145/260zł; 🅿) The Jubilat is conveniently located next to the bus station. Its exterior appearance does little to recommend it, but inside you'll find a fitness centre, restaurant and recently refurbished bathrooms. Despite its lack of internet access, the Jubilat offers better value than more central options.

Hotel Arkadia (☎ 084 638 6507; makben@wp.pl; Rynek Wielki 9; s/d/tr 100/150/190zł; 🅿) With super prices and a superlative location on the Rynek, Arkadia fills up fast. The scruffiness of this tiny seven-room establishment only lends it charm – and keeps the prices reasonable.

Hotel Renesans (☎ 084 639 2001; www.hotelrene sans.pl in Polish; ul Grecka 6; s/d/apt 125/170/200zł; 🅿 🖥) From the people who brought you the Jubilat comes the Renesans. The exterior is something of a train wreck, and doesn't seem worthy of the three stars it wears, but the rooms are comfortable, clean and central. Prices drop if you skip breakfast.

Hotel Senator (☎ 084 638 9990; www.senatorhotel
.pl; ul Rynek Solny 4; s/d/ste 164/229/334zł; P 🖃 ☒ ⚅)
The recently opened Senator offers impressive
value and more charm than its chain-hotel
competition. Rooms have a tasteful aesthetic
with even standard rooms offering impressive space. The onsite restaurant, with its own
fireplace, aims for medieval mellow (and looks
just a bit like a medieval theatre set). The expansive breakfast buffet costs 25zł. Weekend
discounts add to the ambience.

Orbis Hotel 'Zamojski' (☎ 084 639 2516; zamojski
@orbis.pl; ul Kołłątaja 2/4/6; s/d/ste 190/264/389zł;
P ☒ 🖃 ⚅) Occupying three interconnected
houses, the Orbis is a reliable choice that offers conventional professionalism. Some
rooms are bigger than others, some have more
reliable internet access, and some offer better
views. The downfall of the Orbis is that the
old-world charm of the hotel's exterior has
not been matched with modernised interiors.
There is an onsite fitness club.

Eating & Drinking

There is a growing number of eateries scattered throughout the Old Town, most with
dining areas in cellars downstairs and on
the Rynek upstairs. Many of them magically
pumpkin-pop into bars or clubs at night.

Bohema (☎ 084 638 1414; ul Staszica 29; ⏰ 11am-
late) This super-slick underground bar (also
with Rynek seating) not only offers live music
but also turns out some sophisticated food;
pancake concoctions are the breakfast of
champions. Poetry could be written about the
unsurpassable hot chocolate with chilli (possibly the best 7zł you'll spend in Poland).

Corner Pub (☎ 084 627 70 694; www.corner.boo.pl;
ul Żeromskiego 6; ⏰ 11am-last customer) Every town
needs an Irish pub, and this brand new place
has already become Zamość's. It's far classier
than the real deal, and has regular live music.

Bar Asia (☎ 084 639 2304; ul Staszica 10; mains from
8zł; ⏰ 8am-5pm Mon-Fri, 8am-3.30pm Sat) For some
fast and filling soup/dumplings/cabbage-style
food, head to this old-style milk bar.

The following places offer seating right
on the Rynek or in atmospheric cellars
underneath it:

Restauracja-Kawiarnia Padwa (☎ 084 638 6256;
ul Staszica 23; mains 7-14zł; ⏰ lunch & dinner) Hearty
Polish fare opposite the town hall.

Piwnica pod Rektorską (☎ 084 638 1942; mains 10-
20zł; ⏰ 10am-midnight) Polish-style hamburger/piegoli-
style snacks and sometimes jazz downstairs.

Restauracja Muzealna (☎ 084 638 7300; ul
Ormiańska 30; mains 10-25zł; ⏰ lunch & dinner) A better
class of Polish cuisine. The goulash is an essential order.

Getting There & Away
BUS

The **bus terminal** (☎ 084 638 4986; ul Hrubieszowska
11) is 2km east of the Old Town but well serviced by city buses O and 3. Bus stands along
Partyzantów and at Plac Sfefanidesa are convenient for the latter.

Private minibuses leave for several destinations from the stand right opposite the
bus terminal; check the timetable for details
of departures.

Buses to Lublin (12zł, two hours, every
half-hour) run roughly between 5am and
6pm. There are also plenty of minibuses
(10zł, two hours, every half-hour). There is
an afternoon bus to Puławy (16zł, 2½ hours,
1.15pm) via Lublin.

There are a few buses to Kraków a day
(21zł to 35zł, four to five hours), and there are
four buses daily to Warsaw (32zł, five hours).
There are only three buses to Sandomierz
(20zł, three hours) in the morning.

There are two morning buses to Rzeszów
(16zł, three hours) and one to Przemyśl (17zł,
3½ hours).

There are frequent normal buses and minibuses to Zwierzyniec (3.50zł, 40 minutes,
32km), the entry point for Roztocze National
Park. Alternatively, from ul Akademicka in
the centre of town, take a bus headed to either Biłgoraj or Nisko, which may be passing
through Zwierzyniec.

TRAIN

The **train station** (☎ 084 084 9436; ul Szczebrzeska 11) is
about 1km southwest of the Old Town; walk
or take the city bus. There's a 5.30am train
to Lublin (28zł, 2½ hours, 116km) – there
are others, but they take more than eight
hours. Similarly with the morning trains to
Warsaw (46zł, 5½ hours, 293km), forget the
second one, which takes 11 hours. There are
a few morning trains to Kraków (46zł, seven
hours, 318km).

ZWIERZYNIEC
pop 3800

Given what a raging success Jan Zamoyski's
model city Zamość turned out to be, it's no
surprise that his country getaway also came
up trumps. Zwierzyniec (zvyeh-*zhi*-nyets),

MAŁOPOLSKA

32km southwest of Zamość, is picture perfect. In the 16th century, the visionary Zamoyski created a game reserve in this area, which has since become a national park (see opposite). The family's summer palace was erected soon afterwards, around which a small town began to grow. A chapel was later built on one of the tiny islands opposite the palace, and remains the cherry on the cake of Zwierzyniec (since the palace was dismantled in 1833).

Information

There is a small **tourist office** (☎ 084 687 2660; zokir@poczta.oneta.pl; ul Słowackiego 2; ⏰ 8am-7pm Mon-Sat May & Sep, 8am-7pm Mon-Sat & 9am-5pm Sun Jul & Aug, 8am-4pm Mon-Fri Oct-Apr), located in the centre of town, which may be able to help you find private rooms. Alternatively, ask at the tourist office (p252) in Zamość.

Sights

Today Zwierzyniec is the gateway to the Roztocze National Park. It houses park management and on the southern edge of town, roughly 1km from the bus stop, the **Education and Museum Centre** (Muzeum Przyrodnicze; ☎ 084 687 2066; ul Plażowa 3; adult/concession 3.50/2.50zł; ⏰ 9am-5pm Tue-Sun May-Oct, 9am-4pm Tue-Sun Nov-Apr, closed Mon, public holidays & day after public holidays). The museum can be crowded with hikers beginning their journey and school kids queuing for souvenirs – try to get there early. Many short walks starting here offer a nice slice of the park. A particularly pleasant one is the Bukowa Mount didactic path (2.6km, two hours), which leads through some lush fir forest and fine specimens of Carpathian beech wood.

On the way to the Education and Museum Centre, you may see a striking wooden building that looks something like a Swiss chalet. This **plenipotentiary's villa** was built in the late 19th century as a rendition of the 17th-century gates that once led to the Zamoyski's menagerie. It now houses Roztocze National Park Management.

The only significant and authentic structure remaining from the Zamoyski's residential complex is the **Chapel upon the Water** (Kaplica na Wodzie). The appeal of this chapel is not its interior but its setting. The small Baroque church sits on one of four tiny islets on the small lake of Staw Kościelny (Church Pond), which was allegedly dug by Turkish and Tartar prisoners

in the 1740s. The church is linked to the mainland by a bridge (which would be more fitting if it were rickety and wooden rather than solid concrete). The lake is halfway between the bus station and the museum.

Near the church is the **Zwierzyniec Brewery**, established in 1806 and still producing excellent beer today, predictably named 'Zwierzyniec'. The brewery itself is not open to visitors, but the small bar at the entrance sure is. It should be mandatory for breweries to be situated in such close proximity to walking trails.

Sleeping & Eating

The tourist office will be able to help you find agroturystyka accommodation, well-equipped holiday centres and an abundance of local rooms in and around town. In most, longer stays bring the rates down.

Hotel Jodła (☎ 084 687 2012; fax 084 687 2124; ul Parkowa 3A; d 58-69zł, tr 87zł) In a large timber villa near the bus stop, Jodła offers small doubles that share facilities with occupants of one other room. There is also a café and a tennis court onsite.

Ośrodek Wypoczynkowy Anna (☎ 084 687 2590; www.annazwierzyniec.pl in Polish; ul Dębowa 1; s 60zł, d 80-90zł, tr/q 100/120zł; P) Anna offers exceptionally good value all year round. Simply furnished rooms are neat and cosy and the pleasant modern building has its own restaurant. Only the more expensive rooms have private bathrooms, but shared facilities are clean.

Karczma Młyn (☎ 084 687 2527; ul Wachniewskiej 1A; s/d 60/80zł) The best place for lunch or dinner offers wholesome Polish fare surrounded by the lush green you'd expect of a national park. The terrace is idyllically situated for a postcard-perfect view of the Chapel on the Water.

There are several pleasant budget accommodation options in the area:

Camping Echo (☎ 084 687 2314; ul Biłgorajska 3; camp sites per person 7.50zł, cabins with bathroom per person 20zł, cabins with/without basic per person 16/13zł, cars 2zł; ⏰ May-Sep; P) Basic three- and six-bed cabins and a snack bar serving simple meals.

Youth hostel (☎ 084 687 2175; ul Partyzantów 3B; dm 30zł; ⏰ Jul & Aug) Basic 40-bed place in the local school.

Youth hostel (☎ 084 687 2366; ul Browarna 1; dm 10-12zł) Dorm rooms close to the lake.

Getting There & Away

The bus stop is on ul Zamojska, in the town centre north of the lake (if you're facing the

MAŁOPOLSKA

road with your back to the bus stand, follow the road left to the lake). There is a large town map posted nearby, which will help you get your bearings.

Buses to Zamość (3.50zł, 40 minutes, 32km) pass every half-hour or so. There are infrequent buses to more-distant destinations, including Sandomierz and Rzeszów. The train station is about 1km east of town.

ROZTOCZE NATIONAL PARK

Decreed in 1974, **Roztocze National Park** (Roztoczański Park Narodowy; Park Management Office, Zwierzyniec ☎ 084 687 2066; www.roztoczanskipn.pl in Polish; ul Plażowa 2, Zwierzyniec; ☺ 7.15am-5.15pm Mon-Fri) covers an area of 79 sq km to the south and east of Zwierzyniec. The site was a nature reserve for more than 350 years as part of the Zamoyski family estate. Following the purchase of a vast stretch of land (complete with six towns, 149 villages and about 1600 sq km of forest) in 1589, Jan Zamoyski created an enclosed game reserve named Zwierzyniec (zoological garden). This was a remarkable achievement at that time, given that this was not a hunting ground but a protected area for various animal species to roam in relative freedom.

Today's national park includes much of Zamoyski's original reserve. Occupying undulating terrain – 93% of which is covered with forest – the park retains much of its primeval character. It also remains geologically active, apparently rising by 2mm a year. The park is crossed from east to west by the Wieprz, one of the least polluted rivers in the region.

Flora & Fauna

Because Roztocze National Park is home to a diversity of soil types, topography, climate and water sources, an impressive variety of trees grow here, including fir, spruce, pine, Carpathian beech, sycamore, hornbeam, oak, elm and lime. Fir trees in the park grow bigger than elsewhere in the country, some reaching up to 50m high and 4.5m wide. Closer to the ground, attentive visitors will be able to count some 700 species of vascular plant and more than 1000 species of mushroom.

The park's fauna is just as diverse; it is home to 58 species of mammal including stag, roe deer, boar, fox, marten and badger. Elk, wolves and lynxes have been known to visit from time to time. Look up, and you'll be able to spy some 210 bird species passing overhead; look down and zoom in for a glimpse of some of the 2000 species of beetle inhabiting the park.

Park management has put in place various conservation efforts, including the austerely clad 'Mounted Nature Guards' who patrol the park on horseback. In 1979 the beaver was reintroduced into the park and in 1982 the Polish pony – descendents of the tarpan and now the symbol of the park. There is a Polish pony refuge near Echo Ponds. The world's last specimens of tarpan were kept here in Roztocze in the 19th century until they were given away when the estate fell into disarray under tsarist rule.

Walking Trails

The normal starting point for walks is the town of Zwierzyniec, or more specifically the Education and Museum Centre (opposite), where you can buy booklets and park maps.

The shorter walks (between 20 minutes and two hours or so), called 'educational paths', are clearly marked from the museum. A particularly nice Roztocze sampler is the Bukowa Mount didactic path (2.6km) going south from the museum to the top of Bukowa Góra (Beech Mountain, 306m) along a former palace park lane. The gradient is mild, but there are a couple of hundred steps through the various forest habitats. If you would like to visit the Polish pony reserve near Echo Ponds, there is a very short and easy route (1.2km) from the museum.

The several longer walks are called 'tourist routes', which generally weave from Zwierzyniec through forest terrain to neighbouring villages (such as Florianka, also known for its tarpan breeding). Intersecting paths enable you to return by a different route or cut to another path.

Cycling routes of different durations and arduousness are also marked on tourist maps available from the centre.

MAŁOPOLSKA

The Carpathian Mountains

Effectively the eastern extension of the Alps, the Carpathians (Karpaty) stretch from the southern border with Slovakia into the Ukraine. They make up the highest and largest mountain range in Central Europe and form Poland's most scenic and rugged region. Indeed, their wooded hills and snowy mountains are a beacon for hikers, skiers and cyclists. And because of its remoteness and relative inaccessibility over the centuries, this 'forgotten corner' has been able to preserve its strong regional culture. Even today, you'll still see plenty of picturesque timber houses, rustic shingled churches and scores of tiny roadside shrines.

The region's largest city is Rzeszów, which offers excellent transport links but few real attractions. A much better destination is the popular resort town of Zakopane in the heart of the Tatra Mountains (Tatry), the highest section of the Polish Carpathians. This area offers the best winter sports and mountain walks in the country, and in the Podhale region to the north, folk traditions are still a part of everyday life.

Elsewhere, a mosaic of small, modest towns provide jumping-off points for half a dozen national parks and some of Poland's most rewarding walking trails; laid-back spa resorts present a chance to unwind; and historic regional towns such as Przemyśl, Tarnów and Sanok offer unique insights into the past. Just don't try to hurry things down here in the 'deep south'. Instead, adopt the local pace of life and amble at your leisure through some of Poland's most stunning scenery.

HIGHLIGHTS

- Viewing the natural beauty of the Bieszczady up close by jeep tour from **Ustrzyki Górne** (p281)

- Enjoying a papal cream cake in the happy town where Pope John Paul II was born, **Wadowice** (p261)

- Marvelling at the colours and patterns of the painted houses of **Zalipie** (p265)

- Following the **Icon Trail** (p278) from Sanok and visiting the region's charming timber churches

- Hiking or skiing in the Tatra Mountains above the fashionable resort of **Zakopane** (p306)

- Rafting relaxedly down the **Dunajec Gorge** (p301)

- Taking to the waters and having a treatment (milk bath, anyone?) in peaceful **Krynica** (p296)

- Hitting the town after dark in lively, studenty **Rzeszów** (p265)

Getting There & Away

The main entry points for this region are Kraków in the west and Rzeszów in the east. Both have air links with Warsaw, plus some direct international flights (see p206 and p269). Most of the larger towns have bus or train links with other Polish cities and beyond.

Getting Around

Although most of the main towns in the region can be reached by train, buses are usually the fastest and most convenient mode of public transport. Getting around more isolated areas, particularly the Bieszczady, can be a slow and frustrating exercise so it's best to be under your own steam.

THE CARPATHIAN FOOTHILLS

The Carpathian Foothills (Przedgórze Karpackie) form a green and hilly belt sloping from the true mountains in the south to the Vistula and San River Valleys to the north. Except for Kalwaria Zebrzydowska and Wadowice, which are usually visited from Kraków, most sights in the region are located along the Kraków–Tarnów–Rzeszów–Przemyśl road (and are ordered accordingly, west to east, in this section).

KALWARIA ZEBRZYDOWSKA

pop 4475

Poland's second most important pilgrimage site after Jasna Góra in Częstochowa, Kalwaria Zebrzydowska (kahl-*vah*-ryah zeb-zhi-*dof*-skah) is set amid hills 35km southwest of Kraków. The town owes its existence and subsequent fame to the squire of Kraków, Mikołaj Zebrzydowski, who commissioned the church and monastery for the Bernardine order in 1600. Having noticed a resemblance in the area to the topography of Jerusalem, he set about creating a place of worship similar to the Via Dolorosa in the Holy City. By 1617, 24 chapels were built over the surrounding hills, some of which looked as though they'd been brought directly from the mother city. As the place attracted growing numbers of pilgrims, more chapels were erected, eventually totalling 42. In 1999 Kalwaria Zebrzydowska was added to Unesco's list of World Heritage sites.

There is a **tourist office** (☎ 033 876 6101; www .kalwaria-zebrzydowska.pl; Rynek 19; ❤ 8am-5pm Mon-Fri, 8am-1pm Sat) just south of the basilica.

Sights

The original hilltop church north of the centre was gradually enlarged and today is the massive **Basilica of Our Lady of the Angels** (Bazylika Matki Bożej Anielskiej). The holiest image in the church is the icon of Mary in the **Zebrzydowska Chapel** (Kaplica Zebrzydowska) to the left of the high altar. Tradition has it that the eyes shed tears of blood in 1641, and from that time miracles occurred. Pilgrims flock to Kalwaria year-round but especially on Marian feast days, when processions along the **Calvary Trails** (Dróżki Kalwaryjskie) linking the chapels take place.

The basilica is flanked to the north by the equally huge **Bernardine Monastery** (Klasztor Bernadynów; ❤ 7am-7pm), which contains impressive 16th- and 17th-century paintings in its cloister.

What have really made Kalwaria famous are the **Passion plays**, a blend of religious ceremony and popular theatre re-enacting the crucial final days of Christ's life and held here since the 17th century. They are performed by locals, including Bernardine monks, during a two-day-long procession starting in the early afternoon of Maundy (Holy) Thursday during Holy Week.

Sleeping

Hotel Kalwarianka (☎ /fax 033 876 6492; ul Mickiewicza 16; s 39-44zł, d 51-59zł, tr 64-75zł, q 78-96zł; **P**) Located next to the town stadium about 1km south of the Rynek, this 54-bed place is basic but cheap; rooms with private facilities are at the upper end of the price scale. There's a tennis court on site.

Hotel Merkury Tatarscy (☎ 033 867 6277; www .merkury-tatarscy.com.pl; ul Sądowa 11; s 72-92zł, d 124-144zł, tr 171-216zł; **P** 💻) Right in the centre of town, the Merkury has 18 spotless and comfortable rooms in two separate buildings. It's an easy walk up the hill to the church and monastery.

Getting There & Away

There are hourly buses to Kraków (7zł, one hour) and Wadowice (4zł, 30 minutes). Three trains a day pass through Kalwaria on their

THE CARPATHIAN MOUNTAINS

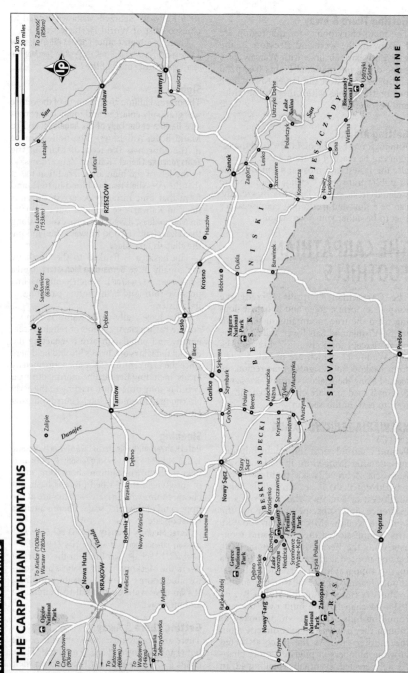

way to/from Kraków (9zł, 45 minutes) and Wadowice (4.50zł, 20 minutes).

WADOWICE
pop 19,100

The birthplace of one Karol Wojtyła (better known to the world as Pope John Paul II), Wadowice (vah-do-*vee*-tsah) is a pretty little town 14km west of Kalwaria Zebrzydowska that today welcomes pilgrims in the tens of thousands. And when – not if – the late pontiff is canonised, it is likely to surpass even Częstochowa as Poland's top pilgrimage centre. Unlike Lourdes and other places where miracles are said to happen, the atmosphere here is not sombre and talk does not come in the form of whispers; indeed, in keeping with the spirit of the man and his vision, Wadowice is a joyous place.

The **tourist office** (☎ 033 873 2365; www.it.wado wice.pl; ul Kościelna 4; ✆ 9am-5pm Mon-Fri, 10am-4pm Sat & Sun) will provide you with all the information you need. The office is opposite the **Family Home of John Paul II** (Dom Rodzinny Jana Pawła II; ☎ 033 823 2662; www.domrodzinnyjanapawla.pl; ul Kościelna 7; donation requested; ✆ 9am-6pm Tue-Sun May-Sep, 9am-4pm Tue-Sun Oct-Apr), where Karol was born in May 1920; to the north is the 18th-century **Lesser Basilica** (Bazylika Mniejska; Plac Jana Pawła II), where he was baptised a month later. Outside the church is a **monument to Pope John Paul II**, which is known as the 'Cream Cake Statue' in some circles. It seems that when the pope visited his hometown in 1999, he sat in almost the same spot and reminisced about how he and his mates would enjoy *kremówki* (cream cakes) from a certain shop 'just over there'. The statue actually depicts the pope in the usual pastoral pose, with his hand raised in a blessing, but it might look to some as though he is pointing.

Naturally, you can't miss trying a *kremówka*, the calorific pastry of cream, eggs, sugar and a dash of brandy. Everyone claims to serve the real McCoy, but to our mind the best is at **Kawiarna Mieszczańska** (☎ 0500 636 842; ul Kościelna 6; cream cakes 4.50zł; ✆ 9am-7pm Apr-Oct, 9am-5pm Nov-Mar), just next to the church.

Getting There & Away

There are hourly buses to Kraków (8zł, 1¼ hours), some of which go via Kalwaria Zebrzydowska (4zł, 30 minutes). There are also half a dozen daily buses to Katowice (12zł, two hours) via Oświęcim (6.50zł, one hour).

Three trains a day go to Kraków (11zł, 1½ hours) via Kalwaria Zebrzydowska (4.50zł, 20 minutes).

NOWY WIŚNICZ
pop 2700

The little town of Nowy Wiśnicz (*no-vi veesh-neech*), 46km east of Kraków and just south of the transport hub Bochnia, boasts a well-proportioned, early Baroque castle designed by Italian architect Matteo Trapola for one of the most powerful men in Poland at the time, Stanisław Lubomirski (1583–1649).

As soon as the castle was completed, Lubomirski commissioned the same architect to build a monastery nearby for the Carmelites. Equally splendid and similarly fortified, the monastery was erected between 1622 and 1635 about 500m up the hill from the castle. After the Carmelites were expelled in the 1780s, the monastery was turned into a prison, and it remains a high-security one to this day.

Sights

With its four distinctive towers in the corners, **Wiśnicz Castle** (Zamek w Wiśniczu; ☎ 014 612 8589; adult/concession 8/5zł; ✆ 9am-2pm Mon, 9am-4pm Tue-Thu, 9am-5pm Fri, 10am-5pm Sat, 10am-6pm Sun Apr-Oct, 9am-2pm Mon-Fri Nov-Mar) is 1.5km uphill from the town centre. The castle was completed in 1621 using the foundations and parts of the walls of a 14th-century stronghold. The new castle was reputedly very well prepared to defend itself: it had food and ammunition to withstand a three-year siege. Despite its enviable defences, the castle surrendered to the Swedes in 1655 in exchange for the promise that they would not destroy it. They indeed kept their word, but nonetheless thoroughly plundered the interior, taking away some 150 wagonloads of art and other valuables. The castle suffered a series of further misfortunes, including a fire in 1831, which left it in ruins. Only after WWII was restoration undertaken, and this is ongoing.

The 50-minute guided tour covers the courtyard and rooms on the two upper floors, including the domed castle chapel, a large hall with a splendid ornate ceiling, the **Knights Hall** (Sala Rycerska) with a coffered ceiling and a huge ballroom measuring 30m by 9m and 9m high. There's also the sarcophagus of Stanisław Lubomirski, a small exhibition displaying three models of the castle from

THE CARPATHIAN MOUNTAINS

different periods and photographic documentation of postwar reconstruction.

Sleeping & Eating

Hotel Atlas (☎ 014 612 9125; www.hotelatlas.pl; Stary Wiśnicz 410; s/d/ste 100/140/160zł; P ▢) The charming Atlas offers 10 spotless rooms in a country setting, with a delightful garden and its own detached restaurant and pub done up like a traditional old barn. It's in Stary Wiśnicz, 2.5km north of Nowy Wiśnicz on the road from Bochnia.

Hotel Cold (☎ 014 612 2802; www.hotel.cold.pl; ul Storynka 5, Bochnia; s/d/apt 115/160/200zł; P ✕ 🎯 ▢ ⅄) The reception at this friendly 19-room hotel in Bochnia is anything but what its name suggests. It's a very smart, modern hotel with a restaurant, pub, tennis court and – wait for it – ten-pin bowling alley right in the heart of town.

Getting There & Away

Nowy Wiśnicz is well served from Bochnia (2.40zł, 15 minutes) by either the hourly suburban bus 12 or the PKS buses running every quarter of an hour or so. Bochnia is on the main Kraków–Tarnów route and has frequent buses and trains to both destinations.

DĘBNO
pop 1500

Lying roughly halfway between Bochnia and Tarnów, the small village of Dębno contains a relatively little-known castle that is a good example of a small defensive residence.

Dębno Castle (Zamek w Dęnie) was built in the 1470s on the foundations of a previous knights' stronghold and was gradually extended until the 1630s. It was plundered several times since, but the structure survived without major damage.

The castle consists of four two-storey buildings joined at the corners to form a small rectangular courtyard, all surrounded by a now-dry moat that's still spanned by a footbridge. The structure is adorned with fine corner towers, oriels, bay windows and doorways.

The castle is now a **museum** (☎ 014 665 8035; adult/concession 8/4zł, 9/5zł Sun, free Fri; ⏱ 10am-4pm Tue & Thu, 9am-3pm Wed & Fri, 11am-3pm Sat & Sun, to 6pm Sat & Sun Jun-Aug). The rooms have been refurnished and contain paintings and weaponry. Larger rooms include the knights' room,

the chapel and the concert hall, which hosts piano recitals from time to time.

Agawa (☎ 014 665 8317; www.agawa.noclegiw.pl; ul Wola Dębińska 278; d 130zł; P), a motel and restaurant at the petrol station 1km east of Dębno on the highway towards Tarnów, offers budget food and has 15 rooms upstairs.

Getting There & Away

The castle is an easy stopover on the Kraków–Tarnów highway. There are regular buses on this road that will let you off at the village centre, from which the castle is about 300m south.

TARNÓW
pop 116,500

Though you probably wouldn't guess it while strolling about its pleasant, finely restored Old Town, Tarnów (*tar-noof*) is an important regional industrial centre and transport hub. With just the right number of attractions and of a manageable size, it's the perfect place to stay put for a while.

The town layout – an oval centre with a large square in its middle – is unusual, suggesting that the town was planned in medieval times. Tarnów is indeed an old city: its municipal charter was granted in 1330. Developing as a trade centre on the busy Kraków–Kyiv route, the town enjoyed good times in the Renaissance period. But a fire in the 15th century completely destroyed the medieval city, which was not rebuilt for almost 200 years.

Not uncommonly for the region, Tarnów had a sizable Jewish community, which by the 19th century accounted for half the city's population. Of 25,000 Jews living here in 1939 (45% of the town's population), only a handful survived the war. To remind itself and others of its past, Tarnów uses a stylised yellow Star of David in its tourist office logo. The city is one of the major centres for Poland's relatively small Roma population.

Information

Bank BPH (ul Wałowa 10; ⏱ 8am-6pm Mon-Fri)
Bank Pekao (Plac Kazimierza Wielkiego 3a; ⏱ 9am-5pm Mon-Fri, 9am-1pm Sat)
PTTK office (☎ 014 622 2200; ul Żydowska 20; ⏱ 9am-1pm & 5-8pm Mon & Thu, 9am-3.30pm Tue, Wed & Fri) Travel agency.
Salon Multimedialny Maestro (Plac Kazimierza Wielkiego 5; per hr 3zł; ⏱ 8am-9pm Mon-Sat, noon-9pm Sun) Internet access.

THE CARPATHIAN MOUNTAINS

Café Forum (☎ 014 620 1111; ul Wekslarska 9; mains 9-28zł; ☾ 11am-11pm Mon-Fri, noon-11pm Sat, 1-10pm Sun) This is a convivial place in the Old Town offering a menu of cheap pizzas, salads and drinks.

Bombay Music (☎ 014 627 0760; www.bombay.rix .pl; ul Krakowska 11a; mains 14-40zł; ☾ 9am-11pm Mon-Sat, 11am-11pm Sun) The Bombay serves up some-what less-than-authentic Indian dishes (plus a few European ones) in elegant surrounds. And the Music part? Photos of jazz musicians on the walls hint at the occasional live set (but not in August).

Pasaż (☎ 014 627 8278; www.pasaz.tarnow.pl; Plac Kazimierza Wielkiego 2; mains 15-38zł; ☾ noon-11pm) Probably Tarnów's finest restaurant, the Pasaż, in a passageway leading west from the Rynek, serves rather exotic international (crab) and Polish (venison) dishes in a very chichi dining room.

Alkohole Świata (Alcohols of the World; ul Targowa 4; ☾ 8am-midnight Mon-Sat, noon-8pm Sun) Late-night shop selling various foodstuffs and drinks.

Two very similar milk bars serve dishes (mains 3zł to 10zł) that are nothing to write home about but are cheap and filling. **Bar Łasuch** (☎ 014 627 7123; ul Sowińskiego 4; ☾ 8am-7pm Mon-Fri, 9am-3pm Sat) is southwest of the Old Town near the Ethnographic Museum, while **Bar Sam** (☎ 014 627 7119; ul Lwowska 12; ☾ 8am-7pm Mon-Fri, 9am-3pm Sat) lies to the east.

Drinking

Café Piano (☎ 014 621 9248; Rynek 9; ☾ 10am-midnight) Set in beautifully decorated cellars, this stu-denty place offers plenty of drinks, a few budget dishes and live jazz on some weekends.

Studio Café (☎ 0603 555 695; ul Żydowska 3; ☾ noon-11pm Mon-Sat, 4-11pm Sun) Where else could you get sloshed, look at artsy photos and have your portrait taken? This pub/gallery/photography studio can see to all your needs.

Getting There & Away

The train and bus stations are next to each other, just over 1km southwest of the Old Town. Bus 9 (2zł) will take you to the Rynek.

There are frequent buses west to Kraków (14zł, two hours) and regular departures southeast to both Jasło (9zł, 1½ hours) and Krosno (12zł, two hours). For Sandomierz (17.50zł, three hours), take any of the Tarnobrzeg (15zł, 2½ hours) buses, which depart every two hours, and then change.

Trains to Kraków (13zł, 1½ hours) and Rzeszów (13zł to 20zł, 1½ hours) run every hour or so. There are departures every other hour to Nowy Sącz (14zł to 22zł, two hours). Two or three direct trains go to Warsaw (84zł, 4½ hours) daily.

ZALIPIE
pop 800

The village of Zalipie, 36km northwest of Tarnów, has been known as a centre for folk painting for more than a century, since its inhabitants started to decorate both the inside and outside of their houses with colourful floral designs. Today about 20 such houses can be seen in Zalipie, with another dozen or so in the neighbouring villages of Kuzie, Niwka and Kłyż.

The best-known painter was Felicja Curyłowa (1904–74), and since her death her three-room farmhouse has been opened to the public as the **Felicja Curyłowa Farmstead Museum** (Muzeum Zagroda Felicji Curyłowej; ☎ 014 641 1912; adult/concession 3/1.50zł; ☾ 10am-4pm Tue-Sun). If you find it locked, ask for the keys from the house (Zalipie 196) across the road. Every flat surface is painted with colourful flow-ers, and on display are painted dishes, icons and costumes.

In order to help maintain the tradition, the Painted Cottage (Malowana Chata) contest for the best decorated house has been held annually since 1948, during the weekend after Corpus Christi (late May or June).

At the **House of Painters** (Dom Malarek; ☎ 014 641 1938; Zalipie 128a; ☾ 8am-6pm Mon-Fri, 11am-6pm Sat & Sun Jun-Aug, 8am-4pm Mon-Fri Sep-May), which serves as a centre for the village's artists, you can watch the women painters at work. There's also a gift shop here, with guides and maps.

Getting There & Around

There are only a few daily buses daily from Tarnów (6.50zł, 1½ hours), and the village spreads over a relatively large area, so it's use-ful to have your own transport.

RZESZÓW
pop 157,800

The chief administrative and industrial cen-tre of southeastern Poland, Rzeszów (zheh-shoof) may at first glance seem to offer little inducement to stay any longer than it takes to get the next bus out. Nevertheless, the town does have a few interesting museums

THE CARPATHIAN MOUNTAINS

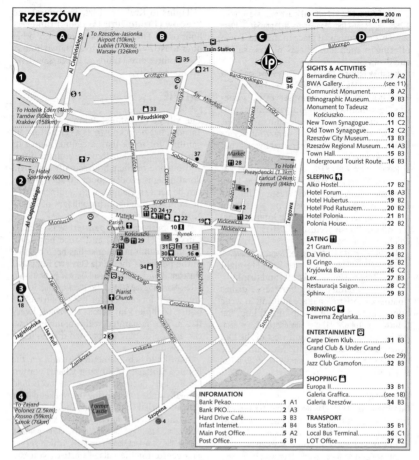

RZESZÓW

and several historic buildings of note. As a major regional transport hub, Rzeszów makes a handy base for exploring the surrounding countryside, and because it is an important university town, the nightlife here is the best in the region.

Rzeszów started life in the 13th century as a remote Ruthenian settlement. It grew rapidly in the 16th century when Mikołaj Spytek Ligęza, the local ruler, commissioned a church and a fortified castle. It later fell into the hands of the powerful Lubomirski clan, but this couldn't save the town from subsequent decline.

Rapid postwar development increased the size of Rzeszów, but with little aesthetic consideration. Fortunately, enough of the his-toric core survived the bulldozers to make a stopover worthwhile.

Information

Bank Pekao (Al Cieplińskiego 1; 8am-6pm Mon-Fri, 9am-4pm Sat)

Bank PKO (ul 3 Maja 23; 8am-6pm Mon-Fri, 9am-1pm Sat) In a lovely neoclassical building.

City of Rzeszów (www.rzeszow.pl/en) Tourist office.

Hard Drive Café (017 852 6141; ul Kościuszki 13; per hr 2.50zł; 8am-11pm Mon-Sat, 10am-10pm Sun) Internet access.

Infast Internet (017 852 3715; ul Szopena 51; per hr 3zł; 9am-5pm Mon-Fri, 9am-1pm Sat) Internet access.

Main post office (ul Moniuszki 1; 7am-8pm Mon-Fri, 8am-2pm Sat)

THE CARPATHIAN MOUNTAINS

Post office (ul Asnyka 9; 7am-8pm Mon-Fri, 8am-2pm Sat)

Sights

Most of the sprawling Rynek has been repaved in recent years. In the centre of the square is a **monument to Tadeusz Kościuszko**, honoured by Poles and Americans alike (see p33). In the southwest corner, the 16th-century **town hall** was wholly remodelled a century ago in overelaborate neo-Gothic style. There are some lovely Art Nouveau townhouses on the square.

Rzeszów's prime attraction is the **Underground Tourist Route** (Podziemna Trasa Turystyczna; 017 875 4199; ul Króla Kazimierza; admission 5.50zł; 9am-3.30pm Tue-Fri, noon-6pm Sun Apr-Oct, 9am-3pm Tue-Fri Nov-Mar). It took 17 years to link 34 old cellars into a 214m-long route, which opened in 2001. The cellars date from various periods (from the 15th to 20th centuries) and are on different levels (the deepest one is nearly 10m below the surface of the Rynek). Visits are by guided tour lasting about 45 minutes. Buy your tickets from the **Rzeszów City Museum** (Muzeum Historii Miasta Rzeszowa; 017 875 4198; www.muzeum.rzeszow.pl; Rynek 12), just around the corner from the entrance.

The **Ethnographic Museum** (Muzeum Etnograficzne; 017 862 0217; Rynek 6; adult/concession 5.50/3.50zł, free Sun; 9am-3pm Tue-Thu & Sun, 9am-5.30pm Fri) has traditional folk costumes and old woodcarvings from the region on permanent display.

The **Rzeszów Regional Museum** (Muzeum Okręgowe w Rzeszowie; 017 853 5278; ul 3 Maja 19; adult/concession 6.50/4.50zł, free Sun; 9am-3pm Tue-Thu & Sun, 9am-5.30pm Fri) is housed in a one-time Piarist monastery complete with frescoed vaulting from the 17th century. It contains Polish paintings from the 18th to 20th centuries and European art from the 16th to 19th centuries, along with glass, faïence and furniture.

Northwest of the Rynek is the **Bernardine Church** (Kościół Bernardynów; ul Sobieskiego), with its opulent furnishings and decoration. It was built for Ligęza as his mausoleum, and there are eight life-sized alabaster effigies of his family in the side walls of the chancel. In the gilded chapel to the right is an early-16th-century statue of the Virgin Mary to which numerous miracles have been attributed; wall paintings on both sides dating from the 17th and 18th centuries showed 100 people who were cured.

Close by, you can't miss the overblown **Communist Monument** (Al Cieplińskiego), erected 'in memory of the heroes of the revolutionary struggles' and now topped with a cross. It towers over a rather arid square and is a rare survivor from the old regime.

To the northeast of the Rynek are two synagogues standing close to each other. Though less attractive from the outside, the 18th-century **New Town Synagogue** (Synagoga Nowomiejska; ul Sobieskiego 18) has more to offer on the inside as it contains the **BWA Gallery** (017 853 3811; admission free; 10am-5pm Tue-Sun). Note the gate to the café on the 1st floor – made of wrought iron and clay, it's the work of the contemporary sculptor Marian Kruczek. The much smaller 17th-century **Old Town Synagogue** (Synagoga Staromiejska; ul Bóźnica 4) now houses the city archives and is also a centre for studies of the history of local Jews.

Sleeping

BUDGET

Alko Hostel (017 853 4430; www.ptsmrzeszow.epodkarpacie.com; Rynek 25; dm 20zł, d/tr from 60/80zł;) This is the cheapest and one of the most central options in town, with 90 beds. It has some doubles and triples, but accommodation is mostly in dormitories with up to 12 beds.

Hotel Sportowy (/fax 017 851 2483; ul Jałowego 23a; s/d 70/95zł;) Located in a long cream-and pink-coloured sports complex roughly 1km west of the Rynek, the Sport is a great budget choice, with good facilities (swimming pool, tennis courts) on site. It also has cheaper doubles/triples without bathrooms or wash-basins for 50/70zł.

Hotelik Eden (017 852 5683; www.hotel.eden.prv.pl; ul Krakowska 150; s/d/tr 75/90/135zł;) The Eden is small, 50-bed hotel that offers reasonable standards, but it's a long way – just over 4km – northwest of the centre. Rooms with washbasins and shared bathrooms cost 60/70/140zł for singles/doubles/quads. To get here, take westbound bus 1 or 22 from Al Piłsudskiego.

Hotel Polonia (017 852 0312; www.hotel-polonia.com; ul Grottgera 16; s/d/tr 110/140/150zł) The 37-room Polonia has been revamped and is just fine for what you'll pay (though its location just opposite the train station is not the most picturesque).

MIDRANGE

Hotel Pod Ratuszem (017 852 9770; www.hotelpodratuszem.rzeszow.pl; ul Matejki 8; s 140zł, d 180-240zł, apt 250zł;

) This modern, perfectly central hotel, not quite 'Under the Town Hall', offers 13 neat (if rather small) rooms.

Polonia House (Dom Polonii; ☎ 017 862 0174; www.wspolnota-polska.rzeszow.pl; Rynek 19; s/d 130/220zł;) Run by an association that looks after the interests of Poles abroad, Poland House is another very central option, but be warned: this guesthouse only has two large single rooms and two even bigger double suites. Book well ahead.

Hotel Forum (☎ 017 859 4038; www.hotelforum.pl; ul Lisa Kuli 19; s/d/apt 190/230/320zł; P ⊠) In the same block as the Galeria Graffica shopping centre, this modernised high-rise offers the best facilities in the city centre, with 34 light and spacious rooms and big bathrooms.

TOP END

Hotel Hubertus ☎ 017 852 6007; www.hubertus.rzeszow.pl; ul Mickiewicza 5; s 190-220zł, d 300-350zł; P ⊠ ⊠) Rzeszów's first and (so far) only boutique hotel is a delightful 13-room hostelry artfully fitted into an 18th-century townhouse on the Rynek. The bathrooms are fabulous and the views of the square from some of the doubles priceless, but the place is decidedly not for animal-rights activists: St Hubert is the patron saint of hunters, and there are trophies and paintings with hunting themes everywhere.

Hotel Prezydencki (☎ 017 860 6500; www.hoteleprezydenckie.com.pl; ul Podwisłocze 48; s/d 250/360zł, ste 515-545zł; P ⊠) Located a little over 1km southeast of the city centre on the opposite side of the Wisłok River, the President is a contemporary 56-room hotel geared towards business travellers. Consequently, it's fairly bland but bright and clean, and it has a sauna, solarium and restaurant.

Eating

Kryjówka Bar (☎ 017 853 2717; ul Mickiewicza 19; mains 3.50-11zł; 9am-10pm Mon-Fri, 10am-10pm Sat) One of the few addresses for a tasty budget meal in the centre of town, the 'Hideaway Bar' is a pleasant place offering an extensive Polish menu as well as that 21st-century European staple, pizza.

Restauracja Saigon (☎ 017 853 3593; ul Sobieskiego 14; mains 11-18.50zł; 11.30am-11pm) It might sound risky trying something as exotic as Vietnamese food in provincial Poland, but the real McCoy is at the helm in the kitchen (we peeked) and dishes are pretty authentic as a result.

El Gringo (☎ 017 864 2118; Rynek 25; mains 12-22zł; noon-midnight Mon-Thu, noon-1am Fri & Sat, 1pm-midnight Sun) Burritos, tacos and enchiladas are on the menu at this colourful sombrero-bedecked Mexican place northwest of the Rynek.

Da Vinci (☎ 017 853 6677; www.davinci.rzeszow.pl; ul Matejki 4; mains 12-24zł; 1-11pm Mon-Thu, noon-midnight Thu-Sun) Tired of pizza but could do with an infusion of something with lots of tomatoes and garlic? Head for this place, where the walls are covered with the drawings, engravings and writings of the great Renaissance man. We love the cosy room with a fireplace in winter. Excellent choice of wines.

Sphinx (☎ 017 853 4598; www.sphinx.pl; ul Kościuszki 9; mains 13.50-30zł) OK, it's a branch of the ubiquitous Egyptian-themed restaurant chain, serving lots of variations on kebabs, cabbage and grilled-meat dishes. But the Sphinx is dependable, if not particularly exciting, and always busy.

21 Gram (☎ 017 853 5350; ul 3 Maja 5; mains 14.50-21zł; 9am-midnight Mon-Wed, noon-1am Thu-Sun) It's not easy to come by vegetarian eateries of any calibre in Poland, but this place, boasting views over pedestrian ul 3 Maja and dishes heavily influenced by the subcontinent, apparently attracts as many meat eaters on holiday as it does vegetarians.

Lex (☎ 017 852 5859; www.restauracjalex.pl; ul 3 Maja 7; mains 18-35zł; 10am-10pm) Rzeszów's finest restaurant, Lex serves continental dishes in the very refined setting of an 18th-century townhouse. A seat on the outside terrace is a coveted spot on a warm summer's evening.

Drinking & Entertainment

Tawerna Żeglarska (☎ 017 862 0239; Rynek 6, enter from ul Króla Kazimierza; 2pm-midnight Mon-Thu, 2pm-1am Fri & Sat, 4pm-midnight Sun) Frequented by students, the 'Sailors' Tavern' is far from the sea but can get pretty stormy when the tide is up on musical evenings.

Jazz Club Gramofon (☎ 0663 440 020; www.jazz.rzeszow.pl; ul 3 Maja 13; noon-1am) A highly recommended venue for cool jazz, this place has live gigs on Friday and Saturday nights.

Grand Club & Under Grand Bowling (☎ 017 853 3035; ul Kościuszki 9; 2pm-midnight Sun-Wed, 2pm-4am Thu-Sat) This super DJ club also has ten-pin bowling (30zł to 60zł per hour) in the basement (Under Grand Bowling – get it?) to lure in the punters.

Carpe Diem Klub (www.carpediem.pl; Rynek 4; 10am-2am) Our favourite new place, this basement DJ club has a fantastic sound-and-light system and some pretty neat motorcycles on display.

Getting There & Around

AIR

Rzeszów-Jasionka Airport (☎ 017 852 0081; www .lotnisko-rzeszow.pl) is at Jasionka, 10km north of the city, and is accessible by bus 14 (3.60zł) from Al Piłsudskiego or by taxi (50zł). There are daily flights to Warsaw as well as to London and Dublin. **LOT** (☎ 017 862 0234; Plac Ofiar Getta 6; ☯ 8am-6pm Mon-Fri, 9am-3pm Sat) makes bookings and sells and issues tickets.

BUS

The bus station is 500m north of the Rynek. Buses depart roughly every hour for Sanok (10.60zł, 1½ hours), Krosno (9zł, 1½ hours), Przemyśl (9zł to 12zł, two hours) and Lublin (24zł, 3½ hours). Buses also go to Ustrzyki Dolne (14.50zł to 16.20zł, 2½ hours, five to seven daily) and Ustrzyki Górne (23zł, 3½ hours, three daily), as well as to Zamość (23zł, three hours, two daily). Buses to Łańcut (4zł, 30 minutes) run roughly every half-hour or so and are more convenient than trains, as they stop near the palace. Eurolines also operates international services, including those to London, Paris, Prague and Lviv. Enquire at **Centrum Eurobus** (☎ 017 852 6498; ☯ 9am-5pm) at the station.

TRAIN

The train station is next to the bus station. Trains depart almost hourly for Przemyśl (22zł to 42zł, 1½ hours) and Tarnów (13zł, one hour). A dozen or so daily trains leave for Kraków (19.50zł, 2½ hours). To Warsaw (88zł, five hours), there are two morning express trains.

ŁAŃCUT

pop 18,600

Just 24km northeast of Rzeszów, Łańcut (*wine*-tsoot) has Poland's largest and richest aristocratic home.

The building started life in the 15th century, but it was Stanisław Lubomirski who turned it into both a mighty fortress and a great residence. Soon after he had successfully completed his castle at Nowy Wiśnicz (p261), he came into possession of the large property of Łańcut and commissioned Matteo Trapola to design a new home even more spectacular than the old one. It was competed in 1641.

A century and a half later the fortifications were partly demolished while the castle was reshaped in Rococo and neoclassical style. The last important alteration, executed at the end of the 19th century, gave the building its neo-Baroque façades, which survive today.

The last private owner, Alfred Potocki, one of the richest men in prewar Poland, accumulated a fabulous collection of art during his tenancy. Shortly before the arrival of the Red Army in July 1944, he loaded 11 railway carriages with the most valuable objects and fled with the collection to Liechtenstein.

Information

Bank Pekao (ul Kościuszki 5; ☯ 9am-4pm Mon-Fri) Opposite the castle entrance.

Post office (ul Królowej Elżbiety; ☯ 7am-8pm Mon-Fri, 8am-1pm Sat)

Sights

Just after WWII the 300-room castle was taken over by the state and opened as the **Castle Museum** (Muzeum Zamek; ☎ 017 225 2008; www .zamek-lancut.pl; ul Zamkowa 1; adult/concession 21/13zł; ☯ noon-3.30pm Mon, 9am-4pm Tue-Fri, 10am-6pm Sat & Sun Jun-Sep, noon-3.30pm Mon, 9am-4pm Tue-Fri, 9am-4pm Sat, 9am-5pm Sun Feb-May, Oct & Nov, closed Dec & Jan). The collection has systematically been supplemented and enlarged to such a degree that it's difficult to take it all in on one visit.

The castle is visited in groups accompanied by a Polish-speaking guide, and the tour takes 1½ hours. The last tour departs one hour before closing time. **Guides** (☎ 017 225 2008 ext 124) speaking English, French and German are available for 240zł per group (plus tickets). Brochures in English are available for a small fee.

You'll be shown around the western wing of the ground floor and the whole of the 1st floor, visiting altogether about two dozen rooms. In the carefully restored interiors – mostly late Baroque and Rococo – you will find heaps of paintings, sculptures and *objets d'art* of all descriptions. Among the highlights are the 17th-century **Grand Hall** (Wielka Sień), the Renaissance-style **Eastern Corridor** (Korytarz Wschodni) and the Rococo **Corner Room** (Pokój Narożny).

After viewing the castle's rooms, you'll be shown around the **Orangery** (Oranżeria) south-west of the castle, with palms and parrots, and then Potocki's collection of 55 carriages and sleighs in the **Coach House** (Powozownia), 300m south of the castle.

You can then individually visit the **stables** (adult/concession 6/3zł; 9am-4pm) north of the Coach House, with a fine collection of more than 1000 icons from the 15th century onwards.

The castle is surrounded by a delightful and very well-kept **park** (admission free; 7am-sunset). Just outside the park and to the west of the castle is the **synagogue** (Plac Sobieskiego; adult/concession 6/3zł; 10.30am-4.30pm Tue-Sun Jun-Aug). Built in the 1760s, it has retained much of its original Rococo decoration and some liturgical items are on display. You can visit it in other months by faxing 017 225 2012 in advance.

Festivals & Events

The **Łańcut Music Festival** (Muzyczny Festiwal w Łańcucie; www.lancut.pl) is held over about 10 days in May, with chamber-music concerts performed in the castle ballroom.

Sleeping

Dom Wycieczkowy PTTK (/fax 017 225 2052; ul Dominikańska 1; beds in d/tr/q 17-25zł; P) This 49-bed hostel, in the former Dominican monastery just off the Rynek, offers simple rooms with shared bathrooms that sleep from two to 10.

Pensjonat Pałacyk (017 225 2043; www.palacyk .emeteor.pl; ul Paderewskiego 18; d/tr 120/150zł; P) About 200m south of the synagogue, the 'Little Palace' is set in a diminutive mansion and is a pleasant place to stay. It has seven rooms as well as its own restaurant.

Hotel Szwadron (017 225 6042; www.szwadron .emeteor.pl; ul Mickiewicza 16; d/tr 120/150zł; P) About 400m southwest of the Rynek in a leafy part of town, the Szwadron is another hotel housed in a historic mansion (this one from 1784 but rebuilt in 1904). It has 10 comfortable rooms and its public areas are an Aladdin's Cave of old photos, antiques and curios.

Hotel Zamkowy (017 225 2671; vena@rze.pl; ul Zamkowa 1; r 100-200zł; P) Located in the castle's southern wing, the 15-room Castle Hotel is quite simple; rooms with a private bathroom are at the top end of the price scale. The hotel's restaurant across the small courtyard has acceptable food at reasonable prices.

Eating

Gospoda Hetmańska (0608 021 210; ul Zamkowa; mains 6-18zł; 8am-10pm) This café-restaurant

is housed in a corner tower in the northeastern wing of the castle. The food is nothing to write home about but you couldn't find a more romantic spot in Łańcut.

Caffé Antico (017 225 6151; Rynek 3; mains 8-20zł; 9am-midnight) With something for everyone (gyros, Polish mains, pizzas), the Antico is the most popular eatery in town, with a wonderful outside seating area overlooking the elongated Rynek.

Getting There & Away

The bus station is 500m northeast of the castle along ul Kościuszki; the train station about 2km to the north. Buses to Rzeszów (4zł, 30 minutes) run about every 30 minutes and to Przemyśl (9zł, 1½ hours) every hour or two.

PRZEMYŚL
pop 66,600

A sleepy town with an impossible name, Przemyśl (*psheh*-mishl) is close to the Ukrainian border and some way off the usual tourist route. It's an agreeable little place though, at the point where the San River leaves the foothills and enters the Sandomierz Plain. Przemyśl has an attractive main square and a couple of worthwhile churches and museums to explore.

Founded in the 10th century on terrain long fought over by Poland and Ruthenia, Przemyśl changed hands several times before being annexed by the Polish crown in 1340. It experienced its golden period in the 16th century and declined afterwards. During the Partitions it fell under Austrian administration.

In around 1850 the Austrians began to fortify Przemyśl. This work continued right up until the outbreak of WWI, and was responsible for producing one of the largest fortresses in Europe. It consisted of a double ring of earth ramparts, including a 15km-long inner circle and an outer girdle three times longer, with more than 60 forts placed at strategic points. This formidable system played an important role during the war, but the garrison surrendered to the Russians in 1915 due to a lack of provisions.

Information

Bank Pekao (ul Jagiellońska 7; 9am-5pm Mon-Fri)
Internet Game Café (016 676 9260; ul Ratuszowa 8; per hr 3zł; 10am-6pm Mon-Fri, 10am-2pm Sat) Internet access.

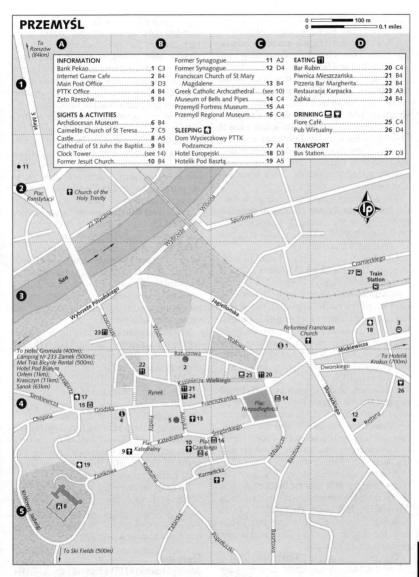

PRZEMYŚL

0 _____ 100 m
0 _____ 0.1 miles

INFORMATION
Bank Pekao............................**1** C3
Internet Game Cafe................**2** B4
Main Post Office....................**3** D3
PTTK Office...........................**4** B4
Zeto Rzeszów........................**5** B4

SIGHTS & ACTIVITIES
Archdiocesan Museum............**6** B4
Carmelite Church of St Teresa...**7** C5
Castle...................................**8** A5
Cathedral of St John the Baptist...**9** B4
Clock Tower.......................(see 14)
Former Jesuit Church.............**10** B4

Former Synagogue.................**11** A2
Former Synagogue.................**12** D4
Franciscan Church of St Mary
   Magdalene.........................**13** B4
Greek Catholic Archcathedral....(see 10)
Museum of Bells and Pipes......**14** C4
Przemyśl Fortress Museum.......**15** A4
Przemyśl Regional Museum......**16** C4

SLEEPING
Dom Wycieczkowy PTTK
   Podzamcze........................**17** A4
Hotel Europejski...................**18** D3
Hotelik Pod Basztą................**19** A5

EATING
Bar Rubin............................**20** C4
Piwnica Mieszczańska............**21** B4
Pizzeria Bar Margherita..........**22** B4
Restauracja Karpacka.............**23** A3
Żabka................................**24** B4

DRINKING
Fiore Café...........................**25** C4
Pub Wirtualny......................**26** D4

TRANSPORT
Bus Station..........................**27** D3

Main post office (ul Mickiewicza 13; ⏰ 7.30am-8pm Mon-Fri, 8am-2pm Sat)

PTTK office (☎ 016 675 2164; www.przemysl.pl; ul Grodzka 1; ⏰ 10am-6pm Mon-Fri, 9am-5pm Sat & Sun) Travel agency that serves as the tourist information office.

Zeto Rzeszów (☎ 016 678 5920; ul Asnyka 4; per hr 3zł; ⏰ 9am-6pm Mon-Fri, 9am-2pm Sat) Internet access.

Sights

Perched on a hillside and dominated by four mighty churches to the south, Przemyśl's Old Town is a picturesque place. The sloping **Rynek** has preserved some of its old arcaded houses, mostly on its north and south sides.

The **Franciscan Church of St Mary Magdalene** (Kościół Franciszkański Św Marii Magdaleny; ul Franciszkańska), southeast of the Rynek, was built between 1754 and 1778 in late-Baroque and classical style, but its monumental façade was remade later. The church has a beautiful Rococo interior with a vaulted and frescoed nave.

Just up the hill behind it stands the **former Jesuit Church** (Kościół Pojezuicki). Built between 1627 and 1659, it's also a Baroque construction. The church now serves the Uniat congregation as the **Greek Catholic Archcathedral** (Archikatedra Grecko-Kałolicka) and is a popular destination for pilgrims from across the border in Ukraine. The enormous and heavily gilded iconostasis dates from the 17th century.

The adjacent former Jesuit college shelters the **Archdiocesan Museum** (Muzeum Archidiecezjalne; ☎ 016 678 2792; Plac Czackiego 2; donation requested; ☯ 10am-4pm May-Oct), which contains religious art, vestments and church plate.

Up the hill is yet another house of worship, the **Carmelite Church of St Teresa** (Kościół Karmelitów Św Teresy). Designed in 1630 by Italian architect Galeazzo Appiani, who also built Krasiczyn castle (opposite), the church has preserved some of its original features, including the classical main gate and the white and gold stucco work on the vaulting. Note the large wooden pulpit in the shape of a boat, complete with mast, sail, rigging, anchor and two saints bearing oars.

Due north of the church is the **Przemyśl Regional Museum** (Muzeum Ziemi Przemyskiej; ☎ 016 678 3325; Plac Czackiego 3; adult/concession 5/3zł, free Sun; ☯ 10.30am-5.30pm Tue, Thu & Fri, 10am-3pm Wed & Sat, 10am-2pm Sun), with a splendid collection of Ruthenian icons and other religious art dating back to the 15th century.

A short walk west along ul Katedralna is the **Cathedral of St John the Baptist** (Katedra Św Jana Chrzciciela; Plac Katedralny), with its 71m-high freestanding bell tower. Originally a Gothic building (note the impressive star vaulting), the church was remodelled and is now predominantly Baroque.

Continue up along ul Zamkowa to what is left of the 14th-century **castle**. Built by King Kazimierz III Wielki (Casimir III the Great) in the 1340s, it mutated into a Renaissance building two centuries later when it acquired its four loopholed towers, two of which have been restored. A local theatre, a city cultural centre and a café now occupy the restored rooms.

The curious **Museum of Bells and Pipes** (Muzeum Dzwonów i Fajek; ☎ 016 678 9666; ul Władycze 3; adult/concession 5/3zł, free Sat; ☯ 10.30am-5.30pm Tue, Thu & Fri, 10am-3pm Wed & Sat, noon-4pm Sun), housed in an 18th-century Baroque clock tower, contains vintage bells as well as elaborately carved wooden and meerschaum pipes and cigar cutters. (Przemyśl has long been famous for manufacturing these items.) The rooftop affords a panoramic view of the town.

Those very interested in military matters may be drawn to the fortifications of the Austro-Hungarian **Przemyśl Fortress** (Twierdza Przemyśl) surrounding the town. As these were mostly earth ramparts, however, they are now overgrown and resemble natural rather than artificial bulwarks. Among the best examples are **Fort I** (Salis Soglio) in Sieliska, **Fort VIII** (Łętownia) in Kuńkowce and **Fort XIII** (San Rideau) in Bolestraszyce. The tourist office can give you information about these sites and transport details. The modest **Przemyśl Fortress Museum** (Muzeum Twierdza Przemyśl; ☎ 016 677 1942; ul Grodzka 8; admission free; ☯ 10am-5pm Wed, Sat & Sun), with photographs, postcards, weapons and commemorative mementos connected with the fortress, will satisfy the curiosities of most.

The only significant relics of the Jewish legacy are two **synagogues** (of four existing before WWII), both dating from the end of the 19th and beginning of the 20th centuries, renovated after the war and put to other uses. One is in Plac Unii Brzeskiej, off ul 3 Maja on the northern side of the river; the other, now housing the city's public library, is on ul Słowackiego.

Bicycles are available for hire from **Mel Tras Bicycle Rental** (☎ 0502 102 950; ul Sanocka 8a; per hr/day 6/40zł), near the camping ground. Ask the staff at the PTTK office for their brochure listing cycle tracks and routes in the area.

Ski fields on the edge of Park Zamkowy, 500m southeast of the castle, have two trails and a downhill slope. During the skiing season the chairlift runs from 9am to 9pm daily and costs 55zł for a day ticket.

Sleeping

Dom Wycieczkowy PTTK Podzamcze (☎ 016 678 5374; http://przemysl.pttk.pl in Polish; ul Waygarta 3; dm 20-24zł, d/tr 58/72zł; P) The nine rooms (containing 46 beds) at this place have seen some wear but have had a new lick of paint. It's just a block west of the Rynek.

Hotelik Pod Basztą (☎ 016 678 8268; ul Królowej Jadwigi 4; s/d/tr 39/59/79zł; P) Enjoying a quiet, central location, this small hotel in an old classical-style building has seven old-fashioned rooms with shared bathrooms, but many have castle or city views. The one en suite double (118zł) boasts a balcony overlooking the Old Town.

Hotelik Krokus (☎ /fax 016 678 5127; ul Mickiewicza 47 & 49; s 50zł, d 80-118zł, tr/q 105/120zł) About 1.3km east of the Rynek, the Krokus provides adequate rooms with private facilities in a nice little villa with garden. It's not far from the train station.

Hotel Europejski (☎ 016 675 7100; www.hotel -europejski.pl; ul Sowińskiego 4; s/d/tr 90/120/140zł; P 🖳) Housed in a renovated old building facing the attractive neoclassical train station (1895), this comfortable place has 29 bright rooms with high ceilings and modern bathrooms.

Hotel Pod Białym Orłem (☎ 016 678 6107; www .podbialymorlem.com.pl; ul Sanocka 13; d/tr/apt 120/145/250zł; P 🖳) Located about 1km west of the Old Town, the 'Under the White Eagle' is an affordable option with 16 spotless rooms with private facilities and a nice (though small) garden.

Hotel Gromada (☎ 016 676 1111; www.hotels.gro mada.pl; Wybrzeże Piłsudskiego 4; s 166-199zł, d 178-249zł; P ✗ 🖳 ⅋) This modern, central but rather soulless hotel has 120 comfortable rooms and its own restaurant. Rates drop significantly at the weekend.

Camping Nr 233 Zamek (☎ /fax 675 0265; Wybrzeże Piłsudskiego 8a; per person/tent/car 7/11/6zł, s/d/tr/q 51/67/80/93zł; P) This camping ground has fairly simple rooms in year-round cabins and is quite close to the centre. Seasonal cabins costing 18zł per person are open from May to September. Get here on bus 2 or 5.

Eating

Żabka (Rynek 10; ☽ 6am-11pm) Branch of the late-night convenience store chain.

Bar Rubin (☎ 016 678 2578; ul Kazimierza Wielkiego 19; mains 5-15zł; ☽ 9am-9pm) This small, friendly, family restaurant, 'where you eat like at mom's', is one of the best places to grab a bite to eat in the Old Town.

Pizzeria Bar Margherita (☎ 016 678 9898; Rynek 4; mains 6-18zł; ☽ noon-midnight Sun-Thu, noon-2am Fri & Sat) This inviting place has a long list of pizzas, plus risotto, pasta and fast food such as hot dogs. It has a lovely terrace right on the Rynek.

Restauracja Karpacka (☎ 016 678 9057; ul Kościuszki 5; mains 6-18 zł; ☽ 10am-10pm) Northwest of the Rynek, this old-fashioned eatery features bow-

tied waiters, a timbered ceiling and yellow stucco walls. It serves a good range of Polish standards, and Ukrainian-style borscht in a nod to the neighbours.

Piwnica Mieszczańska (☎ 016 675 0459; Rynek 9; mains 6-25zł) This beer-cellar restaurant setting is decorated with mini-chandeliers and lace tablecloths. The bourgeoisie platter (22zł), with three types of meat, will excite ardent carnivores.

Drinking

Fiore Cafe (☎ 016 675 1222; ul Kazimierza Wielkiego 17b; ☽ 10am-8pm) If you're looking for ice cream or a slice of something sweet, this modern café on a pedestrian street should be your destination.

Pub Wirtualny (☎ 016 675 1782; ul Dworskiego 12; ☽ 10am-midnight) This very real (not virtual) modern pub south of the stations has a nice back garden.

Getting There & Away

The train and bus stations are next to each other, on the northeastern edge of the town centre, about 600m from the Rynek.

Up to four buses a day depart for Sanok (11zł, 1½ hours), and there are also departures for Ustrzyki Dolne (11zł, two hours, three to four daily) and Rzeszów (9zł, two hours, 10 daily). Buses to Krasiczyn (2.80zł, 20 minutes) run as often as twice an hour.

Trains to Rzeszów (42zł, 1½ hours) depart regularly throughout the day. There are half a dozen fast trains and two express trains a day to Kraków (71zł, 3½ hours). One express and several fast trains go daily to Warsaw (90zł, six hours), and one fast train runs to Lublin (40zł, four hours). International trains to Lviv, Odessa and Kyiv pass via Przemyśl.

KRASICZYN
pop 1000

The **castle** (☎ 016 671 8321; www.krasiczyn.com.pl; adult/concession 8/5zł; ☽ 9am-4pm) in the village of Krasiczyn (krah-*shee*-chin), just 11km south-west of Przemyśl, is called 'the gem of the Polish Renaissance'. It's in a landscaped 14-hectare **park** (adult/concession 1/0.50zł; ☽ dawn-dusk) with almost 100 different species of plants and trees.

Designed by Italian architect Galleazzo Appiani and built between 1592 and 1618 for the wealthy Krasicki family, the castle is more or less square and built around a spacious, partly arcaded courtyard, with four different cylindrical corner towers. The towers were meant to reflect the social order of the period and were named (clockwise from the southeastern corner) after God, the pope, the king and the nobility. The **God Tower** (Baszta Boska), topped with a dome, houses a chapel. The **King Tower** (Baszta Królewska), with its conical roof and little turrets, would make a lovely home for Rapunzel of long-hair fame. On the courtyard side of the castle walls are Renaissance sgraffiti decorations of Biblical scenes and Polish nobility.

The courtyard and three of the corner towers can be visited on a guided tour (in Polish only), which departs on the hour.

Sleeping & Eating

our pick **Hotel Zamkowy** (☎ 016 671 8321; www.krasic zyn.com.pl; Krasiczyn 179; s/d/tr/ste from 140/220/280/500zł; **P** **⊠** **꠸**) This grand hotel, with 36 rooms in a former coach house just north of the castle, is one of the most attractive and evocative places to stay in Poland. It offers elegant and modern rooms in a unique and historic setting. The suites come in blue, pink or green and there's a gym, sauna, solarium and restaurant. Even better, you can also stay in wonderfully restored rooms in the castle itself (doubles/suites 260/500zł). Other accommodation options include the self-contained five-bed Hunter's Pavilion (800zł), which has its own kitchen and garden, and the charming 17th-century Swiss Pavilion (singles/doubles from 140/270zł), which reputedly comes with its own resident ghost. Bikes (per hour 3zł) and fishing equipment can be rented.

Castle Restaurant (☎ 016 671 8321; mains 12-30zł; ☺ 2-10pm Mon, 10am-10pm Tue-Sun) Conveniently located within the castle grounds, this restaurant serves mostly Polish dishes in traditional surrounds.

U Krzycha (☺ noon-midnight Sun & Mon, 4pm-midnight Tue-Sat) In the basement of the castle's northern wing, this is a lively cellar wine bar. The bar usually closes over winter.

Getting There & Away

The castle is am easy trip from Przemyśl (2.80zł, 20 minutes) on one of the frequent PKS buses or the regular bus 40. From Krasiczyn you can also reach Sanok (10zł, one hour, four daily) or Ustrzyki Dolne (10zł, 1½ hours, four daily) by bus.

THE BIESZCZADY

The region around the Bieszczady (byesh-chah-di), in the far southeastern corner of Poland and sandwiched between Ukraine and Slovakia, is one of thick forests and open meadows. Scantily populated and largely unspoilt, it's one of the most attractive areas of the country. As tourist facilities are modest, roads sparse and public transport limited, the Bieszczady retains its relative isolation and makes for an off-the-beaten-track destination. It's very popular with nature-lovers and hikers.

In geographical terms, the Bieszczady is an extension of the Beskids, running east–west for some 60km along Poland's southern frontier, with the lower hills to the north referred to as the Przedgórze Bieszczadzkie (Bieszczady Foothills). In practical terms, the Bieszczady is the whole area to the southeast of the Nowy Łupków–Zagórz–Ustrzyki Dolne railway line, up to the national borders: approximately 2100 sq km, about 60% of which is largely fir and beech forest.

The range's eastern end, the highest and most spectacular part, has been decreed the Bieszczady National Park (Bieszczadzki Park Narodowy), with its headquarters in Ustrzyki Dolne. At 292 sq km it's Poland's third-largest national park after Biebrza and Kampinos. Its highest peak is Mt Tarnica (1346m).

The region was once much more densely populated than it is today, but Ukrainian nationalists devastated it after the war (see the boxed text, opposite). Indeed, many people here say WWII didn't end until 1947.

One of the most exciting developments in recent years is the completion of the 350km bicycle loop known as the **Greenway Bicycle Trail** (Szlak Zielony Rower; www.zielonyrower.pl), which links the Bieszczady towns of Sanok, Lesko, Ustrzyki Dolne and Solina before crossing into Ukraine, Slovakia and back into Poland.

The region around Cisna, Wetlina and Ustrzyki Górne forms part of Unesco's tripartite Eastern Carpathian Biosphere Reserve with Slovakia and Ukraine.

SANOK
pop 39,600

Nestled in a picturesque valley in the Bieszczady Foothills, Sanok, the so-called gateway to the Bieszczady, has been subject to Ruthenian, Hungarian, Austrian, Russian,

BOYKS & LEMKS: A TALE OF TWO PEOPLES

The Bieszczady, along with the Beskid Niski and Beskid Sądecki further west, were settled from about the 13th century by various nomadic Slavic groups migrating up from the south and east. Most notable among them were the Wołosi from the Balkans and the Rusini from Ruthenia. Living in the same areas and intermarrying for centuries, they slowly developed into two distinct ethnic groups known as the Bojkowie and Łemkowie. They are sometimes referred to as Rusyns or Carpathian Russians.

The Bojkowie (Boykos or Boyks) inhabited the eastern part of the Bieszczady, east of Cisna, while the Łemkowie (Lemkos or Lemks) populated mountainous regions stretching from the western Bieszczady up to the Beskid Sądecki. The two groups had much in common culturally, though there were noticeable differences in dialects, dress and architecture. They shared the Orthodox faith with their Ukrainian neighbours.

After the Union of Brest in 1596, most Lemks and Boyks turned to the Uniat Church, which accepted the supremacy of Rome but retained the old Eastern liturgy. From the end of the 19th century, however, the Church began systematically to impose the Latin rite. In response, many Lemks and Boyks chose to return to the more familiar traditions of the Orthodox Church. By WWII both creeds were practised in the region, and the total population of Boyks and Lemks was estimated at 200,000 to 300,000. Ethnic Poles were a minority here.

All this changed dramatically in the aftermath of WWII, when the borders of Poland and the Soviet Union were redrawn. Not everyone was satisfied with the new status quo and some of its opponents didn't lay down their arms. One such armed faction was the Ukrainian Resistance Army, which operated in the Bieszczady region. Civil war continued in the region for almost two years after Germany had surrendered.

In a bid to destroy the rebel base, the postwar Polish government decided to expel the inhabitants of all the villages in the region and resettle the entire area. In the so-called Operation Vistula (Akcja Wisła) in 1947, most of the population was brutally deported either to the Soviet Union or to the 'recovered territories' regained from Germany in northern and western Poland. Ironically, the main victims of the action were the Boyks and the Lemks, who had little to do with the conflict apart from the fact that they happened to be in the way. Their villages were abandoned or destroyed, and those that survived were resettled with inhabitants from other regions. Only about 20,000 Lemks were left in the whole region, and very few Boyks.

Today the most visible reminders of their legacy are the wooden Orthodox or Uniat churches dotting the countryside, many of them dilapidated but others in remarkably good condition. When hiking on remote trails, especially along the Ukrainian border in the Bieszczady, you'll find traces of destroyed villages, including ruined houses, orchards, churches and cemeteries.

German and Polish rule in its eventful history. Although it contains an important industrial zone – Autosan, the bus used in intercity and urban transportation throughout the land, is produced here – it is also a popular base for exploring the mountains. Sanok is also the springboard for the fascinating Icon Trail (p278), a signposted walking or bicycle route taking in the surrounding countryside's wealth of wooden churches.

Information

Bank Pekao (ul Kościuszki 4; ⏲ 9am-6pm Mon-Fri, 9am-2pm Sat)

Bank Zachodni (ul 3 Maja 23; ⏲ 8am-5pm Mon-Fri)

Main post office (ul Kościuszki 28; ⏲ 7am-8pm Mon-Fri, 8am-2pm Sat)

Orbis Travel (☎ 013 463 2859; ul Grzegorza 2; ⏲ 9am-5pm Mon-Fri, 9am-1pm Sat) Information and accommodation.

Prox Internet (☎ 013 464 2250; ul Kazimierza Wielkiego 6; per hr 3.50zł; ⏲ 9am-6pm Mon-Fri, 9am-2pm Sat) Internet access.

PTTK office (☎ 013 463 2512; www.pttk.avx.pl in Polish; ul 3 Maja 2; ⏲ 8am-5pm Mon-Fri) Information about activities; excellent selection of maps.

Tourist office (☎ 013 463 6060; www.sanok.pl; Rynek 14; ⏲ 9am-5pm Mon-Fri, 9am-1pm Sat & Sun)

Sights

One of Sanok's major attractions is the **Historical Museum** (Muzeum Historyczne; ☎ 013 463 0609; ul Zamkowa 2; adult/concession/family 7/10/25zł; ⏲ 8-10am Mon, 9am-5pm Tue-Sun mid-Jun–Sep &

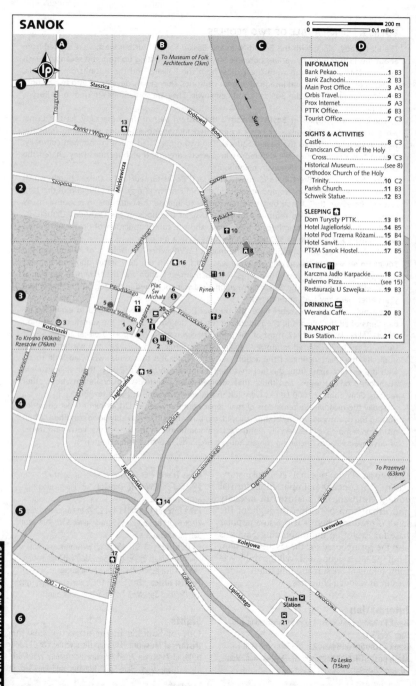

SANOK

0 — 200 m
0 — 0.1 miles

INFORMATION
Bank Pekao..............................1 B3
Bank Zachodni........................2 B3
Main Post Office......................3 A3
Orbis Travel............................4 B3
Prox Internet..........................5 A3
PTTK Office............................6 B3
Tourist Office.........................7 C3

SIGHTS & ACTIVITIES
Castle.....................................8 C3
Franciscan Church of the Holy
Cross....................................9 C3
Historical Museum...............(see 8)
Orthodox Church of the Holy
Trinity................................10 C2
Parish Church.......................11 B3
Schweik Statue.....................12 B3

SLEEPING
Dom Turysty PTTK................13 B1
Hotel Jagielloński.................14 B5
Hotel Pod Trzema Różami....15 B4
Hotel Sanvit.........................16 B3
PTSM Sanok Hostel..............17 B5

EATING
Karczma Jadło Karpackie.......18 C3
Palermo Pizza....................(see 15)
Restauracja U Szwejka...........19 B3

DRINKING
Weranda Caffe......................20 B3

TRANSPORT
Bus Station...........................21 C6

To Museum of Folk
Architecture (2km)

Staszica

Traugutta

Żwirki i Wigury

Królowej Bony

San

Mickiewicza

Szopena

Sobieskiego

Zamkowa

Sanowa

Rybacka

Cerkiewna

Piłsudskiego

Plac
Św
Michała

Rynek

Kazimierza Wielkiego

Kościuszki

To Krosno (40km);
Rzeszów (76km)

Sienkiewicza

Grzegorza

3 Maja

Franciszkańska

Daszyńskiego

Jagiellońska

Podgórze

Jagiellońska

Kochanowskiego

Ogrodowa

Al. Szwajcarii

Zielona

Zielona

To Przemyśl
(63km)

Lwowska

Kolejowa

800 - Lecia

Konarskiego

Kołłątaja

Lipińskiego

Train
Station

Dworcowa

To Lesko
(15km)

Nov-Mar, 8-10am Mon, 9am-5pm Tue & Wed, 9am-3pm Thu–Sun Apr–mid-Jun & Oct). Housed in a renovated 16th-century castle, the museum has several sections, of which the highlight is a 700-piece collection of Ruthenian icons. The selection on display consists of about 260 large pieces dating from the 15th to 18th centuries; most were acquired after WWII from abandoned Uniat churches.

The museum's other treasure is the collection of paintings by Zdzisław Beksiński (1929–2005) exhibited on the top floor. Beksiński, who was born and lived in Sanok, was one of Poland's most remarkable contemporary painters, with a fantastical style all his own. The exhibition features more than 200 of the artist's works.

Sanok is also noted for its unique **Museum of Folk Architecture** (Muzeum Budownictwa Ludowego; ☎ 013 463 1672; ul Rybickiego 3; adult/concession 9/6zł; 8am-6pm May-Sep, 9am-4pm Apr & Oct, 8am-4pm Nov-Mar), a skansen (open-air museum of traditional architecture) about 2km north of the centre. Poland's largest open-air museum, it has gathered about 120 traditional buildings from the southeast of the country and provides an insight into the culture of the Boyks and Lemks (see the boxed text, p275). Among the highlights are four timber churches, an inn, a school and even a fire station. The interiors of many cottages are furnished and decorated as they once were, while some buildings house exhibitions; one of these features a collection of 200 icons.

You can buy a leaflet with short descriptions of the buildings and objects in English or German. In summer there may be some English-speaking guides; enquire at the ticket office or preferably call in advance. Tours cost 30zł per group, in addition to the entry ticket. To reach the skansen, walk north from the town centre for 2km along ul Mickiewicza and ul Białogórska, cross the bridge over the San and turn right. Bus 3 from the Rynek will get you as far as the bridge.

At the southeast corner of the large rebuilt Rynek is the **Franciscan Church of the Holy Cross** (Kościół Franciszkanów Św Krzyża; ul Franciszkanska), the town's oldest, dating back to the 1640s. The neo-Romanesque **parish church** (kościół parafialny; ul Grzegorza), dating from 1886, has Art Nouveau wall paintings and remarkable stained glass behind the main altar. The neoclassical **Orthodox Church of the Holy Trinity** (Cerkiew Św Trójcy; ul Zamkowa) was built in 1784 and initially

served the Uniat congregation. The main door behind the grill is left open for you to admire the modern iconostasis.

The odd little bronze likeness of a soldier sitting on a bench in the centre of ul 3 Maja is the **Schweik statue**, representing the antihero of Czech writer Jaroslav Hašek's polemical novel *The Good Soldier Schweik* (1923). According to the book, Schweik (or Švejk) visited Sanok on 15 July 1915. Fame at last.

Sleeping

PTSM Sanok Hostel (☎ 013 463 0925; soswsanok@op.pl; ul Konarskiego 10; dm 12-15zł; Jul & Aug; P ☐) One of the very cheapest places to stay in town, the local hostel is a modest 60-bed establishment between the bus station and the centre.

Dom Turysty PTTK (☎ 013 463 1413; domturysty@ domturysty.net.pl; ul Mickiewicza 29; s/d/tr/q 70/90/110/120zł; P) This large year-round PTTK hostel offers plenty of beds in 78 rooms. Private bathrooms and low prices may seem an attractive option, but some rooms are on the shabby side.

Hotel Pod Trzema Różami (☎ 013 463 0922; www .podtrzemarozami.pl in Polish; ul Jagiellońska 13; s/d/tr/q 80/100/120/140zł; P) About 200m south of the main square, the cavernous 'Under Three Roses' has only 24 rooms. The accommodation here is in plain but perfectly clean and acceptable rooms.

Hotel Jagielloński (☎ 013 463 1208; jagiellonski sanok@wp.pl; ul Jagiellońska 49; s/d/tr 100/120/140zł; P ☐) The 19-room Jagielloński, with distinctive wooden furniture, parquetry floors and a very good restaurant, is excellent value. Rooms are spacious and have private facilities; we loved the flower-bedecked balcony. Rates don't include breakfast.

Hotel Sanvit (☎ 013 465 5088; www.sanvit.sanok .pl in Polish; ul Łazienna 1; s/d/tr 130/180/230zł, ste from 250zł; P ✕ ☐ ☐) Just west of the Rynek, the Sanvit is far and away Sanok's flashiest accommodation, with 31 bright, modern rooms, shining bathrooms, a restaurant and café, and a wellness centre with sauna, gym and a salt cave.

Eating & Drinking

Restauracja U Szwejka (☎ 013 464 4761; ul 3 Maja 15; mains 5-27zł; 11am-midnight Mon-Fri, 11am-1am Sat, noon-midnight Sun) Just down from the bronze statue of the soldier Schweik (from which it takes its name), this place has something for everyone – Czech dishes, *pierogi* (dumplings), pizza and pancakes.

Karczma Jadło Karpackie (☎ 013 464 6700; Rynek 12; mains 6-18zł; ☼ 9am-10pm) This is an amenable, folksy (but not overly so) bar and restaurant on the main square that serves up unusual Carpathian dishes, including *hreczanyky* (a local dish made with minced pork and buckwheat groats) and *ogórki małosolne* (lightly salted pickles).

Palermo Pizza (☎ 013 464 3979; ul Jagiellońska 13; mains 10-25zł; ☼ 9am-11pm) One of the more popular budget eateries in Sanok, this pizzeria below the Hotel Pod Trzema Różami also does a nice range of pasta dishes and salads.

Weranda Caffe (☎ 0609 741 936; ul 3 Maja 14; ☼ 10am-10pm) This cosy café-bar, with a fireplace glowing in winter and outdoor terrace set up in summer, is a good place to have a drink, alcoholic or otherwise, year-round.

Getting There & Away

The train and bus stations are next to each other, about 1.2km southeast of the Rynek.

There's hourly bus transport to Rzeszów (10.60zł, 1½ hours) and Lesko (3.50zł, 20 minutes, up to 10 daily). Buses also run to Ustrzyki Dolne (7zł, one hour, 12 daily) and Ustrzyki Górne (13zł, 1½ to 2½ hours, seven daily). There are five to six buses to Cisna (8zł, one hour) and Wetlina (12zł, 1½ to two hours), with additional departures in summer. A couple of buses go to Komańcza (7zł, one hour). Five fast buses go directly to Kraków (32zł, three hours), with three heading for Warsaw (47zł, four to five hours).

Two fast trains run to Warsaw daily (57zł, nine hours) while two go to Kraków (46zł, 3½ hours). A dozen ordinary trains serve Jasło (11zł, two hours) via Krosno (7.40zł, 1½ hours).

ICON TRAIL

The environs of Sanok are sprinkled with small villages, many of which still boast old Orthodox or Uniat **churches**. Most of these are traditional wooden ones and a reminder of the prewar ethnic and religious fabric of the region. You can see many of these churches on a pair of marked trails called the **Icon Trail** (Szlak Ikon). The first (and more popular) route is a 70km-long loop that begins and ends in Sanok and wends along the San River valley north of the city. The net walking time is about 15 hours, and it's also suitable for bicycles and mountain bikes.

The trail covers about a dozen churches. Most date from the 18th and 19th centuries, but the route also includes the oldest Uniat timber church in Poland, at **Ulucz**, built in 1510. You can visit all the churches along the way; arrangements have been made with each of the key holders to let visitors in and show them around. A small donation is appreciated.

A longer route follows the Osława River valley south of Sanok into the Bieszczady, and almost to the Slovakian border, although it's not marked in the same way as most of the churches here are close to the main road. One of the more interesting churches on this trail is the wooden Orthodox church at Turzańsk (p285), built in 1803.

Tourist information and PTTK offices stock English-language brochures outlining the trails and briefly describing the churches found along them. They also include details of where to ask for church keys (though that information is not always up to date).

LESKO
pop 5860

Founded in 1470 on the banks of the San River, Lesko had a mixed Polish-Ruthenian population for centuries, a reflection of the region's history. From the 16th century, many Jews arrived from Spain fleeing the Inquisition. Their migration continued and by the 18th century Jews made up half of the town's population.

WWII and the years that followed changed the ethnic picture altogether. The Jews were slaughtered by the Nazis, the Ukrainians were defeated by the Polish military and the Lemks were deported. The town was rebuilt and, without having developed any significant industry, is now a small tourist centre. While it may not be the 'Gateway to the Bieszczady' as it likes to call itself – that distinction really goes to Sanok – it is a pleasant stopover on the way south.

Information

Bank PKO (ul Przemysłowa 11; ☼ 8am-3.30pm Mon-Fri)
Bieszczady Adventure (☎ 013 469 7270; www.kraina wilka.pl; Rynek 1) Specialises in active sport, including rafting, trekking, fly fishing, off-road and mountain biking.
Carpathians Center of Active Tourism (☎ 013 469 6290; www.zielonyrower.pl; Plac Konstytucji 3 Maja 7) Sells the 1:100,000-scale *Greenway Bicycle Trail* (Szlak Zielony Rower; 15zł) map and provides information about the trail.

THE CARPATHIAN MOUNTAINS

WHEN GOD WAS ON VACATION

Based on the number of day tours to Auschwitz on offer, especially out of Kraków, you would be forgiven for thinking that the nightmare of the Holocaust, the time 'when God was on vacation' as some Jews put it, was played out solely in the extermination camps at Oświęcim in Upper Silesia. But even a cursory trip around Galicia, the Austro-Hungarian province that was heavily Jewish and included many of the towns and cities mentioned in this chapter, will dispel that notion. As dozens of plaques, memorials and crude markers point out, hundreds of thousands of Polish Jews – in fact, a quarter of the three million annihilated – were murdered in their fields and forests. And in some respects it is even more horrible to imagine such crimes committed in the idyllic surrounds of a country town or village.

And the cemeteries… You may have wondered why they are so overgrown, their broken stones pitched this way and that. The answer is simple: there are no relatives left. Brothers, mothers, husbands, lovers, nephews, granddaughters – all are dead or have fled.

When a Jew dies a prayer called the Mourner's Kaddish is recited for them. The kaddish is repeated at Yahrzeit, the first anniversary of the death, and annually after that. But virtually no Jews lying in cemeteries like the one at Lesko have anyone to say this prayer for them. You might consider saying kaddish for those whose relatives cannot. Your voice can fill a decades-old void. Download the prayer from www.jewfaq.org/prayer/kaddish.htm.

Main post office (ul Parkowa; ⏲ 7am-8pm Mon-Fri, 8am-2pm Sat)

Tourist office (☎ 013 469 6695; bcit@lesko.pl; ⏲ 8am-4pm Mon-Sat) In a pavilion on the Rynek.

Sights & Activities

Lesko is notable for its Jewish heritage. From the oddly shaped Rynek, with its 19th-century **town hall** in the middle, head 200m north to the town's erstwhile **synagogue** (ul Joselewicza). Built in the Mannerist style in the mid-18th century, the synagogue has an attached tower – a dead giveaway that it was once part of the town's fortifications. Little of the temple's original decoration has survived. The interior houses the **Synagogue Art Gallery** (Galeria Sztuki Synagoga; ☎ 013 469 6649; adult/concession 3/1.50zł; ⏲ 10am-5pm May-Oct), which is supposed to showcase artists from the Bieszczady. In the porch is a list of towns and *shtetls* in the region with Jewish populations of more than 100, a poignant reminder of what the make-up of the region was before the German murderers arrived.

Just west of the synagogue is the **Parish Church of Our Lady** (Kościół Parafialny Najświętszej Marii Panny; ul Kościuszki). It was built in 1539 and its exterior still retains many Gothic features, including the eastern portal. The freestanding Baroque bell tower was added in the mid-18th century.

From the synagogue, follow ul Moniuszki north (and downhill); the stairs on the right lead up to the old **Jewish cemetery** (Kirkut). More than 2000 gravestones, the oldest one dating back to the mid-16th century, are scattered amid trees and ever-consuming ivy, in varying stages of decay. Some of them miraculously retain their rich decoration; others have been defaced.

Sleeping & Eating

Hotelik Ratuszowa (☎ 013 469 8632; s.kaszycki@interia .pl; Rynek 12, enter from ul Parkowa; s/d/tr 60/80/120zł; P) About the only central place in town, the cosy little 'Town Hall Inn' has eight small and rather plain rooms up under the eaves of its restaurant (mains 8zł to 22zł, open 9am to 9pm), which serves Polish favourites and is just about the best venue in town.

Pensjonat Zamek (☎ 013 469 6268; www.gat.pl/98 .php; ul Piłsudskiego 7; s/d/tr 90/110/138zł, apt 300-400zł; P ⓢ) Located about 200m south of the Rynek, in what's left of Sanok's 16th-century castle, this modest guesthouse was once a holiday centre for miners. It's now a regular hotel with 43 rooms, a gym and a swimming pool. It also hires out mountain bikes.

Camping Nad Sanem (☎ 013 469 6689; ul Turystyczna 1; beds per person 20-35zł; ⏲ May-Sep; P) The camping ground is on the riverside below the castle. It has a 15 bungalows with rooms of different sizes, an area where you can pitch your tent and a restaurant.

Pizzeria Kaszyno (☎ 013 469 8680; ul Kazimierza Wielkiego 3; mains 8-30zł; ⏲ 9am-10pm Mon-Sat, 2-10pm Sun) Halfway between the synagogue and the parish church, northwest of the Rynek, the

'Casino' is a no-frills pizzeria that will not send you away hungry.

Getting There & Away

The bus station is on ul Piłsudskiego – the road to Sanok – about 1km west of the Rynek. There are plenty of buses to Sanok (3.50zł, 20 minutes), about 11 of which continue to Krosno (10zł, one hour). A dozen daily buses run to Rzeszów (11.50zł, two hours) and four express buses go directly to Kraków (38zł, three hours).

For the Bieszczady, there are three daily buses to Cisna (7zł, one hour), and some wind up as far as Wetlina (9zł, 1½ hours). As many as 10 buses serve Ustrzyki Górne (11zł, two hours), half of which go via Ustrzyki Dolne.

USTRZYKI DOLNE

pop 9600

An unprepossessing town in the southeastern corner of Poland, Ustrzyki Dolne (oost-*shi-kee dol*-neh) is really only an overnight stop for those heading south into the Bieszczady; the headquarters of the Bieszczady National Park are conveniently located here. If you plan on trekking in the mountains independently, Ustrzyki Dolne is the last reliable place to stock up on a decent range of provisions and exchange money.

Information

Bank Pekao (Rynek 17; ☎ 9am-4.30pm Mon-Fri) Next to the tourist office.

Bieszczady National Park headquarters (☎ 013 461 0650; www.bdpn.pl; ul Bełska 7; ☼ 9am-5pm Tue-Sat, plus 9am-2pm Sun Jul & Aug) In the museum.

Tourist office (☎ 013 471 1130; www.cit.ustrzyki-dolne.pl in Polish; Rynek 16; ☼ 8.30am-4pm Mon-Fri, 9am-2pm Sat)

Sights & Activities

There's not much to see in Ustrzyki Dolne except for the **Natural History Museum** (Muzeum Przyrodnicze; ☎ 013 461 1091; ul Bełska 7; adult/concession 5/3zł; ☼ 9am-5pm Tue-Sat, plus 9am-2pm Sun Jul & Aug) behind the tourist office. It's a good introduction to the geology, flora and fauna of the Bieszczady.

Enquire about horse riding and riding excursions at the **Galop** (☎ 013 471 1151, 0609 940 349; horse@w.polsce.com; ul Chopina 21) shop and travel agency west of the centre.

Sleeping & Eating

Hotelik Bieszczadzki (☎ 013 461 1071; www.bieszczadzka.com; Rynek 19; d/tr with en suite 80/150zł, s/d/tr with shared facilities 35/60/80zł; P) The most central place in town, the 16-room Bieszczadzki is very simple and has a similarly simple budget restaurant (mains 8zł to 20zł, open 8am to 10pm Monday to Thursday, 8am to midnight Friday to Sunday) with pizza and the like.

Hotel Laworta (☎ 013 468 9000; www.laworta.pl in Polish; ul Nadgórna 107; s/d/tr/apt 115/200/240/400zł; P ☐ ☑ ☑) To the north of town, around 1.5km uphill from the train and bus stations, the Laworta is a peaceful 54-room place set in its own parkland. It has good facilities, including tennis courts and a sauna, and its own restaurant.

Getting There & Away

The train and bus stations are in one building. You won't get far by train – Zagórz (7.50zł, 2¾ hours) and Jasło (17zł, 4½ hours) are two of the very few destinations – but bus service is reasonably good. Two dozen daily buses run to Sanok (7zł, one hour), some passing through Lesko (5zł, 30 minutes) on the way. Up to seven buses (several more in summer) go daily to Ustrzyki Górne (7.60zł, 1½ hours) and six to Polańczyk (6.50zł, one hour). Destinations further afield include Przemyśl (11zł, two hours, four daily), Rzeszów (16.20zł, 2½ hours, seven daily) and Kraków (40zł, four hours), which is served by two daily expresses.

LAKE SOLINA

About 30km southwest of Ustrzyki Dolne and accessible by bus is Lake Solina (Jezioro Solińskie), a reservoir 27km long and 60m deep, created in 1968 when the San River was dammed. Today it is the Bieszczady region's most important centre for water sports and recreation.

Polańczyk, the attractive town on the irregularly shaped lake's western shore, offers visitors everything from sailing and windsurfing to fishing and beaches. The **tourist office** (☎ 013 470 3028; www.esolina.pl; ul Wiejska 2; ☼ 8am-6pm Mon-Fri, 10am-6pm Sat), just off Hwy 894 on the way to Lesko, can supply you with all the details.

Ul Zdrojowa, which starts just east of the tourist office, is lined with hotels and sanatoriums offering any number of treatments. Many of them are huge soulless blocks; instead head for **Pensjonat Korona** (☎ 013 469 2201;

www.pensjonatkorona.pl; ul Zdrojowa 29; s/d 60/120zł), a flower-bedecked guesthouse with 40 beds and its own restaurant and pizzeria just over 1km down the peninsula. For budget accommodation close to the water, it's hard to beat the **Centrum Wypoczynkowe Wyspa Polańczyk** (☎ 013 469 2746; www.solina.pl; 4-/6-/8-person cabins 250/300/400zł), which has 20 A-frame cabins on the southwestern cost of the Big Island (Wyspa Duża), accessible by ferry boat across a channel a mere 5m wide.

Getting There & Away

The main bus stop is at the start of ul Zdrojowa, just east of the tourist office. Up to six buses a day head for Ustrzyki Dolne (6.50zł, one hour). Other destinations include Lesko (4.50zł, 30 minutes, hourly), Krosno (12zł, 1½ hours, five daily) and Ustrzyki Górne (11zł, 1½ hours, six daily).

USTRZYKI GÓRNE
pop 120

Ustrzyki Górne, less of a village than a string of houses scattered along the main road, is the Bieszczady's premier hiking base.

Since the Bieszczady loop road opened in 1962, the mountains have become more accessible. But this is still remote country and Ustrzyki Górne is a good example: there are a few mostly basic places to stay and eat, a shop and not much else. The village springs to life in summer, then sinks into a deep sleep for most of the rest of the year, stirring only a little in winter when the cross-country skiers arrive.

Sights & Activities

Bieszczady National Park is full of fascinating sights and sounds: the remnants of villages abandoned or destroyed during Operation Vistula (see the boxed text, p275), ancient cemeteries, peat reserves (complete with quicksand), the cry of a lone wolf in the distance. The best way to see it all is up close with a forest guide. One of the best is **Andrzej Luks** (☎ 013 461 0281, 013 461 0610), who's based at Muczne, 20km northeast of Ustrzyki Górne, and will take you around by jeep.

Horse riding in the national park is offered by **ZHKN** (☎ 0500 207 581; zhkh@bdpn.pl; per hr 25zł, equipment hire 50zł) in Wołosate, 7km southeast of Ustrzyki Górne.

Sleeping & Eating

Villages like Ustrzyki Górne usually don't have street names, but general directions should get you there.

Hotelik Biały (☎ 013 461 0641; www.hotelik-bialy .bieszczady.info.pl; dm 23-26zł; **P**) This 70-bed hostel is run by the Bieszczady National Park; rooms generally have four to five beds. It's on a side road, about 500m from the turn-off next to the shop.

Schronisko PTTK Kremenaros (☎ 013 461 0605; dm 27zł, ⊙ Apr-Oct; **P**) This hostel is in the last house of the village, on the western side of the road heading towards Wetlina and opposite a huge border station. It's old and basic, but the staff is friendly and the atmosphere is good. Rooms have between two and 10 beds. The restaurant has a very short menu but the food is cheap and acceptable.

Hotel Górski (☎ 013 461 0604; www.hotel.ustrzyki .biz; s 75-91zł, d 150-182zł, apt 197-307zł; **P** ✗ ⎚) This PTTK-run hotel, at the northern end of the village on the road to Ustrzyki Dolne and bedecked with flower baskets, is significantly better than anything else around. With 63 clean, comfortable and modern rooms, all with their own bathrooms, it's also the biggest place in town. The hotel has a gym and sauna, and its own reasonably priced restaurant.

Camping Nr 150 PTTK (☎ 013 461 0614; per person/ tent 8/10zł, beds in cabins with/without bathroom 32/21zł; ⊙ May-Sep; **P**) The camping ground next door to the Hotel Górski has some old triple cabins without bathrooms and newer double cabins with en suites.

In addition to the two year-round PTTK eateries listed above, more places open in summer along the main road, including the ever-popular **Bar U Eskulapa** (☎ 0607 139 872; mains 6-16zł; ⊙ 8am-9pm), famous for its *pierogi*, trout and *placek po bieszczadzku* (potato pancake filled with goulash). If you have your own transport, **Wilcza Jama** (Wolf's Lair; ☎ 013 461 0269; mains 10-35zł) in Muczne, 20km northeast of Ustrzyki Górne, is one of the best restaurants in the Bieszczady and specialises in game (boar, venison, pheasant).

Getting There & Away

There are up to seven buses daily to Ustrzyki Dolne (7.60zł, 1½ hours), two to Krosno (16.50zł to 19.50zł, three hours), three to Rzeszów (23zł, 3½ hours) and as many as nine a day to Lesko (11zł, two hours) and Sanok (13zł, 2½ hours). A couple more

HIKING IN THE BIESZCZADY

The Bieszczady region is one of the best places in Poland to go hiking. The region is beautiful and easy to walk around, and you don't need a tent or cooking equipment as mountain hostels are a day's walk apart and provide food. The main area for trekking is the national park, with Ustrzyki Górne and Wetlina being the most popular starting points, followed by Cisna.

Bieszczady National Park counts about a dozen well-marked hiking trails, with a total length of 130km. All three jumping-off points have PTTK hostels, with helpful staff who can provide information, and all have boards outlining the trails, complete with walking times, both up-hill and downhill. Ascending **Mt Tarnica** (the region's highest peak at 1346m) from Wołosate, southeast of Ustrzyki Górne, will take two to three hours. At least one of the trails reaches (but does not cross) the Ukrainian border at one point. Be sure to carry your passport when hiking in this sensitive area.

Mountain hostels will put you up for the night and feed you regardless of how crowded they get. In July and August the floor will most likely be your bed, as these places are pretty small. Take a sleeping bag with you.

Get a copy of Galileos' 1:50,000-scale *Bieszczady* map (9zł), which covers the whole region. Agencja Wit's 1:50,000-scale map showing both the Upper and Lower Bieszczady – *Bieszczady Wysokie i Niskie* – costs 15zł.

buses run in July and August to the above destinations, as well as a couple of buses to Wetlina (4.50zł, 30 minutes) and up to six to Cisna (6.50zł, 45 minutes).

WETLINA
pop 300
Wetlina is another popular jumping-off spot for hiking in the Bieszczady. Like Ustrzyki Górne, it stretches along one main road (in this case Hwy 897) and has a limited choice of simple places to sleep and eat.

Sleeping & Eating
Dom Wycieczkowy PTTK (☎ 013 468 4615; www .wetlinapttk.pl; dm 14zł, d 36-445zł; P ✖) This old and very simple hostel offers beds year-round in doubles as well as dorms sleeping five. In summer you can also stay in cabins (17zł to 25zł per person) or pitch your tent (9zł) on the grounds. There's a rustic restaurant here with rough pine tables and decorated with carved wooden figures.

Zajazd Pod Połoniną (☎ 013 468 4611; www.pod polonina.prv.pl; per person 25-40zł; P) The 45-bed 'Inn below Mt Połonina' has rooms that sleep two to four people, and some come with bathrooms. There is also a budget restaurant. It's at the eastern end of the village, on the way to Ustrzyki Górne.

Pensjonat U Rumcajsa (☎ 013 468 4633; s/d/tr/q 25/40/60/75zł; P) This large pension almost opposite Zajazd Pod Połoniną has 80 beds in basic but serviceable rooms sleeping up to four people.

Camping Górna Wetlinka (☎ 013 468 4776, 0604 172 238; per person/tent/car 7/3/5zł, family cabin 200zł; ✷ May-Oct) This excellent and very friendly camping ground also serves as an information point for Bieszczady National Park. Several hiking trails start from here and the staff can organise horse riding (25zł per hour).

Getting There & Away
Up to 10 buses a day go to Sanok (11zł, two hours) via Lesko (9zł, 1½ hours). Count on up to nine buses a day to Ustrzyki Górne (4.50zł, 30 minutes) to the east and Cisna (4.50zł, 30 minutes) to the west.

CISNA
pop 460
Cisna sits on the borderland between the territories once inhabited by the Boyks to the east and the Lemks to the west. The region was densely populated before WWII but today it counts fewer than 500 inhabitants, yet it's still the largest village in the central part of the Bieszczady. The village is not attractive in itself, but it has a decent choice of accommodation and is a good base for hiking. It is also the place to board the narrow-gauge tourist train.

The **tourist office** (☎ 013 468 6465; www.cisna.pl; ✷ 8am-8pm Mon-Fri, 9am-5pm Sat May-Aug, 8am-4pm Mon-Fri Sep-Apr) is in the county cultural centre in the middle of the village.

Activities

The narrow-gauge train known as the **Bieszczady Forest Railway** (Bieszczadzka Kolejka Leśna; ☎ 013 468 6335; ciuchcianasza@vp.pl), based at the station in Majdan, 2km west of Cisna, was built at the end of the 19th century for transporting timber between Nowy Łupków and Majdan. The line was later extended north to Rzepedź and east to Moczarne, beyond Wetlina. The train on the Majdan–Rzepedź route was in use as recently as 1993, but the line has since been turned into a tourist attraction.

The train makes three runs. The 12km stretch from Majdan to Przysłup (adult/child 11/8zł one way, 18/12zł return), midway between Cisna and Wetlina, operates daily in July and August and at weekends in May, June and September. The other two runs – the 17km one between Majdan and Wola Michowa (14/10zł one way, 22/16zł return) and the 9km stretch between Majdan and Balnica (9/7zł one way, 14/10zł return) – operate at the weekend only in July and August. There's a small museum here as well as a snack bar and shop.

For **cycling** fans, Ośrodek Wczasowy Perełka (below) rents bikes for 4/20zł per hour/day.

Sleeping & Eating

Bacówka PTTK Pod Honem (☎ 0503 137 279; www .podhonem.home.pl in Polish; dm 19zł, d/tr/q 44/63/80zł; **P** **✕**) The 40-bed PTTK mountain hostel is located 668m up on a slope at the eastern end of Cisna; it's about 1km up the hill from behind the Wołosan, along a steep dirt track. It's simple and friendly and serves uncomplicated meals.

Schronisko Turystyczne Okrąglik (☎ 013 468 6349; per person 20-25zł) Handily located on the central crossroads, this hostel has extremely plain rooms with between two and six beds and shared facilities.

Villa Helena (☎ 0502 573 061; Cisna 107; s/d 20/35zł; **P** **✕**) This pleasant little B&B, opposite the road up to the Wołosan and Pod Honem, has 11 neat rooms. It's fairly simple, but comfortable and homely.

Ośrodek Wczasowy Perełka (☎ 013 468 6325; perelka@naturatour.pl; s/d 40/70zł, cabins per person 20zł; **P** **🍴**) This comfortable holiday home, the first house on the left as you enter Cisna from the west, has 34 beds in singles and doubles plus another 54 in seasonal A-frame cabins.

OSW Wołosan (☎ 013 468 6373; www.wolosan.pl; Cisna 87; s/d 190/200zł; **P** **✕** **💻** **♿**) By far the classiest

place in this part of the Bieszczady, the 27-room Wołosan at the eastern end of Cisna is geared towards hunters (thus the trophies and stuffed animals throughout) but can organise any number of activities – from quad bikes and snowmobile excursions to off-road jeep safaris.

Half a dozen eateries near the crossroads open in summer, including the delightful **Demerada** (☎ 013 468 6502; mains 18-22zł; 🕙 9am-10pm), a tearoom and bistro with Carpathian specialities.

Getting There & Away

Half a dozen buses run daily to Sanok (7.80zł, one hour) and Wetlina (4.50zł, 30 minutes). There are more seasonal buses in summer, including up to six to Ustrzyki Górne (6.50zł, 45 minutes).

KOMAŃCZA

pop 880

A village nestled in a valley between the Bieszczady and Beskid Niski, Komańcza is yet another base used by hikers. Though not as popular as Ustrzyki Górne, Wetlina or Cisna, Komańcza offers something different for the traveller. As it somehow escaped Operation Vistula (see the boxed text, p275) in 1947, there's more of an ethnic and religious mix here than elsewhere in the region. There is a sizable community of Lemks living in and around the village.

The **tourist office** (☎ 013 467 7076; www.komancza.pl in Polish; ul Komańcza 166; 🕙 7am-3pm Mon-Fri) is in the county office en route to the Uniat church.

Sights & Activities

Until recently, tiny Komańcza could boast something unique in Poland – Orthodox, Uniat and Roman Catholic churches within walking distance of each other and all in use. Sadly, the oldest of the three, a beautiful wooden Orthodox church dating from 1802 and tucked away on the outskirts of the village on Hwy 897 to Dukla, was burned to the ground in September 2006, leaving only the separate bell tower, dating from 1836. The parish has pledged to rebuild the church and the forestry department has donated the timber, but that won't be nearly enough. If you'd like to make a donation, contact the **Orthodox priest** (☎ 013 467 7224; ul Komańcza 216).

The Uniats make up a significant part of Komańcza's population. In the late 1980s

KEEPING THE BIESZCZADY IN RANGE

Krzystof Krzysta, from Wołosate, is the park ranger of Bieszczady National Park (BNP), home to Poland's largest concentration of wild animals.

Lions and tigers and bears, oh my! Well, bears in the mountains and park, along with wolves, lynx, deer, boar and European bison.

Conservationist equals antihunter, right? In the BNP, of course, but not outside. I was a professional hunter for almost a decade before I joined the park in 1989. There was no great awakening. The area of the park was increased by fivefold and all hunting was forbidden. I had to choose between working in the park or moving on. I chose the former. Now I'm a professional hunter of poachers.

Is that a problem here? No. The human population in the park is tiny; there are just three villages including Wołosate. What is a problem is the growth in the populations of certain animals where the forests cannot sustain the numbers. In Slovakia bears are culled but not in Poland. The problem is, male bears control their own populations by killing off their young as necessary. With male bears being killed, the young population is increasing substantially in areas that cannot sustain those numbers. Wolves also have their own natural birth control. An alpha couple requires 100 sq km of land for roaming and hunting. Otherwise the female cannot conceive or aborts.

How was the park managed under the old regime? Like everything under socialism it was all carefully planned and tightly managed. The animal populations were fattened up over the winter and protected from wolves, especially the best specimens.

Why was that? Hunting was big business, both for government ministers and for their foreign guests. Hunting was always the 'sport of kings' in England and in the rest of Europe, so why should it have been different here? This stag was for the general secretary, that boar was for the minister of the interior. And in those days foreigners might spend up to DM3000 (€1535) just to bag a wolf.

The big bad wolf sure gets a lot of bad press. Is it deserved? Wolves are the smartest animals in the forest and I respect them. Wolves and humans are natural enemies because they have to compete for the same food. But they are no longer afraid of humans and are coming closer and closer to built-up areas. And they've been protected since 1996.

If I were a tourist... I wouldn't run if I saw a wolf. Just stand still. Wolves usually don't attack humans but if you run they may mistake you for a sheep or a dog and pursue you.

they built a **Uniat church** south of the centre. In the basement is a small **Lemk Museum** (Muzeum Łemków; ☎ 013 467 7224) featuring a collection of household items, tools and handicrafts related to the Lemk culture.

Though it looks older, the modest wooden **Roman Catholic church** was built in the early 1950s for newly settled adherents of that creed, which was virtually nonexistent in the region before WWII. The church is opposite the train station, north of the centre on Hwy 892 heading towards Sanok.

Also north of the centre is the **Convent of the Nazarene Sisters** (Klasztor Sióstr Nazaretanek; ☎ 013 467 7056; www.nazaretanki.dir.pl; ul Komańcza 27; ☽ 8am-noon & 1.30-6pm), where Cardinal Stefan Wyszyński (1901–81), primate of Poland, was placed under house arrest for a year in 1955, for his opposition to the arrest and internment of priests and other religious figures. Two rooms in this green clapboard mansion are open to the public, including Wyszyński's bedroom-cum-study and a small chapel. To reach it from the centre, head north for about 1.5km along Hwy 892 and take the narrow track that branches off to the left under the railway bridge. The convent is about 550m up the hill from the car park.

Recently extended, the so-called **Cross Border Cycle Route** (Transgraniczna Trasa Rowerowa; www.komancza.info), a signposted cycling route into Slovakia, now totals 160km. Ask the tourist office for maps, brochures and other practical details.

Sleeping & Eating

Schronisko PTTK (☎ 013 467 7013; www.pttk.komancza .prox.pl; dm 17zł, cabins per person 25-30zł; Ⓟ ⌑) Fully refurbished, this year-round 25-bed hostel, about 250m up the hill from the convent car park, offers a warm welcome and good standards in rooms with two to four beds. It serves simple hot meals and operates five-person cabins when the weather is nice.

Getting There & Away

There are half a dozen daily buses to Sanok (7zł, one hour). One bus goes daily to Cisna (6.50zł, 45 minutes) and there is also sporadic transport to Dukla (8zł, one hour).

The train links Komańcza with Zagórz (7.50zł, 1¼ hours, four daily) via Rzepedź. From Zagórz, there's frequent bus transport to Sanok and Lesko.

AROUND KOMAŃCZA

Scattered around Komańcza are some of the finest Uniat and Orthodox churches in Poland. You'll find the first good example in the village of **Rzepedź**, 5km north of Komańcza and 1.3km west of the main road. This unusually light-coloured wooden structure, with a bell tower in front and topped with three onion domes, dates from 1824 and is now a Uniat church. The key is kept by Sławomir Jurkowski at Rzepedź 26, about 500m from the church, though you might try peering through the keyhole to admire the wonderful polychrome on the walls or attending Mass at 9.45am on Sunday.

A bit different in shape, and perhaps even more attractive, is the church in **Turzańsk**, 1.5km east of Rzepedź. Topped with five graceful onion domes and complemented by a freestanding belfry, the church was built in 1803 and has preserved its internal decoration, complete with an elaborate iconostasis from 1895. Today the church serves the Orthodox community and Divine Liturgy takes place at 10am every second Sunday. If you want to visit at other times, the keys are kept at the house of Teodor Tchoryk,

Turzańsk 63, in the upper part of the village, about 2km from the church.

One more Orthodox *cerkiew* (church) can be found in the village of **Szczawne**, 3km north of Rzepedź and 300m from the main road, just before crossing the railway track. Watch out to the left, as this huge church with green copper domes is well hidden in a cluster of trees. Services are held around 10am every second Sunday. The keys are kept by Jan Walorny, Szczawne 20, in the large brick house near the train station on the road to Bukowsko, 2km northwest of the church.

THE BESKID NISKI

The Beskid Niski, or 'Low Beskid', is a forest-covered mountain range with gentle slopes that runs for about 85km west to east along the Slovakian frontier. It's bordered on the west by the Beskid Sądecki and on the east by the Bieszczady. As its name suggests, it is not a high outcrop: its tallest peak does not exceed 1000m and the range is made for easy walks. Admittedly the Beskid Niski offers less-spectacular vistas than the neighbouring Bieszczady. But its dozens of small Orthodox and Uniat churches, especially in the western half of the region, are a strong draw.

KROSNO

pop 47,600

Founded in the 14th century and prosperous during the Renaissance – it was even nicknamed 'little Kraków' for a time – Krosno slid into decay from the 18th century onwards. It revived with the trade of linen and Hungarian wine, and, in the mid-19th century, with the development of the oil industry. It is especially known for its ornamental and commercial glassworks.

Krosno is unexceptional except for its tiny historic core, perched on a hill, and some interesting sights nearby.

Information

Bank PKO (ul Słowackiego 4; ⓦ 8.30am-4pm Mon-Fri) Northeast of the Rynek.

Jack-Pol (☎ 013 432 7704; Plac Konstytucji 3 Maja 3; per hr 3zł; ⓦ 8am-7pm Mon-Fri, 9am-4pm Sat, 9am-3pm Sun) Internet access south of the Rynek.

Tourist office (☎ 013 432 7707; www.krosno.pl; Rynek 5; ⓦ 9am-5pm Mon-Fri, 10am-2pm Sat & Sun Apr-Sep,

9am-4pm Mon-Fri, 10am-2pm Sat Oct-Mar) At the southeast corner of the main square.

Sights

The Old Town's spacious **Rynek** has retained some of its Renaissance appearance, notably in the houses fronted by wide arcaded passageways that line the southern and northeastern parts of the square. The best example is the **Wójtowska Townhouse** (Kamienica Wójtowska; Rynek 7).

A few steps southeast of the Rynek is the large 15th-century **Franciscan Church of the Holy Cross** (Kościół Franciszkanów Św Krzyża; ul Franciszkańska), today filled with neo-Gothic furnishings. The showpiece here is the **Oświęcim Family Chapel** (Kaplica Oświęcimów), just to the left (north) as you enter the church. Built in 1647 by Italian architect Vincenti Petroni, and embellished with magnificent stucco work by another Italian master, Jan Falconi, the chapel is considered to be one of the best early Baroque chapels in Poland.

Another huge brick structure, the **Parish Church of the Holy Trinity** (Kościół Parafialny Św Trócy; ul Piłsudskiego) is 50m northwest of the Rynek. Founded in 1402, it was almost completely consumed by fire in the mid-17th century (only the chancel survived) and rebuilt. Note the intricate grape pattern on the wrought-iron main gates. Inside, the renovated gilded high altar is 350 years old, as is the elaborate pulpit. The freestanding onion-domed bell tower (1651) houses three bells called Jan, Marian and Urban. The tower is one of the largest in Poland.

One block northwest of the church is the **Subcarpathian Museum** (Muzeum Podkarpackie; ☎ 013 432 1376; www.muzeum.krosno.pl in Polish; ul Piłsudskiego 16; adult/concession 6.50/3.50zł, free Sun; ☼ 9am-5pm Tue-Fri, 10am-5pm Sat & Sun May-Oct, 9am-4pm Tue-Fri, 10am-4pm Sat & Sun Nov-Apr). Installed in the 15th-century former Bishops' Palace, the museum has interesting historical, archaeological and art sections. The highlight, however, is its extensive collection of decorative old kerosene lamps, reputedly the largest in Europe.

Directly opposite is the **Craft Museum** (Muzeum Rzemiosła; ☎ 013 432 4188; www.muzeumrzemiosla.pl in Polish; ul Piłsudskiego 19; adult/concession 5/3zł, free Sat; ☼ 9am-5pm Mon-Fri, 10am-2pm Sat & Sun May-Sep, 9am-3pm Mon-Fri, 10am-2pm Sat Oct-Apr), featuring displays related to such local crafts and trades as clock-making, weaving, saddlery and even hairdressing.

About 1km northwest of the Old Town is the famous **Krosno glassworks** (Krośnieńskie Huty Szkła; ☎ 013 432 8000; www.krosno.com.pl; ul Tysiąclecia 13). There's a **factory shop** (☎ 013 432 8755; ☼ 9am-5pm Mon-Fri) on site selling a range of its products.

Sleeping

Hotelik Śnieżka (☎ 013 432 3449; www.hotelsniezka.prv .pl; ul Lewakowskiego 22; s/d/tr 89/128/169zł; **P** **🖳**) This attractive brick-red Victorian townhouse, hard by the bus and train stations, now counts 14 cosy rooms, all sparklingly modern, with polished wood floors and big bathrooms. The in-house restaurant is pretty stylish.

Pensjonacik Buda (☎ 013 432 0053; www.buda .krosno.pl; ul Jagiellońska 4; d/tr/ste 150/200/250zł; **P** **✕** **🖳**) This friendly B&B sits uncomfortably close to the railroad tracks 800m southwest of the Rynek, but its seven charming rooms and excellent restaurant (below) make it worth consideration.

Hotelik Twist (☎ 013 432 0708; www.krosno-twist .republika.pl; ul Pużaka 37; s 80-150zł, d 140-180zł, tr 200-210zł; **P** **🖳**) It may look boxy from the outside, but this hotel 400m southeast of the train and bus stations offers 29 large and airy rooms in both new and old wings.

Hotel Krosno-Nafta (☎ 013 432 6212; www .hotel.nafta.pl; ul Lwowska 21; s/d/q 180/270/370zł; **P** **✕** **🖳** **♿**) The city's top-end accommodation option, this modern hotel, a little over 1km southeast of the centre on the Sanok road, offers 41 comfortable rooms and its own upmarket restaurant. Prices drop by 30% at the weekend.

Eating & Drinking

Cukierna Santos (☎ 013 431 5127; ul Staszica 16; cakes & pastries 1.50-10zł; ☼ 8am-8pm) This very popular little bakery and café sells a wide range of pastries, cakes and other sweet and savoury snacks.

Marhaba Bar (☎ 013 420 2492; ul Sienkiewicza 2, enter from the Rynek; mains 6-21zł; ☼ 10am-midnight Mon-Sat, 10am-10pm Sun) This vaguely Turkish-sounding eatery offers generic Middle Eastern favourites such as kebabs, koftas and falafel.

Restauracja Buda (☎ 013 432 0053; ul Jagiellońska 4; mains 11-25zł; ☼ 10am-10pm) This charming Polish-style eatery at the pension of the same name is the best restaurant in town. Check out the snarling stuffed monkey on the bar.

Piwnica Wójtowska (☎ 013 432 1532; Rynek 7; mains 6-30zł; ☼ 10am-9pm) Located in the pleasant vaulted cellar of the Rynek's most beautiful Renaissance building, this pub-restaurant offers a variety of Polish dishes as well as basic international fare (think chicken with chips).

Que Pasa (☎ 013 436 5191; ul Słowackiego 14; ☼ 10am-10pm Sun-Thu, 10am-late Fri & Sat) Popular with Krosno's young bloods, this bar has a large outside terrace perfect for watching the day (or night) come to an end.

Getting There & Away
The train and bus stations sit eyeballing one another 1.5km west of the Rynek.

A dozen or so daily buses head eastward for Sanok (7.40zł, 1½ hours), up to four of which continue to Ustrzyki Dolne (17.40zł, two hours) and two to Ustrzyki Górne (16.60zł, three hours). A dozen fast buses depart daily for Kraków (23zł, three hours), and hourly buses go to Rzeszów (9zł, 1½ hours). There are frequent buses south to Dukla (3.20zł, 45 minutes) and regular buses to Bóbrka (2.80zł, 30 minutes). For Haczów (2.80zł, 40 minutes) count on up to 10 buses a day, most of which terminate at Brzozów.

Most trains cover the Zagórz–Jasło route, which can be used for Sanok (7.50zł, 1½ hours, 10 per day) but not much else. There are trains to Warsaw (55zł, eight hours, three daily) and Kraków (42zł, five hours, two daily).

HACZÓW
pop 1175
The village of Haczów (*hah*-choof), 16km east of Krosno, boasts what is considered to be the largest timber Gothic church in Europe. Built around the mid-15th century on the site of a previous church founded by Władysław Jagiełło in 1388, the **Church of the Assumption of Mary and Michael the Archangel** (Kościół Wniebowzięcia Matki Boskiej i Św Michała Archanioła), on Unesco's World Heritage List since 2003, is also one of Europe's oldest timber churches. The walls and coffered ceiling inside are covered in naive paintings dating from the late 15th century and restored in the 1990s.

You shouldn't wait more than an hour for a bus to Krosno (2.80zł, 40 minutes), which goes via Krościenko Wyżne or Miejsce Piastowe.

BÓBRKA
pop 510
The small village of Bóbrka, 17km southwest of Krosno, is the cradle of the Polish oil industry. It was here in 1854 that the world's first oil

well was sunk by Ignacy Łukasiewicz, inventor of the paraffin lamp (see the boxed text, p288), and one of the country's most ambitious (and unusual) skansens marks the achievement.

Sights
Today the site where Łukasiewicz first hit pay dirt is the open-air **Museum of the Oil and Gas Industry** (Muzeum Przemysłu Naftowego i Gazowniczego; ☎ 013 433 3478; www.bobrka.home.pl in Polish; 38-458 Chorkówa; adult/concession 6/3zł; ☼ 9am-5pm Tue-Sun May-Sep, 7am-3pm Tue-Sun Oct-Apr), established in 1961. It's based on a group of early oil wells, complemented by their old drilling derricks and other rigs collected from around the world. The world's oldest surviving hand-dug oil shaft, named Franek and dating back to 1860, can be seen with crude still bubbling below. The Janina shaft (1878) nearby is still used commercially. In all there are more than 50 pieces of machinery and outbuildings here.

The **Ignacy Łukasiewicz House**, which once served as the oil-industry pioneer's office, contains exhibits relating to the oil and gas industries. The collection of kerosene lamps includes decorative and industrial examples. Note the original map of the Bóbrka oil field with the shafts marked on it; the deepest went down as far as 319m. There are more exhibits in the new **Grand Exhibition Pavilion** at the entrance, as well as a library and archives.

Those who can't get enough of the oil industry will be pleased to hear that there is a **Petroleum Trail** (Szlak Naftowy; www.beskidniski.org.pl) in Krosno and neighbouring counties that can be followed by car or bicycle.

Getting There & Away
From Krosno there are about 10 buses daily to Bóbrka village (2.80zł, 30 minutes), though fewer depart at the weekends. The skansen is at Chorkówa, about 2km north of where the bus will let you off.

DUKLA
pop 2140
Dukla, 19km southwest of Krosno, is close to the Dukla Pass (Przełęcz Dukielska), the lowest and most easily accessible passage over the Western Carpathians. In the 16th century this strategic location brought prosperity to the town, which became a centre of the wine trade on the route from Hungary. Its heyday was in the 18th century, when most of its important monuments were built.

THE BLACK GOLD OF BÓBRKA

Natural oil had been known for centuries in the Krosno region and was used by local people for both domestic and medicinal purposes. But it wasn't until 1854, when Ignacy Łukasiewicz (1822–82) sank the world's first oil well at Bóbrka, that oil exploitation at a commercial level began.

Łukasiewicz, a pharmacy graduate from universities in Lwów (now Lviv in Ukraine), Kraków and Vienna, studied the properties of crude oil and was the first to obtain paraffin oil from petroleum. In 1853 he constructed the world's first kerosene lamp, used in a Lwów hospital to light a surgical operation that urgently had to be carried out one night. A year later he lit the world's first kerosene-fuelled streetlamp at Gorlice.

That same year a local landowner pointed out a site in the Bóbrka forest where substantial amounts of oil accumulated in natural hollows. The first approach to get oil out of the soil was by means of a 120m-long, 1.2m-deep ditch. When that proved ineffective Łukasiewicz began to experiment with vertical shafts. By 1858, four years after initial trials, the new Małgorzata shaft was yielding about 4000L of crude oil a day, a milestone that fostered further exploitation.

More shafts, including Franek, were sunk, and in 1861 a primitive refinery was opened at Polanka. The region prospered from the industry, which reached its peak just before WWI. When larger deposits of crude were discovered elsewhere, the importance of the local oil fields diminished. Exploitation on a small scale continues, primarily to preserve the memory of this far-flung village's role in the discovery of a product that changed the world.

In the autumn of 1944 one of the fiercest mountain battles of WWII was fought around the Dukla Pass, in which the combined Soviet and Czechoslovakian armies crushed the German defence, leaving more than 100,000 soldiers dead.

There's a **Bank PKO** (ul Mickiewicza 1; 8am-3.30pm Mon-Fri) south of the parish church.

Sights

Dukla's large Rynek boasts a squat **town hall** in the centre. Across the Krosno road to the northwest and next to the tiny Dukielska River is the mighty **Parish Church of St Mary Magdalene** (Kościół Parafialny Św Marii Magdaleny), built in 1765. With its glorious pink and white stuccoed and marbled wood interior, it's a fine example of late Baroque and Rococo architecture.

Diagonally opposite the church is the **Historical Museum** (Muzeum Historyczne; ☎ 013 433 0085; Trakt Węgierski 5; adult/concession 6/3zł; 10am-6pm Tue-Sun May-Sep, 10am-3.30pm Tue-Sun Oct-Apr), housed in the decaying 18th-century Mniszech Palace (Pałac Mniszchów). It has a permanent display on the battle of 1944 and some temporary exhibitions; note the number of signs in Czech. In the park surrounding the palace are 20 heavy weapons – tanks, big guns, lorries and fighter planes – from WWII on permanent display.

Sleeping & Eating

Dukla Hostel (☎ 013 433 0886, 013 433 0033; ptsmdukla@op.pl; Rynek 9; dm 17-22zł;) A basic and very central option on the Rynek, this year-round hostel has 40 beds.

Dom Wycieczkowy PTTK (☎ 013 433 0046; Rynek 18; dm 20zł, s/tr 30/75zł; P) The local PTTK offers seven stark rooms with bare-bones facilities, and it also has its own pub and cheap restaurant (open 10am to 10pm).

Getting There & Away

There are about a dozen daily buses up to Krosno (3.20zł, 45 minutes) and four south to Barwinek (4.50zł, 40 minutes), near the Czech border and the Dukla Pass. A bus runs from around April to October along the backwoods route from Dukla to Komańcza (8zł, one hour) and on to Cisna (12zł, two hours), which is a short cut to the Bieszczady. Count on four buses to and from Rzeszów (12zł, two hours).

BIECZ

pop 4650

One of the oldest settlements in Poland, Biecz (pronounced byech) was a busy commercial centre from at least the 15th century. It benefited from the wine-trading route heading south over the Carpathians to Hungary, and some 30 crafts developed here. In the 17th century Biecz began to see its prosperity wane when the plague struck and new trade routes appeared. The sleepy atmosphere seems to have remained to this day, though some important historic monuments and a good museum make the town worth a stop.

There's a **Bank PKO** (Rynek 17; ☉ 8.15am-3.30pm Mon-Fri) on the main square.

Sights

The town's landmark is the **town hall** on the Rynek or, more precisely, its huge 56m-high octagonal **tower** (adult/concession 2/1zł; ☉ 8am-3pm Tue-Sat), which you can climb with a ticket purchased from the museum. The tower, which looks a little like a lighthouse, was built between 1569 and 1581, except for the top, which is a Baroque addition. Its original Renaissance decoration and the unusual 24-hour clock face on its eastern side have been restored in recent years.

West of the Rynek is the monumental **Corpus Christi Parish Church** (Kościół Parafialny Bożego Ciała). This mighty Gothic brick structure, evidence of the town's erstwhile affluence, dates from the 15th century and looks vaguely Flemish. Inside, the chancel holds most of the church's treasures, most notably the late-Renaissance high altar and massive stalls, all from the early 17th century. To the side of the altar is a gilded woodcarving depicting the genealogical tree of the Virgin Mary. Further up is an impressive crucifix from 1639.

Near the church are the remains of the **town walls** and what has become known as **Execution Tower** (Katownia). Biecz was allowed to pass death sentences, and there was even a corporation of executioners who appear to have taken their job pretty seriously. In the year 1614 alone, some 120 brigands were executed here.

Most of the collection of the excellent **Biecz Regional Museum** (Muzeum Ziemi Bieckiej; ☎ 013 447 1093; ☉ 8am-5pm Tue-Fri, 8am-4pm Sat, 9am-4pm Sun May-Sep, 8am-3pm Tue-Sat, 9am-2pm Sun Oct-Apr) is housed in two 16th-century buildings, both close to the church. The so-called **House with a Turret** (Dom z Basztą; ul Węgierska; adult/concession 4/2zł) holds the complete contents of an ancient pharmacy including its laboratory, as well as musical instruments, traditional household utensils, equipment from old craft workshops and a cellar for storing Hungarian wine. The **Kromer Townhouse** (Kamienica Kromerówka; ul Kromera 3; adult/concession 3/1.5zł) has more historical exhibits

on the town's past, plus archaeological and numismatic collections.

Sleeping & Eating

Biecz Hostel (☎ 013 447 1014; ptsmbiecz@o2.pl; ul Parkowa 1; dm 22zł; P ✗) This basic but clean hostel with 130 beds is around 1km from the Rynek. It's on the top floor of a large school building and has only doubles and quads, so provides more privacy than most.

Hotel Restauracja Grodzka (☎ 013 447 1121; grodzka@grodzka.info; ul Kazimierza Wielkiego 35; s 60zł, d 65-70zł, apt 90zł; P) This is a just-acceptable, 16-room, budget option not far from the hostel. It's nothing out of the ordinary, but it does have its own bright and airy restaurant (mains 9zł to 17zł, open 8am to 10pm Monday to Saturday, 10am to 10pm Sunday).

Hotel Centennial (☎ 013 447 1576; www.centennial.com.pl; Rynek 6; s/d/ste 182/161/235zł; P ☐) The somewhat over-the-top Centennial – all swag drapes, chrome and leatherette settees – offers the best facilities in town, including suites of different size and design in two historic burghers' houses. The two singles face the Rynek. The hotel's Restauracja Ogród (mains 8zł to 18zł, open 10am to 10pm) next door serves excellent and reasonably priced Polish food and pizza. The hotel offers big reductions at the weekend.

Getting There & Away

All buses pass through and stop on the northeast and southwest sides of the Rynek. Buses to Jasło (4.50zł, 35 minutes) run regularly but only a few buses continue to Krosno (8zł, one hour). Plenty of buses run to Gorlice (1.80zł to 3.50zł, 30 minutes), and there are a couple of daily departures to Nowy Sącz (9zł, 1½ hours), Nowy Targ (19.50zł, 2½ hours) and Zakopane (26zł, 3½ hours).

Biecz's train station, 1km west of the centre, handles a couple of trains a day to Jasło (9zł, 30 minutes), Nowy Sącz (14.50zł, two hours) and Kraków (34zł, three hours). There's a daily departure for Warsaw (54zł, seven hours).

GORLICE
pop 28,400

Like Bóbrka's, Gorlice's name entered the history books (well, the Polish ones anyway) with the beginnings of the Polish oil industry. In 1853, in the local chemist shop, Ignacy Łukasiewicz obtained paraffin (or kerosene) from crude oil. Gorlice was also the site of a

HIKING IN THE BESKID NISKI

Two main trails cover the entire length of the Beskid Niski range. The trail marked in blue originates in Grybów, goes southeast to the border and then eastwards all along the frontier to bring you eventually to Nowy Łupków near Komańcza. The red trail begins in Krynica, crosses the blue trail around Hańczowa, continues east along the northern slopes of the Beskid, and arrives at Komańcza. Both these trails head further east into the Bieszczady.

You need four to six days to do the whole of the Beskid Niski on either of these routes, but there are other trails as well as a number of rough roads that link the two main trails.

A dozen hostels scattered in small villages throughout the region provide shelter, but most are open only in high summer (July and August). There are also a number of agrotourist farms; these are open for a longer season and sometimes year-round. If you plan on more ambitious trekking, camping gear may be useful. You can buy some elementary supplies in the villages you pass, but you're better off stocking up on essentials before you set out.

The major starting points for the Beskid Niski are Krynica, Grybów and Gorlice from the west; Komańcza and Sanok from the east; and Krosno, Dukla and Barwinek for the central part.

The 1:125,000 *Beskid Niski i Pogórze* map (9zł) from PPWK will give you all the basic information you need for hiking. A more detailed map is Galileos' 1:50,000 *Beskid Niski* (8.90zł).

---

great WWI battle, fought for 126 days from May 1915, which ended with the Austrians breaking through the Russian Carpathian front, leaving 20,000 dead.

The town itself has a few tourist sights but the region to the south was once Lemk territory and harbours some lovely old Orthodox and Uniat churches. Gorlice is a major transportation hub for the region, and the helpful tourist office can provide information.

Information

Bank Pekao (ul Legionów 12; ⊙ 7.30am-6pm Mon-Fri) Opposite the tourist office.

Bank Spółdzielczy (ul Stróżowska 1; ⊙ 7.30am-6pm Mon-Fri, 7.30am-1pm Sat) At the northwest corner of the Rynek.

Post office (ul Węgierska 2; ⊙ 8am-6pm Mon-Fri, 8am-12.30pm Sat) Across the river.

Tourist office (☎ 018 353 5091; www.it.gorlice.pl in Polish; ul Legionów 3; ⊙ 9am-5pm Mon-Fri, 9am-1pm Sat)

Toxic Intonet Café (☎ 018 353 6700; ul Piekarska 5; per hr 3zł; ⊙ 9am-5pm Mon-Fri, 9am-1pm Sat) Internet access; southwest of the Rynek.

Sights & Activities

Gorlice's **Old Town** and its unusual two-tiered, sunken Rynek are perched on a rise above the Ropa River. The **PTTK Regional Museum** (Muzeum Regionalne PTTK; ☎ 018 352 2615; ul Wąska 7/9; adult/concession 5/3zł; ⊙ 9am-4pm Tue-Fri, 10am-2pm Sat & Sun May-Sep, 9am-4pm Tue-Fri Oct-Apr), south of the Rynek, has exhibitions on Lemk ethnography, the oil industry and the battle of 1915.

Gorlice claims to have the world's first kerosene **streetlamp**, dating back to 1854. It's attached to roadside shrine of Christ and an unusual umbrella on the corner of ul Kościuszki and ul Węgierska.

There are more than 100 **WWI cemeteries** around Gorlice. Ask at the tourist office for the brochure *Gorlickie Cmentarze z I Wojny Światowej* (Gorlice Cemeteries from the First World War), which contains illustrations and a simple map.

Gorlice sits at the foot of the mountains and is excellent starting point for **hiking** into the Beskid Niski. Two marked trails, blue and green, start near the tourist office and wend southeast from the town up the mountains, joining the main west–east red trail that crosses the range. And while the town is not the main gateway to the 200-sq-km **Magura National Park** (Magurski Park Narodowy; www.magurskipmn.pl) – that honour goes to Krempna, 44km to the southeast – it is easily accessible from here via Sękowa. The tourist office distributes a useful pack of brochures on the park and its flora, fauna and cultural heritage.

Sleeping & Eating

Dwór Karwacjanów (☎ 018 353 5618; www.gorlice.art.pl in Polish; ul Wróblewskiego 10a; d/tr 80/100zł; P) This is a very attractive fortified manor house whose roots reputedly go back to 1417. Extensively renovated, the building now houses the Małopolska Art Gallery, a cellar pub and four cosy (in every sense) rooms. Rates don't include breakfast.

Dom Nauczyciela (☎ 018 353 5231; oupisgorlice@ up.pl; ul Wróblewskiego 10; s/d 60/85zł; P ✗ 🖵) This central student house, next door to the Dwór Karwacjanów, offers a dozen beds in simple but very clean rooms. It's 100m northeast of the Rynek.

Hotelik Dark Pub (☎ 018 352 0238; www.hotelik .gorlice.pl; ul Wąska 11; s/d/tr 90/130/180zł; P 🖵) This amenable little place next to the PTTK Regional Museum has just three rooms, all with bright modern bathrooms. There is a very popular pub-restaurant (mains 5zł to 20zł, open 10am to 11pm Monday to Saturday, and 2pm to 11pm Sunday) with a covered courtyard downstairs.

There are not many other eating options in Gorlice beyond pizzerias. Two tried and tested ones (small/medium/large pizzas from 3.80/5/7.90zł) are **Café Rose** (☎ 018 352 2053; ul Mickiewicza 10; ☾ 10am-10pm Mon-Fri, noon-10pm Sat & Sun), on the way down to the river, and **Pizzeria Oregano** (☎ 018 352 0070; ul Piekarska 14; ☾ 10am-10pm), southwest of the Rynek in the Old Town.

Getting There & Away

The bus and shuttle-train stations are 1.5km northeast of the Rynek. At least six fast buses go to Kraków (12zł, 2½ hours) every day and there are almost hourly departures for Nowy Sącz (6.50zł, two hours). Buses also go to Nowy Targ (13.60zł, two hours) and Krosno (5zł, 1½ hours) three times a day. Buses run every half-hour or so to Biecz (1.80zł, 30 minutes).

The main railway station is at the village of Zagórzany, 5km to the northeast, which is linked with Gorlice by a shuttle train running back and forth every two or three hours. From Zagórzany, there are a couple of daily trains to Jasło (10zł, 40 minutes) and Kraków (19.50zł, three hours).

AROUND GORLICE

Sękowa
pop 240

Lying in the ethnic borderland between the Poles and the Lemks, Sękowa, 6.5km southeast of Gorlice, was one of the southernmost outposts of Roman Catholicism before the war.

The small wooden **Parish Church of SS Philip and James** (Kościół Parafialny Św Filipa i Jakuba) at the start of the village is an exquisite example of timber architecture and was listed by Unesco as a World Heritage site in 2003. The main part of the building dates back to 1522, though the bell tower and *soboty*, the steep arcading that looks like a veranda around the church, were added in the 17th century. The *soboty*, meaning 'Saturdays', were built to shelter churchgoers from distant villages arriving late on Saturday night in time for Mass on Sunday morning.

The church passed through particularly hard times during WWI when the Austro-Hungarian army took part of it away to reinforce the trenches and for firewood, but careful reconstruction has restored its gracious outline. The interior contains an original baptismal font, a Renaissance altar, and wall paintings and portraits, some by Stanisław Wyspiański. The key is held by the affable priest in the house next to the church. If no-one answers ring ☎ 0696 888 454.

From Gorlice take suburban bus 6 (to Ropica Górna), 7 (to Owczary) or 17 (direct to Sękowa; 2.20zł), get off in Siary and continue in the same direction for 50m until the road divides. Take the left-hand fork, cross the bridge 300m ahead and you'll see the church to your right.

Szymbark
pop 3200

Just a scattering of houses that spreads along the Gorlice–Grybów road, Szymbark, 6.5km southwest of Gorlice, contains the **Centre of Folk Architecture** (Ośrodek Budownictwa Ludowego; ☎ 018 351 3114; adult/concession 7/4zł, free Sun; ☾ 9am-4pm Tue-Sun May-Sep, 9am-3pm Mon-Fri Oct-Apr), a skansen of old peasant cottages in the centre. The biggest building is an impressive fortified manor house from the 16th century, adorned with Renaissance parapets.

Buses on the main east–west road run regularly throughout the day to both Gorlice (1.50zł, 20 minutes) and Nowy Sącz (6.50zł, 50 minutes).

THE BESKID SĄDECKI

Fanning out to the south of Nowy Sącz, the Beskid Sądecki (*bes*-keed son-*dets*-kee) is yet another attractive mountain range where you can hike, sightsee or simply have a rest at a mountain spa like Krynica or Muszyna. The mountains are easily accessible from Nowy Sącz by two roads (Hwy 87 and Hwy 75) that head south along the river valleys, joining

THE CARPATHIAN MOUNTAINS

up with Hwy 971 to form a convenient loop; public transport is good along this route.

The Beskid Sądecki consists of two ranges, the Pasmo Jaworzyny and the Pasmo Radziejowej, which are separated by the Poprad River valley. There are a number of peaks over 1000m, the highest being Mt Radziejowa (1261m).

The Beskid Sądecki was the westernmost territory populated by the Lemks, and a dozen of their charming rustic churches survive, particularly around Krynica and Muszyna. *Beskid Sądecki* maps (scale 1:50,000; 9zł) published by three different firms (WiT, Demart and Galileos) are helpful for both hikers and *cerkiew* peepers.

NOWY SĄCZ
pop 84,300

Nowy Sącz (*no*-vi sonch), the economic and cultural centre of the Sącz region, is a laid-back town with an attractive main square and a few decent attractions, most notably its large skansen. It can also be a good base for further exploration of the surrounding countryside.

Founded in 1292 and fortified in the middle of the next century by King Kazimierz III Wielki, Nowy Sącz developed rapidly until the 16th century, thanks to its strategic position on trading crossroads. As elsewhere, decline in the 17th century gave way to a partial revival at the close of the 19th century. Nowy Sącz grew considerably after WWII, and its historic district has been largely restored over recent years.

Information

Bank BPH (ul Jagiellońska 26; ☒ 8am-6pm Mon-Fri)

Bank PKO (Al Wolności 16; ☒ 8am-7pm Mon-Fri)

C@ffe Internet (☎ 018 443 8433; ul Kościuszki 22; per hr 3zł; ☒ 8am-9pm Mon-Sat, 2-8pm Sun) Internet access.

EMPiK (☎ 018 443 7241; Rynek 17; ☒ 9am-6pm Mon-Fri, 9am-4pm Sat) Maps and English-language books and guides.

Klub Mega (☎ 018 443 4727; 1st fl, ul Kościuszki 3; per hr 3zł; ☒ 8am-10pm Mon-Fri, 10am-10pm Sat & Sun) Internet access.

Main post office (ul Dunajewskiego 10; ☒ 9am-5pm Mon-Fri)

PTTK office (☎ 018 443 7457; Rynek 9; ☒ 7am-3pm Mon, Wed & Thu, 11am-7pm Thu & Fri) Travel agency.

Tourist office (☎ /fax 018 443 5597; www.nowy-sacz .info in Polish; ul Piotra Skargi 2; ☒ 8am-6pm Mon-Fri, 9am-2pm Sat)

Sights

Measuring 160m by 120m, Nowy Sącz's **Rynek** is one of the largest in Poland and is lined on all sides by a harmonious collection of historic houses. The large **town hall**, erected in the middle in 1897, incorporates a number of architectural styles, including Art Nouveau. You'll spot more examples of this style south of the Rynek along pedestrian ul Jagiellońska.

The **Collegiate Church of St Margaret** (Kościół Kolegiacki Św Małgorzaty; ul Św Ducha), a block east of the Rynek, dates back to the 14th century but has undergone many additions and changes since then. The small 15th-century image of Christ on the Renaissance main altar suggests a Byzantine influence. Note the remnants of a medieval fresco of the Last Supper on the column to the left as you enter. At the northern end of the same street is the Jesuit **Church of the Holy Spirit** (Kościól Św Ducha) and its massive cloister.

The 15th-century Gothic building to the south of St Margaret's houses the **District Museum** (Muzeum Okręgowe; ☎ 018 443 7708; www .muzeum.sacz.pl; ul Lwowska 3; adult/concession 6/4zł, free Sat; ☒ 10am-3pm Tue-Thu, 10am-5.30pm Fri, 9am-2.30pm Sat & Sun). The museum is dedicated to religious art, with naive religious paintings and folk-art woodcarvings collected from rural churches and roadside chapels throughout the region. The collection of Ruthenian Orthodox icons, which includes a splendid iconostasis of the 17th century, is especially fine.

Two blocks north of the Rynek is the **former synagogue** (ul Joselewicza 12), built in the first half of the 18th century in Baroque style but remodelled in a neo-Moorish style in the 1920s. Partly destroyed in WWII after some 25,000 Jews from around the region were gathered here and shipped off to Nazi concentration camps, it was restored and now houses the **Synagogue Gallery** (☎ 018 444 2370; admission varies, free Sat; ☒ 10am-3pm Wed & Thu, 10am-5.30pm Fri, 9am-2.30pm Sat & Sun), which presents changing exhibitions and a small permanent display of Judaica.

The remains of the **Royal Castle** (Zamek Królewski; ul Kazimierza Wielkiego), built by Kazimierz III Wielki in the 1350s, are 200m further north. The castle was in use till the early 17th century, when a fire destroyed much of it. You can still see doorways, windows, brick vaults and loopholes.

Another 500m north, on the other side of the Kamienica River, is the **Jewish cemetery**

NOWY SĄCZ

0 — 300 m
0 — 0.2 miles

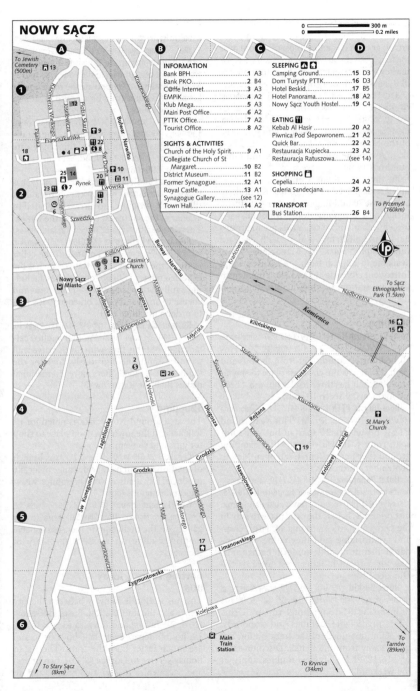

INFORMATION
Bank BPH...................................**1** A3
Bank PKO...................................**2** B4
C@ffe Internet.........................**3** A3
EMPiK.......................................**4** A2
Klub Mega................................**5** A3
Main Post Office.....................**6** A2
PTTK Office..............................**7** A2
Tourist Office..........................**8** A2

SIGHTS & ACTIVITIES
Church of the Holy Spirit.......**9** A1
Collegiate Church of St
  Margaret.............................**10** B2
District Museum....................**11** B2
Former Synagogue................**12** A1
Royal Castle...........................**13** A1
Synagogue Gallery.............(see 12)
Town Hall...............................**14** A2

SLEEPING
Camping Ground....................**15** D3
Dom Turysty PTTK..................**16** D3
Hotel Beskid...........................**17** B5
Hotel Panorama......................**18** A2
Nowy Sącz Youth Hostel........**19** C4

EATING
Kebab Al Hasir **20** A2
Piwnica Pod Ślepowronem....**21** A2
Quick Bar................................**22** A2
Restauracja Kupiecka.............**23** A2
Restauracja Ratuszowa........(see 14)

SHOPPING
Cepelia....................................**24** A2
Galeria Sandecjana...............**25** A2

TRANSPORT
Bus Station.............................**26** B4

To Jewish Cemetery (500m)
To Przemyśl (160km)
To Sącz Ethnographic Park (1.5km)
To Tarnów (89km)
To Krynica (34km)
To Stary Sącz (8km)

Main Train Station

St Mary's Church

St Casimir's Church

Nowy Sącz Miasto

Rynek

(cmentarz żydowski; ul Rybacka), containing a couple of hundred derelict headstones amid overgrown grass. You can see most of it from over the fence, but if you want a closer look, ask for the key to the cemetery gate from the house at ul Rybacka 3, directly opposite the entrance.

Sącz Ethnographic Park (Sądecki Park Etnograficzny; ☎ 018 441 4412; ul Długoszowskiego 83b; adult/concession 10/6zł, free Sat; ⊙ 10am-5pm Tue-Sun May-Sep, 10am-2pm Mon-Fri Oct-Apr), about 3.5km southeast of the centre, is one of the largest and best skansens in the country. Houses and other buildings typical of several ethnic cultures from the Carpathian Mountains and foothills are displayed in 10 groups. All in there are almost 70 buildings and other structures, including a farmhouse, forge, windmill, various churches and so on. Visits are in groups guided in Polish; follow along with *The Sącz Ethnographic Park* by Magdalena Kroh, available in English from the skansen shop. Infrequent city buses 14 and 15 go there from the train station, passing the bus station on the way.

Sleeping

Nowy Sącz Youth Hostel (☎ 018 442 3897; ssmrejtana@ op.pl; ul Reytana 18; dm 17-22zł, tr 66zł; Ⓟ ✗) This 50-bed hostel, equidistant from the bus and train stations, is the cheapest place to stay in Nowy Sącz. It has three triples but most beds are in dorms of six to 10 beds.

Dom Turysty PTTK (☎ 018 441 5012; ul Nadbrzeżna 40; d/tr/q 75/110/150zł; Ⓟ ⓐ) This year-round PTTK hostel is 21 spartan but spic-and-span rooms. It also operates the camping ground (per person/tent 4/7zł, open May to September) next door.

Hotel Panorama (☎ 018 443 7110; htpanorama@ poczta.onet.pl; ul Romanowskiego 4a; s/d/ste 110/176/ 219/310zł; Ⓟ) The recently renovated Panorama, just off the Rynek, is the only place to stay in the Old Town. Its 32 rooms are large, clean and comfortable, and they come with updated furniture and modern bathrooms. Ask for a room looking west towards the Dunajec River.

Hotel Beskid (☎ 018 443 5770; www.orbis.pl; ul Limanowskiego 1; s/d 150/180zł; Ⓟ ✗ ⓐ ⓑ) This uninspiring 81-room hotel run by Orbis offers predictable facilities and standards. It's 300m due north of the train station but quite a way from the Rynek. Discount rates of 116/127zł for singles/doubles apply at the weekend.

Eating

Kebab Al Hasir (☎ 018 440 0580; ul Lwowska 1; mains 3.30-12.40zł; ⊙ 10am-10pm Mon-Sat, 3-10pm Sun) If you just can't handle any more Polish fast food (and we all have our limits), make your way to this Middle Eastern grill opposite the museum for kebabs, *shoarmas* (pita bread with meat and salad) and salads.

Quick Bar (☎ 018 442 1448; ul Piotra Skargi 4; mains 3.50-10zł; ⊙ 9.30am-10pm) Next to the tourist office and just off the Rynek, this small café offers simple Polish fast food. Set lunches are a snip at 9.90zł or 11.50zł.

Piwnica Pod Ślepowronem (☎ 018 443 7921; ul Lwowska 2; mains 6-18zł) This quirky pub-restaurant filled with antiques and curios is located in a cellar at the southeast corner of the Rynek. There's a healthy choice of vegetarian dishes.

Restauracja Ratuszowa (☎ 018 443 5615; Rynek 1; mains 8-20zł; ⊙ noon-11pm) Located in the cellar vaults of the town hall, the Ratuszowa has the expected range of filling Polish dishes, including a full 20 types of *pierogi* – from meat and cheese to strawberry and blueberry. It's best to order a mixture (24zł).

Restauracja Kupiecka (☎ 018 442 0831; Rynek 10; mains 15-40zł; ⊙ noon-11pm) Another vaulted cellar affair, but this time with lovely naive wall paintings and, incongruously, toys for the kiddies, the 'Trader' offers more international dishes than the Ratuszowa.

Shopping

The area around Nowy Sącz is noted for its folk art and the town is a good place to shop for gifts and souvenirs.

Cepelia (☎ 018 442 0045; Rynek 21) This branch of a national chain has a wide range of locally produced folk items as well as ceramics, weavings and religious icons.

Galeria Sandecjana (☎ 018 443 4929; Rynek 12; ⊙ 10am-5pm Mon-Fri, 10am-2pm Sat) This lovely gallery on the main square focuses on naive paintings done on glass, a speciality of the region.

Getting There & Away
BUS

The bus station is midway between the city centre and the train station. Buses to Kraków (16zł, 2½ hours) and Krynica (3.50zł to 6zł, 1½ hours) depart every half-hour or so and are much faster than the train. There's an hourly service to Gorlice (6.50zł, two hours) and Szczawnica (6.70zł, two hours), and up to nine departures to Zakopane (18zł, three hours). Frequent city buses go to Stary Sącz (2.60zł, 20 minutes).

TRAIN

The main train station is 2km south of the Old Town, but city buses run frequently between the two. (The Nowy Sącz Miasto station is much closer to the centre but does not serve destinations useful to most travellers.) There are a few trains to Kraków (34zł, three hours), but buses are more useful for this route. Trains run regularly throughout the day to Krynica (11zł, 1½ hours) and pass Stary Sącz (5.50zł, 10 minutes) on their way. There's a reasonable service to Tarnów (22zł, two hours), with trains departing every couple of hours, and three trains a day to Warsaw (98zł, 5½ hours).

STARY SĄCZ
pop 8950

As the first part of its double-barrelled name suggests, Stary Sącz (*stah*-ri sonch) is the oldest town in the region and owes its existence to 13th-century Princess Kinga, wife of King Bolesław Wstydliwy (Bolesław the Shy), who in the 1270s founded the convent of the Poor Clares here. After the king's death, Kinga entered the convent, where she lived for the last 13 years of her life, becoming its first abbess.

The town's position at the confluence of the Dunajec and Poprad Rivers and on the trade route between Kraków and Buda made it a busy commercial centre, though it gradually lost out to its younger but more progressive sister, Nowy Sącz to the northeast. Today there's no comparison between the two – Stary Sącz is now just a small satellite town, but has been able to preserve much of its old architecture and charm.

Sights

There are not many genuine cobbled market squares left in Poland, but Stary Sącz's **Rynek** is the real thing. The neat houses lining the square are almost all one-storey buildings; for a closer look, walk into the passageway of No 5. The oldest house, at No 6, dates from the 17th century and now contains the **Regional Museum** (Muzeum Regionalne; ☎ 018 446 0094; Rynek 6; admission 3zł; ☷ 10am-5pm Tue-Sun May-Aug, 10am-1pm Tue-Sun Sep-Apr). Its collection of objects relating to the town is reminiscent of a charming old curiosity shop.

The Gothic **Parish Church of St Elizabeth of Hungary** (Kościół Parafialny Św Elżbiety Węgierskiej; ul Kazimierza Wielkiego), two blocks south of the Rynek, dates from the town's 13th-century beginnings but was changed considerably in the 17th and 18th centuries and is now a textbook example of unbridled Baroque, with five large florid altars.

Equally splendid is the **Church of the Poor Clares** (Kościół SS Klarysek; Plac Św Kingi), a short walk east from the parish church. Surrounded by a high defensive wall, this was the birthplace of the town. The church, originally Gothic and completed in 1332, also ended up with opulent Baroque fittings. The traces of its creator are clearly visible: the Baroque frescoes in the nave depict scenes from the life of Blessed Kinga, and her chapel on the south side boasts a 1470 statue of her on the altar. The pulpit (1671) on the opposite wall is an extraordinary piece of art.

Sleeping & Eating

Zajazd Szałas (☎ 018 446 0077; ul Jana Pawła II 77; d 35zł; P) This very basic four-room property with the cutesy name of 'Shed Inn' is smack dab on the Poprad River, 1.5km northeast of town on the way to Nowy Sącz. It has its own restaurant serving inexpensive meals and there is a camping ground, too. Breakfast costs extra.

Motel Miś (☎ 018 446 2451; www.motelmis.pl; Rynek 2, enter from ul Daszyńskiego; s 40-60zł, d 60-80zł, tr 80-100zł; P) This colourful 11-room hostelry on the Rynek's east side has rooms both with and without bathrooms. There's a charming vaulted pub-restaurant and a beer garden covered with rustic canopies made of birch logs.

Restauracja Marysieńka (☎ 018 446 0072; Rynek 12; mains 7.50-22.50zł; ☷ 10am-10pm) Located up the steps of the tallest house in the main square, the Marysieńka is the most pleasant place to eat in town and incorporates quite a nice art gallery within its walls. If the weather is fine, the balcony overlooking the Rynek is *the* spot of choice in Stary Sącz.

Festivals & Events

The town is celebrated for the annual **Stary Sącz Festival of Ancient Music** (Starosądecki Festiwal Muzyki Dawnej; www.festiwal.stary.sacz.pl), held the first week in July.

Getting There & Away

Buses stop in the Rynek. A continuous service to Nowy Sącz (2.60zł, 20 minutes) is provided by both PKS and several city buses, including No 11. The train station is about 2km east of the centre and has a regular service southeast to Krynica (10zł, 1½ hours) and northeast to Nowy Sącz (5.50zł, 10 minutes).

KRYNICA
pop 12,200

Set in attractive countryside amid the wooded hills of the Beskid Sądecki, Krynica (kri-*nee*-tsah), often known as Krynica-Zdrój (Krynica Spa), is Poland's largest spa and mountain health resort. Though the healing properties of the local mineral springs had been known for centuries, the town only really began to exploit them in the mid-19th century. By the end of the century Krynica was a fashionable hang-out for the artistic and intellectual elite and continued to be so right up until WWII. Splendid villas and pensions were constructed during that period, blending into the wooded landscape. Development continued after the war but priorities shifted towards cheap mass tourism, and massive concrete holiday homes and sanatoriums came to occupy the slopes of surrounding hills. Nevertheless, Krynica has managed to retain much of its laid-back, refined atmosphere.

Information

Bank PKO (ul Zdrojowa 1; ❤ 8am-6pm Mon-Fri)
Post office (ul Zdrojowa 28; ❤ 9am-5pm Mon-Fri)
Tourist office (☎ 018 471 6105; www.krynica.org.pl in Polish; ul Piłsudskiego 8; ❤ 9am-5pm Mon-Fri, 9am-1pm Sat) Books accommodation.

Sights & Activities

About 20 mineral springs are exploited in this pretty town and roughly half of them feed the public pump rooms where, for a mere 1zł, the waters can be tried by anybody. The largest of all is the **Main Pump Room** (Pijalnia Główna; ☎ 018 471 2223; Al Nowotarskiego 9; ❤ 6.30am-6pm) on the central pedestrian promenade running parallel to ul Zdrojowa and west of the massive Park Zdrojowy.

There are a number of different waters to choose from in the pump room and displays list the chemical composition of each. By far the heaviest, as you'll notice, is the Zuber, which has over 21g of soluble solid components per litre – a record for all liquids of that type in Europe. It's a sulphurous brew that won't be to everyone's taste.

You'll need your own drinking vessel; a bottle or a plastic cup will do, but if you want to follow local style, buy one of the kitsch porcelain tankards from the water 'bars' themselves, or from the shops downstairs in the pump room. Local practice is to drink the water slowly while walking up and down the promenade.

On a more cultural front, the **Nikifor Museum** (Muzeum Nikifora; ☎ 018 471 5303; ul Bulwary Dietla 19; adult/concession 6/4zł, free Wed; ❤ 10am-1pm & 2-5pm Tue-Sun), located just west of the promenade, displays about 50 works by Epifan Drowniak, better known as Nikifor (1895–1968) and possibly the best-known Polish naive painter. Born in Krynica and Lemk by ethnicity, he produced hundreds of watercolours and drawings that have been exhibited round the world.

You can take a short trip on the **Góra Parkowa Funicular** (Kolej Linowa na Górę Parkową; ☎ 018 471 2262; ul Nowotarskiego 1; adult/concession up 8/5zł, down 5/3zł; ❤ 10am-sunset). The bottom station is near the northern end of the promenade in Park Zdrojowy. The car departs every half-hour or more frequently, depending on the season and the demand. The ascent of 142m takes less than three minutes.

A longer trip can be taken on the modern **Mt Jaworzyna Cable Car** (Kolej Gondolowa na Jaworzynę; ☎ 018 471 3868; ul Czarny Potok 75; adult/concession up 15/12zł, down 13/9zł), which keeps more or less the same hours as the Góra Parkowa funicular. The cable-car system consists of 55 six-person cars that run from the bottom station in the Czarny Potok Valley, about 6km west from the centre of Krynica, to the top of Mt Jaworzyna (1113m). The route is 2210m long and the cable car climbs 465m in seven minutes.

Sleeping & Eating

Krynica has a slew of hotels, pensions and holiday homes – a total of 120 in all. Many places – particularly holiday homes – will offer you half or full board, which can be convenient. There are also plenty of private rooms welcoming guests. The tourist office can arrange private accommodation for around 25/35zł per person without/with private bathroom. Remember that in the high season (July and August, January and February) few owners will be interested in travellers staying just a night or two.

HIKING IN THE BESKID SĄDECKI

Krynica is an excellent springboard for hiking in the Beskid Sądecki. Two marked trails, green and red, head westward from Krynica up to the top of **Mt Jaworzyna**. It takes three hours to walk there by either trail (or you can get there faster by the Mt Jaworzyna cable car, opposite). At the top, you'll get some good views, and may even spot the Tatras on clear days. There's a **PTTK mountain hostel** (☎ 018 471 2171; dm 30-40zł) just below the summit, where you can eat and stay overnight in doubles or cheap dorms, or you can return to Krynica the same day. You can also continue on the red trail northwest to **Hala Łabowska** (1038m), another three hours' walk from Mt Jaworzyna, where you'll find another **PTTK mountain hostel** (☎ 018 447 6453; dm/d 20/60zł) providing cheap beds and food. The red trail continues northwest to **Rytro** (four hours' walk). This route, leading mostly through the forest along the ridge of the main chain of the Beskid Sądecki, is spectacular and easy, and because of the accommodation on the way you can travel light. From Rytro, you can go back to Krynica by train or bus.

BUDGET

Dom Wypoczynkowy PTTK Rzymianka (☎ 018 471 2227; www.halka.ibd.pl; ul Dąbrowskiego 15; per person without/with en suite 40/45zł) The PTTK Rzymianka offers only very basic but comfortable accommodation in 26 rooms. It's up a quiet street about 300m northwest of the tourist office.

Hotel Kasztelanka (☎ 018 471 2945; www.granit .cstnet.pl; ul Piłsudskiego 33; per person 50-70zł; P 🖳) This comfortable and very friendly 33-room hotel is housed in a pretty, vaguely Art Deco building facing Park Zdrojowy, a bit out of the centre. Try to get a room with a balcony. Facilities are minimal but there's an indoor pool (adult/concession 10/6zł, open 9am to 6pm) diagonally opposite on ul Piłsudskiego where you can keep cool or fit or both.

Dom Wypoczynkowy-Leczniczny Jagiellonka (☎ 018 471 5486; jagiellonka@nat.pl; ul Piłsudskiego 8; per person B&B/half board 50/85zł; P ✗ 🖳) This rarest of breeds, a holiday home offering budget accommodation in the heart of Krynica, is a mere 150m north of the tourist office. The 80 rooms offer bare-bones comfort but are tidy, and there's a decent in-house restaurant.

MIDRANGE & TOP END

Pensjonat Witoldówka (☎ 018 471 5577; www.witol dowka-krynica.pl; ul Bulwary Dietla 10; per person 70-150zł; P 🖳) This big wooden hotel looks like a grand Gothic lodge from the outside. It's in a great central location, set along the narrow Kryniczanka River and close to the pump room. The 40 upgraded rooms are comfortable and spacious and there's a bar and restaurant.

Małopolanka (☎ 018 471 5896; www.malopolanka .com.pl; ul Bulwary Dietla 13; s 65-145zł, d 125-185zł, apt 225-315zł; P 🖳 ✗) Just next door to the Nikifor Museum, the Małopolanka is an old-fashioned, somewhat faded 20-room pension and spa dating from the 1930s. It could almost be the setting for an Agatha Christie mystery. Rooms are well equipped (some have hardwood floors) and there's a small spa with sauna, massage and various treatments (goat-milk bath, anyone?). Rates depend on the season and the view.

Ośrodek Panorama (☎ 018 471 2885; www.pano rama.krynica.pl in Polish; ul Wysoka 15; s/d from 110/180zł; P 🖳 🖳) This large, 80-room holiday home, about 500m up the wooded slope east of the tourist office, offers OK standards, but has excellent views and a wealth of fitness and recreational facilities, including a large indoor pool. You may never come down from the mountains.

Hotel Saol (☎ 018 471 5858; www.hotel.saol.com.pl; ul Zdrojowa 16; s 100-120zł, d 200-240zł, tr 270-300zł; P 🖳) This property is one of Krynica's more modern and upmarket hotels. Perched above busy ul Zdrojowa not far from the centre, it offers 82 bright, clean rooms, two of which have fireplaces. Facilities include a sauna, solarium, pub and restaurant.

Hotel Lwigród (☎ 018 472 5800; www.hotel-lwigrod .pl in Polish; ul Nitribitta 6; s 110-150zł, d 195-300zł; P ✗ ♿) Very flash indeed is this newly opened hotel and wellness centre set in a park 150m southeast of the tourist office. Housed in a renovated holiday home dating back to 1928, the hotel has 119 positively shimmering rooms and a spa that will respond to every possible need and/or affliction.

Getting There & Away

The train and bus stations are next to one another on ul Dr Henryka Ebersa in the southern part of town, about 1.2km from the centre.

Buses to Nowy Sącz (3.50zł to 6zł, 1½ hours) run every half-hour to hour. Buses to Grybów (6zł, 50 minutes, six daily) pass through Berest and Polany. There are plenty of buses south to Muszyna (1.50zł, 25 minutes) via Powroźnik, and a fairly regular service to Mochnaczka and Tylicz (2.60zł).

There's a regular train service to Nowy Sącz (11zł, 1½ hours) by a roundabout but pleasant route, passing through Muszyna and Stary Sącz. Half a dozen daily trains go to Tarnów (19.50zł, 3½ hours) and there are several to Kraków (24zł, 4½ hours) as well.

AROUND KRYNICA

The countryside surrounding Krynica, with its beautiful wooded valleys, hills and charming small villages, is worth exploring, particularly for the wealth of old wooden churches still standing. An essential aid for exploring the region is one of the *Beskid Sądecki* maps (see p291), readily available in these parts. Most of the churches – all originally Uniat and Lemk – are accessible by bus, though it's better to be under your own steam in a car or on a bicycle.

To the north of Krynica, 13km and 16km respectively on the road to Grybów, there are good *cerkwie* – that's the plural of *cerkiew* – in **Berest** (1842) and **Polany** (1820). Both retain some of the old interior fittings, including iconostases and wall paintings. Buses ply this route regularly so you shouldn't have problems getting back to Krynica or continuing on to Grybów, from where there's frequent transport west to Nowy Sącz or east to Szymbark and Gorlice.

The 24km loop via Mochnaczka, Tylicz and Powroźnik to the east and south of Krynica is another interesting trip. The 1846 church in **Mochnaczka Niżna** still has its late-17th-century iconostasis, although it's disfigured by a central altar. You can also see the small *cerkiew* 600m down the road towards Tylicz on the other side. Built in 1787, it holds a beautiful tiny iconostasis complete with original icons. If you find the church locked, ask the nuns living in the nearby house to open it. There are several buses from Krynica to Mochnaczka daily, but take an early one if you want to continue along the route.

The next village, **Tylicz**, boasts two churches, a Catholic one and the Uniat *cerkiew* dating from 1743. The latter is used only for funerals. The priest is not eager to open the churches

for visitors, but in July and August he runs a guided tour around their interiors. If you have your own transport head due east for 3km to **Muszynka**, which is almost at the border with Slovakia. The striking *cerkiew* here dates from 1689.

From Tylicz, a spectacular road skirts the Muszyna River valley for 8km to **Powroźnik**, which features yet another *cerkiew*. This one is the oldest in the region (1606) and the best-known. The exterior is beautiful, and inside is an 18th-century iconostasis and several older icons on the side walls. The church can only be visited just before or after Mass, which is held at 7am and 11am on Sunday, and once a day on weekdays: at 6pm on Wednesday and Friday, or at 6.30am on remaining days.

MUSZYNA
pop 5000

Much smaller than its big sister Krynica, 11km to the northeast, Muszyna (moo-*shin*-na) is another spa town that exploits its mineral springs for tourism, and there are a number of old-fashioned sanatoriums in the area.

Information
Bank PKO (ul Kity 1; 9am-4pm Mon-Fri) Southwest of the Rynek.
Post office (Rynek 24; 7am-7pm Mon-Fri, 8am-2pm Sat)
Tourist office (018 477 7922; www.muszyna.pl; Rynek 31; 7.30-11am & 2-3.30pm Mon-Fri)
Vector travel agency (018 471 8003; info@bt vector.com; ul Kity 24; 8am-6pm Mon-Sat year-round, 8am-1pm Sun Jun-Aug) Can provide information, book accommodation and organise tours.

Sights & Activities
Worth a look is the tiny **Regional Museum** (Muzeum Regionalne; 018 471 4140; ul Kity 26; adult/concession 3/1.50zł; 10am-1pm & 2-5pm Mon-Fri May-Sep, 10am-12.30pm Mon-Fri Oct–mid-Nov, 10am-noon Jan-Apr, closed mid-Nov–Dec), in an old inn 300m southwest of the V-shaped Rynek. It displays artefacts and old household implements collected from the area. Otherwise Muszyna has no remarkable sights, though it can be a convenient starting point for trips into the surrounding region. If you can't travel further afield, have a look at the lovely folk houses and gardens lining ul Kościelna, the street running north of the Rynek.

Two **hiking trails** originate in Muszyna and wend their way northward up the mountains.

The green one will take you to **Mt Jaworzyna** (1113m), while the yellow one goes to the peak of **Mt Pusta Wielka** (1061m). You can get to either in three hours, then continue on to Krynica or Rytro. Any one of the *Beskid Sądecki* maps (see p291) has all the details.

Sleeping

Ośrodek Wypoczynkowy Mimoza (☎ 018 471 4023; www.mimoza.pl; ul Nowa 4; per person 20-35zł, full board 35-60zł; **P**) This central 'holiday centre', 300m up from the river, is one of the cheapest places in town. Rooms are fairly plain but they're clean; some have balconies and there are fabulous views.

Pensjonat Jaworzyna (☎ 018 471 4733; www.pensjonat-jaworzyna.pl; ul Polna 24; d/tr 60/90zł; **P**) Jaworzyna is a neat little B&B with 13 modern rooms, on the opposite (northern) side of Muszyna River as you approach the town from Krynica. Keep your eyes open for the narrow bridge beyond the railway tracks and turn right on the other side. Breakfast is an extra 10zł.

Sanatorium Uzdrowiskowe Korona (☎ 018 477 7960; www.sanatoriumkorona.pl in Polish; ul Mściwujewskiego 2; s/d/tr 65/110/220zł; **P** 🖎) Perched on a hill above the Poprad River about 1.5km southwest of the Rynek, this modern hotel-cum-hydrotherapy centre has 120 beds in bright, well-maintained rooms and a good choice of spa treatments.

Hotel Klimek Spa (☎ 018 477 8222; www.hotel-klimek.com.pl; Złockie 107; s/d/tr/ste 300/400/550/700zł; **P** 🍴 🖎 🖵 🖎 🖎) In Złockie, about 3km northwest of the centre of Muszyna, this new 53-room spa hotel is one of the best (and most expensive) places around, with an interminable list of hydrotherapy programmes and treatments on offer, plus a sauna, a steam room and a small water park. You'll also find a well-received restaurant and a pub. Some suites have their own Jacuzzis.

Getting There & Away

Buses to Krynica (1.50zł, 25 minutes) run frequently, and there's also an adequate service to Nowy Sącz (7zł to 9.50zł, 1½ hours). Muszyna is on the rail line linking Krynica (4zł, 20 minutes) and Nowy Sącz (14zł, 1¼ hours), and trains go regularly to both destinations.

AROUND MUSZYNA

Having been in the possession of the bishops of Kraków from 1288 to 1772, Muszyna was traditionally a Polish town; not surprisingly, it has a Catholic church but not a *cerkiew*. The surrounding villages, however, were populated for the most part by Lemks, whose wooden Uniat churches still dot the region. There are at least five within 5km of Muszyna.

Three of the churches are north of the town, at **Szczawnik** (built in 1841), **Złockie** (1872) and **Jastrzębik** (1856). Each boasts its original iconostasis. The *cerkiew* at Złockie has a separate bell tower and is somewhat different in style. The belfry of the Jastrzębik *cerkiew* is home to a colony of lesser horseshoe bats and thus off limits. Krynica suburban buses go via Muszyna to these villages sporadically throughout the day.

Two more wooden churches, in **Milik** (1813) and **Andrzejówka** (1864), are west and southwest of Muszyna and have their original iconostases; you can get there by the regular buses or trains heading for Nowy Sącz. In Andrzejówka, ask for the key in the mustard-coloured house 50m down the road from the church. In Milik, the priest lives in the house at the foot of the *cerkiew*.

THE PIENINY

The Pieniny, the startling beautiful mountain range between the Beskid Sądecki and the Tatras, is famous for the raft trip down the spectacular Dunajec Gorge, which has become one of Poland's major tourist highlights. Yet there's much more to see and do here. Walkers won't be disappointed with the hiking paths, which offer more dramatic vistas than the Beskid Sądecki or Bieszczady, while lovers of architecture will find some amazing old wooden churches here. There's also a picturesque mountain castle in Niedzica, or you can just take it easy in the pleasant spa resort of Szczawnica.

The Pieniny consists of three separate ranges divided by the Dunajec River, the whole chain stretching east-west for about 35km. The highest and most popular is the central range topped by Mt Trzy Korony (Three Crowns; 981m), overlooking the Dunajec Gorge. Almost all of this area is now the Pieniny National Park (Pieniński Park Narodowy), whose headquarters is at at Krościenko. To the east, behind the Dunajec River and south of Szczawnica, lies the Małe

Pieniny (Small Pieniny), while to the west extends the Pieniny Spiskie. The latter outcrop, south of Lake Czorsztyn and including Niedzica, is the lowest and the least spectacular, though the region around it, known as the Spisz, has an interesting blend of Polish and Slovakian cultures.

SZCZAWNICA
pop 7350

Picturesquely located along the Grajcarek River, Szczawnica (shchahv-*nee*-tsah) has developed into a popular summer resort, while its mineral springs have made it an important spa. It's also the disembarkation point for Dunajec Gorge raft trips.

The town spreads for 4km along the main road, ul Główna, and is divided into two suburbs, Szczawnica Niżna (Szczawnica Lower) to the west and Szczawnica Wyżna (Szczawnica Upper) to the east, with the bus station more or less in between. Most of the tourist and spa facilities are in the upper section, which also boasts most of the fine old timber houses.

Information
Bank Spółdzielczy (ul Główna 1; ☯ 7.30am-6pm Mon-Fri, 7.30am-1pm Sat) Next to the PTTK office.
Podhale Tour (☎ 018 262 2727; www.podhale-tour .com in Polish; ul Zdrojowa 3; ☯ 9am-5pm Mon-Fri, 10am-3pm Sat) Organises accommodation.
PTTK office (☎ 018 262 2332; www.pttk.szczawnica.pl in Polish; ul Główna 1; ☯ 8am-4pm Mon-Fri) Organises excursions.
Szewczyk Travel (☎ 018 262 1895; www.szewczyk travel.pl in Polish; ul Zdrojowa 2; ☯ 9am-5pm) De facto tourist office in the centre of town.

Sights & Activities
Try the local version of liquid sulphur at the **Magdalena Jan Pijalnia** (ul Zdrojowa 28; tastings free; ☯ 7am-6pm Mon-Sat, 9am-5pm Sun), the pump room 500m north of Szewczyk Travel.

Szczawnica is a good starting point for **hiking** in both the Pieniny and the Beskid Sądecki ranges. Three trails originate in town and two more begin at Jaworki, 8km to the southeast.

Sleeping & Eating
Accommodation in Szczawnica is the same as in many other mountain resorts: plentiful, usually inexpensive and highly varied depending on the season. There are a few regular year-round hotels as well as a number of small pensions and holiday homes, though most are open in summer only. Plenty of locals also rent out rooms; look for signs along ul Główna and the side streets. Expect to pay from 40zł to 45zł per person for a room with a bathroom (20zł to 30zł without).

Solar Spa Centrum (☎ 018 262 2411; www.solar spa.pl; ul Zdrojowa 4; per person 58-88zł; P ☻) This huge hotel and spa complex, on a hill more or less opposite Szewczyk Travel, has 103 unadorned though spotless rooms in four separate buildings. The list of spa treatments goes on forever. Best of all is the water park complex (Park Wodny; adult/concession from 10/8zł, open 10am to 10pm), with pools and slides and open to nonresidents.

Hotel Batory (☎ 018 262 0207; www.batory-hotel .pl; Park Górny 13; s 90-150zł, d 160-220zł; P ✗ ▯ ☍) This half-timbered hotel dating back to 1874 has had a makeover and is the nicest place in town if you want something on a human scale. The interior décor is a little too standard-issue international, but the 27 rooms are large and airy. The hotel's list of VIP guests includes Nobel laureate Henryk Sienkiewicz, who stayed several times in 1909.

Willa Pokusa (☎ 018 262 0235; ul Zdrojowa 15/16; mains 13-22zł) This restaurant in another wonderful (though new) half-timbered house opposite the Solar Spa Centrum that gets good reviews and offers excellent-value set lunches during the week.

Getting There & Away
Buses to Nowy Targ (7zł, 50 minutes to 1½ hours) depart roughly every hour, as do ones to Nowy Sącz (6.70zł, two hours) via Stary Sącz (5.90zł, 1½ hours). Up to eight fast buses run daily to Kraków (13.50zł, 2½ hours). Buses to Krościenko (2.20zł, 15 minutes) depart frequently.

For the Dunajec Gorge, take a bus (up to four daily in the high season) to Sromowce Wyżne-Kąty (4.40zł, 30 to 40 minutes) – the driver will set you down at the right place. There are also private minibuses that depart when full. Also check with the PTTK, which organises tours to the gorge for 48zł per person.

KROŚCIENKO
pop 3700

A small town at the northern foot of the Pieniny range, founded in 1348, Krościenko is today a local holiday resort that fills up with visitors in summer. Rich mineral springs were discovered here in the 19th century, but the town didn't exploit them and the title of spa went to nearby Szczawnica. But Krościenko remains the number-one hiking base for the Pieniny and is home to the headquarters of the Pieniny National Park.

Information

Pieniny National Park headquarters (Dyrekcja PNP; ☎ 018 262 5601; www.pieninypn.pl in Polish; ul Jagiellońska 107b) West of the Rynek.

PTTK office (☎ 018 262 3059; www.pttk.pl; ul Jagiellońska 28; ☺ 8am-4pm Mon-Fri, 8am-1pm Sat) Books accommodation.

Tourist office (☎ 018 262 3304; www.kroscienko.pl; Rynek 32; ☺ 8am-4pm Mon-Fri) In the town hall.

Sights

Drop into the startling yellow Gothic **All Saints' Church** (Kościół Wszystkich Świętych) at the eastern end of the Rynek to admire the surviving fragments of 14th-century frescoes depicting scenes from the Passion of Christ on the north, south and east walls. Note, too, the Gothic baptismal font and the overblown Baroque gilded pulpit. The long and leafy **Rynek** has some lovely 19th-century wooden buildings, including the **town hall** at No 32.

Sleeping & Eating

Willa Maria (☎ 018 262 6151; www.kroscienko.info; ul Św Kingi 75a; per person 25-30zł; P) On a quiet street 900m south of the Rynek and hard by the Dunajec River, the 10-room Maria is one of the more attractive small hotels in the area. It has a variety of rooms, most with balconies overlooking the river.

Pensjonat Granit (☎ 018 262 5707; www.granit .kroscienko.pl; ul Jagiellońska 70; per person 25-35zł) This delightful 14-room pension just off the main road into town feels like a family home, which is just what it is. There are several others in the immediate area if the 'Granite' is full, but they're not as nice. It has an in-house pizzeria.

Restauracja U Walusia (☎ 018 262 3095; ul Jagiellońska; mains 8-20zł) This is the best restaurant in Krościenko, 800m west of the Rynek along the Nowy Targ road. Specialities include *placki po góralsku* (potato pancakes with goulash), *żurek po pienińsku* (Pieniny-style sour rye soup) and *kwaśnica na żeberkach* (sauerkraut soup with pork spareribs).

Getting There & Away

Buses stop in Krościenko on the southern side of the Rynek. There are regular services to both Nowy Targ (6.50zł, 45 minutes) and Nowy Sącz (9zł, one hour). Buses to Szczawnica (2.20zł, 15 minutes) run every 20 minutes or so. Four buses go to Sromowce Niżne daily (4.50zł, 25 minutes), which is the way to the raft wharf in Sromowce Wyżne (sometimes called Kąty); there are private minibuses that go directly to the wharf in summer. As many as nine buses a day go to Zakopane (11zł, two hours).

DUNAJEC GORGE

The Dunajec Gorge (Przełom Dunajca) is a spectacular stretch of the Dunajec (doo-*nah*-yets) River, which snakes from Lake Czorsztyn (Jezioro Czorsztyńskie) west for about 8km between steep cliffs, some of which are over 300m high. The river is narrow, in one instance funnelling through a 12m-wide bottleneck, and changes incessantly from majestically quiet, deep stretches to shallow mountain rapids. Be advised, however, that this is not a white-water experience but a leisurely pleasure trip.

The gorge has been a tourist attraction since the mid-19th century, when primitive rafts ferried guests of the Szczawnica spa on a day out. Today the raft trip through the gorge attracts hundreds of thousands of people every year, not counting do-it-yourselfers in their own kayaks. The raft itself is a set of five narrow, 6m-long, coffinlike canoes lashed together with rope. It holds 10 to 12 passengers and is steered by two raftsmen, each decked out in embroidered folk costume and armed with a long pole used to navigate.

The raft trip begins in the small village of **Sromowce Wyżne-Kąty**, at the **Raft Landing Place** (Przystań Flisacka; ☎ 018 62 9721; www.flisacy.com.pl; ul Kąty 14; ☺ 8.30am-5pm May-Aug, 9am-4pm Apr & Sep, 9am-3pm Oct, closed Nov-Mar). You'll take an 18km-long trip and disembark in Szczawnica. The journey takes about 2¼ hours, depending on the level of the river. Some rafts go further downstream to Krościenko (23km, 2¾ hours), but there's not very much to see on that stretch of the river.

The trip to Szczawnica costs 35/17.50zł adult/concession, while the one to Krościenko is 44/22zł. You can organise a trip at any travel agency in Zakopane from 71/52zł and in Kraków from 240/220zł, which includes transport, equipment and guides. The

HIKING IN THE PIENINY

Almost all hiking concentrates on the central Pieniny range, a compact area of 40 sq km that now encompasses Pieniny National Park. Trails are well marked and short, and no trekking equipment is necessary. There are three starting points on the outskirts of the park, all providing accommodation and food. The most popular is Krościenko at the northern edge, then Szczawnica on the eastern rim and Sromowce Niżne to the south. Arm yourself with the 1:50,000 *Gorce i Pieniny, Pieniński Park Narodowy* map, which includes a 1:125,000-scale map of the park showing all hiking routes.

Most walkers start from the Rynek in Krościenko. Follow the yellow trail as far as the **Przełęcz Szopka** pass, then switch to the blue trail branching off to the left and head up to the top of **Mt Trzy Korony** (981m), the highest summit of the central range. The reward for this two-hour walk is a breathtaking panorama that includes the Tatras, 35km to the southwest, if the weather is clear. You are now about 520m above the level of the Dunajec River.

Another excellent view is from **Mt Sokolica** (747m), 2km east as the crow flies from Mt Trzy Korony, or a 1½-hour walk along the blue trail. From Mt Sokolica, you can go back down to Krościenko by the green trail in about 1¼ hours, or to Szczawnica by the blue one in less than an hour.

If you plan on taking the raft trip through the Dunajec Gorge, you can hike all the way to Sromowce Wyżne-Kąty, site of the raft landing place. There are several ways of getting there and the park map shows them all. The shortest way is to take the blue trail heading west from the Przełęcz Szopka and winding up along the ridge. After 30 to 40 minutes, watch for the red trail branching off to the left (south) and leading downhill. It will take you directly to the wharf in about half an hour.

tour sponsored by the PTTK in Szczawnica is 48zł.

There are about 250 rafts in operation and they depart as soon as 10 passengers are ready to go. In general you won't have to wait long to get on the raft. Rafts normally operate from April to October; the trips may be suspended occasionally for a day or two when the river level is high.

Just down from the ticket office is a branch office of the **Pieniny National Park** (☎ 018 262 5601; www.pieninypn.pl in Polish; ul Kąty 117b), which keeps the same hours as the ticket office.

Getting There & Away

Sromowce Wyżne-Kąty is serviced by five buses daily from Nowy Targ (10zł, 45 minutes) and, in season, four from Szczawnica (4.40zł, 30 minutes). There's also a seasonal private minibus service from Szczawnica and Krościenko. Another way of getting to Sromowce Wyżne-Kąty is to hike from Krościenko or Szczawnica (see the boxed text, above).

If you have private transport, you'll have to either leave your vehicle in Sromowce Wyżne-Kąty and come back for it after completing the raft trip in Szczawnica, or drive to Szczawnica and leave your vehicle

there, so you'll have it as soon as you complete the trip. There are car parks in both Sromowce Wyżne-Kąty and Szczawnica, and the raft operator provides a bus service between the two locations. The cost from Szczawnica back to the raft wharf is 8/6zł adult/concession.

NIEDZICA
pop 3000

Niedzica, 5km northwest of Sromowce Wyżne-Kąty, is known for its castle. Perched on a rocky hill above the southeastern end of Lake Czorsztyn, the castle was built in the first half of the 14th century as one of the Hungarian border strongholds and was extended in 1601. It remained in private Hungarian hands until the end of WWII. It was partially restored in the 1920s and again 50 years later, but it essentially looks the same as it did in the 17th century, managing to retain its graceful Renaissance shape.

Sights & Activities

The fortress shelters the **Niedzica Castle Museum** (Muzeum Zamkowy w Niedzicy; ☎ 018 262 9480; adult/concession 9/7zł; ⏰ 9am-7pm daily May-Sep, 9am-4pm Tue-Sun Oct-Apr). There's not a tremendous amount to see – some period costumes, furnishings, hunting trophies, a chapel from the late 14th century, and collections on the archaeology and history of the Spisz region – but there are fine views over the lake and surrounding area. An ethnographic section of the museum, including Spisz folk art, is presented in season in an old timber **granary** (spichlerz; admission 2zł; ☺ May-Sep) 150m from the castle. You can also visit the nearby **Coach House** (Powozownia).

Pleasure boats **Biała Dama I** and **Biała Dama II** (☎ 018 275 0121; www.turystyka.wolski.pl) ply the waters of Lake Czorsztyn daily in July and August and at the weekend in May and June. Boats leave the pier at the Harnaś Café beneath the castle to the northwest between 9am and 6pm; the 50-minute trip costs 10/8zł adult/concession. A trip to or from Czorsztyn on the opposite side of the lake costs 4zł.

Sleeping & Eating

Hotel Pieniny (☎ 018 262 9383; www.niedzica.pl; ul Kanada 38; s 55-65zł, d 100-120zł, tr 140-160zł; P 🖳 &) Located halfway between the castle and Niedzica village to the south, this 52-room hotel is a reasonably priced option with plain but comfortable rooms. It also has a tennis court and a sauna, and bikes can be hired for 5/25zł per hour/day.

Hotel Lokis (☎ 018 262 8540; www.lokis.com.pl; Zamek 76; d 180-220zł, tr 240-280zł, apt 280-460zł; P ✗ 🖳) Situated in a wonderful spot overlooking the lake, about 500m from the castle on the road to Nowy Targ, the Lokis is a lovely modern hotel and one of the more attractive places to stay in the Spisz region. It has 23 rooms and a sauna, and there's a big balcony with lake views. Guests can rent bicycles for 15zł a day.

ourpick Zespół Zamkowy (☎ 018 262 9489; shsneed zica@wp.pl; s 200zł, d 180-250zł, tr 200-400zł; ✗ 🖳) Part of the castle has been turned into a hotel, providing 39 beds in 13 rooms, some of which are in the historic castle chambers and decorated with antique furniture. The castle management also offers cheaper rooms (a couple without private bathroom) in the Celnica (double/twin 180/200zł), a fine timber house built in the local style, 200m up the road from the castle. The lovely castle restaurant (mains 9zł to 20zł, open noon to 9pm) is open to all.

Karczma Hajduk (☎ 018 262 9507; Zamek 1; mains 6.50-18.50zł; ☺ 9am-6pm) This little inn, whose name recalls the castle's Hungarian links (the Heyducks were Hungarian mercenaries who fought against the Habsburgs in the 17th and 18th centuries), serves basic Polish dishes right next door to the castle.

Getting There & Away

There are eight or nine buses a day from Nowy Targ (6zł to 4.50zł, 30 to 40 minutes) to Niedzica castle. The village of Niedzica is better serviced from Nowy Targ, with about 10 buses per day, but not all go via the castle. When buying your ticket, make sure to specify 'Niedzica-Zamek' (castle). Bus links between the castle and other towns in the region are sporadic (there are two departures a day to Szczawnica).

CZORSZTYN
pop 310

The village of Czorsztyn (*chor*-shtin), across the lake from Niedzica, boasts **castle ruins** (ruiny zamku; adult/concession 4/2zł; ☺ 9am-6pm May-Sep, 10am-3pm Tue-Sun Oct-Apr) dating from the second half of the 13th century. The fortress was built as the Polish counterpart to the Hungarian stronghold opposite at Niedzica. It's a picturesque ruin: you get to see a 15th-century gatehouse, courtyards and the remains of an old kitchen. Best of all are the excellent views over the lake, the Dunajec River valley and as far as the Tatras. There's a small exhibition on the Pieniny region.

The castle is 2km west of the new village of Czorsztyn (no public transport). The village was built in the 1990s to accommodate residents of old Czorsztyn, further west, which is now flooded by the waters of Lake Czorsztyn. The village is just off the Krośnica–Sromowce Wyżne-Kąty road, accessible by the same buses you take for the Dunajec raft trip at Sromowce Wyżne-Kąty (see opposite).

DĘBNO PODHALAŃSKIE
pop 3000

This small village boasts one of the oldest and most highly rated wooden churches in Poland. The **Church of St Michael the Archangel** (Kościół Św Michała Archanioła) was built in the 1490s on the site of a former church and, like most others, the larch-wood construction was put together without a single nail. The paintings – representing 77 patterns and motifs in 33 brilliant colours – covering the ceiling and most of the walls date from around 1500 and have never been renovated.

A triptych from the late 15th century adorns the high altar, while the crucifix that stands on the Tree of Life rood beam dates from 1380 and was probably transferred from an earlier church. There are some antique furnishings and objects on the side walls, including a wooden tabernacle from the 14th century.

Another curiosity is a small musical instrument, a sort of primitive dulcimer from the 15th century, which is used during Mass in place of an organ. The seemingly illogical thing about it is that the thicker the bars, the higher the notes they produce.

The priest living in the house just across the road at ul Kościelna 42 takes visitors through the church. He expects tourists from 9am to noon and from 2pm to 4.30pm weekdays and on Saturday morning. He will wait until about 10 people turn up, so you may have to wait as well. He can be reached on ☎ 018 275 1797.

THE TATRAS

The Tatras form the highest range of the Carpathians and the only alpine type, with towering peaks and steep rocky sides dropping hundreds of metres to icy lakes. There are no glaciers in the Tatras, but patches of snow remain all year. Winters are long, summers short and the weather unpredictable.

The vegetation changes with altitude, from mixed forest in the lower parts (below 1200m) to spruce woods and stone pine stands higher up (to 1500m), then to dwarf mountain shrubs (to 1800m) and highland pastures (to 2300m). The wildlife is similarly stratified, with deer, roe deer and wildcats living in the lower forests, and marmots and chamois in the upper parts; there is also a small population of bears.

The whole range, roughly 900 sq km, stretches for 60km across the Polish–Slovakian border and is 15km at its widest point. About a quarter of it is Polish territory and forms the Tatra National Park (Tatrzański Park Narodowy), encompassing 211 sq km and headquartered in Zakopane. The Polish Tatras boast two dozen peaks exceeding 2000m, the highest of which is **Mt Rysy** (2499m).

At the northern foot of the Tatras lies the Podhale region, which extends from Zakopane to Nowy Targ. Dotted with small villages populated by *górale* (literally 'highlanders'), the Podhale is one of the few

Polish regions where old folk traditions still form a part of everyday life.

NOWY TARG
pop 34,200

One of the region's oldest settlements, Nowy Targ started life at the foot of the Tatras in the early 13th century. Little of its old architecture survived the 1784 conflagration that all but reduced the town to ashes. Located at the confluence of the Czarny (Black) and Biały (White) Dunajec Rivers, 'New Market' is a busy commercial town and a transport hub on the crossroads between the Tatra, Gorce, Pieniny, Spisz and Orawa ranges.

The town is a possible jumping-off point for travellers wanting to get to the surrounding countryside, though accommodation offerings are poor and there's very little to detain you. You'll find a better selection of lodging options – and a whole lot more to see and do – in Zakopane to the south and even Szczawnica to the east.

Information

Bank Pekao (Al Tysiąclecia 35/37; ⏱ 8am-6pm Mon-Fri, 10am-2pm Sat)

Post office (ul Jana III Sobieskiego 1/3; ⏱ 7am-8pm Mon-Fri, 8am-2pm Sat, 8am-noon Sun)

Sights

The town hall in the Rynek shelters the **PTTK Podhale Museum** (Muzeum Podhalańskie PTTK; ☎ 018 266 7776; Rynek 1; adult/concession 4/2zł; ⏱ 10am-6pm Mon, 8am-3pm Tue-Fri), which features exhibitions related to regional folk art and the history of the region.

One block north of the Rynek is the walled **Parish Church of St Catherine** (Kościół Parafialny Św Katarzyny; ul Kościelna), built in the mid-14th century (the sanctuary still has Gothic features) but extensively reformed in the early 1600s. The interior boasts the usual Baroque overlay. The freestanding **bell tower** was recently renovated.

A bit further northwest, beyond the Czarny Dunajec River, is a cemetery with the shingled **Church of St Anne** (Kościół Św Anny) at its entrance. Local lore has it that it was built by brigands from the Tatras in the 12th century, though it probably went up some four centuries later. The interior is embellished with wall paintings from 1866.

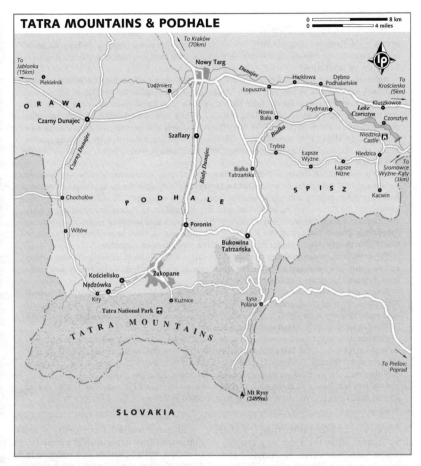

TATRA MOUNTAINS & PODHALE

Nowy Targ's best-known attraction is the **Thursday market**, which has been held here for more than five centuries after the king granted the town the privilege in 1487. But nowadays it's full of mass-produced consumer goods; if you're looking for more traditional items such as hand-knitted sweaters and carved wooden utensils, wait for Zakopane. The market is held on Plac Targowy, a few blocks southeast of the Rynek and facing the Biały Dunajec River.

Sleeping

Dudek (☎ 018 266 2033, 0603 402 033; www.dudek .nowytarg.pl; Al Tysiąclecia 7a; per person 25-60zł; **P**) This popular music club 200m west of the bus station has well-equipped rooms upstairs worthy of consideration for an overnight stay.

Ośrodek Sportowy Gorce (☎ 018 266 2661; www .gorce.nowytarg.pl; Al Tysiąclecia 74; s/d 40/60zł with bathroom, d/tr/q 50/66/88zł with shared facilities; **P**) This simple, 50-bed place a few blocks south of the Rynek has hotel rooms plus four heated cabins. Conditions aren't exactly plush but it's one of the few central places in town.

Getting There & Away

The bus station is about 800m southwest of the Rynek; the train station is about the same distance further along Al Tysiąclecia to the southwest.

All the Kraków–Zakopane traffic passes through Nowy Targ. Buses to Zakopane (4zł to 6zł, 30 to 45 minutes) run frequently. To Kraków, it's faster to go by bus (13zł, two

HIKING IN THE TATRA MOUNTAINS

With a huge variety of trails, totalling around 300km, the Tatras are ideal for walking. No other area of Poland is so densely crisscrossed with hiking paths, and nowhere else will you find such a diversity of landscapes.

Although marked trails go all across the region, the most popular area for hiking is **Tatra National Park**, which begins just south of Zakopane. Geographically, the Tatras are divided into three parts: the West Tatras (Tatry Zachodnie), the High Tatras (Tatry Wysokie) to the east, and the adjoining Belianske Tatras (Tatry Bielskie). All the areas are attractive, though they offer quite different scenery. In general the West Tatras are lower and gentler, and are easier to walk and safer. The High Tatras and Belianske Tatras are completely different: a land of bare granite peaks with alpine lakes at their bases. Hikers will face more challenges here, but will also enjoy much more dramatic scenery.

If you just want to go for a short walk, there are several picturesque and densely forested valleys south of Zakopane, of which **Dolina Strążyska** is arguably the most attractive. It's long been a popular walking and picnic area for locals, and for reasonably fit walkers it should take no longer than 50 minutes to walk all of it by the red trail up to Polana Strążyska. From there you can come back the same way or transfer by the black trail to either of the neighbouring valleys, the **Dolina Białego** to the east being the usual way. It takes around an hour to get to this charming valley and another hour to go all the way down to Zakopane.

The most popular mountaintop climbed in the Tatras is **Mt Giewont** (1894m), the very symbol of Zakopane. You can reach it via the red trail in about 3½ hours from Zakopane. A reasonable level of fitness is required to attempt this climb.

Before you do any walking or climbing, you should get hold of the 1:25,000-scale *Tatrzański Park Narodowy* map (12zł), published by Sygnatura. It shows all the trails in the area, complete with walking times both uphill and downhill. Another option is the 1:20,000-scale *Tatry Polskie* (Polish Tatras) map (8zł), which is divided into two sheets.

You normally won't need a guide for hiking in the Tatras, as trails are well marked, but if you do require this service, the **Tatra Guides Centre** (Centrum Przewodnictwa Tatrzańskiego; ☎ 018 206 3799; www.przewodnik-tatrzanski.pl in Polish; Chałubińskiego 42/44; ☺ 9am-3pm) in Zakopane is able to arrange English- and German-speaking mountain guides for about 330zł per day.

Camping is not allowed in the park, but there are several basic PTTK mountain hostels dotted around the slopes and mountaintops. The tourist office in Zakopane has a list and details.

hours, up to nine a day) as the train (18.50zł, three hours) takes the long way around. Buses to Szczawnica (7zł, 50 minutes) run roughly every hour. There are two daily buses to Niedzica castle (6zł, 30 minutes), via the village of Niedzica.

ZAKOPANE
pop 27,200

Nestled in the foothills of the Tatras, Zakopane is the most fashionable mountain resort in Poland and the country's winter-sports capital. Although Zakopane is essentially a base or springboard for skiing or hiking in the Tatras, the attractive town is an enjoyable enough place to hang about for a while, with a fair number of sights and plenty of facilities. It may resemble a tourist trap at times, but it also has a relaxed, laid-back vibe that makes it a great place to visit.

Zakopane moved from being a small mountain village in about 1870, when it began to attract writers, artists and composers in search of inspiration. Among them were the composer Karol Szymanowski and the writer and painter Stanisław Ignacy Witkiewicz, better known as Witkacy. The father of the latter, Stanisław Witkiewicz (1851–1915), based his so-called Zakopane style of architecture on traditional houses and outbuildings in the area. Some of the buildings he designed still stand to this day and can be visited.

Zakopane grew at a faster pace in the interwar period, and shortly before the outbreak of WWII the town's prime attractions – the cableway and funicular railway – were built. Development continued after the war but it's still reasonably small. Overall Zakopane feels more like an overgrown village than a town, its mainly villa-type houses set informally in their own gardens.

Orientation

Zakopane sits at an altitude of 850m at the foot of Mt Giewont (1894m), which, locals say, resembles the profile of a sleeping giant. The bus and train stations are opposite one another in the northeast part of town. From here, ul Kościuszki leads 800m or so southwest to the pedestrian ul Krupówki, the heart of town and always jammed with strollers.

The funicular to Mt Gubałówka is just beyond the northwestern end of Krupówki. The cable car to Mt Kasprowy Wierch is at Kuźnice, 3km to the southeast.

Information

BOOKSHOPS

Księgarnia Górska (☎ 018 201 2481; ul Zaruskiego 5; ☺ 10am-6pm Mon-Sat year-round, daily Jul & Aug) In the Dom Turysty PTTK, with the best choice of maps and guidebooks on the Tatras.

INTERNET ACCESS

Cyber-Net (☎ 018 201 4040; ul Kościuszki 24a; per hr 4.50zł; ☺ 7am-10pm) Next to the bus station.
Widmo (☎ 018 206 4377; ul Gen Galicy 6; per 30/60min 3/5zł; ☺ 7.30am-midnight Mon-Fri, 9am-midnight Sat & Sun)

INTERNET RESOURCES

Zakopane Life (www.zakopane-life.com) Interactive information portal on every aspect of life and tourism in Zakopane.

LAUNDRY

Pralnia Ekologiczna (☎ 018 206 3637; ul Gen Galicy 8)

MONEY

Bank BPH (ul Krupówki 19; ☺ 8am-6pm Mon-Fri)
Bank Pekao (Al 3 Maja 5; ☺ 8am-6pm Mon-Fri, 9am-1pm Sat)

POST OFFICE

Main post office (ul Krupówki 20; ☺ 7am-8pm Mon-Fri, 8am-2pm Sat year-round, 8am-6pm Sat Jul–mid-Sep & mid-Jan–Feb)

TOURIST INFORMATION

Tourist office (☎ 018 201 2211; www.zakopane.pl; ul Kościuszki 17; ☺ 8am-6pm year-round, 8am-8pm Jan, Feb & Jul-Sep)
Tatra National Park headquarters (Tatrzański Park Narodowy; ☎ 018 202 3288; www.tpn.pl in Polish; ul Chałubińskiego 42/44; ☺ 7am-3pm Mon-Fri)

TRAVEL AGENCIES

Orbis Travel (☎ 018 201 5051; www.orbis.pl; ul Krupówki 22; ☺ 9am-6pm Mon-Fri, 9am-4pm Sat) organises accommodation in private homes. Other useful travel agencies include **Tatra Tourist Centre** (Centrum Turystyki Tatry; ☎ 018 201 3744; www.cttatry.pl; 1st fl, ul Krupówki 50; ☺ 9am-6pm Mon-Fri, 9am-2pm Sat), **Strama** (☎ 018 200 1386; www.nosal.pl; ul Krupówki 58; ☺ 9am-9pm) and **Trip** (☎ 018 202 0200; www.trip.pl; ul Tetmajera 18; ☺ 9am-5pm Mon-Fri, 9am-1pm Sat). They all arrange accommodation, sell transportation tickets and have tours to popular regional destinations, including the Dunajec Gorge (p301).

Sights

Tatra Museum (Muzeum Tatrzańskie; ☎ 018 201 5205; ul Krupówki 10; adult/concession 6/5zł, free Sun; ☺ 9am-5pm Wed-Sat, 9am-3pm Sun), the big wooden pile above the pedestrian mall, has sections on regional and natural history, ethnography and geology, and is a good introduction to the region.

At the northern end of ul Krupówki is the neo-Romanesque **Parish Church of the Holy Family** (Kościół Najświętszej Rodziny), which looks as though it has been imported from suburban Boston in the USA. It was built at the end of the 19th century when the wooden **Old Church** (Stary Kościół; ul Kościelska), 200m to the west and dating from 1851, could no longer cope with the numbers of worshippers. The Old Church has charming carved wooden decorations and pews, and Stations of the Cross painted on glass.

The **stone chapel** standing beside the Old Church is about 30 years older and is in fact the oldest extant structure in Zakopane. Just behind it is the **old cemetery**, with a number of amazing wooden tombs, some dating back to the mid-19th century and resembling giant chess pieces.

Some 300m to the southwest and on the same road is the **Villa Koliba**, completed in 1893 and Witkiewicz's first design in 'Zakopane style'. It now houses the **Museum of Zakopane Style** (Muzeum Stylu Zakopiańskiego; ☎ 018 201 3602; ul Kościeliska 18; adult/concession 5/4zł; ☺ 9am-4.30pm Wed-Sat, 9am-3pm Sun), which examines that school of design through architectural drawings and models as well as interior furnishings.

About 500m to the southeast is **Villa Atma**, the home of Karol Szymanowski from 1930 to 1935. Today it's the **Karol Szymanowski Museum** (Muzeum Karola Szymanowskiego; ☎ 018 206 3493; ul Kasprusie 19; adult/concession 5/3zł, free Sun; ☺ 10am-4pm Tue-Thu & Sat, 10am-6pm Fri, 10am-3pm Sun).

THE CARPATHIAN MOUNTAINS

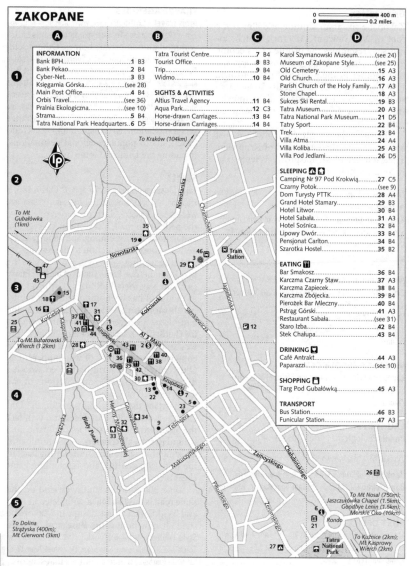

ZAKOPANE

0 — 400 m
0 — 0.2 miles

To Kraków (104km)

To Mt Gubałówka (1km)

Nowotarska

Nowotarska

Chramcówki

Train Station

Jagiellońska

To Mt Butorowski Wierch (1.2km)

Kościeliska

Kościuszki

Sienkiewicza

Krupówki

Al 3 Maja

Zamoyskiego

Chałubińskiego

Krupówki

Heleny Modrzejewskiej

Chramcówki

Tetmajera

Makuszyńskiego

Piłsudskiego

Żeromskiego

To Mt Nosal (750m);
Jaszczurówka Chapel (1.5km);
Goodbye Lenin (1.5km);
Morskie Oko (10km)

To Kuźnice (2km);
Mt Kasprowy Wierch (2km)

Rondo

To Dolina Strążyska (400m);
Mt Giewont (3km)

Tatra National Park

Biały Potok

Strążyska

Just under 2km southeast and next to the large roundabout is the **Tatra National Park Museum** (Muzeum Tatrzańskiego Parku Narodowego; ☎ 018 206 3203; ul Chałubińskiego 42a; admission free; ☿ 8am-3pm Mon-Sat), with displays on local flora and fauna and the natural history of the park.

A short walk northeast up the hill takes you to **Villa Pod Jedlami**, another splendid

Zakopane-style house built in 1897 for the Pawlikowski family (interior closed to the public). But Witkiewicz's greatest achievement is **Jaszczurówka Chapel** (Kaplica w Jaszczurówka), built in 1907 and about 1.5km further east. The folk interior alone is worth the trip.

The emerald-green lake called **Morskie Oko** (Eye of the Sea), about 12km southeast of

Zakopane, is a popular day trip. Buses and minibuses regularly depart from ul Kościuszki for Polana Palenica (30 minutes), from where a 9km-long road continues uphill to the lake. Cars, bikes and buses are not allowed up this road, so you'll have to walk (allow about two hours each way). Alternatively, take a horse-drawn carriage (about 40zł) to within 2km of the lake. The last minibus to Zakopane returns between 5pm and 6pm. Most travel agencies organise day trips here (from 140zł).

Activities

CYCLING

Cycling can be a pleasant and convenient means of getting around the Zakopane region, including some of the less-steep parts of the Tatras. Bikes are permitted only on designated routes in Tatra National Park. These include the Dolina Chochołowska and Dolina Suchej Wody, both picturesque and attractive for biking. Droga Pod Reglami, the service road that marks the northern boundary of the park, also offers some good riding. Note that the access road to Morskie Oko is not open to cyclists; they can go only as far as the car park at Polana Palenica.

Bicycles are available for hire from a number of companies in Zakopane, including **Tatry Sport** (☎ 018 201 4423; ul Piłsudskiego 4; ⏰ 10am-6pm) and **Trek** (☎ 018 201 2555; ul Tetmajera 8; ⏰ 10am-8pm). Expect to pay from 10/40zł per day/week.

SKIING

Zakopane is Poland's capital of winter sports. The town's environs have a number of ski areas, ranging from flat surfaces for cross-country touring to steep slopes – suitable for everyone from beginners to advanced – served by 50 ski lifts and tows in all.

Mt Kasprowy Wierch (1985m) offers some of the most challenging ski slopes in the area, as well as the best conditions, with the spring skiing season sometimes extending as late as early May. You can get to the top in 20 minutes by **cable car** (return adult/concession 30/20zł; ⏰ 7am-9pm Jul-Aug, 7.30-5pm Mar-Jun & Sep-Oct, 8am-4pm Nov-Feb), then stay in the mountains and use the two chairlifts, in the Goryczkowa and Gąsienicowa valleys, on both sides of Mt Kasprowy. The view from the top is spectacular (clouds permitting) and you can stand with one foot in Poland and the other in Slovakia.

Mt Gubałówka is another popular skiing area and it, too, offers some pistes and good conditions. It's easily accessible from central Zakopane by **funicular** (one way/return adult 8/14zł, concession 6/10zł; ⏰ 8am-10pm Jul & Aug, 8.30am-7.30pm Sep, 8.30am-6pm Apr, May & Oct-Dec, 7.30am-10pm Jan-Mar, 9am-8pm Jun), covering the 1298m-long route in 3½ minutes and climbing 300m from the lower station just north of ul Krupówki. An all-day pass for skiers costs 70zł; a one-day pass at other times for 10 rides costs 50zł.

Some 2km to the west is **Mt Butorowski Wierch**, with its 1.6km-long chairlift making it yet another good skiing area.

One more major ski area is at the slopes of **Mt Nosal**, on the southeastern outskirts of Zakopane. Facilities include a chairlift and a dozen T-bars.

Ski-equipment hire is available from outlets throughout Zakopane, including **Tatry Sport** (☎ 018 201 4423; ul Piłsudskiego 4; ☎ 10am-6pm) and **Sukces Ski Rental** (☎ 018 206 41 97; ul Nowotarska 39). Complete kits for skiing/snowboarding average 35/40zł a day.

OTHER ACTIVITIES

A half-hour whirl around Zakopane in a **horse-drawn carriage** (or, in winter, a sleigh) seating four people will set you back from 40zł. They gather near Tatry Sport on ul Piłsudskiego.

The **Altius Travel Agency** (☎ 018 201 53 99; www.horsebacktouring.com; ul Piłsudskiego 4) offers horse riding, as well as riding holidays and excursions into the surrounding countryside.

An excellent place to cool off on a warm summer's day is **Aqua Park** (☎ 018 200 1122; www.aquapark.zakopane.pl; ul Jagiellońska 31; per hr/day adult 16/80zł, child 9/50zł; ⏰ 8am-10pm), with indoor and outdoor pools, slides, various saunas and – incongruously – bowling.

Festivals & Events

The **International Festival of Mountain Folklore** (Międzynarodowy Festiwal Folkloru Ziem Górskich; www.zakopane.pl) held in August is the town's leading cultural event. In June and July, a series of **piano concerts** (usually 35zł) presenting the music of Karol Szymanowski and other composers is held in the Villa Atma.

Sleeping

Zakopane has no shortage of places to stay and, except for occasional peaks, finding a bed is no problem. Even if the hotels and hostels are full, there will always be private

THE CARPATHIAN MOUNTAINS

rooms around, which provide some of the most reasonable and best-value accommodation in town. Check at the tourist office for details (rooms should cost around 40zł to 50zł per person) or look for signs reading 'pokoje', 'noclegi' or 'zimmer frei' outside private homes.

As with all seasonal resorts, accommodation prices in Zakopane fluctuate between the high and low seasons, peaking in late December, January and February, and then again in July and August. Prices given here are for the high season.

BUDGET

Szarotka Hostel (☎ 018 201 3618; www.szarotkaptsm .republika.pl; ul Nowotarska 45g; dm/d 35/100zł) This friendly and homely place with 62 beds gets packed in the high season and is on a busy road. But it's friendly and there's a kitchen and washing machine on site.

Goodbye Lenin (☎ 018 200 1330; www.goodbyelenin .pl; ul Chłabówka 44; dm 30-50zł, d 110-120zł) A branch of the popular Kraków hostel, this five-room place with 30 beds in a century-old farmhouse is as chilled a place as you'll find. The welcome is warm, the barbecues free and the mountain views priceless. It's 2.5km southeast of the centre; the hostel will pick you up from the stations or you can take any bus headed for Morskie Oko and Polana Palenica.

Dom Turysty PTTK (☎ 018 206 3281; www.domturysty .z-ne.pl; ul Zaruskiego 5; with bathroom s 55-70zł, d 100-140zł, with shared bathroom d 60-80zł, tr 75-105zł; P □) The very central PTTK hostel has 350 beds in lots of rooms of different sizes, including 'suites' for up to five people. It can often be swamped with school excursion groups.

Camping Nr 97 Pod Krokwią (☎ 018 201 2256; www.podkrokwia.pl in Polish; ul Żeromskiego 34; camping per person/tent 12/12zł, beds in bungalows 40-45zł; P) The camping ground has large heated bungalows, each containing several double and triple rooms. They are often full in the July/ August period. To get here from the bus/train stations, take any bus heading south and get off at the roundabout.

MIDRANGE & TOP END

Pensjonat Carlton (☎ 018 201 4415; www.carlton .pl; ul Grunwaldzka 11; s 65-90zł, d 130-190zł; P □) This 21-room pension in a grand old house away from the main drag features light-filled rooms with modern furniture. There's an impressive shared balcony overlooking the road, a big comfy lounge lined with potted plants, and lovely grounds.

Lipowy Dwór & Hotel Sośnica (☎ 018 206 6796; www.lipowydwor.gat.pl; ul Heleny Modrzejewskiej 7; s 60-170zł, d 180-220zł, apt 250-380zł; P ☒ □ ☑) On a quiet street south of the centre and opposite one another, these sister hotels could not be more different. The Lipowy Dwór is a charming, wooden, chalet-style hotel with 15 small, well-maintained rooms. The larger Sośnica, with all the facilities (including reception), is a little dated, but some of the 38 rooms have been renovated and have mountain views.

Hotel Sabała (☎ 018 201 5092; www.sabala.zakopane .pl; ul Krupówki 11; s 245-295zł, d 320-390zł, ste from 660zł; P □ ☑ ☒) Built in 1894 but thoroughly up to date, this striking timber hotel has a superb location overlooking the picturesque pedestrian thoroughfare. The hotel offers 51 cosy, attic-style rooms, and there's a sauna, solarium and swimming pool.

Czary Potok (☎ 018 202 0204; www.czarnypotok .pl; ul Tetmajera 20; s/d from 250/350zł; P □ ☑) The 'Black Stream', set upon a pretty brook amid lovely gardens, is a 36-room pensionlike hostelry along a quiet street just south the pedestrian mall. It has a great fitness centre with two saunas.

Grand Hotel Stamary (☎ 018 202 4510; www.stamary .pl; ul Kościuszki 19; s/d/ste 340/440/690zł; P ☒ □ ☑ ☒) As posh as a hotel as you'll find in the Tatras, this massive 54-room gingerbread house was the bee's knees when it opened in 1905 and is just that now after a total makeover. The emphasis here is on style and health; the spa/wellness centre is among most attractive and best equipped we've seen in Poland.

Hotel Litwor (☎ 018 202 4200; www.litwor.pl; ul Krupówki 40; s/d 450/600, ste 625-840zł; P □ ☑ ☒) This is a sumptuous four-star place, with large, restful rooms and all the usual top-end facilities, including a gym and sauna. It has an excellent restaurant serving traditional Polish dishes.

Eating

Pierożek Bar Mleczny (☎ 018 206 6257; ul Weteranów Wojny 2; mains 2.50-7zł; ⏱ 9am-8pm) Set in a little wood cabin with folk décor just off the main pedestrian street, this place serves the best *pierogi* in Zakopane.

Bar Smakosz (☎ 018 206 4049; ul Krupówki 22; mains 5.90-11.90zł; ⏱ 8am-9pm) Serving Polish fast food at its most basic and cheapest, the ironically named 'Gourmet' is for early birds at both ends of the day.

Pstrąg Górski (☎ 018 206 4163; ul Krupówki 6; mains 12-28zł; ☺ 9am-10pm) This self-service fish restaurant, done up in traditional style and overlooking a narrow stream, serves some of the freshest trout, salmon and sea fish in town. It's excellent value.

Karczma Zbójecka (☎ 0512 351 739; ul Krupówki 28; mains 12-36zł; ☺ 10am-midnight) An attractive basement eatery, this place offers regional dishes and meats grilled on a huge wood-burning rotisserie. There's always a buzzy atmosphere and decent local folk music on some evenings.

Restaurant Sabała (☎ 018 201 5092; ul Krupówki 11; mains 12-45zł; ☺ 10am-midnight) This delightful candlelit restaurant at the hotel of the same name (opposite) serves both local specialities and international favourites. The views up and down the pedestrian street below are enviable.

Karczma Czarny Staw (☎ 018 201 3856; ul Krupówki 2; mains 16-31zł; ☺ 10am-midnight) Though under the same management as Zbójecka, the 'Black Pond' is more upmarket. It offers a tasty range of Polish dishes, including fish, much of it cooked before your very eyes on the central grill. There's a good salad bar, with home-preserved vegetables and mushrooms.

A large number of the traditional (and similar-looking) restaurants lining ul Krupówki are owned by the same group and offer the exact same *jadło karpackie* (Carpathian cuisine), accompanied by rather hokey alpine music performed by a *kapela góralska* (folk-music ensemble). Still, there are a few diamonds in the rough: try any of the following.

Karczma Zapiecek (☎ 018 201 5699; ul Krupówki 43; mains 10-22zł) Arguably the pick of the lot, with great food, old stove and terrace.

Staro Izba (☎ 018 201 3391; ul Krupówki 28; mains 14-35zł) Serves lots of excellent lamb dishes, including *kiełbasa* (Polish sausage) and *kwaśnica*, a kind of sauerkraut soup.

Stek Chałupa (☎ 018 201 5918; ul Krupówki 33; mains 12-33zł) Good for grilled sausages and steaks in all their guises.

Drinking & Entertainment

Paparazzi (☎ 018 206 3251; ul Gen Galicy 8; ☺ 4am-1pm Mon-Fri, noon-1am Sat & Sun) This branch of the popular chain with a media theme keeps both the après-ski crowd and tourists well lubricated into the wee hours. Great cocktails – try anything mixed with *miód pitny* (mead).

Café Antrakt (☎ 018 201 7302; ul Krupówki 6; ☺ 11am-midnight) A mellow venue for an alcoholic or caffeine-laden drink, hidden away above a mineral shop with an ambient old-meets-new décor. It occasionally hosts live jazz.

Shopping

Targ Pod Gubałówką (☺ 9am-5pm) This large market at the northern end of ul Krupówki and in front of the funicular's lower station is the place to come for woollen goods and knits, handicrafts such as carved wood kitchen utensils, cheap clothing and food. This is also the place to try *oscypki*, the round and stamped sheep's cheese that comes plain or smoked.

Getting There & Away

Most regional routes are covered by bus. The train is better for long-distance travel (eg to Warsaw).

BUS

Fast buses run to Kraków (16zł, two hours) run every 30 to 40 minutes. There are also two private companies, **Trans Frej** (www.trans-frej.com.pl) and **Szwagropol** (www.szwagropol.pl), that run services roughly hourly to Kraków (15zł, 1¾ hours), departing from the front of the Grand Hotel Stamary at ul Kościuszki 19. There are two daily buses to Nowy Sącz (18zł, three hours) and daily buses to Przemyśl (38zł, 4½ hours), Rzeszów (38zł, 4½ hours), Łódź (48zł, six hours), Katowice (28zł, three hours) and Nowy Targ (4zł, 30 minutes). There are also two direct buses to Sromowce Wyżne-Kąty (8zł, 1½ hours) for the Dunajec Gorge raft trip in summer.

In the region around Zakopane, bus transport is relatively frequent. PKS buses can take you to the foot of the Kościeliska and Chochołowska valleys, as well as to Polana Palenica (5zł), the gateway to Morskie Oko. There are also private minibuses that ply the most popular tourist routes, including Gubałówka (3zł), Polana Palenica (6zł) and Poprad (17zł), departing across the road from the bus station.

TRAIN

There are a number of trains to Kraków (19.50zł, 3½ hours), but buses are faster and more frequent. One train (a few more in the high season) runs daily to Warsaw (100zł, 6½ hours).

Silesia

Occupying the whole of southwestern Poland, Silesia, or Śląsk (pronounced shlonsk) in Polish, can claim both the most tumultuous history and the most distinct identity of all the country's regions. The area was defined long before the modern-day Polish state, and parts now fall within the borders of Germany and the Czech Republic. Most of Polish Silesia is comprised of the *voivodeships* (provinces) of Upper Silesia (Górny Śląsk), whose major city is industrial Katowice, and Lower Silesia (Dolny Śląsk), the capital of which is picturesque Wrocław. The names refer to altitude rather than geographical location.

The culture of Silesia is not the result of continuous development, but rather the last vestiges of a stronger regional tradition largely obliterated by forced population shifts after WWII. Silesia had a German majority throughout much of its history, and memories of those communities and their mass 'repatriation' still linger. Wrocław is a historical gem and well worth a visit. But the real draw is the Sudetes Mountains, a strip of natural beauty and idyllic resort towns stretching along the Czech border, and a boon to hikers, bikers and spa fans alike.

The rich history of the region underpins its charm, with architecture ranging from medieval fortresses to Baroque cathedrals. Importantly, this is the site of the Auschwitz-Birkenau extermination camp complex, a grim memorial that has been listed as a Unesco World Heritage site (1979) and is compulsory viewing. Silesia may afford plenty of opportunities for fun and relaxation, but it also takes a glimpse at the dark side to appreciate the significance of this once-turbulent corner of Europe.

HIGHLIGHTS

- Getting out and about on the lively streets of **Wrocław** (p325) after dark

- Eyeballing cranium after cranium at the macabre **Chapel of Skulls** (p343) near Kudowa-Zdrój

- Visiting the tranquil and phenomenally con-structed **Church of Peace** (p329) in Świdnica

- Ogling the frescoed ceiling and opulent Baroque decoration in the Princes' Hall at the **Cistercian monastery** (p327) at Lubiąż

- Hiking along the red trail linking Mt Szrenica with Mt Śnieżka in **Karkonosze National Park** (p336)

- Observing a moment's silence at the harrow-ing but must-see Nazi extermination camp at **Auschwitz-Birkenau** (p357) in Oświęcim

- Reliving the past at the wonderful **skansen** (p363) near Opole

- Splashing about on a hot day in the artificial lake at **Nysa** (p351)

Karkonosze National Park ★
★ Lubiąż
★ Wrocław
Świdnica ★
★ Opole
Kudowa-Zdrój ★
★ Nysa
Oświęcim ★

- POPULATION: 7.5 MILLION | - AREA: 45,000 SQ KM

WROCŁAW

pop 638,000

Everyone loves Wrocław (*vrots*-wahf) and it's easy to see why. A more manageable Kraków, with all the cultural attributes and entertainment, the capital of Lower Silesia has a character all its own.

Having absorbed Bohemian, Austrian and Prussian influences, the city has a unique architectural and cultural make-up, best seen in its magnificent market square. Wrocław's location on the Odra River, with its 12 islands, 130 bridges and riverside parks, is idyllic, and the beautifully preserved ecclesiastical district is a treat for lovers of Gothic architecture. Fans of Wrocław are in good company. Pablo Picasso said he found the postwar reconstruction of the city a powerful inspiration on a visit in 1948, and the British historians Norman Davies and Roger Moorhouse used Wrocław as the model for their highly readable *Microcosm: A Portrait of a Central European City* (2003).

But Wrocław is not just a pretty face. It is Poland's fourth-largest city and the major industrial, commercial and educational centre for the region; virtually everything in southwestern Poland starts, finishes or is taking place in Wrocław. At the same time it is a lively cultural centre, with several theatres, some major festivals, rampant nightlife and a large student community.

HISTORY

Wrocław was originally founded on Cathedral Island (Ostrów Tumski). The first recorded Polish ruler, Duke Mieszko I, brought the town, together with most of Silesia, into the Polish state. It must have been a fair-sized settlement by the turn of the first millennium, as it was chosen, along with Kraków and Kołobrzeg, as one of the Piast Poland's three bishoprics.

During the period of division in the 12th and 13th centuries, Wrocław was the capital of one of the principalities of the Silesian Piasts. Like most settlements in southern Poland, Wrocław was burned down by the Tatars. The town centre was then moved to the river's left bank.

Wrocław continued to grow under Bohemian administration (1335–1526), reaching perhaps the height of its prosperity in the 15th century and maintaining trade and cultural links with the Polish Crown. This speedy development led to the construction of new fortifications at the beginning of the 16th century, and the remains of the Fosa Miejska (City Moat) show where they were once positioned.

The Habsburgs, who ruled the city for the next two centuries, were less tolerant of the Polish and Czech communities, and things got even worse for the Slavic populations after 1741, when Wrocław fell to Prussia. For the next two centuries the city was increasingly Germanised and became known as Breslau.

As one of the major eastern outposts of the Reich, Breslau was given a key defensive role in the last stages of WWII, converting the whole city into a fortified compound. Besieged by the Red Army in February 1945, the Nazis defended their last bastion, Fortress Breslau, until May, executing anyone who refused to fight. During the battle, 75% of the city was razed to the ground.

Of the prewar population of more than 600,000, an estimated 30% died, mostly as a result of the fighting and the botched evacuation that preceded it. The handful of Germans who remained were expelled to Germany, and the ruined city was resettled with people from Poland's prewar eastern regions, mostly from Lviv (Lwów in Polish), which had been ceded to the Soviet Union.

The difficult reconstruction of Wrocław continued well into the 1980s, when the city surpassed its prewar population level for the first time.

ORIENTATION

The roughly oval-shaped Old Town is about 800m north of the neo-Moorish train station on ul Piłsudskiego. The bus station is just behind the train station, on ul Sucha. Almost all major sights and most forms of accommodation are within easy walking distance of the central area.

INFORMATION
Bookshops

EMPiK Rynek (☎ 071 343 4016; www.empik.com; Rynek 50; ☻ 9am-10pm Mon-Sat, noon-9pm Sun); Plac Kościuszki (☎ 071 344 8862; Plac Kościuszki 21/23; ☻ 10am-8pm Mon-Fri, 10am-6pm Sat, 10am-4pm Sun) Best for newspapers and magazines.

PolAnglo (www.polanglo.pl in Polish) Rynek (☎ 071 341 7960; Rynek 7); ul Kuźnicza (☎ 071 341 9760; ul Kuźnicza 49a)

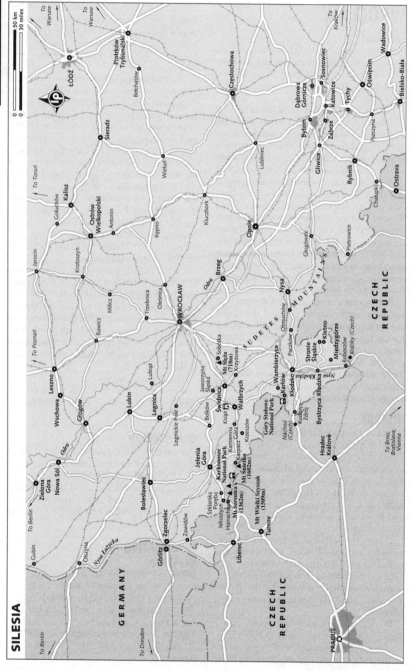

Świat Podróżnika (☎ 071 346 0071; ul Wita Stwosza 19/20; ◷ 10am-6pm Mon-Fri, 10am-3pm Sat) Maps and guidebooks.

Internet Access

Intermax (☎ 071 794 0573; ul Psie Budy 10/11; per hr 4zł; ◷ 9am-11pm)

Internet Netvigator ul Igielna (☎ 071 344 5962; ul Igielna 14; per 15/30/60min 1/2/3zł; ◷ 9am-midnight); ul Kuźnicza (☎ 071 343 7069; ul Kuźnicza 11/13; ◷ 9am-10pm)

W Sercu Miasta (☎ 071 342 4675; Przejście Żelaźnicze 4, Rynek-Ratusz; per 10/30/60min 1/3/4zł, per 3hr 10zł; ◷ 9am-midnight Mon-Sat, noon-midnight Sun)

Internet Resources

City of Wrocław (www.wroclaw.pl) Informative official site direct from city hall.

Wrocław Life (www.wroclaw-life.com) Interactive information portal on every aspect of life and tourism in Wrocław.

Laundry

Foka (☎ 071 355 0176; ul Żubrza 18; ◷ 6am-10pm Mon-Fri, 6am-2pm Sat)

Money

Bank Pekao (ul Oławska 2; ◷ 8am-7pm Mon-Fri, 9am-2pm Sat)

Post

Main post office (ul Piłsudskiego 12; ◷ 8am-7pm Mon-Fri, 9am-2pm Sat)

Post office (Rynek 28; ◷ 6.30am-6pm Mon-Fri, 9am-1pm Sat)

Telephone
MOBILE PHONES

Orange (☎ 071 344 7166; www.orange.pl; ul Kazimierza Wielkiego 19-23; ◷ 9am-8pm Mon-Fri, 11am-5pm Sat)

Plus GSM (☎ 071 343 4910; www.plusgsm.pl; ul Szewska 74; ◷ 10am-8pm Mon-Fri, 10am-2pm Sat)

Tourist Information

Lower Silesia Cultural Information Centre (☎ 071 342 2291; www.okis.pl; Rynek-Ratusz 24; ◷ 10am-6pm Mon-Fri, 9am-5pm Sat)

Tourist office (☎ 071 344 3111; www.itwroclaw.pl; Rynek 14; ◷ 9am-9pm Apr-Oct, 9am-8pm Nov-Mar)

Travel Agencies

Almatur (☎ 071 343 4135; www.almatur.pl; ul Kościuszki 34)

Orbis Travel (☎ 071 344 4408; www.orbis.pl; Rynek 29; ◷ 9am-6pm Mon-Fri, 10am-2pm Sat)

PTTK office (☎ 071 343 8331; www.pttk.pl; 1st fl Rynek-Ratusz 11/12; ◷ 9am-5pm Mon-Fri, 9am-2pm Sat)

SIGHTS
Old Town

Wrocław's extensive Old Town is so full of historic buildings that you could wander round for weeks and still feel like you hadn't seen everything.

RYNEK

Wrocław's market square is Poland's second biggest after the one in Kraków. The central **town hall** complex is so large that it incorporates three internal streets. The main structure took almost two centuries (1327–1504) to complete, and work on the 66m-high tower and decoration continued for another century.

The eastern façade reflects the stages of the town hall's development, split into three distinct elements. The segment to the right, with its austere early-Gothic features, is the oldest, while the delicate carving in the section to the left shows elements of the early Renaissance style. Prisoners' sentences were once read aloud from the little loggia. The central section dates from the 16th century and is topped by an ornamented triangular roof adorned with pinnacles. The astronomical clock, made of larch wood and showing the time and phases of the moon, was built in 1580.

The southern façade, dating from the early 16th century, is the most elaborate, with three projections, a pair of ornate bay windows and carved stone figures. The cellar on this side holds a popular pub-restaurant called Piwnica Świdnicka.

The western elevation is the most austere, apart from the early-Baroque portal (1615) leading to the **City Dwellers' Art Museum** (Muzeum Sztuki Mieszczańskiej; ☎ 071 347 1693; www.mmw.pl; Sukiennice 14/15, Rynek-Ratusz; adult/concession 10/5zł; ◷ 11am-5pm Wed-Sat, 10am-6pm Sun). The museum's Gothic interiors are every bit as magnificent as the building's exterior, particularly the **Great Hall** (Sala Wielka) on the 1st floor, with carved decorations from the second half of the 15th century. Adjoining it is the **Princes' Room** (Sala Książęca), which was built as a chapel in the mid-14th century. The historic rooms house several exhibitions, including the **Wrocław Treasury** (Wrocławski Skarb) of gold and silverware from the 16th to 19th centuries.

WROCŁAW

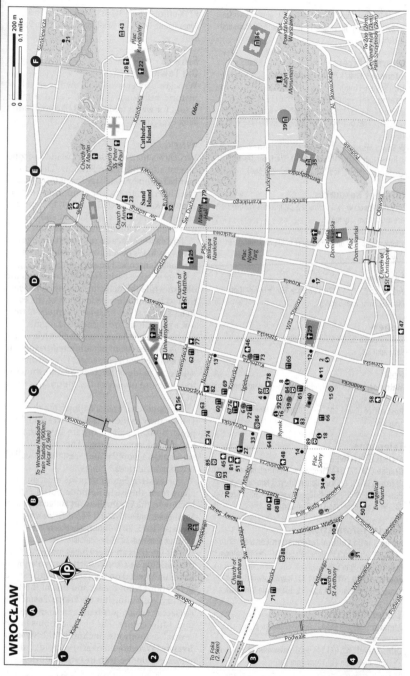

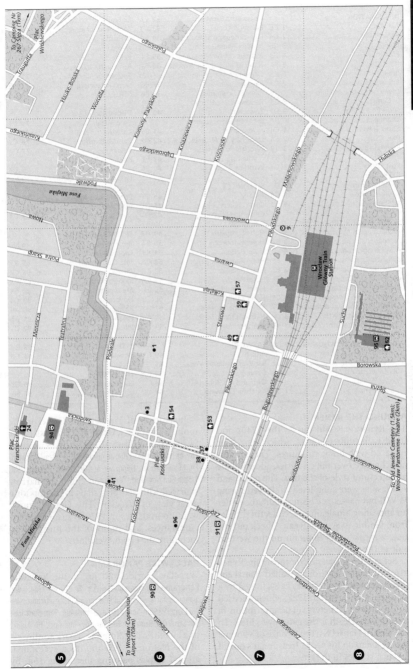

AROUND THE RYNEK

The Rynek was laid out in the 1240s and lined with timber houses, which were later replaced with brick structures. They gradually changed over the centuries, adopting the architectural style of the day. The north and south sides were completely destroyed during WWII but have since been rebuilt; they offer an appealing amalgam of architectural styles from Gothic to Art Nouveau. Check out the new wavelike glass fountain on the western side of the square.

Set in the northwestern corner of the Rynek are two charming houses called **Hansel and Gretel** (Jaś i Małgosia; ul Odrzańska 39/40), linked by a Baroque archway from 1728, which once led to the church cemetery. (The inscription in Latin reads 'Death is the gateway to life.') To the west of Hansel is a tiny bronze of a gnome taking a nap on his secret treasure; it's one of 15 such statues in the city.

Just north of Hansel and Gretel is the monumental brick **Church of St Elizabeth** (Kościół Św Elżbiety; ul Św Elżbiety 1/2), with its 83m-high **tower** (☎ 071 343 7204; admission 5zł; 9am-7pm Mon-Fri, 11am-5pm Sat, 1-5pm Sun Apr-Oct, 10am-5pm Mon-Sat, 1-5pm Sun Nov-Mar). You can climb the narrow stairwell with 250-plus steps to the top for a great view of Wrocław. This Gothic church went up in flames in 1976 in suspicious circumstances, and many of the furnishings, including the organ, were lost.

RACŁAWICE PANORAMA

Wrocław's pride and joy is the **Racławice Panorama** (Panorama Racławicka; ☎ 071 344 2344; www .panoramaraclawicka.pl; ul Purkyniego 11; adult/concession 20/15zł; 9am-5pm daily mid-Apr–Aug, 9am-5pm Tue-Sun Sep & Oct, 9am-4pm Tue-Sun Nov–mid-Apr). Housed in a cylindrical building in a park southwest of the National Museum, it's a cyclorama, a giant canvas painting measuring 15m by

A 360-DEGREE VIEW OF HISTORY

Filip Tarczewski is a steward and guide at Wrocław's most visited sight, the Racławice Panorama (opposite), a huge cyclorama depicting an 18th-century battle with the Russians.

Why do Poles come to see the panorama? It awakens something in our national spirit. It's about victory. The Polish people were under Russian subjugation then and later. They like to see our soldiers getting back at the Russians.

Foreigners? Are they interested? Until recently most of our foreign guests were English and German. Now with so many Koreans working [at the LG Electronics factory] nearby, we're getting a lot of them. Koreans like the fighting scenes.

Hmmm...English. Any problems with overenthusiastic stags? Not necessarily English. But some drunken people have tried to climb over the barrier. Maybe they think the panorama is real and they want to take part!

Do you like the panorama? Yes, and I like my job. I come from a very patriotic family. Every time I look at the picture I see something new.

On my perfect day, find me... Having coffee with friends at Pożegnanie z Afryką (p324). I also like to visit the Church of St Adalbert (p320). It's a very special place for the people of Wrocław and miracles happen here. Blessed Czesław prayed for Wrocław during the Mongol invasion and the church survived. And only Czesław's chapel remained standing after the war.

When I'm away I miss... The women of Wrocław. The women of Poland are the best in the world and the women of Wrocław the best in Poland.

114m and wrapped around the internal walls of the rotunda. It is viewed from an elevated central balcony. Three-dimensional items (tree trunks, plants, weapons, roads), special lighting and sound effects bring it to life.

The picture depicts the battle of Racławice (a village 40km northeast of Kraków), fought on 4 April 1794 between the Polish insurrectionist army of regulars and peasants led by Tadeusz Kościuszko and Russian troops under General Alexander Tormasov. One of the last attempts to defend Poland's independence, the battle was won by the Poles, but it was all for nought: months later the nationwide insurrection was crushed by the tsarist army and the Third Partition put into effect. Poland ceased to exist as a nation until WWI, yet the battle lived on in Polish hearts and minds as the most glorious engagement of the rebellion.

A century after the battle, a group of patriots in Lviv (then the Polish city of Lwów) commissioned the panorama. The two main artists, Jan Styka and Wojciech Kossak, were helped by seven other painters who did the background scenes and details. They completed the monumental canvas in just over

nine months, using 750kg of paint. The picture was on display until 1944, when a bomb damaged the canvas.

After the war the painting was sent to Wrocław, but since it depicted a defeat of the Russians, Poland's official friend and liberator, the communist authorities were reluctant to put it on display. The pavilion built for the panorama in 1967 sat empty until 1985, when the canvas was shown for the first time in more than four decades.

Visits are by 30-minute guided tours, which depart every half-hour. You move around the balcony to inspect each scene in turn while a handheld audioguide provides recorded commentary. The **Small Rotunda** (Mała Rotunda), behind the ticket office, features a model of the battlefield and the uniforms of forces engaged in the battle. A panorama ticket allows entry to the National Museum on the same day.

NATIONAL MUSEUM IN WROCŁAW

The **National Museum** (Muzeum Narodowe w Wrocławiu; ☎ 071 372 5150; www.mnwr.art.pl; Plac Powstańców Warszawy 5; adult/concession 15/10zł, free Sat; ⊙ 10am-4pm Wed, Fri & Sun, 9am-4pm Thu, 10am-6pm Sat) is a treasure-trove of fine art on three floors, with extensive permanent collections and a stunning skylit atrium. It's a lot to take in, but the café on the 1st floor is good for alleviating museum fatigue.

The Silesian art collection is a highlight of the museum. Medieval stone sculpture is displayed on the ground floor; exhibits include the Romanesque tympanum from the portal of the Church of St Mary Magdalene (right), depicting the Dormition (or Assumption) of the Virgin Mary, and 14th-century sarcophagi from the Church of SS Vincent and James (below). The medieval wooden sculpture on the 1st floor features some powerful Gothic triptychs and statues of saints. There are also collections of Silesian paintings, ceramics, silverware and furnishings from the 16th to 19th centuries.

The 2nd floor holds Polish art, mainly paintings, from the 17th century to the present. The collection covers most of Poland's big names, including Jacek Malczewski, Stanisław Wyspiański, Witkacy (Stanisław Ignacy Witkiewicz) and Jan Matejko; be prepared for moody portraits and massive battle scenes. Among the modern painters, Władysław Hasior, Eugeniusz Stankiewicz-Get and Tadeusz Makowski are names to look out for, especially for their humorous takes on war and religion.

UNIVERSITY QUARTER

This area occupies the northernmost part of the Old Town, between the riverfront and ul Uniwersytecka. Walking west from the National Museum, the first important historic building you see is the Gothic **Church of SS Vincent and James** (Kościół Św Wincentego i Św Jakuba; Plac Biskupa Nankiera 15a), originally a Romanesque basilica founded in the early 13th century. The largest church in the city, it's now used by the Uniat (Eastern Rite Catholic) faithful.

The Baroque-Rococo **Church of the Holy Name of Jesus** (Kościół Najświętszego Imienia Jezus; Plac Uniwersytecki), the university church and arguably the city's most beautiful, was built in the 1690s on the site of the former Piast castle. Its spacious interior, crammed with ornate fittings and adorned with fine illusionist frescoes of the life of Jesus on its vaulting, is quite spectacular.

The monumental building adjoining the church is the main edifice of the **University of Wrocław** (Uniwersytet Wrocławski; Plac Uniwersytecki 1), built between 1728 and 1742. Enter through the grand blue and gold Rococo gate at the western end and go up to the 1st floor to see the **Aula Leopoldinum** (☎ 071 375 2245; Plac Uniwersytecki; adult/concession 4.50/2.50zł; 🕐 10am-3.15pm Thu-Tue). Embellished with elaborate stucco work, sculptures, paintings and a trompe l'œil ceiling fresco, it's the city's best Baroque interior. The more modest **Oratorium Marianum**, on the ground floor, is included in the admission fee. Classical music concerts are occasionally held here. You can climb the **Mathematical Tower** (Wieża Matematyczna; adult/concession 4.50/2.5zł), topped with a sphere and decorated with allegorical figures.

OTHER SIGHTS

One block east of the Rynek is the **Church of St Mary Magdalene** (Kościół Św Marii Magdaleny; ul Szewska 10), a mighty Gothic brick building constructed during the city's heyday in the 14th century. Its showpiece is a copy of a Romanesque portal from around 1280 on the south wall, which originally adorned the Benedictine Abbey in Ołbin, but was moved here in 1546 after the abbey was demolished. The original tympanum is on display in Wrocław's National Museum. You can climb the 72m-high **tower** (☎ 071 344 1904; adult/concession 4/3zł; 🕐 10am-8pm Apr-Oct) and cross the so-called **Penance Footbridge** (Mostek Pokutnik).

A 16th-century former Bernardine church and monastery contains the **Museum of Architecture** (Muzeum Architektury; ☎ 071 344 8278; www.ma.wroc.pl; ul Bernardyńska 5; adult/concession 7/5zł, free Wed; 🕐 10am-4pm Tue, Wed, Fri & Sat, noon-6pm Thu, 11am-5pm Sun). The collection features stone sculptures and stained-glass windows from various historic buildings of the region. The oldest exhibit, a Romanesque tympanum on the ground floor, dates from 1165. The museum also has a 12th-century Jewish tombstone, a 1:500 scale model of Wrocław (1740) and a delightful cloister garden.

The church to the west of the museum and opposite the Galeria Dominikańska shopping centre is the single-nave Gothic **Church of St Adalbert** (Kościół Św Wojciecha; Plac Dominikański 2). The highlight here is the 18th-century Baroque chapel adjoining the southern transept, with its Rococo alabaster sarcophagus of the Blessed Czesław, founder of the original monastery here. Wrocławians are devoted to this chapel as it remained unscathed during WWII while the rest of the church was almost demolished.

Cathedral & Sand Islands

The erstwhile Cathedral Island (Ostrów Tumski) – it was connected to the mainland in the 19th century – was the cradle of Wrocław. It was here that the Ślężanie, a tribe of West Slavs who gave their name to the region, constructed their stronghold in the 7th or 8th century. After the town was incorporated into the Polish state and a bishopric established in 1000, Wrocław's first church was built here. Over time a number of churches, monasteries and other religious buildings were constructed, giving a distinctive, markedly ecclesiastical character to the district.

The centrepiece is the mammoth, twin-towered **Cathedral of St John the Baptist** (Katedra Św Jana Chrzciciela; Plac Katedralny 18). This three-aisled Gothic basilica was built between 1244 and 1590. Seriously damaged during WWII – shrapnel scarring is still visible on the exterior walls – it was reconstructed in its previous Gothic form, complete with dragon guttering. The high altar boasts a gold and silver triptych from 1522 attributed to the school of Veit Stoss, and the western portico is a medieval gem. For once you don't need strong legs to climb the 91m-high **tower** (☎ 071 322 2574; adult/concession 4/3zł; ☽ 10am-6pm Mon-Sat) as there is a lift.

In contrast to the enormous cathedral, the **Church of St Giles** (Kościół Św Idziego; Plac Św Idziego) is barely a cupboard. Built between 1218 and 1230, this is the oldest surviving church in Wrocław, and has an original Romanesque portal.

A few steps east of St Giles is the **Wrocław Archdiocesan Museum** (Muzeum Archidiecezji Wrocławskiej; ☎ 071 327 1178; Plac Katedralny 16; adult/concession 3/2zł; ☽ 9am-3pm Tue-Sun), with a large collection of sacred art.

If you've had enough of bricks and mortar – sacred or otherwise – Cathedral Island also contains the city's **Botanical Gardens** (Ogród Botaniczny; ☎ 071 322 5957; ul Sienkiewicza 23; adult/concession 7/5zł; ☽ 8am-6pm Apr-Oct, 10am-6pm Nov-Mar), a charming patch of greenery with palm houses.

To the west is Sand Island (Wyspa Piasek), a real island in the Odra connected to Cathedral Island by the Cathedral Bridge (Most Tumski) and to the Old Town by the Sand Bridge (Most Piaskowy). The main monument here is the **Church of Our Lady on the Sand** (Kościół Najświętszej Marii Panny na Piasku), a lofty 14th-century building that dominates this tiny islet. Almost all the fittings were destroyed during WWII and the half-dozen old triptychs you see inside have been collected from other Silesian churches. The wonderful Romanesque tympanum in the south aisle is the only remnant of the original 12th-century church that once stood here. There's a mechanised *szopka* (Nativity scene) in the first chapel to the right; make a small donation when one of the assistants turns it on.

West & South of the Old Town

Just outside the ring road encircling the Old Town, the squat brick **Arsenal** (Arsenał), with two towers and an enormous courtyard, is the most significant remnant of the 15th-century fortifications. It now houses the **Military Museum** (Muzeum Militariów; ☎ 071 347 1696; www.mmw.pl; ul Cieszyńskiego 9; adult/concession 7/5zł, free Wed; ☽ 11am-5pm Wed-Sat, 10am-6pm Sun), featuring old weapons, uniforms and lots of helmets. This is also the home of the **Archaeological Museum** (Muzeum Archeologiczne; ☎ 071 347 1698), which opens the same hours and charges the same admission fee.

About 750m south of the Arsenal is the partially restored **White Stork Synagogue** (Synagoga Pod Białym Bocianem; ul Włodkowica 7), built in 1829. Another reminder that this city was once home to more than 20,000 Jews is the **ul Łąkowa synagogue memorial.** Formerly a synagogue built in 1872, it was the country's second largest until it was torched on Kristallnacht (9 November 1938). The **Old Jewish Cemetery** (Stary Cmentarz Żydowski; ☎ 071 791 5904; www.mmw.pl; ul Ślężna 37/39; adult/concession 7/5zł; ☽ 8am-6pm), founded in 1856, is about 1.5km south of the train and bus stations. Take tram 9 or 16.

The massive Gothic affair located just south of the Old Town is the Franciscan **Church of SS Stanislaus, Wenceslas and Dorothy** (Kościół Franciszkanów Św Stanisława, Wacława i Doroty; Plac Franciszkanski), founded in 1351 to commemorate the meeting between Polish King Kazimierz III Wielki (Casimir III the Great) and his Bohemian counterpart, Charles IV, at which they agreed to leave Silesia in Bohemia's hands. Note the sizable Rococo tomb at the start of the south aisle.

About 500m south of the church on the corner of ul Świdnicka and ul Piłsudskiego is a fascinating sculpture called **Passage** (Przejście), which shows a group of seven bronze pedestrians literally being swallowed into the pavement, only to re-emerge on the other side of the street. It's by Jerzy Kalina and was

SILESIA

unveiled in 2005 to mark the 24th anniversary of the declaration of martial law.

Eastern Suburbs

Wrocław can boast Poland's largest (and supposedly best) **zoo** (Ogród Zoologiczny; ☎ 071 348 3025; www.zoo.wroclaw.pl in Polish; ul Wróblewskiego 1; adult/concession 10/4zł; ☾ 9am-6pm Apr-Oct, 9am-4pm Nov-Mar), with some 6000 animals representing more than 600 species and spread over 100 hectares. It's 2km to the east; take tram 2 or 10 from Plac Dominikański.

Across the street to the north is the **Centennial Hall** (Hala Stulecia; ☎ 071 347 5113; www.halaludowa.wroc .pl; ul Wystawowa 1; admission 10zł; ☾ 8am-7pm), also called the People's Hall (Hala Ludowa). It's a huge, round, 6000-seat auditorium, built in 1913 and added to Unesco's World Heritage List in 2007. Designed by German architect Max Berg and opened to mark the centenary of Napoleon's defeat by allied European forces in 1813, the hall is topped with a huge dome measuring 65m in diameter – a remarkable achievement in its day. The unusual 96m-high steel **Spire** (Iglica) in front of the entrance was built in 1948 on the occasion of the Exhibition of the Regained Territories.

Behind the hall to the northeast is **Park Szczytnicki**, Wrocław's oldest and largest 'English park' (ie wooded area), encompassing 112 hectares with 400 species of trees. A short walk north along the pergola will bring you to the small **Japanese Garden** (Ogród Japoński; ☎ 0662 169 226; adult/concession 3/2zł; ☾ 9am-7pm Apr-Oct), while further east is the 16th-century wooden **Church of St John Nepomuk** (Kościół Św Jana Nepomucena; Al Dąska), brought here from the Opole region in 1914.

COURSES

Link Language School (☎ 071 372 5335, 0604 649 554; www.link.szkola.pl; 2nd fl, Plac Solny 13; ☾ 9.30am-5pm Mon-Fri) offers numerous Polish-language courses of varying intensities, from 30zł to 80zł per hour, depending on class size (generally up to six people) and frequency of the lessons.

TOURS

Wrocław Tours (☎ 071 727 1534, 0602 115 349; www .wroclawtours.pl; Plac Solny 14/14a) has a three-hour guided bus and walking tour of Wroclaw (adult/ concession 100/50zł) in English departing at 9.30am on Monday, Wednesday and Friday. It also offers a five-hour tour to Świdnica (p329) and Książ (p332) at 1.30pm on Tuesday and Saturday (adult/concession 150/75zł).

In the warmer months a boat called **Gucio** (☎ 0609 200 867; ☾ 11am-7pm) has 40-minute cruises (8zł) on the Odra departing hourly from the southern end of Sand Island. Hour-long sailings (15zł) depart at 8pm and 9pm on Friday and Saturday.

FESTIVALS & EVENTS

Wrocław hosts some exciting events.

Musica Polonica Nova (www.musicapolonicanova.pl in Polish) Contemporary music festival held biannually (2008, 2010, 2012 etc) in February.

Jazz on the Odra (www.jnofestival.pl in Polish) One of Poland's foremost jazz festivals, held in April.

Wrocław Nonstop (www.wroclawnonstop.pl) Five-day open-air pop and rock music festival held in June.

Arsenal Nights (www.wieczory-w-arsenale.pl) Chamber music festival at the Arsenal in June/July.

Wratislavia Cantans (www.wratislaviacantans.pl) Wrocław's top international music and fine-arts festival, now in its 4th decade, is held for a week in June and a week in September annually.

SLEEPING
Budget

In addition to the places listed here, the Hotel Tumski (opposite) also offers dormitory accommodation.

MDK Kopernik Hostel (☎ 071 343 8857; mdkko pernik1@wp.pl; ul Kołłątaja 20; dm 19-28zł, d 60zł; ✗) Not far from the train station, this is a basic, recently renovated official hostel with 59 beds, located in a grand mustard-coloured building. Some dorms are huge and beds (five to seven) are packed close together. Prices are cheaper after the first night.

Bursa Nauczycielska (☎ 071 344 3781; www.dodn .wroclaw.pl/bursa; ul Kotlarska 42; s/d/tr/q 65/110/110/120zł; ✗) Wrocław's most central teachers' dorm is basic but clean, with shared bathrooms. There's a lot of brown in the colour scheme, but the rooms are quite cosy and it's ideally located just one block northeast of the Rynek.

our pick **Stranger Hostel** (☎ 071 344 1206; www .thestrangerhostel.com; 2nd fl, ul Kołłątaja 16; dm 45-60zł, tw 120zł; ✗ ▣) A tatty old staircase in a vintage building just opposite the train station leads to Wrocław's best budget accommodation. Dorms (four to 10 beds) are set in six renovated apartment rooms with ornate lamps and wooden floors. Bathrooms are sparkling, and guests have free access to a kitchen and washing machine. There's a DVD projector with big screen for rainy days. There's also an apartment available in the same building.

Cinnamon Hostel (☎ 071 344 5858; www.cinnamon hostel.com; ul Kazimierza Wielkiego 67; dm 45-60zł, d 135zł; ✗ 🖳) Right on the ring road and within spitting distance of pedestrian ul Świdnicka, this charming and upbeat place run by a Polish/ English couple has nine large rooms (two to 10 beds) named for spices and herbs – basil, sesame, chilly (sic) – a bright kitchen and a common room with flat-screen PC. Doubles have their own toilet and shower.

Hotel Savoy (☎ 071 344 3071; www.savoy.wroc.pl; Plac Kościuszki 19; s 100-170zł, d 120-150zł, tr 150-180zł, ste 160-200zł) It may not look like much, but the 27-room Savoy is one of your best shots at a bargain. Pot plants, half-decent furniture and little balconies liven up the best rooms. Reception is up the steps on the 1st floor. Cheapest prices are at the weekend.

Hotel Podróżnik (☎ /fax 071 373 2845; ul Sucha 1; s/d/ tr/q 98/146/186/228zł; 🅿) Staying at the bus station isn't just a last resort for tired travellers: this skylit establishment has 23 bright, clean and comfortable rooms worthy of a night or two. Student discounts of 20% are available.

Midrange
Nathan's Villa Hostel (☎ 071 344 1095; www.nathans villa.com; ul Świdnicka 13; dm 45-60zł, s & d 150-190zł; ✗ 🅇 🖳) Sister to Kraków's most established hostel, this 96-bed place 150m south of the Rynek just had to be a success when it opened in 2006. Along with the expected free laundry and flat-screen TVs, expect your bunk to have its own locker and reading lamp. A full 20 bathrooms over three floors reduce waiting time for a shower.

Hotel Europejski (☎ 071 343 1071; www.odratourist .pl; ul Piłsudskiego 88; s 139-199zł, d 169-209 zł; ✗) In the same stable as the Hotel Polonia, this 31-room hotel is handy for the train and bus stations, but don't expect the Ritz at these prices. The pricier 'renovated' rooms are large and comfortable, though the décor is rather tired.

Hotel Polonia (☎ 071 343 1021; www.odratourist.pl; ul Piłsudskiego 66; s 159-209zł, d 189-229zł; ✗ 🖳) There's little spectacular about this 145-room place, but it's close to the stations, and weekend and summer promotions (singles/doubles from 109/159zł) make it decent value. Room prices depend on size and quality of decoration.

Hotel Zaułek (☎ 071 341 0046; www.hotel.uni.wroc.pl; ul Garbary 11; s 203-240zł, d 245-320zł; 🅿 🖳) Run by the university, this is a very personal guesthouse at the upper end of the scale, accommodating just 18 visitors in a dozen homely

rooms. The 1pm checkout is a boon for heavy sleepers, and weekend prices are a snip.

Hotel Europeum (☎ 071 371 4500; www.europeum .pl; ul Kazimierza Wielkiego 27a; s/d 240/275zł; 🅿 ✗ 🅇 🖳 🖭) Prices might just edge the motel-like Europeum out of the comfortable mid-range bracket, but it's more attractive at the weekend when the 20 singles/doubles drop to 220/255zł.

Art Hotel (☎ 071 787 7100; www.arthotel.pl; ul Kiełbaśnicza 20; s 250-400zł, d 270-440zł, ste 300-520zł; 🅿 ✗ 🖳 🖭) A bit frayed but all the more attractive for that, the Art features 78 rooms with tastefully restrained décor, quality fittings and gleaming bathrooms. Within the arched brick cellar is a top-notch restaurant, and there's a fitness room for working off any extra weight gained therein.

Top End
Dwór Polski (☎ 071 372 3415; www.dworpolski.wroclaw.pl; ul Kiełbaśnicza 2; s/d/ste 265/325/470zł; 🅿 ✗ 🖳) You couldn't ask for more character than this: a restored 16th-century house, complete with 28 idiosyncratic rooms, some original dark-wood fittings and fixtures, and a popular restaurant (enter from Rynek 5). The atmospheric internal courtyard is a plus, as are the weekend rates – 20% off the standard ones.

Hotel Patio (☎ 071 375 0400; www.hotelpatio.pl; ul Kiełbaśnicza 24; s 300-330zł, d 330-360zł, ste from 395zł; 🅿 ✗ 🖳 🖭) The 49-room Patio offers pleasant lodgings a short hop from the main square, within two buildings linked by a covered sunlit courtyard. Rooms are clean and light, sometimes small but with reasonably high ceilings. At weekends singles/double/ suites are priced from 240/260/290zł.

Hotel Tumski (☎ 071 322 6099; www.hotel-tumski .com.pl; Wyspa Słodowa 10; s 250-270zł, d 350zł, ste 480zł; 🅿 ✗ 🖳 🖭) Located on one of the islets in the Odra and within easy walking distance of both the Old Town and Cathedral Island, this neat 57-room hotel has a nice riverside setting and is set back from a busy road. Rates at the weekend drop to as low as 210/300/440zł for singles/doubles/suites. For the more budget-conscious, part of the hotel is an official HI hostel, with some three dozen dorm beds costing 23zł to 68zł per person.

EATING
Delikatesy U Roberta (ul Odrzańska 11/12; ⏱ 24hr) This grocery and sundries shop is open round the clock.

STP (☎ 071 344 5449; www.szybkotaniopysznie.pl; ul Kuźnicza 10; mains from 2.40zł; ☷ 10am-9pm) Short for 'Szybko, Tanio, Pysznie', the name says it all: 'Fast, Cheap, Delicious'. This is one of those cafeteria-style eateries that sells food by weight – 2.40zł for 100g – and it's surprisingly good.

Bar Wegetariański Vega (☎ 071 344 3934; Sukiennice 1/2, Rynek-Ratusz; mains 3.60-5.40zł; ☷ 8am-7pm Mon-Fri, 9am-5pm Sat & Sun) This is a cheap cafeteria on two floors in the centre of the Rynek, offering vegetarian dishes in a light green space. There's a good choice of soups and crepes.

Amalfi (☎ 071 343 6784; ul Więzienna 21; mains 9.50-25.50zł; ☷ 12.30pm-midnight) This pizzeria with a wood-burning stove and sunny disposition is just north of the Rynek. It's a good choice for a simple, low-cost meal.

Mexico Bar (☎ 071 346 0292; www.mexicobar.com; ul Rzeźnicza 34; mains 12.50-38zł; ☷ noon-11pm Sun-Thu, noon-midnight Fri & Sat) This is a compact, warmly lit restaurant featuring sombreros and backlit masks on the walls and all the Mexican favourites. There's a small bar to lean on while waiting for a table.

Pekin (☎ 071 787 8784; ul Kotlarska 24/1a; mains 15-25zł; ☷ 11am-10pm Mon-Thu, noon-11pm Fri & Sat, noon-10pm Sun) OK, Chinese but *kuchnia sichuańska* (Sichuan cuisine)? Uh-uh. Still, it's one of Wrocław's very few Chinese eateries and relatively authentic.

Mercado (☎ 071 344 4040; ul Więzienna 30; mains 18-65zł; ☷ 11am-11pm Mon-Thu, noon-midnight Fri & Sat, noon-11pm Sun) This offspring of the prodigious Sphinx chain has a more rustic feel to it, with rough-hewn walls and handmade ceramics. The menu's a familiar mix of Middle Eastern and Italian platters, plus a smattering of Greek, Syrian and Asian efforts.

Darea (☎ 071 343 5301; ul Kuźnicza 43/45; mains 25-100zł; ☷ 11am-10pm) With management at the LG Electronics factory in Kobierzyce (south of Wrocław) top-heavy with Koreans, it was inevitable that they'd demand their own place for authentic Korean dishes like *bibimbab* and *bulgogi*. You won't find better Korean anywhere in Poland.

Sankt Petersburg (☎ 071 341 8084; www.sankt petersburg.pl; ul Igielna 14/15; mains 29-85zł; ☷ noon-late) If you thought Russia's culinary traditions were limited to stroganoff and blinis, then this slightly formal restaurant will be a revelation. Meat, fish and game prop up the high-powered menu, along with the requisite *kaviar* (65zł).

our pick Restauracja JaDka (☎ 071 343 6461; www .jadka.pl; ul Rzeźnicza 24/25; mains 38-81zł; ☷ noon-11pm) Behind what is arguably the best restaurant in town is Magda Gessler, the country's top female chef. Expect impeccable modern versions of Polish classics and silver-service table settings (candles, crystal, linen) in delightful Gothic surrounds. The set lunch available Monday to Saturday is a snip at 35zł.

Restauracja Vincent (☎ 071 341 0520; www.vincent .wroclaw.pl; ul Ruska 39; mains 40-68zł; ☷ 9am-midnight Mon-Sat, 1-10pm Sun) Situated in a historic building with a café, cellar restaurant and main dining room, quirky but charming Vincent has lovely interiors and unusual offerings. Anything from shashlik to seafood risotto can pop up on the menu, and there's live accordion music from time to time.

The Rynek is lined with restaurants on every side, but not all of them offer the highest quality for the highest złoty. If you're intent on being in the thick of things, choose one of the following – they're tried and tested.

Karczma Lwowska (☎ 071 343 9887; www.lwowska .com.pl; Rynek 4; mains 21-40zł; ☷ noon-midnight) Meaty Polish standards in a space with a rustic rural look.

La Scala (☎ 071 372 5394; Rynek 38; mains 32-68zł; ☷ 10am-midnight) Offers authentic Italian food at relatively high prices; go for pizza (13.50zł to 19zł) or pasta (16zł to 32zł).

Maru Restauracja (☎ 071 343 2678; www.maru.pl; Rynek16/17; mains 20-50zł; ☷ noon-11pm) Toned down but tasty hybrid Korean and Japanese dishes, including sushi (9zł to 25zł).

DRINKING
Cafés

Café Artzat (☎ 071 373 3766; ul Malarska 30; ☷ 11am-midnight Sun-Thu, 11am-2am Fri & Sat) This low-key café just north of the landmark Church of St Elizabeth is one of the best places in town to recharge the batteries over coffee or tea and a good book.

Pożegnanie z Afryką (☎ 071 341 7732; ul Kiełbaśnicza 24; ☷ 9.30am-10pm Mon-Thu, 9.30am-11pm Fri & Sat, 11am-10pm Sun) An independent chain of fair-trade coffeehouses in Poland, 'Out of Africa' blows its big-business rivals out of the (hot) water with a superb selection of imported beans and lovely 'front parlour' décor.

Café Uni (☎ 071 375 2838; Plac Uniwersytecki 11; ☷ 11am-midnight Sun-Thu, 11am-1am Fri & Sat) As the name suggests, this is student central, a traffic-cone's throw from the main university buildings. Semi-slick décor – red leather chairs, glass bricks, neon, fake palms – and noncheesy music set it apart.

Czekoladziarnia (☎ 071 797 5716; ul Więzienna 30; ⏰ noon-8.30pm Mon-Sat, noon-8pm Sun) This little place sells its own shop-made chocolate in both solid and liquid (5zł to 8zł) forms.

Kawiarnia Pod Słodką Borówka (☎ 071 343 6856; Rynek 45; ⏰ 9am-10pm) If you're after a heart-starter, try the *kawa* (coffee) and cakes here. It serves great apple strudel (9.90zł) and there's a curious collection of old hats on the wall.

Pubs & Bars

PracOFFnia (☎ 0603 585 496; ul Więzienna 6; ⏰ 3pm-2am) Housed in what was a prison in the Middle Ages, below a well-concealed court-yard, this eclectic place crammed with old cameras and projectors is Wrocław's most interesting boozer.

La Luz (☎ 0661 927 476; www.laluz.pl; ul Kraińskiego 14; ⏰ noon-2am Tue-Fri, 5pm-2am Sat-Mon) This American-owned wine bar and pub is housed in a 13th-century guard tower and is a superb retreat from the hubbub of the Rynek.

Kalogródek (☎ 0501 778 346; ul Kuźnicza 29b; ⏰ 10am-midnight Sun-Thu, 10am-2am Fri & Sat) Hidden behind some rough-looking wooden hoardings, the big, stepped terrace here is like a playground for students. Darts and cheap beer (the local brew Piast) make sure it's generally heaving, even when the weather's uncooperative.

Paparazzi (☎ 071 341 0485; www.paparazzi.com.pl; ul Rzeźnicza 32/33; ⏰ noon-1am Mon-Thu, noon-2am Fri, 4pm-2am Sat, 4pm-1am Sun) Paparazzi are sprouting up throughout Poland but this particularly spacious branch is a cut above the rest, with its designer décor, huge rectangular bar and incomparable cocktails.

Spiż (☎ 071 344 7225; www.spiz.pl; Rynek-Ratusz 2; ⏰ 10am-midnight Sun & Mon, 10am-2am Tue-Thu, 10am-3am Fri & Sat) Poland's first microbrew-ery bar-restaurant is buried in a basement under the town hall, with harassed staff scurrying around the copper vats to serve the voracious clientele.

ENTERTAINMENT

Wrocław is an important cultural and night-life centre, and there's a lot of stuff going on all year round. The monthly freebies *Aktivist* (www.aktivist.pl) and *Moveout* (www.moveout.pl) have listings in Polish; you can pick up copy of the bimonthly English-language *The Visitor* (www.the

visitor.pl) from the tourist office. For a more detailed rundown of clubs, bars and the like, seek out the reliably forthright *Wrocław in Your Pocket* (www.inyourpocket.com; 5zł) or consult the excellent Wrocław Life (www.wroclaw-life.com) website.

Theatre

Wrocław is internationally known for its avant-garde Laboratory Theatre (Teatr Laboratorium), created by radical director Jerzy Grotowski (1933–99). Founded in 1990 in the theatre's former home, the **Grotowski Institute** (☎ 071 344 5320; www.grotowski-institute.art.pl; Rynek-Ratusz 27) has a complete archive and several documentaries on the Laboratory Theatre and invites various experimental groups, often from abroad, to give performances in its small theatre. Enter from Przejście Żelaźnicze.

Polish Theatre (Teatr Polski; ☎ 071 316 0777; www.teatrpolski.wroc.pl in Polish; ul Zapolskiej 3; ⏰ box office 11am-2pm & 3-7pm Mon-Sat) Housed in a modern glass and concrete building, the Polish Theatre is the major mainstream venue in town, staging classic Polish and foreign plays.

Wrocław Pantomime Theatre (Wrocławski Teatr Pantomimy; ☎ 071 337 2103; www.pantomima.wroc.pl in Polish; Al Dębowa 16) Created by impresario Henryk Tomaszewski, this is Wrocław's principal ambassador for contemporary theatre. Tickets are generally available from the box office at the Polish Theatre (above).

Wrocław Contemporary Theatre (Wrocławski Teatr Współczesny; ☎ 071 358 8940; www.wteatrw.pl in Polish; ul Rzeźnicza 12; ⏰ box office noon-7pm Mon-Fri) Near the centre of town, Teatr Współczesny tends more towards contemporary productions from modern Polish and international playwrights.

Opera & Classical Music

Philharmonic Hall (Filharmonia; ☎ 071 342 2001; www.filharmonia.wroclaw.pl; ul Piłsudskiego 19; ⏰ box office 11am-6pm Mon-Fri) If you are interested in hearing the Wrocław Philharmonic, Friday and Saturday evenings are your best bets.

Wrocław Opera (Opera Wrocławska; ☎ 071 344 5779; www.opera.wroclaw.pl; ul Świdnicka 35; ⏰ box office 10am-6pm Mon, 9am-7pm Tue-Fri, 10am-2pm Sat) This venerable and recently restored music theatre is the traditional venue for opera and ballet performances.

Jazz

Jazz Club Rura (☎ 071 799 0907; www.jazzklubrura.art.pl; ul Łazienna 4; ⏰ 1pm-2am Mon-Wed, 1pm-4am Thu-Sat,

4pm-2am Sun) Finally plugging Wrocław into the Western jazz craze, this bright modern space has live gigs of different flavours most nights.

Clubs

There are two areas to head for if you fancy a night on the town: the Rynek, where cheese predominates; and Pasaż Niepolda, just off ul Ruska west of the Old Town, which offers a bit more variety. Entry charges vary (up to 20zł) depending on the night, the time you arrive, your gender and anything else the promoters can think of.

Bezsenność (☎ 071 792 8048; ul Ruska 51; 6pm-1am Sun-Thu, 6pm-4am Fri & Sat) With its alternative/rock/dance line-up and distressed décor, 'Insomnia' attracts a high-end clientele and is probably the best club in town currently.

Klub Radio Bar (☎ 071 372 5013; www.radio-bar .pl; Rynek 48; 9pm-3am) Loud, proud and oh-so-central, the Radio Bar is an essential stop for first-timers and anyone aiming to dig the scene.

PRL (☎ 071 342 5526; www.prl.wroc.pl; Rynek-Ratusz 10; noon-4am) The dictatorship of the proletariat is alive and well in this tongue-in-cheek venue inspired by communist nostalgia. Disco lights play over a bust of Lenin, propaganda posters line the walls and red-menace memorabilia is scattered through the maze of rooms. Descend to the basement – beneath the portraits of Stalin and Mao – if you'd like to hit the dance floor.

Jazzda (☎ 071 346 0825; www.jazzda.pl; Rynek 60; 9am-3am Mon-Sat, 10.30am-2am Sun) Looking for a John Travolta kind of evening? This central café-club with a lit-up, multicoloured dance floor and strobe lights will fit the bill.

Novocaina (☎ 071 343 6915; www.novocaina.com; Rynek 16; 10.30am-2am) Another Rynek café-restaurant that dons its party duds late in the evening, this neo-Gothic wet dream with plasma screens and intimate nooks and crannies attracts a fashion-conscious crowd.

Metropolis (☎ 071 794 5162; www.metropolis.wroc.pl; ul Ruska 51; 9pm-3am) This humungous place has two dance floors, one on the ground floor with dance and techno, and a piano bar in the cellar. It's something of a meat market.

GETTING THERE & AWAY
Air

Wrocław Copernicus Airport (☎ 071 358 1100; www .airport.wroclaw.pl) is in Strachowice, 13km west of the city centre. There are currently direct connections with Warsaw (up to seven times daily) as well as Dublin (daily), Frankfurt am Main (daily), London Gatwick and London Stansted (each daily), Munich (twice daily) and Rome (four times weekly).

LOT (☎ 0801 703 703; ul Piłsudskiego 36) has an office near the train station.

Bus

The most useful buses are those to Trzebnica (6.50zł, 40 minutes), Sobótka (5.50zł, one hour), Świdnica (5zł, 1½ hours), Lubiąż (9zł, 1½ hours) and Nysa (12zł to 16zł, two hours), none of which is served by direct train. From Wrocław you can also reach Warsaw (46zł to 50zł, five to 6½ hours), Poznań (35zł, 2½ hours), Częstochowa (28zł, three hours) and Białystok (62zł, seven hours), but the train is usually more convenient. Note that some regional buses arriving from the north terminate at Wrocław Nadodrze train station on Cathedral Island instead of at the main bus station.

There are a number of international bus routes (go to window 3) to places including Prague (from 110zł, 4½ hours, daily) and plenty of cities in Western Europe.

Train

Fast trains to Katowice (36zł, 2¾ hours) depart every two hours or so and pass via Opole (22zł, 1¼ hours) on their way. Most continue to Kraków (34zł, 4½ hours). There are at least half a dozen fast trains plus three express trains to Warsaw (50zł, five to 6½ hours); some call at Łódź (42zł, 3¾ to 4½ hours) en route. Wrocław also has regular train links with Poznań (34zł, two to 2½ hours, roughly hourly), Wałbrzych (13zł, two hours, every two hours), Jelenia Góra (18.50zł to 31zł, 3½ hours, up to 15 daily), Legnica (11zł, 1½ hours, roughly hourly) and Kłodzko (15.50zł, 1¾ hours, every two hours).

GETTING AROUND
To/From the Airport

The airport can be reached on bus 406 from the main train station (3zł, 30 minutes, every 20 to 40 minutes). A taxi to the airport will cost just under 40zł.

Bicycle

Both the **tourist office** (☎ 071 344 3111; Rynek 14; per hr/day 10/50zł; 9am-9pm Apr-Oct, 10am-8pm

Nov-Mar) and **W Sercu Miasta** (☎ 071 342 4675; Przejście Żelaźnicze 4, Rynek-Ratusz; per hr/day/24hr/week 6.50/28/32/145zł; ☺ 9am-midnight Mon-Sat, noon-midnight Sun) rent bicycles.

Car & Motorcycle

Micar (☎ 071 325 1949; www.micar.pl; ul Kamieńskiego 12) has Fiat Seicentos with unlimited kilometres from 80zł and Ford Fiestas from 130zł.

Public Transport

Wrocław has an efficient network of trams and buses covering the city centre and suburbs. Journeys within the centre cost 2.50zł; longer trips 3zł. Night buses (numbered over 200) and fast services cost 5zł. Useful routes include trams 8 and 9, which link the bus and train stations, Cathedral Island and the Botanical Gardens.

Taxi

Should you need a taxi, these are some of the better-known companies:

Mini Radio Taxi (☎ 96 26, 071 322 4800)
Nova Radio Taxi (☎ 96 86)
Super Taxi (☎ 96 63)

AROUND WROCŁAW

TRZEBNICA
pop 12,300

A small town 25km north of Wrocław, Trzebnica (tsheb-*nee*-tsah) is noted for its former Cistercian abbey *(opactwo cysterskie)*. It's an impressive site and a pleasant half-day trip from Wrocław.

The Cistercian order was brought to Poland in 1140 and established its first monastery in Jędrzejów, from where it expanded rapidly, counting some 40 abbeys throughout the country within a century. Trzebnica (Trebnitz in German) was the site of the first Cistercian convent in Poland, founded in 1202 by Henryk I Brodaty (Henry I the Bearded), the duke of Lower Silesia, at the request of his wife, Princess Jadwiga (Hedwig). After the hirsute duke's death in 1238, the pious Jadwiga entered the abbey and lived an ascetic life till her death in 1243; just 24 years later, she was canonised as St Hedwig of Andechs (Św Jadwiga Śląska). She is the patron saint of Silesia, and the abbey church where she and Henryk were buried is now a pilgrimage site, particularly on her feast day, 16 October.

Sights

The **abbey church** (☎ 071 312 1118; ul Jana Pawła II 3) is thought to be one of the first brick buildings erected in Poland. Though it was rebuilt in the 18th century, the structure has preserved much of its original Romanesque shape and, importantly, still boasts two **portals** from that time. The one next to the main entrance, partly hidden behind the Baroque tower added in the 1780s, is particularly fine; on the tympanum, which dates from the 1220s, you can still make out King David on his throne playing the harp to Queen Bathsheba and her lady-in-waiting.

The church's showpiece is **St Hedwig's Chapel** (Kaplica Św Jadwigi), to the right of the chancel. It was built soon after the canonisation of the princess, and the graceful, ribbed Gothic vaulting has been preserved unchanged. Its central feature is the saint's Gothic sarcophagus, an elaborate work in black marble and alabaster created in stages between 1680 and 1750. To the left of the tomb is the entrance to the three-nave crypt, the oldest part of the church.

The rest of the chapel is full of gilded and marbled altars; in the nave are 18 scenes from Jadwiga's life. The beautiful black organ is striking against the white walls and pastel colours of the ornamentation.

Getting There & Away

Buses to Wrocław (6.50zł, 40 minutes) run once or twice an hour, depending on the time of day. There are extra services and hourly private minibuses to Wrocław Nadodrze, north of the Old Town on Cathedral Island.

LUBIĄŻ
pop 2300

The small village of Lubiąż (*loo*-byonsh), 52km northwest of Wrocław, boasts a gigantic **Cistercian monastery** *(klasztor cysterskie)*, one of Europe's largest monastic complexes. Founded in 1163, the modest original abbey was gradually extended as the order grew. After the Thirty Years' War the monastery entered a period of prosperity, and it was then that the magnificent Baroque complex here was built. Construction took almost a century, finishing in 1739. It has a 223m-wide façade and 365 rooms. A team of distinguished artists, including the painters Michael Willmann and Franz Heigel, were commissioned for the monumental project.

In 1810 the Cistercians were expelled from Lubiąż (Leubus in German) by the king of

SILESIA

Prussia and the abbey shut down. The buildings were subsequently occupied, used and abused by a bizarre range of tenants: at various times the complex was a horse stud, a mental hospital, an arsenal, a Nazi military plant (during WWII), a Soviet army hospital (1945–48) and finally a storehouse for the state book publisher.

In 1991 a Polish-German foundation began to restore the abbey. A few rooms, including the **summer refectory** (*refektarz lełnie*; 1706), have been renovated and are open to the public as a **museum** (☎ 071 389 7166; www.fundacja lubiaz.org.pl in Polish; adult/concession 10/6zł; ⓨ 9am-6pm Apr-Sep, 10am-3pm Oct-Apr). The showpiece is the huge **Princes' Hall** (Sala Książęca), with its 15m-high frescoed ceiling and opulent Baroque decoration from the 1730s. The statues of the arts and virtues and the Atlas supporting the enormous balcony are impressive, but we're smitten by the figures in the four corners representing Europe, Africa, Asia and America.

The work on some other rooms is in progress; at the time of writing the phenomenally decorated **library** (*biblioteka*) above the refectory was a forest of support beams as its frescoes were being restored. The mighty **Church of the Blessed Virgin** (Kościół Najświętszej Marii Panny) and adjoining chapel will probably take longer. As yet they have no decoration apart from some surviving portals and fragments of frescoes. The crypt beneath the church, which cannot be visited, holds 98 mummified bodies, including that of Willmann himself.

There is only one daily bus to Lubiąż at 4.20pm from Legnica (5zł, 45 minutes), and two from Wrocław (9zł, 1½ hours) at 8.10am and 4.40pm.

SOBÓTKA & MT ŚLĘŻA
pop 6800

Some 34km southwest of Wrocław, the solitary forested cone of Mt Ślęża rises to 718m above the surrounding open plain. Mt Ślęża was one of the holy places of an ancient pagan tribe that set up cult sites in the area from at least the 5th century BC till the 11th century AD, when Christianity put a halt to it. The summit was circled by a stone wall marking off the sanctuary where rituals were held, and the remains of these ramparts survive to this day. Mysterious votive statues were carved crudely out of granite,

and several of them are scattered over the mountain's slopes. The Ślęża Massif is surrounded by the 15,640-hectare **Ślęża Landscape Park** (Ślężański Park Krajobrazowy).

At the northern foot of the mountain is the small town of Sobótka, the starting point for a hike to the top. The town's irregularly shaped Rynek is dominated by the massive **Church of St James** (Kościół Św Jakuba), originally Romanesque but repeatedly remodelled over the years. Note the Romanesque stone figure of a lion incorporated into the front wall. Nearby, to the northwest on Plac Wolności, is the Baroque'd 13th-century pink and white **Church of St Anne** (Sanktuarium Św Anny). Beside it is a pagan stone statue known as the Mushroom (Grzyb) and another Romanesque lion.

About 200m south of the Rynek is the small **Ślęża Museum** (Muzeum Ślężańskie; ☎ 071 316 2622; www.sleza.sobotka.net in Polish; ul Św Jakuba 18; adult/concession 2/1zł; ⓨ 9am-4pm Wed-Sun, last Tue of month), recognisable by its fine Renaissance doorway from 1568. The museum displays some of the finds of archaeological excavations in the region.

Proceed south along the same street for another 300m and take ul Garncarska to the right (west), heading uphill. After crossing the main road, turn left and take the red route up to **Mt Ślęża**, a hike that should take you about two hours. You'll find two more statues called the Bear (Miś) and the Fish (Ryba) on the way, plus a tall TV mast and a 19th-century church at the top.

Coming down, you can take the steeper but faster (1¼ hours) yellow route directly to the PTTK hostel, about 800m west of your starting point. There's a **viewing tower** (wieża; adult/concession 3/2zł; ⓨ 10am-4pm Sat & Sun) about halfway down, and on the road back into town you'll pass another stone statue, called the Monk (Mnich) but resembling an urn to our untrained eyes.

Sleeping & Eating

Dom Turysty Pod Wieżą (☎ 071 316 2857; ul Armii Krajowej 13; without/with bathroom s 40/60zł; d 60/80zł; Ⓟ ⓧ) The PTTK hostel, at the foot of Mt Ślęża 1.5km from the Rynek, is very simple but pleasant enough, and also has a restaurant (open 9am to 9pm). The yellow mountain trail starts here.

Zajazd Pod Misiem (☎ 0664 273 015; www.pod misiem.emeteor.pl; ul Mickiewicza 7/9; s/d/ste 60/100/140zł)

The 'Inn Under the Bear', southeast of the Rynek, is crying out for a revamp but it's as central a spot as you'll find.

Restauracja Pod Jeleniem (☎ 071 390 3237; Rynek 8; mains 4-18.50zł; ☷ 9am-7pm) This homely, very welcoming eatery on the northeast side of the Rynek serves traditional Polish fare but keeps bankers' hours. Plan a late lunch.

Getting There & Away

Sobótka is easily accessible by bus from Wrocław (5.50zł, one hour, twice hourly) and Świdnica (5zł, 40 minutes, up to 14 daily). Buses drop you in the town centre just north of the Church of St Anne.

THE SUDETES MOUNTAINS

The Sudetes Mountains are the northernmost part of the Sudentenland, a part of the world familiar to anyone who has studied WWII history. They run for more than 250km along the Czech–Polish border, and the highest part of this old and eroded chain of mountains is the Karkonosze, reaching 1602m at Mt Śnieżka. Though what are called the Sudetes in English, Sudety in Polish and Sudeten in German don't offer much alpine scenery, they are amazingly varied and heavily covered in forests, with spectacular geological formations such as those at the Góry Stołowe (p344) to break the monotony.

To the north, the Sudetes gradually decline into a belt of gently rolling foothills known as the Sudetes Foothills (Przedgórze Sudeckie). This area is more densely populated, and many of the towns and villages in the region still boast some of their centuries-old timber buildings. Combining visits to these historic settlements with hikes into the mountains and the surrounding countryside is the best way to explore the region.

ŚWIDNICA

pop 59,800

One of the wealthiest towns in Silesia in the Middle Ages, Świdnica (shfeed-nee-tsah) was founded in the 12th century. In 1290 it became the capital of the Duchy of Świdnica-Jawor, one of myriad Silesian Piast principalities but among the most powerful, thanks to its two gifted rulers: Bolko I, who founded it, and his grandson Bolko II, who extended it significantly.

The capital itself was a flourishing commercial centre, well known for its beer, which ended up on the tables of Kraków, Prague and Buda. Until the Thirteen Years' War (1454–66) it was one of the largest Polish towns, with 6000 inhabitants. By 1648, however, the population had dropped to 200, and Świdnica has never managed to become a city, remaining way behind its former rival, Wrocław.

Świdnica (Schweidnitz in German) escaped major damage in WWII and has kept some important historic buildings. It's an agreeable place for a stopover and a convenient springboard for the castle at Książ (p332).

Information

Bank Pekao (Rynek 30)

Café Internet (☎ 074 852 0463; ul Spółdzielcza 14; per hr 3zł; ☷ 10am-10pm Mon-Sat, noon-8pm Sun) Internet access.

Post office (Al Niepodległości; ☷ 8am-8pm Mon-Fri, 8am-1pm Sat)

Tourist office (☎ 074 852 0290; www.um.swidnica.pl; ul Wewnętrzna 2, Rynek-Ratusz; ☷ 9am-5pm Mon-Fri, 8am-4pm Sat, 9am-2pm 1st Sun of month May-Sep, 9am-5pm Mon-Fri, 8am-4pm 1st & 2nd Sat of month Oct-Apr)

Sights

The timbered **Church of Peace** (Kościół Pokoju; ☎ 074 852 2814; www.kosciolpokoju.pl in Polish; Plac Pokoju 6; adult/concession 6/3zł; ☷ 9am-1pm & 3-5pm Mon-Sat, 3-5pm Sun Apr-Oct, by reservation Nov-Mar) was erected between 1656 and 1657 in just 10 months. The builders were not trying to set any records; the so-called Peace of Westphalia of 1648 allowed the Protestants of Silesia to build a total of three churches as long as they went up in less than a year, had no belfry and used only clay, sand and wood as building materials. The churches at Świdnica and at Jawor, 18km south of Legnica, still stand, though the one at Głogów burned down in 1758. The Świdnica church is a shingled structure laid out in the form of a cross and contains not a single nail. The Baroque decoration, with paintings covering the walls and coffered ceiling, has been preserved intact. Along the walls, two storeys of galleries and several small balconies were installed, allowing some 3500 seated worshippers and 4000 standees. The church was added to Unesco's World Heritage List in 2001.

SILESIA

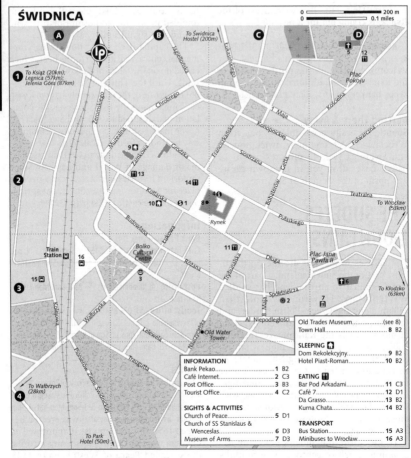

ŚWIDNICA

| 0 | 200 m |
| 0 | 0.1 miles |

To Świdnica
Hostel (200m)

To Książ (20km);
Legnica (57km);
Jelenia Góra (87km)

Plac
Pokoju

Train
Station

Bolko
Cultural
Centre

Old Water
Tower

To Wrocław
(53km)

Plac Jana
Pawła II

To Kłodzko
(63km)

To Wałbrzych
(28km)

To Park
Hotel (50m)

Old Trades Museum..................(see 8)	
Town Hall.....................................**8** B2	
SLEEPING	
Dom Rekolekcyjny......................**9** B2	
Hotel Piast-Roman.....................**10** B2	
EATING	
Bar Pod Arkadami......................**11** C3	
Café 7..**12** D1	
Da Grasso....................................**13** B2	
Kurna Chata................................**14** B2	
TRANSPORT	
Bus Station..................................**15** A3	
Minibuses to Wrocław..............**16** A3	

INFORMATION	
Bank Pekao.................................**1** B2	
Café Internet...............................**2** C3	
Post Office...................................**3** B3	
Tourist Office..............................**4** C2	
SIGHTS & ACTIVITIES	
Church of Peace..........................**5** D1	
Church of SS Stanislaus &	
Wenceslas..................................**6** D3	
Museum of Arms........................**7** D3	

The Old Town's **Rynek** has everything, from Baroque to postwar architecture, the cumulative effect of rebuilding after successive fires and the damage caused by Austrian, Prussian and Napoleonic sieges. Most of the façades have been thoroughly revamped over recent years, though beyond the main market square you'll see a fair amount of decay.

The bright yellow **town hall** dates from the 1710s, and looks a bit squat without its tower, which collapsed in 1967. It contains the **Old Trades Museum** (Muzeum Dawnego Kupiectwa; ☎ 074 852 1291; Rynek 37; adult/concession 3.50/2.50zł, free Fri; ☉ 10am-3pm Tue-Fri, 11am-5pm Sat & Sun), with reconstructions of an old tavern – Świdnica was always famous for its beer – pharmacy and shop, and a collection of historic scales and

balances. A bugle call sounds from the town-hall tower at 10am, noon, 2pm and 4pm but, alas, this is not the live *hejnał* of Kraków (see the boxed text, p183) but a recording.

The parish **Church of SS Stanislaus and Wenceslas** (Kościół Św Stanisława i Wacława; ☎ 074 852 2729; Plac Jana Pawła II 1), east of the Rynek, is a massive Gothic stone building whose façade is adorned with four elegant 15th-century doorways and an 18m-high window (the stained glass is not original). The tower, completed in 1565, is 103m high, making it Poland's tallest historic church tower after that of the basilica in Częstochowa (106m). The spacious interior has the familiar Gothic structure and ornate Baroque decoration and furnishings. The original church was accidentally burned down in

1532 by the town's *burmistrz* (mayor) Franz Glogisch, who fled Świdnica pursued by angry townsfolk who beat him to death in Nysa.

The **Museum of Arms** (Muzeum Broni; ☎ 074 852 5234, 0606 458 908; Al Niepodległości 21; adult/concession 3/2zł; ⏰ 11am-2pm Tue-Sun), practically a fortified compound in itself, displays arms, artillery and weapons from the 19th and 20th centuries.

Sleeping

Dom Rekolekcyjny (☎ 074 853 5260; ul Muzealna 1, enter from ul Zamkowa; s/d/tr 49/79/99zł, apt 140zł; P X) Conveniently positioned just one block west of the Rynek, this facility run by the Pentecostal Church is excellent value and nowhere near as monastic as you might expect. Breakfast not included.

Świdnica Hostel (☎ 074 852 2645; www.ssm.swidnica .pl; ul Kanonierska 3; dm 22zł, s/d 70/100zł; P X 💻) This friendly 90-bed hostel, 700m north of the Rynek, offers above-average HI-type accommodation in dorm rooms with three to five beds, as well as private rooms with bathroom.

Hotel Piast-Roman (☎ 074 852 1393; www.hotel -piast-roman.pl; ul Kotlarska 11; s/d 120/160zł; P 💻) The award-winning Piast-Roman, just off the Rynek, isn't quite as swish as the ground-floor restaurant might lead you to believe, but it's a good three-star, the 27 rooms are spic and span and you can't top the location.

Park Hotel (☎ 074 853 7098; www.park-hotel.com.pl; ul Pionierów Ziemi Świdnickiej 20; s/d/tr 120/160/200zł, ste 300-350zł; P X 💻) A modern turreted affair on a lovely leafy street within easy walking distance of the Old Town, the 18-room Park is a slightly smarter alternative to its more central rival and offers some big suites with shower or bath tub. The restaurant stays open relatively late.

Eating

Café 7 (☎ 074 640 6364; Plac Pokoju 7; dishes 3-9zł; ⏰ 11am-12.30am) In summer this café is hands-down the most attractive place for a drink or light meal in town, occupying a half-timbered building with a lovely walled garden right by the Church of Peace.

Bar Pod Arkadami (☎ 074 853 4902; ul Trybunalska 2; mains 3.50-8zł; ⏰ 9am-6pm Mon-Sat) This tiny snack bar 'Under the Arcade' is the place to get your lips round some proper *barszcz* (beetroot soup) and a *pasztecik* (hot pastry filled with meat, cheese or cabbage with mushrooms).

Kurna Chata (☎ 074 851 3488; Rynek 35; mains 8-20zł; ⏰ 10am-midnight) Tucked away within the Rynek's main pub, this charming sunken restaurant is modelled on a rustic hut, with old crockery, hefty home cooking and a hanging menu written on sackcloth (the English version comes in a rather pedestrian laminated form).

Da Grasso (☎ 074 851 4065; ul Zamkowa 9; pizza 12-25zł; ⏰ 11am-10pm Mon-Thu, 11am-midnight Fri & Sat, noon-midnight Sun) Another pizzeria, you might think, but this place is a slice or two above the usual.

Getting There & Away

The train station is a convenient five-minute walk southwest from the Rynek. The PKS bus station is behind it, but you have to go the long way round via the level crossing to reach it.

Direct train services are to Legnica (10zł, 1½ hours, twice daily); change at Jaworzyna Śląska or Kamieniec Ząbkowicki (departures every two hours) for Wrocław (10zł, 1½ hours), Jelenia Góra (21zł, three hours) and other regional destinations.

Hourly buses run to Wrocław (5zł, 1½ hours), while eight buses a day depart for Kłodzko (11zł, 1¾ hours) and the same number for Legnica (12zł, 1½ hours). Private minibuses to Wrocław depart from the front of the train station, as do ones headed for Wałbrzych via Książ (4.50zł, 30 minutes, every 20 minutes).

KRZYŻOWA
pop 500

This village 11km south of Świdnica was once the private estate of the Von Moltke family, whose 19th-century patriarch was the brilliant military strategist Prussian Field Marshal Helmuth von Moltke (1800–91). More importantly, Krzyżowa (Kreisau in German) and the estate were the nerve centre of the so-called Kreisau Circle (Kreisauer Kreis), the anti-Nazi resistance group led by the field marshal's great-grandnephew, Count Helmuth James von Moltke (1907–45), who was executed for his alleged role in the plot against Hitler in 1944 (see boxed text, p332).

Today the estate's 10 renovated buildings house the **Foundation for European Understanding** (☎ 074 850 0300; www.krzyzowa.org.pl; Krzyżowa 7), a nonprofit organisation dedicated to keeping alive the spiritual heritage of the Kreisau Circle and the humanistic teachings of Count von Moltke and his fellow resistance fighters. The centre has a small but interesting exhibition in the central **Krzyżowa Palace** (Pałac w Krzyżowej; adult/concession 4/2.50zł; ⏰ 8am-10pm), and surrounding it are fields, a river, a lake and ancient groves offering many opportunities for walking and hiking. You can also visit the **House on the Hill** (Domek na Wzgórzu), about 500m to the northeast, from where the circle operated during the war (the conspirators used a small train station near the house to avoid being seen by the German villagers); and **Cemetery Hill** (Wzgórze Cmentarne), containing the graves of the von Moltke family.

The centre contains an **information office** (❧ 8am-10pm) to the northwest of the main entrance. There is a couple of cafés and, just south, a fully fledged **restaurant** (mains 24-54zł; ❧ 10am-10pm). Should you want to spend the night, the 24-room **Hotel Spichlerz** (☎ 074 850 0200; s 120-150zł, d 150-180zł; P ✗ ✗ ⬚ ⬚) next to the main entrance is surprisingly well equipped and even has a sauna and fitness room.

You can reach Krzyżowa from Świdnica via city bus 12 (3.60zł, 20 minutes, five to eight daily), which will drop you near the main entrance, or by train (3zł, 10 minutes, four daily). The train station is 300m west of the centre.

KSIĄŻ

With its 415 rooms, the **castle** at Książ (pronounced kshonzh) is the largest in Silesia. It was built in the late 13th century by the Silesian Piast Duke Bolko I, acquired by the aristocratic von Hoberg (later Hochberg) family in 1509 and continuously enlarged and remodelled until well into the 20th century. It's thus an amalgam of styles from Romanesque onwards; the central portion, with three massive arcades, is the oldest. The eastern part (to the right) is an 18th-century Baroque addition,

while the western segment was built between 1908 and 1923 in a neo-Renaissance style.

During WWII Hitler planned to use the castle as a shelter and a huge bunker was hewn out of the rock directly beneath the courtyard. The Soviets used it as a barracks until 1949, after which it was pretty much abandoned. Part of the complex has now been restored and turned into a **museum** (☎ 074 664 3834; www.ksiaz.walbrzych.pl; ul Piastów Śląskich 1; adult/concession 10/7zł, with 30min tour 11/9zł, with 60min tour 13/10zł; ❧ 10am-5pm Mon-Fri, 10am-6pm Sat & Sun Apr-Oct, 10am-3pm Tue-Sun Nov-Mar).

Approaching the castle from the car park, you will pass under a large, decorative, freestanding **gateway** that now contains a restaurant on its upper floor and offers superb views of the castle, majestically perched on a steep hill amid lush woods.

While you follow a prescribed (and rather convoluted) route and only get to see a dozen or so rooms, the showpiece is **Maximilian Hall**, built in the first half of the 18th century. It's the largest room in the castle and only one completely restored to its original lavish form, including the ceiling (1733) painted with mythological scenes. The identical fireplaces on either side of the room are sublime. Along with the main rooms, including 'themed' salons (Baroque, Chinese, white etc) on the 1st floor, there are all kinds of temporary, rotating and hobby exhibits – from model aeroplanes and porcelain to medieval archery *en costume* in the basement – squirreled away in the many smaller chambers, most with separate admission charges. The corridors often hold displays of historical paintings and photos – look for the castle's last owners, Duke Bolko VI and his wife Daisy

---

COUNT VON MOLTKE & THE KREISAU CIRCLE

One of the few instances of united German resistance to the Nazi regime, the so-called Kreisau Circle was centred on the Krzyżowa estate of Count Helmuth James von Moltke. An attorney of German–South African parentage, Moltke opposed Hitler from early days, declining the chance in 1935 to become a judge as he would have been obliged to join the National Socialist Party. Even in 1940, when Germany was winning on all fronts, the circle was convinced that Germany would lose the war. Its members, from different political circles, prepared for a future democratic Germany integrated into Europe. Moltke, not necessarily in agreement with all members of the Kreisau Circle, opposed the plot of 20 July 1944 to assassinate Hitler. He argued that if the plot succeeded Hitler would become a martyr, and if it failed resistance leaders, the only ones who could help build a democratic Germany after the collapse of the Third Reich, would be decimated. Sadly the latter was what happened and, in the aftermath of the attempted coup, some 5000 of Hitler's opponents, including Moltke, were executed. 'What shall I say when I am asked: "And what did you do during that time?"' he wrote to his wife in 1941. Countess Freya von Moltke attended the opening of the first phase of the Foundation for European Understanding at Krzyżowa in 1994.

von Pless, who apparently featured in Britain's *Country Life* magazine often in the 1920s.

The dozen terraced **gardens** on the slopes to the left as you approach the castle were laid out gradually as the medieval fortifications were dismantled from the 17th century onwards.

A five-minute walk east of the castle is the **Sudetes Stud Farm** (Sudeckie Stadnina Ogierów; ☎ 074 840 5860; ul Jeździecka 3; adult/concession 3/2zł; ☺ 10am-6pm), once the castle stables. It has horses for hire (per hour 35zł) from Sunday to Tuesday and on Thursday.

Sleeping & Eating

Hotel Przy Oślej Bramie (☎ 074 664 9270; www.mirjan .pl; ul Piastów Śląskich 1; s 145-160zł, d 210-250zł, ste 215-300zł; Ⓟ ⊠ ⌨) 'Before the Donkey Gate' has 28 rooms contained in four pretty little stone buildings to the right as you pass under the gateway to the castle. Even better are the two suites in the castle watchtower. For dyed-in-the-wool romantics only.

Hotel Książ (☎ 074 664 3890; www.zamekksiaz.pl; ul Piastów Śląskich 1; s/d/tr 170/260/300zł, ste 360-480zł; Ⓟ ⊠ ⌨ ☒) This hotel occupies several out-buildings in the castle complex to the left as you walk up the main path, providing varied standards and facilities, though sadly little of the historical character seems to have rubbed off on the 46 rooms. There are also two restaurants and a café on the site.

Getting There & Away

The castle is some 7.5km from Wałbrzych; reach it from there on city bus 8 (2.20zł, 15 minutes), which runs every 30 to 50 minutes. Alternatively, private buses ply the Wałbrzych–Świdnica route (4.50zł, 30 minutes) every 20 minutes or so and will let you off on the main road, a 10-minute walk from the castle.

JELENIA GÓRA
pop 86,100

Set in a beautiful valley surrounded by the Western Sudetes, Jelenia Góra (yeh-*lane*-yah goo-rah) is a deceptively quiet place with a fair bit of history and important architecture. Founded in 1108 by King Bolesław Krzywousty (Boleslaus the Wry-Mouthed) – legend has it that the witty royal had been following a wounded deer and was so taken by the beauty of the place that he named it 'Deer Mountain' – the border stronghold came under the rule of the powerful Duchy of Świdnica-Jawor. Gold mining in the region

gave way to glass production around the 15th century, but weaving gave the town a solid economic base, and its high-quality linen was exported all over Europe.

Unlike many other towns in Silesia, Jelenia Góra (Hirschzunge in German) survived WWII pretty much unscathed, and it makes a great base for trips into the Karkonosze Mountains.

Information

Amigos (☎ 075 753 2601; ul Długa 4; ☺ 8.30am-6pm Mon-Fri, 8.30am-2pm Sat) Travel agency.
Bank Pekao (Plac Wyszyńskiego 35; ☺ 8am-6pm Mon-Fri)
Bank Zachodni (Plac Niepodległości 4; ☺ 8am-6pm Mon-Fri)
Internet C@fe (☎ 0506 996 365; ul Marii Konopnickiej 3; per hr 3zł; ☺ 10am-10pm Mon-Sat) Internet access.
Main post office (ul Pocztowa 9/10; ☺ 7am-9pm Mon-Fri, 9am-3pm Sat)
Sigmar (☎ 075 752 5304; ul Klonowica 3; per hr 2zł; ☺ 10am-6pm Mon-Fri, 10am-2pm Sat) Internet access.
Tourist office (☎ 075 767 6925; www.jeleniagora.pl; ul Grodzka 16; ☺ 9am-6pm Mon-Fri, 10am-2pm Sat, 10am-2pm Sun Jul & Aug only) In the 15th-century Grodzka Tower.

Sights & Activities

Jelenia Góra's main attraction is the massive **Church of the Holy Cross** (Kościół Św Krzyża), built in 1718 for a Lutheran congregation, though it has served a Catholic one since 1947. The three-storey galleries plus the dark, densely packed ground floor can accommodate 4000 people. The ceiling is embellished with illusionist Baroque paintings of scenes from the Old and New Testaments, while the magnificent organ over the high altar dates from 1729.

The **Karkonosze Museum** (Karkonoskie Muzeum Okręgowe; ☎ 075 752 3465; www.muzeumkarkonoskie .pbox.pl in Polish; ul Matejki 28; adult/concession/family 6/3/6zł, free Sun; ☺ 9am-4pm Tue-Fri, 9am-5pm Sat & Sun) is renowned for its extensive collection of glass dating from medieval times to the present; the Art Nouveau pieces are wonderful. On the museum grounds is a small skansen (open-air museum of traditional architecture) of traditional mountain huts typical of the Karkonosze Mountains.

The elongated **Rynek** (Town Sq), also called Plac Ratuszowy, is lined with a harmonious group of 17th- and 18th-century houses. Much of their charm is due to their porticoes and ground-floor arcades, which provide a covered passageway all around the square. The

SILESIA

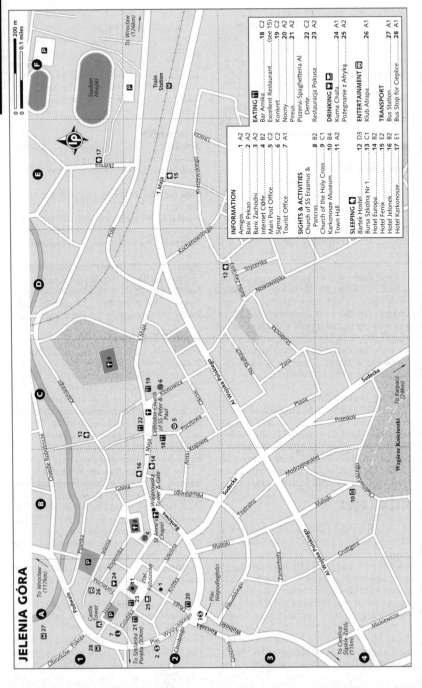

JELENIA GÓRA

INFORMATION	
Amigos......................................1 A2	
Bank Pekao..............................2 A2	
Bank Zachodni..........................3 A2	
Internet C@fe............................4 B2	
Main Post Office........................5 C2	
Sigmar.....................................6 C2	
Tourist Office............................7 A1	

SIGHTS & ACTIVITIES	
Church of SS Erasmus &	
Pancras.................................8 B2	
Church of the Holy Cross............9 C1	
Karkonosze Museum.................10 B4	
Town Hall...............................11 A2	

SLEEPING	
Bartek Hostel..........................12 D3	
Bursa Szkolna Nr 1...................13 C1	
Hotel Europa...........................14 B2	
Hotel Fenix.............................15 E2	
Hotel Jelonek.........................16 B2	
Hotel Karkonosze....................17 E1	

EATING	
Bar Arnika.............................18 C2	
Excellent Restaurant...........(see 15)	
Konkret................................19 C2	
Nocny..................................20 A2	
Pireus..................................21 A1	
Pizzeria-Spaghetteria Al	
Dente..................................22 C2	
Restauracja Pokusa.................23 A2	

DRINKING	
Kurna Chata...........................24 A1	
Pożegnanie z Afryką................25 A2	

ENTERTAINMENT	
Klub Atrapa...........................26 A1	

TRANSPORT	
Bus Station............................27 A1	
Bus Stop for Cieplice...............28 A1	

town hall on the square was built in the 1749, after its predecessor collapsed.

The **Church of SS Erasmus and Pancras** (Kościół Św Erazma i Pankracego), northeast of the Rynek, was erected in the 15th century; note the Gothic doorway in the southern entrance portraying Mary and St John at the foot of the Cross. The interior, with its theatrical 22m-high Rococo main altar crafted from brick-red marble, boasts mostly Baroque furnishings, including a richly decorated organ.

Sleeping

Bursa Szkolna Nr 1 (☎ 075 752 6848; www.bursa1jg .new.pl; ul Kilińskiego 5/7; dm 15-20zł; 🕑 Jul & Aug; **P**) This very basic school dormitory rents out its 130 beds in quad rooms during the summer holidays, though some space may be available in term time as well, mostly on weekends.

Bartek Hostel (☎ 075 752 5746; ssm.bartek@wp.pl; ul Bartka Zwycięzcy 10; dm 12.50-14.50zł, d 50zł; **P**) Modest but pleasant and housed in a cabinlike wooden building, the 42-bed hostel southeast of the Old Town has dorm rooms with between four and 10 beds as well as a few doubles.

Hotel Karkonosze (☎ 075 752 6756; www.hotel karkonosze.com.pl in Polish; ul Złotnica 12; d/tr 100/120zł; **P**) Out towards the train station, this is one of the better sports dorms you'll come across in Poland, despite the tartan carpets. Sadly you don't get to see into the adjacent stadium from the 20-odd rooms.

Hotel Europa (☎ 075 649 5500; www.ptkarkonosze.pl in Polish; ul 1 Maja 16/18; s/d/ste 139/195/274zł; **P**) The large block opposite the Jelonek can't compete in terms of ambience and charm, but the 49 rooms are huge, there's a budget restaurant on site and rates are 20% lower at weekends. Back rooms look on to the car park.

ourpick **Hotel Jelonek** (☎ 075 764 6541; www .hotel-jelonek.com.pl; ul 1 Maja 5; s/d 165/215zł, ste 250-450zł; **P** 🖳) Situated in a fine 18th-century burgher's house, this appealing 12-unit hostelry is the nicest in Jelenia Góra. Concentrate on the old prints and antiques in the public areas and turn a blind eye to the Pizza Hut downstairs with its separate entrance. The eight rooms are stylishly modern; the four enormous suites ideal for self-pampering.

Hotel Fenix (☎ 075 641 6600; www.hotelefenix .pl; ul 1 Maja 88; s/d/tr/q 189/249/289/329zł; **P** 🗙 🖳) More convenient for the train station than the centre, the town's flashest hotel offers 36 ultramodern rooms, and a spa and wellness centre with massage and treatments. It

also boasts the excellent Excellent Restaurant (below). Weekend rates drop by 15%.

Eating

Nocny (ul Długa 12; 🕑 24hr) This central shop open round the clock sells all the staples, including booze.

Bar Arnika (☎ 075 767 6124; ul Pocztowa 8; mains 5.50-15zł; 🕑 10am-5pm Mon-Fri, noon-3pm Sat) One of the cheapest central options, Arnika is a tiny cafeteria serving basic Polish dishes.

Konkret (☎ 075 645 7256; ul 1 Maja 44; mains 8-44zł) Probably the most popular (though not necessarily the best) pizzeria in town, 'Concrete' won't slam you with its food but the outside seating and music are both draws.

Pizzeria-Spaghetteria Al Dente (☎ 0501 682 383; ul 1 Maja 31; mains 9-24zł; 🕑 10am-10pm) Nestled in the foyer of the local cinema, Al Dente offers competent versions of all the Italian standards, though pizza (9zł to 24zł) and pasta (9zł to 16zł) are its forte. Good selection of vegetarian dishes.

Restauracja Pokusa (☎ 075 752 5347; Plac Ratuszowy 12; mains 15-28zł; 🕑 9am-10pm) With outdoor tables in the arcaded passageway encircling the Rynek, Pokusa is a very agreeable place, with upbeat surrounds and a repertoire mostly based on Polish food.

Pireus (☎ 075 767 6600; Plac Ratuszowy 10; mains 16-38zł; 🕑 10am-10pm) This ever-popular Greek(ish) taverna in the Rynek arcade does everything from *avgolemono* (egg and lemon soup) and gyros to moussaka, and almost hits the target. Service is a bit frazzled.

Excellent Restaurant (☎ 075 641 6600; ul 1 Maja 88; mains 21-55zł; 🕑 10am-10pm) This aptly named restaurant in the Hotel Fenix, decorated in comforting peach and blue tones, blows its own trumpet with theme weeks and good set lunches.

Drinking & Entertainment

Pożegnanie z Afryką (☎ 075 755 0376; Plac Ratuszowy 4; 🕑 10am-6pm Mon-Fri, 10am-5pm Sat, 11am-5pm Sun) Another branch of the serious independent coffeehouse, 'Out of Africa' peddles any number of imported beans and, of course, serves coffee. Sip, savour and stock up your grinder.

Kurna Chata (☎ 075 642 5850; Plac Ratuszowy 23/24; 🕑 10am-late) A small, cosy café with a pub feel and folksy décor (think mountain hut and bales of hay), Kurna Chata is a good place on the Rynek for a drink and light meal.

Klub Atrapa (☎ 075 642 4784; www.klubatrapa.com; ul Forteczna 1; ⊙ 6pm-4am Mon-Sat) One of the most attractive haunts in the centre, Atrapa is a great club with a dance floor, cheap beer and occasional live music.

Getting There & Away

The train station is about 1.5km east of the Rynek, while the bus station is on the opposite side of town, just northwest of the ring road.

Trains service Szklarska Poręba (12zł, one hour, up to 12 daily) and Wrocław (18.50zł to 31zł, 3½ hours, up to 15 daily); there are several daily to Kraków (46zł, 7½ hours) and Warsaw (106zł, 10¼ hours).

Buses to Karpacz (5zł to 6.40zł, one hour) and Szklarska Poręba (5zł, 45 minutes) run every hour or so. There's also regular bus service to Kamienna Góra (7zł, one hour), Legnica (13zł, 2½ hours) and Wrocław (20zł, 3½ hours). In summer there are buses to Prague and Berlin; contact the travel agency **Amigos** (☎ 075 753 2601; ul Długa 4; ⊙ 8.30am-6pm Mon-Fri, 8.30am-2pm Sat) for information about Eurolines.

CIEPLICE ŚLĄSKIE-ZDRÓJ

pop 8000

As its suffix 'Śląskie-Zdrój' suggests in Polish, Cieplice (cheh-plee-tseh), 11km south of the centre of Jelenia Góra, is a 'Silesian spa' – the oldest in the region. The local sulphur hot springs have probably been used for a millennium, and the first spa house was established as early as the late 13th century. The curative properties of the springs, which come out of the ground at a scalding 90°C, were only recognised in the late 18th century, paving the way for the building of the resort and spa town.

The helpful **tourist office** (☎ 075 755 8844; www.karkonosze.it.pl; Plac Piastowski 36; ⊙ 9am-5pm Mon-Fri, 9am-2pm Sat) in the centre can supply you with a map and brochures, including one with four area walks lasting between one and two hours.

Sights

The town's core is made up of a large **Spa Park** (Park Zdrojowy), with an embarrassment of lovely *fin-de-siècle* pavilions and buildings, including the domed **Spa Theatre** (Teatr Zdrojowy) and the wooden open-air **Concert Shell** (Muszla Koncertowa). At the western end of pedestrian Plac Piastowski is the 18th-century **Church of St John the Baptist** (Kościół Św Jana Chrzciciela), which contains an altarpiece painted by Michael Willmann. Should

you wish to sample the local waters, the **Pump Room** (Pijalnia; ul Ściegiennego) between the church and the tourist office serves water from four of the town's eight springs.

South of the spa park, in the timbered **Norwegian Pavilion** (Pawilon Norweski), is the **Natural History Museum** (Muzeum Przyrodnicze; ☎ 075 755 1506; www.muzeum-cieplice.com; ul Wolności 268; adult/concession 3.50/2.50zł; ⊙ 9am-6pm Tue-Fri, 9am-5pm Sat & Sun May-Sep, 9am-4pm Tue-Sun Oct-Apr). Its display of birds and butterflies from all over the world stems from the collection of the prominent Schaffgotsch family, local nobles who established the museum in 1876.

Sleeping & Eating

Hotel Caspar (☎ 075 645 5001; www.caspar.urlop.info.pl; Plac Piastowski 28; s 100zł, d 130-170zł, tr 190-220zł; P 🖵) What was once a rather tired budget place has metamorphosed into one of the most attractive boutique hotels in Silesia. Boasting its own spa and wellness centre, the Caspar has 29 beautifully designed rooms with hardwood floors and Oriental carpets; vaulted ceilings give the lounge a cathedral feel.

Hotel Pod Różami (☎ 075 755 1453; www.podrozami.pl; Plac Piastowski 26; s/d 120/170zł, ste 200-250zł; P 🖵) If you want to stay in Cieplice and make the most of the spa facilities, 'Under the Roses' is a sophisticated, 22-room option with sizable doubles. We love the café filled with old Victrolas and other antiques. It's set directly opposite the former Schaffgotsch Palace, part of which now serves as a school.

Café Sonata (☎ 075 755 7212; Plac Piastowski 13; dishes 7.50-15.50zł; ⊙ 11am-10pm) Arguably the best of Cieplice's limited eating options, Sonata is housed in a traditional detached house at the eastern end of the pedestrian mall, with suitably refined interiors and homemade cakes.

Getting There & Away

To get to Cieplice from Jelenia Góra, take any of the frequent urban buses (2.25zł, 20 minutes) from the stop near the bus station, including bus 4, 6, 9 or 14.

KARKONOSZE NATIONAL PARK

Karkonosze National Park (Karkonoski Park Narodowy; ☎ 075 755 3348; www.kpnmab.pl; adult/concession 4/2zł) is a 5563-hectare belt that runs along the Polish–Czech border for some 25km. The two main settlements here are the resort towns of Szklarska Poręba and Karpacz.

The range is divided by the Karkonosze Pass (Przełęcz Karkonoska; 1198m). The highest summit of the eastern section is Mt Śnieżka (1602m), while the western portion is topped by Mt Wielki Szyszak (1509m). The park is predominantly spruce forest up to an altitude of about 1250m.

The characteristic features of the Karkonosze landscape are *kotły* (cirques), huge hollows carved by glaciers during the ice age and bordered with steep cliffs. There are six cirques on the Polish side of the range, the most spectacular being Kocioł Małego Stawu and Kocioł Wielkiego Stawu near Mt Śnieżka, and Śnieżne Kotły at the foot of Mt Wielki Szyszak.

The Karkonosze range is known for its harsh climate, with heavy rainfall (snow in winter) and highly variable weather, including strong winds and mists at any time of year. Statistically, the best chances of good weather are in January, February, May and September.

The national park is the most popular **hiking** territory in the Sudetes and boasts 33 trails covering 100km. The two main gateways are Szklarska Poręba and Karpacz, from where most tourists ascend Mt Szrenica and Mt Śnieżka respectively. For longer walks, the red trail runs right along the ridge between the two peaks, with excellent views on both sides. The trail also passes along the upper edges of the *kotły*. You can walk the whole stretch in six to seven hours. If you start early enough, it's possible to do the Karpacz–Szklarska Poręba (or vice versa) trip within a day, preferably by using the chairlift to Mt Szrenica or Mt Kopa to speed up the initial ascent.

You can break the walk by taking any of the trails that branch off from the main route, or by stopping at one of the half-dozen mountain hostels. The **Odrodzenie mountain hostel** (☎ 075 752 2546; www.karkomega .pl/schronisko_odrodzenie in Polish; dm 25zł, d/q 120/180zł), with 112 beds, is roughly halfway between Mt Szrenica and Mt Śnieżka, while the **Samotnia hostel** (☎ 075 761 9376; www.samotnia .com.pl; dm 22-29zł, s/d/tr/q 37/70/105/128zł) at Kocioł Małego Stawu has the best views in the park. Book in advance.

Whatever you're into, take warm, waterproof clothes to deal with the unpredictable weather and get a detailed map of the area. The best one is the 1:25,000 *Karkonosze i Góry Izerskie* (6zł), which also includes the Izera Mountains of the Western Sudetes to the northeast of Szklarska Poręba.

SZKLARSKA PORĘBA
pop 7100

At the foot of Mt Szrenica (1362m) at the western end of Karkonosze National Park, Szklarska Poręba (*shklahr*-skah po-*rem*-bah) is, with Karpacz on the eastern side, one of a pair of major health resorts and ski centres in the Sudetes. The main street, ul Jedności Narodowej, skirts Kamienna River on its way into the hills; the bus station is at the south end and train station at the north end. Szklarska Poręba (Schreiberhau in German), 21km southeast of Jelenia Góra, is usually a lively little place, full of walkers, skiers and souvenir *cudgels* (mini tomahawks), and makes a good base for the region's many outdoor activities.

Information

Bank Zachodni (ul Jedności Narodowej 16; ⏲ 9am-4pm Mon-Fri)

Biuro Turystyki WNW (☎ 075 717 2100; www.szklar ska.com.pl in Polish; ul Wzgórze Paderewskiego 4) Travel agency for accommodation, hiking and cycling.

Post office (ul Jedności Narodowej 8; ⏲ 8am-6pm Mon-Fri, 9am-3pm Sat)

Sudety IT (☎ 075 717 2939; www.sudetyit.com.pl in Polish; ul Turystyczna 26; ⏲ 9am-4pm Mon-Sat, 9am-1pm Sun) Travel agency specialising in snow sports.

Tourist office (☎ 075 754 7740; www.szklarskaporeba .pl; ul Pstrowskiego 1; ⏲ 8am-6pm Mon-Fri, 9am-5pm Sat & Sun Apr-Oct, 8am-4pm Mon-Fri, 9am-5pm Sat & Sun Nov-Mar)

Sights & Activities

The **Mt Szrenica chairlift** (☎ 075 717 3035; www .sudetylift.com.pl; ul Turystyczna 25a; one way/return 24/27zł; ⏲ 9am-4.30pm May-Oct) rises 603m in two stages and deposits you at the top in about 25 minutes; it's used by skiers and snowboarders to reach five trails and two slopes in winter and by hikers the rest of the year. The lower station is 1km south of the centre, uphill along ul Turystyczna. Different prices and times apply during the ski season.

There are some attractions in easy walking distance of town. The road to Jelenia Góra winds east in a beautiful valley along Kamienna River. Some 3km down the road (or along the green trail on the right bank of the river) is the 13m-high **Szklarka Waterfall** (Wodospad Szklarki). From here the blue trail heads to the mountains and you can follow it to Mt Szrenica in two to three hours.

The road that heads west 4km to the Czech border at Jakuszyce passes rocky cliffs called **Ravens' Rocks** (Krucze Skały). About 500m further on, a red trail branches to the left. It's a 1.5km walk along this trail to **Kamieńczyk Waterfall** (Wodospad Kamieńczyka), the highest (843m) in the Polish part of the Sudetes. Continue for about 1½ hours along the same trail to get to Mt Szrenica. It is possible to hike across the border and join the yellow trail heading south to Vosecká in the Czech Republic, but make sure to carry your passport or EU national identity card with you.

The national park counts 19 mountain-bike trails totalling some 450km. You can rent bikes from **SG-Sport** (☎ 075 717 2074; ul Wzgórze Paderewskiego 5; ☻ 9am-8pm) for 5/25zł per hour/day. It also has scooters for 25/150zł and rents skis and snowboards in winter.

The **Bata farmhouse** (☎ 075 717 3234; www.agro turystyka.ig.pl/bata; ul Wolności 19) has horses for riding (25zł to 30zł per hour) and gives lesson for 50zł per hour.

Sleeping & Eating

Schronisko Na Hali Szrenickiej (☎ 075 717 2421; dm 18-31zł, d from 90zł; ☒ ▯) Just west of the summit of Mt Szrenica itself, this ageing 110-bed wooden hostel is often full of school groups hiding from the weather. The basic two- to 12-bed dorms are perfectly serviceable, and there are a couple of en suite rooms if you prefer privacy. There's a sauna (50zł) for the weary.

Fantazja (☎ 075 717 3935; www.fantazja.com.pl; ul Jedności Narodowej 14; s 80-120zł, d 140-200zł, tr 180-270 zł; ℗ ▯) This very central guesthouse has eight comfortable rooms, a solarium with massage and a popular restaurant (mains 11zł to 17zł, open noon to 10pm) serving international dishes.

OSSiR Mauritius (☎ 075 717 2083; ul Dworcowa 6; s/d 83/150zł; ℗ ▯) At the northern end of town and 100m from the train station, this exotically named 44-room place is a very basic holiday home run by the post office. Rooms with balconies, a gym and a café-bar add to the attraction. Rates are 10% cheaper after the second night.

Hotel Las (☎ 075 717 5252; www.hotel-las.pl; ul Turystyczna 8; s/d 160/220zł, ste 300-600zł; ℗ ▯ ☒) Occupying its own forest clearing about 4km northeast of the centre, the somewhat garish 144-room Las offers an astonishing range of sports and fitness facilities, including a pool (adult/concession 15/10zł, open 8am to 10pm), which nonresidents can use.

Camping Pod Klonem (☎ 075 717 3525; ul Armii Krajowej 2; per person/small tent/large tent/caravan 9/9/12/17zł; ℗) One of several camping grounds in the area, this is a fairly sparse facility but it's just opposite the train station and a mere 500m from the centre of town.

Diavolo Pizza Bar (☎ 075 717 2507; mains 9-16zł; ☻ 10am-10pm) It might not serve the best pizza in the world, but this place does Polish dishes too, and it's just across the bridge from the bus station.

Getting There & Away

Some four daily trains go to Jelenia Góra (12zł, one hour) and another three to Wrocław (33zł, 4½ hours). Buses to Jelenia Góra depart at least hourly (5zł, 45 minutes) and there are five daily buses to Wrocław (27zł, three hours).

For the Czech Republic, take the bus to Jakuszyce (4zł, 15 minutes) and cross the border to Harrachov, the first Czech village, from where there are onward buses.

KARPACZ

pop 5050

Karpacz (kar-pach), 22km south of Jelenia Góra, on the slopes of Mt Śnieżka, is one of the most popular mountain resorts in Poland, as much for skiing in winter as for hiking the rest of the year. Indeed, its reliable snow cover makes Mt Śnieżka one of the country's top winter-sports centres. Karpacz (Krummhübel in German) is a fun place to visit and has some very fine wooden buildings.

Orientation

Karpacz is essentially a village spread over 3km along winding ul Konstytucji 3 Maja without any obvious centre. The eastern part, known as Karpacz Dolny (Lower Karpacz), has most of the places to stay and eat. The western part, Karpacz Górny (Upper Karpacz), is largely a collection of holiday homes. In the middle of the two districts is the main bus station and the landmark Hotel Biały Jar. About 1km uphill from here is the lower station of the chairlift to Mt Kopa (1377m).

Information

Bank Zachodni (ul Konstytucji 3 Maja 43; ☻ 9am-4.30pm Mon-Fri)

Biuro Turystyki Karpacz (☎ 075 761 9547; www .btkarpacz.com.pl; ul Konstytucji 3 Maja 52; ☻ 9am-5pm Mon-Sat, 9am-2pm Sun) Travel agency.

Biuro Turystyki Sudety (☎ 075 761 6392; www
.btsudety.com.pl; ul Konstytucji 3 Maja 31; ☒ 9am-6pm
Mon-Sat, 10am-4pm Sun) Travel agency.
Tourist office (☎ 075 761 8605; www.karpacz.pl; ul
Konstytucji 3 Maja 25a; ☒ 9am-5pm Mon-Sat, 10am-
2pm Sun)

Sights & Activities

Karpacz has a curious architectural gem –
the **Wang Chapel** (Kościółek Wang; ☎ 075 752 8290;
www.wang.com.pl; ul Na Śnieżkę 8; adult/concession 5/4zł;
☒ 9am-6pm Mon-Sat, 11.30am-6pm Sun mid-Apr–Oct,
9am-5pm Mon-Sat, 11.30am-5pm Sun Nov–mid-Apr), the
only Nordic Romanesque building in Poland.
This remarkable wooden structure in Upper
Karpacz was one of about 400 such chapels built at the turn of the 12th century on
the bank of Lake Vang in southern Norway;
only 28 of these 'stave churches' survive there
today. By the 19th century it became too small
for the local congregation, and was put up for
sale to make way for a larger church. King
Friedrich Wilhelm IV of Prussia bought it in
1841, had it dismantled piece by piece and
then had it transported to Karpacz via Berlin.
Not only is it the oldest church in the Sudetes,
it's also the highest situated (886m).

The church is made of hard Norwegian
pine and has been constructed without a
single nail. It's surrounded by a cloister that
helps to protect it from mountain wind. Part
of the woodcarving is original and in excellent shape, particularly the doorways and
the capitals of the pillars. The freestanding
stone belfry was built when the church was
reconstructed here.

Bordered to the south by Karkonosze
National Park, Karpacz is an ideal starting
point for **hiking**. Most tourists aim for Mt
Śnieżka, and there are half a dozen different
trails leading there. The most popular routes
originate from the landmark **Hotel Biały Jar** (ul
Konstytucji 3 Maja 79) and will take you to the top in
three to four hours. When planning a trip to
Mt Śnieżka, try to include in your route two
picturesque postglacial lakes, Wielki Staw and
Mały Staw, both bordered by rocky cliffs. A
couple of trails pass near the lakes.

If you prefer not to walk up Mt Kopa, a **chairlift** (Miejska Kolej Linowa; ☎ 075 761 9284; ul Turystyczna 4;
one way/return 20/23zł; ☒ 8.30am-4.30pm), which caters
for skiers and snowboarders in winter, will
take you up 528m in 17 minutes. From Mt
Kopa, you can get to the top of Mt Śnieżka in
less than an hour via the black trail.

On Kolorowa Hill in the centre of Karpacz,
the **summer sleigh track** (letni tor saneczkowy; ☎ 075
761 9098; www.kolorowa.pl; ul Parkowa 10; 1/2/5/10 rides
5/8/17/30zł; ☒ 9am-late) is more than 1km long
and allows for speeds of up to 30km/h.

Sleeping

The tourist office has a full list of accommodation. Rooms in private houses and holiday
homes can also be arranged through local
travel agencies and cost around 25zł to 40zł
per person without bathroom or 40zł to 60zł
with en suite.

Schronisko PTTK Strzecha Akademicka (☎ 075
753 5275; www.strzecha-akademicka.com.pl in Polish; dm
25zł, s/d/tr 35/60/85zł; ☒) Karpacz' own rugged
mountaintop hostel sits snugly in a shallow
valley atop Mt Złotówka (1258m), next to Mt
Kopa, and is reached by a separate chairlift.
The accommodation's strictly budget stuff,
but you should see it when it snows.

Hotel Karolinka (☎ 075 761 9866; www.karolinka
.karpacz.pl; ul Linowa 3b; r per person 40-60zł; ☒) The
sweeping views from the front rooms make
some amends for this hilltop eyesore of a
hotel, and facilities include a sauna and its
own ski lift.

Hotel Kolorowa (☎ 075 761 9503; www.hotel-kolo
rowa.pl; ul Konstytucji 3 Maja 58; s/d 90/160zł, ste 150-200zł;
☒ ☒) This 26-room hotel-guesthouse oppo-
site the summer sleigh track in Lower Karpacz
offers good standards, the all-important sweet
on pillows and some rooms with restful hillside views. Restaurant and bar on site.

Hotel Rezydencja (☎ 075 761 8020; www.hotel
rezydencja.pl; ul Parkowa 6; s 150-210zł, d 180-240zł; ☒ ☒)
The 14 tastefully decorated rooms of this stunner of a hotel, housed in an 18th-century hilltop
villa overlooking the centre of Lower Karpacz,
are among the most desirable in town. There's
a spa, restaurant and café-bar on site.

Hotel Vivaldi (☎ 075 761 9933; www.vivaldi.pl;
ul Olimpijska 4; s 180-240zł, d 220-300zł; ste 340-420zł;
☒ ☒ ☒ ☒) A pale-yellow building in the
midst of the trees, the 27-room Vivaldi is a
classy proposition on the winding road up
to the chairlift and national-park entrance.
Smart modern rooms add a bit of russet to
the yellow theme, while model planes dogfight
on the bar ceiling. The well-equipped spa has
saunas and a Jacuzzi.

Camping Pod Lipami (☎ 0504 231 039; ul Konstytucji
3 Maja 8; per person/small tent/large tent/caravan 7/5/6/15zł;
☒ ☒) This camping ground close to the bus
station has its own outdoor pool.

Eating

Central Bar 49 (☎ 075 761 8592; ul Konstytucji 3 Maja 49; mains 13-32zł) This atmospheric little cross between a bar and a restaurant serves up simple but better-than-average Polish dishes such as beetroot soup with croquette and grilled *kiełbasa* (Polish sausage).

Pizzeria Verde (☎ 075 761 8194; ul Konstytucji 3 Maja 48; mains 12.50-21.50zł; ⏲ 1-9pm Tue-Sun) Just opposite the Central Bar 49, the Verde (did they mean Verdi?) is a cut above the usual pizzeria, with some decent pasta and meat dishes.

Getting There & Away

Buses run regularly to Jelenia Góra (5zł to 6.40zł, one hour, hourly). They go along Karpacz's main road, and you can pick them up at at least half a dozen points, though fewer go all the way to the Upper Karpacz stop. In July and August there are daily buses to Szklarska Poręba (6.40zł, 50 minutes) at 9.15am and 6.15pm.

KŁODZKO

pop 28,300

One of the oldest settlements in Silesia, Kłodzko (*kwots-koh*) started out as a major trade centre thanks to its location on the Nysa Kłodzka River, a tributary of the Odra. Like most settlements in the region, it changed hands every century or so, with Bohemia, Austria and Prussia all having a crack, and only after WWII did the town revert to Poland.

Due to its strategic position, Kłodzko (Glatz in German) has a long tradition of fortification. The early castles were replaced by a monstrous brick fortress, begun by the Austrians in 1662 and only completed two centuries later by the Prussians. Today it's the dominant, somewhat apocalyptic, landmark of the town and the best reason to pay a visit to Kłodzko, though the Old Town sits on a hillside and its steep winding streets have a special charm all their own.

Information

Bank Pekao (Plac Bolesława Chrobrego 20; ⏲ 9am-5pm Mon-Fri, 9am-1pm Sat)

Bank Zachodni (ul Kościuszki 7; ⏲ 8am-5pm Mon-Fri)

Internet KKO.pl (☎ 074 647 6045; 1st fl, ul Okrzei 17; per hr 3-4zł; ⏲ 10am-midnight Mon-Sat, 3pm-midnight Sun) Internet access, south of the Old Town.

Main post office (Plac Jagiełły 2; ⏲ 7am-8pm Mon-Fri, 8am-3pm Sat)

Orbis Travel (☎ 074 867 2775; Plac Grottgera 1; ⏲ 8am-5.30pm Mon-Fri, 9am-1.30pm Sat) Travel agency that shares an office with Eurolines.

PTTK office (☎ 074 867 3740; ul Wita Stwosza 1; ⏲ 8am-3pm Mon-Fri) Travel agency.

Tourist office (☎ 074 867 7007; www.ziemiaklodzka .it.pl; Plac Bolesława Chrobrego 1; ⏲ 10am-6pm Mon-Fri, 10am-4pm Sat) In the town hall.

Sights & Activities

Mighty **Kłodzko Fortress** (Twierdza Kłodzka; ☎ 074 867 3468; ul Grodzisko 1; adult/concession 7/5zł, with labyrinth 13/9zł; ⏲ 10am-7pm mid-Apr–Oct, 9am-4pm Nov–mid-Apr), begun under Austrian rule in the mid-17th century, was extended, modernised and modified over the next 200 years. Today it covers 17 hectares, making it the largest and best-preserved fortress of its kind in Poland. The walls in the lower parts measure up to 11m thick, and even at the top they are never narrower than 4m.

On entering, you can wander around various pathways and chambers and go to the top of the fortress for a bird's-eye view of town. There are several exhibitions in the grounds, including a **lapidarium** containing old stone sculptures (mostly tombstones) collected from historic buildings around the region.

The real attraction here, though, is the extensive network of defensive tunnels. Guided 40-minute tours of this so-called **labyrinth** (labirynt; adult/concession 7/5zł, with fortress 13/9zł; ⏲ 10am-7pm mid-Apr–Oct, 9am-4pm Nov–mid-Apr) begin on the hour, taking you on a 1km circuit including some passageways that are so low you have to bend over. The average temperature is about 8°C and the humidity very high.

Altogether 40km of tunnels were drilled around the fortress and served two purposes, those under the fortifications were principally for communication, shelter and storage, while the others, running up to 500m away from the fortress, were designed to attack and destroy enemy artillery. They were divided into sectors and stuffed with gunpowder; when the enemy happened to move their guns into a particular sector, the relevant chamber was blown up. This bizarre minefield was initiated in 1743 by a Dutch engineer, and by 1807 an immense labyrinth of tunnels had been built. The system was never actually used – at least not here.

Down the steps from the fortress is one of the entrances to the **Underground Tourist Route** (Podziemna Trasa Turystyczna; ☎ 074 867 3048; ul Zawiszy Czarnego 3; adult/concession 7/5zł; ⏲ 10am-6pm

KŁODZKO

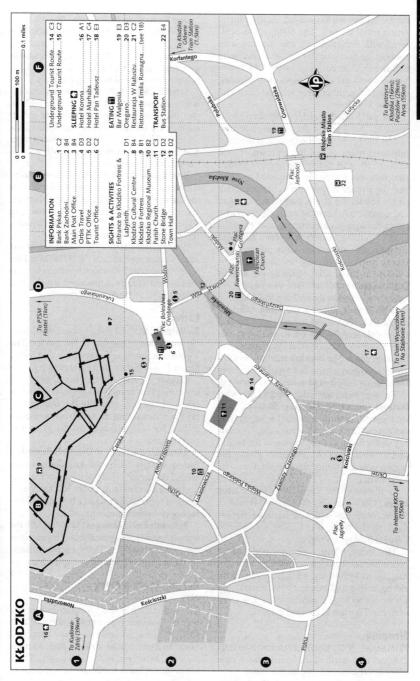

INFORMATION
Bank Pekao.........................	**1** C2
Bank Zachodni....................	**2** B4
Main Post Office.................	**3** B4
Orbis Travel.......................	**4** D3
PTTK Office.......................	**5** D2
Tourist Office....................	**6** C2

SIGHTS & ACTIVITIES
Entrance to Kłodzko Fortress &	
Labyrinth.....................	**7** D1
Kłodzko Cultural Centre......	**8** B4
Kłodzko Fortress................	**9** B1
Kłodzko Regional Museum.....	**10** B2
Parish Church....................	**11** C3
Stone Bridge....................	**12** D2
Town Hall.......................	**13** D2

SLEEPING 🛏
Hotel Korona....................	**16** A1
Hotel Marhaba..................	**17** C4
Hotel Pan Tadeusz.............	**18** E3

EATING 🍴
Bar Małgosia....................	**19** E3
Oregano.........................	**20** D3
Restauracja W Ratuszu........	**21** C2
Ristorante Emilia Romagna....	(see 18)

TRANSPORT
Bus Station......................	**22** E4

Underground Tourist Route...**14** C3
Underground Tourist Route...**15** C2

mid-Apr–Oct, 9am-4pm Nov–mid-Apr), another interesting set of tunnels. The 600m route, scattered with dungeon-type implements, uses some of the medieval storage cellars that were hollowed out under most of the Old Town. You can walk the whole length in 10 minutes, entering from either direction; the other end is in the Old Town.

The **parish church** (kościół parafialny), dedicated to Our Lady of the Assumption and just by the lower tunnel entrance, is the most imposing religious building in town. It took almost 150 years before the massive Gothic structure was eventually completed in 1490, and the overall shape hasn't changed much since. Inside, the altars, pulpit, pews, organ and dozen carved confessionals all blaze with florid Baroque ornamentation, and even the Gothic vaulting, usually left plain, has been sumptuously decorated with plasterwork. Organ recitals are held in the church – enquire at the tourist office or the **Kłodzko Cultural Centre** (☎ 074 867 33 64; www.kok.net.pl; Plac Jagieɫɫy 1; ☷ 10am-6pm Mon-Fri, 2-6pm Sat & Sun).

A short walk uphill is the **Rynek**, officially called Plac Bolesława Chrobrego. Several pastel-coloured houses on its southern side have preserved their original Renaissance and Baroque décor. The **town hall** was built in 1890 after its predecessor was destroyed by fire; only the 17th-century Renaissance tower survived.

To the southwest the **Kłodzko Regional Museum** (Muzeum Ziemi Kłodzkiej; ☎ 074 867 3570; ul Łukasiewicza 4; adult/concession 5/3zł, free Sun; ☷ 10am-4pm Wed-Fri, 11am-5pm Sat & Sun) has a display relating to the history of the town and the region and a collection of contemporary glass – the region is noted for its glass production – by local artists.

Southeast of the Rynek is a Gothic **stone bridge** (1390) spanning the narrow Młynówka River. With half a dozen Baroque statues flanking the sides, it is Kłodko's answer to Charles Bridge in Prague.

The helpful and well-informed tourist office has information on **activities** as wide-ranging rock climbing, hiking, cycling, horse riding, skiing and taking to the waters. Ask for one of its topical brochures or The Land of Active Tourism illustrated map.

Sleeping

PTSM Hostel (☎ 074 867 2524; ul Nadrzeczna 5; dm 18.50-23zł) Just 1km north of the Rynek, this simple place has rooms with two to five beds.

Dom Wycieczkowy Na Stadionie (☎ 074 867 2425; www.noclegi.pop.pl; ul Kusocińskiego 1; d/tr/q 60/90/120zł; ℗ ⛺) The sports centre by the city stadium, 500m south of the Old Town, offers basic accommodation for 38 guests. Rooms have private showers and there's a cafeteria.

Hotel Marhaba (☎ 074 865 9933; www.marhaba.ng.pl; ul Daszyńskiego 16; s 80-90zł, d 90-110zł, tr/ste 120/170zł; ℗) Bedsit-style rooms with shower or full en suite are the mainstay of this unfussy 20-room establishment, on the south side of town and backing on to the narrow Młynówka. Breakfast is 13zł extra.

Hotel Korona (☎ 074 867 3737; www.hotel-korona.pl; ul Noworudzka 1; s/d/ste 100/120/170zł; ℗) Located in the far northwestern part of town, this modern motel-like establishment accommodating 40 people is an option if you're just transiting through Kłodzko for the night.

Hotel Pan Tadeusz (☎ 074 867 0216; www.pantadeusz.com.pl; Plac Grottgera 7; s/d/tr/ste 150/190/230/265zł) This recently reopened 15-room boutique hotel is the choicest address in town and just about as central as you'll find in Kłodzko.

Eating

Bar Małgosia (☎ 074 867 36 40; ul Połabska 2; mains 5-9.50zł; ☷ 7am-7pm Mon-Fri, 8am-6pm Sat, 9am-5pm Sun) The 'Gretel' is a simple self-service bar that serves hearty Polish dishes until early evening.

Oregano (☎ 074 867 1473; ul Daszyńskiego 10; mains 6.90-21.90zł) This branch of a popular Wrocław chain of eateries, opposite the monumental Franciscan church, serves some Polish dishes, but our money is on the pizza and pasta dishes.

Restauracja W Ratuszu (☎ 074 865 8145; Plac Bolesława Chrobrego 3; mains 12-25zł; ☷ 10am-9pm) Kłodko's most formal restaurant, which you may or may not find open after trudging up the hill, has a good range of regional dishes and a tree-shaded terrace open in the warmer months.

Ristorante Emilia Romagna (☎ 074 867 0216; Plac Grottgera 7; mains 15-28zł; ☷ noon-10pm) This excellent eatery at the Hotel Pan Tadeusz serves authentic Italian dishes amid prewar splendour.

Getting There & Away

BUS

The bus station is the transport hub of the region. Buses are frequent to Kudowa-Zdrój (8zł, 50 minutes) and run every couple of hours to Bystrzyca Kłodzka (5.50zł, 30 minutes) and Wrocław (18.40zł, 1¾ hours). There are no direct buses to Kletno; take the bus to

Stronie Śląskie (6.50zł to 7.40zł, 40 to 75 minutes) and change or walk from there.

Czech Republic

From Kłodzko you can travel to the Czech Republic via Kudowa-Zdrój to Náchod (40km west of Kłodzko, on the way to Prague) or via Boboszów to Králíky (45km south of Kłodzko, on the Brno road). Note, there are no longer border posts or border crossing formalities between Poland and the Czech Republic. See boxed text, p514, for more information.

One daily bus goes across the border from Kłodzko to Náchod (11.50zł, 1½ hours), leaving at 1.35pm and travelling via Kudowa-Zdrój. There's also a daily bus to Prague at 1.30pm following the same route. There are a lot more buses to Náchod from Kudowa-Zdrój.

Alternatively, take the daily bus from Kłodzko to Boboszów (9zł, 1½ hours) at just past 9am Monday to Saturday and walk across the border 2km to Králíky.

TRAIN

Kłodzko has two train stations. The centrally located Kłodzko Miasto station, next to the bus station, handles regional services, including trains to Bystrzyca Kłodzka (4.50zł, 20 minutes, five daily), Kudowa-Zdrój (14zł, two hours, four to five daily) and Wrocław (15.50zł, 1¾ hours, eight daily), and many long-distance trains. There are more long-distance trains from the main station, Kłodzko Główne, 2km north.

KUDOWA-ZDRÓJ
pop 10,200

There are three popular spas to the west of Kłodzko and Kudowa-Zdrój (koo-doe-va zdruy) is by far the most attractive, favoured by a mild climate and several mineral springs. It's also the usual jumping-off point for the marvellous Góry Stołowe.

Renowned since the 18th century, Kudowa-Zdrój (Bad Kudowa in German), 37km from Kłodzko, is one of the oldest spas in Europe, with well-preserved spa architecture and a pleasant park lining the single main road. It's the ideal pit stop for recharging in between the more strenuous activities the region has to offer.

Information

Arcom Internet Café (☎ 074 866 3838; ul Słoneczna 3; per 20/60min 1/3zł; 10am-5pm Mon-Fri, 9am-noon Sat) Internet access.

Bank PKO (ul Zdrojowa 23) Southwest of the tourist office.
Góry Stołowe National Park headquarters (Dyrekcja PNGS; ☎ 074 866 1436; www.pngs.pulsar.net.pl; ul Słoneczna 31; 8am-3pm Mon-Fri) Some 650m southeast of the tourist office.
Tourist office (☎ 074 866 1387; www.kudowa.pl; ul Zdrojowa 44; 10am-6pm Mon-Fri, 9am-5pm Sat & Sun May-Sep, 9am-4pm Mon-Fri, 9am-3pm Sat Oct-Apr)

Sights & Activities

You can't miss the macabre **Chapel of Skulls** (Kaplica Czaszek; ☎ 074 866 1754, 0605 540 927; ul Moniuszki 8; adult/concession 4/2zł; 9.30am-1pm & 2-5.30pm Tue-Sun May-Sep, 10am-1pm & 2-4pm Tue-Sun Oct-Apr) in the Church of St Bartholomew (Kościół Św Bartomieja) grounds at Czermna, 1km north of the centre. The length of its walls and ceiling are covered with human skulls and bones – about 3000 of them, with another 20,000 to 30,000 filling the crypt below. The overall effect is stunning and will certainly offer you a reality check (see boxed text, p345).

Kudowa has an attractive 17-hectare **Spa Park** (Park Zdrojowy) but most treatments on offer involve room and board at one of the sanatoria. If you want (literally) a taste of what Kudowa has to offer, the **pump room** (pijalnia; adult/concession 1/0.50zł; 7am-6pm Mon-Fri, 6am-6pm Sat, 9am-6pm Sun) in the southeastern corner of the park serves up two of the local mineral waters. The **Galos salt caves** (☎ 074 868 0481; www.galos.pl in Polish; adult/concession 14/10zł; 9am-9pm) to the west claim to relieve all your ills with their remarkable artificial sea-salt chambers. Their rivals, the **Solana caves** (☎ 074 866 1997; www.solana.pl) near the tourist office, make the same claims. The **Water World Aqua Park** (Aqua Park Wodny Świat; ☎ 074 866 4502; ul Moniuszki 2a; admission 9-12zł; 9am-9pm Mon-Sat, 10am-9pm Sun), on the southern edge of the park opposite where the buses stop, has more active, watery fun.

Fans of the bizarre should hop on over to the Góry Stołowe park headquarters and check out Poland's only **Frog Museum** (Muzeum Żaby; ☎ 074 866 1436; ul Słoneczna 31; admission free; 9am-5pm Mon-Fri, 9am-1pm Sat & Sun). With a collection of some 3000 everyday objects with an amphibian theme, it's probably the only museum in the world where you can bring your own frog-related items to add to the collection. The national park was the first in Poland to build tunnels under roads to allow frogs to return to their ponds to spawn without injury. The aim of the museum is to raise awareness of frog conservation issues.

Sleeping

Recepcja Domów FWP (☎ 074 866 1261; www.fwp.pl in Polish; ul Słoneczna 7/9; s 28-58zł, d 50-106zł; ☺ 8am-7pm) This organisation will book a room in one of its two budget holiday homes on ul Słoneczna, with a total 145 beds.

Recepcja ZUK (☎ 074 868 0401; www.zuk-sa.pl; ul Moniuszki 2; dm 23-29zł, s 35-93zł, d 76-164zł, tr 90-168zł, ste 200-318zł; Ⓟ ⊠ ⬛ ⓖ) The Kłodzko Health Resort Company administers seven fine old villa sanatoriums in the centre of town, providing an unparalleled range of rooms. The emphasis is on medical treatment but they will accept casual guests.

Pensjonat Sudety (☎ 074 866 3756; www.kudowa.net .pl in Polish; ul Zdrojowa 32; s 65-75zł, d 90-100zł, tr 120-135zł; Ⓟ) This 24-room pension could do with a touch of external renovation, but inside you'll find perfectly acceptable budget accommodation, all with en suites.

Pensjonat Akacja (☎ 074 866 2712; www.akacja.info .pl; ul Kombatantów 5; s/d/tr 95/140/180zł; Ⓟ ⬛) This modernised classic villa happens to be one of our favourite places in Kudowa. Pensjonat Akacja is an excellent family-run guesthouse with 21 rooms in a quiet spot with plenty of space. Some of the rooms on the upper floors have balconies.

Willa Sanssouci (☎ 074 866 1350; www.sanssouci .info.pl; ul Buczka 3; s/d/tr/ste 110/140/180/200zł; Ⓟ ⬛) Located in a lovely villa dating back to 1894, the 52-bed Sanssouci has comfortable, ample rooms and good service. If you're feeling lucky, it also has its own wishing well in the garden.

Eating

Cafe Pod Palmani (☎ 074 866 3834; Park Zdrojowy; mains 7-17zł; ☺ 10am-11pm Sun-Thu, 10am-2am Fri & Sat) This brick-lined café in the park is one of the best places in town to grab a light bite, and stays open till late on weekends for a bit of music-bar action.

Pizzeria Tevere (☎ 074 866 1575; ul Zdrojowa 36; mains 7-23zł; ☺ 10am-11pm Mon-Fri, 10am-midnight Sat, 11am-10pm Sun) This large pizzeria next to the Sudety pension has a huge leafy terrace out front, ideal for relaxing after a day of hiking in the Góry Stołowe.

Zagroda w Starym Młynie (☎ 074 866 3601; ul Fredry 10; mains 12-28zł; ☺ 2-10pm Tue-Sun) About 1.5km southwest of the centre en route to Náchod, the 'Old Mill Farmstead' is a bit of a schlep but well worth the trip for its excellent Polish food and attractive surrounds.

Getting There & Away

BUS

Buses depart from the corner of ul 1 Maja and ul Warszawska in the town centre – hourly departures for Kłodzko (8zł, 50 minutes) and seven a day to Wrocław (25zł, three hours).

For the Góry Stołowe, there are half a dozen buses a day to Karłów (5zł, 25 minutes), which pass by the turn-off to Błędne Skały. Private minibuses run along the same route year-round.

Count on up to 10 buses a day on weekdays to Náchod in the Czech Republic and eight at the weekend. Alternatively, go to the border (3km) and cross it on foot to Náchod, 2km behind the frontier, from where there are onward buses and trains.

TRAIN

The train station, 2.5km south of the town centre, isn't much use unless you want to go to Warsaw (55zł, 10½ hours, two direct trains daily). To Kłodzko (14zł, two hours, four to five daily) and Wrocław (31zł, 3½ hours, four daily), it's better to go by bus.

GÓRY STOŁOWE

The Góry Stołowe (goo-ri sto-wo-veh), or 'Table Mountains', are among the most spectacular ranges of all the Sudetes. Lying roughly 10km northeast of Kudowa-Zdrój, they are almost as flat-topped as their name suggests. However, the main plateau is punctuated by remnants of an eroded upper layer, forming secondary 'islands' scattered with fantastic rock formations. This magical landscape was created when the main strata of soft sandstone were eroded, leaving harder rocks behind.

In 1994 the whole area became the Góry Stołowe National Park (Park Narodowy Gór Stołowych). The highlights of the 6300-hectare park are the Szczeliniec Wielki and the Błędne Skały.

Information

The park's headquarters in Kudowa-Zdrój (p343) can provide all the information you need; its *How to Sightsee the Stołowe Mountains?* brochure-map is punctuationally challenged but useful. More detailed are Eko-Graf's 1:50,000-scale *Góry Stołowe* and a new 1:30,000-scale map of the same name from Galileos. Both have all the walking routes and the important rocks are individually marked.

HEAD CASES

The Chapel of Skulls in Czermna was built in 1776 and looks pretty modest from the outside. Inside, however, it's a different story: thousands of neatly arranged skulls and bones decorate the walls, with more suspended from the ceiling. It's the only chapel of its kind in Poland and one of just three in Europe.

The creator of this unusual 'Sanctuary of Silence' was one Václav Tomášek, a Czech parish priest (Czermna belonged to the Prague Archdiocese at that time). He and the local grave-digger spent two decades collecting human skeletons, which they then cleaned and conserved. The 'decoration' of the chapel wasn't completed until 1804. Skulls and bones that didn't fit on the walls and the ceiling were deposited in a 4m-deep crypt.

Since the region was the borderland of the Polish, Czech and German cultures, and Catholic, Hussite and Protestant traditions, many of the bones belonged to victims of nationalist and religious conflicts. The skeletons came mostly from numerous mass graves, the result of two Silesian wars (1740–42 and 1744–45) and the Seven Years' War (1756–63). The cholera epidemic that plagued the region also contributed to such an impressive quantity of raw material.

Several anatomically interesting skulls are displayed on the main altar, including those of a Tatar warrior, a giant and a victim of syphilis. Alongside them are the skulls of the masterminds of the enterprise – the priest and the grave-digger – at one with their work for all eternity.

Sights

SZCZELINIEC WIELKI

At 919m, **Szczeliniec Wielki** (adult/concession 5/2.50zł; 9am-6pm mid-Apr–mid-Oct) is the highest outcrop of the Góry Stołowe range and has been a magnet for visitors for centuries. In 1790 German man of letters and walking enthusiast Goethe was one of the first trail tourists to pass through here. A decade later the man who would become America's sixth president, John Quincy Adams, remarked while touring Silesia that: 'This range of rocks…begins and ends so abruptly that it looks as if it were a crown upon the head of the mountain.'

Indeed, from a distance, the plateau looks like a high ridge adorned with pinnacles, rising abruptly from the surrounding fields. The most popular way to the top is from Karłów, a small village about 1km south of the plateau, from where a short road leads north to the foothills. You then ascend 682 stone steps (built in 1790) to a PTTK snack bar on the top – it takes about 40 minutes to get there.

The trail around the summit skirts the cliff edge (giving excellent views) before turning inland. The 'Long Steps' take you down to the 'Devils' Kitchen', from where, after passing through the chasm of 'Hell' and 'Purgatory', you can climb the narrow rocky steps to 'Heaven', another viewpoint.

The trail continues to two more viewpoints on the opposite side of the plateau and winds back to the starting point, passing a string of rocks carved into a wild array of shapes by time and erosion. Signs tell you the names given to each formation; it takes more than a little imagination to see where some of these came from, but others, such as the Camel and the Horse, will raise a smile when you get them. Don't miss the great Ape overlooking the plains. The whole loop takes about an hour, including scenic stops.

BŁĘDNE SKAŁY

About 4km to the west, the **Błędne Skały** (Errant Boulders; adult/concession 5/2.50zł; 9am-6pm mid-Apr–mid-Oct) are another impressive sight. Hundreds of gigantic boulders were deposited at 852m by glaciers in vaguely geometric shapes, forming a vast stone labyrinth. A trail runs between the rocks, which are so close together in places that you have to squeeze through sideways.

An hour is enough to do the loop. Cars and vans, charged 10zł and 30zł extra respectively, are only allowed in and out within set 15-minute windows every hour. You can stay as long as you like once you're parked.

The Błędne Skały are about 3.5km from the Kudowa-Zdrój–Karłów road, linked to it by a narrow, paved road (no public transport). The turn-off is 7km from Kudowa-Zdrój and 6km from Karłów.

Getting There & Away

The Góry Stołowe covers a fairly small area, and a day trip generally gives enough time to cover the two highlights. There's just one bus a day from Kudowa-Zdrój to Karłów

(4zł, 20 minutes) at 11am, though an earlier one leaves at 8.20am in summer as well. They go along the Road of the Hundred Bends, which snakes spectacularly through the forest. There are lots more private minibuses from Kudowa-Zdrój. Cyclists can take advantage of a cycle path leading through to the Czech Republic.

WAMBIERZYCE
pop 1200

A small village at the northeastern foot of the Góry Stołowe, Wambierzyce (vahm-byeh-*zhi*-tseh) is an important pilgrimage site and one of the oldest in Poland. Legend has it that in 1218 a blind peasant recovered his sight after praying to a statue of the Virgin Mary, which had been placed in the hollow trunk of a lime tree. A wooden chapel was constructed on the miraculous site and was later replaced with a church. The fame of Wambierzyce (Albendorf in German), dubbed the 'Silesian Jerusalem', spread, and a large, two-towered basilica was subsequently built between 1695 and 1711. When this collapsed seven years after its completion, a new sanctuary was built using the surviving Renaissance façade.

The largest numbers of pilgrims arrive on 15 August (Feast of the Assumption) and 8 September (Birth of Mary), as well as on the Sunday closest to those dates.

Sights

A flight of 33 steps – Christ's age when he was crucified – leads to the squat, 50m-wide façade of the **Church of Mary** (Sanktuarium Maryjne; Plac Najświętszej Marii Panny 11), its palatial appearance underwritten by the complete absence of towers. The side entrance takes you into the square cloister running around the church, lined with chapels and Stations of the Cross; the walls are densely adorned with folk paintings of Mary and old votive pictures. In the chapel west of the main altar you'll find a relic of one of Poland's modern saints, Zygmunt Gorazdowski (1845–1920), a native of Polish Lwów (now Lviv in Ukraine) who fought in the 1863 uprising, despite severe pulmonary problems, and later become a pioneering priest, author and educator. He was canonised in 2005.

The church proper, in the centre of the complex, is much smaller than you'd think from the outside, due to the size of the cloister. It's laid out on two ellipses, with the main one being the nave and the other the chancel, each

topped with a painted dome. The Baroque décor includes an unusually elaborate pulpit with the symbols of the four Evangelists. In the sanctuary behind an ornamental grille (1725), the florid high altar displays the miraculous miniature figure (only 28cm high) of the Virgin Mary with Child.

From May to mid-September, at 9pm Friday to Sunday, the church illuminations take place, lighting up the façade dramatically with some serious technical wizardry.

The hill opposite the church is dotted with a motley collection of chapels, gates, grottoes and sculptures connected with the Passion of Christ and collectively known as **Calvary** (Kalwaria). It was established in the late 17th century to mirror the Via Dolorosa in Jerusalem and was subsequently extended to include 74 chapels.

East of the church you'll find the **Bethlehem Crèche** (Szopka Betlejemska; ☎ 074 871 9197; ul Objazdowa; adult/concession 5/2.50zł; ☯ 9am-5.45pm Tue-Sun May-Sep, 10am-1pm & 2-3.45pm Tue-Sun Oct-Apr), a set of mechanised Nativity scenes. The main one includes 800 tiny figurines carved from lime wood, 300 of which move. Other scenes portray the Crucifixion, the Last Supper and the Massacre of the Holy Innocents. The crèche took a local craftsman 28 years to carve.

About 2.5km west of the church is a private **Ethnographic Open-Air Museum** (Skansen Museum Etnograficzne; ☎ 074 871 9184; ul Wiejska 52; ☯ 9am-sunset). The result of 10 years' work by the eccentric packrat owner, this is a museum featuring just about everything you could think of, including antiques, old household implements, minerals, stuffed birds and miners' uniforms, plus a small zoo. It's free, but donations are appreciated.

Sleeping & Eating

Locals, including the owners of the skansen, rent out rooms in their homes for about 20zł per person. The priests, too, offer budget accommodation in rooms with two to four beds. Just follow the sign to the Dom Pielgrzyma Nazaret, south of the Bethlehem Crèche on ul Objazdowa.

Hotel Wambierzyce (☎ 074 871 9186; www.hotel-wambierzyce.pl in Polish; Plac Najświętszej Marii Panny 1; s/d/tr/ste 150/240/280/600zł; Ⓟ) Everything you need in one convenient spot, no more than a one-minute pilgrimage from the church. Rooms have some nice old-style trappings (including a couple of tiled heating stoves), the restaurant is the best in town, and the pool table, minigym and bar should dispose of an evening one way or another.

Karczma Kowala (☎ 074 667 5072; ul Noworudzka 3; mains 7-15zł; ☷ 10am-10pm) This bright little place east of the church, on the way to the crèche, serves hearty Polish fare to hungry pilgrims.

Getting There & Away
There are up to half a dozen regularly scheduled buses to Kłodzko (5zł, 40 minutes) via Polanica-Zdrój, but only three services go direct to Kudowa-Zdrój (6.50zł, one hour).

BYSTRZYCA KŁODZKA
pop 10,500
Bystrzyca Kłodzka (bist-shi-tsah kwots-kah), perched on a hilltop above the Nysa Kłodzka River, is the second-largest town in the Kłodzko region. Since the 13th century, when it was founded, the town has been destroyed and rebuilt several times, though ironically it survived WWII virtually unmolested and still looks like a medieval fortified town. The few attractions here don't really add up to much, but somehow Bystrzyca Kłodzka (Habelschwerdt in German) feels right and you'll certainly enjoy walking around the Old Town.

Information
Bank PKO (ul Okrezi 1; ☷ 10am-5pm Mon-Fri)
Tourist office (☎ 074 811 3731; www.bystrzycak lodzka.pl; ul Rycerska 20; ☷ 8am-5pm Mon-Fri, 10am-4pm Sat) In the Knights' Tower.

Sights
The houses lining the **Rynek**, officially known as Plac Wolności, are a blend of architectural styles. The octagonal Renaissance tower (1567) of the Italianate **town hall** in the centre gives the square an almost southern European feel. Next to the town hall is an elaborate Baroque **plague pillar** (1737) dedicated to the Holy Trinity.

In the 14th century the town was granted municipal status and surrounded by fortified **city walls** (mury miejskie), some of which are still in place. The most substantial structures include the **Water Gate** (Brama Wodna) just south of the Rynek, and the **Kłodzko Tower** (Baszta Kłodzka; adult/concession 2.50/1.50zł; ☷ 9am-5pm Mon-Fri, 9am-3pm Sat, 10am-2pm Sun), which you can climb, on the opposite side of the Old Town to the north.

East of the Rynek, the **Knights' Tower** (Baszta Rycerska) was reshaped in the 19th century and turned into the belfry of a Protestant church that had been built alongside; you'll find the tourist office on the ground floor. After WWII the church was occupied by the rather esoteric **Philumenistic Museum** (Muzeum Filumenistyczne; ☎ 074 811 0637; www.muzeum2.filumenista.pl; Mały Rynek 1; adult/concession/family 4/3/14zł; ☷ 8am-4pm Tue-Sun), which displays lighters, matchbox labels from various countries and other paraphernalia related to the match industry. On the square southwest of the museum stands the old **whipping post** (pręgierz) from 1566; the Latin inscription on its top reads 'God punishes the impious'.

The Gothic **Parish Church of St Michael the Archangel** (Kościół Parafialny Św Michała Archanioła) sits at the highest point of the Old Town, two blocks northwest of the Rynek. It has a nave and just one aisle with a row of six Gothic columns running right across the middle.

Sleeping & Eating
Hotel Piast (☎ 074 811 0322; ul Okrzei 26; s 35-60zł, d 50-80zł; P) About 150m northeast of the tourist office just outside the Old Town, this basic hotel with a mixture of rooms with and without en suite was undergoing renovations when we last visited, so expect better, brighter and more expensive things when you visit.

Hotel Abis (☎ 074 811 0645; www.hotelabis.pl; ul Strażacka 28; s/d/tr/ste 99/166/249/209zł; P ☒ ☐ ☖) About 2km northwest of the centre and just off Rte 388, the Abis has 31 spic-and-span rooms in a modest modern block and offers excellent value for money. The stylish restaurant is worth a visit on its own.

Bistro Bałuszek (☎ 074 811 3899; ul Sienkiewicza 2; mains 5.50-15zł; ☷ 9am-10pm Mon-Sat, 11am-10pm Sun) Unfancy pub grub is available here in a fairly traditional style, with a terrace for summer sipping and nibbling.

Helios (☎ 074 811 0645; Plac Wolności 13; mains 6-16zł; ☷ 11am-10pm Sun-Thu, 11am-11pm Fri & Sat) Facing the Rynek, this pizzeria does a good range of pasta dishes as well.

Getting There & Away
The train station is just east of the tourist office. From here trains go to Kłodzko Miasto (4.50zł, 20 minutes, five daily), Międzylesie (4.50zł, 30 minutes, five daily) via Domaszków and Wrocław (17zł, two hours, five daily).

The bus station, on ul Sienkiewicza 200m north of the Parish Church of St Michael the

Archangel, has services to Kłodzko (5.50zł, 30 minutes) at least once an hour. There are also reasonable bus connections to Międzygórze (4.70zł, 40 minutes, hourly) and five or so buses to Stronie Śląskie (7.40zł, one hour) and Boboszów (8zł, 50 minutes).

MIĘDZYGÓRZE

pop 690

Międzygórze (myen-dzi-*goo*-zheh), 18km southeast of Bystrzyca Kłodzka, is a small, charming village set in a deep valley surrounded by forest. The town was an exclusive German mountain resort called Wolfwlsgrund in the late 19th and early 20th centuries, and still has half a dozen splendid (though rundown) historic villas that look as if they have been dropped in from the Tyrol.

Information

Dom Wczasowy Nad Wodospadem (☎ 074 813 5120; www.miedzygorze.net; ul Wojska Polskiego 12) The reception desk at this hotel doubles as a local tourist office, and the helpful staff can supply you with all manner of maps and brochures.

PTTK office (☎ 074 813 5195; www.pttkmiedzygorze.ta.pl; ul Wojska Polskiego 2; 🕑 8am-4pm Mon-Fri, 8am-2pm Sat) Has information about activities in the area.

Sights & Activities

Międzygórze's countryside is a gold mine for hikers and walkers. If you plan on hiking in the area, get a copy of Compass' *Ziemia Kłodzka* 1:50,000-scale map (10zł).

Northwest of the village is **Mt Igliczna** (845m), with the Baroque **Church of Mary of the Snows** (Sanktuarium Maria Śnieżna) in its shadow. You can get there by any of three different trails – waymarked red, green or yellow – in about 1½ hours.

About halfway up the yellow trail you'll come to the **Fairytale Garden** (Ogród Bajek; adult/concession 4/2.50zł; 🕑 10am-6pm May-Sep, 10am-4pm Oct-Apr), a little hillside plot of models and huts based on Polish fairy stories. It was originally assembled in the 1920s and completely restored in the 1970s and late 1980s.

There are at least five longer trails originating in or passing through the village. The most popular is the hike southeast to the top of **Mt Śnieżnik** (1425m), the highest peak in the region. It will take about 2½ hours to get there by the red trail. The best map to have is the 1:30,000 *Masyw Śnieżnika* (Śnieżnik Massif; 8zł) from Compass.

Northeast of Międzygórze is **Black Mountain** (Czarna Góra), which has an excellent **ski centre** (☎ 074 814 1245; www.czarnagora.pl in Polish) and reliable snow coverage. You can get here via the blue or green trails in about three hours. In Międzygórze the **Centrum Śnieżnik** (☎ 0502 525 564; www.snieznik.omega.pl; ul Wojska Polskiego 6; 🕑 9.30am-6pm) organises ski lessons (four-hour day 150/250zł weekend/weekday) and will kit you out for a day on the slopes for around 130zł.

At the western end of town behind the Dom Wczasowy Nad Wodospadem is the 21m-high **Wilczki Waterfall** (Wodospad Wilczki). The best vantage point is from the bridge right above the drop.

Centrum Śnieżnik rents **bicycles** for 25zł a day.

Sleeping & Eating

Schronisko Na Śnieżniku (☎ 074 813 5130; www.sudety.info.pl/nasniezniku in Polish; dm 21zł; ⊠) If you're climbing Mt Śnieżnik and don't feel like coming back the same day, this 58-bed PTTK hostel awaits you half an hour before reaching the summit.

Chata Lidia (☎ 074 812 5403; www.sudety.info.pl/chatalidia in Polish; ul Wojska Polskiego 27; r from 25zł per person; P ⊠) On the road into Międzygórze from Bystrzyca Kłodzka and just before the Dom Wczasowy Nad Wodospadem, 'Lydia's Hut' is one of the most stylish tourist farms in the Sudetes and can organise horse riding, cycling and skiing tours.

Recepcja FWP (☎ 074 813 5109; www.fwp.pl in Polish; ul Sanatoryjna 2; r per person 25-35zł, with full board 50-60zł; 🕑 7am-11pm) The FWP runs three of the nicest holiday homes in town, offering everything from singles with shared bathroom to full-board suites.

Dom Wczasowy Nad Wodospadem (☎ 074 813 5120; www.miedzygorze.net; ul Wojska Polskiego 12; d 70-100zł, tr/q/ste 90/100/150zł; P) At the western end of the village, right next to the waterfall, Nad Wodospadem offers reasonable rooms one step up from a hostel and has its own café-restaurant. Breakfast is an extra 12zł.

Willa Millennium (☎ 074 813 5287; www.millennium.ta.pl; ul Wojska Polskiego 9; s 75zł, d 95-99zł, ste 135zł; P ⊠ 💻) The 10-room Millennium offers central alpine-style accommodation at bargain prices. It has its own restaurant and a charming communal terrace.

Pizzeria Wilczy Dół (☎ 074 813 5286; ul Sanatoryjna 2; mains 7-15zł; 🕑 1-7pm Tue-Thu, noon-8pm Fri & Sun, noon-9pm Sat) A lot more than a pizzeria (as it bills itself), this rather charming alpine-style eatery also serves hearty rib-sticking Polish main courses.

Getting There & Away
All outbound buses go via Bystrzyca Kłodzka (4.70zł, 40 minutes), with services at least every couple of hours or so. Six buses continue to Kłodzko (8.40zł, one hour).

KLETNO
pop 50

Kletno is an elongated hamlet stretching some 3km. But it's not the smattering of cottages or even the spectacular scenery along the road from Międzygórze, 41km to the southwest, that brings visitors to Kletno (Klessengrudn in German). Poland's most beautiful cave is hidden in the trees beyond the village. Bones belonging to a cave bear, which lived here during the last Ice Age, were found and gave the place its name, the **Bear's Cave** (Jaskinia Niedźwiedzia; ☎ 074 814 1250; www.jaskinia.pl; adult 11-18zł, concession 6-13zł; ⏰ 10am-5.40pm Feb-Apr & Sep-Nov, 9am-4.40pm May-Aug, closed Mon & Thu).

The cave was discovered accidentally during marble quarrying in 1966, and a small 400m section of the 3km labyrinth was opened to the public 11 years later. You enter through a protective pavilion that houses a snack bar and a small exhibition focusing on the cave's history, then proceed into the spectacular corridors and chambers, festooned with stalactites and stalagmites. The humidity inside the cave is nearly 100% and the temperature is 6°C all year, so bring something warm. Visits are by 40-minute tours (Polish only) in groups of up to 15 people, starting every 20 minutes.

Getting There & Away
Kletno is most easily accessed via Stronie Śląskie, which has regular bus connections with Kłodzko (6.50zł to 7.40zł, 40 minutes to 1¼ hours, up to 18 daily) and Bystrzyca Kłodzka (7.40zł, one hour, up to nine daily). From here it's a 9km walk south to the cave by the yellow trail (2½ hours). If this is too much for you, take the bus to Bolesławów (about 11 daily), get off at Stara Morawa and walk the remaining 5km. There's one afternoon bus to Kletno from Stronie Śląskie (3.30zł, 15 minutes) at 3pm, but as it returns straight away you'll either have to walk back or leave

in time to get the last bus from Stara Morawa (around 5pm).

You can also reach the cave by walking for 2½ hours directly from Międzygórze. Take the black-marked ski trail that goes east from the centre along a rough road and switch to the yellow one leading north.

PACZKÓW
pop 8500

More than 750 years of history have left Paczków (*patch*-koof), a sleepy town midway between Nysa and Kłodzko, with one of the most complete sets of medieval fortifications in the country. Within the walls of what the Germans called Patschkau, the tiny Old Town is so attractive that it's been dubbed the 'Polish Carcassonne'.

Information
Bank Zachodni (Rynek 11; ⏰ 8.30am-4.30pm Mon-Fri)
Post office (ul Pocztowa 10; ⏰ 8am-6pm Mon-Fri, 8am-2pm Sat)
Tourist office (☎ 077 431 6790; www.paczkow.pl; ul Słowackiego 4; ⏰ 8am-4pm Mon, 7am-3pm Tue-Fri)

Sights
The oval ring of Paczków's **defensive walls** was built around 1350 and surrounded by a moat. This system protected the town for a time, but when firearms arrived in the 15th century, an additional, external ring of defences was erected outside the moat (it was pulled down in the 19th century). The original walls were fortunately retained and, as the town escaped major destruction during WWII, they still encircle the historic quarter. They were initially about 9m high for the whole of their 1200m length and had a wooden gallery for sentries below the top.

Four gateways were built, complete with towers (all of which still stand) and drawbridges, and there were two dozen semicircular towers built into the walls themselves (19 have survived, though most are incomplete). The most interesting is the round **Kłodzko Gate Tower** (Wieża Bramy Kłodzkiej), with its irregular loopholes; the oldest is the 14th-century **Wrocław Gate Tower** (Wieża Bramy Wrocławskiej; adult/concession 3/2zł; ⏰ 6am-6pm), which can be climbed. Buy your ticket at the kiosk opposite.

The Rynek occupies a good part of the Old Town. The **town hall** (Rynek 1) was built in the mid-16th century but only its tower is original; the main building was largely modernised

SILESIA

in the 1820s. You can climb to the top of the **tower** (adult/concession 3/2zł; 10am-5pm May-Sep), which provides much better views than the Wrocław Gate Tower.

The **Parish Church of St John the Evangelist** (Kościół Parafialny Św Jana Ewangelisty), just south of the Rynek, is a squat Gothic cube built in the second half of the 14th century. Even the Renaissance parapets are heavy and unattractive, though the Gothic doorway is some compensation. Inside, the church now has predominantly neo-Gothic furnishings, and only a few fittings from earlier times remain. The most unusual feature is the well in the right-hand aisle, which provided drinking water during times of siege.

A short walk north of the Rynek is the interesting **Gas Industry Museum** (Muzeum Gazownictwa; ☎ 077 431 6834; ul Pocztowa 6; admission free; 8am-2pm Mon-Fri), installed in an old redbrick gas works that operated from 1902 to 1977. The museum gives an insight into the gas production process, featuring the machinery and various related products such as heaters, irons, lamps and stoves, as well as Europe's largest collection of gas meters.

Sleeping

PTSM Hostel Pod Basztą (☎ 077 431 6441; ul Kołłątaja 9; dm 20-30zł; Jul & Aug) This seasonal hostel is on the 3rd floor of a school located on the west side of the walled town. The entrance is at the back of the building, via ul Narutowicza.

Korona Paczkowa Hotel (☎ 077 431 6277; ul Wojska Polskiego 31; d 80-110zł, tr 100-145zł, q 120-180zł; P) Korona is a small 10-room hotel about 300m southeast of the Rynek. Decent rooms, friendly owner-staff and a homely atmosphere are capped off by a lovely garden and terrace.

Camping Nr 258 (☎ 077 431 6509; ul Jagiellońska 8; camp site/cabin/apt 6/45/90zł; Jun-Sep; P) This camping ground about 1km south of the Old Town has a collection of rustic cabins and a tent area. It's in the local sports centre, which has a swimming pool.

Getting There & Away

The bus station, on the northeastern edge of the Old Town, has services to Nysa (4zł to 6.90zł, 45 minutes) and Otmuchów (3.70zł, 30 minutes) at least twice an hour, and to Opole (20zł, two hours) about six times a day. In the opposite direction, buses run to Kłodzko (6.90zł, 50 minutes) every two to three hours.

OTMUCHÓW
pop 5300

If you're travelling from Kłodzko to Nysa, you may want to stop at Otmuchów (ot-*moo*-hoof), about 12km short of Nysa. The town was founded around AD 1000 by King Bolesław Chroby, who built a fortified castle here to repel invasions by the Germans, Czechs and Moravians. The town passed into the hands of Wrocław bishops for over 500 years and came to be an important ecclesiastical centre. Set between two lakes – Lake Otmuchów to the west and Lake Nysa to the east – Otmuchów has now become a local holiday spot and is worth a stop.

Sights & Activities

The sloping Rynek retains little of its former character apart from the 16th-century **town hall**, which has a Renaissance tower and a lovely double **sundial** dating from 1575 on the south side. The Baroque **Parish Church of St Nicholas** (Kościół Parafialny Św Mikołaja), overlooking the Rynek from the west, was built at the end of the 17th century and most of its internal decoration, including frescoes by Dankwart and paintings by Willmann, dates from that period.

Just south of the church, atop the hill, is the massive **Bishops' Castle** (Zamek Biskupi), erected in the 13th century but much extended and remodelled later. It's now a hotel (see below), but you can climb the tower year-round.

Just 1.5km west of the Rynek and across fields and marshland is the 29-hectare **Lake Otmuchów** (Jezioro Otmuchowskie). This artificial body of water was created between 1928 and 1933 and today it is a regional centre for water sports, including sailing, kayaking, windsurfing and swimming. Most of the lake-related action happens along ul Plażowa.

Sleeping & Eating

Ośrodek Wypoczynkowy Sandacz (☎ 077 431 5581; ul Plażowa 1; r per person from 20zł) This holiday home on the water with direct access to a small beach offers basic accommodation in 12 rooms with shared facilities.

Gościniec Zamek (☎ 077 431 4691; www.zamek .otmuchow.pl; ul Zamkowa 4; s 100-130zł, d/tr/ste 160/190/ 200zł; P) If you're going to stick around, you should make this place a priority. The 35-room 'Castle Guesthouse' has no end of character, with a vine-covered restaurant, lots of greenery, the odd cannon and farming implements all over the place. Breakfast is 15zł extra.

Getting There & Away

Otmuchów lies on the road linking Paczków (3.70zł, 30 minutes) to the west with Nysa (3.50zł, 20 minutes) to the east and buses run about twice an hour. The Otmuchów bus station is just south of the castle hill on ul Mickiewicza.

NYSA

pop 47,900

For centuries Nysa (*ni-sah*) was one of the most important religious centres in Silesia. In the 17th century it became a seat of the Catholic bishops, who were in flight from newly 'Reformed' Wrocław. The bishops soon made Nysa a bastion of the Counter-Reformation; so strong was their hold that the town came to be known as the Silesian Rome.

Around 80% of Nysa's buildings were destroyed during fierce battles in 1945, and some of the postwar reconstruction leaves a lot to be desired in aesthetic terms. Visit Nysa for the dramatic cathedral, the little-big town vibe and one unique hotel.

Information

Bank Zachodni (ul Krzywoustego 7/9; ⌚ 9am-4pm Mon-Fri)

Omnibus (☎ 077 433 5927; Rynek 32; ⌚ 8am-6pm Mon-Sat, 10am-2pm Sun) Free internet access next door to the tourist office.

Post office (ul Krzywoustego 21; ⌚ 8am-7pm Mon-Fri, 8am-2pm Sat)

PTTK office (☎ 077 433 4171; ul Bracka 4; ⌚ 9am-5pm Mon-Fri)

Tourist office (☎ 077 433 5927; Rynek 32; ⌚ 8am-6pm Mon-Sat, 10am-2pm Sun)

Sights

There's no mistaking Nysa's powerful **Cathedral of SS James and Agnes** (Katedra Św Jakuba i Agnieszki), with its imposing blackened bulk and fine stone double portal. Built in 1430, it was remodelled after a fire in 1542, but hasn't changed much since then. The cathedral's 4000-sq-metre roof, supported by 18 brick columns inside, is one of the steepest church roofs in Europe.

The vast interior, much of it dating from the late 19th century, looks distinctly sober and noble, its loftiness being the most arresting feature. On closer inspection, however, you'll see that its side chapels (a total of 18) boast wonderful stained glass and a wealth of tombstones, funeral monuments and epitaphs, making up the largest collection of funerary sculpture in any Silesian church.

The freestanding block next to the cathedral is the **bell tower** (*dzwonnica*), which was begun 50 years after the church was built and originally intended to be over 100m high. Despite 40 years' work it only reached half that height, and consequently looks truncated and odd, especially with the tiny turret tacked on to it.

To the east of the cathedral is the 17th-century **Bishops' Palace** (Pałac Biskupi), a spacious double-fronted former Episcopal residence now housing the **Nysa Museum** (Muzeum w Nysie; ☎ 077 433 2083; ul Jarosława 11; adult/concession 5/3zł, free Sat; ⌚ 9am-5pm Tue-Fri, 10am-3pm Sat & Sun). Exhibits range from archaeological finds to photos documenting war damage, plus a model of the town in its heyday. The museum also features European paintings from the 15th to the 19th centuries, mostly from the Flemish and Dutch schools.

Stretching out from the foot of the cathedral, the vast **Rynek** shows the extent of the war damage. Only the southern side of the square is anything like it used to be, with its restored houses originally dating from the 16th century. The detached building facing them, the **Town Weighing House** (Dom Wagi Miejskiej; 1604), retains fragments of 19th-century wall painting on a side wall. Just round the corner, on ul Bracka, there are more historic houses and a 1701 copy of the Baroque **Triton Fountain** by Bernini in Rome.

Just past the fountain is the twin-towered **Church of SS Peter and Paul** (Kościół Św Piotra i Pawła), built in the 1727 for the Hospitallers of the Holy Sepulchre. It has one of Silesia's best Baroque interiors, complete with an opulent high altar, organ and *trompe l'œil* wall paintings.

The only significant traces of the medieval defences are two 14th-century brick towers: the **Ziębice Tower** (Wieża Ziębicka; ul Krzywoustego), with unusual turrets and dragon guttering; and the white-plastered **Wrocław Tower** (Wieża Wrocławska; ul Wrocławska). About 1.5km to the northwest and across the Nysa Kłodzka River are the remains of **Nysa Fortress** (Twierdza Nysa; ul Obrońców Tobruku), an enormous citadel built by Prussian King Frederic II and site of the annual **Nysa Fortress**

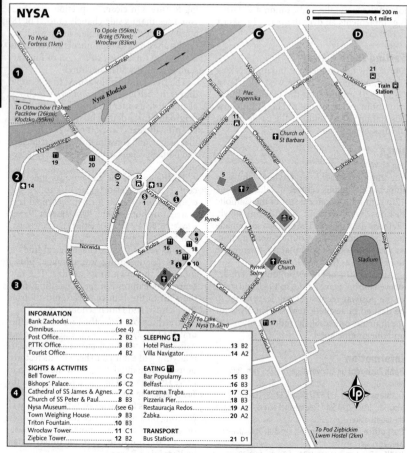

NYSA

INFORMATION	
Bank Zachodni	1 B2
Omnibus	(see 4)
Post Office	2 B2
PTTK Office	3 B3
Tourist Office	4 B2

SIGHTS & ACTIVITIES	
Bell Tower	5 C2
Bishops' Palace	6 C2
Cathedral of SS James & Agnes	7 C2
Church of SS Peter & Paul	8 B3
Nysa Museum	(see 6)
Town Weighing House	9 B3
Triton Fountain	10 B3
Wrocław Tower	11 C1
Ziębice Tower	12 B2

SLEEPING	
Hotel Piast	13 B2
Villa Navigator	14 A2

EATING	
Bar Popularny	15 B3
Belfast	16 B3
Karczma Trąba	17 C3
Pizzeria Pier	18 B3
Restauracja Redos	19 A2
Żabka	20 A2

TRANSPORT	
Bus Station	21 D1

Days (www.twierdzanysa.pl) held for three days in late July/early August.

Like nearby Otmuchów, Nysa has its own artificial body of water, the 20-hectare **Lake Nysa** (Jezioro Nyskie), formed in 1972 when the Nysa Kłodzka River was dammed. The sandy **lido** (🕘 9am-7pm May-Sep) in the lake's northeast corner, 3.5km from the centre of town, is particularly popular in season.

Sleeping

Pod Ziębickim Lwem Hostel (☎ 077 433 3731; www .kadett.d.pl/nysa; ul Krakiecka 28; dm 13-15zł; P ✕) About 2km south of the Old Town, this 48-bed hostel has small but smart dorms of two to four beds, providing a little more privacy than many other hostels.

Villa Navigator (☎ 077 433 4170; www .villanavigator.pl; ul Wyspiańskiego 11; s 70-150zł, d 100-180zł; P 🖳) This charming 12-room establishment run by an loquacious couple is exactly what a guesthouse should be, from the antique furniture, oil paintings and potted plants to the sociable breakfasts in the family parlour. Mansard rooms on the 3rd (top) floor are smaller and simpler but still thoroughly serviceable. For a real treat, ask for the Danzig (No 4) or Secessionist (No 3) room.

Hotel Piast (☎ 077 433 4084; www.hotel-piast .com.pl; ul Krzywoustego 14; s/d/tr/ste 135/170/255/230zł; P 🖳) Good tourist-class standards, a fridge in each room and small balconies entice guests into what could easily be overlooked as yet another concrete city block.

Eating

Żabka (ul Krzywoustego 29; 6am-11pm) A branch of the late-night convenience store chain.

Bar Popularny (077 433 3015; Rynek 23/24; mains 2.30-8zł; 8am-6pm Mon-Fri, 8am-4pm Sat) This un-reformed milk bar–cafeteria looks drab and basic, but the food is predictably acceptable. Set meals are a snip at 9.30zł.

Restauracja Redos (077 433 4972; ul Wyspiań-skiego 1a; mains 8-20zł; noon-1am Mon-Thu, noon-2am Fri & Sat, noon-midnight Sun) A pavilion near the river and the Villa Navigator holds this lively bar-restaurant, whipping out pizza and other modern staples for a youngish crowd.

Karczma Trąba (077 433 8974; ul Prudnicka 1; mains 8.80-17.80zł; 11am-2am) The 'Trumpet' attracts a chilled crowd with its enlightened Polish and international dishes (good choice of vegetarian ones), intimate seating, easy-listening canned jazz and eclectic décor.

Pizzeria Pier (077 433 5560; Rynek 39; mains 10-19zł; 11am-midnight Mon-Thu, 11am-1am Fri & Sat, noon-midnight Sun) Drinkers and diners alike congregate in this den of pasta and pizza clutching the hindquarters of the Town Weighing House.

Belfast (077 433 4880; Rynek 24/25; mains 10-38zł; 8am-midnight) Taking its name from the brewery sign on the outside, the Belfast is Nysa's most stylish place, serving inventive Italian and Polish dishes and – wait for it – green beer.

Getting There & Away

The bus and train stations face one another on ul Racławicka, a 500m walk northeast of the Rynek. Getting around the area is easiest by bus; there are services to Paczków (4zł to 6.90zł, 45 minutes, up to 10 daily), Kłodzko (10zł, 1¾ hours, up to six daily), Opole (10zł, 1½ hours, hourly) and Wrocław (12zł to 16zł, two hours, hourly). Trains are less frequent but may be useful when travelling to Opole (17zł, 1½ hours, eight daily).

UPPER SILESIA

After the idyllic villages and unfettered nature of the Sudetes, arriving in Upper Silesia (Górny Śląsk) may feel like stepping into a cold shower. Heavily developed and industrialised, the area occupies just 2% of Poland's territory, yet it's home to a full 9% of the population. Thanks to large deposits of coal, it's traditionally been the nation's centre of heavy industry and the most densely urbanised area in Central Europe. Under socialism this region was the 'reddest' in Poland and relatively well treated as a result.

Few people come to Upper Silesia for the sights. But whatever your feelings on urban sprawl, there are some important destinations in the region, including the unmissable Auschwitz extermination camp complex. Upper Silesia is also an easy port of call if you're heading to Kraków or the Czech Republic.

KATOWICE

pop 311,500

Katowice (kah-to-*vee*-tseh), the centre of the so-called Upper Silesian Industrial District (Górnośląski Okręg Przemysłowy), is a difficult child to love. The GOP contains 14 cities and a number of neighbouring towns, forming one vast conurbation with a population of well over three million. It's one of the biggest industrial centres in Europe, and one of the most outdated, though EU money is now helping to modernise the area and the work done here.

Historically, Katowice is a product of the 19th-century industrial boom, but it only became a city in the interwar period. After WWII, at the height of the Stalinist cult craze, the city was renamed Stalinogród, but reverted to its old name soon after Comrade Joe died in 1953. Katowice has few significant historical monuments, but it's a major commercial and cultural centre.

Information

BOOKSHOPS

EMPiK (032 203 7201; www.empik.com; ul Piotra Skargi 6; 8am-8pm Mon-Sat, 10am-2pm Sun) Best for newspapers and magazines.

INTERNET ACCESS

Eurocafé (032 710 5361; www.café.katowice.pl in Polish; per 15/30/60min 1.50/2.50/3.50zł; 24hr) At the train station.

Internet Bob Café (0501 406 567; ul Chopina 8; per 15min 1zł; 10am-midnight Mon-Thu, 10am-5am Fri & Sat, 2-10pm Sun)

Kino Helios Internet Café (032 603 0101; Altus Shopping Centre, ul Uniwersytecka 13; per 15/30/60min 1/2/3.50zł; 9.30am-10pm) The city's best, at Helios Cinema.

Wic Internet Café (032 259 9523; www.wic.pl in Polish; ul Opolska 5; per 15/30/60min 1/1.50/3zł; 24hr)

SILESIA

LAUNDRY

Eko Express (☎ 032 603 0200; Altus Shopping Centre,
ul Uniwersytecka 13; ⏰ 7.15am-8pm Mon-Fri, 9am-8pm
Sat, 10am-3pm Sun)

MONEY

Bank Pekao (ul Św Jana 5; ⏰ 8am-6pm Mon-Fri,
9am-2pm Sat)
Bank Zachodni (Al Korfantego 5; ⏰ 8am-6pm Mon-Fri)

TOURIST INFORMATION

Tourist office (☎ 032 259 3808; www.um.katowice. pl;
ul Młyńska 2; ⏰ 9am-5pm Mon-Fri)

TRAVEL AGENCIES

Orbis Travel (☎ 032 355 9960; ul Staromiejska 21; ⏰ 8am-
6pm Mon-Fri, 9am-2pm Sat)

Sights

The central **Rynek** is not lined with historic
burghers' houses as you'd find elsewhere in
Silesia but encircled by drab postwar blocks.
It's a showpiece of the 'early Gierek style' –
the term Poles sarcastically give to architecture spawned during the fleeting period
of apparent prosperity in the early 1970s,
when Edward Gierek's government took out
hefty loans from the West to make Poland a
'second Japan'.

North of the Rynek, the **Silesian Museum**
(Muzeum Śląskie; ☎ 032 258 5661; www.muzeumslaskie
.pl; Al Korfantego 3; adult/concession/family 9/4.50/12zł, free
Sat; ⏰ 10am-5pm Tue-Fri, 11am-5pm Sat & Sun) features
one permanent exhibition – Polish paintings
from 1800 to 1939 – as well as various tempo-

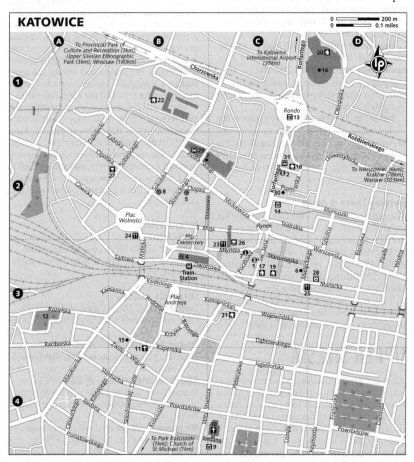

rary displays from its vast collections (fine art, archaeology, ethnography and local history and culture).

Some 350m further north is the large roundabout called the Rondo, which now houses the new **Rondo Art Gallery** (Galeria Rondo Sztuki; www.rondosztuki.pl in Polish; Rondo Gen Jerzego Ziętka 1; 11am-7pm Tue-Fri, 10am-6pm Sat & Sun). Facing it to the northeast is the landmark **Spodek** (032 258 3261; www.spodek.com.pl; Al Korfantego 35), a sports and concert stadium built in 1971 that truly deserves its name of 'Flying Saucer'.

The enormous **Provincial Park of Culture and Recreation** (Wojewódzki Park Kultury i Wypoczynku) is possibly Katowice's most popular attraction and the conurbation's most important recreation area. It includes a large stadium, zoo, amusement grounds, planetarium and the **Upper Silesian Ethnographic Park** (Górnośląski Park Etnograficzny; 032 241 0718; www.chorzow.pl/skansen; ul Parkowa 25; adult/concession 7/4zł; 9am-5pm Tue-Fri) with scores of traditional wooden buildings spread over 20 hectares. The park is about 3km northwest of the centre; reach it from the Rondo on tram 6, 11 or 23.

Some 800m south of the Rynek is the **Cathedral of Christ the King** (Katedra Chrystusa Króla; ul Plebiscytowa 49a), Poland's largest cathedral, measuring 89m by 53m. The massive sandstone structure was erected between 1927 and 1955. The spacious interior is topped with a large dome rising 59m from the floor, but apart from colourful stained-glass windows and an unusual 'wheel' crucifix it's fairly plain.

Behind it, the **Archdiocesan Museum** (Museum Archidiecezjalne; 032 608 1452; ul Jordana 39, enter from ul Wita Stwosza 16; admission free; 2-6pm Tue & Thu, 2-5pm Sun) has a collection of sacral art from the late 14th century, including some beautiful Gothic altarpieces.

About 1.5km further to the southwest, in **Park Kościuszki**, is the lovely, timber-shingled **Church of St Michael** (Kościół Św Michała), dating from 1510 and brought from the Upper Silesian village of Syrynia in 1939.

Katowice has Silesia's best-preserved **Jewish Cemetery** (Cmentarz Żydowski; 032 251 2826, 032 253 0209; ul Kozielska 16; 8am-5pm Sun-Thu, 8am-noon Fri). Established in 1868, it's divided into two parts, of which the front one is the older.

Just east of the cemetery is the **Skyscraper** (Drapacz Chmur; ul Żwirki i Wigury 15), Poland's first such building when completed in 1934 and considered the best example of functionalism in Poland. The 14-storey, 60m-tall tower was the highest building in the country until 1955. Just opposite is the lovely Art Deco **Garrison Church of St Casimir** (Parafia Wojskowa Św Kazimierza; ul Skłodowskiej-Curie 20), which opened just a year before Skyscraper.

Those with time on their hands should head for the suburb of **Nikiszowiec**, which is about 6km to the southeast, where there is a unique housing estate built for miners (and their families) who worked at the nearby Nickisch (now Poniatowski) shaft between 1908 and 1924. Built of attractive red brick, with a network of streets between them, the nine blocks are interconnected by gateways, and the complex was totally self-sufficient, with everything from shops, restaurants and a swimming pool to a hospital, a school and a detention centre. Bus 12 (2.40zł) goes here from the centre.

Sleeping

Ślązaczek Hostel (032 351 1956; www.sltzn.katowice .pl; ul Sokolska 26; dm 20-30zł) This 50-bed HI hostel is an 800m walk north of the train station, offering the usual basic accommodation in dorms of up to eight people.

SILESIA

Hotel Olimpijski (☎ 032 258 1233; www.hotelspodek
.katowice.pl; Spodek, Al Korfantego 35; s 120zł, d 160-180zł,
ste 220zł; ▣) Don't expect much from this step
up from a hostel in the Spodek stadium, apart
from a great location and lots of traffic. Still,
it's probably the best deal in town.

Hotel Polonia (☎ 032 251 4051; www.hotelpolonia
.katowice.pl; ul Kochanowskiego 3; s/d/tr 120/190/270zł;
Ⓟ ✕ 🐾 ▣) This 81-bed hotel, while of-
fering nothing special beyond bare-bones
comfort, is just a five-minute walk south
of the train station. The welcome here is
always warm.

Hotel Katowice (☎ 032 258 8281; www.hotel-katowice
.com.pl; Al Korfantego 9; s/d/tr 180/224/298zł, ste 272-292zł;
Ⓟ ▣ 👤) A typical communist-era product,
this 230-bed block has little character, lots
of broken things and some downright nasty
rugs. But it's not short on amenities (bar, restaurant, cake shop) and the town centre's a
light stroll away. Prices go down by 25% at
the weekend.

Hotel Diament (☎ 032 231 2244; www.hoteldiamentul
.pl; ul Dworcowa 5; s/d/ste 269/359/439zł; Ⓟ ✕ ▣ 👤)
This 43-room link in a small local chain is just
a stone's throw from the Monopol. It's comfortable, convenient and reliably friendly.

Hotel Monopol (☎ 032 782 8282; www.hotel.com.pl;
ul Dworcowa 5; s/d 490/560zł, ste 650-790zł; Ⓟ ✕ 🐾
▣ 🍽 👤) The 114-room Monopol is a
tasteful reincarnation of Katowice's most
celebrated prewar hotel: modern and full
of stylish walnut and chrome surfaces, with
friendly, informed staff, huge shower heads,
two restaurants, and a fitness centre with
two saunas and swimming pool. There's a
fabulous 19th-century floor mosaic under
glass in the lobby.

Eating

Several pedestrian strips hold Katowice's
highest concentrations of eateries: ul
Stawowa, just north of the train station, has
plenty of snack bars and unfussy restaurants;
while the areas around ul Staromiejska and
ul Wawelska, northeast of the station, are a
bit more cosmopolitan and upmarket.

Złoty Osioł (☎ 032 203 5005; ul Mariacka 1; two-course
set meal 8.90zł; ☯ 10am-10pm Mon-Sat, noon-10pm Sun) A
cheerful, popular vegetarian café of the kind
you'd expect in health-conscious Western
Europe, the 'Golden Donkey' has hippy décor
(think psychedelic walls and distressed furniture) and meat-free dishes, including some
vegan dishes.

La Grotta (☎ 032 206 8166; ul Wawelska 3; mains
12-40zł; ☯ 9am-10pm) On a short but heaving
pedestrian street by the train station, this
charming two-floor trattoria is Katowice's
best Italian eatery and reaches far beyond
the usual pizza and pasta offerings.

Restauracja A Dong (☎ 032 258 6662; ul Matejki 3;
mains 24-42zł) With the university having just
added Chinese to its curriculum, there is a
need for authentic Chinese food in Katowice
and this is your baby.

Drinking & Entertainment

Gaudi Café (☎ 032 253 8775; ul Wawelska 2) In tribute
to the acclaimed Spanish architect, this is the
coolest café on the centre's coolest pedestrian
street. The coffee and cakes are good, but it's
the out-there interior that'll leave you in awe.

Dekadencja (☎ 032 203 4433; ul Mariacka 20;
☯ noon-5am Mon-Sat, 4pm-1am Sun) Arguably the
best dive on a street of dives. Decadence is the
kind of place you'll come to and never leave.
Legendary club nights.

Spiż (☎ 032 781 1132; www.spiz-katowice.pl; ul Opolska
22; ☯ 10am-midnight Sun-Thu, 10am-2am Fri & Sat) This
branch of the Wrocław microbrewery bar-
restaurant has live music some nights.

Getting There & Away

AIR

Katowice International Airport (☎ 032 392 7200; www
.gtl.com.pl) is in Pyrzowice, 35km north of the city.
Domestic flights currently cover just Warsaw
(three daily), with international services to
30 or so European cities, including Frankfurt
(up to three daily), London (up to five daily),
Munich (daily) and Paris (three weekly). **LOT**
(☎ 032 206 2462; ul Piastowska 1; ☯ 9am-6pm Mon-Fri, 9am-
3pm Sat) has an office near the Hotel Katowice.

BUS

The bus station, on ul Piotra Skargi some
500m north of the train station, handles a couple of buses a day to most destinations around
the region, with plenty of long-distance and
international services as well.

Polski Express buses depart from in front
of Hotel Katowice. There are two buses a day
to Kraków (23zł, 1½ hours) at 10.40am and
9.40pm, and one to Warsaw (69zł, 6½ hours)
at 7.50am via Częstochowa and Łódź.

TRAIN

Trains are the main means of transport in
the region and beyond. The train station is

in the city centre and trains depart hourly for Oświęcim (15.50zł, one to 1½ hours), Pszczyna (7.50zł, 45 minutes), Kraków (20zł, 1½ hours), Opole (28zł, 1¾ hours), Wrocław (36zł, 2¾ hours), Poznań (42zł, five hours), Częstochowa (14zł to 17zł, 1½ hours) and Warsaw (46zł, 2¾ hours). International destinations include Berlin, Bratislava, Budapest, Hamburg, Prague and Vienna.

OŚWIĘCIM

pop 40,650

Oświęcim (osh-*fyen*-cheem) is a quiet, medium-sized industrial town on the border between Silesia and Małopolska, about 30km southeast of Katowice and about 40km west of Kraków. The Polish name may be unfamiliar to most foreigners, but the German one is not. This is Auschwitz, the scene of the largest attempt at genocide in human history and the world's largest cemetery.

The Auschwitz extermination camp was established in April 1940 by the Germans in the prewar Polish army barracks on the outskirts of Oświęcim. Auschwitz was originally intended for Polish political prisoners, but the camp was 'repurposed' as a dedicated centre for the wholesale extermination of the Jews of Europe. For this purpose, the much larger camp at Birkenau (Brzezinka), also referred to as Auschwitz II, was built 2km west of the original site in 1941 and 1942, followed by another one in Monowitz (Monowice), several kilometres to the west.

It is now estimated that in total this death factory eliminated some 1.6 million people of 27 nationalities, including 1.1 million Jews, 150,000 Poles and 23,000 Roma.

The name Auschwitz often describes the whole Auschwitz-Birkenau complex. In 2007, its Unesco world heritage listing was changed from 'Auschwitz Concentration Camp' to 'Auschwitz-Birkenau: German Nazi Concentration & Extermination Camp (1940–45)'. Both Auschwitz and Birkenau are open to the public as the **State Museum Auschwitz-Birkenau** (Państwowe Muzeum Auschwitz-Birkenau; ☎ 033 843 2022; www.auschwitz.org.pl; ul Więźniów Oświęcimia 20; donation requested; 🕑 8am-7pm Jun-Aug, 8am-6pm May & Sep, 8am-5pm Apr & Oct, 8am-4pm Mar & Nov, 8am-3pm Dec-Feb). The museum's visitors centre is at the entrance to the Auschwitz site.

There's also a **tourist office** (☎ 033 843 0091; www.cit.oswiecim.neostrada.pl; ul Leszczyńskiej 12; 🕑 8am-6pm Mon-Fri, 8am-4pm Sat & Sun Apr-Sep, 8am-5pm Mon-Fri, 8am-3pm Sat & Sun Oct-Mar) near the Auschwitz site.

Sights

AUSCHWITZ

Auschwitz was only partially destroyed by the fleeing Nazis, and many of the original brick buildings stand to this day as a bleak testament to the camp's history. Some 13 of the 30 surviving prison blocks now house museum exhibitions, either general or dedicated to victims from particular countries or races that lost citizens at Auschwitz.

During the communist era, the museum at Auschwitz-Birkenau was conceived as an antifascist exhibition – the fact that most of the victims were Jewish was played down, and undue prominence was given to the Poles killed here. This approach has changed: block 27, once dedicated to the 'suffering and struggle of the Jews', now presents Auschwitz more correctly as a place of the 'martyrdom of the Jews'.

From the visitors centre in the entrance building, you enter the barbed-wire encampment through the infamous gate, still displaying the grimly cynical legend *Arbeit Macht Frei* (Work Brings Freedom). Visit the exhibitions in the prison blocks, then go to the gas chamber and crematorium.

A 17-minute **documentary film** (adult/concession 3.50/2.50zł) about the liberation of the camp by Soviet troops on 27 January 1945 is screened in the visitors centre every half-hour, with a foreign-language soundtrack a few times a day (the English version is normally at 10am, 11am, 1pm and 3pm).

Photography and filming are permitted throughout the camp, though visitors should be discreet when using such equipment. There's a self-service snack bar by the entrance as well as a *kantor* (private currency-exchange office), free left-luggage room and several bookshops with publications about the place.

Get a copy of the museum-produced *Auschwitz Birkenau Guidebook* (3zł), available in many languages, including English. It has plans of both camps and gets you round the grounds. **English-language tours** (26zł) of both camps, including entry to the documentary film, last 3½ hours and depart at 10.30am, 11.30am and 1.30pm, with an additional one at 3.30pm from April to September.

BIRKENAU

It was actually at Birkenau, not Auschwitz, that the torture and murder of more than a

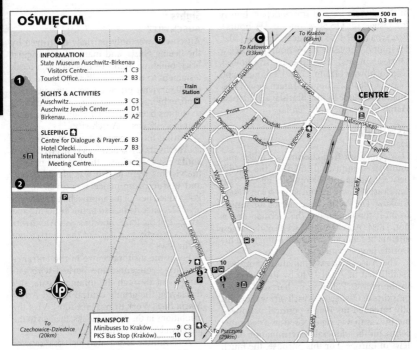

OŚWIĘCIM

million Jews took place. Massive (175 hectares), purpose-built and typically 'efficient', the camp had more than 300 prison 'barracks'. (They were actually stables built for 52 horses but housed 300 people each.) Birkenau also had four huge gas chambers complete with crematoria. Each could asphyxiate 2000 people at one time, and there were electric lifts to raise the bodies to the ovens. The camp could hold up to 200,000 inmates – and often did.

Though much of Birkenau was destroyed by the retreating Nazis, the size of the place, fenced off with long lines of barbed wire and watchtowers stretching almost as far as your eye can see, will give you some idea of the scale of the crime; climb the tower at the entrance gate to get the full effect. Some of the surviving barracks are open to visitors for viewing, silent contemplation and prayer (p279). Make sure to leave enough time (at least an hour) to walk around the camp.

AUSCHWITZ JEWISH CENTRE
In the centre of the town of Oświęcim, the excellent **Auschwitz Jewish Center** (☎ 033 844 7002; www.ajcf.org; Plac Skarbka 5; admission free; ⏰ 8.30am-8pm

Sun-Fri Mar-Oct, 8.30am-6pm Sun-Fri Nov-Feb) approaches the Holocaust from another angle, with permanent exhibitions building up a picture of Oświęcim's thriving Jewish community in the years before WWII. While the restored synagogue (1913), archive photos and Judaica found beneath the town's Great Synagogue in 2004 are much less harrowing than the camps' displays, trying to reconcile the family portraits here with the museum's ranks of mug shots quickly brings home the realities of what happened. It's hard to forget you're looking at the last remnants of Polish Jewry, an all-but-exterminated culture.

Sleeping & Eating
Centre for Dialogue and Prayer (Centrum Dialogu i Modlitwy; ☎ 033 843 1000; www.centrum-dialogu .pl; ul Kolbego 1; camping per person 20zł, bed per adult/ student 88/68zł; Ⓟ ▣) This 50-bed centre is a Catholic facility 500m southwest of the tourist office, providing comfortable and quiet accommodation in rooms of two to 10 beds (most with en suite) and a restaurant.

International Youth Meeting Centre (Międzynarodowy Dom Spotkań Młodzieży; ☎ 033 843 2107; www

.mdsm.pl; ul Legionów 11; camping 15zł, s 110-120zł, d 150-170zł, tr 180-210zł; P ☐ ⚑) This German-built centre, 1km east of the train station, is essentially for long-staying groups, but they'll take anyone if there are vacancies. Meals and cheaper rooms with shared bathroom are available.

Hotel Olecki (☎ 033 847 5000; www.hotelolecki .pl; ul Leszczyńskiej 12; s/d/tr 150/180/200zł, ste 300-350zł; P ☐) This spanking new 29-room hotel, just opposite the tourist office and entrance to Auschwitz, is the most comfortable and centrally located accommodation in Oświęcim.

Getting There & Around

For most tourists, the jump-off point for Oświęcim is Kraków. Buses (8zł, 1½ hours, up to 10 daily) can be a more convenient option than trains, as they drop you off in the parking lot opposite the entrance to Auschwitz. Minibuses, which are even more frequent, arrive at and depart from ul Więźniów Oświęcima, northeast of the museum. Take note that the last minibus goes back to Kraków at 7pm and the last bus 15 minutes later.

If you want to stay beyond that time you'll need to take a train back to Kraków (11zł, 1½ hours, up to 12 a day). If Katowice is your starting point, there are five daily trains (15.50zł, one hour) and twice as many buses (6zł, 1½ hours), though only one stops near the museum. If you want to go to Pszczyna (10zł) from Oświęcim, take the train to Czechowice-Dziedzice (up to 12 daily) and change there. The whole journey should take about 1½ hours.

To get from the train station to the museum, take any of the southbound city buses (2.40zł), including the 24, 25, 28 and 29. Taxis will take you to either camp for 10zł to 15zł.

From mid-April to late October, there is a free bus linking Auschwitz with Birkenau. It departs hourly, from 10.30am to 5.30pm (11am to 6pm from Birkenau), from outside the entrance to the visitors centre. Alternatively, you can walk (2km) or take a taxi (10zł to 15zł).

There are no buses from Birkenau to the train station; walk the 2km or take a taxi. Alternatively, catch the free shuttle bus back to Auschwitz and change there for one of the frequent buses to the station.

PSZCZYNA

pop 25,000

One of the oldest towns in Silesia (its origins go back to the 11th century), Pszczyna (*psh-chi-nah*), the 'pearl of Silesia', was home for centuries to the Piasts. In 1847, after centuries of changing ownership, it became the property of the powerful Hochberg family of Prussia.

In the last months of WWI, Pszczyna was the flashpoint of the first of three consecutive Silesian uprisings in which Polish peasants took up arms and demanded that the region be incorporated into Poland. Their wishes were granted in 1921, following a plebiscite held by the League of Nations.

Information

Bank Zachodni (ul Piastowska 2; ⏰ 9am-5pm Mon-Fri)

Post office (ul Batorego 1; ⏰ 7am-8pm Mon-Fri, 7am-1pm Sat)

PTTK office (☎ 032 210 3530; www.pttk-pszczyna .slask.pl in Polish; Rynek 15; ⏰ 8am-5pm Mon-Fri, 9am-1pm Sat)

Tourist office (☎ 032 212 9999; www.pszczyna.info.pl; Brama Wybrańców 1; ⏰ 8am-4pm Mon-Fri, 10am-4pm Sat, noon-6pm Sun) Just inside the castle gate.

Sights

On the western side of the Old Town, Pszczyna's grandiose **castle** dates back to the 12th century, when the Opole dukes built a hunting lodge here. It has been enlarged and redesigned several times, most recently in 1870.

The Hochbergs, who owned the castle until 1945, furnished their home according to their status – they were among the richest families in Europe, ruling vast swathes of land from their Silesian family seat, the castle at Książ (p332). Priceless works of art completed the scene, but most were lost during WWII.

Today the palace houses the **Castle Museum** (Muzeum Zamkowe; ☎ 032 210 3037; www.zamek-pszczyna .pl; adult/concession/family 12/7/28zł; ⏰ 11am-3pm Mon, 10am-3pm Tue, 9am-5pm Wed-Fri, 10am-5pm Sat, 10am-6pm Sun Jul & Aug, 11am-3pm Mon, 10am-3pm Tue, 9am-5pm Wed, 9am-4pm Thu & Fri, 10am-4pm Sat, 10am-5pm Sun Apr-Jun, Sep & Oct, 11am-3pm Tue, 9am-4pm Wed, 9am-3pm Thu & Fri, 10am-3pm Sat, 10am-4pm Sun Nov-Mar), with about a dozen rooms open over three floors. Those wanting more detailed information should pick up a copy of the English-language guidebook *The Castle Museum in Pszczyna* (14zł) from the ticket office.

The castle's interiors feature bedchambers, drawing rooms and salons filled with

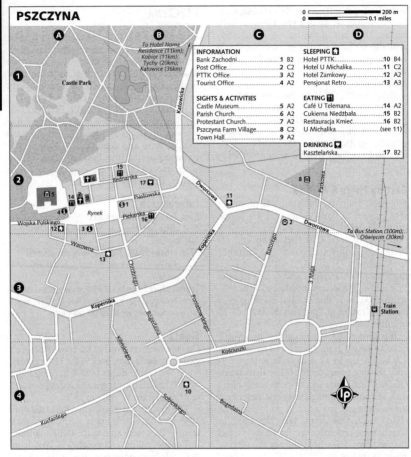

PSZCZYNA

0   200 m
0   0.1 miles

INFORMATION
Bank Zachodni.........................1 B2
Post Office...............................2 C2
PTTK Office..............................3 A2
Tourist Office...........................4 A2

SIGHTS & ACTIVITIES
Castle Museum.........................5 A2
Parish Church..........................6 A2
Protestant Church.....................7 A2
Pszczyna Farm Village..............8 C2
Town Hall................................9 A2

SLEEPING
Hotel PTTK.............................10 B4
Hotel U Michalika....................11 C2
Hotel Zamkowy.......................12 A2
Pensjonat Retro.......................13 A3

EATING
Café U Telemana.....................14 A2
Cukiernia Niedźbała.................15 A2
Restauracja Kmieć...................16 B2
U Michalika..........................(see 11)

DRINKING
Kasztelańska..........................17 B2

tapestries, ceramics, paintings and hunting trophies. Unforgettable are the **library** (biblioteka; adult/concession 4/2zł), panelled entirely in walnut, and the stunning **Mirror Chamber** (Sala Lustrzana), which hosts occasional chamber music concerts. Some of the palace's rooms also contain themed exhibitions, including a **collection of armour** (zbrojownia) in the basement and one of miniscule portraits in the **Cabinet of Miniatures** (Gabinet Miniatur; adult/concession 2.50/1.50zł) on the 3rd floor. Behind the castle is the extensive English-style **Castle Park** (Park Zamkowy) along the Pszczynka River.

The castle gives on to the elongated and leafy **Rynek**, lined with old burghers' houses dating mostly from the 18th and 19th centuries. On its northern side is the **Protestant church** and, next to it at No 2, the **town hall**, both remodelled early this century. Behind the town hall is the 14th-century **parish church**, extensively rebuilt over the years, with a typically lavish interior featuring a ceiling painting of the Ascension.

A five-minute walk east of the Rynek is the small but interesting **Pszczyna Farm Village** (Zagroda Wsi Pszczyńskiej; ☎ 0603 131 186; ul Parkowa; adult/concession 5/2.50zł; ☀ 10am-3pm Tue-Sat, 10am-sunset Sun Apr-Nov), a small but interesting skansen with half a dozen 200-year-old timber houses – including a mill, smithy and barn – collected from the region.

The town of **Tychy**, some 20km north of Pszczyna, 16km south of Katowice and on the same train line, has been famous for its beer for four centuries, and a tour of the **Tyskie Browary Książęce** (Tychy Prince's Brewery; ☎ 032 327 8430; wycieczki.tyskie.kp.pl; ul Mikołowska 5; ☑ 2-6pm Mon, 10am-2pm Tue, noon-6pm Wed, 10am-6pm Thu, 10am-8pm Fri, 10am-5pm Sat) is well worth a stopover. The tours last about 2½ hours and include a visit to the Tychy Brewing Museum (Tyskie Museum Piwowarstwa) and, of course, a beer tasting in the pub. They are free and conducted in six languages, including English, but you should book in advance by phone or email.

Sleeping

Hotel PTTK (☎ 032 210 3833; www.pttk-pszczyna.slask .pl in Polish; ul Bogedaina 16; s 45-75zł, d 60-99zł; **P**) The PTTK hotel, south of the Rynek, is charmingly situated in a former redbrick prison, though the last inmate left in 1975. There's nothing cell-like about the rooms now, though the cheaper rooms share facilities. Breakfast is not included.

Pensjonat Retro (☎ 032 210 2245; retro@retro.pl; ul Warowna 31; s 95-110zł, d 120-140zł, tr 160zł; **P** ▣) Named (and decorated) long before retro became a byword for cool, this guesthouse with 15 rooms in two buildings is a friendly and central choice.

Hotel U Michalika (☎ 032 210 1355; umichalika@post .pl; ul Dworcowa 11; s/d/tr 110/150/190zł; **P**) This hotel is owned and operated by local chef-turned-entrepreneur Stefan Michalika and offers 16 modern and upbeat rooms. It is located east of the Old Town. The in-house restaurant is very good.

Hotel Zamkowy (☎ 032 449 1720; www.hotel zamkowy.eu; Rynek 20; s/d/tr 200/240/320zł) Also known by its English name, the Castle Hotel is a stunner of a new 10-room boutique caravanserai housed in a renovated 18th-century burgher's house. If the marble floors in the public areas and the guestrooms' enormous bathrooms don't impress, the views of the Rynek and the castle will. Rates come down between 10% and 15% at the weekend.

Hotel Noma Residence (☎ 032 219 4678; www .promnice.com.pl; ul Promnicka; r 300-540zł, ste 600-740zł; **P** ✕ ▣ ⬩) Housed in a half-timbered royal hunting lodge at Kobiór, 9km south of Tychy and on the train line linking Katowice with Pszczyna, this 13-room hostelry is a destination in itself and must be seen to be believed. Built in 1868, it retains many of its original features and all of its character. The two rooms in the Hunting Cottage 100m from the main building are cosy and romantic;

the pair of Duke's Suites extravagant beyond your dreams.

Eating & Drinking

Cukierna Niedźbała (☎ 032 210 3691; ul Bednarska 10; ☑ 7am-5.30pm Mon-Fri, 7am-2pm Sat, 9.30am-2pm Sun) Probably Pszczyna's best bakery (judging from the queues) and famous for its poppy-seed pastries.

Café U Telemana (☎ 032 449 1520; www.utelemanna .roy.pl; dishes 5-12zł; ☑ 9am-9pm Mon-Thu, 9am-11pm Fri & Sat, 10am-9pm Sun) Located in the courtyard of the castle, this is a good pit stop for a drink or a snack after viewing the castle. The café is named after 18th-century composer Georg Philip Telemann (1681–1767), who lived here for four years in the early 18th century.

Restauracja Kmieć (☎ 032 210 3638; www.kmiec .pna.pl; ul Piekarska 10; mains 15-27zł; ☑ noon-9pm) Set in a historic townhouse dating from 1756, this long-established family restaurant has a solid range of old-fashioned Polish food and is hugely popular for it.

U Michalika (☎ 032 210 1355; ul Dworcowa 11; mains 14-26zł; ☑ 11am-10pm Tue-Sat, noon-10pm Sun & Mon) Located at the hotel of that name, this is said to be the best restaurant in Pszczyna.

Kasztelańska (☎ 032 210 3638; ul Bednarska 3; ☑ noon-10pm Mon-Thu, noon-midnight Fri & Sat, noon-11pm Sun) This pub is a bit more relaxed than the places on the Rynek and makes a good spot for a leisurely beer.

Getting There & Away

The bus and train stations are to the east of the centre, about 200m apart. Trains to Katowice (7.50zł, 45 minutes) via Tychy and Kobiór run roughly every hour. To Oświęcim (10zł, 1½ hours), take any of the frequent trains to Czechowice-Dziedzice and change there. There's only one bus to Oświęcim (6zł, 40 minutes) but four to Kraków (15zł, 2¼ hours). If you want to get to Kraków and there's no bus due, go by train to Katowice, from where trains leave every hour or so.

LOWER SILESIA

A fertile lowland extending along the upper and middle course of the Odra River, Lower Silesia (Dolny Śląsk) was settled relatively early on, and is full of old towns and villages. Architecture buffs will have a field day with the wide assortment of castles and churches preserved in some unlikely spots, and the area's larger towns have more than enough to tempt those with partying on their minds.

OPOLE

pop 126,700

Halfway between Katowice and Wrocław, Opole lies on the border of Upper and Lower Silesia, but generally considers itself part of its own Opole Silesia (Śląsk Opolski) and is the capital of its own voivodeship called Opolskie. The region is known for an active German minority, one of the few communities of its kind to survive the war. They number about 45,000 and are represented in local government.

The first Slav stronghold was built here in the 9th century. In the 13th century Opole became the capital of its principality and was ruled by a line of Silesian Piasts until 1532, even though it was part of Bohemia from 1327. Later, Opole fell to Austria, then to Prussia, and after significant destruction in WWII returned to Poland in 1945.

Today Opole is a fairly large regional industrial centre best known for the **National Festival of Polish Song** (Krajowy Festiwal Piosenki Polskiej), which has taken place annually in June since 1963 and is broadcast nationwide on TV.

Information

Bank Pekao (ul Osmańczyka 15; 8am-6pm Mon-Fri, 9am-1pm Sat)

Bank Zachodni (ul Ozimska 6; 8am-6pm Mon-Fri)

EMPiK (077 400 1715; www.empik.com; ul Krakowska 45/47; 9am-10pm Mon-Sat, noon-9pm Sun) Good for newspapers and magazines.

HMS Computers (077 453 1200; ul Krakowska 26; per hr 4zł; 9am-6pm Mon-Fri, 8am-2pm Sat) Internet access.

Main post office (ul Krakowska 46; 24hr)

Orbis Travel (077 453 9730; www.orbis.opole.pl; ul Krakowska 31; 9am-6pm Mon-Fri, 10am-2pm Sat) Eurolines is based at this travel agency.

PTTK office (077 454 5113; ul Krakowska 17; 9am-5pm Mon-Fri, 9am-1pm Sat) Travel agency.

Tourist office (077 451 1987; www.opole.pl; ul Krakowska 15; 10am-6pm Mon-Fri, 10am-1pm Sat Jul & Aug, 10am-5pm Mon-Fri, 10am-1pm Sat Sep-Jun)

Sights

Opole's **Rynek**, badly damaged during WWII, has been rebuilt. It is lined with attractive sand-coloured Baroque and Rococo houses and, particularly on the west side, pubs and

bars. The 64m-high tower of the oversized **town hall** in the middle was modelled after the one at the Palazzo Vecchio in Florence and looks a little out of place here. The original, dating from 1864, collapsed in 1934 but was rebuilt in the same style.

Opole is even madder than most Polish municipalities about matching up with towns and cities worldwide, judging from the **twinned-cities post** southeast of the town hall; it lists 13 twins of Opole – from Roanoke in the American state of Virginia to Grasse in France and Carrara in Italy.

The **Franciscan Church of the Holy Trinity** (Kościół Franciszkanów Św Trójcy; Plac Wolności 2), off the southern corner of the Rynek, was built of brick around 1330, but the interior was reshaped later on various occasions. It boasts an ornate high altar, an 18th-century organ, and a domed Renaissance chapel in the left-hand aisle, separated by a fine, late-16th-century wrought-iron grille. The highlight of the church is the **Chapel of St Anne** (Kaplica Św Anny), which is accessible from the right-hand aisle through a doorway with a tympanum. The Gothic-vaulted chapel houses a pair of massive double tombs (interring the local dukes) carved in sandstone in the 1380s. They were originally painted but the colour has almost disappeared. There are 13 more coffins in the crypt below.

Two blocks east of the Rynek, a former Jesuit college (1698) houses the **Opole Silesian Museum** (Muzeum Śląska Opolskiego; 077 453 6677; Mały Rynek 7; adult/concession 3/1zł, free Sat; 10am-4pm Tue-Fri, 10am-3pm Sat, noon-5pm Sun). The permanent display features the prehistory and history of the surrounding area and city, and there are always temporary exhibitions.

The Gothic **Holy Cross Cathedral** (Katedra Św Krzyża; ul Katedralna 2), a short walk north of the Rynek, features 73m-high towers and mostly Baroque interior furnishing. The chapel in the right-hand aisle shelters the red-marble tombstone of the last of the Opole dukes, Jan II Dobry (John II the Good), who popped his ducal clogs here in 1532. A Gothic triptych (1519), the last survivor from the church's original collection of 26 pieces, is also displayed in this chapel. The lovely bronze gate at the western entrance was erected in 1995 to mark the church's 700th year.

The only vestige of the dukes' castle is the 33m-tall **Piast Tower** (Wieża Piastowska; 077 453 6121; ul Piastowska 14; adult/concession 4/2zł; 10am-1pm

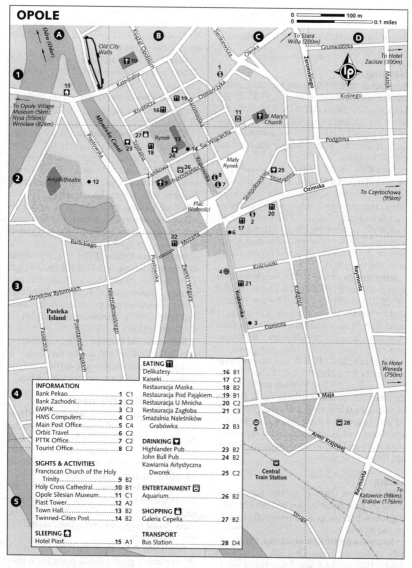

OPOLE

& 2-6pm Tue-Sun), a sturdy watchtower with 3m walls and foundations 6m deep. Built in the 14th century, the castle was pulled down in the 1920s to make room for office buildings. You can climb the 163 steps to the top for a panoramic view over the city.

Opole also has an excellent skansen, the **Opole Village Museum** (Muzeum Wsi Opolskiej; ☎ 077 474 3021; ul Wrocławska 174; adult/student 6/3zł, free Mon; ☼ 10am-6pm Tue-Sun mid-Apr–mid-Oct, 10am-3pm Mon-Fri mid-Oct–mid-Apr). Located in the suburb of Bierkowice, 5km west of the centre, the 20-hectare skansen has a variety of rural architecture from the region. A shingled church from 1613, a windmill from 1734, a smithy from 1726 and a couple of large granaries are among the showpieces. Several houses are fully furnished and decorated and can be visited. It's accessible by bus 9 with 'Bierkowice' written in front.

Sleeping

Hotel Zacisze (☎ 077 453 9553; www.hotel-zacisze.opole.pl; ul Grunwaldzka 28; s 70-120zł, d 130-220zł; P ✕ ▢ ⅋) Located about 500m east of the Rynek, the 18-room Zacisze has a range of small but acceptable single and double rooms in a wonderfully leafy residential area. Cheaper rooms have shared facilities.

Szara Willa (☎ 077 441 4560; www.szarawilla.pl; ul Oleska 11; s 160-280zł, d 180-290zł; P ✕ ▢) Opole's first and only boutique hotel, the 'Gray Villa' has a crisp modern feel and design elements that are clearly Asian influenced. The 19 rooms are generously sized, with high ceilings, and four rooms in front give on to a large terrace. A plus is the attached fitness centre with bowling alleys.

Hotel Weneda (☎ 077 442 1000; www.hotel-weneda .opole.pl; ul 1 Maja 77; s 180-220zł, d 220-270zł, ste 280-320zł; P ✕ ▢) Don't be put off by the slightly shabby block – this is a decent mid-category hotel with 29 rooms and substantial weekend discounts. It's a 750m walk from the bus station, with plenty of city buses going past.

Hotel Piast (☎ 077 454 9710; www.hotelpiast.com.pl; ul Piastowska 1; s/d 239/288zł, ste 272-316zł; P ✕) Commanding the best location in the centre, the Piast sits on the northern tip of Pasieka Island, a short trot away from the Old Town. As you'd expect for these prices, the 29 rooms are classy and comfortable, and the house restaurant and bar do good business. Rooms are 199zł at the weekend.

Eating

Delikatesy (Rynek 13/14; ☯ 7am-11pm Mon-Thu, 7am-midnight Fri, 8am-midnight Sat, 8am-10pm Sun) This late-night sundries shop is conveniently located on the Rynek.

Smażalnia Naleśników Grabówka (☎ 077 454 1796; ul Mozarta 2; crepes 5.50-9.50zł; ☯ 10am-7pm Mon-Fri, 11am-7pm Sat & Sun) Enjoying a riverside location and gorgeous terrace, this tiny place offers authentic-tasting sweet and savoury crepes with a choice of two dozen different fillings.

Restauracja Maska (☎ 077 453 9267; Rynek 2/4; mains 9-30zł; ☯ 10am-2am) Maska is a charming establishment divided into a pub and restaurant, so you can dine on varied Polish cuisine to an incongruous soundtrack of funky house classics. Jerzy Grotowski's Theatre of 13 Rows (see p325) operated in this house from 1959 to 1964.

Kaiseki (☎ 077 441 9100; ul Ozimska 4; dishes 9-39zł; ☯ noon-10pm Mon-Sat, noon-9pm Sun) This very stylish and very Japanese eatery in a modern shopping mall in the centre serves sushi by the piece as well as more substantial mains such as tempura.

our pick **Restauracja Zagłoba** (☎ 077 441 7860; www.zagloba.pl; ul Krakowska 39; mains 14-35zł; ☯ noon-midnight) One of our favourite restaurants in provincial Poland, this cellar eatery serves inspired modern Polish food in historic vaults and has won several local awards. Try the excellent Casimir's Delight (pork loin with wild mushroom sauce). Brunch is served from noon to 4pm at the weekend and is popular: make sure you book ahead.

Restauracja U Mnicha (☎ 077 454 5234; ul Ozimska 10, enter from ul Kołłątaja; mains 17.50-29zł; ☯ 9am-11pm) This modern, monk-themed basement restaurant (modernised with air conditioning) serves up sandwiches, pizzas and hefty salads and holds regular summer barbecues in its small garden area.

Restauracja Pod Pająkiem (ul Książąt Opolskich 2/6; mains 18-30zł; ☯ 11am-9pm) 'Under the Spider' is a large Hungarian restaurant northeast of the Rynek that has live music on some nights.

Drinking & Entertainment

John Bull Pub (☎ 0502 634 922; Rynek-Ratusz; ☯ 10am-late) This facsimile of a pub from provincial Britain (right down to the busy carpet and fruit machines) has a huge 'African-style' terrace (go figure) on the Rynek that stays open till midnight in the warmer months.

Kawiarnia Artystyczna Dworek (☎ 077 454 3606; ul Studzienna 1; ☯ noon-2am) A leafy terrace tucked out the back of the Old Town, the 'Arts Palace Café' shelters a pub, art gallery and music club.

Highlander Pub (☎ 077 456 5528; ul Szpitalna 3; ☯ 11am-late) A good central place for a beer and a bop, the friendly but not-very-Scottish Highlander hosts DJs playing anything from tribal house to Latin and dancehall.

Aquarium (ul Franciszkańska 1; ☯ 5pm-4am) Soaked in UV light, the basement Aquarium brings on some top dance nights, including an entertaining kitsch funk party. It's serious clubbing for over-21s.

Shopping

Galeria Cepelia (☎ 077 454 1408; Rynek 5/6) Opole is famed for its porcelain hand-painted with fine floral motifs, and Cepelia is where you'll find the widest selection.

Getting There & Away

The train station and bus station face each other, not far south of the Old Town; you can walk to the Rynek in 10 minutes.

Opole is on the main line between Katowice (28zł, 1¾ hours, hourly) and Wrocław (22zł, 1¼ hours, hourly). Most Katowice trains continue to Kraków (36zł, 3½ hours). There are also frequent trains to Częstochowa (14zł, 1¾ hours), as well as morning and late-afternoon fast trains to Warsaw (84zł, 4½ hours).

Buses go regularly to Nysa (10zł, 1½ hours, up to 12 daily) and Kłodzko (15zł, three hours, five daily), a route not so well serviced by trains.

LEGNICA

pop 105,400

Some 79km west of Wrocław, the origins of Legnica (leg-*nee*-tsa) go back to the 10th century, but it wasn't until the 13th century that real development began, when it became the joint capital of the Duchy of Legnica-Brzeg. In the 16th century the town saw golden days under Bohemian rule as an active centre of culture; the first university in Silesia was established here at that time. After the last Piast duke died in 1675, the town fell to the Habsburgs. In 1742 the Prussians took control.

Badly damaged during WWII, Legnica (Liegnitz in German) has revived as an industrial centre following the discovery of copper and nickel deposits in the region. Much of the city is drab and feels only partly constructed, but the few surviving historic buildings in the centre make for an interesting diversion.

Information

Bank Pekao ul Wrocławska (ul Wrocławska 26/28; ◔ 8am-6pm Mon-Fri, 10am-2pm Sat); Plac Klasztorny (Plac Klasztorny 1; ◔ 8am-6pm Mon-Fri)
Bank Zachodni (ul Gwarna 4a; ◔ 8am-6pm Mon-Fri)
Post office (ul Dworcowa 4; ◔ 7am-9pm Mon-Sat, 8am-3pm Sun) Near the train and bus stations.
Tourist office (☎ 076 851 2280; www.legnica.pl in Polish; Rynek 29; ◔ 9am-5pm Mon-Fri, 9am-1pm Sat) Under the arcade next to the theatre.

Sights

The brick **Piast Castle** (Zamek Piastowski) on the northern edge of the Old Town should be your first port of call. Erected in the 13th century, it was rebuilt in Gothic style (two towers from that period survive), then thoroughly modernised in the 1530s as a Renaissance residence, and again in 1835 when the noted German architect Karl Friedrich Schinkel gave it a neoclassical look. Enter through the main gate, which is embellished with a Renaissance portal (1533), the only significant remnant of the 16th-century renovation. A glass pavilion in the middle of the courtyard shelters the foundations of the 13th-century Romanesque **Castle Chapel** (Kaplica Zamkowa; admission 2.50zł; ◔ 9.30am-5pm Tue-Sat). The castle is now part of the city university.

The Baroque **Franciscan Church of St John the Baptist** (Kościół Franciszkanów Św Jana Chrzciciela; ul Partyzantów), southwest of the castle and north of the Rynek, is Legnica's most important church. The chapel off the right-hand (east) wall is actually the sanctuary of the former Gothic church, set at right angles to the existing one. Richly decorated, with a spectacular painted ceiling, the chapel also houses the extravagant **Legnica Piasts mausoleum** (◔ 9am-4pm). Enquire at the **Museum of Copper** (Muzeum Miedzi; ☎ 076 862 4949; ul Św Jana 1; ◔ 11am-5pm Wed-Sat) nearby and they will open the chapel for you and show you around.

At the southern end of the Rynek, the **Cathedral of SS Peter and Paul** (Katedra Św Piotra i Pawła; Plac Katedralny) retains two original Gothic doorways. The one on the northern side (facing the Rynek) has a splendid (though recut) tympanum depicting the Adoration of the Magi, while that on the west depicts Mary with the infant Jesus. The interior has the usual hotchpotch of furnishings, of which the oldest piece, the bronze baptismal font with bas-reliefs in the chapel off the left aisle, dates from the late 13th century and is reputedly the oldest metal font in Poland.

The **Marian Church** (Kościół Mariacki; ul Biskupia) is another notable building, one of the oldest churches in Silesia but refurbished in mock-Gothic style in the 19th century. It's used today by the small Protestant community for Sunday services and doubles as a venue for cultural events, such as organ and chamber music concerts. Have a look at the luridly coloured **new townhouses** along ul Szpitalna and ul Środkowa to the southwest, which are trying to blend in with the older ones.

Sleeping

Legnica Hostel (☎ 076 862 5412; ssmlegnica@02.pl; ul Jordana 17; dm/d/tr 22/62/81zł; P ☒) The hostel, an 800m walk southeast of the centre and through City Park (Park Miejski), offers 50 beds, most of which are in five- to 10-bed dorms.

Hotel Kamieniczka (☎ 076 723 7392; www.hotel -kamieniczka.pl; ul Młynarska 15/16; s 85-145zł, d 125-210zł, tr/q/ste 275/365/405zł; P ☒ ▢ ⬧) Central and sensitively modernised, this 17th-century townhouse hotel on the edge of the Old Town and opposite City Park is the pick of Legnica's scant accommodation offerings. The two dozen rooms are smart but not overdone, there are a couple of spacious suites and the house restaurant consolidates the touch of class. Rooms 3 and 4 on the 1st floor have large balconies.

Qubus Hotel (☎ 076 866 2100; www.qubushotel .com; ul Skarbowa 2; s 235-265zł, d 280zł, ste 345-535zł; P ☒ ▢ ⬧) A branch of the ever-growing chain of hotels, this 219-room business hotel is housed in a towering modern edifice that seems totally overblown for Legnica's modest needs. Still, if it's comfort you want you won't be complaining, and some hefty discounts – 25% to 35% – are available at the weekend.

Eating

Efez (☎ 076 727 7464; ul Najświętszej Marii Panny 9; mains 6.90-29.90zł; ☒ 9.30am-11pm Mon-Thu, 9.30am-midnight Fri, 9.30am-1am Sat, 10am-11pm Sun) This modern and bright Turkish place, in the central Galeria Piastów shopping centre, has excellent doner kebabs and *dürüm* (kebab wrapped in very thin, flat wheaten bread) for 6.90zł to 12.90zł, as well as lots of salads.

Restauracja Tivoli (☎ 076 862 2304; ul Złotoryjska 21; mains 7-25zł; ☒ 10am-9pm) This low-key traditional restaurant, 200m southwest of the Rynek, has served hearty Polish fare since 1957. We love the plates and old photos on the walls as well as the open buffet of *zakąski* (hors d'oeuvres).

Antica Roma (☎ 076 722 5060; ul Skarbowa 1; mains 12-28zł) This comfortable eatery a short distance southwest of the castle has pizza (12zł to 15zł), pasta (13zł to 18zł) and more ambitious Italian main courses.

Getting There & Away

The train and bus stations are next to each other on the northeastern edge, just over ul Pocztowa from the Old Town. Take the bus to regional destinations such as Legnickie

Pole (3.70zł, 30 minutes, up to 15 daily), Jelenia Góra (13zł, 2½ hours, up to 11 daily), Świdnica (12zł, 1½ hours, up to eight daily) and Kłodzko (22zł, three hours, up to four daily). There are hourly trains to Wrocław (11zł, 1½ hours) and several trains a day to Warsaw (107zł, 7½ hours).

LEGNICKIE POLE
pop 4950

The small village of Legnickie Pole (leg-*neets*-kyeh *po*-leh), or 'Legnica Field', holds its place in folk history due to the great battle of 9 April 1241. Silesian troops under the command of Duke Henryk Pobożny (Henry the Pious) were defeated by the Tatars. The duke was killed and beheaded; the enemy stuck his head on a pole and proceeded to Legnica, but failed to take the town. In the absence of his head, the duke's wife, Princess Anna, identified his body by the six toes on his left foot.

Henryk's mother, Princess Hedwig (Księżna Jadwiga; see p327), built a small commemorative chapel on the site of his decapitation, later replaced by a Gothic church. The church now shelters the **Museum of the Battle of Legnica** (Muzeum Bitwy Legnickiej; ☎ 076 858 2398; adult/concession 4.50/2.50zł; ☒ 11am-5pm Wed-Sun). The modest exhibition features weapons, armour and a copy of the duke's tomb – the original is in the National Museum in Wrocław – in the nave on the ground floor, and a miniature model of the battle (commentary in German and Polish only) on the 1st floor.

Across the road from the museum is the former Benedictine Abbey. Its central part is occupied by the **Church of St Hedwig** (Kościół Św Jadwigi), a masterpiece of Baroque art dating from the 1730s and designed by Bohemian architect Kilian Ignaz Dientzenhofer, who also did the sublime Minorite church in Eger in northern Hungary. Inside, the vaulting has splendid frescoes by Bavarian painter Cosmas Damian Asam. The fresco over the organ loft shows Princess Anna with the body of her husband after the battle.

Sleeping & Eating

Jurta Motel (☎ 076 858 2094; www.rmjurta.webpark.pl; ul Kossak-Szczuckiej 7; s 55-70zł, d 65-90zł, tr/ste 90/140zł; P) The only year-round place to stay in central Legnickie Pole, the 32-bed Jurta has rooms with or without en suite, and there's a simple in-house restaurant to keep you from starving.

Camping Nr 234 (☎ 076 858 2397; ul Henryka Brodatego 7; per person/small tent/large tent/caravan 11/9/12/20zł; ⏱ May-Sep; [P] [🛇]) This basic camping ground has 10 triangular cabins and a tent area. Nonguests can use the site's pool for 5zł (child 3zł).

Getting There & Away

Up to 15 daily buses run to Legnica (3.70zł, 30 minutes), though most leave in the morning. There are also a number of private minibuses (3zł).

ZIELONA GÓRA

pop 118,750

Like the majority of other towns in the region, Zielona Góra (zhyeh-*lo*-na *goo*-rah) was founded by the Silesian Piasts. It was part of the Głogów Duchy, one of the numerous regional principalities, before it passed to the Habsburgs in the 16th century and to Prussia two centuries later. Unlike most other Silesian towns, however, Zielona Góra, or 'Green Mountain', came through the 1945 offensive during WWII with minimal damage, which is why prewar architecture is well represented here.

Zielona Góra also stands out as Poland's only wine producer. The wine-making tradition runs all the way back to the 14th century, but the climate is less than ideal and viticulture was never a very profitable endeavour here. Though the output today is merely symbolic, the city still holds the **Feast of the Grape Harvest** (Święto Winobrania) at the end of September, as it has for the past century and a half.

Information

Bank Pekao (ul Pieniężnego 24; ⏱ 8am-5pm Mon-Fri)
Bank Zachodni (ul Sikorskiego 9; ⏱ 8am-5pm Mon-Fri)
Internet Café (☎ 068 324 6369; www.ipub.pl; ul Kupiecka 28; per hr 5zł; ⏱ 10am-6pm Mon-Fri, 10am-2pm Sat) In the basement, down the steps below the graffiti.
Post office (ul Bohaterów Westerplatte 21; ⏱ 7am-8pm Mon-Fri, 8am-5pm Sat, 9am-2pm Sun)
Tourist office (☎ 068 327 0323; www.zielona-gora.pl; ul Kupiecka 15; ⏱ 9am-5pm Mon-Fri, plus 10am-2pm Sat & Sun mid-Jun–mid-Sep)

Sights

Lined with brightly painted houses, the renovated **Stary Rynek** (Old Market Sq) is a pleasant and harmonious square at the end of the long pedestrian stretch of Al Niepodległości

and ul Żeromskiego. The 18th-century **town hall**, complete with a slim 54m tower, has escaped being over-modernised in spite of changes over the years.

The **Lubuski Regional Museum** (Muzeum Ziemi Lubuskiej; ☎ 068 327 2345; www.zgora.pl/muzeum in Polish; Al Niepodległości 15; adult/concession 6/3zł, free Sat; ⏱ 11am-5pm Wed-Fri, 10am-3pm Sat, 10am-4pm Sun) has a large collection of Silesian sacral art from the 14th to 18th centuries, a fascinating Clock Gallery and a permanent exhibition of works by Marian Kruczek (1927–83). Kruczek used everyday objects – anything from buttons to spark plugs – to create some striking assemblages, and this is the largest collection of his work in Poland. In the same building (and included in the ticket price) you'll find the new **Wine Museum** (Muzeum Wina), which illustrates the history of wine-making in the region, as well as the **Museum of Torture** (Muzeum Dawnych Tortur), Poland's largest exhibition on the history of criminal law, the penalty system and torture methods employed from the Middle Ages until the 18th century.

Next door to the museum is the **BWA Art Gallery** (☎ 068 325 3726; www.bwazg.pl in Polish; Al Niepodległości 19; admission varies; ⏱ 10am-5pm Tue, 11am-5pm Wed-Fri & Sun, noon-4pm Sat), which hosts changing exhibitions of contemporary art. On the same street to the south, don't miss the fabulous Art Deco **Lubuski Theatre** (Teatr Lubuski; ☎ 068 452 7272; Al Niepodległości 3/5), designed by the Berlin architect Oskar Kaufmann in 1931.

There's a **skansen** (Muzeum Etnograficzne Skansen; ☎ 068 321 1591; www.muzeum-etnog.zielman.pl; ul Muzealna 5, adult/concession/family 7/5/16zł; ⏱ 10am-5pm Tue-Sun Apr-Oct, 10am-3pm Tue-Sun Nov-Mar) in Ochla, 7km south of the city, served by bus 27. About three dozen traditional buildings – half of them residential – have been reassembled over 13 hectares of land.

Sleeping

CKUiP Hostel (☎ 068 453 0139; www.cku.zgora.pl; ul Długa 13; dm 26-33zł, s/d 100/140zł; [🛇]) This spotless hostel, 800m west of the Stary Rynek over the ring road, has place for 70 travellers, mostly in good six-bed dorms.

Hotelik Przy Kinie Wenus (☎ 068 327 1329; Al Konstytucji 3 Maja 6; r 80-120zł; [P]) This family house 'By the Venus Cinema' on the southern ring road has been converted somewhat haphazardly into a four-room guesthouse. It's noisy but very inviting.

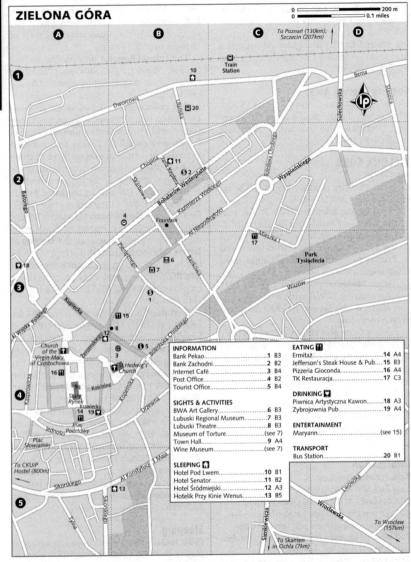

ZIELONA GÓRA

To Poznań (130km);
Szczecin (207km)

To CKUiP
Hostel (800m)

To Skansen
in Ochla (7km)

To Wrocław
(157km)

INFORMATION
Bank Pekao................................**1** B3
Bank Zachodni...........................**2** B2
Internet Café.............................**3** B4
Post Office................................**4** B2
Tourist Office............................**5** B4

SIGHTS & ACTIVITIES
BWA Art Gallery.........................**6** B3
Lubuski Regional Museum...........**7** B3
Lubuski Theatre.........................**8** B3
Museum of Torture...............(see 7)
Town Hall..................................**9** A4
Wine Museum.......................(see 7)

SLEEPING
Hotel Pod Lwem.......................**10** B1
Hotel Senator..........................**11** B2
Hotel Śródmiejski....................**12** A3
Hotelik Przy Kinie Wenus..........**13** B5

EATING
Ermitaż...................................**14** A4
Jefferson's Steak House & Pub...**15** B3
Pizzeria Gioconda....................**16** A4
TK Restauracja.........................**17** C3

DRINKING
Piwnica Artystyczna Kawon.......**18** A3
Zybrojownia Pub......................**19** A4

ENTERTAINMENT
Maryann.............................(see 15)

TRANSPORT
Bus Station.............................**20** B1

Hotel Śródmiejski (☎ 068 325 4471; www.srodmiejski
.maxmedia.pl; ul Żeromskiego 23; s 100-180zł, d 120-300zł, tr
270zł; P ☐ ♿) Slightly institutional corridors
don't detract from the comfortable rooms (with
or without en suite) at this very central place.
Generous weekend discounts available.

Hotel Pod Lwem (☎ 068 324 1055; www.hotelpod
lwem.emeteor.pl; ul Dworcowa 14; s 120zł, d & tr 160-190zł;

☐) Convenience of a different kind, the 18-
room 'Under the Lion' sits just opposite the
bus station, looking like a rural guesthouse
that somehow woke up between a main road
and a train line. Cosy furnishings expand on
the homely theme.

Hotel Senator (☎ 068 324 0436; www.hotelsenator
.net; ul Chopina 23a, enter from ul Jana Keplera; s 220-260zł,

d 260-320zł; ⓟ ⓧ ⓛ) Prices may seem a little steep here, but that's mainly because they include half board (breakfast and dinner) and two nonalcoholic drinks. At the weekend room-only rates are heavily reduced, with singles/doubles from 143/169zł. Either way it's a great little 43-bed establishment, with eager service and comfortable rooms.

Eating

Pizzeria Gioconda (☎ 068 324 6565; ul Mariacka 5; mains 6.50-15.50zł; ☾ 11am-11pm Mon-Sat, noon-10pm Sun) Tuck into the fastest Italian food on the Stary Rynek under the inscrutable gaze of Mona Lisa. Gourmet it ain't, but you'll certainly encounter worse pizzas than these.

TK Restauracja (☎ 068 451 2626; www.kasyno.zgo.pl; ul Bolesława Chrobrego 35/41; mains 12-30zł; ☾ noon-8pm Mon-Sat, 11am-5pm Sun) Discreetly removed from the centre, TK's is so unobtrusive you barely notice it's there – quite an achievement for a 20-foot glass-fronted restaurant.

Jefferson's Steak House & Pub (☎ 068 329 3939; www.jeffersons.pl; Al Niepodległości 3/5; mains 13.90-32.90zł; ☾ 10am-midnight Mon-Thu, 10am-2am Fri & Sat, noon-midnight Sun) This pleasant place with comfortable 'living room' décor in the theatre building has a good range of steaks and stays open late enough to permit at least a couple of post-performance nightcaps. But just what the third president of the US (yes, that's Tom all right) has to do with it remains a mystery.

Ermitaż (☎ 068 329 0443; Plac Pocztowy 16; mains 28-55zł; ☾ 8am-10pm Mon-Sat, 10am-10pm Sun) The new kid on the block, this café-restaurant attracts ZG's movers and shakers with its stylish décor, Mediterranean-tinged cuisine (lots of pasta dishes for 19zł to 22zł), excellent coffee and large terrace.

Drinking & Entertainment

Piwnica Artystyczna Kawon (☎ 068 324 4386; ul Zamkowa 5; ☾ 11am-2am Mon-Sat, 5pm-midnight Sun) Weird beer-bottle installations, tables made from sewing machines, rusty swords, old dust-covered lanterns – it may sound like a cliché, but you really do need to see this place to believe it.

Zbrojownia Pub (☎ 0669 337 319; ul Krawiecka 7/9; ☾ 4pm-4am Mon-Sat, 4pm-1am Sun) This basement bar boasts the best opening hours in town. Insomniacs, barflies and plenty of part-timers gather to take in occasional gigs and admire the random décor.

Maryann (☎ 068 329 3939; Al Niepodległości 3/5; ☾ 8pm-4am Thu-Sun) This hugely popular club one floor down from Jefferson's Steak House & Pub tries to be everything to everyone: 'music club, drink bar, party, TV, talk/comment, chill out'. On Friday night, when karaoke is on offer, it decidedly ain't for us.

Getting There & Away

The bus station is about 1km northeast of the city centre, and the train station just across ul Dworcowa. Major destinations by bus include Poznań (22zł, 2¾ hours, up to seven daily) and Wrocław (23zł, 3½ hours), with between seven and nine departures a day. There are also up to seven buses to Jelenia Góra (26zł, four hours), which is a more convenient way of getting there than by train, and five buses to Legnica (17.50zł, 2½ hours).

There are six trains to Wrocław daily (36zł, 3½ hours), one to Kraków (50zł, eight hours), four to Szczecin (38zł, five hours) and six to Poznań (31zł to 53zł, 2½ hours). For Warsaw (88zł, 5½ hours), there's one morning express train and one fast afternoon train.

Wielkopolska

If you want to distil the essence of Poland's eventful history, head for Wielkopolska. The region's name means Greater Poland, and with good reason – this is where the Polish state was founded in the Middle Ages, when warring Slavic tribes united to become the original Poles. Centuries later, the local population has an understandable pride in its history. Every city, town and village has treasured relics that have escaped the upheavals of the past millennia and help to define them.

Despite this distinct identity, Wielkopolska is often overlooked by visitors focusing on the high-profile attractions of Poland's coast and its mountainous south. Though Poznań is a city focused on commerce, it has a lively character and plenty of sights; and outside the city, the Wielkopolska countryside offers a selection of charming heritage towns and attractive rural scenery. Among the province's sights are eccentrically constructed castles, steam trains, palaces, churches, nature reserves and a memorable Iron Age settlement. And at the heart of it all is the great cathedral of Gniezno, the birthplace of Catholic Poland.

It's an impressive menu – but Wielkopolska is also a great place to depart from the tourist trail, and strike out on your own. When you've had your fill of its major cities and towns, choose a destination from the bus or train station departure board and head on out. Wherever you end up, you'll be sure to find something of historic interest…it's that kind of place.

HIGHLIGHTS

- Sampling the **historic buildings** (p373) and lively **entertainment** (p384) of Poznań's Old Town
- Going back to the Iron Age at the fortified village of **Biskupin** (p394)
- Exploring Gniezno's monumental historic **cathedral** (p391)
- **Cycling** (p380) through the Wielkopolska countryside
- Visiting the small, distinctive castles at **Kórnik** (p386) and **Gołuchów** (p399)
- Encountering meteorite craters at **Morasko** (p388)
- Dancing the night away at the **Ekwador club** (p385) in Manieczki
- Catching a steam train to **Wolsztyn** (p389)

- POPULATION: 3.4 MILLION
- AREA: 30,000 SQ KM

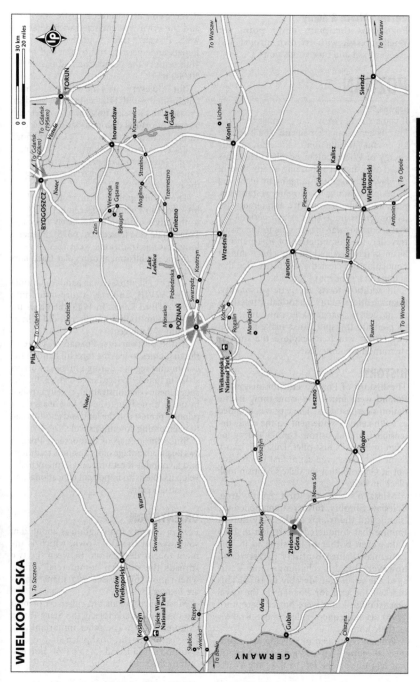

Getting There & Away

Poznań is the main entry point for Wielkopolska, with its own airport and excellent rail and bus connections.

POZNAŃ

pop 568,000

If you arrive in Poznań any evening and stroll into its central market square, you'll receive an instant introduction to the characteristic energy of Wielkopolska's capital. The city's Old Town district is buzzing at any time of the day, and positively jumping by night, full of people heading to its many restaurants, pubs and clubs. Though it's also famous for its numerous trade fairs, which periodically make Poznań near-inaccessible to the casual traveller, the combination of international business travellers and the city's huge student population has created a distinctive vibe that is quite independent of tourism.

In addition to its energetic personality, Poznań offers many historical attractions in its centre, particularly museums, and its plentiful transport links make it a great base from which to explore the quieter surrounding countryside.

HISTORY

The history of Poznań and the history of Poland were much the same thing in the nation's earliest days. The city was founded as a 9th-century settlement on the easily defensible island of Ostrów Tumski, during the reign of Poland's first ruler, Duke Mieszko I. Some historians even claim that it was here, not in Gniezno, that the duke's baptism took place in 966.

Mieszko's son, the first Polish king, Bolesław Chrobry, further strengthened the island, and the troops of the Holy Roman Empire that conquered the region in 1005 didn't even bother to lay siege to it. The Bohemian Prince Bratislav (Brzetysław), however, liked a challenge and damaged the town considerably in 1038. This marked the end for Poznań as the royal seat (though kings were buried here until 1296), as subsequent rulers chose Kraków as their home.

Poznań continued to develop as a commercial centre – in 1253 a new town centre was laid out on the left bank of the Warta

River. Soon afterwards a castle was built and the town was encircled with defensive walls. Poznań's trade flourished during the Renaissance period, and by the end of the 16th century the population had passed the 20,000 mark.

But into every city's life a little rain must fall. From the mid-17th century on, Swedish, Prussian and Russian invasions, together with a series of natural disasters, battered the city. In the Second Partition of 1793, Poznań fell under Prussian occupation and was renamed Posen, later becoming part of Germany and experiencing steady industrial growth up to the outbreak of WWI.

The Wielkopolska Insurrection, which broke out in Poznań in December 1918, led to the city's addition to the newly reformed Polish state (see boxed text, p375). Poznań's long trading traditions were then revived with the establishment of regular trade fairs in 1921.

The city fell into German hands once more during WWII, and was incorporated into Hitler's Third Reich. In 1945, the battle for its liberation took a month and did a huge amount of damage.

In the postwar era, Poznań was one of the first cities to feel the forceful hand of the communist regime, during a massive workers strike in June 1956 (see boxed text, p379). The spontaneous demonstration, cruelly crushed by tanks, turned out to be the first of a wave of popular protests on the long and painful road to overcoming communist rule.

Since the return of democracy, Poznań has taken advantage of its business traditions and favourable location near Germany to develop its role as an important educational and industrial centre.

ORIENTATION

Poznań Główny train station is about 2km southwest of the Old Town, which is the main tourist destination. Between the two spreads the modern commercial centre, where most businesses and many hotels are located.

Most tourist sights are either on or near the medieval marketplace, the Stary Rynek (Map pp376–7). The other important area for visitors is the birthplace of the city, Ostrów Tumski island (Map p374), 1km east of the Old Town, beyond the Warta River.

Maps

Poland's major publishers produce good, detailed maps of Poznań, which are readily available in the city. The tourist offices also provide free plans of the Old Town and central area.

INFORMATION
Bookshops

Bookseller (Map pp376–7; ☎ 061 856 0279; ul Powstańców Wielkopolskich; ⏰ 9am-5pm) Big stock of Lonely Planet guides.

EMPiK Megastore (Map pp376–7; ☎ 061 852 6690; ul Ratajczaka 44; ⏰ 9am-10pm Mon-Sat, 11am-6pm Sun)

Globtroter (Map pp376–7; ☎ 061 853 2915; Stary Rynek 98/100) Enter from ul Żydowska.

Księgarnia Kawiarnia Bookcrossing (Map pp376–7; ☎ 0664 139239; ul Ratajczaka 18; ⏰ 11am-8pm) Down the arcade towards the Apollo Cinema. Has a shelf of used books you can swap with your own, and free internet access.

Omnibus (Map pp376–7; ☎ 061 853 6182; ul Św Marcin 39; ⏰ 10am-7pm Mon-Fri, 10am-2pm Sat)

Cultural Centres

Centrum Kultury Zamek (Castle Cultural Centre; Map pp376–7; ☎ 061 646 5200; www.zamek.poznan.pl; ul Św Marcin 80/82) Active cultural hub located in the Kaiserhaus, hosting cinema, art and music events.

Internet Access

Adax (Map pp376–7; ☎ 061 850 1100; ul Półwiejska 28; per hr 2.50zł)

E24 (Map pp376–7; ☎ 061 859 6303; Stary Browar; per hr 1.50-4.50zł; ⏰ 24hr)

Internet C@ffe (Map pp376–7; ul 23 Lutego 7; per hr3zł; ⏰ 9am-9pm Mon-Sat, noon-8pm Sun)

Kawiarenka Internetowa (Map p374; Rondo Kaponiera; per hr 3zł; ⏰ 8am-8pm Mon-Fri) Beneath the underpass.

Tunel (Map p374; ☎ 061 863 5305; Poznań Główny, ul Dworcowa 1; per hr3zł; ⏰ 24hr)

Money

Bank BPH (Map pp376–7; Stary Rynek 97/98)

Bank Pekao (Map pp376–7) Northern Old Town (ul Maszталarska 8A); Western Old Town (ul Paderewskiego 3); Station area (ul Św Marcin 52/56)

Bank Zachodni (Map pp376–7; Plac Wolności 16)

Post

Main post office (Map pp376–7; ul Kościuszki 77; ⏰ 7am-9pm Mon-Fri, 9am-5pm Sat, 10am-4pm Sun)

> ### DISCOUNT CARD
>
> The **Poznań City Card** (Poznańska Karta Miejska; www.poznan.pl; 1/2/3 days 30/40/45zł) provides free entry to major museums, sizable discounts at restaurants and recreational activities, and free public transport. It's available from tourist offices.

Tourist Information

City Information Centre (CIM; Map pp376–7; ☎ 061 851 9645; www.cim.poznan.pl; ul Ratajczaka 44; ⏰ 10am-7pm Mon-Fri, 10am-5pm Sat)

Glob-Tour (Map p374; ☎ 061 866 0667; Poznań Główny, ul Dworcowa 1; ⏰ 24hr)

Tourist office (Map pp376–7; ☎ 061 852 6156; www.city.poznan.pl; Stary Rynek 59/60; ⏰ 9am-6pm Mon-Fri, 10am-4pm Sat Jun-Sep, 9am-5pm Mon-Fri, 10am-2pm Sat Oct-May)

Travel Agencies

Almatur (Map pp376–7; ☎ 061 855 7633; ul Ratajczaka 8)

LOT (off Map p374; ☎ 061 849 2261) At the airport.

Orbis Travel (Map pp376–7; ☎ 061 851 2000; Al Marcinkowskiego 21)

SIGHTS
Stary Rynek

The heart of the city, the **Stary Rynek** (Old Market Sq) was laid out in 1253 and contains a vibrant mix of sights, restaurants and entertainment outlets.

TOWN HALL

Poznań's Renaissance **town hall** (Map pp376–7), topped with a 61m-high tower, instantly captures your attention. Its graceful form replaced the 13th-century Gothic town hall, which was consumed by fire in the early 16th century, along with much of the town. It was designed by Italian architect Giovanni Battista Quadro and constructed from 1550 to 1560; only the tower is a later addition, built in the 1780s after its predecessor collapsed. The crowned eagle on top of the spire, with an impressive wingspan of 2m, adds some Polish symbolism.

The main eastern façade is embellished with a three-storey **arcade**. Above it is a painted frieze depicting kings of the Jagiellonian dynasty, and a clock. Every day at noon two metal goats appear through a pair of small doors above the timepiece and butt their horns together 12 times, in deference to an old legend. Apparently two goats intended

WIELKOPOLSKA

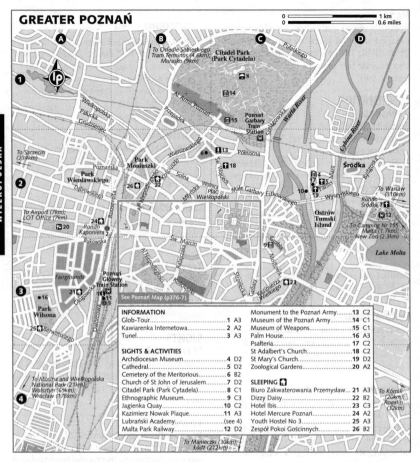

for a celebratory banquet escaped and ended up clashing horns above the about-to-be-unveiled clock, much to the amusement of the assembled dignitaries. The clockmaker was duly ordered to add the errant animals' images to his piece.

The **Historical Museum of Poznań** (Muzeum Historii Miasta Poznania; Map pp376–7; ☎ 061 856 8000; Stary Rynek 1; adult/concession 5.50/3.50zł, free Sat; ⏰ 9am-4pm Tue, Thu & Fri, 11am-6pm Wed, 10am-4pm Sat, 10am-3pm Sun) is inside the town hall. There's an interesting and well-presented exhibition on the town's history, despite the lack of English text, and the building's original interiors are worth the entry price on their own.

The Gothic vaulted **cellars** are the only remains of the first town hall. They were initially used for trade but later became a jail. At the time of research they were under renovation, but previously they've housed exhibits on medieval Poznań.

The 1st floor is home to three splendid rooms. The largest, the richly ornamented **Renaissance Hall** (Sala Renesansowa), is a real gem, with its original stuccowork and paintings from 1555. The 2nd floor contains artefacts from the Prussian period, documents illustrating city life in the 1920s and '30s, and a collection of photos showing the devastation of the city in WWII.

In front of the building, near the main entrance, is the **whipping post** (pręgierz), once the site of public floggings – and of more serious penalties, as the miniature model executioner on top suggests. The original, dating from 1535, is on display in the museum.

AROUND THE SQUARE

Behind the town hall is the **Weigh House** (Waga Miejska; Map pp376–7), a postwar replica of the 16th-century building designed by Quadro, which was dismantled in the 19th century. South of it are two discordant postwar structures on the site of the old arsenal and cloth hall.

The arsenal site now houses the **Arsenal City Art Gallery** (Galeria Miejska Arsenał; Map pp376–7; ☎ 061 852 9501; Stary Rynek 3; adult/concession 3/2zł; ⓨ 11am-6pm Tue-Sat, 11am-3pm Sun), which partly atones for its external design sins by hosting temporary exhibitions of modern art. Its eastern neighbour is the **Wielkopolska Military Museum** (Wielkopolskie Muzeum Wojskowe; Map pp376–7; ☎ 061 852 6739; Stary Rynek 9; adult/concession 3.50/2.20zł, free Sat; ⓨ 10am-4pm Tue-Sat, 10am-3pm Sun), and in the old Guardhouse on the western side of the cluster of buildings you'll find the **Museum of the Wielkopolska Uprising** (Muzeum Powstania Wielkopolskiego; Map pp376–7; ☎ 061 853 1993; Stary Rynek 3; adult/concession 4/2zł, free Sat; ⓨ 10am-5pm Tue, Thu & Fri, 10am-6pm Wed, 10am-3pm Sat & Sun), which details the battles waged by Polish fighters seeking independence from Germany after the end of WWI (see boxed text, below). It's an interesting if compact institution with displays of military uniforms, weaponry, photographs and documents created for the newborn Polish state that the Uprising hoped to help create. There's a brochure in English.

On the eastern side of the two monstrosities is a much more endearing row of small, arcaded buildings, known as the **Fish Sellers' Houses** (Domki Budnicze; Map pp376–7). They were built in the 16th century on the site of fish stalls and later reconstructed after major WWII damage.

Directly opposite is the **Museum of Musical Instruments** (Muzeum Instrumentów Muzycznych; Map pp376–7; ☎ 061 852 0857; Stary Rynek 45; adult/concession 5.50/3.50zł, free Sat; ⓨ 11am-5pm Tue-Sat, 10am-3pm Sun). It houses hundreds of instruments, from whistles to concert pianos, but it's less interesting than it should be. One room on the ground floor is filled with intriguing musical devices including a typewriter for musician notation, and a polyphon, the precursor of the record player. Upstairs, however, it's like an antiques clearance sale – rooms of pianos, rooms of violins, and so on, with little creative attempt to give them a context.

Southeastern Old Town

Off the southeastern corner of the Rynek, inside the 16th-century **Górka Palace** (Pałac Górków), is the **Archaeological Museum** (Muzeum Archeologiczne; Map pp376–7; ☎ 061 852 8251; ul Wodna 27; adult/concession 6/3zł, free Sat; ⓨ 10am-4pm Tue-Fri, 10am-6pm Sat, 10am-3pm Sun). Before going in, stop and

---

LINE IN THE SAND

Europe breathed a deep sigh of relief on 11 November 1918, the day the guns fell silent in WWI. But for Poles living in Wielkopolska, the fight was just beginning.

Germany had sued for peace in the west, but in the east it had been militarily successful against newly communist Russia, and still held firm authority in the ethnically Polish portions of its empire. However, change was in the wind – US President Woodrow Wilson had foreshadowed the creation of an independent Poland as a buffer state between Germany and Russia.

But where would the border of a new Poland fall? The Polish-majority inhabitants of Wielkopolska were unwilling to risk Poland's oldest province staying within Germany, and on 27 December 1918 a full-scale rebellion, the Wielkopolska Uprising, broke out in Poznań. Sparked by a stirring speech by acclaimed pianist Ignacy Paderewski (who later became prime minister of the new nation), the Uprising was led by Polish soldiers who had been drafted into the German army in the war, and was endorsed by underground citizens' committees.

The insurrection quickly escalated into a full-blown civil war that raged across Wielkopolska through the winter, as Polish forces liberated town after town. Their successful capture of Poznań's airport in early January 1919 even enabled them to launch airborne bombing raids on German targets in Frankfurt an der Oder a few days later.

Though a ceasefire was signed in February, skirmishes continued over the following months. But the Uprising had achieved its aim: on 28 June 1919, just over six months after hostilities had broken out, the Treaty of Versailles awarded Wielkopolska to the newly-formed Poland.

WIELKOPOLSKA

WIELKOPOLSKA

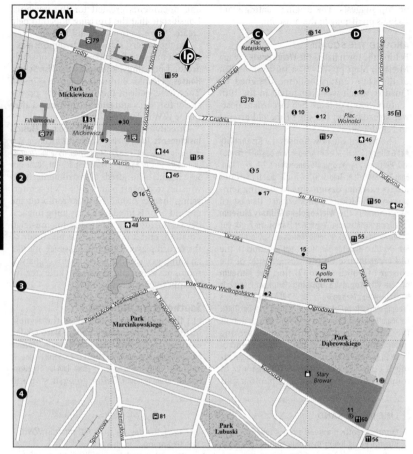

POZNAŃ

have a look at the fine Renaissance doorway on the building's eastern façade. The museum itself presents the prehistory of the region, from the Stone Age to the early medieval period, as well as an extensive Egyptian collection.

A few steps south of the museum is the **Parish Church** (Kościół Farny; Map pp376–7; ul Gołębia), originally built for the Jesuits by architects from Italy. After more than 80 years of work (1651–1732), an impressive baroque church was created, with an ornamented façade and a lofty interior supported on massive columns and crammed with monumental altars.

A five-minute walk east from here is the **Ethnographic Museum** (Muzeum Etnograficzne; Map p374; ☎ 061 852 3006; ul Grobla 25; adult/concession 5.50/3.50zł, free Sat; ☽ 10am–4pm Tue, Wed, Fri & Sat,

10am–3pm Sun). It has a good collection of folk woodcarving – of note are the large roadside posts and crosses – and traditional costumes of the region.

Western Old Town

Plac Wolności, one of the main squares of contemporary Poznań, marks the western edge of the Old Town. Its chief attraction is the **National Museum** (Muzeum Narodowe; Map pp376–7; ☎ 061 856 8117; Al Marcinkowskiego 9; adult/concession 10/6zł, free Sat; ☽ 10am–6pm Tue, 9am–5pm Wed, 10am–4pm Thu & Sun, 10am–5pm Fri & Sat; ⬤), where an extensive collection of Polish and European art is displayed in countless rooms. The building's architecture isn't much to look at, but the art is displayed to best advantage in the spacious and light-filled

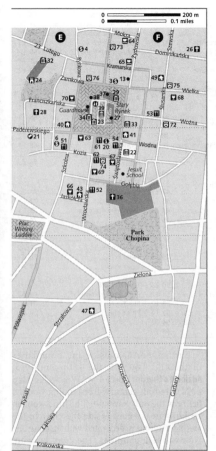

WIELKOPOLSKA

Sztuk Użytkowych; Map pp376–7; ☎ 061 852 20 35; Góra Przemysława 1; adult/concession 5.50/3.50zł; free Sat; ☻ 10am-4pm Tue-Sat, 10am-3pm Sun). The collection includes furniture, gold and silverware, glass, ceramics, weapons, clocks, watches and sundials from Europe and the Far East. Exhibits date from the 13th century to the present.

Just south of the castle is the richly decorated baroque **Franciscan Church** (Kościół Franciszkanów; Map pp376–7; ul Franciszkańska 2). Its **Chapel of the Virgin Mary** (Kaplica NMP), in the left transept, has a carved oak altar and a tiny, reputedly miraculous image of St Mary.

Station Area

Further west towards the train station along ul Św Marcin, on **Plac Mickiewicza**, you'll find one of Poznań's most significant memorials, the **Monument to the Victims of June 1956** (Pomnik Poznańskiego Czerwca 1956; Map pp376–7), which commemorates the ill-fated workers' protest (see the boxed text, p379). The monument, consisting of two 20m-tall crosses bound together, was unveiled on 28 June 1981, the 25th anniversary of the strike, at a ceremony attended by more than 100,000 people. It's a huge, evocative landmark, similar to the Monument to the Fallen Shipyard Workers (p416) in Gdańsk. At the time of research, an accompanying **Museum of Poznań June 1956** (Map pp376–7; ☎ 061 852 9464; ul Św Marcin 80/82) was under construction next door within the neo-Romanesque **Kaiserhaus** (Map pp376–7), built from 1904 to 1910 for Emperor Wilhelm II.

In addition to the Kaiserhaus, there are copious examples of Prussian architecture in this area. Notable specimens include the **Teatr Wielki** (p385), the **Collegium Maius** (Map pp376–7) and the **Collegium Minus** (Map pp376–7).

West of here, across the railway line and past the Hotel Mercure Poznań, are the **Zoological Gardens** (Ogród Zoologiczny; ☎ 061 848 08 47; ul Zwierzyniecka 19; adult/concession 9/6zł; ☻ 9am-7pm Apr-Sep, 9am-4pm Oct-Mar), Poznań's original zoo, and one of the oldest in Poland. Animal lovers can breathe reasonably easily: the oldest enclosures are no longer occupied, with most larger animals having been relocated to the New Zoo (p380). Those that remain include giraffes and zebras in a sizable open space. The remaining faded, but decorative, 19th-century facilities are populated by birds, otters, lemurs, alpacas, reptiles and amphibians, including some vividly coloured poisonous frogs.

interior and, unusually for Polish museums, it has disabled access throughout.

Polish painting of the last two centuries is represented by almost all the big names, including Jan Matejko, Stanisław Wyspiański and Jacek Malczewski. Look out for the distinctive work of Tadeusz Makowski, a 20th-century artist who created curious human figures from basic geometric shapes. An older noteworthy curiosity is the museum's collection of coffin portraits.

Between Plac Wolności and the Rynek stands Poznań's **castle** (Map pp376–7), though the residence you see today is the postwar reconstruction of a late-18th-century building, which hardly looks like a castle at all. It now houses the **Museum of Applied Arts** (Muzeum

WIELKOPOLSKA

Further south, a five-minute walk from the main train station along ul Głogowska, is the large **Park Wilsona**, which contains the **Palm House** (Palmiarnia; Map p374; ☎ 061 865 8907; ul Matejki 18; adult/concession 5.50/4zł; ⌚ 9am-4pm Tue-Sun Mar-Oct, 9am-3pm Tue-Sun Nov-Feb). Constructed in 1910, this is one of the biggest greenhouses in Europe. Inside, 19,000 species of tropical and subtropical plants are housed, including the continent's largest cactus collection and its tallest bamboo trees. The adjacent aquarium is home to exotic fish. Curiously, there's a surviving wartime air-raid shelter within the grounds, which you can pay 2zł to inspect.

North of the Old Town

Before WWII, the area north of the Rynek was populated mainly by Jews, though there's little trace of their community now.

The oldest surviving monument on this side of the river is the former **Dominican Church** (Kościół Podominikański; Map pp376–7), now belonging to the Jesuits. Built in the mid-13th century, it was repeatedly reshaped and redecorated in later periods, but the fine early-Gothic doorway at the main entrance is still in place.

Further north, outside the boundaries of the Old Town, is the 15th-century **St Adalbert's Church** (Kościół Św Wojciecha; Map p374). Its 16th-century, freestanding wooden belfry is the only substantial historic wooden building in Poznań. Inside the church, the Gothic vaulting is decorated with striking Art Nouveau wall paintings. The crypt beneath, open to visitors, has become a mausoleum for the most eminent Poles from Wielkopolska, among them Józef Wybicki, who wrote the lyrics of the national anthem.

During the Christmas period, the mechanised *szopka* (Nativity scene) is open in the church. It includes several dozen movable figures that depict the history of the region, from Mieszko I to the present day.

Not far from the church you'll find the stark, modern **Monument to the Poznań Army** (Pomnik Armii Poznań; Map p374), dedicated to the local armed force that resisted the German invasion of 1939 for almost two weeks. It's just opposite the sloping **Cemetery of the Meritorious** (Cmentarz Zasłużonych; Map p374), the oldest existing graveyard in the city (1810).

STRIKING OUT

The June 1956 industrial strike in Poznań was the first mass protest in the Soviet bloc, breaking out just three years after Stalin's death.

It originated in the city's largest industrial plant, the Cegielski metalworks (then named after Stalin), which produced railway stock. When the workers demanded the refund of an unfairly charged tax, the factory management refused and simply threw the workers' delegates out of the meeting room. This sparked a spontaneous strike the next day, in which the metalworkers, joined by workers from other local industrial plants, headed for Plac Mickiewicza (then named Plac Stalina).

The 100,000-strong crowd that gathered (a quarter of the city's total population) demanded 'bread and freedom', insisting that changes had to be introduced to improve working conditions, and requested that authorities come and discuss the issue. The demonstration was disregarded by city officials.

Matters soon got out of hand. The angry crowd stormed police headquarters and the Communist Party building, and released 257 prisoners from the local jail after disarming the guards. Shortly afterwards, a battle for the secret-police headquarters broke out, and it was there that the bloodshed began, when police started firing at people surrounding the building. Tanks were introduced into the action, and troops were hastily brought from Wrocław and told they were there to pacify a German riot.

Fierce street battles continued for the whole night and part of the next day, resulting in a total of at least 76 dead and 900 wounded. More than 300 people were arrested, 58 of whom were indicted.

These figures make the protest the most tragic in communist Poland, yet it was underreported and for a long time underestimated. The historic importance of the revolt has only recently been appreciated and given the status it deserves, as an event on par with the internationally famous shipyard strikes in Gdańsk.

Further north is the large **Citadel Park** (Wzgórze Cytadela; Map p374), laid out on what was once a massive Prussian fortress known as the **Citadel** (Cytadela). It was involved in one major battle, when the Germans defended themselves for four weeks in 1945; it was destroyed apart from a few fragments.

Today Citadel Park incorporates two museums: the **Museum of Weapons** (Muzeum Cytadeli Poznańskiej; ☎ 061 820 4503; adult/concession 4/2zł, free Fri; ☒ 9am-4pm Tue-Sat, 10am-4pm Sun) and the **Museum of the Poznań Army** (Muzeum Armii Poznań; ☎ 061 820 4503; adult/concession 4/2zł, free Fri; ☒ 9am-4pm Tue-Sat, 10am-4pm Sun). There are also cemeteries for Polish, Soviet, British and Commonwealth soldiers, all on the southern slopes of the hill.

Ostrów Tumski

To the east, over the Warta River, is the island of **Ostrów Tumski** (Map p374). You're walking through deep history here, the place where Poznań took its first steps, and with it the Polish state. The original 9th-century settlement was gradually transformed into an oval stronghold surrounded by wood-and-earth

ramparts, with an early stone palace. Mieszko I added a cathedral and further fortifications, and by the end of the 10th century Poznań was the most powerful stronghold in the country.

In the 13th century, when Poznań had spread beyond the island and the newly designed town was laid out, Ostrów lost its trade and administrative importance, but remained the residence of the Church authorities.

Today it's a tiny, quiet ecclesiastical quarter radiating an air of history, dominated by Poznań's monumental, double-towered **cathedral** (Map p374; ul Ostrów Tumski; adult/concession 2.80/1.80zł). Basically Gothic with additions from later periods, most notably the baroque tops of the towers, the cathedral was badly damaged in 1945 and took 11 years to rebuild.

The aisles and the ambulatory are ringed by a dozen chapels containing numerous tombstones. The most famous of these is the **Golden Chapel** (Złota Kaplica), behind the high altar, its golden ceiling decorated with various saints. For the princely sum of 2zł, the church attendant will turn on the chapel illumination for you. Dating from the 15th century, the chapel was completely rebuilt in the 1830s as the mausoleum of the first two Polish rulers, Mieszko I and Bolesław Chrobry. Enveloped in Byzantine-style decoration are the double tomb of the two monarchs on one side and their bronze statues on the other.

The rulers' original burial site was the **crypt**, accessible from the back of the left-hand aisle, though it's robbed of atmosphere by the bright lighting and wooden walkways. Apart from the fragments of what are thought to have been their tombs, you can see the relics of the first pre-Romanesque cathedral dating from 968 and of the subsequent Romanesque building from the second half of the 11th century, along with dozens of coins tossed in by more recent Polish visitors. A diorama explains the development of the cathedral over the centuries, with some English captioning.

Opposite the cathedral is **St Mary's Church** (Kościół NMP; Map p374; ul Panny Marii), built in the mid-15th century. Just behind the church is the early-16th-century **Psałteria** (Map p374), which was home to the choristers. Below here on the riverbank, the paddleboat **Jagienka** (Map p374; ☎ 061 827 0589; adult/concession 1hr cruise 12/9zł, 2hr cruise 22/16zł; ☼ 11am-5pm May-Sep) sets off for regular pleasure cruises.

North of the cathedral is **Lubrański Academy** (Akademia Lubrańskiego), also known as the Collegium Lubranscianum, the first high school in Poznań (1518). Within the walls you will find the **Archdiocesan Museum** (Map p374; Muzeum Archidiecezjalne; ☎ 061 852 6195; ul Lubrańskiego 1; adult/concession 6/3zł; ☼ 10am-5pm Tue-Fri, 9am-3pm Sat), a collection of sacred art from the 12th century onwards.

Lake Malta

If you venture east from Ostrów Tumski, over the bridge that stretches over the Cybina River, and beyond the Rondo Środka, you'll discover the **Church of St John of Jerusalem** (Kościół Św Jana Jerozolimskiego; Map p374; ul Świętojańska 1). One of the oldest brick churches in the country, this late-12th-century building was extended in the Gothic period and later acquired a baroque chapel. The interior contains beautiful Gothic star vaults, and the Romanesque doorway in the main western entrance is magnificent.

South of the church is the terminus of the **Malta Park Railway** (Kolejka Parkowa Maltanka; Map p374; ☎ 061 877 2612; ul Jana Pawła II; adult/concession 4.50/3zł; ☼ 10am-6.45pm Mon-Fri, 10am-6.30pm Sat & Sun

May-15 Oct), which runs miniature trains along the shoreline of the 70-hectare artificial **Lake Malta** (Jezioro Maltańskie; Map p374), a favourite summer spot for families, picnickers and boating enthusiasts. During the Malta International Theatre Festival (opposite) in June, the lake's banks are used for outdoor theatre productions and other events, creating a lively atmosphere. At other times there are sailing regattas and outdoor concerts by the lake, and in winter there's a ski slope in operation.

The railway terminates at the **New Zoo** (Nowe Zoo; off Map p374; ☎ 061 877 3517; ul Krańcowa 81; adult/concession 9/6zł; ☼ 9am-7pm Apr-Sep, 9am-4pm Oct-Mar). This sprawling institution covers 116 hectares at the eastern end of the lake, and houses diverse species including Baltic grey seals, in a leafy pine forest environment.

ACTIVITIES

If you're challenged for time in Poznań, a good way to get a feel for the city's history is to follow one or more of the 10 self-guided **walking routes**, outlined in free brochures available from the tourist office. Each walk takes two hours, and leads you past selected historic and scenic locations, with the brochure explaining their significance in English. A more ambitious stroll is the **Royal-Imperial Route**, mapped out in another free brochure, which takes you from the shores of Lake Malta to the city's west, passing 56 sights along the way.

Poznań is also good for **cycling**, with plenty of bike trails through the city and beyond. To get started, ask the tourist office for the brochure *Poznań on Two and Four Wheels*, and its map of Wielkopolska's major marked bicycle routes. Bicycles can be hired from **MPK** (☎ 061 869 9361; ☼ 6.30am-9pm Mon-Fri, 7am-9pm Sat, 7am-4pm Sun) at the Osledle Sobieskiego tram terminus to the north of the Old Town, reached via trams 12, 14, 15 or 16.

FESTIVALS & EVENTS

Poznań's trade fairs are its pride and joy, though few are of interest to casual visitors. The main ones take place in January, June, September and October, with dozens of other trade shows of varying size throughout the year. July, August and December are almost completely free of fairs.

Major cultural events:

Poznań Jazz Festival (☎ 061 813 2566; www.jazz.pl) Held in March.

St John's Fair (Jarmark Świętojański; ☎ 061 853 6081) A handicraft and antiques fair, held on the Stary Rynek in June.

Malta International Theatre Festival (☎ 061 646 5243; www.malta-festival.pl) Fringe and alternative theatre, held in late June.

Wieniawski International Violin Competition (☎ 061 852 2642; www.wieniawski.pl) Held every five years in October (next due in 2011).

SLEEPING

Try not to arrive in Poznań during one of the numerous trade fairs – they wreak havoc on the city's accommodation range, doubling prices and reducing available beds. Outside trade fair periods, room prices drop significantly on weekends. Prices given here are standard weekday rates for 'off-fair' periods. Unless otherwise specified, prices include breakfast. The tourist offices and Glob-Tour (p373) are knowledgeable about lodging options and should be able to help you find a bed.

Budget
HOSTELS & HOTELS
Youth Hostel No 3 (off Map p374; ☎ 061 866 4040; ul Berwińskiego 2/3; dm 29zł, tr 102zł) The closest hostel to the train station, a 550m walk southwest along ul Głogowska. It's the smallest and most basic of the lot and fills up fast. Most of the 52 beds here are in eight- to 10-bed dorms.

Dizzy Daisy (Map p374; ☎ 061 829 3902; www.dizzy daisy.pl; Al Niepodległości 26; dm/s/d/tr 40/65/100/135zł; ☼ Jul-Sep; P 🖳) A sociable summer backpacker haunt within easy reach of the centre. The standards are basic but it's got everything you need, including kitchen and laundry for guest use.

Frolic Goats Hostel (Map pp376-7; ☎ 061 852 4411; www.frolicgoatshostel.com; ul Wrocławska 16/6; dm 50-65zł, d/ste 140/200zł; ✕ 🖳) Named after the feisty goats who fight above the town hall clock, this shiny new hostel is aimed squarely at the international backpacker. The pleasant green lounge complements tidy, reasonably uncrowded dorms, bike hire is available for 25zł per day, and room rates are unaffected by trade fairs. Enter from ul Jaskółcza.

Mini Hotelik (Map pp376-7; ☎ 061 633 1416; Al Niepodległości 8; s 80zł, d 107-135zł, ste 187zł; P) As it says on the label, this is a small hotel between the train station and the Old Town. It's basic but clean, and a step up from hostel accommodation with colourfully painted rooms (though breakfast isn't included). Enter from ul Taylora.

PRIVATE ROOMS
Biuro Zakwaterowania Przemysław (Map p374; ☎ 061 866 3560; www.przemyslaw.com.pl; ul Głogowska 16; s 43-65zł, d 65-96zł; ☼ 8am-6pm Mon-Fri, 10am-2pm Sat) This private-accommodation agency is opposite the train station, and will diligently hunt you down a place to stay. Rooms are almost always available, but at trade fair times there may be less choice; the price ranges given here run from ordinary days up to trade-fair periods.

CAMPING
Camping Nr 155 Malta (off Map p374; ☎ 061 876 6155; www.posir.poznan.pl; ul Krańcowa 98; camp sites per person 7zł, bungalows 130-350zł; P ♿) Malta is the best of Poznań's three camping grounds and the closest to the centre – it's on the northeastern shore of Lake Malta, 3km east of the Old Town. Sixty-six heated bungalows, including five specially adapted for disabled guests, provide good all-year shelter.

Midrange
Capital Apartments (☎ 061 852 5300; www.toppoznan hotels.com; apt 180-200zł) This company maintains a number of renovated apartments dotted around the city centre, most within walking distance of the Rynek. Call to discuss available options (staff will meet travellers at apartments). They're a good-value option if you're tired of hotel breakfasts and want to prepare your own food, or if the lack of laundrettes in Poland is making you desperate for a washing machine.

Zespół Pokoi Gościnnych (Map p374; ☎ 061 851 6841; www.ibch.poznan.pl; ul Wieniawskiego 17/19; s/d/ste 140/220/250zł; P ✕) Don't be confused by the unlikely looking building – this accommodation is indeed part of the Poznań Institute of Biochemistry, though the lack of signage classifies it as a well-kept scientific secret. From ul Wieniawskiego, ignore the main doors and walk along the building to the right, then left towards a door at the back.

Dom Polonii (Map pp376-7; ☎ 061 852 7121; Stary Rynek 51; s/d 140/230zł) Dating from 1488, the Dom Polonii occupies one corner of Poznań's market square, offering just two double rooms to anyone who's organised enough to book sufficiently in advance. The only way you could get more central would be by tunnelling under the town hall.

Hotel Lech (Map pp376-7; ☎ 061 853 0151; www.hotel -lech.poznan.pl; ul Św Marcin 74; s/d/tr/ste 162/244/336/254zł) A comfortable, good, standard three-star, with slightly worn furniture but high ceilings. It's set in a convenient location, midway between the train station and the Old Town, and the accommodating staff are used to dealing with tourists. Flash your ISIC card for a substantial discount.

Hotel Rzymski (Map pp376–7; ☎ 061 852 8121; www.hotelrzymski.com.pl; Al Marcinkowskiego 22; s/d/tr 195/250/300zł, ste 280–430zł; P X Q &) If walls could talk, this hotel would have a story worth listening to. It began life as the German-owned Hotel de Rome, changed to Polish ownership, was used in WWII as a hotel for the German military, then became Polish-owned once more, still with the same name (Rzym is Rome in Polish). The décor is overly brown and old-fashioned, but the rooms are comfortable and the multilingual staff helpful.

Rezydencja Solei (Map pp376–7; ☎ 061 855 7351; www.hotel-solei.pl; ul Szewska 2; s/d/ste 189/289/359zł; Q) Temptingly close to the Rynek, this tiny hotel offers small but cosy rooms in an old-fashioned residential style, with wallpaper and timber furniture striking a homely note. The attic suite is amazingly large and can accommodate up to four people.

Brovaria (Map pp376–7; ☎ 061 858 6868; www.brovaria.pl; Stary Rynek 73/74; s 250zł, d 290–350zł, ste 410zł; P X X) This multitalented hotel also operates as a restaurant and bar, but most impressive is its in-house boutique brewery, whose operations you can view within the building. The elegant rooms have tasteful dark timber tones, and some have views onto the Rynek.

our pick **Hotel Stare Miasto** (Map pp376–7; ☎ 061 663 6242; www.hotelstaremiasto.pl; ul Rybaki 36; s 215zł, d 295–325zł, ste 350–450zł; P X Q) Stylish value-for-money hotel with a tasteful chandeliered foyer and spacious breakfast room. Rooms can be small but are clean and bright with lovely starched white sheets. Some upper rooms have skylights in place of windows.

Hotel Ibis (Map p374; ☎ 061 858 4400; www.ibishotel.com; ul Kazimierza Wielkiego 23; s/d 287/315zł; P X X Q) A typical hotel in this reliable business chain, Poznań's Ibis offers a multitude of predictably well-maintained rooms within an easy walk of the historic centre. If you don't like surprises, this is a good place to hang your hat.

Top End

Hotel Royal (Map pp376–7; ☎ 061 858 2300; www.hotel-royal.com.pl; ul Św Marcin 71; s 320zł, d 420–450zł, ste 500zł; P X) Tasteful terracotta tones predominate

in this smart, refined hotel, situated on the main road leading into the centre. Spring for the spacious suite for extra elbow room, or just hang around the lobby perusing the photos of famous Polish TV stars who've stayed here.

Hotel Mercure Poznań (Map p374; ☎ 061 855 8000; www.orbisonline.pl; ul Roosevelta 20; s/d from €111/123; P X Q &) In a gigantic modern building just off a busy main road, this hotel offers all the expected facilities for business travellers, including a gym, a restaurant and a bar. The 'big box' look is softened by musical designs on bedspreads and curtains, a reference to the nearby Philharmonic Hall. It's handy for the train station and Zoological Gardens.

Domina Prestige (Map pp376–7; ☎ 061 859 0590; www.dominahotels.com; ul Św Marcin 2; apt 560–840zł; P X X Q &) Some hotels try to make you feel like you're at home – the Domina makes you wish your home was a bit more like this. The luxury serviced apartments come with stylish interiors, kitchens with full facilities and more mod cons than a New York penthouse.

EATING

Poznań's sophisticated dining scene centres on the Old Town, whose narrow streets contain eateries offering every cuisine imaginable. There are also notable concentrations of restaurants around ul Św Marcin and ul 27 Grudnia.

Bar Mleczny Apetyt (Map pp376–7; ☎ 061 852 1339; ul Szkolna 4; mains 4–8zł; 8am-10pm Mon-Sat, 10am-10pm Sun) The latest-closing *bar mleczny* (milk bar) in town enjoys a good, central location. The food is exactly what you'd expect, and none the worse for that, with *naleśniki* (crepes) choices galore.

Pancake Square (Map pp376–7; ☎ 061 835 3642; ul Półwiejska 45; mains 4–9zł; 10am-9pm Mon-Sat, 11am-8pm Sun) No prizes for guessing which dish takes centre stage here. The modern café ambience suits the lightness of the raw materials, but be prepared for busy workday crowds sharing your enthusiasm for the fare.

Bar Mamamija (Map pp376–7; ☎ 061 665 8508; ul Św Marcin 12; mains 4–11zł; 11am-8pm Mon-Fri, 11am-5pm Sat) Dragging the traditional *bar mleczny* firmly into the 1970s, students and snackers alike dig this retro joint's rainbow paint job and kidney-shaped tables. Pasta, stroganoff and other fads join the usual suspects on the budget menu. Head downstairs off the street to find it.

Bar Wegetariański (Map pp376-7; ☎ 061 852 1255; ul Wrocławska 21; mains 5-12zł; ☒) This cheap vegetarian eatery is in a cellar off the main road, bedecked with plant life around the walls, and offers the usual meat-free dishes. The low prices keep it popular with the masses.

Stary Browar Food Court (Map pp376-7; ☎ 061 850 10 76; ul Półwiejska 42; ☟ 9am-9pm) The dining section of this gigantic shopping mall offers decent food in chic surrounds, from Ottoman Turkish cuisine to seriously good wine. There are also cafés scattered through the complex, and the building's spectacular old-meets-new architecture is worth a visit in its own right.

Mezzoforte (Map pp376-7; ☎ 0511 784288; ul Piekary 5; mains 8-35zł; ☟ 9.30am-midnight Sun-Thu, 9.30am-2am Fri & Sat) Funky restaurant with a mosaic-tiled bar and bright orange walls decorated with giant poppy designs. The menu contains an array of pizzas and pastas, alongside photos of two customers enjoying their meal together just a little *too* much. From 9pm you can trek downstairs to enjoy Poznań's smallest nightclub – good luck finding enough space to dance!

Restauracja W-Z (Map pp376-7; ☎ 061 665 8801; ul Fredry 12; mains 12-39zł; ☟ 11am-midnight) Short for Wielkopolska Zagroda (Wielkopolskan Farm), the W-Z takes its rustic theme to the limit – the building contains a re-creation of a country cabin, complete with timber roof, allowing diners to feast on excellent Polish cooking either inside or round the edge. The attached W-Z Café is a good place to grab a quick coffee.

Restauracja Sphinx (Map pp376-7; ☎ 061 852 5362; ul Św Marcin 66/72; mains 15-50zł; ☟ 11am-11pm Sun-Thu, 11am-midnight Fri & Sat) Firmly installed on the Poznań food map, the all-conquering kebab chain offers reasonable-value grills and salads, amid ancient Egyptian décor and colourful lampshades.

Cymes (Map pp376-7; ☎ 061 851 6638; ul Woźna 2/3; mains 18-26zł; ☟ 11am-10pm) If you're tired of pork for dinner, this ambient Jewish restaurant is the logical place to go. The interior is warm and cosy, done out like a residential dining room with ceramic plates on the walls. On the menu are various poultry and fish dishes, including a whole goose for eight people, to be ordered 24 hours beforehand.

Deserovnia (Map pp376-7; ☎ 061 852 5029; ul Świętosławska 12; mains 18-34zł; ☟ 11am-11pm) One side of this split-personality venue is a sporty bar, all dark timber, beer and photos of sports

stars. The other side is a gracious restaurant serving classy Polish cuisine. Heads or tails?

Trattoria Valpolicella (Map pp376-7; ☎ 061 855 7191; ul Wrocławska 7; mains 21-66zł; ☟ 1-11pm) Serves a wide variety of pasta and other Italian specialities, well suited to a glass of vino, in convincingly rustic Mediterranean surroundings.

our pick Tapas Bar (Map pp376-7; ☎ 061 852 8532; Stary Rynek 60; mains 31-54zł; ☟ noon-midnight) This atmospheric place dishes up authentic tapas and Spanish wine in a room lined with in-triguing bric-a-brac, including jars of stuffed olives, Mediterranean-themed artwork and bright red candles. Most tapas dishes are 17zł to 19zł, so forget the mains and share with friends. There's a nightclub downstairs for post-prandial dancing.

Restauracja Delicja (Map pp376-7; ☎ 061 852 1128; www.delicja.com.pl; Plac Wolności 5; mains 47-85zł; ☟ noon-11pm) One of Poznań's top restaurants, tucked away off Plac Wolności, the Delicja has its own miniature courtyard and an illustrious reputation for top-notch international cuisine along French-Italian lines. Refinement and elegance are *de rigueur*.

DRINKING

Once you've done the rounds of the beer gardens on the Rynek, there are plenty of places elsewhere in town worth seeking out for a drink. Ul Woźna and ul Nowowiejskiego have plenty of student-oriented bars, while ul Żydowska caters for a more mature audience and the southern Old Town has a bit of everything.

Proletaryat (Map pp376-7; ☎ 0508 173608; ul Wrocławska 9; ☟ 1pm-late Mon-Sat, 3pm-late Sun) Bright red communist-nostalgia bar with an array of socialist-era gear on the walls, including military insignia, portraits of Brezhnev and Marx, and the obligatory bust of Lenin in the window. Play 'spot the communist leader' while sipping a boutique beer from the Czarnków Brewery.

Alter Ego (Map pp376-7; ☎ 061 853 1347; Stary Rynek 63; ☟ 11am-late Mon-Sat, 7pm-late Sun) The base-ment of the Powszechna bookshop conceals an intriguing narrow bar with a lively dance-music policy. Look closely at the portholes separating the seating booths, and you may find something alive within their depths…

Nargila Klub (Map pp376-7; ☎ 061 855 1026; ul Kozia 5/4; ☟ 2pm-midnight) If you don't know what a *narghile* is, one look at the generic Turkish-Arabic décor here should give you a clue. Whether you call it a sheesha, hookah, hubble-bubble or water pipe, you can bung in some flavoured tobacco and puff away on the snug cushions and carpets.

Czarna Owca (Map pp376-7; ☎ 061 855 3240; ul Jaskółcza 13; ☺ from 4pm Mon-Fri, from 6pm Sat) Calling your pub the 'Black Sheep' hardly encourages good behaviour, so sipping a quiet pint is seldom on the agenda here. When you've finished boozing in the dark, intimate bar, join the herd on the downstairs dance floor for DJs playing house, pop, rock, Latin or retro sounds, depending on the night.

Piwnica 21 (Map pp376-7; ☎ 061 852 2926; ul Wielka 21; ☺ from 5pm) On busy weekend nights this brick basement bar is packed with music fans taking in DJs, or classic live pub gigs in a jazz-blues vein, helped on by table football and draft stout.

Room 55 (Map pp376-7; ☎ 061 855 3224; Stary Rynek 80/82; ☺ 9am-midnight Mon-Thu, 9am-2am Fri & Sat, 11am-midnight Sun) This well-placed bar, bang on the Rynek, features mellow red chairs and banquettes, with a mezzanine area for observing the beautiful people below. There's also a food menu.

Bodega (Map pp376-7; ☎ 061 851 0094; ul Żydowska 4; ☺ 11am-11pm Sun-Thu, 11am-midnight Fri & Sat) On a street populated with cafés, Bodega's sleek modern lines stand out. The geometrically sharp interior is composed of mellow chocolate and gold tones, with candles on the tables, and chatting locals enjoying the relaxed vibe. Good coffee is accompanied by snacks and sweet temptations.

Atmosfera (Map pp376-7; ☎ 061 851 0399; ul Mokra 2; ☺ noon-11pm) If you're on the run from the Foreign Legion, or just trying to escape the hordes in the Stary Rynek, you could do worse than head for this hidden-away café in tiny ul Mokra. The décor is a faded blue showcase of floral wreaths and abstract art, just worn enough to give it character. To become even more unfindable, head to the upstairs room.

ENTERTAINMENT

Poznań's comprehensive monthly *iks* (4zł) contains listings on everything from museums to outdoor activities, with a short summary of the most important events in English. It's available from Ruch kiosks and the tourist offices (p373). The free monthly *Aktivist* can also be helpful, especially for nightlife, and *In Your Pocket* (5zł) pulls no punches with its colourful descriptions of local clubs.

Live Music & Clubs

OUR PICK Johnny Rocker (Map pp376-7; ☎ 061 853 6232; ul Wielka 9; ☺ from 5pm) This super-smooth basement venue with a curvy bar is crammed with happy drinkers sitting cabaret-style in front of a stage that features live blues, jazz or rock acts every weekend. If the sounds are overwhelming, you can always retreat to the stylish 'red room'.

Lizard King (Map pp376-7; ☎ 061 855 0472; Stary Rynek 86; ☺ noon-2am) Simultaneously happening and laid-back, this venue is easily located by the big guitar on its outside wall. Friendly crowds sit drinking and eating in the split-level space, casting the occasional glance at the lizard over the bar. There's live music most nights, usually from 9pm, including rock, jazz and blues.

Czerwony Fortepian (Map pp376-7; ☎ 061 852 0174; www.czerwony-fortepian.pl; ul Wroniecka 18; ☺ 5pm-late Mon-Sat, 2-10pm Sun) This smart bar-restaurant and jazz joint takes its name from an antique red piano, played by an array of visiting guest artists. A place for upscale aficionados who know their swing from their skiffle.

Charyzma (Map pp376-7; ☎ 061 851 7948; ul Ślusarska 6; ☺ 6pm-late) No overbearing personality here, just an intelligent, low-key sense of cool and some well-chosen, left-field music, covering various bases from emo to blues. Believe it or not, the club occasionally runs tango courses on Monday, complete with Argentinian wine.

Deep (Map pp376-7; ☎ 061 855 7302; ul Wrocławska 5; ☺ 8pm-late) One for the townies, this underground den is a hotbed of sportswear, short skirts and bumpin' black music. Deep is the kind of place that is good for rowdy nights out with your mates.

As well as the Dubliner, Balzac and Bogota pubs, the Centrum Kultury Zamek is also home to the **Blue Note Jazz Club** (Map pp376-7; ☎ 061 851 0408; www.bluenote.poznan.pl; ul Kościuszki 76/78), a major live jazz spot and occasional dance club, which holds regular concerts and jam sessions by local groups and occasional big-name gigs.

Classical Music, Opera & Ballet

Philharmonic Hall (Filharmonia; Map pp376-7; ☎ 061 853 6935; www.filharmonia.poznan.pl; ul Św Marcin 81) This musical institution holds concerts at least weekly, performed by the house symphony orchestra, often featuring visiting artists. Poznań also has Poland's best boys' choir, the

> **GET OUT OF TOWN!**
>
> Poznań has a reasonable selection of dance venues, but for dedicated clubbers around the country there's only one place to go for a real weekender: Manieczki. Never heard of it? Hardly surprising – but this tiny town south of the Wielkopolska National Park is a nightlife mecca.
>
> Roll up at the weekend, and you'll discover why. Manieczki is home to **Ekwador** (☎ 061 282 0850; www.ekwador.com.pl in Polish; ul Wybickiego; ☼ 9.30pm-late Fri & Sat), possibly the most famous club in Poland and a consistent ambassador for dance music at home and abroad. The list of visiting DJs, both Polish and international, is stellar.
>
> If you can't make it to the club itself, parties are held in more accessible venues around the country. In summer the management is partial to holding special events in beach venues on the Baltic coast – check the hyperactive website for details of the latest.
>
> It's easiest to get here with your own transport, but there are also nine buses from Poznań to Manieczki on Friday, and five on Saturday (7.40zł, 1¼ hours).

Poznańskie Słowiki (Poznań Nightingales), who can be heard here.

Teatr Wielki (Map pp376-7; ☎ 061 659 0280; www.opera .poznan.pl; ul Fredry 9) The usual stage for opera, ballet and various visiting performances. The annual Verdi festival in October is a particular highlight, and you should also look out for productions by the renowned **Polski Teatr Tańca** dance group.

Theatre

Teatr Polski (Map pp376-7; ☎ 061 852 5628; www.teatr -polski.pl; ul 27 Grudnia 8/10) The Polish Theatre is Poznań's main repertory stage, with a sound reputation and plenty of classics such as Chekhov and Kafka on the programme, alongside newer Polish works.

Teatr Biuro Podróży (☎ 0605 217668; www.teatrbiuro podrozy.ipoznan.pl) At the more avant-garde end of the scale, the Travel Agency Theatre is an innovative theatre group that has gained international acclaim for its spectacular new work and imaginative rejigging of the classics. The theatre has no fixed venue (contact the group for location info).

GETTING THERE & AWAY
Air

Poznań's **airport** (off Map p374; ☎ 061 849 2343; www .airport-poznan.com.pl; ul Bukowska 285) is in the western suburb of Ławica, 7km from the centre. There are flights from Poznań to Warsaw (four to five daily) via LOT; Barcelona (three weekly) on Ryanair; Bristol (three weekly) via Ryanair; Copenhagen (daily) via SAS; Dortmund (three weekly) on Wizz Air; Dublin (five weekly) via Ryanair or Aer Lingus; East Midlands (three weekly) on Ryanair; Frankfurt (daily) on LOT; Liverpool

(three weekly) via Ryanair; London (twice daily) on Ryanair or Wizz Air; Munich (four daily) via LOT or Lufthansa; and Stockholm (six weekly) on Wizz Air.

Bus

The bus terminal (Map pp376–7) is about 750m east of the train station. Buses run half-hourly to Kórnik (6.30zł, 40 minutes) and every couple of hours to Rogalin (6.30zł, one hour) on weekdays, but only twice daily on weekends. You can also get to Kórnik by hourly suburban buses from ul Św Marcin. Buses to Gniezno (10.50zł, 1½ hours) depart at least hourly and go via either Kostrzyn or Pobiedziska; the latter pass Lake Lednica (6.30zł). On longer routes, you could use buses to get to Kalisz (20zł, 2½ hours, 12 daily) and Zielona Góra (22zł, 2¾ hours, seven daily), as they run more frequently than trains.

Train

Poznań is a busy railway hub. From **Poznań Główny train station** (Map p374) there are about 20 trains to Warsaw daily (InterCity/ fast 89zł/46zł, three to four hours). Equally frequent services run to Wrocław (35zł, 2½ hours) and Szczecin (38zł, 2½ hours), and there are 10 to 12 direct trains to Kraków (50zł, seven hours).

Trains to Gdańsk (46zł, 4¾ hours, seven daily) and Toruń (33zł, 2½ hours, five daily) all pass through Gniezno (16zł, 45 minutes, hourly). Six trains depart for Zielona Góra daily (31zł to 53zł, 2½ hours). There are also five daily trains to Wolsztyn (14zł, 1¾ hours), including one steam train (see boxed text, p389).

WIELKOPOLSKA

HAVE BIKE, WILL TRAVEL

Since communism fell and took its travel restrictions with it, Poles have been making up for lost time, journeying to more far-flung locales each year. But they'd have to put in some serious trekking to catch up with their compatriot Kazimierz Nowak.

In 1931, this Poznań resident fetched up in Tripoli, Libya, as a press correspondent, covering the Italian military campaign there. When his colleagues returned to Europe, however, Nowak stayed behind. He had a dream: to travel the entire length of Africa by bicycle.

On 4 November 1931 he set off, passing through Egypt before heading south. On his journey, he often shared stories with locals around their campfires, and cast a critical eye on colonial settlers from Europe. He also took photographs, which he sold to Polish and German newspapers to supplement his funds.

Nowak reached Cape Town in May 1934. Then, amazingly, he turned his bike around and rode the entire length of the continent again, on a western route this time. In November 1936, five years after his odyssey had begun, he reached the Mediterranean at Algiers. He had covered 40,000km on bicycle and foot along the way.

Returning to Poznań, Nowak wrote a book about his exploits and gave ethnographic lectures at the Apollo Cinema, while planning a new expedition in Asia. It was not to be: on 13 October 1937 Kazimierz Nowak died of malaria, no doubt contracted on his epic trek. The great traveller was gone, but not forgotten – nowadays you can see a **plaque** (Map p374) commemorating his journey, with a map of the route, on the far wall of the concourse at Poznań Główny train station.

Seven international trains run to Berlin daily (113zł), including three EuroCity services taking just three hours. There are also direct trains to Cologne, Kyiv and Moscow.

Tickets and couchette reservations are handled by the train station, travel agencies and the **PKP office** (Map pp376-7; ☎ 061 863 1290; Al Niepodległości 8a).

GETTING AROUND
To/From the Airport

Poznań's airport is accessible via city buses 59, 77 and 78 (2.60zł, 25 minutes), which all run into town as far as Rondo Kaponiera, near the train station (the stop's called Bałtyk). A taxi should cost around 20zł to 30zł (15 minutes).

Public Transport

Poznań's public-transport system uses both timed and distance-based tickets. Timed tickets cost 1.30zł for a 10-minute ride, 2.60zł for half an hour, 3.90zł for up to one hour, and 5.20zł for 1½ hours. Approximate journey times are posted at stops. Distance-based tickets for buses cost 1.90zł for a ride of up to 10 stops and 3.20zł for any longer trip. A day ticket for all transport costs 11.40zł (and is far less complicated to work out!).

AROUND POZNAŃ

KÓRNIK
pop 6900

The town of Kórnik, 20km southeast of Poznań, is proof that mad German kings didn't have a monopoly on eccentric castle design. Its unconventional **castle** was built by the powerful Górka family in the 15th century. Nowadays it's more like a mansion than a castle; anyone who's visited a stately home in the English countryside will experience *déjà vu* (it even has tasteful tea rooms outside the main gate).

Its present-day appearance dates from the mid-19th century, when its owner, Tytus Działyński, gave the castle a somewhat outlandish mock-Gothic character, partly based on a design by German architect Karl Friedrich Schinkel. The building now looks as though two halves of completely different castles were spliced together, perhaps by force, and provides some interesting photos from varying angles.

The interior, too, was extensively (though more consistently) remodelled to provide a plush family home and accommodate the owner's vast art collection. On the 1st floor a spectacular Moorish hall was created (clearly influenced by the Alhambra in Granada) as a memorable setting for the display of armour and military accessories. The collection was expanded by Działyński's son Jan and his nephew Władysław Zamoyski; the latter donated the castle and its contents to the state in 1924.

The castle luckily survived the war and, miraculously, so did its contents. Part of it is now open as a **museum** (☎ 061 817 0081; ul Zamkowa 5; adult/concession 9/5zł; ⏰ 10am-5pm Tue-Sun). You can wander through its fully furnished and decorated 19th-century interiors, dotted with items collected by the family. The collection is well presented in a surprisingly light-filled space, and includes some intriguing pieces like elaborately designed furniture, medieval weaponry and centuries-old books, including a copy of Copernicus' masterwork, *De Revolutionibus Orbium Coelestium*. Make sure you don the slippers handed out at the entrance – scuff marks are not appreciated on the original wooden floors.

Behind the castle is a large, English-style park known as the **Arboretum** (☎ 061 817 0033; adult/concession 3.50/2.50zł; ⏰ 9am-6pm), which was laid out during the castle's reconstruction, and stocked with exotic species of trees and shrubs from Europe's leading nurseries. Today the Arboretum is run by a scientific research institute and has some 2500 plant species and varieties; the best times to visit are May to June and September to October, when the greatest number of specimens come into flower.

Some of the castle's outbuildings are also used for exhibitions. **Galeria Klaudynówka** (adult/concession 2/1zł; ⏰ 10am-4pm Tue-Sun), a servants' house from 1791, displays contemporary paintings, while the **powozownia** (coach house; admission free; ⏰ 11am-4pm Tue-Sun), on the opposite side of the road, holds three London coaches, brought from Paris by Jan Działyński in 1856.

Getting There & Away

There's frequent bus transport from Poznań to Kórnik (6.30zł, 40 minutes). You can either take the PKS bus from the central bus terminal (departing every half-hour or so) or go by suburban bus from ul Św Marcin (hourly). Both deposit you at the Rynek in Kórnik, a three-minute walk from the castle. Follow the road as it veers to the right past the town hall and becomes ul Zamkowa.

If you plan to continue on to Rogalin (4.30zł, 25 minutes), there are approximately two buses a day from Monday to Friday (check the timetable before visiting the castle).

ROGALIN
pop 800

The tiny village of Rogalin, 12km west of Kórnik, was the seat of yet another Polish aristocratic clan, the Raczyński family, who built a **palace** here in the closing decades of the 18th century, and lived in it until WWII. Plundered but not damaged during WWII, the palace was taken over by the state. In 1991, Count Edward Raczyński, who had been Polish ambassador to Britain at the outbreak of WWII and a leading figure in the Polish government in exile, reaffirmed the use of the palace as a branch of Poznań's **National Museum** (☎ 061 813 8030; adult/concession 8/5.50zł, free Wed; ⏰ 10am-4pm Tue-Sat & 10am-6pm Sun May-Sep, 10am-4pm Tue-Sun Jan-Apr, Oct & Nov).

Less visited than Kórnik's castle and much more Germanic in its appearance, the Rogalin palace consists of a massive, two-storey, baroque central structure and two modest symmetrical wings linked to the main body by curving galleries, forming a giant horseshoe around a vast forecourt. Within the main house, you can peruse art and furniture from the different ages of the mansion, and also an exact replica of the London study of Count Raczyński.

Just beyond the left wing is the **Gallery of Painting** (Galeria Obrazów), an adapted greenhouse displaying Polish and European canvases from the 19th and early 20th centuries. The Polish collection includes some first-class work, with Jacek Malczewski best represented. The dominant work, though, is Jan Matejko's *Joan of Arc*.

In the **coach house**, near the front courtyard, are a dozen old coaches, including Poznań's last horse-drawn cab, and a restaurant.

Opposite the main house is a small French garden, which leads into the larger **English landscaped park**, originally laid out in primeval oak forest. Not much of the park's design can be deciphered today, but the ancient oak trees are still here, some of them centuries old. The three most imposing specimens have been fenced off and baptised with the names Lech, Czech and Rus, after the legendary founders of the Polish, Czech and Russian nations.

One more place to see is the **chapel**, on the eastern outskirts of the village, built in the 1820s to serve as a mausoleum for the

WIELKOPOLSKA

Raczyński family. It's a replica of the Roman temple known as the Maison Carrée in Nîmes, southern France.

Getting There & Away

There are several buses from Poznań to Rogalin (6.30zł, one hour), going by various routes. Buses back to Poznań pass through every couple of hours until late afternoon.

WIELKOPOLSKA NATIONAL PARK

Just a few kilometres southwest of Poznań's administrative boundaries is the 76-sq-km **Wielkopolska National Park** (Wielkopolski Park Narodowy; ☎ 061 813 2206; www.wielkopolskipn.pl). About 80% of the park is forest – pine and oak being the dominant species – and its postglacial lakes give it a certain charm.

Hiking is the main attraction here, and a good point to start your stroll is the town of Mosina (21km from Poznań), which is served regularly by both train and bus from Poznań. From Mosina, follow the blue-marked trail heading northwest to Osowa Góra (3km). Once you reach small Lake Kociołek, switch to the red trail, which winds southwestwards. After passing another miniature lake, the trail reaches Lake Góreckie, the most beautiful body of water in the park. The trail then skirts the eastern part of the lake and turns northeast to bring you to the town of Puszczykowo, from where trains and buses can take you back to Poznań. It's about a 17km walk altogether, through the most attractive area of the park.

If you want to do more walking, there are four more trails to choose from. Get a copy of the TopMapa *Wielkopolski Park Narodowy* map (scale 1:35,000), which has all the details.

Accommodation is available in Puszczykowo and Mosina, if you decide on a longer stay. The two towns sit conveniently on the eastern edge of the park, just 4km apart on the Poznań-Wrocław railway line. There are regular slow trains from Poznań Główny to Puszczykowo (4zł, 15 minutes) and Mosina (4.50zł, 25 minutes).

MORASKO

Great balls of fire! Just 10km from the centre of Poznań is the **Morasko Meteorite Reserve** (Rezerwat Meteoryt Morasko), one of just two registered impact sites in Europe. The idea of flaming space rock crash-landing in the peaceful forest here may seem bizarre, but that's exactly what happened roughly 10,000 years ago, and eight craters are still clearly visible, some filled with water. The largest is over 100m across and 13m in depth, and while it's overgrown enough not to look like the surface of the moon, the extent of the dent is still pretty impressive.

To get here you can catch tram 12, 14, 15 or 16 from the train station to the Osledle Sobieskiego tram terminus and follow the 4km walking trail, or change at Szymanowskiego for bus 88 to Morasko village.

THE PIAST ROUTE

The Piast Route (Szlak Piastowski) is a popular tourist trail, winding from Poznań to Kruszwica. It weaves together a selection of sites related to Poland's early history, along with other historic curios like the Iron-Age village of Biskupin. Following the route is a great way to gain insights into the formative years of the nation.

LAKE LEDNICA

Lake Lednica, 30km east of Poznań, is the first important point on the Piast Route. The 7km-long elongated postglacial lake has four islands.

The largest, Ostrów Lednicki, was one of the major settlements of the first Piasts. In the 10th century a stronghold was built here, along with a stone palace and a church, and the route between Poznań and Gniezno ran across two wooden bridges linking the island to the lake's western and eastern shores.

The settlement was overrun by the Bohemians and destroyed in 1038, and though the church and the defensive ramparts were rebuilt, the island never regained its importance. Between the 12th and 14th centuries a large part of it was used as a graveyard. Some 2000 tombs have been found here, making the site the largest cemetery from that period discovered in Central Europe.

Sights

On the lakeshore facing the island of Ostrów Lednicki is the **Museum of the First Piasts** (Muzeum Pierwszych Piastów; ☎ 061 427 5010; ul Dziekanowice 32, Lednogóra; adult/concession 6/3zł; ⏲ 9am-6pm Tue-Sat & 10am-5pm Sun Apr-Oct, 9am-3pm Tue-Sat & 10am-3pm Sun Nov-Mar). Among the build-

---

ALL STEAMED UP

Almost everywhere in Europe, the grand age of steam is over. The steam trains that still operate are confined to picturesque tourist railways, functioning as museum pieces on wheels. But not in the town of Wolsztyn, 65km southwest of Poznań.

Thanks partly to the enthusiasm of British trainspotters, PKP still runs regular steam-train services between Poznań Główny and Wolsztyn. Each day between one to three steam trains haul passengers along the route – check at the station for the current timetable (*pociąg parowy* means 'steam train').

In addition to the Poznań services, there's one steam train a day in each direction between Wolsztyn and Leszno, which is also linked directly by rail to Poznań. PKP also operates special one-off steam services throughout the warmer months, including an annual Wolsztyn–Wrocław train.

So where do those train enthusiasts come in? They're the eager customers of the **Wolsztyn Experience** (☎ 068 384 2543; www.wolsztyn.co.uk), a steam-train course that instructs would-be drivers and gives them a chance to actually drive a train on its regular run.

Also, in May each year Wolsztyn is home to the Steam Parade, a festival featuring steam locomotives from across Europe. And if too much steam is never enough, the town also offers a steam-train museum, within its working engine depot south of the train station at ul Fabryczna 1.

---

ings in the grounds is the oldest windmill in Poland (built in 1585), and an 18th-century granary, which has a display of excavated human remains.

The main exhibition is in the churchlike building, which has two floors of finds from excavations on and around the island. Among the exhibits, most of which date from the 10th and 11th centuries, are weapons, household items and implements, pottery, ornaments, and a dugout canoe, which is one of the very few wooden objects to have survived for almost a millennium.

Between mid-April and October, a small boat takes visitors from the museum's jetty to the island of Ostrów Lednicki, 175m away, where you can see what is left of the palace and the church. The foundations and lower parts of the walls are still in place and this gives a rough idea of how big the complex was.

Each May, the medieval atmosphere gets turned up to 11 at the **International Festival of Early Medieval Culture** (☎ 061 427 5040), with numerous historically themed events involving costumes and axes.

Two kilometres south of the museum, also on the lakeshore, is the **Wielkopolska Ethnographic Park** (Wielkopolski Park Etnograficzny; ☎ 061 427 5040; Dziekanowice; adult/concession 6/3zł; 9am-6pm Tue-Sat & 10am-5pm Sun Apr-Oct, 9am-3pm Tue-Sat & 10am-3pm Sun Nov-Mar). It's on the eastern side of the lake, 500m north of the Poznań–Gniezno road. The skansen features a good

selection of 19th-century rural architecture from Wielkopolska in a village setting.

A combined ticket covering entry to the museum and the skansen costs 10zł for adults and 5zł concession.

Getting There & Away

The lake lies on the Poznań–Gniezno road and there's a regular bus service between the two cities – up to 12 daily to/from Poznań (6.30zł) and to/from Gniezno (4.30zł). From whichever end you start, take the bus that runs via Pobiedziska, not via Kostrzyn. Coming from Poznań, you'll see three old windmills on the hill to the left of the road; stay on the bus for another 2.5km and get off at the turn-off to Komorowo (the bus stop is just by the turn-off). From here it is about a five-minute walk to the skansen, then you need to walk for another 2km along a sealed road to the museum.

GNIEZNO
pop 70,000

Appearances can be deceptive – on first glance at the relaxed centre of Gniezno (*gnyez*-no), you'd never guess the huge part it played in the founding of Poland. Its Old Town, attractively renovated on the 1000th anniversary (in 2000) of the establishment of the city's historic bishopric, is a charming collection of winding streets and colourful, slope-roofed buildings centred on a pleasant cobblestone square and the city's famous cathedral.

WIELKOPOLSKA

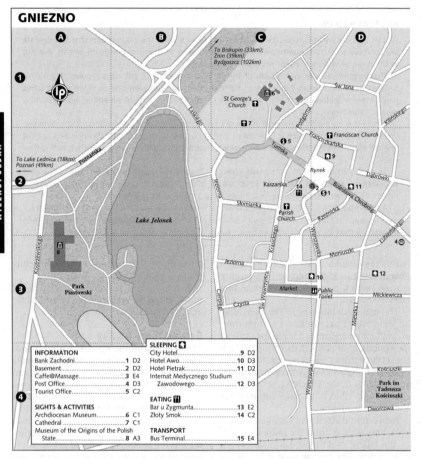

GNIEZNO

To Biskupin (33km);
Znin (39km);
Bydgoszcz (102km)

St George's
Church

To Lake Lednica (18km);
Poznań (49km)

Lake Jelonek

Rynek

Kaszarska

Park
Piastowski

Słomianka

Parish
Church

Jeziorna

Market

Public
Toilet

Franciscan Church

Dąbrówki

Mickiewicza

Park im
Tadeusza
Kościuszki

Kościuszki

Dworcowa

INFORMATION
Bank Zachodni...................................1 D2
Basement..2 D2
Caffe@Massage.................................3 E4
Post Office..4 D3
Tourist Office....................................5 C2

SIGHTS & ACTIVITIES
Archdiocesan Museum......................6 C1
Cathedral...7 C1
Museum of the Origins of the Polish
State...8 A3

SLEEPING
City Hotel...9 D2
Hotel Awo..10 D3
Hotel Pietrak....................................11 D2
Internat Medycznego Studium
Zawodowego..............................12 D3

EATING
Bar u Zygmunta...............................13 E2
Złoty Smok.......................................14 C2

TRANSPORT
Bus Terminal....................................15 E4

It may be slow-paced now, but in its day Gniezno has been both a royal and a religious seat. It is also considered to be the cradle of the Polish state, as it was here that the various tribes of the region were first united as Poles in the 10th century. Its historic cathedral is well worth a visit, and it is also a great place to catch your breath after the hustle of Poznań.

History
Legend has it that Gniezno was founded by the mythical Lech, the grandson of the original legendary Piast and the grandfather of Mieszko I. While hunting in the area, young Lech found the *gniazdo* (nest) of a white eagle, giving the town its name and the na-

tion its emblem (the man himself had to settle for having a beer named after him).

In historical terms, Gniezno was already fortified with wood and earth ramparts by the end of the 8th century, and had regular trade links with commercial centres far outside the region. In a key development, Duke Mieszko I is thought to have been baptised here in 966, thus raising the autonomous region of Wielkopolska from obscurity to the rank of Christianised nations.

Despite this, Mieszko seems to have favoured Poznań as a city, and some historians have argued that Gniezno was never officially Wielkopolska's capital – the first cathedral was, after all, built in Poznań, and the ruler was buried there.

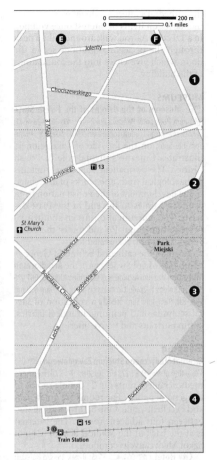

Information

Bank Zachodni (Rynek 4)
Basement (☎ 0607 538684; Rynek 5; per hr 2zł; ☽ 9am-11pm) Internet access.
Caffe@Massage (☎ 061 633 4365; ul Dworcowa 7; per hr 2.50zł; ☽ 7.30am-9.30pm) Internet access (and massage!) at the train station.
Post office (ul Bolesława Chrobrego 36)
Tourist office (☎ 061 428 4100; ul Tumska 12; ☽ 8am-6pm Mon-Fri, 9am-3pm Sat, 10am-2pm Sun May-Sep, 8am-4pm Mon-Fri Oct-Apr)

Sights

CATHEDRAL

Gniezno's history and character are inextricably intertwined with its **cathedral** (☎ 061 424 3820; ☽ 9am-5.30pm Mon-Sat, 1-5.45pm Sun), an imposing, double-towered, brick Gothic structure. The present church, which you may recognise from a common 2zł postage stamp, was constructed after the 1331 destruction of the previous Romanesque cathedral by the Teutonic Knights (see boxed text, p451). It changed a lot in later periods: chapels sprouted all around it, and the interior was redecorated in successive styles. After considerable damage in WWII, it was rebuilt according to the original Gothic structure.

Aside from its historic value, the cathedral's interior has an unusually soothing atmosphere, perhaps due to its relatively compact size and graceful curves. It's a good place to sit and contemplate.

Its focal point is the elaborate silver **sarcophagus of St Adalbert**, which is in the chancel. The baroque coffin was the work of Peter van der Rennen and was made in 1662 in Gdańsk. It's topped with the semi-reclining figure of the saint, who looks remarkably lively considering his unfortunate demise.

Adalbert was a Bohemian bishop who passed through Gniezno in 997, on a missionary trip to convert the Prussians, a heathen Baltic tribe inhabiting what is now Masuria in northeastern Poland. The pagans were less than enthusiastic about accepting the new faith and terminated the bishop's efforts by cutting off his head. Bolesław Chrobry recovered the bishop's body, paying its weight in gold, then buried it in Gniezno's cathedral in 999. In the same year, Pope Sylvester canonised the martyr. This contributed to Gniezno's elevation to an archbishopric a year later, and also led to the placing of several important memorials to the saint in the church.

Gniezno came to the fore again in the year 1000, when the archbishopric was established here, and then Gniezno's position was further strengthened in 1025 when Bolesław Chrobry was crowned in the local cathedral as the first Polish king. Only 13 years later, the Bohemians invaded, devastating the entire region. This prompted the Poles to shift their seat of power to the more secure Kraków, though kings were still crowned in Gniezno until the end of the 13th century.

The town retained its status as the seat of the Church of Poland and is still the formal ecclesiastical capital, despite the fact that the archbishops are only occasional guests these days.

One example is the pair of Romanesque **bronze doors** from about 1175, in the back of the right-hand (southern) aisle, at the entrance from the porch. Undeniably one of the best examples of Romanesque art in Europe, the doors depict, in bas-relief, 18 scenes from the life of St Adalbert.

Framing the doors is the exquisite 15th-century **Gothic portal** with the scene of the Last Judgement in its tympanum. In the opposite porch, right across the nave, is another elaborate **Gothic portal**, dating from the same period, this one with the scene of the Crucifixion in its tympanum.

The nearby entrance in the back wall of the church leads downstairs to the **basement**, where the relics of the previous Romanesque cathedral can be seen, along with the Gothic tombstones of the bishops.

Also on this back wall are two carved tombstones. To the left is the red-marble **tomb of Primate Zbigniew Oleśnicki**, attributed to Veit Stoss, and to the right is the late-15th-century bronze **tomb of Archbishop Jakub** from Sienna. Also note an expressive wooden crucifix from around 1440, placed high on the rood beam at the entrance to the chancel.

All along the aisles and the ambulatory are **chapels**, built from the 15th to 18th centuries, and separated from the aisles by decorative wrought-iron screens. There are 17 screens in all, ranging in style from Gothic and Renaissance to baroque, and constituting one of the most beautiful collections of its kind to be gathered in a single church in Poland. Inside the chapels are some fine tombstones, altarpieces, paintings and wall decorations – well worth a closer look.

One interesting modern artwork sits in the body of the church: a **statue of Cardinal Stefan Wyszyński**, the Polish primate credited with persuading the Soviets to relax their antireligious stance during the communist era. The panelled piece shows various scenes from the cardinal's eventful life and career.

You can look around the interior free of charge, except for the **tower** (adult/concession 3/2zł; 9.30am-5.30pm Mon-Sat, 1-6pm Sun), and the **bronze doors and basement** (adult/concession 2/1.50zł; 9am-5pm Mon-Sat, 1-5.45pm Sun), the latter two visited with a guide. English- or German-speaking guides may be available for 45-minute cathedral tours at around 80zł per group – enquire at the office in the porch opposite the doors. There are also machines scattered through

the cathedral's interior, which produce commentaries on items of interest once you pop in a 1zł coin. As you walk around, take a peek through the occasional gratings set in the floor, which give views into the foundations of the building.

MUSEUMS

The **Museum of the Origins of the Polish State** (Muzeum Początków Państwa Polskiego; ☎ 061 426 4641; ul Kostrzewskiego 1; adult/concession 5.50/3.50zł; 10am-5pm Tue-Sun), on the far side of Lake Jelonek, illustrates Gniezno's pivotal role in Polish history. The permanent collection contains archaeological finds and works of art related to the development of the Polish nation from pre-Slavic times to the end of the Piast dynasty. The museum also runs an audiovisual presentation about Poland under the Piasts (English soundtrack available).

North of the cathedral behind St George's Church (Kościół Św Jerzego), the **Archdiocesan Museum** (Muzeum Archidiecezji Gnieźnieńskiej; ☎ 061 426 3778; ul Kolegiaty 2; adult/concession 4/3zł; 9am-5.30pm Mon-Sat, 9am-4pm Sun) holds a collection of sacral sculpture and painting, liturgical fabrics, coffin portraits and votive offerings.

Sleeping

Internat Medycznego Studium Zawodowego (☎ 061 426 3409; ul Mieszka I 27; s/d 30/60zł; P) Gniezno's medical college rents out 24 double rooms to the general public. The rooms are quiet, neat and excellent value. One bathroom is shared between four adjacent rooms. The Internat is at the back of the Medical School (Zespół Szkół Medycznych) compound.

City Hotel (☎ 061 425 3535; Rynek 15; s/d 80/90zł) This hotel doesn't make much effort to live up to its prestigious position on the Rynek – inside its rooms, you'll find sofa beds and a dodgy green-brown colour scheme. But the price is right, the rooms and the café look out onto the square, and you can't get much closer to the cathedral. Enter via the City Bar.

Hotel Awo (☎ 061 426 1197; www.hotel-awo.pl; ul Warszawska 32; s/d/tr/q/ste 150/190/230/280/300zł;) A midrange place with neat, clean rooms, a pleasant courtyard with a beer garden, and a restaurant and nightclub on the premises. It's right by the city market, making it potentially noisy for south-facing rooms.

Hotel Pietrak (☎ 061 426 1497; www.pietrak.pl; ul Bolesława Chrobrego 3; s/d/ste 180/210/250zł; P) Located in two 18th-century burghers' houses, just shy of the Rynek, the Pietrak provides the best facilities in town, including a fitness centre with a spa. The restaurant (mains 8zł to 45zł) serves up quality food, and operates a colourful beer garden in the street during summer.

Eating

Bar u Zygmunta (☎ 061 426 3774; ul Wyszyńskiego 20; mains 2-7zł; 🕑 9am-6pm Mon-Fri, 9am-4pm Sat) In the more modern part of town, this self-service cafeteria has a good claim to being the cheapest budget eatery in the central area, and has a fine grasp of classic milk-bar standards.

Złoty Smok (☎ 061 426 7804; ul Kaszarska 1; mains 13-23zł; 🕑 11am-2am) The Golden Dragon is a pretty standard Chinese restaurant, but stands out as the most adventurous eating choice in the town centre. It's popular with locals, and the menu has a dash of authenticity thanks to the Vietnamese chef.

Getting There & Away

BUS

Buses travel to Poznań (10.50zł, 1½ hours) from the bus terminal at least hourly; if you want to stop at Lake Lednica (4.30zł, 35 minutes), take one that goes via Pobiedziska (up to 12 daily). There are six daily buses running to Żnin (8zł, one hour), where you can change for the narrow-gauge train to Biskupin.

TRAIN

Trains run regularly throughout the day to Poznań (16zł, 45 minutes). There are also departures to Bydgoszcz (28zł, 1½ hours, six daily), Toruń (24zł, 1½ hours, six daily), Gdańsk (43zł, 4½ hours, seven daily) and Wrocław (38zł, 3¾ hours, seven daily).

ŻNIN

pop 14,000

This sleepy town, 39km north of Gniezno, is well off the international tourist trail, with only a handful of buildings of historical interest. However, as it's the terminus of a narrow-gauge tourist railway that links a bundle of disparate sights, it's a worthwhile day-trip from Gniezno.

Sights & Activities

The town's **Pałuki Lands Museum** (Muzeum Ziemi Pałuckiej; ☎ 052 302 0293; Plac Wolności 1; adult/concession 5/3zł; 🕑 9am-4pm Tue-Fri, 10am-3pm Sat & Sun) is housed within the town hall and the nearby 15th-century Gothic tower, located across the canal to the west of the bus station. It displays historical and ethnographic exhibits related to the town and the historical Pałuki region around it. If religious art is your thing, you can also visit the **Sacred Art Museum** (Muzeum Sztuki Sakralnej; ☎ 052 302 8344; ul 700-lecia 24; adult/concession 5/3zł; 🕑 9am-5pm Tue-Fri), south of the bus station.

Then step aboard a train running along the **Żnin District Railway** (Żnińska Kolej Powiatowa; ☎ 052 302 0492; www.paluki.pl/ciuchcia; ul Potockiego 4; one-way/return 9/17zł), a narrow-gauge line that was opened in 1894 to carry sugar beets to the local sugar factory, and which also functioned as public transport. The passenger service was cancelled in 1962, but the line lives on as a tourist attraction. You'll find the station across the park east of the bus terminal.

Once the train leaves the dinky narrow-gauge station at Żnin, it trundles very slowly through a succession of low green hills covered with crops, pausing briefly at a stop serving the village of Wenecja before reaching the **Wenecja Narrow Gauge Railway Museum** (Muzeum Kolei Wąskotorowej w Wenecji; ☎ 052 302 5150; adult/concession 5/3zł; 🕑 9am-6pm May-Oct, 10am-2pm Nov-Apr), a showcase of narrow little engines, carriages, and their associated memorabilia. Across the rails from the museum are the **ruins** of a 14th-century castle.

The next stop on the line is the Archaeological Reserve at Biskupin (see p394); then the train finally reaches the village of Gąsawa. The main sight of interest here is **St Nicholas' Church** (Kościół Św Mikołaja; ☎ 052 302 5030; ul Żnińska 1; admission free), a 17th-century wooden structure with an unusual mix of architectural styles: Gothic, baroque, neoclassicist and more modern additions all jostling together. When the church was renovated in 1999, the workers discovered original frescoes that had been covered up by a mixture of reeds and plaster. The paintings depict saints and other Biblical figures, and have been gradually revealed by ongoing 'excavation'.

If you take an early train from Żnin, it's perfectly possible to stop off at the railway museum, Biskupin and Gąsawa, then return to Żnin by the last train of the day.

Getting There & Away

BUS

From the bus station on ul Towarowa in the centre of town, buses run every hour or two between Żnin and Gniezno (8zł, one hour). There are twice-hourly buses to Gąsawa (3.40zł, 25 minutes), though only eight of these run through Biskupin (3.40zł, 20 minutes, Monday to Friday). Seven services a day head to Poznań (16.30zł, 2¼ hours), passing through Gniezno. There are hourly services to Bydgoszcz (9zł, one hour), and one bus a day to Toruń (11.60zł, 1½ hours).

TRAIN
The narrow-gauge tourist train operates from May to September, from Żnin to Gąsawa (one-way/return 9zł/17zł, one hour), passing Biskupin on the way (40 minutes). Five trains depart from Żnin daily between 9am and 2.40pm (in July and August there's an extra departure at 4pm), then make the return journey from Gąsawa. In Żnin, the station is 150m east of the bus station; in Gąsawa it's 700m southwest of the Rynek on the Gniezno road.

BISKUPIN
Forget static museum displays in dimly lit rooms – Biskupin's recreated Iron Age town site, with its wooden palisades, thatched roofs and costumed historical re-enactors, is a stimulating way to learn about the distant pre-Polish past.

The fortified lake town was built about 2700 years ago by a tribe of the Lusatian culture, then accidentally rediscovered in 1933 by a school teacher who noticed some wooden stakes poking out of the lake. The town's remnants were then unearthed from beneath a thick layer of turf. It is the only known surviving Iron Age town in Poland, and proves that the region was already inhabited by well-organised social groups more than 1600 years before the Polish state was born.

Sights & Activities
The Iron Age town is situated within the **Archaeological Reserve** (Rezerwat Archeologiczny; ☎ 052 302 5420; www.biskupin.pl; adult/concession 7/5zł; ⏰ 8am-6pm, closes at dusk in winter). You can just wander through the grounds, but it's also possible to hire an electronic audio tour for 15zł, or organise an English-speaking guide in advance for 80zł. The ticket office also sells some publications about the site in English.

Once past the gate, follow the path to the **museum**, which presents finds excavated on and

around the island, together with background information (there's some English signage) about the place and the people. There's also a model of the town as it once looked.

The **Iron Age town** lies further along, on the peninsula in the northern end of the park. The gateway, a fragment of the defensive wall and two rows of houses have been reconstructed to give some idea of what the town once looked like. The interiors of a few houses have been fitted out as they may have been 2700 years ago. Within the thatched structures you'll find various stalls selling handcrafted arrows, jewellery and replica coins, and a man in period garb giving hatchet-throwing demonstrations out front. From the wharf near the gateway, a **pleasure boat** (trips 5zł) departs several times a day for a short trip around the lake.

In September each year, an **archaeological festival** is held at the reserve. In addition to demonstrations of ancient cultures including dance, handcrafts and food, it's an annual excuse to stage rousing re-enactments of battles between Germanic and Slavic tribes, providing a colourful (and photogenic) spectacle.

Getting There & Away
BUS
From the bus stop at the entrance to the Archaeological Reserve, buses run every hour or two north to Żnin (3.40zł, 20 minutes, Monday to Friday) and south to Gąsawa (2.60zł, five minutes, Monday to Friday). From either of these places, regular buses go to Gniezno (8zł, one hour). If you miss your bus, Gąsawa is an easy 2km walk away.

TRAIN
See the Żnin Getting There & Away section (left) for details of the narrow-gauge tourist train that passes through Biskupin from May to September. The station is right by the entrance to the reserve.

STRZELNO
pop 6100
Strzelno (*stshel-*no) boasts two of the best Romanesque churches in the region and a museum. It's a good side trip for architecture buffs and church-art fans.

Sights
Strzelno's attractions are all next to each other, 200m east of the Rynek.

IRON LIFE

The Iron Age settlement of Biskupin was built around 740–730 BC, taking just a few years to be constructed. Following a highly organised plan, the island was encircled by a 6m-high barricade consisting of a wooden framework filled with earth and sand. The island's shores were then reinforced with a palisade of about 20,000 oak stakes that were driven into the lake bottom, which served as a breakwater and an obstacle for potential invaders. The only access to the town was through a gateway topped with a watchtower and connected to the lake shore by a 250m-long bridge.

Within the defensive walls, 13 parallel rows of houses were laid out with streets between them, and encircled by a street running inside the ramparts. More than 100 houses were built, each inhabited by one family of seven to 10 members. The total population of the settlement was about 800 to 1000 people, which probably constituted a big city for its inhabitants. The town was essentially self-sufficient but also benefited from nearby trade routes.

Around 400 BC the town was destroyed, most likely by the Scythians, and was never rebuilt. This was essentially because of climatic changes, which caused the lake's level to rise, making the island uninhabitable. The remains of the wooden structure were preserved in mud and silt for 2300 years. Early in the 20th century the water level began to drop and the island re-emerged, eventually turning into a peninsula, as it is today.

A lot of effort was put into reconstructing the houses and the ramparts when the town was rediscovered, and the results haven't just impressed the steady trickle of tourists who come here. The authenticity and location of the site have made it a favourite with Polish filmmakers, and Biskupin has already appeared in Jerzy Hoffman's historical epics *Stara Baśń* (2003) and *Ogniem i Mieczem* (1999), as well as the TV series *Sagala*. In a small way, the Iron Age is back.

Built of red stone in around 1150, **St Procopius' Church** (Kościół Św Prokopa; ☎ 052 318 9281; Plac Św Wojciecha; adult/concession 2/1.50zł; ⊙ 9am-5pm Mon-Sat, 1.30-5pm Sun) has preserved its austere Romanesque form remarkably well, even though its upper part was rebuilt in brick after damage in the 18th century. The interior, almost free of decoration, looks admirably authentic. By the entrance is the original 12th-century font.

Built a decade or two after its neighbour, the larger **Church of the Holy Trinity** (Kościół Św Trójcy; ☎ 052 318 9281; Plac Św Wojciecha; adult/concession 3/2.50zł; ⊙ 9am-5pm Mon-Sat, 1.30-5pm Sun) acquired a Gothic vault in the 14th century and a baroque façade four centuries later. The interior is a remarkably harmonious composition of baroque furnishings, Gothic vaulting and four original Romanesque columns. These columns, revealed only during postwar restoration, are the most precious treasure of the church, particularly the two with elaborate figurative designs. There are 18 figures carved in each column; those on the left-hand column personify vices, while those on the right are virtues.

The door at the head of the right-hand aisle leads to St Barbara's Chapel, its fine palmlike vault resting on yet another delicately carved Romanesque pillar.

Next door, the **museum** (☎ 052 318 9281; Plac Św Wojciecha; adult/concession 2/1.50zł; ⊙ 9am-5pm Mon-Sat, 1.30-5pm Sun) presents some architectural remains (including a Romanesque portal with a tympanum depicting the scene of the Teaching of Christ) and archaeological finds.

Getting There & Away
The bus terminal is at the western end of town, and has regular services to Gniezno (8.50zł, 50 minutes).

KRUSZWICA
pop 9400
Set on the northern end of Lake Gopło, Kruszwica (kroosh-*fee*-tsah) existed from at least the 8th century as a fortified village of the Goplanie, one of the Slav tribes living in the area. The Goplanie were eventually wiped out by the Polanie, forerunners of the medieval Poles, who made considerably more of a mark on history.

Today Kruszwica is an undistinguished, small industrial town notable for its remnants of the Piast legacy and a few strange legends about the region's early days (see boxed text, p396).

THE LEGEND OF DUKE POPIEL

Once upon a time, a duke named Popiel lived in the castle of Kruszwica. He was a cruel and despotic ruler but was terrified of being overthrown. To remove any competitors to the throne, he decided to kill all his relatives and leading members of the community.

To put his diabolical plan into effect, the duke organised a great party in the castle, inviting his family and other distinguished guests. Once the initial toasts had been made, a poisonous wine was served to selected invitees, who died in a great deal of pain. Popiel then threw the bodies out of the castle and refused to bury them, as an example to others.

But, as fate would have it, the decomposing corpses attracted thousands of mice, which soon infested the castle. Popiel sought refuge high up in the castle's tower, but the mice cornered him there and devoured him. Since then the tower has been known as the Mouse Tower.

Following Popiel's death, a modest peasant, Piast, was chosen by the people and proclaimed the new ruler. He was the first leader of the Piast dynasty, which ruled Poland for many years and made it great and prosperous. And the mice lived happily (and plumply) ever after…

Sights & Activities

The 32m-high **Mouse Tower** (Mysia Wieża; ☎ 052 351 5303; adult/concession 3.60/2.90zł; ☺ 8am-6pm May-Sep), near the Rynek, is the only remainder of the 14th-century castle built by King Kazimierz III Wielki. You can go to the top for a view over the town and lake. From the foot of this octagonal tower, a **tourist boat** (adult/concession 8.50/7zł) sails several times a day in summer for an hour-long trip around Lake Gopło.

The early-12th-century stone Romanesque **collegiate church** (ul Kolegiacka) was altered in later periods but returned more or less to its original form during postwar restoration. The interior fittings include the 12th-century baptismal font. The church is on the northeastern outskirts of town, an 800m walk from the Rynek.

Getting There & Away

The main bus stop is on the Rynek. Buses to Strzelno (4zł, 10 minutes) depart every other hour or so. You can take a bus to Inowrocław (4zł, 20 minutes, hourly) for transport further afield.

SOUTHEASTERN WIELKOPOLSKA

KALISZ

pop 109,000

Given how little the average traveller knows about Kalisz (kah-leesh), its centre comes as a pleasant surprise, revealing a charming collection of city parks, gently curving streets and simple but harmonious architecture. This provincial city still has the feel of a small market town, so it's easy to avoid urban stresses while taking full advantage of the city's facilities. Kalisz is also a good point from which to leave the tourist trail and investigate the quieter rural backwaters of Wielkopolska.

History

Kalisz has the longest documented history of any town in Poland: it was mentioned by Claudius Ptolemy in his renowned *Geography* of the 2nd century AD as Calisia, a trading settlement on the Amber Route between the Roman Empire and the Baltic Sea. In the 9th century a stronghold was built in the present-day suburb of Zawodzie. Burnt down in 1233, the town was rebuilt further to the north, in its present location.

During the reign of Kazimierz III Wielki, Kalisz acquired defensive walls with 15 watchtowers and a castle. From the 16th century it began to decline. A huge fire in 1792 left only the churches standing, and almost all the fortifications were taken down in the early 19th century.

The greatest blow to civic pride, sometimes compared to Warsaw's annihilation in 1944, came in WWI – in August 1914 Kalisz was razed to the ground by the invading Germans. Within a month, the population dropped from 70,000 to 5000 and most buildings were reduced to ruins, though the churches once again miraculously escaped destruction. The town was rebuilt on the old street plan, but in a new architectural style. Luckily, given the circumstances, most of the new buildings survived WWII without much damage.

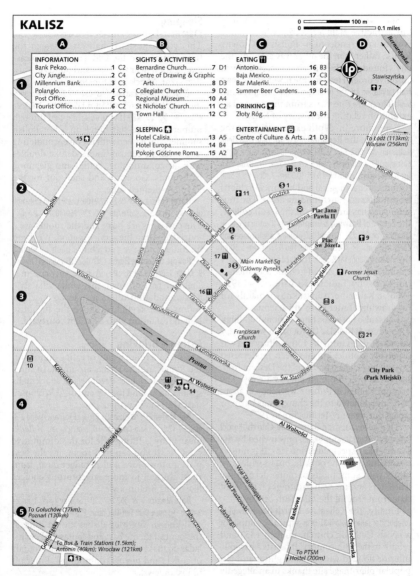

KALISZ

0 ———— 100 m
0 ———— 0.1 miles

INFORMATION
Bank Pekao..................1 C2
City Jungle..................2 C4
Millennium Bank...........3 C3
Polanglo.....................4 C3
Post Office...................5 C2
Tourist Office...............6 C2

SIGHTS & ACTIVITIES
Bernardine Church.............7 D1
Centre of Drawing & Graphic
Arts.........................8 D3
Collegiate Church.............9 D2
Regional Museum............10 A4
St Nicholas' Church..........11 C2
Town Hall...................12 C3

SLEEPING
Hotel Calisia..................13 A5
Hotel Europa..................14 B4
Pokoje Gościnne Roma.....15 A2

EATING
Antonio......................16 B3
Baja Mexico..................17 C3
Bar Maleński.................18 C2
Summer Beer Gardens......19 B4

DRINKING
Złoty Róg....................20 B4

ENTERTAINMENT
Centre of Culture & Arts....21 D3

Labels on map: Stawiszyńska, Bernardynka, 3 Maja, To Łódź (113km); Warsaw (256km), WIELKOPOLSKA, Niecała, Grodzka, Plac Jana Pawła II, Zamkowa, Plac Sw Józefa, Kanonicka, Piskorzewska, Garbarska, Złota, Główny Rynek (Main Market Sq), Martańska, Former Jesuit Church, Kolegialna, Łazienna, Sukiennica, Piekarska, Franciscan Church, Browarna, Kazimierzowska, Prosna, Sw Stanisława, City Park (Park Miejski), Chopina, Ciasna, Babina, Paczeyskiego, Targowa, Złota, Kościelna, Narutowicza, Franciszkańska, Wodna, Al Wolności, Kościuszki, Śródmiejska, Al Wolności, Theatre, Wał Staromiejski, Wał Piastowski, Bankowa, Częstochowska, To Gołuchów (17km); Poznań (130km), To Bus & Train Stations (1.5km); Antonin (40km); Wrocław (121km), To PTSM Hostel (700m), Puławskiego, Fabryczna, Górnośląska

Information

Bank Pekao (ul Grodzka 7)
City Jungle (☎ 062 767 6700; Al Wolności 6; per hr 3zł; ☺ 9am-10pm Mon-Sat, 10am-10pm Sun) Internet access.
Millennium Bank (Główny Rynek 3)
Polanglo (☎ 062 502 9898; ul Złota 1) Bookshop.
Post office (ul Zamkowa 18/20)

Tourist office (☎ 062 598 2731; www.kalisz.pl; ul Garbarska 2; ☺ 10am-5pm Mon-Fri, 10am-2pm Sat)

Sights

The Old Town sits in the angle between the Prosna and Bernardynka Rivers, with a dozen small bridges and the **City Park** (Park Miejski) stretching to the southeast.

Start your sightseeing in the low-key but attractive **Main Market Sq**, whose name is unusually rendered in Polish as Główny Rynek, rather than the other way around – the city's founders valued a certain eccentricity in adjective order. Head for the tower of the **Town Hall** (admission 4zł; ☻ 10am-2pm Mon-Fri, 10am-1pm Sat & Sun). There are fine views from the top, and an exhibition relating the history of Kalisz.

For a more in-depth examination of the city's story, the **Regional Museum** (Muzeum Ziemi Kaliskiej; ☎ 062 757 1608; www.muzeum.kalisz.pl; ul Kościuszki 12; adult/concession 4/2zł, free Sun; ☻ 10am-3pm Tue & Thu, noon-5.30pm Wed & Fri, 10.30am-2.30pm Sat & Sun) features archaeological and historical exhibits from Kalisz and surrounding areas. The museum also has an annexe in the Jesuit college, the **Centre of Drawing & Graphic Arts** (Centrum Rysunku i Grafiki; ☎ 062 757 2999; ul Kolegialna 4; adult/concession 4/2zł, free Sun; ☻ 10am-3pm Tue, Thu & Fri, 10am-5.30pm Wed, 10am-2.30pm Sat & Sun). It displays temporary exhibits of drawings and graphic arts, including works by Tadeusz Kulisiewicz (1899–1988), a Kalisz-born artist known mainly for his drawings. Enter from ul Łazienna.

Kalisz also has some fine religious buildings. The oldest, **St Nicholas' Church** (Kościół Św Mikołaja; ul Kanonicka 5), dates from the 13th century and was originally Gothic, but has been modernised several times. The painting of the Descent from the Cross over the high altar is a copy. The original, painted in Rubens' workshop in about 1617 and donated to the church, was burnt or stolen during a mysterious fire in 1973.

The 1607 former **Bernardine Church** (Kościół Pobernardyński; ul Stawiszyńska 2), now owned by the Jesuits, has a spectacular interior. It is unprepossessing from the outside, but its wide nave glows with sumptuous baroque decoration. The altars and the wall paintings on the vault date from around the mid-18th century.

Finally, the **Collegiate Church** (Sanctuary of St Joseph; Plac Jana Pawła II 3) is a typical example of a lavish Catholic church, built in 1353 and rebuilt in the 18th century. It boasts a baroque interior flooded with gilt and glitter and is a popular pilgrimage site thanks to an allegedly miraculous picture of the Holy Family, dating from the 17th century.

Festivals & Events

Kalisz Theatre Meetings (☎ 062 502 3222; www .mojkalisz.pl/kst in Polish) Held at the beginning of May.
International Piano Jazz Festival (☎ 062 765 2500) In late November.

Sleeping

PTSM Hostel (☎ 062 757 2404; ul Handlowa 30; dm 15zł) This youth hostel is halfway between the train station and the Old Town, in a pleasant location near the trees and ponds of Park Przyjaźni. Check in before 9pm.

ourpick Hotel Europa (☎ 062 767 2032; www.hotel -europa.pl; Al Wolności 5; s 155zł, d 135-210zł, tr 230zł, ste 450zł; P ✗ ☒ ☐) If you've schlepped through numerous three-star hotels in a hot Polish summer, you'll weep with joy on encountering this excellent central hotel's deluxe doubles with air-conditioning, kettles and gleaming bathrooms. Go crazy and shell out for the Egyptian-themed suite.

Hotel Calisia (☎ 062 767 9100; www.hotel-calisia.pl; ul Nowy Świat 1-3; s/d/tr/ste 160/220/260/400zł; P ☐) The corridors are boxy and the rooms are a touch faded, but the service is good. Weekend discounts can save you a bit of cash as well.

Pokoje Gościnne Roma (☎ 062 501 7555; ul Chopina 9; s/d/tr 160/220/280zł; P) A nice surprise in a shabbier part of town, this white villa-style accommodation offers just seven spacious rooms with skylights, above the in-house Italian restaurant with a garden courtyard.

Eating & Drinking

As usual, there are plenty of eating options on the Rynek and the streets around it. In summer a gaggle of beer gardens and snack stalls springs up around the top end of Al Wolności, near the Hotel Europa.

Bar Maleńki (☎ 062 501 9303; ul Parczewskiego 2-3; mains 4-12zł; ☻ 8am-6pm Mon-Fri, 9am-3pm Sat) *Maleńki* means tiny, a fitting title for this diminutive cafeteria. If you can find room, it's the best place in town for an ultrabudget meal, from roast chicken to more adventurous choices like beans Breton-style.

Baja Mexico (☎ 062 767 5504; Główny Rynek 3; mains 5-45zł; ☻ noon-9pm Sun-Thu, noon-11pm Fri & Sat) All the well-known Tex-Mex dishes are on offer at this central theme bar, and fajitas and enchiladas do make a change from the usual rounds of cutlets and *pierogi* (dumplings). Enter off ul Piskorzewska.

ourpick Antonio (☎ 062 757 4690; ul Śródmiejska 21; mains 15-59zł; ☻ noon-11pm) If you're not hungry after smelling the garlic aroma drifting up to the street from this cellar restaurant, you may be deceased. The dining area features red-checked tablecloths, candlelight, roses, Renaissance-inspired artwork and quality Italian food.

A good place for a drink is **Złoty Róg** (☎ 062 599 7171; Al Wolności 3; ☽ 11am-11pm Mon-Thu, 11am-midnight Fri & Sat, 1-11pm Sun), right next to the Hotel Europa. Sample one of the four boutique beers brewed out the back, and recuperate from sightseeing within the cool timber interior.

Entertainment

The **Centre of Culture & Arts** (Centrum Kultury i Sztuki; ☎ 062 765 2500; www.ckis.kalisz.pl; ul Łazienna 6) is an active institution hosting a variety of events, which include regular screenings of arthouse movies.

Getting There & Around

The bus and train stations are close to each other, about 2km southwest of the Old Town. To get to the centre, take bus 18 from the station, or bus 2, 4, 11, 12, 18 or 19 from the nearby main road (2.20zł).

BUS

There are 12 buses to Poznań daily (21zł, 2½ hours) via Gołuchów (7zł, 25 minutes), seven to Wrocław (22zł, 2½ hours) via Antonin (11zł, one hour), and one to Toruń (34zł, four hours). The hourly suburban bus 12A to Pleszew Szpital also passes through Gołuchów (4.40zł, 40 minutes); it stops in Kalisz centre on Plac Jana Pawła II.

TRAIN

Trains to Łódź (28zł, 1¾ hours) run about every two hours throughout the day. There are fast trains to Warsaw (42zł, 5¼ hours, three daily), Wrocław (31zł, 2¼ hours, three daily) and Poznań (31zł, 2½ hours, six daily).

GOŁUCHÓW
pop 1200

Is it a castle, a mansion or a palace? Whichever way you slice it, the castle in the small village of Gołuchów (go-*woo*-hoof) is an attractive sight, somewhat resembling the châteaux of France's Loire Valley. A bonus is the expanse of landscaped garden surrounding the building, dotted with museum exhibitions and a mini-herd of bison.

Sights

CASTLE

Gołuchów's castle began life around 1560 as a small fortified mansion with four octagonal towers at the corners, built by the Leszczyński family. Some 50 years later it was enlarged and reshaped into a palatial residence in late-Renaissance style. Abandoned at the end of the 17th century, it gradually fell into ruins until the Działyński family, the owners of Kórnik castle (p386), bought it in 1856. It was completely rebuilt between 1872 and 1885, and it was then that it acquired its French appearance.

The castle's stylistic mutation was essentially the brainchild of Izabela Czartoryska, daughter of Prince Adam Czartoryski and wife of Jan Działyński. She commissioned the French architect Viollet le Duc to reinvent the residence; under his supervision many architectural bits and pieces were brought from abroad, mainly from France and Italy, and incorporated into the building.

Having acquired large numbers of works of art, Izabela crammed them into her new palace, which became one of the largest private museums in Europe. During WWII the Nazis stole the works of art but the building itself survived relatively undamaged. Part of the collection was recovered and is now once more on display in its rightful home.

Inside the building is the **museum** (☎ 062 761 5090; ul Działyńskich 2; adult/concession 8/5.50zł, free Sat; ☽ 10am-4pm Tue-Sun), exhibiting a wealth of furniture, paintings, sculptures, weapons, tapestries, rugs and the like. One of the highlights is a collection of Greek vases from the 5th century BC. You enter the castle through a decorative 17th-century doorway, which leads into a graceful arcaded courtyard; admission is strictly limited, with tours running for a set number of visitors every half-hour.

CASTLE PARK

The vast 160-hectare, English-style **park** (admission free; ☽ 8am-8pm) surrounding the castle was laid out during the last quarter of the 19th century and holds several hundred species of trees and shrubs. Its oldest part is the 350m-long lime-tree alley, planted in 1856.

To the south of the castle is the **Museum of Forestry** (Muzeum Leśnictwa; ☎ 062 761 5046; ul Działyńskich 2; adult/concession 5/3zł; ☽ 10am-3pm Tue-Fri, 10am-4pm Sat & Sun), housed in a former distillery, which was considerably extended in 1874 and adapted as a residence. It contains displays on the history of Polish forestry and the timber industry, along with a collection of contemporary art on the subject.

East of the castle, the museum's **annexe** (adult/concession 6/3zł; ☽ 10am-4pm Tue-Fri, 10am-

4.30pm Sat & Sun) displays ecological exhibits in an old coach house. The collection includes a number of curious *księgi drzewne* (wooden books), boxes shaped like books, which were used to collect seeds and other plant matter.

Another outpost, in the far north of the park, is the **Museum of Forest Techniques** (Muzeum Techniki Leśnej; ☎ 062 761 5046), 750m beyond the castle. It contains tools and machinery used in forestry, but at the time of research was closed, pending an update of the collection.

Seven bison live relatively freely in a large, fenced-off **bison enclosure** (☼ 7am-sunset), west of the park, 500m beyond the forestry techniques museum (follow the Żubry signs).

Sleeping & Eating

Dom Pracy Twórczej (☎ 062 761 5044; ul Borowskiego 2; r 100zł; **P**) If you're taken enough with the estate to want to stay over, this place offers comfortable rooms in a historic building inside the park, just a short amble from the castle beyond the Museum of Forestry's annexe. Its restaurant (mains 9zł to 15zł) does a good line in Polish specialities.

Getting There & Away

Suburban bus 12A goes roughly hourly to/ from Kalisz (4.40zł, 40 minutes). Get off at the bus stand next to the cemetery, cross the main road, and walk around the church to find the park entrance. About 12 PKS buses run to Poznań daily (15zł, 2¼ hours).

ANTONIN

pop 500

Before WWII, Antonin was the summer residence of the Radziwiłł family, one of the richest and most famous aristocratic clans in Poland. Today it's a small lakeside resort, popular with wedding photographers and a pleasant place for a quick stopover or a slightly longer break.

Sights & Activities

Prince Antoni Radziwiłł gave his name to Antonin, having put it on the map by building his **Hunting Palace** (Pałac Myśliwski; ☎ 062 734 8300; admission free; ☼ 8am-10pm) here from 1822 to 1824. This handsome wooden structure is still the town's showpiece; it was designed by Karl Friedrich Schinkel, one of the outstanding German architects of the period, who was also responsible for numerous monumental buildings in Berlin and Prussia.

The palace has an unusual structure. The main part is a large, octagonal, three-storey hall, called the Chimney Room, with a column in the middle supporting the roof and also functioning as a chimney for the central fireplace. There are four side wings, originally designed as living rooms for the owner and his guests. One such guest, Frédéric Chopin, stayed here a couple of times, performing concerts and composing.

The Centre of Culture & Arts (p399) in Kalisz now runs the palace as a hotel, and there is also a small museum and 'creative work centre' that is available for casual visitors. Regular piano recitals are held here, with special buses laid on from Ostrów Wielkopolski and Kalisz.

The palace is surrounded by a 46-hectare **nature reserve**, which offers some pleasant walks of up to 25km. You can also go **fishing** or **boating**, or take up any number of activities on the lake, which borders the main road.

Festivals & Events

The **Chopin Festival** (☎ 062 765 2500) is a prestigious four-day festival held at the Hunting Palace; in September.

Sleeping & Eating

Lido (☎ 062 734 8191; ul Wrocławska 6; camp sites per person 10zł; cabins 55-90zł; s/d 100/120zł; **P**) If you can't stretch to the palace (or are beaten to it by a bride), the Lido has decent motel rooms and a range of camping, cabin and leisure facilities, all on the lakeside next door to the palace.

Hunting Palace (Pałac Myśliwski; ☎ 062 734 8300; s 140zł, d 180-260zł; **P**) How could you stay anywhere else? This is the most romantic option for miles, even if you're just grabbing a bite in its stylish restaurant in the Chimney Room. Advance booking is recommended; it's invariably swamped with wedding parties on Saturday in summer.

Getting There & Away

The train station is about 1km from the palace, beyond the lake. Three trains run to Poznań daily (18.50zł, 2¾ hours). There are no direct trains to Kalisz – change in Ostrów Wielkopolski.

There are seven daily buses to Wrocław (15zł, two hours), and seven to Kalisz (11zł, one hour). About 10 buses go to Ostrów Wielkopolski (5zł, 30 minutes), from where suburban buses run regularly to Kalisz.

LICHEŃ
pop 1500

Licheń (*lee*-hen) is reputedly Poland's second most visited pilgrimage site after Częstochowa. The pilgrims' destination, a sizable **ecclesiastical complex**, occupies the village's centre and includes three churches, a fairy-tale stone fortress (Golgotha) depicting the Way of the Cross in model tableaux, chapels, grottoes and statues scattered all over the grounds, and more images of the Virgin Mary than you can swing a censer at. About 1.5 million pilgrims pass through here annually, coming to pay tribute to a reputedly miraculous icon of Mary in the main church. (It's tucked away in the high altar if you're interested – follow the queue of people shuffling on all fours.)

The most recent church is the one that instantly grabs your attention. Built to celebrate two millennia of Christianity, the gigantic **Church of Our Lady of Licheń** (Bazylika Matki Bożej Licheńskiej) was begun in 1994, and the monumental building was officially consecrated in 2004.

The resulting building is Poland's largest place of worship, and the golden dome can be spotted from miles away in the flat countryside. The interior is resplendent with gilded ornamentation, chandeliers, paintings, two massive triptychs and no fewer than 50 confessionals.

Beneath the main hall is an underground level containing the round **Golden Chapel**, which is a good-sized church in itself. Completed in 1996, it's crammed full with crystal chandeliers and golden stucco. The floor is of marble, imported from all over the world, forming a multicoloured design. The side rooms down on this level are used for exhibitions on various pious themes.

Give yourself at least half a day for a visit here. There's a lot to see in the basilica and the gardens, and the never-ending influx of pilgrims really adds to the atmosphere. Local guidebooks (some in English) are sold at various locations and have full details of the diverse attractions.

Sleeping

Dom Pielgrzyma Betania (☎ 063 270 8162; www .lichen.pl; ul Klasztorna 4; dm 10-32zł, d 64zł, tr 45-75zł, q 60-100zł) This budget accommodation operated by the church is a cheap and flexible option; its chambers can operate as dorms or private rooms.

Dom Pielgrzyma Arka (☎ 063 270 8162; www.lichen .pl; ul Klasztorna 4; s/d/tr/q 70/130/100/100zł) The main lodging facility is also within the sanctuary. Simple, immaculate rooms for one to 10 people are available to pilgrims and anyone else wanting to sleep over. The complex also has its own chapel, café and restaurant.

Getting There & Away

To get to Licheń you'll need to go via Konin, a fair-sized town, 13km to the southwest, which sits on the busy Poznań–Warsaw rail line. There are hourly buses between Konin and Licheń (6zł, 30 minutes).

WIELKOPOLSKA

Pomerania

The diverse region of Pomerania (Pomorze) could be summarised by the three Bs – beaches, beer gardens and bricks. Although Poland isn't often regarded as a beach destination by outsiders, for the Poles this area is prime summer-holiday territory. The shores of the Baltic Sea are blessed with fine white sand, and during the warmer months you'll find its numerous seaside towns heavily populated by Polish and German visitors enjoying the sunshine on the sands, or seated in the beer gardens that materialise the moment the weather heats up.

The German connection isn't just recreational – Pomerania has switched hands between Germanic and Polish rulers many times over the centuries. The region's character is also tinged with influences from Swedes, Danes and other past invaders; and its magnificently eventful history is symbolised by the stunning historic city of Gdańsk.

This is where the bricks come in – the red bricks that comprise central Pomerania's wealth of Gothic architecture, an enduring legacy of its medieval conquerors. Castles, churches and ancient granaries loom large amid the region's well-worn towns and cities, lending it a distinctive visual identity. Every name on the map has its own architectural keepsake, and its areas of natural beauty provide even more reasons to visit.

With its unique mix of sea, sand and unforgettable historic sights, Pomerania is both very Polish and possessed of a character all its own. From its bustling major cities to its beachside villages and attractive inland towns, the region is a fascinating destination.

HIGHLIGHTS

- Strolling past the breathtaking historic buildings lining Długi Targ in **Gdańsk** (opposite)

- Chilling out at a cool bar or café in sensational **Sopot** (p425)

- Following the astronomical footprints of Copernicus in **Frombork** (p453)

- Visiting the Teutonic past at **Malbork's castle** (p448)

- Munching gingerbread among the Gothic architecture of **Toruń** (p436)

- Having a dip in the Baltic (or a spa treatment) at **Kołobrzeg** (p462)

- Tramping up the shifting dunes of **Słowiński National Park** (p457)

- Absorbing the charms of **Chełmno's walled town** (p445)

- Taking a day trip on a ferry from **Elbląg** (p451)

- Going to **Hel** (p433) and back to meet a rare seal

- POPULATION: 6.5 MILLION
- AREA: 59,000 SQ KM

POMERANIA

Getting There & Away

Gdańsk is the principal transport hub for the region, with its own international airport and connections to other Polish and European cities by road, rail, bus and boat. In the west, Szczecin offers easy access to Germany and western Poland.

GDAŃSK

pop 458,000

There's a special atmosphere about Gdańsk, a unique look and feel that's very different from that of other Polish cities. It could be something to do with its historic role as a port city, visited by and fought over by people from diverse nations. It's definitely connected to its distinctive architecture, which is strongly influenced by its historic maritime connections. And the knowledge that its stunning centre was rebuilt from rubble after the devastation of WWII is breathtaking and inspiring.

Whatever the source of its appeal, visitors are always delighted by the grand, elegant buildings of the Main Town district, and charmed by its decorative narrow side streets with their cafés and amber shops. Popular maritime pleasures include cruising downriver on a pleasure boat, or sipping a beverage at a dockside beer garden while admiring the mix of medieval and Renaissance rooftops on the skyline.

Though it's an old city with a tumultuous past, and the historic scars to prove it, 21st-century Gdańsk is a vibrant destination packed with diverse sights and entertainment options, and also makes a great base for journeys into the surrounding countryside.

HISTORY

Describing Gdańsk's past as 'eventful' would be a major understatement. The official history of the much fought-over city is counted from the year 997, when the Bohemian Bishop Adalbert arrived here from Gniezno and baptised the inhabitants. The settlement developed as a port over the following centuries, expanding northwards into what is today the Old Town. The German community then arrived from Lübeck in the early 13th century, the first in a succession of migrants, who crafted the town's cosmopolitan character.

In 1308 the Teutonic order (see boxed text, p451) seized Gdańsk and quickly turned it into a major trade centre, joining the Hanseatic League (see boxed text, p413) in 1361. In 1454 the locals decided on a spot of regime change, razing the Teutonic Knights' castle, and pledging allegiance to the Polish monarch instead.

From here, the only way was up: by the mid-16th century, the successful trading city of 40,000 was Poland's largest city, and the most important trading centre in Central Europe. Legions of international traders joined the local German–Polish population, adding their own cultural influences to the city's unique blend.

Gdańsk was one of the very few Polish cities to withstand the Swedish Deluge of the 1650s, but the devastation of the surrounding area weakened its position, and in 1793 Prussia annexed the shrinking city. Just 14 years later, however, the Prussians were ousted by the Napoleonic army and its Polish allies.

It turned out to be a brief interlude – in 1815 the Congress of Vienna gave Gdańsk back to Prussia, which became part of Germany later in the century. In the years that followed, the Polish minority was systematically Germanised, the city's defences were reinforced and there was gradual but steady economic and industrial growth.

After Germany's defeat in WWI, the Treaty of Versailles granted the newly reformed Polish nation the so-called Polish Corridor, a strip of land stretching from Toruń to Gdańsk, providing the country with an outlet to the sea. Gdańsk itself was excluded and designated the Free City of Danzig, under the protection of the League of Nations. With the city having a German majority, however, the Polish population never had much political influence, and once Hitler came to power it was effectively a German port.

WWII started in Gdańsk when the German battleship *Schleswig-Holstein* fired the first shots on the Polish military post in Westerplatte. During the occupation of the city, the Nazis continued to use the local shipyards for building warships, with Poles as forced labour. The Russians arrived in March 1945; during the fierce battle the city centre virtually ceased to exist. The German residents fled, or died in the conflict. Their

POMERANIA

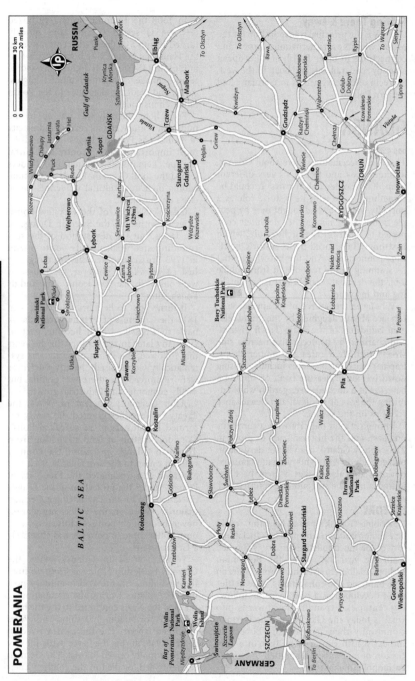

place was taken by Polish newcomers, mainly from the territories lost to the Soviet Union in the east.

The complex reconstruction of the Main Town took over 20 years from 1949, though work on some interiors continued well into the 1990s. Nowhere else in Europe was such a large area of an historic city reconstructed from the ground up.

In December 1970 a huge strike broke in the shipyard and was 'pacified' by authorities as soon as the workers left the gates, leaving 44 dead. This was the second important challenge to the communist regime after that in Poznań in 1956 (see boxed text, p379). Gdańsk came to the fore again in 1980, when another popular protest paralysed the shipyard. This time it culminated in negotiations with the government and the foundation of Solidarity. Lech Wałęsa, the electrician who led the strike and subsequent talks, later became the first freely elected president in postwar Poland.

In the postcommunist era, Gdańsk has consolidated its role as the leading administrative and industrial city in Pomerania, with some diversification into high-tech products and processes; and tourism has increased enormously. In 1997 the city hosted a range of cultural events and architectural projects commemorating its millennium – a worthy celebration of a great historical survivor.

ORIENTATION

Most visitors arrive at Gdańsk Główny train station, on the edge of the Old Town and just a 10-minute walk to the heart of the historic quarter. If you come by bus, you arrive just behind the train station. City buses and trams also operate on the outskirts of the centre, but don't go through it.

The city centre consists of three historic districts: the Main Town in the centre, the Old Town to the north, and the Old Suburb to the south. To the east of the Main Town, beyond the Motława River, are two island components of the historic city: Spichlerze Island, once crammed with over 300 granaries; and Ołowianka Island, connected to the Main Town by a daytime ferry. Beyond Spichlerze Island is the Lower Town district.

A string of suburbs runs north up the coast, linking Gdańsk with Sopot and Gdynia. The efficient SKM commuter train means it's easy to negotiate your way up and down the Tri-City.

Maps

Free maps of central Gdańsk can be obtained from the tourist offices and certain travel agencies. These usually include some detail on Sopot and Gdynia. For full-size commercial maps covering the whole Tri-City, go to the tourist offices or any of the bookshops in town; the Demart map of Gdańsk, Gdynia and Sopot is particularly useful as it contains clear details of city tram and bus routes, including stops.

INFORMATION
Bookshops
Book Crossing Point (Map p408; ul Garncarska 30; ☼ 11am-8pm) Inside the doorway of the Lokomotywa

café, these shelves contain secondhand books that are available free of charge as long as you swap them with your own pre-read gems.

EMPiK Megastore (Map p408; ☎ 058 301 7244; ul Podwale Grodzkie 8; ☯ 9am-9pm Mon-Sat, 11am-8pm Sun)

English Unlimited (Map p408; ☎ 058 301 3373; ul Podmłyńska 10)

Księgarnia Muza (Map p408; ☎ 058 690 8002; ul Rajska 10) Inside the Madison Centre; stocks good range of maps.

Discount Cards

Pomeranian Tourist Card (Pomorska Karta Turystyczna; www.przystanekpomorza.pl) Discounts to attractions across the region; valid for 14 days (14zł).

Tri-City Tourist Card (Karta Turystyczna Trójmiasta; www.przystanekpomorze.pl) Discounts of 5% to 50% on sights, restaurants and boat trips; valid for three days (8zł).

Internet Access

Flisak (Map p408; ☎ 058 301 8562; ul Chlebnicka 9/10; per hr 4zł) In a downstairs pub-restaurant.

Jazz'n'Java (Map p408; ☎ 058 305 3616; ul Tkacka 17/18; per hr 5zł; ☯ 10am-10pm)

Kawiarnia Internetowa (Map p408; ☎ 058 320 9230; Cinema City, ul Karmelicka 1; per hr 5zł; ☯ 9am-1am Mon-Sat, 9.30am-1am Sun) Free coffee over 30 minutes' access.

PTTK Tourist Office (Map p408; ☎ 058 301 9151; ul Długa 45; per hr 6.50zł; ☯ 9am-6pm Mon-Fri, 10am-6pm Sat & Sun May-Sep, 9am-5pm Mon-Fri Oct-Apr)

Internet Resources

http://guide.trojmiasto.pl Detailed Tri-City tourist guide.

www.gdansk.pl Excellent city information site.

www.gdansk-life.com News, accommodation and events.

www.inyourpocket.com/city/gdansk.html Opinionated reviews of bars, restaurants and accommodation.

www.virtualtourist.com Gdańsk section contains a range of tips and comments posted by travellers.

Medical Services

Provincial Hospital (Map p407; ☎ 058 302 3031; ul Nowe Ogrody 1/6)

Swissmed (☎ 058 524 1584; www.swissmed.pl) clinic (Map p407; ul Skłodowskiej-Curie 5); hospital (Map p407; ul Wileńska 44) Private medical care.

Money

Bank Millennium Eastern Main Town (Map p408; Długi Targ 17/18); Western Main Town (Map p408; ul Wały Jagiellońskie 14/16)

Bank Pekao (Map p408; ul Garncarska 23)

PBK Bank (Map p408; ul Ogarna 116)

Post

Post office (Map p408; ul Długa 23/28)

Tourist Information

City tourist office (Map p408; Gdańska Organizacja Turystyczna, ☎ 058 301 4355; www.got.gdansk.pl; ul Heweliusza 27; ☯ 8am-4pm Mon-Fri)

PTTK Tourist Office (Map p408; ☎ 058 301 9151; www.pttk-gdansk.pl; ul Długa 45; ☯ 9am-7pm Jul-Aug, 9am-6pm Mon-Fri, 9am-2pm Sat & Sun May-Jun & Sep, 9am-5pm Mon-Fri Oct-Apr)

Tourist information booths Train station (Map p408; ☎ 058 301 9151; ul Podwale Grodzkie; ☯ 8am-6pm Mon-Fri, 9am-5pm Sat & Sun Jul-Aug, 9am-5pm Mon-Fri Sep-Jun); Old Town (Map p408; ☎ 058 320 8512; ul Targ Rybny 6a; ☯ 10am-6pm Jul-Sep, 8am-4pm May-Jun); Oliwa (Map p407; ☎ 058 301 4818; ul Cysterów 5; ☯ 10am-6pm Jul-Sep); Airport (Map p407; ☎ 058 348 1368; ul Słowackiego 200; ☯ 8am-6pm Jun-Aug, 9am-5pm Sep-May)

Travel Agencies

Almatur (Map p408; ☎ 058 301 2931; Długi Targ 11)

Lauer (Map p408; www.lauer.com.pl; ☎ 058 305 8986; ul Piwna 22/23) Organises trips over the border to Kaliningrad in Russia.

Orbis Travel (www.orbistravel-gda.com.pl) Old Town (Map p408; ☎ 058 301 2132; Hotel Mercure Hevelius, ul Heweliusza 22); Main Town (Map p408; ☎ 058 301 4425; ul Podwale Staromiejskie 96/97)

PTTK (Map p408; ☎ 058 301 6096; www.pttk-gdansk.pl; ul Długa 45) Above the tourist office; arranges foreign-language tours and other excursions.

DANGERS & ANNOYANCES

In general Gdańsk is perfectly safe, though pickpocketing can be a problem at busy times. Believe it or not, shady money-changers still hang around Długi Targ, Długie Pobrzeże and the train station offering foreigners marginally attractive rates; the mark-up's not that impressive, and it's not worth the chance of being ripped off. During the peak tourist season there's a noticeable police presence around the Main Town, which will either reassure or unsettle you, depending on your attitude to the sight of uniformed officers.

SIGHTS
Main Town

Gdańsk's jewel in the crown is its Main Town (Główne Miasto; Map p408), which looks much as it did some 300 to 400 years ago, during the height of its prosperity. As the largest of the city's historic quarters, and the richest architecturally, it was the most carefully restored after WWII. Prussian additions

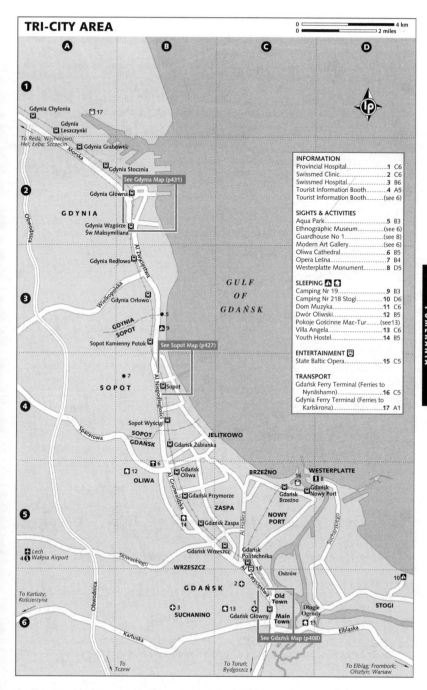

TRI-CITY AREA

0 — 4 km
0 — 2 miles

GDYNIA

Gdynia Chylonia
Gdynia Leszczynki
To Reda; Wejherowo; Hel; Łeba; Szczecin
Gdynia Grabówek
Gdynia Stocznia
See Gdynia Map (p431)
Gdynia Główna
Gdynia Wzgórze Św Maksymiliana
Gdynia Redłowo
Gdynia Orłowo
GDYNIA SOPOT
Sopot Kamienny Potok
See Sopot Map (p427)

GULF OF GDAŃSK

SOPOT
Sopot Wyścigi
SOPOT GDAŃSK
JELITKOWO
Gdańsk Żabianka
Gdańsk Oliwa
OLIWA
Gdańsk Przymorze
BRZEŹNO
WESTERPLATTE
Gdańsk Brzeźno
Gdańsk Nowy Port
ZASPA
Gdańsk Zaspa
NOWY PORT
Gdańsk Wrzeszcz
Gdańsk Politechnika
WRZESZCZ
Ostrów
Lech
Wałęsa Airport
To Kartuzy; Kościerzyna
GDAŃSK
SUCHANINO
Gdańsk Główny
Old Town
Main Town
Długie Ogrody
STOGI
Elbląska
See Gdańsk Map (p408)
To Tczew
To Toruń; Bydgoszcz
To Elbląg; Frombork; Olsztyn; Warsaw

INFORMATION
Provincial Hospital...........................1 C6
Swissmed Clinic................................2 C6
Swissmed Hospital..........................3 B6
Tourist Information Booth................4 A5
Tourist Information Booth............(see 6)

SIGHTS & ACTIVITIES
Aqua Park..5 B3
Ethnographic Museum..................(see 6)
Guardhouse No 1..........................(see 8)
Modern Art Gallery......................(see 6)
Oliwa Cathedral.............................6 B5
Opera Leśna....................................7 B4
Westerplatte Monument................8 D5

SLEEPING
Camping Nr 19................................9 B3
Camping Nr 218 Stogi....................10 D6
Dom Muzyka..................................11 C6
Dwór Oliwski.................................12 B5
Pokoje Gościnne Mac-Tur...........(see13)
Villa Angela..................................13 C6
Youth Hostel.................................14 B5

ENTERTAINMENT
State Baltic Opera........................15 C5

TRANSPORT
Gdańsk Ferry Terminal (Ferries to Nynäshamn)..................................16 C5
Gdynia Ferry Terminal (Ferries to Karlskrona)...................................17 A1

POMERANIA

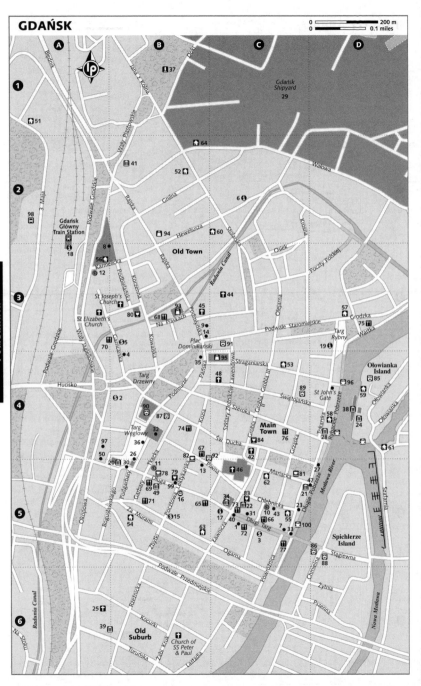

GDAŃSK

POMERANIA

POMERANIA

from the Partition period were airbrushed out of this remarkably impressive recreation, so the result is a snapshot of Gdańsk up to the end of the 18th century.

The town was originally laid out in the mid-14th century along a central axis consisting of ul Długa (Long St) and Długi Targ (Long Market). The latter was designed for trading, which would have taken place in the Rynek (Main Market Sq). This axis is also known as the Royal Way.

ROYAL WAY

Unrelated to the 'royal we' or even the royal wave, the Royal Way was the thoroughfare along which the Polish kings traditionally paraded during their periodic visits. Of the three Royal Ways in Poland (Warsaw, Kraków and Gdańsk), the Gdańsk one is the shortest – only

500m long – but it's architecturally perhaps the most refined.

The traditional entry point for kings was the **Upland Gate** (Brama Wyżynna; Map p408), at the western end of Royal Way. The gate was built in 1574 as part of the city's new fortifications, which were constructed outside the medieval walls to strengthen the system. The authorities weren't happy with the original structure, so in 1586 they commissioned a Flemish artist, Willem van den Block, to embellish it. It was covered with sandstone slabs and ornamented with three coats of arms: Prussia (with unicorns), Poland (with angels) and Gdańsk (with lions). Gdańsk's shield, invariably featuring heraldic lions, is on countless public buildings throughout the city.

Just behind the Upland Gate is a large 15th-century construction known as the **Foregate**

(Przedbramie; Map p408). It consists of the **Torture House** (Katownia) to the west and a high **Prison Tower** (Wieża Więzienna) to the east, linked to one another by two walls.

When the Upland Gate was built, the Foregate lost its defensive function and was turned into a jail. The Torture House then had an extra storey added as a court room and was topped with decorative Renaissance parapets. A gallows was built on the square to the north, where public executions of condemned foreigners were held (locals had the 'privilege' of being hanged on Długi Targ). The Foregate was used as a jail till the mid-19th century. It was damaged during WWII and the restoration that began in 1951 is still ongoing. Nowadays it's the home of the **Amber Museum** (Muzeum Bursztynu; Map p408; ☎ 058 767 9128; adult/concession 10/5zł, free Tue; ◷ 10am-3pm Tue, 11am-4pm Wed-Sun), wherein you can marvel at the history of Baltic gold (see boxed text, p423).

Further to the east is the **Golden Gate** (Złota Brama; Map p408). Designed by Abraham van den Block, son of the decorator of the Upland Gate, and built in 1612, it's a sort of triumphal arch ornamented with a double-storey colonnade and topped with eight allegorical statues. The four figures on the side of the Prison Tower represent Peace, Liberty, Wealth and Fame, for which Gdańsk was always struggling to achieve against foreign powers (sometimes including the Polish kings). The sculptures on the opposite side symbolise the burghers' virtues: Wisdom, Piety, Justice and Concord. Today's figures are postwar copies of the 1648 originals.

Adjoining the gate to the north is the **Court of the Fraternity of St George** (Dwór Bractwa Św Jerzego; Map p408), a good example of late-Gothic secular architecture, dating from the 1490s. The roof is topped with a 16th-century octagonal tower, with St George and the Dragon on the spire (the 1556 original is in Gdańsk's National Museum).

Once you pass the Golden Gate, you are on the gently curving **ul Długa**, one of the loveliest streets in Poland, which, despite its name, is only 300m long. In 1945 it was just a heap of smoking rubble. Stop at the **Uphagens' House** (Dom Uphagena; Map p408; ☎ 058 301 2371; ul Długa 12; adult/concession 8/4zł, free Tue; ◷ 10am-3pm Tue, 10am-4pm Wed-Sat, 11am-4pm Sun) to see the restored historic interior, a collection of sumptuously decorated rooms with period furniture from the 18th century. As you pass beyond the kitchen, take a minute to browse the family tree and history of the Uphagen family, outlined in English.

TOWN HALL

As you reach the eastern end of ul Długa, look up to the pinnacle of the **town hall** (Map p408). This tall slim tower, the highest in Gdańsk (81.5m), has a life-sized gilded figure of King Zygmunt II August on top – a reward for his generosity in granting privileges to the city.

The town hall has both Gothic and Renaissance elements. The first building was reputedly put up in the 1330s, but it grew and changed until the end of the 16th century. In 1945 it was almost completely burnt out and the authorities were on the point of demolishing the ruin, which was eventually saved thanks to local protests.

After serving as a municipal seat for over half a millennium, it today houses the **Historical Museum of Gdańsk** (Muzeum Historii Miasta Gdańska; Map p408; ☎ 058 301 4871; ul Długa 47; adult/concession 8/4zł, free Tue; ◷ 10am-3pm Tue, 10am-4pm Wed-Sat, 11am-4pm Sun). Enter the building by twin flights of balustraded stairs and go through an ornate Baroque doorway (1766), which is topped by the city's coat of arms guarded by two lions that, unusually, are both looking toward the Golden Gate, supposedly awaiting the arrival of the king. The doorway was the final addition to the external decoration of the building.

Inside are several rooms decked out in period decoration, either original or re-created from old drawings, engravings and photographs. The showpiece is the **Red Room** (Sala Czerwona), done up in Dutch mannerist style from the end of the 16th century, which was once the setting for the town council's debates. There's a large, richly carved fireplace (1593) and a marvellous portal (1596), but your eyes will immediately be attracted to the ornamented ceiling – 25 paintings dominated by the oval centrepiece entitled *The Glorification of the Unity of Gdańsk with Poland*. The painter, Isaac van den Block, yet another member of the Flemish family of artists, incorporated various themes in the painting, from everyday scenes to the panorama of Gdańsk on the top of the triumphal arch. All the room's decoration is authentic; it was dismantled in 1942 and hidden outside Gdańsk.

POMERANIA

The 2nd floor houses exhibitions related to Gdańsk's history, including photos of the destruction of 1945. From here you can enter the **tower** (admission 4zł; ☉ 10am-4pm Wed-Sat, 11am-4pm Sun) for great views across the city.

DŁUGI TARG

Packed with buskers, street stalls and restaurants, Długi Targ (Long Market) was once the main city market and is now the major focus for visitors.

According to legend, the **Neptune Fountain** (Fontana Neptuna; Map p408), next to the town hall, once gushed forth with the trademark Gdańsk liqueur, Goldwasser. As the story goes, it spurted out of the trident one merry night and Neptune found himself endangered by crowds of drunken locals. Perhaps that's why, in 1634, the fountain was fenced off with a wrought-iron barrier. The bronze statue itself was the work of another Flemish artist, Peter Husen; it was made between 1606 and 1613 and is the oldest secular monument in Poland. A menagerie of stone sea creatures was added in the 1750s during the restoration of the fountain.

The nearby 1618 **Golden House** (Złota Kamienica; Map p408), designed by Johan Voigt, has the richest façade in the city. In the friezes between storeys are 12 elaborately carved scenes interspersed with busts of famous historical figures, including two Polish kings. The four statues waving to you from the balustrade at the top are Cleopatra, Oedipus, Achilles and Antigone.

The Long Market is flanked from the east by the **Green Gate** (Zielona Brama; Map p408), marking the end of the Royal Way. It was built in the 1560s on the site of a medieval defensive gate and was supposed to be the residence of the kings. But they never stayed in what turned out to be a cold and uncomfortable lodge; they preferred the houses nearby, particularly those opposite the Artus Court.

ARTUS COURT

Not many houses have a brand of vodka named after them, but the **Artus Court** (Dwór Artusa; Map p408; ☎ 058 346 3358; Długi Targ 43/44; adult/concession 8/4zł, free Tue; ☉ 10am-3pm Tue, 10am-4pm Wed-Sat, 11am-4pm Sun) behind the Neptune fountain is perhaps the single best-known house in Gdańsk. The court has been an essential stop for passing luminaries ever since its earliest days, and a photo display in the entrance shows an enviable selection of famous visitors, from King Henry IV of England to a host of contemporary presidents.

Built at the end of the 15th century, the court was given its monumental façade by Abraham van den Block in the 1610s. Inside there's a huge hall, topped by a Gothic vault supported on four slim granite columns, decorated with hunting murals and dominated by a vast painting depicting the Battle of Grunwald. There are also large models of masted sailing ships suspended from its ceiling! Wealthy local merchants used the building as a communal guildhall, holding meetings, banquets and general revelries in the lavishly decorated interior.

Like most of the centre, the court was comprehensively destroyed in WWII, but has been painstakingly restored from old photographs and historical records, recapturing at least a glimpse of its remarkable past. The hall is still the undisputed centrepiece, but the adjoining chambers hold historical artefacts and some exquisite pieces of classic Danzig furniture in the dark-wood style synonymous with the city's golden age.

The plainly renovated upper floors hold a selection of historical exhibits, including a photographic 'simulacrum' of how the great hall would have looked at its peak – even in two dimensions it's a breathtaking space, filled from top to bottom with paintings, models and stuffed animals.

One unique feature of the interior is its giant Renaissance **tiled stove**, standing in the corner of the hall and almost touching the ceiling. It's reputedly the highest tiled stove in Europe. Looking like a five-tier tower, 10.65m high, the stove is also lavishly ornamented, with a wealth of decoration portraying, among other things, rulers, allegorical figures and coats of arms. Built in 1546 by George Stelzener, the stove survived virtually unchanged until 1943, when local conservators dismantled the upper part and hid it outside the city. The fragments were collected after the war, and after a long and complex restoration, the stove was eventually put together and revealed to the public in 1995. It contains 520 tiles, 437 of which are original.

WATERFRONT

Beyond the Green Gate is the Motława River. There once was a busy quay along here, crowded with hundreds of sailing ships

POMERANIA

loading and unloading their cargo, which was stored either in the cellars of the burghers' houses in town or in the granaries on the other side of the river, on Spichlerze Island. Today it's a popular tourist promenade lined with cafés, art galleries and souvenir shops.

In medieval times, the parallel east–west streets of the Main Town all had defensive gates at their riverfront ends. Some of them still exist, though most were altered in later periods. Walking north along Długie Pobrzeże (literally, Long Waterfront), you first get to the **Bread Gate** (Brama Chlebnicka; Map p408), at the end of ul Chlebnicka. It was built around 1450, still under the Teutonic order, as shown by the original city coat of arms consisting of two crosses. The crown was added by King Kazimierz Jagiellończyk in 1457, when Gdańsk was incorporated into the kingdom.

Enter the gate and walk a few steps to see the palatial **House Under the Angels** (Dom Pod Aniołami; Map p408), which is also known as the English House (Dom Angielski) after the nationality of the merchants who owned it in the 17th century. At that time it was the largest burgher's house in Gdańsk. Today it's a student dorm, which says a lot about changing standards!

At No 14 stands the late-Gothic **Schlieff House** (Map p408) of 1520. It's a replica built after the emperor of Prussia, Friedrich Wilhelm III, fell in love with its predecessor in the 1820s and had it taken apart brick by brick and rebuilt in Brandenburg. The original is in Potsdam, near Berlin.

The tiny ul Grząska will take you to **ul Mariacka**, the most atmospheric of all the streets in Gdańsk and unique in Poland. It was reconstructed after the war, almost from the ground up, with the utmost piety on the basis of old documents and illustrations, and every detail found in the rubble was incorporated. It looks amazingly authentic. It's the only street with a complete row of terraces, which gives it enormous charm, and is a trendy place lined with shops selling amber jewellery. You'll also find some of the best stalls here during the Dominican Fair (p418).

The street ends at **St Mary's Gate** (Brama Mariacka; Map p408), similar to the Bread Gate but constructed later, as you'll see from its coats of arms. Next to it is the fair-sized Renaissance **House of the Naturalists' Society** (Dom Towarzystwa Przyrodniczego; Map p408), which houses the **Archaeological Museum**

(Muzeum Archeologiczne; Map p408; ☎ 058 301 5031; ul Mariacka 25/26; adult/concession 5/4zł, free Sat; ☯ 9am-5pm Jul-Aug, 9am-4pm Tue, Thu & Fri, 10am-5pm Wed, 10am-4pm Sat & Sun Sep-Jun). The extensive collection stresses the Polish cultural and ethnic roots of the region; if you haven't had your fill of views elsewhere, you can also go to the top of the building's **tower** (admission 2zł; ☯ 8am-4pm Mon, 10am-5pm Tue-Sun).

GDAŃSK CRANE & CENTRAL MARITIME MUSEUM

Back on the waterfront, just beyond the modest **Gate of the Holy Spirit** (Brama Św Ducha; Map p408), is the conspicuous and world-renowned **Gdańsk Crane** (Żuraw Gdański; Map p408; ☎ 058 301 5311; ul Szeroka 67/68; adult/concession 6/4zł; ☯ 10am-6pm Mon-Fri, 10.30am-6.30pm Sat & Sun Jul-Aug, 10am-4pm Tue-Fri, 10.30am-4.30pm Sat & Sun Sep-Jun). Built in the mid-15th century as the biggest double-towered gate on the waterfront, it also served to move heavy cargoes directly onto or off the vessels. For this purpose two large wheels – 5m in diameter – were installed as a hoist with a rope wound around the axle; it was put in motion by people 'walking' along the inner circumference of the wheels as a treadmill. It could hoist loads of up to 2000kg, making it the biggest crane in medieval Europe. At the beginning of the 17th century another set of wheels was added higher up, for installing masts.

The crane suffered considerable damage in 1945 but was carefully rebuilt; it's the only fully restored relic of its kind in the world, and is administered by the Central Maritime Museum. The interior has exhibits relating to the history of shipping, plus a collection of shells, corals and other marine life, and there's English commentary available via laminated sheets. You can also climb up into the section overlooking the water and have a closer look at the hoisting gear.

Next door to the crane, the main annexe of the **Central Maritime Museum** (Centralne Muzeum Morskie; Map p408; ☎ 058 320 3358; www.cmm .pl; ul Szeroka 67/68; adult/concession 6/4zł; ☯ 10am-6pm Jul-Aug, 10am-4pm Tue-Sun Sep-Jun) is a featureless modern building displaying traditional rowing and sailing boats from various countries: there's a Venetian gondola as a centrepiece in the foyer. English captioning is at its most minimal here.

The museum continues in three reconstructed **granaries** (Map p408; ☎ 058 301 8611; ul

IN A LEAGUE OF ITS OWN

It wasn't easy being a merchant in the Middle Ages, without the benefit of chambers of commerce or Rotary Clubs, and very little respect from the ruling classes. Travelling salesmen were seen as easy pickings by local lords, paying heavy tolls as they moved from province to province in Central Europe. Taking to the sea wasn't much better, as merchants' slow-moving boats were subject to attack by pirates.

The answer to their problems was to band together in the Hanseatic League, a group of trading ports that formed in the late 13th century and wielded unprecedented economic power. The Hansa (from a German word for 'association') was centred on Germany, making good use of its central location, with members also scattered throughout Scandinavia, across the Baltic to Russia, and west to the Netherlands. The League also had trading posts in cities like London and Venice. As a result, it could trade wax from Russia with items from English or Dutch manufacturers, or Swedish minerals with fruit from the Mediterranean.

The League took a far more muscular approach than that of today's business councils. It bribed rulers, built lighthouses and led expeditions against pirates, and on one memorable occasion raised an armed force that defeated the Danish military in 1368.

At its height the League had over a hundred members, including major cities now within Poland such as Danzig (Gdańsk), Stettin (Szczecin), Thorn (Toruń) and Elbing (Elbląg).

But it was all downhill from there. As it had no standing army and no government beyond irregular assemblies of city representatives, the League was unable to withstand the rise of the new nation states of the 15th century, and the shift of trade to Atlantic ports after the discovery of the New World. Its assembly met for the last time in 1669, and its membership had been reduced to the core cities of Hamburg, Bremen and Lübeck by the time of its final disintegration in 1863.

The memory of the League lives on, however, in the **New Hanse** (www.hanse.org), founded in 1980 and bringing together the former Hansa member cities in a body promoting cultural cooperation and civic pride.

Ołowianka 9/13; adult/concession 6/4zł) just across the Motława, on Ołowianka Island. The museum's own ferry service shuttles between the crane and the island. The exhibits illustrate the history of Polish seafaring from the earliest times to the present and include models of old sailing warships and ports, a 9th-century dugout, navigation instruments, ships' artillery, flags and the like. An interesting exhibit is a collection of salvaged items from the *General Carleton*, a British ship that disappeared mysteriously in the Baltic in 1785. In 1995 Polish scuba divers happened upon the wreck, and the museum's later excavation turned up the ship's bell with its name engraved, thus solving the mystery.

Offshore, there's the **MS Sołdek** (Map p408; adult/ concession 6/4zł; 10am-6pm Jul-Aug, 10am-3.30pm Sep-Jun), a museum ship moored in front of the granaries. Once you're on board and past the fairly dull introductory video, you can test the limits of your claustrophobia and vertigo in the lower and higher sections of the vessel.

Set aside three hours to visit all the sites – there's a lot to see. Combined entry to all four sections, including the crane, costs 15/9zł for adult/concession tickets; tours in English and other languages cost 20zł to 40zł, depending on numbers.

ST MARY'S CHURCH

Set right in the middle of the Main Town, **St Mary's Church** (Bazylika Mariacka; Map p408) is believed to be the largest old brick church in the world. It's 105m long and 66m wide at the transept, and its massive squat tower is 78m high. About 25,000 people can be easily accommodated into its 5000-sq-metre (0.5-hectare) interior. It's a fascinating building to look at even from a few streets away, as its weathered red brickwork looms in a somewhat sinister manner over the much smaller, more thoroughly redecorated buildings at its feet.

The church was begun in 1343 and reached its present gigantic size in 1502. It served as the parish church for the Catholic congregation until the Reformation blew into Gdańsk, and it passed to the Protestants in 1572, to be used by them until WWII.

The church didn't escape the destruction of 1945; half of the vault collapsed and the interior was largely burnt out. Fortunately, the most valuable works of art had been removed and hidden before the battle front arrived. They were brought back after a long and complex reconstruction.

The church's elephantine size is arresting and you feel even more antlike when you enter the building. Illuminated with natural light passing through 37 large windows (the biggest is 127 sq metres in area) the three-naved, whitewashed interior, topped by an intricate Gothic vault, is astonishingly bright and spacious. It was originally covered with frescoes, the sparse remains of which are visible in the far right corner. Imagine the impact the church must have made on medieval worshippers.

On first sight, the church looks almost empty, but walk around its 30-odd chapels to discover how many outstanding works of art have been accumulated. In the floor alone, there are about 300 tombstones. In the chapel at the back of the left (northern) aisle is a replica of Memling's *The Last Judgment* – the original is in the National Museum. Note the extraordinary Baroque organ.

The high altar boasts a Gothic polyptych from the 1510s, with the Coronation of the Virgin depicted in its central panel. Large as it is, it's a miniature in this vast space. The same applies to the 4m crucifix high up on the rood beam. Directly below it is a lofty wooden sacrarium from 1482, elaborately carved in the shape of a tower.

One object that does stand out, in terms both of its size and rarity, is the 15th-century **astronomical clock**, placed in the northern transept. Another attraction of the church is its **tower** (adult/concession 3/1.50zł; ☉ 9am-5.30pm Mon-Sat, 1-5.30pm Sun), offering a sweeping bird's-eye view from its tiny viewing platform, 405 steps above.

ROYAL CHAPEL

Just to the north of St Mary's Church, and completely overshadowed by its massive neighbour, sits the small **Royal Chapel** (Kaplica Królewska; Map p408), which is squeezed between two houses. The only Baroque church in old Gdańsk, it was built between 1678 and 1681 to fulfil the last will of the primate of Poland of the time, Andrzej Olszowski.

The chapel was designed by famous royal architect Tylman van Gameren. Its façade is its more attractive feature, and bears the coats of arms of Poland, Lithuania and King Jan III Sobieski (the founder of the chapel).

GREAT ARSENAL

To the west of St Mary's Church, ul Piwna (Beer St) ends at the **Great Arsenal** (Wielka Zbrojownia; Map p408). This being Gdańsk, even such an apparently prosaic building as an armoury is an architectural gem. It's the work of Antoon van Opberghen, built at the beginning of the 17th century and, like most of Gdańsk's architecture, clearly shows the influence of the Low Countries. The main eastern façade, framed within two side towers, is floridly decorated and guarded by figures of soldiers on the top. Military motifs predominate, and the city's coat of arms guards the doorways. A small stone structure rather like a well, in the middle of the façade, is the lift that was used for hoisting heavy ammunition from the basement. Above it stands Athena, goddess of warfare.

The armoury is now home to a decidedly nonmartial supermarket. Walk through to the Coal Market (Targ Węglowy) square on the opposite side, to see the western façade – though not as heavily ornamented as the eastern one, it's a fine composition that looks like four burghers' houses.

Slightly to the south, toward the Foregate, is a curious metal sculpture known as the **Millennium Tree**. It was erected in 1997 to commemorate Gdańsk's thousandth anniversary.

NORTHERN MAIN TOWN

The main attraction of this sector is **St Nicholas' Church** (Bazylika Św Mikołaja; Map p408), one of the oldest in town. It was built by the Dominican order on its arrival from Kraków in 1227, but only reached its final shape at the end of the 15th century. Amazingly, it was the only central church to escape damage in WWII – according to one story the attacking Russian soldiers deliberately avoided shelling it, due to Orthodox believers' high regard for St Nicholas. Unlike most of the other Gothic churches in the city, the interior of St Nick's is very richly decorated. The magnificent late-Renaissance high altar of 1647 first catches the eye, followed by the imposing Baroque organ made a century later. Don't miss the bronze rosary chandelier (1617), which features the Virgin and Child carved in wood, hanging in the nave in front of the entrance to the chancel.

Just behind the church is the large **Market Hall** (Hala Targowa; Map p408; 🏷 9am-7pm Mon-Fri, 9am-5pm Sat May-Sep, 9am-6pm Mon-Fri, 9am-3pm Sat Oct-Apr), constructed in the late 19th century after the Dominicans were expelled by the Prussian authorities and their monastery standing on this site was pulled down. Wander through to check out the various shops and their contents, including food and clothing.

In front of the market hall is the tall octagonal **Hyacinthus' Tower** (Baszta Jacek; Map p408), one of the remnants of the medieval fortifications. It was built around 1400 and, apart from its defensive role, it also served as a watchtower. Today it houses a photo shop.

Old Town

Despite its name, Gdańsk's Old Town (Map p408) was not the cradle of the city. The earliest inhabited site, according to archaeologists, was in what is now the Main Town area. Nonetheless, a settlement existed in the Old Town from the late 10th century and developed parallel to the Main Town.

Under the Teutonic order, the two parts merged into a single urban entity, but the Old Town was always poorer and had no defensive system of its own. One other difference was that the Main Town was more 'German' while the Old Town had a larger Polish population. During WWII it suffered as much as its wealthier cousin but, apart from a handful of buildings (mainly churches) it was not rebuilt in its previous shape. The most interesting area today is along the Radunia Canal, between ul Garncarska and ul Stolarska.

The largest monument of the Old Town is **St Catherine's Church** (Kościół Św Katarzyny; Map p408), which is the oldest church in Gdańsk, begun in the 1220s. It was the parish church for the whole town until St Mary's was completed. As is common, the church evolved over centuries and only reached its final shape in the mid-15th century (save for the Baroque top to the tower, added in 1634).

The vaulted Gothic interior was originally covered with frescoes, fragments of which were discovered under a layer of plaster. Note the huge painting (11m long) depicting the entry of Christ to Jerusalem, placed under the organ loft in the left-hand aisle, and the richly carved enclosure of the baptismal font (1585) in the opposite aisle. The astronomer Johannes Hevelius was buried in the church's chancel, an 18th-century epitaph is above the grave.

The church is home to the **Tower Clocks Museum** (Muzeum Zegarów Wieżowych; Map p408; ☎ 058 305 64 92; ul Wielkie Młyny; adult/concession 4/2zł; 🏷 10am-5pm Tue-Sun), which features a collection of old tower clocks from the 15th century onwards. The church tower also houses a **carillon** (admission 3zł), a set of 49 bells that plays a selection of familiar melodies every hour.

Unfortunately, a major fire in May 2006 collapsed the church roof and caused damage to its interiors. Restoration work was in progress at the time of research, with some areas inaccessible to visitors, including the museum and tower, which were expected to be closed for some time.

Set immediately behind St Catherine's is **St Bridget's Church** (Kościół Św Brygidy; Map p408). Founded 700 years ago, the building was almost completely destroyed in 1945, and until 1970 only the walls were left standing. There's almost nothing left of the prewar furnishings within, but amber fans will be interested in seeing the spectacular 174cm-high amber monstrance depicting the tree of life and the monumental high altar, a recent construction, which comprises a record-breaking 6500kg of the stuff.

Lech Wałęsa attended Mass here when he was an unknown electrician in the nearby shipyard. With the wave of strikes in 1980 the church became a strong supporter of the dockyard workers, and its priest, Henryk Jankowski, took every opportunity to express their views in his sermons. The church remains a record of the Solidarity period, with several contemporary craftworks related to the trade union and to modern Polish history in general. You'll find the tombstone of murdered priest Jerzy Popiełuszko, the Katyń epitaph, a collection of crosses from the 1980 and '88 strikes, and a door covered with bas-reliefs of scenes from Solidarity's history – all in the right-hand (northern) aisle.

The peculiar seven-storey building opposite St Catherine's Church is the **Great Mill** (Wielki Młyn; Map p408). Built in around 1350 by the Teutonic Knights, it was the largest mill in medieval Europe at over 40m long and 26m high, and equipped with a set of 18 millstones, each 5m in diameter. The mill operated until 1945 and just before WWII produced 200 tonnes of flour per day. It now houses a modern shopping mall.

Behind the mill, across a small park, is the **Old Town Hall** (Ratusz Staromiejski; Map p408), once the seat of the Old Town council. A well-proportioned Renaissance building crowned with a high central tower typical of its Flemish provenance, it was designed at the end of the 16th century by Antonius van Opbergen, the architect later responsible for the Great Arsenal. The brick structure is delicately ornamented in stone, including the central doorway and a frieze with the shields of Poland, Prussia and Gdańsk.

The Old Town Hall now houses the Baltic Sea Culture Centre and an exhibition hall. Go upstairs to see the foyer, notable for its rich decoration, which was partly assembled from old burghers' houses. Note the arcaded stone wall (1560) with three Roman gods in bas-relief. This composition, older than the town hall itself, was moved here from one of the houses in the Main Town. One of the doors leads to the Great Hall, which can also be visited. Concerts are held here – check the programme for details. There's also a café downstairs if you feel like a quick coffee or beer.

SHIPYARD

Gdańsk's **shipyard** (Map p408) is not just an industrial zone, it's an important fragment of 20th-century history. It was here that discontent with the communist regime boiled over into strikes and dissent, which were stamped out by armed force in 1970; 10 years later an electrician named Lech Wałęsa sprang up to address crowds of strikers here, leading to the formation of the Solidarity movement and ultimately to democracy for Poland.

Since the heady times of Wałęsa's presidency, however, the yard has largely lost its protected status; the vast area is now slated to be partly redeveloped as the site of offices and shops, though structures with historic significance will remain in place.

Just in front of the shipyard gates, on Solidarity Sq, the **Monument to the Fallen Shipyard Workers** (Pomnik Poległych Stoczniowców; Map p408) commemorates the workers killed in the riots of 1970. Unveiled on 16 December 1980, 10 years after the massacre, the monument is a set of three 42m-tall steel crosses, with a series of bronze bas-reliefs in their bases. One of the plates contains a fragment of a poem by late Nobel laureate Czesław Miłosz: 'You who wronged a simple man/Do not feel safe. A poet remembers./You can kill one, but another is born.'

The first monument in a communist regime to commemorate the regime's victims, it became an instant symbol and landmark.

Back toward the Old Town is the **Roads to Freedom exhibition** (Droga do Wolności; Map p408; ☎ 058 308 4712; www.fcs.org.pl; ul Wały Piastowskie 24; adult/concession 6/4zł; ☿ 10am-5pm Tue-Sun), a collection of multimedia displays and artefacts illustrating Poland's turbulent path to democracy, from the 1956 uprisings to martial law and the collapse of communism. At the time of research it was about to move from its former home in the shipyards to this location, attached to the Solidarity HQ. The exhibition is a poignant reminder of just how much has changed over the last 60 years, and of just how much dedication and sacrifice went into achieving that change. It's well captioned in English, and is something every visitor to Gdańsk should see – it rounds out the Main Town's Renaissance splendour with the knowledge of recent events that shaped the city.

Old Suburb

The Old Suburb (Stare Przedmieście; Map p408), south of the Main Town, was the product of the expansion of the city between the 15th and 17th centuries. Reduced to rubble in 1945 and rebuilt in the familiar bland postwar fashion, the suburb has little charm but boasts some notable sights.

The most significant of these is the **National Museum's Department of Early Art** (Muzeum Narodowe Oddział Sztuki Dawnej; Map p408; ☎ 058 301 6804; ul Toruńska 1; adult/concession 10/6zł; ☿ 10am-5pm May-Sep, 9am-4pm Oct-Apr), located in the vaulted interiors of the former Franciscan monastery. Among the best museums in the country, it covers the broad spectrum of Polish and international art and crafts, boasting extensive collections of paintings, woodcarvings, gold and silverware, embroidery, fabrics, porcelain, faience, wrought iron and furniture. It has the original figure of St George from the spire of the Court of the Fraternity of St George, an assortment of huge, elaborately carved Danzig-style wardrobes (typical of the city, from where they were sent all over the country) and several beautiful ceramic tiled stoves.

The 1st floor is given over to paintings, with a section devoted to Dutch and Flemish work. The jewel of the collection is Hans Memling's (1435–94) triptych of the *Last Judgment,* one of the earlier works of the artist, dating from 1472 to 1473. You'll also find works by the younger Brueghel and Van Dyck, and the beautifully macabre *Hell* by Jacob Swanenburgh, who was the master of the young Rembrandt.

Adjoining the museum from the north, and formerly belonging to the Franciscan monastery, is the **Church of the Holy Trinity** (Kościół Św Trójcy; Map p408), which was built at the end of the 15th century, when the Gothic style had already reached its late decorative stage. After St Mary's Church it's the largest in town, with a spacious and lofty whitewashed interior topped with a superb, netlike vault.

Note the high altar's assembly of panels from triptychs of different origins, the old tombstones paving the floor, and the spidery Baroque chandeliers from the mid-17th century.

Westerplatte

Westerplatte (Map p407) is a long peninsula at the entrance to the harbour, 7km north of the historic town. When Gdańsk became a free city after WWI, Poland was permitted to maintain a post at this location, at the tip of the port zone. It served both trading and military purposes and had a garrison to protect it.

WWII broke out here at dawn on 1 September 1939, when the German battleship *Schleswig-Holstein* began shelling the Polish guard post. The garrison, which numbered just 182 men, held out for seven days before surrendering. The site is now a memorial, with some of the ruins left as they were after the bombardment, plus a massive **monument** (Map p407) put up in memory of the defenders. The surviving **Guardhouse No 1** (Wartownia Nr 1; Map p407; ☎ 058 343 6972; ul Sucharskiego; adult/concession 3/2zł; ♨ 9am-4pm May-Sep) houses a small exhibition related to the event, including a model of the battle labelled in English.

Bus 106 goes to Westerplatte from the main train station, but a more attractive way to get here is by boat. Ferries, paddle steamers and a replica galleon depart several times daily for Westerplatte from the wharf next to the Green Gate (p424).

Oliwa

Oliwa (Map p407), a desirable suburb about 9km from the historic centre, boasts a fine cathedral set in a quiet park, and provides an enjoyable half-day break from the dense attractions of the Main Town. To get here, take the commuter train from central Gdańsk and get off at Gdańsk Oliwa station, from where it's a 10-minute walk.

The beginnings of Oliwa go back over 800 years, when the Pomeranian dukes who then ruled Gdańsk invited the Cistercians to settle here in 1186 and granted them land together with privileges, including the revenues of the port of Gdańsk.

The abbey didn't have an easy life. The original church from around 1200 was burnt out by the pagan Baltic Prussians, then by the Teutonic Knights. A new Gothic church, built in the mid-14th century, was surrounded by defensive walls, but that didn't save it from further misfortunes. When in 1577 the abbots supported King Stefan Batory in his attempts to reduce the city's independence, the citizens of Gdańsk burned the church down in revenge. The monks rebuilt their holy home once more, but then the Swedish wars began and the church fell prey to repeated looting, losing its organ and pulpit among other things. The monks' troubles came to an end in 1831, when the Prussian government decided to expel them from the city. The church was given to the local parish and, in 1925, raised to the rank of **cathedral** (Map p407). It came through the war almost unscathed, and is an important, and unusual, example of ecclesiastical architecture.

The first surprise is its façade, a striking composition of two slim octagonal Gothic towers with a central Baroque portion squeezed between them. You enter the church by going downstairs, for its floor is more than a metre below the external ground level. The interior looks extraordinarily long, mainly because of the unusual proportions of the building – the nave and chancel together are 90m long but only 8.3m wide. At the far end of this 'tunnel' is a Baroque high altar (1688), while the previous oak-carved Renaissance altar (from 1606) is now in the left-hand transept. Opposite, in the right transept, is the marble tombstone of the Pomeranian dukes (1613).

The showpiece of the church is the **organ**. The instrument, begun in 1763 and completed 30 years later, is noted for its fine tone and the mechanised angels that blow trumpets and ring bells when the organ is played. In July and August, recitals take place on Tuesday and Friday evenings, but 20-minute performances are held daily every hour or two between 10am and 3pm or 4pm (in the afternoon only on Sunday). Check the schedule with the tourist offices before setting off.

Behind the cathedral is the 18th-century abbots' palace that now accommodates the **Modern Art Gallery** (Wystawa Sztuki Współczesnej; Map p407; ☎ 058 552 1271; ul Cystersów 18; adult/concession 9/6zł; ⏰ 9am-5pm Tue-Fri, 10am-6pm Sun), a branch of the National Museum of Gdańsk. The old granary opposite the palace houses the **Ethnographic Museum** (Muzeum Etnograficzne; Map p407; ☎ 058 552 4139; ul Cystersów 19; adult/concession 8/5zł; ⏰ 9am-5pm Tue-Fri, 10am-6pm Sun) and its interesting collection of rural household implements and crafts from the region. The 18th-century **park**, with its lakes, old exotic trees, a palm house, a greenhouse and a small formal French garden, supplies a fine natural setting for the historic complex.

FESTIVALS & EVENTS

The oldest and most important event that takes place in the city is the **Dominican Fair** (Jarmark Dominikański; ☎ 058 554 9348; www.mtgsa .pl), which dates back to 1260, when the local Dominican monks received the papal privilege of holding a fair on the feast day of their saint. The fair was initially held on Plac Dominikański, the square next to St Nicholas' Church, but today it takes up 6000 sq metres of the Main Town for three weeks from the last Saturday of July. There's no shortage of tacky crap on offer, but you'll still find plenty of antiques, bric-a-brac and craft items. The fair is accompanied by various cultural events, including street theatre, concerts, races and parades.

Other major events:

International Festival of Open-Air & Street Theatre (FETA; ☎ 058 557 4247; www.feta.pl) Held in July.

International Organ, Choir & Chamber Music Festival (☎ 058 620 7633) Held on Friday in July and August in St Mary's Church.

International Organ Music Festival (☎ 058 305 2040; www.filharmonia.gda.pl in Polish) Held in the Oliwa cathedral, with twice-weekly organ recitals from mid-June till the end of August.

International Shakespeare Festival (☎ 058 305 6800; www.teatr-szekspir.gda.pl) Held in August.

Sounds of the North Festival (☎ 058 301 1051; www .nck.org.pl) Held in August, featuring traditional folk music from the northern hemisphere, particularly northern Europe.

World Amber Trawling Championship (☎ 058 247 8293) Unusual all-comers contest held each July in the Mierzeja Wiślana region (see boxed text, p455), east of Gdańsk.

SLEEPING
Budget

For accommodation listed in this category, bathrooms are shared unless otherwise indicated.

HOSTELS & HOTELS

Youth Hostel Old Town (Map p408; ☎ 058 301 2313; www .mokf.com.pl; ul Wałowa 21; dm/s/d/tr/q 17/30/60/60/80zł; ⓟ ✗); Wrzeszcz (Map p407; ☎ 058 341 1660; Al Grunwaldzka 244; s 53zł, d 80-106zł, q 104zł; ⓟ ✗ ▢ ✆) Old-fashioned hostel in a quiet, old building on the doorstep of the Gdańsk Shipyards. Rooms are brown and basic, but clean. Smoking and drinking are strictly forbidden, reception is closed between 10am and 5pm, and there's a midnight curfew. Book ahead, particularly in summer. Another, more modern branch is located within a sports complex 6km northwest of the centre in the Wrzeszcz district; take the SKM to Gdańsk Zaspa and walk northwest.

Dom Studenta ASP (Map p408; ☎ 058 301 2816; ul Chlebnicka 13/16; adult/student dm 32/29zł; ⏰ Jul–mid-Sep) This is the dorm of the Academy of Fine Arts, ideally located in the historic House Under the Angels in the Main Town. It's basic, but you won't find cheaper lodgings in a more central location.

Baltic Hostel (Map p408; ☎ 058 721 9657; www.baltic hostel.com; ul 3 Maja 25; dm 35zł, r 100zł; ✗ ▢) This budget accommodation is just north of both train and bus stations; the entrance is at the far end of the block on the right. The building's foyer has a touch of 'Alfred Hitchcock meets the Addams Family' about it, but the rooms are reassuringly cheerful and brightly coloured, though the dorm beds are placed fairly close together. A laundry service is available, along with bike and kayak hire.

Hostel Targ Rybny (Map p408; ☎ 058 301 5627; www.gdanskhostel.com.pl; ul Grodzka 21; dm 50zł, s/d/tr/q 200/200/240/280zł; ⓟ ✗ ▢) This waterfront hostel sits within a picturesque old building with a sloping roof. Both the dorm area and rooms are a bit squeezy, but that's made up for by their neat and tidy appearance and soothing tones. There's also a friendly lounge area filled with backpackers relaxing after a day about town. Bike and kayak rental is available, and there's a washing machine on site.

Dizzy Daisy (Map p408; ☎ 058 301 3919; www.dizzy daisy.pl; ul Gnilna 3; dm/s/d/tr 55/110/150/195zł; ⏰ Jul & Aug; ⓟ ▢) Hostel open at the height of summer only, housing visitors within basic student rooms. The location's good, and there's a laundry and kitchen available for guest use.

Dom Harcerza (Map p408; ☎ 058 301 3621; www.dom harcerza.prv.pl; ul Za Murami 2/10; s 50zł, d120-220zł, tr 150-260zł, q 160zł) It may be housed within a former cinema, but the Dom Harcerza has a decidedly un-Hollywood feel. The simple, snug rooms are nothing fancy, but they're clean and tidy. Downstairs there's an old-fashioned restaurant serving standard Polish dishes. The hotel is popular with student groups, so it can be noisy and energetic, but it's in a great location near ul Długa.

PRIVATE ROOMS

Grand-Tourist (Map p408; ☎ 058 301 1727; www.gt.com .pl; ul Podwale Grodzkie 8; s 60-70zł, d 100-110zł, apt 180-350zł) Opposite the train station, this is the main agency handling private rooms, and it also offers a selection of apartments for up to six people. When making your choice, don't worry too much about the distance from the centre – work out how close the place is to the SKM commuter train.

CAMPING

Camping Nr 218 Stogi (Map p407; ☎ 058 307 3915; www .kemping-gdansk.pl; ul Wydmy 9; camp sites per adult/child 10/7zł, cabins 100zł; ☼ May-Sep) Located in a pine forest in the suburb of Stogi, about 5.5km northeast of the centre, this is the most convenient of Gdańsk's three camping grounds. Just 200m away is one of the city's best beaches, with the cleanest water you'll find for miles. Tram 8 from the main train station passes here.

Midrange

Gdańsk's long-running shortage of mid-priced accommodation in the historic centre is still evident, but some new places have arisen to fill the gap, including conveniently located apartments for hire. Suchanino, a suburb a short bus ride west from the main station, also contains some handy options. You could also consider staying in Sopot (p425) or Gdynia (p430) and using the ever-useful SKM trains to commute to Gdańsk.

Old Town Apartments (☎ 022 351 2260; www .warsawshotel.com; apt €55-93) This Warsaw-based firm offers a selection of one- and two-bedroom apartments scattered around the Main Town, suitable for up to four people. Rates are competitive with hotel accommodation, and cheaper by the week.

Pokoje Gościnne Mac-Tur (Map p407; ☎ 058 302 4170; www.mactur.gda.pl; ul Beethovena 8; s/d/tr 200/220/250zł; P ⊠ 🖳) West of the city centre, the Mac-Tur is a guesthouse full of unfussy character. Rooms are brightly painted, with pine furniture and parquetry floors. Downstairs there's an attractive spacious breakfast room, along with a garden, barbecue and table tennis. To get here take buses 115, 130, 184, 384 or night bus N6 to the first stop past the service station on ul Beethovena, or you can grab a taxi (20zł to 25zł).

our pick **Kamienica Gotyk** (Map p408; ☎ 058 301 8567; www.gotykhouse.eu; ul Mariacka 1; s/d 250/280zł) This Gothic guesthouse claims to be Gdańsk's oldest house, and its narrow red brick façade is flanked by angels carved onto large stone tablets. Inside, the compact rooms are compact but neat, with clean, shiny bathrooms. The location is impressive, with St Mary's Church and the cafés and shops of ul Mariacka just outside the door.

Dom Muzyka (Map p407; ☎ 058 326 0600; ul Łąkowa 1/2; s 200zł, d 280-300zł, ste 420zł; P ⊠ 🖳 ♿) During the day, this smart accommodation within a music college has a background soundtrack of random musical sounds. Its light-filled rooms feature high ceilings and are discreetly decorated with old prints. Gleaming bathrooms complete the elegant look, and there's a classy restaurant and bar off the foyer.

Kamienica Zacisze (Map p408; ☎ 0508 096 221; www.apartments.gdansk.pl; ul Ogarna 107; apt 300-440zł; P ⊠ 🖳 ♿) Set within a quiet courtyard off the street, this communist-era workers dormitory building has been transformed into a set of light, airy apartments for up to six people. Each apartment has high ceilings, a fully equipped kitchen and loads of space.

Villa Angela (Map p407; ☎ 058 302 2315; www.villa angela.pl; ul Beethovena 12; s 250zł, d 310-350zł, tr/ste 420/580zł; P ⊠ 🖳) There's a whiff of the Mediterranean about this suburban hotel with a splash of terracotta and stucco in its décor. Rooms are stylish and comfortable, and most have balconies with sweeping views from the hotel's hilly location, just next door to the Pokoje Gościnne Mac-Tur.

Dom Aktora (Map p408; ☎ 058 301 5901; www .domaktora.pl; ul Straganiarska 55/56; s/d 230/320zł, apt 380-520zł; P 🖳) Affordable set of apartments with simply equipped kitchens, along with some straightforward single and double rooms. The apartments supposedly reflect an Italian style, but it's hard to see it, and the décor is showing its age. However, these quibbles are offset by its excellent location. Guests can hire bicycles (5/30zł per hour/day).

Top End

In keeping with the restored splendour of the Main Town, Gdańsk has some superb accommodation options for those who can afford the finer things in life. Look out for serious discounting at weekends and out of season.

Hotel Królewski (Map p408; ☎ 058 326 1111; www .hotelkrolewski.pl; ul Ołowianka 1; s 350zł, d 400-450zł, ste 560-700zł; P X 🖳 🕭) This hotel is set in an amazing old granary building on the opposite bank of the river from the Main Town, and oozes history from its worn redbrick exterior. Rooms are modern and attractive, and there's a lovely outdoor dining area overlooking the water.

Hotel Mercure Hevelius (Map p408; ☎ 058 321 0000; www.mercure.com; ul Heweliusza 22; r 503zł, ste 990zł; P X 🖳 🕭) This towering hotel would be included in anyone's short list of 'ugliest buildings of Gdańsk', but its rooms and facilities are reassuringly consistent in quality. There are various in-house options to take advantage of, including a restaurant, bar and massage.

Dwór Oliwski (Map p407; ☎ 058 554 7000; www .dwor-oliwski.com.pl; ul Bytowska 4; s/d €149/184, ste €330; P X 🖳 🕭) If you're inclined to treat yourself to a little luxury, this magnificent manor house provides a compelling reason to head for Oliwa. The five-star accommodation is housed in traditional buildings set amid extensive gardens, and offers sophisticated rooms and sauna facilities. The restaurant has a fantastic reputation for its French cuisine.

Hotel Podewils (Map p408; ☎ 058 300 9560; www .podewils.pl; ul Szafarnia 2; s €183-220, d €224-247, ste €271; P X 🖳) The view from the Podewils across the river to the Main Town can't be beaten. Its cheery Baroque exterior comes straight from the 18th century, and contains rooms filled with elegantly curved timber furniture, classic prints and distinctive wallpaper. There's also a restaurant, a bar and a choice of Turkish or Finnish saunas.

Hotel Hanza (Map p408; ☎ 058 305 3427; www .hotelhanza.pl; ul Tokarska 6; s/d 695/745zł, ste 985-1190zł; P X 🕭 🖳 🕭) This luxurious establishment's modern structure blends seamlessly with the old-world architecture of the waterfront. The rooms are simple and classy, featuring beds with polished timber head-

boards, wide-screen televisions and spotless bathrooms. A riverside terrace allows the sipping of a leisurely drink while taking in the attractive old granaries across the water.

EATING

There are plenty of eateries throughout the centre catering to every budget. As you may expect, fish is plentiful, but you'll have to hunt around for ethnic cuisines.

Bar Mleczny Neptun (Map p408; ☎ 058 301 4988; ul Długa 33/34; mains 2-12zł; ⏲ 7.30am-6pm Mon-Fri, 10am-5pm Sat & Sun) Ultrabudget dining in an original communist-era milk bar, though this joint is a cut above your run-of-the-mill *bar mleczny*, with potted plants, lace curtains, decorative tiling and old lamps for décor.

Green Way (Map p408; ☎ 058 301 4121; ul Garncarska 4/6; mains 4-9zł; ⏲ 10am-8pm Mon-Fri, noon-7pm Sat & Sun; X) Folksy blue-and-yellow space serving vegetarian and organic dishes ranging from soy cutlets to Mexican goulash. As the ultimate accolade, even nonveggies come to eat here. There's another, more central, branch at ul Długa 11.

Bar Pod Rybą (Map p408; ☎ 058 305 1307; Długi Targ 35/38; mains 6-20zł; ⏲ 11am-9pm Jul-Aug, 11am-7pm Sep-Jun) You wouldn't expect much from a budget eatery at the heart of the tourist trail, but this neat central bar turns out great baked potatoes with a variety of fillings. The old photos of Gdańsk give you something to look at while eating.

Kuchnia Rosyjska (Map p408; ☎ 058 301 2735; Długi Targ 11; mains 9-32zł; ⏲ 11am-11pm) Brilliantly coloured Russian restaurant with a folkloric interior, serving lots of traditional snacks, soups and mains.

Gospoda Pod Wielkem Młynem (Map p408; ☎ 058 302 1779; ul Na Piaskach 1; mains 13-44zł; ⏲ noon-11pm) A sure-fire tip for summer, this charming half-timbered building behind the Great Mill has the city's best restaurant garden, straddling the tip of an island on the Radunia Canal. Romantics will lap up the secluded atmosphere, surrounded by shady trees and rustic wagon wheels. There's also a cheaper snack menu with Polish standards such as *bigos* (sauerkraut dish, see boxed text, p61; 5zł).

Kansai (Map p408; ☎ 058 324 0888; ul Ogarna 124/125; mains 15-43zł; ⏲ noon-9pm Mon-Sat, noon-8pm Sun) You'd expect to find fish in a seaport, but Kansai adds an exotic twist by serving sushi in full-on Japanese ambience. Waiters are dressed in traditional robes, there's a samurai sword on the counter, and the menu has dishes made from tuna, salmon and butterfish, along with classic California rolls.

Restauracja Kubicki (Map p408; ☎ 058 301 0050; ul Wartka 5; mains 15-43zł; ⊗ noon-11pm; ⊠) This family firm has served solid, tasty Polish food from its waterfront location since the last days of the German Empire in 1918, making it Gdańsk's oldest continuously operated restaurant. There's plenty of fresh fish on the menu, priced by weight, and a wide-ranging wine list including several Bulgarian drops. There's a great river view from the outdoor seating.

Czerwone Drzwi (Map p408; ☎ 058 301 5764; ul Piwna 52/53; mains 18-65zł; ⊗ noon-10pm) Step through the Red Door into a relaxed, refined café atmosphere, which helps you digest the small but interesting menu of Polish and international meals.

Restauracja Gdańska (Map p408; ☎ 058 305 7671; ul Św Ducha 16; mains 24-110zł; ⊗ noon-midnight) Eating here is a memorable experience: the five banquet rooms and salons are crammed to the rafters with antique furniture, paintings, model ships, random *objets d'art* and nimble waiters in epaulettes. The upper-end traditional cooking makes a visit doubly worthwhile.

Piwnica Rajców (Map p408; ☎ 058 300 0280; ul Długi Targ 44; mains 25-110zł; ⊗ 10am-midnight) The gods are smiling on this excellent cellar-restaurant, near the Neptune fountain and below a striking entrance topped by a statue of the god Mercury. The menu features some of the finest Polish cuisine to be had in Gdańsk, particularly its wild boar, and extends to more exotic dishes like springbok fillet.

Tawerna (Map p408; ☎ 058 301 4114; ul Powroźnicza 19/20; mains 29-119zł; ⊗ 11am-late) A historic eatery within a dark, restfully gloomy interior. It's nautically themed, serves a Polish menu with plenty of fish, and has a great location just inside the Green Gate, which is handy for a bite between city sightseeing and river cruising.

Restauracja Pod Łososiem (Map p408; ☎ 058 301 7652; ul Szeroka 52/54; mains 49-95zł; ⊗ noon-10pm) Founded in 1598 and particularly famous for its salmon dishes, this is one of Gdańsk's oldest and most highly regarded restaurants. Red leather seats, brass chandeliers and a gathering of gas lamps fill out the sombre interior. The speciality drink here is Goldwasser, a thick, sweet liqueur with flakes of gold floating in it, and invented and produced in its cellars from the end of the 16th century till the outbreak of WWII.

DRINKING

The photogenic ul Mariacka has several romantic little café-bars, with tables on their charming front terraces. You'll find plenty of open-air summer bars amid the fancy restaurants on the waterfront, especially at the Targ Rybny end.

Punkt (Map p408; ☎ 058 301 2535; ul Chlebnicka 2; ⊗ 4pm-late) Popular with a hipper brand of student, the murky stained glass here conceals a den of wannabe urban chic, complete with cutting-edge music and fashionable ennui. Look for the permanent gaggle of people on the steps outside.

Irish Pub (Map p408; ☎ 058 320 2474; www.irish.pl in Polish; ul Korzenna 33/35; ⊗ 3pm-late Mon-Sat, 4pm-late Sun) Set in the vast vaulted cellars of the Old Town Hall, this sort-of Irish pub is famous for its cheap booze and shamelessly naff sessions of the dreaded karaoke. There's some kind of music most nights – see the very green website for details.

Celtic Pub (Map p408; ☎ 058 301 2999; ul Lektykarska 3; ⊗ 5pm-late) Another Hibernian-themed cellar bar with late-night parties, and it's exactly the kind of messy, crowded, chaotic dive you need to round off a hard day's drinking. The surface-level entrance leads to DJs playing music every night, ranging from karaoke to chill-out tunes.

our pick **Spiritus Sanctus** (Map p408; ☎ 058 320 7019; ul Grobla I 13; ⊗ 2-11pm) If you're tired of beer and vodka, head for this stylish wine bar opposite St Mary's Church. There's no wine list to peruse – instead, the knowledgeable waiters suggest suitable tipples from unfamiliar regions of the Balkans. While you're enjoying your Slovenian white or Croatian red, you can marvel at the amazing décor, a jumble of abstract art and classic *objets d'art*.

Café Ferber (Map p408; ☎ 058 301 5566; ul Długa 77/78; ⊗ 8am-2am) It's startling to step straight from Gdańsk's historic main street into this very modern café-bar, dominated by bright red panels, a suspended ceiling and boxy lighting. The scarlet décor contrasts with its comfy brown armchairs, from which you can sip well-made coffee, international wines, and cocktail creations such as the *szary kot* (grey cat). On weekends, DJs spin house and chill-out music into the wee small hours.

Pi Kawa (Map p408; ☎ 058 309 1444; ul Piwna 5/6; ⊗ 10am-10pm) This café on Beer Street has a relaxed interior with a country kitchen feel, sporting timber tables, original artwork for sale, and a fish tank. It's a good hide-out from the tourist crowds on ul Długa.

Kamienica (Map p408; ☎ 058 301 1230; ul Mariacka 37/39; 🕑 10am-11pm) The pick of the bunch on Mariacka is this excellent two-level café with a calm, sophisticated atmosphere and the best patio on the block. It's as popular for daytime coffee and cakes as it is for a sociable evening beverage.

ENTERTAINMENT

Check the local press for up-to-date cultural and entertainment listings. *Gdańsk in Your Pocket* provides comprehensive and usefully opinionated reviews of the city's nightlife options. But, as anyone in town will tell you, Sopot is the place to go for a serious night out.

Clubs & Live Music

Soda (Map p408; ☎ 058 305 1256; ul Chmielna 103/104; 🕑 7pm-late) Cool, laid-back venue with a split identity – upstairs it's a mellow pot plant–strewn bar and restaurant during the day, while downstairs it's a club after dark. Musical styles change from night to night, and can include anything from house to '70s and '80s classics.

Miasto Aniołów (Map p408; ☎ 058 768 5831; www .miastoaniolow.com.pl; ul Chmielna 26; entry 10zł; 🕑 9pm-late) The City of Angels covers all the bases – late-night revellers can hit the spacious dance floor, crash in the chill-out area, or hang around the atmospheric deck overlooking the Motława River. Nightly DJs play disco and other dance-oriented sounds.

Parlament (Map p408; ☎ 058 320 1365; www.parla ment.com.pl; ul Św Ducha 2; admission 5-10zł; 🕑 8pm-late Wed-Sat) Hardly a talking shop, this high-profile club plays host to big dance events punctuated by anything from industrial to Asian beats. There's hip-hop on Friday, disco on Saturday…oh, and karaoke on Thursday.

Yesterday (Map p408; ☎ 058 301 3924; ul Piwna 50/51; 🕑 7pm-late) Groovy cellar venue decked out in 1960s flower-power décor, including cartoon characters and a fluorescent portrait of Chairman Mao. DJs play a variety of sounds from 9pm every night, and there's the occasional live gig.

Leisure Activities

U7 (Map p408; ☎ 058 305 5577; www.u7.pl; Plac Domini-kański 7; 🕑 9am-1am) Taking the American under-one-roof concept to extremes, U7 of-fers much more than your average bowling alley: a snack bar, a gym, a sauna, a solarium, pool tables, darts and even a shooting range are packed into the subterranean space by the market hall. Unsurprisingly, the heady combination of tenpin and live ammo is a magnet for Gdańsk's younger citizens.

Opera, Classical Music & Theatre

Baltic Philharmonic Hall (Map p408; ☎ 058 305 2040; www.filharmonia.gda.pl in Polish; ul Ołowianka 1) This is the usual home of chamber music concerts, and also organises many of the major music festivals throughout the year.

State Baltic Opera (Map p407; ☎ 058 763 4906; www .operabaltycka.pl; Al Zwycięstwa 15) Founded in 1950, Gdańsk's premier opera company resides in this opera house in the Wrzeszcz district, next to the Gdańsk Politechnika train station. Alongside the usual operatic repertoire, it stages regular ballets. Symphonic concerts are also held here.

Teatr Wybrzeże (Map p408; ☎ 058 301 1328; www .teatrwybrzeze.pl; Targ Węglowy 1) The main city stage, next to the Arsenal in the Main Town. The theatre features mostly mainstream fare, including some top productions of great Polish and foreign classics.

St John's Centre (Centrum Św Jana; Map p408; ☎ 058 301 1051; www.nck.org.pl; ul Świętojańska 72) Housed within the massive Gothic interior of the former St John's Church in the heart of the Main Town, this spectacular venue is administered by the Baltic Sea Culture Centre as an exhibition space and auditorium, showcasing everything from classical concerts to world music. Check the posters outside for upcoming events.

SHOPPING

Gdańsk is widely known for its amber, nicknamed 'Baltic gold' (see boxed text, opposite). It's sold either unset or in silver jewellery, some of which is high quality. Amber shops are concentrated around ul Mariacka, Długi Targ and Długie Pobrzeże, with dozens more stalls springing up around the Dominican Fair in August. Beware of souvenir shops preying on clueless tourists with overpriced jewellery.

Beyond amber, a good place to buy craft items and paintings created by local artists is **Galeria Piękny Świat** (Map p408; ☎ 058 306 5253; ul Długa 22/27; 🕑 9am-9pm), within the main post office building.

POMERANIA

AMBER: TRUE OR FALSE?

Just as oil is nicknamed black gold, amber richly deserves its title of Baltic gold. This 'precious stone' is actually a fossilised tree resin. It's always been highly prized for decorative purposes, and the largest deposits are found along the Baltic shores of Poland and Russia.

Andrzej Gierszewski works as an amber salesman in a small shop on the riverfront in Gdańsk's Main Town. As he's also a history graduate, he has a keen interest in the substance's back story. 'The history of the amber industry is well recorded,' he says. 'We know amber figures of warriors were transported 4000 years ago to northeast Turkey and even further. They've even found amber in Egypt.'

Maintaining its historic success, amber has become one of the most popular 'stones' used in Polish jewellery. But the buyer need beware…at some smaller, less-reputable stalls, you may not be getting the real deal.

Andrzej shares an insider's tips: 'There are three main tests to differentiate between real and fake amber. If you have a lighter, and you put amber into the heat, it has a characteristic smell, like incense, and emits distinct squeaks,' he says. 'But only try this on the usual cognac-coloured amber, not white amber. Also, amber floats in 20% salt water, while plastic or synthetic amber won't.'

And the third test? 'If one rubs amber against cloth, the static electricity produced attracts tiny pieces of paper.'

It's hard to imagine producing a box of matches or a lighter at an amber stall, but Andrzej disagrees. 'If a salesman doesn't have anything to hide, he will allow you to do so. When I worked at a very small stand near the Gdańsk Crane, we did lighter tests for our customers.'

Somehow, though, the static electricity test seems the option with the least stress.

Gdańsk is also a good place for Western-style multiplex shopping, with several massive malls in town – the centres in the Great Mill (see p415) and Market Hall (see p415) are worth a look just for the architecture, while the modern **Madison Centre** (Map p408; ☎ 058 766 7541; www.madison.gda.pl; ul Rajska 10) provides four floors of international brands, food and a gym, not to mention free public toilets. Self-caterers can head for the supermarket in the Great Arsenal building (see p414).

GETTING THERE & AWAY
Air
Lech Wałęsa airport (Map p407; ☎ 058 348 1163; www .airport.gdansk.pl) is in Rębiechowo, 14km west of Gdańsk. The **LOT office** (Map p408; ☎ 058 301 1161; Wały Jagiellońskie 2/4) is next to the Upland Gate.

The only domestic flights are with LOT to Warsaw (at least four times daily), but the airport has seen a massive increase over the last few years in international flights, particularly those operated by low-cost European airlines. Destinations served by more than one airline are Frankfurt via LOT and Ryanair (at least twice daily); Munich via LOT and Lufthansa (at least twice daily); Dublin via Centralwings and Ryanair (up to six weekly); and London via Wizz Air and Ryanair (up to three daily).

There are also direct international connections via SAS to Copenhagen (up to three daily); via LOT to Hamburg (daily); with Wizz Air to Cologne (three weekly), Cork (three weekly), Dortmund (daily), Glasgow (three weekly), Hamburg (four weekly), Liverpool (five weekly), Malmö (three weekly), Sheffield (four weekly) and Stockholm (four weekly); via Centralwings to Edinburgh (up to four weekly), Rome (three weekly) and Shannon (twice weekly); and via Norwegian to Oslo (three weekly).

Bus
Gdańsk's PKS terminal (Map p408) is right behind the central train station, and linked by an underground passageway. Buses are handy for regional destinations, which seldom, or never, have trains.

There's one morning bus directly to Frombork (16zł, three hours); alternatively, you can take any of the frequent buses to Elbląg (13zł, 1½ hours) and change there. Five buses head to Krynica Morska via Sztutowo (11zł, 1½ hours), with an additional eight departures per day from July to October. Four fast buses go to Olsztyn daily (26zł, four hours) and one to Lidzbark Warmiński (22zł to 26zł, three to 3½ hours). From June to August there are three fast buses daily to Łeba (22zł, 2½ hours); otherwise head for Lębork (19zł, 2¼ hours, five daily) and change there.

For the Kaszuby region, there are regular buses travelling to Kartuzy (12zł, one hour) and 15 daily services to Kościerzyna (9zł, 1¾ hours).

The private bus company Polski Express also connects to Warsaw twice a day (42zł to 48zł).

There are plenty of connections from Gdańsk to Western European cities; travel agencies (including Almatur and Orbis, p406) have information and sell tickets. PKS buses travel twice-daily (except Sunday) to Kaliningrad (32zł, five hours), and daily to Vilnius (149zł, 16 hours) via Olsztyn.

Ferry

Polferries (☎ 058 620 8761; www.polferries.pl) operates car ferries from Gdańsk Nowy Port (Map p407) to Nynäshamn in Sweden (adult/concession Skr670/560, 18 hours, up to four times weekly). Information, bookings and tickets can be obtained from Orbis and other travel agents. See also p520.

Train

The main train station, Gdańsk Główny (Map p408), on the western outskirts of the Old Town, handles all incoming and outgoing traffic. Note the station building itself, with the distinctive 'winged wheels' atop its roof; it's another historic monument that has been restored to its former glory.

Almost all long-distance trains to/from the south originate and terminate in Gdynia, while trains running along the coast to western destinations start in Gdańsk and stop at Gdynia en route. Timetables show departure times from all the main Tri-City stations – ensure you look at the correct column.

Gdańsk is a busy railway junction, with 18 services to Warsaw daily (82zł, 4½ hours). Trains go at least twice an hour to Malbork (16zł, 45 minutes), including seven fast trains daily to Olsztyn (34zł, 2½ hours). If you're travelling these routes and don't plan on stopping in Malbork, make sure your camera is ready as you pass the castle.

There are four fast trains to Wrocław (52zł, 7½ hours); they all go through Bydgoszcz (33zł, two hours) and Poznań (46zł, four hours). There are also six trains to Toruń (38zł, 3½ hours), and five to Szczecin (49zł,

5½ hours). For Łeba, take one of the frequent trains to Lębork (20zł, 1½ hours) and change there.

GETTING AROUND
To/From the Airport

Bus B goes to the airport up to twice hourly from Gdańsk Główny station (35 minutes), or you can take bus 110 from Gdańsk Wrzeszcz (35 minutes).

Boat

From April until October **Żegluga Gdańska** (Map p408; ☎ 058 301 4926; www.zegluga.gda.pl) runs pleasure boats and hydrofoils from Gdańsk's wharf, near the Green Gate, to Sopot (one way/return 44/60zł), Gdynia (52/70zł), Westerplatte (29/43zł) and across the Gulf of Gdańsk to the fishing village of Hel (60/76zł). Concession tickets cost about two-thirds of the normal fare, but are not available on the hydrofoils.

Another way to go to Hel is aboard the **Ferry Tram** (Tramwaj Wodny; Map p408; www.ztm.gda .pl/ferry), which departs from a point further up the wharf to Sopot (adult/concession 8/4zł, four daily) and Hel (16/8zł, three daily) each weekend during May and June, then daily from July to August. Bicycles cost an extra 2zł to transport.

The paddle-steamer company **Żegluga Pomeranka** (☎ 058 301 1300), leaving from a similar location, also runs regular boats to Westerplatte (one way/return 20/30zł) from May to September, usually including a visit to the port.

From the same departure point, **Ustka-Tour** (☎ 0501 571 383) operates cruises to Westerplatte (adult/concession return 30/20zł, six daily) aboard the *Galeon Lew*, a replica 17th-century galleon.

Car

Gdańsk's busy traffic isn't much fun to drive in, but if you'd like to hire a car for some day trips in the surrounding region, contact **Pol-Rent** (Map p408; ☎ 0601 502 501; www.polrent.com; ul Długa 67/68; per day from €25).

Train

A commuter train, known as the SKM (Szybka Kolej Miejska; Fast City Train), runs constantly between Gdańsk Główny and Gdynia Główna (4zł, 35 minutes), stopping at a dozen intermediate stations, including

Sopot (2.80zł). The trains run every five to 10 minutes at peak times and every hour or so late at night. You buy tickets at the stations and validate them in the big yellow boxes at the platform entrance (not in the train itself), or purchase them prevalidated from vending machines on the platform.

Tram & Bus

These are a slower means of transport than the SKM but cover more ground, running from 5am until around 11pm, when a handful of night lines take over. Fares depend on the duration of the journey: 1.40zł for up to 10 minutes, 2.80zł for 30 minutes and 4.20zł for one hour. A day ticket costs 9.10zł. Remember to validate your ticket in the vehicle, so it's stamped with the date and time.

AROUND GDAŃSK

SOPOT
pop 40,000

Prepare yourself for a shock if arriving in Sopot after a tour of Pomerania's rural districts – this is 21st-century Poland, writ large. As the favoured playground of citizens of neighbouring Gdynia and Gdańsk, along with plentiful international visitors, Sopot is sophisticated and cosmopolitan, and isn't afraid to show it. Unlike its rival seaside towns to the west, Sopot offers both beachfront attractions and cutting-edge urban style, being well populated with stylish bars, clubs and restaurants.

Sopot's incarnation as a fashionable resort arose in 1823 when Jean Georges Haffner, a former doctor in Napoleon's army, popularised sea bathing here. The settlement, originally established in the 13th century as a fishing village, rapidly became the beach destination of the rich and famous, particularly after WWI when it was included in the territory of the Free City of Danzig.

The resort life continues today, with Sopot attracting large numbers of visitors to its long, sandy beach and varied nightlife. Despite being at the centre of the Tri-City, Sopot has managed to maintain an identity separate from its two bigger neighbours. Though pricey in places, it's a fantastic place for some R&R and a splurge or two.

Information

Gamer (Map p427; ☎ 058 555 0183; ul Chopina 1; per hr 4zł; ⏰ 9am-10pm) Internet access.

Millennium Bank (Map p427; Plac Konstytucji 3 Maja 1)
NetCave (Map p427; ☎ 058 551 1183; www.netcave
.coco.pl; ul Pułaskiego 7A; per hr 4zł; ⏰ 10am-9pm)
Internet access.
Post office (Map p427; ul Kościuszki 2)
Sopot School of Polish for Foreigners (Map p427;
☎ 058 550 3284; www.ssp.edu.pl; Al Niepodległości 763)
Offers Polish language courses; arranges accommodation.
Tourist office (Map p427; ☎ 058 550 3783; www
.sopot.pl; ul Dworcowa 4; ⏰ 9am-8pm Jun-Sep, 10am-
6pm Oct-May)

Sights & Activities

Sopot's unavoidable pedestrian spine is **ul Bohaterów Monte Cassino**, an attractive and invariably crowded mall stretching from the railway line to the pier. On your way down the street, you can't fail to notice the warped, modern **Crooked House** (Krzywy Domek; Map p427; ☎ 058 555 5123; ul Bohaterów Monte Cassino 53), a building well worth investigating. Concealed within its twin-level innards are a dozen bars and restaurants, and several shops, including a wine outlet.

At the end of Monte Cassino, beyond Plac Zdrojowy, is the famous **Molo** (Map p427; ☎ 058 551 0002; www.molo.sopot.pl; adult/concession Mon-Thu 3/1.70zł, Fri-Sun 3.80/2zł), Europe's longest wooden pier, built in 1928 and jutting 515m out into the Gulf of Gdańsk. Various attractions along its length come and go with the seasons.

North of the pier is the landmark 1927 **Grand Hotel**, adjoining the long waterfront **spa park** that first popularised the town. The park backs directly onto the **beach**, arguably the finest in the Tri-City area and Sopot's *raison d'être* in the all-too-short summer season. Towards the northern end of this stretch is the large **Aqua Park** (Map p407; ☎ 058 555 8555; www.aqua parksopot.pl; ul Zamkowa Góra 3/5; per hr 10zł; ⏰ 9am-8pm), which has tubes, slides, spas and a wild river ride, guaranteed to keep the kids happy.

At the southern end of the beachfront, the **Sopot Museum** (Muzeum Sopotu; Map p427; ☎ 058 551 2266; www.muzeumsopotu.pl; ul Poniatowskiego 8; adult/concession 7/5zł; ⏰ 10am-4pm Tue-Fri, 11am-5pm Sat & Sun) showcases 19th-century furniture and fittings within a grand villa of that era, including some enormous, ornately carved wardrobes. There's an English-language brochure detailing the history of the house, and its attractive architecture is worth a look in its own right.

If you wander about Sopot's back streets, you'll find more fine **villas** (Map p427) from Sopot's 19th-century heyday as the German resort town Zoppot; some of the best examples are on ul Obrońców Westerplatte.

The western part of Sopot, behind the railway track, consists of newer suburbs, which ascend gradually, finally giving way to a wooded hilly area. Here is the **Opera Leśna** (Opera in the Woods; Map p407; ☎ 058 555 8440; www .bart.sopot.pl; ul Moniuszki 12), an amphitheatre that seats 5000 people, and where the prestigious **International Sopot Festival** (☎ 058 555 8440; www .sopotfestival.onet.pl) has been held in late August for over 40 years. The festival began life as a Eurovision-style song contest and still draws crowds to its competing mix of local and international artists.

Sleeping

If you're a budget traveller, you may find Sopot a bit traumatic – there are few low-cost options, and none in the centre of town. As it's a seaside resort, accommodation varies hugely in price and quantity between the high and low seasons. Year-round facilities are supplemented by a variety of pensions and holiday homes in summer. Prices listed are for the high season, which peaks in July and August and can be very, very busy – so book ahead and prepare for high prices. Alternatively, stay in Gdańsk or Gdynia and commute to Sopot via the SKM commuter train.

A good place to start is the tourist office, whose friendly staff keep track of accommodation options, from private rooms and student dorms to holiday homes and villas. There are always locals hanging around the verandah of the office (even when it's closed), offering rooms in their own houses, which start from 25zł per person. Competition can be fierce, and some of the old ladies, in particular, market their lodgings very forcefully!

Pensjonat Eden (Map p427; ☎ 058 551 1503; www .hotel-eden.com.pl; ul Kordeckiego 4/6; s 100-180zł, d 170-260zł, tr/q/ste 320/360/410zł; P) It may not be paradise in the strictest sense of the word, but the Eden's comfortable rooms are attractively decked out with vintage touches such as wooden furniture, lace tablecloths and artfully old-fashioned radios, though the place could do with a coat of paint to freshen its appearance.

Willa Zacisze (Map p427; ☎ 058 551 7868; www .apartamenty.gda.pl; ul Grunwaldzka 22a; apt 240zł; P ✗) These apartments with modern furniture and fittings allow some savings on meals, as they're fitted out with kitchens, and they're in a great location close to both the beach and entertainment options.

Pensjonat Wanda (Map p427; ☎ 058 550 3037; www .bsw-hotele.pl; ul Poniatowskiego 7; s 200-250zł, d 250-390zł, tr 410zł; P ☐) Ambient three-star pension offering tastefully traditional accommodation, though the curious moulded leather artwork on the walls adds a quirky note to the décor. Its light-filled rooms are decorated with pine tones and yellow wallpaper, and some have balconies overlooking the sea and sand. There's also a restaurant and sauna.

Willa Karat II (Map p427; ☎ 058 550 0742; www .willakarat.pl; ul 3 Maja 31; s/d/tr/q 170/270/290/300zł, ste 340-380zł; P) Though it's tucked away at the end of a scrappy laneway full of parked cars, the Willa Karat has light, spacious rooms vividly decorated with bright colours and simple timber furniture, lending a homely touch. Say hello to the budgie as you pass in and out.

Zhong Hua Hotel (Map p427; ☎ 058 550 2020; www .hotelchinski.pl; Al Wojska Polskiego 1; s/d 470/500zł, apt 620-740zł) Unique hotel housed within a vast timber pavilion in Chinese style; even the receptionists are clad in cheongsams. The rooms are located literally on the beach, and are small but contain elegant lacquered furniture, and bathrooms with marble fittings. The onsite restaurant also offers Baltic vistas, and a range of Chinese dishes.

Hotel Rezydent (Map p427; ☎ 058 555 5800; www .hotelrezydent.pl; Plac Konstytucji 3 Maja 3; s 530-580zł, d 650-990zł, ste 2500zł; P ✗ ✗ ☐ ☐) The Rezydent is the most elegant hotel in town, though you'll need an inelegantly fat wallet to stay here. Its rooms' tasteful tones are set-off by stylish carpets, timber furniture and gleaming bathrooms. When you've finished luxuriating, there's a classy restaurant and pub downstairs, along with an art gallery, a sauna and massage services.

Camping Nr 19 (Map p407; ☎ 058 550 0445; ul Zamkowa Góra 25; camp site per adult/child 12/6zł, tent additional 5zł, bungalows 90-160zł; ☼ May-Sep; P) Located in the northern end of town (a five-minute walk from the Sopot Kamienny Potok train station), Camping Nr 19 is a good big camping ground right by the Aqua Park and the beach.

Eating

Much of Sopot's cuisine scene is seasonal, particularly in the beach area, but there's no shortage of good options that stay open all year.

SOPOT

0 ————— 200 m
0 ————— 0.1 miles

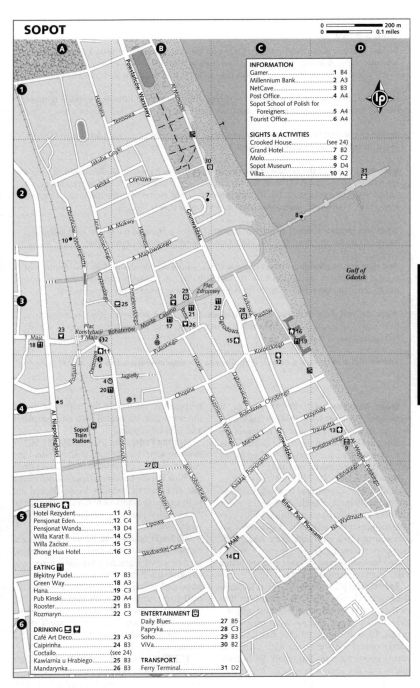

INFORMATION		
Gamer	1	B4
Millennium Bank	2	A3
NetCave	3	B3
Post Office	4	A4
Sopot School of Polish for		
Foreigners	5	A4
Tourist Office	6	A4

SIGHTS & ACTIVITIES		
Crooked House	(see 24)	
Grand Hotel	7	B2
Molo	8	C2
Sopot Museum	9	D4
Villas	10	A2

Gulf of Gdańsk

POMERANIA

Plac Zdrojowy

Plac Konstytucji 3 Maja

Sopot Train Station

SLEEPING		
Hotel Rezydent	11	A3
Pensjonat Eden	12	C4
Pensjonat Wanda	13	D4
Willa Karat II	14	C5
Willa Zacisze	15	C3
Zhong Hua Hotel	16	C3

EATING		
Błękitny Pudel	17	B3
Green Way	18	A3
Hana	19	C3
Pub Kinski	20	A4
Rooster	21	B3
Rozmaryn	22	C3

DRINKING		
Café Art Deco	23	A3
Caipirinha	24	B3
Coctailo	(see 24)	
Kawiarnia u Hrabiego	25	B3
Mandarynka	26	B3

ENTERTAINMENT		
Daily Blues	27	B5
Papryka	28	C3
Soho	29	B3
ViVa	30	B2

TRANSPORT		
Ferry Terminal	31	D2

VARIED MENU

Bogdan Grabarczyk has lived in the Tri-City all his life, and in Sopot for the past quarter-century. A former shipyard worker turned restaurateur, he's in the thick of the seasonal action each year in the seaside town. Author Tim Richards talks to him about his home and colourful career.

How is Sopot different from Gdańsk or Gdynia? It's still a small fisherman's village between two big towns…but it isn't a village and there aren't any fishermen. Well, maybe a few.

What's the atmosphere of Sopot? It's like a magic village. Heavy industry doesn't exist in Sopot. There are a lot of old houses, they create a special atmosphere.

But what's it like in the middle of the season? Sometimes it's too much. Thousands of people are walking up and down ul Bohaterów Monte Cassino, just one street. Yeah, Sopot means Monte Casino Street to most people. But it's concentrated – a few metres from the main road it's totally empty. The back streets have atmosphere and a special style.

What was the most recent restaurant you ran? It was a seasonal restaurant, with coffee and cakes and vodka and beer. And fast food, Chinese food. We had a Chinese chef.

And now you're planning a new restaurant? Yes, on the seaside about 70km from Sopot, past Gdynia, with Chinese and Indian food. My wife Gosia was on holiday in India, and she met these Indian chefs and organised visas for these guys to come to Poland. Lots of paperwork!

What did you do before you ran these places? I built and renovated ships in shipyards in Poland and Lithuania. And I also exported fish products, and was deputy manager in a paint factory, and worked in a sand quarry.

You've had a very varied career. Why did you become interested in restaurants? I like to cook. So why not?

Green Way (Map p427; ☎ 0502 309 744; Al Niepodległości 786; mains 6-12zł; ⏰ 10am-7pm Mon-Fri, noon-7pm Sat & Sun; ✗) Similar to its franchise siblings in Gdańsk and the rest of Poland, this is a simple green-hued eatery trading on its excellent budget vegetarian food.

Hana (☎ Map p427; 058 550 2020; ul Wojska Polskiego 1; mains 9-95zł; ⏰ 1pm-midnight) Japanese food has arrived in Poland, muscling aside the older Chinese and Vietnamese outlets. This restaurant presents a selection of quality sushi and sashimi in a compact space lined with rice-paper screens. The set menus (90zł to 150zł) include several courses and are better value than ordering à la carte.

Rooster (Map p427; ☎ 058 550 7404; ul Bohaterów Monte Cassino 54; mains 12-57zł; ⏰ 11am-midnight Mon-Fri, 11am-1am Sat, 11am-11pm Sun) Feast on burgers, shawarmas, salads and pastas at reasonable prices, though the proprietor has unfortunately issued the waitresses with shiny red shorts about six sizes too small. Sit outside and watch the tourist hordes go by, or stay within and marvel at the barn-like Texan diner interior, decorated with number plates and telephone poles.

Błękitny Pudel (Map p427; ☎ 058 551 1672; ul Bohaterów Monte Cassino 44; mains 19-37zł; ⏰ 9am-11pm) A cosy place in the middle of the main drag, the Blue Poodle features a front room looking like an eccentric nanna's house, decked out with a strange assortment of random objects. As an added plus it serves German Paulaner wheat beer.

Pub Kinski (Map p427; ☎ 058 802 5638; ul Kościuszki 10; mains 25-30zł; ⏰ 1pm-3am) The house and birthplace of legendary German actor and psychopath Klaus Kinski (see boxed text, opposite) has been converted into an off-beat bar-restaurant, with film posters and decadent crimson tablecloths within a cosy, candle-lit setting. The man himself probably would have trashed the place, but in a loving way.

ourpick Rozmaryn (Map p427; ☎ 058 551 1104; ul Ogrodowa 8; mains 36-99zł; ⏰ 2-11pm Mon-Fri, 1-11pm Sat

& Sun) It may be the most pricey restaurant in town, but there's a reason – the Italian food served here is excellent, as is the tasteful décor. In addition to the soups, pastas and salads, there are more exotic dishes such as curries. Service and presentation is top class, and there's a way to enjoy it without breaking the budget: dine here between 1pm and 5pm on weekends, when all the dishes are discounted by 50%.

Drinking

ourpick Mandarynka (Map p427; ☎ 058 550 4563; www .mandarynka.pl; ul Bema 6) This very cool confection of timber tables, scarlet lampshades and huge orange cushions, is about as loungey as it gets. The bartenders seem to be on first-name terms with all the patrons, and are superbly nonchalant to boot. There's a food menu, and a DJ in action upstairs most nights.

Coctailo (Map p427; ☎ 0696 501 462; ul Haffnera 6; ☽ 10am-2am) Bright little drinking space hidden from ul Bohaterów Monte Cassino at the back of the Crooked House, with a cosy light-filled interior and a peaceful outdoor seating area. The drinks list contains Italian wines by the glass (6zł to 15zł), along with good coffee, smoothies and ice cream sundaes.

Caipirinha (Map p427; ☎ 058 555 5380; ul Bohaterów Monte Cassino 53; ☽ 10am-midnight) Another good bar set within the surreal façade of the Crooked House, it serves plenty of cocktails, including local creations like the Sopot Special Night, featuring peach liqueur. It also has a decent selection of nonalcoholic drinks and light meals.

Café Art Deco (Map p427; ☎ 058 555 0160; ul Bohaterów Monte Cassino 9a; ☽ 11am-10pm; ✗) Tucked away at the quiet western end of Monte Cassino in a small courtyard back from the street, the tiny Art Deco serves some alcoholic tipples, but it's the coffee that makes it special. It's an atmospheric update of the classic Polish *kawiarnia* (café) that defies the current onslaught of cookie-cutter café chains.

Kawiarnia u Hrabiego (Map p427; ☎ 058 550 1997; ul Czyżewskiego 12; ☽ 10am-10pm) The oldest family home in Sopot now houses a charming little café and art gallery, far from the madding summer crowds. The quaint interior is perfect

POMERANIA

FEELING KINSKI

If you've ever seen a Klaus Kinski film, you won't have any difficulty believing the many outlandish stories about the actor. Kinski's wild, piercing eyes and unruly blonde hair gave him the look of an Aryan angel gone bad, and the manic intensity he brought to his roles was merely a muted version of his off-screen persona. He was arguably the ultimate Method actor, seeing his body as a conduit for the souls of the characters he portrayed.

The actor's finest work came in his collaborations with equally idiosyncratic German New Wave director Werner Herzog. The two met while sharing an apartment in Munich in the 1950s, when 13-year-old Herzog watched Kinski destroying everything around him in a spectacular outburst of rage. Their working relationship involved much the same volatility – one classic archive photo shows Kinski attacking the director with a machete, while on another occasion Herzog put a gun to his star's head to persuade him to keep working. The roll call of Kinski's memorable work with Herzog includes *Aguirre, Wrath of God* (1972), *Nosferatu the Vampyre* (1979) and *Cobra Verde* (1987).

Kinski refused to distinguish between art-house and commercial projects, accepting work regardless of its audience or quality. He memorably described his chosen profession as 'prostitution', basing decisions purely on who he was selling himself to, and for how much – busking French poetry in a Berlin bar for pfennigs was the same to him as performing *Hamlet* for a lucrative private client.

Alongside acting and money, Kinski's main obsession was women. Considering himself a reincarnation of the legendary 'devil violinist', composer and philanderer Niccolò Paganini, Kinski threw himself into the constant pursuit of sexual conquests, with breathtaking success. Towards the end of his life the great actor finally completed his 20-year ambition to make a film biography of Paganini; the end product was cut to shreds by distributors and censors due to its highly explicit content, but remains a unique, fragmented, glorious chaos, saying as much about Kinski as it does about his idol. Of all his films, this is perhaps the greatest expression of his truly twisted genius.

for cake and conversation, and there's seating in the garden terrace.

Entertainment

Sopot has a vibrant club and live music culture that's always changing; ask the locals about the current hot favourites. The scene here is also notably gay-friendly: check www.gay poland.pl for updates on local venues.

Papryka (Map p427; ☎ 058 551 7476; www.klub papryka.pl; ul Grunwaldzka 11; ☺ 3pm-late) This appealing timbered villa near the beach buzzes on all levels – the two floors, balcony and beer garden are set in an attractive park surrounding the club. Music includes house, dub and alternative sounds. You must be 21 or older to enter.

Soho (Map p427; ☎ 058 551 6927; ul Bohaterów Monte Cassino 61; ☺ noon-3am Sun-Thu, noon-5am Fri & Sat) This long-time hot spot still hasn't lost it. Haunt of the cool people, including scenesters, celebs and fashionistas, Soho goes for a surprisingly rough-cut retro style: brown walls, pink and yellow stripes, and red lighting fixtures to set off the glamorous crowds.

ViVa (Map p427; ☎ 058 551 6268; www.vivaclub.pl; Al Mamuszki 2; admission free-25zł; ☺ 9pm-late; P) The self-proclaimed 'Number One in the Tri-City' is still a top spot around for all-out spectacle, hosting vast beachfront dance nights with all the eye candy and hi-tech wizardry it can muster.

Daily Blues (Map p427; ☎ 058 551 3939; www.daily blues.com.pl; ul Władysława IV 1a; ☺ 4pm-3am) Hidden away in a quiet residential street, this laid-back venue sings the blues daily, with jam sessions on Mondays, Wednesdays and Sundays. Join the happy crowd in its squeezy confines.

Getting There & Away

All trains that service Gdańsk go to Gdynia and stop in Sopot – see p424. Commuter trains to Gdańsk and Gdynia (2.80zł) run every five to 10 minutes at peak times.

A regular ferry service dubbed the **Ferry Tram** (Tramwaj Wodny; www.ztm.gda.pl/ferry) heads from Sopot to Hel or Gdańsk (see p424). Other boats connect Sopot to Gdynia (p432). The landing site is at the pier.

GDYNIA

pop 252,000

You couldn't say Gdynia shares the charms of its southern neighbours in the Tri-City.

As a relatively modern city, it lacks the historic touch and has a little too much concrete for most tastes. However, its broad, straight streets lend the place a look unlike any other Polish city, and it has enough interesting sights to justify a day trip.

Gdynia wasn't always an industrial city; it managed to progress from the 14th century to the early 20th century as a humble fishing village. However, in the aftermath of WWI, when Poland was reconstituted without regaining Gdańsk, the Polish government decided to build a new outlet to the sea. By the 1930s, Gdynia was the largest and most modern port on the Baltic.

The port was badly damaged during WWII, but was rebuilt and modernised and is now the base for much of Poland's merchant and fishing fleet.

Information

Baltic Information Point (Map p431; ☎ 058 620 7711; Molo Południowe; ☺ 9am-6pm Mon-Fri, 10am-5pm Sat, 10am-4pm Sun)

Bank Pekao (Map p431; ul 10 Lutego 8)

C@fluna Internet (Map p431; ☎ 058 661 2209; ul Armii Krajowej 13; per hr 4zł; ☺ 10am-9pm Mon-Sat) Internet access.

Orbis Travel (Map p431; ☎ 058 620 4844; ul 10 Lutego 2) Travel agent.

Post office (Map p431; ul 10 Lutego 10)

Silver Zone (Map p431; ☎ 058 628 1800; ul Waszyngtona 21; per hr 6zł; ☺ 10am-10pm) Internet access, part of the Silver Screen cinema within the Centrum Gemini building.

Tourist information booth (Map p431; ☎ 058 628 5466; www.gdynia.pl; Gdynia Główna train station; ☺ 8am-6pm Mon-Fri, 9am-4pm Sat, 9am-3pm Sun May-Sep, 10am-5pm Mon-Fri, 10am-3pm Sat Oct-Apr)

Sights & Activities

Gdynia's tourist zone is anchored at its **Southern Pier** (Molo Południowe; Map p431). Moored on the northern side are two museum ships, a highlight for visitors. The beautiful three-masted frigate **Dar Pomorza** (Map p431; ☎ 058 620 2371; adult/concession 6/3zł; ☺ 9am-6pm daily Jun-Sep, 10am-4pm Tue-Sun Oct-May) was built in Hamburg in 1909 and used as a training ship for German sailors. Check out the information in English on the dockside before you step aboard.

Next door, the destroyer **Błyskawica** (Map p431; ☎ 058 626 3658; adult/concession 8/4zł; ☺ 10.10am-1pm

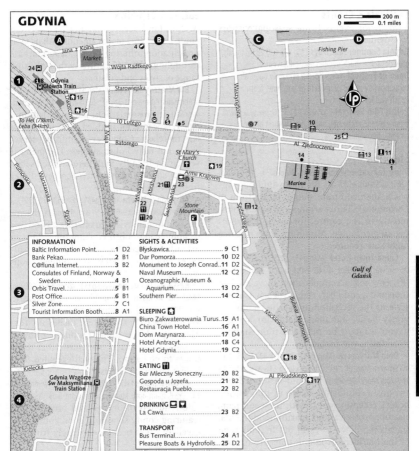

GDYNIA

0   200 m
0   0.1 miles

Fishing Pier

Gulf of
Gdańsk

POMERANIA

INFORMATION
Baltic Information Point..........**1** D2
Bank Pekao.............................**2** B1
C@fluna Internet..................**3** B2
Consulates of Finland, Norway &
  Sweden...............................**4** B1
Orbis Travel.........................**5** B1
Post Office..........................**6** B1
Silver Zone..........................**7** C1
Tourist Information Booth......**8** A1

SIGHTS & ACTIVITIES
Błyskawica.............................**9** C1
Dar Pomorza........................**10** B2
Monument to Joseph Conrad..**11** D2
Naval Museum......................**12** C2
Oceanographic Museum &
  Aquarium.........................**13** D2
Southern Pier.......................**14** C2

SLEEPING
Biuro Zakwaterowania Turus.**15** A1
China Town Hotel................**16** A1
Dom Marynarza....................**17** D4
Hotel Antracyt.....................**18** C4
Hotel Gdynia.......................**19** C2

EATING
Bar Mleczny Słoneczny.........**20** B2
Gospoda u Józefa................**21** B2
Restauracja Pueblo..............**22** B2

DRINKING
La Cawa..............................**23** B2

TRANSPORT
Bus Terminal.......................**24** A1
Pleasure Boats & Hydrofoils...**25** D2

& 2-5pm Tue-Sun May-Sep) has a fascinating story. Escaping capture in 1939 by the German invaders, it went on to serve successfully with Allied naval forces throughout WWII. In 1987 it was awarded the Golden Cross of Military Virtue, the only Polish ship to receive this honour. Now it's a floating museum, and you can buy an informative English language booklet (5zł) from the on-board shop which outlines its history.

Near the tip of the pier is the **Oceanographic Museum & Aquarium** (Muzeum Oceanograficzne i Akwarium Morskie; Map p431; ☎ 058 621 7021; www.akwarium.gdynia .pl; Al Zjednoczenia 1; adult/concession 11/7zł; ☼ 9am-7pm daily May-Aug, 10am-5pm Tue-Sun Sep-Apr), a minimally interesting institution that improves once you encounter its bigger residents such as

moray eels and a green turtle. Beyond it is a large **monument** (Map p431) to Józef Konrad Korzeniowski, better known to the English-speaking world as author Joseph Conrad.

South of the pier, on Bulwar Nadmorski, is the **Naval Museum** (Muzeum Marynarki Wojennej; Map p431; ☎ 058 626 3984; ul Sędzickiego 3; adult/concession 4/2zł, free Fri; ☼ 10am-4pm Tue-Sun). It has a display of guns, fighter planes, helicopters and rockets, mostly of interest to militaria aficionados.

Behind the museum is a 52m-high hill called **Stone Mountain** (Kamienna Góra; Map p431), which provides views over the beach, the city centre and the harbour from its pretty parkland summit. Keen cyclists or walkers can follow the Bulwar Nadmorski beach road down to Sopot and Gdańsk.

Festivals & Events

Two major events bring seasonal visitors to Gdynia:

Gdynia Summer Jazz Days (☎ 058 620 2836) In July, provides some much-needed musical flavour.

Open'er Festival (www.opener.pl) Lively open-air contemporary music event held in late June, featuring Polish and foreign bands.

Polish Film Festival (☎ 058 621 1509; www.festiwal filmow.pl) In September; highlights the best of the national film industry.

Sleeping

Biuro Zakwaterowania Turus (Map p431; ☎ 058 621 8265; ul Starowiejska 47) Behind a building opposite the main train station (enter from ul Dworcowa), Turus arranges private rooms, mostly in the centre, for around 40/80zł per single/double. Minimum stays of three nights are required.

China Town Hotel (Map p431; ☎ 058 620 9221; ul Dworcowa 11a; s 90zł, d 140-190zł, tr 240-260zł, q 280zł; ⓟ) Low-cost accommodation above a kebab shop and a sushi bar, with a vaguely Chinese style in the reception area. The rooms are pretty basic, but manageable for a night if you want to be near the train station. Breakfast is not included.

Dom Marynarza (Map p431; ☎ 058 622 0025; dom marynarza@wp.pl; Al Piłsudskiego 1; s/d/tr/q/ste 160/200/245/260/360zł) The old-fashioned but curiously comforting décor in this seaside hotel's reception area, with its wood panels supporting various maritime oddments, signals the down-to-earth but friendly tone of the Mariner's Home. Rooms are reasonable, and there's a beer garden out front in summer.

Hotel Antracyt (Map p431; ☎ 058 620 6571; www .hotel-antracyt.pl; ul Korzeniowskiego 19; s/d/tr/ste 180/260/320/400zł; ⓟ ⊠ ▣) Located on a pleasant leafy hill, the Antracyt offers spacious comfortable rooms with views over the sea, just a stagger from the beach. Ask for one with a balcony.

Hotel Gdynia (Map p431; ☎ 058 666 3040; www.orbis .pl; ul Armii Krajowej 22; r €90, ste €150; ⓟ ⊠ ▣ ▣) The hideous concrete exterior of the local Orbis complex evokes the worst architectural excesses of postwar Poland, and the abstract lime-green lightshades in the foyer don't help. However, it has the best range of facilities in Gdynia, and good views from the upper floors.

Eating & Drinking

Architectural beauty may not be its strong point, but Gdynia makes amends with its food presentation, offering plenty of restaurants throughout the city centre with a pleasing range of styles and cuisines.

Bar Mleczny Słoneczny (Map p431; ☎ 058 620 5316; ul Abrahama 60; mains 1-5zł; ⏱ 6.30am-7pm Mon-Fri, 9am-4pm Sat) Surprisingly light and airy, within a pale yellow interior studded with curious pillars, this classic Cold War-era milk bar serves cheap but tasty Polish staples. The menu is vegetarian-friendly, and there's a good selection of soups and *naleśniki* (crepes). Enter from ul Władysława IV.

Gospoda u Józefa (Map p431; ☎ 058 620 3051; ul Świętojańska 49; mains 9-65zł; ⏱ 8am-11pm) A charming traditional-style café offering a good line in homemade Polish cooking, including an extensive choice of sweet and savoury pancakes, along with *pierogi* (dumplings), soups and salads.

Restauracja Pueblo (Map p431; ☎ 058 621 6007; ul Abrahama 56; mains 15-40zł; ⏱ noon-11pm) Next to Bar Mleczny Słoneczny and entered from ul Władysława IV, this eatery dishes up Tex-Mex with all the usual trappings: primary colours, funky lamps and music that really wants to be Latino. The well-executed food is an unexpected bonus.

La Cawa (Map p431; ☎ 058 782 0640; ul Świętojańska 35; ⏱ 8.30am-8pm Mon-Fri, 9am-8pm Sat) Mellow café rendered in orange and brown tones featuring comfy sofas and good coffee. The excellent cakes beckon enticingly from the display cabinet.

Getting There & Away

BOAT

Stena Line (☎ 058 660 9200; www.stenaline.pl) operates ferries to/from Karlskrona, Sweden (adult 155zł to 185zł, concession 130zł to 155zł, 10½ to 12 hours, two or three daily). Services depart from the **Ferry Terminal** (Terminal Promowy; Map p407; ul Kwiatkowskiego 60), 5km northwest of central Gdynia. Information, bookings and tickets can be obtained from Orbis and other travel agents. See also p520.

There are pleasure boats/hydrofoils to Gdańsk (one way/return 52/70zł), Sopot (35/20zł) and Hel (48/35zł) from May to September, departing from the southern pier. One-hour boat excursions go several times daily from April to October (15zł to 23zł).

BUS

The bus terminal (Map p431) is next to the train station. Regional routes include Hel (13zł, 2½ hours, hourly) and Łeba (15zł, three hours, three daily). Polski Express runs services twice a day to Warsaw (45zł to 59zł), calling at Sopot and Gdańsk on the way.

TRAIN

For long-distance trains, see p424. There are several trains daily to Hel (13zł, 1¾ hours, hourly in summer). Roughly hourly trains run to Lębork (16zł, 50 minutes), where you can change for Łeba.

HEL PENINSULA

Located north of the Tri-City and arcing out into the Baltic Sea, the Hel Peninsula (Półwysep Helski) is a 34km-long, crescent-shaped sandbank. The peninsula is only 300m wide at the base and no wider than 500m for most of its length. Only close to the end does it expand out, reaching a breadth of about 3km. The highest point of the peninsula is 23m above sea level. Much of the landscape is covered with trees – picturesque, wind-deformed pines predominate – and there's also a number of typical coastal plant varieties including sand sedge and dune thistle.

The peninsula was formed over the course of about 8000 years by sea currents and winds, which gradually created an uninterrupted belt of sand. At the end of the 17th century, as old maps show, the sand bar was still cut by six inlets, making it a chain of islands. In the 19th century the peninsula was cut into separate pieces several times by storms. The edges have been strengthened and the movement of the sand has been reduced by vegetation, but the sand bar continues to grow.

The peninsula is bookended by two fishing ports: Hel at its tip and Władysławowo at its base. Between them is a third port, Jastarnia, and three villages: Chałupy, Kuźnica and Jurata. All are tourist resorts during the short summer season (July and August). There's a railway and a good road running the whole length of the peninsula.

All along the northern shore stretch beautiful sandy beaches and, except for small areas around the resorts (which are usually packed with holidaymakers), they are clean and deserted.

The Hel Peninsula is easily accessible from the Tri-City by train, bus and boat. The bus and train can take you anywhere you want, while boats and hydrofoils sail from Gdańsk, Sopot and Gdynia to Hel. A boat trip is the most popular way of getting a feel for the peninsula.

Hel
pop 3900

Let's face it…this town has a name that amuses English speakers, prompting gags about 'when Hel freezes over', 'a cold day in Hel' and 'to Hel and back'. When the clever wordplay is out of the way, however, what remains is a pleasant, relaxed holiday town. At the end of its long slender sand bar, it feels like it's a million miles from the worries of the wider world.

Dependent on seasonal influxes of visitors, Hel is almost dead in winter. In summer, it transforms into a cheerful, lively beach town, its main street full of holidaymakers browsing souvenir stands or having a drink in the numerous beer gardens.

Throughout history, the town benefited from its strategic location at the maritime gateway to Gdańsk. By the 14th century Hel was a prosperous fishing port and trading centre. However, it was constantly threatened by storms and the shifting coastline, and declined in importance in the 18th century before reinventing itself as a popular seaside resort.

SIGHTS

As you walk from the train station to the town centre, you'll notice a park containing a **memorial** to the 1939 defence of the town during the Nazi invasion. Hel was the last place in Poland to surrender; a garrison of some 3000 Polish soldiers defended the town until 2 October. The peninsula became a battlefield once more on 5 April 1945, when about 60,000 Germans were caught in a bottleneck by the Red Army and didn't lay down their arms until 9 May; this time it was the last piece of Polish territory to be liberated.

Just off the beach in the centre is the **Fokarium** (☎ 058 675 0836; www.fokarium.com; ul Morska 2; admission 2zł; ☺ 8.30am-dusk), Hel's signature attraction, and the place to see Baltic grey seals. It has three large tanks housing half a dozen of the creatures, and feeding takes place at 11am and 3pm. The grey seal is the largest and most populous seal species in the Baltic, numbering about 20,000, but it's under threat from development and pollution. Even in the Fokarium itself, the seals have been endangered by the superstitious Polish habit of throwing coins into any body of water; one of the older animals actually died in 2001 after eating massive amounts of small change over several years. Grisly posters warn visitors against repeating the incident. On your way in and out of the facility, there's no shortage of stallholders willing to sell you plush seals dressed as pirates or sailors, and other such amusing tourist tat.

Elsewhere in town, a dozen 19th-century, half-timbered **fishing houses** on the main street, ul Wiejska, managed to survive Hel's various battles. The oldest building in town is the Gothic church dating from the 1420s, which is now the **Museum of Fishery** (Muzeum Rybołówstwa; ☎ 058 675 0552; Bulwar Nadmorski 2; adult/concession 5/3zł; ☺ 10am-6pm daily Jul & Aug, 10am-4pm Tue-Sun Sep-Jun). It features exhibits on fishing and boat-building techniques, plus a collection of old fishing boats. Though it's attractively laid out, with picturesque fishing boats, dioramas and stuffed sea birds, the lack of English captions robs it of context. Go up to the **tower** for good views over the town, the peninsula and the Gulf of Gdańsk.

There's a beautiful 100m-wide beach on the sea coast, 1km north of town, and you can visit the 42m-high brick **lighthouse** (☎ 058 675 0617; ul Bałtycka 3; adult/concession 3/2zł; ☺ 10am-2pm & 3-7pm Jul & Aug, 10am-2pm & 3-6pm Sep).

SLEEPING & EATING

The town has a reasonable array of places to stay and eat, most of which only open in summer. Many locals rent out rooms in their homes – just ask around. The usual price is about 65zł per double room, but you'll probably find that few locals will want to rent out a room for just one night.

Some of the tourist restaurants on ul Wiejska also offer rooms. Try the **Captain Morgan Pub Hotel** (☎ 058 675 0091; ul Wiejska 21) or **Admiral Nelson** (☎ 058 675 1155; ul Wiejska 62) – a double room costs 100zł at either of them.

GETTING THERE & AWAY

Hel can be reached by road and rail; even in the off-season there are fairly regular services by train and bus from Gdynia. When you arrive by rail, follow the brick footpath 500m to the town centre.

You can also get to Hel via the **Ferry Tram** (Tramwaj Wodny; www.ztm.gda.pl/ferry) from Gdańsk or Sopot (see p424).

Another waterborne option is the pleasure boat/hydrofoil from May to September from Gdańsk (p424) and Gdynia (p432).

If you arrive by train and don't feel like walking to the sights, electric-car operators tout for business at the train station as services arrive, and will happily drive you to Hel and back (5zł one way to the town centre, other places negotiable).

Around Hel

For a change from Hel, you may like to stroll along the beach to **Jurata** (12km) or 2km further to **Jastarnia** and take the train back from there, or stay for the night. Both are lively holiday resorts and have camping grounds, places to eat, some nightlife and a range of holiday homes.

Further northwest are two tiny ports, **Kuźnica** and **Chałupy**, which have retained more of their old atmosphere than other places on the peninsula. Finally you get back to the base of the peninsula at **Władysławowo**, which is a large fishing port and town of some 13,000 people, and has a good wide beach. The town has a number of accommodation options and an array of restaurants.

Between Chałupy and Władysławowo, there are several camping grounds that have windsurfing centres. One place you can hire windsurfing gear and catamarans from May to October is **Camp Solar** (☎ 058 677 8967; www .obozy-windsurfingowe.pl; ul Droga Helska, Chałupy; per hr from 30zł).

Around 8km west along the coast from Władysławowo is the **Rozewie Cape** (Przylądek Rozewie), the northernmost tip of Poland. Its 33m-high cliff-top lighthouse has a small **museum** (☎ 058 674 9542; ul Leona Wzorka 1, Jastrzębia Góra; adult/concession 5/3zł; ☺ 9.30am-2pm & 3-7pm Jul & Aug, 10am-2pm & 3-6pm Sep); you can go to the top for sweeping views.

KASHUBIA

If you believe the legend, the region of Kashubia (Kaszuby) was created by giants, whose footprints account for the many hills and lakes that characterise the landscape. Stretching for 100km southwest of Gdańsk, it's a picturesque area noted for its small, traditional villages, and its lack of cities and industry.

In contrast to most of the other groups who gradually merged to form one big family of Poles, the Kashubians have managed to retain some of their early ethnic identity, expressed in their distinctive culture, dress, crafts, architecture and language.

The Kashubian language, still spoken by some of the old generation, is the most distinct dialect of Polish; other Poles have a hard time understanding it. It's thought to derive from the ancient Pomeranian language.

The area between Kartuzy and Kościerzyna is the most topographically diverse part of the region, including the highest point of Kashubia, Mt Wieżyca (329m). This is the most touristy area of Kashubia, with an array of facilities. Public transport between Kartuzy and Kościerzyna is fairly regular, with buses running every hour or two.

Unless you have your own transport, you miss out on some of the region by being limited to the major routes. Public transport becomes less frequent the further off the track you go. Visiting the two regional destinations Kartuzy (below) and Wdzydze Kiszewskie (right) will give a taste of the culture of Kashubia, though less of its natural beauty.

Kartuzy
pop 15,000

The town of Kartuzy, 30km west of Gdańsk, owes its birth and its name to the Carthusians, a religious order that was brought here from Bohemia in 1380. Originally founded in 1084 near Grenoble in France, the order was known for its austere monastic rules – its monks passing their days in the contemplation of death, following the motto 'Memento Mori' (Remember You Must Die).

When they arrived in Kartuzy the monks built a church and, beside it, 18 hermitages laid out in the shape of a horseshoe. The **church** (☎ 058 681 2085; ul Klasztorna 5) seems to be a declaration of the monks' philosophy; the original Gothic brick structure was topped in the 1730s with a Baroque roof that looks like a huge coffin. On the outer wall of the chancel there's a sundial and, just beneath it, a skull with the 'Memento Mori' inscription.

The maxim is also tangibly manifested inside, on the clock on the balustrade of the organ loft. Its pendulum is in the form of the angel of death armed with a scythe. The clock is tactfully stopped if there's an unusual number of funerals in town.

The interior fittings are mainly Baroque, and the richly carved stalls deserve a closer look. There's some unusual cordovan (painting on goat leather) decoration (1685) in the chancel, while the church's oldest artefact, an extraordinary panel from a 15th-century Gothic triptych, is in the right-hand chapel.

Another attraction is the **Kashubian Museum** (Muzeum Kaszubskie; ☎ 058 681 1442; www.muzeum -kaszubskie.gda.pl; ul Kościerska 1; adult/concession 7.50/5.50zł; ⏰ 8am-4pm Tue-Fri, 8am-3pm Sat year-round, 10am-2pm Sun May-Sep), south of the train station near the railway track. It depicts the traditional culture of the region, with everything from curious folk instruments to typical household implements and furniture.

There's only one hotel in town, but you can easily leave on one of the hourly buses to Gdańsk (12zł, one hour).

Wdzydze Kiszewskie
pop 1000

The small village of Wdzydze Kiszewskie, 16km south of Kościerzyna, boasts an interesting **skansen** (Kaszubski Park Etnograficzny; ☎ 058 686 1288; www.muzeum-wdzydze.gda.pl; adult/concession 8/6zł; ⏰ 10am-6pm Jul & Aug, 9am-4pm Tue-Sun Apr-Jun & Sep, 10am-3pm Tue-Sun Oct, 10am-3pm Mon-Fri Nov-Mar) featuring typical Kashubian architecture. Established in 1906 by the local schoolmaster, this was Poland's first open-air museum of traditional architecture. Pleasantly positioned on the lakeside, it now contains a score of buildings collected from central and southern Kashubia, including cottages, barns, a school, a windmill and an 18th-century church used for Sunday Mass. Some of the interiors are fitted with authentic furnishings, implements and decorations, showing how the Kashubians lived a century or two ago.

In the village, there are a few budget pensions that provide around 100 beds in all. Wdzydze is linked to Kościerzyna by several buses daily.

LOWER VISTULA

The fertile land within the valley of the Lower Vistula, bisected by the wide, slowly flowing river, was prized by invaders for centuries. Flat, open and dotted with green farms, this region developed during the 13th and 14th centuries into a thriving trade centre, via the many ports established along the Vistula's banks from Toruń to Gdańsk. The history of these towns is intertwined with

POMERANIA

that of the Teutonic order (see boxed text, p451), the powerful league of Germanic knights who by then occupied much of the valley. Remnants from the order's heyday now comprise some of the most prominent sights in the region.

Though the Lower Vistula suffered much destruction in the closing months of WWII, what survived is a rich cultural inheritance of great depth and interest.

TORUŃ
pop 208,000

In some ways, Toruń is the city that time forgot – the low-rise centre of the former Hanseatic port has a slow-paced country-town feel, and its Old Town has avoided excesses of commercial signage and tourist tat. On the other hand, it's not *too* sleepy, and the vicinity of the central square buzzes with bars, restaurants and music venues.

But Toruń's entertainment options pale into insignificance compared with its spectacular Gothic architecture, an impressive collection of redbrick churches, residences and fortifications that justify the town's promotional slogan 'Gotyk na dotyk' (Touch Gothic). Undamaged in WWII, Toruń's Old Town was included on Unesco's World Heritage List in 1997.

Beyond architecture, Toruń is best known as the birthplace of Nicolaus Copernicus (1473–1543). His name (Mikołaj Kopernik in Polish) is all over town, and you can even buy gingerbread shaped in his image. Which is another Toruń icon – its *pierniki* (gingerbread) is famous across Poland. It may not have the international profile of Gdańsk or Kraków, but Toruń should be high on any visitor's must-see list.

History

Toruń was kickstarted into prominence in 1233, when the Teutonic Knights (see boxed text, p451) transformed the existing 11th-century Slav settlement into one of their early outposts. The knights surrounded the town, then known as Thorn, with walls and a castle. Rapid expansion as a port meant that newly arriving merchants and craftspeople had to settle outside the city walls and soon built what became known as the New Town. In the 1280s Toruń joined the Hanseatic League (see boxed text, p413), giving further impetus to its development.

Toruń later became a focal point of the conflict between Toruń and the Teutonic order, and when the Thirteen Years' War finally ended in 1466, the Treaty of Toruń returned a large area of land to Poland, stretching from Toruń to Gdańsk.

The following period of prosperity ended with the Swedish wars, and the city fell under Prussian domination in 1793, later becoming part of Germany. Toruń didn't return to Poland until the nation was recreated after WWI.

After WWII, which fortunately did relatively little damage to the city, Toruń expanded significantly, with vast new suburbs and industries. Luckily, the medieval quarter was unaffected and largely retains its old appearance.

Orientation

The historic sector of Toruń sits on the northern bank of the Vistula, made up of the Old Town (Stare Miasto) to the west and the New Town (Nowe Miasto) to the east. All the major attractions are in this area.

The bus terminal is a five-minute walk north of the historic quarter, while the main train station is south across the river, a short bus ride away. When coming from the station over the bridge, you'll get a fine view of the Gothic silhouette of the city.

Information

Bank Pekao (ul Wielkie Garbary 11)
EMPiK Megastore (☎ 056 622 4895; ul Wielkie Garbary 18) Bookshop.
Ksero Uniwerek (☎ 056 621 9279; ul Franciszkańska 5; internet per hr 3zł; ☽ 8am-7pm Mon-Fri, 9am-4pm Sat)
Orbis Travel (☎ 056 658 4221; ul Mostowa 7)
Post office (Rynek Staromiejski 15)
Pralnia Wiatka (☎ 0601 512 358; ul Szeroka 37/37a; from 5zł; ☽ 10am-7pm Mon-Fri; 10am-4pm Sat) A rare Polish laundrette.
Tourist office (☎ 056 621 0931; www.it.torun.pl; Rynek Staromiejski 25; ☽ 9am-4pm Mon & Sat, 9am-6pm Tue-Fri year-round, 9am-1pm Sun May-Aug)
U Zibiego (☎ 056 621 0191; ul Szewska 6; per hr 4zł; ☽ 10am-10pm Mon-Sat, noon-6pm Sun) Internet access.

Sights
OLD TOWN

The usual starting point on Toruń's Gothic trail is the **Old Town Market Sq** (Rynek Staromiejski), dominated by its massive redbrick town hall and lined with fine restored houses, many graced by intricate decorative façades.

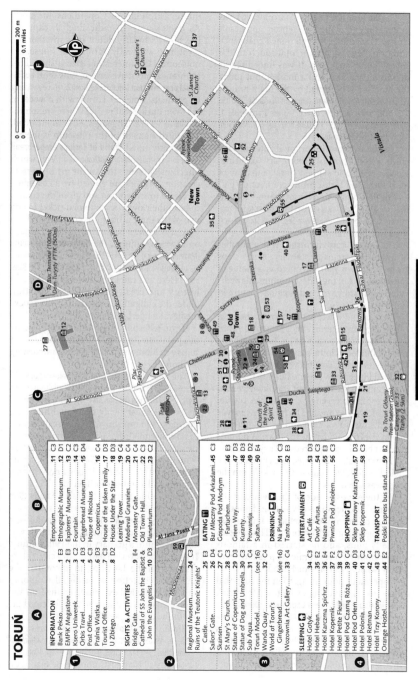

TORUŃ

POMERANIA

The **Old Town Hall** (Ratusz Staromiejski) was built at the end of the 14th century and hasn't changed that much, though some Renaissance additions lent an ornamental touch to the sober Gothic structure. It was once used as the municipal seat and a market, but today the building is occupied by the main branch of the **Regional Museum** (Muzeum Okręgowe; ☎ 056 622 7038; www.muzeum.torun.pl; Rynek Staromiejski 1; adult/concession 10/6zł; 10am-6pm Tue-Sun May-Sep, 10am-4pm Tue-Sun Oct-Apr).

Displays within its original interiors include a collection of Gothic art (painting, woodcarving and stained glass), a display of local 17th- and 18th-century crafts, and a gallery of Polish paintings from around 1800 to the present. You can go up the **tower** (adult/concession 10/6zł; 10am-8pm May-Sep, 10am-5pm Oct-Apr) for a fine panoramic view.

The square is also furnished with a number of interesting items of statuary. A few steps from the town hall entrance is a **statue of Copernicus**, one of the oldest monuments dedicated to the stargazer and a regular feature in holiday snaps.

West of the town hall, opposite the post office, is an intriguing small **fountain** built in 1914. Bronze-cast frogs sit on its rim, admiring a statue of a violin-playing boy known as Janko Muzykant, Toruń's very own answer to the Pied Piper story. Legend has it that a witch once came to the town, but wasn't welcomed by the locals. In revenge, she invoked a curse, and the town was invaded by frogs. The mayor offered a sackful of gold and his daughter to anyone who would rescue the town. A humble peasant boy then appeared and began to play his rustic fiddle. The frogs, enchanted by the melodies, followed him to the woods and the town was saved.

On the opposite side of the Rynek, at the corner of ul Chełmińska, you'll find another curious critter-related **statue** at knee-level, depicting a dog and umbrella. The pooch's name is Filus, and he starred in a famous long-running Polish comic strip as the pet of brolly-wielding Professor Filutek.

Copernicus pops up again in the Regional Museum's second big attraction, the brick Gothic **House of Nicolaus Copernicus** (Dom Mikołaja Kopernika; ☎ 056 622 7038; ul Kopernika 15/17; adult/concession 10/7zł; 10am-6pm Tue-Sun May-Sep, 10am-4pm Tue-Sun Oct-Apr). Unfortunately it's an institution suffering from an identity crisis, unsure of whether its exhibits should focus on old fur-

niture, astronomy or Copernicus' life story. As there's only sporadic English captioning, amid scholarly doubt over whether the great man was really born in this house, the museum is less interesting than it should be. More engaging, if overpriced, is its short **audiovisual presentation** (adult/concession 12/7zł) regarding Copernicus' times in Toruń, with a **model** of the town during that period. There are soundtracks in several languages, English included. The third element of the museum is the extravagantly titled **World of Torun's Gingerbread** (Świat Toruńskiego Piernika; adult/concession 10/6zł), which offers insights into the arcane art of *pierniki* creation. Visitors are guided by a costumed medieval townswoman and given the chance to bake their own. A combined ticket to any two of the three attractions costs 18/11zł.

A street away is another facility focused on the same subject, the **Gingerbread Museum** (Muzeum Piernika; ☎ 056 663 6617; www.muzeumpiernika .pl; ul Rabiańska 9; adult/concession 8.50/6.50zł; 9am-6pm). Here you can learn about gingerbread's history and create even more of the stuff, under the enlightened instruction of a mockmedieval gingerbread master.

If you're feeling sated with gingerbread by this point, the Regional Museum presents less sugary exhibitions inside several interesting old houses.

The **House Under the Star** (Kamienica Pod Gwiazdą; ☎ 056 622 7038; Rynek Staromiejski 35; adult/concession 7/4zł; 11am-5pm Tue-Sun May-Sep, 10am-4pm Tue-Sun Oct-Apr), the most richly decorated house on the main square, showcases a small but elegant collection from Asia, including Japanese swords, Indian statues and Chinese pottery from the Tang dynasty. The building's ornate Baroque fittings include striking polychrome ceilings and a statue of Minerva.

The Gothic **House of the Esken Family** (Dom Eskenów; ☎ 056 622 8680; ul Łazienna 16; adult/concession 7/4zł; 11am-5pm Tue-Sun May-Sep, 10am-4pm Tue-Sun Oct-Apr), set behind the cathedral, was converted into a granary in the 19th century. It's worth persevering past the dry city history displays on the 1st floor, to encounter the 2nd floor collection of medieval weaponry and archaeological exhibits from the Iron and Bronze Ages, including a human skeleton buried in the distant pre-Poland past.

Finally, the **Explorers' Museum** (Muzeum Podróżników; ☎ 056 622 7038; ul Franciszkańska 11; adult/concession 8/5zł; 11am-5pm Tue-Sun May-Sep, 10am-4pm Tue-Sun Oct-Apr) is an institution to be placed on every die-hard traveller's itinerary. It contains artefacts from the collection of inveterate wanderer Antonio Halik, comprising hats, travel documents and souvenirs of his journeys – including a vast array of hotel keys!

Of the historical buildings outside the museum's administration, the largest and most impressive is the giant Gothic **Cathedral of SS John the Baptist & John the Evangelist** (Katedra Św Janów; ul Św Jana; donation adult/child 2/1zł, tower 6/4zł). Work started around 1260 and was only completed at the end of the 15th century, by which time the church dominated the town's skyline, as it still does today. Its massive tower houses Poland's second-largest historic bell (after the one in the Wawel Royal Cathedral of Kraków), the Tuba Dei (God's Trumpet). Cast in 1530, it weighs 7238kg and is rung for significant religious and national events. On the southern side of the tower, facing the Vistula, is a large 15th-century clock; its original face and single hand are still in working order. Check out the dent above the VIII – it's from a cannonball that struck the clock during the Swedish siege of 1703.

The interior is a light-filled environment with elaborate altars resting beneath the whitewashed vaulting. Its most striking murals are the monochrome paintings set high at the back of each aisle, which depict a monk and a devil or plague figure; created by an unknown artist, the black-and-white style is highly unusual for this kind of church art.

The high altar, adorned with a Gothic triptych and topped with a crucifix, has as a background a superb stained-glass window in the best medieval style. The last chapel in the right-hand aisle holds the oldest object in the church, the font where Copernicus was baptised. To one side is his epitaph.

The third great Gothic structure in the old town is **St Mary's Church** (Kościół NMP; ul Panny Marii), erected by the Franciscans at the end of the 13th century. Austere and plain from the outside, it has a lofty interior with tall, intricate stained-glass windows and a prominent golden altarpiece, framed by a wooden archway depicting a complete crucifixion scene.

History buffs should also take the opportunity to check out the remnants of the town's original medieval fortifications. To the east, in a triangle squeezed between the Old and New Towns, are the **ruins of the castle**, built by the Teutonic Knights. It was destroyed by the town's inhabitants in 1454 as a protest against the order's economic restrictions (they must have been really ticked off – those Teutonic castles were solidly built).

Following the old city walls east around from the castle, you'll come to the first of three surviving city gates, the **Bridge Gate** (Brama Mostowa). A 700m-long bridge was built here between 1497 and 1500 and survived for over three centuries. Continue along the walls to find the other two gates, the **Sailors' Gate** (Brama Żeglarska) and the **Monastery Gate** (Brama Klasztorna). At the far western end are a few medieval granaries and the **Leaning Tower** (Krzywa Wieża).

Amid all the history, Toruń presents more modern cultural diversions. The **Wozownia Art Gallery** (☎ 056 622 6339; ul Rabiańska 20; adult/concession 5/3zł, free Tue; ☉ 10am-6pm Tue-Fri, 11am-6pm Sat & Sun) has changing displays of contemporary art, while aspiring astronomers can see what Copernicus was on about at the **Planetarium** (☎ 056 622 6066; ul Franciszkańska 15/21; adult/concession 8.50/6.50zł; ☉ 9.30am-3.30pm Mon, 9.30am-5.30pm Tue-Fri, 11.30am-3pm Sat & Sun), which usually has two daily shows in English.

NEW TOWN
North of the castle lies the New Town, centred on the **New Town Sq** (Rynek Nowomiejski). The building in the middle is a former Protestant church, erected in the 19th century after the town hall was pulled down. It's a quieter, more tourist-free part of town, and the square hosts irregular art and craft markets.

OTHER SIGHTS
In a park just to the north of the Old Town is the **Ethnographic Museum** (Muzeum Etnograficzne; ☎ 056 622 8091; Wały Sikorskiego 19; adult/concession 8.50/5.50zł, free Mon; ☉ 9am-4pm Mon, Wed & Fri, 10am-6pm Tue, Thu, Sat & Sun mid-Apr–Sep, 9am-4pm Tue-Fri, 10am-4pm Sat & Sun Oct–mid-Apr). It focuses on traditional fishery, with all sorts of implements, boats and nets. Admission also lets you visit the small but good **skansen** in the grounds, which contains examples of the traditional rural architecture of the region and beyond.

Activities
Beyond succumbing to Gothic mania in the Old Town, you can enjoy the great outdoors by getting out on the water. Below the

POMERANIA

Monastery Gate you'll find the **Wanda** (☎ 0601 625 682; adult/concession 8/6zł; ☒ 9am-7pm), a pleasure boat which will take you for a 40-minute cruise along the Vistula, once 15 passengers can be rounded up.

Not far away, **Sub Aqua** (☎ 056 652 1008; ul Bankowa 14/16) arranges diving excursions. Bicycles can be hired from **Emporium** (☎ 056 657 6108; ul Piekary 28; per hr 5zł; ☒ 10am-6pm Mon-Fri, 10am-4pm Sat year-round, 10am-4pm Sun Jun-Jul), which offers discounts to ISIC card holders. If you fancy a drive in the countryside, contact **Bonus** (☎ 056 648 0747; janusz_nalaskowski@poczta .onet.pl) to hire a car.

Festivals & Events

Probaltica Music & Art Festival of Baltic States (☎ 056 648 8647) Held in May.

Kontakt International Theatre Festival (☎ 056 622 5597; www.teatr.torun.pl) Held in May/June, productions have audio translation in English.

International Meetings of Folk Bands (☎ 056 622 8091) Held in early June.

Music & Architecture International Summer Festival (☎ 056 655 4929; www.tos.art.pl) Held from late June to August.

Toruń Days City festival held on 24 June.

Sleeping

Toruń has plenty of central places to stay, but as hotels tend to be small, finding a room can be tricky in busy times; weekdays are busiest, and many places offer substantial weekend discounts.

BUDGET

Orange Hostel (☎ 056 652 0033; www.hostelorange.pl; ul Prosta 19; dm/s/d/tr 30/50/90/120zł; ℙ ☒ ☐) The wave of Polish hostels for the international backpacker has finally swept over sleepy Toruń. Orange is in a handy location, its décor tends toward the brightly coloured and cheerful, and its kitchen is an impressive place to practise the gentle art of self-catering.

Dom Turysty PTTK (☎ 056 622 3855; www.pttk .torun.pl; ul Legionów 24; s/d/tr/q 60/76/99/112zł) The 65-bed PTTK hostel is in a residential house, a 10-minute walk north of the Old Town (five minutes from the bus terminal), with 24-hour reception and a snack bar. Rooms are simple but clean and practical.

Hotel Trzy Korony (☎ 056 622 60 31; www.hotel 3korony.pl; Rynek Staromiejski 21; s 95-155zł, d 130-200zł, tr 165-245zł) This budget hotel is by no means luxurious, but the simple rooms are neatly furnished with pine furniture, blue sofas and sunny yellow wallpaper. The hotel's glorious history includes stopovers by three distinguished monarchs (hence the 'three crowns' in the name).

Hotel Kopernik (☎ 056 652 25 73; www.hotel -kopernik.torun.pl; ul Wola Zamkowa 16; s 110-150zł, d 135-190zł, ste 200-260zł; ℙ ♿) It may have once been an army hostel, but the military edges have since rubbed off this attractively priced hotel in the New Town. Its basic but comfortable rooms are equipped with pine furniture, chunky radio sets, and pot plants with fake blooms.

Hotel Pod Orłem (☎ 056 622 5024; www.hotel.torun .pl; ul Mostowa 17; s 110zł, d 140-180zł, ste 200zł; ℙ ☐) The Pod Orłem is one of Toruń's oldest hotels, with a history going back more than a century. Leather-padded doors hide some pretty spacious rooms; the cheaper ones are strangely like staying at your grandma's. Breakfast is an extra 15zł.

Camping Nr 33 Tramp (☎ 056 654 71 87; www.tramp .mosir.torun.pl; ul Kujawska 14; camp sites per adult/child 8/4zł, per tent 5zł, d/tr/q 65/80/100zł, cabins 40-80zł; ☒ May–mid-Sep; ℙ) This camping ground, a five-minute walk from the main train station, has simple hotel-style rooms, a collection of basic cabins, a tent/caravan area and an onsite bar serving food. Some triple rooms have their own bathrooms.

MIDRANGE & TOP END

For some mysterious reason, Toruń has a vast number of three-star hotels housed within historic buildings in the centre of town, and competition keeps standards gratifyingly high.

Hotel Polonia (☎ 056 657 1800; www.polonia.torun .pl; Plac Teatralny 5; s 150zł, d 190-220zł, tr 245zł, q 280zł; ☐) The Polonia has a curious topography, with a *kantor* (private currency-exchange office) on the 1st floor and the breakfast room in the basement. These oddities aside, its rooms are a comfortable option, though they can vary considerably in dimensions.

Hotel Retman (☎ 056 657 4460; www.hotel retman.pl; ul Rabiańska 15; s 160-190zł, d 210zł) Simply furnished hotel with tasteful dark timber furniture and red carpets, highlighting the simplicity of its white walls. Downstairs there's a restaurant and a pub, handy for that post-sightseeing restorer.

Hotel Pod Czarną Różą (☎ 056 621 9637; www .hotelczarnaroza.pl; ul Rabiańska 11; s/d/tr 170/210/250zł; ☐) 'Under the Black Rose' is spread between a historic inn and a new wing facing the river, though its interiors present a uniformly clean up-to-date look. Some doubles come with small but functional kitchens.

Hotel Gotyk (☎ 056 658 4000; www.hotel-gotyk.com.pl; ul Piekary 20; s 150-180zł, d 250-300zł) Yet another restored town-house hotel. Pass the suit of armour in the foyer and up green carpeted stairs, to find individually decorated rooms and classic furniture.

Hotel Petite Fleur (☎ 056 663 4400; www.petitefleur.pl; ul Piekary 25; s 190-270zł, d 250-290zł; ☐) The Petite Fleur is one of the best midrange options in Toruń, with elegantly appointed rooms containing smoothly polished timber furniture and elegant prints. It also has an impressive French restaurant downstairs in its cellar, and a memorable lounge.

ourpick Hotel Karczma Spichrz (☎ 056 657 1140; www.spichrz.pl; ul Mostowa 1; s/d 190/250zł, ste 300-350zł; P ✗ ☐ ⬤) Situated within a historic granary on the waterfront, this hotel's rooms are well supplied with personality, featuring massive exposed beams above elegant timber furniture. There's a restaurant and bar within the establishment, along with a billiards room.

Hotel Heban (☎ 056 652 1555; www.hotel-heban.com.pl; ul Małe Garbary 7; s/d 190/300zł, ste 350-500zł; P ✗) Luxuriously restored town house with elegant touches. The foyer is a collection of classic ornamentation, including brass fireplace hoods, statues of lions, and marble floors. Upstairs, the rooms feature lots of timber elements. The onsite restaurant is also a pleasant place to dine.

Eating

Bar Mleczny Pod Arkadami (☎ 056 622 2428; ul Różana 1; mains 2-6.50zł; ⏰ 9am-7pm Mon-Fri, 9am-4pm Sat & Sun) Toruń's most central milk bar is just off the Old Town Sq, offering sturdy bites at silly prices. The outdoor window serves up waffles, ice cream and northern Poland's best *zapiekanki* (Polish pizza).

Green Way (☎ 056 621 1056; ul Żeglarska 18; mains 6-12zł; ⏰ 10.30am-8.30pm Mon-Sat, noon-7pm Sun) Another instalment in the national vegetarian chain, it serves cheap animal-free food in a cheery orange stucco interior.

ourpick Sułtan (☎ 056 621 0607; ul Mostowa 7; mains 7-18zł; ⏰ noon-midnight Sun-Thu, noon-2.30am Fri & Sat) Light, bright venue with an Arabian motif, it cooks up Middle Eastern cuisine in an space decorated with colourful lanterns. The menu contains many variants of kebabs, along with soups, salads, pizzas and a scattering of decent vegetarian options.

Prowansja (☎ 056 622 2111; ul Szewska 19; mains 10-18zł; ⏰ noon-10pm Sun-Thu, noon-11pm Fri & Sat) This charming eatery does a convincing impersonation of a Provence restaurant and wine bar. Quiche, crepes and salads add to the Frenchness of it all, but it's the wine list that's the highlight. There's an ISIC card discount available.

Kuranty (☎ 056 662 5252; Rynek Staromiejski 29; mains 12-49zł; ⏰ 11am-2am) The menu is firmly based on the three Ps: pizza, pasta and *pierogi* (including a rather tasty baked version which looks suspiciously like the Italian calzone). Random photos and extraordinary Art Nouveau lights add to the atmosphere. Be warned: sports-playing TVs hang off the walls.

Gospoda Pod Modrym Fartuchem (☎ 056 622 2626; Rynek Nowomiejski 8; mains 16-29zł; ⏰ 10am-10pm) This atmospheric 15th-century eatery on the New Town Sq modestly claims to be 'probably the oldest restaurant in the world', and has served Polish kings and Napoleon. Polish standards are joined by more adventurous choices involving tortillas and Indian spices, on the vegetarian-friendly menu.

Drinking

ourpick Tantra (☎ 0697 133 569; ul Ślusarska 5; ⏰ noon-midnight Sun-Thu, noon-2am Fri & Sat) Forget those Gothic bricks – this bar takes the colour red to new heights in its astonishingly decorated interior. It's done out in an Indian and Tibetan theme and layered with cloth and other artefacts from the subcontinent, including some tastefully rendered images of erotic temple statuary. Sit on the cushion-strewn divans, order a drink from the long list and meditate on the infinite.

Na Plantacji (☎ 056 655 0231; Rynek Staromiejski 23; ⏰ 10am-10pm) Was it ever this civilised down on the plantation? Genteel ladies sip tea while waiters glide past bearing orders from the voluminous menu of hot beverages. This might be the place to order that great Polish refresher – *herbata z rumem* (tea with rum).

Entertainment

Dwór Artusa (☎ 056 655 4929; Rynek Staromiejski 6) The Artus Court, one of the most impressive mansions on the main square, is now a major cultural centre and has an auditorium hosting musical events, including concerts and recitals.

Art Café (☎ 056 652 2076; ul Szeroka 35; ☻ 9pm-late) The insider's address for everything new and cool in electronic music, from house to hardcore, with occasional hip-hop nights thrown in. Posters outside the door outline upcoming acts.

Piwnica Pod Aniołem (☎ 056 622 70 39; www.pod aniolem.art.pl in Polish; Rynek Staromiejski 1) This splendid, spacious pub in the town hall cellar is one of the old quarter's most popular live music venues – check the big posters at street level for the latest gigs.

our pick **Nasze Kino** (☎ 056 652 2372; www.naszekino .pl in Polish; ul Podmurna 14; admission 12zł) A cool little arthouse cinema embedded within part of the old city walls, its single screen showing a range of non-Hollywood films. Double features and movie marathon screenings are cheaper.

Shopping

Toruń is famous for its *pierniki*, which has been produced here since the town was founded. The confection comes in a variety of shapes, though some are intended for decorative purposes only – they're too hard to be eaten. Good places to buy it are **Sklep Firmowy Katarzynka** (☎ 056 622 37 12; ul Żeglarska 25) and **Sklep Kopernik** (☎ 056 645 07 34; Rynek Staromiejski 6).

Getting There & Away
BUS

The PKS terminal, close to the northern edge of the Old Town, handles regular bus services to Chełmno (8.50zł, 1½ hours), Golub-Dobrzyń (8.50zł, 1½ hours) and Bydgoszcz (9zł, one hour). Polski Express runs departures every hour or two to Bydgoszcz (12zł, one hour) and Warsaw (32zł to 54zł, 3¾ hours), and two a day to Szczecin (59zł, six hours), leaving from a stand on ul Mickiewicza.

TRAIN

The Toruń Główny train station is about 2km south of the Old Town, on the opposite side of the Vistula. Buses 22 and 27 (2zł, 10 minutes) link the two.

Trains head to Grudziądz (11zł, 1¾ hours) and Bydgoszcz (16zł, one hour) at least every other hour. There are also departures to Malbork (34zł, 2½ hours, three daily), Gdańsk (38zł, 3½ hours, seven daily), Olsztyn (34zł, 2½ hours, eight daily), Poznań (33zł, 2½ hours, five daily) and Warsaw (40zł, three hours, five daily).

GOLUB-DOBRZYŃ
pop 13,000

Golub-Dobrzyń may sound like a minor character in *The Lord of the Rings*, but it is in fact a town about 40km east of Toruń. Dobrzyń, on the southern bank of the Drwęca River, is newish and not worth a mention, but Golub was founded in the 13th century as a border outpost of the Teutonic Knights (see boxed text, p451), who left behind an impressive castle.

Castle

Golub's sturdy, square castle is its most prominent feature, looming over the town from a central hill. The structure consists of a massive Gothic brick base topped with a slightly more refined Renaissance cornice, which was added in the 17th century. The whole building was extensively restored after WWII. Its small **museum** (☎ 056 683 24 66; adult/concession 10/8zł; ☻ 9am-7pm May-Sep, 9am-4pm Oct-Apr) is interesting more for the original Gothic interiors than for its modest ethnographic collection.

Festivals & Events

Every July the castle hosts the **International Knights' Tournament** (☎ 056 683 2455), a big mock-medieval jamboree including jousting, music and lots of costumes.

Sleeping & Eating

Dom Wycieczkowy PTTK (☎ 056 683 24 55; zamek@zamek golub.pl; hostel dm/d 30/80zł; hotel s/d/tr 150/200/250zł; **P** **P** **👜**) The castle's upper floor houses some of the cheapest fortification accommodation in Poland. There are two standards on offer: one a hostel style with dorm beds and simple doubles, the other consisting of hotel-type rooms. A pleasant café in the vaulted cellar serves snacks and drinks.

Getting There & Away

The town has a regular bus service to Toruń (8.50zł, 1½ hours) and Grudziądz (10.50zł, two hours, four daily). There's a bus stop at the foot of the castle, but not all incoming services stop there – you may have to walk 1.5km from the bus station in Dobrzyń.

BYDGOSZCZ
pop 366,000

It's hard to imagine why you'd head to Bydgoszcz (*bid*-goshch) for an extended stay – though it's one of Poland's largest cities, the majority of the city is a postwar industrial zone

POMERANIA

with little character. However, it's not without its charms, particularly in the centre where local authorities have spent time and money regenerating the city's older quarters.

Lying outside the territory of the Teutonic Knights (see boxed text, p451), Bydgoszcz developed over time into a trading centre, beer producer and military base. Becoming part of Prussia in the First Partition of 1772, Bydgoszcz returned to Poland in 1919 and underwent intensive industrial development.

Since it's only an hour from Toruń and has its own international airport, you may find yourself here on the way to or from its sexier Gothic sister, and there's enough of interest to fill a pleasant few hours. It would also make a reasonable day trip from Toruń, if you fancy a change of scene.

Information
Bank Pekao (ul Dworcowa 6)
Main post office (ul Jagiellońska 6)
Tourist office (☎ 052 321 4595; www.it.byd.pl; Stary Rynek 1; ☻ 9am-6pm Mon-Fri, 9am-2pm Sat)

Sights & Activities
The Old Town is on the southern bank of the Brda River, a 20-minute walk from the train station. Its heart, **Stary Rynek**, is dominated by the palatial **town hall** and a large Modernist **monument** to the victims of fascism. It was here that the Nazi invaders kept hostages at gunpoint for two days in September 1939, shooting 40 of them. Nowadays the grim monument seems somewhat at odds with the life of the square and the surrounding streets.

To the west, just off the Rynek, the metal front door of the 16th-century brick **parish church** depicts scenes from the city's 1000-year history. Within is a gilded Baroque high altar with a 1466 painting of the Virgin Mary. What's really surprising, however, is the church's colour scheme – its interior is done out in vivid purple and orange shades that would have appealed to adherents of 1960s flower power. You may want to keep your sunglasses on! The illustrations on the walls date from the 1920s when the church was redecorated, having been commandeered in the 19th century for use as storage by various passing military forces.

The Regional Museum has branches in several interesting buildings around town. The most important of these is the 18th-century

White Granary (Biały Spichrz; ☎ 052 585 9812; ul Mennica 1; adult/concession 6/4zł; ☻ 10am-6pm Tue-Fri, noon-4pm Sat & Sun), west of the Rynek on Mill Island (Wyspa Młyńska). Displays here outline the region's history, and illustrate traditional arts and crafts.

In the newer part of town, a block north of Hotel Pod Orłem on ul Gdańska, you can find a seated **statue** of celebrated Bydgoszcz citizen and mathematician Marian Rejewski (see boxed text, p444).

For a more relaxing perspective on the city, the **Water Tram** (Tramwaj Wodny; ☎ 052 323 3201; www .tramwaywodny.byd.pl; adult/concession 2.20/1.10zł) runs up and down the river from the Fish Market (Rybi Rynek) on the Old Town waterfront, up to four times daily from May to October. One stop is on the riverbank below the bus station, if you want to enter or depart the centre by less conventional means.

Sleeping & Eating
Youth hostel (☎ 052 322 7570; www.ssm.bydgoszcz.pl; ul Sowińskiego 5; dm 20-60zł, s 50-60zł, d 70-80zł; ☒ ☐) This 100-bed youth hostel, just five minutes' walk from the station, has everything from singles to 10-bed dorms available all year. ISIC card holders receive discounts. Note that reception is closed between 10am and 5pm, and there's an 11pm curfew.

Hotel Ratuszowy (☎ 052 339 8400; www.hotel ratuszowy.com.pl; ul Długa 37; s 160-250zł, d 230-300zł, ste 280-450zł; ☒ ☐) This is the only option for visitors wishing to stay in the Old Town. Luckily it's a nice, low-key place in a quiet, central location, and the rooms are just homely enough to be welcoming.

Hotel Brda (☎ 052 585 0100; www.hotelbrda.com .pl; ul Dworcowa 94; s 150-250zł, d 260-350zł, ste 390-440zł; P ☒ ☐ ☒) Unexciting but reliable, the Brda is a standard conference-class block near the station with neat rooms and a good range of facilities.

Hotel Pod Orłem (☎ 052 583 0530; www.hotel podorlem.pl; ul Gdańska 14; s 300-350zł, d 440zł, ste 530-640zł; P ☒ ☐ ☒) This elegant hotel, with its ornate façade, has been the city's most prestigious inn ever since it opened in 1898, hosting Prussian and Polish VIPs alike. It was restored to its prewar Art Nouveau elegance towards the end of the communist period. The fanciest option here is the Rubenstein Suite, named for famous Polish-born pianist Artur Rubenstein.

ADVENTURES OF A CRYPTOLOGIST

Mathematicians are usually stereotyped as bookish, unworldly creatures. But not so Bydgoszcz-born Marian Rejewski (1905–1980), who took on the Nazi ciphers to become one of the heroes of WWII.

Rejewski was teaching at Poznań University in 1932, a year before Hitler came to power, when he was seconded to the Polish army's Cipher Bureau. Using a mix of intuition and mathematical equations, he soon deciphered the inner workings of the Enigma machines, which encrypted German military traffic, years before the famous British Ultra project began its work at Bletchley Park outside London.

In 1939, with war imminent, Rejewski's team decided to reveal all to the astonished cryptology teams of France and Britain. This data was to be of invaluable assistance to Poland's allies, as periodic upgrading of the German devices meant the decryption work was an ongoing project.

When Poland was overrun, Rejewski's team fled to France via Romania, evacuating again to Algeria when France was invaded. Returning to work undercover in unoccupied Vichy France, Rejewski fled to Spain in 1943, where he was promptly robbed by his pistol-wielding guide and imprisoned by the Spanish police. Released after a few months, he headed through Portugal and Gibraltar, to finally end up in Britain. Here he resumed his code-breaking efforts, though relegated to relatively minor projects.

In 1946, Rejewski returned to Bydgoszcz to be reunited with his family. In the mid-1970s the story of the Polish role in cracking Enigma broke, and Rejewski was feted both internationally and at home. He died a national hero in 1980.

Bydgoszcz is intensely proud of its mathematical prodigy: nowadays you can encounter a statue of Marian Rejewski on ul Gdańska, a block north of the Hotel Pod Orłem. Conservatively depicted in suit and glasses, the great mathematician is seated modestly on a bench. Next to him is the likeness of an Enigma machine, the device he once defeated.

Restauracja Kaskada (☎ 052 324 9332; ul Mostowa 2; mains 10-18zł; ⏱ 11am-8pm) You can spot this big, modern, multilevel eatery from almost any point on the Rynek. Indecisive diners can ponder their options inside, outside or in the adjoining snack bar; if all else fails, the kiosk here is open 24 hours.

Gallery Restaurant (☎ 052 322 6023; Stary Rynek 15/21; mains 13-72zł; ⏱ 1pm-midnight) Fine food is the watchword in the two gracious dining rooms occupying Gallery's cellar, with a bar, and dancing on Friday and Saturday nights. The street-level café provides a more relaxed alternative.

Getting There & Away

IJ Paderewski airport (☎ 052 365 4650; www.plb .pl; Al Jana Pawła II 158) is located 3km south of the city centre, accessible via bus 80 (2.20zł, hourly, 20 minutes) from the Old Town. A taxi should cost about 30zł (15 minutes). There are domestic flights to Warsaw via LOT (up to three daily), and international flights via Ryanair to London (daily) and Dublin (twice weekly).

The main train station is 1.5km northwest of the Old Town, while the bus terminal is 1km east; city buses 54 and 94 link the two stations, passing through the centre.

Trains go frequently to Toruń (16zł, one hour), and there are also services to Gdańsk (33zł, 2¼ hours, 15 daily), Poznań (33zł, 2½ hours, 11 daily) and Warsaw (46zł, four hours, seven daily).

Buses head to Toruń regularly through the day (9zł, one hour). Polski Express also runs buses every hour or two to Warsaw (42zł, 4½ hours) via Toruń and Płock, leaving Bydgoszcz from a stand 150m west of the bus station on ul Jagiellońska.

CHEŁMNO
pop 20,000

The bus journey to Chełmno (*heum*-no), around 40km north of Toruń, makes you feel you're heading for a forgotten place far from urban pressures. Then, after passing through green fields and tiny villages, you're suddenly confronted by mighty Gothic city walls and imposing churches, set high on a hilltop. The town's compact size and intact Old Town are an atmospheric combination.

Like Toruń, Chełmno was once an important centre in the territories of the Teutonic

Knights (see boxed text, p451). Though it had been a Polish settlement since the late 10th century, the Teutonic Knights bookmarked it as a potential capital when they arrived in the late 1220s. Their castle was completed by 1265, bolstering Chełmno's profitable position on the Vistula trade route, and its lucrative affiliation to the Hanseatic League (see boxed text, p413).

After the Treaty of Toruń, Chełmno was returned to Poland, but a devastating plague and a series of wars left the town an unimportant place by the time it was annexed by Prussia in 1772. Though it was returned to Poland in 1920 and survived WWII without major damage, things stayed quiet. Today it's a relaxed, attractive town whose historic atmosphere and visual appeal make it well worth a visit.

Information

Bank Gdański (ul Dworcowa 3)
Kredyt Bank (ul Dworcowa 24A)
Tourist office (☎ 056 686 2104; Ratusz, Rynek; ☼ 8am-3pm Mon & Sat, 8am-4pm Tue-Fri)

Sights & Activities

Walking along ul Dworcowa from the bus terminal, you'll enter the Old Town through the **Grudziądz Gate** (Brama Grudziądzka), the only surviving medieval gateway. It was remodelled in the 17th century to incorporate a chapel. Note an expressive pietà in the niche in the gate's eastern façade.

Past the gate, you'll find yourself on a chessboard of streets, with the Rynek at its heart. In the middle stands the graceful Renaissance **town hall**, built around 1570 on the site of the previous Gothic structure and now home to the **Regional Museum** (Muzeum Ziemi Chełmińskiej; ☎ 056 686 16 41; adult/concession 3/2zł; ☼ 10am-4pm Tue-Fri, 10am-3pm Sat, 11am-2pm Sun). Its collection relates to the town's history within its original interiors, including a spectacular courtroom.

Outside, affixed on the rear wall of the town hall is the old Chełmno measure, the 4.35m-long *pręt chełmiński*. The entire town was laid out according to this measure, setting all the streets exactly the same width apart. It is divided into 'feet' a little smaller than an English foot. This unique system was used until the 19th century, and the town also had its own weights.

Just off the Rynek is the massive, late-13th-century Gothic **parish church**. The magnificent interior is crammed with ornate Baroque and Rococo furnishings, and also holds some supposed relics of St Valentine, patron saint of lovers, locked within the right-hand pillar as you face the altar.

The **Church of SS John the Baptist & John the Evangelist** (Kościół Św Jana Chrzciciela i Jana Ewangelisty), in the western end of the Old Town, was built between 1266 and 1325 and has a richly gilded high altar with an ornate organ to the side. Underneath the organ is a black-marble tombstone from 1275, one of the oldest in the region.

The town's other churches are less spectacular but are worth a peek just for their original Gothic structures. They're open to visitors between 10am and 6pm, from May to September.

Finally, you may want to inspect the 2.2km-long **fortified walls**, which have survived almost in their entirety. There once were 23 defensive towers in the walls and some still exist, though they're not all in good shape.

If you want to see more of the surrounding countryside, the tourist office can arrange bicycle or walking **tours**, and supply details of **sightseeing flights** by light aircraft or balloon.

Sleeping & Eating

Europejskie Centrum Wymiany Młodzieży (☎ 056 686 1256; ul Jastrzębskiego 5; s/d/tr 60/100/130zł; ☼ May-Sep) On Lake Starogrodzkie, 2km west of the walled town, the European Centre of Youth Exchange offers basic rooms and a camping ground.

Hotel Centralny (☎ 056 686 0212; www.hotelcentralny .pl; ul Dworcowa 23; s/d/tr/q 90/120/150/200zł) Outside the city walls, the Centralny is simple but perfectly pleasant, and very convenient for the bus station. Its worthwhile restaurant (mains 5zł to 22zł) is an air-conditioned oasis on a hot summer day.

Hotelik (☎ 056 676 2030; ul Podmurna 3; s/d/tr 100/140/160zł; ▣) Located in a quiet corner of the Old Town, right near the Grudziądz Gate, the half-timbered Hotelik offers good value for money and a late-opening restaurant.

Karczma Chełmińska (☎ 056 679 0605; www .karczmachelminska.pl; ul 22 Stycznia 1b; s/d/tr/q/ste 150/190/240/260/280zł; P ▣) This tourist-friendly courtyard hotel, in the southwestern corner of the Old Town, is a little cheesy at times (see the big wooden figure outside) but offers neat rooms with great stone-effect bathrooms. The courtyard restaurant, with waiters in traditional garb, serves up good food (mains 7zł to 55zł), including interesting seasonal dishes.

POMERANIA

Restauracja Spichlerz (☎ 056 686 9912; ul Biskupia 3; mains 4-13zł; ☺ 9am-midnight Mon-Fri, 10am-midnight Sun) Full of farmhouse beams and fantasy murals, the combination of pub-restaurant and youth hang-out makes for an interesting atmosphere. It's just off the Rynek.

Getting There & Away
Buses depart roughly hourly to Bydgoszcz (7.70zł, 1½ hours), Toruń (8.50zł, 1½ hours) and Grudziądz (6.50zł, 50 minutes). There are also 12 buses a day to Gdańsk (25zł, 2½ hours).

GRUDZIĄDZ
pop 99,000
The wave of urban renewal sweeping Pomeranian cities doesn't seem to have yet reached Grudziądz (*groo*-jonts), located some 30km down the Vistula River from Chełmno. Its Old Town is a mass of peeling façades and haphazard cobblestones, and trams still run through its market square. Despite the decay, there's something intriguing about its weathered architecture, as if you're being given a glimpse of how Polish cities must have looked a few decades ago.

Grudziądz may not be too focused on appearances, but its history is certainly colourful. It started life as an early Piast settlement, came under the rule of the Teutonic Knights (see boxed text, p451) as Graudenz in the 1230s, then returned to the Polish crown in 1466. The city was caught up in the 17th-century wars with Sweden – it was burnt down while being liberated by Polish troops in 1659. In the First Partition of 1772, Grudziądz was swallowed by Prussia, developing as an industrial centre before returning to Poland in the aftermath of WWI.

Grudziądz was severely damaged in 1945 but was rebuilt and developed into a bustling, if fairly unremarkable, urban centre.

Information
Bank Millennium (ul Sienkiewicza 19)
Bank Pekao (ul Chełmińska 68)
Tourist office (☎ 056 461 2318; www.it.gdz.pl; ul Skłodowskiej-Curie 19; ☺ 9am-5pm Mon-Fri, 9am-2pm Sat, 10am-2pm Sun Jul-Aug, 9am-5pm Mon-Fri, 9am-2pm Sat May, Jun & Sep, 9am-5pm Mon-Fri Oct-Apr)

Sights
The extraordinary row of crumbling **granaries** (*spichrze*) was built along the whole length of the town's waterfront to provide storage and protect the town from invaders. Begun in the 14th century, they were gradually rebuilt and extended until the 18th century, and some were later turned into housing blocks by cutting windows in the walls. These massive buttressed brick buildings – most of them six storeys high – are an impressive sight.

The town's other drawcard is its regional **museum** (☎ 056 465 9063; www.muzeum.grudziadz .pl; ul Wodna 3/5; adult/concession 6/3zł; ☺ 10am-4pm Tue, 10am-3pm Wed-Sat, 10am-2pm Sun), based in a former Benedictine convent at the southern end of the old quarter. The main building houses contemporary paintings from the region and temporary exhibitions, with further sections on local archaeology and history in two old granaries just to the west.

A few other buildings in the centre retain their historical significance, the most impressive of which is the **Church of St Francis Xavier** (Kościół Św Franciszka Ksawerego; ul Kościelna), built in 1715. Most of the church's narrow interior is taken up by a beautiful Baroque high altar, and the surrounding ornamentation includes some unusual chinoiserie, a decorative style drawing on Chinese art.

At the top of the hill that slopes up from the granaries, you'll find the remnants of the Teutonic order's 13th-century **castle** and a great view over the Vistula.

Sleeping & Eating
Youth hostel (☎ 056 643 5540; ul Hallera 37; dm 17-20zł) This 150-bed hostel is in a large, nondescript, 11-storey block, part of the Bursa Szkolna (School Dorm), 1.5km south of the Old Town. Its small dorms provide more privacy than usual.

Ośrodek Wypoczynkowy Rudnik (MORiW; ☎ 056 462 2581; www.moriw.pl; ul Zaleśna 1; bungalows 45-100zł; P ♿) This two-star camping ground, on a lake 5km south of town, has an enviable selection of facilities, including restaurants, sports equipment, boats, a children's playground, and a paddling pool. In summer, the R bus runs here from a stop near the tourist office.

Hotel Teatr (☎ 056 462 0900; ul Focha 19; s/d/tr/apt 49/98/147/122zł; P) Reasonably priced accommodation hidden inside a cultural complex, cheek-to-cheek with a theatre. The apartment is a good-value self-catering option, and the hotel is on the tram 1 route between the train station and Old Town.

POMERANIA

Hotel Kowalkowski (☎ 056 461 3480; www.hotel
.grudziadz.net; ul Chopina 1/3, s/d/tr/ste 139/179/219/290zł;
P) South of the Old Town and west of the
train station, this is a comfy three-star choice
with a restaurant and bar on the premises.

Da Grasso (☎ 056 643 4444; Rynek 13; mains 13-23zł;
11am-10pm) Facing the market square and
its dramatic military statue, this cheap-and-
cheerful pizzeria serves up all the usual suspects, with a generous vegetarian selection.

Getting There & Away

The train station is about 1km southeast of the
Old Town, a 15-minute walk or a quick trip
on tram 1. The bus terminal is a short walk
north of the station. Seven trains run daily to
Toruń (11zł, 1½ hours), and five very slow
trains limp to Kwidzyn (7.50zł, one hour),
continuing further north to Malbork (13zł,
1¾ hours). Buses to Bydgoszcz (12zł, 1¾
hours) and Chełmno (6.50zł, 50 minutes)
leave roughly every hour. There are also eight
buses to Kwidzyn (10zł, 45 minutes).

KWIDZYN

pop 37,000

Kwidzyn is a tranquil town containing a surprisingly massive Gothic castle and cathedral.
Located 40km downriver from Grudziądz,
it's yet another medieval stronghold of the
Teutonic order (see boxed text, p451), and
was formerly known as Marienwerder. Under
the rule of German authorities for most of
its history, the town became part of Poland
after 1945.

Information

Tourist office (☎ 055 79 5812; ul Katedralna 18;
8am-4pm) Next to the cathedral.

Sights

The square **castle**, with its central courtyard,
was built in the first half of the 14th century.
It experienced many ups and downs in subsequent periods and suffered a serious loss
in 1798 when the Prussians pulled down two
sides (eastern and southern) and the main
tower. It passed almost unscathed through WWII.

Most of the building is now the **Kwidzyn
Museum** (☎ 055 646 3797; ul Katedralna 1; adult/con-
cession 7/5zł; 9am-5pm Tue-Sun May-Aug, 9am-4pm
Tue-Sun Sep-Apr), which has several sections
including displays on medieval sacred art,
regional folk crafts and plenty of farming
implements, as well as a display in the cellar

detailing the German-funded archaeological
excavations around the site. There are some
grim sets of manacles hanging off the dun-
geon walls for effect, and some inexplicably
placed cannons beside them. You won't find
any English labelling, but the fine original
interiors justify a visit, and there are some
good views over the countryside from some
of the windows.

The most curious feature of the castle is
the two unusual towers standing some distance away from the western and southern
sides, linked to the main building by arcaded
bridges. The smaller tower held a well, while
the western one was the *gdanisko* (knights'
toilet), and later also served as the execution
ground. You can visit both while wandering
around the interior, but it's also worth walking around the outside.

The **cathedral** attached to the castle is the
familiar Gothic brick blockbuster, which has
a suitably defensive appearance, thanks to its
19th-century tower. Look for the interesting
ceramic mosaic (from around 1380) in the
external wall above the southern porch.

Sleeping & Eating

Hotel Kaskada (☎ 055 279 3731; www.hotelkaskada.eme
teor.pl; ul Chopina 42; s/d/tr/q 135/160/215/250zł; P ▣)
Right opposite the train station, the Kaskada
has been recently redone in bright colours
and also has a simple restaurant, making it a
good option if you decide to stay over.

Pensjonat Miłosna (☎ 055 279 4052; www.milosna
.emeteor.pl; ul Miłosna 2; s/d/tr/q 220/250/280/310zł;
P ▣) Miłosna is a stylish villa set in the
woods off the Grudziądz road; about 4km
from Kwidzyn, it's only a practical proposition for motorists. Rooms are cosy and comfortable, and there's also a good restaurant.

Getting There & Away

The bus and train stations are set 200m apart,
both around a 10-minute walk from the castle. Seven trains head to Malbork (7.50zł, 45
minutes), four to Grudziądz (7.50zł, one hour)
and two to Toruń (15.50zł, 2¾ hours). There
are 10 buses daily to Malbork (8.80zł, 50 minutes), five to Elbląg (13zł, 1½ hours) and four
to Gdańsk (17zł, two hours).

GNIEW

pop 6800

Not to be outdone, the small town of Gniew
(pronounced gnyef) has an equally prominent

and remarkably well-maintained castle in its location on the other side of the Vistula. The town has also retained its original medieval layout in its tiny old centre. With few interruptions from modern life, it's a charming place to visit for a couple of hours.

Sights

The first stronghold of the Teutonic order (see boxed text, p451) on the left bank of the Vistula, the **castle** was built in the late 13th century and is a massive, multistorey brick structure with a deep courtyard. In 1464 it came under Polish rule and remained so until the First Partition of 1773. The Prussians remodelled it to accommodate a barracks, a jail and an ammunition depot. It was seriously burnt out in 1921, but the 2m-thick walls survived and it was later restored.

The castle now houses the **Archaeological Museum** (☎ 058 35 2537; www.zamek-gniew.pl; Plac Zamkowy 2; adult/concession 8/5zł; ⏰ 9am-5pm Tue-Sun May-Sep, by appointment Oct-Apr). The archaeological exhibition is in two rooms, but you will also get to see the chapel and temporary exhibitions in other rooms, and wander through most of the castle. All visits are guided and the tour takes up to 1½ hours; unless you pay 50zł for a foreign-language guide, this will mean tagging along with a Polish group and hanging around through some fairly lengthy explanations of each display (including a dramatic account of the Battle of Grunwald). At weekends historical performances are held twice a day.

Sleeping & Eating

Dormitorium (☎ 058 535 2162; dm 33zł) In part of the castle, the 90-bed Dormitorium offers bunk accommodation in spacious vaulted dorms, which are heated in winter. It's simple but clean and has character, and offers some of Poland's cheapest castle beds. Breakfast is an extra 15zł.

Pałac Marysieńki (☎ 058 535 2162; Plac Zamkowe 3; s/d/tr/ste 100/150/240/250zł; Ⓟ) The Pałac is a large, imposing building set next to the castle, fully renovated and offering a fine range of comfortable accommodation. The house restaurant is of equally good value.

Getting There & Away

Gniew's bus terminal is about 200m northwest of the Rynek. There are roughly hourly services to Tczew (10zł, 45 minutes), six to

Gdańsk (15.50zł, 1½ hours), one to Grudziądz (13zł, one hour) and two to Toruń (23zł, 2½ hours).

MALBORK

pop 38,000

It's not hard to figure out what the tourists streaming out of Malbork's train station every day are heading towards – this quiet hamlet's spectacular castle. The top dog among Polish fortifications, the magnificent Unesco-listed structure is a classic example of the medieval fortress, and Europe's largest Gothic castle as well. In summer it's at its busiest, playing host to crowds of both local and international visitors. Malbork is an easy day trip from Gdańsk, but you could also stay overnight to appreciate the town and its famous stronghold in a less hectic atmosphere.

Information

Bank Pekao (ul Piłsudskiego 9)
Post office (ul 17 Marca 38)
Tourist office (☎ 055 273 4990; ul Piastowska 15; ⏰ 10am-6pm Mon-Fri, 10am-2pm Sat & Sun Jun-Sep)

Sights

Malbork's showpiece *extraordinaire* is the massive castle that sits on the bank of the Nogat River, an eastern arm of the Vistula. Built by the Teutonic Knights (see boxed text, p451), the **Marienburg** (Fortress of Mary) was the main seat of the order for almost 150 years, and its vast bulk is an apt embodiment of its weighty history.

The immense castle took shape in stages. First was the so-called High Castle, the formidable central bastion that was begun around 1276 and finished within three decades. When Malbork became the capital of the order in 1309, the fortress was expanded considerably. The Middle Castle was built to the side of the high one, followed by the Lower Castle still further along. The whole complex was encircled by three rings of defensive walls and strengthened with dungeons and towers. The castle eventually spread over 21 hectares, making it the largest fortress built in the Middle Ages.

The castle was only seized by the Polish army in 1457, during the Thirteen Years' War, when the military power of the knights had started to erode. Malbork then became the residence of Polish kings visiting Pomerania, but from the Swedish invasions onwards it

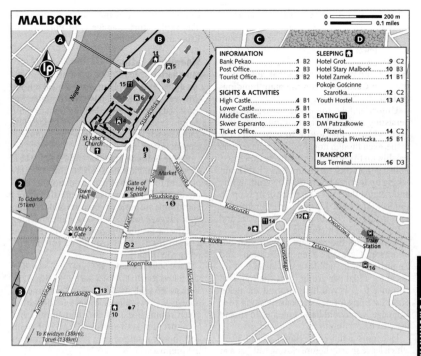

MALBORK

0 ——— 200 m
0 ——— 0.1 miles

INFORMATION	
Bank Pekao..........................1	B2
Post Office..........................2	B3
Tourist Office......................3	B2

SIGHTS & ACTIVITIES	
High Castle.........................4	B1
Lower Castle.......................5	B1
Middle Castle.....................6	B1
Skwer Esperanto.................7	B3
Ticket Office.......................8	B1

SLEEPING	
Hotel Grot..........................9	C2
Hotel Stary Malbork..........10	B3
Hotel Zamek......................11	B1
Pokoje Gościnne	
Szarotka.........................12	C2
Youth Hostel.....................13	A3

EATING	
DM Patrzałkowie	
Pizzeria..........................14	C2
Restauracja Piwniczka......15	B1

TRANSPORT	
Bus Terminal....................16	D3

POMERANIA

gradually went into decline. After the First Partition in 1772, the Prussians turned it into barracks, destroying much of the decoration and dismantling sections of no military use.

In the 19th century the Marienburg was one of the first historic buildings taken under government protection, becoming a symbol of medieval German glory. Despite sustaining damage during WWII, almost the entire complex has been preserved, and the castle today looks much as it did six centuries ago, dominating the town and the surrounding countryside. The best view is from the opposite side of the river (you can get there by footbridge), especially in the late afternoon when the brick turns an intense red-brown in the setting sun.

The fortress now operates as the **Castle Museum** (Muzeum Zamkowe; ☎ 055 647 0802; www.zamek .malbork.pl; ul Starościńska 1; tours adult/concession 30/17.50zł; ⌚ 9am-7pm Tue-Sun May-Aug, 10am-5pm Tue-Sun Apr & Sep, 10am-3pm Tue-Sun Oct-Mar) and access is strictly controlled. Most of the rooms and chambers are open to visitors, housing dozens of exhibitions on various historical and archaeological topics.

The entrance to the complex is from the northern side, through what used to be the only way in. From the main gate, you walk over the drawbridge, then go through five iron-barred doors to the vast courtyard of the **Middle Castle** (Zamek Średni). On the western side (to your right) is the **Grand Masters' Palace** (Pałac Wielkich Mistrzów), which has some splendid interiors. Alongside is the **Knights' Hall** (Sala Rycerska), which is the largest chamber in the castle at 450 sq metres. The remarkable ceiling has its original palm vaulting preserved. The building on the opposite side of the courtyard houses a collection of armour and an excellent display of amber.

The tour proceeds to the **High Castle** (Zamek Wysoki), over another drawbridge and through a gate (note the ornamented 1280 doorway) to a spectacular arcaded courtyard that has a reconstructed well in the middle. You'll then be taken around the rooms on three storeys, including the knights' dormitories, kitchen, bakery, chapterhouse and refectory. The entrance to the **castle church** is through a beautiful Gothic doorway, known as the Golden Gate. Underneath the church's presbytery is St Anne's Chapel, with the grand masters' crypt below its floor.

Finally, you can climb the castle's main square **tower** for an excellent view over the whole complex and the flat countryside around, and visit the terraces that run around the High Castle between the main buildings and the fortified walls.

Unfortunately, the castle management is persisting with its long-standing policy that every visitor must join a tour to enter the castle, even though non-Polish language tours are thin on the ground or relatively expensive. Polish guides pick up groups every half-hour, taking up to three hours to go around; in July and August there are also three daily tours in English (at 11am, 1.30pm and 3.30pm) and four in German (at 10am, noon, 1.30pm and 3.30pm), for 35zł including entry.

If you miss the relevant slot or visit out of season, German-, French-, Russian- and English-speaking guides are available on request for 150zł per group (plus the standard entrance fee). If you hang around the ticket office listening for new arrivals speaking your language, you could band together to spread the cost of a group tour.

Late tours (adult/concession 17.50/11.50zł), which leave shortly before closing time, run at breakneck speed and miss some exhibitions. Access to the grounds on Monday, when all the buildings and exhibition rooms are closed, costs just 5zł.

During the warmer months a sound-and-light show, **Cross and Sword** (Krzyżem i Mieczem; ☎ 055 647 0978; adult/concession 15/8zł; ☼ shows at 10pm Jun-Jul, 9.30pm mid-Apr–May & 1-15 Aug, 9pm 16-31 Aug, 8pm 1-15 Sep), is held at the castle, but only in Polish. Still, it's a good chance to see the building in a different light. Another onsite spectacle is the **Siege of Malbork**, a week-long medieval fair in mid-July that includes craft workshops, concerts, outdoor movies and a dramatic staged siege of the castle.

If you've seen the castle and have more time to kill in Malbork, walk south along the line of the river, past impressive remnants of the old city walls, to **Skwer Esperanto** (Plac Zamenhofa), behind the Hotel Stary Malbork. This scrappy park isn't much to look at, but around its edge are commemorative stones placed by keen international speakers of Esperanto from as far away as Korea and Congo, in honour of the world language invented by Ludwig Zamenhof. There's a monument

to the great man in the middle of the park. The explanatory signage is in Polish…and Esperanto, naturally.

Sleeping & Eating

Youth hostel (☎ 055 272 2408; ul Żeromskiego 45; dm 25-30zł, d 51zł; ℗ ✗ 🖳) Housed in a local school, this year-round hostel has a few doubles, but most beds are in dorms sleeping eight or more people. Internet access is only available in July and August. If you arrive when reception is closed, just press the buzzer.

Pokoje Gościnne Szarotka (☎ 055 612 1444; ul Dworcowa 1a; s/d/tr/q 25/45/65/80zł) Surprisingly pleasant rooms near the train station are simple but well maintained, though the shared bathrooms are basic. If you just want to dump your luggage for a few hours while checking out the castle, the obliging staff will rent you a room for 10zł per two hours (no, it isn't what you think!).

Hotel Stary Malbork (☎ 055 647 2400; www.hotel starymalbork.com.pl; ul 17 Marca 26/27; s 210-250zł, d 250-360zł, ste 550-650zł; ℗ ✗ 🖳 ⅋) This graceful hotel is the best value in town, with delightful green rooms boasting excellent fittings and furniture. The staff are friendly and efficient, and there's a sauna, café and restaurant on the premises.

ourpick Hotel Grot (☎ 055 646 9660; www.grot hotel.pl; ul Kościuszki 22d; s/d/tr/ste 199/289/379/399zł; ℗ ✗ 🖳 ⅋) British and Australian travellers will laugh at the name, but there's nothing unhygienic about this brand-new three-star hotel. It's very classy for its price range, with contemporary furniture and an impressive restaurant. It's located back from the street down an unnamed dead-end laneway opposite the unrecommended Hotel Zbyszko.

Hotel Zamek (☎ 055 272 3367; biuro@hotelzamek .pl; ul Starościńska 14; s/d/tr/q/ste €72/86/112/138/170; ℗ ✗) Nestled in a restored medieval building in the Lower Castle, a former hospital, the Hotel Zamek isn't as palatial as you might expect. The interiors are dark and a bit drab, but the location's great. The in-house restaurant is good, though often crowded with tour groups.

DM Patrzałkowie Pizzeria (☎ 055 272 3991; ul Kościuszki 25; mains 9-16zł; ☼ 10am-9pm Sun-Thu, 10am-10pm Fri & Sat) At the station end of town, this eatery's friendly staff serves pizza, pasta, *pierogi*, salads and soups to a mixed crowd of locals and tourists, including some decent vegetarian options.

A THOUSAND AND ONE KNIGHTS

It's impossible to travel anywhere in Pomerania without encountering the ghosts of the Teutonic Knights, the military monks who ended up ruling great swathes of modern-day Germany and Poland.

Their rise is a spectacular tale worthy of a big-budget Hollywood treatment, involving foreign origins, holy war, conquest, defeat and an unexpected sideline in charitable works.

The Order of the Hospitalers of Saint Mary of the Teutons in Jerusalem, as it was formally known, was founded in Palestine in 1190, as a medical body to treat Germanic knights fighting in the Crusades.

In this religion-infused landscape, the order attracted many fighters wanting to take holy orders. From this potent military and spiritual mix emerged the Teutonic Knights, warrior monks who wore a distinctive white habit with a black cross.

Back in Europe, their big break came when the Polish Duke Konrad I of Mazovia needed help subduing the pagan Prussians of the Lower Vistula.

By the end of the 13th century, the Teutonic Knights had conquered all of Prussia. They then set about consolidating their rule by building castles, importing German peasants to build up the population, and developing trade. Towns such as Thorn (Toruń) and Elbing (Elbląg) became important Teutonic centres, and the castle at Marienburg (Malbork) was a potent symbol of the order's might.

Inevitably, territorial tensions arose with the neighbouring and newly resurgent Kingdom of Poland. After a century of friction, the Knights fell to combined Polish and Lithuanian forces at the Battle of Grunwald (1410). But their greatest defeat at Polish hands was yet to come – the Thirteen Years' War saw the order's own subjects turn against it, and the Treaty of Toruń in 1466 forced it to give up much of Pomerania, Warmia and the banks of the Vistula.

The Teutonic Knights were on the way out. In 1525 the order's Grand Master Albert transformed Prussia into a secular state, ending the knights' rule and naming himself duke. Then, after centuries of decline, Napoleon declared the Teutonic order dissolved in 1809.

Curiously though, the order refused to die. In 1834 the Austrian Emperor Franz I re-established the Teutonic order as a religious body, restricted to charitable and nursing activities – neatly returning the body to its medieval roots. Nowadays the Grand Master holds office at Singerstrasse 7 in Vienna, where the Teutonic order operates a museum and archive. It even has a website: www.deutscher-orden.at (in German).

POMERANIA

Restauracja Piwniczka (☎ 055 273 3668; ul Starościńska 1; mains 10-80zł; ☻ 10am-7pm) Situated in an atmospheric cellar beneath the west wall of the castle, facing the river, this restaurant dishes up excellent, flavoursome Polish standards along with specials like Castle's Pot Soup (pork and mushroom) and The Knight's Plate (two kinds of pork and a chicken shashlik).

Getting There & Away

The train station and bus terminal are at the eastern end of the town centre, 1km from the castle. Malbork sits on the busy Gdańsk–Warsaw railway route, so there are plenty of trains to Gdańsk (16zł, 45 minutes) and Warsaw (express 74zł, 3¾ hours). There are also frequent links with Elbląg (10zł, 20 minutes) and seven daily services to Kwidzyn (7.50zł, 45 minutes), four to Grudziądz (13zł, 1¾ hours), and seven to Olsztyn (31zł, 1¾

hours). There's also one train to Kaliningrad (4¼ hours). PKS buses also serve most regional destinations.

Coming from Gdańsk by train, you'll catch a splendid view of the castle; watch out to your right when crossing the river.

ELBLĄG
pop 127,000

Elbląg (*el*-blonk) is something of a revelation. Though being low on sights, and not an obvious place for either Poles or international travellers to visit, its innovatively rebuilt Old Town is an intriguing slice of 21st-century Poland. The unexpectedly harmonious blend of old buildings and recently created modern structures catches the eye and gives the city a unique look. Though it's still a work in progress, Elbląg is fast becoming an attractive place to drop into.

Centuries before WWII turned its historical centre into a heap of rubble, Elbląg became a stronghold and port of the Teutonic Knights (see boxed text, p451). In the 13th century, the Vistula Lagoon (Zalew Wiślany) extended further south than it does today, allowing the town to develop as a maritime centre and a member of the Hanseatic League (see boxed text, p413). When Elbląg came under Polish rule after the Treaty of Toruń, it was a major gateway to the sea. Later, Swedish invasions and the gradual silting up of the waterway capsized the town's prosperity, though a partial revival came with industrial development in the late 19th century.

The port may have gone, but the city still enjoys favourable geography – it's a gateway to Frombork, the starting/finishing point of the Elbląg-Ostróda Canal (see p486) and a jumping-off point for the Russian region of Kaliningrad.

Information

Bank Pekao (Stary Rynek 18a)
Lobos (☎ 055 642 1952; ul Nitschmana 20/22) Travel agency.
Nell@ (☎ 055 643 6855; ul Słoneczna 19u; per hr 2zł; ☼ 8am-8pm Mon-Fri, noon-10pm Sat, noon-8pm Sun) Internet access northeast of the Old Town.
Orbis Travel (☎ 055 236 8555; ul Hetmańska 24)
Post office (Plac Słowiański 1)
Tourist office City centre (☎ 055 232 4234; www .it.elblag.com.pl; ul Czerwonego Krzyża 2; ☼ 7.30am-3.30pm Mon-Fri); Market Gate (☎ 055 611 0820; Brama Targowa; ☼ 10am-6pm Jun-Jul, 8am-4pm Mon-Fri Aug-May)

Sights & Activities

In the early 1990s work started on a project combining modern and traditional elements with the city's Old Town area, creating a stylised **New Old Town** harking back to the merchants' quarters of the great Hanseatic cities. Though construction is ongoing, the area has already acquired a distinctive character, aided by the flurry of new restaurants, bars and hotels cashing in on the increasingly attractive neighbourhood.

One blast from the past still dominates this evolving site: **St Nicholas' Church** (Kościół Św Mikołaja) is a sturdy, redbrick concoction, noted for its 95m-high, carefully reconstructed tower. Within, you'll find some of the original woodcarving, including several triptychs, which escaped war damage.

Some 200m to the north is the **Galeria El** (☎ 055 232 5386; ul Kuśnierska 6; adult/concession 4/2zł; ☼ 10am-6pm Mon-Sat, 10am-5pm Sun), formerly St Mary's Church. Another massive Gothic brick structure, the original church was gutted and now houses a gallery of contemporary art, with occasional concerts and events. It's worth a visit just to see the imposing, lofty interior, and the large modern art objects dotted through the grounds.

A few steps from here is the **Market Gate** (Brama Targowa), the only surviving gate of the medieval fortifications. In front of it is a **statue** of a baker who legendarily saved the town in the 16th century when he spotted the approaching Teutonic Knights, bent on invasion, and cut the ropes that held the gates open. It's good luck to touch his nose as you pass. You can climb to the top of the gate for free, and check out city views.

A five-minute walk south along the river bank is the **Elbląg Museum** (☎ 055 232 7273; Bulwar Zygmunta Augusta 11; adult/concession 9/5zł, free Sat; ☼ 9am-5pm Tue-Sun May-Sep, 8am-4pm Tue-Sun Oct-Apr). Occupying two large buildings, the museum has sections on archaeology and the city's history, plus a photographic record of the town from the 19th century to WWII.

For some physical activity in the great outdoors, head for **Nurwid** (☎ 0601 617 008; Bulwar Zygmunta Augusta; ☼ daylight) near the canal boat quay. These enterprising gentlemen will happily hire you kayaks, boats and bicycles, from 5zł per hour.

Sleeping

Hotel Sowa (☎ 055 233 7422; ul Grunwaldzka 49; s 125-145zł, d 165-180zł; ℗) The centre's a bit of a walk from this two-star, but the bus station is right across the road, making it ideal if you want an early start out of town. There's a restaurant on site, and bicycles available for 5zł per hour.

Pensjonat Boss (☎ 055 239 3728; www.pensjonat boss.pl; ul Św Ducha 30; s/d/tr/ste 150/220/300/300zł) One of several small hotels in the Old Town, Pensjonat Boss offers 13 comfortable rooms above its own bar. The building is a nicer example of the new-look architecture, especially when the window boxes bloom.

Hotel Viwaldi (☎ 055 236 2542; www.viwaldi .m.walentynowicz.pl; Stary Rynek 16; s/d/ste 230/300/385zł; ℗ ▢) Though the blue-grey exterior is a little off-putting, this well-organised hotel has no problem satisfying its demanding target market. There's a restaurant, nightclub and 10% discount at weekends.

POMERANIA

Camping Nr 61 (☎ 055 641 8666; www.camping61 .com.pl; ul Panieńska 14; camp sites per adult/child 12/6zł; d/q 60/100zł; ☺ May-Sep; Ⓟ) Elbląg's pleasantly shaded camping ground occupies an unusually convenient spot on the Elbląg River, close to the Old Town and about 1km west of the train and bus stations.

Eating & Drinking

Café Carillon (☎ 055 232 5295; ul Mostowa 22; mains 8-18zł; ☺ 10am-10pm) This stylish venue has a small patio with a view of St Nicholas' Church, while the interior is an amazing pastiche of Art Deco–style stained glass on a musical theme. The extensive drinks menu is a bit pricey, however.

Roma (☎ 055 237 5555; ul Wieżowa 15; mains 8-21zł; ☺ 11am-10pm) Attractive pizzeria and café a few doors from the Hotel Viwaldi. Pizza, pasta, soups and fish dishes are served within its brown-and-white pseudo-Mediterranean interior.

Złoty Żuraw (☎ 055 642 2233; Stary Rynek 35C; mains 14-16zł; ☺ noon-11pm) On a strategic corner of the Old Town, this Chinese restaurant is decorated in red and gold, with trellises covered in greenery between its booths. Spot the Buddha statue on the way in.

Restauracja Pod Aniołami (☎ 055 236 1726; ul Rybacka 23/24B; mains 17-30zł; ☺ noon-midnight) Tempting tourists and hip locals alike, the Latin American menu here adds a welcome dash of chilli. It's hard not to say olé.

Getting There & Away

BOAT

Boats heading for the Elbląg-Ostróda Canal depart from the quay next to the Old Town. Information and tickets are available from **Żegluga Ostródzko-Elbląska** (☎ 055 232 4307; www.zegluga.elblag.com.pl; ul Wieżowa 14) near the Hotel Viwaldi.

The neighbouring wharf is the departure point for cruises operated by **Żegluga Gdańska** (☎ 055 232 7319; www.zegluga.gda.pl). They depart at 7am daily from May to September, calling at Krynica Morska (return adult/concession 43/30zł, 2½ hours), then continuing to Frombork (86/60zł, four hours), before returning to Elbląg. At the time of research, the company was not running services to Kaliningrad due to tensions between Poland and Russia; no doubt they will resume when the political ice thaws.

BUS

The bus terminal is next to the train station; PKS buses to Gdańsk (13zł, 1½ hours) and Braniewo, for Frombork (8zł, 40 minutes), operate at least hourly. Private minibuses serve the same Braniewo via Frombork route. Polski Express also runs two services a day to Warsaw (38zł).

TRAIN

The train station is 1km southeast of the centre. There are regular trains to Malbork (10zł, 20 minutes, roughly hourly), Gdańsk (20zł, 1¼ hours, 14 daily) and Olsztyn (24zł, 1½ hours, nine daily).

FROMBORK

pop 2500

It's an adventure getting to Frombork by bus, tucked away as it is near the northeast edge of coastal Poland. Roads narrow as you pass through stands of forest, interrupted only by dot-on-the-map villages. The payoff is worth it, however, as you arrive beneath the impressive walled complex that overlooks the tranquil town and the water beyond.

What looks like a castle is, in fact, a cathedral, established by the Warmian bishops (see p479) in the 13th century after a forced departure from nearby Braniewo, following an uprising of pagan Prussians. Later, from 1466 to 1772, Frombork was part of Poland, before it shifted to Prussian control as Frauenburg.

In WWII the town was devastated, but the cathedral somehow survived, and Frombork became repopulated by Poles exiled from territories annexed by the Soviet Union.

The complex is an attractive reason to visit Frombork, but the icing on the cake is its association with Nicolaus Copernicus. It was here that he spent the latter half of his life and conducted most of the observations and research for his heliocentric theory. Copernicus was buried in the cathedral, having survived just long enough to have the first printed copy of his great work placed in his hands – or so the legend goes.

Sights

CATHEDRAL HILL

The Cathedral Hill complex (Wzgórze Katedralne) is today the **Nicolaus Copernicus Museum** (Muzeum Mikołaja Kopernika; ☎ 055 244 0075; www.frombork.art.pl). It covers several sights within the fortified complex, each visited

POMERANIA

on a separate ticket. The entrance is from the southern side through the massive **Main Gate** (Brama Główna), where you'll find the ticket office.

The **cathedral** (adult/concession 4/2zł; 9.30am-5pm Mon-Sat May-Sep, 9am-4pm Mon-Sat Oct-Apr), in the middle of the courtyard, is a huge brick Gothic construction embellished with a decorated western façade and a slim octagonal tower at each corner. Built from 1329 to 1388, it was the largest church ever built by the Warmian bishops, and became a model for most of the subsequent churches they founded throughout the region.

The Baroque organ within, dating from 1683, is a replacement for the one looted by the Swedes in 1626. The instrument is noted for its rich tone, best appreciated during the Sunday recitals held annually from late June to late August, as part of Frombork's **International Festival of Organ Music** (www.frombork -festiwal.pl in Polish).

Note the large number of tombstones within the cathedral's interior, and look for the two intriguing Baroque marble epitaphs, each with the image of a skeleton and a skull: one is on the first northern column (near the chancel), the other on the fifth southern column.

In the southeastern corner of the courtyard is the **Old Bishops' Palace** (Stary Pałac Biskupi; adult/concession 4/2zł; 9am-4.30pm Tue-Sun May-Sep, 9am-4pm Tue-Sun Oct-Apr), now the museum's main exhibition space. On the ground floor are objects discovered during postwar archaeological excavations, while the other levels are largely devoted to the life and work of Copernicus, along with temporary displays and a collection of old telescopes.

The most interesting section is on the first floor, where modern artists' interpretations of the great man, in sculpture and oils, are presented, before you pass into the room containing books and other artefacts from his time.

Though Copernicus is essentially remembered for his astronomical achievements (supplanting the old geocentric Ptolemaic system with his revelation that the earth revolves around the sun), his interests extended to many other fields, including medicine, economy and the law. Apart from an early edition of his famous *De Revolutionibus Orbium Coelestium* (On the Revolutions of the Celestial Spheres), there are copies displayed of his treatises and manuscripts on a range of subjects, together with astronomi-

cal instruments and a copy of Jan Matejko's painting depicting the astronomer at work. The exhibits are well lit and creatively placed, though there's no English captioning.

The high tower at the southwestern corner of the defensive walls is the former cathedral **belfry** (dzwonnica; adult/concession 4/2zł; 9.30am-5pm May-Sep, 9am-4pm Oct-Apr), which has a **planetarium** (adult/concession 6/4zł) at its base presenting half-hour shows in Polish. Go to the top of the tower for views of the cathedral, town, and the Vistula Lagoon and Vistula Spit (see boxed text, opposite).

At the northwestern corner of the complex is the 14th-century **Copernicus Tower** (Wieża Kopernika). It's believed that the astronomer took some of his observations from here, and the top floor is set up to re-create his study; if he'd looked down, he could also have seen his own house, which was just across the road. At the time of research the tower was indefinitely closed to visitors; check with the ticket office to see if it's open when you arrive.

OTHER SIGHTS

The 15th-century **Hospital of the Holy Ghost** (☎ 055 243 7562; ul Stara; adult/concession 4/2zł; 10am-6pm Tue-Sat May-Sep, 9am-4pm Tue-Sat Oct-Apr), formerly St Anne's Chapel, contains exhibitions of religious art and medical history. It's a short walk east of the cathedral.

The **Water Tower** (Wieża Wodna; ☎ 055 243 7500; ul Elbląska 2; adult/concession 3/2zł; 9am-7pm May-Sep, 9am-3pm Oct-Apr), across the main road from the cathedral, was built in 1571 as part of one of the first water-supply systems in Europe and was used for two centuries to provide Cathedral Hill with water through oak pipes. The admission fee lets you climb to the top of the tower.

Sleeping & Eating

In addition to the following options, several private homes around town rent rooms to visitors at reasonable prices – look out for the *kwatery prywatne* signs.

Kwatery Prywatne Koczergo (☎ 055 243 7357; ul Kapelańska 5; s/d 40/70zł; P) Convenient, nicely turned-out lodgings in a residential house just off the Rynek. You can cook meals in the kitchen and relax in the garden – an excellent pick.

Hotelik Dom Familijny Rheticus (☎ 055 243 7800; www.domfamilijny.pl; ul Kopernika 10; s 80-88zł, d 100-120zł, apt 150-200zł; P) This fine family villa contains

---

DIY TRAVEL: MIERZEJA WIŚLANA

If you want to escape the tourist hordes of Gdańsk, head east to the Mierzeja Wiślana (Vistula Spit). This long, narrow sand bar is flanked by the Gulf of Gdańsk to the north and the Zalew Wiślany (Vistula Lagoon) to the south, a vast estuary which stretches all the way to Kaliningrad in Russia. The peninsula is also part Russian, being neatly bisected by the international border.

On the route from Gdańsk to the spit is Sztutowo, some 30km from the city. Here you'll find Stutthof, the former extermination camp in which the Nazis disposed of Polish resisters from the beginning of WWII, and which later became part of their Final Solution against Jews. Nowadays it's a sombre museum presenting exhibitions and documentaries about the Nazi occupation of the region.

Continuing on to the Mierzeja Wiślana, there's a wealth of natural attractions, including pine forests, giant sand dunes, a cormorant reserve in Kąty Rybackie, and places to hire sailboats, yachts and catamarans. Krynica Morska is the major town on the peninsula, with a popular swimming beach, accommodation in old-fashioned villas, and a lighthouse open to visitors. You can reach Krynica Morska by bus or car from Gdańsk, or by ferry from Elbląg (p453).

For that all-over Baltic tan, there's even a nude beach near Piaski, 12km east of Krynica Morska on the far Polish end of the spit. And while you're enjoying the Mierzeja Wiślana beaches, don't forget to have a look for fragments of amber on the shore, washed up by storms in the colder months…

---

nine spacious apartments with various configurations sleeping up to five people. The onsite solarium, hairdresser and florist all add to the informal character of the place. Breakfast is an extra 7zł.

Hotel Kopernik (☎ 055 243 7285; www.hotelkopernik.pl; ul Kościelna 2; s/d/tr 120/170/210zł; P ⓘ ⓖ) The modern Hotel Kopernik has 37 reasonable rooms, its own budget restaurant and the only *kantor* in town. The motel look doesn't sit well with Frombork's more traditional buildings, but some south-facing rooms have great views of the cathedral.

Camping Nr 12 (☎ 055 243 7744; ul Braniewska 14; camp sites 5zł & per person 10zł, dm 25zł, d/tr 50/75zł; ⓨ May-Sep) This privately owned camping ground is at the eastern end of town, on the Braniewo road. It has basic cabins and a snack bar on the grounds.

Restauracja Akcent (☎ 055 243 7275; ul Rybacka 4; mains 5-29zł; ⓨ 10am-11pm; ⓘ) An alternative to the hotel eateries listed above, this is a decent place with a sightline to the castle and a menu that goes beyond the basics.

Getting There & Away

The bus station is in the western part of town, near the waterfront. Buses run to Elbląg (8zł, 40 minutes, hourly) and Gdańsk (16zł, three hours, five daily).

Just north of the station is the marina; from here pleasure boats go to Krynica Morska (return adult/concession 42/30zł, 1½ hours) and on to Elbląg (86/60zł, four hours; see p453).

NORTHERN & WESTERN POMERANIA

Stretching northwest from Gdańsk, the Baltic coast is Poland's key summer holiday strip. It may not be as well known as Spain's Costa del Sol, but it's an attractive coastline of dunes, woods and coastal lakes, fronted by pristine white sandy beaches.

The numerous resort towns stretching all the way from Hel to Świnoujście are engaging places to spend some time. Often blessed with historic architecture, they also contain pleasant green parks and a good mix of restaurants, bars and other diversions. Outside the urban centres, there are also two interesting national parks on the Pomeranian coast.

As you move around, you'll notice that northern and western Pomerania is basically a rural, sparsely populated region, with compact towns and little industry. This blend of natural beauty with the delights of low-key resort towns makes it a pleasing region to explore, whatever the season.

ŁEBA
pop 3800

In the summer months, Łeba (*weh*-bah) is an uber-resort town, taken over by Polish and German holidaymakers. There's a relaxed, good-humoured buzz in the air, generated by the vacationing crowds and the various eateries and amusements that spring up to keep them diverted. Outside the high season, however, Łeba reverts to its off-peak persona of a small, quiet fishing port.

Life wasn't always this relaxed here – in the 16th century the town moved from the western to the eastern bank of the Łeba River after a huge storm flattened the settlement. Even then, Łeba was prey to the exotic peril of shifting sand dunes, which threatened to cover its buildings and disrupt shipping. However, at the end of the 19th century a new port was constructed and forests were planted to impede the sands.

Nowadays it's a great place for a seaside jaunt, boasting a generous expanse of wide sandy beaches and clean water for swimming. It's also within day-trip distance from Gdańsk, and the attractive Słowiński National Park is just next door.

Orientation

The train and bus stations are next to each other in the southwestern part of Łeba, two blocks west of ul Kościuszki, the main drag. This shopping street crosses the Chełst canal then runs north to the port, on a brief stretch of the Łeba River that joins Lake Łebsko to the sea. The river divides Łeba's beachfront into two sections – the east and the quieter west.

Information

Bank Pekao (ul Kościuszki 87)
Biuro Wczasów Przymorze (☎ 059 866 1360; ul Zawiszy Czarnego 8) Information and accommodation; arranges guides to the national park.
Post office (ul Kościuszki 23) Postal services and *kantor*.
Tourist office (☎ 059 866 2565; www.leba.pl; ul 11 Listopada 5a; ⏰ 8am-8pm Mon-Fri, 8am-6pm Sat, 10am-4pm Sun Jul-Aug, 8am-4pm Mon-Fri Sep-May)
Town library (☎ 059 866 1723; ul 11 Listopada 5a; per hr 2zł; ⏰ noon-7pm Mon-Sat) Internet access, next to the tourist office.

Sleeping & Eating

As in most seaside resorts, the accommodation and culinary picture varies wildly between the high season and the rest of the year. Most places have their own eating facilities, and there's a particular concentration of eateries along and around ul Kościuszki.

All prices given here are for the peak season, July to August. At other times of the year, you'll be amazed how much the rates drop.

Dom Turysty PTTK (☎ 059 866 1324; ul Kościuszki 66; dm 40zł) A surprisingly good entry in the ultrabudget category, the PTTK is often virtually empty between groups, so you may even get a room to yourself. The shared bathrooms reflect the pressures of mass occupation, but the price includes breakfast so you can't really quibble.

Mazowsze (☎ 059 866 1870; www.zwmazowsze.pl; ul Nadmorska 15; s/d/tr 140/160/230zł; P X 🖳 ⑤) A stiff walk east of the centre, but just 150m from the beach, the Mazowsze complex accommodates up to 250 people in comfortable rooms. As its main function is as a health resort, all kinds of interesting treatments and fitness activities are available, from cryotherapy to tennis.

Arkun (☎ 059 866 2419; www.arkun.interleba.pl; ul Wróbleskiego 11; s/d/tr 100/200/300zł; P 🖳) The mixed modern-traditional building by the fishing wharf looks like it ought to be pretty fancy, but in fact rooms here are a reasonable lower-midrange standard. Prices come down if you stay for more than one night, though breakfast costs an extra 20zł. Six rooms have balconies facing the canal.

Hotel Gołąbek (☎ 059 866 2175; www.hotel-golabek .leba.pl; ul Wybrzeże 10; s/d/tr/ste 240/330/390/700zł; P X) It may be named after a cabbage roll, but the Gołąbek exudes style on the edge of the wharf, with charming old fishing boats and port views. The sauna, solarium and waterfront restaurant all add to the value. In summer the hotel hires out bicycles (5zł per hr).

Hotel Neptun (☎ 059 866 1432; www.neptunhotel.pl; ul Sosnowa 1; s 455zł, d 455zł, tr 645-685zł, ste 875-1160zł; P X 🖳 ⑤) With super-elegant rooms and an impeccably tasteful restaurant, this spectacular castle-like villa sets the Baltic standard for class and refinement. Located right on the seashore, it has a terrace pool area overlooking the beach, and a bar with great views of the sunset.

Camping Nr 41Ambré (☎ 059 866 2472; www.ambre .leba.pl; ul Nadmorska 9a; camp sites per adult/child 13/8zł, bungalows 240-400zł) This camping ground has a handy range of rooms, a restaurant and delicatessen, and neat, cared-for grounds and facilities. It's open for caravans all year (30zł supplement). And for dogs (3zł).

Relaks (☎ 059 866 1250; ul Nadmorska 13; cabins 280-460zł, r 210-320zł; P X 🖳 ⑤) An upmarket camping ground with full amenities, beach access, charming wooden Toblerone cabins (sleeping up to six people) and some spacious rooms. Warning: the cabins' gardens are populated by garden gnomes.

Maat (☎ 059 866 2977; ul Kościuszki 30a; mains 11-39zł; ☺ 10am-midnight) For casual dining overlooking the canal in the town centre, try this place. Its upstairs timber balcony with a fishy motif has water views, and the staff serve up excellent pizzas, and a range of salads, pasta and fish dishes.

Getting There & Away

The usual transit point to/from Łeba is Lębork, a town 29km to the south, offering good connections with Gdańsk, Gdynia and some other destinations. Trains to Lębork (7.50zł, 50 minutes) depart up to 18 times daily in summer, but only twice daily the rest of the year. Buses (5zł, 35 minutes) head to Lębork at least every hour, supplemented by private minibuses, including those of **Boguś Bus** (☎ 059 862 9300), which runs the route twice-hourly. There's one direct bus between Łeba and Gdynia in summer (18zł, three hours), and two to Słupsk (10zł, 1½ hours).

SŁOWIŃSKI NATIONAL PARK

The 186-sq-km **Słowiński National Park** (Słowiński Park Narodowy; ☎ 059 811 7204; adult/concession 4/2zł; ☺ 7am-9pm May-Sep, 8am-4pm Oct-Apr) takes up the 33km stretch of coast between Łeba and the fishing tourist village of **Rowy**, complete with two large lakes, the Łebsko and the Gardno, and their surrounding belts of peat bog, meadows and woods. It's named after the Slav tribe of the Slovincians (Słowińcy), a western branch of the Kashubians whose descendants inhabited this part of the coast right up until the 19th century. In 1977 the park was included on Unesco's list of World Biosphere Reserves.

Sights

SHIFTING DUNES

The most unusual feature of the national park are the **shifting dunes** (wydmy ruchome), which create a genuine desert landscape (see boxed text, p458). They're on the sand bar separating the sea from Lake Łebsko, about 8km west of Łeba. Rommel's Afrika Korps trained in this desert during WWII, and the site was also a secret missile testing ground from 1940 to 1945.

The dunes are easily reached from Łeba: take the road west to the hamlet of **Rąbka** (2.5km), where there's a car park and the gate to the national park. Private minibuses, open-sided electric cars and motorised trains (5zł) ply this road in summer, from a stop on Al Wojska Polskiego, north of the canal. It's also an easy walk. The sealed road continues into the park for another 3.5km to the site of the rocket launcher, now an outdoor **museum** (adult/concession 6/5zł). From here a wide path goes on through the forest for another 2km to the southern foot of the dunes, where half-buried trees jut out of the sand. As you walk round the bend from the woods, it's quite a sight – the pale, immense dunes open up in front of you like a desert dropped into the middle of a forest, with a striking contrast at the line where the trees meet the sand. Continue up the vast dunes for a sweeping view of desert, lake, beach, sea and forest.

No cars or buses are allowed beyond the car park. You can walk to the dunes (45 minutes), buy a ticket on one of the small electric cars (10zł one way), or rent a bicycle (6zł per hour). There are also large electric cars (5zł one way) and boats (12zł), but both only go as far as the launcher, so you'll still have 2km to walk to the dunes. Coming back, you can either retrace your steps or walk to Łeba along the beach (8km), perhaps stopping for a swim – something you certainly can't do in the Sahara.

LAKES

There are four lakes in the park, two large and two small. They are shallow lagoons that started life as bays and were gradually cut off from the sea by the sand bar. With densely overgrown, almost inaccessible marshy shores, they provide a habitat for about 250 species of birds, which live here either permanently or seasonally. Large parts of the lake shores have been made into strict no-access reserves, safe from human interference.

About 16km long and 71 sq km in area, **Lake Łebsko** is the biggest in Pomerania and the third-largest in Poland, after Śniardwy and Mamry in Masuria. It's steadily shrinking as a result of the movement of the dunes, the growth of weeds, and silting.

KLUKI

Set on the southwestern shore of Lake Łebsko, the tiny isolated hamlet of Kluki was the last holdout of Slovincian culture, now showcased in the centrally located **skansen** (Muzeum Wsi Słowińskiej; ☎ 059 846 3020; adult/concession 7.50/4.50zł; ☺ 9am-3pm Mon, 9am-6pm Tue-Sun Jun-Aug, 9am-3.30pm

POMERANIA

Tue-Sun Sep-May). It's modest but authentic, comprising original *in situ* buildings. The long, two-family, whitewashed houses are fitted with traditional furniture and decorations.

Regular bus transport to Kluki runs from Słupsk (7.50zł, one hour, six daily). During summer there are three daily buses between Łeba and Kluki, or you could try negotiating the hire of a private minibus. Summer boat tours go twice-weekly to the skansen (adult/concession 45/39zł), including admission and an English-speaking guide, making a six-hour round trip.

SMOŁDZINO

West of Kluki, outside the park's boundaries, Smoldzino boasts a fine **Natural History Museum** (Muzeum Przyrodnicze; ☎ 059 811 7204; adult/concession 3/1.50zł; ☷ 9am-5pm daily May-Sep, 7.30am-3.30pm Mon-Fri Oct-Apr), which features collections of flora and fauna from the park's various habitats.

Just 1km southwest of the village is **Mt Rowokół**, the highest hill in the area at 115m above sea level. On its top is a 20m **observation tower**, providing sweeping views over the forest, the lakes and the sea. The path up the hill begins next to the petrol station and you can get to the top in 15 minutes.

Buses to Słupsk (7.50zł, 45 minutes) go fairly regularly through the day. There's one morning bus to Łeba in the summer holidays.

SŁUPSK

pop 98,000

Less visited by tourists, Słupsk (pronounced swoopsk) is a regional service centre with a country town pace. Though its façades are a little cracked and faded, the city centre is home to some broad, attractive thoroughfares containing well-maintained gardens, and some grand 19th-century buildings. There's a distinct sense of civic pride, and a lot of pro-European signage about the city – even

the local PKS affiliate has a logo resembling the EU stars painted on its buses.

Like all Pomeranian cities, Słupsk's history involves a complex list of owners: it began life in the 11th century as a Slav stronghold on the Gdańsk–Szczecin trading route, then was ruled by Gdańsk dukes from 1236, passed to the Brandenburg margraves in 1307 and later became part of the West Pomeranian Duchy. In 1648 it reverted to the Brandenburgs, and became part of Prussia, then Germany, until returning to Polish rule after WWII.

Today, Słupsk is a pleasant alternative to the busier centres on the coast, and is a good base for visiting the seaside resorts of Darłowo and Ustka.

Information

Bank Pekao (ul 9 Marca 6)

Kawiarnia Internet (☎ 0601 641 003; per hr 4zł; ☷ 10am-10pm Mon-Sat) Upstairs at the train station.

Net Arena (☎ 059 841 4700; ul Staszica 14; per hr 2.50zł; ☷ 10am-10pm Sun-Thu, Fri & Sat 24hr) Internet access.

Post office (ul Łukasiewicza 3)

Tourist office Plac Zwycięstwa (summer tourist info booth; Plac Zwycięstwa); ul Sienkiewicza (☎ 059 842 4326; www.slupsk.pl; ul Sienkiewicza 19; ☷ 8am-6pm Mon-Fri, 9am-3pm Sat Jun-Aug, 8am-4pm Mon-Fri Sep-May) Ask the helpful staff about tours to Słowiński National Park.

Sights

The **Museum of Central Pomerania** (Muzeum Pomorza Środkowego; ☎ 059 842 4081; ul Dominikańska 5; admission 4.50zł; ☷ 10am-3pm Mon, 10am-5pm Tue-Sat, 10am-6pm Sun) is housed within Słupsk's main attraction, its commanding 16th-century **castle**. Beyond its impressive blocky tower are sacral woodcarvings, historic furniture and other exhibits illustrating the town's history. The highlight is a 200-piece collection of portraits by Stanisław Ignacy Witkiewicz (1885–1939), the controversial writer, photographer and painter popularly known as Witkacy.

SHIFTING SANDS

The 'walking' dunes in the Słowiński National Park are composed of sand thrown up on the beach by waves. Dried by wind and sun, the grains of sand are then blown away to form dunes that are steadily moving inland. The 'white mountain' progresses at a speed of 2m to 10m a year, burying everything it meets on its way. The main victim is the forest, which is gradually disappearing under the sand, to reappear several decades later as a field of skeletal trees.

The process started at least 5000 years ago, and so far the dunes have covered an area of about 6 sq km and reached a height of 30m to 40m, with the highest peak at 42m. They continue to spread inland over new areas, maintaining their miniature Sahara-by-the-Sea.

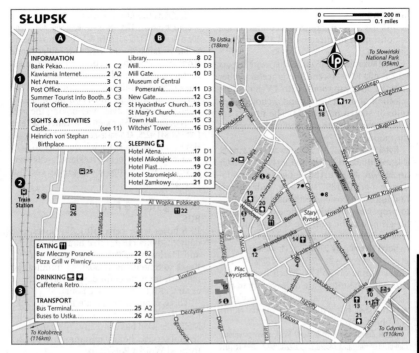

SŁUPSK

0 —————— 200 m
0 —————— 0.1 miles

INFORMATION		
Bank Pekao	1	C2
Kawiarnia Internet	2	A2
Net Arena	3	C1
Post Office	4	C3
Summer Tourist Info Booth	5	C3
Tourist Office	6	C3

SIGHTS & ACTIVITIES		
Castle	(see 11)	
Heinrich von Stephan Birthplace	7	A2

Library	8	D2
Mill	9	D3
Mill Gate	10	D3
Museum of Central Pomerania	11	D3
New Gate	12	C3
St Hyacinthus' Church	13	C3
St Mary's Church	14	C3
Town Hall	15	C3
Witches' Tower	16	D3

SLEEPING		
Hotel Atena	17	D1
Hotel Mikołajek	18	D1
Hotel Piast	19	C2
Hotel Staromiejski	20	C2
Hotel Zamkowy	21	D3

EATING		
Bar Mleczny Poranek	22	B2
Pizza Grill w Piwnicy	23	C2

DRINKING		
Caffeteria Retro	24	C2

TRANSPORT		
Bus Terminal	25	A2
Buses to Ustka	26	A2

To Ustka (18km)
To Słowiński National Park (35km)
Train Station
Al Wojska Polskiego
Plac Zwycięstwa
Stary Rynek
To Kołobrzeg (116km)
To Gdynia (110km)

POMERANIA

The building opposite the castle gate is the 14th-century **mill** (admission 4.50zł; 10am-3pm Mon, 10am-5pm Tue-Sat, 10am-6pm Sun), an annexe to the museum. Its three floors contain colourful displays of traditional decorative arts including costume, embroidery and pottery, with a small amber display in the basement. There's not an English caption in sight, but a combined entry ticket to both sections of the museum is available at 7.50zł.

Next to the mill is the 15th-century **St Hyacinthus' Church** (Kościół Św Jacka). The main body of the church is often closed outside service times, but its fine organ can be heard at regular summer concerts, held midweek in July and August.

Only two remnants of the 15th-century fortified walls that once encircled the town survive: the **Mill Gate** (Brama Młyńska), beside the mill, and the **Witches' Tower** (Baszta Czarownic; ☎ 059 841 2621; ul Nullo 8; admission free; 9am-5pm Tue-Sun), a bit further north. The latter has had a sensational career, having been a 17th-century jail for women suspected of witchcraft; in total, 18 women were executed here up to 1714. Nowadays the tower is a showroom

for the Baltic Gallery of Art, exhibiting funky contemporary works.

One more enduring element of the fortifications is the **New Gate** (Brama Nowa), facing the elaborate Renaissance-Gothic **town hall**. You can climb the castle-like hall's impressive main **tower** (adult/concession 2/1zł; 9am-5pm Mon, 9am-3pm Tue-Sun Jun-Sep) for a full Słupsk panorama. Fans of red brick and stained glass should also check out the chunky Gothic **St Mary's Church**, with its vibrantly coloured windows, and the restored city **library** (built between 1276 and 1281), itself formerly a house of God.

Not far from the library is an untidy **park** with signage commemorating the birthplace of Heinrich von Stephan (1831–97), the reputed inventor of the postcard. Pause for a moment and pay homage to the creator of the indispensable travel accessory.

Festivals & Events
Polish Piano Festival (☎ 059 842 4960) Held in September.
Komeda Jazz Festival (☎ 059 842 1396) Held in November, and dedicated to the father of Polish jazz, Krzysztof Komeda.

Sleeping

Słupsk has a decent range of accommodation options, most in attractive old 19th-century buildings.

Hotel Mikołajek (☎ 059 842 2902; ul Szarych Szeregów 1; s 70zł, d 80-100zł) Ascend the graceful timber staircase to cheap rooms with TV, a random selection of duvet covers and a choice of en suite or shared bathrooms. The fittings are a bit shabby, but the very high ceilings lift the mood.

Hotel Piast (☎ 059 842 5286; www.hotelpiast.slupsk.pl; ul Jedności Narodowej 3; s 132-190zł, d 149-240zł, tr 240zł, ste 390-490zł; P) Affordable accommodation in a grand 1897 structure, with options ranging from basic guesthouse-style rooms to proper luxury suites. The corridors are a bit grim, but the staff are friendly and the rooms are pleasantly light and airy.

Hotel Atena (☎ 059 842 8814; www.hotel.atena .at.pl; ul Kilińskiego 7; s/d 120/150, tr 180-240zł; P) The Greek theme doesn't go much beyond the name, but the rooms are quite comfy in this classic lemon-coloured building. They're of variable size, but with neat parquetry floors and pine furniture.

Hotel Zamkowy (☎ 059 842 5294; www.przymorze .com.pl; ul Dominikańska 4; s/d/tr 150/220/250zł; P) Right next to the castle, this is a good, unfussy option, with rooms ranging from tiny singles to spacious two-room doubles, with lovely clean bathrooms. Choose between the church side (views of St Hyacinthus') and the road side (garden views).

Hotel Staromiejski (☎ 059 842 8464; www.przy morze.com.pl; ul Jedności Narodowej 4; s 130-190zł, d 220-250zł, tr 270zł) Right next door to the Piast, the Staromiejski is posh and smart. The newly renovated rooms feature vibrant carpets and timber furniture. The fancy in-house restaurant (mains 12zł to 35zł) dishes up quality Polish food.

Eating & Drinking

All the hotels listed under Sleeping have their own restaurants, but there are plenty of eateries scattered around the city centre, including the following.

Bar Mleczny Poranek (☎ 059 844 3397; Al Wojska Polskiego 46; mains 1-6zł; 8am-6pm Mon-Fri, 9am-5pm Sat & Sun) Serves up all the Polish standards and their trimmings (along with pizzas) in a plain, unreconstructed *bar mleczny* setting.

ourpick Pizza Grill w Piwnicy (☎ 059 841 0440; ul Bema 9; mains 5-17zł; noon-10pm Sun-Mon, 11am-10pm Tue-Thu, 11am-11pm Fri & Sat) Atmospheric cellar restaurant and bar, with tables made from massive cross-sections of tree trunks. Menu choices include good pizzas and various grilled meat dishes. Try not to meet the gaze of the stuffed animals on the walls.

For a drink in style, overlooking the gardens of broad Al Sienkiewicza, **Caffeteria Retro** (☎ 059 841 4235; Al Sienkiewicza 3; 9am-midnight Mon-Fri, noon-midnight Sat & Sun) is the place to park yourself. If you're feeling reckless, it sells beers flavoured with syrups such as mint, coconut or Irish cream.

Getting There & Away

BUS

PKS buses serve Łeba (10zł, 1½ hours, two daily), Gdynia (15zł, three hours, two daily) and Darłowo (8.50zł, 1½ hours, 11 daily). Buses to Smołdzino (7.50zł, 45 minutes) go regularly throughout the day, and six continue as far as Kluki (6.80zł, one hour).

Three companies operate buses to Ustka (3.80zł, 30 minutes): PKS, Nord Express and MZK, the local bus company. You can expect several services hourly in summer, departing from Al Wojska Polskiego.

TRAIN

The PKP station has trains roughly every two hours east to Gdańsk (31zł, two hours). Eight trains head west to Szczecin (42zł, 3½ hours). Three trains go straight to Warsaw (53zł, seven hours), with two extra services in summer.

USTKA

pop 16,000

This fishing port is an ambient inclusion in the list of Baltic resort towns, with a pleasant, neatly maintained centre and some impressive, elegant architecture. It's been popular with German sun-seekers since 19th-century; 'Iron Chancellor' Otto von Bismarck built an elaborate beach shack here, and their enthusiasm shows no sign of abating. As a result, the town offers a lively seaside promenade, a good quantity of parkland and some appealing accommodation options.

Information

Bank Pekao (ul Marynarki Polskiej 81c)
Doma Ustka (☎ 059 814 5623; www.doma.ustka.pl; ul Wilcza 22) Accommodation-finding service.

Post office (ul Marynarki Polskiej 47)

Tourist office (☎ 059 814 7170; www.ustka.pl; ul Marynarki Polskiej 87; ☻ 8am-8pm Jul & Aug, 9am-5pm Mon-Sat Sep-Jun) Can provide information on fishing tours, horse riding, canoeing and hiking in the area.

Sleeping & Eating

The helpful tourist office staff can help find you a place in a hotel, pension, holiday home or private house, starting from 55zł per person.

Baltic Art Gallery (Bałtycka Galeria Sztuki; ☎ 059 814 6089; www.hotel.baltic-gallery.art.pl; ul Zaruskiego 1a; d/tr 60/75zł; ☐) Art imitates life at this 19th-century granary, which is right by the port, and doubles as a contemporary art gallery. The art is downstairs, the budget travellers up above.

Pensjonat Oleńka (☎ 059 814 8522; ul Zaruskiego 1; d 250, ste 400-550zł) Just next door, in the middle of the granary row, the Oleńka has just three rooms and four suites, all elegantly stylish.

Hotel Rejs (☎ 059 814 7850; www.hotelrejs.com in Polish; ul Marynarki Polskiej 51; s/d 190/260zł, ste 260-320zł; ☐ ☐) Swish central hotel, just minutes from the beach and offering spiffy modern standards. It has an excellent house restaurant with a geographically diverse wine list.

Villa Red (☎ 059 814 8000; www.villa-red.pl; ul Żeromskiego 1; s/d/tr/ste 260/340/370/580zł; ☐ ☐) A grand old redbrick pile built in 1886 for Otto von Bismarck, Ustka's most prominent beachside villa is crammed with antique furniture. There's also a restaurant and nightclub in the grounds.

Camping Słoneczny (☎ 059 814 5586; ul Grunwaldzka 35; dm 35zł, cabins 100zł) The most convenient of the two seasonal camping grounds, about 1.2km away from the beach. Cabin space disappears like snow in summer.

Getting There & Away

The train station is diagonally opposite the tourist office. The bus station is a five-minute walk further north along Al Marynarki Polskiej. Trains to Słupsk depart about every other hour (4.50zł, 25 minutes) in summer, and there are three or four buses per hour (3.80zł, 30 minutes). Regular buses also go to Rowy (6.80zł, one hour), on the edge of Słowiński National Park. In July and August, Polski Express runs daily to Warsaw (81zł, nine hours).

DARŁOWO

pop 14,000

This spread-out coastal settlement west of Ustka falls into three easy parts: inland Darłowo, and the western and eastern sections of Darłówko, a beachfront settlement divided by the Wieprza River. The result is an interesting contrast of the historic and the hedonistic – represented by the medieval character of Darłowo and the prosaic seaside feel of Darłówko.

Darłowo, 2.5km from the Baltic, was yet another successful Hanseatic trading port (see boxed text, p413) in medieval times, with a familiar chessboard of streets laid out in 1312. It also has several venerable buildings worth a look.

Darłówko, by contrast, was once a small fishing port but has developed into a popular seaside resort, its western and eastern sides linked by a pedestrian drawbridge that opens when boats go into or out of the bay. The two towns are linked by local buses that run regularly along both sides of the river.

Information

Post office (ul Morska 3)

Tourist office (☎ 094 314 2902; ul Zamkowa 4; ☻ 10am-6pm Mon-Fri, 10am-4pm Sun & Sat) Near the castle.

Sights

South of Darłowo's central Rynek is its well-preserved 14th-century **castle**, erected in 1352 and renovated in 1988. It was the residence of the Pomeranian dukes until the Swedes devastated it during the Thirty Years' War, and the Brandenburgs took it following the Treaty of Westphalia. The dethroned King Erik, who ruled Denmark, Norway and Sweden between 1396 and 1438 and became known as the 'last Viking of the Baltic', lived in the castle for the last 10 years of his life. He is believed to have hidden his enormous ill-gotten treasure here; so far it remains undiscovered, so keep your eyes peeled as you wander about!

The castle's resident **museum** (Muzeum Zamku Książąt Pomorskich; ☎ 094 314 2351; www.muzeumdarlowo .pl; ul Zamkowa 4; adult/concession 8/4zł; ☻ 10am-4pm) features well-restored period interiors packed with folk carvings, portraits of Pomeranian princes, original Danzig furniture, sacred art, armour, quite a few paintings of ships at sea, and even some exhibits from the Far East. No English captions, but it's still worth a look. Poke around the claustrophobic brick basement to see the former beer cellars and medieval central heating.

Besides the main body of the castle, there is a **Nautineum** (admission 3zł) holding seafaring artefacts, just under the ramparts. Other sections house temporary exhibitions, including the castle's main **tower** (admission 2zł).

The western side of the Rynek is occupied by the **town hall**, a largish Baroque building, lacking a tower and fairly sober in decoration except for its original central doorway, and a rather fetching nautical fountain out front. Right behind it rises the massive brick **St Mary's Church**. Begun in the 1320s and enlarged later, it has preserved its Gothic shape pretty well.

Worth special attention are the three **tombs** placed in the chapel under the tower. The one made of sandstone holds the ashes of King Erik, who died in Darłowo in 1459. His tombstone, commissioned in 1882 by the Prussian Emperor Wilhelm II, isn't as impressive as the two mid-17th-century, richly decorated tin tombs standing on either side of it, which contain the remains of the last West Pomeranian duke Jadwig and his wife Elizabeth.

A few hundred metres north of the Rynek is the marvellous **St Gertrude's Chapel** (Kaplica Św Gertrudy). The most unusual building in town, it is 12-sided and topped with a high, shingled central spire. It's been renovated and looks amazing, but is usually only open for Mass.

Sleeping

Accommodation is highly seasonal, with summer lodgings operating mainly in Darłówko. Many locals rent out rooms in their homes, from 30zł per person.

Hotel Irena (☎ 094 314 3692; Al Wojska Polskiego 64, Darłowo; s/d/tr/ste 70/120/130/150zł) One of a handful of options in central Darłowo, the Irena is a decent pension, with neat, clean rooms and easy access to the castle and the bus station.

Róża Wiatrów (☎ 094 314 2127; www.rozawiatrow .pl; ul Muchy 2, Darłówko; camp sites per adult/child 10/8zł, d 230-320zł, tr 270-400zł, cabins 60-100zł, apt 420zł; ☯ May-Oct, camping Jun-Aug) This multifaceted holiday complex near the sea has camping space for 100 bodies and offers plenty of other accommodation, from plain to glam.

Klub Plaza (☎ 094 314 2407; ul Słowiańska 3, Darłówko; s/d/q 185/370/800zł; Ⓟ 🖳 🖳) Complex situated bang on the beachfront, offering a staggering range of facilities. Prices include breakfast (even with self-catering facilities), the huge penthouse apartments sleep up to six people, and you get a choice of sea or park views.

Getting There & Away

The bus terminal is at the southwestern end of Darłowo, a 10-minute walk from the Rynek. Buses run twice a day to Ustka (7.30zł, 50 minutes) and Słupsk (8.50zł, 1½ hours).

KOŁOBRZEG

pop 44,000

If like lying on the beach but quickly get bored, Kołobrzeg (ko-*wob*-zhek) may appeal. This atmospheric seaside town, with its long clean beach, spa treatments, beer gardens and relaxed strolling crowds of German tourists, is big enough to offer urban distractions on top of the delights of sea and sand. It's actually one of Poland's oldest settlements, having been founded in the 7th century when salt springs were discovered here. In 1000 it became a seat of the Polish bishopric, putting it on a par with Kraków and Wrocław.

The good times couldn't last, unfortunately, the town became a popular destination for military invaders, including Swedes, Brandenburgs, Russians and the French forces under Napoleon. Once this phase was over, Kołobrzeg reinvented itself as a sunny spa resort, only to be demolished by the two-week battle for the city in the closing months of WWII.

With the war well behind it, Kołobrzeg is once again a popular seaside city and busy working port, and some effort has been made to rebuild it in a style sympathetic with its history. Factor in its plentiful parks and lively beachfront area, and you have a coastal city that well repays a few days' visit.

Information

Albatros (☎ 094 354 2800; www.albatros.turystyka.pl; ul Morska 7A; ☯ 9am-4pm Mon-Fri, 9am-1pm Sat) Accommodation service.

Bank Pekao (ul Źródlana 5)

BPH Bank (ul Łopuskiego 6)

Net Spin (☎ 094 354 7366; Giełdowa 7C; per hr 4zł; ☯ 10am-9pm) Internet access.

Post office (ul Armii Krajowej 1)

PTTK (☎ 094 352 2311; butpttk@interia.pl; Baszta Prochowa, ul Dubois 20; ☯ 7.30am-3.30pm Mon-Fri, 8am-noon Sat) Accommodation and information.

Tourist office train station (☎ 094 352 7939; www.kolo brzeg.pl; ul Dworcowa 1; ☯ 8am-5pm Jul & Aug, 8am-4pm Mon-Fri Sep-Jun); city centre (☎ 094 354 7220; Plac Ratuszowy 2/1; ☯ 8am-5pm)

Vobis (☎ 094 354 0891; ul Armii Krajowej 20; per hr 4zł; ☯ 10am-6pm) Internet access.

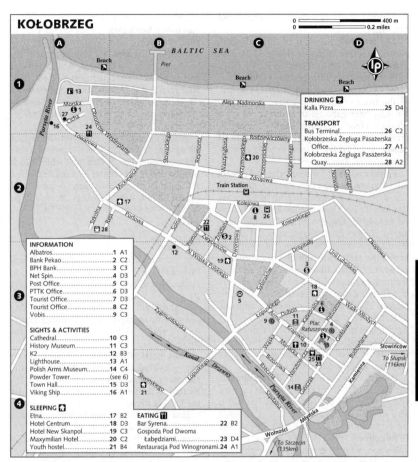

KOŁOBRZEG

BALTIC SEA

INFORMATION
Albatros.....................................1	A1
Bank Pekao.............................2	C2
BPH Bank.................................3	C3
Net Spin...................................4	D3
Post Office...............................5	C3
PTTK Office.............................6	D3
Tourist Office..........................7	D3
Tourist Office..........................8	C2
Vobis.......................................9	C3

SIGHTS & ACTIVITIES
Cathedral.................................10	C3
History Museum......................11	C3
K2..12	B3
Lighthouse...............................13	A1
Polish Arms Museum...............14	C4
Powder Tower..................(see 6)	
Town Hall................................15	D3
Viking Ship..............................16	A1

SLEEPING
Etna...17	B2
Hotel Centrum.........................18	D3
Hotel New Skanpol..................19	C3
Maxymilian Hotel....................20	C2
Youth hostel............................21	B4

EATING
Bar Syrena...............................22	B2
Gospoda Pod Dwoma	
Łabędziami...............................23	D4
Restauracja Pod Winogronami..24	A1

DRINKING
Kalla Pizza...............................25	D4

TRANSPORT
Bus Terminal...........................26	C2
Kołobrzeska Żegluga Pasażerska	
Office......................................27	A1
Kołobrzeska Żegluga Pasażerska	
Quay.......................................28	A2

POMERANIA

Sights & Activities

Not much remains of Kołobrzeg's old quarter, but the area around the central Rynek has been rebuilt as what you might call the **New Old Town**, an interesting blend of old and new architecture.

The 14th-century **cathedral** is the most important historic sight in town. Though badly damaged in 1945, it has been rebuilt close to its original form. For such a massive building, it has a surprisingly light-filled interior, illuminated by its extremely tall and narrow windows. Its colossal two conjoined towers occupy the whole width of the building, and the façade is a striking composition of windows placed haphazardly – a bizarre folly of its medieval builders and rebuilders.

The five-naved interior is impressively spacious. Its most striking feature is the leaning columns on the right side of the nave, which give the impression that the cathedral is on the point of collapsing. Don't worry – they have been leaning since the 16th century.

Old fittings include three 16th-century triptychs and a unique Gothic wooden chandelier (1523) in the central nave. There are some even older objects such as the bronze baptismal font (1355) featuring scenes of Christ's life, a 4m-high, seven-armed candelabrum (1327) and the stalls in the chancel (1340). Outside is a striking modern monument celebrating 1000 years of Polish Catholicism; the design, a symbolic split cross joined by a peace dove, depicts influential rulers Bolesław Chrobrego and Otto III.

The **town hall**, just east of the cathedral, is a neo-Gothic structure designed by Karl Friedrich Schinkel and erected in the 1830s after the previous 14th-century building was razed by Napoleon's forces in 1807. The area in the front of the main entrance is populated by beer gardens in summer, so it's a pleasant place to sit and admire the architecture. One of its wings houses a **modern art gallery** (☎ 094 352 4348; ul Armii Krajowej 12; adult/concession 4/2zł; ⏰ 10am-5pm Tue-Sun).

Prepare yourself for a surprise – the **Polish Arms Museum** (Muzeum Oręża Polskiego; ☎ 094 352 5254; ul Gierczak 5; adult/concession 7/5zł; ⏰ 9.30am-5pm Mon, Tue & Thu-Sun, 9.30am-noon Wed Jun-Aug, 10am-4pm Tue, Wed & Fri-Sun, 11am-5pm Thu Sep-May, outdoor display only Tue) is more interesting than you'd expect. Its displays cover the history of weaponry across the ages, with examples of swords, armour, halberds and more modern military technology, including an outdoor display of suitably daunting weapons and vehicles. Its vast display of cannonballs is courtesy of Kołobrzeg's various battles, and the 1945 destruction is impressively depicted via war wreckage against a panorama of the burning city. It's well worth buying the English language guidebook for 6zł.

Its sister institution, the **History Museum** (☎ 094 352 5253; ul Armii Krajowej 13; adult/concession 7/5zł; ⏰ 10am-4pm Wed, Fri & Sat, 11am-7pm Thu) is also worth a look, partly because it's housed in a gracious old merchant's house, the Braunschweig Palace. It has a neatly presented collection, with an emphasis on weights and scales. Head downstairs for an interesting audiovisual presentation (in English on request) about the city's history, using images of old postcards.

Around the corner, near the Hotel Centrum, is the **Powder Tower** (Baszta Prochowa; ul Dubois 20). This 15th-century survivor from the original city walls was given this name in 1945, in honour of an earlier tower that exploded into oblivion in 1657 when its gunpowder store caught fire. Occasional medieval fairs are held around its base.

In the seaside sector, the **beach** itself is the attraction, supplemented by the usual seasonal stalls, games, novelty boat trips, buskers and other street life. There are also various outlets offering **spa treatments**, though for some odd reason they're rarely available on weekends. At intervals along the sands you can hire a **beach chair** (per hour 8zł) for two, to sunbathe in comfort. Walk out 200m over the sea on the **pier**, an obligatory trip for holidaymakers. To the west, by the harbour and its newly constructed cluster of waterside apartments, stands the **lighthouse** (Latarnia Morska; ☎ 0502 058 767; adult/concession 3/2zł; ⏰ 10am-4pm daily, ⏰ until sunset Jul & Aug), which you can climb for panoramic views.

A fun excursion is a ride on the replica **viking ship** (☎ 0604 189 120; cnr ul Towarowa & ul Cicha; adult/concession 20/15zł; ⏰ 10am-5pm), which heads into the Baltic for regular 45-minute cruises. If you fancy more active exercise, head to **K2** (☎ 094 354 7874; Al Wojska Polskiego 28h; per hr 5zł, per day 30zł; ⏰ 10am-6pm Mon-Fri, 10am-3pm Sat) to hire a bicycle.

Sleeping

The summer crowds can make a real dent in Kołobrzeg's substantial accommodation range, though private rooms are on offer from locals hanging around the tourist office and train station brandishing *wolne pokoje* (rooms free) signs. You can expect to pay about 30zł to 35zł per person for these rooms.

Youth hostel (☎ 094 352 2769; ul Śliwińskiego 1; dm 60zł; ⏰ Jul & Aug) Basic accommodation in the summer months, set up in a local school. It's located to the west of the city centre, across the Parsęta River.

Etna (☎ 094 355 2525; www.hoteletna.pl; ul Portowa 18; s/d/ste 160/200/300zł; P X X &) This massive beach-area building looks plain from the outside, but the rooms are spacious and bright, and you can indulge in a full range of spa treatments here (even Polynesian massage!).

Hotel Centrum (☎ 094 354 5560; www.centrum.info.pl; ul Katedralna 12; s/d/tr/ste 130/210/260/300zł; P X 🖳) Popular with tour groups, the Hotel Centrum provides comfortable accommodation right in the city centre, with its own restaurant, café and nightclub. The large rooms, with relaxing timber tones, often have park or garden views.

Hotel New Skanpol (☎ 094 352 8211; www.newskanpol.pl; ul Dworcowa 10; s/d/ste €50/69/95; P X 🖳) The communist-era Skanpol has recently been given a 21st-century make-over, and is now an attractive option with loads of facilities, including in-house health treatments. Though its blocky 1960s styling makes this hotel stand out like a sore thumb, its height creates good views over the city.

ourpick Maxymilian Hotel (☎ 094 354 0012; www .maxymilian-hotel.pl; ul Borzymowskiego 3; s/d 185/280zł; ste 380-430zł; Ⓟ ⌨ 🐾) The splendidly classy Maxymilian revels in a quiet location and quality rooms – a touch more elegant than those usually found in resort hotels. The restaurant and spa facilities mean you don't have to go far to relax. Breakfast is an extra 25zł, and full board is available.

Eating & Drinking

In the beach district, most holiday homes provide meals for their guests (and often for nonguests); half and full board is often possible. There are also seasonal fast-food outlets and cafés everywhere, as well as some good year-round options.

ourpick Restauracja Pod Winogronami (☎ 094 354 7336; www.winogrona.pl; ul Towarowa 16; mains 12-52zł; ☽ 11am-midnight) In the harbour area, 'Under the Grapes' has a slightly French air, but the hearty menu draws mainly on the Polish and German rule books, with a few intriguing items such as 'trapper's cutlet with mushrooms'.

Bar Syrena (☎ 094 352 3188; ul Zwycięzców 11; mains 7-13zł; ☽ 11am-6pm Mon-Fri, 11am-5pm Sat, 11am-4pm Sun) Modern take on the classic *bar mleczny*, serving up Polish standards in a spick-and-span tiled dining room with abstract prints on the walls. There's a reasonable selection of salads, and the *placek po węgiersku* (Hungarian potato cake and goulash) is to die for.

Gospoda Pod Dwoma Łabędziami (☎ 094 354 7126; ul Armii Krajowej 30b; mains 14-32zł; ☽ 11am-9pm) Downstairs eatery with a stone floor and rustic décor, and drawings of Kołobrzeg buildings on the walls. Hearty Polish food is on the menu, including some excellent soups.

Kalla Pizza (☎ 094 354 0330; ul Armii Krajowej 32; mains 10-31zł; ☽ 10am-11pm) A great place for a drink is this beer garden operated by Kalla Pizza in the warmer months, in the square in front of the town hall. It's a cut above its rivals, with floral décor and a miniature Neptune fountain among the timber tables. You can order pizza from the nearby shopfront and eat it alfresco.

Getting There & Away

The train and bus stations are next to each other, halfway between the beach and the historic centre. The harbour is 1km northwest.

There are seven trains daily east to Gdańsk (42zł, four hours) and six west to Szczecin (18.50zł, 2¾ hours). Six fast trains head to Warsaw (57zł, 9¼ hours).

Buses head to Świnoujście (22zł, 2½ hours, four daily) and Słupsk (22zł, 2¾ hours, twice daily). Polski Express runs one bus a day to Warsaw (69zł, 7½ hours).

Kołobrzeska Żegluga Pasażerska (☎ 094 352 8920; www.kzp.man.pl; ul Morska 2) operates regular catamaran cruises to Nexo on Bornholm Island, Denmark (one way/return 100/150zł, 4½ hours). The service sails daily from May to September, and three times a week from October to April.

KAMIEŃ POMORSKI
pop 9100

On paper, this small town doesn't seem promising: it was devastated in the battles of WWII, and very little was restored in a sympathetic style. However, the breathtakingly ugly buildings that fill the town centre are more than made up for by the attractive historic fragments that remain, and its waterfront location on Kamień Bay gives the sleepy centre a touch of scenic beauty.

Information

Bank Pekao (ul Gryfitów 2a)
Post office (ul Pocztowa 1)

Sights

Kamień's **cathedral** is well worth stopping for as you journey along the coast. Begun by the Wolinian bishops in a Romanesque style, it was then thoroughly revamped in the 14th century in the Gothic fashion, which has basically survived to this day. Inside is an impressive triptych on the high altar, thought to derive from the school of Veit Stoss, the maker of the famous pentaptych in the Basilica of the Assumption of Our Lady (p182) in Kraków.

While you're in the church, don't miss the cloister **pleasure garden** (admission 2zł) – the entrance is through a door from the left-hand aisle. This retreat from the woes of the medieval world is a beautiful, serene space that retains its power to calm the nerves. Stand in the centre of the garden, next to the 1124 baptismal font, and breathe deeply. Once you're done, check out the old tombstones along the walls of the cloister, which were moved here in 1890 from the church's floor to preserve their carved images.

POMERANIA

Going west through the centre of town you'll reach the **Wolin Gate** (Brama Wolińska), part of the 14th-century city walls. It now houses the **Museum of Precious Stones** (Muzeum Kamieni; ☎ 0609 358 205; ul Słowackiego 1; adult/concession 8/5zł; ⌚ 10am-6pm Jun-Sep, 10am-5pm Oct-May), which features semiprecious rocks and baubles, along with dinosaur bones and other fossils. It's a refreshingly interesting exhibition that's well laid out and well lit, despite the lack of English captions. Be aware that the steps to each new level of the building get steeper and narrower!

Festivals & Events

The **Festival of Organ & Chamber Music** (☎ 091 382 0541) is held from mid-June to late August, with concerts every Friday evening, and shorter organ performances twice daily.

Sleeping & Eating

Youth hostel (☎ 091 382 0841; Plac Katedralny 5; dm 15-20zł; ⌚ Jul & Aug, reception 7-10am & 5-10pm) In a school across the road from the cathedral, this 60-bed hostel has large dorms only, though the impressive redbrick edifice doesn't lack character.

Hotel Staromiejski (☎ 091 382 2644; www.hotel-staromiejski.pl; ul Rybacka 3; s/d/tr 112/160/204zł; P ⊠ 💻) A smart, service-oriented hotel, though it lacks the character and charm of the neighbouring Hotel Pod Muzami. However, you can't beat its terrace café for views over the water.

Hotel Pod Muzami (☎ 091 382 2241; www.podmuzami.pl; ul Gryfitów 1; s/d/tr 115/164/200zł) In a beautiful historic timbered house on the corner of the central Rynek, the Pod Muzami is a breath of fresh air. Friendly staff offer 12 reasonably spacious rooms within sight of the water, plus a good house restaurant (mains 6zł to 29zł).

Between the Rynek and the cathedral, **Kawiarnia o Poranku** (☎ 091 382 2425; ul Gryfitów 14; mains 8-12zł; ⌚ 10am-11pm) is a pleasant place for a hot drink or light meal after sightseeing. Its menu contains multiple variants of hot chocolate and tea, along with wine, beer, and great garlic bread.

Getting There & Away

The bus terminal, 600m south of the centre, has services every two hours or so to Szczecin (18zł, two hours), and up to three an hour to Międzyzdroje (14zł, 1½ hours) and Świnoujście (15zł, 1¾ hours). There are also two fast buses daily to Kołobrzeg (19zł, 1½ hours) and two to Gdynia (45zł, seven hours) via Słupsk. From the nearby sleepy train station, two to three services a day head to Szczecin (14zł, 1½ hours).

MIĘDZYZDROJE

pop 5500

Międzyzdroje (myen-dzi-*zdro*-yeh) almost shuts down and rolls up its main street in winter. However, blessed with warm seas and clean beaches, it's a thriving seaside resort in the warmer months. A long sandy shoreline and a picturesque coastal cliff occupy the northeast of town, and the attractive Wolin National Park stretches to the southeast. Parks and gardens in the centre of town link the two, and provide a pleasant place to while away a few leisurely hours.

Information

Internet Café (☎ 091 328 0421; ul Norwida 17a; per hr 5zł; ⌚ 11am-7pm Mon-Fri, 11am-6pm Sat & Sun)
PTTK (☎ 091 328 0382; www.pttk-miedzyzdroje.com; ul Kolejowa 2) Can arrange guides to natural attractions.
Tourist office (☎ 091 328 2778; www.miedzyzdroje.pl in Polish; ul Bohaterów Warszawy 20; ⌚ 10am-5pm)
Viking Tour (☎ 091 328 0768; www.vikingtour.com.pl; ul Niepodległości 2a) Accommodation bookings and tours.
Wolin Travel (☎ 091 328 2774; www.wolin-travel.com; ul Turystyczna 2/22) Accommodation bookings.

Sights

The **Natural History Museum** (Muzeum Przyrodnicze; ☎ 091 328 07 27; ul Niepodległości 3; adult/concession 5/3zł; ⌚ 9am-5pm Tue-Sun) is a taxidermist's heaven, displaying dozens of stuffed examples of the fauna of Wolin National Park, via a fairly dull set of static displays in gloomily lit rooms. There are also exhibits of minerals, along with amber, and a marginally more engaging fossil display upstairs. Though unexciting, the museum's collection is a good overview of the park's wildlife.

Outside, two large bird cages can be found on either side of the museum building; one holds two long-eared owls, the other a genuine (if slightly scruffy-looking) white-tailed eagle, said to be the model for Poland's national emblem. The national park's headquarters are just opposite the eagle.

Sleeping & Eating

Międzyzdroje is crammed with accommodation – the best approach is to contact one of the specialised local travel agencies (see opposite). Private rooms start at 30zł per person in July and August, 20zł in other months. Pensions/holiday homes will cost from 40/30zł per person.

There are cafés, restaurants and snack bars liberally scattered through the town, many in pleasing proximity to parks or the sea.

Dom Turysty PTTK (☎ 091 328 0462; ul Kolejowa 2; s/d 35/70zł; P) This old-fashioned hostel is one of the cheapest places to stay in Międzyzdroje, though its room standards and location won't knock your socks off. It is handy for the main bus stop and the museum, however.

FWP Posejdon (☎ 091 328 0567; www.fwp.pl; Promenada Gwiazd 4; s/d/tr 110/200/300zł; P ✕ ▣) Though the main building of this complex is downright ugly, and the rooms somewhat scuffed, you can't beat its location just a stone's throw from the sea. In addition to the hotel-standard rooms in its three main buildings, the FWP offers 500 beds spread over 11 budget holiday homes.

Hotel Amber Baltic (☎ 091 328 1000; www.hotel -amber-baltic.pl; Promenada Gwiazd 1; s/d €93/132, ste €205-250; P ✕ ▣ ☎ ⟨⟩) If you fancy a splurge, you're in the right place – this is one of the best resort hotels on the coast, with great views over the Baltic and various amenities including a Jacuzzi, solarium and gym. Golfers can catch a shuttle bus to the hotel's own course, a short distance outside town.

Camping Nr 24 Gromada (☎ 091 328 0275; ul Polna 10a; tents per person 13-15zł; ⟨⟩ Jun-Sep) At the southwestern end of town, Gromada is the largest camping facility here; there are another two camping grounds slightly closer to the beach.

Restauracja Bursztynowy Szlak (☎ 091 328 0649; ul Niepodległości 4; mains 8-22zł; ⟨⟩ 10am-10pm) Across the road from the museum, this eatery offers good-value dishes in a soothingly rustic setting. There's a decent selection of salads, *pierogi* and omelettes among the menu choices.

Getting There & Away

The train station is at the southern end of town, with a PKS stop outside. Międzyzdroje is on the Szczecin–Świnoujście railway line and all trains stop here, providing roughly 20 daily services in each direction. There are also four daily trains to Wrocław (52zł, seven hours) and three to Warsaw (57zł, 8½ hours).

The main bus stop is on ul Niepodległości, opposite the museum. PKS and private buses run to Świnoujście (4.80zł, 15 minutes) up to five times an hour. Two fast buses go daily to Kołobrzeg (22zł, 2½ hours) and two as far as Gdynia (54zł, eight hours). In summer there are hourly buses to Kamień Pomorski (14zł, 1½ hours).

WOLIN NATIONAL PARK

Set in the far northwestern corner of the country, Wolin National Park (Woliński Park Narodowy) occupies the central section of Wolin Island, just southeast of Międzyzdroje. With a total area of about 50 sq km, it's one of the smaller Polish parks, yet it's picturesque enough to warrant a day or two's walking.

The park's northern edge drops sharply into the sea, forming an 11km-long sandy cliff nearly 100m high in places.

Back from the coast are a number of lakes, mostly on the remote eastern edge of the park. The most beautiful is the horseshoe-shaped **Lake Czajcze**. Away from the lakeland, there's **Lake Turkusowe** (Turquoise), named after the colour of its water, at the southern end of the park, and the lovely **Lake Gardno** close to the seashore, next to the Międzyzdroje–Dziwnów road. The lakes are surrounded by mixed forest, with beech, oak and pine predominating. The flora and fauna is relatively diverse, with a rich bird life. The last wild bison in Pomerania were wiped out in the 14th century, but there's a small **bison reserve** (adult/concession 5/3zł; ⟨⟩ 10am-6pm Tue-Sun) inside the park, 2km east of Międzyzdroje.

Activities

The best way to explore the park is by **hiking**, and the small area means a good walk needn't be too taxing. Three marked trails wind into the park from Międzyzdroje. The red trail leads northeast along the shore, then turns inland to **Wisełka** and continues through wooded hills to the small village of **Kołczewo**. The green trail runs east across the middle of the park, skirts the lakeland and also ends in Kołczewo. The blue trail goes to the southern end of the park, passing the Turquoise Lake on the way. It then continues east to the town of **Wolin**.

All the trails are well marked and easy. Get a copy of the detailed *Woliński Park Narodowy* map (scale 1:30,000), and consult the park headquarters in Międzyzdroje for further information.

POMERANIA

ŚWINOUJŚCIE
pop 40,000

As far northwest as you can get in Poland without leaving the country, Świnoujście (shvee-no-*ooysh*-cheh) is an attractive seaside town with a touch of faded grandeur along its waterfront promenade, and a relaxed atmosphere despite its role as a major port and naval base. There are plenty of green parks and a choice of water views over sea or river, something that may have inspired its famous literary residents from its 19th-century German past, including novelist and travel writer Theodor Fontane and poet Ernst Schrerenberg. Other notable visitors included Kaiser Wilhelm II and Tsar Nicholas II, who met here in 1907, sparking fruitless hopes that their friendship would avert a European war.

Swinoujście's location makes the city a handy entry point for travellers across the Baltic, via ferry services from Sweden and Denmark; it also has a border crossing with Germany.

Orientation

Świnoujście straddles two islands at the mouth of the Świna River. The eastern part of town, on Wolin Island, has the port and transport facilities; the main town is across the river on Uznam Island (Usedom in German), linked by a frequent shuttle ferry. Here you'll find the town centre and, 1km further north, the beach resort; the two are separated by a belt of parks.

Information

Bank Pekao ul Monte Cassino (ul Monte Cassino 7) ul Piłsudskiego (ul Piłsudskiego 4)

Biuro Podróży Partner (☎ 091 322 4397; ul Bohaterów Września 83/14) Information and ferry tickets; enter via Pasaż Żeglarski.

M & M Internet Café (☎ 0602 797 510; ul Piastowska 1/4a; per hr 3zł; ☽ 10am-9pm) Internet access.

Morskie Biuro Podróży PŻB (☎ 091 322 4396; mbp .swinoujscie@polferries.pl; ul Bema 9/2) Information and ferry tickets.

Post office (ul Piłsudskiego 1)

Tourist office (☎ 091 322 4999; www.swinoujscie.pl; ul Wybrzeże Władysława IV; ☽ 9am-5pm Mon-Fri, 10am-2pm Sat)

Sights & Activities

The **beach** is one of the widest and longest in Poland, and a major tourist attraction. Back from the sands, the waterfront resort district still retains a certain *fin-de-siècle* air in places, with some elegant villas, and the main pedestrian promenade is packed with stalls and amusements in summer. If you fancy cycling along the quiet, flat roads in this part of town, you can hire a bike from **Wypożyczalnia Rowerów Jakub** (☎ 0602 230 688; ul Matejki 19; per hr 4zł, per day 20zł; ☽ 9am-6pm).

The town centre has received a good deal of beautification in recent years, though its attractive small-scale buildings are still rudely interrupted by the odd concrete monstrosity. The marina waterfront is a good place for a stroll, and you can drop into the **Museum of Sea Fishery** (Muzeum Rybołówstwa Morskiego; ☎ 091 321 2426; Plac Rybaka 1; adult/concession 5/3zł; ☽ 9am-5pm Tue-Sun) on your way. If you're keen on stuffed sea life, you'll be delighted by the static displays of albatrosses, sharks and seals, along with fishing paraphernalia and model boats. The museum's saving grace is its three tanks of exotic fish, including a real live piranha. There are also displays on the town's history, including historic official seals of a nonaquatic nature, but no captions in English.

A curious remnant from WWII is the **Air Raid Shelter** (ul Wyspiańskiego 51), which was once used by residents sheltering from heavy Allied bombing of then German Swinemünde. The shelter's exterior is inexplicably decorated with nautical memorabilia including anchors and ropes. It's not open for viewing, but there's an explanatory plaque in English.

Festivals & Events

At the end of September, just as the tourist season is waning, Świnoujście takes part in the **Four Corners Culture Week** (☎ 091 321 3705; www .four-corners.org), a series of concerts and exhibitions held in conjunction with similar events on Bornholm (Denmark), Rügen (Germany) and Southeast Skåne (Sweden). The main stage is the whimsically designed open-air Concert Mussel (Muszla Koncertowa; Map p469), near the beach.

Sleeping & Eating

As in other Baltic beach resorts, the high season is in July and August. The tourist office keeps an eye on what's available in all categories.

There are a few year-round restaurants, mostly in the centre, but the majority of places are seasonal. Three loosely defined food cen-

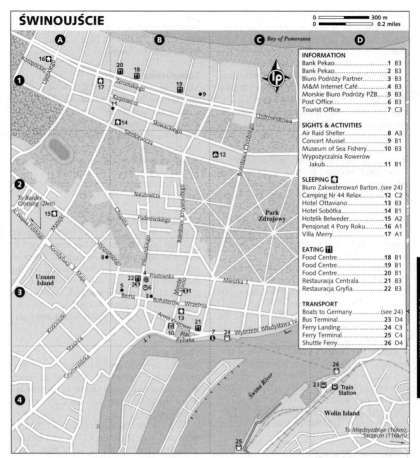

ŚWINOUJŚCIE

0 —— 300 m
0 —— 0.2 miles

Bay of Pomerania

Park Zdrojowy

Uznam Island

Świna River

Wolin Island

To Międzyzdroje (16km);
Szczecin (116km)

To Border
Crossing (2km)

POMERANIA

---

tres on the beach promenade, ul Żeromskiego, have convenient clusters of eating options.

Biuro Zakwaterowań Barton (☎ 091 321 1155; www.barton.com.pl; Wybrzeże Władysława IV) For private rooms, head to this small office by the ferry landing. Prices start from 25zł and average around 40zł to 60zł per person; note that most are in the southwestern suburbs, with almost none in the beach area.

Villa Merry (☎ 091 321 2619; www.villa-merry.com; ul Żeromskiego 16; d €18-23, apt €26-90; P) One of the top self-catering options in town, Merry's two swish Art Nouveau buildings contain several kitchen-equipped apartments with an accent on white tiles and cool blue tones.

Pensjonat 4 Pory Roku (☎ 091 321 1694; www .4poryroku.com.pl; ul Ujejskiego 8; d 230-270zł, tr/q/ste 345/410/395zł; P X 💻) Hidden gem off the main promenade, offering beautiful light-filled rooms with parquetry floors. Breakfast is served in the sociable communal kitchen, and the pension also smokes its own fish.

our pick Hotelik Belweder (☎ 091 327 1678; www .hotel-belweder.pl; ul Wyspiańskiego 1; s/d/tr/ste 180/240/330/380zł; P 💻 &) Small hotel in a leafy neighbourhood, within walking distance of both the town centre and the beach. Spacious rooms are done out in bright orange tones, with lofty ceilings and well-maintained fittings. A good place to escape the summer bustle.

Hotel Ottaviano (☎ 091 321 4403; www.ottaviano.pl; ul Monte Cassino 3; s/d/tr 168/254/278zł; P X 💻 &) Well located in the town centre, and handy for the ferry crossing, the Ottaviano is good value. There's a hint of Scandinavian in the décor, via loads of blonde wood and a light and airy look. The in-house restaurant has views across the attractive paved street.

Hotel Sobótka (☎ 091 321 4964; www.sobotka.uznam .net.pl; ul Sienkiewicza 13; d/tr 264/360zł, ste 310-570zł; P ✕ 🖳) The Sobótka is a plain-looking sanatorium hotel, with the scents of mysterious therapeutic agents hovering in the air. It offers dozens of health treatments, many of which you'll never have heard of before (magneto-stimulation anyone?). Full board available.

Camping Nr 44 Relax (☎ 091 321 3912; www.camping -relax.com.pl; ul Słowackiego 1; camp sites per adult/student/child 12/10/7zł, bungalows 110-190zł) This large, popular camping ground is superbly located between the beach and the spa park, and has a good selection of year-round bungalows, though you'll need a miracle to get one in July or August.

Restauracja Gryfia (☎ 091 321 2578; ul Piłsudskiego 10; mains 10-30zł; ✆ 10am-3am) This eatery's black interior makes for a sombre atmosphere, but it's relieved by hearty serves of Polish standards. Every evening except Wednesday, the Gryfia's clientele trips the light fantastic via music and dancing.

Restauracja Centrala (☎ 091 321 2640; ul Armii Krajowej 3; mains 10-45zł; ✆ 10am-midnight) Chilled-out space with a gorgeous burnt orange interior, and striking frescoes featuring primitive figures; grab a seat for marina views. The apple strudel with vanilla cream is particularly good, and there's live jazz here at regular intervals.

Getting There & Away

The most convenient overland crossing to/from Germany is 2km west of town. The first town on the German side, Ahlbeck, handles transport further into the country.

BOAT

Tickets for all boat services are available at the terminals and from most travel agencies around town.

Germany

The German company **Adler-Schiffe** (☎ 091 322 4288; www.adler-schiffe.de) runs boats from Świnoujście to Ahlbeck, Heringsdorf and Bansin in Germany, up to four times daily. A return ticket, including a stopover, costs €7.50 for adults and €3.80 concession. The company also operates weekly ferries to German Altwarp (one-way adult/child €10/5, 2½ hours) and Zinnowitz (one way adult/child €9.50/4.80, five hours).

Scandinavia

Major carrier **Polferries** (☎ 322 61 40; www.polferries .pl) operates ferries to Ystad, Sweden (adult/concession Skr540/460, seven hours, daily), Rønne, Denmark (250/220kr, 5¼ hours, weekly) and Copenhagen (450/380kr, nine hours, four to five weekly). **Unity Line** (☎ 359 55 92; www.unityline.pl) also runs daily ferries to Ystad (Skr470/390, seven hours).

All ferries depart from the ferry terminal on Wolin Island.

CAR & MOTORCYCLE

If you're arriving with your own transport, you can only use the shuttle ferry at weekends and after 10pm on weekdays; otherwise you'll have to head for the crossing serving Karsibór Island, 7km south of Świnoujście. Expect to wait during the peak season (usually no longer than a couple of hours). Passage for both vehicles and passengers is free.

TRAIN & BUS

The bus terminal and train station are next to each other on the right bank of the Świna River. Passenger ferries shuttle constantly between the town centre and the stations (free, 10 minutes).

All trains go via Międzyzdroje (7.50zł, 15 minutes) and Szczecin (28zł, two hours), with departures every hour or two. There are also trains to Warsaw (fast/express 58/97zł, 8¾ hours, three daily), and to Kraków (63zł, 12½ hours, four daily) via Poznań (46zł, five hours) and to Wrocław (54zł, seven hours).

There are two daily buses that run to Szczecin (25zł, 2½ hours), but plenty of services cover the coast, including 10 buses to Kamień Pomorski (15zł, 1¼ hours) and two buses to Kołobrzeg (22zł, 2½ hours). All routes go via Międzyzdroje, which is also served by half-hourly private buses (4.80zł, 15 minutes).

Europa-Linie buses (€1.90) link the Polish and German sides of the island. A day pass valid for six single journeys costs 10zł, or €4 in Germany. City bus 8 also runs to the border (2zł, 10 daily).

SZCZECIN
pop 411,000

When you first encounter the western port city Szczecin (*shcheh*-cheen), the impression is of an unaesthetic muddle of architecture inherited from wildly different ages. But on a sunny day you can't help noticing the rough-edged beauty of the crumbling German-era apartment buildings and mansions, and the city's unkempt but spacious parks, and reflect on its past splendour and future potential. Though a busy working port, there's plenty of scope for play, with enough entertainment and sights to warrant a stopover.

History

Szczecin's beginnings go back to the 8th century, when a Slav stronghold was built here. In 967 Duke Mieszko I annexed the town for the newborn Polish state, but was unable to hold or Christianise it. It was Bolesław Krzywousty who recaptured the town in 1121 and brought the Catholic faith to the locals.

Krzywousty died in 1138 and the Polish Crown crumbled; Pomerania formally became an independent principality. Periods of allegiance to Germanic and Danish rulers followed, before Western Pomerania was unified by Duke Bogusław X in 1478, with Szczecin being chosen as the capital.

The next major shift in power came in 1630, when the Swedes conquered the city. Sweden then ceded Szczecin to the kingdom of Prussia in 1720, which as part of Germany held the region until WWII. Under Prussian rule, Szczecin (Stettin in German) grew considerably, becoming the main port for landlocked Berlin. By the outbreak of WWII the city had about 300,000 inhabitants.

In April 1945 the Red Army passed through on its way to Berlin, leaving 60% of the urban area in ruins. Only 6000 souls remained of the former population, most of the others having fled.

With new inhabitants, mostly drawn from territories lost by Poland to the Soviet Union, the battered city started a new life, developing into an important port and industrial centre for the postwar nation.

Information

INTERNET ACCESS

Bondi (☎ 091 433 5933; Al Wyzwolenia 1; per hr 3zł; 9am-11pm)

Internet Café (☎ 091 433 0319; ul Obrońców Stalingradu 12; per hr 3zł; 10am-10pm) Enter from ul Śląska.
Portal (☎ 091 488 4066; ul Kaszubska 52; per hr 4zł; 24hr)

MONEY

Bank Pekao West (Al Wojska Polskiego 1); Northwest (ul Obrońców Stalingradu 10/11); East (ul Grodzka 9); Northeast (Plac Żołnierza Polskiego 16)
Deutsche Bank (Al Wyzwolenia 12)

POST

Post office main post office (Al Niepodłegości 41/42); station branch (ul Dworcowa 20b)

TOURIST INFORMATION

Cultural & Tourist Information Centre (☎ 091 489 1630; www.zamek.szczecin.pl; ul Korsarzy 34; 10am-6pm) In the castle.
PTTK (☎ 091 434 5624; Al Jedności Narodowej 49A)
Tourist office (☎ 091 434 0440; Al Niepodległości 1; 9am-5pm Mon-Fri, 10am-2pm Sat Jun-Aug, 9am-5pm Mon-Fri Sep-May)

TRAVEL AGENCIES

Orbis Travel (☎ 091 434 7563; Plac Zwycięstwa 1)

Sights & Activities

Rome wasn't built in a day, and Szeczin's historic heart won't be rebuilt overnight. Gradually, however, the local authorities are building up the city's tourist infrastructure. A prime example is the **Red Tourist Route**, a 7km walking circuit around town covering 42 important historic sights and buildings; pick up the explanatory map at one of the tourist offices and look for the red arrows sprayed graffiti-style on the pavement. It's a great overview of Szczecin's attractions if you have limited time in the city.

The mother of all Szczecin monuments is the **Castle of the Pomeranian Dukes** (Zamek Książąt Pomorskich). This vast, blocky building looms over the Old Town, but the square central courtyard and simple Renaissance-style decoration atop the walls have a certain understated grace (spot the repeated circular pattern that resembles the Yin and Yang symbol). The castle was originally built in the mid-14th century and grew into its current form by 1577, but was destroyed by Allied carpet bombing in 1944 before being extensively restored. Admire the colourful historic clockface from the courtyard, with its jester

SZCZECIN

0 — 200 m
0 — 0.1 miles

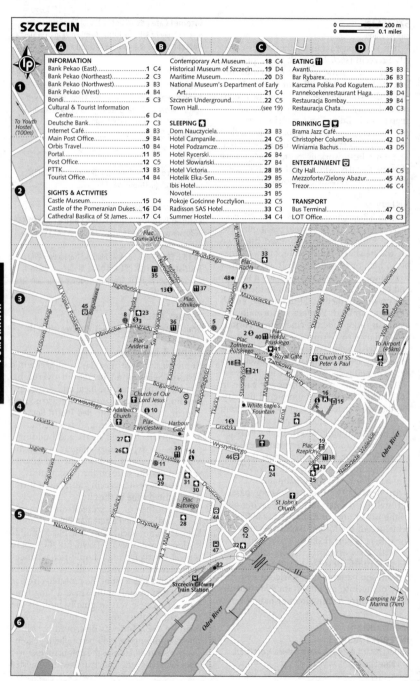

figure chiming in each new hour, then climb to the top of the 58.6m **bell tower** (adult/concession 4/3zł) for a view of the city.

The castle also accommodates the **Castle Museum** (Muzeum Zamkowe; ☎ 091 489 1630; www .zamek.szczecin.pl; ul Korsarzy 34; adult/concession 6/3zł; ☒ 10am-6pm Tue-Sun). Its star exhibits are six spectacular sarcophagi of the Pomeranian dukes. These large tin boxes are decorated with a fine engraved ornamentation, and were made between 1606 and 1637 by artists from Königsberg. Following the death of the last Pomeranian duke, Bogusław XIV, the crypt was walled up until the sarcophagi were discovered during restoration work in 1946, after the castle's wartime destruction. The remains of the dukes were deposited in the cathedral, while the least-damaged sarcophagi were restored for display.

Various temporary exhibitions are presented in other rooms of the castle, including art shows. In summer, concerts are held on Sunday in the courtyard or the former chapel, which occupies nearly half the northern side.

A short walk south will bring you to the 15th-century Gothic **town hall**, one of the finest buildings in the city. This is the only relic of the Old Town, having miraculously survived the near-total destruction of the district in WWII. Szczecin never enjoyed the meticulous postwar reconstruction of other Polish cities, but the Old Town is finally being pieced back together: an attractive line of stylised burghers' houses has been constructed right behind the town hall, in striking contrast to the unbecoming communist-era blocks opposite. As the renewal inches along, the area has started to fill with fashionable cafés and upmarket bars. The day the market square in front of the town hall ceases to be an open-air car park, you'll know the Old Town has finally (re)arrived.

Within the town hall is the **Historical Museum of Szczecin** (Muzeum Historii Miasta Szczecina; ☎ 091 431 5258; Plac Rzepichy 1; adult/concession 6/3zł; ☒ 10am-6pm Tue-Fri, 10am-4pm Sat & Sun), which is well laid out within the airy light-filled interior. The star exhibit is a medieval treasure trove unearthed in 2001 during building works elsewhere in the city, a multimillion dollar collection of silver coins, buttons, rings and other jewellery – and the small iron pot the loot was stashed in. At time of research there were plans to add English captions.

Not far away is the **Cathedral Basilica of St James** (Bazylika Katedralna pw Św Jakuba Apostoła; ul Wyszyńskiego; requested donation €1; ☒ groups 2-5pm Mon-Sat) a historic church built in the overwhelming fortress-like style favoured by the medieval religious authorities, which dominates the view toward the city centre. It was consecrated in 1187 but only reconstructed in 1972. On one side of the cathedral is the 15th-century vicarage and on the other a huge bell weighing almost 6 tonnes, dating from 1681.

The **National Museum's Department of Early Art** (Dział Sztuki Dawnej; ☎ 091 431 5200; www.muzeum.szczecin .pl; ul Staromłyńska 27; adult/concession 6/3zł; ☒ 10am-4pm Tue-Sun) is located two blocks north in an 18th-century palace that formerly served as the Pomeranian parliament. It features a collection of religious art, particularly woodcarving from the 14th to 16th centuries, and you can also ogle the Pomeranian crown jewels. The **Contemporary Art Museum** (Muzeum Sztuki Współczesnej; ☎ 091 431 5200; www .muzeum.szczecin.pl; ul Staromłyńska 1; adult/concession 6/3zł; ☒ 10am-4pm Tue-Sun), another National Museum campus directly across the street, hosts changing displays of modern art. In both buildings the captions are primarily in Polish, but there is a general brochure available in English. A joint ticket to the two institutions is 10/5zł.

A third National Museum outpost is the grand **Maritime Museum** (Muzeum Morskie; ☎ 091 431 5200; www.muzeum.szczecin.pl; ul Wały Chrobrego 3; adult/concession 6/3zł; ☒ 10am-6pm Tue-Sun), on a hill next to the Naval Academy, above the waterfront. The maritime exhibits are a bit dull, but the regional archaeology displays and ethnographical artefacts present more interest. There are minimal English captions throughout the permanent exhibitions.

A recently opened attraction near the train station is **Szczecin Underground** (☎ 091 434 0801; www.schron.szczecin.pl; ul Kolumba 1; adult/concession single tour 15/14zł, both tours 25/23zł; ☒ 10am-6pm Mon-Sat, noon-4pm Sun). This sprawling set of concrete tunnels beneath the city streets was designated as a bomb shelter in the 1940s and as a fallout shelter thereafter. Tours alternate between a WWII or Cold War theme approximately every hour, and attract a 3zł surcharge after 5pm on a weekday, after 2pm Saturday and all day Sunday. English-language tours are only scheduled for 3pm and 4pm on Saturday, but can be booked for groups of 10 or more.

Sleeping

BUDGET

Summer hostel (☎ 091 433 2924; ul Grodzka 22; dm 16-25zł; ☽ Jul & Aug) A super-cheap central option for the summer months.

ourpick **Youth hostel** (☎ 091 422 4761; www.ptsm .home.pl; ul Monte Cassino 19A; dm 20-22zł, s/d 50/56/96zł; **P** ✗ 🖳) Everything is pleasant about this place, with its simple but bright rooms located in a leafy neighbourhood. There's a laundry for guest use, and out in the well-kept garden there are concrete table tennis tables! It's 2km northwest of the centre; take tram 3 from the station to Plac Rodła and change for the westbound tram 1 to the 'Piotra Skargi' stop.

Pokoje Gościnne Pocztylion (☎ 091 440 1209; ul Dworcowa 20b; dm 42zł; **P**) Talk about well-kept secrets…you have to pass a guard box to reach this unmarked accommodation. It's worth the effort as this post office facility is surprisingly nice inside, with spacious bright rooms containing fridges and TVs. There's also a kitchen and a spectacular communal lounge with enormous potted palms and a pool table.

Hotelik Słowiański (☎ 091 812 5461; ul Potulicka 1; s 73-108zł, d 88-120zł, tr 117-135zł) This former police dorm is modest and neat, if a little plain. The swirly brown carpets are a blast from the past, but the high ceilings add perspective to the smallish rooms. There's a choice of en suite or shared bathrooms.

Camping Nr 25 Marina (☎ 091 460 1165; www.camping marina.pl; ul Przestrzenna 23; adult/child 15/7zł, cabins 60-100zł; ☽ May-Sep) Good camping ground with cabins on the shore of Lake Dąbie in Szczecin Dąbie, about 7km southeast of the city centre. If you are coming by train, get off in Szczecin Dąbie and continue by urban bus 56 or walk 2km.

MIDRANGE

Dom Nauczyciela (☎ 091 433 0481; www.dn.szczecin .pl; ul Śląska 4; s 100zł, d 120-140zł, tr 150zł) Quiet, neat and central, this is an unpretentious residential establishment that has light-filled rooms with stucco walls, an international bookshop, home-cooked food and massive discounts for students. Breakfast is an extra 15zł.

Hotelik Elka-Sen (☎ 091 433 5604; www.elkasen .szczecin.pl; Al 3 Maja 1a; s/d/tr/q 120/140/160/200zł; **P** ✗ ⬤) Strange name, strange location: the Elka-Sen has a lift as its front door and occupies a basement space in the School of Economics, itself next door to the local prison. The foyer's a little gloomy but the rooms receive natural light and the bathrooms shine.

Ibis Hotel (☎ 091 480 1800; www.ibishotel.com; ul Dworcowa 16; r 189zł; **P** ⬤ ⬤) This business-style hotel is housed in the Novotel building but is more affordable, with straightforward neat rooms and a bar and restaurant downstairs.

Hotel Victoria (☎ 091 434 3855; Plac Batorego 2; s/d 140/190zł; **P**) Just uphill from the bus terminal and train station, this determinedly old-fashioned accommodation has friendly staff and lashings of brown in its décor, and sits opposite an unkempt park in a quieter part of the city centre. Rooms vary in size so have a look first. The downstairs Tango nightclub plays up-to-date 'boompah boompah' music, according to a staff member.

Hotel Campanile (☎ 091 481 7700; www.campanile .com.pl; ul Wyszyńskiego 30; r 199zł; **P** ✗ ⬤ 🖳 ⬤) This hotel is in pole position for sightseeing, as it's an easy walk from the castle, the Old Town, the train and bus stations, and the city's main drag. Rooms are compact but tidy and comfortable, with tea- and coffee-making facilities. There's a bar and restaurant off the foyer, with a bright – some might say clashing – colour scheme.

Hotel Podzamcze (☎ 091 812 1404; ul Sienna 1; s/d 190/240zł, ste 240zł; **P**) On the corner of the partially reconstructed Old Town, this small guesthouse offers cosy modern rooms with unfussy fittings above a traditional restaurant and pub. The quality buffet breakfast adds value to the tariff, and there are a bundle of good bars and restaurants just around the corner.

Hotel Rycerski (☎ 091 814 6601; www.hotelrycerski .pl; ul Potulicka 2a; s/d/ste 180/240/360zł; **P** ⬤) It's all swords, breastplates and suits of armour in the reception area of this imposing redbrick pile, tucked away within its own walled grounds. The rooms are soothing with their timber furniture and green tones, and there's a smart restaurant on site.

TOP END

Novotel (☎ 091 480 1400; www.novotel.com; Al 3 Maja 31; s/d €88/90; **P** ✗ ⬤ 🖳 ⬤) A four-star option containing lots of spacious white rooms with parquetry on the bathroom floors, and the full complement of in-house facilities. The location is useful for transport links.

Radisson SAS Hotel (☎ 091 359 5595; www.radisson sas.com; Plac Rodła 10; s from €94, d from €106, ste from €209; **P** ✗ ⬤ 🖳 ⬤ ⬤) Szczecin's fanciest option, if not its prettiest, features slick rooms within a salmon-pink complex. The hotel also comes complete with its own shops, two restaurants, a sauna, a gym, bars and smart little fruit-scented gels and shampoos in its bathrooms.

Eating

Bar Rybarex (☎ 091 434 3222; ul Obrońców Stalingradu 6; mains 3-15zł; ۝ 9am-7pm Mon-Fri, 9am-5pm Sat) This budget fish cafeteria has a reasonable range of piscine dishes to choose from. From the vibrant red and blue interior, you can watch Szczecin life go by through the large plate-glass windows.

Restauracja Chata (☎ 091 434 1338; Plac Hołdu Pruskiego 8; mains 8-45zł; ۝ 12-10pm Mon-Fri, noon-3am Sat) Charming place serving traditional Polish food in rustic timber surroundings, decked out with folkloric items from peasant dresses to carved mirror frames. Some interesting specials tempt the curious, like joint of boar in a wild mushroom sauce.

ourpick Pannekoekenrestaurant Haga (☎ 091 812 1759; ul Sienna 10; mains 10-21zł; ۝ 11am-10pm Mon-Thu, 11am-11pm Fri & Sat, noon-10pm Sun) Haga specialises in very filling Dutch pancakes – over 400 varieties of 'em, served up in a dining room decorated with old wall clocks and porcelain plates. There's also soup served within a bread loaf, which can be eaten afterwards – don't try to tackle both this and a pancake unless you're ravenous.

Karczma Polska Pod Kogutem (☎ 091 434 6873; Plac Lotników 3; mains 12-55zł; ۝ 11am-midnight Sun-Thu, 11am-1am Fri & Sat) The rustic barn look is enduringly popular with restaurants serving traditional Polish food, and Karczma Polska doesn't disappoint – there's even a mock pigsty on the way downstairs to the toilets. Its external wooden deck is a great vantage point over the picturesque square opposite, and the menu offers plenty of options. Roast rabbit in hazelnut sauce, anyone?

Avanti (☎ 091 434 6410; Al Jedności Narodowej 43; mains 15-89zł; ۝ noon-10pm Sun-Thu, noon-11pm Fri & Sat) Serious and authentic Italian food served in a refined, atmospheric interior that wouldn't be out of place in any sophisticated city – if you excuse the scale model of the Leaning Tower of Pisa housing the wine selection.

Restauracja Bombay (☎ 091 812 1171; www.india .pl; ul Partyzantów 1; mains 25-45zł; ۝ 1-11pm; ✗) This would be quite a treat in any country – quality Indian food, including items such as thali meals, served in tastefully exotic surrounds by waiters with impeccable English. It's owned by a former Miss India (1973 vintage), and boasts an appropriately international wine list.

Drinking

Szczecin's drinking hot spots are the Old Town area, for sophisticated tipples and conversation, and the funkier pedestrian strip of ul Bogusława, for terrace lounging and decent music.

Winiarnia Bachus (☎ 091 488 3721; ul Sienna 6; ۝ noon-11pm Mon-Fri, 3pm-midnight Sat, 3-10pm Sun) Classy wine bar offering outdoor seating overlooking the square in front of the town hall and it serves up beer, spirits and wine, though the selection isn't as broad as you'd expect. There's also fine food on the menu, including snails.

Christopher Columbus (☎ 091 489 3401; ul Wały Chrobrego 1; ۝ 10am-1am Sun-Thu, 10am-2am Fri & Sat) This bar-restaurant, boasting an attractive timber-lined interior, overlooks the river and its less than fascinating dockyards, but you can always turn your chair to face the nearby Naval Academy. The curved bar resembles a boat, and there's a vast beer garden. Jazz and swing music is on Monday and Tuesday evenings, respectively.

Brama Jazz Café (☎ 0660 765 211; Plac Hołdu Pruskiego 1; ۝ 10am-midnight) Housed in the Baroque Royal Gate, another fragment of lost history, the Brama has a DJ playing different styles of jazz on Tuesday nights. Have a drink in the relaxed outdoor area beneath a stern circle of carved Prussian eagles.

Entertainment

Check the local press and flyers for the latest nightlife listings, or visit www.clubbing.szn .pl (Polish only).

Mezzoforte/Zielony Abażur (☎ 091 814 4144; ul Bogusława 8; mains 8-38zł; ۝ 10am-midnight Sun-Thu, 10am-2am Fri & Sat) This Italian restaurant leads a double life as one of Szczecin's hippest bar-clubs, with a different musical flavour on the upstairs stereo every day, and guest artists laying beats in the basement at night. The outdoor seating on the cobblestone mall is a great place to sip a beer.

City Hall (☎ 091 440 3288; www.cityhall.pl; Czerwony Ratusz, ul Dworcowa; admission 5-10zł; ۝ 6pm-late) The basement of the massive Red Town Hall packs in up to 400 mad-for-it clubbers for some of the biggest nights in town, featuring rhythms from soul to house to R & B. The best night is Saturday, when Berlin DJs often hop over the border to play here.

Trezor (☎ 091 812 55 52; www.trezor-club.pl; ul Wyszyńskiego 14; admission 10-15zł; ۝ 9pm-4am Wed-Fri,

POMERANIA

9pm-5am Sat) An unpromising entrance with an appearance halfway between the Tardis and a Portaloo, hidden in the courtyard back from the street, leads down into three floors of good old-fashioned hedonism. For over-20s only.

Getting There & Away

AIR

The **airport** (☎ 091 484 7400; www.airport.com.pl) is in Goleniów, about 45km northeast of the city. A shuttle bus (11.90zł) operated by **Interglobus** (☎ 091 485 0422; www.interglobus.pl) picks up from stops outside the LOT office and the train station before every flight, and meets all arrivals. **LOT** (☎ 0801 703 703; Al Wyzwolenia 17) runs a similar service via a minibus; enquire about tickets at its office. Alternatively, a taxi should cost around 120zł.

There are services to Warsaw (up to four daily) via LOT, London (four weekly) via Ryanair, Dublin (four weekly) via Centralwings, and Oslo (twice weekly) via Norwegian.

BUS

The bus terminal is uphill from the train station and handles frequent departures to Stargard Szczeciński (7zł, 50 minutes, twice hourly) and Kamień Pomorski (18zł, two hours, up to 14 daily). There are regular summer buses to nearby beach resorts, but limited services to Świnoujście and Międzyzdroje – go by train instead. Polski Express runs two buses daily from here to Warsaw (69zł to 83zł, 9½ hours).

Evatrans (☎ 091 484 2010; www.evatrans.pl) runs daily minibuses to Berlin (one way/return 83/128zł, 2½ hours), as does **Interglobus** (☎ 091 485 0422; www.interglobus.pl), starting from 45zł one way. Enquire at the bus terminal or the train station for details.

TRAIN

The main train station, Szczecin Główny, is on the bank of the Odra River, 1km south of the centre. There are trains to Poznań (38zł, 2¾ hours, 12 daily), Gdańsk (49zł, 5½ hours, five daily), Kołobrzeg (18.50zł, 2¾ hours, six daily) and Zielona Góra (38zł, five hours, one or two daily). There are up to eight daily services to Warsaw (54zł, 7½ hours), including two InterCity trains (96zł, 5¾ hours). Trains to Stargard Szczeciński (12zł, 30 minutes) depart at least every 30 minutes, and to Świnoujście (28zł, two hours) every hour or so (fewer in winter). Two to three services a day head to Kamień Pomorski (14zł, 1½ hours).

STARGARD SZCZECIŃSKI
pop 70,000

Believe it or not, slow-paced Stargard Szczeciński was once a prosperous port city and member of the Hanseatic League (see boxed text, p413), so wealthy it could afford to fight Szczecin for control of the Odra River trade route. The fierce competition between the two ports even led to a war in 1454. The conflict was conducted with no holds barred, and included regular battles, complete with the ransacking and sinking of the enemy's ships.

But that was then. Today Stargard has no port at all, and is content to be a satellite town of its old rival. WWII added to its decline by destroying over 70% of its buildings, and the resultant reconstruction left the town a modern urban sprawl with a fair amount of industry. However, its remaining medieval walls, and the massive churches that dominate the skyline, are worth a day trip from Szczecin or a quick break in transit.

Information

For information head to the **Tourist office** (☎ 092 578 5466; www.cit.stargard.com.pl; Rynek Staromiejski 4; ☯ 9am-5pm Mon-Fri, 10am-2pm Sat).

Sights

As in so many Pomeranian cities, one of Stargard's main attractions is a mighty brick church. **St Mary's Church**, one of the largest in the region, was begun in 1292. It was extended several times by the end of the 15th century, then the townspeople left the structure alone for another five centuries, at which point the church was destroyed during WWII. Its rich external decoration of glazed bricks and tiles, with three elaborate doorways, was restored between 1946 and 1962. Step inside and look up at the amazing painted columns and ceiling vault.

Next door is the guardhouse formerly accommodating the city guards, now the **City Museum** (☎ 092 578 3835; Rynek Staromiejski 2/4; adult/concession 6/3zł, free Sat; ☯ 10am-4pm Tue-Fri & Sun, 10am-2pm Sat). It was also once a library and a weights and measures office, which explains the exhibits on weights and measures among those depicting local history and archaeology. Adjoining the museum is the **town hall**, a late-Gothic building with a beautifully ornamented Renaissance gable.

St John's Church, on the opposite side of the Old Town, has the highest tower in Western

Pomerania (99m). It was constructed in the 15th century but has been modified significantly over the years.

The city's **fortified walls** were once 2260m long, having been built between the late 13th century and the beginning of the 16th century. Once hailed as the most elaborate system of fortified walls in Pomerania, they're now just over a kilometre in length, with three surviving gates and five towers. In summer the towers occasionally hold exhibitions administered by the museum, and you can generally climb them for the view.

Sleeping & Eating

Hotel PTTK (☎ 092 578 3191; www.hotelpttk.pl; ul Kuśnierzy 5; s 50-80zł, d 65-150zł, tr 80-140zł; P) Just a few minutes' walk from the cathedral, the PTTK occupies one of the few old buildings, a gabled house overlooking the small canal, to have survived in the area. The oddly shaped rooms are pretty good value, though breakfast costs an extra 10zł.

Hotel Staromiejski (☎ 578 22 11; ul Spichrzowa 2; s 72-90zł, d 95-130zł, tr 117zł, ste 170zł; P) This large apartment block is geared towards coach parties, offering a greater choice of rooms (with shared or en suite bathroom). Rooms are cheaper for stays of more than one night.

Getting There & Away

The train and bus stations are close to each other, 1km west of the Old Town.

Szczecin is easily reached by bus (7zł, 50 minutes) and train (12zł, 30 minutes), both running twice hourly. You can also pick up most eastbound rail services from Szczecin here.

Warmia & Masuria

If ever two regions were ruled by water, they are Warmia and Masuria. This swath of land bordering Russia's isolated Kaliningrad is Poland's lakeland, riven throughout with rivers, canals, wetlands, swamps and ever-present lakes. It's an aquaphile's dream come true, with more water-bound fun than the rest of the country put together.

Watery action is centred on the Great Masurian Lakes. The region may not contain the thousand lakes that tourist brochures proudly proclaim, but who cares? The lakes' natural beauty is breathtaking, and there's enough space for all yachties to find their own sheltered bay. That's not to say there isn't any life here – in summer the resort towns are abuzz, and every harbour and wharf packed with locals and visitors.

Canoeists and kayakers will find ample opportunity to buff up their shoulder muscles. Aside from lake kayaking, there's the celebrated Krutynia River to explore, along with the lesser-known Łyna River. If you prefer less strenuous excursions, passenger boats ply the main lakes, and there's always the Elbląg-Ostróda Canal to experience.

Culturally, Warmia and Masuria have plenty to offer. The legacy of the powerful Teutonic Knights dots the landscape in the shape of redbrick Gothic castles, and Nazi occupation has left behind the secret bunker headquarters of Wolf's Lair and Mauerwald.

This is a place many locals only dream of visiting, so count your blessings you've made it this far. And however you choose to spend your time, you'll quickly realise that this is a beautiful spot, remote enough to be peaceful and developed enough to be accessible.

HIGHLIGHTS

- Kicking back with a coffee or beer in Olsztyn's **Old Town** (opposite)
- Letting your partner kayak you down the **Krutynia River** (p481)
- Slipping and sliding down (or up) the unique **Elbląg-Ostróda Canal** (p486)
- Wandering the halls of Lidzbark Warmiński's proud Gothic **castle** (p487)
- Joining the throngs in admiration of Święta Lipka's Baroque **Church of Our Lady** (p489)
- Exploring the **Wolf's Lair** (p492), Hitler's now-overgrown secret headquarters
- Sailing on the **Great Masurian Lakes** (p490)

- POPULATION: 4.1 MILLION
- AREA: 24,000 SQ KM

History

Despite being lumped together administratively today, Warmia and Masuria have always been separate entities with separate populations, and their histories, though broadly similar, are largely independent.

Warmia is imaginatively named after its original inhabitants, the Warmians, who were wiped out by the Teutonic Knights (see p451) in the 13th century. The Knights then set up a Teutonic province. For more than five centuries this was largely an autonomous ecclesiastical state run by Catholic bishops.

The Warmian diocese was the largest of four that were created by the papal bulls of 1243. Though administratively within the Teutonic state, the bishops used papal protection to achieve a far-reaching autonomy. Their bishopric extended from the north of Olsztyn up to the present-day national border, and from the Vistula Lagoon in the west to the town of Reszel in the east. Following the 1466 Treaty of Toruń, Warmia was incorporated into the kingdom of Poland, but the bishops retained much of their control over internal affairs, answering directly to the pope. When the last grand master adopted Protestantism in 1525, Warmia became a bastion of the Counter-Reformation. In 1773 the region fell under Prussian rule, along with swaths of western Poland.

Meanwhile, Masuria was dealing with its own upheavals. The Jatzvingians (Jaćwingowie), the first inhabitants, belonged to the same ethnic and linguistic family as the Prussians, Latvians and Lithuanians. For farmers they were unusually warlike, and caused plenty of headaches for the Mazovian dukes, as they invaded and ravaged the northern outskirts of the principality on a regular basis and even pressed as far south as Kraków. In the second half of the 13th century, however, the Teutonic Knights expanded eastwards over the region, and by the 1280s they had wiped them out too.

The region quickly became a bone of contention between the Teutonic order and Lithuania, and remained in dispute until the 16th century. At that time the territory formally became a Polish dominion, but its colonisation was slow. Development was also hindered by the Swedish invasions of the 1650s and the catastrophic plague of 1710.

In the Third Partition of 1795, the region was swallowed up by Prussia, and in 1815 it became a part of the Congress Kingdom of Poland, only to be grabbed by Russia after the failure of the November Insurrection of 1830. After WWI Poland took over the territory, though not without resistance from Lithuania, but the region remained remote and economically unimportant. Warmia was finally restored to Poland after WWII, and the two halves became a single administrative zone.

THE OLSZTYN REGION

The Olsztyn region is principally Warmia and the land to the south of the region's main city, Olsztyn. Like its more famous cousin to the east, its landscape is dotted with lakes and sporadically cloaked in forest. There are several important architectural monuments here and relics of the bishops that once ruled the area. Of particular note is the castle of Lidzbark Warmiński and the church in Święta Lipka; more secular highlights include the impressive skansen at Olsztynek and the unique Elbląg-Ostróda Canal.

OLSZTYN

pop 174,000

After so many bruised and battered Polish towns, Olsztyn (*ol*-shtin) comes as a pleasant surprise. Its reconstructed **Old Town**, complete with gabled houses, cobblestone streets, and a refined, café-style culture (with plenty of bars thrown in – this is Poland after all), is as attractive as any in the country, and it's worth lingering for at least a day, exploring its historical sites. Nature is also close at hand; there are 11 lakes within the city borders.

The town was founded in the 14th century as the southernmost outpost of Warmia, and only came under Polish control following the Treaty of Toruń in 1466. With the First Partition of Poland in 1772, Olsztyn became Prussian (renamed Allenstein) and remained so until the end of WWII.

Information

Bank Pekao (ul Staromiejska 13)
Biblioteka (Library; ☎ 089 535 9781; ul Stare Miasto 33; ◷ 10am-7pm Mon-Fri, 9am-2pm Sat) Internet access on 1st floor 3zł per hour; also between 10am and 3pm Monday to Friday free internet access on 2nd floor.
Main post office (ul Pieniężnego 21)
Orbis Travel (☎ 089 535 1678; ul Dąbrowszczaków 1; ◷ 9am-6pm Mon-Fri, 9am-3pm Sat) Can help with accommodation and onward travel.

WARMIA & MASURIA

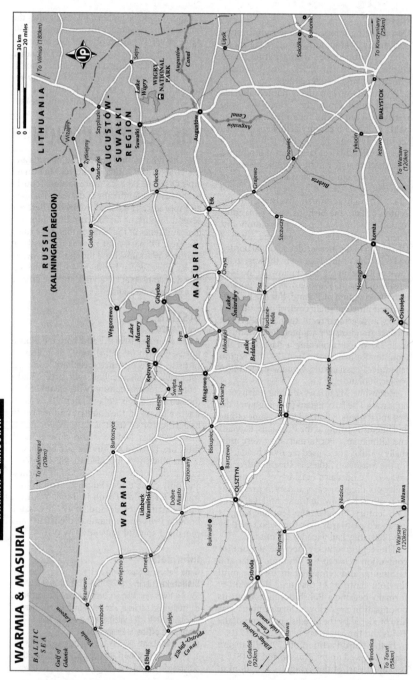

PBK Bank (ul Mickiewicza 2)
Pralnia (☎ 089 526 7677; www.automatica.republika
.pl; ul Toruńska 1a; laundry loads up to 5.5kg 12zł;
internet per hr 3.50zł; ☼ 8am-6pm Mon-Fri, 11am-3pm
Sat) Laundry (!!!) and internet café.
Regional tourist office (☎ 089 535 3565; www
.warmia.mazury.pl; ul Staromiejska 1; ☼ 8am-6pm
Mon-Fri year-round, 10am-3pm Sat & Sun Jul & Aug)
Helpful and knowledgeable; stocks the handy *Warmia i
Mazury* map (7zł), which has cycling and walking tracks,
and waterways of the region.

Sights

The most important historic building in town
is the massive, redbrick 14th-century **castle**.
Despite its age, it's in excellent shape and now
houses an art gallery, restaurant and open-
air theatre, along with the **Museum of Warmia
& Masuria** (Muzeum Warmii i Mazur; ☎ 089 527 9596; ul
Zamkowa 2; adult/concession 8/5zł; ☼ 9am-5pm Tue-Sun
Jun-Sep, 10am-4pm Tue-Sun Oct-May). Two rooms
on the 1st floor are dedicated to astronomer
Nicolaus Copernicus, who was the administ-
trator of Warmia and lived in the castle for
more than three years (1516–20). He made
some of his astronomical observations here,
and you can still see the diagram he drew on
the cloister wall to record the equinox and
thereby calculate the exact length of the year.
Models of the instruments he used are on
display in his former living quarters, and a
set of narrow steps lead up to his toilet – a
dark, uninviting place, but at least private. A
third room was used as a chapel by the great
astronomer, and traces of the original 14th-
century ceiling pattern can still be seen above
the alcoves. The rest of the 1st floor has displays
of silverware and religious icons, and the 2nd
floor houses temporary exhibitions, normally
of a contemporary nature. The castle tower
affords views of the town through narrow gaps
in the brickwork.

The **High Gate**, the historic gateway to the
Old Town, is the only remainder of the 14th-
century city walls. Just to the west, on the
quiet old fish-market square, is the **Museum
of Warmia & Masuria main annexe** (☎ 089 534 0119;
Targ Rybny 1; adult/concession 8/5zł; ☼ 9am-5pm Tue-Sun
Jun-Sep, 10am-4pm Tue-Sun Oct-May), housed in the
former *Gazeta Olsztyńska* newspaper building. The paper was famed for its outspoken
politics under occupation, which swiftly led
to the arrest and execution of its publisher
in 1940 and the destruction of the offices.
Reconstructed, the building now has exhibi-

tions about the city's and region's past, and
the political role of journalism.

A block south is the **Rynek** (formally called
ul Stare Miasto), which was destroyed during
WWII and rebuilt in a grandiose style only
superficially referring to the past. It's best seen
at night, when the town hall is lit up with dazzling spotlights and half the population turns
out for an evening drink.

The Gothic **cathedral** on the other side of the
Old Town dates from the same period as the
castle, though its huge 60m tower was only
added in 1596. Here, as in the castle, crystal-
line vaults can be seen in the aisles. However,
the nave has netlike arches dating from the
17th century. Among the remarkable works
of art are the 16th-century triptych at the head
of the left aisle, and a shimmering gold and
silver altarpiece of the Virgin Mary.

For a dramatic look at the heavens, the
planetarium (☎ 089 533 4951; www.planetarium.olsztyn
.pl; Al Piłsudskiego 38; adult/concession 8/6zł) has shows and
occasional temporary exhibits. Soundtracks
in English, German, French and Russian are
generally offered during two shows a day, at
noon and 2pm.

Copernicus fans can get a bit more hands-
on at the **astronomical observatory** (☎ 089 527 6703;
ul Żołnierska 13), located in an old water tower out
to the east of town. It was enjoying a much-
needed renovation at the time of writing;
check with the tourist office for observation
hours and prices.

Activities

KAYAKING

The travel agency **PTTK Mazury** (☎ 089 527 4059;
www.mazurypttk.pl in Polish; ul Staromiejska 1; ☼ 8am-4pm
Mon-Fri) runs 10-day kayaking tours along the
Krutynia River route (known as Szlak Kajakowy
Krutyni). The 103km trip begins at **Stanica
Wodna PTTK** (☎ 089 742 8124) in Sorkwity, 50km
east of Olsztyn, and goes down the Krutynia
River and Lake Bełdany to Ruciane-Nida
(p500). It's regarded as Poland's top kayak
trip and few come away disappointed. Tours
depart daily from May to October, and the
price (around 950zł) includes kayak, food,
insurance, lodging in cabins and a Polish-,
English- or German-speaking guide.

You can also do the trip on your own, hiring a kayak (25zł to 40zł per day) from the
Stanica Wodna PTTK in Sorkwity, but check
availability in advance. You can use the same
overnight bases as the tours but you can't

always count on cabins, so be prepared to camp. It's easier to secure a kayak and shelter in June or September than in July and August.

Brochures in English and German, with a detailed description and maps of the Krutynia route, are available at the Mazury office. Information in German is also available online (www.masuren-online.de).

PTTK Mazury also organises kayak trips on the river that slices through the heart of Olsztyn, the Łyna. Trips begin in Ruś 10km south of the town, and end as far north as the border to Kaliningrad. For a short taster of the river, rent a kayak from Camping 173 Dywity (opposite) and set out from the centre of town to the camping ground. The trip takes approx-

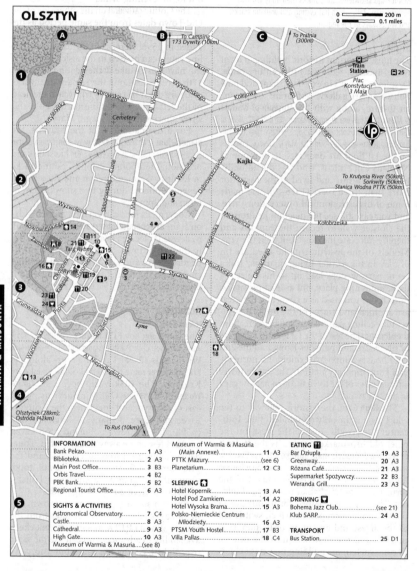

OLSZTYN

imately two hours, and pick-ups and drop-offs can be organised through the camp.

Festivals & Events

Summer of Arts (Olsztyńskie Lato Artystyczne, OLA; ☎ 089 527 0964; www.mok.olsztyn.pl in Polish) Poland's longest-running arts festival, held from mid-June to mid-September.

Olsztyn Blues Nights (☎ 089 527 0964; www.mok .olsztyn.pl in Polish) One of Poland's oldest blues festivals, held in mid-July.

Sleeping

PTSM Youth Hostel (☎ 089 527 6650; schronisko@ ssmolsztyn.pl; ul Kościuszki 72/74; dm/s/d 25/65/62zł; **P**) This well-run hostel has a kitchen, bike hire and large rooms with private bathrooms that sleep up to six. Secure parking is available at the back.

Hotel Wysoka Brama (☎ 089 527 3675; www.hotel wysokabrama.olsztyn.pl in Polish; ul Staromiejska 1; dm/s/d 18/50/68zł) The 70-bed PTTK hotel is superbly located on the edge of the Old Town, actually occupying a section of the High Gate with its mid-sized dorms. The newer annexe has slightly scrappy private rooms and a handful of much nicer en suites. Predictably, it's crammed with backpackers in summer.

Polsko-Niemieckie Centrum Młodzieży (☎ 089 534 0780; www.pncm.olsztyn.pl in Polish & German; ul Okopowa 25; s/d 190/200zł; **P** 🖳 ♿) The Polish-German Youth Centre is ideally located next to the castle; you don't have to be Polish, German or a youth to stay here, though speaking some Deutsch would make things easier. Everything is appropriately shipshape and orderly, and there's a good restaurant on the premises.

Villa Pallas (☎ 089 535 0115; www.villapallas.pl in Polish & German; ul Żołnierska 4; s 150-210zł, d 180-240zł, ste 280-380zł; **P** 🖳) The best of several options east of town, this sophisticated villa is named for the Greek goddess Athena, whose statue makes up part of the mix 'n' match décor. Negotiate the maze of stairways to find refined, spotless rooms and some great suites (just ignore the red-vinyl sofas). A smart restaurant and small spa centre complete the look, and rooms are cheaper on weekends.

Hotel Kopernik (☎ 089 522 9929; www.kopernik .olsztyn.pl; ul Warszawska 37; s/d 190/225zł, ste 300-350zł; **P** 🖳 ♿) Done up in shades of blue you never knew existed, plus a few other cheerful tones, the Copernicus is a sprightly mid-class option away from the action to the south of the Old Town.

Hotel Pod Zamkiem (☎ 089 535 1287; www.hotel -olsztyn.com.pl; ul Nowowiejskiego 10; s/d 170/240zł; **P**) Set in a large historic villa, once the home of the influential Sperl family, this is a stylish traditional inn with character in spades. Wooden beams, murals and lots of pine provide atmosphere, and the park setting puts you right by the castle and the Old Town. It's on a busy road so request a room at the back.

Camping 173 Dywity (☎ 089 512 0646; www.dywity .com.pl; ul Barczewskiego 47; camp sites per person/car/tent 12/8/10zł, cottages 17-60zł; ⏰ May-Sep) Dywity is perfectly situated on a peaceful, isolated bend of the Łyna River. There are tent sites aplenty, well-equipped bungalows that sleep between four and six persons, and bicycles and kayaks for hire. It's 10km north of Olsztyn and best reached with your own transport.

Eating

Bar Dziupla (☎ 089 527 5083; ul Stare Miasto 9/10; mains 5-12zł; ⏰ 8am-10pm Mon-Sat, 9am-10pm Sun) Dziupla takes on the milk-bar mantle to provide some of the best budget meals in the Old Town, including delicious *pierogi* (Polish dumplings) and *chłodnik* (cold beetroot soup).

Greenway (☎ 089 535 0640; ul Prosta 10/11; mains 7.50-10zł; ⏰ 10am-8pm Mon-Thu, 10am-9pm Fri & Sat, noon-8pm Sun) Another branch of the popular Polish chain. Pick up a large portion of the usual offerings, such as Mexican goulash, enchiladas and spinach quiche. Grab a real fruit shake and head for the quiet outdoor patio at the rear.

Weranda Grill (☎ 089 527 6266; ul Kołłątaja 15; mains 16-30zł; ⏰ 11am-midnight) Meat lovers will flock to this large restaurant for a menu packed with loin chops, grilled ribs and sausages; vegetarians will be disappointed with a small selection of salads. A compromise is easy to find though; grab a beer and kick back on the enormous summer terrace along the banks of the Łyna River.

Różana Café (☎ 089 523 5039; Targ Rybny 14; mains 20-50zł; ⏰ 11am-midnight) A well-translated trilingual menu, with just a dash of humour, introduces you to this refined selection of Polish dishes, while waiters in braces gently woo you with extras. The portions won't blow you away, but it's a good excuse to stick around for dessert or one last drink.

Self-caterers can head to **Supermarket Spożywczy** (Al Piłsudskiego 16; ⏰ 9am-9pm Mon-Sat, 10am-8pm Sun) on the ground floor of the new Alfa Centrum shopping mall.

WARMIA & MASURIA

Drinking

Bohema Jazz Club (☎ 089 525 7051; Targ Rybny 15; ☻ 3pm-2am) Sidling up to Różana Café is Bohema, Olsztyn's best jazz club. It has a reputation for quality live jazz and well-mixed cocktails, and may also be the only basement club in Poland with a lift.

Klub SARP (☎ 089 535 9649; ul Kołłątaja 14; ☻ 11am-midnight) The riverside area around the southern end of the Old Town is a hotbed of pubs, clubs and restaurants, and SARP is a top contender. This split-level setup in a former granary is run by the local Association of Polish Architects and, with its blackened wooden beams and whitewashed walls, looks as though it's been transplanted from Tudor times.

Getting There & Away

The busy bus and train stations are both in a big L-shaped building on Plac Konstytucji 3 Maja. You can walk to the Old Town in 15 minutes or take one of the frequent city buses that drop you off in front of the High Gate.

BUS

Buses to Olsztynek (5zł, 50 minutes), Ostróda (5zł, 1¼ hours), Lidzbark Warmiński (6zł, one hour) and Kętrzyn (14zł to 19zł, 2¼ hours) go at least every hour. There are regular departures to Giżycko (18zł, three hours, 10 daily), Elbląg (20zł, 2¼ hours, seven daily) and Gdańsk (26zł, four hours, six daily). Half a dozen fast buses run to Warsaw daily (32zł to 34zł, four to 4½ hours).

International buses serve a number of European countries. Among the most frequent are PKS' daily departure at 12.45pm to Kaliningrad in Russia (25zł, four hours) and 9.30pm Friday service to Vilnius in Lithuania (80zł, nine hours).

TRAIN

Six direct trains leave for Gdańsk daily (22zł to 34zł, 2½ hours), four of which go via Elbląg (24zł, 1½ hours). Four fast trains go to Warsaw (43zł, 3½ hours) daily and another four to Toruń (21zł to 34zł, three hours).

OLSZTYNEK

pop 7600

Around 25km southwest of Olsztyn, Olsztynek is a small town with one big attraction: the **Museum of Folk Architecture** (Muzeum Budownictwa Ludowego; ☎ 089 519 2164; ul Sportowa 21; adult/concession May-Aug 8/5.50zł, Sep 7/5zł, Oct 6/4.50zł; ☻ 9am-3.30pm Tue-Sun mid-Apr–end-Apr, to 5.30pm Tue-Sun May & Tue-Fri Jun-Aug, to 6pm Sat & Sun Jun-Aug, to 4.30pm Sep, to 3pm Oct). Tucked away on the northeastern outskirts of town, this skansen features about 40 examples of regional timber architecture from Warmia and Masuria, and also has a cluster of Lithuanian houses. There's a variety of peasant cottages complete with outbuildings, various windmills and a thatch-roofed church. A number of buildings have been furnished and decorated inside, and it's been done really well.

Above the skansen's rustic restaurant is a small museum that is split in two; one half is filled with the usual collection of folk art and farming tools, while other contains a detailed account (in Polish) of Stalag 1B Hohenstein, a POW camp located on the outskirts of the village during WWII. Some 650,000 captured soldiers passed through the camp, consisting mostly of French, Belgian, Italian and Russian nationals.

The 14th-century Protestant church, on the pretty Rynek, was rebuilt after suffering damage in WWII and is now an **art gallery** (☎ 089 519 2491; Rynek 1; adult/concession 3/2zł; ☻ 9am-5pm Tue-Sun May-Sep, to 4pm Tue-Sun Oct-Apr). It's a good spot to see current folk art; displays include hand-painted ceramic tiles, fine lace work, and iconic wooden figures that run from comical to moving.

The area to the south and east of the town is popular with Poles for its lakes and horse riding. Agrotourist accommodation is common here, and information on them, and local activities, can be picked up at the friendly **tourist office** (☎ 089 519 2756; it@olsztynek.com.pl; Ratusz, Rynek; ☻ 8am-5pm Mon-Fri, 10am-2pm Sat) near the art gallery.

The train station is 1km northeast of the centre, close to the skansen. At least six trains run to Olsztyn (7.50zł to 12zł, 30 minutes) daily.

The bus terminal is 250m south of the Rynek, but many regional buses call in at the train station. You can travel from either to Olsztyn (5zł, 50 minutes, once or twice hourly), Grunwald (4zł, 30 minutes, up to eight daily) and Ostróda (7zł, one hour, seven daily). Private minibuses duplicate many of the local lines.

GRUNWALD

Grunwald is hard to find even on detailed maps, yet the name is known to every Pole.

WARMIA & MASURIA

Here, on 15 July 1410, the combined Polish and Lithuanian forces (supported by contingents of Ruthenians and Tatars) under King Władysław II Jagiełło defeated the army of the Teutonic Knights (see p451). A crucial moment in Polish history, the 10 hours of carnage left the grand master of the Teutonic order, Ulrich von Jungingen, dead and his forces decimated. This was reputedly the largest medieval battle in Europe, with an estimated 70,000 troops aiming to hack each other to bits.

The battlefield is an open, gently rolling meadow adorned with three monuments. Built on the central hill is the **Museum of the Grunwald Battlefield** (Muzeum Bitwy Grunwaldzkiej; ☎ 089 647 2228; adult/concession 6/3zł; ☒ 8am-6pm 1 May-15 Oct), which has a miniscule display of period armour, maps and battle banners. Its redeeming feature is a small cinema that plays scenes from *Bitwa pod Grunwaldem* (1931), a classic Polish flick about the battle. Five hundred metres from the museum are the ruins of a **chapel**, erected by the order a year after the battle, on the spot where the grand master is supposed to have died. All signs are in Polish, but the shop by the entrance to the battlefield sells brochures in English and German.

Frequently visited by Poles, Grunwald is essentially a memorial to this glorious moment in Poland's history, and nonpartisan foreigners may find it less interesting. The best time to visit the place is in July during the **Days of Grunwald festival** (www.republika.pl/grunwald), a medieval extravaganza with lots of stalls, tournaments, concerts and costumed characters, culminating in a huge re-enactment of the battle itself. Watched by almost as many people as attended the original skirmish, it's one of the biggest and most colourful spectacles of its kind in Poland, which is saying something in a country that's so marked by its Middle Ages.

Year-round at least four or five daily buses go to Olsztynek (4zł, 30 minutes) and Olsztyn (9zł, 1½ hours) from the battlefield, with another two or three departing the battlefield for Ostróda (7.60zł, 45 minutes).

OSTRÓDA

pop 33,500

Ostróda is one of the region's many lakeside towns popular with Poles but unknown to others. It's also the southern terminus of the Elbląg-Ostróda Canal, and if you take a boat in either direction you're likely to spend a night here. Apparently Napoleon once ruled Europe from this deceptively sleepy place; he wouldn't look twice at it now, but the leisurely pace of life seems to suit holidaymakers.

For information on Ostróda and its surrounding lakes, head to the regional **tourist office** (☎ 089 642 3000; www.mazury-zachodnie.pl; Plac 1000-lecia Państwa Polskiego 1A; ☒ 9am-6pm Mon-Fri, 10am-4pm Sat, 10am-2pm Sun Jun-Aug, 9am-5pm Mon-Fri Sep-May) near the town's small castle.

Sleeping & Eating

The tourist office has an extensive list of agrotourism options in the region.

Hotel Promenada (☎ 089 642 8100; www.hotel promenada.com.pl; ul Mickiewicza 3; s/d 120/180zł; ℗) The Promenada offers the best accommodation in town, close to the lake. Rooms are modern and clean, if a tad soulless; ask for one facing the lake, as the hotel is located on a busy corner.

Taverna (Gen Roji 1; mains 15-30zł; ☒ 11am-11pm) Taverna occupies a lovely spot on a small lake inlet at the northern end of town. Its large wooden deck is the perfect place for a sundowner or a hearty Polish meal, and kayaks are available for the energetic at 5/25zł per hour/day.

Zakątek (☎ 0603 579691; ul Czarnieckiego 38a/51; per car/person/tent 4/4/4zł; ℗) This tiny, basic camping ground sits at the northern tip of the 18km-long Lake Szeląg, some 12km north of Ostróda on the 530 road to Dobre Miasto. It's pretty much all by itself with only the forest and lake for company, but the owner has had the good sense to supply a small shop, beer on tap and kayak rental (5zł per hour) for guests. It's best reached with your own transport.

Getting There & Away

The train and bus stations are next to each other, 500m west of the wharf. Nine trains run to Olsztyn (7.50zł, 30 minutes) and there are four daily trains to Toruń (19zł to 30zł, two to 2½ hours). For Warsaw (40zł, 3¼ hours) a change is usually required at Iława, but there is one direct train daily at 9.14am.

There are buses to Olsztyn (5zł, 1¼ hours, 10 daily), Olsztynek (7zł, one hour, seven daily), Grunwald (7.60zł, 45 minutes, two or three daily) and Elbląg (15zł, 1¾ hours, 11 daily).

From May to September a boat to Elbląg leaves daily at 8am (p486).

ELBLĄG-OSTRÓDA CANAL

The 82km Elbląg-Ostróda Canal is the longest navigable canal still in use in Poland. It's also the most unusual: the canal deals with the 99.5m difference in water levels by means of a unique system of **slipways**, where boats are physically dragged across dry land on rail-mounted trolleys (opposite).

The canal follows the course of a chain of six lakes, most of which are now protected conservation areas. The largest is the considerably overgrown **Lake Drużno** near Elbląg, left behind by the Vistula Lagoon, which once extended deep into this region.

The five slipways are on a 10km stretch of the northern part of the canal. Each slipway consists of two trolleys tied to a single looped rope, operating on the same principle as a funicular. They are powered by water.

Boat Excursions

From May to September, pleasure boats operated by **Żegluga Ostródzko-Elbląska** (☎ in Ostróda 089 646 3871; www.zegluga.com.pl; ☾ 7am-7pm May-Sep) sail the main part of the canal between Ostróda and Elbląg. They depart from both towns at 8am and arrive at the opposite end at about 7pm (adult/under 18 85/65zł). Luggage and bicycles can be taken on free of charge.

If you don't feel like committing to the full 11-hour stretch, take the boat from Elbląg as far as Buczyniec (70/50zł, five hours), which covers the most interesting part of the canal, including all five slipways. This is a good solution for motorists leaving their vehicles in Elbląg as the company puts on buses to transport passengers back to Elbląg. There are no buses from Buczyniec on to Ostróda, but a taxi (100zł to 120zł) can be organised through the boat office in Ostróda – simply call ahead of time.

The boats, which have a capacity of 65, only run when at least 20 passengers turn up. You can expect regular daily services in July and August (sometimes two boats are required to meet the demand) and on hot summer days it may be an idea to reserve a place via phone or email. Outside this period there may be some days off. It's worth ringing Żegluga Ostródzko-Elbląska a couple of days in advance to find out about the availability of tickets and the current timetable status. Boats have snack bars on board, which serve some basic snacks, as well as tea, coffee and beer.

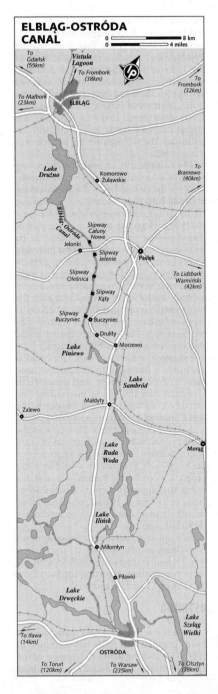

WARMIA & MASURIA

If you're not going to take the boat trip, but have your own transport and want to have a look at the slipways, head to **Buczyniec** between noon and 2pm to see the boats pass on their way north and south. There's a small **museum** (☎ 055 248 7092) here and you can see the impressive machinery that powers the trolleys.

LIDZBARK WARMIŃSKI
pop 16,500

Lidzbark Warmiński, 46km north of Olsztyn, is a rough and ready town with a massive Gothic castle. Its past is certainly more glorious than its present; it was the capital of the Warmian bishopric for over four centuries. In 1350 the bishops chose it as their main residence; a castle and a church were built and the town swiftly became an important religious and cultural centre. Copernicus lived here between 1503 and 1510, serving as doctor and adviser to his uncle, Bishop Łukasz Watzenrode.

When the Reformation arrived in the 16th century, Lidzbark, along with most of the province, became a citadel of Catholicism, and it remained so until the First Partition of 1772. Deprived of his office, the last bishop, Ignacy Krasicki, turned to literature, becoming an outstanding satirist and all-round man of letters.

Today there's little trace of the town that was reputedly the richest and most cultured in Warmia, but the castle alone is enough to justify a day trip.

Castle

This mighty square redbrick structure, adorned with turrets on the corners, is the most important sight in Lidzbark and one of Warmia's most significant cultural gems. Enter from the south through the palatial, horseshoe-shaped building surrounding Plac Zamkowy, which was extensively rebuilt in the 18th century. A wide brick bridge runs up to the main castle gate.

The castle was constructed in the second half of the 14th century on a square plan with a central courtyard, the whole surrounded by a moat and fortified walls. When the bishops' era ended with the Partitions, the castle fell into decline and served a variety of purposes, including use as barracks, storage, hospital and orphanage. Restoration was undertaken in the 1920s and within 10 years the building had been more or less returned to its original form. Miraculously, it came through the war unharmed, and today it is easily one of Poland's best-preserved medieval castles.

Most of the interior, from the cellars up to the 2nd floor, now houses the **Warmian Museum** (Muzeum Warmińskie; ☎ 089 767 2111; Plac Zamkowy 1;

BARGING IN

The rich forests of the Ostróda region have attracted merchants from Gdańsk and Elbląg since medieval times, yet until the 19th century the only way of getting timber down to the Baltic was a long water route along the Drwęca and Vistula Rivers via Toruń. Engineers considered building a canal as a short cut but quickly found that the terrain was rugged and too steep for conventional locks.

In 1836 Prussian engineer Georg Jakob Steenke (1801–82), from Königsberg, produced a sophisticated design for an Elbląg-Ostróda Canal incorporating slipways, but Prussian authorities rejected the project as unrealistic and too costly. Steenke didn't give up, however, and eventually succeeded in getting an audience with the king of Prussia. With typical kingly shrewdness, the monarch approved the plan, not because of its technical or economic aspects but because nobody had ever constructed such a system before.

The part of the canal between Elbląg and Miłomłyn, which included all the slipways, was built between 1848 and 1860, and the remaining leg to Ostróda was completed by 1872. The canal proved to be reliable and profitable, and it cut the distance of the original route along the Drwęca and Vistula almost fivefold. Various extensions were planned, including one linking the canal with the Great Masurian Lakes 120km to the east, but none were ever built.

The canal was damaged during the 1945 Red Army offensive but was repaired soon after liberation and opened for timber transport in 1946. A year later, the first tourist boat sailed the route. It remains the only canal of its kind in Europe and continues to operate, though the timber boats are a distant memory.

adult/concession 8/5zł, courtyard & cellar only 2zł; 9am-5pm Tue-Sun Jun-Aug, 10am-4pm Tue-Sun Sep–May). The first thing you'll notice is a beautiful courtyard with two-storey arcaded galleries all round it. It was constructed in the 1380s and has hardly been altered since then.

The castle's two-storey vaulted cellar, cool on even the hottest of days, is largely empty aside from a few marble fireplaces and cannon barrels. The cannons once belonged to the bishops, who had their own small army – an essential ecumenical accessory at that time.

Most of the attractions are housed on the 1st floor, which boasts the main chambers; the vaulted **Grand Refectory** (Wielki Refektarz) is quite remarkable. The chessboard-style wall paintings, dating from the end of the 14th century, feature the names and coats of arms of bishops who once resided here. In stark contrast is a tiny room centred on a dank, dark pit off the beautiful chamber, once used as a prison cell. Exhibitions on this floor include medieval art from the region, such as some charming Madonnas and fine silverware. The adjoining chapel was redecorated in rococo style in the mid-18th century and is quite overbearing compared to the rest of the castle.

The top floor contains several exhibitions, including cubist and surrealist 20th-century Polish painting, a collection of icons dating from the 17th century onward, and spiffy army uniforms and evening gowns from the early 1800s.

Sleeping & Eating

There is no reason to stay here unless transport connections force you to. If you happen to require a bed for the night, try **Gościniec Myśliwski** (089 767 5259; ul Spółdzielców 2B; d with/without bath 90/120zł; P), halfway between the bus station and the castle. This hunting lodge, complete with animal pelts and antlers adorning the walls, has passable rooms and its own restaurant.

Getting There & Away

The bus terminal occupies the defunct train station, about 500m northwest of the castle. Buses to Olsztyn (6zł, one hour) depart at least hourly, and are supplemented by private minibuses. There are five express buses a day to Gdańsk (22zł to 26zł, three to 3½ hours) and two to Kętrzyn (11zł, 1½ hours), passing Reszel and Święta Lipka on the way.

RESZEL
pop 5100

Like Lidzbark Warmiński, the big drawcard of Reszel (reh-shel) is its castle. It easily dominates the tiny market town from a slightly elevated position, and is testament to Reszel's long history: the town began life as the easternmost outpost of the Warmian bishopric in the 13th century and remained a prosperous craft centre until the wars of the 18th century. Today it's quite the backwater, though its minuscule centre still boasts the original street plan and a fine parish church.

Sights

Reszel's tiny Old Town is centred on the Rynek and its low-key town hall, which houses the local **tourist office** (089 755 0097; Rynek 24; 10am-5pm Mon-Fri, 10am-3pm Sat May–mid-Sep, 7.30am-3.30pm Mon-Fri mid-Sep–May). One block east is the 14th-century brick **castle** (089 755 0216; ul Podzamcze 3; adult/concession 3/2zł), built at the same time as that in Lidzbark. It has retained much of its original form, except for the southern side, which was turned into a Protestant church in the 19th century, with a belfry and a jarring concrete gable added to the top. Today the complex is open to the public and houses a hotel, a restaurant, some function rooms and an **art gallery** (adult/concession 6/3zł; 10am-4pm Tue-Sun). Go to the top of the castle's massive cylindrical tower for some views over the red-tiled roofs of the Old Town.

The other main building in town is the 14th-century **parish church** (9am-6pm), a large Gothic brick construction with a tall square tower. It was refurnished and redecorated in the 1820s after fires that devastated much of the centre, and has a harmonious though not outstanding interior. If you'd like a birds-eye view of the town with the castle as a backdrop, ascend the church's **tower** (adult/concession 4/2zł).

At the entrance to the Old Town, when arriving from Kętrzyn, is the unusually massive brick **Fishing Bridge** (Most Rybacki), also known as the Gothic Bridge (Most Gotycki), built in the 14th century and recently so extensively restored that it looks like new. Don't be fooled by the name – you'd need a long line and a lot more river before you could actually catch anything!

Sleeping & Eating

If you're going to stay anywhere in Reszel, it may as well be the castle. The big suite-like rooms of the **Kreativ Hotel** (089 755 0109; www

HIGH STAKES

Reszel may have the dubious distinction of being the last place in Europe to sentence a woman to death as a witch. Where most such cases had died out by the early 18th century, massive fires in 1806 and 1807 incensed the townspeople here to such a degree that they accused unfortunate local woman Barbara Zdunk of sorcery and imprisoned her in the castle. The case reached the attention of Prussia's highest authorities and was referred to several courts and even to King Frederick Wilhelm II himself – incredibly, all of them upheld the guilty verdict. In 1811 Zdunk was burned at the stake, though legend has it that the executioner mercifully strangled her before torching the wood. Not what you'd expect from the Age of Enlightenment.

.zamek-reszel.com; ul Podzamcze 3; s/d/q 210/280/440zł; **P**) are big on atmosphere, with brick flooring, whitewashed walls, and large, comfy beds. Its vaulted **restaurant** (mains 9-30zł; 8am-11pm) takes over the central courtyard in warm weather.

Getting There & Away

Trains no longer call in at Reszel. The bus terminal is by the old station, a five-minute walk north of the Old Town. There are plenty of buses east to Kętrzyn (5zł to 6zł, 30 minutes), passing via Święta Lipka (3.50zł, 10 minutes). A dozen buses go to Olsztyn daily (12zł, 1½ hours). Two buses run west to Lidzbark Warmiński (9zł, one hour), one of them a fast service to Gdańsk (35zł, four hours).

ŚWIĘTA LIPKA

Polish Catholics flock to this tiny hamlet for one reason alone – to visit its celebrated church. The origins of Święta Lipka (*shfyen-tah leep-kah*), which means 'Holy Lime Tree', are linked to one of Poland's most famous miracle stories. Apparently a prisoner in Kętrzyn castle was visited the night before his execution by the Virgin Mary, who presented him with a tree trunk so he could carve an effigy of her. The resulting figure was so beautiful that the judges took it to be a sign from heaven and gave the condemned man his freedom. On his way home he placed the statue on the first lime tree he encountered, which happened to be in Święta Lipka.

Miracles immediately began to occur, and even sheep knelt down while passing the shrine. Pilgrims arrived in increasing numbers, including the last grand master of the Teutonic order, Albrecht von Hohenzollern, who walked here barefoot (ironically, he converted to Lutherism six years later). A timber chapel was built to protect the miraculous figure, and was later replaced with the present building. It's perhaps the most magnificent Baroque church in northern Poland, a huge attraction and still a major pilgrimage site.

Church of Our Lady

Built between 1687 and 1693, and later surrounded by an ample rectangular cloister, the **church** (089 755 1481; www.swlipka.pl; admission free; 8am-6pm except during Mass) was built around four identical corner towers, all housing chapels. The best artists from Warmia, Königsberg (Kaliningrad) and Vilnius were commissioned for the furnishings and decoration, which were completed by about 1740. Since then the church has hardly changed, either inside or out, and is regarded as one of the purest examples of a late-Baroque church in the country.

The entrance to the complex is an elaborate wrought-iron **gateway**. Just behind it, the two-towered cream façade holds a stone **sculpture** of the holy lime tree in its central niche, with a statue of the Virgin Mary on top.

Once inside (appropriate clothing is required to enter), the visitor is enveloped in colourful and florid, but not overwhelming, Baroque ornamentation. All the frescoes are the work of Maciej Mayer of Lidzbark, and display trompe l'œil images, which were fashionable at the time. These are clearly visible both on the vault and the columns; the latter look as if they were carved. Of course Mayer also left behind his own image – you can see him in a blue waistcoat with brushes in his hand, in the corner of the vault painting over the organ.

The three-storey, 19m-high **altar**, covering the whole back of the chancel, is carved of walnut and painted to look like marble. Of the three paintings in the altar, the lowest one depicts the Virgin Mary of Święta Lipka with the Christ child, which is lit with subtle lighting for effect.

The pulpit is ornamented with paintings and sculptures. Directly opposite, across the nave, is a **holy lime tree** topped with the figure of the Virgin Mary, supposedly placed on the spot where the legendary tree itself once stood.

The pride of the church is its breathtaking **organ**, a sumptuously decorated instrument of about 5000 pipes. The work of Johann Jozue Mosengel of Königsberg, it is decorated with mechanical figures of saints and angels that dance around when the organ is played, much like an astronomical clock. Short demonstrations are held every hour on the half-hour from 9.30am to 5.30pm May to September and at 10am, noon and 2pm in October.

The cloister surrounding the church is ornamented with frescoes, also masterminded by Mayer. The artist painted the corner chapels and parts of the northern and western cloister, but died before the work was complete. It was continued in the same vein by other artists, but without the same success.

Święta Lipka is hugely popular with tourists and pilgrims alike; don't expect too much peace and serenity inside the church. The main religious celebrations fall on the last Sunday of May, and on 11, 14 and 15 August.

Sleeping & Eating

Dom Pielgrzyma (☎ 089 755 1481; Święta Lipka 29; dm 25zł) This simple pilgrims' place, in the monastery complex next to the church, provides 85 beds in rooms for up to five people, but it can often be full to overflowing in July and August. Full and half board is available if requested in advance.

Hotel w Świętej Lipce (☎ 089 755 3737; www.swieta lipka.hotel500.com.pl; Święta Lipka 16; s/d 190/220zł; P) Big, modern and a pale imitation of a traditional timbered farmhouse, the town's biggest tourist venture is instantly redeemed by a leafy setting and perfect views of the church. The rooms are good and staff are eager to please. It's also known as Hotel 500.

Getting There & Away

There are buses to Kętrzyn (5zł, 20 minutes) and Reszel (3.50zł, 10 minutes) every hour or so. There are several to Olsztyn (12zł, 1¾ hours) and a couple to Lidzbark Warmiński (10zł, 1¼ hours).

THE GREAT MASURIAN LAKES

The Great Masurian Lake district (Kraina Wielkich Jezior Mazurskich), east of Olsztyn, is a verdant land of rolling hills dotted with countless lakes, healthy little farms, scattered tracts of forest and small towns. The district is centred on Lake Śniardwy (114 sq km), Poland's largest lake, and Lake Mamry and its adjacent waters (an additional 104 sq km). Over 15% of the area is covered by water and another 30% by forest.

The lakes are well connected by rivers and canals, to form an extensive system of waterways. The whole area has become a prime destination for yachtspeople and canoeists, and is also popular among anglers, hikers, bikers and nature-lovers. Any boating enthusiast worth their (freshwater) salt should make Masuria their first port of call.

The main lakeside centres are Giżycko and Mikołajki, with two minor ones, Węgorzewo and Ruciane-Nida, at the northern and southern ends of the lakeland, respectively. Visitors arrive in great numbers in July and August, though after mid-August the crowds begin to thin out.

Getting Around

Yachties can sail most of the larger lakes, all the way from Węgorzewo to Ruciane-Nida. These larger lakes are interconnected and form the district's main waterway system. Kayakers will perhaps prefer more intimate surroundings alongside rivers and smaller lakes. The best established and most popular kayak route in the area originates at Sorkwity and follows the Krutynia River and Lake Bełdany to Ruciane-Nida (see p481).

If you're not up for doing everything yourself, you can enjoy the lakes in comfort from the deck of one of the pleasure boats operated by the **Żegluga Mazurska** (☎ 087 428 5332; www.zeglugamazurska.com.pl) in Giżycko. These large boats have an open deck above and a coffee shop below, and can carry backpacks and bicycles.

Theoretically, boats run between Giżycko, Mikołajki and Ruciane-Nida daily from May to September, and to Węgorzewo from June to August. In practice, as trips can be cancelled if too few passengers turn up, the service is most reliable from late June to late August. Schedules are clearly posted at the lake ports.

The detailed *Wielkie Jeziora Mazurskie* map (scale 1:100,000; 8zł), produced by Copernicus, is a great help for anyone exploring the region by boat, kayak, bike, car or foot. The map shows walking trails, canoeing routes, accommodation options, petrol stations and much more.

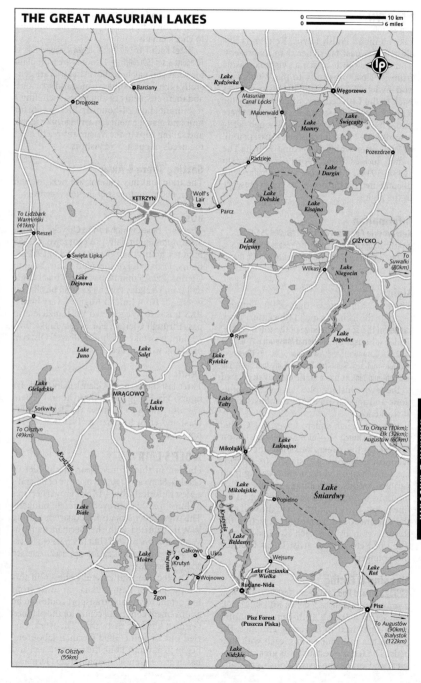

THE GREAT MASURIAN LAKES

KĘTRZYN

pop 28,100

Like so many Polish towns, Kętrzyn (kent-shin) has a past far richer than its present. Today there's little to attract visitors – aside from its close proximity to the Wolf's Lair and Święta Lipka – but its history dates back to the 14th century, when the Teutonic Knights (see p451) founded a settlement here under the name of Rastenburg. Though partly colonised by Poles, it remained Prussian until WWII, after which it became Polish. The name derives from Wojciech Kętrzyński (1838–1919), a historian and scholar who documented the history of the Polish presence in the region.

Information

Kętrzyńskie Centrum Kultury (☎ 089 751 4765; it@ketrzyn.com.pl; Piłsudskiego 1; ☒ 8am-6pm Mon, 7.30am-3.30pm Tue-Fri) Small information office in the heart of town.

Sights

There are still some vestiges of the Teutonic legacy in the form of a mid-14th-century brick **castle** on the southern edge of the town centre. Today it houses the **Regional Museum** (☎ 089 752 3282; Plac Zamkowy 1; adult/concession 5/3zł; ☒ 10am-5pm mid-Jun–mid-Sep, 9am-4pm Tue-Fri, 9am-3pm Sat & Sun mid-Sep–mid-Jun). It has a static display dedicated to the town's history, plus temporary exhibitions and regular medieval demonstrations at weekends.

With its squat, square tower, the Gothic **St George's Church** (Kościół Św Jerzego), a bit further up the street, looks like the town's second castle from a distance. Its interior has furnishings and decoration dating from various periods, indicating a number of alterations over time. Of particular note is the fine pulpit, three tombstones in the wall near the entrance, and a painting depicting the Resurrection by Heinrich Königswieser, a pupil of Reformation artist Lucas Cranach the Younger.

Sleeping & Eating

ourpick Zajazd Pod Zamkiem (☎ 089 752 3117; www .zajazd.ketrzyn.pl; ul Struga 3; s/d/t/q 100/150/190/250zł; P) Set in a stylish 19th-century country house right next to the castle entrance, the Zajazd has just four rooms, each with four beds. The terrace restaurant is great in summer, and offers the usual Polish grub and plenty of shade. Ask the owner about internet cafés in town; he may let you use his computer to check emails.

Hotel Koch (☎ 089 752 2058; www.masuren2.de; ul Traugutta 3; s/d 150/200zł; P) Rooms are a bit plain for what you pay here, but standards are generally high, bathrooms are nice and spacious, and there are plenty of amenities, including a restaurant and a 24-hour bar. Bicycles are for hire, and management can arrange bike, kayak and sailing trips in the Masurian area to meet the needs of guests and visitors.

Getting There & Away

The train and bus stations are next to each other, 600m southeast of the town centre.

BUS

There are buses which run to Giżycko (6.90zł, 40 minutes, eight daily), Węgorzewo (8zł, 55 minutes, hourly) and Olsztyn (14zł to 19zł, 2¼ hours, 17 daily). For the Wolf's Lair, head to Gierłoż (2zł, 15 minutes) with city bus 1 (nine daily) on weekdays or the Zielona bus line at weekends from June to August (every hour). PKS buses to Węgorzewo via Radzieje also pass through Gierłoż. For Święta Lipka (5zł, 20 minutes), take any bus to Reszel, Olsztyn, or Mrągowo via Pilec.

TRAIN

Three fast trains run to Gdańsk daily (43zł, 4½ hours) via Elbląg (36zł, three hours). There are four trains to Giżycko (6.50zł, 30 minutes) and eight to Olsztyn (14zł to 22zł, 1½ hours) daily.

WOLF'S LAIR

Hidden in thick forest near the hamlet of Gierłoż, 8km east of Kętrzyn, is one of Poland's eeriest historical relics – 18 overgrown hectares of huge, partly destroyed concrete bunkers. This was Hitler's main headquarters during WWII, baptised with the German name of Wolfsschanze, or **Wolf's Lair** (Wilczy Szaniec; ☎ 089 752 4429; www.wolfsschanze.home.pl; adult/concession 8/5zł; ☒ 8am-sunset).

The location was carefully chosen in this remote part of East Prussia, far away from important towns and transport routes, to be a convenient command centre for the planned German advance eastwards. The work, carried out by some 3000 German labourers, began in autumn 1940; the cement, steel and basalt gravel were all brought from Germany.

THE HIT ON HITLER

Hitler used to say that the Wolf's Lair was one of the very few places in Europe where he felt safe. Ironically, it was here that an assassination attempt came closest to succeeding. It was organised by a group of pragmatic, high-ranking German officers who considered the continuation of the war to be suicidal, with no real chance of victory. They planned to negotiate peace with the Allies after eliminating Hitler.

The leader of the plot, Colonel Claus von Stauffenberg, arrived from Berlin on 20 July 1944 under the pretext of informing Hitler about the newly formed reserve army. A frequent guest at the Wolf's Lair, he enjoyed the confidence of the staff and had no problems entering the bunker complex with a bomb in his briefcase. He placed the case beneath the table a few feet from Hitler and left the meeting to take a prearranged phone call. The explosion killed two members of Hitler's staff and wounded half a dozen others, but the Führer himself suffered only minor injuries and was even able to meet Mussolini later the same day. Stauffenberg and some 5000 people involved directly or indirectly in the plot were executed.

Had the outcome been different, it could have radically changed the final course of WWII. A peace treaty between the Germans and the Allies in 1944 might well have saved the lives of some five million people and prevented the devastation of vast parts of Poland and Germany.

About 80 structures were finally built, including seven heavy bunkers for the top leaders: Martin Bormann (Hitler's adviser and private secretary), Hermann Göring (Prussian prime minister and German commissioner for aviation) and Hitler himself were among the residents. Their bunkers had walls and ceilings up to 8m thick.

The whole complex was surrounded by multiple barriers of barbed wire and artillery emplacements, and a sophisticated minefield. An airfield was built 5km away and there was an emergency airstrip within the camp. Apart from the natural camouflage of trees and plants, the bunker site was further disguised with artificial vegetation-like screens suspended on wires and changed according to the season of the year. The Allies did not discover the site until 1945.

Hitler arrived in the Wolf's Lair on 26 June 1941 (four days after the invasion of the Soviet Union) and stayed there until 20 November 1944, with only short trips to the outside world. His longest journey outside the bunker was a four-month stint at the Ukraine headquarters of the Wehrmacht (the armed services of the German Reich) in 1942, overseeing the advancing German front.

As the Red Army approached in 1944, Hitler left the Wolf's Lair and the headquarters were evacuated. The army prepared the bunkers to be destroyed, should the enemy have attempted to seize them. About 10 tonnes of explosives were stuffed into each heavy bunker. The complex was eventually blown up on 24 January 1945 and the Germans retreated. Three days later the Soviets arrived, but the extensive minefield was still efficiently defending the empty ruins. It took 10 years to clear the 10km of mines within the complex; about 55,000 were detected and defused.

Today, the site has succumbed to Mother Nature; bunkers are slowly disappearing behind a thick wall of natural camouflage. It's best to pick up a site map or booklet (12zł), sold from stands in the parking area. If you're in a group organise a guide to show you around; English-, German- and Russian-speaking guides charge 50zł per 1½-hour tour, but you may be able to negotiate a lower price if things are slow. All structures are identified with numbers and marked with big signs telling you not to enter the ruins, advice that many people ignore, including some guides (bunker 6 appears the most popular to enter). Of Hitler's bunker (13) only one wall survived, but Göring's 'home' (16) is in relatively good shape. A memorial plate (placed in 1992) marks the location of Colonel Claus von Stauffenberg's 1944 assassination attempt on Hitler (see boxed text, above) and a small exhibition room houses a scale model of the original camp layout.

You can also continue 200m past the entrance towards Węgorzewo, and take a small road to the right signposted 'Kwiedzina (5km)'. On either side of this narrow path is a handful of crumbling bunkers that can be explored free of charge.

Whichever direction you head, it's worth bringing insect repellent in summer.

EXPLORING MAUERWALD

The Wolf's Lair may be the most famous example of Germany's wartime presence in Masuria, but it's not the only one. A second bunker complex, known as **Mauerwald** (☎ 089 752 4283; www .mauerwald.com in German; adult/concession 5/3zł; ☺ 8am-dusk May-Oct), was built 18km northeast of Hitler's secret headquarters. The 30 bunkers and accompanying buildings, which were occupied from 1941 to 1944, were home to a handful of the Nazis' top military commanders, including Field Marshall Paulus, General Guderian and Colonel von Stauffenberg (p493).

The bunkers are in exceptional condition and range from small huts to solid two-storey blocks with 7m thick walls. Bunker 6 is the largest, and sports a wooden tower atop its roof that affords partial views of the surrounding bunkers (trees obscure most buildings). Unlike the Wolf's Lair, almost all of the bunkers can be entered, and it's a creepy experience exploring such dark, damp places. If you've a flashlight bring it along, otherwise hire one at the ticket desk for 2zł. Be sure to bring insect repellent too.

About 4km northwest of Mauerwald along the Masurian Canal are more solid concrete edifices in the shape of two unfinished **locks**. Begun in 1911 by the Prussians, these massive structures standing 21m high and 46m long were part of a series of 10 locks, planned to connect the Masurian lakes with the Baltic Sea. WWI halted work, but construction began again in 1934, only to be stopped once more by war. One of the locks is now used as an adult playground by **S-Borg** (☎ 087 427 4939; www.s-borg.pl in Polish), a local extreme-sports company that's set a rope bridge (10zł), swing bridge (15zł), flying fox (40zł) and giant swing (40zł) for the adventurous to play on.

For Mauerwald, take any bus between Kętrzyn and Węgorzewo and ask to be let off at Mamerki; the bus stop is about 300m north of the bunkers. To reach the locks, hop on a bus from Węgorzewo heading in the direction of Srokowo and tell the driver to drop you at Lake Rydzówka.

Sleeping & Eating

Hotel Wilcze Gniazdo (☎ 089 752 4429; s 70zł, d 80-90zł, tr 130zł; Ⓟ) The former officers' hostel at the entrance to the complex has been refurbished to serve as a basic hotel, but it's certainly a lot more comfortable than the dank remains of the bunkers. There're also a snack bar and a budget restaurant on the site. Hotel guests can enter the bunker complex for free.

Getting There & Away

PKS buses between Kętrzyn (2zł, 15 minutes) and Węgorzewo (6.30zł, 45 minutes) stop here several times a day. You can also go to Kętrzyn by city bus 1.

WĘGORZEWO
pop 11,700

The small but busy town of Węgorzewo (ven-go-*zheh*-vo) on Lake Mamry is the northernmost lakeside centre for both excursion boats and independent sailors. The main town itself isn't quite on the lake shore but is linked to it by a 2km river canal.

It's less overrun by tourists than its southern cousins, except on the first weekend of August when the town hosts a large craft fair, which is 25 years old and attracts plenty of artisans from the region and beyond.

Information

PKO Bank (Plac Wolności 18)
Tourist office (☎ 087 427 4009; www.wegorzewo.pl; Plac Wolności 11; ☺ 9am-5pm mid-Jun–mid-Sep, 8am-4pm Mon-Fri mid-Sep–mid-Jun) Has information on lake and biking activities.

Sleeping & Eating

As the focus of activity is on the lake area, you won't find too many places to stay around the centre. There are dozens of pensions and larger leisure facilities spread out in the surrounding area, particularly in the lakeside suburb of Kal, but they can be tricky to get to and usually only open in summer.

Pensjonat Nautic (☎ 087 427 2080; www.nautic.pl; ul Słowackiego 14; s 110zł, d 190-210zł, apt 240-500zł; Ⓟ ⌨) An excellent and versatile family guesthouse near the canal and the boat wharf. Rooms range from comfortable standard en suites with blue wood fittings to a pair of amazing apartments with their own kitchenettes and terraces. The restaurant here also comes recommended.

Camping Nr 175 Rusałka (☎ 087 427 2191; www .cmazur.pl; ul Leśna 2; camp sites per adult/child 9/7zł, cabins 100-180zł; ☺ May-Sep) With its pleasant wooded grounds, a restaurant, and boats and kayaks for hire, Rusałka is a good place and well run, though most cabins are pretty basic. It's on Lake Święcajty, 4km from Węgorzewo off the Giżycko road. Infrequent PKS buses go there in season; if you don't want to wait, take any bus to Giżycko, get out at the Lake Święcajty turn-off and walk the last 1km.

Getting There & Away

Trains no longer operate here, but the bus terminal, 1km northwest of the centre, provides reasonable transport to Giżycko (6.70zł, 55 minutes, at least hourly) and Kętrzyn (8.30zł, 55 minutes, hourly); buses to Kętrzyn via Radzieje will drop you at the entrance to the Wolf's Lair. Several buses go to Gołdap (8.70zł, 1½ hours) and two to Suwałki (15.50zł, 3½ hours). Four fast buses run directly to Warsaw (36zł, 5½ hours); book in advance in the high season.

From July to August, a boat sails from the wharf at Lake Mamry for Giżycko at 3pm (adult/concession 40/32zł, 2½ hours).

GIŻYCKO

pop 29,800

Positioned on the northern shore of Lake Niegocin, Giżycko (ghee-*zhits*-ko) is the largest sailing centre in the lakes, and the focal point of the seasonal tourist trade. It's not an aesthetically pleasing town, with a lake frontage more tacky than tasteful, but it's one of the few Masurian towns with a buzz and its huge fortress is worth at least an hour of your time.

The town started life under the Teutonic Knights (see p451) but was destroyed on numerous occasions by Lithuanians, Poles, Swedes, Tatars, Russians and Germans in turn. Today it's essentially a transport hub and provision base for the holiday homes and water-sports centres that have grown up outside the town, and for the hordes of lake-bound holidaymakers who arrive en masse in the short summer season.

Information

Bank Pekao ATM (ul Olsztyńska 15A)
Main post office (ul Pocztowa 2)
Orbis Travel (☎ 087 428 3112; ul Dąbrowskiego 3; ☼ 9am-5pm Mon-Fri, 9am-3pm Sat)
Romix Internet (☎ 087 429 2997; ul Olsztyńska 11B; per hr 4zł; ☼ 9am-5pm Mon-Fri, 10am-2pm Sat)
Tourist office (☎ 087 428 5265; www.gizycko.turystyka .pl; ul Wyzwolenia 2; ☼ 9am-6pm Mon-Fri, 10am-4pm Sat & Sun Jun-Sep, 8am-4pm Mon-Fri Sep-May) Loads of info on the entire lake region and free internet access.

Sights

Named after the then Prussian minister of war, General Hermann von Boyen, the **Boyen Fortress** (Twierdza Boyen; adult/concession fortress & museum 5/3zł) was built between 1844 and 1856 to protect the kingdom's border with Russia. Since the frontier ran north–south along the 90km string of lakes, the stronghold was strategically placed in the middle, on the isthmus near Giżycko.

The fortress, which consists of several bastions and defensive towers surrounded by a moat, was continually modified and strengthened, and successfully withstood Russian attacks during WWI. In WWII it was a defensive outpost of the Wolf's Lair, given up to the Red Army without a fight during the 1945 offensive. The fortifications have survived in surprisingly good shape, and some of the walls, bastions and barracks can safely be explored. One of the barracks houses a youth hostel at one end and a small **museum** (☼ 9am-8pm mid-Apr–mid-Nov) at the other. Inside the museum you'll find a scale model of the fortress and a few odd items, such as a section of wall painted with a Russian soldier, used as target practice by the Prussians.

Built in 1900 in neo-Gothic style, Giżycko's seven-storey **Water Tower** (☎ 087 428 5170; adult/ concession 10/5zł; ☼ 9am-11pm) supplied the city with running water until 1997. Today the tall red-brick structure houses a café and an assortment of memorabilia related to the region, but its big attraction is of course the views it provides over the town and surrounding lakes.

Giżycko's working **rotary bridge** on ul Moniuszki was built in 1889 and is the only one of its kind in the country. Despite weighing more than 100 tonnes, it can be turned by one person, and is opened six times daily to allow boats through, closing to traffic for between 30 minutes and 1¾ hours each time. If you're travelling by car, circumvent the wait and take the long way round via ul Obwodowa.

Activities

YACHT CHARTERS

Giżycko has the largest number of yacht-charter agencies in the area, and accordingly offers the widest choice of boats. The town is also a recognised centre for disabled sailors, with regular national regattas, and many companies provide specialist equipment, advice and training.

WARMIA & MASURIA

With yachting such a huge business here, the boat-charter market is highly volatile and operators often change. The tourist office is likely to have the current list of agents (sometimes up to 40) and can provide advice. It's also worth getting a copy of the monthly yachting magazine *Żagle*, in which plenty of firms advertise, or the multi-lingual *Informator Żeglarski*.

Finding anything in July and August without advance booking can be difficult. Securing a boat in early June or late September is much easier, but shop around, as prices and conditions vary substantially and bargaining is possible with some agents.

In July and August, expect to pay somewhere between 180zł and 400zł per day for a sailing boat large enough to sleep around four to five people. Prices depend on the size of cabins, toilet and kitchen facilities and so on. Prices are significantly lower in June and September – often half of the high-season prices. You pay for your own petrol, though most firms throw in a few litres for free. A boat with skipper included costs on average 250zł per day.

Check the state of the boat and its equipment carefully, and report every deficiency and bit of damage in advance to avoid hassles when returning the boat. Come prepared with your own equipment, such as sleeping bag, sturdy rain gear and torch.

The following are local charter operators:

Bełbot (☎ 087 428 0385; www.marina.com.pl in Polish)

Grzymała (☎ 087 428 6276; http://czarter.mazury.info .pl in Polish)

Osmolik Romuald (☎ 087 428 86; www.osmolik.trinet .pl in Polish)

PUH Żeglarz (☎ 087 428 2084; www.zeglarz-czartery .pl in Polish)

Sygnet (☎ 060 462 8201; www.sygnet-czarter.com.pl)

ICE SAILING

The Masurian Lake district is one of Poland's coldest regions in winter; lake surfaces often freeze over from December to April. During this time the lakes support ice sailing and ice windsurfing, mostly on crisp, clear days. The tourist office has a list of operators renting boats and giving lessons if you're interested.

DIVING

CK Diver (☎ 087 428 4362; www.ckdiver.suw.pl in Polish; ul Mickiewicza 9; 🕙 9am-5pm Mon-Fri) offers scuba-diving courses for all levels throughout the

year, in groups or on an individual basis. Prices start at 100zł for a taster session, going up to 1600zł for advanced tuition.

Festivals & Events

St John's Night (Noc Świętojańska; ☎ 087 428 4326) Street festival in honour of the apostle, held in late June.

Giżycko Festival (☎ 087 428 4326) Concerts, performances and special events, held in the fortress in July.

St Bruno's Fair (☎ 087 428 4326) Held in July.

Sleeping

The tourist office has a long list of accommodation options available in town, most of which consists of holiday cottages, pensions and private rooms. The majority only open in July and August – outside these months few places are open and prices are notably lower than those listed below.

Youth hostel (☎ 087 428 2959; ul Turystyczna 1; dm 20zł; **P**) Stripped-back dorms at this simple youth hostel are far too reminiscent of the army barracks they once were, but this can be forgiven as you're staying within the thick walls of Boyen Fortress.

Almatur (☎ 087 428 5971; www.sail-almatur.pl in Polish; ul Moniuszki 24; cabins 70-360zł, d 99zł; **P**) Almatur is a large waterside centre with a full spectrum of leisure activities run by the Almatur student travel agency. It also offers yacht charters and specialises in sailing for the disabled.

Centralny Ośrodek Sportu (COS; ☎ 087 428 2335; recepcja@gizycko.cos.pl; ul Moniuszki 22; camp sites/s/d/cabins 10/80/120/170zł; **P**) The COS is a large activity centre on Lake Kisajno, offering accommodation in a variety of cabins and hotel rooms, plus a handful of camping sites. It's crowded with eating and sports facilities, including boat and bicycle hire and yacht charters.

Gościniec Jantar (☎ 087 428 5415; pawelczyk@ rydzewo.com; ul Warszawska 10; s/d 120/180zł; **P**) Stacked above its own traditional restaurant in the centre of town, this is an excellent little guesthouse with 12 pine-filled rooms, thick rugs and personable staff. Rooms at the rear have balconies, though there's not a whole lot to see.

Hotel Cesarski (☎ 087 428 1514; www.cesarski.pl in Polish; Plac Grunwaldzki 8; s/d 160/220zł; **P**) This new hotel couldn't be more central, with its location on the main town square. Rooms are all creamy and cosy, but best of all is the large roof terrace where breakfast can be taken.

Hotel i Camping Zamek (☎ 087 428 2419; www.cmazur .pl; ul Moniuszki 1; camp sites per person 25zł, s/d 134/180zł; **P**)

GIŻYCKO

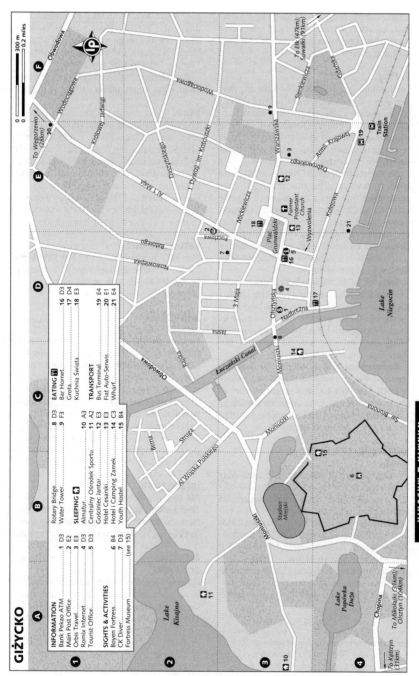

INFORMATION
Bank Pekao ATM	**1** D3
Main Post Office	**2** E2
Orbis Travel	**3** E3
Romix Internet	**4** D3
Tourist Office	**5** D3

SIGHTS & ACTIVITIES
Boyen Fortress	**6** B4
CK Diver	**7** D3
Fortress Museum	(see 15)

SLEEPING
Almatur	**10** A3
Centralny Ośrodek Sportu	**11** A2
Gościniec Jantar	**12** E3
Hotel Cesarski	**13** E3
Hotel i Camping Zamek	**14** C3
Youth Hostel	**15** B4

EATING
Bar Hornet	**16** D3
Grota	**17** D4
Kuchnia Świata	**18** E3

TRANSPORT
Bus Terminal	**19** E4
Fiat Auto-Serwis	**20** E1
Wharf	**21** E4

WARMIA & MASURIA

One of a gaggle of options on the fortress peninsula, Zamek is a rather dire motel with bland rooms, but it manages the town's most central camping ground.

Eating

In the high season you only have to wander down to the waterfront to find dozens of temporary cafés, stands and snack bars catering for the holiday crowds. Outside these times you'll have to choose from the hotel restaurants and a handful of other year-round eateries in the centre.

Bar Hornet (☎ 087 428 1267; Plac Grunwaldzki 12; mains 8-25zł; ☺ 8am-11pm) The enterprising Hornet splits itself into two sections, a self-service cafeteria and a smarter sit-down restaurant. The only difference between them is the waiters, but it's nice to have a choice! The food's decent value anyway, with a fine selection of quick eats and a salad bar, and the wooden deck is good for warm evenings.

Grota (☎ 066390 1868; ul Nadbrzeżna 3a; mains 15-30zł; ☺ 11am-midnight) Restaurants on the marina may draw the crowds with their lake-front views, but Grota gets the locals' vote for its food. Wood oven–baked pizzas and a mix of Polish and German cuisine fill the menu, and there's seating along the canal in summer.

Kuchnia Świata (☎ 087 429 2255; Plac Grunwaldzki 1; mains 10-40zł; ☺ 11am-11pm Sun-Thu, 11am-midnight Fri & Sat) The only bar-restaurant worthy of the name in town. A varied menu (Polish to Chinese via Italian) and a massive summer terrace see it full most nights of the week.

Getting There & Away

BOAT

Żegluga Mazurska boats operate from May to September, with extra services in July and August. There are two daily departures to Mikołajki at 9am and 3pm (adult/concession 48/35zł, three hours) via Rydzewo and Szymonka, and one daily trip north to Węgorzewo at 10.30am (40/32zł, 2½ hours). If you want to stay around town, you can take a spin around Lake Niegocin (25/20zł, 80 minutes) or an evening dancing cruise (50zł, two hours). The wharf is near the train station.

BUS

Next to the train station, the bus terminal offers hourly services to Węgorzewo (6.70zł, 55 minutes) and Olsztyn (18zł, three hours), and regular buses to Mikołajki (9.30zł, one hour,

nine daily), Kętrzyn (6.90zł, 40 minutes, eight daily) and Suwałki (16zł, two hours, seven daily). Two buses go to Lidzbark Warmiński (16zł, 1¾ hours), and up to 12 fast buses serve Warsaw (35zł to 48zł, five hours).

An international overnight bus to Vilnius (50zł, eight hours) leaves daily at 11.50pm.

TRAIN

The train station is on the southern edge of town near the lake. Trains run to Ełk (9zł to 14zł, 50 minutes, five daily) and Olsztyn (17zł to 28zł, two hours, seven daily) via Kętrzyn (6.50zł to 10zł, 30 to 40 minutes), and three fast trains go to Gdańsk (46zł, five hours) and two to Białystok (33zł, 2½ hours). Trains to Warsaw (47zł, six hours) take a roundabout route – it's faster to go by bus.

Getting Around

Car hire is available from **Fiat Auto-Serwis** (☎ 087 429 4294; gizycko@elk.com.pl; Al 1 Maja 21; ☺ 8am-4pm Mon-Fri). It is in the northern part of town.

MIKOŁAJKI

pop 3800

Perched on picturesque narrows crossed by three bridges, Mikołajki (mee-ko-wahy-kee) is a lively lakeside town and second only to Giżycko in the popularity stakes. Tourism has all but taken over here, and its waterfront is filled to overflowing with promenade plodders and pleasure boats in summer.

Like most resorts of this kind, Mikołajki lives a frenetic life in July and August, takes it easy in June and September, and retires for a long nap the rest of the year.

Information

PKO Bank (Plac Wolności 7)

Tourist office (☎ 087 421 6850; www.mikolajki.pl in Polish; Plac Wolności 3; ☺ 10am-8pm Jul & Aug, 10am-5pm May, Jun, Sep & Oct) Excellent source of information.

Activities

BOAT HIRE

As in Giżycko, yacht hire is big business here in summer, and around 10 companies vie for the seasonal trade. The **Wioska Żeglarska** (☎ 087 421 6040; www.wioskazeglarskamikolajki.pl; ul Kowalska 3), on the waterfront, has sailing boats for hire, or staff may be able to advise you on other companies if it's booked out. See p495 for more information on yacht charters.

For shorter-term excursions, **Port Rybitwa** (☎ 087 421 6163; www.portrybitwa.pl; ul Okrężna 5) hires out low-powered motorboats (from 85zł per hour, 425zł per day) from near the town's swimming beach. The owner can suggest plenty of DIY excursions on the connecting lakes.

Sleeping & Eating

The centre of town is largely reserved for 'proper' hotels. In the outer areas, small pensions (50zł to 80zł per person) do a roaring trade and dozens of private rooms (30zł to 50zł per person) become available in summer; the tourist office can provide a full list. There are plenty of places for food along the waterfront, and enough year-round restaurants to keep you from starving if you happen by out of season.

Król Sielaw (☎ 087 421 6323; ul Kajki 5; s/d/tr 80/150/180zł; P) Rustic beams and twee crafts provide the usual touch of colour in these very reasonable rooms. The country theme continues in the unpretentious fish restaurant downstairs. The location is supremely central and the lake is only a block away.

Pensjonat Mikołajki (☎ 087 421 6437; www .pensjonatmikolajki.prv.pl; ul Kajki 18; s/d from 120/180zł, ste 360zł) This lovely, timbered modern villa offers some superb lake views to the select few who book earliest. Otherwise you'll have to settle for the views from the private terrace, which aren't that bad either.

Hotel Mazur (☎ 087 421 6941; www.hotelmazur .republika.pl; Plac Wolności 6; d 200zł; P) Stylish and refined, the Mazur dominates Mikołajki's main square – unsurprising, considering it used to be the town hall. Luckily, you don't have to dabble in politics to enjoy the discreet rooms and ample facilities. The hotel also offers car rental for 100zł to 140zł per day.

ourpick Hotel Zamek Ryn (☎ 087 429 7000; www .zamekryn.pl; Plac Wolności 2; s/d/ste/apt 345/395/550/650zł; P 🖥 🍸 &) This brand spanking new hotel fills one of the largest 14th-century Teutonic castles in Europe, completely dominating the town of Ryn. Its facilities include a heated indoor pool, a sauna, Turkish baths, a restaurant, a wine cellar and a nightclub. Rooms are modern but a tad small, while apartments are massive (as is the medieval banquet hall). Ryn is 17km north of Mikołajki and connected by regular daily buses (6zł, 40 minutes).

Camping Nr 2 Wagabunda (☎ 087 421 6018; www .wagabunda-mikolajki.pl; ul Leśna 2; camp sites per person/ car/tent 12/10/12zł, cabins from 145zł; 🕑 May-Sep) The Wagabunda is the town's main camping ground. It's across the bridge from the centre and a 600m walk southwest. In addition to the camping area it has plenty of small cabins that vary in standard and price, and bicycles, boats and canoes are available for hire.

Restauracja Prohibicja (☎ 087 421 9919; Plac Handlowy 13; mains 15-340zł; 🕑 11am-midnight) Of all the gin joints in all the world, Mikołajki is the last place you'd expect to find a gangster-themed bar-restaurant. If you fancy sleeping with the fishes, there's also a fistful of hotel rooms upstairs. Despite the name, alcohol is sold over the counter, and it's all family-friendly, of course.

Getting There & Away

BOAT

From May to September, boats leave Mikołajki for Giżycko (adult/concession 48/35zł, three hours) at 10.30am and 3pm and Ruciane (40/32zł, 2½ hours) at 10am and 2.20pm. Round trips on Lake Śniardwy (25/18zł, 1½ hours) sail on a regular basis, and there are also combination routes available (eg Mikołajki–Lake Śniardwy–Ruciane–Mikołajki; 62/50zł, five hours).

BUS

The bus terminal is in the centre, near the Protestant church. Buses to Mrągowo (6.20zł, 40 minutes) run every couple of hours; change there for Olsztyn (15zł) or Kętrzyn (10zł). Ten buses go to Giżycko daily (8zł, one hour) and there's one service to Suwałki (15.50zł, 1¾ hours). Six buses depart daily to Warsaw (35zł to 50zł, five hours) in summer.

TRAIN

The sleepy train station is 1km from the centre, on the Giżycko road. It handles just a few trains a day to Ełk (11zł, 1¼ hours) and Olsztyn (14zł, two hours).

ŁUKNAJNO RESERVE

The shallow 700-hectare **Lake Łuknajno**, 4km east of Mikołajki, shelters Europe's largest surviving community of wild swans (*Cygnus olor*) and is home to many other birds – 128 species have been recorded here. The 1200- to 2000-strong swan population nests in April and May but stays at the lake all summer. A few observation towers beside the lake make swan viewing possible.

A rough road from Mikołajki goes to the lake, but there's no public transport. Walk 3.5km until you get to a sign that reads '*do wieży widokowej*' (to the viewing tower), then continue for 10 minutes along the path to the lake shore. The track can be muddy in spring and after rain, so choose your shoes wisely. Depending on the wind, the swans may be close to the tower or far away on the opposite side of the lake. Accommodation is available near the lake at **Folwark Łuknajno** (☎ 087 421 6862; www.luknajno.pl; s/d 120/180zł, camp sites per person/tent 10/15zł; P), a lovely country house with its own restaurant and pier on Lake Śniardwy. Bicycles and canoes are available for rent.

RUCIANE-NIDA
pop 4900

Ruciane-Nida (roo-*chah*-neh *nee*-dah) is the southernmost base for the Great Masurian Lakes. As the name suggests, it consists of two parts: Nida, an unremarkable collection of apartment blocks, and the tacky main lakeside resort of Ruciane, 2km northeast. The halves are linked by Al Wczasów, which runs through woods and is lined with holiday homes. About 1.5km north of Ruciane is the Śluza Guzianka, the only working lock on the Great Masurian Lakes.

The town's biggest drawcard is its location; it's surrounded by forest and set on the banks of two lakes, **Lake Guzianka Wielka** and **Lake Nidzkie**. There's also lots of quality accommodation options here, making it a grand base for exploring the region. To the southeast is the **Pisz Forest** (Puszcza Piska), a vast area of thick woodland. There are no marked trails, but dirt tracks and paths crisscross the woods; most are OK for bikes.

Sleeping

ourpick **Klasztor Wojnowo** (☎ 087 425 7030; www .klasztor.com.pl in Polish & German; Wojnowo 76; s/d 35/70zł; P) At the southern edge of tiny Wojnowo village, 6km west of Ruciane-Nida, stands a former Old Believers cloister overlooking a small lake. Its living quarters now house accommodation in the form of three basic rooms with shared facilities, and hearty home-cooked breakfasts are available for 10zł. Even if you're not staying, pop in and take a peek at the gorgeous religious icons.

ourpick **Knajpa u Targowiczan** (☎ 087 425 7073; www.galkowo.pl; Gałkowo 46; s 50-80zł, d 70-120zł, apt 200zł; P) A peaceful rural setting, renovated farm cottages with simple, stylish rooms, camp-fire sites, a superb restaurant only a minute away, and horse riding and walking options on your doorstep – what more do you need? The occasional raucous party? Got it. Targowiczan is located in Gałkowo, about 10km west of Ruciane-Nida.

Ośrodek Wypoczynkowy NBP Guzianka (☎ 087 424 0600; www.guzianka.pl in Polish; ul Guzianka 7; s/d/tr/cabins 84/156/234/312zł; P) This large complex, owned by the National Bank of Poland, is an excellent place for families, with playgrounds, tennis courts, private beaches and bicycle rental. Rooms are modern and comfortable, and cabins sleep up to four. It's about 2km north of the station, near the Guzianka lock.

Hotel Nidzki (☎ 087 423 6401; www.hotel .nidzki.oit.pl in Polish & German; ul Nadbrzeżna; s/d/tr/apt 200/235/292/675zł; P ▣) Rooms at the three-star Nidzki are a little overpriced for the facilities they provide, but it's their balcony views over Lake Nidzki (particularly at sunset) that makes them worth the money. The hotel restaurant is the finest in town and its terrace is a wonderful spot for an early-evening tipple.

PTTK Camping No 7 (☎ 087 423 1012; Al Wczasów 17; camp sites per person/car 10/6zł, cabins 44-80zł, d 100zł, d 130-150zł; ☼ May-Sep) The resident PTTK site is close to Nida and has just about every type of accommodation you could think of, making the most of its tree-lined setting.

Getting There & Away
BOAT

One daily Żegluga Mazurska excursion boat operates to Mikołajki (adult/concession 36/27zł, two hours, 2.10pm) in summer, with a second going via Lake Śniardwy (40/32zł, 2½ hours) and continuing on to Giżycko (74/54zł, 7½ hours, 10.30am). Four boats a day depart for round trips south around Lake Nidzkie (18/14zł, one hour). Local rival **Faryj** (☎ 087 423 1006; www.faryj.pl in Polish) does similar routes, including a Lake Nidzkie tour (10/8zł, one hour) and Mikołajki (40/30zł, 1½ hours).

BUS

There are nine buses to Mrągowo (8zł, 45 minutes) daily and five to Mikołajki (8zł, 35 minutes). One or two buses go as far east as Suwałki daily.

TRAIN

Very few trains pass through Ruciane-Nida; you're better off relying on the bus.

Directory

CONTENTS

ACCOMMODATION

Poland has a wide choice of accommodation options to suit most budgets. And while prices have risen in recent years, they're still low compared to Western Europe. Cheap, however, doesn't always mean good value – standards can vary greatly from one place to the next, with one hotel offering excellent facilities and the next god-awful rooms for around the same price.

Room prices are usually displayed at the reception desk. You are most likely to find listings for *pokój 1-osobowy* (single rooms) and *pokój 2-osobowy* (double rooms), possibly *z łazienką* (with bathroom) or *bez łazienki* (without bathroom), or *z umywalką* (with basin only). Rates normally include value-added tax (VAT), so you will be charged the rate shown, unless indicated otherwise.

Warsaw is the most expensive place to stay, followed by Kraków, Poznań and other major cities. The further away from the big cities you go, the cheaper accommodation gets. The summer resorts, particularly those on the Baltic coast, on the Masurian lakes and in the mountains, have higher prices in the high season (July and August). Similarly, the mountain ski centres put their prices up in winter. The price of accommodation is the same for foreigners as for Poles, except in some youth hostels, which charge foreigners marginally more.

In this book, budget listings generally include anything costing less than 150zł for a double room; midrange covers hotels priced from approximately 150zł to 300zł a double, and anything over 300zł is considered top end. In Warsaw and Kraków the midrange category is between 200zł and 400zł. Parking almost always costs extra, and can be anything from 5zł to 30zł, while breakfast is generally included in the price. Sleeping options in this book are listed from lowest to highest by double-room price.

Note that the wheelchair icon has only been used if a place is accessible to mobility-impaired people. This could mean a lift or ramps for easy access to reception and rooms, or that there are no stairs to contend with.

Agrotourist Accommodation

Known as *kwatery agroturystyczne,* agrotourist accommodation refers to rooms in farms, country houses and cottages. Meals can normally be provided on request, and sometimes

---

BOOK YOUR STAY ONLINE

For more accommodation reviews and recommendations by Lonely Planet authors, check out the online booking service at www.lonelyplanet.com/hotels. You'll find the true, insider lowdown on the best places to stay. Reviews are thorough and independent. Best of all, you can book online.

DIRECTORY

there are opportunities for horse riding, fishing, canoeing, cycling and such. They're a great way to meet locals on their own turf, sample home-cooked regional food and enjoy a bit of country lifestyle. In most cases, rooms are simple and rarely have private bathrooms, but prices are reasonable, usually between 20zł and 50zł per bed.

The owners of these places are affiliated with *stowarzyszenia agroturystyczne* (agrotourist associations), which have 30-plus regional offices around the country; contact local tourist information centres for more details.

While this accommodation type is generally not included in this book (as most require your own transport to get to), information is easy to track down – most local tourist offices have a list of places in their region.

Apartments

In recent years fully equipped apartments in larger cities such as Warsaw and Kraków have become handy accommodation options. They range from simple studios to two-bedroom luxury establishments, and are often centrally located. Prices vary wildly, but a little internet research can save a fair amount of cash. Be sure to check the size of the apartment before making a booking, as some are so tiny you could be sleeping standing up.

Camping

Poland has over 500 camping and bivouac sites registered at the **Polish Federation of Camping & Caravanning** (www.pfcc.info). The sites are distributed throughout the country, and can be found in all the major cities (usually on the outskirts), in many towns and in the countryside.

About 40% of registered sites are camping grounds with full facilities, including lighting, electricity, running water, showers, kitchen and caravan pitches. Many places also have wooden cabins for rent, which are similar to very basic hotel rooms. The remaining 60% are bivouac sites, the equivalent of very basic camp sites, usually equipped with toilets and not much else. The *Campingi w Polsce* map, available from bookshops, has details of registered camping and bivouac sites.

Private camping grounds also exist in Poland. They range from small back gardens with a bathroom in the owner's house to large grounds with bungalows, cafés, shops, bike and boat hire, and so on.

Most camping grounds are open from May to September, but some run only from June to August. The opening and closing dates given here are a rough guide only: sites may open and close earlier or later in the season, depending on factors such as the weather, flow of tourists or the owner's whim.

Fees are usually charged per tent site, plus an extra fee per person and per car.

Holiday Homes

In popular holiday areas, such as the mountains or the coast, you'll come across workers' holiday homes, known to Poles as *domy wcza-sowe* or *domy wypoczynkowe*. In communist times, these large establishments either served the employees of a company or were

---

PRACTICALITIES

■ Catch up on Polish current affairs in the *Warsaw Voice* (www.warsawvoice.pl), a weekly available from major newsagencies. Foreign newspapers can be found at EMPiK stores, foreign-language bookshops and newsstands in the lobbies of upmarket hotels.

■ The state-run Polskie Radio is the main radio broadcaster, operating on AM and FM in every corner of the country; all programmes are in Polish. You can pick up BBC World Service on short wave on 6195KHz, 9410KHz and 12095KHz.

■ Poland has two state-owned, countrywide TV channels: TVP1 and the more educational and culture-focused TVP2. There are also several private channels, including the countrywide PolSat.

■ Video recorders use the PAL system.

■ Electrical sockets are 220V, 50Hz, and plugs with two round pins are used, the same as in the rest of continental Europe.

■ Poland uses the metric system. There's a conversion table on the inside front cover of this book.

directed centrally by the Fundusz Wczasów Pracowniczych (FWP; Workers' Holiday Fund). Nowadays they welcome everybody. Most are open in summer only, but some run year-round. They tend to be full in July and August, but it's relatively easy to get a room in June or September. Their standards vary but on the whole they're not bad, and prices are usually reasonable. Almost all houses have their own dining rooms. Full board is usually optional but in some homes it can be compulsory.

Hostels

YOUTH HOSTELS

Poland has just under 600 *schroniska młodzieżowe* (youth hostels), which are operated by the **Polskie Towarzystwo Schronisk Młodzieżowych** (PTSM; Polish Youth Hostel Association; ☎ 022 849 8128; www.ptsm.org.pl; ul Chocimska 14, Warsaw), a member of Hostelling International (HI). Of this 600 hostels, around 20% open year-round and the rest in July and August only; all are listed in *Informator PTSM* (8zł), a PTSM-produced guidebook available at hostels throughout the country.

The all-year hostels have more facilities, including showers, a place to cook and a dining room. Some hostels are in poor shape, while others are good and modern. Hostels are normally marked with a sign, featuring a green triangle with the PTSM logo inside, placed over the entrance.

The PTSM also runs seasonal hostels, which are usually located in schools while pupils are on holidays. These schools are in no way adapted to being hostels – they hardly ever have showers or kitchens, and hot water is rare.

Youth hostels are open to all, members and nonmembers alike, and there is no age limit. Curfew is normally 10pm, and almost all hostels are closed between 10am and 5pm. A dorm bed in a hostel costs from 15zł to 40zł, depending on the hostel's category. Singles, doubles and triples, if there are any, cost about 20% to 50% more. A hostelling card gives a 10% to 25% discount off these prices for nationals and, in some places, for foreigners. Bed sheets are available for 4zł to 6zł (not available in some seasonal hostels).

PRIVATE HOSTELS

Private hostels are making inroads into Poland, but at present are restricted to the bigger cities – Kraków, and to a lesser extent Warsaw, are awash with them. They normally market themselves to backpackers, providing kitchens, laundry facilities, plenty of tourist information and sometimes a lounge and bar. Standards are normally high, and staff are young, multilingual, knowledgeable and friendly.

PTTK & MOUNTAIN HOSTELS

The **Polskie Towarzystwo Turystyczno-Krajoznawcze** (PTTK; Polish Tourist & Countryside Association; www.pttk .pl) has built up a network of its own hostels, called *dom turysty* or *dom wycieczkowy*. They are aimed at budget travellers, providing basic accommodation for hikers and backpackers throughout the country. Single rooms are a rarity, but you'll always have a choice of three- and four-bed rooms, usually with shared facilities, where you can often rent just one bed (not the whole room) for around 20zł to 40zł. Some PTTK hostels, particularly those in the cities, are now under private management and cost more.

PTTK also runs a network of *schroniska górskie* (mountain hostels). Conditions are usually simple but prices are low and hot meals are available. The more isolated mountain hostels are obliged to take in all-comers, regardless of how crowded they get, which means that in the high season (summer and/or winter) it can sometimes be hard to even find a space on the floor. These hostels are open all year, though it's best to check at the nearest regional PTTK office before setting off.

STUDENT HOSTELS

From July to late September many student dormitories in schools, universities and even kindergartens become student hostels. These are run by the schools themselves. Standards are basic but good and facilities are usually shared, although some hostels have rooms with private bathrooms. Expect to pay anything between 60zł and 120zł for a double room. Note that some dorms have a limited number of rooms available year-round.

Hotels

Most accommodation in Poland falls under this category. It is also the most diverse group, encompassing an immense variety of old and new places ranging from ultrabasic to extraplush.

The old generation of hotels, dating from before the fall of communism, was graded from one to five stars, intended to reflect the quality and price. The rudimentary one-stars are mostly confined to the smaller provincial towns, whereas the upmarket five-star establishments, now monopolised by **Orbis** (www.orbis .pl), dot the central areas of big cities.

Orbis runs 63 hotels across the country. Focusing on affluent tourists and locals, Orbis hotels keep their prices high – about 170zł to 370zł a single and 250zł to 550zł a double, or even more in some establishments in Warsaw, Kraków and Wrocław. Various international hotel chains have also entered the market, mostly building places in the bigger cities with standards equivalent to Western Europe.

There are also plenty of small, mostly private hotels, many of which cater to the middle-priced market. Standards can vary wildly, so if possible check the room before accepting. Don't be fooled by the hotel reception areas, which may look great in contrast to the rest of the establishment. If you ask to see a room, you can be pretty sure that they won't give you the worst one, which may happen otherwise.

Close to the bottom rung of the hotel ladder are sports hotels and workers' hotels. Sports hotels were built in sports centres in order to create facilities for local and visiting teams. In many aspects they are similar to the PTTK hostels: they seldom have singles, offer mostly shared facilities and you can usually pay just for your bed, not the whole room. Expect to pay 30zł to 60zł per head. Sports hostels are usually located next to the local sports stadium, often well away from the town or city centre. Most commonly, they are called *hotel sportowy*, *hotel OSiR* or *hotel MOSiR*, and some offer camping grounds in summer.

Workers' hotels mushroomed in the post-war period of industrial development, when large factories and other enterprises had to provide lodging facilities for their workers, many of whom came from other regions. These hotels are generally found in the cities, particularly industrial ones. They are almost always large, drab apartment blocks, often a long way from the city centre. They are called *hotel pracowniczy* or *hotel robotniczy*, though most have disguised themselves under a proper name. Their standards are usually low, but so is the price (20zł to 40zł per bed in a double, triple or quad). Singles are rare, as are private bathrooms. They are just about the cheapest hotels you can find and, judging by their facilities, could be classified as hostels.

Pensions

Pensjonaty (pensions) are small, privately run guesthouses that provide bed and half- or full board. By and large, pensions are clean, comfortable, friendly and good value: singles/ doubles cost around 80/120zł. Some of them are aimed specifically at Western European tourists, particularly Germans, and may have higher prices.

Private Rooms

These are rooms in private homes. They are available in some major cities and many smaller tourist hot spots, and can be arranged through specialist agencies or directly with the owners. They're often a lottery: you don't know what sort of room you'll get or who your hosts will be. It's therefore a good idea to take the room for a night or two and then extend if you decide to stay longer.

Staff in agencies will show you what's available, you then decide, pay and go to the address given to you. Be sure to check the location before forking over cash as some places are frustratingly far from the centre.

In the large cities (such as Warsaw or Kraków), rooms cost from 60zł to 80zł for singles and from 100zł to 120zł for doubles. In popular holiday resorts, you'll find plenty of signs saying '*pokoje*' (rooms) or '*noclegi*' (lodging) at the entrances to private homes. They are usually cheaper than in the cities – 30zł to 60zł a head in most cases.

ACTIVITIES

See Activities (p75) at the beginning of the book for details.

BUSINESS HOURS

Consider the following as a rough guide only; hours can vary considerably from shop to shop (or office to office) and from the city to the village.

Most grocery shops open from 7am or 8am to 6pm or 7pm on weekdays and to around 2pm on Saturday. Delicatessens and supermarkets usually stay open longer, until 8pm or 9pm (and are often open on Sunday from 9am to 7pm), and there's at least one food shop in every major town and every district of the city that opens for 24 hours. Shops normally open at 10am and close at

6pm (at 2pm or 3pm on Saturday). The office working day is theoretically eight hours long, Monday to Friday, and there's usually no lunch break.

In the larger towns and cities, banks keep their doors open from 8am to 6pm Monday to Friday and 9am to 1pm Saturday, and in smaller hamlets from 9am to around 4.30pm weekdays only.

Larger city post offices are normally open from 8am to 8pm weekdays and 8am to 1pm Saturday, and one will usually stay open 24 hours. In smaller localities, business hours may only be until 4pm weekdays.

Restaurants tend to open between 11am and 11pm, while opening hours for bars vary greatly; it is, however, a given that most stay open well after midnight on Friday and Saturday.

There are no standard opening hours for museums and other attractions. Most museums are closed on Monday; some of them also stay closed on the day following a public holiday. Many museums close one or two hours earlier in the low season, and usually stop selling tickets half an hour (sometimes even one hour) before their official closing time.

Churches are a bigger puzzle. The major churches in the main cities are often open all day long. On the other hand, rural churches in small villages will almost always be locked except during Mass, which may be only on Sunday morning.

CHILDREN

Travelling with children in Poland doesn't create any specific problems: children enjoy privileges on local transport, and with accommodation and entertainment; age limits for particular freebies or discounts vary from place to place, but are not often rigidly enforced; and basic supplies for children are easily available in cities. There are quite a few shops devoted to kids' clothes, shoes and toys, and you can buy disposable nappies (diapers) and baby food in supermarkets and pharmacies. For general suggestions on how to make a trip with kids easier, pick up a copy of Lonely Planet's *Travel with Children*, by Cathy Lanigan.

CLIMATE CHARTS

Poland's climate is influenced by a continental climate from the east and a maritime climate

from the west. As a result, the weather is changeable, with significant differences from day to day and from year to year. Winter one year can be almost without snow, whereas another year very heavy snows can paralyse transport for days. Summer can occasionally be cold, wet and disappointing.

The seasons are clearly differentiated. Spring starts in March and is initially cold and windy, later becoming pleasantly warm and often sunny. Summer, which begins in June, is predominantly warm but hot at times, with plenty of sunshine interlaced with heavy rains. July is the hottest month. Autumn comes in September and is at first warm and usually sunny, turning cold, damp and foggy in November. Winter lasts from December to March and includes short or long periods of snow. High up in the mountains, snow stays well into May. January and February are the coldest months. The temperature sometimes drops below -15°C, or even -20°C.

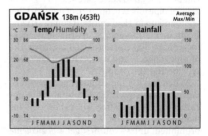

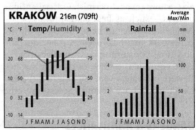

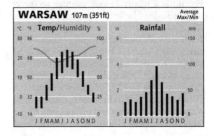

DIRECTORY

COURSES

Polish language courses are available in a number of spots across the country, such as Sopot (p425), Kraków (p195), Warsaw (p103) and Wrocław (p322). They last anywhere between one week to an entire summer, and can be tailored to fit student needs.

Train buffs can learn to drive a steam train in Wolsztyn (p389) and foodies can learn to cook proper *pierogi* (Polish dumplings) in a handful of places, including Warsaw (p65).

CUSTOMS

As with other EU countries, you're allowed to bring duty-free articles for your personal use while you travel and stay in Poland. Unlimited amounts of foreign currency can be brought into the country, but only up to the equivalent of €10,000 can be taken out by a foreigner without a declaration.

Travellers arriving from non-EU countries can bring in up to 200 cigarettes, 50 cigars or 250g of pipe tobacco, up to 2L of nonsparkling wine, and up to 1L of spirits. If you're arriving from an EU member state, the allowances increase to 800 cigarettes, 200 cigars or 1kg of pipe tobacco, and up to 110L of beer, 90L of wine and 10L of spirits.

When leaving the country, you may take out gifts and souvenirs of a total value not exceeding €90, duty free. The export of items manufactured before 9 May 1945 is strictly prohibited, unless you first get a *pozwolenie eksportowe* (export permit). Official antique dealers – such as **Desa Unicum** (www.desa.pl in Polish) – may offer to help you out with the paperwork, but the procedure is bureaucratic and time-consuming, and involves paying a fee equivalent to 25% of the item's value. Beware of dealers who tell you that the law has changed since Poland's accession to the EU – it has not.

DANGERS & ANNOYANCES

Poland is a relatively safe country to travel in, but it does have its fair share of crime. Always keep your eyes open and let common sense prevail. Problems mostly occur in big cities, with Warsaw being perhaps the least safe place in Poland. Take care when walking alone at night, particularly in the suburb of Praga, and be alert at Warszawa Centralna (Warsaw Central) train station, the favourite playground for thieves and pickpockets. Other large cities appear to be quieter, but keep your

wits about you. By and large, the smaller the town, the safer it is.

Keep a sharp eye on your pockets and your bag in crowded places such as markets or city buses and trams. Beware of being short-changed at train stations, taxis, restaurants etc. Always have some smaller bills in order to make change more easily. Hotels are generally safe, though it's better not to leave valuables in your room. In most places you can deposit them at the reception desk.

While car theft is on the decrease, those travelling in cars with foreign number plates should use secure parking at night. 'Pirate' or 'mafia' taxis can be a problem in Warsaw (see p119) and some other large cities. Poles have an aversion to stopping at zebra crossings – be very careful when stepping out into the road.

If your passport, valuables and/or other belongings are lost or stolen, report it to the police. They will give you a copy of the statement, which serves as a temporary identity document; if you have insurance, you'll need to present the statement to your insurer in order to make a claim. English-speaking police are rare, so it's best to take along an interpreter if you can. Don't hold high hopes of having your possessions returned to you, for the police earn next to nothing and can be rather cynical about a 'rich' foreigner complaining about losing a few dollars.

Heavy drinking is a way of life in Poland and drunks may at times be disturbing. Poles smoke a lot and so far there has been little serious antitobacco campaigning. Polish cigarettes are of low quality and the smoke they produce is barely tolerable for anyone not used to them, let alone a nonsmoker.

Slow and impolite service in shops, offices and restaurants is slowly being eradicated, though you can still occasionally experience it. By the way, if a couple of young boys offer to bag your shopping at a supermarket, they're not begging or scamming – they're boy scouts collecting for charity.

Since WWII Poland has been ethnically an almost entirely homogeneous nation, and Poles, particularly those living in rural areas, have had little contact with foreigners. As a result, travellers racially different to the average Pole may attract some stares and a few giggles from the locals. In most cases, this is just a curiosity, without any hostility in mind. While there have been some acts of racism in the cities, it's still not a social problem by any definition.

DISCOUNT CARDS

There are numerous tourist-oriented discount cards for Polish cities, including Warsaw (p87), Poznań (p373) and Kraków (p166). The Tri-City Tourist Card covers Gdańsk, Sopot and Gdynia (p406). The Pomerania region is also covered by the Pomeranian Tourist Card (p406).

Hostel Cards

A HI membership card can gain you 10% to 25% discount on youth hostel prices, though some hostels don't give discounts to foreigners. Bring the card with you, or get one issued in Poland at the provincial branch offices of the PTSM in the main cities. Go to www.ptsm .org.pl to find an office.

Student Cards

Students receive great discounts in Poland, such as 50% on museum admissions, 20% on Polferry ferries, 10% on LOT domestic flights, 50% on urban transport in Warsaw and 33% on InterCity trains. These discounts normally only apply to students under the age of 26 with an International Student Identity Card (ISIC), but not always – museums generally don't stick to this rule and will give discounts to students of any age with or without an ISIC card. ISIC cards are available in Poland at the **Almatur Student Bureau** (www.almatur.pl), which has offices in most major cities. The card costs 30zł and requires you to submit a photo.

EMBASSIES & CONSULATES

Australia (Map pp88-9; ☎ 022 521 3444; www.australia .pl; 3rd fl, ul Nowogrodzka 11, Warsaw)

Belarus Białystok (Map p140; ☎ 085 664 9940; ul Elektryczna 9, Białystok); Gdańsk (☎ 058 341 0026; ul Noakowskiego 9, Gdańsk); Warsaw (☎ 022 742 0990; www.belembassy.org/poland; ul Wiertnicza 58, Warsaw)

Canada (Map pp88-9; ☎ 022 584 3100; www.canada.pl; ul Matejki 1/5, Warsaw)

Czech Republic Katowice (☎ 032 609 9960; ul Stalmacha 21, Katowice); Warsaw (Map pp88-9; ☎ 022 525 1850; www.mfa.cz/warsaw; ul Koszykowa 18, Warsaw)

France (Map p84; ☎ 022 529 3000; www.ambafrance -pl.org; ul Piękna 1, Warsaw)

Germany Gdańsk (☎ 058 340 6500; Al Zwycięstwa 23, Gdańsk); Kraków (☎ 012 424 3000; ul Stolarska 7, Kraków); Warsaw (Map p84; ☎ 022 584 1700; www

.ambasadaniemiec.pl; ul Dąbrowiecka 30, Warsaw); Wrocław (☎ 071 377 2700; ul Podwale 76, Wrocław)

Ireland (Map p84; ☎ 022 849 6633; www.irlandia.pl; ul Mysia 5, Warsaw)

Japan (Map p84; ☎ 022 696 5000; www.pl.emb-japan .go.jp; ul Szwoleżerów 8, Warsaw)

Latvia (Map p84; ☎ 022 617 4389; embassy.poland@ mfa.gov.lv; ul Królowej Aldony 19, Warsaw)

Lithuania Sejny (☎ 087 517 3790; ul 22 Lipca 9, Sejny); Warsaw (Map p84; ☎ 022 625 3410; ambasada@lietuva .pl; Al Ujazdowskie 14, Warsaw)

Netherlands (Map p84; ☎ 022 559 1200; war@ minbuza.nl; ul Kawalerii 10, Warsaw)

New Zealand (Map pp88-9; ☎ 022 521 0500; nzwsw@ nzembassy.pl; Al Ujazdowskie 51, Warsaw)

Russia Gdańsk (☎ 058 341 1088; ul Batorego 15, Gdańsk); Kraków (☎ 012 422 2647; ul Biskupia 7, Kraków); Poznań (☎ 061 841 7523; ul Bukowska 53a, Poznań); Warsaw (Map p84; ☎ 022 621 3453; www .poland.mid.ru; ul Belwederska 49, Warsaw)

Slovakia (Map p84; ☎ 022 525 8110; www.ambasada -slowacji.pl; ul Litewska 6, Warsaw)

South Africa (Map pp88-9; ☎ 022 625 6228; saembassy @supermedia.pl; 6th fl, ul Koszykowa 54, Warsaw)

UK Katowice (☎ 032 206 9801; ul PCK 10, Katowice); Kraków (☎ 012 421 7030; ul Św Anny 9, Kraków); Szczecin (☎ 091 487 0302; ul Starego Wiarusa 32, Szczecin); Warsaw (Map pp88-9; ☎ 022 311 0000; www.british embassy.pl; Al Róż 1, Warsaw); Wrocław (☎ 071 344 8961; ul Oławska 2, Wrocław)

Ukraine (Map p84; ☎ 022 629 3446; www.ukraine -emb.pl; Al Szucha 7, Warsaw)

USA Kraków (☎ 012 424 5183; ul Stolarska 9, Kraków); Poznań (Map pp376-7; ☎ 061 851 8516; ul Paderewskiego 8, Poznań); Warsaw (Map pp88-9; ☎ 022 504 2000; poland.usembassy.gov; Al Ujazdowskie 29/31, Warsaw)

FESTIVALS & EVENTS

Apart from some well-established national or international festivals of film, theatre and music, there are plenty of small local feasts, fairs, contests, meetings and competitions, some of which involve local folklore. Add to this a lot of religious celebrations. The following are some of Poland's biggest festivals and events.

Festivals

FEBRUARY

Shanties (www.shanties.pl in Polish; Kraków) Celebration of old sailors' songs, accompanied by copious quantities of beer.

Musica Polonica Nova (www.musicapolonicanova.pl in Polish; Wrocław) International festival of contemporary music.

MARCH
Poznań Jazz Festival (www.jazz.pl; Poznań) Week-long event with local and international jazz stars.

MAY
Juvenalia Student carnival with fancy dress held in Kraków, masquerades and dancing in the street.
Gaude Mater (www.gaudemater.pl; Częstochowa) Week-long international festival of religious music.

JUNE/JULY
Jewish Culture Festival (www.jewishfestival.pl; Kraków) Biggest festival of its kind in Europe.
Mozart Festival (www.operakameralna.pl; Warsaw) Performances of all 26 of Mozart's stage productions.
Summer Jazz Festival (www.cracjazz.com; Kraków) Best of modern Polish jazz.

AUGUST
International Festival of Mountain Folklore (www .zakopane.pl; Zakopane) Poland's oldest and biggest festival of folk culture.

SEPTEMBER
Warsaw Autumn (www.warsaw-autumn.art.pl; Warsaw) Ten-day international festival of contemporary music.

OCTOBER
JVC Jazz Festival Warsaw (www.festivalproductions.net; Warsaw) One of the most prestigious jazz festivals in Europe, this three-day festival attracts some of the greatest jazz musicians on the planet.
Warsaw International Film Festival (www.wff.pl; Warsaw) A packed programme of art-house film premieres, lectures and screen-writing workshops.

NOVEMBER
Camerimage (www.camerimage.pl; Łódź) An international festival celebrating the art of cinematography in late November/early December.

Religious Events
Given the strong Roman Catholic character of the nation, religious feasts are much celebrated in Poland, especially in the more conservative countryside areas. The Church calendar is marked by two major cycles, which culminate in Boże Narodzenie (Christmas) and Wielkanoc (Easter). There are also a number of feast days devoted to particular saints, of whom the Virgin Mary is the most widely celebrated.

CHRISTMAS
The Christmas cycle begins with Adwent (Advent), a four-week period that precedes Christmas, and is characterised by the preparation of Nativity scenes in churches. Kraków is particularly notable for this, holding a competition for the best scenes.

As for Christmas itself, Wigilia (Christmas Eve) is the day most celebrated in Polish homes, culminating in a solemn supper that begins when the first star appears in the evening sky. Before the meal the family shares *opłatek* (holy bread), wishing each other all the best for the future. Then the supper, which traditionally consists of 12 courses, including some of the best of traditional Polish cuisine, begins. An extra seat and place setting are left prepared for an unexpected guest. Kids will find their gifts under the *choinka* (Christmas tree), or sometimes they will be handed out by Święty Mikołaj (Santa Claus) himself.

In the more traditional rural homes, there will still be much magic and witchcraft involved in Christmas Eve ceremonies, the forms differing from region to region. It's believed, for example, that animals speak with human voices on that one night, and that at midnight the water in wells turns into wine.

After supper is finished, the family set off for church for the specially celebrated Pasterka (Christmas Mass) at midnight. The service is held by most churches, and all are packed.

Christmas Day is, like the previous day, essentially a family day, featuring Mass, eating and relaxing. The holiday atmosphere continues for the remaining days of the year up until Sylwester (New Year's Eve), when the action starts with a variety of formal balls and private parties, held principally among urban communities.

On 6 January comes Dzień Trzech Króli (Epiphany), marked by groups of carol singers, usually armed with a small portable crib or other religious images, who go from door to door. On this day people have a piece of chalk consecrated in church, then use it to write 'K+M+B' (the initials of the three Magi) on their front doors, to ensure Heaven's care over the home.

EASTER
Easter is a moveable feast falling on the first Sunday following the first full moon after 21 March (which can be any day between 22 March and 25 April). It's preceded by Wielki Post (Lent), the season of fasting and penitence, which begins on Środa Popielcowa (Ash Wednesday), 40 weekdays prior to Easter.

Wielki Tydzień (Holy Week) commences with Niedziela Palmowa (Palm Sunday), a reminder of the triumphal entry of Christ into Jerusalem, where he was welcomed with date-palm branches. Today the most common substitutes are willow branches overspread with white catkins, though there are still some villages, notably Rabka, Tokarnia (which is near Rabka) and Łyse (in the Kurpie region), where the tradition is taken quite seriously: the 'palms' made there are elaborate works of art stretching up to 10m in height.

Palm Sunday also marks the beginning of the famous ceremony in Kalwaria Zebrzydowska (p259) near Kraków, which reaches its zenith on Wielki Czwartek (Maundy Thursday) and Wielki Piątek (Good Friday), when a Passion play is performed, re-enacting the last days of the life of Christ. In a blend of religious rite and popular theatre, local amateur actors take the roles of Roman soldiers, apostles, Jewish priests and Christ himself, and circle 20-odd Calvary chapels, representing the stages of the Way of the Cross, accompanied by a crowd of pilgrims and spectators.

On Good Friday people visit the Holy Sepulchres set up in churches, while on Wielka Sobota (Holy Saturday) the faithful go to church with baskets filled with food, such as bread, sausage, cake and eggs, to have them blessed. The eggs are decoratively painted, sometimes with elaborate patterns. Inspired by this tradition, eggs made of wood are painted and sold as souvenirs.

Niedziela Wielkanocna (Easter Day) begins with Mass, which is usually accompanied by a procession. After that, the faithful return home to have a solemn breakfast, at which the consecrated food is eaten. Before breakfast, family members share eggs while wishing each other well.

Lany Poniedziałek (Easter Monday) is when Polish people sprinkle each other with water, which can be anything from a symbolic drop of perfumed water to a bucket of water over the head, or even a dousing from a fire engine.

Zielone Święta (Pentecost) falls on the 50th day after Easter Day (hence its name), and 10 days later comes Boże Ciało (Corpus Christi). The latter is characterised by processions held all over the country, of which the best known is that in Łowicz (p131).

OTHER FEASTS

Among the feasts related to the Virgin Mary, the most important is the Święto Wniebowzięcia Najświętszej Marii Panny (Assumption) on 15 August, celebrated throughout Poland, but nowhere as elaborately as in the Monastery of Jasna Góra in Częstochowa (p215), where pilgrims arrive on that very day, sometimes after a journey of several days on foot.

Dzień Wszystkich Świętych (All Saints' Day) on 1 November is a time of remembrance and prayers for the souls of the dead. On no other day do cemeteries witness so many people leaving flowers, wreaths and candles on graves, and they look most spectacular at night. The celebrations continue to a lesser extent on the following day.

FOOD

The eating listings in this book are ordered from lowest to highest by the price of the average main course. In general, mains are less than 15zł (20zł in Warsaw) for budget places, from 15zł to 40zł (25zł to 50zł in Warsaw) for midrange, and more than 40zł (50zł in Warsaw) for top end. For more on Polish food and drink see p60.

GAY & LESBIAN TRAVELLERS

Homosexuality is legal in Poland; the age of consent is 15, which is the same as for heterosexual sex. Despite the fairly liberal legal situation, Polish society is overwhelmingly conservative and, for the most part, deeply hostile towards homosexuality.

The Polish gay and lesbian scene is fairly discreet; Warsaw and Kraków are the best places to find bars, clubs and gay-friendly accommodation, and Sopot is noted as gay-friendly compared to the rest of Poland (which isn't saying much). The best source of information for Poland's scene is http://warsaw.gayguide.net and www.innas trona.pl.

HOLIDAYS

The following are public holidays in Poland:

New Year's Day 1 January
Easter Monday March or April
Labour Day 1 May
Constitution Day 3 May
Corpus Christi A Thursday in May or June
Assumption Day 15 August
All Saints' Day 1 November
Independence Day 11 November
Christmas 25 and 26 December

INSURANCE

Insurance can cover you for medical expenses, theft or loss, but also for cancellation of, or delays in, any of your travel arrangements. There's a variety of policies and your travel agent can provide recommendations.

Make sure the policy includes health care and medication in Poland. See p530 for information on health insurance and p523 for car insurance.

Always read the small print of a policy carefully. Some policies specifically exclude 'dangerous activities' such as scuba diving, motorcycling, skiing, mountaineering and even trekking.

Not all policies cover ambulances, helicopter rescue or emergency flights home. Most policies exclude cover for pre-existing illnesses.

INTERNET ACCESS

A growing number of Poland's citizens are savvy internet users, which is having a positive knock-on affect for travellers – all large towns and cities (and a growing number of smaller ones) now have at least one internet café. But the life span of said cafés is often short, with many going out of business within a few months. Other options include tourist offices, hotels and public libraries, which sometimes have internet terminals for public use.

There are also an increasing number of hot spots in Polish cities where you can access the internet with a wi-fi-enabled laptop. Many cafés and top-end hotels provide network access for free; http://intel.jiwire.com is a good starting point for tracking places down, but there are many more unlisted locations.

If you're travelling with a laptop, you should be able to log on via a hotel room phone socket for the cost of a local call by registering with an internet roaming service such as **MaGlobe** (www.maglobe.com), which has access numbers for Poland. Most newer midrange and top-end hotels have telephone jacks (usually US-standard RJ-11), which you can plug your modem cable into.

Buy a line tester (a gadget that goes between your computer and the phone jack) so that you don't inadvertently fry your modem. Get on and off quickly, as calls from hotels are expensive. For more information on travelling with a laptop see www.kropla.com.

Major internet-service providers, such as **AOL** (www.aol.com), **CompuServe** (www.compuserve

.com) and **AT&T** (www.attbusiness.net), have dial-in nodes in Poland. If you have an account with one of these ISPs, you can download a list of local dial-in numbers before you leave home.

For a list of useful Polish internet resources, see p21.

LEGAL MATTERS

Foreigners in Poland, as elsewhere, are subject to the laws of the host country. While your embassy or consulate is the best stop in any emergency, bear in mind that there are some things it can't do for you, like getting local laws or regulations waived because you're a foreigner, investigating a crime, providing legal advice or representation in civil or criminal cases, getting you out of jail and lending you money.

A consul can, however, issue emergency passports, contact relatives and friends, advise on how to transfer funds, provide lists of reliable local doctors, lawyers and interpreters, and visit you if you've been arrested or jailed.

MAPS

Poland has plenty of good quality, inexpensive maps that are readily available. Apart from the state-run map producer, the **PPWK** (www.ppwk .pl), there are also a number of private map publishers. Polish maps are also easy to decipher. Most symbols are based on international standards, and they are explained in the key in three foreign languages, English included.

The selection of maps is extensive too. You can buy a single map covering the whole country or a set of four or eight sheets (sold separately) that feature fragments of the country on a larger scale and provide greater

---

WHEN YOU'RE LEGAL

In Poland the following are the minimum legal ages:

- drinking alcohol: 18
- driving: 17
- heterosexual/homosexual sex: 15*
- marriage: 18
- voting: 18

*Travellers may be subject to the laws of their own country in regard to sexual relations.

detail. The book-format *Atlas Samochodowy* (Road Atlas) is also available, including sketch maps of major cities, Polish road signs and a full index.

All cities and most large towns have their own city maps; the **Demart** (www.demart.com.pl) city plans, with orange covers, are excellent. These maps include tram and bus routes, alphabetical lists of streets, post offices, hotels, hospitals, pharmacies and the like. They often cover a number of towns on a single map. On city maps, the word for street, *ulica* or its abbreviated version ul, is usually omitted, but *Aleje* or *Aleja*, more often shortened to Al, is placed before the names of avenues to distinguish them from streets.

Other very useful maps are the large-scale tourist maps (usually between 1:50,000 and 1:75,000) of the most popular destinations. They cover a relatively small sector, a single mountain range or a group of lakes, and are very detailed. These maps show marked hiking routes and practically everything else you may be interested in when hiking, driving, biking etc. They are a must if you plan on doing any serious walking.

All maps mentioned above are easy to find in the larger urban centres; buy them there (at bookshops and/or tourist offices), as they may be hard to come by in the smaller towns. Maps (including city maps) cost anywhere between 5zł and 15zł.

MONEY

Following its accession to the EU, Poland declared its intention to adopt the euro as its currency as soon as possible, but due to the poor state of the economy it probably won't happen before 2012.

The official Polish currency is the złoty (literally, 'golden'), abbreviated to zł and pronounced *zwo*-ti. It is divided into 100 groszy, which are abbreviated to gr. Banknotes come in denominations of 10zł, 20zł, 50zł, 100zł and 200zł, and coins in 1gr, 2gr, 5gr, 10gr, 20gr and 50gr, and 1zł, 2zł and 5zł. The banknotes feature Polish kings, come in different sizes and are easily distinguishable.

Try to keep some small-denomination notes for shops, cafés and restaurants – getting change for the 100zł notes that ATMs often spit out can be a problem.

For an indication of costs in Poland, see p18. For exchange rates, see the inside front cover of this book.

ATMs

Most towns in Poland have a couple of *bankomaty* (ATMs), and the majority accept Visa, MasterCard, Cirrus and Maestro cards.

The easiest and cheapest way to carry money is in the form of a debit card, with which you can withdraw cash either over the counter in a bank or from an ATM. Charges are minimal at major Polish banks (typically from zero to about 2%) and some home banks charge nothing at all for the use of their cards overseas. Check with your bank about transaction fees and withdrawal limits.

Cash

The ubiquitous *kantor* (private currency-exchange office) is the place to exchange cash. They are either self-contained offices or just desks in travel agencies, train stations, post offices, department stores and the more upmarket hotels. The further out from the cities you go, the less numerous they are, but you can be pretty sure that every medium-sized town will have at least a few of them. *Kantors* are usually open between 9am and 6pm on weekdays and to around 2pm on Saturday, but some open longer and a few stay open 24 hours.

Kantors change cash only and accept major world currencies. The most common and thus the most easily changed are US dollars, euros and UK pounds. Most other currency is somewhat exotic to Poles and not all *kantors* will change them. There's no commission on transactions – the rate you get is what is written on the board (every *kantor* has a board displaying its exchange rates). The whole operation takes a few seconds and there's no paperwork involved. You don't need to present your passport or fill out any forms.

Kantors buy and sell foreign currencies, and the difference between the buying and selling rates is usually not larger than 2%. Exchange rates differ slightly from city to city and from *kantor* to *kantor* (about 1%). Smaller towns may offer up to 2% less, so it's better to change money in large urban centres if you can.

To avoid hassles when exchanging currency, one important thing to remember before you set off from home is that any banknotes you take to Poland must be in good condition, without any marks or seals. *Kantors* can refuse to accept banknotes that have numbers written on them (a common practice of bank cashiers totalling bundles of notes) even if they are in otherwise perfect condition.

Credit Cards

Credit cards are increasingly widely accepted for buying goods and services, though their use is still limited to upmarket establishments, mainly in major cities. Among the most popular cards accepted in Poland are Visa, MasterCard, Amex, Diners Club, Eurocard and Access.

Credit cards can also be used for getting cash advances in banks – the best card to bring is Visa, because it's honoured by the largest number of banks, including the Bank Pekao, which will also give cash advances on MasterCard.

International Transfers

You can have money sent to you through the **Western Union** (www.westernunion.com) money transfer service. Money is received within 15 minutes of the sender transferring it (along with the transaction fee) at any of the 30,000 Western Union agents scattered worldwide. Western Union outlets can be found in all Polish cities and most large towns. Information on locations and conditions can be obtained toll-free on ☎ 0800 120 224.

Taxes

Poland's VAT is calculated at three levels: zero (books, press, some basic food products); 7% (most food); and 22% (fine food, hotels, restaurants, petrol, luxury items). The tax is normally included in the advertised price of goods and services.

Tipping & Bargaining

Tipping in hotels is essentially restricted to the top-end establishments, which usually have decent room service and porters, who all expect to be tipped. Taxi drivers are normally not tipped, unless you want to reward someone for their effort.

Bargaining is not common in Poland, and is limited to some informal places such as flea markets, fruit bazaars and street stalls.

For information and advice on tipping in restaurants, see p64.

POST

Postal services are provided by **Poczta Polska** (www.poczta-polska.pl). In large cities there will be a dozen or more post offices, of which the *poczta główna* (main post office) will usually have the widest range of facilities, including poste restante and fax.

Letters and postcards sent by air from Poland take about one week to reach a European destination and up to two weeks if sent to anywhere else. The cost of sending anything up to 50g costs 2.40zł to any destination in the world. Packages and parcels are reasonably cheap if sent by surface mail but they can take up to three months to reach their destination. The cost of sending airmail packages is comparable to that in Western Europe.

You can receive mail care of poste restante in large cities such as Warsaw, Kraków and Gdańsk. Mail is held for 14 working days, then returned to the sender. Amex customers can receive poste restante mail via the Warsaw Amex offices (p86).

SHOPPING

Folk art and handicrafts can be seen and bought across Poland. Common crafts of the country include paper cut-outs, woodcarving, tapestries, embroidery, paintings on glass, pottery and hand-painted wooden boxes and chests. Look for **Cepelia** (www.cepelia.pl) shops, with branches in all large cities, which specialise in local handicrafts.

Amber is typically Polish. It's the fossil resin of ancient pine trees, and occurs as translucent nuggets in earthy hues ranging from pale yellow to reddish brown. You can buy amber necklaces in Cepelia shops, but if you want a designer look, check out specialist jewellery shops or commercial art galleries. Prices vary with the quality of the amber and the level of craftwork. You'll find the best choice of amber jewellery in Gdańsk (p422).

Polish contemporary painting, original prints and sculpture are renowned internationally and sold by commercial art galleries. Galleries in Warsaw and Kraków have the biggest and the most representative choice. Polish posters are among the world's finest (a tempting souvenir). The best selection is, again, in Warsaw and Kraków.

The main seller of art and antiques is a state-owned chain of shops called **Desa Unicum** (www.desa.pl in Polish). These shops often have an amazing variety of old jewellery, watches, furniture and whatever else you can imagine. Remember that it's officially forbidden to export any item manufactured before 9 May 1945, works of art and books included, unless you've got a permit (see p506).

Poland publishes an assortment of well-edited and lavishly illustrated coffee-table books about the country, many of which are also available in English and German. Polish music (pop, folk, jazz, classical and contemporary) is available on CD and easily purchased.

SOLO TRAVELLERS

Travelling by yourself in Poland is easy and fairly hassle-free. Note, though, that solo hitching anywhere in Poland isn't wise. The biggest nuisance for solo travellers is the extra cost of single rooms in hotels and pensions, compared with sharing a double. The easiest places to meet other people, be it English-speaking locals or other travellers, is in hostels and internet cafés. Outside the big metropolises however, don't assume you'll meet travel companions along the way.

See p514 for information on women travelling alone.

TELEPHONE

The state telecommunications provider is **Telekomunikacja Polska** (TP; www.tp.pl in Polish), which usually has a telephone centre near or inside a town's main post office. Card-operated public phones can be found pretty much everywhere. The international code for Poland is ☎ 48.

Local & International Calls

All land-line numbers throughout the country have seven digits, preceded by a two-digit area code. To make a local call, dial 0, then the area code, then the seven-digit subscriber number – this applies even when you're making a call within the same town or city. Cheap rates on long-distance calls operate from 6pm to 8am daily.

To call abroad from Poland, dial the international access code (☎ 00), then the country code, then the area code (minus any initial zero) and number. You can also use the Home Country Direct service to make reverse-charge (collect) calls, or credit- or charge-card calls, or to connect to an operator in your home country. Inquire at any TP office for the toll-free number for the country you want to call, then call from any public or private telephone (you'll still need a phone card, though it will only be charged one unit – around 50gr).

Mobile Phones

Codes for mobile phones usually begin with ☎ 05, ☎ 06, ☎ 07 or ☎ 09. Poland uses the GSM 900/1800 network, which covers the rest of Europe, Australia and New Zealand, but isn't compatible with the North American GSM 1900 or the totally different system in Japan (though some North Americans have GSM 1900/900 phones that will work in Poland). If you have a GSM phone, check with your service provider about using it in Poland, and beware of calls being routed internationally (very expensive for a 'local' call). Those with a European phone can check prices online by going to www.roaming.gsmeurope.org.

A cheaper – and often better – option is to buy a Polish prepaid SIM card. They sell for as little as 9zł and can be organised relatively quickly and painlessly at any provider shop (GSM, Orange etc). No ID is required, and top-ups can be bought at phone shops, newspaper kiosks and even some ATMs. Before purchasing a SIM card be sure your phone is unlocked (able to accept foreign SIM cards).

Phonecards

There are no coin-operated public phones in Poland; all of them work using a phonecard, which you can buy from post offices, newspaper kiosks, and some tourist offices and hotel reception desks. TP cards cost 9/15/24zł for a 15-/30-/60-*impuls* (unit) card. A 60-*impuls* card is enough for an 11-minute call to the UK, or an eight-minute call to the USA.

Alternatively, you can buy a calling card from a private telephone service provider, such as **Intrafon** (www.intrafon.pl), whose international rates are much cheaper – 0.67zł a minute to the UK and 0.59zł to the USA.

TIME

All of Poland lies within the same time zone, GMT/UTC+1, the same as most of continental Europe (see the World Time Zones map on pp546–7). Poland observes Daylight Saving Time (DST), and puts the clock forward one hour at 2am on the last Sunday in March, and back again at 3am on the last Sunday in October.

The 24-hour clock is used for official purposes, including all transport schedules. In everyday conversation, however, people commonly use the 12-hour clock.

DIRECTORY

TOILETS

Toilets are labelled '*toaleta*' or simply 'WC'. The gents will be labelled '*dla panów*' or '*męski*' and/or marked with a triangle, and the ladies will be labelled '*dla pań*' or '*damski*' and/or marked with a circle.

Public toilets in Poland are few and far between and often in a sorry state of disrepair – and cleanliness. A better option is to nip into the nearest eatery, museum or hotel and ask nicely to use the facilities. If you do use public toilets, the fee is usually 1zł, which is collected by a toilet attendant sitting at the door. It's a good idea to bring your own toilet paper, just in case.

TOURIST INFORMATION
Local Tourist Offices

Larger cities – and an ever-increasing number of smaller towns – have local tourist offices, which are usually good sources of information; most also sell maps and tourist publications. Most staff members speak a small amount of English and/or German.

In places where there are no general tourist offices, look for a PTTK office (see p503). PTTK was once a helpful organisation, focusing on outdoor activities such as hiking, sailing, cycling and camping. Today it's just another travel agency, but many of its offices are wellstocked with maps and trekking brochures, can arrange guides and accommodation, and provide tourist information.

SHIFTING BORDERS

Since Poland's entry into the Schengen zone of EU countries in December 2007, there have been no border posts or border crossing formalities between Poland and Germany, the Czech Republic, Slovakia and Lithuania. Thus, having legally entered Poland, a traveller can continue on to any of the Schengen countries without encountering further checks. However, it's worth noting that the 90-day, visa-free entry period into Poland has now been extended to all the Schengen countries; so if travelling from Poland through Germany and France, for example, you can't exceed 90 days in total. Once your 90 days is up, you must leave the Schengen zone for a minimum 90 days before you can once again enter it visa-free.

Tourist Offices Abroad

Polish tourist offices abroad include the following:

France (☎ 01 42 44 19 00; www.tourisme.pologne.net; 9 rue de la Paix, 75002 Paris)
Germany (☎ 30-210 09 2-0; www.polen-info.de; Kurfürstendamm 71, 10709 Berlin)
Netherlands (☎ 20-625 35 70; www.members.tripod .com/~poleninfo; Leidsestraat 64, 1017 PD Amsterdam)
UK (☎ 0870 067 5010; www.visitpoland.org; Level 3, Westec House, West Gate, London W5 1YY)
USA (☎ 201-420 9910; www.polandtour.org; 5 Marine View Plaza, Hoboken NJ 07030)

TRAVELLERS WITH DISABILITIES

Poland is not well equipped for people with disabilities, even though there has been a significant improvement over recent years. Wheelchair ramps are available only at some upmarket hotels and restaurants, and public transport will be a challenge for anyone with mobility problems. Few offices, museums or banks provide special facilities for the disabled traveller, and wheelchair-accessible toilets are few and far between.

Those with some Polish language skills can go to www.niepelnosprawni.pl for up-to-date information on the current situation for disabled people in Poland. In the USA, travellers with disabilities may like to contact the **Society for Accessible Travel & Hospitality** (☎ 212-447 7284; www.sath.org; Ste 610, 347 Fifth Ave, New York, NY 10016) before departing, while in the UK a useful contact is the **Royal Association for Disability & Rehabilitation** (☎ 020-7250 3222; www.radar.org.uk; 12 City Forum, 250 City Rd, London EC1V 8AF).

VISAS

Citizens of EU countries do not need visas to visit Poland and can stay indefinitely. Citizens of the USA, Canada, Australia, New Zealand, Israel and Japan can stay in Poland for up to 90 days without a visa.

Other nationalities should check current visa requirements with the Polish embassy or consulate in their home country. Alternatively, check the **Ministry of Foreign Affairs** (www.mfa.gov.pl) website.

WOMEN TRAVELLERS

Women are unlikely to have any particular problems travelling in Poland (our wonderful female author found Poland to be a 'freakishly hassle-free clockwork country of smooth sailing all the way'), although common-sense caution should always be observed, especially in towns and cities. Women can enter most pubs alone, but there are still a few places where this may attract undesirable attention. Cosmopolitan city pubs are fine – you'll get a pretty good idea as soon as you enter. Sticking to pubs frequented by travellers or populated by an even spread of both sexes is always a safe bet.

On the other hand, a woman travelling alone, especially in remote rural areas, may expect to receive more help, hospitality and generosity from the locals than would a man on his own.

WORK

Without a high standard of Polish, most people will need to arrange a job in Poland through an international company or be prepared to teach English. English teachers are currently in hot demand, with schools popping up in cities and towns across the country. Teacher standards are generally high, however, and you'll probably need a TEFL (Teaching English as a Foreign Language) certificate to secure a job.

English-language supplements, such as the *Warsaw Voice* (www.warsawvoice.pl), sometimes advertise jobs in various fields.

Transport

CONTENTS

GETTING THERE & AWAY

ENTERING THE COUNTRY
Passport

See p514 for which countries require a visa to travel to Poland. Theoretically, the expiry date of your passport should not be less than three months after the date of your departure from Poland.

AIR
Airports & Airlines

The vast majority of international flights to Poland arrive at **Warsaw-Frédéric Chopin Airport** (Port Lotniczy im F Chopina, WAW; Map p84; ☎ 022 650 4220; www.lotnisko-chopina.pl), although there is an increasing number of international car-

---

THINGS CHANGE

The information in this chapter is particularly vulnerable to change. Check directly with the airline or a travel agent to make sure you understand how a fare (and ticket you may buy) works and be aware of the security requirements for international travel. Shop carefully. The details given in this chapter should be regarded as pointers and are not a substitute for your own careful, up-to-date research.

---

riers choosing to land at the country's other international airports:

Gdańsk – Lech Wałęsa (GDN; ☎ 058 348 1154; www.airport.gdansk.pl)
Katowice (KTW; ☎ 032 392 7385; www.gtl.com.pl)
Kraków-Balice (KRK; ☎ 012 639 3000; www.lotnisko-balice.pl)
Wrocław (WRO; ☎ 071 358 1381; www.airport.wroclaw.pl)

Poland's national carrier **LOT** (LO; ☎ 0801 703 703, from mobile phones 022 9572; www.lot.com) flies to all major European capitals as well as most major cities in Germany. Outside Europe it has direct flights to/from Chicago, Istanbul, New York, Tel Aviv and Toronto. Competition is currently fierce in the Polish market, with a wave of budget airlines, including CentralWings, EasyJet, GermanWings, SkyEurope, Ryanair and Wizz Air, moving in and offering cheap flights to not only Warsaw but also Wrocław, Kraków, Gdańsk, Poznań, Bydgoszcz, Katowice, Łódź, Szczecin and Rzeszów.

Fares vary greatly depending on what route you're flying and what time of year it is. Poland's high season (and that of Europe in general) is in summer (June to August) and a short period around Christmas. The rest of the year is quieter and cheaper.

The following are the Polish contact details for airlines flying to and from Poland:

Aeroflot (SU; ☎ 022 628 1710; www.aeroflot.ru; hub Moscow)
Air France (AF; ☎ 022 556 6400; www.airfrance.com; hub Paris)
Alitalia (AZ; ☎ 022 692 8285; www.alitalia.it; hub Rome)
British Airways (BA; ☎ 0800 4411 592; www.ba.com; hub London)
CentralWings (C0; ☎ 0801 080 112; www.centralwings.com; hub Warsaw)
EasyJet (EZY; www.easyjet.com; hub London)
GermanWings (4U; www.germanwings.com; hub Cologne/Bonn)
KLM (KL; ☎ 022 556 6444; www.klm.com; hub Amsterdam)
Lufthansa (LH; ☎ 022 338 1300; www.lufthansa.com; hub Frankfurt)
Malev (MA; ☎ 022 697 7474; www.malev.hu; hub Budapest)

Ryanair (FR; www.ryanair.com; hub Dublin)
SkyEurope (NE; www.skyeurope.com; hub Bratislava/ Vienna)
WizzAir (W6; ☎ 022 351 9499; www.wizzair.com; hub Katowice)

Tickets

Fierce competition on most European routes has resulted in price wars between no-frills carriers and full-service airlines. Discounted web fares offer the best deals, and one-way tickets make it easy to fly into one city and out of another. Note that if you're booking on short notice (that is, less than around three or four weeks before departure), national carriers often offer better prices than the budget airlines.

On transatlantic and long-haul flights your travel agent is probably still the best source of cheap tickets, although there is an increasing number of online booking agencies. Be sure to check the terms and conditions of the cheapest fares before booking.

Australia

There are no direct scheduled flights between Australia and Poland; generally it's cheapest to fly into London, Frankfurt or Amsterdam and continue to Warsaw from there. Round-the-world (RTW) tickets are another good bet and are often better value than standard

DEPARTURE TAX

The departure tax is included in your ticket when flying out of Poland.

return fares. There are a number of well-known travel agencies in Australia; **STA Travel** (☎ 1300 733 035; www.statravel.com.au) and **Flight Centre** (☎ 133 133; www.flightcentre.com.au) have offices throughout the country. For online bookings, try www.travel.com.au.

Continental Europe

Both LOT and other carriers fly to Warsaw from all major European capitals, and the list of regional airports supported by budget airlines is constantly growing – check their websites, opposite, for the latest destinations.

The following are recommended travel and ticket agencies:

FRANCE
Anyway (☎ 08 92 30 23 01; www.anyway.fr)
Lastminute.com (☎ 08 99 78 50 00; www.fr.lastminute .com)
Nouvelles Frontières (☎ 08 25 00 07 47; www.nou velles-frontieres.fr)
Voyageurs du Monde (in Paris ☎ 08 92 23 56 56; www.vdm.com)

TRANSPORT

CLIMATE CHANGE & TRAVEL

Climate change is a serious threat to the ecosystems that humans rely upon, and air travel is the fastest-growing contributor to the problem. Lonely Planet regards travel, overall, as a global benefit, but believes we all have a responsibility to limit our personal impact on global warming.

Flying & climate change

Pretty much every form of motorised travel generates CO_2 (the main cause of human-induced climate change) but planes are far and away the worst offenders, not just because of the sheer distances they allow us to travel, but because they release greenhouse gases high into the atmosphere. The statistics are frightening: two people taking a return flight between Europe and the US will contribute as much to climate change as an average household's gas and electricity consumption over a whole year.

Carbon offset schemes

Climatecare.org and other websites use 'carbon calculators' that allow travellers to offset the level of greenhouse gases they are responsible for with financial contributions to sustainable travel schemes that reduce global warming – including projects in India, Honduras, Kazakhstan and Uganda.

Lonely Planet, together with Rough Guides and other concerned partners in the travel industry, support the carbon offset scheme run by climatecare.org. Lonely Planet offsets all of its staff and author travel.

For more information check out our website: www.lonelyplanet.com.

GERMANY
Expedia (www.expedia.de)
Just Travel (☎ 0897 473 330; www.justtravel.de)
Lastminute.com (☎ 01805 777 257; www.de.last
minute.com)
STA Travel (☎ 069 743 032 92; www.statravel.de)
Specialises in student travel.

ITALY
CTS Viaggi (☎ 199 501 150; www.cts.it)

NETHERLANDS
Airfair (☎ 0900 7717 717; www.airfair.nl)

SPAIN
Barceló Viajes (☎ 902 11 62 26; www.barceloviajes.com)

UK & Ireland

Flights on the London Heathrow–Warsaw route are offered daily by both LOT and British Airways. LOT also has direct flights from Manchester and Dublin to Warsaw.

Budget airline Ryanair offers the most comprehensive coverage of Poland, connecting 10 of the country's largest cities with London Stansted, Bristol, Liverpool, East Midlands, Glasgow, Dublin and Shannon. CentralWings comes a close second, covering eight Polish cities with flights to London, Edinburgh, Dublin, Shannon and Cork. No-frills flyer EasyJet has flights from London Luton and Bristol to Warsaw and Kraków, along with Liverpool, Belfast and Newcastle to Kraków, and London Gatwick, Bristol, Belfast and Edinburgh to Gdańsk. Sky Europe flies between Kraków and Manchester, Birmingham and Dublin, while WizzAir has expanded its coverage and now connects Warsaw, Katowice, Gdańsk, Wrocław and Poznań with a plethora of destinations in the UK and Ireland.

Discount air travel is big business in London. Advertisements for many travel agencies appear in the travel pages of the weekend broadsheet newspapers, in *Time Out*, the *Evening Standard* and in the free magazine *TNT*.

The following are recommended travel agencies:
ebookers (☎ 0871 223 5000; www.ebookers.com)
Flight Centre (☎ 0870 499 0040; www.flightcentre.co.uk)
North-South Travel (☎ 01245-608 291; www.northsouthtravel.co.uk) Donates part of its profit to projects in the developing world.

STA Travel (☎ 0871 230 0040; www.statravel.co.uk) For travellers under the age of 26.
Trailfinders (☎ 0845 050 5945; www.trailfinders.com)
Travel Bag (☎ 0870 814 4441; www.travelbag.co.uk)

USA & Canada

LOT (☎ in USA 212-789 0970, in Canada 416-236 4242) has direct flights from New York, Chicago and Toronto to Warsaw.

Agents often use indirect connections with other carriers such as British Airways, Lufthansa, KLM or Air France. Not only may these work out cheaper, but they can also let you break the journey in Western Europe for the same price or a little extra – a bonus if you want to stop en route in London, Paris or Amsterdam.

Travel Cuts (☎ 1866-246 9762; www.travelcuts.com) is Canada's national student travel agency. For online bookings try www.expedia.ca and www.trave locity.ca.

In the USA, a reputable discount travel agency is **STA Travel** (☎ 800-781 4040; www.sta.com). The following agencies are recommended for online bookings:
American Express (www.itn.net)
CheapTickets (www.cheaptickets.com)
Expedia (www.expedia.com)
Lowestfare.com (www.lowestfare.com)
Orbitz (www.orbitz.com)
Travelocity (www.travelocity.com)

LAND
Border Crossings

Sitting in the middle of Europe and sharing its borders with seven countries, Poland has plenty of rail and road crossings. Border crossings are more numerous with Germany to the west, and the Czech and Slovak republics to the south, than they are with the Ukraine, Belarus, Lithuania and Russia to the east and northeast.

Remember that Poland's eastern border is now one of the external borders of the EU. If you're travelling overland to Russia, be aware that you may need a Belarusian transit visa, which must be obtained in advance.

The following is a list of 24-hour border crossings for heading east out of Poland by road:
Belarusian border (south to north): Terespol, Kuźnica Białostocka
Lithuanian border (east to west): Ogrodniki, Budzisko
Russian border (east to west): Bezledy, Gronowo
Ukrainian border (south to north): Medyka, Hrebenne, Dorohusk

THEFT ON TRAINS

Rumours abound regarding theft on Polish trains; these rumours are mainly a result of the rise in thefts in the '90s (after the fall of communism). These days gangs of thieves are known to work the trains sometimes, but this is becoming less and less frequent due to increased security on the part of Polskie Koleje Państwowe (PKP; Polish State Railways). Reports of theft still surround the Kraków–Prague overnight train though, and travellers should be particularly alert when taking this route.

As with travel in general, common sense should prevail. Don't tempt fate by sitting alone in a compartment; join other passengers. On overnight trains sleepers are the safest way to go as cabin doors have a lock and security chain and there is a sleeper attendant on duty. Watch your luggage and your pockets closely when you are getting on or off the train, as these are the most convenient moments for pickpockets to distract you. Warsaw's central train station is a favourite stalking ground for thieves – be particularly alert when passing through.

Belarus, Lithuania & Russia

BUS

Eurolines Polska (www.eurolinespolska.pl) has daily buses to Warsaw from Minsk (85zł, 12 hours) in Belarus and Vilnius (125zł, 12 hours) in Lithuania. Polish State Railways also operate an overnight bus between Warsaw and Vilnius (€22, 10 hours).

TRAIN

Warsaw has direct trains to Kyiv (from €47, 15 hours) in the Ukraine and Minsk (from €36, 10 hours) in Belarus. These trains are sleeper only, and you'll be automatically sold a sleeping berth when buying your ticket.

The fastest option from Warsaw to Vilnius (€21, 9½ hours) in Lithuania travels through Suwałki and requires a change in Šeštokai across the border. It's a good option as there is no need to arrange a transit visa for Belarus.

Travel to Russia, however, requires a Belarusian transit visa. Without one you'll be sent back to Warsaw by Belarusian border guards. One direct train daily over summer travels between Warsaw and St Petersburg (from €69, 30 hours), while three daily head year-round for Moscow (from €62, 20 hours); both are sleeper trains and pass through Minsk.

Czech Republic

BUS

Eurolines-Sodeli CZ (☎ 245 005 245; www.eurolines .cz; Senovážné nám 6, Nové Město, Prague) runs buses from Prague to Warsaw (125zł, 14 hours) via Wrocław (110zł, five hours).

TRAIN

There are daily express trains from Prague to Warsaw (€56, 9½ hours) via Katowice, and to Kraków (€45, 8½ hours).

UK

BUS

Eurolines (☎ 08705 808080; www.eurolines.co.uk) runs buses from London to Warsaw (one way UK£62, 26½ hours) via Poznań and Łódź, and to Kraków (UK£62, 26¾ hours) via Wrocław and Katowice. The frequency of the service varies depending on the season: it's as often as daily in summer and slows down to twice weekly the rest of the year. Tickets can be bought from any National Express office and a number of travel agencies.

TRAIN

You can travel from London to Warsaw via the Channel Tunnel, with a single change of train at Brussels (20 hours). The normal 2nd-class, one-way fare is around €170.

Western Europe

BUS

Eurolines (www.eurolines.com) operates an extensive network of bus routes all over Western Europe. Standards, reliability and comfort may vary from bus to bus, but on the whole are not too bad. Most buses are from the modern generation, and come equipped with air-conditioning, toilet facilities and a video.

As a rough guide only, average one-way fares and journey times between some Western cities and Warsaw are as follows:

To	One-way fare	Time
Amsterdam	€78	21hr
Brussels	€78	21hr
Cologne	€61	20hr
Frankfurt	€69	19hr
Hamburg	€49	16hr
Munich	€71	20hr
Paris	€77	27hr
Rome	€110	27hr

TRANSPORT

TRANSPORT

TRAIN

A number of German cities are linked by train (direct or indirect) with major Polish cities. Direct connections with Warsaw include Berlin, Cologne, Dresden and Leipzig. There are also direct trains between Berlin and Kraków (via Wrocław; €50, 9½ hours).

The Warsaw–Berlin route (via Frankfurt/Oder and Poznań; €39, six to 8½ hours) is serviced by five trains a day.

There are no direct trains from Brussels (Bruxelles-Nord) to Warsaw (from €91, 14½ hours); if making this trip the quickest route is via Cologne. From Paris to Warsaw (€160, 16½ hours), a change is required in Cologne and Brussels.

SEA

Poland has regular car-ferry services plying the routes from Denmark and Sweden to Gdańsk and Świnoujście on the coast of Poland. The fares quoted here are for a foot passenger throughout the year.

Denmark

Polferries (www.polferries.pl) From Copenhagen to Świnoujście (410kr to 450kr, 10 hours, five times a week in summer).

Sweden

Polferries (www.polferries.pl) Operates the Ystad–Świnoujście (490kr to 540kr, seven hours, daily), Nynäshamn–Gdańsk (560kr to 670kr, 18 hours, daily) and Rønne–Świnoujście (250kr, 5¼ hours, Saturday only) routes.

Stena Line (www.stenaline.com) From Karlskrona to Gdynia (from Skr290, 11 hours, daily).

Unity Line (www.unityline.pl) From Ystad to Świnoujście (Skr470 to Skr790, seven to nine hours, daily).

GETTING AROUND

AIR

LOT (www.lot.com) operates a comprehensive network of domestic routes. There are daily flights between Warsaw and Bydgoszcz, Gdańsk, Katowice, Kraków, Łódź, Poznań, Rzeszów, Szczecin, Wrocław and Zielona Góra. All flights between regional cities travel via Warsaw and connections aren't always convenient. Currently there is no domestic competition, but this may change if **DirectFly** (www.directfly.pl) resumes operations in the future.

The regular one-way fare on any of the direct flights to/from Warsaw starts at 116zł and can reach up to 500zł. Tickets can be booked and bought at any LOT or Orbis office, and from some other travel agencies.

Senior citizens over 60 years of age pay 80% of the full fare on all domestic flights. Foreign students holding an ISIC card get a 10% discount. There are attractive standby fares (about 25% of the regular fare) for people aged between 20 and 24; tickets have to be bought right before scheduled departure. There are also some promotional fares on selected flights in certain periods (eg early or late flights, selected weekend flights); they can be just a third of the ordinary fares and are applicable to everybody.

Most airports are a manageable distance – between 10km and 20km – from city centres and are linked to them by public transport. Only Szczecin and Katowice airports are further out. You must check in at least 30 minutes before departure. Have your passport at hand – you'll be asked to show it as ID. There's no departure tax on domestic flights.

BICYCLE

Poland has great potential as a place to tour by bicycle – most of the country is fairly flat and you can throw your bike on a train to cover long distances quickly. Camping equipment isn't essential, as hotels and hostels are usually no more than an easy day's ride apart, although carrying your own camping gear will give you more flexibility.

Major roads carry pretty heavy traffic and are best avoided. Instead, you can easily plan your route along minor roads, which are usually much less crowded and in reasonable shape. Stock up on detailed tourist maps, which feature all minor roads, specifying which are sealed and which are not, and which also show marked walking trails. Some of these trails are easily travelled by bike, giving you still more options.

On a less optimistic note, the standard of driving in Poland may not be what you're used to at home. Some drivers hug the side of the road, thus giving cars and trucks more room to overtake, but pass perilously close to cyclists. Note that in Poland cyclists are not allowed to ride two abreast.

Cities are often not the most pleasant places to cycle either; dedicated cycle paths are few and far between, some drivers don't give a damn about two-wheeled travellers, city roads are often in poor shape, and cobbled streets are not uncommon. More than likely (simply for safety's sake) you'll end up sharing the footpath with pedestrians and local cyclists.

Hotel staff will usually let you put your bike indoors for the night, sometimes in your room. Bikes, especially those in good condition, are attractive to thieves, so it's a good idea to carry a solid lock and chain (for the frame and both wheels), and always use them when you leave the bike outdoors, even if only for a moment.

Some long-distance trains have a baggage car where you can store your bicycle. If this is the case, you should normally take your bike to the railway luggage office, fill out a tag and pay a small fee. They will then load the bike and drop it off at your destination. It's a good idea to strip the bike of anything easily removable and keep an eye out to be sure it has actually been loaded on the train. You can also take your bike straight to the baggage car (which is usually at the front or the rear of the train), but this can be difficult at intermediate stations where the train may only stop for a few minutes.

Bikes are not allowed on express trains or on those that take reservations, since these trains don't have baggage cars. Many ordinary trains don't have baggage cars either, but you can try to take the bike into the passenger car with you as some Poles do. Check at the baggage window in the station before you do so. Buses don't normally take bikes.

Cycling shops and repair centres are popping up in large cities, and in some of the major tourist resorts. Western bikes for sale are on the increase, as are some popular spare parts. For rural riding, you should carry all essential spare parts, for it's unlikely there'll be a bike shop close at hand. In particular, spare nuts and bolts should be carried.

Bike-hire outlets are growing in number, but they still aren't numerous. They seldom offer anything other than ordinary Polish bikes, the condition of which may leave a little to be desired.

BOAT

Poland has a long coastline and lots of rivers and canals, but passenger-boat services are limited and operate only in summer. There are no regular boats running along the main rivers or along the coast. Several cities, including Szczecin, Gdańsk, Toruń, Poznań, Wrocław and Kraków, have local river cruises during the summer, and a few coastal ports (Kołobrzeg and Gdańsk) offer sea excursions. There are also trips out of Elbląg to Frombork and Krynica Morska.

On the Masurian lakes (p490), excursion boats run in summer between Giżycko, Mikołajki, Węgorzewo and Ruciane-Nida. Tourist boats are also available in the Augustów area where they ply part of the Augustów Canal (p154). The most unusual canal trip is the full-day cruise along the Elbląg-Ostróda Canal (p486).

BUS

Poland has a comprehensive bus network (far greater than the rail network) covering most villages accessible by road. They are often more convenient than trains over a short distance and occasionally longer ones when, for instance, the train route involves a long detour. The frequency of service varies greatly: on the main routes there may be a bus leaving every quarter of an hour or so, whereas some small, remote villages may get only one bus a day. Ticket prices also vary greatly due to fierce competition between bus companies, so shop around. In the mountains you'll often travel by bus because trains are slow and few. Almost all buses run during the daytime, sometimes starting very early in the morning.

Most of Poland's bus transport is operated by the former state bus company, PKS (Państwowa Komunikacja Samochodowa), although deregulation of the country's bus system has made room for a plethora of private operators. What this means for travellers is a broader range of options and frequent promotions; don't automatically assume PKS offers the lowest prices and best service.

PKS can be a good code word when seeking directions to bus stations – it's now a term for buses in general.

You can find details of their services online at their various websites, which mostly take the form www.pks.warszawa.pl, www.pks.krakow.pl etc. Just insert the city or town you will depart from before '.pl' in the web address. Very few sites have English versions, but with a little time and effort it's easy enough to find timetables.

Normally the *dworzec autobusowy PKS* (local PKS bus station) is found alongside the train station, but in some towns it's centrally located. Save for large terminals in major cities, bus stations have pitiful facilities (no left-luggage service or even a place for coffee) but most do have some sort of information counter with surprisingly helpful staff. They close at night.

PKS' main competitor is **Polski Express** (www .polskiexpress.net), a joint venture with Eurolines National Express based in the UK. It runs several long-distance routes out of Warsaw serving most of the country's large cities. Its buses are faster and more comfortable than PKS ones, but cost much the same.

Minibuses are an additional option to the bigger buses of PKS and Polski Express. They are generally more frequent and much faster than their bigger brothers, and service more routes. There is rarely any sort of information counter at minibus stands, but schedules are clearly displayed. Minibus stations are usually in the vicinity of the PKS station.

Costs

The approximate fares for intercity bus journeys are as follows:

Distance	Fare
20km	6-7zł
40km	9-10zł
60km	11-12zł
80km	13-15zł
100km	15-18zł
150km	21-24zł
200km	26-29zł
250km	30-35zł
300km	36-40zł

Note that while prices listed were accurate at the time of research, don't be surprised to find them a few złoty different when you hit the road. The entire bus system is still in a state of flux.

Tickets

The only place to buy PKS tickets is at the bus station itself, either from the information/ticket counter or the bus driver. Tickets on long routes serviced by fast buses can be bought up to 30 days in advance and are best bought from ticket counters – tickets are numbered, and buying one at the counter assures you of a seat – but those for short, local routes are only available the same day and are just as easily purchased from the driver. If you get on the bus some-

where along the route, you buy the ticket directly from the driver.

Tickets for Polski Express buses can be bought at the bus stations and from some Orbis Travel offices.

Timetables

Timetables are posted on boards either inside or outside PKS bus terminal buildings. There are also notice boards on all bus stops along the route (if vandals haven't damaged or removed them). The timetable of *odjazdy* (departures) lists *kierunek* (destinations), *przez* (the places passed en route) and departure times.

Keep in mind that there may be more buses to the particular town you want to go to than those that are mentioned in the destination column of the timetable under the town's name. You therefore need to check whether your town appears in the *przez* column on the way to more-distant destinations. If you want to circumvent a long wait grab a bus to another hub and travel on from there – it may end up saving loads of time.

Also check any additional symbols that accompany the departure time. These symbols can mean that the bus runs only on certain days or in certain seasons. They're explained in the key at the end of the timetable.

You can find online bus timetables at www .polskibus.pl.

Types of Bus

There are two types of PKS bus service: ordinary and fast. The *autobusy zwykłe* (ordinary or local buses) stop at all stops en route and their average speed barely exceeds 35km/h. The standard of these buses is sometimes barely satisfactory. Their departure and arrival times appear in black on timetable boards. The *autobusy pospieszne* (fast buses), marked in red, mainly cover long-distance trips and manage an average speed of 45km/h to 55km/h. As a rule, they take only as many passengers as they have seats, and the standards are better than that of the ordinary buses.

CAR & MOTORCYCLE
Automobile Associations

The **Polski Związek Motorowy** (PZM, Polish Automobile & Motorcycle Federation; ☎ 022 849 9361; www.pzm.pl in Polish; ul Kazimierzowska 66, 02-518 Warsaw) is Poland's national motoring organisation. It provides a 24-hour national **roadside assistance** (☎ 9637) service and if you are a member of an affiliated automobile association, will help you on roughly the same terms as your own organisation would. If not, you must pay for all services.

Bring Your Own Vehicle

Many Western tourists, particularly Germans, bring their own vehicles into Poland. There are no special formalities: all you need at the border is your passport (with a valid visa if necessary), your driving licence, vehicle registration document and third-party insurance (called a Green Card). If your insurance isn't valid for Poland, you can buy an additional policy at the border (depending on the size of the engine, this costs from 67/95zł for 15 days/one month). Fines are severe if you're caught without insurance. A nationality plate or sticker must be displayed on the back of the car.

If you do decide to bring your own vehicle to Poland, remember that life will be easier for you if it's not brand-new. Expensive recent models are favourite targets for gangs of organised car thieves in large cities. The shabbier your car looks, the better.

Driving Licence

Foreign driving licences are valid in Poland for up to 90 days. Strictly speaking, licences that do not include a photo ID need an international driving permit as well, although this rule is rarely enforced.

Fuel & Spare Parts

Benzyna (petrol) is readily available at petrol stations throughout the country. There are several different kinds and grades of petrol available; most hire cars run on *bezołowiowa* (98-octane unleaded) or *diesel* (diesel). The price of fuel can differ from petrol station to petrol station by up to 10%. An increasing number of petrol stations accept credit cards.

Virtually all petrol stations have adopted a self-service system and offer services commonplace in the West. Air and water are usually available, as well as oil, lubricants and basic spare parts such as light bulbs or fuses. An increasing number of new stations also offer food and drink. Many stations located along main roads and in the large cities are open round the clock.

There's a widespread network of garages that specialise in fixing Western cars (though not many for motorcycles), but they mostly deal with older, traditional models with mechanical technology. The more electronic and computer-controlled bits your car has, the more problems you'll face having something fixed. These parts can be ordered for you, but they'll usually take a while to arrive.

Hire

Car-hire agencies will require you to produce your passport, a driving licence held for at least one year, and a credit card. You need to be at least 21 or 23 years of age (depending on the company) to hire a car, although hiring some cars, particularly luxury models and 4WDs, may require a higher age.

One-way hire within Poland is possible with most companies (usually for an additional fee), but most will insist on keeping the car within Poland. No company is likely to allow you to take its car beyond the eastern border.

High insurance premiums mean that car hire in Poland is not cheap, and there are seldom any promotional discounts. As a rough guide only, economy models offered by reputable local companies can be as low as 120/800zł per day/week (including insurance and unlimited mileage). Rates at the big international agencies start at around 225/1000zł per day/week. It's usually cheaper to book your car from abroad or over the internet.

LOCAL & INTERNATIONAL CAR-HIRE AGENCIES

Avis (☎ toll-free 0801 120 010; www.avis.pl; ul Łopuszańska 12a, Warsaw)
Budget (☎ in Warsaw 022 650 4062; www.budget.pl; Terminal 1, Warsaw-Frédéric Chopin Airport)
Europcar (☎ in Warsaw 022 650 2564; www.europcar .com.pl; Terminal 1, Warsaw-Frédéric Chopin Airport)
Hertz (☎ in Warsaw 022 650 2896; www.hertz.com; Terminal 1, Warsaw-Frédéric Chopin Airport)
Local Rent-a-Car (Map pp88–9; ☎ 022 826 7100; www.lrc .com.pl; ul Marszałkowska 140, Warsaw)

Insurance

Bring along a good insurance policy from a reliable company for both the car and your possessions. Car theft is a major problem in Poland, with organised gangs operating in the large cities. Some of them cooperate with Russians in smuggling stolen vehicles across the eastern border, never to be seen again.

TRANSPORT

TRANSPORT

Road Distances (km)

	Białystok	Bydgoszcz	Częstochowa	Gdańsk	Katowice	Kielce	Kraków	Łódź	Lublin	Olsztyn	Opole	Poznań	Rzeszów	Szczecin	Toruń	Warsaw	Wrocław	Zielona Góra
Białystok	---																	
Bydgoszcz	389	---																
Częstochowa	410	316	---															
Gdańsk	379	167	470	---														
Katowice	485	391	75	545	---													
Kielce	363	348	124	483	156	---												
Kraków	477	430	114	565	75	114	---											
Łódź	322	205	121	340	196	143	220	---										
Lublin	260	421	288	500	323	167	269	242	---									
Olsztyn	223	217	404	156	479	394	500	281	370	---								
Opole	507	318	98	485	113	220	182	244	382	452	---							
Poznań	491	129	289	296	335	354	403	212	465	323	261	---						
Rzeszów	430	516	272	642	244	163	165	306	170	516	347	517	---					
Szczecin	656	267	520	348	561	585	634	446	683	484	459	234	751	---				
Toruń	347	46	289	181	364	307	384	159	375	172	312	151	470	313	---			
Warsaw	188	255	222	339	297	181	295	134	161	213	319	310	303	524	209	---		
Wrocław	532	265	176	432	199	221	268	204	428	442	86	178	433	371	279	344	---	
Zielona Góra	601	259	328	411	356	422	427	303	542	453	245	130	585	214	281	413	157	---

Even if the car itself doesn't get stolen, you may lose some of its accessories, most likely the radio/cassette/CD player, as well as any personal belongings you've left inside. Hide your gear, if you must leave it inside; try to make the car look empty. If possible, park your car in a guarded *parking strzeżony* (car park). If your hotel doesn't have its own, the staff will tell you where the nearest one is, probably within walking distance.

In the cities, it may be more convenient and safer to leave your vehicle in a secure place (eg your hotel car park), and get around by taxi or public transport.

Road Conditions

The massive increase in traffic over recent years, along with a lack of maintenance, has led to a deterioration in road surfaces, with some in better shape than others. However, the injection of EU funds has seen an explosion in road works: in 2007 alone 1700km of national roading was marked for upgrade. What this means for the average driver is plenty of delays, but the future of Polish roads looks smooth and well sealed.

Poland currently has only a few motorways in the proper sense of the word, but an array of two- and four-lane highways crisscross the country. Secondary roads are narrower but they usually carry less traffic and are OK for leisurely travel. The sealed minor roads, which are even narrower, are also often in acceptable condition, though driving is harder work as they tend to twist and turn, are not so well signposted and pass through every single village along the way.

Road Hazards

Drive carefully on country roads, particularly at night. There are still horse-drawn carts on Polish roads, and the further off the main routes you wander, the more carts, elderly cyclists, tractors and other agricultural machinery you'll encounter. These vehicles are often lit poorly or not lit at all.

Road Rules

Road rules are the same as in the rest of Europe. A vehicle must be equipped with a first-aid kit, a red-and-white warning triangle and a nationality sticker on the rear; the use of seat belts is compulsory. Drinking and driving is strictly forbidden – the legal blood alcohol level is 0.02%. Police can hit you with on-the-spot fines for speeding and other traffic offences (be sure to insist on a receipt).

Polish speed limits are 20km/h to 50km/h in built-up areas (to 60km/h from 11pm to 5am), 90km/h on open roads, 110km/h on dual carriageways and 130km/h on motorways. At level crossings over rail lines the speed limit is 30km/h. From October to February, car lights must be on at all times while driving, even during a sunny day; and motorcycle lights must be on all year round. Motorcyclists should remember that both rider and passenger must wear helmets.

Unless signs state otherwise, cars and motorcycles can be parked on pavements, as long as a minimum 1.5m-wide walkway is left for pedestrians. Parking in the opposite direction to the flow of traffic is allowed.

The following are traffic signs that may be unfamiliar to Britons and non-European visitors:

Blue disc with red border and red slash No parking on the road, but you still can park on the footpath; if the sign is accompanied by a white board below saying 'doty-czy również chodnika' or 'dotyczy także chodnika' (meaning 'it also refers to the footpath'), you can't park on either the road or the footpath.

Yellow diamond with white border You have right of way; a black slash through it means you no longer have right of way.

Yellow triangle (point down) with red border Give way.

When driving in cities be aware of trams. You may overtake a tram only on the right, and only if it's in motion. You must stop behind any tram taking on or letting off passengers where there's no pedestrian island. If there's a pedestrian island, you don't have to stop. A tram has right of way when making any signalled turn across your path.

HITCHING

Autostop (hitching) is never entirely safe anywhere in the world. Travellers who decide to hitch should understand that they are taking a small but potentially serious risk. Those who choose to hitch will be safer travelling in pairs, and letting someone know where they are planning to go.

That said, hitching does take place in Poland; locals can often be seen thumbing a ride from one small village to the next. Car drivers rarely stop though, and large commercial vehicles (which are easier to wave down) expect to be paid the equivalent of a bus fare.

LOCAL TRANSPORT
Bus, Tram & Trolleybus

In most cities you can travel on the *autobus* (bus) and *tramwaj* (tram), and some also have a *trolejbus* (trolleybus). Warsaw is the only city with a metro. Public transport operates from around 5am to 11pm and may be crowded during the rush hours (7am to 9am and 4.30pm to 6.30pm Monday to Friday). The largest cities also have night-time services, on either buses or trams. Timetables are usually posted at stops, but don't rely too much on their accuracy.

In many cities there's a flat-rate fare for local transport so the duration of the ride and the distance make no difference. If you change vehicles, however, you need another ticket. The ordinary fare is usually around 2.40zł. In some cities the fare depends on how long you travel, with the ticket valid for a certain period of time, such as 30 minutes or one hour. Night services are more expensive than daytime fares.

There are no conductors on board; you buy tickets beforehand and punch or stamp them in one of the little machines installed near the doors. You can buy tickets from Ruch or Relay newspaper kiosks or, in some cities, from street stalls around the central stops, recognisable by the *bilety* (tickets) boards they display. Buy enough tickets on Saturday morning to last you until Monday, as few kiosks are open on Sunday. Note that tickets purchased in one city cannot be used in another.

Plain-clothed ticket inspectors are always on the prowl and foreign backpackers are not exempt. These inspectors tend to be officious, dogged and singularly unpleasant to deal with.

If you are caught without a ticket, it's best to pay the fine straight away. Never give an inspector your passport, even if they threaten you with police intervention if you don't.

Taxi

Taxis are easily available and not too expensive. As a rough guide, a 5km taxi trip will cost around 15zł, and a 10km ride shouldn't cost more than 25zł. Taxi fares are 50% higher at night (10pm to 6am), on Sunday and outside the city limits. The number of passengers (usually up to four) and the amount of luggage doesn't affect the fare.

There are plenty of taxi companies, including the once monopolistic, state-run **Radio Taxi** (☎ 9191), which is the largest and operates in most cities. Taxis are recognisable by large signs on the roof with the company's name and phone number. There are also pirate taxis (called 'mafia' taxis by Poles), which usually have just a small 'taxi' sign on the roof with no name or phone number. These are best avoided.

Taxis can be waved down on the street, but it's easier to go to a *postój taksówek* (taxi stand), where you'll almost always find a line of them. There are plenty of stands and if you ask around somebody can usually tell you where the nearest is. Taxis can also be ordered by phone, and there's usually no extra charge for this.

When you get into a taxi, make sure the driver turns on the meter. Also check whether the meter has been switched to the proper rate: '1' identifies the daytime rate, and '2' is the night-time rate. A typical scam against foreigners is to drop the flag to the higher night-time rate during the daytime.

Remember to carry small bills, so you'll be able to pay the exact fare. If you don't, it's hard to get change from a driver who's intent on charging you more. It's always a good idea to find out how much the right fare should be by asking hotel staff or an attendant at the airport before you leave.

TOURS

The following Polish agencies offer organised tours in Poland:

Fabricum (p123) Specialises in tours of Poland's Unesco sights and following in the footsteps of the country's beloved John Paul II.

Jarden Tourist Agency (p195) A Jewish-interest agency that organises tours of Kraków and its surrounds.

Kampio (p87) Focuses on ecotourism, organising biking tours in Masuria, bird-watching in Białowieża and kayaking in Biebrza National Park.

Mazurkas Travel (p104) Major tour operator with tours of Warsaw plus trips to Kraków, Gdańsk and Białowieża.

Our Roots (p104) Specialises in tours of Jewish sites, including trips around Warsaw and sites throughout the country.

PTTK Mazury (p481) Runs kayak tours along the country's best rivers in and around the Great Masurian Lakes.

TRAIN

Trains will be your main means of transport, especially when travelling long distances – they are good value and usually run on time. Outside peak holiday periods in July and August, it should be no problem finding a seat.

The railways are administered by the **Polskie Koleje Państwowe** (PKP; Polish State Railways, www.pkp .pl in Polish). With over 27,000km of lines, the railway network is extensive and covers most places you might wish to go to. Predictably, the network covers less of the mountainous parts of southern Poland, and trains are slower there.

Costs

Tickets for fast trains (see p528 for information on train types) are about 60% more expensive than those for ordinary trains, and an express train costs 50% more than a fast train. First class is 50% more expensive than 2nd class. Fares are dependent on distance; fares in the following table are approximate prices for 2nd-class tickets.

Distance	Ordinary	Fast
50km	10zł	16zł
100km	15.50zł	24zł
150km	19.50zł	33zł
200km	22zł	36zł
250km	25zł	42zł
300km	27zł	46zł
350km	28zł	47zł
400km	29zł	49zł
450km	31zł	52zł
500km	32zł	54zł

A reservation costs an additional 10zł (25zł on InterCity trains) regardless of distance. A 2nd-class couchette sleeping 3/6 persons costs an additional 50/70zł, while a sleeper for two is 130zł. A 1st-class compartment on an overnight train costs an additional 240zł.

The approximate fares on InterCity trains (including the compulsory seat reservation) from Warsaw to either Gdańsk, Katowice, Kraków or Poznań are 96/132zł in 2nd/1st class.

Discounts

Foreign students under the age of 26 receive a 33% discount on InterCity trains but still must pay the 25zł reservation fee. Persons over 60 can purchase a *legitymacja seniora* (senior concession) card for 75zł which provides 50% discount on 1st- and 2nd-class seats on all Polish trains.

Tickets

Since most train-station ticket offices have been computerised, buying tickets is now less of a hassle than it used to be, but queuing is still a way of life. Be at the station at least half an hour before the departure time of your train and make sure you are queuing at the right ticket window. As cashiers rarely speak English, the easiest way of buying a ticket is to have all the relevant details written down on a piece of paper. These should include the destination, the departure time and the class – *pierwsza klasa* (first) or *druga klasa* (second). If seat reservation is compulsory on your train, you'll automatically be sold a *miejscówka* (reserved-seat ticket); if it's optional, you must state whether you want a *miejscówka* or not.

If you are forced to get on a train without a ticket, you can buy one directly from the conductor for a small supplement – 4zł on ordinary and fast trains, and 6zł express and InterCity trains. On ordinary and fast trains you must seek out the conductor otherwise you'll be fined for travelling without a ticket; on express and InterCity trains you'll be sold the ticket when the conductor comes by.

Couchettes and sleepers can be booked at special counters at larger stations; it's advisable to reserve them in advance. Advance tickets

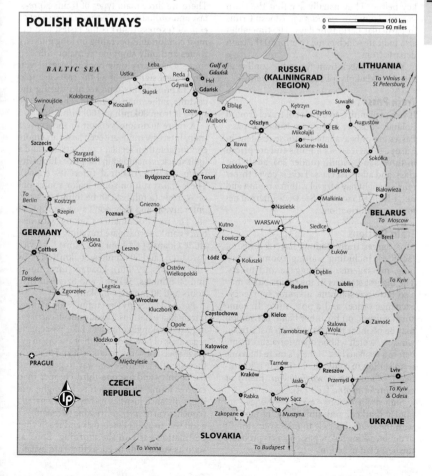

POLISH RAILWAYS

for journeys of over 100km and couchette and sleeper tickets can also be bought at any Orbis Travel office and some other agencies – perhaps a quicker option.

Timetables

Rozkład jazdy (train timetables) are displayed in stations, with *odjazdy* (departures) on yellow boards and *przyjazdy* (arrivals) on white.

Ordinary trains are marked in black print, fast trains in red, and if you spot an additional 'Ex', this means an express train. InterCity trains are identified by the letters 'IC'. The letter 'R' in a square indicates a train with compulsory seat reservation. There will be some letters and/or numbers following the departure time; always check them in the key below. They usually say that the train *kursuje* (runs) or *nie kursuje* (doesn't run) in particular periods or days. The timetables also indicate which *peron* (platform) the train departs from.

You can check train timetables online at http://rozklad.pkp.pl/bin/query.exe/en?.

Train Passes

If you're planning to do a lot of travel around Poland, consider buying an InterRail pass. Passes are only available to those resident in Europe for at least six months and are priced in three bands: youth (under 26), adult 2nd class, and adult 1st class. Tickets cover three/four/six/eight day's travel within a month and range from €45 to €188. See www.interrail.net for more information.

Train Stations

Most larger train stations have a range of facilities, including waiting rooms, snack bars, newsagents, left-luggage and toilets. The biggest stations in the major cities may also have a restaurant, a *kantor* (currency-exchange office) and a post office. In some small villages, on the other hand, the station may be no more than a shed with just a ticket window, which will be open for a short time before a train arrives. If there's more than one train station in a city, the main one is identified by the name *główny/główna* (main) or *centralny/centralna* (central).

Some train stations – even major ones – are poorly marked, and, unless you're familiar with the route, it's easy to miss your stop. If in doubt, asking fellow passengers is probably the best plan of action.

All large stations have *przechowalnia bagażu* (left-luggage rooms), which are usually open round the clock. You can store your luggage there for up to 10 days. There's a low basic daily-storage charge per item (3zł), plus 1% of the declared value of the luggage as insurance. One thing to remember is that they usually close once or twice a day for an hour or so. The times of these breaks are displayed over the counter. If you've put your baggage in storage, be sure to arrive at least half an hour before your departure time to allow time for some queuing and paperwork. You pay the charge when you pick up your luggage, not when you deposit it.

Types of Train

There are three main types of train: express, fast and ordinary. The *pociąg ekspresowy* or *ekspres* (express train) is the fastest and the most comfortable, operating on long intercity routes and only stopping at major cities en route. They carry only bookable seats; you can't travel standing if all the seats are sold out. Express trains tend to run during the daytime, rather than overnight. Their average speed is from 80km/h to 100km/h.

A more luxurious version of the express train, InterCity trains are even faster and more comfortable than regular express trains, and a light snack is included in the price (EuroCity trains are international InterCity trains). These trains run on some major routes out of Warsaw (a full list can be found on www.intercity.pl) and they don't stop en route at all. The main destinations (along with distances and approximate travelling times) include Gdańsk (4½ hours, 333km); Katowice (two hours and 50 minutes, 303km); Kraków (three hours, 297km); Poznań (three hours and 50 minutes, 311km); and Szczecin (five hours and 30 minutes, 525km).

Pociąg pospieszny (fast trains) stop at more intermediate stations. Usually not all carriages require booking; some will take passengers regardless of how crowded they are. At an average speed of between 60km/h and 80km/h, they are still a convenient way to get around the country and are one-third cheaper than express trains. They often travel at night, and if the distance justifies it they carry *kuszetki* (couchettes) or *miejsca sypialne* (sleepers) – a good way to avoid hotel costs and reach your destination early in the morning. Book as soon as you decide to go, as there are usually only a couple of sleeping cars and beds may sell out fast.

The *pociąg osobowy* (ordinary or local train) is far slower as it stops at all stations along the way. These trains mostly cover shorter distances, but they also run on longer routes. You can assume that their average speed will be between 30km/h and 40km/h. They are less comfortable than express or fast trains and don't require reservations. They are OK for short distances, but a longer journey can be tiring.

Almost all trains have two classes of carriage: 2nd class and 1st class. The carriages of long-distance trains are usually divided into compartments: the 1st-class compartments have six seats, while the 2nd-class ones contain eight seats. Smoking is only allowed in designated compartments, but in practice some people still smoke in corridors and outside toilets; smoking is banned on InterCity trains. Chain smoking is not uncommon in Poland and a journey in a designated smoking compartment can be almost unbearable. It's better to book a seat in a nonsmoking compartment and go into the smoking corridor if you wish to smoke.

The 2nd-class couchette compartments have six beds, with three to a side; the 1st-class compartments have four beds, two to a side. Sleepers come in both 2nd and 1st class; the former sleep three to a compartment, the latter only two, and both have a washbasin, sheets and blankets.

TRANSPORT

Health Dr Caroline Evans

CONTENTS

Travel health depends on your predeparture preparations, your daily health care while travelling and how you handle any medical problem that does develop. There's a popular Polish saying: 'To be ill in Poland, it helps to be healthy'. It's a wryly humorous reference to the poor state of health care in the country; political mismanagement and lack of investment have seen the health service decline in the last five years. Fortunately, there are private hospitals and clinics in the main cities where the level of care is the same as you'll find in the West (see Medical Services, p86 and p166).

BEFORE YOU GO

Prevention is the key to staying healthy while you are abroad. A little planning before your departure, particularly for pre-existing illnesses, will save trouble later: see your dentist before a long trip, carry a spare pair of contact lenses and glasses, and take your optical prescription with you. Bring medications in their original, clearly labelled containers. A signed and dated letter from your physician describing your medical conditions and medications, including generic names, is also a good idea. If carrying syringes or needles, be sure to have a physician's letter documenting their medical necessity.

INSURANCE

If you're an EU citizen, a European Health Insurance Card (EHIC), available from health centres or, in the UK, post offices, covers you for most medical care. It will not cover you for nonemergencies or emergency repatriation. Citizens from other countries should find out if there is a reciprocal arrangement for free medical care between their country and Poland. If you do need health insurance, strongly consider a policy that covers you for the worst possible scenario, such as an accident requiring an emergency flight home. Find out in advance if your insurance plan will make payments directly to providers or if they'll reimburse you later for overseas health expenditures. The former option is generally preferable, as it doesn't require you to pay for services in a foreign country.

RECOMMENDED VACCINATIONS

The World Health Organization (WHO) recommends that all travellers should be covered for diphtheria, tetanus, measles, mumps, rubella and polio, regardless of their intended destination. Since most vaccines don't produce immunity until at least two weeks after they're given, visit a physician at least six weeks before your departure.

INTERNET RESOURCES

International Travel and Health, a publication of the WHO, is revised annually and is available online at www.who.int/ith. Other useful websites include www.mdtravelhealth.com (travel health recommendations for every country, which are updated daily), www.fitfortravel.scot.nhs.uk (general travel advice for the layperson), www.ageconcern.org.uk (advice on travel for the elderly) and www.mariestopes.org.uk (information on women's health and contraception).

It's also a good idea to consult your government's travel health website before departure:

Australia (www.dfat.gov.au/travel)
Canada (www.travelhealth.gc.ca)
United Kingdom (www.dh.gov.uk)
United States (www.cdc.gov/travel)

IN TRANSIT

DEEP VEIN THROMBOSIS (DVT)

Blood clots may form in the legs during plane flights, chiefly because of prolonged immobility. The longer the flight, the greater the risk. The chief symptom of DVT is swelling or pain of the foot, ankle or calf, usually but not always on just one side. When a blood clot travels to the lungs, it may cause chest pain and breathing difficulties. Travellers with any of these symptoms should immediately seek medical attention.

To prevent the development of DVT on long flights you should walk about the cabin, contract the leg muscles while sitting, drink plenty of fluids and avoid alcohol and tobacco.

JET LAG & MOTION SICKNESS

To avoid jet lag (common when crossing more than five time zones) try drinking plenty of nonalchoholic fluids and eating light meals. Upon arrival, get exposure to natural sunlight and readjust your schedule (for meals, sleep and so on) as soon as possible.

Antihistamines such as dimenhydrinate (Dramamine) and meclizine (Antivert, Bonine) are usually the first choice for treating motion sickness. A herbal alternative is ginger.

IN POLAND

AVAILABILITY & COST OF HEALTH CARE

High-quality medical care is not always readily available outside of major cities, but embassies, consulates and five-star hotels can usually recommend doctors or clinics. In some cases, medical supplies required in hospital may need to be bought from a pharmacy and nursing care may be limited. Note that there can be an increased risk of hepatitis B and HIV transmission via poorly sterilised equipment.

INFECTIOUS DISEASES

Tick-borne encephalitis is spread by tick bites. It is a serious infection of the brain, and vaccination is advised for those in risk areas who are unable to avoid tick bites (such as campers, forestry workers and walkers). Two doses of vaccine will give a year's protection, and three doses will cover you for up to three years.

ENVIRONMENTAL HAZARDS
Insect Bites & Stings

Mosquitoes are found in most parts of Europe. They are a particular pest around the region of the Great Masurian Lakes. They may not carry malaria but can cause irritation and infected bites. Use a DEET-based insect repellent.

Bees and wasps only cause major problems to those with a severe allergy (anaphylaxis). If you have a severe allergy to bee or wasp stings carry an 'EpiPen' or similar adrenaline injection.

Bed bugs lead to very itchy, lumpy bites. Spraying the mattress with crawling insect killer after changing bedding will get rid of them.

Scabies are tiny mites that live in the skin, particularly between the fingers. They cause an intensely itchy rash. Scabies are easily treated with lotion from a pharmacy; other members of the household also need treating to avoid spreading scabies between asymptomatic carriers.

TRAVELLING WITH CHILDREN

All travellers with children should know how to treat minor ailments and when to seek medical treatment. Make sure the children are up-to-date with routine vaccinations, and discuss possible travel vaccines well before departure, as some vaccines are not suitable for children under one year of age.

In hot, moist climates any wound or break in the skin is likely to let in infection. The area should be cleaned and kept dry.

Remember to avoid contaminated food and water. If your child has vomiting or diarrhoea, lost fluid and salts must be replaced. It may be helpful to take rehydration powders for reconstituting with boiled water.

Children should be encouraged to avoid and mistrust any dogs or other mammals because of the risk of rabies and other diseases. Any bite, scratch or lick from a warm-blooded, furry animal should immediately be thoroughly cleaned. If there is any possibility that the animal is infected with rabies, medical assistance should be sought immediately.

WOMEN'S HEALTH

Travelling during pregnancy is usually possible but always consult your doctor before planning your trip. The most risky times for

HEALTH

travel are during the first 12 weeks of pregnancy and after 30 weeks.

SEXUAL HEALTH

Emergency contraception is most effective if taken within 24 hours after unprotected sex. The **International Planned Parent Federation** (www.ippf.org) can advise about the availability of contraception in different countries.

When buying condoms, look for a European CE mark, which means that they have been rigorously tested, and then keep them in a cool, dry place or they may crack and perish.

Language

CONTENTS

Polish is a western variety of the Slavonic languages found in Central and Eastern Europe, such as Croatian, Czech, Russian, Serbian, Slovak and Slovene.

Ideally, everyone who wants to travel in Poland should know some basic Polish – the more you know the easier your travel is likely to be and the more you'll get out of your time in the country. For a more comprehensive guide to the language, get a copy of Lonely Planet's *Polish Phrasebook* or *Small Talk Eastern Europe*.

THE POLISH ALPHABET

Polish letters with diacritical marks are treated as separate letters, and the order of the Polish alphabet is as follows:

a ą b c ć d e ę f g h i j k l ł m n ń o ó p (q) r s ś t u (v) w (x) y z ź ż

The letters **q**, **v** and **x** appear only in words of foreign origin.

PRONUNCIATION

Written Polish is phonetically consistent, which means that the pronunciation of letters or clusters of letters doesn't vary from word to word. The stress almost always falls on the second-last syllable.

Vowels

Polish vowels are pure, consisting of one sound only, and are of roughly even length. Their approximate pronunciations are as follows:

a	as the 'u' in 'cut'
ą	a highly nasalised vowel; a cross between the 'awn' in 'lawn' and the 'ong' in 'long'
e	'e' in 'ten'
ę	also highly nasalised; like the 'eng' in 'engage' (where the 'ng' is one sound, not 'n' followed by 'g'); pronounced as **e** when word-final
i	as in 'police' but shorter
o	as in 'not'
ó	the same as Polish **u**
u	as in 'put'
y	as the 'i' in 'bit'

Consonants

Most Polish consonants are pronounced as in English. However, there are some very fine distinctions between certain consonants in Polish, which English speakers may find difficult to produce. The following guide only gives approximations of the correct pronunciation – your best bet is to listen to and learn from native speakers:

c	as the 'ts' in 'its'
ch	as the 'ch' in Scottish *loch*
cz	as the 'ch' in 'church'
ć	similar to **c** but pronounced with the tongue a little further back on the roof of the mouth; pronounced as 'tsi' before vowels
dz	as the 'ds' in 'adds up'
dź	similar to **dz** but pronounced with the tongue a little further back on the roof of the mouth; pronounced as 'dzi' before vowels
dż	as the 'j' in 'jam'
g	as in 'get'
h	the same as **ch**
j	as the 'y' in 'yet'
ł	as the 'w' in 'wine'
ń	as the 'ni' in 'onion'; written as **ni** before vowels

r   always trilled
rz   as the 's' in 'pleasure'
s   as in 'set'
sz   as the 'sh' in 'show'
ś   a soft 'sh' sound, similar to **sz**; written
         as **si** before vowels
w   'v' in 'van'
ź   as the 's' in 'pleasure'; written as **zi**
         before vowels
ż   the same as **rz**
szcz   the most obtuse-looking consonant
         cluster; pronounced as the 'shch' in
         'fresh cheese'

The following consonants are unvoiced
when they are word-final: **b** is pronounced
as 'p', **d** as 't', **g** as 'k', **w** as 'f', **z** as 's' and **rz**
as 'sz'.

Finally, here's the favourite Polish
tongue-twister for you to test your pronunciation skills on:

Chrząszcz brzmi w trzcinie.
The cockchafer buzzes in the weeds.

ACCOMMODATION

Where can I find a ...?
Gdzie mogę znaleźć ...?   gjye *mo*·ge *zna*·leshch ...
  camping ground
  camping   *kam*·peenk
  guesthouse
  pensjonat   pen·*syo*·nat
  hotel
  hotel   *ho*·tel
  youth hostel
  schronisko młodzieżowe sro·*nees*·ko mwo·jye·*zho*·ve

Where is a cheap hotel?
Gdzie jest tani hotel?   gjye yest *ta*·nee *ho*·tel
What is the address?
Jaki jest adres?   ya·kee yest *ad*·res
Please write down the address.
Proszę to napisać.   pro·she to na·*pee*·sach
Do you have any rooms available?
Czy są wolne pokoje?   chi som *vol*·ne po·*ko*·ye

I'd like (a) ...
Poproszę o ...   po·*pro*·she o ...
  bed
  łóżko   *woosh*·ko
  single room
  pokój jednoosobowy   po·kooy yed·no·o·so·*bo*·vi
  double bed
  podwójnym łóżkiem   pod·*vooy*·nim *woosh*·kyem
  room
  pokój   po·*kooy*

twin room with two beds
pokój dwuosobowy   po·kooy dvoo·o·so·*bo*·vi
room with a bathroom
pokój z łazienką   po·kooys s wa·*zhen*·kom
to share a dorm
łóżko w sali zbiorowej   *woosh*·ko *fsa*·lee zbyo·*ro*·vey

MAKING A RESERVATION

(for written and phone inquiries)

from ...	*od ...*
to ...	*do ...*
date	*data*
surname	*nazwisko*
I'd like to book ...	*Chcę zarezerwować ...*
price	*cena*
credit card	*karta kredytowa*
number	*numer*
expiry date	*data ważności*

How much is it per night?
Ile kosztuje za noc?   ee·le kosh·*too*·ye za nots
May I see it?
Czy mogę go zobaczyć?   chi *mo*·ge go zo·*ba*·chich
Where is the bathroom?
Gdzie jest łazienka?   gjye yest wa·*zhen*·ka
Where is the toilet?
Gdzie są toalety?   gjye som to·a·*le*·ti
I'm leaving today.
Wyjeżdżam dziś.   vi·*yesh*·jyam jyeesh

CONVERSATION & ESSENTIALS

Hello.	*Dzień dobry.*	jyen *do*·bri
Goodbye.	*Do widzenia.*	do vee·*dze*·nya
Yes.	*Tak.*	tak
No.	*Nie.*	nye
Please.	*Proszę.*	*pro*·she
Thank you.	*Dziękuję.*	jyen·*koo*·ye
You're welcome.	*Proszę.*	*pro*·she
Excuse me.	*Przepraszam.*	pshe·*pra*·sham
Sorry.	*Przepraszam.*	pshe·*pra*·sham
I like ...	*Lubię ...*	*loo*·bye ...
I don't like ...	*Nie lubię ...*	nye *loo*·bye ...
Just a minute.	*Chwileczkę.*	hfee·*lech*·ke

What's your name?
Jak masz na imię?   yak mash na *ee*·mye
My name is ...
Mam na imię ...   mam na *ee*·mye ...
I'm from ...
Jestem z ...   *yes*·tem s ...
Where are you from?
Skąd pan/pani jest?   skont pan/*pa*·nee yest (pol, m/f)
Skąd jesteś?   skont *yes*·tesh (inf)

DIRECTIONS

Where is ...?
Gdzie jest ...?   gjye yest ...
Go straight ahead.
Proszę iść prosto.   pro·she eeshch pros·to
Turn left.
Proszę skręcić w lewo.   pro·she skren·cheech fle·vo
Turn right.
Proszę skręcić w prawo.   pro·she skren·cheech fpra·vo
at the corner
na rogu   na ro·goo
at the traffic lights
na światłach   na shfya·twah

SIGNS

Wejście	Entrance
Wyjście	Exit
Informacja	Information
Otwarte	Open
Zamknięte	Closed
Wzbroniony	Prohibited
Posterunek Policji	Police Station
Toalety	Toilets/WC
Panowie	Men
Panie	Women

---

behind	*za*	za
in front of	*przed*	pshet
opposite	*naprzeciwko*	na·pshe·cheef·ko
far (from)	*daleko*	da·le·ko
near (to)	*blisko*	blees·ko
beach	*plaża*	pla·zha
bridge	*most*	most
castle	*zamek*	za·mek
cathedral	*katedra*	ka·te·dra
church	*kościół*	kosh·choow
island	*wyspa*	vis·pa
lake	*jezioro*	ye·zho·ro
main square	*plac główny*	plats gwoov·ni
market	*targ*	tark
old city (town)	*stare miasto*	sta·re mya·sto
palace	*pałac*	pa·wats
ruins	*ruiny*	roo·ee·ni
sea	*morze*	mo·zhe
square	*plac*	plats
tower	*wieża*	vye·zha

HEALTH

I'm ill.
Jestem chory/a.   yes·tem ho·ri/a (m/f)
It hurts here.
Tutaj mnie boli.   too·tay mnye bo·lee

EMERGENCIES

Help!
Na pomoc!   na po·mots
It's an emergency.
To jest nagły przypadek.   to yest na·gwi pshi·pa·dek
I'm lost.
Zgubiłem się.   zgoo·bee·wem she (m)
Zgubiłam się.   zgoo·bee·wam she (f)
Leave me alone!
Proszę odejść!   pro·she o·deyshch

Call ...!   *Proszę wezwać ...!*   pro·she vez·vach ...
a doctor   *lekarza*   le·ka·zha
the police   *policję*   po·lee·tsye

I'm asthmatic/epileptic.
Mam astmę/epilepsję.   mam as·tme/e·pee·lep·sye
I'm diabetic.
Jestem diabetykiem.   yes·tem dya·be·ti·kyem

I'm allergic to ...
Mam uczulenie na ...
mam oo·choo·le·nye na ...

antibiotics	*antybiotyki*	an·ti·byo·ti·kee
penicillin	*penicylinę*	pe·nee·tsi·lee·ne
bees	*pszczoły*	pshcho·wi

antiseptic	*antyseptyczny*	an·ti·sep·tich·ni
aspirin	*aspiryna*	as·pee·ri·na
condoms	*kondomy*	kon·do·mi
contraceptive	*środek anty-*	shro·dek an·ti·
	koncepcyjny	kon·tsep·tsiy·ni
diarrhoea	*biegunka*	bye·goon·ka
medicine	*lek*	lek
nausea	*mdłości*	mdwosh·chee
sunblock cream	*krem do opalania*	krem do o·pa·la·nya
tampons	*tampony*	tam·po·ni

LANGUAGE DIFFICULTIES

Do you speak English?
Czy pan/pani mówi   chi pan/pa·nee moo·vee
po angielsku?   po an·gyel·skoo (m/f)
Does anyone here speak English?
Czy ktoś tu mówi   chi ktosh too moo·vee
po angielsku?   po an·gyel·skoo
How do you say ...?
Jak się mówi ...?   yak she moo·vee ...
What does it mean?
Co to znaczy?   tso to zna·chi
I understand.
Rozumiem.   ro·zoo·myem
I don't understand.
Nie rozumiem.   nye ro·zoo·myem

LANGUAGE

Could you write it down, please?
Proszę to napisać.   *pro*·she to na·*pee*·sach
Can you show me (on the map)?
Proszę mi pokazać   *pro*·she mee po·*ka*·zach
(na mapie).   (na *ma*·pye)

NUMBERS

0	zero	ze·ro
1	jeden	ye·den
2	dwa	dva
3	trzy	tshi
4	cztery	chte·ri
5	pięć	pyench
6	sześć	sheshch
7	siedem	she·dem
8	osiem	o·shem
9	dziewięć	jye·vyench
10	dziesięć	jye·shench
11	jedenaście	ye·de·nash·che
12	dwanaście	dva·nash·che
13	trzynaście	tshi·nash·che
14	czternaście	chter·nash·che
15	piętnaście	pyent·nash·che
16	szesnaście	shes·nash·che
17	siedemnaście	she·dem·nash·che
18	osiemnaście	o·shem·nash·che
19	dziewiętnaście	jye·vyet·nash·che
20	dwadzieścia	dva·jyesh·cha
21	dwadzieścia jeden	dva·jyesh·cha ye·den
22	dwadzieścia dwa	dva·jyesh·cha dva
30	trzydzieści	tshi·jyesh·chee
40	czterdzieści	chter·jyesh·chee
50	pięćdziesiąt	pyen·jye·shont
60	sześćdziesiąt	shesh·jye·shont
70	siedemdziesiąt	she·dem·jye·shont
80	osiemdziesiąt	o·shem·jye·shont
90	dziewięćdziesiąt	jye·vyen·jye·shont
100	sto	sto
1000	tysiąc	ti·shonts

PAPERWORK

given names	imiona	ee·myo·na
surname	nazwisko	naz·vees·ko
nationality	narodowość	na·ro·do·voshch
date of birth	data urodzenia	da·ta oo·ro·dze·nya
place of birth	miejsce	myey·stse
	urodzenia	oo·ro·dze·nya
sex/gender	płeć	pwech
passport	paszport	pash·port
visa	wiza	vee·za

QUESTION WORDS

Who?	Kto?	kto
What?	Co?	tso
What is it?	Co to jest?	tso to yest
When?	Kiedy?	kye·di
Where?	Gdzie?	gjye
Which?	Który?	ktoo·ri
Why?	Dlaczego?	dla·che·go
How?	Jak?	yak

SHOPPING & SERVICES

I'd like to buy ...
Chcę kupić ...   htse *koo*·peech ...
How much is it?
Ile to kosztuje?   ee·le to kosh·*too*·ye
I don't like it.
Nie podoba mi się.   nye po·*do*·ba mee she
May I look at it?
Czy mogę to zobaczyć?   chi *mo*·ge to zo·*ba*·chich
I'm just looking.
Tylko oglądam.   til·ko o·*glon*·dam
It's expensive.
To jest drogie.   to yest *dro*·gye
I'll take it.
Wezmę to.   *vez*·me to
Can I pay by credit card?
Czy mogę zapłacić   chi *mo*·ge za·*pwa*·cheech
kartą kredytową?   *kar*·tom kre·di·*to*·vom

more	więcej	vyen·tsey
less	mniej	mnyey
smaller	mniejszy	mnyey·shi
bigger	większy	vyenk·shi

Where's ...?
Gdzie jest ...?   gjye yest ...
  a bank
  bank   bank
  the church
  kościół   kosh·choow
  the city centre
  centrum   tsen·troom
  the ... embassy
  ambasada ...   am·ba·*sa*·da ...
  the hospital
  szpital   shpee·tal
  the hotel
  hotel   ho·tel
  an internet café
  kawiarnia internetowa   ka·*vyar*·nya een·ter·ne·*to*·va
  the market
  targ   tark
  the museum
  muzeum   moo·ze·oom
  the police station
  posterunek policji   pos·te·*roo*·nek po·*lee*·tsyee
  the post office
  poczta   *poch*·ta
  a public phone
  automat telefoniczny   aw·*to*·mat te·le·fo·*neech*·ni

a public toilet
toaleta publiczna to·a·*le*·ta poo·*bleech*·na
the tourist information office
biuro informacji byoo·ro een·for·*ma*·tsyee
turystycznej too·ris·*tich*·ney

POLISH COMPUTER JARGON

If you surf the web at a Polish internet café you may have to do it in Polish. The following is a bit of useful Polish cyberspeak:

Bookmark	*Zakładka*
Close	*Zamknij*
Copy	*Kopiuj*
Cut	*Wytnij*
Delete	*Usuń*
Edit	*Edycja*
Exit	*Zakończ*
File	*Plik*
Help	*Pomoc*
Insert	*Wstaw*
New	*Nowy*
Open	*Otwórz*
Paste	*Wklej*
Print	*Drukuj*
Save	*Zapisz*
Save As	*Zapisz Jako*
Search	*Szukaj*
View	*Widok*

TIME & DATES
What time is it?
Która jest godzina? ktoo·ra yest go·*jee*·na
It's 10 o'clock.
Jest dziesiąta. yest jye·*shon*·ta

in the morning	*rano*	*ra*·no
in the afternoon	*po południu*	po po·*wood*·nyoo
in the evening	*wieczorem*	vye·*cho*·rem
today	*dziś* or *dzisiaj*	jeesh/*jee*·shay
tomorrow	*jutro*	*yoo*·tro
yesterday	*wczoraj*	*fcho*·ray
Monday	*poniedziałek*	po·nye·*jya*·wek
Tuesday	*wtorek*	*fto*·rek
Wednesday	*środa*	*shro*·da
Thursday	*czwartek*	*chfar*·tek
Friday	*piątek*	*pyon*·tek
Saturday	*sobota*	so·*bo*·ta
Sunday	*niedziela*	nye·*jye*·la
January	*styczeń*	*sti*·chen
February	*luty*	*loo*·ti
March	*marzec*	*ma*·zhets

April	*kwiecień*	*kfye*·chen
May	*maj*	may
June	*czerwiec*	*cher*·vyets
July	*lipiec*	*lee*·pyets
August	*sierpień*	*sher*·pyen
September	*wrzesień*	*vzhe*·shen
October	*październik*	pazh·*jyer*·neek
November	*listopad*	*lees*·to·pat
December	*grudzień*	*groo*·jyen

TRANSPORT
Public Transport
What time does the ... leave/arrive?
O której odchodzi/przychodzi ...?
o *ktoo*·rey ot·*ho*·jee/pshi·*ho*·jee ...

boat		
łódź		wooch
bus		
autobus		aw·*to*·boos
plane		
samolot		sa·*mo*·lot
train		
pociąg		po·chonk
tram		
tramwaj		tram·vay

I'd like a ... ticket.
Poproszę bilet ...
po·*pro*·she *bee*·let ...

one-way		
w jedną stronę		*fyed*·nom *stro*·ne
return		
powrotny		po·*vrot*·ni

I want to go to ...
Chcę jechać do ... htse *ye*·hach do ...

1st class	*pierwsza klasa*	*pyer*·fsha *kla*·sa
2nd class	*druga klasa*	*droo*·ga *kla*·sa
cancel	*odwołać*	ot·*vo*·wach
delay	*opóźnienie*	o·poozh·*nye*·nye
the first	*pierwszy*	*pyer*·fshi
the last	*ostatni*	os·*tat*·ni
platform	*peron*	*pe*·ron
ticket office	*kasa biletowa*	*ka*·sa bee·le·*to*·va
timetable	*rozkład jazdy*	ros·kwat *yaz*·di
train station	*dworzec kolejowy*	*dvo*·zhets ko·le·*yo*·vi

Private Transport
I'd like to hire a ...
Chcę wypożyczyć ...
htse vi·po·*zhi*·chich ...

bicycle		
rower		*ro*·ver

car
samochód   sa·mo·hoot
motorbike
motocykl   mo·to·tsikl

Where's the nearest petrol station?
Gdzie jest najbliższa   gjye yest nay·bleesh·sha
stacja benzynowa?   sta·tsya ben·zi·no·va
Please fill it up.
Proszę napełnić bak.   pro·she na·peoo·neech bak
I'd like ... litres.
Poproszę ... litrów.   po·pro·she ... leet·roof

petrol   benzyna   ben·zi·na
unleaded   bezołowiowa   be·so·wo·vyo·va
diesel   diesel/   dee·sel
              olej napędowy o·ley na·pen·do·vi

```
┌─────────────────────────────────────────┐
│ ROAD SIGNS                               │
│                                          │
│ Objazd                    Detour         │
│ Parkowanie Wzbronione     No Parking     │
│ Uwaga                     Caution        │
│ Wjazd                     Entry          │
│ Wjazd Wzbroniony          No Entry       │
│ Wyjazd                    Exit           │
└─────────────────────────────────────────┘
```

Is this the road to ...?
Czy ta droga prowadzi   chi ta dro·ga pro·va·jee
do ...?   do ...
Can I park here?
Czy można tu parkować?   chi mozh·na too par·ko·vach
How long can I park here?
Jak długo można   yak dwoo·go mozh·na
tu parkować?   too par·ko·vach

I need a mechanic.
Potrzebuję mechanika.   pot·she·boo·ye me·ha·nee·ka
The car has broken down.
Samochód się zepsuł.   sa·mo·hoot she zep·soow
It won't start.
Nie zapala.   nye za·pa·la
I have a flat tyre.
Złapałem gumę.   zwa·pa·wem goo·me (m)
Złapałam gumę.   zwa·pa·wam goo·me (f)
I've run out of petrol.
Zabrakło mi benzyny.   za·brak·wo mee ben·zi·ni

TRAVEL WITH CHILDREN
Where can I find a baby-sitter?
Gdzie można znaleźć opiekunkę do dziecka?
gjye mozh·na zna·leshch o·pye·koon·ke do jyets·ka
Can you put an extra bed in the room?
Poproszę o dodatkowe łóżko w pokoju.
po·pro·she o do·dat·ko·we woosh·ko fpo·ko·yoo
I need a car with a child seat.
Potrzebuję samochód z fotelikiem dla dziecka.
pot·she·boo·ye sa·mo·hoot sfo·te·lee·kyem dla jyets·ka
Do you have a children's menu?
Czy są jakieś dania dla dzieci?
chi som ya·kyesh da·nya dla jye·chee
Could you make it a child's portion?
Czy mogę prosić o porcję dla dziecka?
chi mo·ge pro·sheech o por·tsye dla jyets·ka
Are children allowed to enter?
Czy dzieci mogą wejść?
chi jye·chee mo·gom veyshch
Are there any facilities for children?
Czy są jakieś udogodnienia dla dzieci?
chi som ya·kyesh oo·do·go·dnye·nya dla jye·chee

Glossary

The following is a list of terms and abbreviations you're likely to come across in your travels through Poland. For food and drink terms, see p60.

Aleja or Aleje – avenue, main city street; abbreviated to Al in addresses and on maps
apteka – pharmacy

bankomat – ATM
bar mleczny – milk bar; a sort of basic self-service soup kitchen that serves very cheap, mostly vegetarian dishes
bazylika – basilica
bez łazienki – room without bathroom
biblioteka – library
bilet – ticket
biuro turystyki – travel agency
biuro zakwaterowania – office that arranges private accommodation
brama – gate
britzka – horse-drawn cart

Cepelia – a network of shops that sell artefacts made by local artisans
cerkiew (cerkwie) – Orthodox or Uniat church(es)
cukiernia – cake shop

Desa – chain of old art and antique sellers
dom kultury – cultural centre
dom wycieczkowy – term applied to PTTK-run hostels; also called dom turysty
domy wczasowe – workers' holiday homes
dwór – mansion

góra – mountain
gospoda – inn, tavern, restaurant
grosz – unit of Polish currency, abbreviated to gr; plural groszy; see also *złoty*

jaskinia – cave

kancelaria kościelna – church office
kantor(s) – private currency-exchange office(s)
kawiarnia – café
kemping – camping
kino – cinema
kolegiata – collegiate church
komórka – literally, 'cell'; commonly used for cellular (mobile) phone
kościół – church
księgarnia – bookshop

kwatery agroturystyczne – agrotourist accommodation
kwatery prywatne – rooms for rent in private houses

miejscówka – reserved-seat ticket
muzeum – museum

na zdrowie! – cheers!; literally, 'to the health'
noclegi – accommodation

odjazdy – departures (on transport timetables)
ostrów – island
otwarte – open

park narodowy – national park
parking strzeżony – guarded car park
pchać – pull (on door)
pensjonat(y) – pension or private guesthouse(s)
peron – railway platform
piekarnia – bakery
PKS – Państwowa Komunikacja Samochodowa; former state-run company that runs most of Poland's bus transport
Plac – Sq
poczta – post office
poczta główna – main post office
pokój 1-osobowy – single room
pokój 2-osobowy – double room
przechowalnia bagażu – left-luggage room
przez – via, en route (on transport timetables)
przyjazdy – arrivals (on transport timetables)
PTSM – Polskie Towarzystwo Schronisk Młodzieżowych; Polish Youth Hostel Association
PTTK – Polskie Towarzystwo Turystyczno-Krajoznawcze; Polish Tourist & Countryside Association

rachunek – bill or check
riksza – bicycle rickshaws
rozkład jazdy – transport timetable
Rynek – Town/Market Sq

sanktuarium – church (usually pilgrimage site)
schronisko górskie – mountain hostel, providing basic accommodation and meals, usually run by the *PTTK*
schronisko młodzieżowe – youth hostel
Sejm – the lower house of parliament
skansen – open-air museum of traditional architecture
sklep – shop
stanica wodna – waterside hostel, usually with boats, kayaks and other water-related facilities
stare miasto – old town/city
Stary Rynek – Old Town/Market Sq

stołówka – canteen; restaurant or cafeteria of a holiday home, workplace, hostel etc
święty/a (m/f) – saint; abbreviated to Św
szopka – Nativity scene

teatr – theatre
toalety – toilets

ulica – street; abbreviated to ul in addresses (and placed before the street name); usually omitted on maps

Uniat – Eastern-rite Catholics

wódka – vodka; the number one Polish spirit

z łazienką – room with bathroom
zajazd – inn (sometimes restaurant)
zamek – castle
zdrój – spa
złoty – unit of Polish currency; abbreviated to zł; divided into 100 units called *grosz*

The Authors

NEAL BEDFORD
Coordinating Author; Warsaw, Mazovia & Podlasie, Warmia & Masuria

After travelling extensively through Eastern Europe, but only spending a handful of weekends in Poland, Neal thought it time to properly uncover the country that first 'farewelled' the Soviet Union. What he initially took to be a simple task of 'seen it, done it' turned into a moving journey through a land full of surprises – some happy, some sad. Whether it was clubbing in Warsaw, kayaking on Lake Wigry, or paying respects at Treblinka, Neal was always inspired by the country and its resilient people. But, despite his best efforts, he'll never get his head around Polish pronunciation.

STEVE FALLON
Kraków, The Carpathian Mountains, Silesia

A long time ago, when dragons lived at Wawel Castle, Steve packed his Bachelor of Science in modern languages and a Polish phrasebook and headed for Katowice to teach English at the University of Silesia. Never mind that this was still the 'People's Republic of Poland', people spoke of WWII as if VE Day happened the day before, and basic stuff (toilet paper, anyone?) was in short supply. He'd never be the same. Steve returned with some trepidation to help update *Poland* but was overjoyed to discover that the *Polska dusza* (Polish soul) remains passionate, brave and true and the *pierogis* are even better. *Niech żje Polska! Niech żje Polska na zawsze!* (Long live Poland! Long live Poland forever!)

MARIKA MCADAM
Małopolska

Marika is a lawyer and writer who has knack for finding herself in places that are off the beaten track, or just plain off-beat. After an epic road trip from Gdynia to Zakopane, Marika wasn't sure whether Poland got under her skin or just on her nerves. This opportunity to return to Małopolska gave her the chance to figure it out once and for all. After meeting a painting coroneted as a Queen, discussing scare-tactics with a ghost in an underground chalk tunnel and being shooed off a bus by an exasperated driver, Marika now knows that she'll never be able to pronounce 'Zwierzyniec' but that the heart of Europe beats in Poland.

TIM RICHARDS
Wielkopolska, Pomerania

Tim spent a year teaching English in Kraków in 1994–95, on transfer from a two-year teaching stint in Egypt. He was fascinated by the massive post-communism transition affecting every aspect of Polish life, and by surviving remnants of the Cold War days. He returned to Poland in 2006 to research Lonely Planet's *Eastern Europe* book, and in 2007 for this book, and has been delighted by his re-acquaintance with the beautiful, complex country. When he's not on the road for Lonely Planet, Tim is a freelancer living in Melbourne, Australia, writing on various topics: travel, lifestyle, the arts, technology and pets. You can see more of his work at www.iwriter.com.au.

Behind the Scenes

THIS BOOK

This book is the 6th edition of Lonely Planet's *Poland* and was updated by Neal Bedford, Steve Fallon, Marika McAdam and Tim Richards. The first four editions were written by Krzysztof Dydyński. Neil Wilson coordinated the 5th edition, with contributions from Tom Parkinson and Richard Watkins. Dr Caroline Evans wrote the Health chapter. This guidebook was commissioned in Lonely Planet's London office and produced by the following people:

Commissioning Editor Will Gourlay
Coordinating Editor Anna Metcalfe
Coordinating Cartographer Valentina Kremenchutskaya
Coordinating Layout Designer Jim Hsu
Managing Editor Bruce Evans
Managing Cartographer Mark Griffiths
Managing Layout Designer Celia Wood
Assisting Editors Sarah Bailey, Susie Ashworth, Pete Cruttenden, Victoria Harrison, Stephanie Pearson
Assisting Cartographers Tony Fankhauser, Sam Sayer, Peter Shields, Amanda Sierp
Cover Designer Pepi Bluck
Project Manager Eoin Dunlevy
Language Content Coordinator Quentin Frayne
Talk2Us Coordinator Lisa Knights, Trent Paton

Thanks to Piotr Czajkowski, Ryan Evans, James Hardy, Adam McCrow, Wayne Murphy

THANKS
NEAL BEDFORD

So many people helped make *Poland* a memorable experience, but a few went that extra mile, for which I am truly grateful. Thanks to the Lonely Planet team of Will Gourlay, Marika McAdam, Steve Fallon and Tim Richards for their ideas, energy and support, Tony Ludlam for his outstanding help with Warsaw's nightlife, Ania Piekut of WWF for showing me the ropes in Warsaw and Patrycza Fotek for her insider's take on the capital.

Those who lent their considerable Polish expertise to the book include Stefan Laudyn, Bogdan Łukowscy, Ernest Mikołajczuk, Krzysztof Niedziałkowski, Agnieszka Spryszyńska, Jacek Winiarski and Gosia Znaniecka – thanks again. The hardworking souls in Poland's tourist offices, bus stops and train stations made my life that much easier, but Gosia Barecka of the Polish Chamber of Tourism and Maciej Hotowko and Anna Krajewska of Polish State Railways require special mention. Thanks also to Christian Cummins for passing on one Polish article after the next and Paulina Radon-Tanewska for serving up her Polish friends for me to annoy.

THE LONELY PLANET STORY

Fresh from an epic journey across Europe, Asia and Australia in 1972, Tony and Maureen Wheeler sat at their kitchen table stapling together notes. The first Lonely Planet guidebook, *Across Asia on the Cheap,* was born.

Travellers snapped up the guides. Inspired by their success, the Wheelers began publishing books to Southeast Asia, India and beyond. Demand was prodigious, and the Wheelers expanded the business rapidly to keep up. Over the years, Lonely Planet extended its coverage to every country and into the virtual world via lonelyplanet.com and the Thorn Tree message board.

As Lonely Planet became a globally loved brand, Tony and Maureen received several offers for the company. But it wasn't until 2007 that they found a partner whom they trusted to remain true to the company's principles of travelling widely, treading lightly and giving sustainably. In October of that year, BBC Worldwide acquired a 75% share in the company, pledging to uphold Lonely Planet's commitment to independent travel, trustworthy advice and editorial independence.

Today, Lonely Planet has offices in Melbourne, London and Oakland, with over 500 staff members and 300 authors. Tony and Maureen are still actively involved with Lonely Planet. They're travelling more often than ever, and they're devoting their spare time to charitable projects. And the company is still driven by the philosophy of *Across Asia on the Cheap*: 'All you've got to do is decide to go and the hardest part is over. So go!'

STEVE FALLON

A number of people assisted me in the research and writing of my chapters of *Poland*, in particular my dear friends the Karłaszewski family – Marek, Barbara and Agata – of Katowice. Others to whom I'd like to say *dziękuję bardzo* include Ewa Binkin of the Polish National Tourist Office in London; Emil Nowak of the Goodbye Lenin Hostel in Zakopane; Duncan Rhodes of www.cracow-life.com; and Danuta Rożek and Anita Singh of the Stranger Hostel in Kraków. Thanks to my Lonely Planet colleague Daniel Robinson for his helpful words on *kaddish*. The *Poland* team of authors – coordinator Neal Bedford, Tim Richards and Marika McAdam – was among the funnest I've ever worked with.

Two people's life travels ended during the research of this book: fellow author Tom Parkinson, who worked on the previous edition of *Poland*, and Chris Schwarz, founder of the Galicia Museum in Kraków and both a good Jew and a Righteous Gentile. The former was my friend, the latter my hero. May they both rest in peace.

As always, my share of the book is dedicated to my partner – and it's official! – Michael Rothschild, so close to – and yet so far from Polska.

MARIKA MCADAM

Researching Poland would have been a lot more difficult if it hadn't been for Piotr Wójcik in Kielce, Zofia Wymnocka in Zamość and Patricia and her colleagues in Lublin. Writing about Poland would have been a lot less fun if it hadn't been for Will Gourlay, Neal Bedford, Steve Fallon and Tim Richards. The whole experience would have been a lot less memorable if it hadn't been for my globetrotting sister Lorina, who wandered into my 2007 and helped make Poland one of its highlights. And life would be a lot less wonderful if it wasn't for Jo – what could be more supportive than a busy man who makes time to build a desk for a geek like me?

TIM RICHARDS

Vast amounts of gratitude to my wife, Narrelle Harris, who accompanied me and was very helpful at spotting interesting new places to research (sorry about all the fishing museums, though). Many thanks to the Grabarczyk family for their hospitality in sensational Sopot. As always, I'm extremely grateful to the professional, helpful staff of Poland's tourist offices, particularly Tom and Ewa in Szczecin, Joanna in Kołobrzeg, Sławomir in Słupsk, Szymon in Ustka, Iwona in Łeba, Magdalena in Sopot, Katarzyna in Gdańsk, Marzena and Klaudia in Elbląg, Małgorzata and Monika in Kwidzyn, Aleksandra in Grudziądz, Maciej in Toruń, Katarzyna in Bydgoszcz, Karina in Chełmno, Włodzimierz and Anna in Poznań, Artur in Gniezno, and Piotr in Kalisz. Thanks also to Poznań tour guide Agnieszka Rutkowska for her help with translation. I'm indebted to the staff of PKP who nearly always kept the trains running on time (and that two-hour delay at a rural siding in Wielkopolska gave me the chance to finish typing up my notes anyway). A final thanks to the Poles who shyly sidled up to me on station platforms to chat about their time working in Britain, only to discover I was from much, much further away; I appreciated the conversation!

OUR READERS

Many thanks to the travellers who used the last edition and wrote to us with helpful hints, useful advice and interesting anecdotes:

Melissa Addey, Andreas Aichner, Paul Allen, Cathrin Andersson, Victor Ashe, Victoria Baghdjian, Anna Bandurska, Nicolai Bangsgaard, Marta Barbosa, Maria Jose Sanchez Barillas, Pauline Beaton, Mirza Benca, Mike Binder, Emma Brown, David Brulotte, Rosella Bruni, John Brunton, Filip C, Antonio Caimano, Tom Callaghan, Sonia Calza, Shun-Kuei Chang, Kerry Clarke, Laly Coulomb, Catherine Crittenden, Grant Cura, Paolo Davi, Carla De Beer, Marek De van Watering, Reinhart Eisenberg, M S Evans,

SEND US YOUR FEEDBACK

We love to hear from travellers – your comments keep us on our toes and help make our books better. Our well-travelled team reads every word on what you loved or loathed about this book. Although we cannot reply individually to postal submissions, we always guarantee that your feedback goes straight to the appropriate authors, in time for the next edition. Each person who sends us information is thanked in the next edition – and the most useful submissions are rewarded with a free book.

To send us your updates – and find out about Lonely Planet events, newsletters and travel news – visit our award-winning website: **www.lonelyplanet.com/contact**.

Note: we may edit, reproduce and incorporate your comments in Lonely Planet products such as guidebooks, websites and digital products, so let us know if you don't want your comments reproduced or your name acknowledged. For a copy of our privacy policy visit www.lonelyplanet.com/privacy.

Brian O Flynn, Warwick Gardiner, John Gilroy, David Gledhill, Kate Griffiths, David Halford, Katherine Handley, Marc Hawey, Lyn Haynes, Jan Heeringa, Arnaud Hesselink, James Hewison, Rebecca Heys, Adam Hippmann, Urszula Jaremba, Anders Jeppsson, P Jeuken, Daniel Jinnefalt, Inge Jooris, Anna Kaminska, Jennie Karalewich, Suzanne Kenyon, Tono Khula, Christian Kirsch, Stefan Kolb, Klaus Kuhl, Ann Labro, John Lahann, Ed Lambert, Luke Leafgren, Brent Lewin, Stephen Lower, Paolo Mari, Dori Martinez, Alonso Martos, Charles McDonald, Jon Miller, Paul Mollatt, Marjon Mur, Bartosz Nabrdalik, David Negev, Matt Nicklos, Markus Nilsson, Martin Nowak, Brendan O'Brien, Danny Orbach, Andrew Ould, Mark Palatucci, Roger Parris, James Perkins, Mark Pulletz, Thomas Pullosseril, Zsofia Réger, F Rees, Greg Rinker, Julie Riso, Lars Ritterhoff, Mark Rodgers, Daniel Rodríguez, Joanna Rokicka, Eva Romo, Gail Ryan, Marcin Sadurski, Daniel Rodríguez San José, Keno Schulte, Gerhard Schweng, Frits Simonis, Darin Stanley, Ian Story, Mariola Swioklo, Marit Taylor, Ryan Taylor, Fab Tomlin, Philippe van Bellinghen, Michael van Laake, Jeff & Charlotte Vize, Marek Wasinski, Grzegorz Wegiel, Kristi Weidlein, Sieuwe Westerweel, John Woods, Gregg Young, Karol Zemek, Dario Zito.

ACKNOWLEDGMENTS

Many thanks to the following for the use of their content:

Globe on title page ©Mountain High Maps 1993 Digital Wisdom, Inc.

Internal photographs p8 (#1) by FCL Photography / Alamy; p9 (#2) by Brotch Travel / Alamy; p11 (#2) lookGaleria / Alamy. All other photographs by Lonely Planet Images, and by Bruce Bi p5, p175 (top), p179 (top); Mark Daffey p10 (top); Krzysztof Dydynski p6 (top), p7, p8 (bottom), p10 (bottom), p173, p174, p175 (bottom), p176 (bottom), p178, p179 (bottom), p180; Craig Pershouse p6 (bottom), p12 (bottom); Witold Skrypczak p9 (top), p11 (top), p12 (top), p177; Wayne Walton p176 (top).

ACKNOWLEDGMENTS

Index

INDEX

INDEX

554 Index (G-I)

INDEX

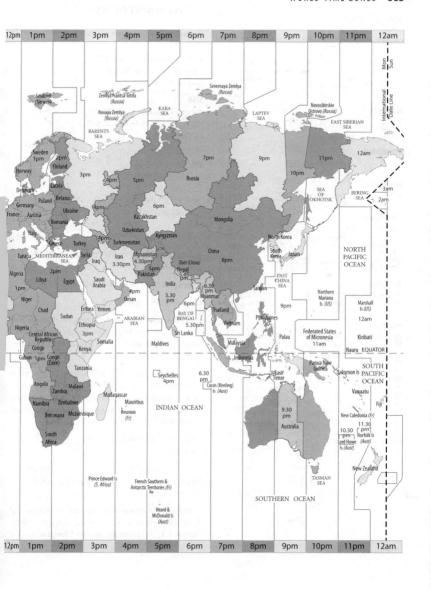

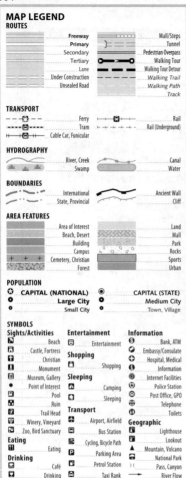

MAP LEGEND

ROUTES

Freeway
Primary
Secondary
Tertiary
Lane
Under Construction
Unsealed Road

Mall/Steps
Tunnel
Pedestrian Overpass
Walking Tour
Walking Tour Detour
Walking Trail
Walking Path
Track

TRANSPORT

Ferry
Tram
Cable Car, Funicular

Rail
Rail (Underground)

HYDROGRAPHY

River, Creek
Swamp

Canal
Water

BOUNDARIES

International
State, Provincial

Ancient Wall
Cliff

AREA FEATURES

Area of Interest
Beach, Desert
Building
Campus
Cemetery, Christian
Forest

Land
Mall
Park
Rocks
Sports
Urban

POPULATION

● CAPITAL (NATIONAL)
● Large City
● Small City

◉ CAPITAL (STATE)
● Medium City
● Town, Village

SYMBOLS

Sights/Activities
Beach
Castle, Fortress
Christian
Monument
Museum, Gallery
Point of Interest
Pool
Ruin
Trail Head
Winery, Vineyard
Zoo, Bird Sanctuary

Eating
Eating

Drinking
Café
Drinking

Entertainment
Entertainment

Shopping
Shopping

Sleeping
Camping
Sleeping

Transport
Airport, Airfield
Bus Station
Cycling, Bicycle Path
Parking Area
Petrol Station
Taxi Rank

Information
Bank, ATM
Embassy/Consulate
Hospital, Medical
Information
Internet Facilities
Police Station
Post Office, GPO
Telephone
Toilets

Geographic
Lighthouse
Lookout
Mountain, Volcano
National Park
Pass, Canyon
River Flow

LONELY PLANET OFFICES

Australia
Head Office
Locked Bag 1, Footscray, Victoria 3011
☎ 03 8379 8000, fax 03 8379 8111
talk2us@lonelyplanet.com.au

USA
150 Linden St, Oakland, CA 94607
☎ 510 893 8555, toll free 800 275 8555
fax 510 893 8572
info@lonelyplanet.com

UK
2nd Floor, 186 City Road,
London EC1V 2NT
☎ 020 7106 2100, fax 020 7106 2101
go@lonelyplanet.co.uk

Published by Lonely Planet Publications Pty Ltd
ABN 36 005 607 983

© Lonely Planet Publications Pty Ltd 2008

© photographers as indicated 2008

Cover photograph: View of busy street through an archway in Stare Miasto (old town), Izzet Keribar/Lonely Planet Images. Many of the images in this guide are available for licensing from Lonely Planet Images: www.lonelyplanetimages.com.